TENNESSEANS IN TEXAS

Compiled by:
Helen & Timothy Marsh

Southern Historical Press, Inc.
Greenville, South Carolina

Please direct all correspondence and orders to:

www.southernhistoricalpress.com
or
SOUTHERN HISTORICAL PRESS, Inc.
PO BOX 1267
Greenville, SC 29601
southernhistoricalpress@gmail.com

ISBN #0-89308-561-8

Printed in the United States of America

FOREWORD

This publication is presented as a useful research tool for those who are researching their Tennessee-Texas ancestry. It was compiled as the results of a detailed study of the 1850 Federal Census of Texas. It gives the researcher a detailed and concentrated view of the Tennessee-Texas relationship in 1850 as well as prior to that date, giving the birth place and dates of the inhabitants living in Texas in 1850 and by interpretation gives a clear picture of the migration route and time structure of the journey to Texas, many times covering a period of years through several states. After a study of this book it becomes clear that the often used statement that "Tennessee is the mother of Texas" has some validity. The fact that there has been a close historical and genealogical relationship between the two states from before the formation of the Republic strengthened our conviction that a comprehensive presentation of these records should be made available to the researcher.

By - Helen C. and Timothy R. Marsh, 1985

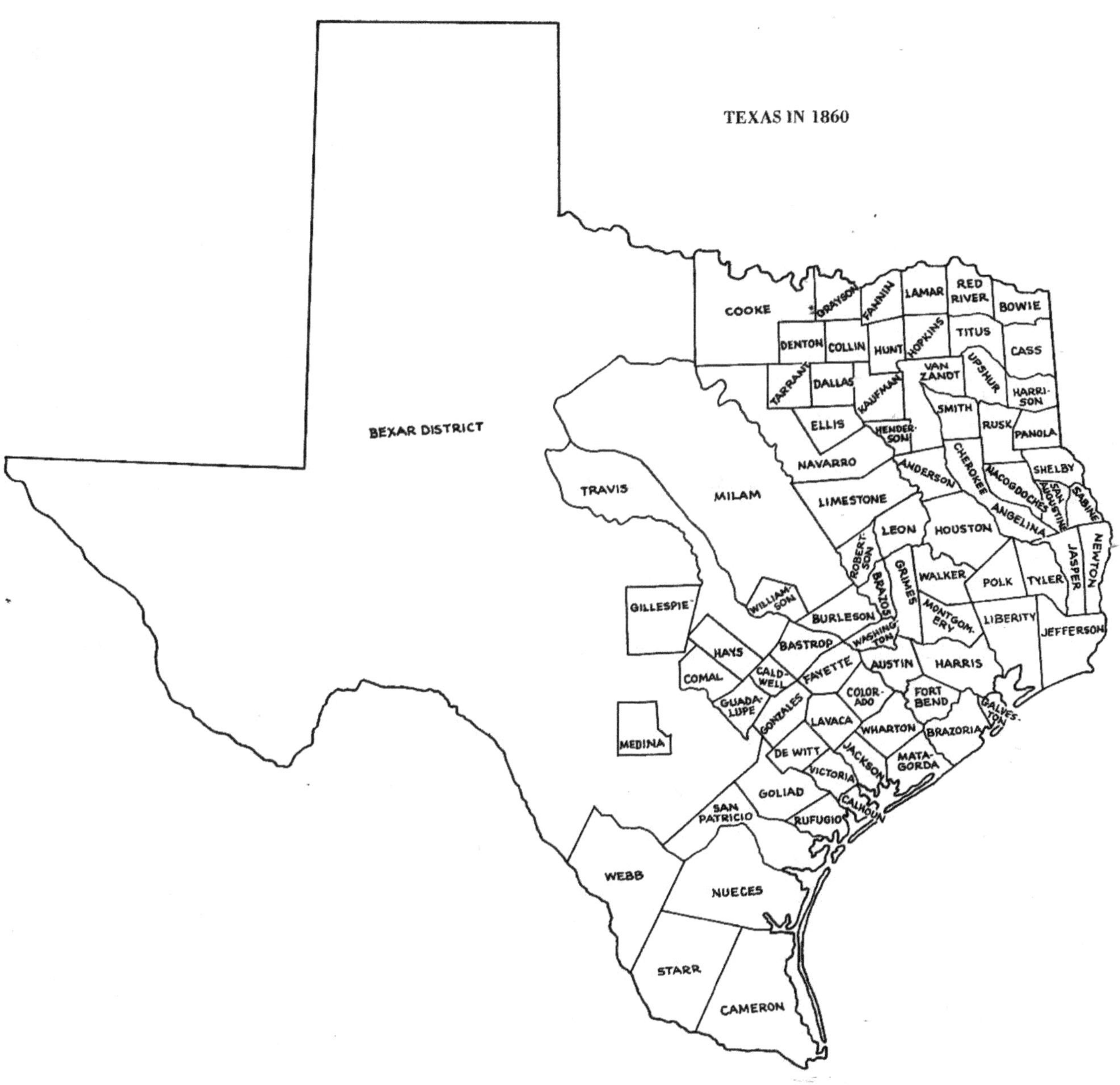

TEXAS IN 1860

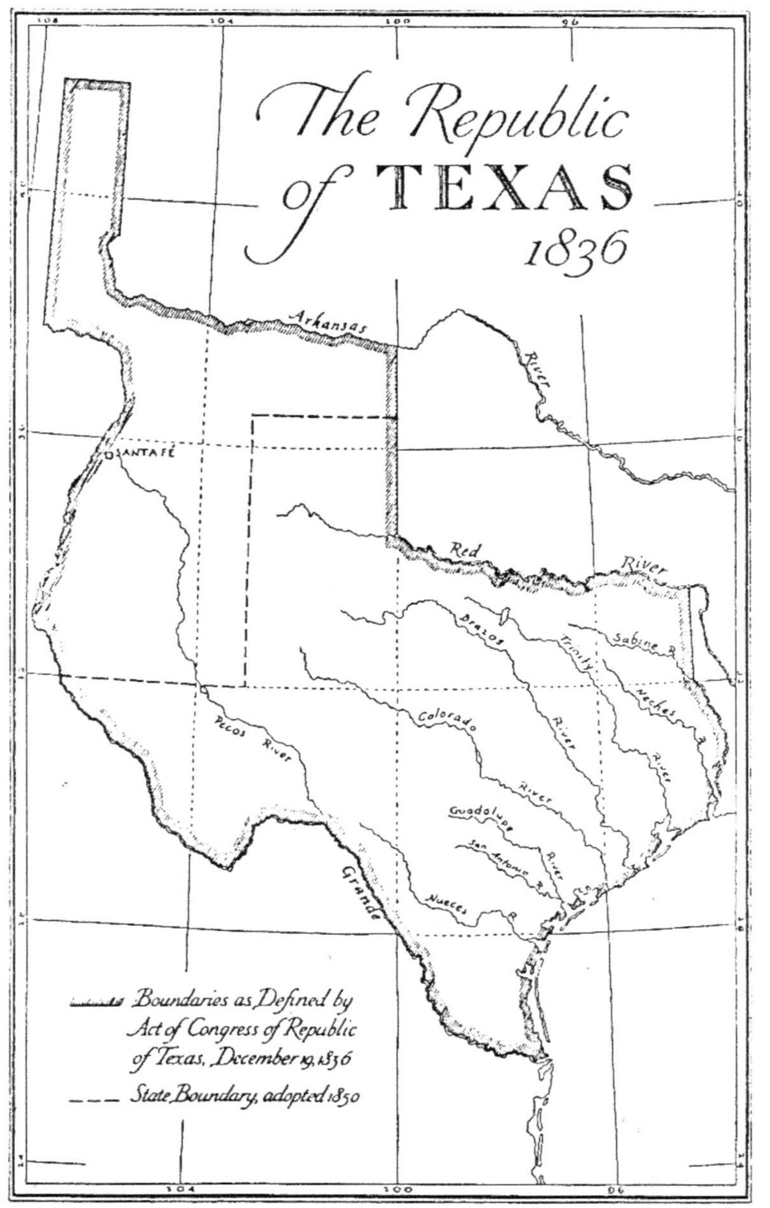
The Republic
of TEXAS
1836
Boundaries as Defined by
Act of Congress of Republic
of Texas, December 19, 1836
State Boundary, adopted 1850

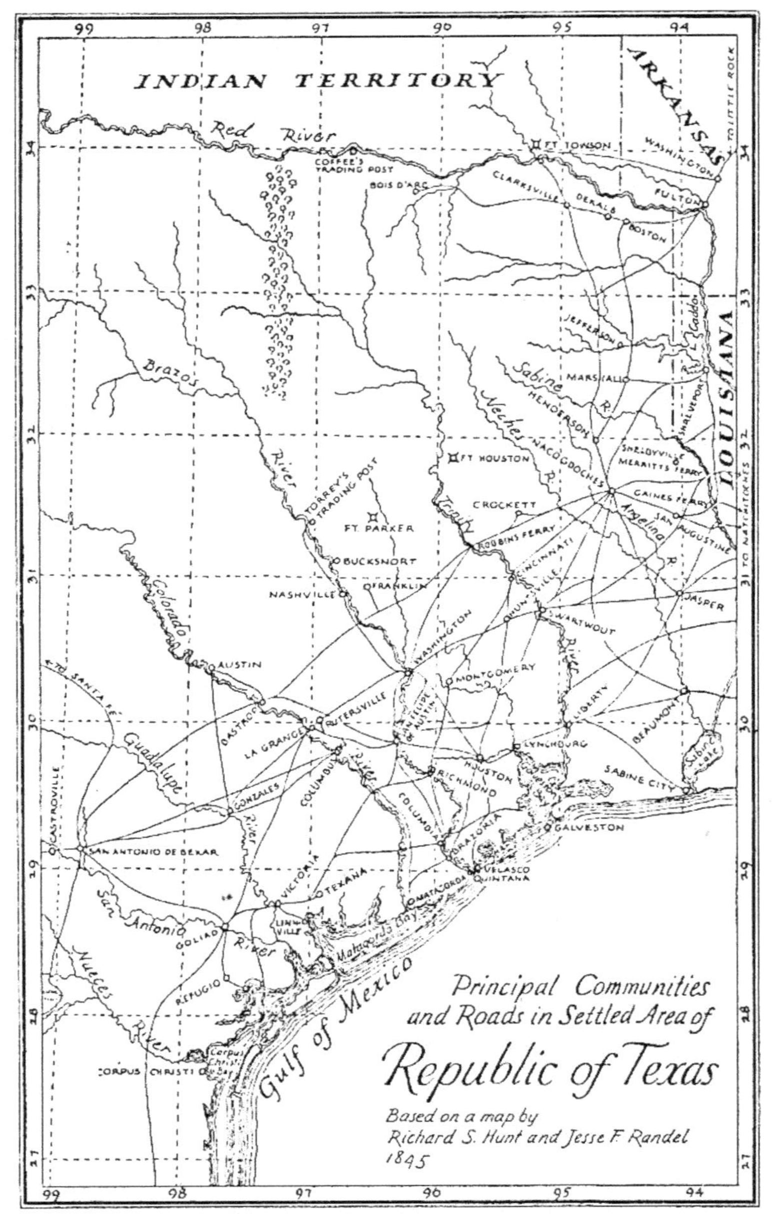
INDIAN TERRITORY
ARKANSAS
LOUISIANA
Gulf of Mexico
Principal Communities
and Roads in Settled Area of
Republic of Texas
Based on a map by
Richard S. Hunt and Jesse F. Randel
1845

ANDERSON COUNTY, TEXAS

Name	Age	Sex	Occupation	Birthplace
Hunt, David C.	55	M	Physician	SC
Achsah	45	F		TN
Julia A.	17	F		TN
Henry J.	13	M		GA
John D.	7	M		GA
Link, Henry H.	29	M	Physician	TN
Scott, T. W.	43	M	Merchant	NC
Criss, George W.	24	M	Clerk	IN
Scott, John	17	M	Clerk	TN
Cravens, John E.	32	M	Lawyer	KY
Iglehart, Ethelbert J.	29	M	Merchant	MD
Wortham, Thomas J.	29	M		TN
Eliza J.	24	F		LA
Albert J.	4	M		LA
William J.	1	M		TX
Howard, George R.	33	M	Merchant	NC
Murcat, William H.	28	M	Clerk	TN
Gramer, Joseph C.	25	M	Blksmith	TN
Sarah	18	F		TN
Andrew J. H.	2/12	M		TX
Galloway, Frances J.	16	F		AR
Owens, Nathaniel T.	29	M	Miller	TN
Mary	24	F		IL
Robert B.	7	M		TX
Rebecca	1	F		TX
Galloway, George R.	24	M		TN
Rogers, William R.	46	M	Hotel Keeper	TN
Joycy A.	47	F		TN
Eliza J.	15	F		MS
William G.	10	M		MS
James A.	6	M		MS
Mary F.	8	F		MS
Joshua H.	4	M		TX
Christopher L.	2	M		TX
Smith, Joseph W.	36	M	Hotel Keeper	KY
Masters, Robert	38	M	Tailor	MA
Hackpole, E. M.	22	M	Merchant	ME
Perry, James M.	32	M	Lawyer	TN
Givins, William T.	25	M	Tanner	TN
Broocks, Thomas W.	--	M		??
Kirksey, Walter T. A.	30	M	Physician	AL
Margaret M.	25	F		TN
Sophia A.	4	F		TX
John G.	2	M		TX
Givins, George W.	20	M	Grocer	TN
Mar (?), Jasper	23	M	Editor	IL
John	16	M	Printer	IL
Borren, James C.	22	M	Printer	TN
Perkins, John D.	28	M	Physician	TN
Margarett A.	22	F		TN
Mabray, David M.	20	M	Student	TN
Debard, Elisha	40	M	Physician	KY
Julia	25	F		TN
Chilton A.	12	M		TX
Elvira C.	10	F		TX
Flora J.	2	F		TX
Mary	8/12	F		TX
Horn, Andrew J.	36	M	Black Smith	KY
Heal, Jane	45	F		GA
John M.	12	M		MS
Margarett A. M.	9	F		MS
Ema E.	7	F		MS
Bremer, John M.	30	M	Carpenter	TN
Massey, John F.	31	M		KY
Mary	24	F		TN
Louisa	6	F		KY
William	4	M		TN
America	2	F		TX
Erwin, Nancy	48	F		VA

Name	Age	Sex	Occupation	Birthplace
Cox, James B.	33	M	Merchant	GA
Alzira J.	21	F		TN
Ida E.	2/12	F		TX
Aaron	25	M	Clerk	GA
Moses, Jr.	23	M	Merchant	GA
Dixon, John M.	26	M	School Teacher	TN
Jane M.	20	F		TN
Robert W.	3	M		TN
Nancy J.	1	F		TN
Jordan, Anderson H., Jr.	48	M	Bapt. Min.	TN
Sarah R.	44	F		TN
Pleasant A.	10	M		TN
Mead, Markus P.	42	M	Farmer	TN
Elizabeth	28	F		AR
William M.	17	M		AL
Mary E.	16	F		AL
Nancy S. J.	14	F		AL
Mead, James R.	1	M		TX
Grigsby, James	21	M		IL
Robert H.	18	M		IL
Moore, Hooper A.	25	M	Farmer	TN
Gibson, Samuel C.	23	M	Farmer	TN
Catharine	25	F		AL
James M.	2	M		TX
Hanks, Hansford	43	M	Farmer	TN
Susan	37	F		TN
Daniel D.	21	M		TN
Harper H.	16	M		MS
Susan E.	14	F		MS
Hansford S.	10	M		TX
Joicey T.	7	F		TX
Exen J.	5	F		TX
Brusellar A.	3	F		TX
Prudy	1	F		TX
Morgan, Daniel	30	M	Farmer	KY
Caroline	25	F		TN
Catharine	6	F		TX
Nancy	5	F		TX
William H.	3	M		TX
Lewis C.	5/12	M		TX
Box, Rowlin W.	46	M	Farmer	SC
Mary	48	F		TN
Faris	22	M		AL
John	19	M		AL
Eliza J.	10	F		TX
Rolin H.	7	M		TX
Mary T.	5	F		TX
Rogers, Elbert M.	32	M	Farmer	TN
Elizabeth C.	26	F		TN
Albert G.	4	M		MS
Sarah A. M.	2	M		TX
Henderson P.	5/12	M		TX
Ashmoore, James N.	27	M	Carpenter	TN
Nancy J.	16	F		AL
John	1	M		TX
Fuller, James R.	35	M	Farmer	VA
Salina	22	F		TN
Sarah J.	2	F		TX
Gardner, James	25	M		TN
Parker, James S.	36	M	Farmer	NC
Lous	29	F		TN
Sarah E.	8	F		TX
Candass E.	5	F		TX
Clementine C.	2	F		TX
Mary E.	1/12	F		TX
Parker, John	40	M	Farmer	TN
Cuthberson, Thomas M.	46	M	Farmer	NC
Phelpenah	45	F		TN
Martha	22	F		TN
Thomas	21	M		TN
Phelpenah	19	F		TN
Caroline	17	F		TN

(Continued)

ANDERSON COUNTY, TEXAS

Name	Age / Sex	Occupation	Birthplace
Cuthberson, Jesse D.	15 M		TN
J--dus	13 F		TX
Jane	83 F		NC
Lawrence, William H.	38 M	Farmer	SC
Clarisa M.	29 F		TN
Connell, James T.	22 M		NC
Joins, Elizabeth M.	20 F		TN
Johnson, James W.	53 M	Cabinet Maker	KY
Eve	47 F		NC
John W.	24 M		TN
Dowthet, James W.	53 M	Farmer	NC
Ellen	42 F		KY
Elizabeth	22 F		TN
Evin	21 M		TN
Sarah	18 F		IL
Ellen J.	16 F		TN
James	13 M		TN
Nancy	10 F		TN
Polly A.	8 F		TN
Martha	2 F		TX
Malinda	4 F		LA
Roberts, Mark	31 M	Farmer	TN
Emily J.	21 F		TN
James F.	1 M		TX
Smith, Sarrah	14 F		TN
John W.	32 M	(Idiot)	TN
Davis, Jackson J.	36 M	Farmer	SC
Elizabeth	36 F		TN
William J.	17 M		AL
Pleasant J.	15 M		MS
Frances M.	12 M		MS
Martha J.	4 F		TX
Nancy A.	2 F		TX
Cantrell, Catharine	43 F		IL
Carroway, Richard	24 M	Farmer	TN
Lucy A.	18 F		--
James M.	1 M		TX
Hassell, David D.	35 M	Farmer	TN
Julia A.	22 F		AL
Charity	4 F		TX
George W.	2 M		TX
Mary E.	2/12 F		TX
Cone, William	25 M	Farmer	TN
Virginia A.	18 F		TN
Hansford S.	3 M		TX
Susan E.	2 F		TX
Richardson, Jonathan	45 M	Farmer	TN
Christina	44 F		VA
Mary E.	15 F		TN
Orlena	13 F		AR
Colinda	10 F		AR
William	6 M		AR
Grooms, Lewis	32 M	Laborer	TN
Elizabeth	28 F		TN
Elizabeth	8 F		LA
William	6 M		TX
Henry Lewis	4 M		TX
Cynthia A.	7/12 F		TX
Leman, Wilmuth	28 F		TN
Ann E.	10 F		TX
William	8 M		TX
Reneau, Elijah B.	32 M	Farmer	TN
Winne	33 F		AL
John C.	15 M		AL
William G.	14 M		AL
Celia A.	13 F		AL
James M.	17 M		TX
Marshall	3 M		TX
Elijah B.	1 M		TX
Knox, James	45 M	Farmer	TN
Sarah R.	41 F		TN
Elizabeth D.	20 F		TN
(continued)			
Knox, Rachel E.	18 F		TN
Elvira	15 F		TN
Marion A.	11 M		TX
Joseph H.	8 M		TX
Amanda J.	5 F		TX
James	1 M		TX
Moore, Shadrack A.	39 M	Farmer	TN
Elizabeth	38 F		AL
William J.	4 M		MS
Shadrack H.	1 M		TX
Shomburger, George W.	18 M	(Idiot)	MS
Augustus E.	17 M		MS
Frances S.	12 F		MS
Lewis, James	19 M		MS
Canady, Martha	28 F		AL
Duval, John	52 M	Farmer	VA
Nancy	32 F		TN
Susan V.	8 F		MS
Samuel G.	6 M		MS
Wagoner, Daniel	39 M	Farmer	TN
Frances	35 F		VA
John	13 M		MO
Lucy A.	9 F		MO
Mary A.	7 F		MO
David J.	5 M		MO
Elizabeth F.	3 F		TX
Wagoner, Mary	76 F		NC
Sinclair, James	24 M		AR
Capps, Dimon	36 M	Farmer	TN
Thirsey	29 F		??
Anderson	10 M		MS
James	8 M		TX
Thomas	5 M		TX
Mary J.	3 F		TX
Tabitha C.	4/12 F		TX
Hopkins, Levi	30 M	Farmer	TN
Sarah G.	38 F		SC
Carpenter, Eliza	18 F		TN
Mary A.	13 F		TX
Hopkins, Francis M.	8 M		TX
Sophronia P.	6 F		TX
Sarah	1 F		TX
Box, James E.	36 M	Farmer	TN
Mary	31 F		TN
William H.	10 M		TX
John W.	8 M		TX
James K. P.	6 M		TX
Robert D.	4 M		TX
Margaret A.	4/12 F		TX
Wolverton, John	43 M	Farmer	KY
Matilda	31 F		??
Mary J.	19 F		TN
Martha A.	17 F		TN
John N.	15 M		TN
Nancy E.	10 F		TN
William J.	7 M		TN
Thomas B.	5 M		TN
Green C.	3 M		TX
Baker, Andrew	29 M	Farmer	AR
Belinda	26 F		TN
Lucena	4 F		AR
Mary L.	3 F		TX
Mooney, William B.	30 M	Farmer	TN
Nancy	29 F		TN
Eliza J.	7 F		IN
Thomas B.	5 M		IN
John D.	1/12 M		TX
Wolverton, Bird	35 M	Farmer	TN
Anna J.	31 F		GA
James H.	12 M		TN
William B.	10 M		TN
Jackson, Robert J.	27 M		VA
Mary J.	23 F		TN
Margarett T.	4 F		TN

Name	Age	Sex	Occupation	Birthplace
Thompson, James J.	42	M	Farmer	NC
Elizabeth	34	F		TN
Jane M.	20	F		NC
Chancy C.	14	F		KY
Anna	6	F		KY
Martha	3	F		KY
Malinda	1	F		TX
Johnson, Chapman	27	M	Farmer	VA
Frances	25	F		TN
William L.	6	M		TN
Pinkney M.	4	M		TN
Frances	2	F		TN
Dodson, Pinkney	18	M	Farmer	TN
Tucker, Joseph R.	55	M	Farmer	SC
Mary	57	F		NC
Lewis	22	M		TN
Sarah	18	F		TN
Jeptha	17	F		TN
Joseph	16	M		TN
Martha	14	F		TN
Henry H.	12	M		TN
Elizabeth	10	F		TN
Wolverton, William	47	M	Farmer	KY
Pansey	46	F		VA
Susan A.	18	F		TN
Mary M.	16	F		TN
Shelton, Thomas	18	M		TN
Cantrell, Newton T.	11	M		??
Hanks, Joshua B.	31	M	Farmer	TN
Arabel	21	F		TN
Joseph T.	2	M		TX
Hanks, Thomas	64	M	Baptist Min.	VA
Golahun(?), Charles	6	M		AR
Willett, Nathan A.	23	M	School Teacher	TN
Green, Samuel T	28	M	Farmer	AL
Lonnie J.	21	F		TN
Mary A. E.	3	F		TX
Louisa F	2	F		TX
George	2/12	M		TX
Montgomery, James M.	26	M	Brick Mason	KY
Mary E.	19	F		IL
McKenzey, James	23	M		--
Harriett	16	F		IL
Collins, John E.	25	M		TN
Roberson, Larkin	38	M	Farmer	TN
Permenta	36	F		KY
William A.	14	M		TX
Lousa J.	12	F		TX
Elias B.	9	M		TX
Selina	5	F		TX
Joanna	1	F		TX
Nutt, William M.	23	M		AL
Magara	31	F		VA
Mary J. E.	1	F		TX
Smith, David S.	10	M		AR
George H.	7	M		TN
Arabella	5	F		TN
Duncan, Mary	75	F		VA
Susan	15	F		TN
Shipley, John	38	M	Farmer	TN
Mary	37	F		IL
Lewis, William T.	27	M	Farmer	IL
Roberts, Franklin	19	M	Farmer	TN
Martha	22	F		TN
Elizabeth	69	F		TN
Rachel	25	F	(Idiot)	TN
Usury, Lafayette	21	M		MS
Gipson, William M.	49	M	Farmer	NC
Cynthia	42	F		TN
James	19	M		TN
Thomas	14	M		TN
George	12	M		TN
Maria A.	9	F		TX
Sarah J.	2	F		TX
Hannah, John	32	M		TN
Wright, William	43	M	Farmer	NC
Nancy	45	F		GA
Leander H.	17	M		GA
Elizabeth	15	F		GA
Charles	13	M		GA
Frances	12	F		GA
Emeline	8	F		TX
George A.	6	M		TX
Susan	2	F		TX
Smith, James	14	M		TN
Prater, Issabella	16	F		IN
Cynthia	14	F		IN
Orpha	12	F		IN
Mallard, John B.	29	M	Attorney	TN
Susan S.	21	F		TN
Marcus M.	6	F		MS
Mary E.	1	F		TX
Dale, Williamson	28	M	Carpenter	TN
Phillips, William	26	M	Carpenter	TN
Bunda, James T.	--	-	Carpenter	--
McClure, Alexander E.	36	M	Clerk, D.C.	TN
Ann E.	28	F		VA
Robert	10	M		TX
Mary E.	4	F		TX
Georgiana V.	7/12	F		TX
Cravens, Samuel	21	M	Clerk, C.C.	MS
Fields, John W.	--	M	M. E. Min.	--
Winna A.	--	F		--
Cole, Michael F.	--	M	M. E. Min.	--
Dalton, Samuel	31	M	School Teacher	TN
Mary	26	F		KY
William F.	8	M		TX
Sarah M.	6	F		TX
Nancy	3	F		TX
Payne, Poindexter	26	M	Farmer	TN
Martha H.	17	F		TN
Sandis, Samuel	40	M	Pump Maker	KY
Frances	19	F		TN
Cordelia J.	2/12	F		TX
Holmes, John	39	M	Farmer	TN
Sarah	27	F		AL
James F.	9	M		TX
Sarah A.	8	F		TX
Mary L.	4	F		TX
George L.	2	M		TX
Killion, John A.	44	M	Farmer	TN
Nancy	45	F		TN
John N.	18	M		AL
Frances C.	16	F		AL
Jackson, William S.	39	M	Farmer	VA
Ann V.	28	F		VA
Thomas E.	7	M		TN
Greene	5	M		MS
Charles M.	2	M		MS
Blackwell, John	32	M	Farmer	TN
Elizabeth	30	F		GA
Martin T.	10	M		TN
Jonathan M.	9	M		TN
William H.	6	M		TN
Mary R.	4	F		TN
Lewis T.	1	F(M)		TN
Mosley, Robert	36	M	Farmer	GA
Emily	30	F		TN
Lucinda	12	F		TN
James	10	M		TN
Mary	4	F		TN
Dickson	2	M		TX
Billings, John	34	M	Gin Maker	GA
Rutha	28	F		TN
Martha A.	12	F		AL
Joseph D.	11	M		AL
Alabama	6	F		AL
Thomas	3	M		TX
Susan	1	F		TX

(continued)

ANDERSON COUNTY, TEXAS

Lowrie, John B.	29 M	Gin Maker	GA
Willett, Robert W.	26 M	Gin Maker	TN
Hagood, Wiley B.	26 M	Gin Maker	SC
Cartright, Rufus	31 M	Gin Maker	TN
Green, George W.	21 M	Gin Maker	GA
Oneal, James R.	29 M	Gin Maker	TN
Payne, William K.	28 M	Gin Maker	AL
Tedford, Robert J.	24 M	Teamster	TN
Woverton, Thomas	45 M	Gin Maker	KY
Lorana	25 F		GA
John L.	7 M		TN
Robert W.	6 M		TN
James T.	5 M		TN
Mary E.	4/12 F		TX
Tannyhill, Benjamin H.	61 M	Farmer	SC
Elizabeth	47 F		TN
Louisa J.	20 F		TN
William	14 M		TN
Sarah	12 F		AR
Rachel	10 F		AR
Robert P.	8 M		AR
Nancy	5 F		AR
Fleming, Monroe	24 M	Farmer	TN
Elizabeth	22 F		TN
Leonidas	4 M		TN
Martha	2 F	(Navarro Co.)	TX
Guthrie, Alexander	16 M		TN
McCarty, Jas. M.	47 M	Farmer	GA
Nancy	47 F		NC
Nancy	18 F		TN
Jacob	16 M		MS
James	14 M		MS
John	10 M		MS
Joseph J.	4 M	(Anderson Co.)	TX
Glass, Martha	6 F		AR
Richardson, Lewis	41 M	Farmer	TN
Elizabeth	41 F		AR
Mary N.	16 F		TN
Mansey	13 F		AR
Laticia J.	12 F		AR
Martha A.	10 F		AR
Eliza A.	5 F	(Navarro Co.)	TX
Lucy	2 F	(Anderson Co.)	TX
Richardson, Joshua	41 M	Farmer	TN
Elizabeth	42 F		TN
Sarah J.	16 F		TN
William L.	14 M		AR
John	11 M		AR
Rachael	9 F		AR
Mary	8 F		AR
Thomas	6 M		AR
Elizabeth	2 F	(Navarro Co.)	TX
James T.	2/12 M	(Anderson Co.)	TX
Richardson, Thomas	32 M	Farmer	TN
Eliza	23 F		IA
William P.	6 M		AR
Richardson, Mary	65 F		VA
Rebecca	34 F		TN
Jacob, John	42 M	Farmer	NC
Laticia	38 F		TN
William P.	20 M		TN
Mary C. F.	14 F		AR
John M.	6 M		AR
Davis, Oliver	32 M	Farmer	GA
Mary	26 F		TN
Arthur	10 M		AL
Emily	8 F		AL
James	5 M		AL
Savannah	4 F		AL
Miles	3 M		AL
Laticia	2/12 F	(Anderson Co.)	TX
Parks, John	51 M	Farmer	NC
Mary	19 F		TN

(continued)

Parks, William C.	17 M		TN
John	15 M		MS
Bedford	12 M		MS
Martha	10 F		MS
Mosley, Johnathan	77 M	Farmer	GA
Lucy	65 F		VA
Newsom, Nancy	10 F		TN
Mosly, John	38 M	Farmer	GA
Elzira	33 F		TN
Catharine	16 F		TN
Nancy	15 F		TN
Frances	13 F		TN
Caldona	11 F		TN
John W.	8 M		TN
Lucy	7 F		TN
Mary	4 F		TN
Jane	1 F	(Anderson Co.)	TX
Mosley, Absolum	26 M	Farmer	TN
Minerva	22 F		TN
Joseph	5 M		TN
Nancy	3 F	(Red River Co.)	TX
Adria	5/12 M	(Anderson Co.)	TX
Clark, John H.	41M	Black Smith	TN
Nancy	39 F		SC
William C.	17 M	Farmer	TN
Mary A.	15 F		TN
Malinda M.	12 F		TN
George	11 M		TN
Ann C.	7 F		TN
Peters, James W.	32 M	Farmer	VA
Medlina	22 F		TN
Calantha	1 F		TN
Harden, Samuel D.	28 M	Farmer	TN
Harden, Margaret B.	59 F		TN
Petters, Martha	30 F.		VA
Sarah	23 F		TN
Mosley, James	43 M	Farmer	GA
Mary A.	35 F		TN
Lucy	16 F		TN
Harriet	12 F		TN
Larna	19 F		TN
Thomas	2 M		TN
Hollis, John T.	26 M	Farmer	TN
Mary A.	21 F		TN
Margaret F.	3 F		MS
William H.	2 M	(Anderson Co.)	TX
Gallcha, Easther	12 F		AR
Roberson, Mathew N.	22 M	Farmer	TN
Hollis, Harvy	30 M	Farmer	TN
Mary A.	25 F		AL
Bluford	4 M	(Anderson Co.)	TX
Harriet	2 F	(Anderson Co.)	TX
John	3/12 M	(Anderson Co.)	TX
Galleha, Martha	9 F		AR
Wylie, Thomas	23 M	Farmer	AL
Lucy C.	21 F		TN
Elenor J.	1 F	(Anderson Co.)	TX
Richardson, John	24 M	Farmer	TN
Highnote, John H.	25 M	Farmer	IA
Britt Anna	25 F		TN
Lucy C.	2 F	(Navarro Co.)	TX
Mary J.	1 F	(Anderson Co.)	TX
Cantrell, William B.	24 M	Farmer	AL
Lydia	21 F		TN
Elizabeth	2 F	(Anderson Co.)	TX
Cynthia	3/12 F	(Anderson Co.)	TX
Cantrell, Elisha	42 M	Farmer	TN
Elizabeth	41 F		TN
William C.	20 M		TN
Malissa	17 F		TN
Herman	13 M		TN
Louiza J.	7 F		AR

Cantrell, Hazel	28	M	Farmer	TN
Cynthia	23	F		AR
Sarah J.	3	F		AR
William C.	1	M	(Anderson Co.)	TX
Collins, Wilson	32	M	Blacksmith	TN
Mary	29	F		TN
Elizabeth E.	11	F		AL
Edie A.	10	F		TN
William P.	8	M		TN
Nancy	7	F		TN
Jasper	5	M		TN
Julia A.	3	F		TN
Sarah	1	F	(Henderson Co.)	TX
Hodge, Robert	45	M	Farmer	TN
Melissa B.	36	F		MS
Hardin A.	19	M		MS
Robert H.	16	M		MS
Aurelia	12	F		MS
Richard S.	10	M		MS
Margaret H.	8	F		MS
Magnes H.	6	M		MS
Harman H.	4	M		MS
Roena S.	2	F		MS
Henderson, Joseph B.	23	M		SC
Hanks, James S.	41	M	Merchant	TN
Isabella	32	F		NC
Mary E.	11	F		TN
Elijah T.	10	M		TN
Joshua B.	6	M		TN
Gallaha, Rice	15	M		AR
Morrow, Jacob S.	37	M	Farmer	TN
Louisa A.	26	F		AL
Mary J.	10	M(F)	(Houston Co.)	TX
Margaret A.	8	F	(Houston Co.)	TX
Celista P.	4	F	(Anderson Co.)	TX
Vaughn, Murphy	34	M	Farmer	AL
Louisa	28	F		TN
Mary C.	9	F		MS
Jane B.	8	F		MS
James B.	6	M		MS
Samuel H.	1	M	(Anderson Co.)	TX
Duke, George W.	50	M	Farmer	NC
Darcus	39	F		TN
James C.	24	M		TN
William W.	22	M		TN
Mary W.	16	F		AL
Melissa A.	14	F		AL
George M.	10	M		MO
Albert P.	8	M	(Houston Co.)	TX
Georgian	1	F	(Anderson Co.)	TX
Smith, Samuel	22	M		TN
Gaston, Robert	38	M	Farmer	TN
Lettitia E.	30	F		SC
George A.	12	M		AL
William H.	9	M		AL
Robert H.	7	M		MS
Priscilla	5	F		MS
John H.	2	M		MS
Pruitt, Ira	35	M	Farmer	SC
Mahala A.	18	F		TN
Montgomery, Samuel A.	16	M		MS
Carpenter, George W.	39	M	Farmer	TN
Julia A.	25	F		TN
Nancy J.	4	F		TN
Sarah E.	2	F		TN
John B.	1/12	M	(Anderson Co.)	TX
Carpenter, George	79	M		VA
Jane	72	F		VA
Hopkins, William	38	M	Farmer	SC
Carolina	32	F		SC
Robert A.	14	M		TN
Mary J.	11	F		TN
Margaret E.	6	F		TN
(continued)				
Hopkins, Susan C.	3	F	(Anderson Co.)	TX
William T.	6/12	M	(Anderson Co.)	TX
Clark, Samuel	25	M	Farmer	TN
Mary	21			TN
Payne, Thomas	62	M	Farmer	TN
Esther	38	F		TN
Thomas J.	22	M		AL
John H.	16	M	(San Augustine)	TX
Andrew J.	14	M	(San Augustine)	TX
Sarah	7	F	(San Augustine)	TX
Sam H.	5	M	(San Augustine)	TX
Pinah J.	4	F	(Anderson Co.)	TX
Isaac R.	1	M	(Anderson Co.)	TX
Marks, Charles F.	31	M	Carpenter	ENG
Mary	20	F		TN
Susan	1/12	F	(Anderson Co.)	TX
Garrett, Thomas	41	M	Farmer	TN
Sinia	34	F		TN
Catherine	3	F	(Anderson Co.)	TX
James	1	M	(Anderson Co.)	TX
Cornelison, Eliza	16	F		AR
Jesse	14	M		AR
Miles	10	M		AR
Benjamin	6	M		AR
Garret, Mary	15	F		TN
Jasper	9	M	(Houston Co.)	TX
Fulton, Lorensa D.	29	F	Farmer	AL
Susan F.	18	F		MS
Fulton, Nancy J.	51	F		TN
Nancy M.	27	F		AL
Lowery, Alfred P.	26	M	Black Smith	TN
Mary	25	F		NC
Robert B.	5	M		TN
Alexander	4	M	(Rusk Co.)	TX
Amanda J.	2	F	(Rusk Co.)	TX
Alfred	4/12	M	(Anderson Co.)	TX
Lester, William S.	37	M	Farmer	GA
Emily E.	19	F		TN
Francina	2/12	F	(Anderson Co.)	TX
Gallaha, John C.	10	M		AR
Fitzgerald, William A.	30	M	Farmer	TN
Joycy H.	24	F		TN
James C.	8	M	(Shelby Co.)	TX
John C.	6	M	(San Augustine)	TX
Nancy K.	4	F	(Anderson Co.)	TX
William J.	1	M	(Anderson Co.)	TX
Condry, Stephen P.	31	M	Farmer	TN
Mary	21	F		VA
William M.	1	M	(Anderson Co.)	TX
Holt, William	32	M	Farmer	AL
Mary	32	F		TN
Willis	7	M		MS
Richard	5	M		MS
Thomas	3	M	(Anderson Co.)	TX
James	1	M	(Anderson Co.)	TX
Fitzgerald, Michael R.	24	M	Farmer	TN
Matilda	28	F		TN
Clayton	3	M	(San Augustine)	TX
William A.	1	F(?)	(Harrison)	TX
Linsy, Thomas H.	11	M	(Sabine Co.)	TX
Amanda	10	F	(Harrison)	TX
Owen H.	8	M	(San Augustine)	TX
Fitzgerald, George W.	37	M	Farmer	TN
Christian	34	F		NC
Nancy	15	F		TN
Nelson	13	M		TN
John	12	M		TN
Christopher	10	M		TN
Alexander	8	M		TN
Jane	6	F		TN
James	5	M		TN
George	2	M		TN
Fitzgerald, Christopher	31	M		TN

ANDERSON COUNTY, TEXAS

Name	Age	Sex	Occupation / County	State
Grey, William	42	M	Farmer	NC
Sarah	38	F		TN
Michael	20	M		IL
Sarah A.	11	F		IL
John	6	M		IL
Paulina	1	F	(Anderson Co.)	TX
Malvina	1	F	(Anderson Co.)	TX
Woodson D.	15	M		IL
Sinclair, John	42	M		MO
McKenzie, Elizabeth	47	F		KY
Francis M.	17	M		TN
Carter T.	11	M	(Houston Co.)	TX
Larkin G.	9	M	(Houston Co.)	TX
Merchison, John	33	M		SC
Paulina H.	24	F		AL
Carter P.	3	M	(Anderson Co.)	TX
Amanda E.	1	F	(Anderson Co.)	TX
Gardiner, James W.	30	M	Farmer	KY
Harris, William R.	27	M		--
Gardiner, Elmira W.	22	F		AL
Harris, America E.	14	F	(Shelby Co.)	TX
Gwinn, William W.	25	M	Farmer	TN
Louisa M.	21	F		TN
Susan M.	1	F	(Anderson Co.)	TX
Gibson, Samuel	32	M		TN
Catharine	27	F		AL
James	2	M	(Anderson Co.)	TX
Reed, Richmond C.	30	M	Farmer	AL
Leonora	33	F		TN
James B.	10	M		MS
Eliza J.	8	F		MS
Margarett	6	F		MS
Caliafornia	1	F	(Anderson Co.)	TX
Meredith, William T.	31	M		TN
Mildred	25	F		MS
Indiana	5	F		MS
Mississippi	1	F	(Anderson Co.)	TX
Meredith, Washington	37	M	Farmer	TN
Louisa	30	F		AL
Margaret	10	F		MS
George B.	8	M		MS
Martha	4	F	(Henderson Co.)	TX
Mary	4	F	(Henderson Co.)	TX
Robert N.	1	M	(Anderson Co.)	TX
Reed, Ann	60	F		KY
Lunsden, Elijah	49	M		GA
Sutton, Jacob	28	M	Farmer	TN
Rhoda H.	27	F		TN
William S.	4	M		TN
Leciel J. N.	2	M		TN
Montgomery, Robert C.	28	M	Farmer	TN
Martha C.	20	F		TN
Sarah E.	5	F		MS
Marcus	1	M	(Anderson Co.)	TX
Earnest, Alfred B.	19	M		AL
Amanda S.	19	F		TN
Rushing, William R.	33	M	Farmer	--
Rebecca	39	F		TN
Martha G. J.	12	F		AL
Elizabeth	7	F		MS
William A.	4	M		TX
Vannoy, John	48	M	Farmer	NC
Tabitha	40	F		SC
Mary H.	17	F		TN
John H.	13	M		TN
Joel	25	M		TN
Green, Ira N.	39	M	Farmer	VA
Rebecca A.	36	F		VA
William L.	6	M		TN
Lewis F.	1	M	(Anderson Co.)	TX
Hodges	-	M		--

Name	Age	Sex	Occupation / County	State
Bruce, Hannah E.	22	F		VA
Frederick J.	1	M		TN
Jackson, Temperance	58	F		VA
Shelton, George A.	34	M	Farmer	TN
Mary	29	F		TN
Nancy A.	12	F		TN
Martha J.	10	F		TN
Mary E.	8	F		TN
Eliza M.	6	F		TN
Lucretia E.	2	F	(Anderson Co.)	TX
Caldwell, Wylie	43	M	Farmer	GA
Kizzie	39	F		TN
William T.	22	M		TN
Eliza J.	20	F		TN
Cynthia C.	16	F		TN
Sarah F.	14	F	(Angelina Co.)	TX
Wylie	8	M	(Angelina Co.)	TX
Debilla B.	6	F	(Angelina Co.)	TX
James J.	1	M	(Angelina Co.)	TX
Anderson, John C.	21	M	Farmer	MS
Mary A.	18	F		TN
Margaret J.	2	F	(Angelina Co.)	TX
Rushing, James A.	30	M	Farmer	TN
Cornelia	25	F		NC
William T.	7	M		AL
Elvy A. M.	4	F		MS
John P.	2	M	(Anderson Co.)	TX
Berry, Thomas	30	M	Farmer	AL
Allen	27	F		TN
Daniel	10	M	(Houston Co.)	TX
Dick	2/12	M	(Anderson Co.)	TX
Robertson, William R.	27	M		MO
Mary A.	25	F		GA
Elizabeth M.	2	F	(Leon Co.)	TX
Sarah J.	5/12	F	(Anderson Co.)	TX
Snow, Sarah	65	F		SC
Eliza	16	F		TN
George W.	14	M		TN
Rucker, Ransom	60	M	Farmer	SC
Calvin	31	M		TN
Tabitha A.	26	F		KY
Amanda	3	F	(Anderson Co.)	TX
Malissa	1	F	(Anderson Co.)	TX
Roberts, David	46	M	Farmer	TN
Eliza J.	26	F		PA
William E.	5	M	(Houston Co.)	TX
John A.	2	M	(Anderson Co.)	TX
Martin, James M.	27	M	Farmer	AL
Martha M.	27	F		TN
Frances	2	F	(Anderson Co.)	TX
Metcalf, Sarah T.	8	F		TN
Cantrell, James	39	M	Farmer	TN
John	17	M		TN
Elizabeth	15	F		TN
Thederick	12	M		TN
Stephen J.	11	M	(Sabine Co.)	TX
Mary J.	7	F	(Augustine Co.)	TX
Nancy E.	6	F	(Augustine Co.)	TX
Easter A.	3	F	(Anderson Co.)	TX
Cantrell, Nancy	39	F		TN
Vaughn, Melkizah D.	30	M	Farmer	MS
Elizabeth	21	F		TN
William M.	5	M	(Houston Co.)	TX
Amanda M.	3	F	(Anderson Co.)	TX
Scarberry, Martha	19	F		AL
Miller, John D.	44	M	Farmer	TN
Eliza A.	30	F		TN
John T.	8	M	(Houston Co.)	TX
Amanda	6	F	(Houston Co.)	TX
Seldon J.	3	M	(Anderson Co.)	TX
Roach, Robert	39	M	Farmer	TN
Martha	27	F		AR

(continued)

ANDERSON COUNTY, TEXAS

Name	Age	Sex	Occupation / Remarks	Birthplace
Roach, Benjamin F.	6	M		AR
Mary M.	4	F		AR
Robert C.	2	M	(Anderson Co.)	TX
Martha J.	4/12	F	(Anderson Co.)	TX
Miller, William T.	41	M	Farmer	TN
Malinda J.	30	F		TN
Robert C.	20	M		AL
Mary F.	16	F		AL
William T.	12	M		AL
Ann A.	7	F	(Houston Co.)	TX
Laticia J.	5	F	(Houston Co.)	TX
Warden, Louisa L.	37	F		GA
Franklin A.	17	M		TN
Mary A.	13	F		TN
Pamelia S.	12	F		TN
George F.	9	M	(Houston Co.)	TX
Eliza A.	6	F	(Houston Co.)	TX
Elizabeth E.	4	F	(Anderson Co.)	TX
Webb, William	26	M		TN
Martha	21	F		AL
Isabella	4	F		MS
Lemuel	2	M		MS
Martin, John S.	35	M	Farmer	VA
Lucinda C.	25	F		TN
Mary A.	7	F	(Houston Co.)	TX
Lucinda	3	F	(Anderson Co.)	TX
Elizabeth	1	F	(Anderson Co.)	TX
Murry, Benjamin	50	M		NC
Bradshaw, William	54	M	Farmer	VA
Malinda	49	F		TN
Pleasant W.	23	M		AL
Martha	19	F		AL
Nancy A.	15	F		AL
Margaret C.	12	F		AL
King, Littleberry	22	M		TN
Walker, Robert	33	M	Farmer	VA
Melvina	18	F		TN
Thomas	4/12	M	(Anderson Co.)	TX
Berry, Morgan	45	M	Farmer	NC
Elizabeth	33	F		TN
John	18	M		AL
Martin	15	M		AL
Mary	14	F		AL
Emily	12	F		AL
Pamelia	10	F	(San Augustine)	TX
Sarah	8	F	(San Augustine)	TX
Rosalee	6	F	(San Augustine)	TX
Nancy	5	F	(Houston Co.)	TX
William	3	M	(Anderson Co.)	TX
Dartha	1	F	(Anderson Co.)	TX
Reynolds, John	23	M		TN
Thomas, Penelope	39	F		TN
Andrew C.	19	M		TN
James M.	16	M		MS
Nancy J.	14	F		MS
Pleasant N.	12	M		MS
Jennet A.	10	F		MS
Sarah C.	8	F		MS
Adams, Briton H.	35	M	Farmer	IA
Emily C.	27	F		TN
Sydney N.	8	M	(Houston Co.)	TX
John W.	5	M	(Houston Co.)	TX
Somerville	3	M	(Anderson Co.)	TX
Blair, Ryly J.	19	M		TN
Adams, Dorothea	46	F		NC
Newton C.	21	M		TN
William C.	19	M		TN
Dorothea	17	F		TN
Benjamin F.	15	M		TN
Missouri E.	11	F	(Houston Co.)	TX
Allen, John	46	M	Farmer	GA
Margaret	47	F		TN

(continued)

Name	Age	Sex	Occupation / Remarks	Birthplace
Hatton, Newton J.	18	M		TN
James M.	15	M		TN
William F.	13	M		MS
Jefferson L.	10	M	(Houston Co.)	TX
Eliza J.	7	F	(Houston Co.)	TX
Allen, Francis M.	1	M	(Anderson Co.)	TX
John E.	20	M		AL
Ethon	18	M		AL
Humphrey W.	15	M		AL
Horton, Sam W.	40	M	Farmer	NC
Isabell	36	F		TN
Susan E.	16	F		MS
Nancy R.	15	F		MS
William W.	13	M		MS
Henry P.	11	M	(San Augustine)	TX
John C.	9	M	(San Augustine)	TX
Lucinda A.	7	F	(San Augustine)	TX
Susan F.	6	F	(San Augustine)	TX
Sandy A.	2	M	(Nacagodaches)	TX
Allen, Jesse E.	24	M		AL
Stewart, William	64	M	Farmer	NC
Martha	27	F		TN
Isaah	5	F(M)		TN
Martha J.	5	F		TN
Leathy A.	3	F		TN
Caleb	2	F(M)	(Anderson Co.)	TX
Lovett, Enoch	39	M	Farmer	TN
Elizabeth	29	F		TN
Wesley	19	M		MS
Melchesadick	12	M		MS
Lidea	9	F		MS
William T.	2	M		AR
Rice, James	50	M	Farmer	TN
Jane	45	F		SC
Albert T.	25	M		AL
Gormery, Elizabeth	23	F		AL
Rice, Jonathan	20	M		AL
Nancy	18	F		AL
Emily	15	F		AL
Martha	12	F		MS
Eliza	8	F	(Houston Co.)	TX
Caledonia	5	F	(Houston Co.)	TX
Gormery, Elmira	6	F	(Houston Co.)	TX
Melvina	6	F	(Houston Co.)	TX
Lewis, Robert B.	43	M	Farmer	VA
William D.	15	M		AL
Mary E.	12	F		TN
Robert M.	11	M		TN
Ann B.	8	F	(Houston Co.)	TX
Martha F.	6	F	(Houston Co.)	TX
Alice A.	5	F	(Houston Co.)	TX
James B.	2	M	(Houston Co.)	TX
McCullough, Alexander	38	M	Farmer	TN
Lucretia	39	F		TN
James H.	10	M		TN
Eliza	5	F		TN
Nancy P.	3	F		TN
Robert F.	5/12	M	(Anderson Co.)	TX
Stewart, William M.	26	M	Farmer	AL
Melissa	25	F		TN
Charles	7	M		TN
John G.	5	M		AL
Sarah	2	F	(Anderson Co.)	TX
Henry	1/12	M	(Anderson Co.)	TX
Jones, Augustus A. K. W.	36(6)	M	Mechanic	CT
Catherine	25	F		AL
Ann E.	10	F		AL
Martha F.	7	F		AL
Wood, (illegible)	39	M		AL
Lowe, Emmett L.	30	M		TN
Hemby, John	30	M	Farmer	TN
Margaret C.	24	F		TN
Adams, William D. F.	23	M	Farmer	TN
Sarah A	17	F		LA
Maden, Sarah	56	F		SC

(continued)

ANDERSON COUNTY, TEXAS

Maden, Elizabeth A. 20 F LA
Cynthia A. 15 F LA

Terry, Jessee 50 M Farmer TN
Elizabeth 43 F TN
Emily 22 F AL
James W. 21 M AL
Masel L. 18 M AL
Isaac L. 12 M (San Augustine Co) TX
Elizabeth 14 F (San Augustine Co) TX
Palmira 10 F (San Augustine Co) TX
Sarah J. 3 F (Anderson Co.) TX

Ross, James C. 25 M Farmer MS
Isabella 23 F TN
Mary 3 F MS
Isabella 1 F MS

Shipman, Calvin S. 37 M Farmer TN
Sarah 29 F LA
Julia A. 10 F MO
Mary 8 F (Houston Co.) TX
Martha 2 F (Anderson Co.) TX
Kilgore, William 36 M TN

Crawford, Joseph 60 M Farmer SC
Mary 57 F NC
John E. 20 M TN
Thomas H. 16 M TN
George W. 14 M TN
Narcissa 12 F TN
Robert 7 M (Houston Co.) TX

Crawford, James M. 25 Farmer NC
Nicie Ann 21 F TN
Green F. 1 M (Anderson Co.) TX
James W. 2/12 M (Anderson Co.) TX

Ferguson, William M. 22 M Farmer AL
Nancy 18 F TN
Mary E. 2/12 F (Anderson Co.) TX

Self, Ervin 39 M Farmer AL
Malinda 33 F TN
James E. 13 M IL
Tabitha E. 11 F IL
George W. 9 M AR
Martha E. 7 F AR
Mariah E. 3 F AR
Levi W. 4/12 M (Anderson Co.) TX

Parks, George 53 M Farmer NC
Sarah 50 F TN
Robert 20 M TN
Benjamin 18 M IL
George W. 13 M IL
Joseph 9 M IL
Thomas J. 7 M IL
Sarah 11 F IL
Neal, Mariah 39 F TN
William 8 M IL
James 5 M IL
Nancy 14 F IL

Bateman, John 48 M Farmer TN
Leah 44 F NC
John P. 18 M IL
Abram 14 M IL
Mary 9 F MO
Emily 8 F MO

Douthet, James 38 M TN
Mary 32 F TN
Celey A. 12 F (Nacogdoches Co.) TX
James C. 9 M (Houston Co.) TX
Eveline 6 F (Houston Co.) TX
John R. 4 M (Anderson Co.) TX
Sarah 1 F (Anderson Co.) TX

Starr, John 52 M Farmer NC
Susannah 42 F TN
Daniel P. 18 M IL
Perry 13 M IL
(continued)

Starr, Sarah E. 10 F IL
Elsey 8 F IL
James N. 3 M IL

Parlmer, John E. 20 M Farmer MO
Sarah A. 18 F IL
Elizabeth E. 10/12 F (Anderson Co.) TX
Conniway, James 61 M SC
Mary 48 F TN
Greenberry 22 M TN
James 20 M MS
Lewellen 18 M MS
Franklin 15 M MS
Martha 13 F MS
Mary 12 F MS
Amanda M. 10 F MS
Susan 7 F MS
Hannah, James 32 M TN

ANGELINA COUNTY, TEXAS

Ewing, J. L. 56 M Farmer GA
Betsey 58 F KY
John 22 M None TN
James 20 M TN
McKnight, Joseph H. 23 M Farmer TN
Mary 18 F TN

Goodwin, George 32 M Farmer AL
Elizabeth 32 F TN
Martha 11 F TX
William 10 M TX
Tabitha 8 F FL
Sarah 6 F FL
Henry 5 M FL
Mary 4 F FL
Leanor 2 F FL
(not named) 11/12 M LA

McElroy, George R. 44 M Farmer GA
Martha 26 F TN
William 17 M GA
Francis 12 M GA
Catharine 8 F GA
John 6 M AR
Roger 3 M TX
Fany 1 F TX
Reynolds, Mary 13 F AR
Causter, Deloraus 22 M Laborer MEX

Cheatham, Archibald 54 M Farmer VA
Mary 55 F VA
Francis 19 M None TN
Edmund 17 M None TN

Walker, Thomas J. 22 M None MS
Elizabeth A. 25 F TN
Nancy A. 17 F MS
Polly 10 F MS

Hall, Henry 29 M Farmer TN
Minerva 29 F TN
Elizabeth A. 5 F TN
William F. 2 M TX
Martha 4/12 F TX

Griphian, Wilson 44 M Farmer TN
Elizabeth 42 F NC
Newton 18 M None TN
Jasper 17 M None TN
Mary 14 F TN
Jacob 10 M LA
Unice 6 F TX
Ann 4 F TX
(not named) 2/12 F TX

Crawford, Thomas 44 M Farmer TN
Martha 36 F TN
Jane 16 F MS
William 14 M TN
Mary 11 F TX
Narcissa 10 F TX
Amanda 8 F TX
Matilda 6 F TX
(continued)

ANGELINE COUNTY, TEXAS

Name	Age	Sex	Occupation	Birthplace
Crawford, Rebecca	4	F		TX
Thomas	2	M		TX
Jesse	1 1/12	M		TX
Paschal, John	25	M		TN
Rachael	21	F		IL
Brown, William	22	M	Laborer	NY
Stephens, Thomas	9	M		TX
Alldridge, Joel H.	29	M	Farmer	TN
Frances	20	F		LA
Jeremiah	10/12	M		TX
Evans, John	37	M	Carpenter	MS
Mary H.	26	F		TN
John A.	7	M		TX
William A.	4	M		TX
Joel H.	2	M		TX
Sarah L.	6	F		TX
Mary A.	7/12	F		TX
Gann, Nathan W.	29	M	Black Smith	TN
Aletha L.	25	F		MS
James D.	7	M		TX
Nathan A.	5	M		TX
Sarah L.	2	F		TX
Wesley D.	17	M	Laborer	TN
White, James L.	22	M	Laborer	MS
Massingill, Henry	32	M	Farmer	TN
Frances	31	F		NC
Martha	12	F		TX
Shedrick	7	M		TX
Jemima	5	F		TX
Sally	3	F		TX
William	1	M		TX
Vincent, Archibald	58	M	Farmer	NC
Jane	61	F		NC
John	27	M	None	TN
Rowin, Milton	30	M	Farmer	OH
Mary	35	F		TN
Goodwin, Francis M.	17	M	None	TN
Isaac	15	M		TX
John H.	10	M		TX
Wilson	13	M		LA
Moore	9	M		TX
Sarah J.	6	F		TX
Martha A.	4	F		TX
Hiram	6/12	M		TX
James, John	46	M	Farmer	TN
Barbary	46	F		SC
Culbert	12	M	Stock Keeper	AL
Weakes, Zedic	25	M	Farmer	NC
Lucinda	36	F		TN
James	14	M		MS
William A.	10	M		MS
Anderson	9	M		LA
Francis	7	M		AR
Lavina	3	F		MS
Ritter, John	41	M	Carpenter	NC
Elender	36	F		TN
Amanda C.	8	F		IN
Lewis J.	7	M		TX
Levi M.	5	M		TX
Susan A.	3	F		TX
Elmira C.	6/12	F		TX
Gann, Solomon	52	M	Stock Keeper	TN
Malinda	38	F		TN
Mary P.	17	F		TN
Nathan	13	M		TN
Isaac	12	M		TX
Matilda	10	F		TX
John	8	M		TX
Elizabeth	6	F		TX
Samuel	6/12	M		TX

Name	Age	Sex	Occupation	Birthplace
Massingill, Isaac	27	M	Farmer	TN
Elizabeth	25	F		TN
Joshua G.	5	M		TX
Page M.	2	M		TX
Mary E.	1/12	F		TX
Brown, Sarah	40	F		NC
Baty, Newton	21	M	Farmer	TN
Brown, William	4	M		TX
Thaddeus S.	1	M		TX
Massingill, Willie	20	M	Farmer	TN
Louisa A.	17	F		TX
Mary	11/12	F		TX
Massingill, John	32	M	Farmer	TN
Mary Ann	29	F		TN
George	13	M		TN
Sarriah	9	F		TX
William	7	M		TX
Tennessee	4	F		TX
Mary Ann	2	F		TX
Cheatham, William	24	M	Farmer	TN
Mary	26	F		TN
Mary	2	F		TN
William	3/12	M		TX
Massingill, George	45	M	Farmer	TN
Mary	45	F		TN
Rutha	17	F		TN
Vincent, Mary	19	F		TN
Lucinda	14	F		TX
George	2	M		TX
Clover, John	26	M	Farmer	AR
Susan	24	F		TN
Polly	5	F		TX
Sally	2	F		TX
Evans, Elisha	35	M	Carpenter	TX
Rutha	24	F		TN
William B.	7	M		TX
Sarah	6	F		TX
Rutha A.	4	F		TX
Elisha	3/12	M		TX
Mantieth, Daniel	31	M	Farmer	TN
Mary A.	24	F		TN
John A.	6	M		TX
Daniel	5	M		TX
Mary	3	F		TX
Mathew	2	M		TX
Gann, John D.	30	M	D. C. Clerk	TN
Malinda	18	F		AL
Sarah E.	2	F		TX
Malinda J.	11/12	F		TX
Finley, Ephraim	37	M	Farmer	SC
Martha	25	F		TN
William	11	M		LA
Lafayette	8	M		TX
Mary Ann	6	F		TX
Benjamin	4	M		TX
Andrew	1	M		TX
Russell, Phillip	25	M	Farmer	TN
Martha	27	F		GA
Thadius	11	M		MS
Cordelia	8	F		AR
Louisa	6	F		AR
Bruce, Jesse	40	M	Farmer	SC
Rachael	30	F		GA
James L.	13	M		AL
Jesse M.	11	M		AL
George N.	8	M		AL
Jasper Y.	6	M		AL
Morehead, Lucinda	22	F		AL
George W.	3	M		MS
Hardee, James T.	20	M	Farmer	AL
Anderson, William	51	M	Farmer	GA
Askins, Calvin	25	M	Methodist Min.	TN
Martha C.	24	F		TN

ANGELINE COUNTY, TEXAS

Name	Age	Sex	Occupation	Birthplace
Moony, Thomas	25	M	Farmer	TN
Norna	18	F		TN
William H.	1	M		TX
Hobb, Elizabeth	26	F		TN
Jones, John F.	30	M	Farmer	AL
Sarah A.	18	F		TN
James P.	9	M		TX
John H.	5	M		TX
William A.	2	M		TX
Holt, Benjamin	53	M	Farmer	NC
Elizabeth	56	F		NC
Elizabeth	22	F		TN
Sarah	13	F		MS
Anderson, Nancy	30	F		TN
Jourdon	14	M		MS
Nearen, John	23	M	Boatsman	TN
Davis, Ashburn	44	M	Black Smith	NC
Hetta	41	F		TN
George A.	20	M	Farmer	TN
Levi	16	M		TN
William	13	M		TN
Nancy A.	12	F		MS
John	7	M		TX
Susana	4	F		TX
Francis B.	6/12	M		TX
Brown, Francis	24	M	Store Clerk	AL
Davis, Martha	20	F		AL
Fulcher, Joshua	36	M	None	AR
Rebecca D.	36	F		TN
Jane J.	15	F		TX
John S.	13	M		TX
James B.	12	M		TX
Radford B.	10	M		TX
William J.	8	M		TX
Sarah A.	6	F		TX
Nancy M.	4	F		TX
Camaluke(?)	1	F		TX
Long, W. G.	33	M	Co. Surveyor	OH
Nancy	35	F		TN
Margaret	7	F		TX
Miami	5	F		TX
Elmira	3	F		TX
Hariet	2	F		TX
Thomason, T. A.	36	M		KY
Duncan G.	15	M	Farmer	TN
Frances H.	14	F		AL
Gardenshire, William	30	M	Farmer	TN
Nancy A.	28	F		TN
Lewis	3	M		TX
Martha A.	6/12	F		TX
McClure, F.	29	M	Farmer	TN
Sibbe A.	22	F		MS
Harriet E.	3	F		TX
Susana M.	2	F		TX
Donigan, Isaac	58	M	Cooper	KY
Roads, T. A.	43	M	Farmer	GA
Elizabeth	43	F		VA
James	18	M	None	TN
Susana	16	F		TN
Mary J.	14	F		TX
Elizabeth	13	F		TX
Thomas	9	M		TX
Sarah	6	F		TX
Isaac	5	M		TX
William	3	M		TX
Elender	1	F		TX
Robinson, Thomas J.	13	M		LA
James	11	M		LA
Lagens, Carter	30	M	Stock Keeper	TN
Lucinda	26	F		TN
William	8	M		TX
Samuel	7	M		TX

(continued)

Name	Age	Sex	Occupation	Birthplace
Lagens, Robert	6	M		TX
John	4	M		TX
Oto	1	M		TX
Gilliam, Eli	63	M	Stock Keeper	TN
James	30	M	Stock Keeper	TN
John	27	M	Stock Keeper	TN
Rebecca	21	F		TN
Eli	2/12	M		TX
Odle, John	15	M	Stock Keeper	TX
Mary	16	F		TX
Ciciah	14	F		TX
Stovall, John N.	27	M	Farmer	KY
Elizabeth	22	F		TN
Mary	4	F		TX
Colwell, Mary	65	F		??
George	20	M	Farmer	TN
Stanly, S. J.	37	M	Farmer	MS
Mary	31	F		AR
James	9	M		TX
Eliza	8	F		TX
William	6	M		TX
Stephen	4	M		TX
Sariah	2	F		TX
Tennessee	3/12	F		TX
Smith, William	--	-		--
Edwards, E.	31	M	Farmer	NC
Martha	20	F		TN
Elizabeth	12	F		AR
Sariah	4	F		TX
James	1	M		TX
Latham, James	32	M	Farmer	LA
Margaret	33	F		TN
Martha	13	F		LA
Sarah	12	F		LA
James	9	M		LA
Lewis	8	M		LA
Elizabeth	5	F		TX
John	1	M		TX
Step, Solomon	34	M	Farmer	TN
Jane	67	F		VA
Crocket	11	M		TN
Sarah	8	F		TX
Martha	9/12	F		TX
Hill, Francis	40	M	Farmer	VA
Sarah	36	F		TN
Frances	17	F		TN
Martha	13	F		TN
Lucy	12	F		TX
James	10	M		TX
Benjamin	6	M		TX
Nathan	3	M		TX
California	1	F		TX
Hill, Henry	73	M	None	VA
James	28	M	Farmer	TN
Needham, Enoch	52	M	Farmer	NC
Johnson, Susan	25	F		TN
Polly	6	F		TX
Enoch	2	M		TX
Gillon, Samuel	41	M	Farmer	TN
Ally	34	F		TN
Samuel	12	M		TX
James	9	M		TX
Martha	6	F		TX
Mary	3	F		TX
William	1	M		TX
Step, J. D.	38	M	Farmer	TN
Mary	30	F		AL
Martha C.	10	F		TX
Elisha	8	M		TX
Mary M.	6	F		TX
Lucy	4	F		TX
John	2	M		TX
Franklin	3/12	M		TX

ANGELINE COUNTY, TEXAS

Name	Age	Sex	Occupation	Birthplace
Needham, Samuel	47	M	Farmer	NC
Peggy	45	F		TN
Lewis, Elizabeth	10	F		IN
Kellsy, Mary A.	6	F		TX
William	8	M		TX
Hankes, W. W.	36	M	Farmer	TN
DeVella	36	F		TN
Franklin	11	M		TX
Martha	8	F		TX
(not named)	1	F		TX
Hankes, B. ?.	45	M	Merchant	TN
Cochran, J. B.	46	M	Farmer	NC
Sarah	46	F		NC
Abraham	21	M	Farmer	NC
Elias	18	M	Farmer	NC
Catharine	16	F		TN
Sarah	12	F		TN
Jane	7	F		MS
Calvin	6	M		MS
Joshua	5	M		MS
Alexander, W. B.	45	M	Farmer	TN
Susan	42	F		TN
James	17	M	Farmer	TN
Sarah	11	F		TN
Susan	9	F		TN
John	7	M		TN
Burkes, S. D.	38	M	Farmer	TN
Unity	23	F		GA
William	10	M		AR
Rody	5	F		AR
Napoleon	2	M		TX
Marguil(?)	1	M		TX
Nash, J. M.	25	M	Teacher	MS
Beshears, J.	39	M	Farmer	TN
Mary M.	37	F		TN
Malinda	17	F		AR
John	15	M		AR
Lucinda	12	F		AR
Walker	13	M		AR
Rody	8	F		AR
Fetna	4	F		AR
Robert	3	M		TX
Bery	10	M		AR
Nash, Elvira	17	F		AR
Shoftner, S. L.	26	M	Farmer	TN
Elzira	23	F		TN
Elvira	6	F		TX
Evaline	2	F		TX
Calidonia	7/12	F		TX
Hearn, Joseph	35	M	Farmer	GA
Nancy	20	F		TN
Thomas	4	M		TX
Susan	7/12	F		TX
Barnes, David	35	M	Farmer	GA
Sinia	33	F		TN
John	12	M		TX
Green	7	M		TX
William	4	M		TX
McCralley, Mrs. Margaret	36	F		TN
James	20	M		AL
Caroline	16	F		TN
Julian	12	F		TX
William	9	M		TX
John	6	M		TX
George	4	M		TX
Chumbley, A.	44	M	Stock Keeper	AR
Harriet	45	F		TN
Martha	18	F		TX
Thomas	16	M		TX
John	14	M		TX
Alexander	9	M		TX
Richardson, John	24	M	Farmer	SC

(continued)

Name	Age	Sex	Occupation	Birthplace
Richardson, Casandra	20	F		TN
Mary	1	F		TX
Richardson, H. S.	21	M	Farmer	SC
Mary	21	F		TN
James	7/12	M		TX

AUSTIN COUNTY, TEXAS

Name	Age	Sex	Occupation	Birthplace
McNutt, Robert	55	M	Farmer	TN
Mary	54	F		NC
Catharine	19	F		TN
Tabitha	15	F		TX
Hamilton	13	M		TX
Sanders, Robert	14	M		TX
George	11	M		TX
Nancy	8	F		TX
Levy, Parker	30	M	Farmer	TN
Mary	20	F		TN
Josiah	2	M		TX
McNutt, Robert B.	24	M	Farmer	TN
Elizabeth	26	F		TN
Sarah	1/12	F		TX
German, Augusta	21	M	Laborer	GER
Bush, W. ?.	31	M	Farmer	TN
Zillah	30	F		KY
Eudorah	9	F		TN
Catharine	7	F		KY
Cloud, James	38	M	Farmer	GA
Jane	38	F		GA
Francis, Joseph	31	M	Farmer	TN
Mary	20	F		AL
George	11	M		TX
Susan	4	F		MO
Alfred, Mary	62	F		VA
Meek, James	31	M	Farmer	TN
Harriet	36	F		AL
Christopher	11	M		TX
Francis, Miller	40	M	Farmer	TN
Nancy	30	F		OH
Margarette	10	F		TX
James	6	M		TX
Lidia Ann	4	F		TX
Francis, Elizabeth	65	F		VA
Elizabeth F., Jun.	22	F		TN
McKey, Mary	21	F		LA
Ahrent, John	14	M		GER
Washam, Lucinda	45	F		TN
John	23	M	Laborer	MO
Woodson	18	M	Laborer	MO
Thomas	15	M	Laborer	MO
William	13	M		MO
Lafayette	8	M		MO
Francis, James	45	M	County Clerk	TN
Claracy	42	F		TN
Woodson	18	M	Laborer	MO
Jonathan	14	M		MO
William	11	M		MO
James	6	M		MO
Narcissa	17	F		MO
Missouri	9	F		MO
America	7	F		MO
Jane	8/12	F		TX
Alexander, Robert	39	M	Methodist Preacher	TN
Eliza P.	29	F		NY
Fanny	4	F		TX
Harvey, George	19	M	Laborer	AL
Grimes, F. M.	41	M	Farmer	TN
Elmira	30	F		AL
Mary	11	F		TX
Martha	8	F		TX
Thomas	6	M		TX
Samuel	5	M		TX
Henry	2	M		TX
Frederick	7/12	M		TX

AUSTIN COUNTY, TEXAS

Name	Age	Sex	Occupation	Birthplace
Anderson, D. B.	34	M	Doctor	NC
T. N.	24	F		KY
George	6	M		TN
James	4	M		TN
John	2	M		TX
Ragland, N. T.	22	M	Medical Student	TN
Dotson, James	31	M	Farmer	TN
Mary	28	F		TN
Priscilla	11	F		TN
Nancy	9	F		TN
Campbell	7	M		TX
Mary	4	F	(prob. TX)	TN
Rebecca	2	F		TX
Shelton, James	38	M	Farmer	TN
Mary	35	F		TN
Leroy	15	M		TX
Mary	11	F		TX
John	7	M		TX
James	4	M		TX
Sarah	1	F		TX
Collins, T. W.	46	M	Farmer	NC
Malinda	42	F		NC
William	20	M	Student	TN
Kinchen	15	M	Student	MS
Mary	13	F		TN
Japhet	10	M		TX
Eustalia	8	F		TX
Malinda	5	F		TX
John	2	M		TX
Daughtery, Elisha	10	M	Student	TX
Slater, William	34	M	Laborer	IRE
Harrison, B. S.	29	M	Constable	TN
Lucinda	18	F		TN
William	2	M		TX
Cheek, Benjamin	35	M	Carpenter	KY
Emily	24	F		TN
Martha	9	F		TX
Mary	2	F		TX
Bachman, John	28	M	Methodist Min.	AL
Elizabeth	24	F		AL
Mary	4	F		MS
Elizabeth	1	F		MS
Talbert, G. B.	26	M	Doctor	NY
Wade, John	43	M	Farmer	TN
Martha	30	F		TN
John	17	M	Laborer	TX
Mary	13	F		TX
Jonathan	10	M		TX
Josh	8	M		TX
Robert	7	M		TX
Charles	3	M		TX
Hampton	6/12	M		TX
Cyntha	6/12	F		TX
Campbell, Siras	40	M	Farmer	NC
Manerva	26	F		KY
William	13	M		TX
Siras, Jr.	11	M		TX
Mary	9	F		TX
Ann	1	F		TX
Whitehead, N.	55	M	Carpenter	VA
Radford, John	27	M	Farmer	TN
Longley, Caleb	29	M	Farmer	TN
Ardella	24	F		NC
Marion	7	M		TN
George	6	M		TN
Oliver	2	M		TX
Caleb, Jr.	5/12	M		TX
Longley, Campbell	33	M	Farmer	TN
Sarah	29	F		PA
Mary	11	F		TX
Martha	9	F		TX
Caroline	7	F		TX
Alexander	5	M		TX
George	1	M		TX
Simons, William	46	M	Farmer	KY
Rebecca	25	F		TN
Sarah	7	F		TX
James	3	M		TX
Mary	1≠ 2	F		TX
Glyn, Alexander	38	M	Farmer	GA
Glenn, Sarah	30	F		TN
William	8	M		TX
Jane	6	F		TX
Culperner	4	F		TX
Whitly, T.	45	M	Farmer	TN
Cloe	43	F		NC
Isaac	14	M		MO
Sarah	12	F		MO
Thomas	8	M		TX
Nathan	5	M		TX
Randolph	1	M		TX
Radford, James	56	M	Farmer	VA
Sarah	49	F		VA
Silas	30	M	Farmer	TN
Sarah	18	F		TN
Nancy	16	F		TN
Ruth	14	F		TN
Samuel	12	M		AL
Benjamin	8	M		AL
Tom, James	32	M	Farmer	TN
Frances E.	28	F		AL
George	12	M		AR
William	4	M		TX
Susan	2	F		TX
Tom, William	34	M	Carpenter	TN
Shelborn, Samuel	51	M	Farmer	VA
Nancy	45	F		TN
Henry	21	M	Farmer	AL
Samuel, Jr.	19	M	Laborer	AL
Mary	16	F		AL
John	13	M		AL
Wood, William	22	M	Farmer	TN
Nelson, Sarah	20	F		MD
Bluford	2	M		AL
Barnett, G. O.	28	M	Farmer	TN
Betsy	25	F		AL
Carothers, George	63	M	Farmer	IRE
Susanah	64	F		GA
Simeon	25	M	Farmer	AL
Jane	23	F		TN
Dunford, David	28	M	Farmer	MS
Arish, E. ?.	23	M	Laborer	GER
Shelborn, Samuel	33	M	Farmer	TN
Adline	26	F		AL
James	5	M		TX
Juliet	3	F		TX
Sarah	1	F		TX
Shelborn, J. R.	59	M	Farmer	VA
Nancy	53	F		VA
Henry	24	M	Farmer	TN
Tennessee	16	F		AL
Andrew	14	M		AL
Dunkin, Jane	80	F		VA
Shelborn, Mariah	16	F		TX
G. F.	22	M	Farmer	TN
C.	28	M	Farmer	SC
Virginia	18	F		AL
Mathias	2	M		TX
Minters, Alfred	47	M	Farmer	SC
Jane	34	F		TN
Robert	17	M	Laborer	AL
Samuel	9	M		TX
Merica	6	F		TX
Virginia	3	F		TX
Bell, J. T.	50	M	Farmer	NC
Jane	43	F		TN
Catherine	20	F		TX
George	18	M	Laborer	TX

(continued)

Bell, Jo.	8	M		TX
Julia	7	F		TX
Adline	4	F		TX
Wily	1	M		TX
Davis, Thomas	23	M	Laborer	NC
Ward, John	30	M	Farmer	NC
Tabitha	22	F		TN
Joseph	2	M		TX
Abner	3/12	M		TX
Logan, A. M.	40	M		TN
Elizabeth	25	F		AL
Lee, John F.	35	M	Farmer	PA
Atkinson, John	56	M	Farmer	NC
Mariah	49	F		SC
John	25	M	Waggoner	AL
Alexander	22	M	Farmer	AL
Solomon	10	M		TX
Catharine	23	F		AL
Nancy	19	F		AL
Martha	18	F		AL
Jane	13	F		TX
Jones, Alen	21	M	Waggoner	TN
Bell, Thomas	48	M	Farmer	NC
Abigail	40	F		TN
Alford, Jane	5	F		TX
Granville, Benjamin	61	M	Farmer	ENG
Nancy	36	F		TN
Abigail	12	F		TX
Margarette	10	F		TX
Jane	9	F		TX
Caroline	7	F		TX
George	19	M	Laborer	TX
Alford, Wright	30	M	Farmer	NC
Susan	29	F		TN
Amos	10	M		TX
George	7	M		TX
Martha	5	F		TX
Isaac	4/12	M		TX
Felps, Micajah	33	M	Farmer	TN
Martha	17	F		FL
Susan	1/12	F		TX
Louis, William W.	47	M	Farmer	TN
Sophia	32	F		SC
Mary	15	F		AL
Sophronia	11	F		AL
Lavonia	9	F		AL
James	7	M		AL
John	5	M		AL
Joel	2	M		TX
Logsden, Alben	52	M	Farmer	TN
Sarah	40	F		IL
Ambrose	19	M	Laborer	IL
John	16	M		MO
Julia	12	F		TX
Finnetta	10	F		TX
Perry	7	M		TX
Ira	3	M		TX
Waddle, Federick	40	M	Farmer	TN
Susan	30	F		TN
Samuel	11	M		TX
George	9	M		TX
Martha	6	F		TX
William	3	M		TX
Bell, Thomas H.	36	M	Farmer	TN
Jemimah	36	F		KY
William	12	M		TX
James	10	M		TX
Thomas	8	M		TX
Sarah	5	F		TX
Robert	3	M		TX
Finis	1	M		TX
Howell, William	23	M	Laborer	PA

Reams, Ann	62	F		SC
T. J.	22	M		TN
R. B.	18	F		TN
Eviot(?), T. F.	36	M	Waggoner	TN
Cole	32	F		AL
Hue	13	M		MS
Margarette	9	F		TX
Thomas	1	M		TX
Mary	2	F		TX
Eviot(?), Samuel	40	M	Carpenter	TN
Mary	39	F		KY
James	18	M	Laborer	TX
Elizabeth	16	F		TX
Frances	11	F		TX
Susan	9	F		TX
George	8	M		TX
Samuel	6	M		TX
Mary	4	F		TX
William	2	M		TX
Mariah	1	F		TX
Eviot(?), Milton B.	20	M	Laborer	TN
Grimes, Anda	25	M	Farmer	TN
Elen	21	F		TX
Fanny	2	F		TX
Terrell, Charles M.	27	M	Farmer	MS
Lucinda	24	F		AR
Samuel	6	M		TX
Hunt	4	M		TX
Charles	6/12	M		TX
Hamilton, Elizabeth T.	23	F		TN
Studerville, James	36	M	Tending Stock	KY
Mary A.	25	F		TN
Martha E.	6	F		TX
Mary J.	4	F		TX
James	2	M		TX
Eviot, William	11	M		TX
Mexican, Olza	40	M	Laborer	MEX
Henely, Joel	24	M	Farmer	TN
Alcy	21	F		AL
Edward	1	M		TX
Baxter, Thomas	37	M	Farmer	SC
Rebecca	43	F		TN
Henely, William	18	M	Laborer	TX
Jasper	16	M	Laborer	TX
Amanda	13	F		TX
Cooper, Louis	24	M	Farmer	TN
Cooper, Enos	37	M	Laborer	MO
Martha	28	F		TN
John	11	M		TX
Ashly	8	M		TX
Susan	6	F		TX
Charles	3	M		TX
Annett	1	F		TX
Cooper, William	68	M	Farmer	TN
Sarah	64	F		PA
Benjamin	21	M	Attending Stock	TX
Sashel	18	M	Laborer	TX
William	15	M	Laborer	TX
Cooper, Thomas	24	M	Farmer	TX
Delana	23	F		TN
Sarah	2	F		TX
Velsey, James	30	M	Carpenter	GA
Robert	24	M	Carpenter	GA
Bell, William G.	27	M	Attending Stock	TN
Martha A.	18	F		TN
Perryhouse, Preston	35	M	Farmer	AR
Sirena	24	F		TN
Miney	8	F		TX
James	1/12	M		TX
Penrice, H. R.	27	M	Farmer	TN
Elizabeth	60	F		NC
W. S.	1	M		TX

AUSTIN COUNTY, TEXAS

Name	Age	Sex	Occupation	Birthplace
Effinger, F. A.	24	M	Doctor	VA
Susan E.	24	F		TN
Mary	5	F		TX
Thompson, James	38	M	Doctor	KY
Jane	25	F		TN
James	6	M		TX
Whitehart, Sarah	4	F		TX
Federick	34	M	Teamster	NC
Bird, William	20	M	Teamster	TN
Bets, Samuel S.	45	M	Farmer	NY
Ann	21	F		IN
Sarah	3	F		TX
Philip	1	M		TX
Lester, William	70	M	None	TN
Samuel	30	M	Laborer	KY
Hiram	14	M		IN
Lucinda	14	F		IN
Ivey, Wyatt	37	M	Farmer	NC
Abby	38	F		NC
Angeline	15	F		NC
Martha	13	F		NC
Mary	10	F		TN
Isaac	8	M		TN
Thomas	5	M		TX
Elijah	5/12	M		TX
Balsom, Hiram	21	M		NY
Stevenson, Elizabeth	33	F		VA
Nancy	16	F		TN
Moss, F.	28	M	Laborer	SC
Ann	20	F		TN
John	3	M		TX
Ann	1	F		TX
Decker, Henry	26	M	Laborer	NY
Long, George	22	M	Teamster	MD
Francis, James B.	37	M	Carpenter	OH
Nancy	39	F		AL
McFerson, Martha	16	F		TN
Susan	12	F		TX
Francis, Richard B.	5	M		TX
Mary E.	3	F		TX
Amanda	1	F		TX
Jones, William F.	37	M	Mail Rider	TN
Rebecca W.	34	F		SC
Nancy	16	F		TN
Sarah	13	F		TN
John	10	M		TN
Martha	1	F		TX
Whitfield, William B.	48	M	Farmer	TN
Verlinella	35	F		LA
William	2	M		TX
Bell, James	54	M	Farmer	NC
Margarette	36	F		TN
Rebecca	17	F		TX
Dicy	16	F		TX
Jane	14	F		TX
Thomas	12	M		TX
Margarette	8	F		TX
Mathew	6	M		TX
Elijah	3	M		TX
Elizabeth	1	F		TX
Cloyd, Neverot(?)	28	M	Farmer	AL
Johns, Stephen H.	30	M	Farmer	TN
Gross, Leonard W.	45	M	Farmer	GA
Courtney	34	F		LA
G---(?)	18	M	Student	TX
William	13	M		TX
Henrietta	10	F		TX
Eliza	8	F		TX
Leonard	6	M		TX
John	4	M		TX
Martha	2	F		TX
Pue, James	23	M	Attending Stock	TN

(continued)

Name	Age	Sex	Occupation	Birthplace
Wright, Elenor	24	F		NH
Barbee, W. T.	28	M	School Teacher	NC
Hill, David S.	35	M	Farmer	NC
Louisiana	27	F		TN

BASTROP COUNTY, TEXAS

Name	Age	Sex	Occupation	Birthplace
Lawhon, H. M.	45	M	Farmer	NC
Anna	44	F		GA
Frances	23	F		AL
William C.	21	M	Farm Hand	TN
E. M.	17	F		AL
L.	14	F		AL
D. W.	13	M		AL
M. A.	9	F		AL
John W.	5	M		AL
R. L.	2	F		AL
Moore, James W.	55	M	Farmer	GA
M.	40	F		TN
H.	22	M	Farm Hand	AR
J. A.	20	M	Farm Hand	AR
D. E.	17	M	Farm Hand	TX
R. C.	16	M	Farm Hand	TX
E.	14	F		TX
B.	10	M		TX
Z.	8	M		TX
N. J.	7	F		TX
A. E.	5	F		TX
M. E.	4	F		TX
Priest, Joseph	32	M	Farmer	AL
E.	28	F		AL
George W.	10	M		MS
William R.	8	M		MS
M. C.	6	F		MS
L. B.	4	M		MS
N. J.	2	F		TN
Cherry, Joel	51	M	Farmer	TN
R.	48	F		SC
James	19	M	Farm Hand	TN
M. L.	21	F		TN
N. L.	17	F		TN
N.	14	M		TN
J.	12	M		TN
R.	10	M		TN
Nickolson, James	34	M	Merchant	ENG
R. H.	30	F		TN
William	13	M		NY
Mary A.	11	F		TX
H.	9	M		TX
R.	7	F		TX
Samuel	1	M		TX
Ploger, Charles	26	M.	M.D.	GER
Smith, M. J.	33	M	Clerk	NC
Schnyder, Philip	14	M		GER
Claiborne, Phil	33	M	Lawyer	VA
Mary C.	24	F		MO
John M.	11	M		TN
Martha A.	9	F		TN
Austin	6	M		TN
Myriam J.	7	F		TX
Redding, William R.	42	M		TN
J. M.	27	F		TN
J. W.	4	M		TX
William R. (twin)	2	M		TX
T. J. (twin)	2	M		TX
Mitchell, John	40	M	None	VA
Castleman, A. E.	47	M	Farmer	TN
M.	15	F		TN
R.	13	M		TN
R.	11	M		TN
R.	9	M		TX
Barnet, E. D.	36	M	Merchant	SC
A. N.	24	F		VA
E. J.	1	F		TX
Gloser, J.	28	M	Merchant	TN

BASTROP COUNTY, TEXAS

Name	Age	Sex	Occupation	Birthplace
Cunningham, L. C.	40	M	Merchant	TN
Ann	40	F		KY
J. L.	11	M		TX
A. D.	8	M		TX
M. C.	6	F		TX
H. J.	4	F		TX
V. F.	1	F		TX
Harris, L. B.	37	M	M.D.	TN
Lucy	34	F		TN
S. F.	13	F		TX
G. W.	10	M		TX
Morgan, R. W.	47	M		KY
Gillespie, Hiram	32	M	Merchant	TN
Morgan, E.	18	F		TN
Hiram S.	15	M	Clerk	TN
J. H.	12	M		TN
C. L.	10	M		TX
Moore, A. W.	32	M	Farmer	TN
M. C.	23	F		AL
Thomas	5	M		AL
William J. W.	3	M		MS
James	1/12	M		TX
McClish, Porter	26	M	Farm Hand	TN
Maria	19	F		AL
Petty, John	25	M	Farm Hand	NC
Benton, John T.	26	M	Farm Hand	NC
Gaines, James	74	M	Hotel Keeper	VA
Susan	52	F		MD
James S.	23	M	None	TX
E.	20	F		MO
William D.	16	M		TX
Baugh, R.	35	M	Carpenter	VA
Gray, A.	38	M	Carpenter	TN
Hanson, G.	30	M		GER
Cameron, M.	40	M	Clerk	PA
Johnson, N.	31	M	Teamster	VA
Brindly, B.	29	M	Carpenter	AR
Riley, J. B.	24	M	Gun Smith	TX
Shrimp, N.	26	M	Carpenter	GER
Brindly, M.	31	M	Carpenter	TN
Baugh, William A.	37	M	Carpenter	VA
Macon, H.	36	M	M.D.	NC
Scales, Samuel	39	M	Farmer	TN
S.	27	F		AL
N.	8	F		AL
William	7	M		AL
N.	6	M		TN
P.	4	M		TX
Samuel	4/12	M		TX
Johnson, James	52	M	Carpenter	NC
O.	42	F		NC
Baker, E.	13	F		AR
Johnson, A.	10	F		AR
O.	8	M		AR
Price, J. R.	26	M	Carpenter	TN
Cornelisson, John	43	M	Farmer	KY
L.	32	F		KY
Robinson, Jane	50	F		SC
White, A. H.	23	M	Teamster	TN
Massey, William L.	35	M	Lawyer	SC
S.	32	F		TN
Nott	8	M		MS
Texana	4	F		TN
Cad	2	M		TX
Nolen, S. C.	39	M	Butcher	TN
M. A.	31	F		TN
Virginia	13	F		TN
M. T.	9	F		TN
Alexander	3	M		MS
John	1	M		MS
Rogers, Mark	34	M	Sheriff	TN
Mary J.	20	F		TX
John	2	M		TX

Name	Age	Sex	Occupation	Birthplace
Young, Alexander H.	35	M	Wagon Maker	TN
C.	36	F		TN
James	16	M	Day Laborer	KY
M.	8	F		TX
E.	4	F		TX
William H.	6/12	M		TX
Dunbar, William	31	M	Clerk County Court	TN
N.	20	F		KY
John S.	1	M		TX
Taylor, C.	37	M	Grocery Keeper	NC
Payne, M.	50	F	School Teacher	ENG
K.	30	F		ENG
Conley, Preston	45	M	Deputy Sheriff	TN
Washington, F.	13	F		AL
Caldwell, M.	13	F		TX
McGehee, M.	12	F		AL
Jackson, S.	40	M	Farmer	TN
A.	36	F		KY
A.	19	M	Farm Hand	IL
J.	16	M	(Criple)	AR
William R.	1	M		AR
Allen, J.	44	M	Farmer	NC
E.	43	F		TN
J. T.	19	M	Farm Hand	TN
Sarah	12	F		TN
George	10	M		TN
Texana	2	F		TN
Gill, R. R.	41	M	Farmer	TN
S. M.	31	F		TN
N.	16	F		TN
L.	14	F		TN
Thomas A.	12	M		TN
E. A.	10	F		TN
J.	8	M		TN
R.	6	M		TN
P.	4	M		MS
A.	2	M		MS
Donald, William P.	28	M	Farmer	TN
Susan	25	F		TN
William	8	M		MO
W. M.	6	M		MO
M. E.	1	F		MO
Stewart, D. K.	36	M	Sadler	TN
M. A.	35	F		TN
M. L.	17	M	Day Laborer	AR
S. J.	14	M		AR
M. E.	8	F		AR
R.	7	M		AR
Robbinson, A. C.	21	M	Farm Hand	TN
Hill, G. L.	45	M	Farmer	NC
M. J.	36	F		VA
Thomas	17	M	Farm Hand	NC
M. W.	12	F		MS
A. V.	10	F		MS
S.	8	M		MS
G. J.	6	M		TN
C. S.	5	M		TN
H. W.	4	F		TX
J. L.	2	F		TN
Hill, John C. F.	32	M	Farmer	TN
M.	24	F		TN
E.	11	F		TN
E.	8	M		TN
John	6	M		TN
W. H.	2	M		TX
McCady, James N.	41	M	Teamster	TN
Isabella	38	F		SC
Nancy J.	17	F		TN
Elizabeth A.	15	F		TN
Amanda	14	F		TN
John C.	7	M		TX
James N.	5	M		TX
William C.	2	M		TX
Melinda C.	5/12	F		TX
Neely, Wilson	26	M	Teamster	TN

(continued)

Name	Age	Sex	Occupation	Birthplace
Forrester, John	21	M	Farm Hand	TN
Thornton, William S.	39	M	Farmer	GA
Willoughby, Francis	44	M	Farmer	VA
Elizabeth	34	F		TN
William	16	M		IL
Lewis	11	M		IL
Elizabeth	7	F		IL
Andrew	4	M		IL
Margaret J.	3	F		IL
Hill, Middleton	47	M	Black Smith	GA
Julia F.	39	F		GA
Robert	18	M		AL
Thomas	16	M		AL
John	13	M		AL
Martha	11	F		TX
James	8	M		TX
Mary	6	F		TX
Middleton	2	M		TX
Long, Minus M.	26	M	Overseer	TN
Owen, John	27	M	Farmer	AL
Elizabeth	24	F		TN
Sarah J.	7	F		TN
John	5	M		MS
Volly	4	F		TN
Mary	1	F		TX
Owen, James	30	M	Farmer	AL
Jane	28	F		NC
Thomas J.	10	M		TN
Rebecca J.	8	F		TN
Melissa A.	6	F		TN
James	4	M		TN
Jonathan	2	M		TX
Owen, Ezekiel	21	M	Farmer	TN
Julia	21	F		TN
Martha	1	F		TX
Wilkes, James	24	M		TN
Owen, Ezekiel	63	M	Farmer	SC
Volley	55	F		NC
Edward	18	M		TN
Sarah	15	F		TN
Hunt, Lydia	59	F		NC
Alexander	26	M	Farmer	TN
Palmyra	17	F		AL
Hall, Alfred	27	M	Farmer	IL
Elizabeth	21	F		TN
George A.	2	M		TX
Priest, Richard	56	M	Farmer	VA
Mary	51	F		TN
John B.	17	M	Farm Hand	AL
Marilda	15	F		AL
Meason W.	13	M		AL
Aaron	10	M		MS
Jones, William D. C.	50	M	Farmer	VA
Rachael	47	F		AL
George W.	21	M	Farm Hand	AL
Maria	18	F		TN
Charles H.	16	M	Farm Hand	TN
William H.	14	M		TN
Benjamin	12	M		TN
Patsy	9	F		TN
Alston, James	43	M	Farmer	TN
Scoggins, David C.	33	M	Farmer	GA
Mary A.	38	F		GA
John A.	12	M		GA
Gilliam	4	M		MS
Mary	3	F		MS
Telemachus(?)	2/12	M		TX
Martha A.	20	F		GA
William J.	26	M		GA
Rice, John	21	M	Teamster	TN
Hunt, Benjamin B.	20	M	Farm Hand	NC
Alford, Thomas	44	M	Merchant	GA
Mary	34	F		AL
Samuel	19	M	Farm Hand	AL
Baldy	17	M	Farm Hand	AL
Sally	12	F		AL
Martha J.	1	F		TX
Gage, James T.	9	M		TX
Marion	7	M		TX
Monroe	5	M		TX
Tate, Reuben	21	M	Farm Hand	MO
Wilkes, John	22	M	Teamster	TN
Gray, Joseph L.	25	M	Farmer	TN
Mary J.	21	F		TN
Naomi	7/12	F		TX
McDonald, Martha A.	16	F		TX
Dancer, Mary	52	F		TN
James H.	13	M		TX
Rebecca	7	F		TX
Wood, Joseph	48	M	Farmer	SC
Elizabeth	36	F		TN
John E.	18	M	Farm Hand	TN
William D.	11	M		TN
Mary R.	7	F		TN
Samuel R.	4	M		TX
Calhoun, Julian C.	35	M	Gun Smith	TN
Genette	32	F		TN
Charles	14	M		AR
James R.	10	M		TX
Louiza J.	8	F		TX
Parmelia	5	F		TX
William C.	3	M		TX
Thomas C.	5/12	M		TX
Rector, Fielding L.	38	M	Lawyer	TN
Benjamin	83	M		VA
Sarah	82	F		VA
Clara	45	F		TN
Rector, Nelson	28	M		TN
Harriet	25	F		AL
Lee	4	M		TX
James N.	2	M		TX
Alsup, Horrace	24	M	Farmer	MS
Della E.	23	F		TN
Harriet E.	2	F		MS
Turner, William A.	24	M	Farmer	AL
Melinda	20	F		AL
Susan	1	F		AL
Turner, James S.	21	M		TN
Emily A.	26	F		MS
Marcellus	7	M		MS
Claudius	5	M		MS
Leonidus	3	M		MS
Della	3/12	F		TX
Turner, James L.	61	M	M.D.	NC
Julina	42	F		NC
Wade H.	18	M	Farm Hand	TN
Calvin	14	M		TN
Mary	12	F		AL
Henry	9	M		TN
Julina	8	F		AL
John	6	M		AL
Wallace	4	M		AL
Curtis, Rebecca	43	F		NC
Perkins, William	22	M	Day Laborer	TN
John	19	M		TN
James W.	8	M		TN
Barke, Nicholas	35	M	Farmer	NOR
Gage, Shirley	27	M	Farmer	TN
Martha	15	F		AL
George W.	6/12	M		TX
Gage, Jonas	42	M	Farmer	TN
Jane	41	F		TN
Mary	18	F		TN
James	16	M	Farm Hand	AR

(continued)

BASTROP COUNTY, TEXAS

Name	Age	Sex	Occupation	Birthplace
Gage, Abigail	15	F		AR
Rozanah	12	F		TX
Marilda	10	F		AR
Rebecca	8	F		AR
Nancy	6	F		AR
Moses	1	M		TX
Gage, Henry	21	M	Farm Hand	TN
Hiram	18	M	Farm Hand	AR
Thomas	15	M	Farm Hand	AR
Gage, Jesse	34	M	Farmer	TN
Martha A.	31	F		TN
Mary J.	9	F		AR
Parmelia E.	4	F		TX
Lucinda	1	F		AL
Gage, Moses	54	M	Farmer	TN
Elizabeth	49	F		GA
Sarah A.	20	F		TN
Moses	15	M		TN
Elizabeth	12	F		TN
John	10	M		TX
George	8	M		TX
Martha	5	F		TX
Blair, Joseph	46	M	Carpenter	ME
Gage, Abigail	78	F		NC
Rector, Ludwil L.	50	M	Farmer	TN
Agnes	38	F		GA
Kenner	14	M		AL
John	12	M		AL
Jenette	6	F		AL
Black, John	36	M	Farmer	GA
Gabrilla	22	F		TN
Elisha	7	M		TX
John	5	M		TX
Mary A.	3	F		TX
Martin, William O.	24	M	Farmer	MS
Martha J.	18	F		TN
Edward	1	M		MS
Willson, Walker B.	55	M	Farmer	VA
Jane	36	F		AL
Elizabeth	12	F		TN
Sarah J.	9	F		MS
Margaret	7	F		MS
Gage, Isaac	18	M	Farm Hand	TN
Willson, Volley Ann	3	F		AR
Ezekiel O.	2	M		TX
Grimes, Robert H.	35	M	Farmer	NC
Elizabeth	27	F		MO
Mary J.	12	F		TX
Elizabeth	9	F		TX
Jesse (twin)	2	M		TX
William H. (twin)	2	M		TX
Highsmith, Deborah	55	F		MA
Benjamin	29	M	Teamster	MO
Smith, John	26	M	Teamster	TN
Curtis, Elijah	33	M	Farmer	TN
Eliza	19	F		AR
Eliza J.	1	F		TX
Gray, Thomas	39	M	Farmer	TN
Nancy	27	F		TN
Sarah J.	4	F		TX
Daniel D.	2	M		TX
John M.	5/12	M		TX
Shelton, Samuel H.	30	M		TN
Mary A.	23	F		AL
Lucinda	3	F		TX
James W.	1	M		TX
Foster, James	44	M	Grocery Keeper	SC
Harrison, Mary	55	F		GA
Jackson	32	M	Farmer	TN
William	22	M	Farm Hand	TN
Marion	20	M	Farm Hand	TN
John	14	M		AL

Name	Age	Sex	Occupation	Birthplace
Harrison, Charles	27	M	Farmer	AL
Mary	18	F		TN
Woods, Alfred	26	M	Teamster	TN
Alvarina	23	F		TN
William	6	M		TX
Catherine	3	F		TX
John	1	M		TX
Higgins, Jacob C.	35	M	Farmer	VT
William T.	5	M		TX
Erastus F	4	M		TX
Gamble, William T.	48	M	Merchant	TN
George	25	M	Clerk	AL
Maria	20	F		AL
Rudder, Edward H.	37	M	Farmer	VA
Minerva	32	F		AL
Samuel	14	M		TN
Francis	12	M		TN
Arabella	8	F		TN
Mary	6	F		TN
Sarah	4	F		TN
Johnson, William R.	25	M	Farmer	TN
Amanda	27	F		MO
Phillips, William H.	8	M		IL
Martha J.	6	F		IL
Davis, Jonathan	32	M	Farmer	TN
Mary A.	23	F		NC
Martin V.	5	M		TX
Parmelia	3	F		TX
James B.	1	M		TX
Baysmore, Freeman	28	M	Day Laborer	NC
Jackson, Squire	30	M	Day Laborer	TN
Rowlet, John	49	M	Farmer	KY
Sarina	36	F		TN
William	17	M	Farm Hand	KY
Mary	13	F		TN
James	11	M		TN
Eliza	9	F		TN
Lee, Leroy	23	M	Tailor	TN
Jemima	15	F		TN
Reynolds, David	32	M	Carpenter	TN
Tabitha	28	F		MO
Mary A.	5	F		TX
John	3	M		TX
Martha E.	8/12	F		TX
Young, Michael	48	M	Farmer	GA
William	23	M	Farm Hand	AL
Anderson	22	M	Farm Hand	AL
Perry	16	M	Farm Hand	TX
Thomas	12	M		TX
Price, Anderson J.	26	M	Day Laborer	TN
Fisher, David	48	M	Day Laborer	OH
Carty, Thomas	48	M	School Teacher	IRE
Lilly, William G.	23	M	Farmer	TN
Susan	26	F		LA
Hufman, Mary A.	10	F		TX
Eliza	6	F		TX
Lilly, Newton A.	1	M		TX
Young, Francis	37	M	Farmer	TN
Sarah	35	F		NC
Amanda E.	11	F		MS
Mary E.	10	F		MS
Parlee	9	F		AR
James	5	M		AR
Robert	4	M		AR
Francis	2	M		AR
Diapa	7	F		AR
Lee, Levi	58	M	Farmer	TN
Mary	52	F		NC
Andrew P.	16	M	Farm Hand	AR
Mary J.	9	F		MO
Izilla E.	7	F		MO
George	19	M	Farm Hand	AR

BASTROP COUNTY, TEXAS

Biggs, Dorsey W.	42	M	Farmer	NC
Catherine	38	F		TN
Seth W.	18	M	Farm Hand	TN
Henry	8	M		TX
Amanda J.	4	F		TX
Standeford, William	37	M	Farmer	TN
Nancy	18	F		TN
William A.	10	M		TX
Jacob S.	8	M		TX
Arinda	7	F		TX
James	5	M		TX
Thomas J.	2	M		TX
Sarah J.	7/12	F		TX
Standeford, James	40	M	Farmer	TN
Sarah	38	F		TN
William	17	M		TX
Thomas	14	M		TX
Richard	12	M		TX
Jane	10	F		TX
Sarah	8	F		TX
James	7	M		TX
Elvira	5	F		TX
Arminta	2	F		TX
Arinda	8/12	F		TX
Williams, James M.	20	M	Farm Hand	AR
Meeks, William	22	M	Farmer	TN
Sarah A.	21	F		TN
Nathan F.	1	M		MS
Stanly, Elias	43	M	Farmer	NC
Lavina	36	F		TN
Adeline	17	F		TN
Mary E.	16	F		TN
Narcissa	14	F		MS
James	12	M		MS
Martha	10	F		MS
William H.	8	M		MS
John T.	6	M		MS
Elias K.	4	M		MS
Lavina C.	1	F		TX
Moore, Larkin B.	49	M	Farmer	TN
Judith	43	F		TN
Elizabeth	15	F		AR
Albert	9	M		AR
Robert	6	M		AR
Charlotte A.	4	F		AR
Paralee	2	F		TX
Clopton, William A.	35	M	Farmer	TN
Kissiah	17	F		TN
Clopton, Benjamin M.	42	M	Black Smith	TN
Justina A.	35	F		NC
Anthony	13	M		TN
Hoggatt	11	M		TX
Agness	8	F		TX
Mary E.	5	F		TX
William	8/12	M		TX
Gressham, John	19	M	Day Laborer	IL
Burlesson, Jonathan	33	M	Farmer	TN
Nancy	33	F		KY
Edward	11	M		TX
John	9	M		TX
Aaron	2	M		TX
Dover, Eliza A.	17	F		AL
Burlesson, Jacob	11	M		TX
Osborne, Thomas	37	M	Farmer	TN
Mary A.	29	F		MD
Augusta A	7	F		TX
Leah M.	4	F		TX
Mariah	2	F		TX
Thomas	1	M		TX
Wells, Wayman T.	35	M	Farmer	TN
Emily E.	30	F		TN
Amanda	1	F		TX
Bacon, Jonathan	48	M		TN
Bacon, Julia A.	64	F		TN
Stanly, John	43	M	Farmer	SC
Edith	46	F		GA
John T.	21	M	Farm Hand	TN
Elizabeth	16	F		MS
Angeline	14	F		MS
Elias S.	11	M		MS
Benjamin A.	6	M		MS
Mary A. C.	4	M(F)		MS
Josiah J.	8/12	M		MS
Holly, Jackson	27	M	Farmer	TN
Martha S.	23	F		TN
Sarah E.	4	F		MS
Davidson A.	2	M		MS
Stanly, Sarah	76	F		SC
Blair, Thomas	42	M	Farmer	TN
Margaret	37	F		TN
Walters, Elizabeth	13	F		TX
Martin T.	10	M		TX
Blair, Eleanor D.	7	F		TX
Margaret	5	F		TX
John W.	2	M		TX
McLane, John	29	M	Farmer	TN
Sarah	32	F		TN
Mary J.	7	F		TN
Moses B.	4	M		TN
Sarah A.	1	F		TX
Smith, John	30	M	Farmer	TN
Mary	26	F		TN
James	2	M		TX
McDuff, John M.	34	M	Farmer	TN
Canziddy	20	F		AL
Bryant, William B.	24	M	Farmer	TN
Nancy	20	F		MO
Sarah J.	1	F		TX
James L.	3/12	M		TX
Falty, John H.	24	M	Farm Hand	GER
Alexander, Pleasant D.	39	M	Farmer	TN
Margaret	35	F		TN
Stephen	4	M		TX
Elizabeth	1	F		TX
Mars, John	30	M	Ferryman	KY
Daniel, Cornelius	40	M	Farm Hand	CT
McGehee, Charles L.	44	M	Farmer	GA
Caroline	25	F		TN
Mary A.	13	F		AL
Charles L.	11	M		AL
Sarah	4	F		AL
Flint, Jeremiah	36	M	Overseer	AL
Rogers, Nancy	44	F		TN
Jonathan	25	M	Farm Hand	TN
Joseph	16	M		TX
James	14	M		TX
Nancy A.	12	F		TX
Grimes, James	54	M	Farmer	NC
Sidney	45	F		TN
Samuel	22	M	Farm Hand	TN
Thomas	18	M	Farm Hand	TN
James	15	M	Farm Hand	TN
John	12	M		TN
Felix	9	M		TN
Robert	7	M		TN
Pinckney	5	M		TN
Andrew	3	M		TN
Jefferson	2	M		TN
Rogers, James	44	M	Farmer	TN
Rachael	48	F		TN
Mary E.	20	F		TN
Nancy L.	15	F		TX
Edward	13	M		TX
Joseph	10	M		TX
Rogers, Jeremiah	34	M	Farmer	TN
Thirsey	37	F		KY
Mary E.	13	F		MO

(continued)

Name	Age	Sex	Occupation	Birthplace
Rogers, Susan K.	11	F		MO
Richard C.	10	M		MO
Ann E.	8	F		MO
John T.	6	M		MO
James	3	M		MO
Sarah J.	3/12	F		TX
Porter, Samuel	31	M	Farmer	TN
Julia A.	27	F		TN
Fonville, Emily	9	F		TN
Asa E.	5	M		TN
Adkins, Richard	26	M	Farm Hand	VA
Whitehead, Richard	41	M	Farmer	VA
Elizabeth	26	F		TN
Ann E.	7	F		TX
Jeremiah	5	M		TX
George	3	M		TX
Joseph	1	M		TX
Emerson, Albert	26	M	Farm Hand	NH
Coulson, David	35	M	Farmer	TN
Letitia	35	F		TN
Sarah E.	8	F		TN
Olive O.	7	M		TN
Wood, Hadacia	17	F		TN
Jackson, James A.	41	M	Black Smith	NC
Jemima	40	F		AL
William	15	M		TN
Joseph	13	M		TN
Sarah	12	F		TN
John	9	M		TN
Robert	6	M		TN
Mary	5	F		TN
Nancy J.	3	F		TN
Daniel, William	29	M	Farmer	TN
Elzira	19	F		MO
Virginia	1	F		TX
Thena	63	F		NC
Frederick	24	M		TN
Cartwright, Charles W.	37	M	Farmer	TN
Susannah	37	F		TN
Mary J.	14	F		TN
John N.	10	M		TN
Levin E.	9	M		TN
Lucy A.	6	F		TN
Charles W.	2	M		TN
William H.	4/12	M		TX
Craft, Samuel, Jr.	29	M	Farmer	TN
Jesse	7	M		TX
William L.	5	M		TX
McKinney, Richard L.	32	M	Farmer	TN
Naomi J.	24	F		TN
Albert	2	M		MS
Findly, Margaret A.	12	F		TN
Kincaid, George J.	23	M	Farmer	IL
Mary A.	21	F		TN
Isaac	20	M	Farm Hand	IL
Toney, Edward	27	M	Teamster	MS
Melinda	15	F		TN
Reed, Rhoda	61	F		SC
McClure	22	M	Farm Hand	SC
John P.	18	M	Farm Hand	TN
Perkins, Jacob H.	45	M	Farmer	NC
Maria	43	F		NC
Derinda J.	18	F		TN
James W.	16	M		TN
William H.	14	M		TN
Martha	12	F		TN
Harriet	11	F		TN
Franklin	9	M		TN
Elizabeth	7	F		TN
Maria T.	4	F		TN
Perkins, John W.	22	M	Farmer	TN
Margaret	16	F		TN
Naomi J.	5/12	F		TX
Ray, Samuel	25	M	Farmer	MO
Ealeanor	33	F		TN
Doss, Amelia	8	F		TX
Mary F.	7	F		TN
Gill, John	3	M		TX
Rector, Thomas B.	43	M	M.D.	TN
Eliza	35	F		AL
Penelope	6	F		AL
Margaret	4	F		AL
Caldwell, Edward H.	34	M	Carpenter	TN
Kissiah	26	F		IN
James C.	3	M		TX
Francis J.	4/12	M		TX
Duncan, Jane A.	29	F		TN
Martha A.	12	F		AR
Sarah E.	10	F		TX
John J.	8	M		TX
William D.	3	M		TX
Boyce, Mahala	47	F		KY
Anderson, Hendrick	21	M	Farm Hand	TN
Robert A.	16	M		TN
Mathew A.	14	M		TN
Sally	13	F		TN
Garrett, Alexander	26	M	Farmer	VA
Nancy	19	F		TN
Holderman, David	41	M	Farmer	KY
Candis	32	F		TN
Mary E.	11	F		TX
John T.	4	M		TX
Thomas J.	1	M		TX
Hemphill, Cornelius M.	40	M	Farmer	GA
Elizabeth	30	F		TN
Margaret	4	F		TX
Cornelius W.	1	M		TX
Ambrose B.	25	M	Tax Collector	GA
Snoddy, George C.	30	M	Farm Hand	TN
Hemphill, Zeno J.	30	M	Farmer	GA
Elizabeth	24	F		TN
Ellen	5	F		TX
Joseph	3	M		TX
Lycurgus	1	M		TX
Hemphill, Lafayette	35	M	Farmer	GA
Mary	25	F		TN
Cordelia	7	F		TX
Ann	5	F		TX
Mary A.	3	F		TX
Perkins, Washington E.	30	M	Farmer	TN
Martha A.	20	F		TN
John F.	1	M		TX
Gray, Anderson A.	22	M	Farm Hand	TN
Rice, Thomas J.	40	M	Farmer	GA
Margaret	34	F		TN
Rebecca A. A.	14	F		AL
Martha	11	F		AL
Sarah	7	F		AL
Mary	2	F		TX
Bogle, Joseph	28	M	Farm Hand	TN
Caldwell, John	47	M	Farmer	KY
Lucinda W.	40	F		TN
Margaret	21	F		AL
John A.	17	M		TX
Mary F.	12	F		TX
Charles C.	10	M		TX
Walter H.	8	M		TX
Lucinda P.	6	F		TX
Oliver B.	4	M		TX
Orlando	3/12	M		TX

BASTROP COUNTY, TEXAS

Name	Age	Sex	Occupation	Birthplace
Goff, Felix	36	M	Shingle Maker	TN
Harris, Estler	15	M	Day Laborer	TN
Garner, John	22	M	Day Laborer	TN
Leroy	25	M	Day Laborer	TN
Moore, Howard	22	M	Day Laborer	TN
Stewart, John	35	M	Farmer	TN
Abby	24	F		AL
Samuel	9	M		TX
James	7	M		TX
John	5	M		TX
Cassy	3	F		TX
Beverly	1	M		TX
Stewart, James	31	M	Farmer	TN
Sally	23	F		TN
Curtis, Sarah A.	7	F		TX
Perkins, James R.	37	M	Farmer	TN
Nancy E.	24	F		TN
Thomas W.	8	M		TN
Martha T.	5	F		TX
Missouri J.	3	F		TX
Sarah T.	7/12	F		TX
Wolfenberger, Samuel	46	M	Wagon Maker	VA
Caroline	44	F		TN
Elizabeth	20	F		TN
Susan	15	F		TX
Charles	13	M		TX
Ann	11	F		TX
William	9	M		TX
Guy	6	M		TX
Waldrip, Wiley B.	40	M	Farmer	TN
Elizabeth	32	F		AR
Sylvester J.	15	M	Farm Hand	TX
Martha	12	F		LA
William W.	9	M		LA
Onisimus	4	M		TX
Daniel	1	M		TX
Armstrong, James	10	M		TX
Ferrel, Hiram	49	M	Farmer	NC
Mournin	46	F		TN
William	21	M		AL
Stephen	19	M		AL
Hiram	17	M		AL
Columbus	15	M		AL
Eliza	13	F		AL
Kelly, Ann	14	F		AL
Billingsly, Jesse	39	M	Farmer	TN
Eliza A.	21	F		IL
Jeptha	1	M		TX
McGill, Samuel	3	M		TX
Denson, Archibald J.	35	M	Farmer	NC
Ann B.	32	F		TN
John T.	7	M		TX
Eliza A.	2	F		TX
Bunton, John W.	43	M	Stock Raiser	TN
Mary H.	35	F		TN
Elizabeth	11	F		TN
Joseph	9	M		TN
Thomas	8	M		TN
Desha	4	M		TN
William	1	M		TN
Bowie, Daniel M.	37	M	Day Laborer	NC
Conway, William H.	38	M	Farmer	TN
Catherine C.	33	F		TN
Bunton, Desha	42	M	Farmer	TN
Eliza	37	F		KY
John	14	M		KY
Joel	8	M		TX
Robert D.	5	M		TX
McGehee, William	27	M	Farmer	AL
Louiza	25	F		TN
Mary	8	F		TX
(continued)				
McGehee, Thomas	6	M		TX
Hiram	4	M		TX
William	2	M		TX
Hall, Constant K.	32	M	Merchant	CT
Margaret M.	30	F		NY
Kate	4	F		TX
Berry, Richard M.	25	M	Clerk	TN
Miller, John	57	M	Farmer	IL
Mary	48	F		IL
Carroll	16	M	Farm Hand	AR
Andrew	13	M		AR
George W.	10	M		AR
Eliza	7	F		AR
Gage, Joseph	26	M		TN
Mary J.	23	F		IL
Tempy	1	F		TX
Allison, Jonathan	47	M	Farmer	SC
Celia	42	F		TN
James T.	22	M	Farmer	AL
Eveline	17	F		MS
Susan C.	20	F		AL
Martha A.	15	F		MS
Jacob	12	M		MS
Lucinda	11	F		MS
Thomas	8	M		MS
Mary	4	F		MS
Jonathan	2	M		MS
Murtt, Sterling	26	M	Farmer	AL
James V.	1	M		MS
Owen, David F.	59	M	Farmer	SC
Sarah	44	F		TN
Sarah	11	F		TX
Richard	9	M		TX
Mordicai Y. (twin)	6	M		TX
Harriet N. (twin)	6	F		TX
Weeks, Robert	14	M		TX
Lucinda	10	F		TX
Mabry, Evans	48	M	Farmer	TN
Sarah	47	F		TN
Seth	18	M		TN
Lucy	14	F		TN
James	11	M		TN
Robert E.	5	M		TX
Billingsly, Elisha	4-	M	Farmer	TN
Martha	36	F		TN
Jeptha L.	17	M	Farm Hand	TN
William C.	16	M	Farm Hand	TN
America P.	15	F		TN
Jesse P.	13	M		TN
Thomas C.	11	M		TN
John C.	9	M		TN
Lock K.	6	M		TN
Osena M.	2	F		TN
Smith, Temperance J.	37	F		TN
Martha J.	19	F		TN
Peyton	18	M	Farm Hand	AR
Thomas	15	M		AR
Francis	13	M		AR
Mary	11	F		AR
Fanny	10	F		AR
Tennessee	3	F		TX
Temperance	1/12	F		TX
Rutherford, Wright H.	40	M	Farmer & Cambelite Parson	TN
Artena	30	F		MO
William J.	3	M		TX
Carroll R.	1	M		TX
McGill, Naomi	11	F		TX
William	37	M	None	KY
Mayes, Andrew	50	M	Farmer	GA
Harriet	35	F		TN
John	5	M		TX
Bell, Thomas	20	M	Farm Hand	GA
Webber, Mark	28	M	Farm Hand	GA
Markisson, Alexander	44	M	Farmer	NC
Mary	40	F		NC
(continued)				

BASTROP COUNTY, TEXAS

Name	Age	Sex	Occupation	Birthplace
Markisson, Isabella	16	F		NC
Mary C.	14	F		TN
Kenneth	8	M		TX
Peter	7	M		TX
Alexander	2	M		TX
Nicholson, Daniel	28	M	Farm Hand	NC
Smith, Walter	22	M	Teamster	MS
Catherine	16	F		TN
Shepherd, John G.	45	M	Farmer	IRE
Rebecca J.	24	F		TN
William E.	6	M		TX
Mary J.	5	F		TX
Daniel W.	3	M		TX
Malvina A.	1	F		TX
Julia A.	5/12	F		TX
Gray, Wesley	38	M	Farmer	TN
Mary	33	F		IRE
Franklin K.	15	M		TN
John D.	12	M		TN
Cymantha	10	F		TN
Sarah L. E.	6	F		TN
McAfee, William	8	M		TN
John F.	2	M		TX
Eastland, Robert M.	40	M	None	KY
Eliza J.	26	F		TN
Maria G.	5	F		TN
Mary F.	1	F		TX
Eastland, Nicholas W.	47	M	Farmer	KY
Famy F.	46	F		TN
Thomas	23	M	Stock Raiser	TN
Mary E.	14	F		TX
Eliza M.	11	F		TX
William M.	7	M		TX
Jenkins, John H.	28	M	Farmer	AL
Mary J.	24	F		MO
William E.	3	M		TX
Evans, Mary	16	F		TN
Northcross, James C.	14	M		TX
Harvey, John	40	M	Farmer	TN
Sinia	31	F		SC
Barton, Wilford	19	M	None	TX
Bradly, James C.	32	M	Day Laborer	SC
Harvey, Thomas	24	M	Day Laborer	TN
Faulkner, James	45	M	Farmer	IRE
Sarah	44	F		IRE
Mary J.	16	F		TN
Amanda E.	14	F		TN
Nancy R.	11	F		TN
John T.	9	M		TN
William M.	7	M		TN
Neil B.	6	M		TN
Robert C.	3	M		TN
McGehee, Francis M.	35	M	Farmer	AL
Nancy	34	F		SC
John G.	11	M		MS
Thomas J.	9	M		MS
Edward	7	M		MS
Christina	5	F		MS
Mary	3	F		TX
Francis N.	7/12	M		TX
Baxter, Thomas	23	M	Farm Hand	TN
Yancy, Napoleon B.	30	M	Farmer	VA
Nancy A.	21	F		TN
Burlesson, Joseph	43	M	Farmer	TN
Alley M.	43	F		TN
George W.	17	M	Farm Hand	TN
Joseph	16	M	Farm Hand	TX
Sarah J.	13	F		TX
Marion W.	12	M		TX
Susan M.	8	F		TX
James M.	7	M		TX
John F.	5	M		TX
Murry	1	M		TX
Hardiman, Thomas J.	62	M	Farmer	TN
Eliza	40	F		MO
Sarah E.	8	F		TX
Thomas J.	2	M		TX
Laura	1/12	F		TX
Sullivan, Jesse	32	M	Herdsman	TN
Eliza	31	F		AL
Thomas	8	M		AR
Ann A.	6	F		AR
John	3	M		TX
Joseph	2	M		TX
Sorrel, James	37	M	Farmer	GA
Minerva	28	F		TN
Samuel	10	M		TN
William	7	M		TX
Mary	2	F		TX
Alfred	4/12	M		TX
Lewis, Lycurgus	12	M		KY
Grasmyer, Frederick W.	49	M	Farmer	GER
Redfield, Henry	30	M	Black Smith	NH
Sarah	24	F		TN
Frances	6	F		TX
Susan	3	F		TX
Mary A.	6/12	F		TX
Fontaine, John	14	M		MS
Alsup, Newton G.	35	M	Farmer	TN
Mary	32	F		MO
Samuel H.	8	M		TX
Sarah	6	F		TX
Drury	1	M		TX
Thompson, William	18	M	Farm Hand	TX
John	11	M		TX
Alsup, James	23	M	Farmer	MS
Harriet L.	22	F		TN
James S.	1	M		TX
Sims, Samuel W.	32	M	Sawyer	MO
Julia J.	27	F		TN
John W. T.	9	M		TX
Laura A.	7	F		TX
Nancy O.	5	F		TX
James O.	3	M		TX
Billingsly, Jeptha	70	M	Farmer	TN
Mariam	64	F		TN

BEXAR COUNTY, TEXAS
(San Antonio)

Name	Age	Sex	Occupation	Birthplace
McIntire, Joseph	21	M	Carpenter	VA
Mary	20	F		TN
Crigler, Ruben	28	M	Carpenter	VA
Thompson, John	20	M	Carpenter	MS
Thomas, Benjamin	41	M	Merchant	AL
Penelope	22	F		TN
William	10	M		TX
Miles, Edward	34	M	Clerk	MS
Rier, A. J.	31	M	Saddler	TN
Grier, Robert	22	M	Messemger	IRE
Shehan, John S.	25	M	Clerk	IRE
Henry, Isaac	37	M	Black Smith, V.M.D.	TN
Elizabeth	33	F		KY
Samuel	5	M		TX
Meliciann	1	F		TX
McDonald, J. S.	35	M	Dist. Surveyor	TN
Clintenie	17	F		MO
Samuel, Letitia	47	F		TN
McDonald, James G.	27	M	Surveyor	TN
Samuel, William	27	M	Farmer	MO
Russell, John	29	M	Painter	TN
Minna	16	F		GER
Day, Jesse L.	46	M	Tavern Keeper	TN
Sarah	44	F		TN

(continued)

BEXAR COUNTY, TEXAS

Name	Age	Sex	Occupation	Birthplace
Day, John W.	20	M		GA
Nancy E.	19	F		GA
William	18	M		GA
James	12	M		MO
Charles	10	M		MO
Joseph	8	M		MO
Addison	6	M		MO
Emma	4	F		MO
Antonio	11/12	M		TX
Osmon, John B.	28	M	Wagon Master QRM	PA
Boyle, Andrew	28	M	Black Smith	ME
Hall, J. W.	29	M	Black Smith	SC
Grieupe, Samuel	40	M	Sadler	POL
Hour, Steven D.	26	M	Black Smith	FRA
Reed, Jacob	26	M	Black Smith	OH
McMurray, J. G.	28	M	Carpenter	TN
Ekins, S. B.	23	M		MO
Horner, George	23	M		GER
Dougherty, John D.	23	M		PA
Browders, Frederick	34	M		GER
Seffel, Stephen	22	M	Black Smith	GER
Lebhart, Frederick	23	M	Laborer	GER
McLain, Samuel	42	M	Baker	PA
Frederick, John	24	M	Night Watchman	FRA
Childress, Solomon	31	M	Saddler	GA
Mary	26	F		TN
James K.	6	M		MS
Samuel	4	M		MS
Sarah	26	F		AL
Wood, Mary C.	26	F	Boarding House	MO
Frances	2	M		TX
Mary J.	1	F		TX
Dale, James	35	M	Stable Keeper	TN
Hickison, John	28	M	Stable Keeper	IL
Navaro, Jefferson	21	M	Clerk	TX
Swimm, John	50	M	Druggist	OH
Rivara, John	19	M	Printer	NY
Gilbert, William E.	27	M	Clerk	KY
Monhart, Barbara	12	F		GER
Evans, Arisumus	43	M	Dry Goods Merch.	TN
Eliza	35	F		GA
Mary	17	F		TN
Lemuel	12	M		AR
Nancy	10	F		AR
John	6	M		AR
Sarah	4	F		TX
Alfred	2	M		TX
Munsey, Helick	26	M	Clerk	TN
Coleman, Alexander	35	M	Tavern Keeper	IRE
Shaw, Thomas	33	M	Bar Keeper	IN
Bowman, Phillip	35	M	Billiard Table Kpr.	NY
Pittman, H. M.	40	M	Billiard Table Kpr.	TN
Rivers, Miguel	35	M	Servant	MEX
Lyttle, William	46	M	Black Smith	PA
Mary	39	F		TN
Samuel	19	M		TN
Lyttle, Charles	22	M	Assessor, Collector	TN
Sarah	16	F		TN
Leslie, Andrew J.	34	M	Bar Keeper	TN
Zimmerman, Joseph	28	M	Bar Keeper	FRA
Newele, Jonathan K.	40	M	Bar Keeper	MA
McDermott, Michael K.	31	M	Laborer	IRE
Lege, Charles L.	19	M	Clerk	GER
Driskill, Jesse L.	23	M	Tavern Keeper	TN
Nancy E.	21	F		TN
James A.	3	M		TX
Orlando	1	M		TX
Taylor, William	38	M	School Teacher	IN
Ruther, John C.	48	M	Merchant	NY
Rowden, Joseph	38	M	Wagoner	TN
Adams, Warren	44	M	Tavern Keeper	KY
Sarah	40	F		SC
Clemments, Mary F.	19	F		AL

(continued)

Name	Age	Sex	Occupation	Birthplace
Clemments, Ruben E.	34	M	General Trader	TN
Jackson, East	12	M		AL
Sarah	10	F		TX
Adams, Clifton R.	7/12	M		TX
Cooley, Simon S.	35	M	Farmer	TN
Alsette	26	F		VA
Simmen	6	M		TN
Garner, Charles J.	42	M	Dry Goods Merchant	TN
Sarah J.	25	F		TN
Mary	8	F		AR
Leroy	6	M		AR
Harriett	4	F		AR
Margaret	5/12	F		TX
Sappington, Benjamin R.	36	M	Livery Stable Kpr.	TN
Margaritta	28	F		PA
Davis, James	33	M	Sergeant, U.S.A.	ENG
Brien, John	26	M	Private, "	NJ
Buchanon, John E.	20	M	Private, "	TN
Murphy, James	22	M	Private, "	IRE
Derrett, Thomas	23	M	Private, "	ENG
Miller, Thomas	17	M	Musician, "	NY
Dunn, Michael	24	M	Private, "	IRE
Johnston, Charles	23	M	Private, "	ENG
Key, John	21	M	Private, "	IRE
McConnel, Isaac	24	M	Private, "	DE
McIntosh, Daniel S.	25	M	Corporal, "	NY
Farral, William	23	M	Sergeant, "	IRE
Gilbert, Henry D.	23	M	Private, "	IRE
Stokes, Joseph P.	23	M	Private, "	IRE
Algoe, Lewis	26	M	Private, "	IRE
Buller, John	23	M	Private, "	ENG
Bending, George A.	23	M	Private, "	OH
COllings, Dennis	32	M	Private, "	IRE
Collett, Jules	23	M	Private, "	FRA
Harrigan, Timothy	32	M	Private, "	IRE
Looby, Lawrence	25	M	Private, "	IRE
Neu-Schaeffer, Charles	23	M	Private, "	GER
Neill, William	24	M	Private, "	IRE
Spelane, Jeremiah	32	M	Private, "	IRE
Weison, Joseph	23	M	Private, "	IRE
Barrett, James	24	M	Private, "	IRE
Kennedy, Richard	23	M	Private, "	IRE
Wilson, James	20	M	Private, "	IRE
Martin, Abner H.	39	M	Private, "	VT
Christopher, Francis	36	M	Private, "	IRE
Beissinger, Constine	27	M	Private, "	GER
Dennis, William	28	M	Private, "	KY
Malloy, JOhn	17	M	Private, "	IRE
Donnelly, Michael	28	M	Private, "	IRE
Murphy, John	23	M	Private, "	IRE
Lewis, John	21	M	Private, "	VA
Brown, John	30	M	Private, "	IRE
Bride, Patrick	26	M	Private, "	IRE
Byrne, Andrew	20	M	Private, "	IRE
Christie, Francis C.	21	M	Private, "	IRE
Dougherty, Patrick	21	M	Private, "	IRE
Hardin, Thomas	23	M	Private, "	KY
Lewis, Edward	23	M	Private, "	IRE
McGrath, Charles	22	M	Private, "	NY
Maslin, Thomas	25	M	Private, "	NY
Morken, John	28	M	Private, "	IRE
Murphy, Daniel	24	M	Private, "	IRE
O'Malley, Michael	21	M	Private, "	IRE
Poogle, Samuel	25	M	Private, "	GER
Kanna, John	24	M	Sergeant, "	NY
Colford, John	28	M	Sergeant, "	IRE
Walch, Daniel	32	M	Private Soldier	IRE
Dunn, William	28	M	Private Soldier	PA
Reilly, Patrick	27	M	Corporal	IRE
Ahern, William	27	M	Private Soldier	IRE
Robertson, Robert	24	M	Private Soldier	IRE
Wheeler, David	37	M	Butcher	SC
Margaret	11	F		TN
Martha	9	F		TX
Rufus	6	M		TX
John	34	M	Butcher	TN
Persia	18	F		TN
Shaw, Peter	50	M	Gardner	GER
Franseva, Meleano	20	M	Butcher	FRA
Schsneider, John	15	M	Herdsman	GER

Name	Age	Sex	Occupation	Birthplace
Small, Sarah J.	37	F		TN
Martha A.	12	F		TX
Leslie, Andrew J.	40	M	Deputy Sheriff &	TN
Canteberry, Harvey	30	M	Clerk Clerk	KY
Rions, Nicholas J.	34	M	Ranging Company	IRE
Hays, Robert B.	28	M	Surveyor	TN
Bonds, Jefferson	36	M	Ranging Company	GA
Young, John	27	M	Ranging Company	MD
Rossman, Mathew	27	M	Carpenter	NY
Willington, William	30	M	Carpenter	TN
Shelley, James	40	M	Laborer	TN
Cherry, Samuel	28	M	Telegraphy in Depot	SC
King, Edward	29	M	Herdsman	TN
Alexander, John	28	M	Herdsman	AL
Neide, John	21	M	Herdsman	NY
Peacock, James	35	M	Herdsman	NY
Wheeler, William	28	M	Herdsman	MA
Pearson, Wiley H.	20	M	Wagonmaster, QrM.	MS
Angel, William	23	M	Wagoner, QrM.Depot	PRU
Norcole, Carl	20	M	Wagoner, QrM.Depot	GER
Reil, Adolph	25	M	Wagoner, QrM.Depot	GER
Abels, William	29	M	Wagoner, QrM.Depot	GER
Barklow, Thomas	19	M	Wagoner, QrM.Depot	KY
Wheat, James	18	M	Wagoner, QrM.Depot	MO
Driscoll, William	20	M	Wagoner, QrM.Depot	KY
Robertson, A. C.	24	M	Wagoner, QrM.Depot	TN
Norman, William	19	M	Wagoner, QrM.Depot	GER
Bowser, James	22	M	Wagoner, QrM.Depot	AL
Estrada, Francisco	40	M	Wagoner, QrM.Depot	NM
Curley, James	26	M	Wagoner, QrM.Depot	NJ
Farmer, Harrison	30	M	Wagoner, QrM.Depot	GA
Walker, John	26	M	Wagoner, QrM.Depot	MO
Blessing, Michael J.	24	M	Wagoner, QrM.Depot	AL
White, Henry B.	24	M	Wagoner, QrM.Depot	NY
Cooper, James F.	21	M	Wagoner, QrM.Depot	TN
Miller, Harman	31	M	Wagoner, QrM.Depot	GER
Benton, Samuel	31	M	Wagoner, QrM.Depot	PA
Butler, Starling G.	38	M	Wagoner, QrM.Depot	GA
Dwyer, John	30	M	Wagoner, QrM.Depot	IRE
Pogue, Mark B.	22	M	Wagoner, QrM.Depot	AR
Sutter, Jacob	45	M	Wagoner, QrM.Depot	FRA
McLaughlin, John	29	M	Wagoner, QrM.Depot	PA
Rose, Francis	19	M	Wagoner, QrM.Depot	ITA
Cocherel, Green	19	M	Wagoner, QrM.Depot	MO
Oldham, Richard F.	19	M	Wagoner, QrM.Depot	TN
Pogue, William C.	19	M	Wagoner, QrM.Depot	AR
Parker, Mary Ann	50	F	Tavern Keeper	TN
William	19	M	Tavern Keeper	CT
Irby, William	33	M	Farmer	TN
Benjamin	30	M	Farmer	TN
Charles	25	M	Wagoner	TN
Evans, Robert B.	28	M	Farmer	TN
Garrison, William E.	20	M	Farmer	TN
Wolf, Alfred	49	M	Clerk	W.IND
Pulley, I. C.	28	M	Attorney at Law	CAN
McClellan, A. J.	30	M	Merchant	IRE
King, Charles F.	39	M	Merchant	NH
Hammock, John	26	M	Ranging Company	TN
Blanchard, Joseph C.	30	M	Ranging Company	MS
Roper, Mark R.	36	M	Carpenter	TN
Otwell, William M.	40	M	Millwright	NY
McCarthy, Daniel E.	28	M	Clerk	TN
Veramindo, Jose A.	25	M	Merchant	TX
Marcos	30	M	Merchant	TX
Dury, William L.	38	M	Merchant	VA
Tatman, Thomas	35	M	Ranging Company	TN
Parkes, William	27	M	Ranging Company	TN
Chevalie, Michael	33	M		--
Dean, William	40	M	Farmer	TN
Brush, Gilbert R.	25	M	Ranging Company	NY

This Company is now engaged examining the Rio Grande River San Antonio their residence.

Name	Age	Sex	Occupation	Birthplace
Cloud, James R.	24	M	Wagon Survey Co.	TN
Angeling, William	25	M	Wagon Survey Co.	TN
Sisk, Daniel J.	25	M	Wagon Survey Co.	TN
Ellington, G. M.	25	M	Wagon Survey Co.	TN
Shelton, Thomas	23	M	Wagon QM Depot	TN
Browser, George	22	M	Wagon QM Depot	TN
Hall, John B.	35	M	Wagon QM Depot	TN
Evans, Edward D.	26	M	Wagon QM Depot	TN
Cauddle, John	23	M	Wagon QM Depot	TN

Fort Inge on the Leona River.

Name	Age	Sex	Occupation	Birthplace
Sanders, Jules	57	M	Farmer	TN
Francis M.	24	M		KY
James	19	M	Farmer	AR
Robinson, William	24	M	Musician	TN
Miller, Robert	17	M	Musician	GA
Reynolds, William	26	M	Farrier	GER
Adams, Robert	22	M	Ranger	AR
Baker, William	21	M	Ranger	MO
Bennett, William C.	20	M	Ranger	GA
Bissell, Auguste	28	M	Ranger	GER
Berry, Peter	30	M	Ranger	GER
Bird, James G.	19	M	Ranger	MO
William	20	M	Ranger	MO
Carson, John	22	M	Ranger	MS
Clary, Jackson	28	M	Ranger	AR
Doane, Joseph A.	32	M	Ranger	KY
Hilburn, Nicholas	41	M	Ranger	TN
Richard, Jr.	20	M	Ranger	TN
Isham, James	32	M	Ranger	TN
Jetts, William	27		Ranger	TN
Johnson, Robert T.	23	M	Ranger	TN
Mitchell, Thomas	25	M	Ranger	TN
Owen, David	23	M	Ranger	TN
Pepper, Alexander	22	M	Ranger	TN
Smith, William	22	M	Ranger	TN
Etheridge, James	35	M	Ranger	TN

(On West Side of Leona River)

Eagle Pass on the Rio Grande River.

Name	Age	Sex	Occupation	Birthplace
McGraw, Daniel L.	26	M	Butcher	TN
Fitzgerald, William	21	M	General Trader	VA
Taylor, James H.	23	M	Clerk	PA
William	23	M	Trader	IN
Haber, Simon	22	M	Merchant	GER
Parez, Ramon	18	M	Cook	MEX
Matson, Henry	37	M	Liquor Mch.	NY
Kelsoe, William	21	M	Bar Keeper	TN
McCoy, Thomas	25	M	Trader	ME
Montgomery, William	24	M	Labor QM Corp.	NY
Robert	26	M	Labor QM Corp.	IRE
Gee, Claiborne C.	24	M	Labor QM Corp.	TN
Miller, Thomas	35	M	Labor QM Corp.	NY
Richardson, Thodore	19	M	Labor QM Corp.	NY
Payne, Campbell	25	M	Laborer	TN
Eliza	17	F		TN
Morgan, Ann	40	F		WAL
Hicks, James E.	27	M	Private Soldier	TN
Duff, Berry	20	M	Private Soldier	TN

Medina River.

Name	Age	Sex	Occupation	Birthplace
Allen, George	45	M	Farmer	TN
Sina	45	F		VA
William	16	M	Wagoner	TX
Rufus	15	M		TX
Eliza	9	F		TX
Virginia	5	F		TX
Warren	1½	M		TX

BEXAR COUNTY, TEXAS

Name	Age	Sex	Occupation	Birthplace
Hammer, Thomas B.	32	M	Farmer	PA
Martha J.	23	F		TN
Evelissa	2	F		TX
Jett, William G.	28	M	Farmer	TN
Price, George W.	43	M	Farmer	TN
Baker, Mitz	30	M	Farmer	GER
Kerr, William P.	52	M	Farmer	SC
Rachel	35	F		NC
Thomas	17	M		TN
Isaac N.	14	M		TN
Frances C.	10	F		TX
Mary J.	8	F		TX
Hernandez, Patrenel	20	M	Laborer	MEX

East Side of San Antonio River.

Name	Age	Sex	Occupation	Birthplace
James, John T.	35	M	Farmer	TN
James K.	18	M		IL
Melesa	11	F		TX
Nathan	8	M		TX
Smythe, Peyton	21	M	Farmer	TN
Louisa A.	16	F		TN

Mission St. Jose.

Name	Age	Sex	Occupation	Birthplace
Kerr, William H.	29	M	Farmer	TN
Matilda M.	19	F		TN
McHenney, James	30	M	Laborer	IRE
Sidebottom, George	35	M	Laborer	KY
Lullwan, Willis	35	M	Laborer	KY
Sligh, George	35	M	Laborer	MD
Small, Lehigh	17	M	Laborer	KY

Mission St. Juan.

Name	Age	Sex	Occupation	Birthplace
Lackey, Mary	38	F		TN
Jackson	19	M	Farmer	TN
Jane	17	F		TN
Sally	14	F		TN
James	12	M		TN
Nancy	9	F		MO
Melinda	1	F		TX
Brown, Edward	35	M	Farmer	TN
Lareta	30	F		TX
Waddy T.	2	M		TX
Lalida	8/12	F		TX

On Salado River.

Name	Age	Sex	Occupation	Birthplace
Doss, John E.	38	M	Farmer	VA
Rachell	20	F		GA
Sam	4	M		TX
Nancy	3	F		TX
Mary	4/12	F		TX
Doss, Benjamin H.	35	M	Farmer	VA
Tuttle, James E.	40	M		TN
Martin, William	33	M	Farmer	TN
Polly	31	F		KY
Mary C.	14	F		AR
Joseph	10	M		AR
Frances	6	F		AR
William	3	M		AR
Elizabeth	4/12	F		TX
White, Joseph E.	42	M	Farmer	TN
Mary A.	37	F		TN
Benjamin	14	M		LA
Schoonover, Isaac	22	M	Butcher	IN
Benjamin	47	M	Wagoner	PA
Gunn, John B.	21	M	Laborer	TN
Thomas, Wiley S.	39	M	Farmer	NC
Julianna	32	F		NC
Smith, William	15	M		NC
Andrew J.	14	M		TN
Thomas, Samuel H.	10	M.		TX
John A.	8	M		TX

(continued)

Name	Age	Sex	Occupation	Birthplace
Thomas, Eleanor T.	6	F		TX
James C.	3	M		TX
Elonzo	9/12	M		TX
Dougherty, Ann	13	F		TX
Thomas, Ann	36	F		NC
Gossett, James	40	M	Wagoner	TN
Precilla	39	F		NC
John	14	M		TX
James H.	12	M		TX
Precilla E.	10	F		TX
Thomas J.	8	M		TX
Levi	4	M		TX
Mary	3	F		TX
Andrew	1	M		TX
Gossett, William	19	M	Laborer	TN
Mary E.	18	F		AL

Mission Consepcion, Cibilo and Sulpher Springs.

Name	Age	Sex	Occupation	Birthplace
Rector, Pendleton	43	M	Farmer	TN
Mary J.	19	F		IL
Margaret	1	F		TX
Leoines, William	23	M	Laborer	TN
Beard, Thomas	14	M		TX
Southerland, David K.	30	M	Farmer	TN
Emelia	20	F		MS
Deana	1½	F		TX
Mays, William D.	42	M	Farmer	TN
Mary A.	28	F		NC
Alvarado	8	M		TN
Florida	4	F		TN
Garland L.	1	M		LA
Taylor, Creed	42	M	Farmer	TN
Nancy	35	F		SC
John H.	8	M		TX
Phillip	7	M		TX
Caroline	6	F		TX
Eliza	4	F		TX
Goodbred, Phillip	25	M	Stock Raiser	SC
West, Martin	41	M	Stock Raiser	TN
Sarah	35	F		SC
Phillip	10	M		TX
Martin	2	M		TX
Peacock, James K.	30	M	Farmer	TN
Colguohn, William	40	M	Laborer	SCO
Deares, Francis	17	M	Laborer	MEX
Bird, Daniel	45	M	Farmer	TN
Minerva	35	F		SC
William	20	M		AL
Houston	18	M		AL
Richard	16	M		AL
Elizabeth	11	F		TX
George	8	M		TX
Daniel	6	M		TX
Minerva	1	F		TX

Cililo Creek and Clato.

Name	Age	Sex	Occupation	Birthplace
Rector, Claiborne	45	M	Farmer	TN
James P.	13	M		TX
Emilia A.	6	F		TX
Emeale C.	4	F		TX
Harmon, John	49	M	Farmer	TN
Emeline	40	F		TN
Benjamin S.	17	M	Student	TX
Mary	12	F		TX
John	3	M		TX
William	1	M		TX
McClellan, John S.	40	M	Farmer	TN
Susan	32	F		MO
Gregg, Jacob	23	M	Farmer	MO
Head, James	58	M	Farmer	VA
Sarah	54	F		VA

(continued)

BEXAR COUNTY, TEXAS

Pullins, Sarah M.	35	F		KY
Benjamin	37	M	Farmer	MO
Head, Martha	18	F		TN
Pullins, Martha	12	F		MO
James D.	10	M		MO
Pernella	8	F		MO
Sarah A.	6	F		MO
Oscar	4	M		MO
Frances	2	F		MO
Mary	6/12	F		TX
Harrison, Jonas	27	M	Black Smith	TN
Crowson, Lucretia	59	F		NC
Nelson, Elizabeth	30	F		TN
Harrison, William	12	M		AR
Nelson, John	8	M		TX
Jane	6	F		TX
Roland	4	M		TX
Lorenzo D.	8/12	M		TX
Nichols, Roland	45	M	Black Smith	TN
Jane	35	F		TN
Nancy K.	14	F		AR
Mary J.	12	F		AR
Eliza	10	F		AR
Fanny	8	F		TX
Elizabeth	5	F		TX
John	2	M		TX
Greenwood, William	30	M	Farmer	AL
Caroline	20	F		TN
Maryan	3	F		TX
Turner, William R.	26	M	Farmer	TN
Martha A.	22	F		TN
Matilda H.	3	F		TX
Elizabeth	10/12	F		TX
Allen, Hugh	49	M	Farmer	SC
Caroline	48	F		VA
James M.	18	M	Student	TN
Hugh	16	M		TN
Mary	14	F		TN
Elizabeth	12	F		TX
Daniel	10	M		TX
Sarah	8	F		TX
Rebecca	2	F		TX
Watters, William	28	M	School Teacher	KY
Wiscowy, Emanuel	30	M	(illegible)	HOL
Ware, William	49	M	Farmer	KY
Richard	22	M	Farmer	AR
Sarah	13	F		TX
John	10	M		TX
Eliza	9	F		TX
Amanda	8	F		TX
Clarisy E.	4	F		TX
Susan T.	2	F		TX
Betsy	1	F		TX
Crane, Narcisy	21	F		TN
John H.	14	M		TX
William A.	11	M		TX

Commanche Spring and Leon Creek.

McIntire, Joseph	30	M	Farmer	TN
Mary	19	F		TN

BOWIE COUNTY, TEXAS

Hays, William J.	42	M	Farmer	TN
Emily	40	F		GA
Malvina	14	F		TN
Sophia C.	9	F		TX
Moss, Azriah	32	M	Farmer	TN
Christiana J.	18	F		AL
Epperson, Mark	55	M	Ferryman	TN
Margaret	40	F		TN
Elizabeth	16	F		TX

(continued)

Epperson, Indenia	14	F		TX
Susan	11	F		TX
Mark	8	M		TX
Walker, Elijah	23	M	Farmer	TN
Mary Ann	16	F		AR
William	19	M	Farmer	TN
Bingham, Benton	29	M	Farmer	TN
Rachel	26	F		NC
Frances	8	F		TX
Martha A.	3	F		TX
Allen, John	30	M	Laborer	NC
Scott, James	25	M	Laborer	NC
Bingham, Elizabeth	63	F		NC
Rodgers, William	11	M		TN
Elisha	8	M		TX
Minor, Henry	28	M	Farmer	TN
Caroline	20	F		LA
McAdams, George	46	M	Carpenter	SC
Jerusha	40	F		TN
George H.	16	M		AL
James H.	14	M		AL
Mary E.	12	F		AL
Penelope	10	F		AL
Andrew J.	7	M		TX
Louisa	3	F		TX
Hannah	10/12	F		TX
Duke, Wood	26	M	Farmer	TN
Harriet	20	F		AL
John	2/12	M		TX
Elizabeth	6	F		TX
Pair(?), Martin	42	M	Farmer	NC
Nancy	39	F		NC
Lucius J.	16	M		TN
Solomon D.	12	M		TX
Sarah	8	F		TX
Catherine	7	F		TX
Elizabeth	6	F		TX
Dannell, Jessee	61	M	Planter	TN
Sally C.	50	F		TN
Jessee	14	M		TN
Henry	10	M		TX
Duke, Thomas	15	M		MS
Jessee	12	M		TX
Martha	10	F		TX
Elizabeth	8	F		TX
Hensly, Burwell	25	M	Overseer	NC
Yeats, J. M. C.	34	M	Gin Wright	OH
Harriet	22	F		MS
Wright, George	18	M	Printer	TN
Yeats, Mary J.	7	F		LA
Lisbey, Wiley	24	M	Carpenter	AL
Lackey, J. C.	35	M	Carpenter	MS
Lindsey, R. M.	32	M	Sawyer	TN
Mary E.	30	F		AL
George M.	12	M		AL
Martha V.	10	F		TX
-----	8	F		TX
William J.	6	M		TX
John Newton	4	M		TX
Ball, Isaac M.	25	M	Physician	AL
Irvin, A. M.	27	M		AL
Freeman, George	29	M	Carpenter	ME
Gains, H. H.	27	M	Dist. Court Clerk	VA
Jarrett, David	56	M	County Sheriff	VA
Betsey E.	40	F		NC
David, Jr.	17	M	None	TN
Minerva	15	F		TN
Martha	13	F		TN
Wright, J. P.	26	M	Merchant	TN
Sarah E.	16	F		AR
Puckett, Douglass	29	M	Shoemaker	TN
Bethula	19	F		TN
John Douglass	4	M		TX
Arraminta	3	F		TX
Sophia Ann	7/12	F		TX

BOWIE COUNTY, TEXAS

Name	Age	Sex	Occupation	Birthplace
Job, Jonathan	27	M	Shoemaker	TN
Narcissa	24	F		TN
Aron A.	6	M		AL
Rice, S. M.	49	M	Planter	NC
Elizabeth	42	F		TN
William M.	14	M		TX
Martin K.	12	M		TX
Henry D. M.	10	M		TX
Edward S. V.	5	M		TX
Collum, George	7	M		TX
Talbot, John A.	35	M	Merchant	VA
Sarah J.	32	F		TN
Ann E.	11	F		TX
John William	10	M		TX
Virginia H.	10	F		TX
Martha F.	8	F		TX
Sarah Eliza	4	F		TX
Mary Jane	2	F		TX
Hanly, John R.	27	M	Laborer	NC
Vicey	23	F		NC
James	7	M		TN
Leonard	5	M		TN
Margaret	3	F		TN
Sarah	10/12	F		TN
Perky, S. H.	36	M	Attorney	VA
A. L.	22	F		VA
R. R. R.	3	M		TN
Bryan	2/12	M		TX
Lafayette C.	2	M		TX
Davis, Julia Love	40	F		TN
Emily	18	F		MO
John	17	M		MO
William A.	13	M		MO
George	7	M		TX
Love, Ben Franklin	5	M		TX
Thomas Jefferson	5	M		TX
Moss, James	66	M	Planter	VA
J. Robert	33	M	Planter	NC
Lucy A.	19	F		VA
Hester	17	F		VA
Ottanay	14	M		TN
Sion	11	M		TN
Mary E.	21	F		AL
Sarah	5	F		MS
William J.	3	M		TX
Infant	2	F		TX
Greenshaw, Bazzell	46	M	Farmer	TN
Hannah	37	F		TN
C. Augustus	18	M	Farmer	TN
William A.	12	M		TN
Alfred, James P.	30	M	Farmer	TN
M. C.	22	F		TN
Sophia C.	5	F		TX
M. A.	3	F		TX
Infant	4/12	F		TX
Durham, Henry	28	M	Farmer	SC
Mauldin, Catherine	47	F		NC
James	21	M	Farmer	TN
John	18	M	Farmer	TN
Taylor	17	M	Farmer	TN
William	13	M		TX
Nancy Ann	11	F		TX
Elizabeth	6	F		TX
Morris, Lew	41	M	Farmer	TN
Sabrenia	28	F		TN
Richard C.	4	M		TX
Hill, Martha	30	F		TN
Armetta	31	F		TN
Newton, Susan	25	F		TN
Richard	6	M		AR
Morris, George	35	M	Farmer	MO
Arramanda	31	F		TN
M. J.	12	M		TX
Harrison	5	M		TX
Lafayette	1½	M		TX
Jeans, H. S.	34	M	Planter	AR
Elizabeth	21	F		TN
Virginia	2	F		TX
John H.	14	M		TX
M. H.	7	M		TX
Echols, James	17	M	Farmer	AL
Knoun(?), George W.	21	M	Farmer	AL
Berry, George B.	17	M	Farmer	TX
Hoskins, A. G.	39	M	Carpenter	VA
Mary R. L.	27	F		NC
Mary C.	12	F		TN
Isabella J.	9	F		TN
Mary Eliza	6	F		LA
Henryanna	2	F		TX
Johnson, William H.	24	M		VA
Getwood, Joseph B.	23	M		VA
Stewart, Benjamin T.	18	M	Farmer	TN
George H.	16	M	Farmer	TN
Mary L.	17	F		TX
Sam M.	9	M		TX
Emma	7	F		TX
Read, Jonas	31	M	Carpenter	KY
Susan	31	F		KY
Martha J.	17	F		KY
William H.	13	M		KY
Mary E.	12	F		KY
B. A.	10	M		KY
Abraham	8	M		KY
Isabella	5	F		KY
Joseph	1	M		KY
Millikin, John	25	M	Carpenter	TN
Harris, C. B.	51	M	Farmer	VA
Mary	46	F		VA
James	21	M		VA
Sarah	17	F		TN
Mary	16	F		TN
Gilbert	8	M		TN
Mat.	6	M		TN
C. B., Jr.	3	M		TX
Jeans, Sarah	40	F		TX
Massee, Richard	27	M	Farmer	IL
Martha	23	F		TN
Anders, Philip	67	M	Farmer	NC
Massee, Sarah Agness	19	F		IL
McWhirter, James	41	M	Farmer	TN
Saranah	26	F		MO
Mary	12	F		TX
Thomas J.	8	M		TX
Hugh	4	M		TX
Paulina	2	F		TX
Moore, James C.	35	M	Merchant	SC
Jane R.	30	F		SC
Mary Eliza	6	F		TX
Frances	4	F		TX
Jane R.	2	F		TX
Murphy, William	24	M	Overseer	TN
Wilson, Nancy	35	F		TN
John W.	16	M		AR
Henrietta	9	F		AR
William Delaney	5	M		LA
Moores, Charles	74	M	Planter	NC
Elizabeth	65	F		SC
William H. H.	19	M	Planter	SC
R. H.	16	M	Planter	SC
Thomas E.	20	M		SC
Julia	14	F		TN
Rain, George W.	22	M	Overseer	SC
Elliott, William M.	59	M	Minister P.M.	VA
Rebecca	57	F		TN

(continued)

Name	Age	Sex	Occupation	Birthplace
Elliott, Samuel	26	M	Farmer	TN
Andrew J.	24	M	Farmer	TN
Elgin D.	22	M	Farmer	TN
Thomas	19	M	Farmer	TN
Richard	13	M		TN
Sherwood, J. W.	32	M	Farmer	TN
Polly	19	F		AR
Benjamin	1	M		TX
McAdams, Samuel	74	M	Farmer	TN
Sarah	67	F		NC
Lupton, J. W.	35	M	Farmer	VA
Lucy J.	37	F		VA
Joseph W.	4	M		TX
Richard Archer	2	M		TX
Bradshaw, John	16	M	Farmer	IL
Elliott, Samuel D.	19	M	Farmer	TN
Weldin, Peter	40	M	Farmer	NJ
Moores, Andrew R.	28	M	Planter	SC
Pauline T.	27	F		TN
Alex Ross	8	M		TX
Virginia	7	F		TX
Gorday, L.	28	M	Laborer	GA
Jane	24	F		KY
Mary Ann	1/12	F		TX
Morris, Mary	63	F		TN
Morris, Richard	19	M	Farmer	VA
Fergeson, Joseph	37	M		TN
Margaret	24	F		VA
Isabella	5	F		TX
William Tom	3	M		TX
Day, Elijah	68	M	Farmer	NC
Isabella	38	F		TN
Nancy Ann	20	F		TN
Towry, Isac	41	M	Farmer	SC
Jane	29	F		TN
M. J.	5	M		AR
Eliza J.	5/12	F		TX
Durham, John	13	M		TN
Almond B.	12	M		IL
Jemima	31	F		TN
Timmons, William	30	M	Physician	GA
Virginia	23	F		TN
Fort, John W.	55	M	Planter	TN
Deanna C.	53	F		VA
Joseph M.	22	M	Planter	TN
Deanna C.	16	F		TN
Killingsworth, Robert	22	M	Overseer	NC
Burnsides, Sam	18	M	Farmer	TX
Fort, J. Ann	20	F		TN
Millikin, John	24	M	Carpenter	TN
Fort, William W.	24	M	Planter	TN
Mary G.	19	F		TN
Mary C.	1	F		TX
Battle, Robert	29	M	Planter	TN
Susan	25	F		TN
Sarah	6	F		TX
William	4	M		TX
Josiah	10/12	M		TX
Susan	3	F		TX
Derryberry, -----	32	M	Overseer	TN
Battle, James	28	M	Planter	TN
Orum	63	M	Planter	NC
Rummell, Richard	27	M	Planter	MS
Thompson, Alfred	24	M		TN
Stephenson, Susan	5	F		AL
Mary	28	F		AL
Murphy, William	28	M	Farmer	TN
Mary	24	F		TN
Mary	1	F		TN
Jas. H.	7	M		TN

Name	Age	Sex	Occupation	Birthplace
Whites, Peter	45	M	Farmer	TN
Nancy	42	F		TN
Giddon	21	M	Farmer	TN
Enock	18	M	Farmer	TN
Mary	16	F		TN
Samuel	14	M		TN
Elizabeth	13	F		TN
Aramintia	12	F		TN
Ira	10	M		TN
Asken	8	M		TN
Barnwell	7	M		TN
Peter	2/12	M		TX
Fort, John	44	M	Planter	NC
Sarah	44	F		NC
Tempe	21	F		TN
James	16	M		TN
Cordilla	13	F		TN
Collum, Jacob	23	M	Constable	TN
Mary W.	28	F		LA
Charles	8	M		TX
Catherine	6	F		TX
Sarah	3	F		TX
Dannell, William	30	M	Planter	TN
Elizabeth	28	F		TN
William, Jr.	9	M		TX
Sarah Jane	8	F		TX
Susan E.	6	F		TX
Mary Caroline	4	F		TX
Frances	2	F		TX
Lucy	6/12	F		TX
Searsey, M.	52	M	Farmer	KY
Martha	37	F		TN
George	16	M	Farmer	TN
William	14	M		TN
Henry	10	M		TN
Berrey	7	M		TX
Payton	5	M		TX
Ellis, N. D.	40	M	Planter	VA
Sarah	1/12	F		TX
Frances	29	F		VA
N. D., Jr.	1 10/12	M		
Wyatt, William	13	M		TX
Hays	5	M		AL
Wise, James K.	7	M		TX
Matilda G.	3	F		TX
Infant of Maj.	3/12	M		TX
Lawrence, John	25	M	Overseer	TN
Timmons, Wilkins	34	M	Farmer	MO
Elizabeth	22	F		TN
Susan	1	F		TX
McCaulish, Charles	30	M	Farmer	VA
Brown, H.	22	M	Overseer	TN
Bird, Able	50	M	Farmer	TN
Hester	50	F		NC
Francis Marion	23	M	Farmer	MS
Alfred	21	M	Farmer	MS
Rhabecca J.	19	F		MS
Enock	15	M		MS
Sarah R.	14	F		MS
Mary E.	12	F		MS
Walker, Jeremiah	46	M	Farmer	NC
Elizabeth	21	F		IL
William	17	M	Farmer	NC
Mary	13	F		TN
Washington	8	M		TX
Elizabeth	8	F		TX
Jesse	6	M		TX
Jane	2	F		TX
Martha	5/12	F		TX
Searsey, Isaac	52	M	Farmer	KY
Martha	42	F		KY
Richard H.	20	M	Farmer	TN
James	18	M	Farmer	KY
Samuel T.	16	M	Farmer	KY

BOWIE COUNTY, TEXAS

Name	Age	Sex	Occupation	Birthplace
Patton, N. B.	27	M	Farmer	TN
Lucinda	25	F		VA
Charles E.	7	M		TX
Mary J.	4	F		TX
Ann	1	F		TX
Lucy A.	2	F		TX
Parham, James	28	M	Saddler	TN
Ann E.	3	F		TX
Darnell, James	32	M	Farmer	TN
Margaret	25	F		TN
James	6/12	M		TX
Roshell, John	22	M	Merchant	SC
Julia	19	F		TN
Parton, H.	30	M	Planter	TN
Martha A.	23	F		TN
Nunly, Nancy	18	F		TN
Birdwell, Elijah	47	M	Farmer	TN
Mary Elizabeth	45	F		TN
James	23	M	Farmer	TN
Mary Ann	17	F		TN
Margaret	15	F		TN
Robert	13	M		TN
William Henry Harmon	9	M		TN
Elijah	2	M		TX
Moore, Sam	39	M	Physician	TN
Narcissa	16	F		TN
E. Amanuel	12	F		TN
Mariah	9	F		TX
Earness, Daniel	25	M	Farmer	TN
Legg, S. D. C.	34	M	Farmer	TN
Jane	22	F		VA
Susan	14	F		AL
James A.	9	M		TX
William W.	4	M		TX
Eliza J.	2	F		TX
Bird, David E.	22	M	Farmer	MS
Rachael	22	F		TN
Elijah A.	8/12	M		TX
Philips, Alpherd	33	M	Farmer	NC
Jane	30	F		NC
John	8	M		TN
Sarah Jane	6	F		TN
Mary A.	5	F		TN
Jefferson	2	M		TX
Duke, Alex.	40	M	Farmer	TN
Martha	26	F		AL
Sarah F.	12	F		AL
Josephus	8	M		AL
Susan Jane	6	F		AL
Aramanda E.	4	F		AL
John	1	M		TX
Stewart, Bluit	40	M	Farmer	NC
Caroline M.	40	F		TN
L. Ann R.	20	F		NC
Mary E.	18	F		NC
Martha A.	16	F		NC
Davison W.	14	M		TN
Joseph A.	12	M		TN
Columbus T.	5	M		TX
McMillin, Johnson	27	M	M.E. Minister	TN
Wise, James	47	M	Planter	NH
William	19	M		LA
Mary E.	17	F		TN
Martha Ann	16	F		MS
Caroline F.	13	F		MS
Sarah Jane	11	F		MS
Henry H.	8	M		TX
Searsey, William	26	M	Overseer	KY
Collum, Catherine	52	F		TN
Spencer	17	M	Waggoner	TX

(continued)

Name	Age	Sex	Occupation	Birthplace
Collum, William C.	15	M		TX
Charles	12	M		TX
Jesse	10	M		TX
Elizabeth	12	F		TX
Sanders, J. H.	34	M	Farmer	TN
Helena	44	F		AL
Thompson, Mary J.	19	F		TN
Sanders, William Wiley	8	M		AL
Joseph Alex.	5	M		TX
Rea, Aaron	59	M	Farmer	TN
Rebecca	41	F		KY
DeCalb	13	M		TN
Benge, Thomas O.	35	M	Planter	TN
Mariah L.	23	F		AL
L. Holmes	6	F(?)		TX
Robert T.	4	M		TX
Charles	10≠ 2	M		TX
James M.	17	M	Farmer	TN
Margaret	18	F		TN
William B.	24	M		TN
Rucker, Clarisy	29	F	Teacher	IN
Dolby, W. K.	44	M	Planter	NC
Joseph G.	19	M	Farmer	TN
Green D.	17	M	Farmer	TN
F. M.	16	M	Farmer	TN
Benjamin B.	14	M		TN
Jesse K.	11	M		TN
Thomas W.	9	M		TX
Bailey, William	32	M	Farmer	TN
Martha	30	F		TN
William	9	M		TN
Alonzo	3	M		TX
James A.	9/12	M		TX
Robert	9/12	M		TX
Parks, William M.	31	M	Farmer	TN
Elizabeth	26	F		TN
Blount, James	2	M		TX
Parks, Thomas	1	M		TX
Walker, Sally	37	F		NC
John T.	17	M	Farmer	TN
William H.	11	M		TN
Mary J.	8	F		TX
Missouri	3	F		TX
Jesse T.	6/12	M		TX
Demick, John	44	M	Farmer	GER
Rhoda	23	F		TN
Sanders L.	1	M		TX
Walker, Elisha	60	M	School Teacher	VA
Jane	56	F		VA
William	18	M		TN
Martha	14	F		TN
Edwards, James	43	M	Farmer	NC
Betsey	39	F		NC
George	18	M	Farmer	TN
Margaret	16	F		TN
Mary Jane	14	F		TN
John	12	M		TN
Lydia	10	F		TN
Cornelius	8	M		TN
Joannah	7	F		TN
James	5	M		TN
Fro	2	F		TN
Womble, John	25	M	Farmer	NC
Jane	18	F		TN
Joannah	65	F		VA
Shafer, C. L.	35	M	Potter	GER
Sarah Jane	17	F		TN
Joshua	6/12	M		TN
Rice, George C.	44	M	Farmer	NC
Lucindia	39	F		SC
Thomas	21	M		NC
Mary	17	F		NC

(continued)

Name	Age	Sex	Occupation	Birthplace
Rice, Joseph S.	18	M	Farmer	NC
William J.	14	M		NC
Martha	13	F		TN
Nancy	10	F		MS
Texana	8	F		TX
Levi	4	M		TX
John	1	M		TX
Bayliss, H., Jr.	60	M	School Teacher	TN
Mary	57	F		TN
Mary G.	26	F		AL
R. H.	24	F		AL
Sarah H.	20	F		AL
Allison B.	15	M		AL
Julia Ann	13	F		AL
Cornelius, Martin	27	M	Physician	AL
Lucy Ann	18	F		TN
Cooley, James	41	M	Farmer	TN
Mariah	37	F		TN
James W.	17	M	Farmer	TN
Jesse T.	7	M		TX
William B.	3	M		TX
Mary E.	3	F		TX
Smith, Sarah A.	3	F		TX
Ormh, Loyd	28	M	Merchant	TN
Cleresy	24	F		AL
Jestus, Cathrine	55	F		GER
Henry	20	M	Farmer	GER
C.	22	F		GER
Cathrine	15	F		TN
Franklin	14	M		TN
Gerard	27	M	Farmer	GER
Epperson, C.	49	M	Planter	TN
Polly	29	F		MS
F. S. E.	15	F		TN
Elizabeth	15	F		TN
Sarah	13	F		TN
James	9	M		TN
Richard	6	M		TX
Cleveland	3	M		TX
Isadora	1	F		TX
Calvins, Parker	36	M	Farmer	TN
Wilkins, John	29	M	Farmer	TN
Thomas	4	M		TX
Graw, George A.	35	M	Carpenter	GER
Nancy H.	27	F		TN
C. Frederick	1	M		TX
Estle, William H.	23	M	Cabinet Worker	TN
Mary Jane	[illegible]	F		TN
William J.	4	M		TN
Elizabeth	2	F		TN
Charlotte	26	F		TN
Kimble, John M.	38	M	Black Smith	TN
Sarah E.	24	F		MS
Elizabeth J.	7	F		TX
Julia R.	5	F		TX
Mary E.	3	F		TX
Matilda	1	F		TX
Groomes, R. E.	27	M	Black Smith	KY
Job, E. B.	28	M	Farmer	TN
Eliza Ann	25	F		TN
George Allen	5	M		AL
Robert J.	1	M		AR
Poir, John	26	M	Farmer	NC
Elizabeth	22	F		TN
Tisdale, John	50	M	Farmer	NC
D. Ann	34	F		NC
Margaret E.	17	F		NC
Isabella T.	14	F		TN
Robert H.	13	M		TN
John R.	11	M		TX

(continued)

Name	Age	Sex	Occupation	Birthplace
Tisdale, William B.	10	M		TX
Charles G.	6	M		TX
Clem R.	4	M		TX
Andrew D.	1	M		TX
Darnell, James	33	M	Overseer	TN
Margaret	26	F		TN
James	5/12	M		TX
Webb, Bethnay	35	F		AL
James M.	18	M	Farmer	TN
Shaw, M. L.	5	M		TX
Webb, William M.	11/12	M		TX
Booth, Jane	23	F		TN
Mary Elizabeth	5	F		TX
James	2	M		TX
Cowan, John S.	22	M	Farmer	AL
Eliza	22	F		TN
Mary	9/12	F		TX
Estill, James	25	M	Farmer	TN
Martha	22	F		TN
Thomas W.	10/12	M		TX
Poir, James	77	M	Farmer	NC
John C.	16	M	Farmer	TN
Daniel	17	M	Farmer	TN
Allen, Mark	56	M	Ironside Bapt. Min.	TN
E.	11	M		AL
L. R.	8	F		AL
Walker, Lewis	40	M	Farmer	TN
N. Ann	18	F		TN
Famer	40	F		NC
Elisha J.	17	M	Farmer	TN
James T.	14	M		TN
A. H.	12	M		TN
William H.	10	M		TN
Lewis A.	8	M		TN
Crossland, Levi M. R.	3	M		TN
Elliott, B. E.	28	M	Merchant	MS
Lucilla	28	F		TN
Edward P.	10	M		TN
William Richard	12	M		TN
Rhabecca	7	F		TX
Samuel	5	M		TX
Rosella	3	F		TX
Infant	--	-		TX
Askin, John W.	32	M	Farmer	TN
Mary	25	F		AL
Margaret Ann	6	F		TX
Martha A.	4	F		TX
B. G.	2	M		TX
Looney, David	55	M	Cabinet Maker	SC
Tessy	46	F		NC
William	9	M		TX
Wright, Tessy	24	F		TN
Ann	7	F		TX
Susannah	5	F		TX
Watt, John	20	M	Farmer	TN
Estle, John J.	19	M	Farmer	TN
Jarrell, James	--	M	Farmer	TN
Cannington, Margret E.	12	F		SC
Sarah A.	9	F		SC
Laura	7	F		SC
William R.	5	M		SC
Infant	7/12	M		TX
Susan	3	F		TX
Leigh, John	38	M	Planter	VA
Martha M.	33	F		TN
William L.	14	M		AL
Mary E.	10	F		AL
Charles H.	8	M		AL
Martha A.	6	F		AL
John T.	4	M		AL
Sarah E.	1	F		TX
Hardin, B.	24	M	Overseer	NC

(continued)

BOWIE COUNTY, TEXAS

Name	Age	Sex	Occupation	Birthplace
Richardson, Elizabeth	38	F		NC
Payne, W. W.	17	M	Watch Maker	VA
Richardson, Sam	28	M	Farmer	NC
C. R.	22	F		AL
R. T.	2	M		TX
Darnell, S.	25	M	Farmer	AL
Sylvia	18	F		TN
A. D.	4	M		TN
M.	2	M		TN
Bassett, Martha	43	F		TN
Thomas J.	26	M	Farmer	AR
John W.	14	M		LA
Adaline	11	F		TX
Richard T.	9	M		TX
Mary J.	7	F		TX
Davis, Anthony	23	M	Farmer	TN
Hellen	20	F		AL
Hulin, Alfred L.	41	M	Trader	TN
Alfred, B. D.	42	M	Farmer	NC
Elizabeth	15	F		TN
Mary	12	F		TN
Wiley	9	M		TX
Frances	7	F		TX
Joannah	7	F		TX
Sophia	5	F		TX
Smith, Robert	56	M	Farmer	NC
M----	30	F		TN
James	16	M	Brick Mason	TN
Joseph	7	M		TX
Jane	4	F		TX
Mary	2	F		TX

BRAZORIA COUNTY, TEXAS

Name	Age	Sex	Occupation	Birthplace
Westervelt, Stephen M.	35	M	Merchant	NY
Martha	30	F		TN
Maria	10	F		TX
Sarah	8	F		TX
Stephen, Jr.	6/12	M		TX
Masterson, T. S.	37	M	Mail Contractor	TN
C. ?.	31	F		TN
William	15	M		TN
James B.	12	M		TN
Thomas W.	9	M		TX
Ann G.	7	F		TX
Archibald	5	M		TX
Branch G.	3	M		TX
Laura R.	7/12	F		TX
Roane, Ann C.	60	F		VA
Laura V.	21	F		TN
Harris, Samuel	40	M	None	VA
Mills, David C.	30	M	Planter	KY
William G.	40	M	Overseer	TN
Hassell, J. W.	40	M	Black Smith	MO
Perry, James T.	59	M	Planter	TN
Emily M. B.	55	F		VA
Eliza M.	20	F		MO
Henry A.	18	M		TX
Nelson, John	33	M	Carpenter	NC
Bryan, Guy M.	27	M	None	MO
Luyder, Charles	23	M	Carpenter	GER
Hixt, Joseph	33	M	Overseer	GA
Copal, Charles	25	M	Carpenter	GER
Lyon, S. C.	40	M	Seaman	ENG
Cawhill, John	36	M	Sailor	IRE
House, William	22	M	None	TN
Shapard, L. P.	25	M	Carpenter	TN
Mary R.	3	F		TX
E. S.	25	F		TX
John	1/12	M		TX
Coolgrove, W. C.	31	M	Farmer	NY
Lucretia C.	30	F		TN
Apollo	3	M		TX
Margaretta	10/12	F		TX
Armstrong, George	34	M	Farmer	TN
D. W.	28	M	None	TN
Bond, John	25	M	Overseer	TN
Shannon, E. D.	35	M	Carpenter	PA
Sweeney, P. W.	27	M	Farmer	TN
Mary G.	24	F		KY
Aradella	1	F		TX
Twedy, John R.	23	M	Overseer	VA
Sears, Josiah	24	M	Overseer	VA
Sweeney, Thomas	32	M	Farmer	TN
Frances D.	24	F		AL
Ann Elizabeth	6	F		TX
Edward L.	3	M		TX
Kate	2	F		TX
Sweeney, John	35	M	Farmer	TN
Hert, William	23	M	Overseer	FL
Sweeney, Samuel	22	M	Farmer	TN
Crews, Edward C.	21	M	Overseer	KY
Henry, Whylie	38	M	Overseer	TN
Mary E.	30	F		GA
James	9	M		AL
Charity C.	7	F		AL
Mary F.	4	F		TX
Hortense	1/12	F		TX
Octavia	1/12	F		TX
Westall, H. G.	30	M	Farmer	TN
Andrew	5	M		TX
Eliza M.	3	F		TX
Mason, V.	70	M	Carpenter	DC
Lewis, Ira B.	48	M	Lawyer	PA
Eliza J.	41	F		MS
Louisa E.	20	F		MS
Cora	19	F		LA
Stella	18	F		LA
Arson, Earnest	4	M		TX
Lewis, James C.	30	M	Farmer	TN
Sarah	54	F		TN
Jacob W.	23	M	None	AL
Joseph C.	20	M	None	AL
Hoskins, Isaac C.	51	M	Farmer	TN
Nancy	47	F		VA
Ann	14	F		TX
James E.	11	M		TX
Virginia A.	8	F		TX
Emily G.	5	F		TX
Martha L.	3	F		TX
Isaac C., Jr.	1	M		TX
Cannon, William C.	42	M	Farmer	SC
Matilda I.	31	F		TN
John	11	M		TX
William W.	10	M		TX
Edward B.	8	M		TX
James W.	6	M		TX
Sarah A.	11/12	F		TX
Samuel	2	M		TX
Huey, G. H.	39	M	Farmer	TN
Susanna	37	F		TN
John W.	19	M	None	TN
Barran B.	17	M	None	TN
Delila C.	14	F		TN
Mary C.	13	F		TN
Martha E.	9	F		TX
Louisa T.	7	F		TX
Hutchinson, S. P.	26	M	None	GA
William	45	M	Gardner	ENG
Huey, Willis	42	M	Farmer	TN
William K.	11	M		MS
John S.	8	M		MS
James E.	5	M		TN

(continued)

BRAZORIA COUNTY, TEXAS

Name	Age	Sex	Occupation	Birthplace
Huey, Green W.	2	M		TX
Sarah	35	F		SC
Hodges, R.	35	M	Carpenter	TN
Barbara	18	F		GER
Munsen, M. S.	25	M	Lawyer	TX
Sarah K.	19	F		TN
Sojourner, C. B.	23	M	Farmer	MS
Martha L.	22	F		LA
Pullium, Edward	25	M	Farmer	KY
Elizabeth	18	F		TN
Thomas H.	19	M	Farmer	KY
David S.	22	M	Carpenter	KY
Adin	35	M	Carpenter	KY
Gass, B.	38	M	Planter	IRE
McNeal, B	28	M	Overseer	KY
Winters, A.	39	M	Overseer	TN
Kyle, W. J.	48	M	Farmer	TN
William R.	22	M	Farmer	TN
Coffee, Thomas J.	44	M	Farmer	NC
Malinda G.	39	F		TN
Aaron	17	M	Farmer	MS
Ellen	15	F		MS
Ambros	12	M		MS
Henry	10	M		MS
Rosana	7	F		MS
Edmondson, James	18	M	None	TN
McInnis, Miles	40	M	Overseer	NC
Churchill, Andrew	59	M	Farmer	KY
Margaret	59	F		TN
William	21	M	Farmer	KY
Downing, Lorenzo	28	M	Farmer	VA
Nancy J.	20	F		TN
Huldy Ann	8	F		TX
Isaac A.	6	M		AR
Nancy O.	4	F		TN
McKinney, M. W.	36	M	Carpenter	KY
Tibitha J.	25	F		TN
Nancy N.	3	F		TX
Lorina A. C.	1/12	F		TX
Callihan, T. J.	32	M	Merchant	VA
Mary C.	22	F		AR
William C.	9	M		TX
Louisa S.	6	F		TX
Harriet	4	F		TX
Cleora A.	9/12	F		TX
Talbott, Susan	43	F		TN
Robinson, Andrew	87	M	None	KY
Andrew, Jr.	40	M	Mail Carrier	AR
Harriet	30	F		TN
Andrew, Jr.	19	M	None	TX
James	9	M		TX
John	8	M		TX
David	4	M		TX
Warren	2	M		TX
Jefferson	2	M		TX
Hoskins, John	56	M	Carpenter	NC
Nathan D.	22	M	None	AL
Nancy J.	16	F		TN
Blood, Henry	38	M	Planter	VT
Laura C.	24	F		TN
Mary	2	F		LA
Baker, N. B.	20	M	Overseer	TN
Sweeney, John W.	44	M	Sugar Maker	VA
Peters, William	21	M	Laborer	SWE
Westall, A. E.	37	M	Planter	TN
Elizabeth M.	34	F		OH
Ann E.	10	F		TX
Thomas H.	8	M		TX
Adelia	5	F		TX

(continued)

Name	Age	Sex	Occupation	Birthplace
Westall, Charles K.	3	M		TX
Philson, Perry	35	M	Carpenter	PA
Faulk, George	27	M	Bricklayer	MD
Amens, John	37	M	Bricklayer	ENG
Ward, Hiram	20	M	Laborer	NY
Pie, John	22	M	Overseer	NY
Shattuck, Horice	32	M	Cooper	NH
Corey, Ezra H.	22	M	Cooper	PA
Estes, M. L.	23	M	Cooper	TN
Armstrong, T. A.	31	M	Overseer	TN
Mary E.	22	F		NY
James L.	2	M		TX
Mary	8/12	F		TX
Ginsley, Isaac T.	50	M	Planter	TN
Mary A.	35	F		TN
Caladonia	12	F		TX
Joseph	8	M		TX
Samuel	6	M		TX
Isaac H.	4	M		TX
Ann E.	2	F		TX
Perfont(?), V. S.	16	F		MS
Damhart, Michael	28	M	Butcher	GER
Smelser, John	24	M	Overseer	TN
Snider, Abram	50	M	Farmer	KY
Sarah	45	F		NC
Stephen	22	M	None	TN
Sophia	17	F		TX
Granville	11	M		TX
Robertson, M.	19	F		TX
Sweeney, John, Sr.	53	M	Farmer	VA
Dance, H.	35	M	Carpenter	NC
Spencer	27	M	Carpenter	NC
James H.	27	M	Carpenter	NC
James	23	M	Carpenter	NC
Hornes, Sophia	25	F		TN
Sweeney, F.	20	M	None	TN

DISTRICTS OF BURKESON & BRAZOS COUNTIES

Name	Age	Sex	Occupation	Birthplace
Richerson, Masy F.	27	F	Farmer	TN
Virginia	24	F		TN
Laura Ann	1	F		TX
Webb, Joseph	27	M	Farmer	TN
William	18	M	Farmer	TN
Collins, Christopher C.	33	M	Farmer	TN
Clayton, Charles	26	M	Farmer	TN
Sarah	26	F		TX
Amanda	8	F		TX
Mary	6	F		TX
Nancy	4	F		TX
Warren	2	M		TX
Havens, William	35	M	Farmer	TN
Oma	35	F		OH
William	12	M		TX
Ann	7	F		TX
Elizabeth	6/12	F		TX
Wirson, Tilmon	20	M	Farmer	TX
Midleton, Washington	41	M	Farmer	LA
Mary	62	F		TN
Walker, Amanda	30	F		LA
Midleton, Martha	14	F		LA
Samuel	12	M		TX
Walker, Jackson	6	M		TX
Mary	4	F		TX
Midleton, Samuel P.	24	M	None	LA
Walker, William C.	40	M	Farmer	TN
Nancy	34	F		AL
James	16	M	Farmer	AL
Calvin	12	M		TX
William	9	M		TX
Poly	7	F		TX
Newton	6	M		TX
Susan	1	F		TX

(continued)

DISTRICT OF BURELSON & BRAZOS COUNTIES, TEXAS

Name	Age	Sex	Occupation	Birthplace
Walker, Julietta	9	F		TX
Mary	17	F		??
Hudson, Henry G.	50	M	Gun Smith	TN
Elizabeth	48	F		TN
Catharine	14	F		AL
John	7	M		TX
Bowman, James P.	50	M	Farmer	TN
Eliza	40	F		SC
Sinthanah	23	F		AL
William	18	M		TN
Bowman, Thomas C.	43	M	Farmer	TN
Mary	41	F		TN
Parlee	19	F		TN
Susan	15	F		TN
Henry	13	M		MS
Leandioses	10	M		MS
Albert	8	M		MS
Sarah	7	F		MS
Alexander	5	M		MS
James	2	M		TX
Cornelia	6/12	F		TX
Warren, Alexander	43	M	Farmer	GA
Mary	35	F		TN
Sarah	17	F		AL
Lunnah	15	F		AL
William	14	M		AL
Jeremiah	12	M		AL
Eliza	10	F		AL
Amanda	7	F		AL
Martha	7	F		AL
Jacob	4	M		AL
Nevill, Hardin	45	M	Farmer	NC
Susan	27	F		NC
Minerva	20	F		TN
Sarah	17	F		AL
David	10	M		TX
William	7	M		TX
Nancy	4	F		TX
Caroline	2	F		TX
King, William	35	M	Farmer	TN
Rachael	30	F		AL
James	14	M		AL
Jacob	10	M		AL
John	9	M		AL
Clarine	7	F		AL
Elizabeth	4	F		TX
Jessey	1	M		TX
Wilson, William	22	M	Farmer	GA
Seale, Eli	57	M	Farmer	SC
Sarah	48	F		TN
Thomas	24	M	Farmer	AL
Augustus	19	M	Farmer	AL
Bradford	17	M	Farmer	AL
Mary	15	F		AL
William	9	M		TX
Roark, Mary	22	F		AR
Budgman, Julia Ann	15	F		AR
Lucinda	5	F		TX
Ellison, Isabella	40	F	Farmer	TN
Alexander	19	M	Farmer	AL
George	15	M	Farmer	AL
Louisa	12	F		AL
Jessey	10	M		TX
Joseph	5	M		TX
Sparkes, William C.	52	M	Farmer	GA
Jane	44	F		TN
Claracy	13	F		TX
John	11	M		TX
Elijah	9	M		TX
Minerva	7	F		TX
William	6	M		TX
Samuel	4	M		TX
Stephen	26	M	Farmer	TN
Elizabeth	15	F		TX
McCuny, Thomas	50	M	Farmer	TN
Matilda	45	F		TN
Thomas	18	M	Farmer	MS
Susan	16	F		TX
Joseph	12	M		TX
Minerva	10	F		TX
Matilda	8	F		TX
Sarah	5	F		TX
John	1	M		TX
McChristian, Mary	2	F		TX
Lines, Thomas	23	M	Farmer	KY
Elizabeth	19	F		TN
Isaac	4/12	M		TX
Love, Gilbert H.	29	M	Farmer	TN
Martha	23	F		AL
William	4	M		TX
Joseph	2/ 2	M		TX
McDonald, John	25	M	Farmer	TN
Anne	23	F		PA
Payne, Marshall	33	M	Farmer	TN
Mary	29	F		TN
Ofelia	14	F		TN
Cain	11	M		TN
Permelia	8	F		TN
Richard	5	M		TN
William	2	M		TX
McDonald, Mathew	28	M	Farmer	TN
Nancy	25	F		AL
John	8	M		TN
Elizabeth	5	F		TN
Angline	2	F		TX
Foley, John H.	52	M	None	KY
Pegy	43	F		TN
John	14	M		TN
Margret	13	F		MS
Josephine	10	F		TX
Harvy	5	M		TX
Georgeann	3	F		TX
Johnson, Robert	32	M	Dist. Court Clerk	VA
Josephine	20	F		TN
Eleanor	2	F		TX
Carter, Richard	72	M	Farmer	TN
Elizabeth	59	F		TN
Reed, Wilson	39	M	Farmer	TN
Maryann	33	F		TN
John	13	M		TX
Jeraldine	12	F		TX
Richard	9	M		TX
Wiley	7	M		TX
William	5	M		TX
Elizabeth	1	F		TX
Berton, Samuel	40	M	Farmer	KY
Eveline	34	F		TN
William	13	M		MS
Elizabeth	11	F		TX
Mary	9	F		TX
Wiley	8	M		TX
Penalton	6	M		TX
Nelson	4	M		TX
Nicham, John	40	M	None	SC
McMilan, Andy	34	M	Farmer	IRE
Tabitha	27	F		TN
George	5	M		TX
Hugh	4	M		TX
Mary	2	F		TX
John	1/12	M		TX
Higgs, George	49	M	Farmer	VA
Evy	47	F		NC
Benjamin	24	M	Farmer	TN
James	20	M	Farmer	TN
Thomas	19	M	Farmer	TN
William	17	M	Farmer	TN

(continued)

DISTRICT OF BURLESON & BRAZOS COUNTIES, TEXAS

Name	Age	Sex	Occupation	Birthplace
Higgs, Doctor	15	M		TN
Mary	11	F		TX
Jane	9	F		TX
Minervy	4	F		TX
Samuel	2	M		TX
George	23	M	None	TN
Wilson, William H.	24	M	Farmer	SC
Mary	20	F		TN
Alice	4	F		TX
Danning, Joseph	18	M	Farmer	SC
Spencer, Alexander	30	M	Farmer	TN
Harriet	20	F		TX
Marthey	5	F		TX
William	1	M		TX
Thomas, Alexander	65	M	Farmer	SC
Elizabeth	55	F		GA
Thornton	24	M	Farmer	TN
Caroline	18	F		TN
Sandy	17	M	Farmer	TX
Wilkison, William	26	M	Farmer	TN
Ann	23	F		TN
James	23	M	Farmer	TN
George	21	M	None	TN
Lucy	13	F		TN
John	12	M		TN
Sarah	7	F		TX
Steven	5	M		TX
Frances	3	F		TX
Ray, G----	49	M	Farmer	VA
Mary	42	F		TN
John	21	M	Farmer	TN
Elizabeth	19	F		TN
Lucretia	17	F		TN
James	15	M	Farmer	TN
Thomas	3	M		TX
Reed, Elijah	34	M	Farmer	TN
Martha	31	F		AL
Margaret	9	F		TX
Missouri	8	F		TX
Matilda	6	F		TX
Elizabeth	2	F		TX
Tomkins, Alfred	43	M	Farmer	TN
Nancy	32	F		KY
Vinah	9	F		IL
Lorensa	8	F		IL
Margret	6	F		IL
Routha Ann	5	F		IL
Mary	2	F		IL
Cinthy	6/12	F		TX
Porter, Jerome	27	M	Farmer	TN
Sinia	19	F		TX
Susan	1/12	F		TX
Porter, Susan	49	F	Farmer	TN
Robert	25	M	Farmer	KY
Newel	21	M	Farmer	KY
Milton	20	M	Farmer	KY
John	18	M	Farmer	TN
Bevly	16	M	Farmer	TX
Thomas	12	M		TX
Welch, William	29	M	Farmer	MD?
Mary	23	F		TN
William	19	M	Farmer	TN
Lucinda	17	F		LA
William	2	M		TN
Emma	1/12	F		TX
Carothers, William	28	M	Farmer	TN
Martha	26	F		AL
Marthey	7	F		TX
John	5	M		TX
Eliza	3	F		TX
Margaret	1	F		TX
Thomas D.	14	M		TN
Oldham, John	48	M	Farmer	TN
Mary	40	F		NC
James	22	M	Farmer	TN
Catherine	17	F		TN
John	16	M	Farmer	TN
William	12	M		TN
James	24	M	Farmer	TN
Hord, Perry	25	M	Farmer	NC
Sarah	19	F		TN
Louisa	16	F		TN
Leander	13	M		TN
Nancy	9	F		TX
Edward	19	M	Farmer	TN
Brymer, Amos	39	M	Farmer	TN
Vasti	35	F		TN
Caroline	17	F		TN
Rodia	--	F		--
Dialthe	13	F		TN
William	14	M		TN
John	9	M		TN
Talithia	7	F		TN
Nancy	4	F		TN
Owen	1	M		TX
Roddy, Ephraim	60	M	Farmer	PA
Harriet	50	F		NC
Boyles, Mary	21	F		TN
Elen	20	F		TN
Joseph	18	M	Farmer	TX
Boswell, Ulyses	34	M	Farmer	TN
Elizabeth	23	F		TN
George	6	M		TX
Jane	3	F		TX
Richard	2	M		TX
Marthey	10	F		TX
Guthrie, John	47	M	Farmer	TN
Mary	36	F		TN
Alexander	18	M	Farmer	AL
John	16	M	Farmer	AL
Manerva	14	F		TX
Mary	11	F		TX
Samuel	11	M		TX
Ulysses	8	M		TX
Thomas	6	M		TX
Sarah	4	F		TX
Franklin	1	M		TX
Mitchell, John	55	M	Farmer	KY
Anna	43	F		NY
Caroline	14	F		NY
Sarah	12	F		TN
Francis	6	M		TN
Guthrie, George	26	M	Farmer	TN
Permelia	17	F		FL
John	1	M		TX
Johnston, Adams	37	M	Farmer	MO
Larinda	31	F		TN
Catherine	11	F		MO
Caster	9	M		MO
Cassa Ann	4	F		TX
James	2/12	M		TX
Nathaniel	2/12	M		TX
Ennis	19	M	Farmer	TN
Guthrie, William	21	M	Farmer	TN
Harriet	24	F		SC
Margaret	21	F		SC
Cinthia	19	F		SC
Mahala	7	F		TX
Tompkins, Joseph	51	M	Farmer	??
Celia	48	F		TN
Elias	28	M	Farmer	TN
William	26	M	Farmer	TN
George	17	M	Farmer	TN
Mary	11	F		IL
Elizabeth	9	F		IL
Joseph	7	M		IL

DISTRICT OF BURLESON & BRAZOS COUNTIES, TEXAS

Name	Age	Sex	Occupation	Birthplace
Leeper, Charles	47	M	Farmer	GA
Frances	41	F		TN
Nancy	18	F		AL
Marthey	16	F		AL
George	13	M		AL
James	11	M		AL
Frances	9	F		AL
William	6	M		AL
Inman, John	43	M	Farmer	SC
Mary	42	F		TN
Louiza	23	F		AL
Matilda	21	F		AL
Elizabeth	18	F		AL
Isaac	16	M	Farmer	AL
Johnson	11	M		AL
Bush, Maple	41	M	Farmer	KY
Olevia	24	F		TX
Mary	8	F		TX
Mordica	5	M		TX
Josephine	2	F		TX
Flack, Robert	46	M	Stock Raiser	TN
Cole, Sampson	50	M	Farmer	TN
Virrah	44	F		TN
Andrew	20	M	Farmer	IL
Benjamin	18	M	Farmer	IL
Joseph	12	M		IL
Isaac	10	M		AR
Alfred	3	M		MO
Hampton, Prusia	19	F		LA
Cole, William	44	M	None	KY
Birchett, John	30	M	Farmer	TN
Elizabeth	22	F		TN
Joseph	6	M		AR
Mary ?.	5	F		AR
John	2	M		AR
McCauley, Margaret	33	F	Farmer	NC
Robert	19	M	Farmer	NC
William	16	M	Farmer	TN
Lemuel	12	M		TN
Voss, John	21	M	Clerk	TN
Crunk, Nicholas S.	37	M	Farmer	TN
Emaline	27	F		AL
John	8	M		TX
Lavina	7	F		TX
Ophelia	5	F		TX
Richard	4	M		TX
Chrisman, Oracio	52	M	Farmer	VA
Augustious	44	F		PA
Rector	22	M	Farmer	TX
Elen	15	F		TX
Camelia	12	F		TX
Richard	10	M		TX
Orenth	8	M		TX
Sarah	4	F		TX
Thomas	2	M		TX
Thomson, Thomas C.	26	M	Farmer	TN
Mary	20	F		TX
Oracio	4	M		TX
Rector	2	M		TX
Doak, John	42	M	Farmer	TN
Mary Ann	38	F		VA
Abner	11	M		MS
John	4	M		MS
Maraham	3	F		TX
William	13	M		MS
Martha	1	F		TX
McMurry, Joseph	33	M	Farmer	TN
Elizabeth	30	F		TN
Samuel	12	M		TN
Moses	9	M		TN
Joseph	6	M		TX
John	2	M		TX
Emily	6/12	F		TX

Name	Age	Sex	Occupation	Birthplace
Wyett, John M.	25	M	None	??
Martha	22	F		TN
Young, William	32	M	M.D.	NY
Cina	16	F		TN
John	24	M	Clerk	NY
Dilard, Zachariah W.	26	M	Merchant	TN
Sarah	18	F		GA
Sarah Ann	4	F		TX
William	6/12	M		TX
Dilard, William	18	M	Clerk	TN
William S.	15	M	None	GA
Miller, Simon	40	M	Farmer	TN
Louis	35	M	Farmer	??
Adison, Isaac S.	61	M	Carpenter	MD
Sarah	65	F		ENG
John	21	M		ENG
Margaret	16	F		ENG
Isabella	8	F		TX
Childers, Hugh M	49	M	Farmer	TN
Sarah	41	F		TN
Hugh	15	M	Farmer	TX
Elisha	12	M		TX
Charp, John	36	M	Farmer	TN
Minerva	28	F		TX
Wiley	10	M		TX
Lucinda	7	F		TX
Frances	5	F		TX
Sarah	2	F		TX
Charp, Archable	66	M	Farmer	??
Lucinda	66	F		VA
Graves, James A.	42	M	Farmer	KY
Mary	38	F		TN
George	22	M	Merchant	KY
James	19	M	Farmer	IL
Thomas	14	M		IL
Robert	10	M		IL
Frederick	11	M		TX
Louannah	9	F		TX
Charles	7	M		IL
Washington	6	M		TX
Sarah	5	F		IL
Josiah	1	M		IL
Isaac	1	M		IL
Scott, Phillip	35	M	Farmer	TN
Mary	28	F		TN
William L.	6	M		TX
Phillip	4	M		TX
Hezekiah	3	M		TX
Lorenah	1	F		TX
Howlet, James	45	M	Farmer	MD
Sarah	40	F		TN
James	6	M		TX
Cina	3	F		TX
Susan	1	F		TX
Laurence, Narcissa	20	F		??
Addison, Joseph	35	M	Farmer	TN
Margaret	26	F		AL
Susan	8	F		TX
John	6	M		TX
Sylvia	4	F		TX
Josephine	1	F		TX
Margaret	6/12	F		TX
Dexter, James W.	37	M	None	NY
Nancy	32	F		TN
Eliza	11	F		TX
Sarah	10	F		TX
Allen, Eveline	8	F		TX
Wooldridge, Thomas D.	47	M	Farmer	GA
Nancy	47	F		GA
Fitch, Cabern	40	M	Farmer	TN
Stewart, Leroy	23	M	Mechanic	AL
Green, Mary	11	F		TX

DISTRICT OF BURLESON & BRAZOS COUNTIES, TEXAS

Name	Age	Sex	Occupation	Birthplace
Oldham, William	52	M	Farmer	KY
Mullins, Henry	35	M	None	TN
Casner, John	23	M	Farmer	GER
Vincent, George	35	M	Black Smith	KY
Carter, Ebner H.	31	M	Farmer	TN
Rebecca	24	F		TN
David	4	M		TX
Lebern	2	M		TX
Gill, William	25	M	Merchant	TN
Gill, George	23	M	None	VA
Ryan, William	38	M	Farmer	TN
Nancy	37	F		TN
James	13	M		AR
Caroline	12	F		TX
Mary	9	F		TX
Markaus	7	M		TX
David	6	M		TX
John	2	M		TX
McChristian, Thomas	70	M	Mechanic	??
Swoop, Franklin	32	M	Farmer	TN
Marthey	18	F		AL
William	3	M		TX
Wiley	1	M		TX
Gragg, Lucretia	40	F		TN
Martha	20	F		AL
Mary	18	F		AL
Henry	15	M	None	AL
William	4	M		TX
Elis, Elgia	39	M	School Teacher	TN
Virginia	13	F		AL
James	8	M		AL
Elizabeth	5	F		MS
McClanahan, Milton	54	M	Farmer	TN
Dolly	48	F		GA
James	27	M	Farmer	AL
John	20	M	Farmer	AL
Frances	16	F		AL
Nancy	13	F		AL
Susan	10	F		AL
Marthey	7	F		AL
William	5	M		AL
Rice, Labon	65	M	Farmer	VA
Elizabeth	62	F		TN
Johhanness	22	F		AL
Elvira	20	F		AR
Tharp, Pleasant	40	M	Black Smith	VA
Nancy	28	F		TN
William	[illegible]	M		TN
James	5	M		TX
Henry	2	M		TX
Mary	5/12	F		TX
Thomas, Jessey T.	43	M	Farmer	TN
Sarah	27	F		LA
Eliza	16	F		AL
Frank	13	M	Farmer	AL
James	12	M		AL
Eldridge, Thomas	10	M		TX
Emila	8	F		TX
Gibbs, George	14	M		AL
Miatari	12	F		AL
Mary	5	F		TX
Boswell, Lucinda	40	M		SC
Lucinda	16	F		TN
Nancy	15	F		TN
Martha	9	F		TX
Josephine	7	F		TX
John	5	M		TX
Richard	3	M		TX
Storm, Pleasant	33	M	Farmer	TN
Mary	26	F		TN
William	5	M		TX

Name	Age	Sex	Occupation	Birthplace
Bailey, M. ?.	39	M	Farmer	TN
Clarisa	35	F		SC
John	16	M	Farmer	MS
Celia	13	F		MS
James	9	M		MS
Abigail	7	F		MS
Iria	5	M		MS
Elija(h)	3	M		TX
Bailey, Elija	31	M	None	TN
Teal, Richard	28	M	Farmer	IL
Mannie	21	F		TN
Thomas	26	M	None	IL
Marancis	18	M	Farmer	TX
William	14	M		TX
John	2	M		TX
Standfer, Iseral	68	M	Farmer	VA
Charine	54	F		TN
Abram	31	M	Farmer	TN
Susanner	19	F		TN
John	25	M	Farmer	AR
Charles	21	M	Farmer	AR
Isereal	15	M	Farmer	AL
Thomas	14	M		AR
Tiaton	22	M	Farmer	MEX
Dun, Charles	22	M	School Teacher	AL
Martha	22	F		TN
Cox, Sarah L.	37	F		TN
John	13	M		TX
Fedrick	12	M		TX
Mary	11	F		TX
Scott, Samuel A.	26	M	School teacher	AL
Andrew	23	M	Farmer	AL
Reed, Jacob	66	M	Farmer	TN
Matilda	66	F		NC
Emlia	23	F		AL
John	22	M	Farmer	TN
Henry	6	M		TX
Lothelen, Sandy Y.	33	M	Farmer	TN
Mary	30	F		TN
Lutetia	9	F		TN
Elizabeth	7	F		TN
Brother	2	M		TN
Susan	6/12	F		TX
Tharp, William J.	25	M	Farmer	TN
Mary	23	F		KY
William	1	M		TX
Cinthia	3/12	F		TX
Joslin, Joslin S.	33	M	Farmer	TN
Jane	19	F		AL
Levi	1	M		MS
Morgan, Alen	31	M	Farmer	TN
Sarah	32	F		TN
Parilee	10	F		TN
John	9	M		TN
Sam	7	M		TN
Aron	4	M		TN
Sarah	2	F		TX
Fulcher, James	53	M	Farmer	TN
Mary	29	F		FL
Gee, Nevel A.	34	M	Farmer	VA
Christianna	18	F		TN
Van	12	M		TX
Susan	5	F		TX
Martha	10/12	F		TX
Gee, Elizabeth	67	F		VA
James, Daniel	35	M	Black Smith	VA
Persons, Thomas	21	M	Farmer	AL
Amous	19	M	Farmer	AL
Hill, William W.	42	M	Farmer	KY
Mary	22	F		KY
John	10	M		TX
William	8	M		TX
James	5	M		TX

(continued)

DISTRICT OF BURLESON & BRAZOS COUNTIES, TEXAS

Name	Age	Sex	Occupation	Birthplace
Hill, Mariah	2	F		TX
Phelix	1	M		TX
Nevill, Sarah	18	F		AL
Rice, Porter	32	M	Farmer	TN
Boles, James	34	M	Farmer	KY
Miller, Drewry	23	M	Farmer	TN
Elendear	22	F		TN
Josiah	10	M		TN
Eli	4	M		TX
Charles	1/12	M		TX
McDowell, Ephrom	34	M	Farmer	IRE
Sarah	19	F		TX
Owler, Benjamin	40	M	Farmer	??
Huland, Walter	30	M	Farmer	TN
Waren, Henry	30	M	Farmer	TN
Micke	29	F		AL
Thomas	11	M		TX
James	8	M		TX
Haley, John	40	M	Farmer	??
Sarah	30	F		TN
Martha	12	F		TN
Louisa	9	F		TN
Rodia	7	F		AR
Lorra	5	F		AR
Fulcher, Elizabeth	50	F	Farming	TN
Frank	26	F	Farmer	AR
Thomas	17	M	Farmer	AR
Mullins, Peter	43	M	Farmer	IRE
Elizabeth	37	F		TN
Marcaus	1/12	M		TX
Caroline	10	F		TX
McCuyton, William	24	M	Farmer	TN
Eliza	27	F		TN
Marcaus	8	M		AR
William	1	M		TX
Blair, Edward J.	26	M	Farmer	MO
Mary	25	F		TN
Adaline	9	F		TX
Benjamin	5	M		TX
John	2	M		TX
Bird, Thomas J.	28	M	Farmer	TN
Martha	20	F		AL
John	3	M		TX
Mary	1/12	F		TX
Bird, Nathan	17	M	None	TN
Hunter, Jane	37	F		TN
John	17	M	Farmer	TN
Marse Letha	5	F		TX
Bird, William P.	30	M	Farmer	TN
Calley	19	F		TN
John	10	M		TX
Elizabeth	4	F		TX
Malissa	2	F		TX
Isaack	9/12	M		TX
Fisher, James	69	M	Farmer	NC
Salley	40	F		TN
Polly Ann	20	F		TN
James	18	M	Farmer	TX
Dicy	16	F		TX
Peggy	14	F		TX
Henry	12	M		TX
Horton	10	M		TX
Thomas	8	M		TX
Elit	5	M		TX
Joseph	2	M		TX
Hughes, William C.	26	M	Farmer	TN
Caroline	18	F		IL
Hughes, Marion S.	21	M	Farmer	IL
Powers, John	52	M	Farmer	MA
Sarah	49	F		VA
John	17	M	Farmer	TN
Amanda	12	F		TX
Owen, Shadrick B.	27	M	Farmer	IL
Marthia	24	F		TN
Liddy	4	F		AR
Mary	2	F		TX
Andrew	6/12	M		TX
Kuykendall, Simon	26	M	Farmer	TN
Sarah	16	F		MO
Brown, William	34	M	Farmer	TN
Sarah	22	F		KY
Mary	4/12	F		TX
Oldham, Moses	73	M	Farmer	NC
Christi	53	F		NC
Moses	15	M	Farmer	TN
Ann Eliza	13	F		TN
Conley, Joseph	27	M	Farmer	TN
Mary	20	F		TN

CALDWELL COUNTY, TEXAS

Name	Age	Sex	Occupation	Birthplace
Click, George W.	30	M	Farmer	TN
Rebecca	19	F		LA
Malicki	2	M		TX
William	4/12	M		TX
Click, Andrew J.	30	M	Farmer	TN
Polk, Hedly	35	M	Farmer	NC
Hetty E.	23	F		TN
James D.	5	M		TX
Martha O.	2	F		TX
Daugherty, Heck	26	M	Farmer	TN
Agness M.	21	F		MO
Mary C.	8/12	F		TX
Daugherty, George ?.	12	M		AR
Nathaniel	24	M	Teamster	TN
Eastwood, William	31	M	Farmer	MO
Harris, Austin	21	M		TN
Hardiman, William	34	M	Farmer	TN
Rebecca	44	F		TN
Clara	7	F		TX
Susan	2	F		TX
Homard, Lewis	34	M	Carriage Maker	SWI
Glasscow, James	25	M	Carpenter	SC
Fentress, Lemuel	31	M	Carpenter	VA
Homard, Mary Ann	1	F		TX
Brown, David F.	49	M	Physician	TN
Jane	37	F		TN
Mary A.	18	F		TN
Cordelia	16	F		TN
Clara	14	F		TN
James F.	12	M		TN
Albert P.	9	M		TX
Lichargas M.	7	M		TX
Stewart, Robert E.	26	M	Carpenter	VA
Polk, Warner	18	M	Stock Keeper	AR
Hester, Edward	19	M	Farmer	CAN
Hardiman, Leonidas	24	M	Farmer	TN
McKean, John C.	53	M	Farmer	VA
Helen	26	F		TN
McKean, W. C.	24	M	Farmer	TN
Andrew J.	19	M	Student	TN
Clarisa F.	13	F		TX
Catherine	6	F		TX
Harris, Leslia	23	M	Teamster	TN
Everline	16	F		TX
William	11	M		TX
Thomas F.	8	M		TX
Jones, Edward	19	M	Teamster	TN
McKean, Joseph	11	M		TX
Long, William	21	M	Teamster	TN

CALDWELL COUNTY, TEXAS

Name	Age	Sex	Occupation	Birthplace
Fentress, James	48	M	Farmer	TN
Mary O.	28	F		TN
Thomas	9	M		TX
Francis, George	56	M	Farmer	IRE
Margaret A.	46	F		TN
John	26	M	Laborer	AL
Pendleton	21	M		AL
George	17	M	Student	AL
Joseph	15	M		AL
Edward	13	M		AL
Armadilla	9	F		AL
Wesley	7	M		AL
Arabella	3	F		AL
Martin, Joseph	40	M		RI
Duncan, Mary	23	F		AL
Hudson, James	34	M	Farmer	SC
Amanda	32	F		TN
Margaret R.	11	F		AL
Warren F.	8	M		AL
Thomas	6	M		AL
Richard	2	M		TX
Reese, George W.	49	M	Farmer	GA
Adaline	27	F		VT
Lafayette	24	M	Laborer	TN
William A.	21	M		TN
Nancy C.	19	F		TN
Mary A.	16	F		TN
Sarah A.	11	F		TN
John	8	M		TN
Wood, James T.	52	M	Farmer	SC
Elizabeth	48	F		SC
William R.	29	M	Farmer	TN
Spencer	26	M	Stock Raiser	TN
John	24	M	Farmer	TN
James H.	20	M	Farmer	TN
Henry	18	M		TX
Warren	12	M		TX
George W.	3	M		TX
Mary A.	16	F		TX
Elizabeth	9	F		TX
Reese, Jane	45	F		GA
Finch, Mary J.	24	F		TN
McKensie, Thomas	22	M	Farmer	TN
Martha E.	18	F		TN
Susan E.	17	F		TN
Lavissa A.	12	F		TN
Finch, John M.	3	M		TX
Reese, Thomas J.	47	M	Farmer	SC
Oliver	25	M	Soldier	TN
James	18	M	Farmer	TN
Eliza T.	13	F		TN
Thomas H.	10	M		AL
Weldon, Isaac	53	M		??
Reese, Thomas	69	M	Farmer	SC
Butler, John	30	M	Farmer	MS
Ann	30	F		TN
Washington	8	M		MS
James P.	7	M		MS
Ann Eliza	5	F		MS
Margaret E.	4	F		TX
Dawson, David C.	44	M	Farmer	VA
Martha	40	F		TN
Joshua	8	M		AL
Sarah F.	6	F		AL
Hall, John W.	23	M	Farmer	TN
Mary P.	22	F		TN
William J.	2	M		TX
Leonidas	1	M		TX
Lechen, Jeremiah	49	M	Farmer	IRE
Mary	23	F		TN
Jeremiah	2	M		TX
McCoy, John	55	M	Farmer	KY

(continued)

Name	Age	Sex	Occupation	Birthplace
McCoy, Elizabeth	50	F		TN
Kimber	19	M	Teamster	TX
John	12	M		TX
Green	10	M		TX
Read, Daniel	33	M	Farmer	TN
Margaret	23	F		AL
James K. P.	4	M		AR
Mary E.	3	F		AR
Rebecca	2	F		TX
May, Albert G.	47	M	Farmer	TN
Margaret	44	F		KY
Morris	23	M	Teamster	IL
Milton C.	21	M	Farmer	IL
Albert G.	20	M	Farmer	IL
Leonard	19	M	Farmer	IL
Julia Ann	15	F		IL
Elizabeth	13	F		IL
Caroline	9	F		TX
Emaline	7	F		TX
Joseph	6	M		TX
Margaret	4	F		TX
Fleming, John M.	55	M	Farmer	GA
Abigal	51	F		TN
John M.	19	M	Farmer	AL
Martha E.	15	F		AL
Robert	14	M		AL
Bishop, Oliver	30	M	Farmer	AL
Mariah Catherine	18	F		AL
Roberts, Abraham	44	M	Farmer	TN
Cintha	41	F		TN
Perlina	19	F		AL
Martha J.	15	F		MS
Mary C.	13	F		AL
James	12	M		TX
William	10	M		TX
Daniel	8	M		TX
Thomas	7	M		TX
Caldwell	2	M		TX
Neal, Hester R.	41	F		TN
Robert E.	23	M	Soldier	TN
Marcus A.	18	M	Farmer	TX
Mary J.	17	F		TX
Benjamin F.	9	M		TX
Samuel H.	12	M		TX
Elliott, John N.	46	M	Farmer	NC
Amanda P.	20	F		AL
Louisa A.	14	F		TN
Rhoda E.	12	F		TX
Thomas H. B.	10	M		TX
John R.	8	M		TX
William S.	6	M		TX
Sarah C.	4	F		TX
William M.	9/12	M		TX
Elliott, William M.	35	M	School Teacher	TN
Elliott, Robert L.	40	M	Farmer	TN
Mary E.	35	F		TN
Henry B.	19	M		AL
James C.	12	M		TN
Martha J.	10	F		TN
Thomas W.	8	M		TN
Mary A.	6	F		TN
William N.	3	M		TN
Roberts, Jeremiah	41	M	Farmer	TN
Sarah	28	F		MO
Martha Ann	12	F		TX
Felix	8	M		TX
Ellen	5	F		TX
Benjamin	3	M		TX
Jeremiah	1	M		TX
Sullivan, B. B.	37	M	Farmer	TN
Elizabeth W.	38	F		TN
Bourland	20	M	Farmer	TN
Madora M.	11	F		TN
Adelia F.	11	F		TN
James M.	6	M		TN
Lucy Ann	4	F		TN
Ushula M.	2	F		TX

CALDWELL COUNTY, TEXAS

Name	Age	Sex	Occupation	Birthplace
Hardiman, Owen	31	M	Farmer	TN
Sarah	25	F		TN
Caroline	3/12	F		TX
McNeal, W. W.	28	M	Merchant	TN
Elizabeth	24	F		TN
Thomas	6/12	M		TX
Berry, William	19	M	School Teacher	TN
Hardiman, Thomas M.	35	M	Farmer	TN
Susan	25	F		AL
William S.	4	M		TX
Elizabeth	1	F		TX
Votaw, Elijah	35	M	Laborer	TN
William	10	M		TX
McClerin, Hugh	36	M	Farmer	NC
Susan Ann	37	F		NC
Robert	16	M	Cooper	TN
Sarah J.	8	F		TX
John T.	5	M		TX
James K.	5	M		TX
Pleasant	1	M		TX
English, Levi	33	M	Soldier	AR
Matilda	23	F		TN
John	11	M		TX
Lucinda	8	F		TX
Marilda	6	F		TX
Jonathan	4	M		TX
Elizabeth	1	F		TX
Byers, Ross	35	M	Trader	SC
Henry, William	35	M	Farmer	TN
Isabella	26	F		KY
James	7	M		TX
Eliza	5	F		TX
Martha	3	F		TX
Elm, William	5	M		TX
Reese, Elias	22	M	Farmer	TN
Drucilla M.	19	F		AL
Thomas G.	1	M		AL
Teas, Samuel	42	M	Farmer	TN
Everline	37	F		MO
William B.	19	M	Farmer	MO
Jesse T.	14	M		MO
Mary	10	F		MO
Thaddeus	8	M		MO
Ann Eliza	6	F		TX
Emily	2	F		TX
McCarly, John P.	24	M	Farmer	TX
Amanda	24	F		TN
Frances	7	F		TX
Matilda J.	2	F		TX
John	1	M		TX
Burleson, Rebecca	56	F		KY
Walker, Joseph	54	M	Farmer	SC
Rebecca	48	F		TN
Joseph H.	17	M		LA
Jeremiah W.	10	M		TX
Elbert M.	7	M		TX
Francis M.	3	F		TX
Hankins, Eli	26	M	Farmer	KY
Elizabeth C.	20	F		SC
Arminda	2	F		TX
Hinds, Gongales	23	M	Trader	TN
Mauldin, William P.	45	M	Farmer	SC
James H.	19	M	Farmer	TN
Elizabeth A.	19	F		TN
Margaret L.	14	F		TN
John B.	12	M		TN
Sarah L.	9	F		TX
Susan C.	7	F		TX
William W.	3	M		TX
Hall, Joshua	44	M	Farmer	TN
Sarah	42	F		TN
Frances	13	F		AL

(continued)

Name	Age	Sex	Occupation	Birthplace
Hall, Galveston V.	11	M		AL
Sarah J.	9	F		AL
Claudius	7	M		AL
David W.	4	M		TX
Winter P.	2	M		TX
Bennett, S. C.	38	M	Farmer	NC
Amanda C.	24	F		TN
Eugenia M.	2	M		TX
Ratliff, Joshua	21	M	Farmer	AR
Sarah Ann	18	F		TN
Patton, James M.	39	M	Farmer	TN
Sarah Jane	21	F		AL
Cicero C.	2	M		TX
Miller, Isaac	49	M	Merchant	SC
Susan	41	F		SC
James F.	20	M	Student	TN
Robert L.	16	M	Student	TN
Nicholas F.	14	M		TN
Nancy M.	11	F		TN
Malinda E.	9	F		TN
Lydia B.	7	F		TN
St. Paul, Luther	4	M		TX
Nix, Jonathan	26	M	Grocery Keeper	TN
Mary L.	18	F		TN
John B.	1/12	M		TX
Coffee, William B.	35	M	Merchant	TN
Mary E.	25	F		GA
Daughtery, James	36	M	Grocery Keeper	AL
McThinn, Richard	75	M	Lawyer	VA
Pullen, Asa	28	M	Black Smith	TN
Japhet	5	M		MO
Pullen, T. D.	31	M	Black Smith	NC
Wilson, Samuel	38	M	Trader	TN
Rosa	30	F		TN
Thomas D.	14	M		TN
Mary J.	10	F		TN
Sarah	9	F		TN
Jason C.	7	M		TX
Tennessee	5	F		TX
McMahon, John B.	33	M	Farmer	TN
Mariah	28	F		AL
Margaret	9	F		TX
Ellenor	2	F		TX
James	1	M		TX
Holmes, James C.	20	M	Carpenter	TN
Sarah	24	F		AL
William E.	5	M		MS
Benjamin H.	2	M		TX
Tuttle, John M.	37	M	Farmer	TN
Margaret J.	29	F		AR
Martha J.	13	F		AR
Susan J.	11	F		AR
Mary R.	9	F		AR
James B.	1	M		TX
Sloan, Joseph	27	M	Teamster	??
Borin, William	24	M	Teamster	??
Storey, John T.	54	M	Farmer	GA
Lucy	33	F		NC
Calvin L.	29	M	Trader	GA
Edward F.	21	M	Merchant	GA
Adaline C.	21	F		GA
Julia Ann	6/12	F		TX
James G.	19	M	Student	CA
Leonidas J.	15	M	Student	GA
Horatio E.	13	M		GA
McClester, Harvey	29	M	Lawyer	GA
Hamblin, William	36	M	Trader	TN
Harrison, Thomas	28	M	Trader	VA
Evans, Edward	28	M	Black Smith	OH
Sarah Ann	18	F		LA
David	3/12	M		TX
Williams, Joseph	35	M	Farmer	TN

CALDWELL COUNTY, TEXAS

Name	Age	Sex	Occupation	Birthplace
Lane, P. W.	50	M	Physician	TN
Marcus D. L.	19	M	Farmer	TN
Queentina	14	F		TN
Thomas J.	12	M		TN
Samuel H.	10	M		TN
Malissa	7	F		TN
Duncan, George W.	36	M	Black Smith	TN
Judith	34	F		IL
John R.	11	M		TX
Mary J.	8	F		TX
Arminda	6	F		TX
Sarah J.	4	F		TX
William M.	4	M		TX
Rebecca C.	5/12	F		TX
Montgomery, William	36	M	Farmer	AL
Mary Ann	28	F		TN
Nancy J.	8	F		TX
William F.	6	M		TX
Francis M.	3	M		TX
Lincecum, Garland R.	53	M	Farmer	GA
Emaline	35	F		TN
Brassoria	11	F		MS
Fernandella	9	F		MS
Brassas	7	M		MS
Riodelmorte	5	M		MS
Perlina	3	F		TX
Orleana	10/12	F		TX
Connel, William	33	M	Farmer	TN
Louisa	28	F		TN
David	5	M		TX
James	3	M		TX
William	4/12	M		TX
Graham, John	21	M	Farmer	??
"Hotel"				
Fulgham, George F.	38	M	Landlord	GA
Marian P.	26	F		GA
Ezekiel	17	M	Farmer	MS
John J.	15	M		MS
Benjamin F	11	M		MS
Henry N.	7	M		LA
George S.	1/12	M		TX
Stiner, Granville H.	31	M	Herdsman	TN
Montgomery, John	35	M	Tailor	VA
Eppingstall, Edward	35	M	Merchant	ENG
Oxley, Francis	35	M	Merchant	ENG
Falling, M.	36	M	Lawyer	MD
Roberts, Alexander	36	M	Farmer	TN
Sabra	35	F		SC
James M.	17	M	Farmer	AL
Jacob F.	14	M		MS
John C.	13	M		MS
Daniel W.	9	M		MS
Ann Eliza	6	F		MS
Amanda	3	F		TX
Buck	1	M		TX
Musgraves, Calvin	44	M	Farmer	TN
Mariah	39	F		TN
Mary Ann	19	F		TN
James H.	15	M	Farmer	TN
Edney	13	F		TN
Bennett	12	M		TN
Cansadia(?)	10	F		TN
Daniel	9	M		TX
Elizabeth	8	F		TX
Walden	6	M		TX
Walden, James	61	M	Farmer	TN
Fanny	65	F		SC
Greenberry	29	M	Farmer	AL
John	22	M	Farmer	AL
Rebecca	6	F		AR
Calvin	4	M		AR
Jane	2	F		AR
Covey, Joseph	36	M	Teamster	TN
Mariah	17	F		AL
Charles A.	3	M		TX

CALHOUN COUNTY, TEXAS

Name	Age	Sex	Occupation	Birthplace
Jordon, Caleb	45	M	Farmer	SC
Rutha	35	F		SC
Amos	12	M		AL
Susan	6	F		TN
Laura	3	F		TN
Thomas	3/12	M		TN
Baker, Jno. R.	41	M	Grocer	TN
Avis	20	F		ME
Harriett J.	1	F		TN
Christian	18	F		GER

ISLAND of MATOGORDA

Name	Age	Sex	Occupation	Birthplace
McRainy, James K.	39	M	M.D.	TN
Elizabeth J.	26	F		NC
Mary	6	F		TX
William	5	M		TX
Foley	3	M		TX
Nelson	1	M		TX
Laura	11	F		LA
Elizabeth	9	F		TX
Huntsman, William	26	M	Farmer	TN

TOWN of INDIANOLA

Name	Age	Sex	Occupation	Birthplace
"Hotel"				
Vandevier, C. H.	58	M	Hotel Keeper	NJ
Ann M.	43	F		MD
Julia	17	F		TX
William	8	M		TX
Coburn, James	40	M	US Army	VT
Mary	30	F		TN
Bernard, Frank	40	M	Merchant	AR
Ema V.	20	F		PA
Mainard, C.	25	M	Clerk	LA
Loyd, Lidia	27	F		MO
Glass, W. C.	28	M	Teacher	PA
Oglesby, William	30	M	Merchant	NY
Fromy, Augustus	35	M		GER
Cooke, William M.	40	M	Builder	TN
Wildy, Sophia	30	F		GER
Caroline	13	F		GER
Edward	11	M		GER
Mary	5	F		GER
"Hotel"				
Everly, A. B.	46	M	Tavern Keeper	TN
Cunningham, C. G.	25	M	Merchant	VA
Cochran, James	35	M	Merchant	TN
Seaton, J.	20	M	Clerk	FL
Rumors, Robert	22	M	Herdsman	OH
John	20	M	Herdsman	OH
Parks, Margaret	30	F		ENG
Etter, Chambers	32	M	Merchant	PA
Judith C.	24	F		TN
B. L. D.	3	M		TX
Orr, Green	60	M	Methodist Clergy	NC
Moore, Joseph L.	18	M	Clerk	NY
Lutwich, Josephine	16	F		GER
Hill, Claiborn	44	M	Farmer	TN
Elizabeth	47	F		TN
Simeon	22	M	Farmer	AL
Claiborn	20	M	Farmer	AL
Statesman	18	M	Farmer	AL
Joseph	17	M	Farmer	AL
John	14	M	Farmer	AL
Polly Ann	11(12)	F		AL
William	10	M		AL
James	6	M		AL
Elizabeth	16	F		AL

CITY of LOVACA

Name	Age	Sex	Occupation	Birthplace
"Hotel"				
Staunton, Juliet C.	33	F	Hotel Keeper	IRE
William	6	M		TX
Clon, Robert J.	37	M	Merchant	TN

(continued)

CALHOUN COUNTY, TEXAS

Name	Age	Sex	Occupation	Birthplace
Clon, Elizabeth	27	F		AL
Catharine	1	F		TX
Little, James T.	26	M	Lawyer	SC
Margaret	21	F		TX
O'Riley, James	36	M	Merchant	SC
Clara	34	F		SC
Udora	9	F		KY
James P.	2	M		TX
Brown, Capt.	40	M	Seaman	ME
Dollum, W. H.	27	M	M.D.	MD
Davis, J. C.	28	M	Merchant	ME
Goedse, ----	40	M	Clerk	GER
Turner, B. M.	26	M	Clerk	OH
Hensley, Mary P.	41	F		TN
Alexander F.	26	M	Merchant	IN
Unis M.	21	F		MS
Albert C.	21	M	Clerk	IN
Travis	14	M	Clerk	TX
William	1	M		TX
Selia A.	18	F		IN
Mary	3	F		TX
Ross, Martha A.	28	F		TN
Walace, Eliza B.	8	F		TX
Mary S.	6	F		TX
Dean, Nancy	53	F		TN
John	32	M	Carpenter	TN
William Dean	18	M	Laborer	TN
Elon	16	F		TN
Jesse	13	M		TN
Johnson, Moses	42	M	M.D.	VA
Olevia	32	F		VT
Samuel	9	M		TX
Ann Olevia	4	F		TX
Sidney	1	M		TX
Litle, Samuel	19	M	None	TN

THE RIO GRANDE VALLEY

Name	Age	Sex	Occupation	Birthplace
Finley, Robert	30	M	Carpenter	SCO
Elizabeth	30	F		NY
Archibald	14	M		TX
Looney, Joseph	33	M	Miner	TN
*				
Ruggles, Joseph R.	30	M	Merchant	MA
Cameron, Frank	23	M	Laborer	LA
Holman, Jasper S.	22	M	Clerk	TN
Schultie, Herman	31	M	Clerk	GER
Lankeman, Vincent	24	M	Clerk	GER
Lemue, T.	23	M	Gun Smith	FRA
Brevard, Leon	25	M	Brick Mason	LA
Denton, Roswell D.	36	M	Merchant	TN
Louisa Jane	25	F		TN
Robinson, William M.	28	M	Clerk	TN

CAMERON, STARR & WEBB COUNTIES, TEXAS

RIO GRANDE VALLEY

Name	Age	Sex	Occupation	Birthplace
Miller, James	25	M	Carpenter	TN
Andrea	22	F		MEX
Williamson, David G.	39	M	Carpenter	VA
Ann	30	F		VA
Eliza	10	F		VA
James D.	5	M		TX
Albert (twin)	7	M		TX
Phoebe (twin)	7	F		TX
Davis, James	24	M	Laborer	DEN
Moses, Benjamin	42	M	Merchant	ENG
Anderson, Nelson	17	M	Clerk	TN
Selkirk, James	32	M	Pilot, Rio Grande	SCO
Smith, Charles	27	M	Mariner	DEN
Pomeroy, George	28	M	Mariner	NY
Jackson, James	24	M	Mariner	NY
Clark, William H.	46	M	Mariner	ME
Mary	32	F		TN

(continued)

Name	Age	Sex	Occupation	Birthplace
Clark, Elizabeth	12	F		TN
Mary J.	7	F		TN
Cornelia	4	F		TX
Martha	1	F		TX
Rhea, John S.	44	M	M.E. Rev. Officer	TN
William	19	M	Clerk	AL
Edwin	17	M		AL
Ella Marian	11	F		AL
Trimble, Robert C.	50	M	Surveyor	TN
Hedrick, A. J.	26	M	Corn Merchant	MD
E. Carroll	18	F		FL
E. Kate	1	F		TX
Sevier, B. M.	23	M	Clerk	LA
Yarde, T. C.	23	M	Clerk	TN
Conner, James F.	18	M	Clerk	TN
Thompson, Henry	49	M	Boatsman	DEN
Culler, Margaret	32	F		IRE
McManis, Jose	35	M	Laborer	MEX
Henry, William	34	M	Farmer	TN
Sally	34	F		VA
John	10	M		TX
Louisa	9	F		TX
Sarah	8	F		TX
Jackson A.	5	M		TX
Augustus H.	4	M		TX
Elizabeth	2	F		TX
King, Thomas B.	35	M	Seaman	ENG
Amanda	28	F		PA
Irene	13	F		AL
Henrietta	6	F		TX
Patterson, William S.	26	M	Clerk	SCO
Patton, Robert	45	M	Engineer	SCO
Cobert, A. M.	28	M	Engineer	OH
Lascano, Juan	18	M	Laborer	MEX
Thompson, Robert	21	M	Seaman	SCO
Hayers, Henry	30	M	Seaman	GER
Davis, Fred	23	M	Seaman	ENG
Samuelson, Charles	26	M	Seaman	DEN
Cummins, William	34	M	Seaman	RI
Coggen, Michael	28	M	Seaman	IRE
Thompson, William	28	M	Seaman	SCO
Roberts, R. J.	21	M	Cotton Spinner	CT
Douglas, William	30	M	Clerk	IRE
Kennedy, Mifflin	32	M	Steam Boatman	PA
Kerns, David	32	M	Engineer	OH
Orto, John	21	M	Cook	ITA
Taylor, James	26	M	(B) Barber	--
Henry, Joseph	35	M	Seaman	MD
Henderson, F. M.	39	M	Seaman	TN
Stimpson, George W.	28	M	Seaman	TN
Martinas, Pedro	22	M	Laborer	MEX
Garcia, Ramon	21	M	Laborer	MEX
Garcia, Manuel	23	M	Laborer	MEX
Mannuhassett, James	31	M	Laborer	ENG
Antonia	22	F		MEX
Cresento	6	M		TX
William	3	M		TX
Isabel	1	F		TX
Muny, Pierce	45	M	Carpenter	CT
Fernandez, Ignacio	50	M	Laborer	MEX
Leske, Robert	26	M	Carpenter	TN
Garcia, Juan	23	M	Laborer	TX
Vincenta	20	F		TX
Anderson, Tandy K.	29	M	Clerk	TN
Ramon, Alfonzo	65	M	Hatter	TX
Flores, Frank	50	M	Stone Mason	TX
Maria	40	F		TX
Antonio	14	M		TX
Jose	12	M		TX
Francisca	10	F		TX
Rezes, Rafael	21	M	Laborer	TX
Gueria, Antonio	40	M	Laborer	MEX
Flores, Francisco	18	M		TX
Hernandez, Dorotio	58	M	Laborer	MEX
Davis, William	25	M	Sheriff, Webb Co.	TN
Castillo, Cristobal	35	M	Laborer	TX
Teodore	30	F		TX

(continued)

CAMERON, STARR & WEBB COUNTIES, TEXAS

Name	Age	Sex	Occupation	Birthplace
Castillo, Alberto	12	M		TX
Miguela	5	F		TX
Loza, Jose M.	20	M	Laborer	TX
Plaza, Vincente	45	M	Black Smith	TX
Anderson, Samuel	24	M	Laborer	TN
Garcia, Juan	30	M	Laborer	MEX
Jose	27	M	Laborer	MEX
Carter, Robert C.	26	M	Carpenter	TN
Silvestra	17	F		TX
Robert	1	M		TX
Minon, Crafford	34	M	Merchant	OH
Cauham, Robert	28	M	Laborer	IRE
Lyzgoda	36	F		MEX
Felicita	10	F		TX
Jesua	8	F		TX
Rafael	6	F		TX
Sulegson, Lewis	23	M	Merchant	PA
Henry	21	M	Merchant	PA
Baker, A. P.	36	M	Clerk	IRE
DeSota, B. H.	23	M	Clerk	DEN
Johnson, William G.	24	M	Merchant	TN
Hancock, Joseph	28	M	Carpenter	TN
Ellen	18	F		TX
Campbell, John G.	41	M	Doctor	TN
Sophia	25	F		AL
Sarah	4	F		TX
Hiram S.	2	M		TX
Noud, Andrew	31	M	Carpenter	IRE
Phillips, Lewson D.	28	M	Brick Mason	NY
Castillo, Antonio	50	M	Laborer	MEX
Land, John F.	50	M	Merchant	NY
Jane	30	M		NY
Jane	4	F		TX
David H. S.	28	M	Saddler	KY
McIntyre, James	30	M	Laborer	OH
Dugan, Thomas J.	40	M	Tanner	TN
Cole, Julian	25	M	Carpenter	TN
Simona	17	F		TX

CASS COUNTY, TEXAS

RIO GRANDE VALLEY, Precinct No. 1

Name	Age	Sex	Occupation	Birthplace
Smith, James	53	M	Waggon Maker	TN
John F.	17	M	Student	AL
Ramsey, Richard G.	37	M	Inn Keeper	TN
Balinda	35	F		TN
Robert E.	10	M		MO
John W.	8	M		TN
J. S.	4	F		LA
Pendleton, B.	28	M		TN
Bentley, J. M.	19	M		AR
Dicks, T. A.	--	M		AR
Ussery, Eli	39	M	Farmer	DEN
Faithful	39	F		SC
E. M.	19	M	Student	TN
William C.	17	M	Student	TN
James A.	15	M	Student	TN
Clarinda	12	F	Student	TN
P. H.	10	M		MO
T. A.	7	M		MO
Jack	4	M		TX
M. J.	2	F		TX
Hobbs, J. C.	31	M	Carriage Maker	NC
Frances	22	F		TN
Julia A.	9	F		KY
William C.	5	M		KY
R. M.	2	M		KY
Baker, J. M.	58	M	Physician	MO
Sarah	47	F		TN
William C.	24	M	None	IL
Benjamin R. C.	13	M		LA

(continued)

Name	Age	Sex	Occupation	Birthplace
Baker, A. H.	11	M		TX
M. E.	9	F		TX
Pettitt, James	37	M	Farmer	NC
Martha	35	F		TN
Thomas J.	11	M		TN
L. M.	7	F		TN
John L.	3	M		TN
A. J.	1	M		TX
Baker, Benjamin E.	33	M	Miller(Saw Mill)	IA
E. J.	24	F		TN
Jno. A.	8	M		IA
Nancy J.	6	F		TN
Chilla	6	F		TN
Robert C.	4	M		TN
Indianna	4/12	M		TN
Schlenter, F. A.	31	M	Farmer	TN
Ann T.	23	F		TN
Walter P.	5	M		KY
Ella	2	F		TX
Usery, George	45	M	Clerk	TN
Rebecca	35	F		NC
Thomas A.	17	M	Student	AL
H. L.	13	F		MS
A. E.	10	F		MS
E. J.	6	F		MS
R. D.	3	M		MS
G. A.	6/10	F		TX
"Inn"				
Ellie, S. H.	36	M	Inn Keeper	VA
Graham, P. M.	25	M	Merchant	TN
Everett, J. C.	45	M	Lawyer	TN
Fussett, Henry	40	M	Carpenter	TN
Pendleton, May	21	M	Black Smith	TN
Robinson, C. C.	23	M	Painter	TN
Flynn, F.	30	M	Plaster	TN
Williard, C. J.	33	M	Merchant	NY
R. S.	25	F		AL
A. D.	5	F		TX
George	2	M		TX
Morgan, George F.	29	M	Clerk	TX
Mabane, J. N.	25	M	Clerk	TN
Hughes, James L.	35	M	Farmer	MO
N----	34	F		MO
L. C.	7	F		AR
S. N. B.	5	F		AR
Jno. W.	2	M		TX
F. E.	2	F		TX
Graham, William H.	24	M	Laborer	TN
Kohn, A.	33	M	Clerk	GER
E.	22	F		TN
M.	2	F		LA
S.	5/12	M		LA
Travick, Nelson	40	M	Physician	TN
S. A.	30	F		LA
L. E.	13	F		LA
W. W.	16	M		MS
J. A.	8	F		LA
M. R.	5	F		LA
T. L.	3	F		TX
Adams, A.	13	M		MS
Pogue, A.	28	M	Overseer	AL
Figers, Bartholemew	45	M	Inn Keeper	TN
Caroline	31	F		TN
John M.	14	M		TN
R. A.	13	M		TN
James C.	11	M		TX
T. A.	9	F		TX
Mary	5	F		TX
Sarah	6/12	F		TX
In Hotel				
Woodward, Elisha	27	M	Laborer	TN
Wilson, Emily	30	F		TN
Paulina	20	F		--
S. B.	17	M	Student	AR
John, Jr.	15	M	Student	AR

(continued)

CASS COUNTY, TEXAS

Name	Age	Sex	Occupation	Birthplace
Coldwell, M. E.	3	F		TX
Frazier, K. E.	28	M	Overseer	TN
Warde, M. A.	25	F	(Pauper)	VA
Randolph, Thomas	20	M	Farmer	TN
Jane	18	F		TN
John W.	1	M		TN
Brandon, Felix G.	39	M	Farmer	TN
Lucinda	37	F		TN
Margaret T.	19	F		TN
William L.	17	M		TN
Frances L.	15	F		TN
A. J.	14	M		TN
Sarah J.	13	F		TN
Joseph	11	M		TN
Jacob F.	9	M		TN
Patrick	7	M		TN
Thomas B.	6	M		TN
Caladonia	5	F		TN
Felix	3	M		TN
Allen, Samuel	38	M	Farmer	TN
E. C.	39	F		TN
E. J.	14	F		TN
M. F.	12	M		TN
John P.	2	M		TX
-----	2/12	M		TX
Asher, William	33	M	Farmer	TN
Ford, Sarah	21	F		TN
Mary	3	F		AL
Bryan, William O.	38	M	Farmer	NC
M. S.	38	F		TN
M. E.	16	F		TN
Sarah	14	F		TN
M.	12	F		AR
Jas. H.	10	M		AR
Allice	8	F		AR
William C.	6	M		AR
John P.	4	M		AR
A. J.	1	M		TX
Bryan, H. C.	20	M	Farmer	TN
M. A.	20	F		AL
Starnes, G. W.	34	M	Farmer	TN
Mary	18	F		AL
Simmons, F. G.	35	M	Farmer	KY
Adaline	24	F		TN
W. S.	6	M		MO
J. M.	4	M		MO
P. F.	2	F		TX
Simmons, Isaac	35	M		KY
S. J.	27	F		TN
C. J.	3	F		MO
J. P.	2	M		TX
R. M. E. F.	1	F		TX
McDaniel, John M.	22	M	Laborer	TN
Asher, Samuel S.	53	M	Farmer	TN
Mary	42	F		MO
Delia	18	F		MO
Conner	14	M		MO
Archebald	10	M		MO
Dedana	8	F		MO
Echols, John M.	35	M	Farmer	GA
Mary A.	25	F		TN
Luther	4	M		MS
William	2	M		MS
Hammons, M. R.	38	M	Farmer	TN
York, Keley	24	M	Farmer	NC
Snow, P. R.	40	M	Farmer	TN
Martha	36	F		AL
James	18	M	Laborer	TN
William	16	M		TN

(continued)

Name	Age	Sex	Occupation	Birthplace
Snow, Margarette	12	F		MS
Stephen	10	M		MS
Francis	7	M		MS
Allen, Virginia	15	F		AL
Eliza	11	F		TX
Martha	4	F		TX
Glass, Isaac	50	M	Farmer	TN
Elizabeth	30	F		VA
Elizabeth, Jr.	6	F		TN
J. N.	2	M		TN
Proctor, Hiram	39	M	Farmer	TN
Rebecca	33	F		TN
Samuel M.	13	M		AL
William R.	12	M		AL
Wesley M.	8	M		AL
James N.	10	M		AL
John	6	M		AL
Sarah E.	4	F		LA
Mary J.	2/12	F		TX
Gibson, George	30	M	Laborer	TN
Trimble, Hiram	35	M	Farmer	NY
Anis	25	F		TN
Mary	1	F		TX
Christin, Henry B.	40	M	Farmer	NC
America	35	F		TN
John	7	M		TX
William	4	M		TX
Texana	2	F		TX
Bailey, C. C.	46	M	Farmer	VA
Frances	37	F		VA
Margaret	19	F		TN
William	18	M	Student	TN
Johnson	16	M		TN
Zachariah	14	M		AL
Loranna ?.	12	F		AL
Mary	9	F		MS
Elizabeth	7	F		MS
John	5	M		TX
Gorge	5	M		TX
Henry	3	M		TX
Jane	2	F		TX
Baber, C. C.	30	M	Carpenter	MO
Griffin, Thomas J.	40	M	Farmer	MO
Eliza A.	40	F		MO
Mary	20	F		AL
Ann	18	F		TN
John R.	16	M	Student	AL
Margaret	14	F		AL
Derrick, Jacob	54	M	Farmer	VA
Crow, Elizabeth	36	F	Farmer	TN
Martin	18	M	Laborer	TN
Mansfield	16	M		TN
Franklin	14	M		TN
Mary	12	F		TN
Nancy	7	F		TX
Carson, Nathaniel	27	M	Laborer	TN
Willgrove, B. S.	45	M	Farmer	SC
Wilgrove, Emily	31	F		SC
James	12	M		TN
Sarah	11	F		TN
John	9	M		TN
Shepard	6	M		TN
Martha	3	F		TN
Mary C.	2/12	F		TX
Ury, A.	40	M	Merchant	TN
B. ?.	29	F		TN
Samuel	10	M		TX
George	4	M		TX
Amos	2	M		TX
Ward, M.	37	M	Merchant	AL
Tomlin, H.	23	M	Clerk	TN
Ward, A. M.	20	M	Clerk	TN
Walker, W. C.	28	M	Farmer	TN
Jones, Eliza	18	F		TN

CASS COUNTY, TEXAS

Name	Age	Sex	Occupation	Birthplace
Duncan, Mary	47	F	Farmer	NC
Cox, Tilman D.	29	M	Laborer	TN
Walker, Mary E.	8/12	F		TX
Kelley, John	51	M	Farmer	GA
Elizabeth	44	F		SC
Walker, Samuel	16	M		TN
Rubin	14	M		TN
William	13	M		TN
James	12	M		TN
John	11	M		TN
Joseph	9	M		TN
Jackson, Samuel F.	35	M	Farmer	TN
Martha	25	F		AL
Johnson, Harris	73	M	Farmer	NC
Fanny	40	F		TN
Vaughn, Newton	25	M	Laborer	TN
Johnson, William	40	M	Farmer	TN
Nancy	25	F		TN
Harris	5	M		TX
John	4	M		TX
Mary Jane	3	F		TX
Samuel H.	1	M		TX
Infant	2/12	M		TX
Burnette, James A.	32	M	Farmer	TN
Mary Ann	25	F		AR
Nancy Ann	8	F		TX
Mary E.	5	F		TX
William T.	3	M		TX
Green	1	M		TX
Huff, Benjamin F.	30	M	Laborer	GA
Carlton, Lewis	24	M	Laborer	AL
Panest, James	20	M	Laborer	AL
Armstrong, William T.	35	M	House P----(?)	MD
Dorsh, Robert	22	M	Wheelright	TN
Bowls, Colonel	25	M		TN
Whagan, (blank)	25	M	Carpenter	MS
Mitchel, Alexander	27	M	Carpenter	KY
Sutton, (blank)	28	M	Carpenter	TN
Terrel, William	31	M	House Carpenter	NC
Nancy D.	28	F		VA
Laura F.	2	F		TN
M. E.	7/12	M		TN
Simmons, Robert	32	M	Carpenter	NC
Buchanan, George	33	M	Carpenter	TN
Elizabeth A.	25	F		AL
Lemuel M.	8	M		MO
Helen B.	2	F		AR
Barker, L. W.	30	M	Carpenter	GA
Martha L.	19	F		AL
Barker, Ludwick	18	M	Farmer	GA
Glass, A.	24	M	Carpenter	TN
Northcut, S. W.	35	M	Carpenter	TN
Williams, Duff	25	M	Carpenter	MD
Bryan, E. P.	42	M	Farmer	NC
Mary	40	F		TN
John H.	18	M	Student	TN
William G.	16	M	Student	TN
Thomas	10	M	Student	AR
Fredonia	8	F	Student	AR
Felix	6	M		AR
Sarah E.	2	F		TX
Prewitt, M. M.	51	M	Farmer (Blind)	TN
M. A.	33	F		VA
N. S.	16	M	Student	AL
Milligan, Lakin	24	M		AL
Cordey, Thomas	28	M	Overseer	GA
Dove, J. B.	28	M	Farmer	TN
Martha	21	F		AL
McAdoo, James E.	28	M	Farmer	TN
Jane	20	F		AL

(continued)

Name	Age	Sex	Occupation	Birthplace
McAdoo, Thomas	1	M		TX
McAdoo, Columbus	17	M	Laborer	TN
Prewitt, James	32	M	Farmer	AL
Frances H.	30	F		AL
William H.	12	M		AL
Tolbert F.	6	M		MS
Foster, Daniel	25	M	School Teacher	NY
Perry, John	22	M	Overseer	TN
Price, F. C.	30	M	School Teacher	NY
Durren, James C.	40	M	Physician	SC
Sarah	32	F		NC
Asher	11	M		TN
William	9	M		TX
John	7	M		TX
Samuel	5	M		TX
Sylus	3	M		TX
(unnamed)	1	M		TX
Carpenter, David A.	32	M	Carpenter	TN
Martha	23	F		AL
Nancy	6	F		AL
Mary	4	F		MS
N.	5	F		MS
Caleruia(?)	2/12	F		TX
Bowers, (blank)	30	M	Carpenter	TN
Bohanon, J. M.	37	M	Waggoner	TN
Ellen	32	F		TN
William S.	15	M		TX
John S.	12	M		TX
Thomas	1	M		TX
William	10	M		KY

Precinct No. 2

Name	Age	Sex	Occupation	Birthplace
Dunlap, George W.	39	M	Miller	PA
Malinda	28	F		TN
Elizabeth A.	8	F		TX
Nancy C.	6	F		TX
Reagen, J. B.	41	M	Farmer	TN
Jane	38	F		TN
Abraham	14	M		AL
Mary Ann	11	F		MO
Charles	9	M		TX
William A.	6	M		TX
Thomas J.	3	M		TX
Kirkland, Thomas	30	M	Farmer	TN
Rebecca	20	F		AL
Sarah	3	F		TX
Nancy	2	F		TX
Louisa	1	F		TX
Danbuck, Samuel	26	M	Farmer	TN
Hariet	24	F		TN
Sarah Ann	5	F		TN
John	2	M		TN
Gun(Garr), B. F.	35	M	Farmer	TN
Martha	34	F		NC
William	12	M		TN
Elisha	10	M		TX
James	7	M		TX
Lemuel	3	M		TX
Hanne, Robert	38	M	Farmer	TN
John N.	16	M	Laborer	TN
Charles N.	13	M		TN
Sarah	12	F		TN
Cela	7	F		TN
Cinn	5	F		TN
Terrel, James	47	M	Farmer	GA
Elizabeth	29	F		AL
Sopronia	6	F		TX
John	4	M		TX
A. P.	3	M		TX
James	10/12	M		TX
Burton, Barkley	24	M	Laborer	TN
Hughes, Robert	74	M	Farmer	SC
Sarah	70	F		TN
Henry	13	M		AL

Name	Age	Sex	Occupation	Birthplace
Gilfinn, James	46	M	Farmer	GA
Ann	20	F		TN
Nathan	12	M		TN
Pickens, Bart W.	32	M	Farmer	TN
Catherine	26	F		TN
Thomas	1	M		TX
Thomas J.	2	M		TX
Brigham, W. B.	45	M	Farmer	TN
Rebecca	35	F		TN
Joseph D.	18	M		TN
Henry	11	M		TN
Elizabeth	7	F		TX
Rebecca	5	F		TX
Robert	2	M		TX
Isaac	22	M		TN
Kimble, B. D.	42	M	Farmer	TN
Nelia	20	F		TN
Tennessee	7	F		TX
Edward	1	M		TX
Martin, Andrew	39	M	Farmer	TN
Susania	19	F		AL
Edmondson, Henry	32	M	Laborer	TN
Martin, P. P.	29	M	Farmer	AL
Harriet Jane	19	F		KY
Martin, Joseph J.	27	M	Laborer	AL
Copeland, Thomas	22	M	Laborer	TN
Martin, Andley	30	M	Farmer	TN
Lafaett	21	M	Laborer	TN
Gray, Fanny	53	F		VA
Sarenia C.	29	F		TN
Napeoleon	27	M	Laborer	TN
Victoria	27	F		TN
Alley, James	62	M	Farmer	VA
Katherine	62	F		TN
Frazier, A, D,	32	M	Farmer	GA
Mariah	29	F		TN
Evaline	8	F		MS
Mary A.	4	F		AR
Subrina	1	F		TX
Wait, James	34	M	Carpenter	TN
Martha	23	F		TN
William	6/12	M		TX
Hasty, Johnathan	25	M	Farmer	MO
Cintha	27	F		MO
Leeroy, M.	18	M	Laborer	TN
Beard, A. P.	32	M	Farmer	TN
Mary Ann	28	F		TX
Sarah	12	F		TX
Joseph R.	10	M		TX
Mary E.	8	F		TX
Franklin C.	6	M		TX
Andrew F.	4	M		TX
Dotha J.	1	F		TX
Beard, Elizabeth	65	F	Farmer	NC
Finley, John B.	50	M	Farmer	TN
C.	46	F		NC
Martha	17	F		AL
Palmesia	3	F		TX
John R.	6/12	M		TX
Lawrence, William	12	M		TN
Edward	8	M		TN
Hughes, Joel	40	M	Farmer	TN
C. S.	26	F		AL
J. S.	5	M		AL
J. P.	3	M		IL
S. J.	1	M		KY
Whit, David J.	28	M	Farmer	TN
Elizabeth	23	F		AL

(continued)

Name	Age	Sex	Occupation	Birthplace
Whit, S. M.	2	M		TX
N. A.	4/12	M		TX
Vant, Montgomery	31	M	Farmer	TN
Rosana	22	F		MS
Hanks, Washington	15	M		--
Haney, Adam P.	45	M		SC
A. E.	33	F		VA
Sarah Ann	6	F		TN
N. C. C.	4	F		TX
Nancy P.	1	F		TX
Hayton, Sanford G.	40	M	Farmer	VA
Mary	44	F		VA
William	15	M	Laborer	TN
Virginia	10	F		AR
Charles	8	M		TX
Catherine	6	F		TX
Lucy	2	F		TX
Stayton, Henry	10	M		LA
Robert	7	M		SC
Barhany, Jacob	56	M	Farmer	VA
Mary	47	F		TN
George T.	24	M		AL
Mary L.	21	F		AL
Sarah	16	F		AL
Nancy R.	14	F		MS
Margarett	10	F		KY
Anderson	8	M		KY
Sabina G.	5	F		KY
Rafty, Little	50	M	Farmer	TN
Tabitha A.	38	F		TN
Fanny A.	16	F		TN
Franklin	11	M		--
Porter, David	32	M	Farmer	PA
T.	30	F		PA
Margret S.	6	F		IN
Hannah E.	4	F		IN
Rachael M.	2	F		TX
Porter, Henry E.	24	M	Farmer	PA
Robert H.	1	M		TN
Porter, James L.	29	M	Farmer	TN
Porter, Sarah B.	24	F		TN
Robert	1	M		--

Precinct No. 3

Name	Age	Sex	Occupation	Birthplace
Gamble, Elisha H.	31	M	Farmer	TN
Sarah A.	21	F		AL
F. G.	4	M		TX
A. J.	2	M		TX
Jeremiah	4/12	M		TX
Beaver, William H.	40	M	Farmer	NC
Cintha	40	F		TN
Levi J.	16	M	Student	TN
Carolina	14	F		TN
Amanda	11	F		TN
Micazah	9	F		TX
Sarah	4	F		TX
Moon, James W.	30	M	Farmer	TN
Elizabeth J.	19	F		TN
William J.	10/12	M		TX
Hughes, William V.	43	M	Farmer	TN
Sarally	38	F		TN
James	14	M		AL
Caroline	16	F		AL
George	10	M		TX
Mary	6	F		TX
Susan	2	F		TX
King, David	26	M	Laborer	IL
Baker, John	47	M	Farmer	TN
M. J.	21	F		AL
Sarah A.	19	F		AL
Lewis	14	M		AL

Name	Age	Sex	Occupation	Birthplace
Davidson, G. W.	29	M	Farmer	TN
Mary H.	30	F		TN
Amanda M.	11	F		AL
Nanney A.	9	F		AL
Susan C.	5	F		TX
James R.	3	M		TX
Martha C.	1	F		TX
Hammer, M.	25	M	Laborer	NC
Daniel, Robert	58	M	Farmer	NC
Robert L.	20	M		TN
Julia C.	15	F		TN
Tennessee	12	F		AR
Winey C.	10	F		AR
Kenedy, Lewis	15	M	Laborer	TN
Walker, James C.	37	M	Farmer	TN
Martha B.	32	F		TN
James A.	14	M	Farmer	TN
Lewis N.	12	M		TN
Frances Jane	10	F		TN
Martha A.	8	F		TX
Hawkins, William	34	M	Farmer	TN
Mary	25	F		AL
Mary A.	9	F		MS
Louisiana	7	F		MS
Sophrona E.	6	F		MS
John W.	5	M		TX
David H.	1	M		TX
Blanton, David	50	M	Farmer	TN
Susana	42	F		KY
Alcy	16	F		AL
Malinda	13	F		AL
James E.	9	M		MS
David N.	6	M		MS
Amanda S.	4	F		MS
Martha	2	F		TX
Gorden, John	31	M	Farmer	TN
Tabitha	18	F		AL
Sarah Ann	2	F		TX
Mary	1/12	F		TX
Bockman, Mikeal	35	M	Farmer	TN
Ruth	32	F		TN
William	13	M		GA
John	12	M		GA
Elizabeth	10	F		GA
Lemon	6	M		TX
Ross, John	30	M	Elder	TN
Martha	35	F		GA
William S.	11	M		GA
Mikel C.	9	M		GA
George A.	6	M		GA
Thomas E.	4	M		GA
Mary E.	6/12	F		TX
Hughes, Reece	38	M	Farmer	TN
Elizabeth	23	F		MS
William P.	7	M		TX
Thomas J. R.	5	M		TX
Reece, Jr.	2	M		TX
Drake, Richard S.	58	M	Farmer	VA
Emily	48	F		NC
Eliza J.	16	F		AL
Mary E.	15	F		AL
Arberry W. E.	13	M		TN
Emily P.	11	F		TN
Cleramella	9	F		TN
Thomas B.	8	M		TN
Sarah F.	6	F		TN
Waltham, John A.	32	M	Farmer	VA
Sally Ann	23	F		AL
William F.	9	M		AR
Sarah A.	1	F		TN
Martha	1	F		TN
Wetherfield, William	52	M	Farmer	VA
Catherine C.	47	F		VA
Samuel L.	20	M	Laborer	TN
Sarah A.	17	F		TN
David J.	16	M		TN
William C.	12	M		TN
Phillip D.	6	M		TN
Virginia	3	F		TN
Norwood, William	45	M	Farmer	TN
Elizabeth	43	F		TN
John	18	M	Laborer	TN
William	12	M		TN
James P.	7	M		TN
Hugh	5	M		TX
George T.	3	M		TX
Emaline	19	F		TN
Smart, Thomas	30	M	Farmer	NC
Mary	21	F		TN
Jasper	4	M		TX
William	2	M		TX
Driver, W. J.	49	M	Farmer	TN
Elizabeth	53	F		TN
Margaret	19	F		AL
Smart, David	17	M		AL
James	12	M		TN
Mary	13	F		TN
Logwood, T. J.	23	M	Farmer	TN
Wilson, Mary W.	26	F		TN
John N.	15	M		TN
McKinney, James	43	M	Farmer	TN
Nancy C.	21	F		VA
Marshall L.	12	M		IL
Albert	7	M		IL
Sophia E.	5	F		TX
William	3	M		TX
McKinney, John A.	73	M	Farmer	VA
Taylor, Dunaway W.	25	M	School Teacher	SC
Mexin, Joseph	41	M	Farmer	SC
Lucy	32	F		TN
Robert R. O.	14	M		AL
Elizabeth J.	12	F		AL
Mary	10	F		AL
Chapman H.	8	M		AL
Early	4	M		MS
Sophronia C.	6	F		AL
Richard	1	M		TX
Mosley, William	45	M	Farmer	GA
Harriet	40	F		GA
John C.	21	M	Laborer	TN
William J.	15	M		TN
Noah S.	11	M		TN
Benjamin R.	8	M		TN
George N.	5	M		TN
Lucy F.	2	F		TX

Precinct No. 4

Name	Age	Sex	Occupation	Birthplace
Thomson, William	50	M	Farmer	SC
David	46	M		AL
Joseph C.	5	M		TX
Winter, James E.	15	M	Laborer	MO
Caroline	9	F		TX
Culbreth, Parker	19	M	Laborer	TN
Keley, M. H.	52	M		OH
Foster, Thomas J.	41	M	Carpenter	TN
Elizabeth	20	F		SC
J. ?.	18	M	Farmer	MS
M. J. D.	14	F		MS
J. ?.	11	F		MS
S. E.	8	F		MS
T. T.	5	M		TX
P. S.	3	F		TX
J. C.	2	M		TX
Landrum, T. H.	22	M	Laborer	MO
Haney, Nelson	52	M	Farmer	NC
Mary	50	F		SC

(continued)

CASS COUNTY, TEXAS

Name	Age	Sex	Occupation	Birthplace
Haney, N. B.	22	F		TN
Joseph B.	18	M	Laborer	TN
Josephine	15	F		TN
P. F.	12	M		TN
Haney, Benjamin D.	26	M	Farmer	TN
Mary B.	21	F		GA
R. C.	2	F		TX
A. F. H.	1	M		TX
Hancock, William	47	M	Farmer	SC
Mary	45	F		TN
William P.	16	M		--
Nathan R.	13	M		--
Nancy J.	11	F		--
Paline F.	7	M		--
Loyde	5	M		--
Carter, William	24	M	Farmer	TN
Mary A.	19	F		MS
Elliott, James H.	33	M	Farmer	TN
Elizabeth	30	F		TN
Thursey B.	7	F		TX
Sarah J.	5	F		TX
Charles M.	3	M		TX
Nancy N.	1	F		TX
Norman, William	37	M		TN
Mary	32	F		TN
Bathiah	9	M		TN
Sarah	8	F		AR
Emey(?)	5	M		AR
Jackson	3	M		AR
James	1	M		TN
Brown, James	33	M	Farmer	TN
Cason	31	F		TX
Wermle, Thomas F.	12	M		TX
Short, Malcomb J.	50	M		SCO
Gammill, Miles	28	M	Farmer	TN
J.	25	F		AL
A. A.	5	F		--
James	1	M		--
Stephenson, Elizabeth	42	F		SC
Elinor	19	F		TN
John	14	M		TN
Martha	12	F		TX
Robert	10	M		TX
Harriett	8	F		TX
Forsyth, David	30	M	Ferryman	TN
Voyles, Nicholas	28	M	Farmer	IL
Mary V.	28	F		NC
Oscar F.	4	M		TX
Samuel M.	2	M		TX
Heming, Mordica	20	M	Student	NC
Edwards, Ivy	30	M	Laborer	TN
Fleming, E. H.	28	M	Farmer	NC
Martha	23	F		TN
William W.	4	M		TX
Mary	3	F		TX
Bass(Ball), David L.	48	M	Farmer	SC
L. E.	26	F		TN
Frances L.	8	F		TX
Eliza	6	F		TX
David E.	3	M		TX
W. M.	2	M		TX
McGuire, David J.	25	M	Black Smith	GA
Amanda H.	22	F		TN
Mary E.	1	F		TX
Halcomb, A. F.	33	M	Gun Smith	TN
Sarah	23	F		TN
Lewis	67	M	Gardener	??
Foster, M. B. A.	22	M	Laborer	AL
Paul, Cavin J.	20	M		TN

Name	Age	Sex	Occupation	Birthplace
Hall, Henry	54	M	Farmer	NC
Margarett	45	F		SC
Henry	17	M	Student	TN
Jane	14	F		TN
Jeremiah	13	M		TN
Frances	10	F		TN
Eliza	4	F		TX
Brandon, William	20	M	Laborer	TN
Winter, Wiley B.	27	M	Farmer	AL
Lucinda	20	F		TN
M. J.	1	F		--
Bes, Elizabeth	42	F		NC
Henson, William R.	17	M	Farmer	TN
P. A.	15	M	Laborer	TN
John	13	M		AL
Mahula	11	F		AL
M. J.	9	F		AL

Precinct No. 5

Name	Age	Sex	Occupation	Birthplace
Hamilton, James	49	M	Farmer	TN
Ann	53	F		TN
Sarah Jane	19	F		TN
E. S.	18	F		TN
L. F.	15	F		TN
J. Thomas	12	M		TX
Legg, N. M.	7	F		TX
Wilson, N. A.	21	F		TN
M. S.	5	M		TX
S. E.	3	M		TX
J. T.	1	M		TX
Kitching, Wilson	35	M	Farmer	TN
Julia	19	F		IN
H.	1	-		TX
Kitching, Pharo	47	M		TN
Sarah	40	F		NC
H. H.	16	F		TX
L. H. K.	7	F		TX
Fitzgerald, William	28	M	Farmer	TN
N. A.	25	F		SC
Mary Jane	3	F		SC
P. F.	10/12	M		SC
Fitzgerald, Anderson	55	M	Mill Wright	GA
Charity	51	F		TN
Lesy	22	M		TN
P. L. F.	17	M		TN
M.	12	F		TN
B.	11	M		TN
J.	8	M		TN
L.	6	M		TN
G.	4	M		TN
W.	23	M		--
Fitzgerald, C.	28	M	Farmer	TN
A.	22	F		TN
S.	4	F		TN
S. A.	2	M		GA
Story, P. W.	25	M	Farmer	TN
L. S.	25	F		TN
L. A.	2	F		TX
C. W.	5/12	M		TX
Story, Edward W.	23	M	Farmer	TN
C. A.	20	F		TN
M. H.	2	F		TX
Work, P. M.	46	M	Farmer	SC
Mary	41	F		TN
John	22	M	Student	TN
H. W.	17	M	Student	TN
M. V. B.	14	M	Student	TN
B. P.	12	M	Student	TN
J. P.	9	M	Student	TN
J. R.	6	M	Student	TN
Ross, Daniel	--	M	Student	TN
Baucom, James N.	24	M		TN
Fussell, Martha	19	F		TN

CASS COUNTY, TEXAS

Name	Age	Sex	Occupation	Birthplace
Graham, T. W.	35	M	Farmer	TN
Jane	27	F		TN
C. G. G.	7	M		--
J. P.	5	M		--
R. A.	4	F		--
T. W.	10/12	M		--
John G.	2	M		--
Heanes, John G.	23	M	Farmer	TN
S.	21	F		TN
Sutherland, Mary	45	F	Farmer	TN
Mary Jane	19	F		TN
Nancy M.	12	F		TN
Thomas	9	M		TN
John	7	M		--
Thomas	--	M		--
Staly, Henry	39	M	Farmer	TN
M. E.	32	F		--
S. E.	15	F		--
M. W.	14	F		--
D. F.	12	M		--
N. C.	10	F		--
S. H.	10	M		--
S. H.	8	M		--
R. C.	5	M		--
M. G.	3	M		--
S. A.	8/12	F		--
Ford, M. A.	42	F		TN
O. L.	19	F		TN
Lane	17	M		TN
John	16	M		TN
John William	16	M		AL
Henry	14	M		AL
Julia	12	F		AL
George	10	M		AL
Martha	6	F		AL
M. C.	8	F		AL
M. F.	1	F		AL
Story, Daniel	55	M	Farmer	VA
S. T.	51	F		TN
Sarah	20	F		TN
Serena	19	F		TN
William	18	M	Laborer	TN
D. M.	16	M		TN
Isaac	14	M		TN
Mary	12	F		TN
Thomas	10	M		TN
John	8	M		TN
Martha	6	F		TN
Stark, G. A. M.	29	M	Teacher	TN
F. C.	29	F		TN
M. A. C.	14	F		TX
W. J.	9	M		TN
R. P.	7	M		TN
E. V.	2	F		TX
Johnson, B. W.	32	M	Farmer	TN
E. E.	25	F		TN
A. J.	9	M		MS
D. N.	7	M		MS
P. J.	5	F		TX
P. J.	4/12	F		TX
Campbell, A.	55	M	Farmer	TN
M. A.	45	F		NC
William	18	M		AL
I. L.	14	M		AL
I. W.	6	F		AL
M. P.	20	M		MS
Menal, A. P.	27	M		MS
Willis, W. E.	20	F	Farmer	TN
M. J.	5	M		TN
T. H.	2	M		MO
P. L.	16	M		MO
Barthalmew, E.	60	F	Farmer	??
Jacob	33	M	Farmer	TN

(continued)

Name	Age	Sex	Occupation	Birthplace
Barthalmew, E. B.	19	F		TN
M. B.	18	F		TN
Wilson	33	M	Farmer	NC
John	20	M	Farmer	TN
Charles	22	M	Farmer	TN
Barthalmew, Green	28	M	Farmer	NC
Rosey	20	F		TN
L. B.	11/12	F		TX
Kenedie, S.	15	M		TN
Stone, Thomas P.	55	M	Farmer	TN
Sarah	54	F		VA
P. S. N.	24	M	Farmer	AL
William	21	M		AL
S. D.	17	F		AL
M. A. ?.	15	F		AL
S. M.	10	M		--
Myrs, S. A.	20	M	Laborer	TN
Carlton, Elias	39	M	Black Smith	NC
Callens	39	F		AL
William	13	M		AL
Manda	1	F		AL
Shoemake, Eli	20	M	Laborer	AL
(illegible)	25	M	Farmer	AL
Carlton, John	29	M	Carpenter	TN
Story, B.	49	M	Farmer	NC
Liddy	44	F		NC
C. C.	17	M	Laborer	TN
R. B.	13	M		TN
Maryan	12	F		TN
S. C.	5	F		TN
B. S. C. T.	8	F		TN
S.	1	F		TN
Graham, Charles	58	M	Farmer	NC
Jane F.	50	F		TN
James F.	22	M	Farmer	TN
E. C.	20	F		TN
C. J.	19	F		TN
C. Y.	17	M	Student	TN
S. R.	14	M		TN
M. F.	13	F		TN
A. E. P.	8	F		TN
E.	6	F		TN
R. D. M.	4	M		TX
Frazier, Ebenezer	55	M	Farmer	TN
J. ?.	40	F		TN
S. P.	22	F		TN
E. M.	19	F		TN
L. F.	18	M	Laborer	TN
E. F., Jr.	10	M		TN
M. F.	7	M		TX
H. F.	10	M		TX
B. F.	5	M		TN
?. C.	1	F		TX
Williams, Parthena	28	F	Farmer	TN
Albert	6	M		TX
Sarah	5	F		TX
Thomson, Josiah	25	M	Laborer	AL
Williams, E.	6	F		TX
Davis, Jeptha	25	M	Farmer	TN
Rebecca	24	F		TN
Kemp, F. T.	5	F		TN
Davis, M.	1	F		TN
Bluford	20	M	Laborer	GA
Frazier, Daniel	52	M	Farmer	TN
L. A.	45	F		VA
M. P.	21	F		TN
M. R.	12	F		TN
D. P.	9	M		TX
Clene, J.	31	M	Laborer	GA
Graham, R. ?.	41	M	Farmer	NC
Nancy H.	29	F		TN
Tennessee F.	18	F	Student	TN
James M.	16	M	Student	TN
John F.	14	M	Student	TN
Robert	7	M	Student	TX
Newton C.	5	M	Student	TX

CASS COUNTY, TEXAS

Name	Age	Sex	Occupation	Birthplace
Price, John	68	M	Farmer	SC
Elizabeth	50	F		NC
Elizabeth	20	F		TN
Joel	16	M	Laborer	TN
Tempy	14	F		TN
Sarah S.	12	F		AL
Mahala	10	F		AL
Solomon	6	M		AL
Price, William	24	M	Farmer	TN
Armla Ann	20	F		KY
John	7	M		AL
Margret	5	F		AL
William	2	M		AR
David F.	8/12	M		TX
Nichols, William	34	M	Farmer	MO
M.	23	M		TN
William J.	6	M		TN
William John	4	M		TN
Sarah	2	F		TN
Watson, Hagen	21	M		AR
A.	20	F		NY
Davis, G.	48	M	Laborer	TN
Haynes, William	50	M	Farmer	TN
N.	45	F		--

Precinct No. 6

Name	Age	Sex	Occupation	Birthplace
McAdams, Mortimore	22	M	Farmer	TN
Nancy W.	19	F		TN
Wilson, J.	51	M	Farmer	KY
Susan	33	F		TN
Robinson, Sterling	27	M		TN
R.	27	F		TN
M. E.	2	F		TX
Ledbetter, William	25	M	Farmer	TN
Nancy	20	F		TN
L. M.	6/12	F		TX
Dun, B. W.	35	M	Farmer	SC
Martha	22	F		TN
J.	17	M	Laborer	AL
M. L.	2	F		TX
William	5/12	M		TX
Warnel, R.	40	M	Farmer	KY
M.	40	F		KY
J.	14	M		TN
W. M.	13	M		TN
Richard	12	M		TX
Whitehead, M. P.	1	F		TX
Warnel, P.	38	M	Farmer	TN
M.	33	F		TN
L. C.	9	F		TN
William	8	M		TN
M. C.	6	F		TN
P. A.	4	M		TN
R.	2	M		TN
Smith, Samuel J.	24	M	Farmer	NC
Martha A.	23	F		TN
Almeda	1	F		TX
Buckhatton, Michael	54	M	P. Bapt. Mins.	SC
Jane	52	F		NC
David W.	28	M	Black Smith	TN
E. W.	23	M	Black Smith	TN
W. S.	18	M	Farmer	TN
Pamelia	21	F		TN
Nancy	16	F		TN
Margarett	10	F		TN
Martha J.	8	F		TN
Williams, William A.	20	M	Laborer	TN
Cooper, Hosa	40	M		AL
Malinda	34	F		TN

(continued)

Name	Age	Sex	Occupation	Birthplace
Cooper, Manervy	15	F		AL
Polly	13	F		AL
Burell	8	M		AL
Thomas	6	M		AL
Balie	4	M		TX
Sarah E.	6/12	F		TX
Harrison, Samuel	40	M	Farmer	KY
Sarah A.	27	F		AL
L. A.	12	F		TN
M. J.	10	F		TX
Martha F.	8	F		TX
James Francis	4	M		TX
Hanna S.	3	F		TX
Elizabeth	5/12	F		TX
Clement, James	51	M	Farmer	SC
Nancy A.	19	F		TN
Pinkney W.	24	M	Carpenter	GA
Bird L.	22	M	Laborer	GA
Adam L.	20	M	Laborer	GA
Delila J.	18	F		GA
Martha M.	14	F		GA
James A.	12	M		GA
Mary E.	5	F		TX
Margaret	6/12	F		TX
Davidson, David M.	33	M	Farmer	TN
L. J.	26	F		TN
William C.	5	M		TN
Mary A.	2	F		TX
Wadkins, Fernandez	30	M	Farmer	TN
Matilda	32	F		IN
Samuel J.	14	M		AR
Thomas J.	12	M		AR
Rosann	8	F		AR
William C.	4	M		TX
David H.	3/12	M		TX
Baily, Wesley	48	M	Farmer	TN
Louisa	43	F		TN
A. F.	23	M	Farmer	TN
Lucy E.	20	F		TN
Margaret E.	18	F		TN
Clerinda M.	15	F		AL
Irramenta	13	F		AL
Leonidas M.	11	M		AL
James H.	5	M		AL
Allen, William J.	23	M	Farmer	MS
Elizabeth J.	20	F		TN
Sarah L.	1	F		TX
Baker, John	45	M	Farmer	SC
Nancy	40	F		TN
H. J.	15	F		TN
Cullen	13	M		TN
Eliza J.	12	F		TN
R. J.	3	M		TX
Latamore, Martha	6	F		LA
Reaves, Martin	33	M	Farmer	MO
Martha	30	F		TN
Philip	10	M		TN
Elizabeth	6	F		TN
Bramon	6	M		TN
Petty, Williamson	30	M	Farmer	TN
Mary A.	30	F		AL
Elizabeth	12	F		MS
Mary Ann	10	F		MS
Sarah A.	7	F		MS
Alexander	3	M		AR
Ross, A. J.	34	M	Carpenter	NC
Martha A.	26	F		TN
Charlot	5	F		MS
M. C.	5	F		MS
N. A.	3	F		MS
Robb, James	55	M	Carpenter	GA
Rebecca	37	F		TN
W.	23	M	Farmer	GA
J. F.	19	M	Laborer	GA

(continued)

CASS COUNTY, TEXAS

Name	Age	Sex	Occupation	Birthplace
Robb, A. C.	17	F		GA
L. A.	14	F		GA
E. R.	12	F		AL
J. R.	10	M		TX
Isaac	8	M		TX
Susan	2	F		TX
Boorer, Leonidas	26	M	Merchant	GA
Tyra(?), John	22	M	Waggon Maker	??
Collins, Henry	29	M	Farmer	KY
Nancy A.	23	F		TN
A. J.	3	M		TX
E. C.	1	F		TX
Rhea, John	38	M	Farmer	TN
Elizabeth	36	F		SC
M. B.	12	M		SC
F. R.	10	F		SC
J. B.	8	F		TX
M. A. W.	4	F		TX
T. J. R.	2	M		TX
M.	5/12	F		TX
Warnell, N. G.	64	M	Farmer	SC
Sarah	56	F		GA
N. G., Jr.	19	M		TN
H. M.	16	M		TN
Thomas F.	12	M		TN
Rhea, William B.	36	M	Farmer	TN
M. F.	32	F		AL
R. H.	7	M		TX
A. L.	5	M		TX
M. E.	2	F		TX
C. A.	5/12	F		TX
Allen, R. C.	46	M		NC
M. W.	38	F		TN
Simmons, William	38	M	Farmer	TN
Sintha A.	24	F		AL
James M.	16	M	Student	TX
William C.	12	M		TX
Common, Elizabeth M.	57	F		TN
Vianna	23	F		TN
Patterson, J. M.	33	M	C. P. Mins.	TN
Louvenia W.	32	F		TN
Charles M.	6	M		MS
J. L.	5	M		MS
J. W.	3	M		AR
Serepta A.	1	F		TX
Warde, Louis C.	24	M	Black Smith	TN
Mary	19	F		TN
James M.	1	M		TN
Spell, Marshall	30	M	Merchant	LA
Elizabeth	17	F		TN
Thomas T.	7/12	M		TX
R. H.	14	M		MS
Gilbert, S. H.	22	M	Physician	TN
Hammons, G. H.	31	M	Clerk	KY
Blackwell, Thomas	26	M	Clerk	VA
Ritchie, Thomas G.	45	M	Farmer	KY
Malinda	47	F		KY
Julia Ann	13	F		TN
Mary	9	F		TX
Isabella J.	5	F		TX
Conley, William	22	M	Farmer	GA
Cuney, James	43	M	Weaver	IRE
Blair, W. G.	30	M	School Teacher	TN
Ann	28	F		TN
Givins, G. W.	34	M	Farmer	TN
Mary	23	F		NC
William Y.	3	M		MS
Vey, Florida M.	13	F		TN

Name	Age	Sex	Occupation	Birthplace
Patterson, Edward	35	M	Farmer	TN
Lyday A.	25	F		TN
Nancy A.	8	F		AR
Louisa B.	5	F		AR
Mary C.	3	F		AR
Hester A.	5/12	F		TX
Edgarton, Levy	30	M	Laborer	SC
Patterson, Bluford	37	M	Physician	TN
Hester	30	F		MS
R. R.	12	M		MS
Mary J.	10	F		MS
Eliza A.	9	F		MS
Albert	7	M		MS
W. H. H.	5	M		MS
John L.	2	M		MS
Armsworth, J. H.	21	M	Farmer	NC
Jane	26	F		NC
Andrew	6	M		TN
Rebecca	3	F		TN
Tennessee	5/12	F		TN
Dunn, A. G.	30	M	Farmer	GA
Eliza	34	F		TN
Patience	12	F		AL
Rebecca	10	F		AL
Allen, William	31	M	Farmer	TN
Molley	29	F		NC
Sarah E.	7	F		AL
Nancy E.	2	F		TX
Allen, Jacob	22	M	Farmer	TN
Martha	19	F		MO
James H.	5/12	M		TX
McAdams, H. J.	38	M	Farmer	TN
Susan	39	F		TN
Jane M.	15	F		AL
Samuel	12	M		AL
Sarah	10	F		AL
Harris	8	M		TX
Meredith	5	M		TX
Wesley	3	M		TX
Bethany	2	F		TX
David	1	M		TX
Moores, Thomas B.	29	M	Farmer	SC
Sarah	28	F		TN
Margaret	1	F		TX
Griffee, Isaac	35	M	Farmer	TN
Clerise H.	29	F		TN
Mary J.	11	F		TN
Elizabeth	10	F		TN
E. L.	7	F		TN
W. R.	8	M		TN
Neaman	6	F		TN
M. R.	4	F		TN
C. S.	2/12	F		TX
Burkhalter, W. H.	30	M	Farmer	TN
Mary	29	F		GA
George G.	6	M		TN
Malinda J.	5	F		TN
Emily A.	2	F		AL
John M.	24	M	Farmer	TN
Martha	22	F		TN
Harvey, Samuel	43	M	Farmer	TN
Margarett	42	F		TN
R. C.	9	M		TN
C. J.	7	M		TN
M. E.	5	F		TN
B. F.	3	M		TN
J. M.	2	M		TX
Tennessee	3/12	F		TX
Atchley, William N.	23	M	Farmer	TN
Mary E.	24	F		TN
Hill, William	58	M	Farmer	SC
Jane	58	F		NC
Joseph	25	M	Clerk	TN

(continued)

CASS COUNTY, TEXAS

Name	Age	Sex	Occupation	Birthplace
Hill, Daniel G.	20	M	Laborer	TN
H. L.	16	M		TN
Frazier, Squire	35	M	Farmer	TN
Martha	35	F		TN
Mary	16	F		KY
Susan J.	14	F		KY
E. J.	6	M		TX
Margaret A.	5	F		TX
J. F.	4	F		TX
J. H.	1	M		TX
Lusk, John	47	M	Farmer	TN
Sarah	34	F		AL
Rhoda A.	15	F		AL
Tabitha	9	F		AL
Gibson, William	17	M		KY

Precinct No. 7

Name	Age	Sex	Occupation	Birthplace
Cocke, J. B.	33	M	Merchant	TN
Lavenia	17	F		NC
Gupton, Adolphus	41	M	Merchant	NC
M. E.	32	F		NC
M. H.	5	M		TX
F. S.	3	F		TX
Smith, T. J.	24	M	Physician	TN
Jones, A. L.	24	M	Physician	AL
Godbold, James C.	32	M	Grocer	SC
Reaves, James	21	M	Merchant	SC
(illegible), Benjamin	24	M	Clerk	TN
Russell, William	34	M	Farmer	TN
Nancy A.	30	F		AL
E. A.	11	F		MS
William W.	7	M		TX
J. J. N.	4	F		TX
Smith, F. P.	50	M	Farmer	NC
Susan	43	F		TN
John F.	17	M		TN
James P.	16	M		TN
Mary F.	11	F		TX
B. B.	5	M		TX
B. F.	7	M		MS
E. E.	1	F		TX
Fownsley, John	21	M		TN
Davis, James H.	28	M	Farmer	MS
Elizabeth	22	F		MS
John H.	29	M	Farmer	MS
Josephine	18	F		TN
Crow, William H.	25	M	Farmer	MS
Mary A.	28	F		MS
Mary M.	10	F		TN
Murry, William	36	M	Farmer	TN
E.	26	F		MS
William, Jr.	9	M		TX
P.	6	M		TX
John	4	M		TX
W.	18	M	Laborer	TN
Tanner, E.	23	M	Laborer	TN
Denson, Jesse	57	M	Farmer	TN
Sarah	48	F		NC
Jesse, Jr.	21	M		MS
J. M.	18	M	Laborer	MS
James H.	15	M		MS
B. F.	5	M		TX
William	3	M		TX
Sarah	13	F		MS
Hunt, R. T.	17	M		NC
Richardson, William	70	M	Overseer	VA
Denson, M. H.	12	M		MS
Mitchell, M. M.	39	M	Farmer	LA
Mary	26	F		TN
B. T.	14	M		MS
Dicy	12	F		MS
A.	9	F		MS

(continued)

Name	Age	Sex	Occupation	Birthplace
Mitchell, M. J.	7	F		AR
James A.	5	M		TX
D.	3	F		TX
F. F.	1	F		TX
Rose, William	27	M	Shoemaker	IN
Haygood, William H.	40	M	Farmer	NC
Eliza	30	F		AL
A.	12	F		TN
M.	10	F		MS
R.	8	M		MS
T.	6	F		MS
Joseph	4	M		MS
Eliza	2	F		MS
William	2/12	M		TX
Perkins, Nathan	25	M	Farmer	LA
F.	55	F		TN
Samuel	52	M	Farmer	LA
Frances	18	F		MS
Judel	12	M		TX
Clone, Jacob	33	M	Laborer	GER
Stallcup, William	35	M	Farmer	TN
E. A.	25	F		TN
M. C.	3	M		TX
W. B.	1	M		TX
Scott, T. H.	14	M		MS
James C.	12	M		MS
John M.	9	M		MS
McReynolds, James H.	62	M	Farmer	NC
Ann	48	F		NC
Thomas B.	23	M	Farmer	AL
James H.	21	M	Student	TN
Benjamin O.	17	M	Student	TN
L. A.	12	F		TN
Ames, Charles	40	M	Farmer	MA
H. A.	40	F		NY
Page, James	20	M	Laborer	TN
Potter, John J.	10	M		TX
Ames, Charles, Jr.	7	M		TX
E. York	3	M		TX
F.	1	M		TX
William	5	M		TX
McLoy, A.	45	M	Laborer	NC
Bourgess, B. A.	36	M	Farmer	TN
L. A.	25	F		AL
P. M.	5	M		TN
N. J.	3	M		TN
F. A.	2	F		TX
John	4/12	M		TX
Moore, Martha	9	F		TN
John M.	6	M		TN
Brackens, T. N.	22	M	Clerk	VA
Tucker, Charles W.	28	M	Overseer	AL
Hoozer, S. D.	50	M	Saddler	VA
Dye, B. B.	50	M	School Teacher	GA
N. L.	42	F		GA
B. F.	21	M	Farmer	SC
B. A.	18	M	Laborer	NC
S.	13	M		NC
Charles	10	M		TN
James	7	M		TN
Thomas	6	M		TN
E.	9/12	M		TX
Haris, McNary	45	M	Farmer	TN
M. A.	35	F		TN
Temple	21	M	Laborer	AL
Sarah	11	F		AL
B.	9	M		AL
Joseph	5	M		TX
N.	4	F		TX
Wiley	1	M		TX
James	1	M		TX
Townsley, William	29	M		TN
R. A.	21	F		AL
S. A.	2	F		TX
M. J.	1	F		TX

CASS COUNTY, TEXAS

Name	Age	Sex	Occupation	Birthplace
Huffine, T.	48	M	Farmer	NC
M.	46	F		IL
Sarah	22	F		TN
John	20	M		TN
Martha	18	F		TN
Joseph	15	M		TN
William	14	M		TN
Ward, John C.	50	M	Farmer	GA
Sarah H.	43	F		GA
Robert H.	19	M		AL
John S.	16	M		AL
Sarah E.	11	F		AL
Silas M.	7	M		AL
M. S.	5	F		AL
L. A.	9/12	F		TX
Margret C.	21	F		TN
Taylor, M. D. K.	31	M	Physician	GA
Elizabeth S.	26	F		AL
Anas W.	12	M		AL
Hillary L.	7	M		AL
Francis M.	4	M		AL
Mathias D.	3	M		TX
Miligan, Samuel	16	M	Laborer	TN
Glass, Harvy	52	M	Farmer	KY
R. P.	50	F		TN
R. D.	18	M	Laborer	TN
J. H.	16	M		TN
W. H.	13	M		TN
M. C.	12	F		TN
S. H.	7	F		TN
M. W.	6	F		TN
Frazier, J. H.	29	M	Farmer	TN
Elizabeth J.	26	F		TN
F. C.	3	F		TN
J. A.	2	F		TX
E. M.	4/12	M		TX
Fazus, Moses B.	59	M	Farmer	TN
Tempy	59	F		VA
John B.	25	M	Farmer	TN
Benjamin M.	23	M	Farmer	TN
O. C.	20	M		TN
Thomas D.	16	M	Student	TN
Sarah R.	14	F		TN
Fitzgerald, G. W.	23	M	Farmer	TN
Mary E.	16	F		AL
Catharine J.	6/12	F		TX
Fitzgerald, A.	22	M	Farmer	TN
Frances	24	F		AL
Fitzgerald, Louisa A.	39	F	Farmer	TN
Pride, Sarah	15	F		AL
Joseph M. C.	9	M		AL
Martha A.	7	F		AL
Fitzgerald, L. J. A.	1	F		TX
Joseph M.	20	M	Farmer	TN
Jesse	17	M		TN
Garrett	15	M		TN
Campbell, John P.	47	M	Farmer	NC
Louisa	40	F		TN
Leonidas A.	17	M		MO
Sarah R.	13	F		MO
James C.	11	M		MO
Thomas	9	M		MO
Samuel J.	1	M		MO
McKinney, Louisa	2	F		MO
McCord, James M.	44	M	Mechanic	NC
Roper, Thomas	39	M	Overseer	TN
Roberson, William H.	35	M	Physician	AL
Core, Wiley	38	M	Farmer	NC
Sarah E.	44	F		VA
Blackburn, William	18	M		AL
C. L.	17	M		TN
Eliz.	15	F		TN
Caroline	13	F		TN

(continued)

Name	Age	Sex	Occupation	Birthplace
Blackburn, Francis	11	M		TN
Robert	9	M		TN
Eugene	7	M		TN
Gray	5	M		TN
Core, Charlot	9	F		TX
John W.	7	M		TX
Cherry, Franklin	26	M		TN
Garden, William	26	M	Overseer	TN
Martha	21	F		AL
Susan	3	F		TN
Taggot, William	55	M	Farmer	NC
Edith	50	F		NC
Hampton	18	M	Laborer	TN
Whitfield	16	M	Laborer	TN
Elizabeth J. A.	19	F		TN
Hine, Wiley	47	M	Farmer	TN
Elizabeth	50	F		TN
Joseph	22	M	Farmer	TN
William	20	M	Laborer	TN
Wiley	16	M	Laborer	TN
Taggot, D. F.	27	M	Farmer	TN
William R.	25	M	Farmer	TN
Perry, Elijah	24	M	Laborer	NC
Wood-y, William D.	56	M	Clerk	TN
Ann	45	F		TN
William A.	19	M	Student	AL
Adams, Mary	12	F		AL
Minor	10	M		AL
Cannon, Nancy R.	50	F		TN
Darden, J. H.	30	M	Farmer	TN
Sarah	24	F		TN
Cobb, William	30	M	Farmer	TN
Susan	25	F		TN
Molton, John	29	M	Farmer	FL
Nancy	21	F		TN
Bryan, A. W.	24	M	Farmer	TN
Louisa	20	F		TN
Sarah	6/12	F		TX
Cobb, A.	25	M	Farmer	TN
Mary	20	F		TN
Infant	4/12	F		TX
Mitchell, August	23	M	Physician	TN
Mary	18	F		TN
Andrew	1	M		TX

CHEROKEE COUNTY, TEXAS

Name	Age	Sex	Occupation	Birthplace
Harris, Samuel	56	M	C. P. Minster	KY
Jane B.	41	F		TN
Susan Jane	20	F		TN
Sarah Ann	18	F		AL
James B.	16	M		AL
David M.	14	M		AR
Ruth E.	12	F		AR
Mary C.	10	F		AR
Samuel R.	6	M		AR
McKee, T. L.	32	M	Merchant	TN
L. E.	28	F		TN
William H.	8	M		TX
Sarah A. F.	6	F		TX
Mary E. S.	4	F		TX
Moore, Sarah	58	F		VA
G. C.	19	M		TN
Hughes, Edward	23	M	Black Smith	TN
William	21	M	Black Smith	TN
McKee, Robert J.	1½	M		TX
Hudson, Sarah J.	34	F		TN
Sarah L.	8	F		IN
Thomas J.	1	M		TX

CHEROKEE COUNTY, TEXAS

Name	Age	Sex	Occupation	Birthplace
Goodman, J. B.	36	M	Carpenter	TN
Lucinda	26	F		SC
James D.	6	M		TX
Lewis C.	5	M		TX
John T.	2	M		TX
Georda	1	M		TX
Broughton, D. W.	26	M	Carpenter	AL
Mary L.	23	F		GA
Mary S.	3	F		AR
Priscilla J.	4/12	F		TX
Templeton, L. A. J.	30	M	Carpenter	TN
Lane, G. W.	31	M	School Teacher	TN
Porter, John F.	23	M	Grocer	TN
Broyles, Joseph	35	M	Farmer	TN
Kezia M.	31	F		TN
Mary Ann	4	F		TN
Robert H.	2	M		TN
Butler, Thomas	31	M	Farmer	MD
Mary C.	27	F		TN
Cordelia A. M.	5	F		TN
Mary C.	4	F		TN
James B.	2	M		TN
William T.	9/12	M		TX
Fry, Michael	63	M	Farmer	NC
Sarah	54	F		NC
Almanda S.	20	F		TN
Andrew J.	17	M		TN
Lebanon L.	16	M		TN
Martha V.	14	F		TN
Clemantine C.	12	F		TN
James K. P.	11	M		TN
Davis, A. J.	23	M	Farmer	VA
Caroline J.	25	F		TN
John W.	2/12	M		TN
Fry, William W.	32	M	Farmer	NC
Agnes S.	29	F		TN
Joseph L.	8	M		TN
Sarah J.	7	F		TN
Andrew J.	5	M		TN
Walters, B. C.	48	M	B. Minister	GA
Nancy	43	F		TN
Pleasant H.	14	M		TX
Tillman	12	M		TX
John	10	M		TX
Phelix H.	8	M		TX
Lucinda	6	F		TX
Sarah Jane	4	F		TX
Kirkpatrick, Isaac	23	M	Farmer	TN
Martha M.	24	F		TN
Morrison, M. C. W.	30	M	Carpenter	TN
Charlotte	26	F		TN
William S.	9	M		TN
Mary M.	5	F		TN
Dorothy J.	2	F		TX
Kerr, William	35	M	Physician	NC
Louisa C.	32	F		NC
Mary L.	12	F		MS
Amanda M.	10	F		MS
Laura M.	8	F		TN
William E.	4	M		TN
Catharine M.	1	F		TX
Gideon, L. H.	38	M	Clerk	TN
S. Ann	27	F		AL
Adolphus W.	8	M	Deaf & Dumb	TX
Isaac F.	6	M		TX
Almira E.	4	F		TX
Joseph P.	2	M		TX
Earle, Samuel L.	23	M	Lawyer	AL
Brown, G. R.	21	M	Clerk	AL
Graves, Joseph	24	M	Teamster	SC
Hood, A. J.	26	M	Teacher	SC
McFadden, C(V).	18	M	Clerk	AL

Name	Age	Sex	Occupation	Birthplace
Wadley, E. R.	32	M	Carpenter	TN
E. R.	34	F		TN
Sam P. N.	7/12	M		TX
Denman, F. G.	23	M	Merchant	GA
S. J.	14	F		TN
Philips, Isaac W.	12	M		TN
Webb, W. D.	24	M	Farmer	GA
Wallace, Thomas	66	M	Farmer	TN
Addison S.	21	M		AL
Langston, H. U(V).	32	M	Farmer	AL
Sarah	35	F		TN
Rachel E.	12	F		MS
Isaac Newton	9	M		MS
John	7	M		MS
Mary	5	F		AR
Joannah	4	F		TX
Sarah	4/12	F		TX
Dodson, C.	39	M	Planter	TN
Nancy	39	F		TN
Jasper N.	15	M		AL
Margaret M.	8	F		AL
Joshua P.	6	M		AL
Jonathan L.	4	M		AL
Joel J.	1	M		TX
Hemmen, Josiah	34	M	Planter	TN
Susanna	29	F		TN
Elizabeth J.	9	F		MO
William P.	7	M		TX
Mary Ann	5	F		TX
Amanda	3	F		TX
Oliver	8/12	M		TX
Fain, W. W.	29	M	Merchant	IN
F. O.	24	F		TN
Weir, Hugh	63	M	Physician	VA
Elizabeth	64	F		VA
David M.	26	M	Physician	AL
James J.	23	M	Planter	AL
Ross, Andrew J.	22	M	Planter	TN
Bass, Willis	39	M	Planter	TN
Elizabeth	38	F		SC
Elijah	20	M	Planter	AL
Nancy	17	F		NC
Tillman M.	18	M	Farmer	AL
Sarah F.	13	F		AL
John	12	M		AL
Martha J.	9	F		AL
Jorden	6	M		AL
Elizabeth W.	5	F		AL
Decia B.	2	F		TX
George H.	5/12	M		TX
Bass, Bathenia	90	F		VA
Rose, Henry	30	M	Planter	TN
Sarah H.	32	F		TN
William Jasper	12	M		AR
Elizabeth Ann	10	F		AR
Mary Frances	8	F		AR
John B.	6	M		TX
Christopher C.	4	M		TX
Sarah	3	F		TX
Marandia ?.	1	F		TX
Brandon, Benjamin	20	M	Planter	TN
Ann M.	21	F		TN
Mary C.	7/12	F		TX
Alvis, E. H.	42	M	Farmer	VA
Rebecca T.	29	F		TN
George T.	12	M		AL
Charles J.	11	M		AL
Mary J.	9	F		AL
Henry C.	7	M		AL
Martha Ann	5	F		AL
Eliza R.	3	F		AL
Bingham, Michael	38	M	Farmer	TN
Mahala	28	F		AL
Missouri	10	F		MS

(continued)

CHEROKEE COUNTY, TEXAS

Name	Age	Sex	Occupation	Birthplace
Bingham, Eliza	8	F		MS
Albert G.	6	M		MS
William E.	4	M		TX
Mary G.	1	F		TX
Taylor, E.	25	M	Farmer	TN
Jane F.	21	F		VA
Mary J.	54	F		AL
Williams, F. E.	27	M	Farmer	TN
Ruth	26	F		AR
Keland	6	M		TX
Selvina J.	4	F		TX
Miram T.	2	F		TX
Edgar, A.	74	M	Farmer	VA
Jane	52	F		TN
Isabella	32	F		TN
Catherine	22	F		TN
Thomas	24	M	Farmer	TN
Margarett	17	F		TN
Lockey C.	14	F		TN
Lotta A.	14	F		TN
Sarah A.	9	F		TN
Gwynn, John	25	M	Farmer	TN
Elizabeth	20	F		TN
James	3	M		TN
Charlotte J.	1	F		TX
Baker, W. L.	25	M	Farmer	TN
Lucinda J.	23	F		IL
William Newton	4	M		TN
John Clark	1	M		TX
Hague, A.	57	M	Farmer	NC
S. E.	22	M	Farmer	TN
William F.	20	M		TN
Sarah J.	15	F		TN
Gray, William E.	31	M	Farmer	TN
Catherine	26	F		TN
James R.	5	M		TN
Robert A.	2	M		TN
Myers, D. A.	23	M	Farmer	TN
Lane, J. H., Jr.	25	M	Farmer	TN
Siney	18	F		AL
Hanby, Thomas	35	M	Farmer	NC
Vina	27	F		TN
Hannah	12	F		TN
Thornton	8	M		TN
James	6	M		TN
Jane	4	F		TN
Jesse	1	M		TX
Odle, John	26	M	Grocer	TN
Lucinda	25	F		AR
Alfred C.	6	M		TX
Nancy T.	3	F		TX
Matilda E.	2	F		TX
Kincheloe, G. W.	43	M	Farmer	TN
Matilda	39	F		TN
Mary J.	18	F		KY
Orlena G.	8	F		AR
Guy, W. T. D.	24	M	Merchant	AL
Erwin, Richard	19	M	Clerk	TN
Wooton, R. A.	22	M	Teacher	GA
Tidwell, D. J.	48	M	M. E. Preacher	SC
Sevilla	45	F		SC
Adaline	18	F		TN
Malissa J.	15	F		MS
Margaret E.	12	F		MS
Eliza V.	10	F		MS
Walden ?.	7	M		MS
William Henry	5	M		MS
John W.	21	M	Farmer	TN
Runnels, Isaac	25	M	Farmer	TN
Emily Ann	25	F		SC
(continued)				
Runnels, William A.	5	M		TX
John A.	4	M		TX
Sarah E.	2	F		TX
Martha	3/12	F		TX
Lane, W. J.	32	M	Farmer	VA
Jemima	24	F		TN
Martha	8	F		TN
James K. P.	5	M		TN
Benjamin F.	3	M		TN
Heziah C.	7/12	M		TX
Watson, W.	25	M	Well Digger	NC
Minerva	23	F		NC
Hughes, John	45	M	Merchant	TN
Maples, Calvin	33	M	Merchant	TN
Hogan, Jas. M.	33	M	Stockman	TN
Nancy P.	23	F		AR
Elizabeth C.	8	F		TX
Marguer L.	6	M		TX
John W.	3	M		TX
Henderson, J. W.	35	M	Grocer	SC
Elvira J.	22	F		SC
Nathaniel C.	3	M		TN
John T.	2	M		MS
Frazer, Richard	40	M	Farmer	KY
Agness	38	F		TN
James	12	M		AR
Robert	10	M		AR
Philip	8	M		AR
John	6	M		TX
Mary	4	F		TX
Carter, Benjamin	29	M	Farmer	TN
Elizabeth	29	F		KY
Abel	12	M		MS
Charity	10	F		MS
Tassey J.	4	F		MS
Arthanly	2	F		TX
William F.	4/12	M		TX
Brock, J. W.	33	M	Farmer	KY
Elizabeth	33	F		TN
Malissa C.	11	F		KY
Haden V.	8	M		KY
Melvina E.	6	F		KY
Rebecca E.	4	F		KY
Vestina B.	2	F		KY
Jas. M.	3/12	M		TX
Stockton, E. C.	29	M	Farmer	TN
Amanda F.	23	F		AL
George R.	6	M		MS
William D.	4	M		TX
Mary E.	1	F		TX
Reynolds, Hiram	21	M	Farmer	TN
Nancy J.	21	F		GA
Sivann, J. F.	38	M	Farmer	TN
Mary	35	F		TN
Elizabeth A.	15	F		AL
Harvey R.	12	M		AL
Joseph	10	M		AL
Mary	8	F		AL
Sarah E.	6	F		AL
Samuel C.	1	M		TX
Cunningham, A.	35	M	Farmer	TN
Mary Ann	28	F		TN
Robert L.	5	M		TN
Sarah M.	4	F		TN
Ruth C.	2	F	(Insane)	TN
Samuel A.	6/12	M		TX
Ferguson, Ruth	64	F		VA
Robert A.	24	M	Farmer	TN
Wiggins, J. W.	25	M	Farmer	TN
Mary K.	22	F		TN
Nancy J.	4	F		TN
Hiram	1	M		TN

CHEROKEE COUNTY, TEXAS

Name	Age	Sex	Occupation	Birthplace
Ewing, J. H.	34	M	Farmer	TN
Sarah J.	19	F		TN
Mary E.	1	F		TN
Gann, William	53	M	Farmer	TN
Westley	18	M	Farmer	TN
George W.	14	M		TN
Coker, H.	22	M		GA
Sarah J.	19	F		TN
Becton, F. E.	76	M	Farmer	NC
Allison, S. E. D.	26	F		TN
Alexander, C. B.	26	M	Gin Wright	NC
M. D. A.	20	F		TN
McKee, Thomas	60	M	Farmer	NC
Frances	58	F		VA
Irvine, Rebecca	28	F		TN
Mary C. A.	6	F		TN
Sarah F. R. A.	4	F		TN
McKee, Thomas N.	32	M	C. P. Minister	TN
Mallory, H. H.	41	M	Farmer	GA
Isabella N.	32	F		TN
John	15	M	Farmer	AL
Mary J.	13	F		AL
Henry P.	10	M		AL
Joseph S.	8	M		AL
William C.	6	M		AL
Elizabeth S. A.	2	F		TX
Hunt, Martin	45	M	Farmer	TN
Cole, William	55	M	M. E. Minister	VA
Mary P.	25	F		TN
Henry B.	26	M	Farmer	AL
Francis A.	18	M	Farmer	AL
Mary F.	14	F		AL
Martha	8	F		AL
Griffin, Jas.	5	M		MS
Frances	2	F		MS
Dodson, J.	33	M	Farmer	TN
Lavenia A.	26	F		AL
Elizabeth F.	11	F		AL
Emeline H.	9	F		AL
Louisa	7	F		AL
Julia A.	5	F		AL
Margaret	3	F		AL
Martha P.	2	F		TX
Bearden, J. L.	40	M	Farmer	SC
Elmira	36	F		TN
Mary P.	14	F		TN
John W.	12	M		TN
Joel L.	10	M		TN
William J.	9	M		TN
Minerva A.	7	F		TN
Sarah E.	5	F		TN
Edwin W.	2	M		TX
Cutbarth, E.	38	M	Farmer	TN
Anna	34	F		TN
Sarah J.	12	F		AR
Alvine	10	M		AR
Mary E.	8	F		AR
Daniel	5	M		AR
William	2	M		TX
Riddle, Stephen	29	M	Farmer	TN
Jane	31	F		TN
Sarah A.	9	F		TN
Susan F.	6	F		TN
Mary J.	4	F		TN
John A.	2	M		TN
Alexander	4/12	M		TX
Jones, J. F.	26	M	Farmer	TN
Nancy M.	21	F		TN
Mary A.	3/12	F		TX
Long, Mary A.	17	F		TN
Matilda A.	13	F		AL
Thomas	20	M	Farmer	TN
Rose, Z.	40	M	M. B. Minister	NC
Sarah	48	F		TN
Thomas P.	16	M	Farmer	TN
Emily J.	15	F		TN
William F.	14	M		TN
Sarah C.	13	F		TN
Martha A.	11	F		TN
P---- L.	10	M		TN
Mary M.	8	F		TN
John B.	6	M		TN
Susannah A.	5	F		TN
Johnson, John	47	M	M. E. Minister	SC
Louisa	41	F		TN
Rebecca A.	22	F		IL
William M.	17	M	Farmer	TN
Lucy A.	14	F		TN
John W.	12	M		TN
Jonathan L.	11	M		TN
George W.	9	M		TN
Barbara L.	5	F		TN
Sarah E.	3	F		TN
Caleb R.	1	M		TX
Fulton, Mary	46	F		TN
John W.	25	M	Farmer	TN
Thomas	16	M	Farmer	TN
William	10	M		TN
James S.	8	M		TN
Ephraim W.	4	M		TN
Rebecca B.	18	F		TN
Eleanor C.	13	F		TN
Hightower, Thomas P.	32	M	Farmer	GA
Louisa	33	F		TN
Charnell B.	9	M		MS
Thomas J.	7	M		MS
Emily E.	3	F		TX
Susan J.	7/12	F		TX
Watts, Warren J.	21	M	Farmer	GA
Morton, A. P.	37	M	Mechanic	TN
Elizabeth	39	F		London, ENG
Isaah S.	12	M		AL
John T.	11	M		AL
Hartwell E.	10	M		AL
William D.	9	M		AL
Mary E.	7	F		AL
James	6	M		AL
Joseph	6	M		AL
Samuel C.	3	M		MS
Benjamin P.	2	M		MS
Martha E.	1	F		MS
Philips, G. W.	32	M	Farmer	TN
Sarah R.	28	F		AL
William T.	8	M		AL
Arthur B.	7	F(M)		MS
John T.	5	M		MS
Cinderilla K.	4	F		TX
Indiana	5/12	M(F)		TX
Nancy A. F.	2	F		TX
Ford, C. J.	22	M	Farmer	TN
Evecia	21	F		LA
Crenshaw, H.	32	M	Farmer	SC
Susan J.	28	F		TN
Marticia	7	F		MS
William Thomas	5	M		MS
Elizabeth A.	5/12	F		TX
George, W. E.	32	M	M. E. Minister	TN
Margaret L.	29	F		KY
James H.	6	M		TX
John W.	3	M		TX
Eliza A.	6/12	F		TX
Davis, John E.	35	M	Farmer	KY
James A.	19	M	Farmer	TN
McKinney, John E.	23	M	Farmer	AL
Gwin, John	37	M	Farmer	TN
Lucy	37	F		NC
Mary Ann	14	F		MS
Frances	12	F		TX

(continued)

Name	Age	Sex	Occupation	Birthplace
Gwin, James	7	M		TX
Lucy	5	F		TX
Emaline	3	F		TX
Chisom, E.	34	M	Farmer	TN
Delilah	30	F		IN
Mary E.	7	F		TX
William E.	5	M		TX
John Madison	3	M		TX
India J.	8/12	F		TX
George, William	66	M	Farmer	VA
Delilah	61	F		SC
Eliza	21	F	(Idiot)	IN
J. S.	18	M	Farmer	IN
Chapman, Clarinda	15	F		TN
John W.	12	M		AL
Taylea, Lena	33	F		NOR
Walker, H.	42	M	Farmer	TN
Judah	37	F		IN
Martha J.	12	F		TX
John C.	9	M		TX
Hiram E.	6	M		TX
Delilah C.	2	F		TX
Hanby, William	32	M	Farmer	TN
Nancy A.	28	F		AL
Nancy	6	F		AL
John N.	4	M		AL
Robert	11/12	M		TX
Blanton, James	40	M	Farmer	TN
Belinda M.	34	F		TN
William C.	18	M	Farmer	AL
Benjamin	14	M		AL
Lucinda C.	12	F		AL
Elihu P.	10	M		AL
James F.	7	M		AL
Charles G.	4	M		AL
Mary Jane	2	F		TX
Julian E.	10/12	F		TX
Bell, Richard S.	25	M	Farmer	TN
Nancy E.	25	F		TN
Samuel P.	30	M	Farmer	TN
Mary M.	30	F		TN
Nancy E.	4	F		TN
John T.	1	M		TN
Gourley, William F.	34	M	Farmer	TN
Sarah J.	34	F		TN
James E.	15	M	Farmer	TN
Robert L.	13	M		TN
Mary E.	8	F		TN
Martha E.	7	F		TN
John F.	5	M		TN
Samantha J.	4	F		TN
Copeland, A. J.	36	M	C. P. Minister	TN
Margaret E.	33	F		TN
Samuel H.	12	M		AL
John M.	10	M		AL
Andrew A.	8	M		AL
Charlotte M.	6	F		AL
Margaret E.	4	F		AL
David P.	1	M		TX
Miller, Elizabeth	74	F		VA
Copeland, David D.	63	M	Farmer	NC
Bell, Epps	23	M	Farmer	TN
Nancy M.	19	F		TN
William T.	9/12	M		TX
Norman, Thomas	36	M	Farmer	TN
Margaret C.	33	F		TN
William T.	9	M		TN
Sarah E.	7	F		TN
Lucy Ann	6	F		TN
Richard C.	4	M		TN
Samuel A.	1	M		TN
Bell, Thomas	65	M	Farmer	TN
Eleanor	66	F		GA

(continued)

Name	Age	Sex	Occupation	Birthplace
Bell, Gilbert H.	20	M	Farmer	TN
Jackson, Worldly	20	M	Farmer	TN
Murphy, James A.	29	M	Farmer	TN
Elizabeth B.	19	F		TN
Smith, Jas. B.	30	M	Farmer	TN
Sarah J.	25	F		VA
Mary E.	4	F		TN
William E.	2	M		TN
Darthula P.	8/12	F		TX
Salmon, William W.	51	M	Farmer	VA
Elizabeth	45	F		VA
Nancy L.	14	F		TN
James H.	17	M	Farmer	TN
Isaac F.	13	M		TN
Martha A.	10	F		TN
Robert D.	7	M		TN
Mary H.	7	F		TN
Brooks, Moses	28	M	Farmer	TN
Eliza A.	23	F		VA
Agnes A.	3	F		TN
Mariah E.	1	F		TX
Smith, Charles	26	M	Farmer	TN
Jane	23	F		TN
Mary E.	5	F		TN
Oney	2	F		TN
Nancy J.	2/12	F		TX
Hibbs, Benjamin	23	M	Farmer	TN
Mary	20	F		TN
Stone, G. W.	35	M	Stock Raiser	TN
Pheroby E.	18	F		AL
Martin, R. R.	39	M	C. P. Minister	TN
Elizabeth E.	23	F		AL
William R.	6	M		AL
John F.	4	M		AL
James D.	2	M		TX
Evie J.	1	F		TX
Hill, Benjamin	39	M	Farmer	TN
Piety	41	F		TN
H.	14	F		MS
Nancy J.	13	F		MS
Elizabeth A.	12	F		MS
Lewis	10	M		AL
Sarah	9	F		AL
Mary	7	F		TN
Robert	6	M		AL
John	5	M		AL
Edney	2	F		AL
W. B.	10/12	M		AL
Bloomfield, James T.	29	M	Farmer	AL
Sarah P.	21	F		GA
Jane T.	2	F		TX
Benjamin K.	1	M		TX
Anthony, Peter	35	M	Farmer	TN
Carmichael, P.	65	M	Farmer	PA
Nancy	62	F		TN
Bishop, P. C.	18	M	Farmer	AL
Shelton, Margaret	38	F		TN
A. J. Gee	19	M	Farmer	AL
Carmichael, A.	29	M	Farmer	TN
Emaline A.	8	F		TN
Haynes, Isabella	35	F		TN
Sarah J.	10	F		TN
Frances M.	6	F		AL
Radford, Mary A.	33	F		TN
William	6	M		TN
Friend, Calvin	17	M	Farmer	IL
Carmichael, William	37	M	Clock Agent	TN
Massy, L.	36	M		NC
M.	36	M		NC
James A.	12	M		TN
Stephen L.	10	M		TN
Nancy E.	8	F		TN
Thomas E.	6	M		TN

(continued)

CHEROKEE COUNTY, TEXAS

Massy, Adam P. 3 M TN
Martha J. 1 F TX

Stadler, S. 27 M Farmer NC
James 21 M Farmer NC
Fulton, David 23 M Farmer TN
Lavena A. 17 F TN

Dickey, Moses 44 M Farmer NC
Melvina D. 31 F TN
Elizabeth J. 15 F TN
William R. 13 M TX
Mary A. 10 F TX
Richard 8 M TX
James 6 M TX
Samuel 4 M TX
John S. 1 M TX
Lowe, Abner 25 M Farmer MO

Muse, M. C. F. 41 F SC
Thomas T. 21 M Farmer TN
Wilson H. 19 M Farmer TN
Amanda J. 17 F KY
Sarah E. 14 F TN
Adolphus D. 11 M TX
Freestone, Eli 18 M Farmer IL

Evans, John 38 M Farmer NC
Mariah 28 F NC
Susan F. 8 F TN
William H. 2 M TN

Carson, Seth 53 M Farmer NC
Elizabeth 43 F TN
William 28 M Farmer TN
James M. 23 M Farmer TN
Leathy L. 17 F TN
Margaret 14 F TN
Vanlans 11 M TX
Lucinda 8 F TX
Jasper N. 6 M TX
Artemecia 3 F TX

Braly, Samuel 25 M Farmer TN
Mary 21 F TN
George M. S. 1 M TX

Wiggins, James F. 25 M Farmer TN
Harriet L. 19 F TN

Wiggins, H. 66 M Farmer NC
Nancy 49 F NC
Harriet S. 22 F TN
William C. 18 M Farmer TN
Ransom 16 M TN
Mary E. 13 F TN
Thomas E. 11 M TN
Brown, J. M. 35 M Mechanic TN

Brewer, Henry 22 M Farmer MS
Mary 18 F TN
Rogers, Rebecca 39 F TN
Lafayette 16 M TN
James 12 M TN
Harmon 10 M AL
Francis M. 6 M AL

Christian, Clinton 28 M Farmer TN
Caroline 25 F TN
James 4 M TX
William 3 M TX
John 10/12 M TX

Donaho, William 50 M Farmer SC
Jane 52 F SC
Lewis 20 M Farmer MS
Hiram 18 M Farmer MS
Francis M. 13 M TX
Daniel W. 10 M TX
Evens, William 27 M Farmer TN

Noblett, John 45 M Farmer NC
Martha A. 34 F KY
(continued)

Noblett, Thomas R. 5 M TX
John L. 4 M TX
Charles A. 3 M TX
Brown, H. G. 10 M TX
Muse, K. H. 25 M Farmer TN
Thomas 60 M Mechanic SC

Dalton, Thomas D. 37 M Farmer NC
Martha 31 F TN
Isaac N. 13 M TN
John W. 12 M TN
Seth T. 8 M TX
Martha J. 1 F TX

Hickerson, M. 34 M Black Smith TN
Clarky 18 F TN
Samuel D. 11 M TN
Mary A. 8 F AR
Sarah J. 5 F AR

Parks, Cyrus 49 M Farmer TN
Mahala W. 42 F NC
Samuel L. 26 M (Dumb) AR
Mary J. 14 F AR
Sarah M. 12 F AR
George W. 10 M AR
Nancy C. 8 F TX
Alcy 6 F TX
Rebecca 3 F TX
K. C. A. 1/12 M TX

Stele, H. R. 49 M Farmer SC
Elizabeth 49 F SC
John W. 23 M Farmer TN
Martha E. 20 F KY
Elizabeth L. 17 F KY
Ann E. 13 F TN
Elvira M. 4 F TN
Williams, James 20 M Farmer KY

Williams, A. B. 22 M Farmer TN
Winny 18 F MO
Jesse S. 1 M TX
Mary E. 1/12 F TX
Freestone, Amos 19 M Farmer IL

Meeks, Nancy 46 F TN
Merrit 16 M Farmer MO
Elijah 13 M MO
Rebbecca A. 11 F MO
John W. 8 M MO
Cyrus W. 6 M MO

Ballerus, S. A. 29 M Farmer TN
Lucinda 23 F AL

Myers, A. 28 M Farmer TN
Rachel 25 F AL
Mary E. 3 F TX
John H. 5/12 M TX
Ballerus, Eldridge 28 M Farmer TN

Muse, G. W. 20 M Farmer TN
Minerva 17 F TA

Morris, Stephen 45 M Farmer TX?
Sarah 36 F TX?
Lavenia 14 F TX
Elizabeth 11 F MS
Sarah A. 7 F MS
William 5 M MS
Ruffin L. 2 M TN

Johnson, William 39 M Farmer VA
Clarissa 29 F IA
Joseph B. 11/12 M TN

Holden, Wilson 33 M Farmer TN
Rebecca 25 F AL
Nancy M. 7 F TN
Florinda 5 F TN
Frances A. E. 4 F TN
Sarah C. 1 F TX
Mary A. A. 2/12 F TX

CHEROKEE COUNTY, TEXAS

Muse, H.	31	M	Farmer	TN
Elizabeth	30	F		TN
Kindred H.	10	M		TN
Rubin J.	8	M		TN
George A.	6	M		TN
Samuel S.	3	M		TN
Mansfield H.	1	M		TX
Kirkland, H.	53	M	Farmer	TN
Prudence	27	F		MS
Sarah T.	17	F		AL
Nancy	13	F		AL
Isaac	8	M		AL
Joseph	8	M		AL
William H.	6	M		AL
Tabitha	3	F		AL
Polly Ann	1	F		AL
Walters, A. C.	45	M	Farmer	GA
Mary	42	F		TN
Moses	80	M		VA
Elizabeth	21	F		MS
Anna	19	F		MS
A. C.	18	M	Farmer	MS
Carrol	16	M		MS
Minerva	14	F		TX
Rutha	12	F		TX
Moses	10	M		TX
Sarah	8	F		TX
Rachel	6	F		TX
Eleanor	4	F		TX
California	2	F		TX
Simpson, G. P.	30	M	Farmer	GA
Mary A.	26	F		AL
Retta J.	4	F		TX
Worldly, Richard	24	M	Farmer	TN
Glass, Sarah	34	F		TN
Frederick M.	16	M	Farmer	MS
M. E.	13	M		MS
Nancy D.	11	F		MS
Mary D.	7	F		MS
Henry C.	5	M		TX
David S.	1	M		TX
Miggs, Samuel	25	M	Farmer	AL
Crunk, Paschal	51	M	Farmer	VA
Nancy	44	F		TN
James	21	M	Farmer	AL
Crunk, J. W.	49	M	Farmer	VA
Louna	41	F		TN
Lilly	19	F		MS
John	16	M	Farmer	MS
William	14	M		TX
Bird	9	M		TX
Green	9	M		TX
Jane	7	F		TX
Lucinda	4	F		TX
Dock	2	M		TX
Tyra, E. H.	31	M	Farmer	TN
Rachael E.	28	F		AL
Sarah T.	8	F		MS
Tildmon J.	6	M		MS
Elisha M.	1	M		TX
Blanton, Isaac	66	M	Farmer	NC
Mary	55	F		SC
Gwin, Lucinda	35	F		TN
Blanton, Ellick	15	M	Farmer	AL
Isaac	14	M		AL
Polly Ann	13	F		AL
Louisa Jane	8	F		AR
Pennington, J.	32	M	Farmer	TN
Eliza A.	25	F		KY
Elizabeth J.	4	F		TX
Martha L.	3	F		TX
Richard E.	1	M		TX

Barnet, Josiah	35	M	Bee Hunter	TN
Martha	34	F		AL
Susan E.	14	F		AL
Mary D.	12	F		MS
Richard L.	10	M		MS
Jas. A.	6	M		MS
George A.	3	M		TX
Pagitt, John	31	M	Farmer	LA
Jane	28	F		AL
Susan B.	4	F		TX
Green, Alexander	20	M	Farmer	TN
Newton, G. A.	26	M	Farmer	TN
Mary A.	23	F		TN
William A.	5	M		TN
Thomas E.	3	M		TN
Allis T.	2	F		TX
Dugan, William	26	M	Farmer	TN
Elizabeth	24	F		TN
Martha J.	5	F		TN
Elizabeth	4	F		TN
Vina	3	F		TN
Samuel	2/12	M		TX
Jackson, Edward	10	M		MS
Wallace, James	40	M	Farmer	TN
Mary	37	F		SC
Sarah R.	15	F		AL
Robert R.	12	M		AL
Thomas Knox	6	M		AL
Martha E.	3	F		AL
John M.	10/12	M		AL
Wallace, Thomas	65	M	Farmer	TN
A. S.	21	M	Farmer	AL
Wallace, S. A. G.	35	M	Farmer	TN
Martha E.	31	F		AL
M. Hannah M.	12	F		AL
Mary J.	8	F		AL
James A.	5	M		AL
Margaret A.	5	F		AL
Melissa E.	1	F		AL
Killough, N.	44	M	Farmer	TN
Ursulah	73	F		VA
Eliza J.	12	F		AL
Julian E.	10	F		TX
Wallace, Green	48	M	Farmer	TN
Sarah D.	48	F		NC
Buford A.	23	M	Farmer	AL
Edward S.	21	M	Farmer	AL
Andrew S.	19	M		AL
Sarah J.	17	F		AL
Susannah S.	14	F		AL
John G.	13	M		AL
Francis C.	8	M		AL
Carrel	22	M	Teacher	TN
Joseph	23	M	Farmer	TN
Steinson, Jno.	55	M	Farmer	NC
Milly	45	F		TN
Eliza R.	19	F		AL
James	10	M		TX
John	8	M		TX
William	7	M		TX
Louisa	5/12	F		TX
Artemus	22	M	Farmer	AL
Reeves, A.	24	M	Farmer	TN
Eliza C.	22	F		TN
Gilbert	2	M		KY
Nancy	1	F		TX
Parks, J. B.	25	M	Farmer	TN
Liddia J.	21	F		TN
William A.	3	M		TX
Elizabeth	2	F		TX
Edney	5/12	F		TX

CHEROKEE COUNTY, TEXAS

Name	Age	Sex	Occupation	Birthplace
Phelps, Jacob	43	M	Farmer	TN
Catharine	47	F		TN
Britton	21	M	Farmer	TN
William D.	19	M	Farmer	TN
Riley W.	16	M	Farmer	TN
Thomas C.	14	M		TN
Mary Ann	12	F		TN
Benjamin F.	10	M		TN
Martha J.	3	F		TX
Dunnica(?), John	52		Farmer	TN
Elizabeth	44	F		KY
Sally A.	17	F		MS
Nancy J.	13	F		MS
Thomas J.	11	M		MS
William H. H.	9	M		MS
Theodore L.	6	M		MS
Joshua S.	3	M		TX
Martha E.	1	F		TX
Leona A.	3/12	F		TX
Biggs, David	51	M	Farmer	NC
Martha	38	F		TN
David C.	20	M	Farmer	AR
Benet	16	M	Farmer	AR
Margaret A.	14	F		AR
Mary J.	12	F		AR
John	9	M		AR
David	8	M		AR
Jack------	6	F		TX
Christopher C.	4	M		TX
Narcissa	2	F		TX
Perkins, G.	35	M	Farmer	KY
Sarah	25	F		KY
Elizabeth L.	10	F		KY
Mary J.	7	F		TN
Martha A.	5	F		AR
Sarah E.	2	F		AR
Newman, F. L.	23	M	Farmer	LA
Rhoda	23	F		TN
Sarah J.	3	F		TX
George W.	2	M		TX
Garrison, William	15	M	Farmer	AR
Loyd, Rachel	63	F		VA
Ball, J.	47	M	Farmer	NC
Sarah	49	F		NC
Jane	23	F		TN
Tandy	21	M	Farmer	TN
Abner	19	M	Farmer	TN
Elias	15	M	Farmer	TN
Rufus	12	M		MS
James C.	10	M		MS
William H.	8	M		MS
Mary	6	F		MS
Willis B.	3	M		TX
Lewis	6/12	M		TX
Williams, John	82	M	Farmer	NC
Elbert S.	28	M	Farmer	TN
Elizabeth	35	F		TN
Hardimand L.	16	M	Farmer	TN
Johnson, Jno. B.	44	M	Farmer	NC
Elizabeth	32	F		AL
Joseph L.	15	M	Farmer	AL
William T.	13	M		AL
Jno. R.	10	M		AL
Mary A.	8	F		MS
Napoleon B.	5	M		TN
Stephen H.	3	M		TX
Garret, H. N.	36	M	Farmer	TN
Elizabeth	34	F		NC
Virginia	12	F		AL
Mary J.	11	F		AL
Franklin	7	M		TX
Sarah	5	F		TX
William	3	M		TX
Eliza	1	F		TX

Name	Age	Sex	Occupation	Birthplace
McCracken, George	46	M	Farmer	NC
Mary L.	37	F		TN
Joseph	11	M		TN
Tennessee J.	10	F		TN
George Smith	8	M		TN
William E.	5	M		TX
Columbus C.	4	M		TX
Margaret L.	2	F		TX
Winneford P.	11/12	F		TX
Stovall, John E.	27	M	M.E. Minister	TN
Eliza J.	19	F		AR
Celia C.	4	F		TX
Martha A.	3	F		TX
Susan C.	2	F		TX
Monk, Jonathan	22	M	Teamster	AL
George, William	30	M	Farmer	SC
Nancy Jane	18	F		TN
George M.	3	M		TX
Martha A.	2	F		TX
Mitchel, A. J.	31	M	Farmer	NC
Nancy	28	F		NC
James W.	4	M		TN
Reuben	3	M		TN
Mary	1	F		TN
Barns, John	58	M	Farmer	NC
Sarah	55	F		NC
Polly	19	F		TN
Margaret M.	20	F		TN
Catharine	13	F		TN
Scott, A.	28	M	Farmer	TN
Lucinda	24	F		NC
Sarah T.	5	F		TN
Margaret A.	2	F		TX
Ater(Ates), Thomas	26	M	Farmer	NC
Sarena	23	F		TN
Martha	10/12	F		TX
Griffis, James	24	M	Farmer	NC
Doherty, G. M.	36	M	Farmer	TN
Mary A.	26	F		NC
Sarah C.	7	F		TX
Susan T.	6	F		TX
Frances L.	2	F		TX
Leeth, Margret	14	F		AL
Daniel P.	9	M		TX
Gwinn, R. H.	27	M	Lawyer	TN
Sarah J.	23	F		GA
Heflin S.	2	M		TX
Phillia P.	6/12	M		TX
Patton, George	42	M	C.P. Minister	TN
Jno. F.	20	M	Farmer	TN
Mary A.	20	F		SC
James B.	2	M		TN
Owen, William	23	M	Farmer	TN
Hannah, William	20	M	Farmer	TN
Ragsdale, E. B.	32	M	Farmer	NC
Matilda	21	F		TN
Sally H.	63	F		NC
A. J. Wates	32	M	Farmer	AL
Partlow, William C.	37	M	Farmer	SC
Margaret J.	25	F		AL
John J.	7/12	M		TX
James K. Dye	5	M		AL
Hooten, Joseph	25	M	Teacher	TN
Coker, Jas.	53	M	Farmer	SC
Mary	43	F		SC
Franklin	19	M	Med. Student	TN
Andrew J.	17	M	Farmer	AL
Mariah E.	14	F		AL
Sarah J.	12	F		AL
John	10	M		AL
Joseph	6	M		AL
Mary F.	3	F		AL

CHEROKEE COUNTY, TEXAS

Name	Age	Sex	Occupation	Birthplace
Shepherd, J. D.	35	M	Farmer	GA
Sarah	34	F		TN
Thomas	11	M		MS
Mary A.	9	F		MS
Dillard	7	M		MS
Elizabeth	5	F		MS
James	3	M		TX
Sarah	4/12	F		TX
Hill, C. D.	49	M	Farmer	KY
Mary	49	F		KY
Samuel C.	25	M	Farmer	TN
Robert	21	M	Farmer	TN
Clement	18	M	Farmer	TN
Franklin	14	M		AR
Rachel	13	F		AR
Augustine	11	F		AR
Mary	9	F		TX
Crocket	5	M		TX
Elizabeth	2	F		TX
Miller, William	36	M	Farmer	TN
Andrew L.	6	M		TN
Thomas	24	M	Farmer	AL
Sarah A.	21	F		TN
Kimbro, Jasper N.	12	M		TN
Miller, Mary J.	13	F		TN
Brook, Allen	55	M	Farmer	TN
Rebecca	52	F		TN
Lewis	30	M	Teacher	TN
Martha	22	F		KY
Milly	19	F		KY
Elizabeth	17	F		KY
Granville	14	M		KY
Fountain	11	M		KY
Templeton, D. G.	34	M	Farmer	NC
Mary E.	21	F		TN
James F.	6	M		AR
John A.	4	M		AR
Dickson W.	1	M		TX
Moore, Samuel	65	M	Black Smith	PA
Jane	63	F		NC
Porter, R. H.	26	M	Farmer	TN
Parks, F. G.	25	M	Farmer	TN
Margaret A.	27	F		TN
Frances E.	3	F		TX
Sarah J.	11/12	F		TX
Aaron	21	M	Farmer	TN
Williams, William F.	34	M	Farmer	TN
Amanda	25	F		TN
Nancy A.	7	F		TX
John W.	5	M		TX
Rhoda	2	F		TX
Chisom, Jno.	40	M	Farmer	TN
Mary	32	F		IN
Elijah	10	M		TX
William	8	M		TX
Elizabeth	6	F		TX
Clabourn	4	M		TX
Ann	2	F		TX
Keller, Abram H.	40	M	Farmer	KY
Kincheloe, E.	21	M	Farmer	TN
Mariah S.	16	F		KY
Shirley, Edmond	49	M	Farmer	TN
Synthia	43	F		KY
William H.	20	M	Farmer	TN
Thomas R.	17	M	Farmer	TN
Hiram F.	14	M		TN
Lucinda P.	11	F		AR
Tennessee M.	9	F		AR
Charlotte T.	7	F		TX
Sarah E.	2	F		TX
Hardgrove, T. C.	39	M	Farmer	TN
Eliza A.	35	F		TN
Martha	17	F		TN
(continued)				
Hardgrove, James B.	14	M		AR
Felix G.	12	M		AR
Mary L.	9	F		AR
Francis R.	8	M		AR
Amanda M.	7	F		AR
William N.	5/12	M		TX
DeBard, Hervey	45	M	Farmer	KY
Rebecca P.	18	F		TN
Lane, J. H.	59	M	M.B. Minister	VA
Theodocia	52	F		VA
George W.	28	M	Teacher	TN
Isham H.	25	M	Farmer	TN
Drury H.	23	M	Mechanic	TN
Horatio G.	18	M	Farmer	TN
Susan J.	16	F		TN
Ann	28	F		VA
Rebecca J.	8	F		TN
Angeline	6	F		TN
John H.	2	M		TN
Henderson, John	35	M	Farmer	TN
Isabella	32	F		AL
James W.	12	M		AL
Vanburen	10	M		AL
John	8	M		AL
Mary E.	6	F		AL
George W.	4	M		TX
Mary J.	3	F		TX
Wiley	3	M		TX
F. E.	4/12	M		TX
Daugherty, William	50	M	Farmer	KY
Matilda	51	F		VA
James	23	M	Farmer	TN
Samuel	19	M	Farmer	AR
Nancy	14	F		AR
Joseph	9	M		AR
William	9	M		AR
Pagett, Thomas	18	M	Farmer	IN
Lafayette	15	M	Farmer	IN
Hearn, John	55	M	Farmer	NC
Drucilla	50	F		VA
Thomas B.	31	M	Farmer	TN
James F.	23	M	Farmer	TN
Margaret D.	17	F		TN
Robert A.	16	M	Farmer	TN
Albert W.	12	M		TN
Martha W.	9	F		TN
Alexander G.	5	M		TN
Joseph C.	22	M	Farmer	TN
Miller, Jas. M.	58	M	Farmer	TN
Amanda N.	37	F		TN
Bodo, Mira E.	17	F		MS
Miller, F. C.	15	M	Farmer	MS
Hamilton	12	M		MS
Elizabeth P.	10	F		TX
Granville C.	7	M		TX
Josephine T.	4	F		TX
America	5/12	F		TX
Carter, Mary	47	F	(Idiot)	TN
Bodo, James S.	1	M		TX
Hoover, H. W.	24	M	Farmer	TN
Mary J.	24	F		TN
Thomason, Eli M.	41	M	Farmer	TN
Mariah	20	F		TX
Sarah A.	10	F		TX
Ann H.	8	F		TX
Mary M.	6	F		TX
Lucinda	4	F		TX
James	3	M		TX
John N.	1	M		TX
Margaret A.	1/12	F		TX
Click, Henry	52	M	Farmer	TN
Elizabeth	57	F		SC
Harrison	19	M	Farmer	AL
Martha	15	F		AL
William	12	M		AL
Henry S.	11	M		AL
James A.	7	M		AL

CHEROKEE COUNTY, TEXAS

Name	Age	Sex	Occupation	Birthplace
Jowel, R. R.	42	M	Farmer	SC
Elzira	17	F		TN
Mary A.	13	F		TX
Roark, William	47	M	Farmer	TN
Margaret	42	F		TN
Nancy	21	F		TN
Elizabeth	19	F		TN
Julian	15	F		TN
Franklin	17	M		TN
Frances	12	F		TX
Emaline	8	F		TX
Calvin	10	M		TX
Sarah	5	F		TX
Cannon, B. B.	49	M	Farmer	TN
Charlotte	44	F		TN
Zachariah H.	16	M	Student	TN
Robert T.	14	M		TN
Harriet M. W.	11	F		TN
James H.	9	M		TN
Benjamin B.	6	M		TN
Creswell, A. B.	35	M	Farmer	TN
Nancy C.	7	F		AL
James R.	5	M		AL
William G.	3	M		AL
Narcissa J.	1	F		AL
Paralee	5/12	F		AL
Stephens, H. B.	36	M	Farmer	TN
Martha A.	23	F		AL
Hannah O.	8	F		TX
Cimantha	6	F		TX
Nancy L.	4	F		TX
Susan C.	5/12	F		TX
Ables, J. S.	38	M	Farmer	TN
Margaret	35	F		TN
Levi	13	M		TX
Winfield	10	M		TX
Mary	8	F		TX
Amanda	5	F		TX
Josephine	2	F		TX
Houston, Mary O. W.	7	F		TX
Ables, Mary	85	F		NC
Summers, William	25	M	Farmer	TN
Trimble, James M.	32	M	Surveyor	GA
Nancy C.	22	F		TN
Gibson, Jesse	53	M	Farmer	SC
Elizabeth	47	F		SC
Joseph T.	23	M	Farmer	MS
Absolem C.	21	M	Farmer	TN
George W.	19	M	Farmer	TN
Mahala E.	10	F		TX
Mary J.	8	F		TX
James	5	M		TX
George W. Cannon	1	M		TX
Frizzell, W. W.	39	M	Farmer	MO
Isabella J.	28	F		KY
Ann H.	9	F		TX
Butler, Julian	13	F		TN
Shorter, Bedford	52	M	Farmer	GA
Sarah	37	F		TN
Wiley Riddle	8	M		TX
William H.	4	M		TX
Frances A.	3	F		TX
Blanton, James R.	34	M	Farmer	VA
Synthia L.	39	F		TN
Sarah G.	7	F		TX

Town of Rusk

Name	Age	Sex	Occupation	Birthplace
Boyd, William B.	37	M	Black Smith	TN
Rheanah P.	32	F		TN
John A. M.	12	M		TN
James M.	9	M		TN
Mary R. D.	6	F		TN

(continued)

Name	Age	Sex	Occupation	Birthplace
Boyd, Margaret J. E.	4	F		TN
Eliza S. A.	1	F		TN
McKnight, James	29	M	Black Smith	TN
Jos. P.	21	M	Farmer	TN
Erwin, S. A.	30	M	Lawyer	TN
Elizabeth J.	20	F		TN
William Scott	1	M		TX
Givens, E. L.	38	M	P. Master	TN
Margaret A.	29	F		TN
Sarah J.	10	F		AL
William M.	8	M		AL
Josephine H. L.	6	F		AL
Susan P.	3	F		TX
Long, William S.	29	M	Carpenter	TN
Altha E.	30	F		AL
John B.	5	M		TX
J. Lewis	4	M		TX
Eliza J.	3	F		TX
William P.	10/12	M		TX
Cannon, Daniel N.	26	M	Tailor	SC
Carter, E. G.	27	M	Tailor	TN
Vaught, J. B.	31	M	M.D.	TN
Nancy J.	22	F		TN
Givens, H. L.	33	M	M.D.	TN
Eleanor	18	F		AL
Eleanor B.	2	F		AR
Moore, Thomas G.	30	M	M.D.	TN
Martha J.	20	F		MO
Polk	4	M		TX
Thomas M.	3	M		TX
Mardella	3/12	F		TX
Goans, John M.	35	M	Carpenter	NC
Suttle, M.	25	M	Carpenter	AL
Johnson, William A.	25	M	Carpenter	GA
Leonard, R.	68	F		IRE
Dorset, A.	36	M	Mechanic	TN
Sally	1	F		TX
Page, P. R.	25	M	Brick Layer	VA
Recerson, G.	34	M	Watch Maker	NOR
Carter, G. J.	35	M	Trader	TN
Sarah	31	F		MO
Hamilton	12	M		MO
Mira J.	10	M		AR
Silas E.	6	M		TX
Susan E.	4	F		TX
James H.	1	M		TX
Spencer, William M.	34	M	Grocer	TN
Amanda	32	F		TN
Nancy C.	9	F		MS
Martha A.	6	F		MS
Benjamin A.	4	M		MS

In Hotel

Name	Age	Sex	Occupation	Birthplace
Bracken, A. G.	46	F	Inn Keeper	VA
Ozment, U.	34	M	Merchant	NC
James	7	M		TN
Proby, D. P.	28	M	Grocer	TN
Elizabeth	19	F		TN
Moore, John	16	M	Clerk	TN
Warren, James L.	25	M	Brick Maker	AL
Eliza J.	16	F		MS
Page, P. K.	25	M	Brick Mason	VA
Davis, Morgan	23	M	Farmer	AL
Hicks, W. D.	21	M	Farmer	TN
Henry, William C.	32	M	Attorney	TN
Elmira C.	28	F		AL
John J.	11	M		AL
Ann D.	8	F		AL
Cora	6	F		AL
William C.	3	M		AL
Andrew J.	10/12	M		TX

CHEROKEE COUNTY, TEXAS

Name	Age	Sex	Occupation	Birthplace
Wilson, J. L.	40	M	Wagon Maker	GA
Mariah	45	F		SC
James	14	M		MS
Eleanor A.	13	F		TN
Wallace, Isabella	17	F		MS
Parson, H. A.	20	M	Med. Student	LA
JOhnson, J. H.	27	M	Mechanic	TN
Jane R.	30	F		TN
Sarah L.	4	F		TX
James A.	2	M		TX
Dorset, Phelix	16	M		TX
Matilda P.	6	F		TX
Stevens, L. D.	28	M	Teacher	TN
Sarah P.	19	F		TN
Graham, W. C.	34	M		TN
Green, Robert	49	M	Farmer	GA
Luzana	48	F		NC
Lucinda	20	F		GA
Louisa	18	F		GA
George W. L.	15	M	Carpenter	GA
Henry J.	12	M		GA
Martha	10	F		GA
Marietta	8	F		GA
Larina	6	F		GA
Monk, Columbus H.	21	M	Carpenter	GA
Ragsdale, Francis	19	M	Carpenter	TN
Floyd, William	24	M	Carpenter	TN
Elkins, Asa M.	58	M	Mechanic	SC
Mary M.	17	F		TN
Richard S.	16	M	Student	TN
Martha M.	13	F		TN
Susan	12	F		TN
America	10	F		TN
Thomas	7	M		TN
Henry, J. F.	34	M	Sheriff	TN
Laura M.	32	F		GA
---phlus	12	M		AL
Ezekiel	10	M		AL
Caroline F.	7	F		AL
Charles M. L.	4	M		AL
Judith	3	F		TX
James	8/12	M		TX
Simmons, J. C.	33	M	House Carpenter	GA
Yarborough, Thomas	19	M	Mail Rider	AL
Whaley, W. D.	43	M	Inn Keeper	GA
Berry, J. H.	20	M	Saddler	TN
Yoe, Harrison	25	M	Saddler	TN
Johnson, Samuel	41	M	Mechanic	SC
Mary W.	39	F		SC
Sarah M.	14	F		AL
Patrick H.	12	M		AL
Margaret L.	10	F		AL
John H.	6	M		AL
Henrietta M.	3	F		AL
Samuel	11/12	M		TX
Jacobs, James	25	M	Laborer	TN
Rains, C. B.	42	M	M.D.	VA
Mary A.	34	F		TN
Delila P.	14	F		TN
Martha B.	13	F		TN
Jonathan P.	9	M		TN
Julia M.	6	F		TX
Charles B.	4	M		TX

End of Town of Rusk

Name	Age	Sex	Occupation	Birthplace
Burks, Leroy	56	M	Farmer	SC
Rebecca	54	F		SC
J. W.	26	M	Farmer	TN
Rachael	27	F		TN
James	19	M	Farmer	TN
Charlotte	15	F		TN
Henry, L.	19	M	Teacher	VA
Miller, R. C.	25	M	Farmer	TN
Mary A.	23	F		TN
Cook, William	49	M	Farmer	SC
Mary	32	F		AL
Mary G.	21	F		TN
Emily F.	17	F		TN
Columbus M.	16	M	Farmer	TN
Melvira R.	9	F		AL
James M.	6	M		AL
Nancy A.	3	F		TX
Parks, W. S.	27	M	Farmer	TN
Minerva	21	F		TN
John	5	M		TX
James	4	M		TX
George	2	M		TX
Thomason, James	60	M	Farmer	SC
Ann	41	F		TN
Martha A.	11	F		TX
James H.	9	M		TX
Mary J.	7	F		TX
Francis M.	4	M		TX
Lucinda H.	1	F		TX
Dillard, L. H.	53	M	Farmer	TN
Sythia	49	F		NC
Thomas J.	21	M	Farmer	TN
Lewis B.	20	M	Farmer	TN
Alexander F.	18	M	Farmer	TN
Caroline	15	F		TN
Jane E.	13	F		LA
Synthia A.	10	F		TX
James R.	6	M		TX
James Farrar	10	M		TN
Melinda F.	9	F		TN
John J.	8	M		TX
Dillard, L. S.	46	M	Farmer	TN
Eleanor	48	F		NC
Joel L.	24	M	Farmer	NC
Thomas J.	23	M	Farmer	NC
Margaret	20	F		NC
Manerva	19	F		NC
James C.	17	M	Farmer	NC
Phelix G.	12	M		AL
Archolas L.	8	M		TN
Murry, William	44	M	Farmer	TN
Eliza	43	F		NC
John	21	M	Farmer	TN
William	19	M		TN
Mary Jane	16	F		TN
Thomas J.	14	M		TN
George	12	M		MS
Elem	10	M		AL
Martha A.	7	F		AL
Isabella	5	F		AL
Robert	4	M		AL
Henry	2	M		TX
Murry, James	25	M	Farmer	TN
Martha J.	24	F		AL
Louisiana	4	F		LA
William J.	2	M		AL
Atwood, John	47	M	(Idiot)	TN
Lewis, L. S.	44	M	Farmer	TN
Elizabeth J.	37	F		SC
Susan A.	16	F		GA
William ?.	14	M		GA
John M.	13	M		GA
Amanda E.	12	F		GA
Virgil L. A.	10	M		GA
Sarah S.	8	F		GA
Cynthia J.	7	F		GA
Arabella C.	6	F		GA
Marshall M. J. J.	4	M		GA
Christopher C. A. A.	1	M		LA
Lewis, L.	36	M	Farmer	TN
Sarah A. L.	27	F		AL
James M.	11	M		AL
William W.	9	M		AL
Olevia J.	6	F		AL
Sparta A.	3	F		AL
Thomas M.	1	M		TX

CHEROKEE COUNTY, TEXAS

Name	Age	Sex	Occupation	Birthplace
Gaskey, William	31	M	Farmer	SC
Ann	35	F		TN
Sarah E. J.	8	F		AL
Eliza C.	6	F		AL
Margaret	4	F		AL
Emily	1	F		TX
Pearson, G. W.	34	F(?)	Farmer	TN
Catharine L. D.	30	F		TN
Mary J.	11	F		TN
Jesse W.	9	M		MO
Alfred H.	7	M		MO
Lucinda L.	4	F		TX
Herendon, S. T.	20	M	Farmer	AL
King, Peter	45	M	Farmer	TN
Patience	42	F		TN
James W.	17	M	Farmer	AL
Nancy E.	15	F		AL
John G.	14	M		AL
Lee A.	12	M		AL
Joseph Y.	10	M		AL
Peter B.	7	M		AL
Sarah M. A.	4	F		TX
Leonard, Eliza	64	F		GA
Henderson, J. W.	64	M	Farmer	TN
Moley	55	F		NC
William B.	23	M	Farmer	TN
Cartwright	21	M	Farmer	TN
Alfred	18	M	Farmer	TN
Hannah	14	F		AL
Hill, Jesse	28	M	Farmer	AL
Laura E.	27	F		TN
George B.	5	M		AL
Ann E.	3	F		TX
James L.	1	M		TX
Rozel, Calvin	19	M	Farmer	AL
Rozell, J. A.	23	M	Farmer	TN
Amanda E.	17	F		TN
James H.	10/12	M		TX
Allen, William	49	M	Farmer	NC
Rebecca F.	49	F		NC
Damaris J.	17	F		GA
James S.	16	M		AL
William H.	14	F		AL
Samuel B. C.	12	M	(Idiot)	AL
Sally E.	10	F		AL
Baker, J. H.	26	M	Laborer	TN
Carr, D.	51	M	Farmer	SC
Mary	38	F		TN
James M.	16	M	Farmer	TN
William	14	M		TN
Martha J.	13	F		TN
Sarah	11	F		TN
David C.	9	M		TN
Samuel	7	M		TN
Oliver	5	M		TN
Nancy A.	2	F		TX
Mary D.	1	F		TX
Hill, John	45	M	Farmer	TN
Mary	35	F		NC
James M.	17	M	Farmer	AL
John R.	16	M	Farmer	AL
Martha	14	F		AL
Jesse	8	M		AL
Texanna	4	F		TX
Green B.	2	M		TX
Henderson, Daniel	33	M	Farmer	TX
Mary	29	F		AL
Alfred J.	11	M		AL
James R.	9	M		AL
George W.	7	M		AL
Rebecca J.	4	F		AL
William C.	6/12	M		TX

Name	Age	Sex	Occupation	Birthplace
Allison, J. P.	35	M	Farmer	TN
Jane	31	F		AL
James W.	5	M		AL
Thomas J.	1	M		AL
Collier, Johnathan	56	M	Farmer	NC
Catharine	52	F		TN
James W.	29	M	Farmer	AL
Green S.	24	M	Farmer	AL
Thomas P.	23	M	Farmer	AL
Christopher C.	21	M	Farmer	AL
Jonathan J.	18	M	Farmer	AL
Salina A. C.	13	F		AL
Susan E.	10	F		AL
Mary F.	7	F		AL
Henderson, James P.	36	M	Farmer	TN
Sarah	33	F		TN
Frances C.	13	F		AL
John M.	11	M		AL
Louisa	9	F		AL
Nancy C.	7	F		AL
Sarah E.	5	F		AL
Ramisha J.	2	F		TX
James W.	1/12	M		TX
Shaw, William	66	M	Farmer	TN
Susanna	64	F		TN
John C.	29	M	Farmer	AR
Black, Colbert	16	M	Farmer	AR
James	14	M		AR
Mackleroy, Jas.	31	M	Black Smith	TN
Adaline	29	F		SC
William A.	10	M		AL
Marcus D. Y. L.	7	M		AL
James H.	3	M		AL
Mary T.	10/12	F		AL
Dunning, William A.	34	M	Merchant	NC
Mary J.	31	F		IN
Isaac W.	11	M		IN
James E.	7	M		IN
Hudson, Isaac R.	25	M	Merchant	IN
Moore, Wiley O.	22	M	Farmer	TN
Fain, John N.	25	M	Clerk	TN
Riddle, John	25	M	Clerk	AL
Dunning, A. A.	19	F		IN
Clement, William W.	27	M	M.D.	TN
Person, John	54	M	Farmer	SC
Margarett	64	F		NC
B. Pierce	28	M	Farmer	SC
Martha E.	18	F		AL
Woodall, John	36	M	Farmer	TN
Joel O.	11	M		AL
Rachel C.	10	F		AL
Robert F.	7	M		AL
Cornway, A. F.	30	M	Carpenter	TN
Copeland, David D.	26	M	Farmer	TN
Cameron, John P.	30	M	Farmer	SC
James L.	5	M		TX
Frances O.	3	F		TX
Thomas	2	M		TX
Eveline	2/12	F		TX
Emison, Samuel	45	M	Farmer	SC
Julian A.	43	F		KY
Benjamin C.	20	M	Farmer	AL
Alexander	18	M	Farmer	??
Hugh B.	16	M		??
Eliza J.	13	F		??
Martha A.	11	F		TN
James L.	8	M		TN
Milton J.	11/12	M		TX
Shoemaker, John	67	M	Farmer	NC
Calvin M.	31	M	Farmer	NC
Mary E.	21	F		TN
John S.	1	M		TX
McCracken, Amanda	14	F		AL
Elizabeth	9	F		TX
Gibson, Absalom	46	M	Farmer	SC
Emelia	47	F		SC

(continued)

Name	Age	Sex	Occupation	Birthplace
Gibson, James	24	M	Farmer	MS
George	22	M		MS
Elizabeth	18	F		TN
Elihu E.	8	M		TX
Mary	3	F		TX
Nelson, Elias	50	M	Farmer	GA
Mary P.	41	F		TN
John A.	17	M	Student	AL
William	20	M	Farmer	AL
Durst, James H.	30	M	Farmer	TX
Elizabeth	24	F		TN
Mortimore Y.	2	M		TX
Timmons, J. H.	39	M	Farmer	TN
Mary B.	27	F		TN
Thomas J.	6	M		TX
James ?.	4	M		TX
Mary C.	2	F		TX
McGauhy, S. M.	44	M	Farmer	TN
Florantine	32	F		SC
James H.	16	M	Farmer	AL
Benjamin F.	14	M		--
Thomas B.	9/12	M		TX
John W.	21	M	Merchant	AL
Frances	24	F		AL
Ford, John	40	M	Engineer	TN
Cynthia C.	22	F		TN
Levi M.	7	M		TX
George E.	3	M		TX
William	1	M		TX
Cooper, John	35	M	Farmer	TN
Martha	32	F		TN
James M.	8	M		AL
Thomas C.	6	M		AL
Andrew J.	5	M		AL
Harvey N.	2	M		TX
Thompson, Laura	20	F		AL
Cook, L. A.	61	M	Farmer	LA
Caroline	15	F		TN
Samuel E.	13	M		TN
Elizabeth	9	F		TX
Ellsberry, William	21	M	Farmer	GA
Alston, Philip	28	M	Farmer	FL
Martha E.	23	F		TN
Henry F.	4	M		TX
William T.	2	M		TX
Harris	12	M		MS
Lawrence, J. H.	44	M	M.D., D.D.	GA
Nancy B.	32	F		TN
Indiana E.	4	F		TX
Mary E.	1	F		TX
Angling, Mary	56	F		MS
Hicks, T. L.	57	M	Farmer	TN
Clary	45	F		NC
Stephen D.	19	M	Farmer	GA
Susan	15	F		MS
Minerva	13	F		GA
John	9	M		MS
Mary	4	F		LA
Smith, J. R.	39	M	Farmer	KY
Mary	35	F		KY
William	18	M	Farmer	KY
Mary J.	14	F		TN
Emily	10	F		TN
Eleanor E.	8	F		TN
John	6	M		KY
Robert W.	4	M		TX
James	1	M		TX
Smith, W.	41	M	Carpenter	VA
Permelia J.	25	F		TN
Meader, Henry J.	29	M	Farmer	TN
Hoover, Joel	32	M	Farmer	TN
Rachel	26	F		TN
Mary J.	11	F		TN
William P.	11	M		TN
Jemima C.	9	F		TN
Nancy E.	7	F		TN
Melvill	4	M		TN
Catharine	2	F		TN
Smith, William	45	M	Farmer	SC
Mary	45	F		TN
Abraham	25	M	(Idiot)	TN
John	22	M	Farmer	TN
Allen	21	M		TN
Pary	16	F		TN
Pheba	12	F		MS
Mary	9	F		MS
Dolly	13	F	(Idiot)	MS
William	5	M		MS
White, L. C.	35	M	Farmer	AL
Sally A.	23	F		TN
Nancy E.	5	F		TX
Mary A.	4	F		TX
Melissa	3	F		TX
Rufus	28	M	Farmer	MS
John D. B.	3	M		MS
Criswell, C. M.	30	M	Farmer	TN
Sarah M.	30	F		AL
William D.	10	M		AL
Phelix T.	8	M		AL
Lerory, W.	23	M	Farmer	TN
Mahala	19	F		TN
Melissa	1	F		TX
Schrimsher, James	51	M	Farmer	SC
Vina	45	F		TN
Early H.	25	M	Farmer	TN
Avrey	22	M	Farmer	TN
Ellis	19	M	Farmer	TN
Alfred	18	M		TN
Anna	10	F		TN
Jackson	8	M		TN
Nancy	6	F		TN
Joshua	4	M		TN
Bird	10/12	M		TX
Cartwright, Thomas	45	M	Farmer	NC
Lucinda	39	F		TN
Henry	22	M	Farmer	TN
Martha L.	21	F		TN
Nancy J.	18	F		TN
David	13	M		TN
Fanny L.	6	F		TN
Jones, Austin	42	M	Farmer	TN
Elizabeth	42	F		NC
Francis G.	18	M	Farmer	TN
John J.	16	M	Farmer	TN
Mary G.	14	F		TN
Wiley	10	M		MS
Sarah A.	9	F		MS
Martha E.	9	F		MS
Lucinda G.	8	F		MS
Manerva A.	6	F		MS
Susan R.	5	F		MS
Thomas C.	4	M		MS
Eliza J.	2	F		MS
James A.	1/12	M		TX
Thomison, Victor	39	M	Farmer	SC
Elizabeth	35	F		TN
Sarah	15	F		AL
Eliza J.	12	F		TX
Emily	10	F		TX
Amanda	7	F		TX
James	3	M		TX
Betheney	2	F		TX
Chandlier, A.	26	M	Farmer	AL
Elizabeth	17	F		Al
Cifford, A.	31	M	Farmer	TN
Sarah C.	26	F		TN

(continued)

CHEROKEE COUNTY, TEXAS

Name	Age	Sex	Occupation	Birthplace
Gifford, Louis P.	9	F(M)		TN
Edward	7	M		TN
John	5	M		TN
William	3	M		TN
Murry, J. C.	23	M	Farmer	TN
Nancy	18	F		TN
Latham, Martin	23	M	Farmer	IL
Elizabeth	18	F		TN
James L.	11/12	M		TX
Tubb, P.	35	M	Farmer	TN
S---	31	F		AL
Toliver W.	12	M		MS
Robert	11	M		TX
John	6	M		TX
Thomas	4	M		TX
Milly	3	F		TX
King, John	25	M	Farmer	TN
Irwin, John	25	M	Farmer	MO
Clark, J. E.	27	M	Farmer	SC
Paralee B.	23	F		AL
Judith C.	4	F		AL
Patrick J.	1	M		TX
Burris, H. S. W.	19	M	Farmer	TN
Thompson, M.	48	M	Farmer	NC
Mahala W.	39	F		SC
William R.	18	M	Farmer	AL
Mary E.	11	F		AL
Hood, Andrew M.	24	M	Farmer	TN
Rozell, James	51	M	Mill Wright	NC
Rebecca	42	F		NC
Benjamin	18	M	Farmer	AL
Wiley W.	15	M	Farmer	AL
Mary A.	7	F		AL
Martha P. M. K.	3	F		TX
Calvin	19	M	Farmer	TN
Burk, Willis	50	M	Farmer	SC
Lucinda	34	F		TN
Elizabeth A.	15	F		TN
Martha	12	F		TN
* James W.	11	M		TN
Catherine P.	8	F		TN
Cassender	6	F		TN
Margaret J.	4	F		TN
Robert L.	3	M		TN
John W.	2/12	M		TX
Harris, James B.	40	M	C.P. Minister	TN
Clemantine G.	33	F		TN
David B.	13	M		TN
Jane S.	11	F		AR
Susan M.	10	F		AR
Sam	9	F(M)		AR
James B.	8	M		AR
Benjamin	4	M		TX
Clemantine	1	F		TX
Pendghart, M.	32	F		KY
Glenn, William T.	44	M	Farmer	SC
Nancy	34	F		TN
James B.	14	M		AL
William J.	5	M		TX
Josiah J.	3	M		TX
Henry T.	1	M		TX
Nutt, Willis	40	M	Gun Smith	??
Scott, Calvin	26	M	Farmer	TN
Mary A.	19	F		TN
Butler, Pleasant	43	M	M.D.	TN
Selman, Benjamin	34	M	Farmer	GA
Sarah	37	F		GA
Benjamin F.	15	M	Farmer	TN
Sarah	12	F		AL
Green L.	29	M	Farmer	AL
Benjamin T.	7	M		AL
Ann A.	6	F		MS
Owen, William	19	M	Farmer	AL

Name	Age	Sex	Occupation	Birthplace
McNeal, Jas.	29	M	Farmer	NC
Elizabeth	23	F		TN
Benjamin L.	7	M		AL
John M.	4	M		TX
Mary T.	2	F		TX
Sarah	5/12	F		TX
Boyd, James	35	M	Farmer	TN
Martha	31	F		AL
Benjamin F.	15	M	Farmer	AL
Elizabeth	13	F		AL
Sarah	11	F		AL
Nancy A.	9	F		AL
Martha F.	7	F		AL
John	5	M		AL
William T.	3	M		LA
Louisa A.	1	F		LA
Harper, Washington	25	M	Farmer	AL
Williams, John E.	31	M	Farmer	TN
Cassa	24	F		AL
Mary E.	7	F		AL
Thomas W.	5	M		AL
Tilman, Willis	46	M	Farmer	GA
Anna	38	F		GA
Benjamin T.	19	M	Farmer	TN
Darcus A.	15	F		AL
Mary A.	14	F		AL
Joseph T. L.	12	M		AL
Eleanor F. A.	9	F		AL
Willis E.	7	M		AL
Leonidas	4	M		AL
Virgil J.	2	M		TX
Boulton, J--	54	M	Farmer	ENG
Elizabeth	39	F		MS
Alfred	24	M	Farmer	AL
William	21	M	Farmer	TN
James	17	M	Farmer	TN
Edward	10	M		TX
Young	8	M		TX
Anderson	6	M		TX
Mary	4	F		TX
Augustus	7/12	M		TX
McBee, William W.	29	M	Farmer	TN
Sarah J.	26	F		SC
Adela A.	3	F		AL
Jason	2	M		AL
Armstrong, M. W.	41	M	M.D.	TN
Mary M.	39	F		TN
William A. D.	15	M	Student	TN
Nancy B.	13	F		TN
John B.	11	M		TN
Martha T.	10	F		TN
Martin M.	9	M		TN
Mary M. M.	8	F		TN
Robert J.	22	M		TN
Spruice, Jas.	50	M	Farmer	NC
Director	30	F		NC
Zebulon	24	M	Farmer	NC
Partin, H.	18	M	Farmer	TN
Tilman, Willis	25	M	Farmer	TN
Margaret R.	16	F		AL
Boon, R. H.	25	M	Farmer	NC
Artamecia	21	F		TN
Thomas H.	4	M		AL
Sarah E.	1	F		TX
Spivey, T.	55	M	Farmer	NC
Charity	46	F		NC
Calvin	21	M	Farmer	AL
Joseph	18	M		TN
Henry	16	M		TN
Elizabeth	12	F		MS
Martha	10	F		MS
Isaac	8	M		MS
George	1	M		MS
Mitchell, R. F.	45	M	Merchant	OH
Butler, G. W.	19	M	Clerk	TN

CHEROKEE COUNTY, TEXAS

Name	Age	Sex	Occupation	Birthplace
Jackson, W. E.	24	M	Farmer	NC
Mary A.	23	F		TN
Frances C.	1	F		TX
Culp, D.	29	M	Farmer	KY
Elizabeth S.	25	F		VA
Terrel, James	19	M	Student	TN
Selman, Thomas	59	M	Farmer	SC
Polly	59	F		SC
Benjamin F.	20	M	Farmer	MS
Goodson, George W.	26	M	Farmer	TN
Selman, Joseph	17	M		MS
Sims, William W.	36	M	Carpenter	TN
Rebecca	43	F		GA
Martha L. A.	9	F		TX
Mary J.	7	F		TX
Ferdenand D.	5	M		TX
Virginia A.	1	F		TX
Moody, C. H.	37	M	Farmer	NC
Nancy	28	F		TN
Martha A. J.	11	F		AL
Sarah E.	9	F		AL
Mary A.	7	F		AL
Nancy A.	5	F		TX
Benjamin R.	1	M		TX
Patton, George	17	M	Farmer	AL
Moffett, John	26	M	Black Smith	SC
Martha D.	25	F		TN
James	4	M		TX
John	2	M		TX
Easter, S.	44	M	Farmer	GA
America W.	36	F		TN
Emily F	11	F		AL
Mitus L.	9	M		AL
James	50	M	Farmer	GA
Adam, Hiram	22	M	Farmer	AL
Ivy, Henry	31	M	Carpenter	TN
McBee, S. B.	25	M	Farmer	TN
Margaret	15	F		AL
Crawford, Joseph	11	M		AL
Mercer, Jesse	23	M	Farmer	MS
Mary	26	F		AL
Wilson J.	6/12	M		TX
Easter, Emily	6	F		AL
Caledonia J. V.	3	F		TX
Collier, William	49	M	Farmer	TN
Sarah	47	F		NC
Easter H.	25	F		AL
Barnes, William S.	28	M	Farmer	TN
Mary	28	F		TN
Joseph	4	M		TN
Jeremiah	2	M		TN
James T.	1	M		TN
Martha H.	1/12	F		TX
Law, J. H.	32	M	Farmer	TN
Mary A.	25	F		MS
Eleanor	6	F		TX
Hannah C.	4	F		TX
Mary Jane	2	F		TX
Bone, Enos	50	M	Farmer	NC
Lucy	42	F		NC
William R.	23	M	Farmer	TN
Mary J.	21	F		TN
Rosina D.	19	F		TN
Emily W.	17	F		TN
John Hill	15	M	Farmer	TN
Permely A.	12	F		TN
Thomas Drury	10	M		TN
Martha E.	8	F		TN
Andrew J.	5	M		TN
Henry P.	3	M		TN
Rufus D.	7/12	M		TX
Howard, Jesse	20	M	Farmer	AL
Looney, T. J.	38	M	Farmer	SC
Eliza M.	31	F		TN
Nancy E.	10	F		TN
Margaret J.	9	F		TN
Sally A.	8	F		TN
Mary B.	7	F		TN
Martha S.	5	F		TN
Adaline L.	3	F		TN
Clemantine V.	5/12	F		TX
Hatchett, H. G.	42	M	Farmer	TN
Evaline A.	40	F		NC
Edward A.	17	M	Farmer	TN
Mathew G.	15	M	Farmer	TN
William W.	13	M		TN
Telitha L. E.	9	F		TN
McCowen, H. A.	25	M	Farmer	TN
Holly	27	F		NC
Napoleon B.	6	M		TN
Martha E.	3	F		TN
Mary	1	F		TX
Scarborough, Silas	43	M	Farmer	NC
Martha	43	F		NC
Monroe	25	M	Farmer	NC
Elizabeth	22	F		NC
Amanda	16	F		NC
John	14	M		TN
Tennessee	13	F		TN
Looney, D.	64	M	Farmer	GA
Nancy	64	F		GA
Sarah M.	33	F		TN
Mary	31	F		TN
Noah	29	M	Farmer	TN
Howard, J. L.	30	M	Farmer	NC
Caroline	24	F		TN
Virginia A.	6	F		MS
Mary C.	4	F		LA
Charles	1	M		TX
Eskridge, R.	37	M	Farmer	TN
Mariah D.	40	F		TN
Samuel C.	14	M		TN
Sarah M.	12	F		LA
William B.	10	M		TX
Turner P.	8	M		TX
Gibbons, William	25	M	Farmer	TN
Waggoner, L.	53	M	Farmer	NC
Nancy	53	F		GA
Sarah	18	F		AL
William	16	M	Farmer	TN
Ver--tha	14	F		AL
Cornelison, M.	29	M	Farmer	TN
Spicy	36	F		TN
Mary A.	9	F		TN
Celia E.	8	F		TN
George W.	6	M		TN
Benjamin J.	5	M		TN
Hannah	1	F		TX
Todd, D.	30	M	Farmer	TN
Artena	28	F		TN
Elizabeth J.	7	F		TN
Lucinda E.	6	F		TN
James M.	3	M		TN
William J.	1	M		TN
Hicks, W. A.	52	M	Farmer	TN
Lucy	47	F		SC
Stone, William N.	19	M	Student	AL
Penalton, J.	30	M	Baliff	AL
Johnson, Robert	19	M	Farmer	AL
Hicks, Newton	21	M	Farmer	GA
Cox, Lucy R.	44	F		VA
William S.	22	M	Farmer	TN
Thomas R.	21	M	Farmer	TN
Charles S.	15	M	Farmer	TN
Martha J.	12	F		TN
Mary F.	10	F		TN
Harriett	17	F		TN

CHEROKEE COUNTY, TEXAS

Name	Age	Sex	Occupation	Birthplace
Carson, A. M.	39	M	Farmer	NC
Louisa A.	30	F		TN
Annett E.	10	F		MS
James	8	M		MS
Emma A.	5	F		LA
Thomas	1	M		TX
Cope, Wily	22	M	Farmer	TN
White, C. B.	21	M	Farmer	MS
Elizabeth E.	20	F		TN
James N.	1	M		TX
William Lewis	2/12	M		TX
Hicks, J. D.	46	M	Farmer	TN
Joannah	43	F		PA
William E.	20	M	Farmer	GA
David C.	16	M	Farmer	GA
James M.	1	M		TX
Neal, Lucinda	15	F		LA
Rutherford, Samuel	47	M	Farmer	TN
Elizabeth	46	F		TN
Leona	20	F		TN
Schrimsher, A. S.	22	M	Farmer	TN
Nancy	30	F		TN
Amanda E.	2	F		TN
Rosanna	1	F		TX
Bowen, G. R.	29	M	Black Smith	TN
Mary	29	F		TN
William P.	10	M		TN
Eliza J.	7	F		TN
Florence J.	5	F		TN
Gideon A.	1	M		TN
Rutherford, R. D.	39	M	Farmer	KY
Martha	38	F		KY
Mary A. E.	3	F		TX
Rebecca A.	10/12	F		TX
Wallace, William G.	14	M		TN
Sherod, James H.	31	M	Farmer	GA
Nancy J.	18	F		TN
Johnson, William J.	28	M	Farmer	TN
Mary	24	F		TN
Mary J.	2	F		TN
Benjamin F.	1	M		TN
Elizabeth	26	F		TN
Mich, B. F.	21	M	Farmer	TN
Catharine	20	F		TN
Roberts, E.	27	M	Farmer	TN
Sarah J.	24	F		TN
Sarah E.	6	F		TN
Hugh F.	4	M		TN
Mary L.	2	F		TN
Mandy J.	1	F		TN
Statford, James H.	22	M	Farmer	TN
Walker, D.	38	M	Farmer	TN
Elizabeth	37	F		TN
Thomas	19	M	Farmer	TN
Leah E.	16	F		TN
Milton	14	M		TN
John	12	M		TN
Scotia A.	8	F		TN
Charles A.	5	M		TN
Daniel	1	M		TN
Conly	18	M		TN
Martha	78	F		NC
Walker, A.	43	M	Farmer	TN
Elizabeth	39	F		VA
John	20	M	Farmer	VA
Hazlee	18	M	Farmer	VA
Thomas J.	17	M	Farmer	VA
Laura A. J.	14	F		VA
Margaret	10	F		VA
James K.	6	M		VA
Martha	3	F		VA
Susan	1	F		VA
Brewer, William	37	M	Farmer	MS
Elizabeth	34	F		KY
George H.	16	M	Farmer	MS
William	11	M		TX
Elizabeth	8	F		TX
Martha A.	7	F		TX
Martin H.	4	M		TX
Christian, Catharine R.	15	F		TN
John C.	13	M		TN
William	10	M		TN
Isabel	5	F		TX
Brewer, Clarissa	2	F		TX
Buster, William	29	M	Teacher	TN
Margaret	29	F		TN
Harriet T.	5	F		AL
John C.	4	M		AL
Martha E.	7/12	F		TN
Gray, E. M.	46	M	Farmer	KY
Elizabeth	46	F		NC
Panter, Jane	8	F		??
Swink, William	16	M	Farmer	TN
Medford, Levi	32	M	Farmer	TN
Tebitha	30	F		AL
Albert	6	M		TX
J. Wilbern	5	M		TX
Melissa J.	2	F		TX
Sephrona	14	F		MS
Samuel	10	M		TX
Summers, William	31	M	Farmer	TN
Isabella	29	F		TN
Elizabeth E.	10	F		TN
Martha	7	F		TN
Mary	5	F		TN
James	2	M		TN
Henrietta	10/12	F		TN
Warick, James	32	M	Farmer	VA
Rachel S.	40	F		TN
Sarah E.	10	F		TN
Jefferson D.	8	M		TN
Jacob A.	6	M		TN
William H.	1	M		TN
Mary E.	3	F		TN
West, Houston	19	M	Farmer	TN
Summers, James F.	46	M	Farmer	NC
Louisiana	37	F		TN
Thomas W.	12	M		AL
William	6	M		TN
Robert	3	M		TN
James	2/12	M		TX
Henry, Ezekiel	65	M	Farmer	TN
Judith	53	F		VA
Patrick H.	25	M	Farmer	AL
Clinton ?.	16	M	Farmer	AL
Henry, John	29	M	Farmer	AL
Catharine	24	F		GA
Thomas	8	M		AL
Ezekiel	6	M		AL
Orrelia	5	F		AL
Sephronia	3	F		AL
Paralee	2	F		TX
Burrus, Miller	21	M	Farmer	TN
Henry, Hugh	26	M	Farmer	AL
Charlotte L.	20	F		GA
Woodson F.	3	M		AL
Jeruth C.	2	F		TX
Coffee, William	22	M	Farmer	TN
Thompson, Wily	21	M	Farmer	AL
Celia A.	21	F		TN
William M.	8/12	M		AL
Lowe, C. F.	51	M	Farmer	VA
Celia	49	E		NC
William	26	M	Farmer	TN
James	23	M	Farmer	TN
Henrietta	19	F		TN

(continued)

CHEROKEE COUNTY, TEXAS

Name	Age	Sex	Occupation	Birthplace
Lowe, Eliza J.	14	F		TN
Mary E.	10	F		TN
Melinda	8	F		TN
Robert	7	M		TN
Blackwell, Martha	44	F		GA
Robert B.	21	M	Farmer	TN
Sumner	19	M	Farmer	TN
David C.	16	M	Farmer	TN
Mary	14	F		TN
Jane	12	F		TN
Lafayette	10	M		TN
Isaac	8	M		TN
Blackwell, Zene	23	M	Farmer	TN
Julia	26	F		TN
Robert W.	1	M		TN
Stafford, Samuel	37	M	Farmer	NC
Parthenia	36	F		TN
Harriet	14	F		TN
Thomas	9	M		TN
Mary	7	F		AR
Newton H.	7	M		AR
Clinton	3	M		TX
Pinckney	8/12	M		TX
Summers, A.	47	M	Farmer	NC
Lucinda	44	F		NC
Melinda	20	F		TN
Alfred	18	M	Farmer	TN
William	16	M	Farmer	TN
Jane	13	F		TN
Rebecca	11	F		TN
Thomas	9	M		TN
Mary E.	8	F		TN
Tubb, E.	33	M	Farmer	TN
Sarah E.	26	F		TN
William T.	9	M		TX
Sarah J.	8	F		TX
Martha V.	6	F		TX
John A.	4	M		TX
Elisha	3	M		TX
Martin	1	M		TX
Blessing, Isaac	24	M	Farmer	VA
Blankenship, B. F.	31	M		TN
Elizabeth	25	F		TN
Charles W.	4	M		TN
William R.	3	M		TN
Sarah J.	1	F		TN
Mankins, Charles	34	M	Farmer	TN
Martha	28	F		TN
Willis	12	M		TN
Mary	9	F		TN
Leroy	8	M		TN
Scurlock, John	36	M	Farmer	SC
Catharine	24	F		AL
James W.	10	M		AL
Malcom V.	8	M		AL
Mary A. E.	5	F		AL
Scurlock, Jno. W.	25	M	Farmer	TN
Scurlock, Thomas A.	24	M	Teacher	TN
Anna	64	F		SC
Lucinda A. E.	20	F		TX
Vanzant, A.	46	M	Farmer	KY
Minerva	49	F		NC
Jane E.	23	F		TN
John R.	12	M		AL
Liddy C.	9	F		AL
Arrington, Thomas C.	30	M	Farmer	IL
Milly	22	F		TN
Mary N.	3	F		TX
Amanda	4/12	F		TX
Waggoner, G. W.	29	M	Farmer	TN
Margaret A.	26	F		AL
(continued)				
Waggoner, Elizabeth	4	F		TX
Martha A.	1	F		TX
P. Asten	59	F		TN
Coleman, Frances	37	F		TN
John W.	16	M	Farmer	KY
Martin Y.	13	M		KY
Henry H.	7	M		KY
Josephine	1	F		TX
Francis, James	39	M	Farmer	TN
Sarah	31	F		TN
Christopher C.	16	M		TN
Nancy	12	F		TN
Joseph	7	M		TN
Frances J.	4	F		TN
Ann C.	1	F		TN
McKenny, William	25	M		MS
Lindsey, Thomas J.	35	M	Farmer	GA
Elizabeth	34	F		TN
Mary E.	13	F		MS
Nancy E.	9	F		MS
Susan D.	5	F		MS
Martha	1	F		TX
James M.	7/12	M		TX
Parker, Matthew	49	M	Farmer	GA
Elizabeth	39	F		TN
Perry	21	M	Farmer	TX
Wiley J.	19	M	Farmer	TX
Washington ?.	17	M	Farmer	TX
Andrew J.	15	M	Farmer	TX
Alexander H.	13	M		TX
Sarah E.	11	F		TX
Willis H.	9	M		TX
Amanda	7	F		TX
Mary A. S.	5	F		TX
Rebecca	2	F		TX
Susan	7/12	F		TX
Young, E. A.	50	M	M.D.	VA
Jency	26	F		MS
Eliza H.	23	F	(Blind)	TN
Carterah A. (Casterah)	8	F		MS
Bolten, Mary	65	F		SC
Giffen, Eleanor	65	F		NC
William	28	M	Farmer	TN
Eubulus	26	M	Farmer	TN
Walden, James	53	M	Farmer	VA
Martha	50	F		VA
Ann	23	F		TN
Elizabeth	20	F		TN
Martha	18	F		TN
James	16	M	Farmer	TN
Sally	15	F		TN
Williams, W. V.	21	M	Farmer	TN
John M.	19	M	Farmer	TN
Leath, E.	26	M	Farmer	TN
Lucinda	22	F		AL
Lankford, P. M.	27	M	Stone Mason	TN
Elizabeth	20	F		TN
Eleanor J.	7	F		AL
James M.	4	M		AL
Martha	10/12	F		AL
Burk, C.	38	M	Farmer	TN
Mary F.	27	F		TN
Archibald	10/12	M		TN
Wilbron, William	50	M	Farmer	GA
Pheba	35	F		OH
Ferdinand	23	M	Farmer	TN
Isabella	14	F		IN
John	13	M		IN
Elizabeth	11	F		AR
Mary A.	7	F		AR
Alfred R.	4	M		AR
Lucinda J.	1	F		TX

CHEROKEE COUNTY, TEXAS

Name	Age	Sex	Occupation	Birthplace
Lankford, C.	24	M	Farmer	AL
Mary A.	20	F		TN
William T.	2	M		AL
Wolfanabarger, S.	30	M	Farmer	TN
Margaret	26	F		TN
Elizabeth	9	F		TN
Harvy M.	4	M		TN
Summers, George	23	M	Farmer	TN
Lucinda	23	F		TN
William P.	1	M		TN
Summers, Jno. P.	23	M	Farmer	TN
Schockley, Levi	50	M	Farmer	SC
Elizabeth	48	F		SC
Lemuel	18	M	Farmer	TN
Abigail	16	F		TN
Eliza W.	13	F		AL
Sarah E.	11	F		AL
James	7	M		AL
Phelix G.	5	M		AL
Griner, H. W.	32	M	Farmer	TN
Mary J.	27	F		TN
Noble J.	9	M		MS
Anson P.	7	M		TX
Mary P.	4	F		TX
Hulet	2	M		TX
Eason, Mary	50	F		GA
Griner, Noble L.	32	M		TN
Runnels, Jno.	29	M	Farmer	TN
Martha E.	21	F		AL
Rebecca J.	3	F		TX
Earls, Drury	35	M	Farmer	TN
Polly A.	31	F		TN
John	13	M		AL
Anderson	10	M		AL
Rhody	8	F		AL
Drucilla	7	F		AL
Elijah	5	M		AL
Elisha	3	M		MO
William	1	M		TX
Chesher, A. J.	35	M	Farmer	TN
Nancy	42	F		TN
Jemima J.	7	F		AL
Henderson, R. L.	44	M	Farmer	TN
Elizabeth	42	F		TN
Jasper	18	M	Farmer	AL
Newton	16	M		AL
Leroy	12	M		AL
Sally	10	F		AL
Calvin	9	M		AL
Houston	3	M		TX
Hammons, William	22	M	Farmer	AL
Sarah	26	F		TN
John	3	M		AL
Edy	9/12	F		AL
Runnels, Isaac	57	M	Farmer	SC
Tempy A.	55	F		NC
Doherty, J.	38	M	Farmer	TN
Alzira	37	F		TN
George W.	16	M	Farmer	AL
Mary A. M.	12	F		AL
William	6	M		TX
Chelnessa A.	1	F		TX
Duncan, M.	18	M	Farmer	AL
Matthews, D. R.	41	M	Farmer	TN
Sarah A.	25	F		SC
Liddy J.	2	F		TX
John D.	2/12	M		TX
Liddy	64	F		NC
Swink, Jas.	14	M		MS
Hammons, Charles W.	54	M	Farmer	KY
Eliza	43	F		GA
Thomas P.	23	M	Farmer	AL
John	21	M		AL
Susanah	18	F		AL
Polly	16	F		AL
Stephen S.	12	M		AL
Mary A.	9	F		AL
Elizabeth	5	F		AL
Nancy J.	2	F		AL
Barns, Anderson	21	M	Farmer	TN
Bange, G. C.	46	M	Black Smith	TN
Nancy	51	F		TN
Matilda	23	F		TN
Obediah M.	22	M	Farmer	AL
John	20	M	Farm	AL
William	17	M	Farmer	AL
Catharine	15	F		AL
Samuel T.	13	M		AL
Heigh L.	12	M		AL
Robert	10	M		AL
Jane	20	F		AL
Nancy J.	1/12	F		TX
Goodman, Jacob	31	M	Farmer	TN
Hamilton, Elizabeth	27	F		TN
Rebecca A.	5	F		MO
Slaton, Jno. C.	36	M	Farmer	GA
Lucinda	31	F		TN
Marion E.	13	M		AL
Sarah J.	10	F		AL
John C.	6	M		AL
William T.	16	M	Farmer	AL
George W.	8	M		AL
Canady	3	M		AL
America	1	F		AL
Kimbro, Lemuel	38	M	Farmer	NC
Nancy	36	F		TN
Martin	2	M		TX
Rushing, J. C.	28	M	Farmer	TN
Elizabeth	20	F		TN
Cassander	2	F		TN
Enoch W.	1	M		TX
Rogers, James	55	M	Farmer	TN
Mary	55	F		NC
Elizabeth E.	21	F		AL
Martha E.	18	F		AL
Thomas H.	17	M	Farmer	AL
Mary F.	15	F		AL
Harris, Hamby	27	M	Farmer	NC
Eleanor	29	F		NC
Holding H.	12	M		MS
Eli	9	M		MS
Timothy M.	6	M		MS
Frederick B.	2	M		TN
Lane, J. B.	43	M	Farmer	TN
Jane	43	F		TN
Nancy A.	22	F		TN
Sarah	20	F		TN
John F.	18	M	Farmer	TN
Margaret J.	17	F		TN
Syntha	16	F		TN
Robert	14	M		TN
James	12	M		TN
Emaline	10	F		TN
Martha	8	F		TN
William	3	M		TN
Long, Wiley	44	M	Farmer	KY
Elizabeth L.	34	F		TN
Solomon	18	M	Farmer	IA
Samuel	16	M	Farmer	IA
Jacob	13	M		IA
Elizabeth	8	F		IA
Mary	5	F		TX
Elijah	2	M		TX
Dennison, William	28	M	Black Smith	TN
Wolsey, Jas.	26	M	Farmer	KY

CHEROKEE COUNTY, TEXAS

Name	Age	Sex	Occupation	Birthplace
Winn, Harmon	30	M	Farmer	KY
Martha	26	F		TN
A. Martin	4	M		KY
Nancy E.	2	F		TX
George W.	2/12	M		TX
Andrew J.	2/12	M		TX
Gwin, C. W.	23	M	Farmer	TN
Catharine	21	F		TN
Polly A.	1	F		TN
Pritchet, Calvin	21	M	Farmer	TN
Mullinax, J.	24	M	Farmer	TN
L---	18	F		TN
William	23	M	Farmer	TN
Noland, William	34	M	Farmer	TN
Polly	50	F		NC
Elizabeth	26	F		KY
Lois	22	F		TN
George	14	M		TN
Serena	16	F		TN
Selina	11	F		TN
Patton, Susan M.	1	F		TX
Martha E. C.	8/12	F		TX
Felps, David	47	M	Farmer	NC
William	16	M	Farmer	TN
Susan	14	F		TN
Loretha E.	12	F		TN
Rhoda	10	F		TN
Ezekiel	8	M		TN
Jacob	6	M		TN
Mary J.	2	F		TX
Grissom, Larkin	27	M	Farmer	TN
Harriet	25	F		AL
James M.	5	M		TN
Martha C.	3	F		KY
Ambrose D.	1	M		TX
Felps, Britton	36	M	Farmer	TN
Angeline	29	F		TN
John J.	7	M		TN
Burrow, Jas.	18	M	Laborer	TN
Jarret, Devereux	68	M	Farmer	VA
Mary	65	F		VA
Elizabeth	41	F		VA
Wade	40	M	Farmer	VA
Devereux, Jr.	34	M	Farmer	VA
Henry M.	32	M	Farmer	VA
John W.	23	M	Farmer	TN
Tatum, Mary E.	26	F		TN
Smith, Julian	17	F		TN
Tatum, Jesse W.	8	M		TN
Robert A.	6	M		TN
William H.	4	M		TN
Fountain ?.	7/12	M		TN
Dunlap, Mary V.	17	F		TN
Grissom, Thomas	59	M	Farmer	TN
Rhody	59	F		TN
Nancy	32	F		TN
James	30	M	Farmer	TN
Catharine	20	F		KY
Isaac	18	M	Farmer	TN
Lafayette	16	M	Farmer	TN
Kilpatrick, William A.	30	M	Farmer	SC
Catharine M.	25	F		TN
C--elia J.	7	F		MS
James B.	5	M		MS
John C.	2	M		MS
Simpson, S. C. P.	24	M	Farmer	TN
Hill, F. M.	23	M	Farmer	TN
Fowler, D. P.	45	M	M.D.	SC
Nancy B.	42	F		TN
Lawrence S.	11	M		AL
David R.	9	M		AL
Nancy A. S.	4	F		AL
Martha E.	1	F		MS
Thomison, W.	39	M	Farmer	TN
Susan	40	F		NC
Isaac	15	M	Farmer	AL
George W.	14	M		AL
John	10	M		AL
Mankers, William	40	M	Farmer	TN
Margaret	40	F		TN
Missouri A.	13	F		AR
Marian T.	10	F		AR
James H.	8	M		AR
Samuel H.	7	M		AR
Robert T.	3	M		AR
Charles W.	1	M		TX
Stout, Harrison C.	24	M	Farmer	TN
Elizabeth	17	F		AR
McClelland, P. C.	19	M	Farmer	LA
Thomason, John	36	M	Farmer	TN
Ann	32	F		TN
Sarah E.	12	F		AL
Richard J.	10	M		AL
Frances C.	9	F		AL
John O.	6	M		AR
Mary	3	F		AR
Tucker, Z.	30	M	Black Smith	VA
Malinda	27	F		TN
Elizabeth	6	F		TN
Nancy A.	4	F		TN
Hill, George	43	M	Farmer	TN
Elizabeth	41	F		??
Pharough	20	M	Farmer	AL
Thomas M.	18	M	Farmer	AL
Lusana	16	F		AL
Rachel L.	13	F		AL
Elizabeth S.	11	F		AL
Pelina A.	9	F		AL
Susan C.	7	F		AL
Margaret D.	4	F		TX
Jesse W.	2/12	M		TX
Grissom, John	23	M	Farmer	TN
Sarah	16	F		TN
Mary T.	2	F		TX
Crenshaw, Manerva	33	F		TN
Silas C.	17	M	Farmer	AL
Malinda A.	12	F		TX
Mary C.	9	F		TX
Falknor, Marshal	34	M	Farmer	TN
Ashael T.	27	F		AL
Jeremiah	8	M		AL
Elizabeth	6	F		MS
Banks, Reza	30	M	Farmer	AL
Manerva	26	F		GA
William C.	3	M		TX
Samuel W.	2	M		TX
Joannah	12/24	F		TX
Delany, Wesley	26	M	Farmer	TN
Halbert, Stephen	44	M	Farmer	TN
Sally	45	F		TN
Joshua E. M.	16	M	Farmer	AL
Charles T.	14	M		AL
Stephen M.	10	M		TX
Joseph B.	8	M		TX
Joel T.	6	M		TX
Susanna E.	3	F		TX
Sarah J.	8/12	F		TX
Johnson, Samuel	24	M	Farmer	AL
Mary M.	20	F		AL
Charles S.	5/12	M		TX
Dyarman, William	40	M	Miller	PA
Nancy	35	F		TN
Ansel	4	M		AR
Hiram	2	M		TX
Garrison, Serena	16	F		AR
Phipps, William T.	25	M	Farmer	TN
Sarah F.	31	F		TN

(continued)

CHEROKEE COUNTY, TEXAS

Name	Age	Sex	Occupation	Birthplace
Edgar, G. R.	28	M	Black Smith	TN
Margaret	25	F		TN
Mary E.	2	F		TN
Juliette	2/12	F		TX
Jones, Stephen	35	M	Farmer	TN
Elizabeth	27	F		TN
Mary J.	8	F		AL
Sarah J.	5	F		AL
Martha B.	3	F		TX
Tatum, Joseph	33	M	Farmer	SC
Jennet S.	29	F		VA
Jesse D.	12	M		TN
Joseph H.	6	M		TN
John W.	3	M		TN
Long, Joseph B.	33	M	Farmer	TN
Emaline	31	F		TN
Eliza	8	F		AL
Elizabeth C.	6	F		TN
Margaret	2	F		TX
McCoy, Jno. C.	14	M		AL
Luce, Joseph	47	M	Farmer	KY
Jane	42	F		TN
Hiram	15	M	Farmer	MO
Jane	13	F		AR
Sarah	11	F		MO
Nathan	9	M		MO
Polly A.	5	F		TX
Luce, David	35	M	Farmer	MO
Elizabeth	34	F		TN
Anna	14	F		MO
Zepheniah	12	M		MO
Nancy	10	F		MO
David	8	M		MO
Emaline	6	F		TX
Malinda	4	F		TX
Leonard	2	M		TX
Buchanan, John	46	M	Farmer	KY
William R.	15	M	Farmer	IL
John	14	M		IL
Archillus	13	M		TN
Frances	10	F		TN
Robert	9	M		TN
Eliza	7	F		TN
Peach, Henderson	26	M	Black Smith	TN
Elizabeth B.	30	F		AL
George W. C.	3	M		TN
James A.	2	M		TN
Mary E.	2/12	F		TX
Stephens, G. W.	24	M	Farmer	AL
Elizabeth	22	F		TN
James W.	1	M		TX
Dugger, Caroline	36	F		SC
Hardy A.	17	M	Farmer	TN
Britton A.	15	M	Farmer	TN
Loretta G.	14	F		TN
Wiley K.	12	M		TN
Sarah C.	10	F		TN
Thomas J.	8	M		TN
Ruth T.	7	F		TN
Lucy W.	5	F		TN
Harris, N.	31	M	Farmer	TN
Rachel	32	F		IL
Abner	9	M		AL
Sarah E.	7	F		AL
Ruthy A.	4	F		AL
James N.	2	M		TX
Halcomb, Z.	54	M	Farmer	KY
Catharine	37	F		TN
Joseph	19	M	Teamster	AR
Nancy D.	17	F		AR
John W.	12	M		AR
Joel P.	11	M		AR

(continued)

Name	Age	Sex	Occupation	Birthplace
Halcomb, Samuel A.	7	M		AR
Lewis H.	4	M		AR
Martha J.	1	F		AR
Luce, William	24	M	Laborer	AR
Sarah	17	F		TX
Slaton(Staton), J. Y.	38	M	Farmer	TN
Milder A.	42	F		AL
Polk, Andrew	58	M	Farmer	NC
Martha	57	F		VA
Winniford	16	F		MO
Jackson, Louisa	34	F		TN
Martha A.	12	F		MO
John A.	10	M		MO
Susan M.	8	M(F)		MO
McNabb, David	36	M	Farmer	TN
Elizabeth	34	F		TN
James F.	14	M		AL
Elizabeth	12	F		AL
William H.	6	M		AL
Joel G.	2	M		AL
Elkin, David	37	M	Farmer	TN
Ruth	36	F		TN
Benjamin N.	16	M	Farmer	TN
Joel M.	14	M		TN
Martha J.	12	F		TN
Lewis F.	3	M		AL
Dennis, Matilda	25	F		TN
Halcomb, George	29	M	Farmer	AR
Narcissa	25	F		TN
John L.	8	M		TX
William H.	4	M		TX
Sarah E.	2	F		TX
Halcomb, W. J.	23	M	Farmer	AR
Martha	24	F		TN
Benjamin F.	3	M		TX
Laura A.	11/12	F		TX
Newman, Warren	22	M	Farmer	AR
Thomason, George	31	M	Farmer	TN
Pelina	24	F		AL
Nancy C.	3	F		TX
Jesse	1	M		TX
Hill, Elizabeth	65	F		VA
Powers, H. C.	35	M	Farmer	TN
Priscilla	23	F		TN
George W.	3	M		TX
Eliza	1	F		TX
Christopher C.	22	M	Farmer	AL
Batten, Malinda	30	F		TN
James	16	M	Farmer	TN
Hezekiah	14	M		MO
Jane	12	F		MO
Thomas	10	M		MO
Stephen	8	M		MO
Hamilton, Nathan	33	M	Farmer	TN
Polly	32	F		KY
John E.	5	M		TX
Mary L.	4	F		TX
Amanda	10	F		TX
Nancy J.	2	F		TX
Newton, N.	38	M	Farmer	GA
Sarah	34	F		TN
John R.	16	M	Farmer	TN
Jemima E.	14	F		TN
Sidney J.	12	F		TN
Kindred P.(?)	10	M		TN
Margaret C.	7	F		TN
James K.	6	M		TN
Edwin C.	2	M		TX
William B.	3/12	M		TX
Box, John A.	42	M	Farmer	SC
Letty T.	40	F		TN
Louisa M.	21	F		AL

(continued)

CHEROKEE COUNTY, TEXAS

Name	Age	Sex	Occupation	Birthplace
Box, William C.	18	M	Farmer	AL
Eunice J.	16	F		AL
Sevire D.	11	M		TX
Emily J.	9	F		TX
Alva A.	7	M		TX
Mary M.	5	F		TX
John R.	3	M		TX
Head, James	41	M	Farmer	TN
Elizabeth A.	22	F		AL
Becton, John M.	44	M	O.S.P. Minister	NC
Eleanor E.	40	F		TN
Edwin T.	16	M	Farmer	TN
Joseph J.	5	M		TX
Isabella S.	6	F		TX
John A.	2	M		TX
Ragsdale, P. C.	37	M	L. Speculator	VA
Stevean, Jas. B.	34	M	Farmer	TN
Susan J.	25	F		AL
John A. G.	7	M		TX
George W.	3	M		TX
Allen, Thomas	15	M	Farmer	AL
Harris, Edwin	42	M	Farmer	PA
Martha G.	32	F		TN
Charles M.	10	M		TX
Edwin R.	7	M		TX
Melinda C.	5	F		TX
Luticia M. A.	2	F		TX
Box, Samuel C.	38	M	M.E. Minister	TN
Nancy G.	33	F		TN
Joseph M. R.	14	M		MO
Pigg, Martha J.	13	F		TN
Lewis, William F.	37	M	Farmer	TN
Adaline	30	F		AL
Mary A. E.	14	F		GA
Andrew L.	12	M		GA
Sarah S.	3	F		AL
Martha A.	2/12	F		TX
Cross(Croft), T. W.	49	M	Farmer	VA
Easter	49	F		TN
Alexander	25	M	Farmer	TN
Mary A.	20	F		TN
H----	10	M		TX
Eliza J.	7	F		TX
Harris, S. W.	43	M	Farmer	NC
Evan S.	16	M	Farmer	AL
William P.	15	M	Farmer	AL
Davis, William	23	M	Farmer	TN
Zerelda	23	F		AL
Louisa	4	F		TX
John W.	2	M		TX
Eliza J.	5	F		TX
Barnes, D.	26	M	Farmer	TN
Martha	22	F		TN
William T.	3	M		AL
Jessie T.	2	M		AL
John	24	M	Farmer	TN

COLLIN COUNTY, TEXAS

Name	Age	Sex	Occupation	Birthplace
Whorton, William	28	M	Farmer	TN
Martha	24	F		TN
M.	5	F		AR
E. C.	4	F		AR
Jno. W.	3	M		TX
Elizabeth	1	F		TX
Roberts, Mark R.	52	M	Farmer	TN
Mary E.	42	F		TN
N. B.	21	M	Farmer	TN
T. W.	19	M	Farmer	TN
Eliza	13	F		TX
Samuel	11	M		TX
William	9	M		TX
(continued)				
Roberts, Mark	7	M		TX
Albert	5	M		TX
Evidently Slaves	12	F	(Black)	--
Cahill Exam (?)	35	F	(Black)	--
Arington, Martha	47	F		KY
E.	26	M	Farmer	AL
James	18	M	Farmer	AR
George W.	5	M		TX
Pruett, William	31	M	Farmer	TN
Coleman, Samuel P.	37	M	Black Smith	GA
A. N.	30	F		TN
S. E.	12	F		AL
C. C.	5	M		TX
S. T. J.	2	M		TX
M. J. F.	4/12	F		TX
Walker, J.	36	M	Carpenter	KY
Evidently slaves	16	F(M)		--
Cahill Exam	20	M	(Black)	--
Dawson, Moses	50	M	Farmer	VA
Susanna	44	F		TN
P.	29	M	Farmer	TN
Jno.	19	M	Farmer	TN
William Y.	16	M	Farmer	TN
George	11	M		MO
Moses	9	M		MO
Sarah	6	F		MO
Mark	2	M		TX
Brindle, Hiram	45	M	Farmer	TN
E. A.	39	F		KY
M. L.	16	F		TX
R. M.	14	M		TX
George R.	12	M		TX
Sarah E.	10	F		TX
H. C.	8	M		TX
Davis F.	6	M		TX
Fitch, Mary	41	F		TN
Jno.	15	M		WI
Thomas	15	M		WI
Caroline	14	F		WI
C. J.	5	F		WI
Smith, H.	33	M	Farmer	TN
S.	34	F		VA
Nancy J.	14	F		TN
V. E.	8	F		TN
Jno. E.	5	M		MO
S.	3	M		TX
Throckmorton, James W.	24	M	Physician	TN
Ann	21	F		IL
H. J.	1	M		TX
Bemoss, P.	24	M	Farmer	IL
H.	24	F		IL
Jane	2/12	F		TX
Elliott, William	30	M	Farmer	KY
J. A.	24	F		TN
Nancy	5	F		IL
J.	4/12	M		TX
Coffman, Jno.	46	M	Farmer	TN
Elizabeth	41	F		TN
R. J.	17	F		IL
E. C.	15	F		IL
Adaline	13	F		IL
George W.	10	M		IL
Nancy	8	F		IL
Sarah A.	5	F		TX
Texana	2	F		TX
Jno. H.	4/12	M		TX
Wilson, Adison	44	M	Farmer	TN
Ann	42	F		TN
George	22	M	Farmer	TN
Elizabeth	18	F		TN
Angeline	16	F		TN
Jos. A.	10	M		TN
Thomas B.	8	M		TN
A.	5	M		TN

COLLIN COUNTY, TEXAS

Name	Age	Sex	Remarks	Birthplace
Atkinson, Jas.	45	M	Farmer	VA
Nancy	41	F		VA
Thomas J.	25	M	Farmer	VA
S. J.	20	F		TN
S. A.	15	F		TN
S. S.	12	F		TN
A. J.	9	M		TX
S. T.	6	F		TX
Slaves	1	M	(Black)	--
	3	M	(Black)	--
	6	F	(Black)	--
	9	M	(Black)	--
	23	F	(Black)	--
	49	M	(Black)	--
Foster, Isaac M.	36	M	Carpenter	VA
Sarah	73	F		NY
Jane	45	F		VA
Jas.	33	M	Carpenter	VA
Nancy	30	F		VA
Rachel	23	F		VA
Wyseng, Charles	30	M		VA
Helen	1	F		TX
Jas.	2/12	M		TX
Kelly, Josiah L.	28	M	Farmer	TN
Oglesby, J. G.	38	M	Farmer	TN
Sarah	31	F		TN
E.	12	M		TN
Daniel	10	M		TN
Mary	8	F		TN
Rebecca	6	F		TN
A. J.	5	M		TN
Jas.	3	M		TN
Martha	1	F		TN
Slaves	5	M	(Black)	--
	7	M	(Black)	--
	35	F	(Black)	--
Witt, Eli W.	24	M	Farmer	TN
Strong, Jas.	23	M	Farmer	??
M.	21	F		??
M.	1	M		MS
McKinney, William C.	46	M	Farmer	KY
Margarett	41	F		TN
N. S.	17	F		AR
E. T.	15	F		TX
Elizabeth	11	F		TX
C. E.	9	M		TX
N. G.	4	M		TX
William J.	1	M		TX
Harling, E.	22	M	Carpenter	KY
Douthett, J. P.	21	M	Farmer	AR
Slaves	1	M	(Black)	--
	1	F	(Black)	--
	1	F	(Black)	--
	3	M	(Black)	--
	3	F	(Black)	--
	14	M	(Black)	--
	14	M	(Black)	--
	15	F	(Black)	--
	16	F	(Black)	--
	27	F	(Black)	--
	27	M	(Black)	--
	40	F	(Black)	--
McBride, Jas. R.	39	M	Farmer	TN
Martha	48	F		KY
Collom, Collin McK.	22	M	Farmer	TX
Daniel McK.	21	M	Farmer	TX
B. M.	19	M	Farmer	TX
P. P.	18	M		TX
Slaves	1	M	(Black)	--
	3	M	(Black)	--
	8	F	(Black)	--
	7	F	(Black)	--
	10	M	(Black)	--
	24	F	(Black)	--
	45	M	(Black)	--
Roberts, Z.	39	M	Black Smith	TN
Naoma	39	F		NC

(continued)

Name	Age	Sex	Remarks	Birthplace
Roberts, M. A.	18	F		TN
Mary Ann	16	F		TN
Charles W.	14	M		AL
M.	7	F		AL
Harriet	2	F		TX
Whitaker, J.	24	M	Farmer	TN
J.	21	F		KY
J. A.	4	F		MO
Jno.	2	M		TX
Susan	6/12	F		TX
White, A. C.	25	M	Farmer	TN
Cynthia	25	F		MO
B. A.	5	M		TX
Martha E.	2	F		TX
Jas. A.	3/12	M		TX
White, Benjamin	59	M	Farmer	NC
Amy	45	F		NC
James	30	M	(Idiot)	NC
White, Jno. L.	36	M	Farmer	TN
Elizabeth	29	F		MO
Russell, Redden	37	M	Farmer	TN
Mary	31	F		IL
Hiram	14	M		TX
Tompkins	12	M		TX
Henry	9	M		TX
S.	7	M		TX
Travis	5	M		TX
Mary J.	3	F		TX
King C.	2/12	M		TX
Rattan, Mary	68	F		TN
Dawson, J.	36	M	Farmer	NC
Sarah Ann	34	F		TN
D. D.	14	M		MO
James D.	12	M		MO
Nancy	8	F		MO
George	19	M	Farmer	GA
Wilson, James	36	M	Farmer	TN
Marthann	34	F		SC
E. J.	13	F		TN
W. H.	11	M		TN
Mary C.	8	F		TN
Slaves	4	F	(Black)	--
	17	F	(Black)	--
Reagan, Jno.	27	M	(Blind)	TN
Mary	26	F		KY
Not named	2/12	M		TX
C.	19	M		AR
Slaves	6	F	(Black)	--
	11	M	(Black)	--
Pulliam, William H.	35	M	Farmer	TN
Matilda	27	F		TN
Benjamin	9	M		TX
A.	6	F		TX
M. F.	5	F		TX
Jno. P.	3	M		TX
William M.	1	M		TX
Fitzhugh, Jno.	58	M	Farmer	VA
Sarah	53	F		TN
G.	18	M	Farmer	MO
George W.	16	M		MO
D. C.	14	F		MO
Jno. D.	11	M		MO
Johnson, Robert A.	30	M	Farmer	MO
Elizabeth	25	F		TN
D. A.	2	F		TX
Shelby, Ezra	39	M	Farmer	PA
Allen, M. W.	25	M	Surveyor	AR
Pulliam, Frances	64	F		NC
S. M.	43	M	Farmer	TN
M. S.	31	M	Farmer	TN
Foote, G. A.	21	M	Physician	VA
Jane	19	F		AR

(continued)

COLLIN COUNTY, TEXAS

Name	Age	Sex	Occupation	Birthplace
Foote, L. A.	2	M		TX
E.	6/12	F		TX
Jones, A.	38	M	Farmer	TN
Slaves	2	F	(Black)	--
	25	F	(Black)	--
Wallace, Peter R.	28	M	Black Smith	NC
Martha	19	F		TN
William M.	2	M		TN
Willson, George E.	22	M	Black Smith	TN
Slave	11	F	(Black)	--
Straughn, J. O.	37	M	C.D.C.C.C.	NC
Nancy E.	32	F		NC
E. C.	10	F		TN
Mary J.	4	F		TX
Martha A.	3/12	F		TX
Lassenbee, L. W.	30	M	Carpenter	IL
M. J.	27	F		AR
A.	3	F		TX
Jno. S.	6/12	M		TX
Wagoner, B.	35	M	Carpenter	TN
Gilmon, Charles	22	M	Carpenter	NY
Boswell, H. M.	30	M	Carpenter	TN
Stuart, J. F.	40	M	C.C.C.C.	KY
A.	29	F		TN
D. A.	8	M		MO
A. R.	2	M		TX
G. B.	1	M		TX
Bogart, Sam	52	M	Farmer	TN
R.	51	F		TN
M. E.	15	F		MO
Hale, Richard	25	M	Farmer	TN
Slave	4	F	(Black)	--
Petty, Jonathan	32	M	Farmer	TN
O.	25	F		??
Hubard	12	M		AR
Elizabeth	10	F		AR
M.	7	F		AR
Nathan	2	M		AR
Jonathan	4/12	M		TX
Petty, Joel W.	20	M	Farmer	TN
Drurinda	20	F		MO
Jacob	3/12	M		TX
Carver, Isaac	43	M	Farmer	TN
Mary Ann	33	F		TN
P.	12	F		MO
Eliza J.	7	F		MO
Ephana	5	F		MO
Elizabeth	2	F		MO
Nancy M.	3/12	F		TX
Wilmith, J. B.	42	M	Farmer	NC
Nancy	42	F		TN
M. W.	20	M	Farmer	TN
Martha	18	F		TN
R. M.	16	F		AR
Jas. R.	15	M		AR
Jos. B.	13	M		AR
W. C.	11	M		AR
H. F.	9	M		AR
Nancy Ann	8	F		AR
Jno. F.	7	M		AR
A. J.	5	M		AR
C. M.	2	M		TX
Whilley, E.	34	M	Farmer	TN
L.	34	F		TN
Sarah A.	8	F		AR
M. A.	6	F		AR
H. S.	5	F		AR
E.	3	M		AR
E.	11/12	F		TX
Fitzhugh, Robert	33	M	Sheriff	KY
C.	22	F		MO
M. A.	3	F		TX

(continued)

Name	Age	Sex	Occupation	Birthplace
Fitzhugh, William C.	5/12	M		TX
Franklin, J. W.	20	M	Farmer	TN
Clark, Jos.	16	M		??

City of McKinney

Name	Age	Sex	Occupation	Birthplace
McReynolds, J. M.	30	M	Farmer	TN
F. M.	7	F		TN
C. J.	5	F		TN
Samuel C.	2	M		TN
Standefer, Sarah	50	F		VA
Mary Ann L.	12	F		AR
Turner, Robert C.	15	M		AR
Reed, Jane	79	F		VA
White, George	29	M	Surveyor	MA
Scott, George B.	24	M	Lawyer	KY

End of City of McKinney

Name	Age	Sex	Occupation	Birthplace
Wilson, P.	45	M	Farmer	TN
Mary J.	22	F		TN
Sarah A.	20	F		TN
Howse, Jane	25	F		TN
Robert	8	M		TN
Sarah A.	6	F		TN
Foster, David C.	42	M	Farmer	VA
Susan	45	F		KY
Sarah	14	F		MO
Jos. H.	12	M		MO
James H.	9	M		MO
S. A.	7	F		MO
Hicks, Thomas	19	M	Farmer	TN
Bradley, E.	63	M	Farmer	NC
Nancy	55	F		TN
Thomas ?.	26	M	Constable	MO
Jas. S.	21	M	Farmer	MO
D. S.	17	M	Farmer	MO
Lovelady, Jas.	34	M	Farmer	TN
Elizabeth	33	F		MO
William A.	12	M		MO
Thomas H.	10	M		MO
Jno. L.	7	M		MO
M. C.	5	F		MO
M.	3	M		TX
G. A.	4/12	F		TX
Smith, Jas.	30	M	Farmer	TN
Samuel	25	M	Teacher	TN
Pratt, Z.	50	M	Stone Mason	MA
M.	28	F		TN
Davis, William	38	M	Trader	AR
M.	21	F		TN
N. H.	1	F		TX
Jas.	18	M	Doing nothing	AR
E.	22	F		TN
M. A.	1	F		TX
Tucker, A. J.	24	M	Farmer	MO
Nancy Ann	23	F		TN
E. A.	4/12	F		TX
Campbell, S. R.	38	M	Lawyer	TN
J. A.	39	F		KY
C. J.	13	F		MO
T. D.	10	M		MO
Sam	8	M		MO
Jas. R.	3	M		TX
Rice, William	49	M	Farmer	VA
A.	45	F		SC
Jno.	18	M	Farmer	TN
Margaret	15	F		TN
Alex	13	M		AR
E.	11	F		AR
Julia A.	9	F		AR
William	7	M		AR
M. E.	4	F		TX
C. W. J. P.	2	F		TX
Franklin, D. J.	28	M	Farmer	TN
R. J.	19	F		TN

(continued)

Name	Age	Sex	Occupation	Born
Franklin, P. B.	8	M		AR
Dawser, F.	30	M	Farmer	IN
Mary A.	9	F		IN
George	2	M		TX
Davidson, L. D.	48	M	Farmer	VA
J.	41	F		TN
M. E.	15	F		MO
M. C.	13	F		TN
J. M.	8	F		TN
Wilson, J.	33	M	Farmer	TN
E.	33	F		TN
K. G.	13	M		MO
William H.	11	M		MO
J. N.	9	M		MO
F. M.	5	M		TX
George W.	1	M		TX
Wilson, L.	24	M	Farmer	TN
A. M.	17	F		PA
Naugh, Jacob J.	47	M		PA
Benjamin	19	M	Farmer	PA
Queen, Samuel	30	M	Farmer	TN
Mary	18	F		MO
E. J.	3/12	F		TX
Couldwell, Hezekiah	52	M	Farmer	NC
Mary	49	F		NC
Nancy	18	F		TN
Jas. M.	16	M		AR
Josh	14	M		AR
Martha A.	11	F		AR
H.	8	M		AR
Hines, S.	35	M	Farmer	NC
M.	34	F		TN
Elizabeth	13	F		TN
S. M.	12	F		TX
A. B.	7	M		TX
M. E.	5	F		TX
Martha A.	3	F		TX
S. J.	4/12	M		TX
Snow, F.	26	M	Farmer	TN
M.	22	F		AR
Howard, David	50	M	Farmer	TN
Jane	43	F		KY
Jonathan	22	M		MO
L. G.	8	F		MO
Martha A.	5	F		TX
Jacob	1	M		TX
Bruce, Thomas	39	M	Farmer	TN
J.	21	F		TN
Jno. M.	4	M		AR
Mary E.	2	F		TX
Martha J.	2/12	F		TX
Hicks, Sarah	50	F		NC
Alfred	24	M	Farmer	NC
William R.	23	M	Farmer	NC
Jesse	19	M	Farmer	NC
Henry	13	M		TN
M.	9	M		TN
Mahala	8	F		TN
Thomas	19	M		NC
Blackwell, Benjamin E.	51	M	School Teacher	VA
R. S.	39	F		VA
W. O.	16	M	Farmer	TN
Jos. L.	14	M		TN
A. C.	11	M		TN
Joel H.	6	M		TN
R. A.	4	F		TN
E. J.	1	F		TX
Herron, Martha	45	F		TN
William H.	26	M	Farmer	IL
Rebecca	18	F		TN
Samuel	16	M		TN

(continued)

Name	Age	Sex	Occupation	Born
Myers, M.	8	M		MO
Routh, Hugh C.	37	M	Farmer	TN
Isham	9	M		MO
Jonathan	6	M		MO
Isaac	5	M		MO
Mary E.	1	F		TX
Routh, L.	33	M	Farmer	TN
V.	34	F		VA
E.	10	M		MO
E.	5	F		MO
D. P.	3	F		TX
Horn, Jeremiah	56	M	E.M.S.Preacher	TN
Cynthia	36	F		GA
Jas. ?.	19	M	Farmer	GA
J. C.	17	M		TN
Ruth E.	4	F		TX
C. C.	6/12	F		TX
Ledbetter, Jno. D.	15	M		AR
A.	13	F		AR
Sarah E.	11	F		AR
Horn, George	24	M	Farmer	GA
Stallcup, Thomas	34	M	Farmer	TN
E.	28	F		AR
William M.	11	M		AR
Thomas B.	10	M		AR
George A.	8	M		AR
S. J.	5	F		TX
Jas. F.	2	M		TX
Chandler, Ruhama	80	F		SC
Dotson, M.	20	F		AR
Ashlock, Me-ady	48	M	Farmer	TN
Sarah	37	F		KY
F. M.	13	M		IL
Elizabeth	9	F		IL
M. S.	8	M		IL
E. C.	6	F		IL
A.	4	F		IL
Sarah J.	2	F		TX
McGarrah, Leo	42	M	Farmer	KY
Sarah	35	F		TN
Elizabeth	16	F		AR
M.	14	F		AR
Jas.	18	M		AR
H.	11	F		AR
Manning, John	26	M	Farmer	TN
Martha A.	20	F		AR
Wilmuth, F. C.	44	M	Farmer	NC
A.	22	F		OH
Jno. G.	15	M		TN
Mary A.	11	F		TN
Elizabeth	9	F		AR
Nancy	3	F		TX
F.	1	F		TX
McCoy, E. D.	30	M	Farmer	TN
Sarah	32	F		NC
E.	1	F		TX
Harris, H. W.	8	M		TN
Jas. W.	7	M		TN
George F.	5	M		TN
Philips, Jonathan	55	M	United B. Preacher	NC
Rebecca	54	F		TN
George	23	M	Farmer	TN
M.	22	F		TN
Caleb	18	M	Farmer	TN
William	15	M	Farmer	TN
C.	14	F		TN
Reed, Jas. S.	23	M	Teamster	TN
Sarah J.	20	F		TN
Wilmuth, Jas. A.	18	M	Teamster	TN
Martin, Charles M.	56	M	Farmer	VA
Mariah	54	F		VA
Jno. E.	21	M	Farmer	TN
William B.	21	M	Farmer	TN

(continued)

COLLIN COUNTY, TEXAS

Martin, A.	20	M		TN
Peter	14	M		TN
Malinda	50	F		VA
White, Virginia T.	35	F		KY
J. B.	16	M	Farmer	TN
S. M.	12	M		TN
V. A.	10	F		AR
Jno. H.	8	M		TX
S. D.	5	M		TX
L. S.	40	F		VA
B. H.	51	M	Lawyer	VA
Slave	45	F	(Black)	--
Herring, Isaac	32	M	Farmer	NC
N.	24	F		TN
Jos.	10	M		IL
Daniel	7	M		IL
Martha J.	4	F		TX
William F.	12	M		TX
Fanny	66	F		NC
Phillips, Thomas	30	M	Farmer	TN
Jno.	27	M	(Idiot)	TN
Slave	24	F	(Black)	--
Roberts, Jas. T.	45	M	Farmer	KY
Catharine	38	F		TN
Zunath(?)	17	F		MO
Peter E.	16	M	Farmer	MO
Nancy E.	13	F		MO
B. L.	12	F		MO
Mary C.	4	F		TX
Fisher, Peter	42	M	Farmer	PA
Elizabeth	29	F		TN
N. B.	10	M		TN
J. E.	9	F		TN
E. Jane	8	F		TN
P. S.	5	F		TN
Jose S.	2	M		TX
Slaves	13	M	(Black)	--
	14	M	(Black)	--
	16	F	(Black)	--
	16	F	(Black)	--
	18	M	(Black)	--
Ortean, Henry	32	M	Farmer	TN
Mary Ann	23	F		KY
W. J.	4	M		IL
Martha A.	3	F		IL
Starks, Hiram	40	M	Farmer	TN
Jane	31	F		TN
Elijah H.	7	M		IL
Jas. M.	4	M		IL
Julia A.	1	F		IL
Thomas	23	M	Farmer	IL
Kirby, Jno. A.	32	M	Farmer	TN
M. R.	32	F		KY
William D.	12	M		MO
James G.	9	M		MO
T. E.	3	F		TX
Sparks, Benjamin	33	M	Farmer	IN
Amanda	28	F		TN
William	13	M		IN
Martha J.	10	F		MO
F. H.	7	F		MO
Sarah	4	F		MO
James M.	2	M		TX
Isaac	3/12	M		TX
Gray, George	23	M	Farmer	VA
Allenberry, Allen	26	M	Farmer	KY
Mary J.	22	F		TN
Thomas J.	2	M		TX
Sarah P.	1/12	F		TX
Jos.	18	M	Farmer	KY
West, Aaron	36	M	Farmer	IL
L.	33	F		TN
(continued)				
West, Sarah J.	11	F		AR
Jas. W.	9	M		AR
R. E.	7	F		AR
W. D.	4	M		TX
M. L.	2	F		TX
Goss, Jno. M.	32	M	Farmer	TN
Sarah S.	20	F		TN
D. R.	2	M		TX
Carter, Rachel	12	F		TN
Fisher, Caroline	4	F		TX
Hayes, H. E.	31	M	Farmer	AL
Duprey, M. C.	33	M	Farmer	TN
Mary	28	F		TN
Miles L.	8	M		TN
R.	5	M		AR
E. J.	6	F		AR
Slave	18	F	(Black)	--
Patterson, Robert	49	M	Farmer	TN
Robert H.	11	M		AR
William W.	9	M		AR
Cloud, E. M. S.	11	F		AR
Slaves	8/12	F	(Black)	--
	2	F	(Black)	--
	5	M	(Black)	--
	38	F	(Black)	--
Gotcher, Joshua	22	M	Farmer	MO
L.	25	F		AR
Gotcher, William	42	M	Farmer	TN
Mary	36	F		TN
Joseph	19	M	Farmer	AL
Julia A.	17	F		MO
William A.	14	M		MO
Jno.	11	M		MO
Caroline	8	F		MO
Jos.	5	M		TX
M. A.	2	F		TX
Hoover, Jno.	39	M	Farmer	TN
A.	35	F		TN
T. M.	16	M	Farmer	MO
H. H.	15	M		MO
N. E.	13	F		MO
M. C.	11	F		MO
William T.	9	M		MO
Jas. M.	5	M		TX
Gotcher, Mary	73	F		VA
Gotcher, Hugh B.	37	M	Farmer	TN
M.	35	F		AL
Henry	16	M	Farmer	MO
Sarah	14	F		MO
James A.	8	M		MO
L.	5	F		TX
Mary	2	F		TX
Yeory, Walter	29	M	Farmer	TN
Margaret	17	F		IL
Jas. K.	5	M		TX
Mary E.	10/12	F		TX
Yeory, David	25	M	Farmer	TN
M. J.	20	F		TN
C. J.	2	F		TN
Yeory, J. W.	23	M	Farmer	TN
M. J.	22	F		TN
C.	2	F		TX
Harrick, Martin	30	M	Farmer	IL
M.	28	F		TN
Jno.	7	M		TX
Mary Ann	6	F		TX
Nancy R.	5	F		TX
A.	4	F		TX
Slave	19	M	(Black)	--
Yeory, John	49	M	farmer	VA
Mary	48	F		TN
K.	17	F		AR
John	13	M		AR
(continued)				

Name	Age	Sex	Occupation	Birthplace
Yeory, John	13	M		AR
Elizabeth	11	F		AR
A.	9	F		TX
Slaves	13	M	(Black)	--
	17	F	(Black)	--
Woody, Hugh	28	M	Farmer	TN
P.	26	F		TN
Sarah J.	9	F		TN
Susanna	6	F		TN
Nancy	3	F		TN
Jas.	1	M		TX
McGarrah, John	45	M	Farmer	??
Mary	46	F		??
Randolph	17	M	Farmer	AR
S. M.	15	M	Farmer	AR
Jos. C.	12	M		AR
Mary	10	F		AR
Rankin, M.	17	F		TN
Parsons, Jas. W.	37	M	Farmer	TN
Catharine	29	F		KY
E.	12	F		KY
A.	9	F		KY
Wood, Alfred	50	M	Farmer	TN
Anna	38	F		OH
Abram	22	M		IL
William	16	M		IL
Martin ?.	10	M		IL
Jno. T.	8	M		IL
David M.	13	M		IL
Jonathan	6	M		IL
Nancy A.	3	F		IL
Whisenant, Robert	39	M	Farmer	GA
M.	36	F		TN
Mary E.	17	F		AR
Hugh	15	M		MO
Nancy A.	9	F		MO
Jno.	7	M		MO
Robert B.	6	F(M)		MO
A.	4	F		TX
M.	1	F		TX
Hale, A.	54	M	Farmer	TN
H.	32	F		NC
V. H.	20	F		AL
E. C.	13	F		AL
Jno.	17	M	Farmer	AL
David	9	M		TN
Jas. W.	4/12	M		TX
Maxwell, J. W.	33	M	Farmer	AL
Elizabeth	26	F		TN
Malana	9	F		AR
F. D.	8	M		AR
Sachse, William	29	M	Farmer	PRU
E.	33	F		TN
Mary J.	13	F		MO
William	11	M		MO
Thomas B.	4	M		TX
Jos.	8/12	M		TX
Scott, Mary	43	F		NC
S. A. E.	17	F		TN
M. F.	13	F		TN
E. E.	12	M		IL
McCalles, Henry	56	M	Black Smith	SC
Mary	54	F		PA
Mary A.	19	F		TN
F.	20	M	Farmer	AL
Jno.	19	M	Farmer	AL
Nancy	16	F		MO
Douglass, Jane	46	F		TN
Nancy	10	F		MO
Jos. M.	7	M		MO
Mary A.	6	F		MO
M.	4	M		MO
Walker, M.	21	M	Doing nothing	TN

Name	Age	Sex	Occupation	Birthplace
Vance, Thomas	65	M	Carpenter	GA
R.	56	F		MA
F. J.	25	M	Surveyor	MO
P.	19	F		TN
L. S.	9/12	M		TX
Vance, Jas. W.	21	M	Farmer	MO
Mary P.	17	F		TN
Mary A.	6/12	F		TX
Beverly, James	19	M	Farmer	TN
Beverly, William	43	M	Farmer	TN
Nancy	44	F		GA
C. C.	13	M		TN
G. M.	11	M		TN
A. J.	9	M		TN
William A.	7	M		AL
Thomas J.	5	M		IL
Turney, L.	38	M	Farmer	KY
Beck, Sanford	48	M	Farmer	TN
Mahala	38	F		IL
Manly	21	M	Farmer	IL
Jno.	13	M		IL
Elizabeth	9	F		IL
J. A.	7	F		IL
Margaret	3	F		TX
Matilda	6/12	F		TX
Ballard, Jesse	21	M	Farmer	IL
Tyler, Jas.	20	M	Farmer	??
Clepper, Jos.	45	M	Farmer	TN
Nancy	42	F		TN
Sam S.	21	M	Farmer	TN
Isaac	13	M		IL
W.	10	M		IL
W. D.	7	M		IL
A. J.	2	F		TX
Dye, Henry	20	M	Physician	VA
Beverly, Jno.	21	M	Farmer	TN
J.	18	F		MO
Jos. W.	1/12	M		TX
Witt, Hogan	26	M	Farmer	TN
S.	23	F		IL
Laura A.	1	F		TX
Blanford, Ann	13	F		IL
Baccus, Peter	32	M	Farmer	OH
Orlena	21	F		TN
B. S.	2	M		TX
M. E.	6/12	F		TX
Brown, Samuel H.	41	M	Carpenter	VA
Ann	33	F		KY
Isabella	15	F		KY
A.	12	M		KY
G.	11	M		TN
Samuel	9	M		TN
Mary E.	6	F		TN
Erwin	5	M		TN
Jno.	4	M		TX
C. C.	1	M		TX
Clark, Lancer	38	M	Farmer	TN
Eliza J.	22	F		KY
T.	16	M	Farmer	TN
M.	15	M		TN
Matilda	13	F		TN
A. C.	10	M		TN
Richard	8	M		TN
Elizabeth	6	F		TN
Slave	10	F	(Black)	--
Rogers, William	35	M	Farmer	TN
Frances	26	F		TN
Mary M.	9	F		TN
Nancy R.	7	F		TN
Sarah E.	5	F		TN
Thomas G.	3	M		IL
M. A.	8/12			TX
Rogers, Clayton	30	M	Farmer	TN
Elizabeth	25	F		TN

(continued)

COLLIN COUNTY, TEXAS

Name	Age	Sex	Occupation	Birthplace
Rogers, R.	8	M		TN
Mary J.	7	F		TN
Mathew	2	M		TX
Powell, William	22	M	Farmer	TN
Strong, Martin	42	M		VA
M.	38	F		TN
Jno.	15	M		MO
F.	13	M		MO
H.	11	M		MO
Benjamin	9	M		MO
Levi	7	M		MO
Nancy	5	F		MO
Mary	2	F		MO

COLORADO COUNTY, TEXAS

Name	Age	Sex	Occupation	Birthplace
Beeson, Abel	36	M	Farmer	TN
Doloras	30	F		MEX
Nessey	13	F		TX
Ann	11	F		TX
Benjamin (twin)	5	M		TX
Collins (twin)	5	M		TX
Winningham	3	M		TX
Crawford, William	42	M	Day Laborer	TN
Sarah	28	F		AL
Jesse (twin)	11	M		TX
Georgina (twin)	11	F		TX
Rebecca	7	F		TX
William	5	M		TX
Martha	4	F		TX
Nancy	2	F		TX
Pace, Dempsy	28	M	Grazier	TN
Elizabeth	24	F		KY
Trane	3	M		TX
Robert	2	M		TX
Laura	2/12	F		TX
Beeson, Leander	33	M	Grazier	TN
Rebecca	27	F		PA
Leander	10	M		TX
Nelson, William	26	M		TN
Ramsey, M. D.	40	M	Farmer	TN
Margaret	25	F		KY
Alexander	4	M		TX
Sarah	1	F		TX
Montgomery, James L(S).	62	M	Farmer	TN
Frances	56	F		TN
William	26	M		MS
John	19	M		MS
Salmons, G. W.	28	M	Farmer	KY
Herbert, C. C.	36	M	Farmer	VA
Mary	35	F		AL
Sarah	11	F		MS
William	8	M		MS
Joseph	4	M		TX
Mary	2	F		TX
Reils(?), John	8	M		TX
Mayes, John	28	M	Grazier	TN
Winfree, Charles	48	M	Mechanic	NC
Nancy	44	F		NC
Mary	21	F		TN
Adelia	16	F		TN
John	11	M		TN
Thomas	7	M		TX
Jack	2	M		TX
Robert	2	M		TX
David, William	49	M	Farmer	NC
Elizabeth	36	F		NC
Caroline	16	F		NC
William	14	M		NC
John	11	M		TN
Laura Anne	8	F		TN
Mary	6	F		TX
Adeline	1	F		TX

Name	Age	Sex	Occupation	Birthplace
Payne, Zachariah	54	M	Farmer	TN
Nancy	53	F		TN
Don Fernando	26	M	Merchant	TN
Josiah	24	M	Farmer	TN
Daniel	19	M	Farmer	TN
Neal, William H.	26	M	Wild Horse Breaker	TN
Windal, Peter	27	M	Farmer	TN
Rivers, Robert J.	44	M	Attorney at Law	VA
Susan	33	F		TN
George	19	M	Ranger	TN
Amanda	17	F		TN
Jane	11	F		TN
Richard	8	M		TN
Thomas	6	M		TN
Mildred	2	F		TX
Joines, Caleb	46	M	Farmer	SC
Lucintha	40	F		SC
Jonathan	17	M	Farmer	TN
Edmond	15	M	Farmer	TN
John	13	M		TN
Mayes, Joshua	13	M		TN
Brown, John D.	26	M	Farmer	KY
Mary Anne	17	F		TN
Pearcie	1	M		TX
Crenshaw, O. B.	31	M	Farmer	TN
Mary Anne	19	F		TN
Wilson, J. C.	34	M	Farmer	NC
Sarah	26	F		AL
John	9	M		TN
Elizabeth	5	F		TX
William	2	M		TX
Alexander, Leman	34	M	Farmer	PA
Jane	25	F		TN
William	7	M		GA
Edwin	5	M		TX
Amos	2	M		TX
Izard, Isabella	55	F		TN
Joseph	24	M	Farmer	TN
Nancy	22	F		TN
William	19	M		TN
Fitzgerald, William	63	M	Farmer	VA
Rebecca	57	F		SC
Alexander	28	M	Farmer	AL
Julia	13	F		TN
Daniel, James M.	26	M	Mechanic	MO
Amanda	22	F		TN
Muckleroy, Miche	42	M	Farmer	TN
Elizabeth	39	F		TN
James	18	M		TN
Martha	16	F		TN
Anne Eliza	5	F		TX
William	1	M		TX
Muckleroy, Charles	21	M	Farmer	TN
Mathews, Thomas	18	M	Farmer	NC
Gilbert, Thomas Z.	38	M	Farmer	LA
Mary	35	F		LA
Eliza	8	F		TX
McGowan, W. C.	23	M	Physician	TN
Waddel, Richard	35	M	Farmer	MS
Narcissa	37	F		TN
Jane	15	F		TX
Mary	11	F		TX
Anne	7	F		TX
Martha	6	F		TX
Joseph	4	M		TX
Susan	2/12	F		TX
Curry, Jane	75	F		TN
Gross, Christian	14	M		GER
Folts, A. J.	30	M	Farmer	NC
Mary	21	F		TN
Mary	3	F		TN
Martha	1	F		TX

COLORADO COUNTY, TEXAS

Name	Age	Sex	Occupation	Birthplace
Wright, Elija	54	M	Farmer	TN
Lucy	52	F		KY
Hiram	21	M	Farmer	TN
Mary	18	F		TN
Caroll	17	M	Farmer	TN
Hatch, George C.	50	M	Farmer	NC
Mary	47	F		NC
John	22	M		NC
James	17	M	Farmer	NC
Lemuel	15	M	Farmer	TN
Amos	13	M		TN
William	11	M		TN
Henry	9	M		TX
Seal, James	34	M	Farmer	TN
Mary	33	F		GA
Martha	10	F		TX
Leonidas	9	M		TX
Ophelia	4	F		TX
Virginia	2	F		TX
Cooper, Dillard	35	M	Farmer	SC
Lucinda	34	F		SC
Jasper	16	M	Farmer	AL
Newton	13	M		TN
Adeline	11	F		TX
Elizabeth	3	F		TX
California	1	F		TX
Toliver, John	42	M	Hotel Keeper	TN
Lavinia	42	F		KY
Henry	14	M		AL
Benjamin	10	M		TX
James	6	M		TX
John	2	M		TX
Haughton, Virginia	13	F		TX
Smith, George W.	26	M	Attorney at Law	KY
Roman, Jackson	24	M		TN
Spence, James	30	M		AL
Hawkins, J. M.	30	M		VA
McMillan, James	30	M	Wagoner	AL
Eliza Anne	19	F		TN
Williamson	2	M		TX
McMillan, John	20	M	Wagoner	AL
Elvira	20	F		TN
Harmon, M. D.	28	M	Farmer	TN
Cynthia	32	F		AL
Thomas	11	M		MS
Arebella	5	F		TX
Mary	2	F		TX
Rize, Darcus	30	F	Seamstress	GA
Wilson	11	M		GA
Mackey, John	30	M	Merchant	TN
Eberley	23	F		KY
Julia	2	F		TX
Harris, T. W.	29	M	Physician	VA
Caroline	25	F		TN
Jonathan	2	M		TN
Morgan, R. G.	44	M	Mechanic	NC
Lucy	30	F		KY
Robert	13	M		TN
Sarah	11	F		TN
Daniel	2	M		TX
Bruton, Elizabeth	40	F		SC
Reuben	20	M		TN
Willie	18	M		TN
Rebecca	16	F		TN
Samuel	14	M		MS
Silas	12	M		TX
George	10	M		TX
Elizabeth	6	F		TX
Naill, Jane	29	F		NC
Samuel	16	M		TN
Mary	13	F		TN

(continued)

Name	Age	Sex	Occupation	Birthplace
Naill, Jane	7	F		TX
William	2	M		TX
Windrow, C.	26	M	County Court Clerk	TN
Sarah Anne	17	F		TN
Henry	6/12	M		TX
Coffee, L. M.	42	M	Laborer	KY
Mary	35	F		TN
Mansil	11	M		AL
Araminta	9	F		AL
William	6	M		TX
Cleveland	4	M		TX
Robert	2	M		TX

COMAL COUNTY, TEXAS

Comal Town

Name	Age	Sex	Occupation	Birthplace
Speva, Andrew	49	M	Farmer	IL
Margaret	36	F		TN
James	16	M	Laborer	IL
Stephen	14	M		MO
Eliza	12	F		IA
Jasper	4	M		TX
Mary Anne	1	F		TX

Town of New Bronsfels

Name	Age	Sex	Occupation	Birthplace
Wakeman, Urah	42	M	Farmer	CT
Elizabeth	36	F		CT
Hill, Elen (Hill)	16	F		TN
Andrews, Louisa C.	23	F		CT
Walter A.	35	M	Merchant	CT
Hargomain, Charlotte	15	F		GER
Williams, William	36	M	Carpenter	NH
Millett, Samuel	49	M	Hotel Keeper	ME
Ementine	34	F		TN
Eugene B.	13	M		TX
Mary	11	F		TX
Leonidas (twin)	9	M		TX
Alansa (twin)	9	F		TX
Almyra	6	F		TX
Hiram	4	M		TX
Lora	2	F		TX
Gossett, James L.	40	M	Farmer	IL
Precilla	37	F		NC
Elijah F.	20	M	Farmer	TN
William	19	M		TN
Mary	18	F		AR
John	17	M		TX
Henry	15	M		TX
Ellen	10	F		TX
Jefferson	9	M		TX
Jackson	7	M		TX
Mary	5	F		TX
Handy	1	M		TX

The Mountains

Name	Age	Sex	Occupation	Birthplace
Philips, John	40	M	Carpenter	BOH
Bas----	32	F		GER
Joseph	10	M		GER
Julian	6	M		TX
Antone	1	M		TX
Wells, William	60	M	Farmer	TN

Horton Town

Name	Age	Sex	Occupation	Birthplace
Crawford, Henry	39	M	Farmer	TN
Ann B.	27	F		IRE
John W.	13	M		TN
Felix	7	M		TX
Jane	2	F		TX
Elizabeth	6/12	F		TX
Wilson, James	66	F(M)		IRE
Crenshaw, Elizabeth	64	F		NC
Strickland, M. D.	28	M	Carpenter	NC

COOKE COUNTY, TEXAS

Name	Age	Sex	Occupation	Birthplace
Montague, Daniel	52	M	Farmer	MA

(continued)

COOKE COUNTY, TEXAS

Name	Age	Sex	Occupation	Birthplace
Montague, Jane	30	F		VA
Elizabeth	14	F		LA
Nancy	11	F		TX
Daniel R.	9	M		TX
Broyle, N.	47	M	Carpenter	TN
Twitty, W. C.	28	M	Farmer	KY
C.	3	F		TX
Boutwell, Alexander	25	M	Farmer	AR
A.	24	F		TN
William R.	4	M		TX
Martha A.	3/12	F		TX
Brown, S. D.	25	M	Farmer	TN
Chadwell, Jno.	26	M	Farmer	TN
Mary	21	F		NC
James P.	3	M		TX
George M.	6/12	M		TX
Underwood, E.	27	M	Farmer	NY
M.	20	F		TN
C.	3	M		TX
F.	50	F		CT
William	12	M		MO
L.	9	M		MO
L.	15	F		IL
Teal, William	28	M	Farmer	TN
F.	18	F		IL
Whorley, Jos.	47	M	Farmer	VA
S.	43	F		TN
T. P.	21	M	Farmer	IN
J. H.	18	M	Farmer	IN
J.	15	M		IN
M. A.	14	F		IN
A.	12	M		IN
S. E.	8	F		IN
William	6	M		IN
Sadler, Hiram	42	M	Farmer	TN
Cox, S.	22	M	Farmer	KY
Sarah Ann	17	F		TN
Brown, William C.	55	M	Farmer	TN
Margaret	32	F		VA
Ann	18	F		TN
Elisha	12	M		TN
Panelope	3	F		TX
Almira	9	F		TN
Elbert S.	2/12	M		TX
Demarquis, John	25	M	Farmer	TN
Malinda	21	F		MO
Mary	1	F		TX
Lawson, Jacob	69	M	Farmer	VA
Ruthy	35	F		VA
Berry	22	M	Farmer	TN
Millers	19	M	Farmer	TN
Malinda	40	F		VA
S(L).	13	F		TN
Jonathan B.	8	M		TN
Dixon, James C.	52	M	Farmer	NC
Elizabeth	53	F		VA
James M.	25	M	Farmer	NC
Chadwell, C.	25	M	Farmer	TN
Dixon, T. F.	19	M		NC
B. F.	15	M		IN
Southerland, Amanda	8	F		MO
Lee, L. C.	14	M		TN
Kuykendall, William	37	M	Farmer	TN
Mahala	37	F		TN
Nancy	14	F		TN
John	12	M		MS
Polly	9	F		IL
Abraham	7	M		IL
Jos.	5	M		MO
L.	2	F		MO
McElroy, Jno. C. (continued)	28	M	Farmer	TN
McElroy, Lucy Ann	25	F		TN
R.	7	M		MO
S. L.	5	M		MO
Eubanks, Mary	6	F		AL
Clark, Mary E.	31	F		TN
B. M.	9	M		MO
Chandler, E. E.	6	F		MO
Clark, J. G.	2	M		TX
Jno. M.	2	M		TX
Carpenter, B. F.	35	M	Farmer	TN
Matilda	28	F		NY
P.	10	F		MO
L.	8	F		MO
Sarah	6	F		TX
A.	3	F		TX
Lewis	2	M		TX
Spray, E.	11	M		OH
William	9	M		MO
Mathews, A.	59	M	Farmer	SC
Mary	45	F		TN
Joseph	20	M	Farmer	MO
Mary	14	F		MO
J. M.	8	M		MO
Lucinda	6	F		MO
A.	24	M	Farmer	AR
D. W.	23	M	Farmer	AR
Martin, James	40	M	Farmer	TN
J.	39	F		TN
William W.	20	M	Farmer	IL
M. J.	16	F		IL
A.	14	F		IL
Richard ?.	12	M		IL
W. J.	11	M		IL
Mary Ann	8	F		IL
James T.	6	M		IL
S. J.	4	F		WI
?.	1	F		TX
Carter, William B.	30	M	Farmer	TN
Rachel	29	F		MO
Jasper	7	M		MO
L.	3	M		MO
Carter, D. A.	25	M	Farmer	TN
A.	23	F		MO
E. P.	4	F		MO
W. B.	2	M		MO

DALLAS COUNTY, TEXAS

Name	Age	Sex	Occupation	Birthplace
Jenkins, William	37	M	Farmer	TN
S. A.	32	F		TN
Mary A.	8	F		AR
John T.	5	M		AR
Margaret E.	4	F		TX
Hanah E.	2	F		TX
Barker, Joshua	29	M	Farmer	KY
Sarah	24	F		NC
M. E.	1	F		TN
Cochran, William	43	M	Farmer	SC
Nancy J.	32	F		NC
J. H.	12	M		TN
A. M.	11	M		TN
William P.	9	M		MO
James	3	M		TX
Martha A.	1	F		TX
Hunter, B. J.	53	M	Farmer	NC
Elizabeth	53	F		NC
Leonard	29	M	Farmer	TN
Hariet	22	F		IA
William L.	3	M		IL
Willson, C. ?.	17	M	(Idiot)	KY
Jackson, James E.	24	M	Farmer	TN
Dianah J.	19	F		VA

Name	Age	Sex	Occupation	Birthplace
Jackson, A. S.	50	M	Farmer	TN
Levicy	45	F		GA
James L.	16	M		TN
John	13	M		TN
Nancy A.	7	F		TN
M----	6	M		TN
Harison	4	M		TN
Highs, William	43	M	Farmer	TN
Jane	42	F		TN
Elizabeth	14	F		IL
G. W.	13	M		IL
William A.	11	M		IL
A. Jackson	6	M		IL
S. L.	1	M		TX
Crownover, Benjamin	55	M	Farmer	SC
Nancy	51	F		TN
Rebecca	25	F		TX
Elizabeth	17	F		AR
Benjamin	15	M		AR
Lavina	11	F		TX
S. A.	6	F		TX
Casey, John	37	M	Farmer	TN
Sarah	28	F		VA
J. W.	11	M		AR
S. A.	3	F		TX
F. R.	2/12	F		TX
Langley, John	38	M	Farmer	TN
S. A.	26	F		OH
M. J.	8	F		MO
Elizabeth	6	F		MO
John	5	M		TX
Rebecca	3	F		TX
David	1	M		TX
Turner, J. C.	6	M		KY
Keen, John W.	24	M	Farmer	TN
Nancy	23	F		VA
Turner, G. A.	10	M		KY
McCollough, Robert	33	M	Farmer	TN
Isabel	32	F		IL
John	9	M		MO
Mary A.	7	F		MO
O. J.	4	F		TX
Martha A.	2	F		TX
Frost, Benjamin	49	M	Farmer	TN
Catharine	29	F		AL
John	27	M	Farmer	AL
Parlee	20	F	(Idiot)	AL
Matilda	18	F		AL
Martha A.	16	F		AL
Benjamin	14	M		AL
Lucrecy	12	F		AL
John	11	M		MS
Reagor, Jacob	34	M	Farmer	TN
Julia A.	29	F		AL
Catharine	10	F		MS
Margaret	9	F		MS
Benjamin F.	7	M		MS
John F.	6	M		MS
Mary P.	4	F		MS
Lurinda V.	2	F		TX
Jas. D.	4/12	M		TX
Keen, Abner	50	M	Farmer	VA
Susan	45	F		TN
A. M.	21	M	Surveyor	IA
Elvira L.	19	F		IA
Lavina A.	16	F		IA
Norris W.	12	M		IA
Milton F.	10	M		IA
Silas E.	7	M		IA
Keen, William H.	30	M	Farmer	TN
Susanna	28	F		IA
Emily L.	8	F		IA
Newton A.	6	M		IA
(continued)				
Keen, Jacob M.	4	M		TX
Samuel A.	1/12	M		TX
Marly, Mary	18	F		PA
Jackson, John	52	M	Farmer	TN
Eliza	47	F		TN
Andrew S.	26	M	Farmer	TN
Mary J.	22	F		TN
Nancy L.	16	F		TN
John ?.	14	M		TN
Thomas J.	9	M		MO
Hannah S(L).	7	F		MO
Willson, A. B.	27	M	Farmer	TN
Alcy J.	19	F		TN
Carpenter, Alcy	53	F		NC
Susan	16	F		IL
Leonard B.	10	M		AR
Hiland, Jacob	62	M	Saddle Maker	VA
Horton, John	55	M	Farmer	VA
Elizabeth M.	22	F		TN
Ramsey, Samuel	37	M	Farmer	TN
Salinday	29	F		MO
William	13	M		MO
Elizabeth	11	F		MO
John	9	M		MO
Isaac	7	M		MO
Mary	4	F		TX
James	2	M		TX
Elliott, T. Marion	23	M		TN
Martha J.	15	F		MO
McDowell, Thomas J.	23	M	Farmer	KY
John	10	M	Millwright	TN
Sarah	49	F		??
F. M.	17	M	Farmer	MO
Biffle, Goldman	53	M		NC
Elizabeth	43	F		NC
Mandy	23	F		GA
Jas. M.	22	M	Farmer	GA
Willson	17	M	Farmer	GA
Manerva	15	F		GA
Virginia	12	F		TN
M----	10	F		TN
Barkly M.	8	M		TN
Armstrong, Thomas B.	27	M	Laborer	GA
Ball, James	20	M	Farmer	TN
Sarah C.	20	F		TN
J. Albert	10/12	M		TN
Sargeant, H. F.	30	M	Farmer	NC
Tabitha	25	F		TN
Elizabeth J.	2	F		TX
William	11/12	M		TX
Browder, Edward C.	25	M	Farmer	MO
Elizabeth	19	F		TN
Lucy J.	49	F		VA
Simpson, James A.	30	M	Farmer	TN
Caroline	32	F		TN
Elizabeth B.	9	F		TN
Nancy ?.	7	F		TN
Thomas P.	5	M		TN
William ?.	3	M		TN
Mary J.	5/12	F		TX
Hopkins, J. B.	40	M	Farmer	TN
Margaret	30	F		NC
Henry	17	M	Farmer	TN
John W.	11	M		MO
Miles	7	M		MO
Baird, G. W.	28	M	Tailor	TN
Mary E.	24	F		KY
G. R.	9/12	M		TX
Leonard, G. S. C.	25	M	Farmer	TN
Thomas Ella	15	F		KY

DALLAS COUNTY, TEXAS

Name	Age	Sex	Occupation	Birthplace
Barns, John T.	24	M	Farmer	TN
Mary ?.	23	F		MO
Sarah E.	2	F		MO
Montgomery, J. A.	25	M	Laborer	MO
John	23	M	Laborer	TN
Baird, Allen	30	M	Carpenter	TN
Dellah	28	F		TN
James H.	5	M		MO
John ?.	1	M		TX
Manning, Samuel	57	M	Farmer	NC
Nancy A.	59	F		TN
James H.	13	M		IL
Samuel	11	M		IL
Evans, John	24	M	Farmer	TN
Rebecca J.	17	F		KY
Chenawith, James F.	30	M	Farmer	OH
Matilda	28	F		TN
Casandra	3	F		MO
Mary J.	1	F		TX
Pullens, John L.	40	M	Farmer	TN
Daniel, Francis R.	28	M	Farmer	TN
Mary J.	22	F		VA
William E.	4	M		AL
Milton L.	2	M		AL
Francis A.	2/12	M		TX
Daniel, Jesse L.	30	M	Farmer	TN
Nancy E.	24	F		AL
John W. B.	4	M		AL
Nancy E.	9/12	F		MS
Downing, Robert C.	45	M	None	TN
Susanah	30	F		VA
Andrew J.	13	M		IL
Richard A.	7	M		TX
William H.	4	M		TX
George W.	4/12	M		TX
Holland, Thomas L.	23	M	Farmer	TN
Malinda	18	F		TN
Piles, W. W.	45	M	Farmer	KY
Patience	37	F		TN
John Thompson	16	M	Farmer	TN
Martha	13	F		TN
Emily	11	F		TN
Margaret	8	F		TN
Cely	6	F		TN
James	3	M		TN
John	17	M	Farmer	TN
Mary	15	F		TN
Ann E.	13	F		TN
Allen	8	M		TN
George	6	M		TN
James K.	2	M		TN
Moores, William H.	32	M	Farmer	TN
Easter D.	29	F		IL
James M.	10	M		IL
Samuel A.	8	M		IL
Lorenzo D.	7	M		IL
William P.	4	M		TX
Susan M.	6/12	F		TX
Clark, A. J.	33	M	Farmer	TN
Sarah	21	F		KY
Henry	3/12	M		TX
Petitt, Enoch	41	M	Farmer	TN
Elizabeth	38	F		SC
Newton	14	M		MO
Laura	12	F		MO
Louisa	11	F		MO
Margaret	8	F		MO
William	6	M		MO
Milton	4	M		MO
James R. P.	2	M		MO

Name	Age	Sex	Occupation	Birthplace
Byrd, James	37	M	Farmer	TN
Mary	36	F		TN
William	17	M	Farmer	MO
Martha	14	F		MO
David	12	M		MO
John W.	10	M		MO
Margaret	8	F		MO
Mary A.	6	F		TX
Elizabeth	4	F		TX
Young, John	55	M	Farmer	TN
Jane	42	F		KY
Nancy D.	11	F		MO
William J.	9	M		MO
Martha M.	7	F		MO
Rachel M.	4	F		TX
Wildum, Edward	45	M	Farmer	KY
Nancy	39	F		TN
James	19	M		MO
Rachel M.	15	F		MO
William P. W.	13	M		MO
Francis M.	10	M		MO
John S.	8	M		MO
Martha M.	5	F		MO
Edward	3	F		TX
Aaron D.	7/12	M		TX
Babbit, William	32	M	Plasterer	IA
Temperence	25	F		TN
David	5	M		MO
John	3	M		MO
Thomas, Alexander A.	25	M	Farmer	TN
Mary E.	21	F		TN
Biffle, John A.	28	M	Farmer	GA
Nancy J.	24	F		TN
Elizabeth	5	F		TN
Mary J.	3	F		TN
Harvy E.	5/12	M		TX
Driper, Thomas	20	M	Farmer	AR
Hansell, Ann	16	F		KY
Haphy, Henry	16	M	Farmer	GER
Armstrong, James	49	M	Farmer	NC
Mary	50	F		NC
Martha A.	23	F		TN
Susanah A.	18	F		TN
Nancy	16	F		TN
Sarah	7	F		AR
Barrett, James W.	14	M		TX
Roswell B.	6	M		AR
James, William	36	M	Farmer	VA
Jane	28	F		TN
Eliza	12	F		TN
Thomas	9	M		MO
John	8	M		MO
Emily	5	F		MO
William	1/12	M		TX
Ledbetter, Arthur	51	M	Farmer	TN
Elizabeth	27	F		KY
Lewis B.	19	M	Farmer	TN
Martha J.	15	F		TN
Thomas L.	13	M		TN
Arthur B.	5	M		TN
Parson, Nancy J.	3	F		TX
Sarah A.	2	F		TX
Stewart, William T.	25	M	Farmer	TN
Susan K.	22	F		MO
Mary M.	2	F		TX
Nancy J.	5/12	F		TX
Harwood, Virginia A.	9	F		MO
Phelps, Mary A.	3	F		TX
Lawrence, J. P.	35	M	Farmer	MD
Fanny	22	F		TN
Josephine	1	F		TX
Carver, Solomon	41	M	Farmer	OH
Ellen	30	F		AL
Icy B.	16	F		IL

(continued)

DALLAS COUNTY, TEXAS

Name	Age	Sex	Occupation	Birthplace
Carver, Morgan	14	M		IL
Jerilda	12	F		MO
Jesseffrona	8	F		MO
Willcox, James H.	10	M		MO
Parrline	8	F		MO
Johnson, Thomas	22	M	Farmer	TN
Carver, Albert	22	M	Farmer	IL
Mary	68	F		SC
Pound, B. O. C.	30	M	Saddletree Maker	KY
Louisa	26	F		TN
James T.	3	M		TX
Joseph H.	4/12	M		TX
Thomas, E. C.	27	M	Farmer	TN
Julia A.	20	F		MO
Ann E.	3	F		TX
John H.	1	M		TX
McCommas, S. B.	43	M	Grocer	TN
Mary A.	33	F		TN
Elizabeth	16	F		IL
William	12	M		IL
John	3	M		TX
Morris, Richard	22	M	Clerk	ENG
Harris, R. C.	23	M	Painter	??
Ayers, E. T.	29	M	Black Smith	TN
Nancy	29	F		KY
William H.	8	M		MO
John W.	6	M		MO
Robinson, John	35	M	Farmer	IA
Allen, Joseph	23	M	Farmer	TN
Jane	15	F		TN
Dogget, E. V.	20	M	Farmer	TN
Thomas, John	56	M	Farmer	TN
Hannah	54	F		VA
Sarah A.	15	F		MO
Eliza	12	F		MO
Houx, N. T.	2	M		TX
Wright, John W.	30	M	Farmer	TN
Sarah E.	21	F		TN
George T.	4	M		TX
John W.	2	M		TX
Howell, John	35	M	Farmer	TN
Parthena	40	F		VA
Sarah E.	13	F		MS
E. V.	10	M		MS
Jas. W.	7	M		MS
Margaret S.	6	F		MS
Abram H.	4	M		MS
Charles M.	1	M		TX
Selridge, M. K.	33	M	Farmer	TN
Matildah	31	F		KY
Hannah, Jas. M.	7	M		MO
Benjamin F.	4	M		TX
Louisa	1	F		TX
Buckles, William	34	M	Farmer	KY
McCrackin, Anson	44	M	Farmer	TN
Mahala A.	34	F		KY
James L.	15	M		MO
Phebe A.	13	F		MO
Mary J.	12	F	(Deaf & Dumb)	MO
Sarah W.	10	F		MO
Amanda E.	1	F		TX
Elam, William B.	37	M	Farmer	TN
Mary	27	F		KY
Artemisa	7	F		MO
Isaac N.	5	M		MO
Andrew J.	3	M		TX
Calphrona	1	F		TX
Coombes, L. C.	26	M	Farmer	KY
Emaline	21	F		TN
Lewis H.	1	M		TX

Name	Age	Sex	Occupation	Birthplace
Ferris, W. A.	31	M	Farmer	NY
Frances	21	F		TN
Emily	1	F		TX
James	9/12	M		TX
Laytham, William	70	M	Mill Wright	ENG
Colwell, Timothy	21	M	Farmer	IA
Nancy	16	F		IL
Thorp, William	51	M	Farmer	VA
Beal, A. J.	25	F	Farmer	TN
Susan	25	F		TN
William J.	1	M		TN
Thorp, William A.	23	M	Farmer	TN
Sarah A.	20	F		TN
Eldridge J.	3	M		TN
William O.	7/12	M		TN
Leonard, George L.	61	M	Farmer	SC
Mary A. M.	44	F		NC
John R.	18	M	Farmer	TN
Samuel F.	15	M		TN
Jackson L.	11	M		TN
Washington C.	7	M		TN
Joseph A.	5/12	M		TX
Nanny, A. J.	27	M	Farmer	TN
Susan	24	F		IL
Benjamin	7	M		IL
Amos	5	M		IL
Rebecca	1	F		TX
Walker, A. G.	41	M	Farmer	VA
Louisa	18	F		AR
A. G.	1	M		TN
Dye, William	22	M	Farmer	KY
Mannin, Sarah A.	18	F		AL
Tunnel,-------	30	M	Laborer	TN
Elkins, Adaline	10	F		AR
Harris, A. C.	29	M	Farmer	MS
J--- B.	17	F		TN
Charlotte	1	F		TX
Taylor, Pleasant	34	M	Farmer	TN
Mary P.	32	F		TN
R. A.	13	M		IL
John A.	11	M		IL
Amelia A.	9	F		IL
Joseph F.	7	M		IL
Jas. P.	4	M		TX
Perry K.	4/12	M		TX
Manley, Joseph	36	M	Farmer	KY
Valentine, H. K.	33	M	Farmer	NC
Rebecca C.	30	F		SC
Sarah	2	F		TX
Thomas, Augustus	11	M		TN
Davids(?), Martha	8	F		TN
Scott, John	22	M	Laborer	TN
Green, James	32	M	Farmer	IL
Mary	23	F		IL
John T.	3	M		TX
William R.	1	M		TX
Carr, Silas	24	M	Farmer	TN
Wiley, Isaac	67	M	Farmer	VA
Kesiah	36	F		TN
Jacob	26	M	Farmer	TN
Stacks, Samuel	55	M	Farmer	SC
Elizabeth	38	F		TN
Calvin	20	M	Farmer	IL
F. Marion	18	M	Farmer	TN
Mary A.	11	F		IL
John M.	8	M		IL
Piles, John	40	M	Farmer	TN
Wood, Whorton	52	M	Black Smith	SC
Polly	52	F		KY
Elenor	23	F		TN
William	21	M		IL
Betsy	16	F		IL
Lydia	12	F		IL
Charles	14	M		IL

DALLAS COUNTY, TEXAS

Name	Age	Sex	Occupation	Birthplace
West, Robert J.	37	M	Farmer	TN
Elizabeth H.	9	F		TN
John R.	8	M		TN
Ann R.	6	F		TN
Martha A.	4	F		TX
Robert H.	2	M		TX
Mary C.	5/12	F		TX
Dooley, George W.	37	M	Farmer	VA
Isabella A.	31	F		TN
Elizabeth	11	F		TN
George L.	9	M		TN
William W.	4	M		TX
Frances M.	2	F		TX
Irwin, William	56	M	Farmer	PA
Sarah	55	F		PA
Miller, Elijah	25	M	Farmer	IA
Ann M.	19	F		OH
Sarah E.	1	F		TN
Jacob	22	M	Farmer	TN
Chapman, James	42	M	Farmer	TN
Mildred	46	F		KY
William D.	18	M	Farmer	IA
James M.	16	M	Farmer	IA
Martha	12	F		TX
Mary E.	10	F		TX
Nancy	2	F		TX
John	22	M	Farmer	IA
Katharine	16	F		IL
McCOmmas, Amon	45	M	Farmer	TN
Mary	44	F		VA
Elisha	20	M	Farmer	OH
Amon	18	M	Farmer	IL
Rosanah	15	F		IL
William M.	13	M		MO
Mary E.	10	F		MO
Armilda	3	F		TX
McCommas, Jas. B.	26	M	Farmer	OH
Mary	27	F		TN
Mary E.	6	F		MO
Matilda J.	3	F		TX
Rody A.	1	F		TX
Chenault, William	22	M	Farmer	VA
Ruth A.	20	F		TN
Pruitt, William	47	M	Farmer	TN
Mary	42	F		VA
Silas	17	M	Farmer	IL
James F.	14	M		IL
Sarah J.	13	F		IL
Willis J.	9	M		IL
Lavina E.	8	F		IL
Joshua	5	M		IL
Roberts, Joel	21	M	Farmer	TN
Mary	20	F		TN
Benjamin W.	1	M		TX
Spearman, John M.	23	M	School Teacher	TN
Helvey, Daniel	39	M	Black Smith	VA
Sopha	30	F		TN
Benjamin	11	M		TN
Mary A.	8	F		TN
Sarah A.	6	F		TN
John W.	1	M		TN
Snider, Abraham	45	M	Farmer	DC
Nancy	41	F		TN
John ?.	20	M	Farmer	AR
Samuel	18	M	Farmer	AR
Mary	15	F		IL
Joseph	11	M		IL
James W.	8	M		TX
George M.	2	M		TX
Rilie, Mary	53	F		KY
Sarah E.	21	F		TN
John A.	18	M	Farmer	IL

(continued)

Name	Age	Sex	Occupation	Birthplace
Rilie, Nancy	14	F		IL
Louise	11	F		IL
Snow, William J.	27	M	Farmer	TN
S---	20	F		IL
Fondren, John R. B.	37	M	Farmer	NC
Jane	35	F		TN
Meek	13	M		AL
Katharine	12	F		MS
DeCalb	11	M		MS
Melvina	9	F		MS
Benton	7	M		MS
John S.	5	M		MS
Miranna	1	F		TX
P. R.	1	M		TX
Lunby, Thomas	30	M	Farmer	TX
Rachel	24	F		OH
Amy A.	5	F		IL
James	3	M		TX
Ellen	1	F		TX
Donnell, A. M.	23	M	Farmer	TN
Sarah	21	F		TN
Telitha	3	F		MO
William P.	1	M		TX
Lanier, John	55	M	Farmer	VA
Arch B.	30	M	Farmer	VA
Lucy A.	7	F		TN
Leonidas	6	M		TN
Orlando F.	4	M		MS
Hill, John	36	M	Farmer	TN
Maria	24	F		NY
Mary	10/12	F		TX
Scott, Amzi	12	M		IA
Isabel	9	F		IA
Ledbetter, Oliver V.	23	M	Farmer	TN
Margaret	23	F		TN
Thomas J.	5/12	M		TX
Coats, Thomas D.	23	M	Farmer	SC
Mary A.	19	F		TN
Samuel L.	11/12	M		TX
Coats, Samuel	47	M	Farmer	SC
Nancy	47	F		SC
James	17	M	Farmer	KY
Marion A.	13	M		TN
Martha A.	13	F		TN
John W.	11	M		TN
Sarah M.	9	F		TN
Pernicy K.	5	F		TN
Freeman, Mary A.	46	F		TN
Robert B.	15	M		IL
Willis	13	M		IL
Katharine	3	F		TX
Rowe, William	51	M	Farmer	NC
Mary F.	25	F		NC
Rheubin	25	M	Farmer	TN
William H.	22	M	Farmer	TN
John M.	20	M	Farmer	TN
Harriett A.	11	F		TN
Sarah M.	7/12	F		TX
Banks, Henry A.	30	M	Trader	NC
Stone, Thomas	29	M	Farmer	KY
Elizabeth	19	F		TN
Norris, William	62	M	Wheelwright	SC
Rebecca	58	F		TN
Rebecca	25	F		MO
Juliather(?)	18	F		MO
Eliza A.	16	F		MO
William	13	M		MO
Cox, Mary	32	F		CT
Dike, James	3	M		TX
Condra, John	49	M	Carpenter	TN
Lurring	36	F		TN

(continued)

DALLAS COUNTY, TEXAS

Name	Age	Sex	Occupation	Birthplace
Condra, Robert	16	M	Farmer	IL
Sidney A.	14	F		IL
George S.	12	M		IL
Malinda	10	F		IL
James	9/12	M		TX
Burke, Mary	32	F		TN
William E.	14	M		MO
Matilda	12	F		MO
Aaron	10	M		MO
Francis	8	M		MO
James	5	M		MO
Ervin	2	M		MO
Willson, William B.	28	M	Black Smith	IA
Martha J.	22	F		VA
Charles?_.	7	M		TN
Ophelia A.	1	F		MO
Gill, Thomas	48	M	Farmer	KY
Sarah	47	F		GA
Eldridge	27	M	Farmer	TN
Nancy	15	F		TN
Robert D.	13	M		TN
William T.	11	M		TN
Mary E.	8	F		TN
Garner, Adrew J.	29	M	Farmer	TN
Eliza J.	25	F		KY
Margaret	9	F		AR
Elizabeth J.	2	F		MO
William L.	11/12	M		MO
Sherifield, William	26	M	Farmer	KY
Martha K.	18	F		TN
Hord, William H.	40	M	Farmer	VA
Mary J.	39	F		SC
Thomas A.	8	M		TN
John C.	6	M		TN
Ferninand	3	M		TX
Martha J.	7/12	F		TX
McKenzie, Robert J.	18	M	Farmer	SC
Elijah J.	16	M	Farmer	SC
Miller, William B(?).	43	M	Farmer	KY
Minerva	28	F		KY
Charilaus(?)	20	M	Farmer	AL
Alonzo	11	M		KY
Martha	9	F		TN
Mary	8	F		TN
Virginia	6	F		TN
Susan	4	F		TN
Bettie	1	F		TX
Gamel, James	31	M	Farmer	TN
Caroline	26	F		KY
John	6	M		IL
James	4	M		IL
Caroline	1	F		IL
Sloan, Samuel	31	M	Farmer	TN
Nancy A.	30	F		AR
John F.	12	M		AR
Richard E.	10	M		AR
William H.	8	M		AR
Robert M.	7	M		AR
Ezekiel	5	M		AR
Sarah E.	2	F		TX
Emery	2/12	M		TX
Sloan, Robert	45	M	Farmer	TN
Sprowls, James	26	M	Farmer	KY
Mary A.	21	F		TN
Eliza J.	5	F		MO
Rachel A.	3	F		MO
Sarah E.	7/12	F		TX
North, Isaac	22	M	Laborer	TN
Hickman, Henry H.	25	M	Farmer	TN
Elizabeth	20	F		MO

Name	Age	Sex	Occupation	Birthplace
Fisher, Samuel A.	37	M	Farmer	KY
Margaret	31	F		TN
Mary E.	13	F		IL
John A.	11	M		IL
Joseph L.	8	M		IL
Nancy C.	6	F		IL
Pleasant B.	4	M		IL
William H.	1	M		IL
Campbell, Thomas J.	39	M	Farmer	NC
O---	37	F		TN
Rosanah	18	F		TN
Albert	17	M	Farmer	TN
Mary A.	13	F		TN
Marilla	8	F		IL
Thomas	7	M		IL
George W.	5	M		IL
John A.	1	M		TX
Staback, W. L.	2	M		TX
Weatherford, Nancy	51	F		TN
Thomas	11	M		IL
Elizabeth	8	F		IL
Nancy	5	F		IL
Harding	20	M	Farmer	IL
Mary	15	F		IL
Harrison, Westly	28	M	Farmer	TN
Frances	20	F		IL
John	3	M		TX
Mary	2	F		TX
Weatherford, Jefferson	39	M	Farmer	TN
Mary	39	F		OH
Har---	16	M	Farmer	IL
Burrell	13	M		IL
Thomas J.	9	M		IL
Milbery	6	F		IL
William	2	M		TX
Pruett, Albert S.	32	M	Farmer	NC
Alcy	46	F		GA
Thomas	6	M		AR
Abram	4	M		AR
Smith, Elizabeth	15	F		AR
John J.	12	M		AR
Mary	9	F		TX
Mayfield, Elijah	26	M	Farmer	TN
Parks, Christian	35	F		TN
Patrick	16	M		AR
Susan	12	F		AR
Perry, Middleton	35	M	Farmer	IA
Ellen M.	25	F		IL
Mary J.	5	F		TX
Margaret A.	2	F		TX
Douglass, Jesse	23	M	Farmer	TN
Ellis, Thomas M.	51	M	Farmer	SC
Mary	47	F		TN
Harriet E.	16	F		IL
William F.	13	M		IL
John T.	11	M		IL
James H.	8	M		IL
Louisa	5	F		IL
Parks, Curtis	40	M	Farmer	NC
Amelia	37	F		TN
Sarah L.	18	F		IA
James J.	16	M	Farmer	IA
George M.	15	M		IA
Rebecca J.	13	F		IA
Mary J.	11	F		IA
Nancy K.	8	F		IA
John A.	5	M		IA
Laura M.	3	F		IA
Thomas J.	9/12	M		TX
Parks, Katharine	72	F		NC
Stewart, Samuel	38	M	Farmer	NC
Malinda	32	F		TN
Irene E.	2	F		TX
Sarah A.	1/12	F		TX
McAnnies, Irene E.	18	F		AL

Name	Age	Sex	Occupation	Birthplace
Branson, Benjamin	29	M	Farmer	KY
Patsy	26	F		TN
James W.	7	M		IL
Mary A.	4	F		MO
George W.	3	M		IA
Elmira J.	1	F		IA
James, Amos M.	27	M	Farmer	TN
Margaret	23	F		TN
Amos W.	2	M		TX
Rebecca J.	1	F		TX
James, Michael	36	M	Farmer	TN
Susan	37	F		KY
Sarah A.	13	F		MO
Elizabeth H.	12	F		MO
Margaret ?.	9	F		MO
H. W.	1/12	M		TX
Rhodes, Elisha S.	43	M	Cabinet Maker	NC
Mary E.	22	F		TN
Thomas L.	20	M	Farmer	TN
Margaret E.	16	F		TN
Ming(Wing), William T.	24	M	Farmer	AL
Frances J.	19	F		TN
Horne, William	42	M	Farmer	TN
Elizabeth	42	F		TN
Samuel A.	20	M	Farmer	MO
Mary J.	18	F		MO
Elizabeth	14	F		MO
Lauretta E.	12	F		MO
Alexander F.	10	M		MO
William R.	8	M		MO
Thomas E.	6	M		MO
Susan H.	4	F		TX
James R.	1	M		TX
Rhodes, Frederick	41	M	Farmer	NC
Delpha	36	F		TN
Elizabeth	15	F		TN
Thomas	13	M		TN
James	11	M		TN
Jonathan	9	M		MO
Katharine	6	F		MO
Robert	1	M		TX
Rhodes, Elizabeth	76	F		NC
Anderson, James	55	M	Farmer	VA
Mary	46	F		KY
Thomas K.	34	M	Farmer	TN
Elizabeth J.	7	F		AR
William T.	6	M		AR
McAnnies, Louisa	19	F		AL
Wilson, George	43	M	Farmer	NC
Elizabeth	44	F		TN
Thomas	21	M	Farmer	TN
Joseph	19	M	Farmer	TN
Nancy	18	F		TN
Avrilla	16	F		TN
Jane	14	F		TN
William	12	M		MO
Harrison	11	M		TX
Larinda	5	F		TX
Charles D.	6	M		TX
James K. P.	2	M		TX
O'Guin, William	52	M	Farmer	NC
Mary C.	49	F		NC
Leonidas	21	M	Farmer	TN
Louisa J.	18	F		TN
William R.	15	M		TN
Stephen A.	13	M		TN
Thomas J.	9	M		TN
Frances C. T.	6	F		TN
Stacks, Albert	21	M	Farmer	IL
Mary J.	15	F		TN
Graham, Joseph	58	M	Farmer	PA
Milton H.	22	M	Farmer	TN
Clarissa A.	19	F		IL

Name	Age	Sex	Occupation	Birthplace
Camron, David ?.	44	M	Farmer	TN
Susan	38	F		KY
Nancy J.	20	F		MO
Christopher C.	16	M	Farmer	MO
Franklin D. F.	13	M		MO
Angeline	11	F		MO
Edward W.	9	M		MO
Isabel	7	F		MO
Thomas H.	4	M		TX
Rachel	1	F		TX
Griffin, Thacker V.	49	M	Farmer	SC
Subrina	36	F		TN
Sarah E.	7	F		TN
Joseph M.	5	M		TN
Cole, John P.	41	M	Farmer	VA
Susan H.	28	F		TN
William	16	M	Farmer	TN
James	15	M		TN
Adaline	8	F		TN
George W.	7	M		TN
Susan R.	3	F		TX
John P.	1	M		TX
Hunt, Edward W.	24	M	Farmer	AL
Adeline J.	19	F		TN
Martha E.	7/12	F		TX
Hunt, John L.	20	M	Farmer	AL
Robert J.	18	M	Farmer	AL
Thomas C.	15	M		AL
Lively E.	12	F		AL
Daniel, Frances	54	F		VA
John ?.	25	M	Farmer	TN
Thomas B.	18	M	Farmer	TN
Isabella O.	15	F		TN
Margaret S.	11	F		TN
Leonard, William M.	37	M	Farmer	SC
Elizabeth C.	31	F		TN
George L.	15	M		TN
Thomas T.	13	M		TN
Mary J.	11	F		TN
Elizabeth	4	F		TN
Rebecca M.	2	F		TX
James C.	6/12	M		TX
McDermett, Joseph B.	56	M	Farmer	PA
Mary	23	F		PA
Cora	17	F		TN
William	16	M	Copper & Tin Smith	TN
Samuel	12	M		TN
Henrietta	9	F		TN
Porter	8	M		AR
Edward	7	M		AR
Lucinda	45	F		PA
Walker, William J.	52	M	Farmer	TN
Sarah	47	F		VA
Martha A.	16	F		TN
Marcus	13	M		TN
Sarah	11	F		TN
Haupe, Tressvant ?.	28	M	Farmer	GA
Electa A.	25	F		NY
John R.	5	M		KY
Bethumm, Eliza J.	6	F		MO
Robert P.	4	M		TX
Neely, Charles	30	M	Laborer	TN
Willburn, H---	25	M	Laborer	MO
Couch, Henderson	37	M	Farmer	TN
Sherlotte	24	F		AR
Tennessee E.	2	F		TX
Highty A.	2/12	F		TX
Couch, Peter	22	M	Farmer	TN
Winn, Francis B.	35	M	Farmer	TN
Avarilla	37	F		TN
Sophronia J.	12	F		AL
William M.	10	M		AL
Martha E.	4	F		AL
Francis A.	11/12	M		TX
Harton, Nancy	65	F		VA

Trimble, William C. 70 M Farmer (East) TN
Bethany 58 F NC

Walker, Joel 56 M Farmer TN
Celah 57 F NC
Elijah J. 17 M Farmer TN
Petty, Nancy 68 F (Idiot) NC

Walker, Hubbard 28 M Farmer TN
Elizabeth 23 F KY
James M. 11/12 M TX

Mathews, James 26 M Farmer MO
Sally A. 22 F TN
Tabitha C. 2 F TX
Francis M. 1/12 M TX

Mooneyham, William 40 M Farmer TN
Rachel 31 F MO
James M. 12 M MO
Josiah 10 M MO
Martha A. 9 F MO
Mary A. 6 F MO
Elizabeth 5 F TX
Sarah S. 2 F TX
Louisa 2/12 F TX

Good, Noah 35 M Farmer VA
Sintha 29 F TN
George W. 7 M TN
S--- A. 6 F TN
Mary E. 4 F TN
Martha A. 2 F TX
Fithe(Fike), Archer 27 M Farmer TN

Fike, Elisha 58 M Farmer SC
John 37 M Farmer TN
Mary 24 F TN
Pennirah 19 F TN

Holland, William J. 25 M Farmer TN
Rachel C. 26 F TN
Harriett M. 5 F TN
Rutha E. 1 F TN
John 72 M Farmer NC
Martha 70 F VA
Edgin, John C. 17 M Farmer TN

Holland, John E. 35 M Farmer TN
Martha 30 F NC
Tolbert 10 M TN
Gilbert M. 7 M TN
Arvazena 6 F TN
William C. 5 M TN
Artalissa 3 F TN

Smith, Shelton 55 M Farmer ??
Pleasant M. 22 M Farmer TN
Litha A. 16 F IL
Elizabeth 15 F IL
Shelton L. 12 M IL

Mathews, Benjamin 24 M Farmer MO
Manerva 19 F TN
Nahulda K. 5/12 F TX

Huett, Andrew J. 29 M Farmer AR
Martha A. 25 F TN
Louisa 7 F TX
Solomon 80 M None NC
Charithy 79 F NC
Condra, John 20 M Farmer IL
Thomas 15 M (Mexican) MEX

Massie, George ?. 36 M Farmer MO
Margaret 34 F TN
Charles W. 13 M MO
Talton 12 M MO
Ann 8 F MO
Elizabeth 7 F MO
Nancy 4 F MO
Sarah J. 1 F TX

Minter, Green W. 46 M Farmer VA
Jane 44 F TN
Caroline 17 F TN
Scruch, Joseph 14 M IL

Baker, Charles 23 M Farmer VA
Lucretia 22 F TN
Martha E. 4 F TX
Thomas W. 2/12 M TX

Cate, James 31 M Farmer TN
Elvira 20 F TN
David H. 4 M MO
Louisa J. 1 F TX
William A. 2/12 M TX
Frances C. 2/12 F TX

Shelby, James S. 35 M Farmer TN
Caroline F. 22 F TN
Olevia S. 4 F TX
Sophronia A. 2 F TX

Crutchfield, Thomas F. 47 M Inn Keeper KY
"In Inn"
Harwood, Alexander 29 M Clerk TN
Latimer, J. W. 25 M Editor & Lawyer TN
Corley, Adelbert P. 18 M Clerk TN
Jackson, John A. 26 M Trader TN

Bryan, John N. 39 M Lawyer TN
Margaret 25 F IL
John 5 M TX
Frances C. 3 F TX
Edward T. 1 M TX

Dakano, Perry 29 M Physician PA
Ann R. 18 F TN
Cora E. 4/12 F TX
Burford, Nat. N. 25 M Lawyer TN
Harwood, William 12 M MO

Bryan, James B. 37 M Dentist TN
Elizabeth 25 F IL
William 14 M AL
Louisa 11 F TX
Henrietta 9 F TX
James 7 M TX
Thomas 1/12 M TX
Harter, Louisianna 5 F TX

Cole, Calvin 34 M Farmer TN
Elvira A. 29 F LA
Green A. 10 M AR
John C. 9 M AR
Tenissee C. 8 F AR
Emily 6 F TX
Mary E. 4 F TX
James 3 M TX
Albert 1 M TX

Cope, Iddle A. 40 M Farmer TN
Nancy 40 F TN
Rheubin F. 19 M Farmer TN
Sarah E. 16 F TN
John ?. 13 M TN
Susan A. 10 F IL
William 8 M IL
Margaret H. 5 F IL
Mary A. 3 F IL

Knight, Obediah W. 42 M Farmer VA
Seranah 25 F TN
William 15 M TN
John 14 M TN
Mary 11 F TN
Elizabeth 9 F TN
Gabriel 7 M TN
Laura 3 F TX
Martha 1 F TX
Gabriel B. 44 M Farmer VA

Tilly, Jefferson 34 M Farmer TN
Eliza J. 25 F TN
Stephen 6 M AR
Story, E-- 25 F IL

(continued)

DALLAS COUNTY, TEXAS

Name	Age	Sex	Remarks	Birthplace
Story, Julia	11	F		IL
Cole, Polly	52	F		VA
James M.	27	M	Farmer	TN
John H.	23	M	Farmer	TN
William L.	20	M	Farmer	AR
George W.	16	M	(Insane)	AR
Martha V.	13	F		AR
Joseph L.	8	M		AR
Conover, Rosaniah	23	F		OH
Mary E.	6	F		TN
John V.	4	M		TN
William U.	3	M		TN
Frances E.	1	F		TN
Nancy A.	3/12	F		TN
Fortner, M. Franklin	37	M	Farmer	TN
Margaret G.	34	F		KY
John L.	14	M		MO
Jane	12	F		AR
Mary	10	F		AR
Caroline	8	F		AR
Amos	6	M		TX
Ben F.	4	M		TX
Margaret	1	F		TX
Webb, Isaac	49	M	Farmer	TN
Mary H.	34	F		VA
William D.	14	M		TN
Joshua W.	12	M		TN
Sarah A.	8	F		TN
Mary J.	6	F		TX
Isaac N.	3	M		TX
Nancy A. M.	2/12	F		TX
Williams, Thomas C.	31	M	Farmer	TN
Sarah M.	31	F		NC
George E.	8	M		TN
Alcy E.	1	F		TX

DENTON COUNTY, TEXAS

Name	Age	Sex	Remarks	Birthplace
Langston, Martin	40	M	Farmer	TN
Martha	37	F		VA
Ledington, Thomas	13	M		MO
Jno. M.	10	M		MO
Jas. H.	8	M		MO
Langston, William	2	M		TX
James	20	M	Farmer	MO
Jackson	17	M	Farmer	MO
S.	15	F		MO
Carter, John	40	M	Farmer	VA
Sarah	37	F		TN
Harden	15	M		AR
Joseph	13	M		AR
Ann	12	F		AR
C.	10	M		AR
Jane	7	F		AR
Hall	5	M		TX
Sarah	3	F		TX
Boswell, Miller H.	30	M	Farmer	TN
Withers, S.	25	F		TN
M. F.	8	F		MO
Sarah A.	2	F		TX
Smith, P.	17	F		IL
Levea-, Sophia	47	F		KY
Graham, Spencer	30	M	Farmer	TN
Nancy	32	F		KY
R. C.	8	M		AR
Mary Ann	5	F		TX
Jas. H.	2	M		TX
Brown, Routh	59	F		SC
S.	26	F		TN
Ellis, J. F.	12	M		MO
S. E.	9	F		MO
J.	5	M		MO
Allen, T. J.	48	M	Farmer	NC
Ruth	34	F		SC
E.	22	F		TN
Richard W.	21	M	Farmer	TN
P.	16	F		MO
Robert M.	14	M		MO
L.	12	F		MO
Thomas	10	M		MO
Lucetta	8	F		MO
George W.	6	M		MO
Medlin, Mary	64	F		SC
Delila	34	F		TN
Mary C.	29	F		TN
Slaves	22	F	(Black)	--
	23	M	(Black)	--
	25	M	(Black)	--
Medlin, Charles	43	M	Farmer	SC
Matilda	37	F		TN
R.	18	F		MO
E.	16	F		MO
Sarah	14	F		MO
W. O.	12	M		MO
Nancy	10	F		MO
S.	7	F		MO
M. R.	1	F		TX
J. W.	4	M		MO
Harris, F. L.	25	M	Farmer	TN
Mulkey, Jno.	23	M	Farmer	MO
Harris, Charles S.	3/12	M		TX
Gibson, William	48	M	Farmer	TN
Rebecca	39	F		TN
Thomas B.	2	M		TX
Jno. M.	20	M		TX
George S.	18	M		TX
Nancy A.	15	F		MO
Mary Ann	11	F		MO
Martha ?.	10	F		MO
Ludicy E.	7	F		MO
Stewart, Taylor	40	M	Farmer	KY
Tabitha	36	F		TN
Delila J.	13	F		MO
Mary E.	11	F		MO
Nancy	8	F		MO
M.	5	F		MO
S.	4	F		MO
Harper, Hugh	39	M	Farmer	TN
Mary	40	F		TN
Jane	14	F		TN
A. McCall	12	M		TN
William ?.	8	M		AR
Gibson, William H.	29	M	Farmer	TN
S.	24	F		TN
Jos. W.	5	M		MO
Matilda E.	3	F		TX
Baker, A.	13	M		IL
M.	11	F		IL
Roberts, Rezin	45	M	Farmer	SC
Elizabeth	38	F		AL
John	23	M	Farmer	TN
William	17	M		TN
Sarah J.	15	F		TN
Martha	12	F		TN
Peter	9	M		TN
Isaac	6	M		TN
Joseph R.	3	M		TX
Malone, Perry	36	M	Farmer	KY
Mary	32	F		TN
Anna E.	13	F		MO
Catharine	11	F		MO
M. J.	9	F		MO
M. C.	7	F		MO
M. M.	5	F		MO
R. M.	4	F		TX
O. C.	2	M		TX
Richard	6/12	M		TX
Garvin, Thomas	38	M	Farmer	SC

(continued)

DENTON COUNTY, TEXAS

Garvin, Ann	38	F		IL
William	45	M	Black Smith	TN
Hunter, Burrel	50	M	Farmer	NC
Elizabeth	45	F		TN
L.	17	F		TN
E. A.	10	F		TN
W. H.	7	M		MO
Willey B.	20	M	Farmer	TN
Rogers, Jno.	50	M	Farmer	SC
R.	33	F		TN
R. M.	14	M		TN
Hyatt, Thomas	12	M		IN
Ann	10	F		IN
William	8	M		IN
Jefferson	6	M		IN
R.	4	F		IN
Hamilton	2	M		TX
Hicks, L. J.	36	M	Farmer	NC
Elizabeth	28	F		SC
Jane	9	F		TN
Jno.	6	M		MO
Emily	3	F		MO
Clary, E. F.	40	M		TN
C. M.	25	F		AL
R. M.	9	F		AR
William C.	7	M		TX
Jno. R. M.	4	M		TX
Anna M.	1	F		TX
Wagner, Jno.	49	M	Farmer	TN
Nancy	47	F		KY
William B.	14	M		AL
Mary Ann	11	F		MO
Sutton, Mary	38	F		TN
William D.	16	M	Farmer	IL
Edmund	13	M		IL
Mary E.	5/12	F		TX
French, Nancy	54	F		SC
Oliver	28	M	Farmer	TN
Jas.	22	M	Farmer	TN
M.	20	F		OH
Bainbridge, N. C.	10	F		IL
Sutton, Jesse	37	M	Farmer	IL
Mary	27	F		KY
L.	7	F		IL
E.	6	F		IL
Jas. K. P.	4	M		TX
Rebecca	1	F		TX
Woodruff, Robert W.	29	M	Farmer	TN
Clary, E. C.	43	M	Farmer	TN
C. E.	37	F		TN
E. C.	18	F		AR
Jno. C.	14	M		AR
F. Jane	12	F		AR
William N.	10	M		AR
Solomon B.	8	M		AR
P. A.	6	F		AR
Mary J.	2	F		AR
Morence, Jno.	47	M	Farmer	??
King, Jno. W.	55	M	Farmer	TN
Jane	52	F		NC
R. R.	28	F		TN
Mary G.	27	F		TN
William	24	M	Black Smith	TN
A. C.	22	M	Farmer	TN
A. J.	20	M	Farmer	MO
Jane	18	F		MO
Ellen R.	16	F		MO
E. W.	12	F		MO
S. A.	10	F		MO
Davis, E. A. L.	29	F		TN
Jno. K.	3	M		TX
King, Isham Jane	1	F		TX
Sager, C. F.	20	M	Farmer	GER

Pickett, E.	70	M	Farmer	TN
Nancy C.	24	F		TN
Jno. K.	1	M		TX
Wagner, Thomas	30	M	Farmer	TN
C.	29	F		TN
L.	5	F		TN
M. E.	2	F		TN
King, J. W.	21	M		MO
Loveing, William R.	36	M	Farmer	KY
Malinda	34	F		TN
W. R.	12	M		MO
Jos. B.	10	M		MO
Jno. S.	6	M		MO
S. A.	6	F		MO
Elliot, E. S.	19	M	Farmer	MO
King, Roda	40	F		KY
William E.	22	M	Farmer	TN
E. McDonnal	21	M	Farmer	TN
S. C.	15	M		TN
R. W.	14	M		TN
Judge S.	11	M		TN
Jas. K. P.	7	M		TN
Samuel D.	6	M		MO
Smith, Samuel K.	35	M	Farmer	KY
Slaves	6/12	F	(Black)	--
	23	F	(Black)	--
Roark, William M.	35	M	Sheriff	TN
C.	31	F		TN
Jas.	13	M		MO
Nancy	11	F		MO
Thomas J.	9	M		MO
M. B.	7	M		MO
Isaac N.	5	M		MO
Lutrell, William	23	M	Farmer	IL
Susan A.	30	F		TN
Marsh, Eli	13	M		AR
Mary Ann	12	F		AR
James C.	10	M		AR
Martha Ann	8	F		AR
P. Jane	6	F		AR
Lutrell, E. J.	1	F		TX
Simmons, Jno. W.	35	M	Farmer	TN
Mary	40	F		TN
Thomas W.	13	M		AR
M. A.	11	F		AR
Jno. M.	10	M		AR
Swiney, James	35	M	Farmer	VA
Legon, Thomas D.	39	M	Farmer	TN
Elizabeth	39	F		TN
Jos. F.	16	M	Farmer	AL
Mary Ann	13	F		AL
Margaret L.	8	F		MS
E. B.	7	M		MS
Elizabeth J.	5	F		MS
Jno. M.	3	M		MS
Not named	3/12	F		TX
Howse, Jno.	23	M	Farmer	NC
C.	18	F		TN
William	1	M		TX
Suggs, Charles	33	M	Farmer	TN
Elizabeth	33	F		MO
H. C. C.	15	M		MO
Ara	11	F		MO
Thomas C.	11	M		MO
V.	9	F		MO
William ?.	6	M		MO
Charles L.	3	M		MO
N. C.	2	M		MO
Bridges, Mildred	48	F		NC
William A.	23	M	Farmer	TN
David C.	7	M		IL
Higgins, Philoman	65	M	Farmer	VA
Delila	53	F		NC
P. R.	24	M	Farmer	IL

(continued)

DENTON COUNTY, TEXAS

Higgins, Martha 15 F IL
Samuel 13 M IL
Aites, Jno. 40 M Farmer TN

Harman, Washington 35 M Farmer TN
Rebecca 25 F MO
W. 6 M MO
Irvin 2 M MO
Allen, Franklin 23 M Farmer MO

Peyton, Jno. 50 M Physician KY
Elizabeth 47 F TN
Thomas B. 23 M Farmer MO
M. E. 18 F MO
Mary J. 16 F MO
P. H. 14 M MO
S. E. 11 F MO
W. S. 5 M MO
Freeman, P. 63 M Farmer MA

Ashlot, Josiah 43 M Farmer TN
Elizabeth 38 F AL
Nancy C. 16 F IL
William F. 13 M IL
Mary E. 9 F IL
Sarah J. 7 F IL
Jno. C. 6 M IL
Joshua M. 2 M TX

Downing, J. W. 34 M Farmer TN
Nancy 29 F KY
Martin 12 M IL
Mary J. 7 F IL
Emily 4 F TX
Sarah 1 F TX

Ragland, Jno. W. 39 M Farmer TN
Margarett 30 F TN
A. 14 F TN
L. J. 7 F TN
William M. 5 M TN
Rogers, R. 15 M TN

Teel, Peter 55 M Farmer VA
Sarah 46 F TN
R. F. 22 M Farmer TN
E. A. 21 M Farmer TN
George M. 18 M Farmer TN
Jas. M. 17 M Farmer TN
E. A. 13 F TN
M. E. 11 F TN
A. B. 8 M IL
E. A. 6 M IL
O. F. 3 F IL

Jones, Mathew 27 M Farmer TN
E. J. 25 F TN
Martha A. 5 F IL
Sarah C. 1 F TX

DeWITT COUNTY, TEXAS

Murphree, D. 39 M Farmer TN

Houston, John 24 M Farmer NC
Julia 18 F MS
Robert 1 M TN

Buchanan, John 45 M Teacher CAN
Emily 31 F MO
Mary 12 F TN
Sarah 10 F TN
Alexander 8 M TN
John 6 M TN
Ellen 3 F TN
Amanda 2 F TN

Thomas, William C. 38 M Farmer GA
Caroline J. 31 F NY
Swift, Albert 14 M MO
Almyra 10 F TX
Isabella 8 F TX
(continued)

Thomas, James H. F. 11 M MS
Davis, Jacob A. 42 M Farmer TN

Friar, Daniel 50 M Farmer GA
Ann 40 F SC
Alfred 19 M Farmer TN
Sarah Ann 16 F TX
William 14 M TX
Susan 12 F TX
John 10 M TX
Mary 8 F TX
Frances 3 F TX
Juliet 6/12 F TX
Wright, James C. 18 M Farmer TX

Johnson, John L. 31 M M.D. GA
Mary Ann 26 F GA
Jesse 12 M AL
John 10 M GA
Malisa 8 F GA
James 6 M AL
Nathan 4 M TN
McCall, William M. 20 M Farmer MS

Wright, E. D. 38 M Farmer NC
M. C. 36 F TN
Johnson, William 22 M Carpenter PA

Petty, Theofolus 37 M Farmer TN
Sarah 39 F AL
Margaret 12 F AR
George 10 M AR
Manerva 7 F AR
William 4 M TX
Mary 1 F TX

Petty, Gipson 27 M Farmer TN
Mary 23 F OH
Araminda 1 F TX
Stran, Vanard 49 M Farmer LA

Taylor, Elizabeth 37 F TN
Croder 19 M Farmer TX
Joseph 17 M Farmer TX
John M. 15 M TX
William 13 M TX
Martha Ann 10 F TX
Elizabeth 8 F TX
Eliza Jane 5 F TX
Hapsabeth 4 F TX

Crabb, Mary M. 39 F TN
Joseph A. 14 M TN
Mary J. 11 F TN
John F. 7 M TN
Susan E. 4 F TN

Stephens, Washington 37 M Farmer NY
Nancy 30 F TN
Sarah Ann 8 F TX
Delila 6 F TX
Joseph 4 M TX
Robert L. 1 M TX

Allen, Joseph 30 M Carpenter OH
Sarah 30 F TN
Jones, James 12 M TX
Allen, Lawrence 1 M TX

Moris, William 25 M Farmer TN
Mary 21 F MS
Mary Ann 3 F TX
Safronia 1 F TX

Davis, Perry 33 M Farmer TN
Adeline 4 F TX
Laura 2 F TX

Demoss, Lewis 48 M Farmer MO
Catharine 41 F TN
James 18 M Farmer TX
Catharine 15 F TX
Laura 12 F TX
Eliza J. 4 F TX
Joseph 1 M TX

DeWITT COUNTY, TEXAS

Name	Age/Sex/Occupation	Birthplace
Jordon, John	46 M Farmer	TN
Valuna Ann	23 F	TN
Ann C.	4 F	TX
William W.	2/12 M	TX
Rusworn, George A.	16 M Farmer	GER
George R.	12 M	GER
Blair, James F.	23 M Farmer	TN
Alonzo	22 M Farmer	TN
Smith, James N.	60 M Clerk	TN
Elizabeth	46 F	TN
Martha	14 F	TN
Susan	8 F	TN
Joseph	7 M	TN
Thomas C.	5 M	TN
Cardwell, Crockett	38 M Farmer & Clerk	KY
Ann E.	24 F	TN
Savage, Caroline	10 F	TX
Fudge, Leroy	17 M Farmer	MS
Howard, Franklin	35 M Farmer	TN
Hall, Jacob	35 M Carpenter	NY
Moret, Archabald	22 M Laborer	TN
North, J. R.	34 M Farmer	TN
Martha J.	11 F	MS
Ophelia C.	8 F	TX
William	6 M	TX
Nichols, E.	24 M Farmer	MS
Hatchet, P. H.	24 M Teacher	GA
Priestly, James	34 M Farmer	TN
Elizabeth	30 F	NC
John	10 M	TN
William	8 M	TX
Edward	7 M	TX
J. P.	5 M	TX
Samuel	3 M	TX
Ann J.	6/12 F	TX
Cunningham, John P.	45 M Farmer	AL
Ross, R. E.	30 M Farmer	SC
Doolitle, Susan	31 F	IL
Amanda	12 F	TN
George	5 M	TN
Mary J.	4 F	TN
Clark, Isaac J.	30 M Farmer	TN
Angeline	23 F	AL
Margaret J.	4 F	MS
Hugh L.	2 M	MS
James H.	6/12 M	TX
Rice, William	61 M Farmer	NC
Sarah	60 F	NC
Elizabeth	30 F	AL
William J.	24 M	TN
Davis, Mary J.	9 F	TX
Clayton, John H.	39 M Farmer	TN
Mary Ann	33 F	TN
Nancy E.	14 F	TN
Mary J.	10 F	TN
Margaret A.	8 F	TN
Joseph M.	7 M	TN
Sarah A.	2 F	TX
Tennessee	3/12 F	TX
Craigg, B. M.	36 M Farmer	TN
Safronia	20 F	MS
Babb, James	74 M Farmer	NC
Elizabeth	60 F	TN
Amanda F.	16 F	TN
Hodge, A. J.	26 M M.D.	AL
A. V.	19 F	TN
Samuel B.	5/12 M	TX
Houston, Walter	40 M Farmer	VA
Jane	35 F	TN
William	21 M Farmer	AL
Andrew	18 M Farmer	AL
John	16 M Farmer	AL

(continued)

Name	Age/Sex/Occupation	Birthplace
Houston, Elen	14 F	AL
Mary	11 F	TX
Robert	9 M	TX
Alexander	7 M	TX
Margaret	4 F	TX
Nancy	1 F	TX
Cunningham, Jno. P.	38 M Farmer	TN
Kelsoe, James	49 M Farmer	KY
Mary Ann	37 F	TN
William	19 M Farmer	AL
Sarah	17 F	AL
John	16 M Farmer	MS
Paralee	13 F	MS
Calvin	12 M	MS
Algn	7 M	MS
Jefferson	5 M	MS
Fudge, Almond	21 M Farmer	AL
Barton, Tember	57 M Farmer	KY
Margaret	50 F	IL
Tember L.	13 M	TX
Kelsoe, Henry	22 M Farmer	TN
Penchan, William	26 M Wagon Maker	VA
Nancy Ann	24 F	TN
Renick, Robert B.	19 M Wagon Maker	MO
Andrew R.	17 M Wagon Maker	MO
McFarland, Laughlin	21 M Wagon Maker	TX
North, Mary	24 F	TN
Ann	2 F	TX
Samuel	1 M	TX
McDaniel, N. R.	35 M Farmer	TN
Zelia	33 F	TN
Mary D.	9 F	MS
Martha V.	7 F	MS
Robert P.	4 M	MS
William S.	2 M	MS
Rebecca	1 F	MS
Miles, C. P.	30 M Farmer	TN
R. C.	28 M Farmer	TN
Harwood, John	55 M Farmer	VA
Mary	44 F	VA
Margaret	22 F	TN
James	20 M Farmer	TN
John	18 M Farmer	TN
William	16 M Farmer	TN
Cunningham, Samuel	64 M Farmer	TN
Ellen	47 F	VA
Frank	19 M Farmer	AL
Nancy E.	17 F	AL
Susan A.	14 F	AL
Araminta C.	13 F	AL
Sprees, Cull	12 M	GER
Baker, James M.	54 M Farmer	SC
Mary C.	24 F	TN
James	20 M Farmer	TN
Elizabeth	19 F	TN
William	17 M Farmer	TN
John B.	16 M Farmer	TN
Michael J.	11 M	MS
Eliza A.	7 F	TX
Sarah	5 F	TX
Walace, James	41 M Farmer	TN
Ellen	26 F	KY
Leonadas	13 M	AL
Elizabeth	10 F	MS
Ellen	2 F	AL
Crawford, James A.	50 M Farmer	VA
Rachael	44 F	TN
John A.	22 M Farmer	TN
Archabald W.	18 M Farmer	TN
William H.	17 M Farmer	TN
James L.	16 M Farmer	TN
Pleasant A.	14 M Farmer	TN
Margaret M.	10 F	TN
Rachael E.	7 F	AR
Isaac C.	5 M	AR

(continued)

Name	Age	Sex	Occupation	Birthplace
Crawford, Nancy M. J. E.	3	F		AR
Thomas	1	M		TX
Case, Emanuel	81	M	Farmer	NY
Buget, Mary Ann	45	F		MO
Isaih	21	M	Farmer	MO
John	17	M	Farmer	TN
Margaret	13	F	(Blind)	TN
Barthalamew	12	M		TN
Ann	10	F		TN
Neely, Harvey	28	M	Farmer	TN
Nancy	19	F		NC
Francis W.	1	M		TN
Bennett, Miles S.	32	M	Farmer	NY
Bathsheba	27	F		KY
Mary G.	5	F		TN
Sarah K.	3	F		TN
Samuel	1	M		TN
Spencer, Carroll W.	25	M	Farmer	TN
Frances A.	18	F		AL
Virginia	2/12	F		TX
Peebles, Robert	50	M	Farmer	SC
Mary J.	35	F		TN
Shenolt, Elen P.	7	F		TX
Foster, John R.	50	M	Farmer	TN
Miller, Michael	33	M	Farmer	SC
next to				
Miller, David	31	M	Farmer	AL
Jane	35	F		TN
Jones, Malinda	17	F		TN
Amanda	14	F		TN
Elizabeth	12	F		TN
Milton	8	M		TN
Davis, Rosanna	45	F		TN
Mary Ann	16	F		TX
Viena	15	F		TX
Lavina	10	F		TX
Nancy	9	F		TX
Rosana	8	F		TX
Emaline	5	F		TX
Duran, Wilie	42	M	Farmer	NC
Bunetta	31	F		AL
Sarah J.	13	F		AL
Abraham	9	M		AL
Eliza A.	7	F		AL
Thomas	3	M		TN
James	1	M		TN
Billings, James	30	M	Farmer	TN
Louisa	28	F		MO
W. R.	9	M		TX
Rebecca	7	F		TX
Amon	2	M		TX
John	1	M		TX
Forister, James	55	M		TN
Sarah J.	13	F		TX
Mary Ann	45	F		TN
Barbary A.	12	F		TX
Mary Ann	8	F		TX
Rebecca E.	5	F		TX
James W.	2	M		TX
Ashur, Thomas	50	M	Farmer	TN
James	30	M	Farmer	TN
Thomas	28	M	Farmer	IL
Anastalia	20	F		GA
Robertson	22	M	Farmer	IL
Franklin	14	M	Farmer	TX
Nancy	12	F		TX
John	10	M		TX
Eliza	8	F		TX
Copeland, Marion	18	M	Farmer	TX
Tomlinson, John	44	M	Farmer	TN
Polly	24	F		IL

(continued)

Name	Age	Sex	Occupation	Birthplace
Tomlinson, Amanda	6	F		TX
Ann	6/12	F		TX
Woford, R. B.	42	M	Farmer	TN
Frances J.	30	F		VA
John F.	5	M		TX
Ann E.	1	F		TX
Gilbert, Jasper	41	M	Black Smith	TN
Eliza	32	F		SC
Pleasant L.	10	M		TX
Ba-thy	8	M		TX
Frances	3	F		TX
Templeton, W.	30	M	Farmer	TN
Malinda	24	F		MO
Patterson, Andrew	8	M		TX
James P.	6	M		TX
Letitia F.	4	F		TX
Als.	2	M		TX
Berry, Alfred	50	M	Farmer	TN
Carroll, Demus	26	M	Farmer	NC
Barnhill, Jno. D.	40	M	Farmer	SC
Elizabeth	36	F		TN
Samuel C.	15	M		TN
Calhoun, William P. M.	13	M	Farmer	TN
John	11	M		TN
Elizabeth	10	F		TN
Barnhill, Martha	1	F		TX
Rankin, Moses B.	33	M	Farmer	AL
Christian H.	33	F		TN
Manerva	6	F		MS
Margaret	3	F		MS
Lucy C.	2	F		MS
Read, Doroty M.	38	M	Farmer	TN
Lucy H.	32	F		GA
Mary J.	12	F		MS
Louisa C.	10	F		TX
Thomas J.	8	M		TX
George M.	5	M		TX
Nancy J.	3	F		TX
Rachael V.	2/12	F		TX
Kesiah, John	60	M	Farmer	TN
Frances	50	F		TN
McFall, J.	26	M	Farmer	TN
Sarah	22	F		TN
Albert	1	M		TX
Petty, Martha	43	F		SC
Porter, William J.	23	M	Farmer	TN
Mary J.	18	F		TX
Brown, Palestine	38	M	Farmer	TN
Myrann	33	F		TN
Jesse K.	16	M	Farmer	TN
Josaphine	9	F		TN
Bazel J.	5	M		TN
Joseph	1	M		TX
Scott, Pheby	38	F		TN
Thomas P.	15	M	Farmer	TX
John James	12	M		TX
William A.	11	M		TX
Susan	10	F		TX
Tatum, Nancy	27	F		AL
Edward	10	M		AL
Telly, Andrew	19	M	Farmer	TX
Porter, John T.	57	M	Farmer	TN
Persie A.	43	F		TN
Isaac N.	26	M	Farmer	TN
Emily H.	19	F		TN
John T.	15	M	Farmer	TN
Humphrey, G. W.	33	M	Carpenter	AL
Mary J.	20	F		TN
Elijah J.	4	M		TX
Virginia A.	2	F		TX
John T.	6/12	M		TX

DeWITT COUNTY, TEXAS

King, John A.	48	M	Surveyor	TN
Mary M.	42	F		NC
N. C. T.	21	F		TN
Rufus	14	M		MS
Wilber	10	M		TX
John M. B.	2	M		TX
Hoathaus, Frederick	15	M	Laborer	GER
Snider, Jno.	30	M	Laborer	GER
Tomlinson, Joseph	30	M	Farmer	TN
Elizabeth	30	F		TX
Ann E.	9	F		TX
John J.	2	M		TX
Martha E.	1	F		TX
Stewart, John	38	M	Farmer	SCO
Brown, Daniel	14	M		TX
Elder, James M.	29	M	Farmer	TN
Sarah Ann	20	F		AL
William F.	2	M		MS
Davis, Columbus	22	M	Farmer	AL
Amanda	15	F		MS
Louisa	13	F		MS
Isham	11	M		MS
Calaway, Francis	33	M	Carpenter	TN
Mary A.	31	F		AL
William D.	4	M		TX
Emily F.	2	F		TX
Chisolm, Richard H.	51	M	Farmer	GA
Hardena	46	F		TN
Thornton	19	M	Farmer	TX
Bradford	14	M		TX
Mary Ann	8	F		TX
Richard	7/12	M		TX
Emery, William	25	M	Laborer	MD

ELLIS COUNTY, TEXAS

Navarro District

Johnson, E. R.	30	M	Farmer	VA
F. C.	25	F		TN
Eva-tha L.	7	F		TN
Edwin J.	4	M		TN
Lambeth, Wesley	22	M	Farmer	TN
Julia Ann	16	F		MS
Johnson, Malcolm	45	M	Black Smith	NC
Julia Ann	24	F		LA
John A.	17	M	Farmer	NC
William M.	14	M		AL
Malcolm	13	M		AL
James	9	M		TX
Ellen	4	F		TX
Harriet E.	9/12	F		TX
Johnson, Alexander	21	M	Black Smith	TN
Thomas, John M.	22	M	Farmer	TN
Doods, C. J.	26	F		SC
N. C.	13	F		TN
M. W.	10	F		TN
S. A.	4	F		TN
M. D.	2	F		TN
Thomas, Augustine	11	M		SC
Gibbs, Smith	45	M	Farmer	TN
Sarah	42	F		TN
Samuel R.	21	M	Farmer	TN
Elizabeth	20	F		TN
Mary Ann	17	F		TN
Barbara G.	15	F		TN
Sarah J.	13	F		TN
James P.	11	M		TN
John S.	9	M		TN
Martha R.	7	M		TN
Drucilla E.	5	F		MO
Lucy C.	1	F		TX
Hicks, James	53	M	None	VA

Brock, Joshua	40	M	Farmer	KY
Susanna	32	F		TN
Joseph F.	13	M		MO
Spencer P.	11	M		MO
John R.	8	M		MO
Elisha	2	M		TX
Phipps, William	40	M	Farmer	TN
Rutha	37	F		KY
Charles	19	M	Farmer	KY
Rebecca	18	F		KY
Elizabeth	16	F		KY
Willis	10	M		MO
Benjamin	4	M		MO
Balch, William	47	M	Farmer	NC
Phebe	44	F		TN
William M.	19	M	Farmer	IL
Eliza M.	16	F		IL
James H.	14	M		IL
Phebe A.	12	F		IL
Lucinda	8	F		IL
Mary	3	F		IL
Bell, Robert	33	M	Farmer	VA
Margaret	20	F		TN
Jane Eliza	1	F		TX
Barker, Charles H.	25	M	Farmer	TN
Rebecca A.	19	F		TN
Whittenburg, Joseph N.	30	M	Farmer	TN
Patton, William T.	27	M	Farmer	TN
Catharine	29	F		VA
John C.	7/12	M		TX
Parker, Robert A. M.	24	M	Farmer	TN
Joseph	6	M		IL
Sarah J.	3	F		IL
Balch, Evan R.	26	M	Farmer	TN
John B.	22	M	Farmer	TN
Hickey, Granville L.	20	M	Farmer	TN
Ellen	17	F		AL
Fearis, David P.	25	M	Farmer	IRE
Margaret E.	24	F		TN
Berry, Robert M.	24	M	Farmer	MO
Mathews, John	21	M	Carpenter	TN
Jones, Robert	38	M	Farmer	KY
Eliza Jane	21	F		TN
Ann A.	3	F		TX
Cintha E.	1	F		TX
Williams, F. A.	2	F		TX
Mayfield, Sarah	47	F		AL
Dillard, Susan	15	F		TN
John H.	13	M		TN
Samuel	11	M		TX
Mayfield, Sarah A.	7	F		TX
Henry R.	4	M		TX
Hulda	2	F		TX
Smith, Thomas	41	M	Farmer	NC
Margaret R.	41	F		NC
John A.	19	M	Farmer	TN
William	17	M	Farmer	TN
James L.	15	M	Farmer	TN
Abram M.	12	M		TN
Teressie	10	F		TN
Mary E.	7	F		TN
Margarett A.	5	F		TN
Herron, Mary	60	F		NC
William R.	28	M	Farmer	TN
Thomas	34	M	Farmer	TN
Tarrant, Edward H.	51	M	Farmer	SC
Young, William	72	M	Carpenter	SC
Brooks, N. B.	24	M	Farmer	KY
Gillam, Jesse T.	10	M		TN
Harnicke, Samuel	30	M	Black Smith	ENG
Mitchell, William	55	M	Farmer	TN

ELLIS COUNTY, TEXAS

Name	Age	Sex	Occupation	Birthplace
Trimble, Henry	38	M	Farmer	OH
Barbara	33	F		TN
Mary A.	15	F		AR
Rebecca	14	F		AR
Prudence	10	F		TX
John	8	M		TX
Henry	4	M		TX
Anderson, William	70	M	Peddler	MA
Young, William	22	M	Farmer	TN
Julia	20	F		IL
William H.	4/12	M		TX
Mary	14	F		IL
Samuel	5	M		TX
Wesley	24	M	Farmer	TN
Henry	18	M	Farmer	TN
Young, Harvey W.	21	M	Farmer	TN
Evelina A.	20	F		IL
Nickleson, W. B. M. P. H.	34	M	Mechanic	TN
Eliza	26	F		TN
Mary E. E.	6	F		IL
John G. W.	3	M		TX
J. H. C.	6/12	M		TX
Young, Sarah	16	F		IL
Harriett	8	F		IL
Mary J.	1	F		TX
Bivins, James	35	M	Farmer	TN
Q(O).	30	F		TN
John	10	M		TX
E.	8	F		TX
Samuel	5	M		TX
Williams, James	25	M	Farmer	TN
Sarah	23	F		TN
John	6	M		TN
Lucy	4	F		TN
Jane	2	F		TX
Harris, Martin	18	M	Farmer	TN
Boren, Joseph	40	M	Farmer	TN
Ann S.	32	F		LA
Eliza	13	F		TX
Tarlton	11	M		TX
Joseph	3	M		TX
Mary E.	2/12	F		TX
Nancy	96	F		VA
Whittenburg, Norm. H.	33	M	Farmer	TN
Malvina	32	F		TN
Clementine L.	9/12	F		TX
Boren, Michael	44	M	Farmer	KY
Mary Ann	27	F		AL
Riley	16	M	Farmer	TX
Albert	11	M		TX
John	6	M		TX
J. H. Levina	3	F		TX
Joseph	1	M		TX
Roberson, Jesse	19	M		TN
Apperson, Peter	66	M	Farmer	NC
Eliza	53	F		KY
James P.	21	M	Farmer	TN
Mary	18	F		IL
John T.	8	M		MS
Starr, George W.	37	M	Physician	VA
Rogers, Emory W.	37	M	Farmer	AL
Nancy	39	F		SC
William	15	M	Farmer	AL
Mary C.	13	F		AL
James M.	11	M		AL
Andrew W.	8	M		TX
America B.	6	F		TX
Hansford S.	4	M		TX
Turpen, Edward	21	M	Farmer	TN
Stevens, Thomas	38	M	Farmer	KY
Briggs, William T.	24	M	Physician	KY
Berry, John W.	23	M	Attorney at Law	KY
Prince, Jonathan E.	36	M	Farmer	TN
Irving, William	65	M	Farmer	TN
Prince, Vienna M.	35	F		TN
Margaret E.	10	F		TN
A. J.	8	M		TN
J. L.	6	M		TN
R. J.	2	F		AR
Jonathan J.	2/12	M		TX
Mayfield, Robert F.	21	M	Farmer	TN
Hulda	22	F		AL
George W.	17	M	Farmer	TN
Weaver, Daniel	58	M	Farmer	TN
Milard	48	F		TN
William	17	M	Farmer	AL
James M.	13	M		AL
Teressa A.	11	F		AL
John	7	M		AL
Witherspoon, Jos. H.	26	M	Farmer	TN
Sarah J.	17	F		AR
Finis E.	16	M	Farmer	TN
William	14	M		TN
Francis	12	F		MO
John	9	M		MO
Phillips, Norman	44	M	Farmer	NC
Jane	20	F		TN
Nancy	18	F		IN
Susan	16	F		IN
Theodore	13	M		IN
Margarett	12	F		IN
Nimrod	10	M		IN
Terrel	8	M		IN
Charles F.	6	M		IN
Mary	4	F		IN
Hannah	7/12	F		Western Territory
Clever, Joseph	21	M	Farmer	NC
Kelly, J. L.	33	M	Farmer	TN
Sarah M.	26	F		TN
Sarah A.	6	F		TN
James E.	4	M		TN
Mary J.	2	F		TN
Newton, Elbert C.	35	M	Farmer	TN
Sarah	35	F		NC
Mary J.	11	F		MO
John R.	8	M		MO
William P.	6	M		MO
Benton J.	4	M		MO
Laughlin, James P.	30	M	Farmer	TN
Lealy	29	F		NC
Eli M.	8	M		MO
William M.	6	M		MO
Eliza Jane	5	F		MO
John	3	M		MO
Jordan G.	8/12	M		TX
Butler, Melinda	11	F		TX
Laughlin, Newton	32	M	Farmer	TN
Margarett J.	28	F		TN
Line Ann	9	F		MO
Martha J.	8	F		MO
William M.	6	M		MO
Donald P.	5	M		MO
Paralee J.	3	F		TX
Nancy N.	1	F		TX
Witherspoon, Nancy Ann	19	F		TN
William	14	M		TN
Frances T.	12	F		MO
Morgan, John	21	M	Farmer	TN
Witherspoon, A. D.	26	M	Farmer	TN
Pickens, William M.	24	M	Farmer	KY
Ellis	23	M	Farmer	TN
Thompson P.	2	M		AR
John H.	8/12	M		TX
Gentry, Dulany S.	27	M	Farmer	AL
Martha M.	19	F		TN
John J.	1	M		MO
William H.	3/12	M		TX

ELLIS COUNTY, TEXAS

Name	Age	Sex	Occupation	Birthplace
Billingsly, Robert M.	32	M	Farmer	AR
Eliza J.	28	F		TN
Edna J.	10	F		MO
John L.	8	M		MO
Tempy	5	F		TX
Nancy	1	F		TX
Laughlin, William B.	28	M	Farmer	TN
Butler, Edna J.	13	F		TX
Malissa	9	F		TX
Billingsly, Nathan L.	32	M	Farmer	TN
Nancy	21	F		AR
Elbert G.	25	M	Farmer	TN
Boyd, John H.	52	M	Farmer	TN
Frances	42	F		TN
Margarett T.	18	F		KY
Joseph W.	14	M		KY
Harriet F.	12	F		MO
Tilla A.	8	F		MO
Victoria	6	F		MO
Pernetta E.	2	F		MO
Boyd, William Jasper	23	M	Farmer	TN
Pernetta	18	F		GA
James Allen	1	M		TX
Jordan, Thomas J.	42	M	Farmer	TN
Stacy	31	F		LA
William L.	10	M		TX
Isabella	3	F		TX
Arbel	1	F		TX
Choat, Kener D.	15	F		TX
King E.	16	M	Farmer	TX
Bell, Thomas	28	M	Farmer	PA
Mary	26	F		AR
Thomas	1	M		TX
Hall, B. F.	21	M	Farmer	TN
Skiles, Harvey	41	M	Farmer	TN
Martha	24	F		MO
Mary J.	18	F		IL
James H.	15	M	Farmer	IL
Lydia M.	10	F		IA
William T.	7	M		TX
Drucilla E.	3	F		TX
Parker, Eliza F.	20	F		MO
Andrew J.	18	M	Farmer	MO
Jasper	13	M		MO
Narcissa	10	F		MO
Janetta	9	F		MO
Amanda	3	F		TX
William E.	2	M		TX
Pryor, William A.	23	M	Farmer	LA
Laura E.	17	F		TN
Benjamin	62	M	Farmer	VA
Davis, Charles	24	M	Farmer	VA
Sarah A.	20	F		LA
Mary E.	1	F		TN
James R.	22	M	Farmer	TN
Sevier, George M.	38	M	Farmer	TN
Elizabeth	27	F		AL
Thomas	9	M		TX
John	6	M		TX
Eliza	4	F		TX
Valentine	3	M		TX
Sarah J.	2	F		TX
James	4/12	M		TX
McKey, Elias	26	M	Farmer	TN
Mariah	26	F		TN
Thomas	2	M		TX
Elias	1	M		TX
Landford, James M.	38	M	Farmer	TN
Mary Jane	25	F		AL
Eliza E.	9	F		TX
James D.	1/12	M		TX

Name	Age	Sex	Occupation	Birthplace
Carter, Edward J.	60	M	(M) Grocer	TN
Susanna	70	F		SC
Alex	34	M	(M) Farmer	TN
Eliza Ann	23	F		AL
Willard S.	6	M	(M)	TX
Stokes, Guy	32	M	Farmer	TN
William J.	28	M	Farmer	TN
Mitchell, T. D.	43	M	Farmer	TN
McCulloch, Alex.	50	M	Farmer	TN
Mathews, Robert	26	M	Farmer	AL
Lacy, Joseph	22	M	Farmer	AL
Smith, William	21	M	Farmer	TN
Stokes, Ann	20	F		AL
Howe, Mary Jane	14	F		TN
Ann F.	10	F		TN
William G.	9	M		TN
Chapman, John	31	M	Farmer	KY
Manerva	25	F		TN
Robert	9	M		IN
Elizabeth	6	F		IN
Davis, Joel L.	33	M	Farmer	TN
Catharine K.	23	F		TN
Elizabeth	5	F		TX
John B.	2	M		TX
Younger, George W.	29	M	Farmer	TN
Mary E.	24	F		TN
John A.	3	M		TX
George	5/12	M		TX
Geaslin, William	48	M	Farmer	VA
Ruth L.	39	F		TN
Sarah J.	20	F		TN
Newton J.	18	M	Farmer	TN
William D.	17	M	Farmer	TN
John N.	15	M	Farmer	TN
Rebecca F.	12	F		TN
Melinda	11	F		TN
Mary Ann	8	F		TN
James K.	5	M		TN
Joseph J.	1	M		TN
Pace, John	37	M	Farmer	TN
Sarah	36	F		TN
John L.	14	M		TN
Ibbey	11	F		TN
Lenney	9	F		TN
James T.	7	M		TN
Sarah E.	5	F		TN
William T.	3	M		TN
Greathouse, Archibald	45	M	Farmer	GA
Mary Ann	36	F		TN
Levisa E.	17	F		TN
John B.	16	M	Farmer	TN
George W.	15	M	Farmer	TN
Joel W.	13	M		AR
Malissa A.	11	F		AR
Hubbard	9	M		TX
Elijah J.	5	M		TX
Margaret E.	1	F		TX
Wilson, Samuel S.	35	M	Black Smith	NY
Sarah	29	F		TN
William H.	3	M		IL
Douglas, Nathaniel	49	M	Tailor	SC
Mary	42	F		TN
Jesse	23	M	Tailor	TN
Henry	22	M	Tailor	TN
Warren	20	M	Tailor	TN
Rebecca	18	F		TN
Susanna	14	F		TN
Laura	10	F		TN
Elizabeth	8	F		TN
George	6	M		TN
Mary	4	F		TN
Emily	12	F		TN
Billingsly, Jonathan B.	34	M	Farmer	MO
Susanna	24	F		TN
Martha A.	10	F		MO

(continued)

ELLIS COUNTY, TEXAS

Name	Age	Sex	Occupation	Birthplace
Billingsly, Mary Jane	9	F		MO
Hannah K.	6	F		MO
Dickson, Mary E.	6	F		IL
Isaac J.	3	M		TX
Billingsly, Nancy A.	4	F		MO
Sarah E.	3	F		TX
Dickson, William W.	1	M		TX
Kirkland, Margaret	48	F		TN
Isaac	16	M	Farmer	IL
Emeline	15	F		IL
Thomas J.	12	M		IL
Park, Alfred J.	22	M	Farmer	IN
Lydia A.	22	F		IL
Rocket, Roberson J.	24	M	Farmer	NC
Nancy E.	21	F		TN
Toy W.	1	M		IN
Nugent, John	20	M	Farmer	IRE
Mary Ann	23	F		TN
Thomas M.	1	M		TX
King, William D.	35	M	Physician	TN
Margaret T.	35	F		TN
Mary Ann	16	F		MO
Wallace T.	14	M		MO
Martha E.	12	F		MO
Sarah J.	9	F		MO
Samuel T.	6	M		MO
Narcissa E.	4	F		MO
Margaret A.	1	F		MO
Newton, Asa R.	26	M	Farmer	AR
Mary	22	F		NC
Emily A.	2	F		TX
Robert L.	7/12	M		TX
Eli Lovett	24	M	Farmer	TN
King, Finis E.	30	M	C.P. Minister	TN
Sarah A.	28	F		AL
George G.	4	M		MO
Mary E.	1	F		TX
Billingsly, Martha A.	12	F		MO
Wilson, Joseph	55	M	Farmer	VA
Mary	60	F		TN
Guliver	19	M	Farmer	MO
Anderson, William	33	M		MO
Joseph	8	M		MO
Mary M.	6	F		MO
Ayers, Benjamin P.	49	M	Farmer	KY
Emily	39	F		NC
James H.	17	M	Farmer	TN
Elias M.	15	M	Farmer	TN
John A.	10	M		TX
Mary Jane	7	F		TX
Emily Ann	5	F		TX
Sanderson, W. A.	32	M	Farmer	ENG
Isabella F.	19	F		TN
John B.	5/12	M		TX

TARRANT COUNTY, TEXAS

Navarro District

Name	Age	Sex	Occupation	Birthplace
Allen, Richard F.	35	M	Black Smith	TN
Rosalinda	33	F		GA
Elizabeth	16	F		TN
Mary	14	F		MO
Hugh B.	12	M		MO
Sabrina	10	F		MO
Permelia S.	8	F		MO
Thomas R.	6	M		MO
Linda C.	1	F		TX
Barcroft, Daniel	37	M	Farmer	VA
Mary A.	32	F		TN
William G.	14	M		MO
Charles E.	12	M		MO
Elizabeth A.	8	F		MO

(continued)

Name	Age	Sex	Occupation	Birthplace
Barcroft, Permelia Ann	6	F		MO
Gabriel L.	4	M		MO
Abigail	1	F		TX
Allen, Jesse J.	52	M	Farmer	NC
Nancy	52	F		NC
Richard	23	M	Farmer	TN
Jesse F.	16	M	Farmer	MO
Elizabeth A.	12	F		MO
Durham, Abby Willas	42	M		NC
Joseph A.	23	M		TN
Elizabeth J.	15	F		MO
John H.	13	M		MO
William O.	11	M		MO
Nancy A.	8	F		MO
Abby L.	6	F		MO
Neill, J.	31	M	Farmer	TN
Lucinda L.	20	F		TN
Permelia M.	13	F		MO
James R.	13	M		MO
Madulda	13	F		MO
Amanda J.	8	F		MO
Thomas	6	M		MO
Charles C.	4	M		MO
Abby	2	F		MO
Gibson, Jesse	54	M	Farmer	SC
Thomas B.	14	M		TN
Baker, James M.	30	M	Farmer	TN
Ruth	31	F		TN
Permelia	14	F		TN
James C.	1	M		TX
Benjamin F.	16	M	Farmer	MO
Mahan, Thomas	35	M	Farmer	KY
Sarah M.	29	F		TN
Rachael M.	6	F		MO
James F.	5	M		MO
Charles M.	3	M		TX
Smith, Robert A.	30	M	Saddler	TN
Mary E.	25	F		SC
Ann H.	6	F		MO
William C.	4	M		MO
Louise	1	F		TX
Freeman, John A.	28	M	Baptist Minister	SC
Nancy	24	F		TN
William F.	3	M		TX
Rachael M.	1	F		TX
Foster, Benjamin J.	19	M	Farmer	MO
Mary Ann	18	F		TN
Foster, Susanna	53	F		SC
Jarret	17	M	Farmer	MO
Owen	15	M	Farmer	MO
James L.	13	M		MO
Dyaria	10	F		MO
Throop, Lucinda	36	F		TN
James M.	5	M		TX
Dyaria C.	2	F		TX
Porter, Jno. F.	58	M	Farmer	SC
Euphany	51	F		VA
Josiah	27	M	Saddler	TN
George F.	21	M	Farmer	AL
Susan J.	19	F		TN
John E.	15	M	Farmer	TN
Thomas A.	13	M		TN
David	11	M		IL
Albert B.	8	M		IL
Bernard, Thomas	24	M	Farmer	TN
Holman, William P.	27	M	Farmer	TN
Elizabeth M.	23	F		TN
James P.	4	M		IL
Rufus	2	M		TX
Fogg, William A.	27	M	Farmer	KY
Mitchell, David	46	M	Farmer	IN
Eliza G.	38	F		TN

(continued)

TARRANT COUNTY, TEXAS

Name	Age	Sex	Occupation	Birthplace
Mitchell, Edwin L.	15	M	Farmer	AR
Mary C.	13	F		AR
Ann E.	10	F		AR
Sopronnas E.	5	F		AR
Harriet E.	1	F		TX
Howerton, Jeremiah	59	M	Bl. S.M.E. Mins.	NC
Eliza	44	F		TN
Dorotha A. E.	14	F		MO
Elvira R.	10	F		MO
Josephine	2	F		AR
Howerton, Jane S.	34	F		TN
Lucy A.	10	F		MO
Nancy E.	8	F		MO
Catharine	1	F		AR
Howerton, F. M.	25	M	Farmer	TN
Didamy F.	17	F		AR
Mary E.	1	F		AR
Burford, William J.	38	M	Farmer	TN
Mary E.	30	F		GA
Margaret A. M.	12	F		AL
Rhoda F.	9	F		TX
Sarah M.	7	F		TX
Mary L.	5	F		TX
Ann E.	3	F		TX
Nancy L.	1	F		TX
Standifer, J. M.	36	M	Far. & Physician	GA
Eliza P.	26	F		TN
C. J.	9	F		TX
Eliza	6	F		TX
Julia C.	4	F		TX
Edward, Carol M.	18	F		TN
Edward, Lemuel	44	M	Carpenter	OH
Eliza	37	F		TN
John William	12	M		MO
Thomas B.	8	M		MO
Richard C.	7	M		MO
Sarah J.	4	F		MO
Martha A.	1	F		MO
Johnson, M. T.	40	M	Farmer	SC
Vienna	37	F		SC
Thomas J.	15	M		AL
Benjamin F.	13	M		AL
Elizabeth	11	F		AL
Rhoda	8	F		TX
M. T.	5	M		TX
Fatime	2	F		TX
Fane, Mercer	30	M	Farmer	TN
Parkey, Josiah R.	25	M	Farmer	AL
Swing, Mathias L.	27	M	School Teacher	NJ
Blackwell, Hiram	28	M	Farmer	TN
Sarah E.	7	F		AR
Nancy A.	2	F		TX
Farmer, George P.	33	M	Farmer	TN
Jane	21	F		TN
Susan A.	3	F		TN

Soldier List

Name	Age	Sex	Occupation	Birthplace
Medland, Dell	23	F		TN

End Soldier List

Name	Age	Sex	Occupation	Birthplace
Goodman, James J.	35	M	Farmer	TN
Jane	20	F		AR
William	6	M		AR
James J.	2	M		AR
Vincent	1	M		TX
Linch, John	46	M	Farmer	TN
Horatio G.	21	M	Farmer	TN
Josiah M. C.	19	M	Farmer	IL
William H.	17	M	Farmer	MO
Thomas, Jacob	37	M	Farmer	TN
Drucilla	38	F		TN

(continued)

Name	Age	Sex	Occupation	Birthplace
Thomas, Napoleon B.	16	M	Farmer	MO
Berry F.	14	M		MO
Eliza L.	12	F		MO
Malinda J.	10	F		MO
Jno. H.	8	M		MO
Robert J.	6	M		MO
James K. P.	4	M		MO
William S.	1	M		TX
Walker, Perry F.	40	M	School Teacher	IRE
Conner, William D.	22	M	Farmer	IN
Nancy	21	F		TN
A. H.	2/12	M		TX
Gillmore, L(S)ebern	50	M	Farmer	GA
Celia	45	F		TN
Henry W.	12	M		IL
Francis D.	8	M		IL
Caroline M.	5	F		IL
Martha E.	9/12	F		TX
Halford, James P.	37	M	Farmer	SC
Sarah	37	F		TN
A. J.	15	M	Farmer	MO
Rachael	13	F		MO
W. J.	11	M		MO
John H.	9	M		MO
Jesse R.	7	M		MO
Jasper N.	5	M		TX
Rebecca N.	1	F		TX
Anderson, Joseph	33	M	Farmer	AR
Elizabeth	25	F		TN
Mary E.	3	F		MO
George W.	3/12	M		TX
Rogers, Walling A.	52	M	Farmer	TN
Sarah	50	F		KY
Thomas	21	M	Farmer	KY
Walling D.	16	M	Farmer	KY
Adinston	14	M		MO
Sarah	13	F		MO
Henry	5	M		Mo
Freshour, John	31	M	Farmer	TN
Permelia	29	F		TN
Mary A.	11	F		MO
William J.	8	M		MO
Elizabeth A.	6	F		MO
Emily J.	4	F		MO
John A.	1	M		MO
Allen, Jesse G.	52	M	Farmer	NC
Nancy	52	F		NC
Richard C.	23	M	Farmer	TN
Jesse F.	15	M	Farmer	MO
Elizabeth	11	F		MO
Anderson, A. W.	50	M	Farmer	TN
Mary	45	F		NC
Hall M.	15	M	Farmer	MO
William C.	13	M		MO
Lucetha	11	F		MO
Araminta	8	F		MO
Alvin W.	4	M		TX
Nancy A.	1	F		TX
Gibson, Nancy	52	F		NC
Bluford	13	M		MO
Mark, A------	45	F		TN
Suggs, Henry	30	M	Farmer	TN
Talita	28	F		TN
Winfield, John J.	32	M	Farmer	KY
Nancy K.	26	F		AR
Rebecca C.	5	F		AR
Talita	2	F		TX
Davis, Joseph	22	M	Farmer	TN
Hust, John A.	34	M	Farmer	TN
Christiana	25	F		TN
Hamilton H.	16	M	Farmer	IN
Leana	14	F		IN
Nancy J.	10	F		Mo

(continued)

TARRANT COUNTY, TEXAS

Name	Age	Sex	Occupation	Birthplace
Hust, Mary Ann	8	F		MO
John	6	M		MO
Abigail E.	3	F		MO
James J.	4/12	M		TX
York, John B.	25	M	Farmer	TN
Julia Ann	23	F		TN
William J.	11/12	M		TX
Mooneyham, J. J.	30	M	Farmer	TN
Mary E.	15	F		TN
Sarah Ann	8	F		MO
Julia Ann	4	F		TX
Harriet L.	2	F		TX
Boydston, Jos.	12	M		MO

FANNIN COUNTY, TEXAS

Name	Age	Sex	Occupation	Birthplace
Moore, Carter	50	M	Farmer	SC
Susan	34	F		TN
Jas. E.	17	M	Farmer	MO
Perry	10	M		TX
Caroline	8	F		TX
Carter	6	M		TX
C. A.	4	F		TX
Hilery	1/12	M		TX
Bledsoe, L. A.	32	M	Carpenter	GA
S. C.	21	F		TN
S. G.	1	F		TX
Burleson, B. M.	39	M	Farmer	TN
M. A.	36	F		TN
Jno. M.	17	M	Laborer	TN
E. L.	14	F		TN
William R.	12	M		AL
S. E.	10	F		AL
J. E.	8	M		AL
M. E.	6	F		AL
M. J.	4	F		AL
J. T.	1	M		AL
Self, T. R.	21	M	Laborer	AL
Freeman, William C.	39	M	Farmer	NC
Nancy	38	F		TN
Thomas P.	17	M	Laborer	TN
A. G.	15	M		TN
Jos. L.	13	M		TN
William D.	11	M		TN
Samuel D.	4	M		TN
Britton, Sarah	10	F		IN
Slave	21	M	(Black)	--
Gilbert, Mobel	52	M	Farmer	NC
C.	49	F		NC
Thomas J.	36	M	Farmer	TN
William H.	24	M	Carpenter	TN
R. M.	23	M	Farmer	TN
F. M.	20	M	Laborer	TN
N.	17	M	Laborer	TN
J.	17	M		TN
S.	12	F		TX
L.	10	F		TX
M.	8	M		TX
Slaves	5/12	M	(Black)	--
	3	F	(Black)	--
	4	M	(Black)	--
	6	M	(Black)	--
	7	F	(Black)	--
	15	F	(M)	--
	21	F	(Black)	--
	30	M	(Black)	--
	6	M	(M)	--
McFarland, Sam.	36	M	Farmer	IRE
D.	27	F		TN
Y.	11	M		TX
Sarah	9	F		TX
Jos.	7	M		TX
P.	5	F		TX
Robert	3	M		TX
M. G.	3/12	F		TX
Dennis, Colby	42	M	Farmer	KY
L.	30	F		TN
M. G.	17	F		AR
Jno. W.	12	M		AR
C. B.	10	M		AR
S. E.	4	F		TX
Blanton, L.	40	M	Farmer	SC
M.	34	F		TN
H. E.	17	F		MO
Jno. D.	5	M		TX
Mary F.	8	F		TX
W. H.	3	M		TX
Isaac C.	1	M		TX
Britton, I.	18	M	Laborer	IN
Stephenson, C.	20	M	Laborer	TN
Slave	24	M	(Black)	--
Justus, Jos.	56	M	Farmer	TN
E.	29	F		MO
Jos.	23	M	Farmer	IL
M.	15	M		IL
Daniel	11	M		IL
Stephens, Lewis	50	M	Farmer	SC
E.	43	F		TN
S.	20	F		AL
L.	18	F		AL
M. A.	13	F		AL
G. F.	11	M		AL
H. E.	7	M		TX
Croones, G.	25	M		KY
Z.	20	F		TN
William	4	M		TN
M.	2	F		LA
Daniel, N. A.	28	M	Laborer	TN
Slaves	5/12	F	(Black)	--
	2	M	(Black)	--
	15	M	(Black)	--
	17	M	(Black)	--
	18	F	(Black)	--
	20	F	(Black)	--
	25	M	(Black)	--
	30	F	(Black)	--
Garrison, Thomas ?.	23	M	M.E. Preacher	TN
T. C.	19	F		TN
William D.	1	M		TX
Moores, E.	16	F		TN
Kerr, Y.	36	M	Farmer	TN
M.	22	F		TN
L.	7	M		TX
A. J.	11/12	M		TX
Acles	22	M	Laborer	TN
A.	18	M	Laborer	TN
C. S.	16	M	Laborer	TN
Peterson, Jno.	24	M	Farmer	IL
L.	27	F		KY
M. S. F.	3	F		AR
Killgore, S.	17	F		KY
Payne, W. W.	27	M	Farmer	TN
Mary A.	25	F		KY
Kirk, Peter	39	M	Farmer	TN
C.	35	F		KY
McCarty, Jos. H.	41	M	Physician	VA
M. A.	22	F		TN
Jas. D.	3	M		TX
Galbraith, Alex.	30	M	Laborer	TN
Apple, J.	22	M	Laborer	TN
Christian, S. B.	70	F		GA
Jno. W.	19	M		AR
Slaves	12	M	(Black)	--
	35	M	(Black)	--
Hampton, Jno.	52	M	Farmer	KY
N. A.	27	F		TN
U. S.	22	M	Laborer	KY
William J.	8	M		MO
C. W.	5	M		MO
Keller, M.	11	F		TX

(continued)

FANNIN COUNTY, TEXAS

Name	Age	Sex / Occupation	Birthplace
Morris, L.	20	M	KY
Slaves	5	M (Black)	--
	38	F (Black)	--
Welch, Jas.	33	M Laborer	TN
E.	24	F	TN
M. J.	12	F	MO
William J.	10	M	MO
E.	9	F	MO
T. B.	8	M	MO
R. C.	1	F	MO
Richards, L.	48	M Farmer	TN
M.	38	F	TN
Thomas	16	M	AR
W.	11	M	AR
Mary	8	F	AR
Ann	5	F	AR
A.	2	M	TX
Santo, A.	32	M Laborer	GER
Slaves	2	M (M)	--
	16	F (M)	--
	23	M (Black)	--
Peters, E.	24	M Farmer	TN
M.	20	F	MO
W. A.	3/12	M	TX
Johnson, David	44	M Surveyor	TN
M. W.	31	F	TN
J. B.	13	F	TN
M. J.	11	F	TN
M. E.	6	F	TN
Slaves	6/12	M (M)	--
	6/12	F (M)	--
	2	M (M)	--
	2	F (M)	--
	8	M (Black)	--
	19	M (Black)	--
	22	F (Black)	--
	24	F (Black)	--
	50	F (Black)	--
Williams, Samuel	28	M Farmer	SC
E. C.	26	F	TN
Jno. A.	4	M	TX
T. J.	1	F	TX
Thomas, George G.	38	M C.D.	TN
M. L.	30	F	MO
L. H.	9	M	MO
Jos. S.	5	M	TX
Jno. D.	2	M	TX
A.	16	M Laborer	TN
K.	15	M	TN
D.	14	M	TN
V.	13	M	TN
G.	12	M	TN
William	10	M	TN
B.	8	M	TN
Henry Clay	7	M	TN
Z. Taylor	5	M	TN
White, R.	43	M Farmer	NC
C.	37	F	NC
M.	17	F	TN
Sarah	16	F	TN
George	11	M	TN
D.	9	F	TN
Nancy	7	F	TN
E.	6	F	TN
Jno.	4	M	TN
E.	2	F	TX
Dulany, William	28	M Farmer	IL
E.	26	F	MO
W.	5	M	TX
Jno.	4	M	TX
V. G.	1	F	TX
Carr, William	58	M Farmer	TN
H.	18	M Farmer	IL
Jas.	11	M	IL
M.	9	F	IA

(continued)

Name	Age	Sex / Occupation	Birthplace
Buckley, Mary	19	F	GER
Southerland, Jas.	15	M	AR
Dulany, Jno.	39	M Farmer	KY
W.	12	M	IL
M. E.	10	F	IL
H.	7	M	IL
F. J.	4	F	TX
O.	1	M	TX
Rodgers, J. J.	26	M Farmer	TN
L. A.	20	F	KY
C.	1	F	TX
Slave	40	M (Black)	--
Bush, Sarah A.	28	F	TN
Joseph	5	M	TX
R. J.	5	F	TX
H. B.	2	M	TX
Slave	24	M (Black)	--
Montgomery, S. P.	40	M Farmer	TN
Mary	28	F	IL
E. F.	12	F	IL
Jos. W.	9	M	IL
O. F.	4	M	TX
Southword, William	51	M M.E. Preacher	VA
M.	50	F	TN
H.	21	M Laborer	IL
E.	19	M Laborer	IL
Jas.	17	M Laborer	IL
E.	15	F	MI
Row, E.	24	M Laborer	MO
Lindsy, Thomas	56	M Farmer	TN
R.	50	F	VA
Thomas W.	17	M Laborer	AR
E. A.	14	M	MO
R. M.	10	F	TX
Slaves	3	F (M)	--
	8	F (Black)	--
	12	F (M)	--
	4	M (M)	--
	8	M (Black)	--
	19	F (M)	--
	40	M (Black)	--
	45	M (Black)	--
Crawford, John F.	40	M Farmer	MO
A.	31	F	TN
B. A.	9	M	AR
E. ?.	8	F	AR
Alfred J.	5	M	TX
A. M.	5	M	TX
M. F.	2	F	TX
Gailey, Jas.	34	M Farmer	TN
M.	24	F	KY
Slave	12	F (Black)	--
Laster, Jno. H.	28	M Farmer	TN
E.	28	F	KY
S. C.	7	F	AR
A. J.	6	F	AR
Jas. H.	2	M	AR
Inglish, Bailey	55	M Farmer	SC
Nancy	39	F	TN
W. C.	21	M Laborer	AR
B.	11	M	TX
Alex.	9	M	TX
L.	7	F	TX
R.	5	M	TX
Capt Bragg	4	M	TX
Not named	2	F	TX
Croomes, L.	22	M Laborer	TN
Jane	17	F	TN
Not named	6/12	M	TX
Keller, C. J.	27	M Deputy Sheriff	TN
Slaves	10	F (M)	--
	12	F (M)	--
	23	M (Black)	--
	32	M (Black)	--
	38	F (M)	--

Name	Age	Sex	Occupation	Birthplace
Sampson, Jno. P.	43	M	Farmer	TN
S.	36	F		TN
Elizabeth	16	F		TN
M. A.	15	F		TN
Mary	13	F		TX
Croons, Jno.	14	M		TN
Fawcet, F. G.	34	M	M.E. Preacher PCS	TN
Jane	36	F		TN
Thomas, Jos. A.	28	M	Laborer	VA
Crawford, Robert	9	M		AR
Butler, Reese	43	M	Farmer	TN
Lucy	44	F		KY
Jno.	18	M		MO
S.	15	M		MO
E.	9	M		MO
Weaks, W.	70	M		VA
Wright, L.	23	F		AR
L.	3	F		MO
Slaves	19	M	(Black)	--
	19	M	(Black)	--
	21	M	(M)	--
	50	F	(Black)	--
Jones, William	50	M	Farmer	NC
Polly	51	F		SC
L.	31	F		TN
M-----	17	F		MO
Robert	18	M		MO
Austin, M. A.	20	F		MO
L.	2	F		MO
Slaves	11/12	F	(Black)	--
	40	F	(Black)	--
Lock, R. H.	39	M	Farmer	TN
Nancy O.	34	F		KY
E.	17	F		KY
M. A.	12	F		TX
W. H.	10	M		TX
Mary	6	F		TX
M. D.	2	F		TX
Jones, Charles	22	M	Laborer	KY
Slaves	7	F	(M)	--
	11	F	(M)	--
	35	F	(M)	--
Rogers, E. C.	42	M	Physician	TN
Nancy	24	F		IL
M. A.	4	F		TX
Jane	1	F		TX
Baker, Jas.	59	M	Farmer	SC
S. C.	53	F		VA
S. F.	19	F		TN
A. E.	17	F		TN
V. C.	12	F		TX
Baker, R. P.	24	M	Farmer	TN
M. G.	20	F		TN
McMennamey, Jno.	56	M	Farmer	TN
P.	55	F		NC
L. M.	25	F		TN
Mary A.	23	F		TN
J. J.	21	M	Laborer	IL
J. M.	18	M	Laborer	IL
J. A.	5	M		TX
McMennamey, Isaac A.	29	M	Farmer	TN
N.	22	F		IN
J. F.	5	M		TX
William H.	3	M		TX
M. A.	11/12	F		TX
W. W.	30	M	Farmer	TN
Dyer, James L.	41	M	Farmer	TN
Sally S.	37	F		KY
H. P.	16	M	Laborer	IN
William B.	12	M		IA
Jno.	5	M		IA
Mary	2	F		TX
Jeans, Thomas	43	M	Wheelwright	??

(continued)

Name	Age	Sex	Occupation	Birthplace
Jeans, Nancy	45	F		TN
Roades, A.	11	M		MO
Meeks, M.	38	M	Farmer	??
Sarah	36	F		TN
George	15	M		MO
William	14	M		MO
Morgan	12	M		MO
Robert	10	M		MO
F.	8	M		MO
M. F.	6	F		MO
S. A.	3	F		TX
Williams, Jno.	24	M	Laborer	??
Warden, H.	19	M	Laborer	MO
J. B.	25	F		KY
C.	7/12	F		TX
Hanson, Mary J.	10	F		MO
James	5	M		TN
Watkins, Daniel	35	M	Farmer	TN
L.	25	F		IL
L.	7	F		IL
William A.	4	M		TX
M. C.	10/12	F		TX
Smith, George W.	55	M	Farmer	TN
Elizabeth	47	F		NC
Cantrell, Jane M.	23	F		AL
Jas. R.	5	M		MO
George W.	4	M		TX
M. E.	9/12	F		TX
Blevens, Jno.	35	M	Farmer	KY
S.	28	F		AR
M. E.	11	F		AR
M. J.	8	F		AR
S. A.	7	F		AR
William J.	4	M		TX
L. M.	2	F		TX
Couch, P. H.	21	M	Laborer	TN
Rean-, William	23	M	Laborer	TN
Routh, Jonathan	46	M	Farmer	TN
Jacob	32	M	Laborer	TN
William A.	22	M	Laborer	TN
C. B.	14	F		IL
Watkins, Jos. C.	31	M	Farmer	TN
Nancy J.	25	F		TN
M. R.	3	F		TX
L. C.	1	F		TX
McFarland, Jos. O.	22	M	Laborer	TN
Watkins, Martha	51	F		VA
Ruth	27	F		TN
William	21	M	Laborer	TN
W. R.	18	M	Laborer	TN
Jos. D.	16	M	Laborer	TN
Boutwell, Jno.	46	M	Farmer	TN
Ruth	48	F		SC
E. G.	19	F		AR
Samuel	15	M		AR
Stephen	14	M		AR
Jas. R.	12	M		AR
A. R.	9	M		AR
Sarah M.	9	F		AR
George W.	8	M		AR
Mary	6	F		TX
Martha A.	4	F		TX
Davis, B. S.	50	M	Farmer	TN
Martha	35	F		GA
William P.	18	M	Laborer	AL
P---	10	F		AL
Jno. R.	7	M		AL
Araminta	5	F		AL
G. A.	3	F		TX
Jane C.	68	F		NC
Slaves	11/12	M	(Black)	--
	4	F	(Black)	--
	6	F	(Black)	--
	23	F	(Black)	--
	26	M	(Black)	--

FANNIN COUNTY, TEXAS

Name	Age	Sex	Occupation	Birthplace
Russell, Robert P.	45	M	Farmer	NC
S.	34	F		TN
E. A.	17	F		TN
Ellen	14	F		TN
P. P.	12	F		TN
B.	9	F		TN
James A.	7	M		TN
Robert V.	5	M		TN
Slaves	33	M	(Black)	--
	70	F	(Black)	--
McKee, Jno.	51	M	C.P. Minister	TN
E.	39	F		KY
W. F.	16	M	Laborer	TN
Jas. R. B.	11	M		TN
Jno. E.	10	M		MS
M. L.	8	F		TX
L.	6	M		TX
L.	4	M		TX
M. R.	3	F		TX
B. G.	1	M		TX
Bolton, L.	68	F		TN
Slaves	11	F	(Black)	--
	21	M	(Black)	--
Drigers, William	33	M	Farmer	SC
F.	23	F		TN
Thomas	8	M		TX
Hill, Thomas	47	M	Carpenter	YN
R.	42	F		TN
Alex.	20	M	Laborer	IL
I.	19	M		IL
L.	17	F		MO
W.	15	M		MO
Duckworth, J. F.	24	M	Farmer	TN
M. G.	22	F		IN
Jos. P.	2	M		TX
S. J.	11/12	F		TX
Price, Evan	36	M	Farmer	TN
M. A.	26	F		TN
Jos. O.	5	M		IL
Jno. P.	4	M		TX
Thomas J.	2	M		TX
Finley, Thomas J.	32	M	Farmer	AL
Evaline	35	F		TN
L.	33	F		AL
Wester, A. K.	7	F		MS
Delay, Jos.	25	M	Farmer	TN
Harriett	23	F		TN
J. A.	6	F		AR
J.	4	M		AR
Jno. R.	1	M		TX
Bone, Jno.	28	M	Wheelwright	MO
Amanda	25	F		TN
E. M.	6	F		MO
R. C.	1	F		TX
Bone, A. S.	49	M	Farmer	KY
Rachael	46	F		TN
William A.	21	M	Laborer	MO
Alfred S.	16	M		MO
Y. E.	13	M		MO
J. P.	11	M		MO
George W.	8	M		MO
J. F.	8	M		MO
F. M.	5	M		MO
Doctor	1	M		TX
Harrell, Robert	33	M	Farmer	NC
Mildred	20	F		IL
William O.	1	M		TX
Blanton, William	12	M		TN
Stone, William	42	M	Farmer	SC
H.	40	F		KY
C. E.	18	F		IL
W. R.	14	M		IL
(continued)				
Stone, Jno.	12	M		IL
Walker, J. H.	26	M	Farmer	TN
C. G.	16	F		IL
Harrell, Richard	38	M	Farmer	NC
Nancy L.	27	F		TN
E. P.	6	M		TX
M.	4	F		TX
Charles W.	1	M		TX
Van Cleave, George W.	7	M		KY
William G.	5	M		TN
Culver, William	22	M	Laborer	TN
Blanton, Susan	12	F		TN
Johnson, Enoch	41	M	Farmer	TN
Sarah	41	F		NC
E. A.	20	F		TN
William M.	17	M	Laborer	TN
M. S.	17	F		TN
W. G.	15	F		TN
E. F.	11	F		MO
S. C.	7	F		MO
B. L.	6	M		MO
E. F.	4	F		TX
R. H.	1	M		TX
Isaac	22	M	Farmer	TN
R. M.	20	F		TN
Murphy, Jackson	22	M	Farmer	TN
Wintin, Jno.	39	M	Farmer	TN
F.	32	F		TN
Sarah	14	F		IL
R. E.	13	F		MO
James W.	11	M		MO
Mary	9	F		MO
A.	4	F		AR
Stephen	2	M		AR
Nancy	6/12	F		TX
English, William	26	M	Farmer	TN
M.	27	F		TX
Jos.	6	M		TX
E.	3	M		TX
M. E.	6/12	F		TX
Jas.	57	M	M.E.C.S.	TN
Martha	12	F		TX
Slave	9	F	(Black)	--
Bourden, Nathaniel	52	M	Black Smith	TN
Sarah	42	F		VA
Carrol	19	M	Laborer	MO
Susan	16	F		AR
David	12	M		AR
M.	9	F		AR
Sarah	8	F		AR
George	3	M		TX
Cannon, William	30	M	Laborer	NC
L.	25	F		TN
Sarah	6	F		AR
Ellen	3	F		TX
Nathaniel	5/12	M		TX
Slaves	3/12	M	(Black)	--
	16	F	(Black)	--
	27	F	(Black)	--
	25	M	(Black)	--
Lawson, William	22	M		IL
M. J.	18	F		TN
Z.	4/12	M		TX
Davis, Jos.	50	M	Saddler	??
E.	49	F		??
A.	18	F		TN
P.	13	M		TN
McFarland, Albert	28	M	Farmer	MO
E.	23	F		TN
Elizabeth	3/12	F		TX
Moore, R. R.	22	M	Farmer	TN
Jane	17	F		AR
M. A.	6/12	F		AR
Thomas	28	M	Laborer	TN
Slaves	9	F	(Black)	--
	15	M	(Black)	--
	16	M	(Black)	--

Wood, Jno. M.	37	M	Farmer	TN
L.	33	F		AR
M. F.	4	M		AR
C. G.	2	F		AR
M. E.	3/12	F		TX
Brown, Reubin	55	M	Farmer	NC
William W.	24	M	Laborer	TN
Anna M.	17	F		TN
M. G.	15	F		AL
Elizabeth	13	F		AL
Jno.	11	M		TN
Jos. M.	9	M		TX
Hughs, William	23	M	Laborer	TN
Wilkerson, George	27	M	Laborer	GA
Jane	23	F		TN
Robert	3	M		TX
Jno.	1	M		TX
Sloan, Washington	33	M	Farmer	TN
S.	28	F		AR
J. C.	13	F		AR
E. A.	12	F		AR
J.	11	F		AR
W. B.	9	M		AR
H.	7	M		AR
E. E.	5	F		AR
T. E.	3	F		AR
Braly, Hugh	50	M	Farmer	TN
Nancy	42	F		NC
Elijah	20	M	Stone Mason	MO
E.	18	F		MO
Jno.	17	M	Laborer	MO
Hugh	15	M		MO
M. A.	13	F		MO
B. F.	12	M		MO
N. E.	9	F		MO
Jonah	7	M		MO
William	5	M		TX
Adams, William H.	10	M		MO
M. F.	8	F		MO
Dillingham, Jas. C.	28	M	Merchant	MS
J. M.	18	F		??
Sarah	62	F		TN
S. M.	18	M		TN
Statts, Nancy	32	F		TN
William	4	M		TX
Nelson	3	M		TX
Slaves	2	M	(M)	--
	3	M	(M)	--
	5	M	(M)	--
	27	F	(Black)	--
	1	M	(Black)	--
	6	F	(M)	--
	18	F	(Black)	--
	27	M	(Black)	--
	30	F	(Black)	--
	33	M	(Black)	--
Merrick, William	21	M	Farmer	TN
Mary	20	F		TN
E. C.	2/12	F		TX
Lyday, Mary	32	F		TN
H. R.	15	M		TN
N. A.	13	F		MS
M. E.	10	F		TX
A.	2	F		TX
Slaves	2	M	(Black)	--
	3	M	(Black)	--
	4	M	(Black)	--
	16	F	(Black)	--
	18	F	(Black)	--
	19	F	(Black)	--
	21	F	(Black)	--
	20	M	(Black)	--
	23	M	(Black)	--
	25	M	(Black)	--
Lyday, Isaac	35	M	Farmer	TN

(continued)

Lyday, Jane	25	F		AR
Jos.	12	M		TX
A. E.	9	F		TX
Mary	7	F		TX
Amanda	5	F		TX
Andrew	4	M		TX
Isaac	2	M		TX
McCleary, S. S.	30	M	Farmer	TN
M. G.	27	F		TN
S. R.	10	M		TN
Jno. W.	8	M		TN
H.	5	F		TX
A.	7/12	F		TX
Slaves	10	F	(Black)	--
	15	F	(Black)	--
	16	F	(Black)	--
	38	F	(Black)	--
	14	M	(M)	--
	27	M	(Black)	--
Hamilton, W. E.	38	M	Farmer	TN
E.	32	F		TN
S. M.	9	M		TX
Thomas A.	7	M		TX
William R.	5	M		TX
A. E.	3	F		TX
C. A.	4/12	F		TX
Foreman, E.	11	F		TN
Slaves	2/12	M	(Black)	--
	18	F	(Black)	--
McKee, S. W.	32	M	Physician	TN
C. L.	29	F		TN
McKee, Jane	60	F		NC
D. E.	25	M	Laborer	TN
Richmond, Thomas	63	M	Physician	NC
Slaves	8/12	F	(Black)	--
	3	M	(Black)	--
	3	M	(Black)	--
	5	M	(Black)	--
	7	F	(Black)	--
	9	F	(Black)	--
	13	M	(M)	--
	26	M	(Black)	--
	33	F	(Black)	--
	50	M	(Black)	--
Mullins, Morgan	40	M	Mins. M.E.C.S.	??
E.	40	F		TN
Jno.	21	M	Laborer	TN
Mary	18	F		TN
William	17	M		TN
M.	14	F		TN
Thomas	12	M		TN
M.	10	F		TN
Bone, M. L.	28	M	Farmer	KY
C. C.	23	F		TN
L. R.	3	F		TX
M. C.	10/12	F		TX
Lane, David	53	M	Farmer	NC
Martha	50	F		TN
Elizabeth	30	F		TN
Robert W.	24	M	Merchant	TN
Isaac G.	19	M	Laborer	TN
Jno. W.	15	M		TN
Moores, W.	13	F		TX
W. A.	8	F		TX
William	7	M		TX
Slave	55	F	(Black)	--
McClure, Rebecca	66	F		NC
W. S.	34	M	Minister M.P.	TN
S. A.	23	F		AL
Slave	12	F	(Black)	--
Tucker, Jas. C.	26	M	Farmer	TN
Cynthia A.	20	F		MO
M. A.	1	F		TX
Titus, P. W.	33	M	Farmer	TN
S. T.	30	F		AL
Robert	9	M		TX

(continued)

Name	Age, Sex, Occupation	Birthplace
Titus, M. E.	6 F	TX
T. H.	3 M	TX
Albert	1 M	TX
Butler, J. W.	21 M Laborer	MO
Slaves	4/12 F (Black)	--
	7 F (Black)	--
	12 F (M)	--
	13 F (Black)	--
	13 F (Black)	--
	16 M (Black)	--
	17 F (Black)	--
	7 F (Black)	--
	18 M (Black)	--
	18 F (Black)	--
	22 F (Black)	--
	39 F (Black)	--
	40 F (Black)	--
	22 M (Black)	--
Living next to		
Titus, George	74 M Farmer	VA
Fulgham, E. W.	30 M Farmer	TN
M. L.	26 F	TN
M. B.	6 F	KY
V. C.	3 F	AR
S. M.	11/12 F	TX
Brasland, B. F.	32 M Farmer	KY
Mary E.	25 F	TN
L. B.	10 F	TX
N. M.	8 F	TX
M. G.	6 F	TX
C. A.	3 F	TX
Hanner, J. B.	12 M	KY
Slaves	3/12 M (Black)	--
	4 M (M)	--
	7 M (M)	--
	25 F (Black)	--
Wood, Franklin	36 M Farmer	TN
M. A.	32 F	TN
J. K. E. T.	12 F	TN
M. A. P.	10 F	TN
Jos. W.	8 M	TX
C. L.	4 M	TX
W. C.	2 M	TX
Not named	11/12 M	TX
Slave	12 F (Black)	--
Merrell, W. B.	45 M Farmer	TN
M. A.	36 F	NC
George W.	21 M Laborer	TN
A. F.	19 M Laborer	TN
Elizabeth F.	18 F	TN
B. H.	13 M	MS
Mary	12 F	TX
R. L.	11 M	TX
W. B.	3 M	TX
Not named	4/12 M	TX
Slaves	22 M (M)	--
	55 F (Black)	--
McFarland, Jas.	55 M Farmer	TN
Jane	50 F	KY
Jas.	17 M Laborer	MO
William	16 M Laborer	MO
M. J.	14 F	MO
Newton	10 M	TX
Arthur	5 M	TX
Jackson, Jno. C.	39 M Farmer	KY
Elizabeth	39 F	TN
Jos. E.	17 M Laborer	AR
S. J.	15 F	AR
Sarah A.	12 F	AR
A.	11 M	AR
Thomas J.	7 M	AR
E. M.	6 F	AR
L. M.	5 F	AR
M. B.	1 F	TX
Slave	20 F (Black)	--
Williams, T. D.	27 M Farmer	TN

(continued)

Name	Age, Sex, Occupation	Birthplace
Williams, H.	27 F	MO
M. J.	7 F	MO
Jno.	5 M	MO
E.	3 M	TX
M. E.	1 F	TX
Staudles, E.	28 M Laborer	AR
Martha	22 F	TN
Sabastine, M.	51 M Stone Mason	NC
M.	50 F	NC
J. C.	20 F	MO
F. M.	17 M Laborer	MO
P. A.	14 F	MO
R. A.	10 F	MO
L. S.	7 F	MO
McFarland, Jasper	21 M Farmer	MO
C.	24 F	TN
M.	5/12 M	TX
White, Andrew	28 M Farmer	TN
E.	20 F	MO
William	3 M	MO
M. E.	1 F	TX
McFarland, Jno.	62 M Farmer	TN
Mary	64 F	VA
DeGuiss, F. P.	45 M Miner	MO
Eliza	36 F	NC
J. N.	17 M Laborer	MO
Jno. F.	15 M	MO
Robert	4 M	MO
Slaves	40 F (Black)	--
	46 M (Black)	--
Wall, Samuel	41 M Farmer	TN
A. C.	28 F	MS
Jos.	18 M Laborer	IN
F. A.	16 F	IN
T. M.	15 M	IN
S. L.	13 M	IN
Jno. H.	8 M	MO
William D.	4 M	TX
J. D.	3 M	TX
Charles M.	1 M	TX
Jordan, Aner	10 M	MO
E.	9 M	MO
A. J.	8 F	MO
Self, A. M., Sr.	48 M Farmer	NC
Mahala	45 F	TN
Sarah	28 F	AL
William	20 M Laborer	AL
A. M., Jr.	18 M	AL
M. M.	16 M Laborer	AL
Jane	14 F	AL
Jno. S.	12 M	AL
Dr. F.	11 M	AL
George W.	6 M	AL
Johnson, F. E.	23 M Farmer	GA
Mary	26 F	TN
R. A.	4 F	AR
Jno. R.	2 M	AR
Slave	14 F (Black)	--
Pettit, J. N.	38 M Farmer	MO
E.	26 F	MO
M.	12 F	MO
M.	10 F	MO
E.	6 F	MO
Mary	4 F	TN
Ann	1 F	TX
Slaves	15 F (Black)	--
	16 M (Black)	--
	18 F (Black)	--
	26 M (Black)	--
Latta, Thomas N.	31 M Farmer	TN
E.	34 F	IL
L. E.	8 F	AR
M. A.	7 F	AR
W. F.	5 F(?)	AR
R. A.	3 M	TX
D. W.	6/12 F	TX

Name	Age	Sex	Occupation	Birthplace
Isham, Jas.	33	M	Farmer	TN
S. A.	29	F		TN
J. B. F.	2	M		TX
William	1/12	M		TX
Fitzgerald, M. A.	9	F		TN
E.	7	F		TN
P. B.	5	F		TN
Sadler, E.	24	M	Laborer	TN
Slaves	9	M	(Black)	--
	24	M	(Black)	--
	60	F	(Black)	--
Carr, Jno.	32	M	Farmer	MO
Fanny	24	F		TN
Wells, Jas.	30	M	Farmer	NC
S. J.	26	F		TN
M. F. J.	4	F		TX
M. M. E.	2	F		TX
Jno. W.	1	M		TX
Davis, A. L.	76	M	Unemployed	NC
Jno. M.	30	M	Laborer	TN
E.	28	M	Laborer (Idiot)	TN
N. E.	16	F		TN
(Illegible), Jas. C.	19	M	Laborer	AR
Fowler, Jos.	54	M	Farmer	SC
Lucy	50	F		SC
A.	19	M	Laborer	AR
Stephen	12	M		AR
William	10	M		AR
Jno.	25	M	Farmer	TN
Jas.	22	M	Laborer	AR
C.	18	F		AR
KIlgore, Jonathan	50	M	farmer	KY
J.	33	F		TN
S.	16	F		KY
R.	13	M		KY
C.	9	F		KY
J.	1/12	M		TX
Hanby, Russ	15	M		AR
S. A.	13	F		AR
William	10	M		AR
H. N.	6	M		AR
Woody, William	25	M	Farmer	TN
Elizabeth	27	F		TN
Jos. L.	3	M		TN
George P.	1	M		TX
Davis, Miles H.	23	M	Farmer	TN
M. A.	22	F		KY
A.	1	M		TX
Walker, Benjamin, Sr.	62	M	Minister R.P.B.	NC
Ann	62	F		VA
William	22	M	Laborer	TN
Jas.	19	M		TN
B. L.	26	M	Farmer	TN
L. A.	21	F		MO
S. A.	3/12	F		TX
Highsaw, F.	42	M	Farmer	KY
M. M.	38	F		NC
Elizabeth	15	F		TN
M. M.	8	F		TN
M.	6	F		TX
E. N.	1	F		TX
Cochran, William M.	28	M	Laborer	KY
Tucker, J. M.	41	M	Farmer	TN
L(S).	38	F		KY
Robert R.	21	M	Laborer	TN
R.	14	F		AR
C. G.	17	M	Laborer	TN
Mary	12	F		AR
Andrew	8	M		TX
L(S).	7	F		TX
Jno.	5	M		TX
Jas.	2	M		TX
Margaret	72	F		NC

Name	Age	Sex	Occupation	Birthplace
Page, Benjamin	31	M	Farmer	TN
Mona	27	F		TN
M. E.	2	F		TX
A. W.	7/12	M		TX
Maddin, R. W.	29	M	Farmer	TN
S. J.	23	F		TN
Bland, P. T.	27	M	Farmer	MO
Sarah J.	17	F		TN
M. E.	2/12	F		TX
Slaves	8	M	(Black)	--
	12	F	(Black)	--
Baker, Thomas C.	41	M	Farmer	TN
Mary S. M.	38	F		VA
Jas. D.	13	M		TN
Lucy A.	12	F		TN
William R.	10	M		TN
Thomas P.	3	M		TN
M. H. E.	1	M		TX
Slaves	17	F	(Black)	--
	19	M	(Black)	--
McKee, A. A.	27	M	Farmer	TN
Sarah J.	22	F		KY
Jas. B.	2	M		TX
M. E.	4/12	F		TX
Slave	9	M	(Black)	--
Fitzgerald, William R.	39	M	Farmer	TN
Nancy A.	30	F		GA
F.	14	M		TN
J. E.	8	F		TX
Sarah	6	F		TX
Robert P.	4	M		TX
M. H.	1	M		TX
Boswell, E.	52	F		GA
Fraze, Jacob	50	M	Farmer	NC
Martha	25	F		TN
F. W. E.	19	M	Laborer	KY
H. B.	11	M		KY
Slave	50	F	(Black)	--
Hobbs, Thomas	36	M	Farmer	TN
Mary	32	F		MO
Jno. W.	10	M		IL
Enos M.	10	M		IL
Jas. S.	6	M		IL
R. A.	3	F		TX
N. J.	1	F		TX
Godsey, B. J.	34	M	Stone Mason	TN
Martha	36	F		IL
Ellen	13	F		MO
Mary	11	F		MO
Richard	9	M		MO
Sarah	7	F		MO
William	5	M		MO
Morrison, J. J.	32	M	Farmer	TN
M. M.	28	F		AR
K.	8	F		TX
E.	7	F		TX
A.	5	F		TX
S.	3	F		TX
Jos.	5/12	M		TX
Pennington, E. G.	40	M	Farmer	SC
J. A.	34	F		NC
Jas.	17	M	Laborer	TN
L. E.	15	F		TN
S.	13	F		TN
C. M.	11	F		TN
Jno. P.	10	M		TX
A. R.	8	F		TX
M. D.	6	F		TX
A. J.	4	F		TX
E. G.	2	M		TX
William H.	6/12	M		TX
Crosley, E.	19	M	Laborer	TN
Johnson, Robert B.	37	M	Farmer	??
A.	36	F		TN

(continued)

Name	Age	Sex	Occupation	Birthplace
Johnson, M. M.	13	F		MO
Nancy	11	F		MO
W. G.	9	M		MO
P. A.	8	F		MO
A.	6	F		MO
Robert W.	1	M		MO
Slaves	2	M	(Black)	--
	3	F	(M)	--
	5	M	(Black)	--
	17	M	(Black)	--
	18	M	(Black)	--
	20	F	(Black)	--
Fitzgerald, G., Jr.	45	M	Farmer	TN
Nancy	40	F		SC
W. P.	20	M	Laborer	AL
E. J.	18	F		AL
R. A.	16	F		TN
Thomas	14	M		TN
Jabez	12	M		AL
M. M.	3	F		TX
R.	2	M		TX
C.	6/12	F		TX
Stanford, H.	33	M	Farmer	TN
H.	33	F		SC
Jas. R.	9	M		TX
A.	7	M		TX
N.	5	M		TX
Jane	3	F		TX
Thomas	23	M	Laborer	TN
N.	17	F		TN
Bouldin, Jacob	24	M	Laborer	AL
Stanford, William	11	M		TN
Stanford, Hiram	45	M	Farmer	SC
E.	43	F		TN
Jane	18	F		KY
P.	16	F		KY
Jno.	44	M		TN
E.	12	M		TN
T.	10	M		TN
H.	8	M		TN
T.	7	M		TN
J.	6	M		TN
E.	4	F		TN
C.	3	F		TN
Weaks, F. G.	45	M	Farmer	TN
L.	44	F		TN
Nancy	20	F		TN
William	21	M		TN
Jane	18	F		TN
W.	16	M		TN
E.	14	F		MS
W.	7	F		MS
Crum, H.	21	M	Laborer	KY
F.	20	F		TN
W. H.	10/12	M		TX
Crosley, William	50	M	Farmer	NC
J.	59	F		SC
M. J.	13	F		TN
J.	10	M		TN
E.	9	M		TN
Lloyd, William	26	M	Black Smith	KY
Jane	21	F		TN
Jno. C.	2/12	M		TX
Mary	54	F		VA
Lee, Jno.	53	M	Farmer	VA
Jane	48	F		TN
Jno. C.	24	M	Stone Mason	TN
Jas. A.	23	M	Stone Mason	TN
Reese D.	18	M	Laborer	TN
L. F.	16	M	Laborer	TN
Mary E.	10	F		AR
Hugh C.	8	M		AR
Nancy A.	6	F		AR
Wallace, Hugh	31	M	Stone Mason	TN

(continued)

Name	Age	Sex	Occupation	Birthplace
Wallace, A. L.	22	F		MO
Jno. C.	6	M		MO
M. A.	1	F		TX
Moore, L. P.	26	M	Carpenter	TN
Mary L.	24	F		MO
George N.	4	M		TX
Robert S.	1	M		TX
Stephens, H. R.	28	M	Farmer	MO
A. M.	22	F		TN
A. E. J.	1	F		TX
M. J.	3/12	F		TX
Cross, J. P.	48	M	Farmer	VA
M.	45	F		NC
Thomas B.	19	M	Laborer	AR
Jos. P.	16	M	Laborer	AR
C.	13	F		AR
G.	10	M		AR
E.	8	M		AR
R. J.	6	F		AR
Vaughan, Jos. M.	40	M	Attending to hogs	TN
Spruce, Jos. P.	39	M	Farmer	NC
M. C.	30	F		TN
Baker, M. A.	23	F		SC
A.	16	M	Laborer	LA
Stuart, Jno.	49	M	Farmer	TN
Elizabeth	37	F		TN
H. F.	13	M		TN
Mary	6	F		TX
L. R.	1	M		TX
F. G.	1	M		TX
Sadler, M.	18	M	Laborer	TN
Slaves	4/12	M	(Black)	--
	2	M	(Black)	--
	3	F	(Black)	--
	5	F	(Black)	--
	6	M	(Black)	--
	10	M	(Black)	--
	13	F	(Black)	--
	16	M	(Black)	--
	34	F	(Black)	--
	43	M	(Black)	--
Dial, Jno.	32	M	Laborer	VA
Lucy	33	F		TN
Susan	9	F		TN
Ellen	7	F		TN
H. H.	6	M		TN
S. T.	10/12	F		TX
Fitzgerald, S. W.	35	M	Farmer	TN
M.	31	F		AL
Jos. P.	10	M		TX
A. H.	7	M		TX
J. B.	1	M		TX
Hobby, Travis	26	M	Laborer	TN
Whelly, David	28	M	Laborer	??
Clark, J. C.	19	M	Laborer	TN
Standerfer, J. E.	36	M	School Teacher	??
Slaves	7/12	M	(Black)	--
	7	M	(Black)	--
	14	M	(Black)	--
	7	F	(M)	--
	30	F	(Black)	--
	37	M	(Black)	--
Vandervant, Jno.	35	M	Laborer	??
H.	24	F		TN
Dagley, Thomas A.	33	M	Sheriff	TN
P. M.	30	F		TN
M. J.	2	F		TX
Davis, William R.	14	M		TN
Spencer, William H.	25	M	Lawyer	TN
Slaves	1	M	(Black)	--
	3	F	(M)	--
	21	F	(Black)	--
	41	M	(Black)	--
Provine, William A.	41	M	Minister C.P.C.	TN
N. F.	37	F		TN

(continued)

FANNIN COUNTY, TEXAS

Provine, George A.	18	M	Laborer	TN
A. E.	12	F		KY
William H.	9	M		KY
S. M.	6	M		KY
Thomas C.	5	M		KY
S. E.	3	F		TX
Sadler, Jno.	39	M	Farmer	TN
N. A.	16	F		MO
L. F.	23	M	Laborer	TN
Stanford, Jos.	30	M	Farmer	TN
R. A.	22	F		TN
M. E.	2	F		TX
Caroway, K. F.	31	M	Black Smith	NC
N. A.	31	F		TN
R. M.	14	F		MS
M. A.	12	F		MS
W.	10	M		MS
Jno.	8	M		MS
Nancy	6	F		MS
R. S.	4	M		TX
E. H.	1	M		TX
Burkhart, G.	37	M	Physician	MO
E.	35	F		TN
George F.	18	M	Laborer	MO
D. W.	16	M	Laborer	MO
Jas. C.	14	M		MO
M. L.	12	F		MO
M. R.	10	F		MO
Jos.	8	M		MO
S. E.	3	F		MO
Stennett, J. A.	23	M	Farmer	VA
E.	18	F		TN
E. E.	25	M	Farmer	VA
Hunt, William H.	35	M	Surveyor	NY
Catharine	24	F		TN
Elizabeth	1	F		TX
Beans, Thomas C.	29	M		VA
Slaves	45	F	(Black)	--
	45	M	(Black)	--
Garnett, Jno. R.	36	M	Farmer	KY
Margarett	36	F		TN
James	12	M		TX
Jabez	6	M		TX
William	4	M		TX
Jane	2	F		TX
Jones, Joseph	16	M	Laborer	TN
Stephen	13	M		TX
Garnett, William R.	31	M	Farmer	AL
Slaves	1/12	M	(Black)	--
	3	F	(Black)	--
	4	F	(Black)	--
	11	F	(M)	--
	22	F	(Black)	--
	37	F	(Black)	--
	35	F	(Black)	--
	14	F	(Black)	--
	45	M	(Black)	--
	28	M	(Black)	--
Fletcher, Wilks	25	M	Farmer	TN
Emily	27	F		TN
William	15	M		TN
Elizabeth	8	F		TN
Routh, S.	48	M	Teamster	TN
Demascus, G.	18	M	Teamster	AL
Jeffers, H.	22	M	Teamster	AR
Fletcher, Lucy	16	F		TN
Mary R.	14	F		TN
George	12	M		TN
David	9	M		TN
Mary J.	6	F		TX
Justice, William T.	24	M	Farmer	??
R. M.	19	F		TN
Brown, A. W.	36	M	Farmer	TN

(continued)

Brown, Harriet	27	F		KY
Jas. A.	21	M	Laborer	TN
William B.	18	M	Laborer	IL
Jno. D. M.	16	M	Laborer	IL
Nancy M.	13	F		IL
Journey, Jas. B.	25	M	Laborer	IL
Gatlin, Mary A.	22	F		TN
Henry A.	1	M		TX
Leemore, Jno.	11	M		IL
Hunter, Mary	55	F		SC
Barnett, Martin	24	M	Laborer	TN
Jas. R.	18	M	Laborer	TN
Joel H.	15	M	Laborer	TN
Cormack, T. C.	26	M	Farmer	TN
B. R.	20	F		OH
Susannah S.	4	F		IA
Sarah J.	10/12	F		TX
Fowler, Josiah	26	M		TN
Mary A.	40	F		KY
William	6	M		AR
Wyatt	2	M		TX
Farmer, Hudson	20	M		AR
Compton P.	14	M		AR
Waldrum, Jno. H.	29	M	Farmer	TN
Elizabeth	30	F		TN
Martha M.	7	F		AR
William R.	4	M		AR
Nancy C.	2	F		AR
James R.	1	M		TX
Gibson, Robert A.	37	M	Farmer	TN
Elizabeth	27	F		IL
Wade	13	M		AR
Nancy	8	F		AR
Samuel	6	M		TX
Robert	4	M		TX
Jane	6/12	F		TX
Waldrum, William	50	M	Farmer	SC
Nancy	47	F		NC
Henry H.	24	M	Laborer	TN
Wiley	17	M	Laborer	AR
Emily J.	14	F		AR
Nemrod	10	M		AR
Lucy C.	8	F		AR
Spencer, Charles	31	M	Farmer	TN
Elizabeth	28	F		TN
Matilda	11	F		AR
Sarah	10	F		AR
James K. P.	5	M		AR
Louisa	4/12	F		TX
Coonrod, Mary	50	F		SC
Owen	25	M	Laborer	IL
Eliza J.	10	F		IL
Preston C.	8	M		IL
Boren, Thomas	25	M	Laborer	TN
Sarah R.	20	F		IL
Payne, Preston A.	30	M	Farmer	VA
Mary C.	20	F		AR
Robert	4	M		TX
James F.	1	M		TX
James F.	21	M		TN
Mary S.	19	F		KY
Winchester, Beach	45	M	Laborer	TN
Jane	43	F		TN
Comfort	17	F		TN
Mary A.	15	F		TN
F-----	12	M		TN
Sanders, James	20	M	Laborer	AR
Alexander	13	M		AR
Gage, Calvin	38	M	Farmer	TN
Mary	33	F		AL
Sarah	18	F		AR
Daniel	15	M		AR
Lyda	11	F		AR
Barbary	10	F		AR

(continued)

Name	Age	Sex	Occupation	Birthplace
Gage, Martha	9	F		AR
Elizabeth	7	F		AR
Anna	6	F		AR
Matilda	4	F		TX
Boren, Thomas F.	45	M	Black Smith	TN
Mary	26	F		TN
Nancy	17	F		TN
Jane	20	F		TN
Thomas	13	M		AR
Amanda	11	F		AR
Celia A.	4	F		TX
Eliza	2	F		TX
Sarah	1	F		TX
Samuel W.	22	M	Laborer	TN
Boren, Jno. M.	24	M	Farmer	IL
Eliza	18	F		TN
Savage, Jno.	23	M	Farmer	MO
Letty H.	22	F		TN
Dulaney, Daniel	34	M	Farmer	KY
Mary	34	F		TN
Sarah	13	F		IL
Ormsby	7	M		TX
William	5	M		TX
Andrew	3	M		TX
Carr, William L.	29	M		MO
Taylor, B. W.	28	M	Minister M.E.C.S.	TN
Catharine C.	26	F		MO
Carmack, Jno.	46	M	Stone Mason	TN
Susanah	46	F		VA
Jno.	16	M	Laborer	IL
Elizabeth S.	14	F		IL
Catharine	12	F		IA
Joseph	10	M		IA
David E. K.	5	M		IA
Brotherton, Jno.	25	M	Farmer	TN
Elizabeth	20	F		CT
Martha E.	2	F		TX
Jas. M.	3/12	M		TX
Harris, William	37	M	Farmer	TN
Hulda	25	F		TN
Malissa J.	9	F		IL
Francis M.	7	M		IL
Sarah E.	5	F		TX
Mary A.	3	F		TX
Jas. W.	1	M		TX
Ware, Joseph	27	M	Farmer	TN
Elizabeth	21	F		TN
Jno.	1	M		TX
Norton, A. B.	35	M	Laborer	GA
Black, John D.	--	M	Farmer	??
Lucinda	--	F		AL
Colmore	2	M		C?
Stephenson, William	24	M	Laborer	TN
Brown, John	19	M	Laborer	??
Slaves	15	F	(Black)	--
	20	F	(M)	--
	20	M	(Black)	--
	35	F	(Black)	--
	35	F	(M)	--
	35	M	(Black)	--
Wethersbee, Rubin	53	M	Farmer	SC
Hiley	25	F		TN
Delila	26	F		SC
Elizabeth	21	F		SC
Pricilla	17	F		GA
Darlin	15	M		GA
Mary	13	F		GA
Rubin	10	M		GA
Francina	8	F		GA
Martin, Sarah	6	F		AR
Eliza	5	F		AR
Brotherton, W. W.	28	M	Farmer	TN
(continued)				
Slaves	8/12	M	(Black)	--
	3	M	(Black)	--
	22	F	(Black)	--
	26	M	(Black)	--
	35	F	(Black)	--
	45	M	(Black)	--
Onstott, William	77	M	Farmer	NC
Elizabeth	65	F		NC
William S.	22	M	Farmer	TN
Slaves	3	F	(Black)	--
	34	F	(Black)	--
Smith, Ann	47	F		TN
Ann M.	22	F		IN
George	21	M	Laborer	IN
Dorcas	18	F		IN
Jane	15	F		IN
Philip	13	M		IN
Mary	7	F		TX
Kennedy, Thomas G.	44	M	Black Smith	??
Slave	4	M	(M)	--
Stuart, William F.	21	M	Miller	SC
Caroline	23	F		TN
Ferney G.	1	M		TX
Yates, Albert G.	30	M	Farmer	TN
Ritta	25	F		IL
Mary E.	6	F		TX
Lucinda	4	F		TX
Nancy L.	3	F		TX
Thomas J.	1	M		TX
Dalton, M. L.	29	M	Farmer	TN
Lucinda	32	F		KY
Eliza J.	8	F		TX
John W.	7	M		TX
William C.	5	M		TX
Sarah E.	3	F		TX
James W.	5/12	M		TX
Dennis, John	49	M	Farmer	KY
Elizabeth C.	27	F		TN
Sarah M.	10	F		TX
James S.	7	M		TX
Amanda C.	5	F		TX
Rachel L.	3	F		TX
Samuel M.	6/12	M		TX
Farmer, Mary	50	F		TN
Joseph	26	M	Farmer	TN
David	21	M	Laborer	TN
Milly	18	F		TN
Mary	16	F		TN
Elizabeth	14	F		TN
Thomas, Jesse F.	47	M	Farmer	VA
Elizabeth	47	F		TN
Nancy A.	18	F		TN
Robert M.	16	M	Laborer	TN
William N. A.	6	M		TX
Williamson, Emily	35	F		TN
Richard	6	M		TX
Harriet F.	4	F		TX
Slave	12	M	(Black)	--
Allen, Standmon H.	22	M	Farmer	TN
Bruce, Gilley	64	F		NC
Slaves	5	F	(Black)	--
	8	F	(M)	--
	28	F	(Black)	--
Rainbolt, William	50	M	Farmer	KY
Elizabeth	43	F		TN
Martha J.	18	F		AL
Liberty W.	11	M		AL
William	8	M		MO
James W.	5	M		TX
Fedelia	1	F		TX
Shoat, Gabriel	24	M	Farmer	KY
Mary	20	F		AL
Adaline	3/12	F		TX

FANNIN COUNTY, TEXAS

Name	Age	Sex	Occupation	Birthplace
Choat, Ephraim	49	M	Farmer	KY
Kessiah	48	F		TN
William	20	M	Laborer	TN
John	18	M		TN
Ephraim	14	M		TN
C-------	13	F		TN
Richard	11	M		TN
Jasper	9	M		TN
Ellender	6	F		AL
May, Lebron	36	M	Farmer	TN
Pamela	22	F		OH
Millard B.	2	M		TX
Elizabeth	8/12	F		TX
Young, Eliza	11	F		AR
Green, Paris	40	M	Shoe Maker	TN
Margaret	40	F		TN
William T.	20	M	Boot & Shoe Maker	TN
Martha J.	18	F		TN
Paris B.	16	M	Laborer	TN
Marcus H.	14	M		TN
Adaline V.	12	F		TN
Riley H.	10	M		TN
Caroline V.	7	F		TN
Wesley C.	5	M		TN
Napoleon	11/12	M		TX
Young, Henry	33	M	Farmer	NC
Amanda	21	F		TN
Hamil, J. N.	41	M	Minister M.C.C.S.	TN
Mary A.	30	F		AL
Gilbert J.	7	M		TX
Martha J.	6	F		TX
Pauline C.	4	F		TX
Mary A.	2	F		TX
Allen, David Y.	28	M	Farmer	NC
Sarah	22	F		TN
Standmore	6/12	M		TX
Farmer, Martha	5	F		TN
Morrison, Jos. H.	41	M	Farmer	??
Lucina J.	39	F		SC
Mary H.	18	F		TN
William	3	M		TX
Schrimshire, Jas. W.	32	M	Laborer	TN
Myres, N. T.	28	M	Farmer	KY
Daniel S.	62	M	Farmer	TN
William H.	29	M	Laborer	KY
Slave	20	F	(Black)	--
McKinley, Sarah J.	21	F		TN
Jno. P. H.	2	M		TX
Pleasant F.	4/12	M		TX
Brown, Mourning	50	F		VA
Mary E.	18	F		TN
Reedy, John	48	M	Farmer	TN
Rebecca M.	36	F		VA
David	22	M	Laborer	AL
Thomas	17	M	Laborer	AL
George W.	13	M		AL
Louisiana	11	F		AL
Ivanonio F.	9	M		AL
Benjamin F.	4	M		MS
James K. P.	2	M		MS
Morrison, Joseph	40	M	Stock Raiser	TN
Elizabeth	36	F		MO
Frederick, John	12	M		AR
Malugen, Jos. B.	32	M	Farmer	TN
Martha A.	21	F		IL
Aquiller C.	8/12	M		TX
Southerland, Jos.	15	M		AR
Hallerman, J. B. R.	27	M	Farmer	TN
Prudence A.	31	F		TN
Prudence A.	4	F		TN
Elizabeth F.	2	F		TN
Mary	68	F		NC

Name	Age	Sex	Occupation	Birthplace
Coplin, William	32	M	Farmer	TN
Mary	31	F		IL
Joseph	9	M		AR
Cassanda	8	F		AR
Elizabeth	6	F		TX
Texana	4	F		TX
Mary	11/12	F		TX
James	11/12	M		TX
Bell, Elizabeth	45	F		TN
Stephen	27	M	School Teacher	MS
D. J.	25	M	School Teacher	MS
Albert H.	20	M	Farmer	MS
Andrew J.	16	M	Farmer	MS
Texana	13	F		TX
Charles	10	M		TX
Jesse	6	M		TX
Slaves	6	F	(Black)	--
	27	M	(Black)	--
Cox, Elihu	43	M	Farmer	KY
Jane	38	F		TN
Ephraim	21	M	Laborer	MO
Mary J.	19	F		MO
Sarah Ann	18	F		MO
Margaret J.	15	F		MO
Absella	14	F		MO
Martha	10	F		MO
Joseph C.	8	M		MO
Dice	6	F		MO
John W.	4	M		MO
Rachel R. E.	1	F		MO
McDonald, William	37	M	Farmer	TN
Susanna	35	F		TN
Logan P.	14	M		TN
Mary J.	11	F		TN
James E.	7	M		AL
John W.	3	M		MO
Hollerman, Agnes	39	F		TN
Samuel	17	M		TN
Mary E.	10	F		TN
Finley, Daniel	29	M		TN
Anna	21	F		TN
Joseph	6	M		AR
Mary A.	7/12	F		TX
Jeffers, Almira	30	F		??
Jane	3	F		TX
Caroline	2	F		TX
Wiley, William E.	40	M	Farmer	OH
Ursula	32	F		TN
Sophia C.	8	F		TX
Jerome D.	3	M		TX
Susan B.	2	F		TX
Larkin, Alonzo	35	M	Farmer	RI
Mary	22	F		TN
Geheal	2	M		TX
Sarah E.	1	F		TX
Reeves, Robert O.	26	M	Farmer	TN
Mahala	23	F		AR
John L.	2	M		TX
Rowland, James	34	M	Farmer	TN
Eliza	31	F		MO
Martha	7	F		TX
Susan	6	F		TX
Mary	3	F		TX
Goeley, William J.	29	M	Farmer	IL
Thomas W.	13	M		TN
Louisa A.	11	F		AR
Mary E.	3	F		TX
Martha J.	1	F		TX
Margaret	26	F		VA
McDonnal, William H.	9	M		VA
Andy	7	M		MO
Cynthia	5	F		TX
Clark, Matilda	40	F		KY
Newton	16	F(M)	Laborer	KY

(continued)

Clark, Elizabeth	15	F		KY
Martha J.	12	F		TN
James M.	8	M		MS
Louisa	5	F		MS
Not Named	2	F		TN
Slaves	8	F	(Black)	--
	45	F	(Black)	--
Watson, Thomas	30	M	Farmer	KY
Evelina	18	F		TN
Mary E.	3/12	F		TX
Slaves	3	M	(Black)	--
	7	F	(Black)	--
	9	M	(Black)	--
	9	M	(Black)	--
	13	M	(Black)	--
	15	M	(Black)	--
	17	M	(Black)	--
	22	M	(Black)	--
	22	M	(Black)	--
	38	F	(Black)	--
	38	F	(Black)	--
	19	F	(Black)	--
	50	M	(Black)	--
	75	M	(Black)	--
	50	F	(Black)	--
Hart, Jonathan	51	M	Farmer	TN
Cynthia	48	F		TN
Jonathan	19	M	Laborer	IL
Olevia	16	F		IL
Martha	13	F		IL
James	11	M		IL
Houghton, B. R.	30	M	Farmer	KY
Astelia A.	20	F		TN
Albert	1	M		TX
Baker, Rachel	54	F		KY
Samuel A.	18	M		TN
William R.	37	M	Carpenter	TN
Jane	24	F		TN
Pace, John S.	33	M	Farmer	MO
Rachel J.	19	F		TN
Susan E.	2/12	F		TX
Slaves	2/12	F	(Black)	--
	2	M	(Black)	--
	3	F	(Black)	--
	4	F	(Black)	--
	4	F	(Black)	--
	6	M	(Black)	--
	8	F	(Black)	--
	10	F	(Black)	--
	14	F	(Black)	--
	18	M	(Black)	--
	18	F	(Black)	--
	18	F	(Black)	--
	19	F	(Black)	--
	20	M	(Black)	--
	23	M	(Black)	--
	26	M	(Black)	--
	35	F	(Black)	--
	40	F	(Black)	--
	45	F	(Black)	--
	70	M	(Black)	--
Jouett, Thomas	41	M	Farmer	NC
Mary F.	23	F		TN
Martha A.	6	F		TX
Thomas W.	4	M		TX
Beal, R. R.	38	M	Farmer	NC
James E.	12	M		TX
Sanders, James	50	M	Carpenter	NC
Owens, William	55	M	Farmer	??
Hawley, William	22	M	Laborer	??
Dillingham, Jno. A.	41	M	Wagon Maker	TN
Slaves	4/12	F	(Black)	--
	6/12	F	(M)	--
	1	F	(M)	--
	2	M	(Black)	--
	2	M	(Black)	--
	2	F	(Black)	--
	4	F	(M)	--
	4	M	(Black)	--
	6	M	(Black)	--
	7	F	(M)	--
	8	M	(Black)	--
	4	F	(Black)	--
	10	F	(Black)	--
	11	M	(M)	--
	12	F	(M)	--
	13	M	(Black)	--
	14	M	(Black)	--
	16	M	(Black)	--
	17	M	(Black)	--
	18	M	(Black)	--
	19	F	(Black)	--
	19	F	(Black)	--
	22	M	(Black)	--
	22	F	(Black)	--
	21	F	(Black)	--
	24	M	(Black)	--
	25	M	(Black)	--
	26	F	(Black)	--
	26	M	(Black)	--
	25	F	(Black)	--
	30	F	(Black)	--
	32	F	(Black)	--
	30	F	(Black)	--
	35	M	(Black)	--
	38	M	(Black)	--
	40	F	(Black)	--
	68	M	(Black)	--
Grandstaff, Henry	36	M	Farmer	TN
Abigail	38	F		KY
Jane	11	F		MO
John	8	M		AR
Henry	6	M		AR
Isaac	5	M		AR
Emily	3	F		TX
Richard, Lewis	36	M	Farmer	MO
Arthema	26	F		TN
Levi	15	M		IN
Elizabeth	13	F		AR
George	5	M		TX
Charles	3	M		TX
Mary	8/12	F		TX
Esque, Willis	9	M		AL
Hagueford, Robert	3	M		TX
Dogley, Catharine	22	F		TN
Cagle, M. G.	42	M	Farmer	NC
Susan C.	34	F		TN
Robert	12	M		AR
Frances D.	10	F		AR
Edward	8	M		AR
Martin	6	M		AR
Mary C.	4	F		TX
Slaves	54	M	(Black)	--
	34	F	(Black)	--
Harris, B. C.	34	M	Carpenter	TN
Mary	24	F		TN
Eliza	2	F		TX
DeGraffenreid, William B.	27	M	Teamster	TN
Elizabeth	49	F		VA
Brown, W. W.	11	M		MO
Moore, James	53	M	Farmer	SC
Cynthia	50	F		TN
Barnes	21	M	Laborer	TN
Mahala	22	F		TN
McDonald	19	M	Laborer	TN
Thomas	17	M		TN
William	14	M		TN
Susan	12	F		TN
Sarah	9	F		TN
Cynthia	7	F		TN
James	4	M		TN
Moore, B. C.	25	M	Farmer	TN
Louisa	20	F		TN
Mona	3	F		??

(continued)

FANNIN COUNTY, TEXAS

Name	Age	Sex	Occupation	Birthplace
Moore, Not Named	1/12	M		??
Moore, L.	23	M		TX
Sarah J.	20	F		??
Elias	2	M		TN
Sanders, William T.	38	M	Farmer	TN
Jemima G.	23	F		MO
Morgan J.	12	M		TX
Catharine	11	F		TX
William M.	8	M		TX
John C. C.	6	M		TX
Adaline	4	F		TX
Virginia L.	1	F		TX

Bonham

Name	Age	Sex	Occupation	Birthplace
Record, N. K.	27	M	Merchant	TN
Mary E.	23	F		TN
J. R.	10/12	M		TX
Slaves	13	M	(Black)	--
	15	F	(Black)	--
Nelms, Jno. A.	52	M	Minister M.E.C.S.	VA
Mary	59	F		TN
Jno. L.	30	M	Saddler	TN
C. C.	25	M	Shoe Maker	KY
Philitia L. B.	23	F		KY
Leanderus A.	18	M	Laborer	KY
McGowen, L. K.	30	M	Lawyer	TN
Martha J.	27	F		TN
McKee, Jas. R.	37	M	Physician	TN
Elizabeth	35	F		TN
Mary A. M.	11	F		TN
Isaac M.	7	M		TX
James B.	5	M		TX
Joseph W.	4	M		TX
Slaves	35	F	(Black)	--
	20	M	(Black)	--
	6/12	F	(M)	--
Barney, Robert A.	38	M	Saddler	TN
Delila	39	F		TN
Elvira A.	14	F		MO
Stanford	12	M		AR
Emily J.	10	F		AR
Delila E.	9	F		AR
Manervia A.	2	F		TX
Deason, R.	20	M	Saddler	NC
Alexander, L. C.	23	M	Merchant	KY
Mary J.	16	F		TN
Ritchie, C.	30	M	Clerk	KY
Inglish, Robert	23	M	Clerk	CT
Slaves	28	F	(Black)	--
	16	M	(M)	--
	12	M	(Black)	--
	10	F	(Black)	--
	2	M	(M)	--
	6/12	F	(M)	--
Doss, James W.	40	M	Merchant	VA
Cyrena	25	F		TN
Frances	11	F		TX
Charles	8	M		TX
Ann	5	F		TX
Reese	3/12	M		TX
Doss, Samuel E.	24	M	Merchant	VA
Slaves	45	F	(Black)	--
	16	M	(M)	--
	15	F	(Black)	--
	12	F	(Black)	--
	8	F	(M)	--
	5	F	(M)	--
	13	F	(Black)	--
Alderson, Richard	25	M	Carpenter	TN
Mary K.	32	F		TN
Pharizina	1	F		TX
Painter, William C.	34	M	Black Smith	TN
Edith	33	F		IL

(continued)

Name	Age	Sex	Occupation	Birthplace
Painter, Hiram	11	M		MO
Houston H.	9	M		MO
John	7	M		MO
Joseph	5	M		MO
Rebecca	4	F		TX
Seals, Campbell	38	M	Carpenter	TN
Elizabeth	34	F		NY
Mary	7	F		TX
Emeline	2	F		TX
Burke, William	17	M	Laborer	IN
Aaron	11	M		IN
Allen, Thomas M.	36	M	Baker	VA
Mary A.	27	F		TN
James	2	M		TX
Thornton, Sarah	17	F		TN
William	14	M		TN
Mobley, Thomas G.	30	M	Carpenter	KY
Susan J.	20	F		TN
Sarah E.	3/12	F		TX
DeGraffenreid, Jas. A.	27	M	Teamster	TN
Alpha	18	F		AR
William H.	1	M		TX
Fitzgerald, G.	63	M	Farmer	TN
Margaret	45	F		VA
John D.	23	M	Teamster	AL
Jane E.	17	F		AL
Slaves	22	F	(Black)	--
	2	M	(M)	--
	5/12	F	(Black)	--
Hearn, Jos.	43	M	Teamster	NC
Ellen	37	F		TN
William	20	M	Laborer	MO
Frances	18	F		MO
Nancy	16	F		MO
Levi	14	M		MO
Larkin	9	M		MO
Lyda	7	F		MO
Missouri	1	F		TX
Thornton, C.	20	M	Carpenter	TN
Keltaner, Jas. C.	20	M	Teamster	AR
Clutter, Grant	40	M	Tavern Keeper	KY
Permelia	34	F		IN
Mary Ann	23	F		IN
William	18	M	Laborer	IN
Angeline	16	F		IN
McDonnal	13	M		IN
Fitzgerald, Ira	2	M		TX
Blackwell, Jas. B.	27	M	Stud Horses Keeper	TN

FAYETTE COUNTY, TEXAS

Name	Age	Sex	Occupation	Birthplace
Shults, C. W.	50	M	Farmer	TN
Mary	50	F		KY
Cintha	25	F		TN
Martin	21	M	None	AL
Joseph	20	M	Mechanic	AL
James	6	M		TX
William	4	M		TX
Pe-es, W.	24	M	None	IN
Cracky, F.	18	M	Laborer	GER
Miatts, W.	15	M		GER
Shults, John	28	M	Farmer	AL
Sarah	28	F		IA
Robert	11/12	M		TX
Sutton, Wesly	29	M	Farmer	TN
Malinda	19	F		AR
Elizabeth	7	F		TX
Sellers, Robert	41	M	Farmer	TN
Nancy	38	F		TN
Martha	15	F		TN
Leath	14	F		TN
Elizabeth	13	F		TN
John	12	M		TX
Isaac	8	M		TN

(continued)

Name	Age	Sex	Occupation	Birthplace
Sellers, Nancy	3	F		TX
Robert	11/12	M		TX
Wallace, Laird	19	M	Student	TN
Atkinson, J.	35	M	Farmer	TN
Jane	34	F		TN
Mary	8	F		TX
Julia	5	F		TX
Bacon, Thomas	63	M	None	KY
Cole, W. J.	64	M	Farmer	VA
James	22	M	Farmer	TN
Lebiller(?), H.	42	M	Farmer	NC
Jane	37	F		TN
Alexander	19	M	Student	TN
Albert	17	M	Student	TN
William	15	M	Student	TN
Orelias	13	M	Student	TN
Olivia	11	F		TX
Cecelia	8	F		TX
Adda	6	F		TX
James	3	M		TX
Taylor, C. H.	39	M	Farmer	TN
Elizabeth	60	F		TN
Hill, John	19	M	None	AL
C.	14	M		AL
Lunceford, A.	21	M	Laborer	NC
Adams, H. V.	38	M	Merchant	RI
Rankin, C. R.	28	M	Physician	TN
Mary	24	F		MO
Harrison	1	M		TX
Bell, G.	23	M	Farmer	TN
Mary	18	F		TN
Eliza	10/12	F		TX
Bell, J. P.	28	M	Farmer	TN
Ann	25	F		TN
John	5	M		TN
Rufus	2	M		TN
Laura	7/12	F		TN
Sutton, William	67	M	Farmer	VA
Eliza	45	F		MD
Charles	19	M	Farmer	TN
Elizabeth	17	F		TN
Martha	15	F		TN
Jane	12	F		TN
Hardin, A.	28	M	Chair Maker	TN
Adaline	26	F		KY
Lean	4	F		KY
Andrew	2	M		KY
McMillon, J.	30	M	Farmer	KY
Sarah	34	F		TN
Sophia	6	F		TX
John	2	M		TX
N.	33	M	None	KY
Daniel	28	M	Lawyer	KY
Herald, B.	30	M	Farmer	NC
Eliza	19	F		TN
Mary	1	F		TX
John	27	M	Laborer	NC
Kuykendall, H.	47	M	Farmer	TN
Marie	38	F		KY
William	15	M		TX
Mary	13	F		TX
Mathew	11	M		TX
George	9	M		TX
Ellen	7	F		TX
Robert	5	M		TX
Milldred	3	F		TX
Cliff, J.	55	M	Laborer	KY
Hamilton, C.	24	M	School Teacher	KY
Howell, C.	34	M	Farmer	NC
Mary	30	F		TN

(continued)

Name	Age	Sex	Occupation	Birthplace
Howell, Sarah	9	F		TX
James	7	M		TX
Margaret	4	F		TX
Mary	1	F		TX
Enneann(?), S.	33	M	None	TN
Hill, J. M.	31	M	Farmer	GA
Jane	25	F		TN
James	5	M		TX
John	3	M		TX
Thomas, C. W.	33	M	Meth. Clergyman	CT
Susan	28	F		GA
Henrietta	6	F		TX
Charles	4	M		TX
George	1	M		TX
Wade, D.	55	M	Farmer	VA
Evenline	40	F		TN
David	2	M		TX
Ellis, Mary	13	F		TN
James	10	M		TX
Sewell, G.	37	M	Farmer	TN
Bethany	37	F		TN
Cornelius	8	M		TN
Absalom	5	M		TN
Malissa	4	F		GA
George	2	M		TX
Gregory, A. D.	28	M	Farmer	TN
Margaret	21	F		KY
Texanna	2	F		TX
Amanda	1	F		TX
Essinger, R.	30	M	Farmer	TN
Julia	28	F		TN
George	8	M		TN
Sarah	6	F		TN
Martha	4	F		TN
David	11/12	M		TX
Grayham, A.	60	M	Farmer	??
S.	48	F		TX
James	21	M		TN
Mary	17	F		TN
Texas	14	F		TX
Andrew	1/12	M		TX
Hamilton, A.	45	M	Farmer	NC
Bettsy	38	F		TN
John	20	M	Laborer	TN
Thomas	20	M	Laborer	TN
Nelson	16	M	Laborer	TN
Claricy	14	F		TN
Prudy	12	F		TN
Emily	11	F		TN
Giddeon	9	M		TN
Mary	3	F		TX
Abel	7/12	M		TX
Blackborn, J.	35	M	Farmer	TN
Martha	22	F		MD
Martha	3	F		TX
R. S.	20	M	Laborer	TN
Cox, Thomas	49	M	Lawyer	TN
Franklin	20	M	Laborer	TN
Mary	17	F		AL
Susan	15	F		AL
Sarah	8	F		AL
William	5	M		AL
Malinda	2	F		TX
Breeding, E. J.	25	M	Farmer	KY
Henrietta	20	F		TN
Mary	5	F		TN
George	?	M		TN
Marlow, E. M.	30	M	Farmer	GER
Perry, Thomas	37	M	Farmer	TN
Martha	24	F		TX
William	7	M		TX
Elizabeth	7/12	F		TX
McElyea, James	28	M	Laborer	TN

(continued)

Name	Age	Sex	Occupation	Birthplace
McElyea, Mary	24	F		AL
George	23	M	Student	TN
Gibb, Susan	5	F		TX
Renick, H.	48	M	C.P. Minister	KY
Sarah	44	F		KY
Samuel	21	M		MO
Julia	15	F		MO
Elizabeth	12	F		TN
Martha	10	F		TX
Miller, Nelson	14	M		TX
Estill	5	M		TX
Ann	3	F		TX
Williams, Allen	34	M	Farmer	AL
James	8	M		TX
Hugh	6	M		TX
Stephen	2	M		TX
Stribline, J.	24	M	School Teacher	TN
Barkley, R. A.	33	M	Farmer	TN
Catherine	25	F		MO
Robert	5	M		TX
Frances	1	F		TX
Stradher(?), William	25	M	Laborer	MO
Whipple, S. B.	27	M	Meth. Clergyman	OH
Mary	23	F		TN
Melinda	1	F		TX
Huff, H.	41	M	Farmer	SC
Elizabeth	38	F		TN
William	16	M	Student	TN
Jane	13	F		TN
Josaphine	10	F		TX
Elizabeth	6	F		TX
Ann	4	F		TX
Franklin	1	M		TX
Smith, John	22	M	Laborer	AL
Albrina	23	F		AL
William	11/12	M		TX
Young, William	35	M	Farmer	TN
Elizabeth	22	F		AL
Virginia	1	F		TX
Leo	8	M		TX
Mary	6	F		TX
Martha	4	F		TX
Young, Samuel	63	M	Farmer	IRE
Jane	57	F		KY
Alfred	25	M	Farmer	TN
Wesley	21	M	Farmer	TN
Martha	13	F		TN
Young, J. J.	31	M	Farmer	TN
Lutetia	31	F		TN
Minerva	12	F		TN
William	9	M		TX
Eliza	7	F		TX
Sarah	5	F		TX
John	1	M		TX
Francis, William	34	M	Farmer	TN
Martha	25	F		TN
Frances	10	F		TN
Mary	8	F		TN
Robert	7	M		TN
Julia	6	F		TN
Rhubin	4	M		TN
Lester, J. S.	45	M	Farmer	VA
Richards, S.	22	M	Laborer	TN
Keeling, J. B.	22	M	Laborer	TN
Scott, S. M.	30	M	Laborer	CAN
Hunt, William	35	M	Farmer	TN
Lucinda	30	F		TN
John	12	M		TX
Elizabeth	10	F		TX
Sarah	6	F		TX
Martha	2	F		TX
Daniels, J. O.	37	M	Farmer	SC
Elizabeth	28	F		TN
James	8	M		TX
Mary	6	F		TX
Elizabeth	4	F		TX
Conway, G. B.	34	M	Farmer	GA
Rosanna	33	F		SC
Winney	13	F		TN
Elizabeth	11	F		TN
Matilda	9	F		TN
Wiley	6	M		TN
Sarah	5	F		TN
Mary	3	F		TN
James	1	M		TX
Ragin, A. R.	25	M	Farmer	TN
Sarah	18	F		TX
Josaphine	1/12	F		TX
Drake, O.	38	M	Farmer	NY
Louisa	31	F		TN
Mary	7	F		TX
Ann	5	F		TX
William	8/12	M		TX
J. M.	13	M		TX
Ross, W. B.	25	M	Farmer	AL
Susan	27	F		NC
William	1/12	M		TX
Branch, William	23	M	Farmer	NC
Sarah	14	F		TN
Hearold, James	49	M	Farmer	TN
Sarah	36	F		NC
Martha	15	F		TN
Sarah	14	F		TN
Francis	11	M		TN
Marcellus	8	M		TN
James	6	M		TN
Udora	3	F		TN
Tilfa(?)	73	F		NC
Ragin, G. C.	26	M	Farmer	SC
Martheana	31	F		TN
Rabb, Ullias	24	M	None	TX
Mary	17	F		TX
Rabb, John	25	M	Farmer	TX
Martha	24	F		TN
Elizabeth	1	F		TX
Darbin, S.	45	M	Farmer	MA
Luneany	39	F		TN
James	4	M		TX
William	1	M		TX
Elizabeth Susan	16	F		TN
Henrietta	13	F		TN
Brazill, A.	23	M		TN
Awallt, Jacob	28	M	Farmer	TN
Emeline	26	F		AL
William	5	M		MS
Mary	3	F		MS
Thomas	1	M		MS
Moore, J. H.	50	M	Farmer	TN
Eliza	41	F		TN
William	22	M	Student	TX
Tabitha	17	F		TX
Eliza	13	F		TX
John	11	M		TX
Robert	8	M		TX
Mary	6	F		TX
Bible, Adam	51	M	Laborer	VA
Brazill, Mrs. Elizabeth	48	F		KY
Columbus	23	M	Laborer	TN
Franklin	21	M	Laborer	TN
Jefferson	18	M	Student	TN
Sarah	14	F		TN
John	12	M		TN
Clinton	10	M		TN
Harrison	8	M		TN

FAYETTE COUNTY, TEXAS

Name	Age	Sex	Occupation	Birthplace
Eastland, R.	35	M	None	KY
Eliza	26	F		TN
Josaphine	6	F		TN
Mary	2	F		TX
Crownover, A.	40	M	Farmer	AR
Lurina	38	F		TN
Aaron	19	M	Student	TX
Malissa	17	F		TX
Jasper	14	M		TX
Marion	13	M		TX
Levi	13	M		TX
Rufina	10	F		TX
Rufana	9	F		TX
Mary	5	F		TX
Ann	3	F		TX
Morrow, W.	23	M	Laborer	TX
Nail, Joseph	70	M	Farmer	TN
Alvira	50	F		TN
James	27	M	Laborer	TN
Pleasant	25	M	Laborer	TN
Quincy	23	M	Laborer	TN
Clark	21	M	Laborer	AR
Mary	19	F		TX
Broady	17	F		TX
Thomas, N.	42	M	Farmer	TN
Mary	36	F		KY
Mary	13	F		TN
Sarah	10	F		TX
Susan	8	F		TX
William	6	M		TX
Clinton	4	M		TX
Louisa	2	F		TX
Dorris, G. W.	38	M	Carpenter	TN
Sarah	24	F		SC
Willis	12	M		AL
George	7	M		AL
Sarah	6	F		MS
Joseph	2	M		MS
Moore, C.	15	F		SC
Flack, C. J.	38	M	Merchant	TN
Elizabeth	21	F		GA
Thomas	3	M		TX
Robert	1	M		TX
D----, Louisa	25	F		NJ
Cranes, J.	35	M	Physician	PA
Louisa	26	F		TN
Emily	5	F		MO
Mary	3	F		MO
Ann	1/12	F		TX
Weaver, J. M.	28	M	Carpenter	OH
Haynie, James	37	M	Farmer	TN
Ann	42	F		MA
George	14	M		AL
Mary	11	F		TX
John	8	M		TX
Sarah	5	F		TX
Keys, Henry	40	M	Farmer	VA
Catherine	39	F		TN
Mathew	21	M	Farmer	TN
Calvin	20	M	Farmer	TN
Tolbert	18	M	Farmer	AR
Caswell	17	M	Farmer	AR
Elizabeth	14	F		AR
Indianna	11	F		AR
Tennessee	9	F		AR
Martha	7	F		AR
Henry	4	M		AR
Solomen	2	M		TX
Naiser, William	20	M		GER
Keys, Thomas	24	M	Farmer	TN
Martha	23	F		TN
Calhoun	4	M		AR
Hodge, W. F.	45	M	Farmer	KY
John	14	M		TN
William	9	M		TX
Robert	8	M		TX
Rankin, Mrs. Haniah	60	F		KY
Hanniah	23	M	Farmer	TN
Samuelson	20	M		TN
Robert	15	M		TN
John	9	M		TX
Amanda	7	F		TX
Ann	5	F		TX
Samuel	2	M		TX
Shaw, Joseph	64	M	Merchant	TN
Abigail	65	F		PA
Cook, J.	30	M	Carpenter	OH
Martha	26	F		TN
John	8	M		AR
Sarah	6	F		AR
Joseph	4	M		TX
Emily	1	F		TX
Gregory, A. C.	41	M	Physician	TN
Mary	41	F		TN
Robert	20	M	Druggist	TN
Mary	18	F		TN
Charles	16	M	Student	MO
Thomas	14	M		MO
Julia	10	F		MO
Emeline	8	F		MO
Missouri	5	F		MO
William	2	M		TX
Boyle, A.	40	M	Hotel Keeper	KY
Amanda	34	F		KY
Faison, N. W.	30	M	Clerk Court	TN
Green, J. A.	28	M	Lawyer	TN
Ellis, James	22	M	None	KY
Allen, Alexander	31	M	Dancing Master	VA
Weaver, T.	34	M	None	TN
Cavenaugh, M.	32	M	Merchant	OH
McCain, William	27	M	None	KY
Davis, Mrs. Martha	30	F		TN
Martha	10	F		TN
McClure, M. M.	34	M	Hotel Keeper	TX
Cinda	34	F		SC
Nicks, James	18	M	None	TN
Jane	15	F		TN
John	10	M		TX
Lowden, E. C.	22	M		TN
Sarah	21	F		TN
Martha	1	F		TN
Mayfield, Jos. J.	45	M	Lawyer	TN
Sophia	35	F		TN
Elizabeth	16	F		TN
Martha	15	F		TN
James	12	M		TN
Fanny	10	F		TN
Lucy	6	F		TX
Snicks, Julia	6	F		TX
John	9/12	M		TX
Breeding, G. M.	28	M	None	KY
Bardon, Catherine	51	F		NC
Green	16	M	Laborer	AL
David	13	M		TN
Jancks, A.	40	M	Jeweler	SWE
Madorah	30	F		TN
Albert	7	M		AR
Charles	6	M		AR
Mary	1	F		TX
Kiser, Henrietta	17	F		GER
McFarland, J. B.	31	M	Lawyer	TN
Adaline	36	F		TN
Robert	4	M		TX
Julia	2	F		TX
Bales	7/12	M		TX

FAYETTE COUNTY, TEXAS

Name	Age	Sex	Occupation	Birthplace
Howland, C. P.	35	M	Tailor	NC
Eveline	28	F		TN
Caroline	5	M(F)		TX
Almanda	3	F		TX
Edwin	1	M		TX
Jenks, J.	30	M	Painter	ENG
Ann	20	F		TN
Francis	16	M	Laborer	TN
Thomas	14	M		TN
Andrew	8	M		TX
William	6	M		TX
Farquah, James	40	M	Farmer	TN
Adaline	21	F		TX
Edward	2/12	M		TX
McClure, Wiley	21	M	Farmer	TN
Louisa	20	F		TX
Sophrona	1/12	F		TX
Chester, J.	16	M		TX
Matilda	13	F		TX
Castleman, Jacob	32	M	Farmer	MO
Sophronia	29	F		MO
Charles	10	M		TX
George	7	M		TX
Amanda	3	F		TX
John	1	M		TX
Elizabeth	70	F		TN
Brown, Mrs. Sarah	44	F		TN
Mitchell	27	M	Farmer	TX
Silviana	17	F		TX
Robert	14	M		TX
William	10	M		TX
Minerva	8	F		TX
Cyrus	6	M		TX
Sarah	4	F		TX
Mendley, A.	34	M	Laborer	TN
Harper, Thomas	27	M	Farmer	TN
Lucinda	24	F		AR
Sellers, Stephen	10	M		TX
William S.	5	M		TX
Harper, Francis	1/12	M		TX
Frame, William	29	M	Farmer	TN
Martha	20	F		TN
Carnes, Mrs. E.	48	F		KY
Francis	22	M	Student	TN
William	21	M	Student	TN
George	18	M	Student	TN
Asa	16	M	Student	TX
Tramell, W.	43	M	Farmer	KY
Elizabeth	22	F		TN
Emeline	14	F		AR
Henry	12	M		AR
Eliza	3	F		AR
Mary	1	F		TX
Tramell, T.	26	M	Laborer	MO
Farris, William	44	M	Farmer	SC
Ada	40	F		KY
William	13	M		TX
Richard	9	M		TX
John	7	M		TX
Charles	3	M		TX
Clanton, William	50	M	Laborer	VA
David	14	M		TN
Scallon, William	54	M	Farmer	MO
Allis	52	F		KY
Mary	24	F		TN
Emily	17	F		TN
Ada	13	F		TN
Roberts, L.	25	M	School Teacher	AL
William	19	M	Student	TN
Sorrell, Thomas	38	M	Farmer	GA
Babary	30	F		TN

(continued)

Name	Age	Sex	Occupation	Birthplace
Sorrell, Mary	14	F		AL
Walter	6	M		AL
Charles	4	M		TX
Irvin	2	M		TX
Josaphine	1/12	F		TX
Roberson, James	52	M	Farmer	KY
Robison, Jos.	27	M	Farmer	MO
Elizabeth	22	F		TN
Blackwell, Mrs. Sarah	50	F		MS
George	23	M	Farmer	TN
Josiah	21	M	Farmer	TN
Virginia	17	F		TN
Burleson, Aaron	45	M	Farmer	TN
Rilda	40	F		TN
Elizabeth	15	F		TX
John	12	M		TX
Joanna	10	F		TX
Aaron	8	M		TX
Marilda	3	F		TX
Ringer, Isaac	21	M	Laborer	TX
Burleson, C.	25	M	Farmer	TN
Mary	22	F		TN
Harrison, J.	22	M	Farmer	TN
Nancy	17	F		TN
Tiggs, J.	22	M	Farmer	TN
Mary	18	F		TN
Bishop, Alfred	48	M	Farmer	TN
Delia	43	F		TN
Jane	16	F		IL
Susan	14	F		IL
Andrew	12	M		IL
Emeline	11	F		MO
Rodasky	9	F		MO
Catherine	7	F		MO
Ritty	6	F		MO
Locascka	3	F		MO
Rebecca	9/12	F		TX
Seatson, H.	30	M	Farmer	TN
Eliza	26	F		TN
Minerva	8	F		TN
Pelmeada	3	F		TN
Cane, James	46	M	Laborer	TN
Jane	44	F		TN
Samuel	22	M	Laborer	TN
Elizabeth	20	F		TN
William	18	M		TN
Josiah	14	M		TN
Susan	12	F		TX
Neill	9	M		TX
Gorham, William	52	M	Farmer	CT
Lucinda	36	F		TN
Berry, William	16	M	Student	TX
Thomas	15	M		TX
Daniels, Joel A.	11	M		TX
Kenner, Nancy	64	F		VA
Ross, James	30	M	Farmer	AR
Margaret	26	F		TN
Martha	3	F		TX
Mary	2	F		TX
James	9/12	M		TX
Click, John	45	M	Laborer	VA
Smith, T. C. C.	30	M	Farmer	TN
Mary	27	F		TN
Elizabeth	6	F		TX
Amanda	3	F		TX
Mary	1	F		TX
Trimble, John	16	M	Laborer	IN
McNight, J. C.	30	M	Bapt. Clergyman	MS
Martha	34	F		MS
David	12	M		MS
Elizabeth	6	F		MS
Rebecca	4	F		MS
Armineca	9/12	F		TX
Holland, H. W.	46	M	Bapt. Clergyman	SC

FAYETTE COUNTY, TEXAS

Name	Age	Sex	Occupation	Birthplace
Robbins, J. R.	26	M	Laborer	TX
Martha	22	F		AL
William	3	M		TX
Mary	3	F		TX
John	1	M		TX
Robbins, Mary	45	F		TN
Burleson, James	58	M	Laborer	TN
Sibra	35	F		AR
Joseph	25	M	Laborer	IN
Sarah	17	F		AR
Isaac	15	M		AR
Benjamin	12	M		AR
Mary	11	F		AR
Thomas	9	M		AR
Susan	7	F		AR
William	5	M		TX
Allen	1	M		TX
McMickin, A.	46	M	None	TN
James	10	M		TX
Black, J. S.	32	M	Farmer	KY
Malinda	24	F		TN
Amanda	8	F		AR
William	5	M		AR
John	3	M		AR
Callough, G. T.	13	M		TX
Chriswell, William V.	35	M	Farmer	KY
Mary	21	F		TN
Elizabeth	4	F		TX
Sarah	3	F		TX
Criswell, Leroy V.	37	M	Farmer	KY
Elizabeth	25	F		TN
Eliza	7	F		TN
Mary	6	F		TN
John	4	M		TN
Wayman	3	M		TN
William	1	M		TN
Trimble, Ellen	11	F		IN
Criswell, Joseph	23	M	Laborer	KY
Sarah	19	F		TN
Anderson	1	M		TX
Tuttle, George	30	M	Farmer	NY
Mary	23	F		TN
Ellen	5	F		TX
Noah	3	M		TX
Charles	2	M		TX
Almeana	1	F		TX
Scallorn, W.	31	M	Wagon Maker	AL
Mary	21	F		SC
Glimp, Thomas	25	M	Laborer	TN
Ragsdale, Charles	31	M	Farmer	AR
Sarah	31	F		TN
Robert	9	M		TX
Elizabeth	7	F		TX
Thomas	6	M		TX
Mary	3	F		TX
Moore, Jesse	35	M	Farmer	AL
Narcissa	33	F		TN
John	5	M		MS
Phillip	2	M		MS
Menifee, William	54	M	Farmer	TN
Agnes	56	F		VA
Thomas	30	M	Farmer	AL
William	24	M	Farmer	AL
Quin	20	M	Farmer	AL
Elizabeth	16	F		TX
McClure, Mrs. Susan	35	F		TN
James	20	M	Farmer(Deaf & Dumb)	TN
Phillip	18	M	Farmer	TN
Francis	14	M		AR
Sarah	12	F		TX
Ada	10	F		TX
Albert	6/12	M		TX
Duff, J. C.	40	M		TN
Malvina	43	F		KY
Mary	20	F		TN
Minny	18	F		TN
Marion	17	M	Laborer	TN
Maria	14	F		TX
James	11	M		TX
Louisa	8	F		TX
Martha	7	F		TX
John	5	M		TX
William	4	M		TX
Malissa	2	F		TX
McClure, Levi	45	M	Farmer	TN
Denica	24	F		AL
William	18	M	Farmer	TN
Levi	13	M		AR
Martha	4	F		TX
Albert	1	M		TX
Lowden, E.	35	M	Farmer	TN
Emily	21	F		TN
Mary	1	F		TX
Low, William	50	M	None	MD
Scallorn, S.	63	M	Farmer	MD
Martha	53	F		VA
William	22	M	Farmer	TN
Frances	20	F		TN
Minerva	18	F		TN
Lemuel	14	M		TN
Grall(?),Nancy	12	F	(Idiot)	TX
Trail, James	19	M	Laborer	TN
Fitzgerald, S.	57	M	Farmer	VA
Nancy	55	F		VA
William	19	M	Farmer	TN
Louisa	16	F		TN
Susan	13	F		TN
Mays, Watson	36	M	Farmer	VA
Emeline	21	F		TN
Nancy	8/12	F		TX
Seeves, Thomas	31	M	Farmer	TN
Maria	22	F		TN
Edna	6	F		AR
Washington	5	M		AR
Susan	2	F		TX
Seeves, Nancy	55	F		SC
Francis	17	M	None	AR
Dismukes, G.	25	M	Farmer	TN
Martha	21	F		AL
John	59	M		NC
Mitchell, E. H.	29	M	Carpenter	TN
Nancy	25	F		AL
William	14	M		TN
Amanda	7	F		AL
Archabald	4	M		TX
Brazill, S.	35	M		TN
Jane	30	F		VA
Sarah	9	F		TX
William	8	M		TX
Amanda	6	F		TX
Vansall, Peter	30	M	Farmer	IL
Mary	28	F		TN
McStephen	2	M		TX
John	1	M		TX
N.	23	M		TN
Anderson, W. B.	38	M	Gin Wright	TN
Rosetta	32	F		TN
Julius	12	M		TN
Susannah	10	F		TN
Samuel	7	M		TN
Littleton	6	M		TN
James	4	M		TN
William	2	M		TN
Anderson, Susannah	67	F		TN
Stewart, Isaac	19	M	Laborer	TN
Benthall, Benjamin	18	M	Black Smith	TN

FAYETTE COUNTY, TEXAS

Name	Age	Sex	Occupation	Birthplace
Chadowin, Jesse	50	M	Farmer	VA
Nancy	50	F		TN
George	21	M	Laborer	TN
John	19	M	Laborer	IL
Green	18	M	Laborer	IL
Thomas	17	M		IL
Susan	14	F		IL
Elizabeth	11	F		MO
Mahala	9	F		TX
Peter	7	M		TX
Mary	5	F		TX
Sarah	3	F		TX
Chadowin, Willis	26	M	Farmer	TN
Nancy	19	F		TN
Thompson, Michael	42	M	Laborer	VA
Martha	40	F		TN
Elizabeth	8	F		TX
Lewis	2	M		TX
Alexander	80	M		VA
Burnham, Jesse	58	M	Farmer	KY
Nancy	40	F		TN
Robert	24	M		TX
Burnett	19	M		TX
Eliza	17	F		TX
Emily	12	F		TX
Woddy	4	M		TX
Giddeon	2	M		TX
Samara	1/12	F		TX
Seamen, John	38	M	Carpenter	NY
Lett, John	28	M	Laborer	VA
Townsend, John	15	M		TX
Nancy	13	F		TX
Minerva	11	F		TX
Burnham, Sarah	8	F		TX
Sarah	9	F		TX
James	5	M		TX
Burnham, Sarah	33	F		TN
Jane	7	F		TN
George	6	M		TN
Mary	5	F		TN
William	4	M		TN
James, Nancy	40	F		VA
Rebecca	19	F		TN
Walker, N. H.	30	M	E.P. Clergy	TN
Lucinda	26	F		TN
Mary	9	F		TN
Lucinda	6	F		TN
Robert	4	M		TN
Francis	2	M		TN
Holman, Jno. T.	32	M	Farmer	VA
Amanda	26	F		TX
Nathaniel	8	M		TX
Virginia	3	F		TX
Henry	2	M		TX
Alexander, Jerome	7	M		TX
Walker, George	22	M	Laborer	TN
Taylor, Mrs. Sarah	40	F		GA
James	16	M	Farmer	TN
Lafayette	14	M		TX
Moses	10	M		TX
William	8	M		TX
Wheeler, John	35	M	Farmer	VA
Ann	23	F		TN
David	2	M		TX
Cox, James	35	M	Physician	VA
Elizabeth	35	F		TN
Wilson, W. B.	45	M	Farmer	CAN
Mary	24	F		TN
Richard	8	M		TX
Elizabeth	6	F		TX
William	4	M		TX
Jacob	1	M		TX
White, Richard	19	M	Laborer	TX
Tonage, Walker	30	M	Black Smith	TN
Martha	25	F		TN
Sarah	5	F		TN
James	4	M		TX
Elizabeth	1	F		TX
Simpson, Robert	15	M		TN

FORT BEND COUNTY, TEXAS

Town of Richmond

Name	Age	Sex	Occupation	Birthplace
Carsner, Jacob	27	M	Farmer	TN
Petrina	18	F		MS
Johnson, Samuel	46	M	Clerk in Store	TN
Hannah D.	43	F		TN
Serena Ann	16	F		AL
Martha W.	14	F		AL
Emmett	11	M		AL
Samuel A.	7	M		AL
Mary K.	1	F		TX
Massey, P. N.	50	M	Commission Merchant	VA
Mrs.	47	F		VA
E. W.	22	M		AL
Mary M.	17	F		TN
Gracey Ann	14	F		TN
Pamelia A.	12	F		TN
Clursa(?)	12	M(?)		TN
Caroline	8	M(F)		TN
G. A.	6	M		TN
Dyer, C. C.	50	M	Chief Justice	TN
Sarah	36	F		TN
Foster	22	M	Farmer	TX
Hervey F.	20	M	Farmer	TX
Eli J.	17	M	Farmer	TX
Sarah	14	F		TX
Julia Ann	10	F		TX
Josephine	8	F		TX
Martha Ann	6	F		TX
Penbrook	4	M		TX
Clemance, Jr.	2	M		TX

End of Town of Richmond

Judicial District

Name	Age	Sex	Occupation	Birthplace
Pickens, J. H.	42	M	Farmer	KY
Elizabeth	46	F		TN
Mary C.	20	F		KY
Caroline	15	F		TX
El N.	11	M		TX
John H., Jr.	9	M		TX
Little, John F.	17	M	Farmer	TX
Mary T.	16	F		TX
A.	14	F		TX
Jane S.	12	F		TX
Baker, John	40	M	Black Smith	TN
Mary	22	F		GER
McCloy, R.	49	M		TN
Alexander	25	M		TN
John	22	M		TN
McMahon, Martin	72	M	Farmer	SC
Sarah	45	F		TN
Caldonia	11	F		TX
Lafayette	7	M		TX
Bennett, A.	15	F		AL
Echols, John	53	M	Farmer	TN
Rebecka	53	F		SC
Andrew	25	M	Mail Contractor	TN
David	13	M		TN
Patton, John	50	M	Farmer	SC
Adaline	38	F		TN
Samuel R.	16	M	Farmer	AL
Brookshire, Mary C.	25	F		AL
Garner, Henry J.	29	M	Laborer	TN
Moor, Francis M.	24	M	Black Smith	TN
Broson, Joseph	35	M	Black Smith	GER

(continued)

FORT BEND COUNTY, TEXAS

Name	Age	Sex	Occupation	Birthplace
Weast, Joseph	33	M	Black Smith	GER
Ballman, George	33	M	Wheel Wright	GER
Smith, Adam	35	M	Black Smith	GER
Hill, Richard	14	M		TX
Kemp, E. H.	41	M	Farmer	MD
Harriet	42	F		TN
Roberts, H.	16	M	Farmer	TX
John	13	M		TX
Mary	11	F		TX
Thomas	7	M		TX
Kemp, Susan E.	21	F		--
Simonton, T.	29	M	Farmer	NC
Caroline	21	F		TN
Mary	65	F		NC
James	35	M	Farmer	NC
Austin, David	36	M	Farmer	TN
Mary L.	51	F		SC
George B.	15	M		TX
Ann	12	F		TX
Raceter, R. P.	35	M	Farmer	TN
Lucy	20	F		AL
Sellaton, T.	32	M	Farmer	MS
Louisa	30	F		TN
Lavina	9	F		TX
Samuel	7/12	M		TX
J.	12	M		KY
Elizabeth	10	F		MS
Mary	8	F		MS
Ethris, Josephine B.	15	F		IL
Danahbol, H. B.	38	M	Overseer	IRE
Perkinson, William	27	M	Black Smith	TN
Stephens, Robert	18	M	Laborer	KY
James, Jesse	35	M	Overseer	KY
Brookshire, Joseph	20	M	Hunter	TN
Emma	25	F		MS
E.	2	F		TX
Cynthia	7/12	F		TX
Walker, Edward	26	M	Farmer	MS
Martha	24	F		TX
Rodgers, B. F.	22	M	Mechanic	MS
Gurbeckler, George	22	M	Laborer	TN
Green, William H.	30	M		TN
Falshear, Churchill	42	M	Farmer	TN
Manerva	40	F		TN
Mary A.	18	F		TX
Graves	15	M		TX
Jesse	13	M		TX
John	7	M		TX
Churchill	2	M		TX
Kalegira, Samuel C.	40	M	Overseer	TN
Daniel, G. D.	42	M		SC
Rachael	27	F		AL
Susan	5	F		AL
Charles	4	M		AL
Jones, Hannah	39	F		TX
Daniels, Sarah	2	F		TX
Raider, John	42	M	Farmer	TN
Gracey	35	F		MO
Pilant, E. P.	29	M	Physician	TN
Mary C. M.	29	F		LA
Alexander	10/12	M		TX
Collins, William	10	M		LA
Mary C.	8	F		LA
Ann E.	6	F		LA
T.	5	M		LA
A.	45	M	Laborer	MEX
Kegins, John	33	M	Planter	MS
Varney, Ezekiel, Jr.	4	M		TX
How, Catherine	16	F		LA
Smith, Richard	23	M	Overseer	MS

(continued)

Name	Age	Sex	Occupation	Birthplace
Harrenson, John	48	M	Laborer	IRE
Campbell, C.	33	M		TN
Beall, George	25	M	Physician	MD
Echols, Abner	56	M	Farmer	TN
Sarah Ann	35	F		MD
Rebecca	18	F		TX
Louisa	16	F		TX
John	13	M		TX
Ann	12	F		TX
Ann E.	9	M(?)		TX
James P.	11	M		TX
Gustavus	5	M		TX
Abner	3	M		TX
Allies	2	F		TX
Any E.	12	F		TX
Wheaton, John	27	M	Laborer	PA
Mary	23	F		TN
Henry	4	M		TX
Secrets, W. Henry W.	41	M	Sportsman	TN
Comfort	41	F		NC
Feidder E. C.	12	M		TX
Elizabeth J.	9	F		TX
Jacob W. J.	3	M		TX
Francis A.	17	M	Farmer	AR
Hodge, Archey	59	M	Farmer	GA
Sarah	45	F		SC
Alleot	26	M		AR
Leucenday	14	F		TX
Martha	12	F		TX
Hogan, John	28	M		TN
Einger, E. C.	22	M	School Teacher	NY
Donelary, Frenithy	17	F		TX
Murry, William R.	31	M	Farmer	TN
Mary	30	F		TN
Charles H. W.	15	M		MS
Hammons C.	10	M		TX
Julia C.	8	F		TX
William F.	5	M		TX
Marria J.	2	F		TX
Woodhound, Mary A.	23	F		TN
Henry F.	4	M		TX
William H.	2	M		TX
Fink, James	21	M	Laborer	TN
Marshall, B. G.	36	M	Attorney at Law	TN
Phillip	30	M	Laborer	MEX
Hertiargo, Henry E.	45	M	Farmer	GA
Sarah	25	F		AL
Fink, C.	23	M	Laborer	TN
Carlous, Raffrey	31	M	Planter	VA
Martha C.	20	F		TN
K. S.	5/12	M		TX
Kegins, Washington	30	M	Farmer	MS
Elizabeth	25	F		TN
James	5	M		TX
Elizabeth	2	F		TX
Jameson, John	42	M	Farmer	MS
Evaline	34	F		VA
Ann E.	4	F		MS
J. W.	2	M		MS
McKay, Walter	13	M		MS
Coast, John	24	M	Overseer	TN
Bertrams, Thomas L.	31	M	Planter	TN
Emaly Ann	21	F		TN
Ann W.	3	F		TN
Mary E.	2	F		TN
Caroline	1/12	F		TN
P. E.	22	M	Farmer	TN
Frederick C.	17	M	Farmer	TX
Secrets, T. G.	36	M	Planter	TN
Martha A.	27	F		AL
Nancy S. E.	11	F		TX
Albert C.	6	M		AR
Philix G.	4	M		TX
Martha A.	1	F		TX

FORT BEND COUNTY, TEXAS

Name	Age	Sex	Occupation	Birthplace
Nibbs, Ann B.	38	F	Planter	NC
Mary L.	18	F		AL
Austin	15	M		AL
Mary	85	F		SC
Ratcliff, Jacob	45	M	Overseer	TN
Grey, Thomas M.	45	M	Planter	NY
Nancy	48	F		TN
Robert M.	3	M		TX
Barnett, John	21	M	Asses & Collector	TX
Sarah C.	15	F		TX
James, Jr.	8	M		TX
James, Sr.	40	M		KY

GALVESTON COUNTY, TEXAS

Galveston City

Name	Age	Sex	Occupation	Birthplace
Price, Sophia	40	F		TN
Susan L.	16	F		TN
Eliza J.	14	F		TN
James W.	10	M		TX
Armstrong, Aaron	34	M	Constable	MS
Jane S.	32	F		TN
Frances K.	12	F		TX
Thomas B.	10	M		TX
William	8	M		TX
Mary A.	7/12	F		TX
Yerby, Robert M.	43	M		VA
Jane F.	35	F		TN
Emily T.	18	F		MS
Joseph W.	16	M		MS
Virginia	8	F		MS
Frances	6	F		MS
Edwina	1	F		LA
Bradford, C. T.	22	M	Dry Goods Clerk	TN
Bening, Margaret	22	F		LA
Ashton, William	40	M	Merchant	KY
Elizabeth	32	F		KY
Josephine	15	F		KY
William	13	M		KY
Mary	11	F		KY
Charlotte	2	F		TX
Edmondson, Jas.	19	M	Merchant Clerk	TN
Doke, L. W.	30	M	Merchant	NY
A. A.	20	F		TN
L. W.	2	M		TX
Sarah E.	1/12	F		TX
Sterns, G. W.	15	M		TX
Thompson, James	36	M	Book Keeper	MO
Rebecca A.	30	F		TN
Jane C. S.	12	F		AR
Mary A.	2	F		TX
Carroll, Mrs.	30	F		IN
Jones, Jno. B.	47	M	Attorney at Law	SC
Ann N.	47	F		TN
Gustavus A.	25	M	Attorney at Law	AL
Emmett A.	22	M		AL
Louisa A. N.	15	F		MS
Trimble, Jane	45	F		IRE
Russell, Fanny	12	F		AL
Dixon	8	M		AL
Bryant, Sarah	43	F		VA
Roberts, John	26	M	Carpenter	MD
Dyer, Isadore	35	M	Merchant	MD
Amelia	22	F		CT
John W.	8	M		TX
Emily	6	F		TX
Leon	5	M		TX
Rosanna	4	F		TX
Joseph	2	M		TX
Gee, Louisa	25	F		GER
Brasford, Thomas	23	M	Silversmith	TN
Vedder, J. S.	32	M	Merchant	NY

(continued)

Name	Age	Sex	Occupation	Birthplace
Vedder, Margaret	20	F		TN
Catharine	8/12	F		TX
Scott, Jane	23	F		MO
Browne, H.	25	M	Merchant	NY
Nancy	22	F		PA
Jane	17	F		TN
Elizabeth	10	F		AR
Shepherd, John	38	M	Black Smith	GA
Sarah	23	F		TN
Mary	6	F		MS
Martha	3	F		TX
Pratt, Mary	41	F		TN
Gillespie, Robert	37	M	Black Smith	MA
Vandergriff, P.	65	M		KY
Abbott, H.	47	M	Laborer	SC
George	6	M		TX
Sparks, William	43	M	Sheriff	TN
Lucy	32	F		SC
Arabella	15	F		MS
Sarah	13	F		MS
Mary Ann	12	F		TX
William W.	9	M		TX
John	7	M		TX
Carey, Seth	40	M	Inn Keeper	VT
Rachael	22	F		TX
Sarah E.	3	F		TX
Seth	4/12	M		TX
Ray, Eliza	16	F		TX
Taylor, Adaline	19	F		SWI
Leater, Andrew	29	M	Laborer	NY
Sypert, Thomas S.	26	M	Tinner	TN
Allen, James	32	M	Tailor	IRE
Jemimah K.	35	F		TN
Pace, W.	17	M		TN
Jno.	14	M		TN
Thomas	9	M		TX
Allen, Jno.	4	M		TX
West, Elizabeth	20	F		ENG
Blakeman, E.	33	M	Inn Keeper	CT
Hotel "Palmetto House"				
Anderson, J. A.	24	M	Boatman	TN
Vandergriff, A. B.	57	M	Black Smith	TN
Ann	46	F		SC
George	6	M		TX
Churchill, S.	50	M	Laborer	IRE
Ayres, David	56	M	Land Agent	NJ
Ann M.	51	F		NJ
Parke, Moses	39	M	Merchant	TN
Sarah S.	28	F		NY
Robert A.	9	M		TX
Smith	7	M		TX
Jane Ann	5	F		TX
Frank A.	3	M		TX
Ayres, Theodore	22	M	Merchant Clerk	NY
Peacock, Thomas	33	M	Engineer	PA
Mary C.	29	F		KY
North, Thomas A.	14	M		KY
Peacock, Sarah M.	9	F		TN
Mary A.	7	F		TN
Charles	4	M		TN
Anna	4	F		TN
Richardson, David	31	M		ENG
Eliza	28	F	(Isle of Man)=	IM
Sophia J.	11	F		ENG
Annie	9	F		ENG
David	7	M		ENG
Louisa	6	F		ENG
Eliza	4	F		IM
Frederick	2	M		LA
Higgs, Emma	11	F		ENG
Osmond, Thomas	50	M	Laborer	ENG
Bone, Jno.	30	M	Steamboat Clerk	TN
Pritchard, Thomas	17	M	Steamboat Clerk	ENG
Hughes, Robert	51	M	Attorney at Law	KY

(continued)

GALVESTON COUNTY, TEXAS

Name	Age	Sex	Occupation	Birthplace
Hughes, Archibald M.	25	M	Attorney at Law	TN
Mary E.	20	F		TN
Kraikere, Mary	12	F		GER
Crawford, A. C.	36	M	Merchant	DE
Martha A.	30	F		TN
Elizabeth G.	13	F		PA
Lytle	11	M		TX
Ezekiel C.	7	M		TX
John D.	6	M		TX
Alexander C.	1½	M		TX
Rayburn	1½	M		TX
Shepherd	6/12	M		TX
Boyd, George T.	48	M	Laborer	IRE
Hone, John	60	M	Merchant Clerk	MA
Crawford, Mary	9	F		TX
Kage, K.	28	M	Attorney at Law	TN
Mary	25	F		TN
Fanny	7	F		TN
Marie	3	F		TN
Carey, Celia	38	F	B.	VA
Cooper, Adaline	40	F	B.	RI
Gautier, Nancy	80	F	B.	FL
Cooper, George	27	M	B.	CT
Martha	23	F	B.	TN
Theodore	7	M	B.	TX
Ellen	6	F	B.	TX
George	5	M	B.	NY
Ofelia	2	F	B.	TX
Pell, Mary Ann	35	F	B.	CT
Marone, Josiah	38	M	Laborer	GA
Milbry	33	F		TN
Frances	13	F		TN
William Allston	9/12	M		TX
Marone, Ernst	35	M		KY
Frances	25	F		TN
Matilda O.	1	F		TN
Nicholls, Benjamin P.	32	M	Carpenter	MD
Tabitha	24	F		TN
Amelia	8	F		LA
Amelius	10	M		LA
Washington C.	5	M		LA
John B.	3	M		TX
Althe Ann	3/12	F		TX
Carter, Ellen	2	F		LA
McCullough, John	40	M	Principal of Galv. Seminary. Pupil boarding in the family.	PA
Walker, Nancy	15	F	Pupil	TN
Carr, Mary M.	31	F		TN
Hunter, Catharine	14	F		TN
Nathan	12	M		NC
Smith, Lex	12	F		TN
Walker, Tipton	28	M	Court House Off.	TN
Frances	24	F		PA
Gilbert	6/12	M		TX
Jane H.	49	F		TN
Williams, Mary	12	F		GER
Pilant, J. W.	42	M	None	TN
Leonora J.	33	F		MS
Mary E.	6	F		TX
Josiah W.	4	M		TX
Caroline A.	2	F		TX
Sisson, Nahum S.	39	M	Engineer	NY
Phebe F.	36	F		NH
Mary Emma	14	F		VA
Ellen T.	11	F		TN
George W.	4	M		MS
Nahum W.	15	M		IN
Crone, William	30	M	Carpenter	VA
Felician	30	F		VA
Frenth, William	21	M		TN
Younger, Thomas	20	M		TN
Thrall, H. S.	32	M	Meth. Minister	VT
Amanda J.	24	F		TN
Dragon, James	39	M	Laborer	TN
Mary S.	31	F		TN
Swift, J. A.	40	M	Attorney at Law	VT
Prentice, Mrs. C.	36	F		TN
Helen	18	F		TN
Ashe, Jno. B.	40	M	Attorney at Law	NC
Eliza H.	35	F		NC
William	13	M		TN
Samuel S.	11	M		TN
Gaston R.	8	M		TN
Elizabeth	4	F		TN
Susan	1	F		TX

Clear Creek & Dickinson's Bayou

Name	Age	Sex	Occupation	Birthplace
Tompkins, G.	36	M	Farmer	NY
Maria	24	F		TN
Emma	5	F		TX
Charles	2	M		TX
Underhill, Charles B.	39	M	Farmer	NY
Martha G.	36	F		TN
Robert	12	M		TX
Maria L. C.	8	F		TX
Clarke, Jos. A.	35	M	Printer	IL
Hetty	27	F		TN
Addison	8	M		TX
Randolph	6	M		TX
Eda A.	1	F		TX

GUADALUPE COUNTY, TEXAS

Name	Age	Sex	Occupation	Birthplace
Duggan, Thomas H.	35	M	Farmer	MS
Elizabeth	34	F		MS
Edward	9	M		TX
Thomas	7	M		TX
Alston	5	M		TX
Maria	2	F		TX
Thompson, William H.	30	M	Laborer	TN
Hardiman, Blackstone	60	M	Farmer	TN
Elizabeth	55	F		TN
Peter	19	M	Farmer	TN
Sherer, Francis	43	M	Laborer	FRA
Baker, John	32	M	Farmer	AL
Elizabeth	22	F		MS
Blackstone	3	M		TX
Tate, Sarah	36	F		TN
James	13	M		TX
William	11	M		TX
Elizabeth	8	F		TX
Nicholson, Bonapart B.	31	M	Laborer	TN
Jane	29	F		AR
Martha	13	F		AR
Henry	9	M		TX
Granville	7	M		TX
Priscilla	5	F		TX
Frances	2	F		TX
Daniel, George	47	M	Farmer	GA
Sylvania	43	F		NC
Sharlott	19	F		TN
Arnold	16	M	None	AR
William	14	M		AR
George	11	M		TX
John	9	M		TX
Mahala	7	F		TX
Omega	7	F		TX
Keener, Nancy	48	F		TN
Keener	20	M	Farmer	AL
Mary	18	F		AL
Sarah	18	F		AL
Maria	12	F		AL
Snodgrass, Sarah	26	F		AL

GUADALUPE COUNTY, TEXAS

Happle, Frederick W. 48 M Farmer GER
Rebecca 50 F TN
James 10 M TX
Ann 7 F TX
William 4 M TX
Smith, Louisa 15 F TX
Patterson, Robert 1 M TX
Carter, Vincent 25 M Laborer LA

Chapin, William 26 M Farmer TN
Lucretia 25 F TN
Sarah 4 F AL
Peter 1 M TX

Pettus, Edward C. 40 M Farmer VA
Frances 25 F TN
Rebecca 3 F TX
Frances 1 F TX

Kersey, George W. 31 M Farmer TN
Margaret 28 F TN
Francis 8 M AR
Mary 5 F AR
Andrew 4 M AR
Sarah 3/12 F TX

Winters, Levina 40 F SC
William 40 M None TN
James 20 M None TN
John 16 M None TN
Mary 14 F TX
Leoma 11 F TX
Elisha 9 M TX
William 4 M TX

Waller, Roberson 36 M Farmer TN
Mary 28 F AR
Maria 10 F AR
Mary 9 F AR
James 5 M TX

Swift, Arthur 38 M Farmer VA
Margarett 21 F TN
Mary 4 F TX
Martha 2 F TX
Power, James 30 M Laborer AL
Edrington, Daniel 27 M Laborer MS
Power, Francis 50 M Laborer AL

Tom, William 58 M Farmer SC
Keziah 45 F NC
Houston 21 M Farmer TN
William 17 M Farmer TN
Nancy 15 F TN
George 10 M TX
Dudley 4 M TX
Morehead, Philopa 22 F TX
Jane 2 F TX
Sarah 3/12 F TX

Irvin, Jourdan 28 M Farmer GA
Sarah 24 F TN
William 3 M TX
Mary 1 F TX
Tom, Charles 29 M Farmer TN
Alfred 27 M Farmer TN
Kelley, George 62 M Laborer VA

Tom, John F. 31 M Farmer TN
Mary 29 F PA
Mary 8 M(F) TX
Sarah 5 F TX
Harriett 3 F TX
Emily 6/12 F TX
Gezar, William 38 M Laborer GER

Winsett, John 35 M Farmer TN
Judus 30 F AR
William 9 M TX
Martha 5 F TX
Francis 4 F TX
Levina 3 F TX

Mays, John 57 M Farmer VA
Ann 41 F NC
Elizabeth 16 F TN
Catharine 14 F AR
Watkins 12 M AR
Nelson 10 M AR
William 8 M AR
Allis 6 F AR
Ledora 4 F TX
Tortus, Cicero 16 M Laborer TX

Louis, George W. 35 M Laborer TN

Hunter, Robert H. 36 M Farmer OH
Lamira 30 F MO
Mary 7 F TX
Marcus 6 M TX
Jasgna(?) 2 F TX
Beard, Lewis 25 M Farmer MO
Louis, William 22 M None TN

Smith, Charles A. 39 M Farmer VA
Elizabeth 29 F TN
Ezekiel 9 M TX
Paris 8 M TX
Gertrude 6 F TX
Margarett 3 F TX
Emily 3/12 F TX
Smith, Ezekiel 68 M None VA
Martin, Abraham G. 22 M Laborer GA

Turner, William S. 60 M Farmer VA
Elizabeth 60 F VA
Calvin 24 M Laborer TN
John 17 M Laborer TN
George 5 M TX

Nichols, John W. 33 M Farmer TN
Mary 30 F SC
Elizabeth 9 F TX
Andrew 6 M TX
Mary 2 F TX

Sowell, John N. 30 M Farmer TN
Elizabeth 26 F TN
James 9 M TX
William 2 M TX

Upam, Martha 25 F TN
John 31 M Farmer IN
William 2 M IN

Erskine, Michael 56 M Farmer VA
John 30 M VA
Malinda 20 F VA
Michael 16 M AL
Agnes 11 F MS
Anderson, Ellen ?. 22 F VA
Sophia 2 F TX
Chloe 1 F TX
Hall, Samuel ?. 34 M Laborer TN
Berry, John W. 40 M Laborer VA

Nash, Maria 21 F TN
Luiza 1 F TX
Nichols, Sharlott 19 F AR

West, Claiborn 50 M Farmer TN
Prudence 50 F KY
Larkin 24 M Farmer LA
Lucinda 22 F TX
George 14 M TX
Jefferson 12 M TX
David 9 M TX
William 4 M TX
Kimble, Chester 17 M Farmer TX
Jane 14 F TX
Amanda 14 F TX
Farris, Asenath 7 F TX
Henry, George 25 M Farmer AL
Garner 23 M AL
Crane, William 4/12 M TX
West, Jesse 30 M None VA

Lay, Arnold W. 37 M Farmer SC

(continued)

GUADALUPE COUNTY, TEXAS

Name	Age	Sex	Occupation	Birthplace
Lay, Mary	26	F		AR
William	2	M		TX
James	8/12	M		TX
Beard, Abner	22	M	Farmer	AR
Randolph, Joseph W.	50	M	Farmer	TN
Harris, Harriett	7	F		TX
Abner	5	M		TX
Mary	3	F		TX
Beard, Milam	7	M		TX
Randle, Wilson	35	M	Farmer	TN
Sarah	20	F		GA
Susan	1	F		TX
Williams, David	22	M	Laborer	ENG
Rowton, Edwin S.	32	M	None	TN
Elizabeth	21	F		TN
Siccions(?)	1	M		AR
Rosaline	2/12	F		TX
Hibben, Sarah	45	F		NC
Thomas	48	M	Stockraiser	TN
William	25	M	Stockraiser	TN
John	22	M	Stockraiser	TN
George	20	M	Stockraiser	IL
Daniel	14	M		TN
Alfred	9	M		AR
Julius	5	M		MO
Henry	4	M		MO
Thomas	3	M		MO
Springle, Michael	21	M	Laborer	TN
Jones, Kezziah	27	F		TN
William E.	42	M	District Judge	GA
Willis	19	M	None	GA
James	1	M		TX
William	1	M		TX
Myer, Bartholamew	49	M	Saddler	GER
Powline	35	F		TN
Cary, William	10	M		TX
Sowell, Asa J.	27	M	Farmer	TN
Mary	21	F		TN
Araminter	4	F		TX
Andrew	2	M		TX
Sowell, Rachel	65	F	(Deaf)	NC
Rachel	15	F		TX
Saunders, James F.	38	M	Farmer	TN
Elizabeth	31	F		TN
Samuel	12	M		AL
Feba	6	F		AL
Mary	5	F		AL
Nancy	1	F		TX
Allen, Isaac	51	M	Farmer	TN
Nancy	31	F		TN
David	13	M		AL
Seley, Feba	60	F		VA
Samuel	25	M		TN
King, Henry B.	32	M	Farmer	TN
Mahala	30	F		SC
Rachel	10	F		TX
James	8	M		TX
John	5	M		TX
Elizabeth	3	F		TX
Catharine	2	F		TX
Elliott, Samuel N(A).	26	M	Lawyer	TN
Jane	23	F		OH
Charles	1	M		TX
Cox, Caleb L.	22	M	Farmer	TN
Nancy	63	F		NC
Elizabeth	17	F		TN
King, John G.	24	M	Farmer	LA
Elizabeth	18	F		MS
Drenen, Thomas	26	M	Laborer	TN
Holland, Nelson	51	M	Farmer	NC

(continued)

Name	Age	Sex	Occupation	Birthplace
Holland, Araminta	47	F		TN
Narcissa	26	F		TN
Susan	18	F		TN
Sophia	15	F		TN
Luiza	12	F		TN
Margaret	9	F		TN
Martha	2	F		TN
Holland, William	24	M	Black Smith	TN
Jane	23	F		TN
Catharine	2	F		TN
Martha	6/12	F		TX
Evans, William	22	M	Black Smith	TN
Baxter, William C.	36	M	Black Smith	MA
Caladonia	19	F		TN
William	1	M		TX
Dale, Elijah	40	M	Carpenter	GA
Boyd, John A. M.	47	M	Farmer	TN
Rachel	57	F		SC
Sarah	19	F	(Idiot)	TN
Nancy	18	F		TN
King, John R.	34	M	Farmer	TN
William G.	26	M	Farmer	TN
Ashley, Charity	36	F	(Black)	SC
Matilda	13	F	(Black)	GA
John	11	M	(Black)	GA
Antnett	6	F	(Black)	TX
George	1	M	(Black)	TX
Pharr, Augustus	26	M	Farmer	MS
Meka	16	F		TN
Louis, John	27	M	Farmer	AL
Polley, Joseph H.	54	M	Farmer	NY
Mary	40	F		TN
Mary	21	F		TX
Susan	15	F		TX
Sarah	13	F		TX
Catharine	11	F		TX
Joseph	10	M		TX
Harriett	7	F		TX
Abner	5	M		TX
Jonathan	1	M		TX
Polley, Ellenor A.	6	F		TX
Joseph	5	M		TX
Skinner, William	12	M		TX
James, Richard C.	23	M	Farmer	ENG
Potts, Eliazer	35	M	Farmer	TN
Laura	25	F		IL
Elijah	2	M		TX
James	6/12	M		TX
Butler, Eliza	8	F		TX

GILLESPIE COUNTY, TEXAS

Fredericksburg

Name	Age	Sex	Occupation	Birthplace
Hunter, J. M.	29	M	Merchant	TN
Sofia	18	F		GER
Arnst, Hedwig	50	F		GER
Keyser, Christian	17	M	Clerk	GER
Witman, George	47	M	Merchant	SWE
Cecil, R. W.	45	M	Ass. & Collector	KY
Aukrim, Capt. J. L.	40	M	Surveyor	PA
Strackline, Dina	17	F		GER
Hall, John	40	M	Ranger	TN
Evans, J. L.	26	M	Merchant	TN
Warshouse, William	15	M	Clerk	GER

End of Fredericksburg

Zodiac

Name	Age	Sex	Occupation	Birthplace
Montague, George	48	M	Black Smith	NY
Eliza	37	F		NY
George	21	M	Black Smith	NY
Andrews, Nancy	39	F		TN
Marion	20	M	Farmer	TN
Ann	13	F		TN
Emeline	10	F		TN
Ramora	6/12	M		TX

GILLESPIE COUNTY, TEXAS

Name	Age	Sex	Occupation	Birthplace
Young, John	39	M	Clerk	TN
Pricilla	18	F		IL
Romala	6/12	M		TX
Goodall, Joseph F.	30	M	Cabinet Maker	NY
Elvira	25	F		TN

GOLAID COUNTY, TEXAS

Town of Golaid

Name	Age	Sex	Occupation	Birthplace
Page, John	40	M	Farmer(Hotel Kpr.)	LA
Edey	20	F		AR
Powhatton	1	M		TN
Hughes, William	46	M	Farmer	MO
Warnic, Eliza	13	F		IRE
Stoddard, J. M.	50	M	Farmer	CT
Jane	36	F		TN
Hunter, W. L.	40	M	Farmer	VA
F. E.	29	F		CT
Lipscomb, W.	22	M	M.D.	AL
McCampbell, William B.	62	M	Farmer	TN
Marr, John	25	M	Laborer	IRE
Miller, William	60	M	None	VA
Martha	60	F		VA
Brookin, Joana M.	30	F		TN
Bevean	38	M	None	VA
Hariet	10	F		AR
Martha J.	7	F		AR
Edward M.	3	M		TN
William W.	8/12	M		TN
Campbell, Harrison	30	M	Gin Maker	TN
Susan	25	F		AL
Mary (twin)	3	F		AL
Martha (twin)	3	F		AL
William H.	4/12	M		TX
Whitley, W.	42	M	Farmer	SC
Percy	32	F		SC
M. L. P. K.	12	F		SC
Ann E.	10	F	(Idiot)	SC
Leonora	8	F		TN
William M.	7	M		TN
Phelene	6/12	F		TX
Hord, Jesse	40	M	Teacher	TN
Mary B.	40	F		NC
William J.	8	M		TX
Ann A.	4	F		TX
Jesse	1	M		TX
Hord, James	57	M	Trader	TN
Eucled	14	M		LA
James R.	12	M		LA
Sarah	10	F		LA
Ethelbert	6	M		TX
Vegery, Neopoleon	15	M		NY
Leoton, Joseph A.	14	M		MEX
Bridge, B. S.	48	M	Farmer	MO
Mary	40	F		TN
William B.	8	M		TX
Ann E.	6	F		TX
Samuel P.	3	M		TX
Kiney, Eliza A.	35	F		TN
Samuel H.	10	M		TX
Jno. W.	6	M		TX
Eliza A.	4	F		TX
Sarah J.	1	F		TX
Perkins, T. J.	36	M	Saddler	TN
Dial, William	35	M	Farmer	TN
Fulchive, Elizabeth	48	F		SC
Mathias	50	M	Farmer	PA
Pool, Martha	20	F		MS
William	4	M		TN
Mary Ann	17	F		MS

(continued)

Name	Age	Sex	Occupation	Birthplace
Pool, Catharine	16	F		MS
Philip	13	M		MS
Resenger, Joana	8	F		GER
Lee, Prior	53	M	Lawyer	TN
Mary	35	F		VA
Abraham H.	20	M	None	TN
Julia	15	F		TN
Cintha	13	F		TN
McCampbell, William T.	25	M	Farmer	TN
Joseph W.	23	M	Farmer	TN
Burrus, Bazel	27	M	Farmer	OH
Eliza	30	F		IL
Culver, Martin	14	M		LA
Martha	6	F		TX
Burrus, Mary S.	2	F		TX
Smith, Jediah	28	M	Farmer	OH
Houston, William	21	M	Laborer	TN
Hughes, James	27	M	Farmer	TN
Lucy E.	21	F		SC
Lowery, Susan E.	16	F		SC

End of Town of Golaid

Name	Age	Sex	Occupation	Birthplace
Hurst, John	53	M	Farmer	VA
Nancy	43	F		KY
Brown, Hiram	25	M	Farmer	MS
Lidia	18	F		TN
Hurst, Thonomia(?)	14	F		AR
George W.	10	M		AR
Martha	8	F		TX
Nancy A.	5/12	F		TX
Brown, A. G.	18	M	Farmer	MS
Elzy	15	M	Farmer	MS
Brockman, H. H.	26	M	Farmer	VA
Olive	26	F		MO
William	13	M		(?)GER
Headstrain, John Z.	27	M	Farmer	(?)TN
Delila	18	F		TN
Scott, Richard	18	M	Farmer	NY
Peck, Barton	43	M	Farmer	MA
Francis	31	F		TN
Lucy E.	8	F		TX
Susan M.	6	F		TX
Francis A.	4	F		TX
Barton	2	M		TX
Hill, Robert	33	M	Farmer	NC
Agnes	25	F		TN
Thomas	8	M		TX
Lucy	5	F		TX
Alabama	3	F		TX
Hodges, John W.	49	M	Farmer	TN
Susan L.	31	F		TN
David W.	21	M	Farmer	AL
John S.	15	M	Farmer	AL
Susan A.	12	F		AL
Lucy N.	6	F		TX
William D.	4	M		TX
Robert W.	3	M		TX
Thomas	1	M		TX
Rhynes, George W.	31	M	Farmer	MS
Cinthian	21	F		MS
John F.	2	M		TX
Martha J.	1	F		TX
Hall, Thomas J.	21	M	Farmer	TN
Barbey, James D.	31	M	Capt. Rangers	AL
Edmondson, D. E.	25	M	Ranger	TX
Wood, William	23	M	Ranger	TN
Nolan, Thomas	18	M	Ranger	NY
Lourner, John	40	M	Ranger	TN
Ailes, Jas. S. W.	23	M	Ranger	LA
McFadden, David	20	M	Ranger	MO
Fleming, William	18	M	Ranger	GA
Thomason, Zack W.	22	M	Ranger	TN
Baker, Michael	30	M	Ranger	KY
Bradley, Lewis	20	M	Ranger	AR
Wilson, W. G.	21	M	Ranger	TN

GOLAID COUNTY, TEXAS

Name	Age	Sex	Occupation	Birthplace
Tredwell, James	25	M	Ranger	GA
McLaughlin, Thomas	33	M	Ranger	IRE
Morow, Henry	33	M	Ranger	GER
Jett, Woodson	22	M	Ranger	TN
Smith, A. J.	30	M	Ranger	IL
Roberts, W.	21	M	Ranger	TX
Reace, I. N.	23	M	Ranger	GA
Collins, John	24	M	Ranger	MO
Coy, Antonio	20	M	(Y) Ranger	MEX
Lorenzo	40	M	(Y) Ranger	MEX
Williams, James	20	M	Ranger	TN
Minton, Stephen	28	M	Ranger	GA
Levey, Jac	19	M	Ranger	LA
Southerland, Henry	20	M	Ranger	SCO
Howard, John	21	M	Ranger	TN
Robuck, Rosa	20	M	Ranger	AL
Shackleford, L. D.	21	M	Ranger	KY
Mayfield, W. H.	24	M	Ranger	AL
Smith, Andrew	27	M	Ranger	AR
Birmingham, Giles	20	M	Ranger	TN
Lepsey, S. R.	21	M	Ranger	NC
Nighlin, J. N.	25	M	Ranger	LA
Bush, I. M.	26	M	Ranger	GA
Russell, G. W.	21	M	Ranger	IL

GONZALES COUNTY, TEXAS

Peach Creek

Name	Age	Sex	Occupation	Birthplace
Jones, Augustus H.	39	M		GA
Ann R.	26	F		TN
William	9	M		TX
James	5	M		TX
Sophia	3	F		TX
Augustus	1/12	M		TX
Jones, Sophia	60	F		GA
Anderson, Barry G.	5	M		TX
Berton, A. J.	21	M		TN
Thredgill, Joshua	42	M		NC
Gass, William D.	26	M		TN
Louisa	27	F		MS
William D.	7/12	M		TX
Stewart, Joshua	30	M		AL
Hetty	15	F		TN
Elizabeth	1	F		TX
Beverly	2/12	M		TX
Choat, John	7	M		MS
Harrell, Wilbern	26	M		MO
Malinda	18	F		MO
Leander	24	M		MO
Berry, Joseph	21	M		TN
Wilson, Joseph S.	51	M		TN
Lena	17	F		GA
James	24	M		TN
John E.	22	M		TN
Joseph P.	20	M		TN
Mary C.	12	F		TN
Harvy	7	M		TX
Amelaza	5	F		TX
Loyd, Aaron	30	M	Laborer	??
Blanton, Nancy	33	F		TN
Tabitha	11	F		TX
Margaret	7	F		TX
Nancy	3	F		TX
Texana	1	F		TX
Burlison, Joseph	30	M		TN
Martha	18	F		TN
Burlison, John	50	M		NC
Sarah	17	F		TN
Aaron	17	M		AL
Bayes, John	38	M	(Y)	MEX
Zumwalt, Thomas	30	M		MO

(continued)

Name	Age	Sex	Occupation	Birthplace
Zumwalt, Ele	27	F		TN
Ellen	7	F		TX
Isaac C.	5	M		TX
Andy	5	M		TX
Lucinda J.	3	F		TX
Lucinda Ann	2/12	F		TX
Aplin, Asa	35	M		TN
Elizabeth	70	F		TN
John	23	M		AR
Reames, L. Y.	38	M		TN
Sarah	31	F		AL
Nancy	13	F		TX
Mary	11	F		TX
Clarinda	13	F		TX
Eliza	5/12	F		TX
Ward, William C.	32	M		MO
Sarah	19	F		IN
Mary	1	F		TX
Alford, Winfield	46	M		NC
Eliza	42	F		TN
Leroy	16	M		TX
Julius	11	M		TX
Abraham	1	M		TX
Hart, A. T.	34	M		KY
Nancy	30	F		MO
Malinda	9	F		TX
Mary	7	F		TX
Larmore	2	M		TX
Wheeler, Solemon	24	M		TN

Town of Gonzales

Name	Age	Sex	Occupation	Birthplace
Peck, B. B.	32	M	Merchant	RI
Elizabeth	25	F		TN
Ann E.	1	F		TX
William D. W.	18	M		RI
Cox, John	23	M	Cabinet Maker	IN
Arington, Emma	10	F		TX
Dewitt, C. C.	30	M		MO
P. N.	22	F		TN
Green	7	M		TX
S. E.	5	F		TX
T. J. H.	2	M		TX
T.	6/12	M		TX
Conner, H. C.	35	M	Surveyor	TN
Martha	19	F		AL
Chenault, F.	44	M	Clerk	KY
Eliza	23	F		AR
Alacran	21	M		TN
Steven	18	M		TN
James	4	M		TX
John	2	M		TX
Charles	1	M		TX
Law, Dalton	24	M	Carpenter	TN
Tinsley, John T.	48	M	Physician	TN
Nancy	48	F		KY
Fountin	17	M		TX
Virginia	10	F		TX
Amanda	7	F		TX
John	5	M		TX
Dewitt, C. E.	26	M	Sheriff	MO
S. A. E.	18	F		TN
Nancy	10/12	F		TX
ONeill, J. W.	38	M	Stock Raiser	VA
Mary	40	F		TN
Henry	21	M		TN
William	18	M		TN
George	16	M		MO
Harrison	14	M		MO
John	12	M		MO
Mary Ann	10	F		MO
Miles	4	M		TX
Baupe, William	50	M		TN
Susan	45	F		TN

(continued)

GONZALES COUNTY, TEXAS

Name	Age Sex Occupation	Birthplace
Baupe, William	12 M	MS
Susan	10 F	MS

End of Town of Gonzales

St. Mark River

Name	Age Sex Occupation	Birthplace
Matthews, William	49 M	VA
Nancy	28 F	TN
William C.	15 M	TX
Mary	13 F	TX
Almira	10 F	TX
Alonela(?)	8 F	TX
Alvira	6 F	TX
Thomas	1 M	TX
Bruce, J. T.	31 M Overseer	MO
Tennell, George	28 M Stockraiser	AL
Short, M. H.	42 M Merchant	KY
Putman, William	30 M Stockraiser	TN
Elizabeth	23 F	TN
William	4 M	TX
Jane	2 F	TX
Bailey, Jeremiah	26 M	TN
Martha	23 F	TN
Bailey, Howard	34 M	TN
Elizabeth	23 F	AL
Sarah	1 F	TX
Davis, N.	6 M	AL
Sarah	14 F	AL
Tumblinson, James	6 M	TX
Gay, William	28 M	TN
Sary	24 F	TN
Gay, Quince	24 M	TN
Elizabeth	20 F	TN
Putman, Micael	50 M	TN
Elizabeth	40 F	TN
James	20 M	AL
Hencle	5 M	TX
Lambert, Thomas	37 M	TN
Josiah	13 M	TX
Anthony	11 M	TX
Sarer	7 F	TX
Samuel	4 M	TX
Barrier, Samuel	45 M	TN
Elizabeth	40 F	TN
Toner(?)	20 M	TN
Samuel	18 M	TN
Sarah	15 F	MS
Seth	12 M	MS
Isham	10 M	MS
Hescue, Moses	45 M	GA
Luisa	35 F	TN
Elisa	6 F	TX
Amanda	4 F	TX
William	2 M	TX
Kelly, William	31 M	TN
Amanda	25 F	GA
Coldwell, Mrs.	50 F	TN
Colly, Marinda	30 F	TN
Elizabeth	6 F	TX
Edwin	4 M	TX
William	2 M	TX

End of Town of St. Marks River

Guadaloupe River

Name	Age Sex Occupation	Birthplace
Burman, William	35 M	TN
Caroline	30 F	KY
Sarah	6 F	TX
Mary	4 F	TX
John	2 M	TX
Stringer, Parson	40 M Minister	TN

(continued)

Name	Age Sex Occupation	Birthplace
Stringer, Nancy	35 F	TN
Caroline	18 F	TN
Jula	12 F	TN
Bailey, Howard	36 M	TN
Elizabeth	22 F	AL
Sarah	1 F	TX
Tumlinson, James	7 M	TX
Davis, Sarah	14 F	AL
Nathaniel	10 M	AL
Bailey, Jerry	30 M	TN
Martha	18 F	AL
Nicholes, Latiman	35 M	TN
Mary	25 F	TN
Ralph	7 M	TX
Nancy	3 F	TX
Robert	1 M	TX
Odaniels, J.	50 M Stockraiser	TN
Sarah	40 F	TN
John	21 M	TN
King, J. G.	59 M	SC
Milly	52 F	TN
Thomas	21 M	LA
James	15 M	TX
Eliza	18 F	TX
McCloud, George	21 M	TX
Miller, A. S.	30 M	NC
Permelia	24 F	TX
Mary Ann	7 F	TX
William	4 M	TX
Thomas	2 M	TX
James	3/12 M	TX
Wade, Henry	28 M	TN
Pelham, A. W.	24 M	AL
Mettza, C.	55 M	GER
Joseph	15 M	GER
Adams, Benjamin	35 M	MO
Gay, Thomas	30 M Stockraiser	TN
Eliza	24 F	TX
Allisa	4 F	TX
Baty, M. H.	40 M	TN
Catharine	26 F	NC
Henry	6 M	TX
Rebeccar	4 F	TX
Hunter, Rebeccar	55 F	NC
Bryan, W. C.	25 M Black Smith	TN
Wilson, Thomas	24 M	TN
Foster, William	23 M	TN
Elizar	18 F	TX
William	2 M	TX
Suffield, James	35 M	TN
Cooksey, John C.	35 M	TN
Nancy	32 F	TN
Woodsen	10 M	TX
Sarah	8 F	TX
Mary	6 F	TX
Richmond	4 M	TX
Mandy	2 F	TX
Oliver, John	19 M	TX
Smith, William	17 M	TN
John	29 M	TN
Meredith, James	90 M	VA
Murry, Joseph	23 M (Y)(Mulatto)	MEX
Coe, P. H.	45 M	TN
Sarah	40 F	TN
Jane	25 F	TX
Sarah	23 F	TX
Mary	20 F	TX
William	19 M	TX

End of Guadaloupe River

GONZALES COUNTY, TEXAS

The Sandies Creeks

Name	Age	Sex	Birthplace
Towns, William	30	M	MS
Joel	20	M	TN
Price, Joseph	37	M	TN
Jane	30	F	TN
Elizabeth	4	F	TN
Mary	2	F	TN
William	1	M	TX
Hodges, John S.	28	M	TN
Sophronia	21	F	MO
William	3	M	TX
Elenor	2	F	TX
Hodges, Thomas	40	M	TN
Nancy	42	F	AL
A. J.	22	M	TN
Clement	20	M	TX
John	17	M	TX
Elizabeth	12	F	TX
Nancy	9	F	TX
Breeding, James	30	M	MO
Caroline	22	F	TN
William	4	M	TX
Susan	1	F	TX
Hodges, David	39	M	TN
Jane	25	F	MO
William	5	M	TX
James	4	M	TX
Jane	2	F	TX
David	9/12	M	TX
Hodges, James	45	M	TN
Nancy	44	F	TN
Emeline	25	F	TN
Elizabeth	20	F	TX
William	18	M	TX
John	12	M	TX
Neill, Samuel	35	M	TN
Ruy	34	F	TN
Sarah	5	F	TX
Jane	2	F	TX
Jemima	1	F	TX
Dilworth, Partran	29	M	TN
Elizabeth	24	F	TN
Mary	9	F	TX
Abr. G.	4	M	TX
Nations, Jack	30	M	AL
Mary	24	F	GA
Elvira	5	F	MS
next to			
Nations, John	60	M	TN
Hannah	48	F	SC
Thomas	14	M	MS
Robert	11	M	MS
Mary	9	F	MS
Francis	6	M	MS
Jones, A.	25	M	VA
V. C. J.	8	F	TX
Franklin	6	M	TX
Jones, William H.	28	M	TN
Miller, H. L.	49	M	TN
Catharine	38	F	TN
Malinda J.	14	F	MS
Sarah Jane	12	F	MS
Missouri	10	F	MS
Darling L.	8	M	MS
Ellen J.	6	F	MS
James P.	4	M	MS
Jonithan	2	M	MS

GRAYSON COUNTY, TEXAS

Name	Age	Sex	Occupation	Birthplace
Henderson, John	44	M	Farmer	TN
Sarah	39	F		TN
E.	19	M	Farmer	TN
Parman	17	M	Farmer	TN
Catharine	15	F		TN
E. A.	11	F		MO
John	8	M		MO
A. J.	5	M		MO
N.	2	M		TX
Jackson, William	38	M	Farmer	TN
Sarah	33	F		AL
Martha A.	15	F		AR
Josiah	13	M		AR
Jos. P.	11	M		AR
William A.	9	M		AR
Cynthia C.	6	F		AR
Robert N.	4	M		AR
Mary E.	2	F		AR
Butler, Joab	33	M	Farmer	MO
C.	31	F		TN
H.	13	F		AR
Jesse	11	M		MO
Jos. A.	9	M		MO
William	7	M		MO
Benjamin	5	M		TX
Robert	4	M		TX
Mary E.	3/12	F		TX
Butler, Mary	76	F		NC
Wheat, William W.	30	M	Farmer	AL
C. A.	30	F		TN
P.	10	F		AR
C. C.	8	F		AR
Jos. R.	6	M		TX
E. G(J).	4	F		TX
George A.	8/12	M		TX
Wheat, William	31	M		AL
Smith, Rapel	41	M	Farmer	KY
F. E.	34	F		TN
D. M. W.	19	M	Farmer	AR
A. E.	17	F		AR
Mary Ann	15	F		AR
Robert Lee	13	M		AR
Jno. E.	15	M		AR
Maxwell, J. E.	10	F		AR
Adams, Solomon E.	23	M	Farmer	TN
Stanley, Page	49	M	Farmer	TN
Catharine	43	F		TN
J.	21	M	Farmer	MO
Sarah G.	19	F		MO
William G.	15	M		MO
Miller, John H.	39	M	Farmer	TN
Mary	37	F		TN
J.	19	F		TN
Elizabeth	17	F		TN
Thomas J.	15	M		TN
Joshua	13	M		TN
Martha	11	F		TN
Malinda	9	F		TN
Daniel	7	M		TN
P.	5	F		TN
G.	1	M		TX
Fergerson, Jno. P.	29	M	Farmer	TN
Mary Ann	20	F		TN
Mary Ann	1	F		TX
Hamilton, Fred.	35	M	Farmer	RI
Susan	32	F		TN
Mary J.	8	F		AR
Matilda	5	F		AR
William	4	M		AR
Fred.	1	M		TX
Arington, Mary	56	F		NC
White, Anderson	48	M	Farmer	NC
Mary	53	F		NC
Nancy	20	F		TN

(continued)

GRAYSON COUNTY, TEXAS

Name	Age	Sex	Occupation / Remarks	Born
White, Elizabeth	17	F		TN
Sarah F.	15	F		TN
Dicy E.	13	F		MO
J. B. M.	11	M		MO
Slave	15	M	(Black)	--
Davis, William C.	36	M	Farmer	TN
H. F.	30	F		AL
Sarah J.	13	F		MO
Eliza A.	11	F		MO
William H.	9	M		MO
B. F.	7	F		MO
H. Clay	5	M		MO
Mary E.	3	F		MO
DeSpain, Solomon	44	M	Farmer	KY
Cynthia	42	F		NC
Thomas C.	15	M		TN
Jno. De.	13	M		TN
Benjamin F.	12	F(M)		MO
William H. H.	10	M		MO
George W. M.	8	M		MO
H. Clay	5	M		MO
Samuel F.	2	M		MO
Slaves	7	F	(Black)	--
	14	M	(Black)	--
	25	M	(Black)	--
	30	F	(M)	--
Stark, Isaac ?.	25	M	Farmer	MO
A. R.	18	F		TN
Hayhurst, Jos. W.	30	M	Farmer	VA
Elizabeth	25	F		TN
Mary J.	4	F		AR
Josephine A.	2	F		TX
Thomas A.	6/12	M		TX
Willson, William C.	40	M	Farmer	TN
Eliza	38	F		TN
Martha A.	16	F		TN
M. J.	10	F		TN
William D.	7	M		TN
W. S.	2	M		TX
J. A.	1	F		TX
Willson, David	65	M	Farmer	NC
Sarah A.	48	F		SC
Alex.	20	M	Farmer	TN
Drigers, Sarah Ann	15	F		TN
Jno.	21	M	Farmer	SC
Willson, David C.	31	M	Farmer	TN
Mary	30	F		TN
George W.	9	M		TN
Jane	7	F		TN
S.	5	F		TN
Amanda	2	F		TX
P. A.	6/12	F		TX
Gibson, Levander	46	M	Farmer	SC
Jane	36	F		TN
Robert F.	14	M		MO
Mary C.	12	F		TN
Jno. T.	9	M		TN
Martha E.	8	F		TN
Nancy S.	5	F		TN
Thomas J.	1	M		TX
Paxton, Elizabeth	40	F		TN
Jno. C.	22	M	Farmer	TN
Alice J.	19	F		TN
R. E.	14	F		AR
M. E.	12	F		AR
F. E.	8	F		AR
Robert J.	6	M		AR
Maddin, A. C.	38	M	Farmer	TN
Cartwright, A.	40	M	Preacher C.C.	TN
S.	40	F		VA
S. A.	17	F		TN
S. S.	15	M		TN
M. H.	14	F		TN

(continued)

Name	Age	Sex	Occupation / Remarks	Born
Cartwright, Thomas J.	13	M		MO
S. J.	9	F		MO
E. R.	7	F		MO
F. E.	5	F		MO
Jos. L.	2	M		TX
Blundell, William	55	M	Farmer	VA
E.	44	F		TN
Jno.	22	M	Farmer	KY
Murratt, L. E.	17	F		TN
Mary J.	13	F		IL
J. W. L. M.	6	M		MO
Fox, Jos. T.	6/12	M		TX
Carter, Jno. W.	27	M	Farmer	TN
Mary Ann	22	F		TX
M. E.	5	F		TX
William R.	4	M		TX
Jas. C.	1	M		TX
Thomas, Jesse	25	M	Farmer	TN
L.	16	F		OH
McKinney, M. L.	26	M	Farmer	KY
E. M.	19	F		TN
Francis, Jno.	52	M	Farmer	KY
Frances	48	F		KY
Nancy	22	F		KY
Jas. M.	26	M	Farmer	TN
Elizabeth	20	F		MO
Thomas J.	19	M	Farmer	MO
Jno. W.	17	M	Farmer	MO
E. R.	15	M		MO
H. L.	11	M		MO
William R.	9	M		MO
George W.	6	M		MO
Benjamin L.	2	M		MO
Slave	40	M	(Black)	--
Maddox, Nicholas	55	M	Farmer	TN
Sarah	28	F		TN
J. A.	17	F		AR
William S.	9	M		TX
Benjamin F.	5	M		TX
L. J.	7	F		TX
Jno. W.	3	M		TX
Jas. A. J.	1	M		TX
Templeton, A.	25	M	Black Smith	KY
Mary	30	F		TN
William L.	1	M		MO
A.	35	M	Black Smith	KY
Sarah Ann	28	F		MO
George W.	8	M		MO
David S.	6	M		MO
M. E.	5	F		MO
William A.	2	M		MO
Williams, L. J.	14	F		MO
E.	12	F		MO
M. E.	9	F		MO
J. M.	6	M		MO
Wilson, Jno. H.	27	M	Physician	TN
M.	26	F		MO
V.	8	F		TX
W. E.	7	M		TX
D. R.	3	M		TX
M. J.	1	F		TX
Barton, Jno.	25	M		AL
Govis(?), B. L.	31	M	School Teacher	TN
Slaves	3	F	(Black)	--
	4	F	(Black)	--
	18	F	(Black)	--
	26	M	(M)	--
Lackey, Henry	49	M	Farmer	TN
Nancy	49	F		TN
Jno.	24	M	Farmer	TN
George	22	M	Farmer	TN
Mary J.	19	F		KY
Sarah Ann	17	F		KY
A.	12	M		MO
H.	10	M		MO
Isaac A.	6	M		MO

(continued)

GRAYSON COUNTY, TEXAS

Name	Age	Sex	Occupation	Birthplace
Lackey, Alford	4	M		MO
Lackey, Mary	99	F		VA
Corn, Richard	27	M	Farmer	MO
Mary A.	29	F		AL
Fitch, Mary Craig	49	F		TN
Ann	5	F		AL
Fleck, Isaac	40	M	Carpenter	OH
McCaskle, A. B.	35	M	Saddler	NC
A. M.	27	F		MS
George W.	11	M		AL
William C.	8	M		MO
M. H.	6	F		MO
Porter, William W.	32	M	Trader	TN
Laseter, William L.	34	M	Farmer	TN
S.	33	F		LA
J. A.	13	M		LA
Jno. H.	12	M		LA
S. L.	8	F		LA
G. N.	5	M		MO
M. L.	3	M		TN
A. M.	1	M		TN
Willerbee, D.	40	M	Farmer	TN
Candes	41	F		NC
Willaby, J.	19	F		TN
Jno.	17	M	Farmer	TN
E.	16	F		TN
Mary	9	F		KY
Prudy	4	F		KY
Alex	1	M		TX
Thomas, A.	47	M	Farmer	??
Sarah	34	F		TN
Jas.	12	M		MS
Charles	11	M		TX
William	8	M		TX
R. M.	3	M		TX
Sarah E.	2/12	F		TX
Savage, Mary	53	F		TN
Robert	20	M	Farmer	MO
Thomas	16	M	Farmer	MO
Polly	14	F		MO
A. W.	12	M		MO
Slaves	3/12	F	(M)	--
	3	F	(M)	--
	12	M	(Black)	--
	22	F	(Black)	--
Daniel, Wyatt	29	M	Farmer	TN
R.	22	F		TN
R. J.	4	F		TN
M. M.	3	F		TN
William M.	1	M		TN
Savage, Luke W.	33	M	Farmer (Deaf-Dumb)	MO
Polly	34	F		TN
H. J.	7	F		MO
M. E.	5	F		MO
L. C.	2	M		TX
William F.	5/12	M		TX
Simmons, David P.	34	M	Farmer	TN
E.	31	F		IL
M. J.	12	F		MO
B. F.	8	M		MO
D. S.	7	M		TX
W. J.	4	M		TX
J. B.	2	M		MO
Simmons, Isaac	47	M	Black Smith	TN
E.	48	F		NY
M.	16	F		AR
George	13	M		AR
William	12	M		AR
Sarah	9	F		AR
Bogart, C. E.	13	F		MO
Jones, E. M.	36	M	Farmer	KY
M. A.	36	F		TN

(continued)

Name	Age	Sex	Occupation	Birthplace
Jones, William T.	16	M	Laborer	IL
Jos. B.	11	M		TX
E. G.	9	F		TX
Robert	2	M		TX
Varner, George W.	37	M	Farmer	TN
R.	40	F		TN
Polly	20	F		MO
Mulkey	15	M		MO
George J.	13	M		MO
George W. G.	11	M		MO
L. J.	8	F		MO
A. C.	5	M		MO
N. E.	1	F		TX
Savage, Jos. M.	20	M	Farmer	MO
C. M.	18	F		MO
Carr, B. M.	40	M	Farmer	TN
Mary Ann	29	F		KY
Charles	9	M		TX
Jno.	7	M		TX
E. D.	1	M		TX
B. F.	1	M		TX
Slave	20	F	(M)	--
Wallace, S. S.	34	M	Farmer	TN
Sarah M.	32	F		TN
L.	11	F		TN
E. D.	9	M		TN
Fitch, R. A.	48	M	Farmer	TN
Nancy	28	F		TN
C. H.	2	M		TX
S. L.	5/12	F		TX
Lackey, Jos.	27	M	Farmer	TN
Susanna	24	F		MO
Jas. T.	6	M		MO
William H.	3	M		MO
Savage, William T.	23	M	Farmer	MO
L. G.	22	F		TN
F. M.	1	M		TX
Williams, William	18	M	Laborer	MO
Fitch, Thomas B.	4	M		TX
Shield, George	25	M	Farmer	TN
Nancy	23	F		TN
A. E.	4	F		MO
M. E.	1	F		MO
Mary	14	F		TN
Jane	4	F		MO
Morten, Alex.	41	M	Farmer	TN
Charlotte	37	F		TN
M. P.	17	M	Laborer	IL
Sarah L.	15	F		IL
William J.	12	M		IL
F. M.	10	M		TN
Mary J.	4	F		TX
E. C.	5/12	F		TX
Carter, Charles	33	M	Farmer	TN
V.	26	F		TN
J. William	9	M		MO
E. J.	7	F		MO
V. F.	2	F		TX
Not named	1/12	M		TX
Cardwell, P.	23	M	Farmer	TN
S.	19	F		TN
C.	3	F		TN
L.	1	F		TN
Smith, Jno. B.	26	M	Farmer	TN
H.	24	F		NY
Reaves, George R.	25	M	Ass. & Collector	NY
Jane	21	F		TN
Thomas	4	M		AR
Nancy	2	F		AR
Smith, William B.	17	M	Laborer	TX
Chafin, Jos.	45	M	Farmer	MO
Honor(?)				

(continued)

Name	Age	Sex	Occupation	Birthplace
Chafin, E. P.	20	M	Farmer	TN
E. J.	18	F		TN
N. C.	17	F		TN
M. A.	16	F		TN
M. D.	16	M		TN
Jas. R.	15	M		TN
R. N.	14	M		TN
Jno. H.	14	M		TN
A.	12	F		TN
S. F.	11	M		TN
Thomas	9	M		TN
W. M.	7	M		MO
S. M.	6	F		MO
J. M.	3	M		TX
Jennings, Jno.	36	M	Farmer	TN
E.	34	F		IN
S. A.	14	F		MO
William R.	13	M		MO
M. J.	12	F		MO
V. J.	11	F		MO
C. M.	9	F		MO
Jos. ?.	8	M		MO
C. J.	5	M		MO
N. W.	5	M		MO
M. E.	2	F		TX
R. H.	1/12	-		TX
Watson, Joseph	30	M	Farmer	KY
C. C.	15	F		TN
Watson, M.	26	M	Farmer	KY
R. C.	19	F		TN
N. J.	1	M		TX
Jennings, Hillard	34	M	Farmer	TN
Nancy	22	F		KY
?. J.	10	F		MO
J. D.	7	M		MO
C. A.	2	M		TX
M. E.	5/12	F		TX
Johnson, Jonathan	42	M	Farmer	KY
F.	39	F		KY
Jno.	13	M		AR
F.	9	M		AR
John	6	M		AR
Benjamin	4	M		TX
F. E.	1	F		TX
McMillan, Jno.	25	M	M.E.C.S. Preacher	TN
Atcherson, J. L.	48	M	Farmer	KY
L. R.	43	F		NC
W. C.	21	M	Laborer	TN
H. C.	19	M	Laborer	TN
Jas. M.	17	M	Laborer	MS
L.	15	F		MS
A. W.	14	M		MS
G.	12	M		AR
L. A.	7	F		AR
Not named	2	M		TX
Perdue, Mark	27	M	Farmer	TN
Dorcas	27	F		TN
Luke	7	M		TN
Susannah	6	F		TN
W. C.	5	M		TN
Davis, F. W.	32	M	Black Smith	TN
Elizabeth	19	F		IL
Washburn, Josiah	25	M	Farmer	AR
Davis, Porter M.	21	M	Farmer	TN
E. J.	22	F		OH
Jno. H.	2	M		TX
Browning, E.	21	M	Laborer	TN
E. D.	18	F		TN
Bony, Jos.	17	M		IN
Washburn, Jos.	23	M	Farmer	TN
Sarah	25	F		IL
M. E.	5	F		TX
J. F.	3	M		TX
(continued)				
Washburn, L.	5/12	F		TX
Larkee, M.	16	M		IL
Washburn, Mary	57	F		TN
Jos. W.	16	M	Laborer	MO
Francis	21	F		AR
J. G.	19	M		AR
S. S.	12	M		TX
Everhart, E.	30	M	Farmer	TN
R.	22	F		TN
William	1	M		AL
Slaves	11	F	(M)	--
	13	M	(Black)	--
	21	M	(Black)	--
Allen, Robert	54	M	Farmer	TN
Anna	54	F		TN
O. D.	32	M	Laborer	TN
R. P.	26	M	Laborer	TN
J. A.	17	F		TN
Sidney, Hampton W.	24	M	Farmer	MO
Lindsey, J. E.	24	F		TN
S. E.	5	F		TX
L. G.	4	F		TX
M. A.	3	F		TX
M. A.	7/12	F		TX
Boon, Daniel	34	M	Farmer	NC
J.	30	F		MO
Mary	11	F		MO
E.	9	F		MO
Jno.	7	F(M)		MO
M.	6	F		MO
Daniel	2	M		MO
Next to				
Boon, B. G.	26	M	Farmer	TN
S. A.	21	F		KY
R. P.	2	F		KY
A. P.	1	M		KY
Cochran, George W.	30	M	Farmer	MO
H.	27	F		TN
Jane	16	F		AR
M.	14	F		AR
George	12	M		AR
Jos.	8	M		AR
E.	6	F		AR
H.	4	M		AR
William	1	M		AR
Carothers, William C.	35	M	Stockraiser	TN
D.	30	F		TN
Mary	9	F		TX
L.	6	F		TX
E.	3	F		TX
William	1	M		TX
Atchison, Robert	45	M	C.D.C.G.C.	KY
Mary R.	39	F		IL
L. B.	4	F		TX
William	21	M	Farmer	TN
Mors, Jos. H.	35	M	Surveyor	NY
Slave	15	F	(Black)	--
Bostick, Sol.	36	M	Shoe Maker	TN
E.	31	F		VA
W. N.	12	M		KY
Jno. H.	10	M		TN
Mary	9	F		TN
Robert	7	M		TN
Eliza	5	F		TN
Thomas	2/12	M		TX
Merredith, William	55	M	Black Smith	SC
A.	35	F		TN
Mary Ann	21	F		AR
William H.	11	M		AR
Ala	7	F		AR
Hatcher, Sol.	29	M	Farmer	TN
J.	26	F		TN
T. A.	5	F		MO
Jno. R.	3/12	M		TX

GRAYSON COUNTY, TEXAS

Strickland, Daniel	27	M	J.P.C.C.	MO
L. M.	23	F		TN
Dunham, M.	61	F		MD
Pierce, W. P.	29	M	Farmer	TN
J.	24	F		MO
W.	7	M		MO
William	5	M		MO
M.	3	F		TX
McKay, Margaret	53	F		SC
Pierce, William	21	M	Laborer	IL
Pierce, Thomas M.	31	M	Farmer	TN
K.	29	F		KY
George W.	10	M		MO
Nancy	8	F		MO
E.	5	M		MO
Thomas	3	M		TX
Hill, Jas. O.	28	M	Farmer	SC
L. J.	21	F		TN
George W.	4	M		TX
A. L.	5/12	M		TX
Luker, Jos. H.	17	M	Laborer	TN
Mary Ann	17	F		TN
C. M.	15	F		TN
A. H.	14	M		TN
J. M.	12	M		TN
M. E.	8	F		TN
S. R.	7	M		MS
O'Neal, Jos.	44	M	Chief Justice	TN
Eliza	27	F		KY
R.	5	F		TX
Jno. A.	2	M		TX
Whitlock, R.	56	F		VA
Quillan, Charles C.	24	M	Farmer	??
C.	17	F		TN
William	23	M	Laborer	??
Slaves	3	F	(M)	--
	4	F	(Black)	--
	6	M	(M)	--
	10	M	(Black)	--
	13	F	(Black)	--
	15	F	(Black)	--
Harbolt, James	27	M	Farmer	PA
S. M.	24	F		TN
P. J.	1	F		TX
Hartzog, E.	38	M	Black Smith	NC
M. C.	38	F		SC
George W.	18	M	Laborer	TN
K. E.	14	F		AR
Sarah J.	12	M		AR
R. M.	11	M		AR
M. E.	9	F		AR
S. C.	7	F		AR
A. T.	3	M		TX
A. J.	1	M		TX
Hartzog, Josiah	27	M	Farmer	TN
Sarah	24	F		MO
C.	7	F		AR
Nancy C.	4	F		TX
Jos. M.	2	M		TX
Bruce, P. M.	33	M	Farmer	TN
Sarah	33	F		KY
William W.	11	M		IL
Jno. S.	9	M		IL
F. M.	3/12	M		TX
Walker, Isaac B.	35	M	Farmer	TN
L.	44	F		TN
Richard	17	M	Laborer	IL
Ellen	14	F		IL
L. D.	10	M		IL
Jesse	8	M		IL
Allen	7	M		IL
William	1	M		TX
Deshom, Levi	45	M	Farmer	TN
Polly Ann	44	F		TN
William C.	22	M	Laborer	TN
L. J.	16	F		IL
E. M.	14	F		IL
E. E.	12	M		IL
Jno. B.	9	M		IL
O. M.	7	M		IL
Bonfoot, Jonathan	35	M	Farmer	TN
E. B.	25	F		TN
Deavers, S. E.	1	F		TX
Skidmore, E.	22	M	Farmer	TN
L.	18	F		IL
E.	55	M		??
S.	56	F		GA
Gamson, William A.	24	M		GA
Nancy	58	F		GA
Nancy Ann	22	F		GA
Ellen	17	F		TN
Holbrooks, N. M.	5	F		IL
J. A.	3	M		TX
Peters, Stephen	36	M	Farmer	TN
Margaret	31	F		TN
A. W.	7	M		TX
S. R.	6	M		TX
H. W.	2	M		TX
Slaves	1	M	(Black)	--
	2	F	(Black)	--
	2	F	(Black)	--
	4	F	(Black)	--
	4	F	(Black)	--
	6	M	(Black)	--
	6	F	(Black)	--
	10	F	(Black)	--
	10	F	(Black)	--
	11	F	(Black)	--
	11	F	(Black)	--
	11	M	(Black)	--
	13	M	(Black)	--
	14	M	(Black)	--
	18	F	(Black)	--
	22	F	(Black)	--
	28	F	(Black)	--
	34	F	(Black)	--
	34	F	(Black)	--
	32	M	(Black)	--
	35	M	(Black)	--
Curtis, Ervin	32	M	Farmer	TN
Nancy J.	26	F		TN
Jno. E.	5	M		TX
Sarah E.	3	F		TX
Robert E.	9/12	M		TX
Rease, Moses	52	M	Farmer	NC
Frances	43	F		--
Duke, Jno.	25	M	Farmer	TN
Slaves	5/12	M	(M)	--
	2	F	(Black)	--
	4	M	(Black)	--
	5	F	(Black)	--
	9	F	(Black)	--
	15	F	(M)	--
	28	F	(Black)	--
	30	F	(Black)	--
Inman, S. C.	23	M	Cooper	TN
Martha	20	F		TN
Thomas J.	1	M		TX
Hebbit, William P.	30	M	Cooper	MO
Margaret	27	F		TN
Jos. C.	10	M		MO
Jno. M.	8	M		MO
M. A.	4	F		TX
H. A.	6/12	M		TX
Allen, R.	48	M	Farmer	VA
Eliza	43	F		TN
William H.	21	M	Laborer	TN
Thomas	20	M	Laborer	TN

(continued)

GRAYSON COUNTY, TEXAS

Name	Age	Sex	Occupation	Birthplace
Allen, Thomas P.	18	M	Laborer	TN
Isaac	16	M	Laborer	TN
Harrison	12	M		TN
R.	8	M		TN
M. J.	5	F		TX
Hill, Thomas J.	27	M	Farmer	TN
C. J.	23	F		TN
Mary	5	F		TX
Carter, William	59	M	Farmer	SC
Gilbert, Martha	58	F		VA
Reeves, William T.	56	M	Farmer	SC
Nancy	50	F		NC
William J.	20	M	Laborer	TN
Donada	17	F		TN
L. P.	15	M		TN
M. J.	13	F		AR
Nancy T.	11	F		AR
Talitha A.	8	F		AR
Jno. P.	30	M	Farmer	TN
E. C.	7	F		TX
H. E.	5	F		TX
William J.	2	M		TX
Nancy J.	1	F		TX
Slaves	1	M	(Black)	--
	4	F	(Black)	--
	7	M	(Black)	--
	9	M	(Black)	--
	15	F	(Black)	--
	35	F	(M)	--
Barnes, James	52	M	Carpenter	??
Elizabeth	48	F		TN
Heord, T. B.	21	M	Laborer	MO
J.	18	M		MO
Eliza	16	F		MO
Jno.	14	M		AR
S.	12	M		AR
G. W.	10	M		AR
E.	7	F		AR
M.	5	F		AR
Bishop, Jones	32	M	Farmer	TN
B.	30	F		KY
M. J.	8	F		IL
Richard	20	M	Laborer	IL
Jno.	17	M		IL
Jos.	14	M		IL
M. K.	7	F		AR
Joshua	5	M		AR
William H.	2	M		TX
L. J.	5/12	F		TX
Coffee, Hiram	50	M	Farmer	TN
Elizabeth	52	F		VA
Wash	21*	M	Laborer	IN
Eli	18	M	Laborer	IN
Hiram	16	M	Laborer	IN
Thomas	12	M		IN
Pearce, William	31	M	Farmer	AR
Caroline	33	F		TN
Jno.	11	M		AR
George	7	M		AR
A.	3	F		AR
David	6/12	M		TX
May, Elizabeth	59	F		SC
E.	27	F		TN
Jane	16	F		AR
Covington, Thomas	3	M		AR
Hall, Jno.	50	M	Cooper	PA
Sarah	37	F		TN
Isaac	11	M		IL
William	9	M		IL
Jno.	5	M		IL
Brogden, William H.	46	M	Farmer	NC
Nancy	35	F		TN
T.	16	F		TN
C.	13	F		TN

(continued)

Name	Age	Sex	Occupation	Birthplace
Brogden, William	12	M		TN
L.	9	M		TX
Jno.	5	M		TX
C. M.	4/12	F		TX
S.	36	M	Miller	GER
Martin, Hardy	28	M	Farmer	TN
L.	18	F		AR
Boyd, C. M.	27	M	Farmer	MO
Mary	21	F		TN
Vance, David	34	M	Farmer	TN
Mary	35	F		NJ
Freeman, William	15	M		IN
L. E.	7	F		MO
Vance, Jno.	3	M		MO
L.	11/12	F		TX
Inglish, Jos.	53	M	Farmer	TN
Elizabeth	45	F		KY
Gilmore	4	M		MO
Jos.	2	M		MO
Stamps, Jno.	27	M	Farmer	TN
George W.	23	M	Farmer	TN
Polly	56	F		VA
Mary Ann	22	F		TN
E. J.	17	F		TN
Andy	3	M		TX
Korn, L.	38	M	Carpenter	MD
Maria	23	F		TN
C.	3	M		TX
Eliza	6	F		TX
Mary	1	F		TX
Moss, Jos. F.	29	M	Farmer	AR
Myars, A.	37	M	Farmer	OH
McFall, Robert	30	M	Laborer	AR
Sotherland, Jno.	22	M	Stone Mason	TN
Slave	26	F	(Black)	--
Johnson, William H.	51	M	Farmer	NC
Eliza	40	F		TN
William	20	M	Laborer	AR
Harriet	18	F		AR
Robert	13	M		AR
Sarah	10	F		AR
Mary	8	F		AR
Jane	6	F		AR
Jon	3	M		TX
Slaves	16	F	(Black)	--
	45	M	(Black)	--
Smith, William B.	39	M	Farmer	TN
Elizabeth	48	F		SC
Jos. A.	16	M	Laborer	TN
William B.	13	M		TN
Barnes, Sarah	50	F		SC
Davis, M. C.	64	M	Black Smith	MD
Mary	60	F		GA
Mary C.	22	F		TN
L. N.	20	F		TN
Jane A.	17	F		TN
M. J.	15	M		TN
Bradley, Jos.	22	M	Laborer	TN
Bean, Robert	30	M	Farmer	AR
Nancy M.	24	F		TN
Jno. I.	8	M		AR
Mark	3	M		TX
M. A.	10/12	F		TX
Slaves	1	M	(Black)	--
	3	M	(Black)	--
	5	M	(Black)	--
	11	M	(Black)	--
	23	F	(Black)	--
	24	M	(Black)	--
Beatty, Robert	40	M	Farmer	TN
Slaves	22	M	(M)	--
	25	M	(M)	--
	40	F	(Black)	--

Name	Age	Sex	Occupation	Birthplace
Mays, William T.	31	M	Farmer	TN
Mary D.	27	F		TN
P. V.	8	M		MO
M. A.	6	F		TN
E.	4	F		MO
H. S.	2	F		TN
M. E.	9/12	F		TX
Lankford, William P.	31	M	Farmer	TN
M.	26	F		MO
Ursula	6	F		TX
B. N.	2	F		TX
T. J.	19	M	Laborer	GA
Clark, D. M.	21	M		AR
H. V.	8	F		AR
R. L.	15	M		AR
Jno. S.	12	M		AR
Barnett, E.	32	M	Farmer	TN
M. L.	32	F		TN
M. J.	8	F		TN
T. J.	5	M		TN
Jno. H.	3	M		TN
William E.	8/12	M		TX
Carter, Allen	35	M	Shoe Maker	NC
A.	33	F		TN
T.	8	M		MO
M. A. S.	6	F		MO
T. O.	7/12	M		TX
Hackney, F. N.	28	M	Farmer	TN
K.	26	F		OH
Thomas	1	M		TX
Vaden, Jos.	43	M	Saddler	TN
Elizabeth	37	F		NC
William	17	M	Laborer	TN
Samuel	14	M		TN
Mona	12	F		TN
J.	10	M		TN
Jos.	9	M		TN
E.	5	F		TX
C.	4	F		TX
H.	1	M		TX
Martin, Jno.	32	M	Farmer	TN
M.	32	F		MO
M. A.	13	F		IA
G. W.	8	M		IA
Jennings, Jno.	47	M	Farmer	SC
Sarah	43	F		TN
H.	21	M	Laborer	MO
Jno. M.	19	M	Laborer	MO
Mary Ann	17	F		MO
M. J.	15	F		MO
William E.	13	M		MO
M. E. E.	10	F		MO
Drake, A. H.	34	M	Farmer	TN
Sarah	38	F		TN
W. J.	8	M		IL
L.	7	F		IL
Blagg, Jno.	16	M	Laborer	AL
Jos.	14	M		GA
McConnell, Jno.	40	M	Farmer	??
E. J.	13	F		TN
T. L.	10	M		TX
Glover, Jno.	52	M	Physician	KY
Nancy	45	F		TN
Richard	22	M	Laborer	MO
E.	17	F		MO
M.	13	F		MO
S.	10	F		MO
Jonas	7	M		TX
Samuel	3	M		TX
Killebrough, Jos.	24	M	Laborer	KY
B.	23	M	Laborer	KY
Keele, Sol	55	M	Physician	KY

(continued)

Name	Age	Sex	Occupation	Birthplace
Turley, Jno. S.	50		Farmer	TN
E.	50	F		TN
William M.	19	M	Laborer	IL
A. R.	17	F		IL
Jno.	13	M		IL
E.	11	F		IL
Lankford, Jno. B.	3-	M	Carpenter	TN
L.	27	F		IL
P.	10	F		IL
Sarah	8	F		IL
Jos. A.	6	M		IL
G.	4	M		IL
Ryburn, H. W.	49	M	Farmer	TN
H.	29	F		TN
T.	3	F		TX
N.	8/12	F		TX
Slave	50	F	(Black)	--
Davis, R.	40	M	Farmer	VA
Jane	24	F		AL
M.	14	F		TN
H. E.	13	F		IL
W. T.	11	M		IL
M. V.	9	F		IL
Sarah	6	F		IL
M. J.	2	F		IL
Harris, M.	52	F		KY
L. P.	13	F		TN
J. S.	17	M	Laborer	TN
M. H.	10	M		TN
Jno. M.	28	M	Laborer	TN
R. R.	21	M	Laborer	TN
R. P.	8	M		IL
Allred, R.	47	M	Farmer	NC
L.	30	F		IL
Adaline S.	17	F		TN
J.	13	F		AR
B.	3	F		TX
L.	2	F		TX
Poplin, Jane	9	F		AR
Everhart, Jos.	37	M	Farmer	TN
Jane E.	38	F		MO
William	10	M		MO
Fletcher	7	M		MO
Amanda M.	4	F		TX
Richard	2/12	M		TX
Gilliams, John	49	M	Farmer	NC
Nancy	40	F		TN
John W.	19	M	Laborer	MO
Athalia	16	F		MO
Americus	14	M		MO
Elizabeth	13	F		MO
Mary M.	11	F		MO
Violet L.	9	F		MO
Nancy L.	6	F		MO
Robert A.	4	M		MO

Preston

Name	Age	Sex	Occupation	Birthplace
Bean, William	44	M	Merchant	TN
B. Caroline	33	F		TN
Robert	11	M		AR
Mary L.	9	F		AR
William	7	M		AR
Nancy J.	5	F		AR
S. M.	4	F		TX
Eliza	2	F		TX
Slaves	12	F	(Black)	--
	14	M	(Black)	--
	15	F	(Black)	--
Benge, Ware	30	M	Merchant	TN
Tennessee M.	17	F		TN
Jewell, George	13	M		TX
Walker, William A.	37	M	Grocer	NC
M. M.	32	F		TN
Jno. R.	10	M		MO
M. E.	9	F		MO

(continued)

GRAYSON COUNTY, TEXAS

Name	Age	Sex	Occupation	Birthplace
Walker, W. R.	7	M		MO
Duval, William	25	M	Physician	AR
Alexander, A. M.	30	M	Merchant	KY
J. B.	19	F		KY
Jno. M.	6/12	M		TX
Creel, R.	23	M	Merchant	KY
Thompson, J.	26	M	Merchant	TN
Hanes, A.	31	M		VA
Slaves	2	F	(M)	--
	4	M	(M)	--
	6	M	(M)	--
	22	F	(M)	--

End of Preston

Shermon

Name	Age	Sex	Occupation	Birthplace
Richards, F.	21	M	Merchant	TN
M. J.	20	F		AR
Bean, Jno. B.	34	M		TN
Jane	40	F		KY
A. S.	2	M		TX
Mitchell, Thomas L.	20	M		TN
M. J.	13	F		TN
S. E.	9	F		TN
Slaves	5	M	(Black)	--
	12	F	(Black)	--
	15	F	(M)	--
	21	M	(M)	--
Bradley, B. W.	27	M	School Teacher	TN
M. J.	19	F		TN
Lovell, R. B.	23	M	Laborer	TN
E.	18	F		TN
Beasly, F. G.	34	M	Farmer	TN
S.	30	F		TN
M. A.	13	F		MO
M. J.	10	F		MO
Jos. W.	8	M		MO
Robert	6	M		MO
Susan	4	F		MO
Jordan, E.	39	M	Farmer	TN

End of Shermon

GRIMES COUNTY, TEXAS

Name	Age	Sex	Occupation	Birthplace
Floyd, Elisha	35	M	Farmer	TN
Charles E.	8	M		TX
William	6	M		TX
McGown, Elizabeth Ann	21	F		TN
Margaret J.	15	F		TN
Ferris, John	21	M	Laborer	ENG
Giles, S. B.	41	M	C.C. Clergyman	VA
Elizabeth	33	F		TN
B. C.	11	M		TX
L. B.	9	M		TX
Mary A.	7	F		TX
Black, John S., Sr.	60	M	Shepherd	NC
Mary	53	F		TN
John S. M.	18	M	None	TX
Woods, O. T. H.	30	M	Carpenter	TN
R. J.	25	F		TN
O. K.	8	M		TX
Dan	6	M		TX
S. E.	4	F		TX
J. D.	1	M		TX
Mitchell, William M.	41	M	Farmer	VA
Ann L.	35	F		TN
Bell, Enoch	27	M	Carpenter	AL
Hill, O. R. H.	37	M	Farmer	TN
Caroline	26	F		MS
Martin, William A.	10	M		TX
Winson	9	M		TX
John	7	M		TX
Margaret ?.	4	F		TX
Hill, Ann J.	2	F		TX
Thomas G.	2/12	M		TX
Couch, John	49	M	Farmer	SC
Mary	46	F		TN
Samuel	20	M	None	AL
John M.	17	M	None	AL
William J.	14	M		AL
Mary E.	12	F		AL
M. W.	9	M		AL
N. A.	7	F		AL
J. C. K.	4	M		MS
Burrell, E. A.	26	M	None	AL
M. T.	20	F		VA
Kerr, James H.	30	M	Physician	TN
Boggess, H. H.	42	M	Merchant	TN
Harriet C.	32	F		TN
John A.	6	M		TX
W. R.	4	M		TX
H. C.	1	M		TX
McGown, Samuel	31	M	Farmer	TN
Lusinda N.	18	F		TN
John	9/12	M		TX
Fanthrop, Henry	59	M	Farmer	ENG
Rachael	36	F		TN
John	9	M		TX
Mary	5	F		TX
Goodrich, E. W.	41	M	Farmer	TN
Lucy A.	32	F		TN
Washington	14	M		TN
Jane	6	F		TN
John	1	M		TX
Brigance, Foster	33	M	Carpenter	TN
Evaline M.	27	F		GA
Mary J.	7	F		TX
W. F.	6	M		TX
L. V.	4	M		TX
M. L.	1	F		TX
Kelly, H. B.	32	M	Farmer	GA
H. C.	24	F		TN
P. V.	6	M		TX
T. J.	3	F		TX
J. W.	2/12	M		TX
Glass, Elizabeth	23	F		GER
Hobbs, Robert	25	M	Wagon Maker	TN
Martha	19	F		TX
Ephraim M.	4/12	M		TX
Hobbs, Edward	50	M	Farmer	VA
William E.	24	M	None	TN
Nancy A.	15	F		TN
Collin	12	M		TN
Cawthron, E. W.	39	M	Merchant	NC
Aurela	24	F		AL
S. F.	5	F		TX
J. W.	3	M		TX
C. A.	1	F		TX
Grimes, Jacob	28	M	Clerk	AL
Cawthron, R. H.	37	M	Physician	NC
James P.	22	M	Physician	TN
Jones, Hardy	65	M	Farmer	VA
A. V.	65	F		VA
Benjamin	34	M	(Idiot)	TN
Hambleton	22	M	None	TN
J. N.	19	M	None	TN
Eperson, Mary	30	F		TN
William	8	M		TX
A. J.	6	F		TX
R. C.	5	M		TX
McKissack, Mc. J. D.	35	M	Farmer	GA
Y. W. H.	30	M	Carpenter	GA
Lloyd, Robert	38	M	Farmer	TN
Buffington, A.	44	M	C. Bapt. Clergyman	SC
P. C.	34	F		TN
John F.	15	M		TN

(continued)

GRIMES COUNTY, TEXAS

Name	Age	Sex	Occupation	Birthplace
Buffington, Issabella	13	F		TX
T. C.	10	M		TX
Emily	3	F		TX
Paralee	1/12	F		TX
Holsted, B. H.	46	M	Carpenter	GA
E. W.	40	F		GA
Elizabeth J.	18	F		AL
B. R.	16	M	None	AL
B. H., Jr.	13	M		AL
William	11	M		AL
Epephras(?)	5	M		TX
Brigance, Elias	22	M	None	TN
Brigance, C. N.	55	M	Farmer	TN
Phagan	25	M	Merchant	TN
A. L.	27	M	Carpenter	TN
Saunders, William R.	39	M	Carpenter	TN
Elizabeth R.	33	F		KY
M. L.	11	F		TX
William L.	9	M		TX
Sarah	6	F		TX
Berryman, William	53	M	Farmer	NC
Nancy	30	F		OH
Wesley	30	M	None	TN
William	10	M		TX
Susan	8	F		TX
John	6	M		TX
Gressett, John	11	M		LA
William	6	M		LA
Brigance, Harvy	30	M	Miller	TN
M. J. H.	24	F		AL
M. F.	2	F		TX
C. W.	1	M		TX
Rone, William	35	M	Grocery Keeper	GA
Roan, Martha	30	F		AL
James	5	M		AL
King, John	50	M	Farmer	TN
Ann L.	30	F		GA
William B.	15	M	None	TN
Elizabeth A.	12	F		TN
J. H.	2	M		TX
H. P.	5/12	M		TX
Estes, James M.	23	M	Farmer	TN
M. J.	23	F		NC
L. ?. A.	1	F		TX
Adkins, J. W.	36	M	Farmer	TN
J. W., Jr.	16	M	None	AL
John D.	12	M		AL
Lemuel O.	5	M		TX
Emily M.	34	F		AL
Parum, G. A.	22	M	None	TN
Gilbert, James M	38	M	Farmer	NC
Mary E.	24	F		NC
J. Frands	8	F		NC
Tryce, James H.	23	M	Farmer	NC
Smith, Robert	23	M	Laborer	TN
Montgomery, J. M.	32	M		TN
H. M.	19	F		GA
Black, G. B.	29	M	Sheriff	AL
M. A.	23	F		TN
J. M.	7	M	(Deaf & Dumb)	TX
G. M.	5	M		TX
H. E. P.	3	F		TX
D. H.	2	M		TX
M. A.	2/12	F		TX
Brigance, Franklin	31	M	Assessor	TN
Susan	17	F		MS
Scott, John N.	25	M	Farmer	TN
Susan E.	22	F		GA
Garrett L.	4	M		TX
Mary	2	F		TX
Abram M.	8/12	M		TX

Name	Age	Sex	Occupation	Birthplace
Barry, L. D.	35	M	Saddler	NC
M. M.	33	F		TN
William E.	12	M		TN
J. D.	10	M		TX
L. H.	8	M		TX
T. T.	6	M		TX
R. C.	2	M		TX
Travelsted, E. C.	25	M	Carpenter	TN
Regeon, J. B.	25	M	None	TN
E. J.	21	F		AL
Kannon, Polly King	50	F		GA
Brantley, Blake	52	M	Miller	GA
Margarett	43	F		VA
John H.	20	M	Dresser, Mill Store	TN
S. C.	16	F		TN
M. E.	12	F		TX
Tennessee	9	F		TX
Adaline	6	F		TX
Henry, John	21	M	None	TN
Lurana	18	F		TN
Ganes, M. J.	26	F		TN
Rolly	1	M		TX
Henry, Abigail	42	F		SC
William	21	M	None	TN
Z. P.	15	M	None	TN
G. T.	10	M		TX
Miner	16	M	None	TN
Eberly, John	23	M	Laborer	TX
M. E.	22	F		TN
Harrison, Mary Ann	25	F		AL
Mary Jane	5	F		AL
William E.	2	M		TX
Cassleman, David	16	M	None	TN
Muldrow, M. E.	30	F		SC
Samuel W.	9	M		AL
J. T.	8	M		TX
James H.	6	M		TX
A. B.	4	M		TX
P. F.	2	F		TX
Wilson, R. L.	17	M	Student	MO
Simmons, L. C.	29	M	School Teacher	TN
Howell, Alfred	52	M	Farmer	TN
A. E.	18	M	Student	AL
S. W.	16	F		AL
L. F.	13	F		AL
James	21	M	Overseer	TN
Susan	17	F		TN
Smithey, F. S.	38	M	Farmer	KY
Prudence E.	23	F		TN
W. J.	6	M		TX
F. E.	2	F		TX
Dunham, John H.	22	M	Farmer	TN
Retilda	19	F		AL
J. T.	5/12	M		TX
Johns, M. C.	4	F		TX
Dunham, J. H.	31	M	Farmer	TN
S. C.	26	F		NC
D. T.	36	M	None	TN
Knott, Joseph	48	M	Farmer	NC
Treacy	35	F		TN
Jane	10	F		TN
George W.	5	M		TX
Alfred	2	M		TX
Loftin, William T.	17	M	None	TN
Mary C.	12	F		TN
White, J. C.	31	M	Farmer	GA
Virginia	26	F		TN
E. A. A.	6	F		TX
W. E.	3	M		TX
Gregory, T. J.	33	M	Farmer	TN
Elenor	24	F		MS
M. E.	3	F		TX

GRIMES COUNTY, TEXAS

Walker, Delila	29	F		TN
Amanda	11	F		TX
Elizabeth	7	F		TX
John	4	M		TX
Armor, Denina	20	F		TN
Polly Ann	17	F		TN
Whitesides, T. J.	38	M	Farmer	TN
Elizabeth	38	F		GA
Mary	10	F		TX
Hoxey	7	M		TX
John	3	M		TX
Loftin, W. D.	53	M	Farmer	VA
Mrs. L.	45	F		TN
Urilda	18	F		TN
William	17	M	Student	TN
John	15	M	Student	TX
Donoho	11	M		TX
George	9	M		TX
Balie	7	M		TX
Charles	5	M		TX
Harris, D. L.	45	M	Farmer	GA
S. L.	30	F		NC
Whitfield, T. W.	23	M	School Teacher	TN
Lawrence, M. B.	55	M	Physician	NC
Mariah	45	F		KY
George	26	M	None	MO
Pauline	18	F		AR
Adaline	16	F		TX
Grace	14	F		TX
Emily	12	F		TX
Edward	9	M		TX
Ludwell	7	M		TX
A. W.	4	M		TX
Henrietta	1	F		TX
Turner, Georgia	13	F		??
J. W.	9	M		??
Ellen	4	F		FL
Weaver, Urilda	2	F		TX
Wood, John A.	21	M	Physician	TN
Hargraves, Joseph	34	M	Farmer	LA
Missouri	24	F		TN
Selila	8	F		LA
J. Anna	7	F		LA
S. Ann	2	F		TX
Mary E.	1	F		TX
Cobbs, James H.	69	M	Carpenter	VA
LePoint, Vetal	30	M	Laborer	LA
Owen, A. F.	35	M	Black Smith	TN
Lusinda	32	F		AL
Melvira	11	F		MS
E. A.	9	F		TX
T. J.	7	F		TX
H. C.	5	M		TX
L. J.	3/12	F		TX
Wood, James	65	M	Farmer	KY
Mary	58	F		KY
Rufua	13	M		AL
T--. B.	23	M		AL
Mary	18	F		TN
Wood, R. F.	35	M	Farmer	MO
M. A.	24	F		TN
Ann R.	3	F		TX
Ballon, Seth T.	37	M	Miller	RI
Elizabeth	33	F		TN
T. A.	16	M	None	MA
Lugenid(?)	6	M		TX
Lucretia	4	F		TX
Seth	2	M		TX
Low, William	25	M	Brick Mason	DE
Jones, Beninah	55	M	Farmer	MA
Manda	33	F		TN
William	9	M		TX
Caroline	7	F		TX

(continued)

Jones, T. P.	5	M		TX
Peppecuras(?)	3	M		TX
A. Davis	5/12	M		TX
Perry, T. L.	14	M		TX
Chrenshaw, Charles	32	M	Farmer	TN
Lucinda	29	F		LA
?. B.	5	M		TX
William U.	3	M		TX
J. J. C.	8/12	M		TX
McKerlly, Sela	57	F		NC
Samuel	18	M		TX
Stokes, Samuel	40	M	Farmer	TN
Martha	34	F		AL
E. Ann	11	F		LA
Mary M.	8	F		TX
M. L. A.	6	F		TX
Cartright, Pinky	40	F		AL
Montgomery, Andrew	48	M	Farmer	TN
Mary	28	F		AL
Edmund	4	M		TX
Mary	2	F		TX
William	6/12	M		TX
Slonans, J. D.	52	M		VA
Wilson, J. G.	41	M	Farmer	TN
Mariah	33	F		VA
Robert	17	M	None	TN
Thomas	14	M		TN
Elizabeth	13	F		MS
J. K.	11	M		MS
Richard	9	M		TN
John	7	M		TN
Mary	5	F		TN
Sintha	3	F		TN
Margarett	1	F		TX
Marshall, J. T.	35	M	Farmer	IL
Elvira	27	F		MO
L. T.	4	F		TX
Amanda	2	F		TX
Wallice, J. M.	14	M		TX
S. J.	10	F		TX
M. C.	7	M		TX
Cobbs, Andrew	20	M	None	TN
Sooten(r), William	41	M	None	TN
Myra	26	F		AR
Elizabeth	7	F		TX
Frances	5	F		TX
Grimes, Rufus	28	M	Merchant	AL
Martha	24	F		TN
M. J.	7	F		TX
A. C.	5	M		TX
William R.	3	M		TX
Jesse	1	M		TX
McIntire, Robert	31	M	Farmer	LA
Sarah	25	F		TN
John	9	M		TX
Franklin	5	M		TX
William	3	M		TX
R. L.	11/12	M		TX
Rutledge, Thomas	28	M	Farmer	TN
M. M.	18	F		AL
Bradberry, Thomas C.	50	M	Farmer	ME
Hannah D.	40	F		ME
Cassleman, James	40	M	None	TN
Milly	10	F		TX
Harbeson, Jackson	33	M	Farmer	TN
Susanna	33	F		TN
Mary T.	9	F		TN
John L.	7	M		TN
Josaphine	5	F		TX
(Blank)	2	F		TX
Mott, Adolphus	20	M	Farmer	TN
Nancy E.	32	F		SC
Frances W.	11	F		TX

(continued)

GRIMES COUNTY, TEXAS

Name	Age	Sex	Occupation	Birthplace
Mott, Lucy	6	F		TX
Laura	4	F		TX
Duke, M. J.	35	M	Farmer	TN
Martha	28	F		TN
Josiah	10	M		MS
Hexy R.	7	F		MS
Jackson E.	4	M		MS
Martha J.	2	F		MS
Renfroe, W. A.	40	M	Farmer	TN
Arminda	29	F		TN
Charlotte	9	F		AL
William	60	M	None	TN
Margarett	7	F		AL
Guess, John	50	M	Laborer	TN
Anderson	21	M	Laborer	TN
Brown, Owen	33	M	Farmer	TN
Syntha	30	F		IN
Vilinta	9	F		AR
Pinckney B.	6	M		AR
Victora	4	F		TX
Owen C.	1	M		TX
McGuffin, Joyce U.	45	M		SC
Floyd, David B.	18	M	None	TN
James V.	12	M		AL
Hadley, Joshua	8	M	(Deaf & Dumb)	TX
William	7	M		TX
Anthony D.	5	M		TX
McGuffin, Mary E.	8	F		TX
Stewart, Daniel M.	38	M	Overseer	SC
Kinnard, William E.	34	M	None	TN
Stewart, James A.	3	M		TX
Roe, William C.	34	M	Farmer	MS
Hester A.	24	F		TN
James L.	2	M		TX
Mary F.	2/12	F		TX
Johnson, Jacob	41	M	Farmer	TN
Lucy Ann	21	F		TX
Martha	1	F		TX
Biggers, Willis	56	M	Farmer	NC
Polly	49	F		NC
Martha	25	F		NC
William	18	M	None	NC
Frances	15	F		NC
P--	12	M		TN
Lonzo	9	M		TN
Leonidas	6	M		TN
Arrington, William W.	45	M	Farmer	NC
Mary A.	28	F		MS
James K.	12	M		TX
John W.	7	M		TX
Emine	9	F		TX
P.	4	M		TX
Jane	2	F		TX
Runnells, James	7	M		TX
Cornelius	5	M		TX
Marshall, William	40	M	Laborer	TN
Field, D. H.	42	M	Farmer	VA
Caroline F.	32	F		TN
Frances	11	F		AL
Sarah	9	F		AL
Drury	6	M		AL
Florena	4	F		AL
Hadley, D. P.	25	M	Farmer	TN
Mary	26	F		TN
Harriett C. (Twin)	5	F		TX
Susan C. (Twin)	5	F		TX
Thomas	3	M		TX
Calidona	1	F		TX
Young, Mrs.	29	F		GA
Hadley, Grantham H.	28	M	(Idiot)	TN
Henry T.	17	M	None	TX
Edwards, J. Rush	25	M	Farmer	TN
Mary A. D.	24	F		LA

(continued)

Name	Age	Sex	Occupation	Birthplace
Edwards, Caroline S.	2	F		TX
William	1	M		TX
Edwards, John C.	26	M	Farmer	TN
Sarah H.	18	F		AL
Bartlett R.	10/12	M		AL
Rucker, T. J. R.	32	M	Farmer	TN
Mary H.	26	F		TN
Andrew J.	5	M		TX
Mahala E.	3	F		TX
Thomas H.	1	M		TX
Barker, Robert	42	M	Farmer	NC
Elizabeth	39	F		(?)TX
Adaline	7	F		TX
Mary	4	F		TX
Sarah	1	F		TX
Berlison, Elizabeth	16	F		TN
Marilda	9	F		TX
Crisp, George W.	35	M	Laborer	NC
Vandine, John	45	M	Laborer	??
Ruble, Felding	47	M	Farmer	OH
Frances	37	F		TN
Catharine	16	F		TX
Martha J.	14	F		TX
Amanda T.	11	F		TX
Sarah	10	F		TX
Felding L.	9	M		TX
Mary	6	F		TX
Lucy Ann	5	F		TX
William A.	8/12	M		TX
Burnett, Frances	17	F		TX
Celia	15	F		TX
Lange, Adam	23	M	Laborer	??
Bookman, Jesse	32	M	Farmer	SC
Martha	25	F		SC
Samuel	24	M	Gin Right	SC
McGuffin, William	12	M		TN
Dunn, Madison	23	M	Laborer	AL
Cluckart, Christian	20	M	Laborer	GER
Brixey, Keziah	28	F		TN
Lucy A.	6	F		TN
Jesse	4	M		TN
Nealy, Samuel	44	M	Farmer	TN
Ruth	38	F		KY
Margarett A.	19	F		IL
William P.	14	M		IL
Eliza	12	F		IL
Nancy J.	9	F		MO
Joseph	7	M		TX
Mary	5	F		TX
Sarah	1	F		TX
McCoy, William	41	M	Farmer	GA
Martha	28	F		TN
Caroline V.	8	F		TX
John H.	6	M		TX
Peter J.	4	M		TX
Mary L.	1	F		TX
Parnell, William	29	M	Farmer	SC
Nancy	29	F		TN
John A.	3	M		TX
Moses R.	1	M		TX
Cook, Elias P.	27	M	Laborer	TN
Sophia	20	F		FL
William	4	M		TX
Nancy Ann	2	F		TX
Davis, C. J.	34	M	Farmer	NC
Harriett	27	F		FL
Sarah Ann	13	F		MS
Frances P.	11	F		MS
Elizabeth M.	8	F		MS
James	6	M		TX
Harriett R.	6/12	F		TX
Hadley, Simon P.	45	M	Farmer	GA
Sarah	24	F		TN

GRIMES COUNTY, TEXAS

Name		Age	Sex	Occupation	Birthplace
McIver, Joseph		29	M	Farmer	NC
Alafar		23	F		TN
Elizabeth Ann		6	F		TN
Joseph M.		3	M		TX
John R.		8/12	M		TX
Harmes, Francis W.		35	M	Farmer	VA
Ann C.		22	F		TN
Lee, Robert		35	M	Farmer	TN
Clarissa		28	F		VA
Jeremiah W.		10	M		AL
John F.		7	M		AL
Sarah E.		4	F		AL
Nancy C.		2	F		TX
Davis, Christopher		57	M	Farmer	NC
Frances		57	F		NC
Pool, Balina		18	F		TN
Brown, Warren		28	M	Farmer	TN
Francis		31	F		TN
Roberson, Henry G.		35	M	Laborer	GA
Harris, William		45	M	Farmer	GA
Elizabeth		25	F		TN
Winford ?.		9	M		TX
Caroline		12	F		AL
Sarah J.		6	F		TX
Elizabeth J.		6/12	F		TX
Keer, William		40	M	Farmer	TN
S---		38	F		AR
Darcas		16	F		LA
John		14	M		LA
Nancy		12	F		TX
Mary J.		7	F		TX
James		3	M		TX
Rachael		1	F		TX
Rogers, Stephen		47	M	Farmer	TN
Rebecca		44	F		VA
Robert		22	M	None	MO
Elizabeth		18	F		MO
Polly		15	F		TX
Margarett		9	F		TX
Amanda		4	F		TX
Miller, John		45	M	Farmer	TN
Elizabeth		40	F		TN
Hannah		19	F		MO
Anderson		17	M	None	MO
Polly		12	F		MO
Jackson R.		5	M		MO
Bullock, Allen C.		48	M	Farmer	NC
Luticia		41	F		KY
Gates, James	(Twin)	14	M		LA
Thomas	(Twin)	14	M		LA
Mary E.		12	F		LA
Bullock, Oscar A.		3	M		TX
Aaron H.		20	M	Farmer	TN
Martha E.		20	F		TN
Harrison, J. P.		27	M	Farmer	VA
Melvina D.		22	F		TN
McIver, Daniel		25	M	Farmer	NC
Julia B.		23	F		TN
Mary C.		5	F		TX
Frances Ann		2	F		TX
John R.		5/12	M		TX
Schrighoger, Charles		14	M		GER
Mires, John		35	M	Laborer (Idiot)	GER
Brays, Peter		38	M	Farmer	TN
Delila		35	F		LA
Henry L.		17	M	None	LA
Joseph		13	M		LA
Mitchell, Thomas		26	M	Farmer	TN
Dicy		20	F		TN
James C.		2	M		TX

Name		Age	Sex	Occupation	Birthplace
Mitchell, James T.		24	M	Farmer	TN
Mary Ann		18	F		GA
Floyd, Ann P.		48	F		NC
George A.		27	M	None	TN
McClenny, Mary J.		23	F		TN
Patton, E. B.		22	M	Laborer	TN
McIver, Rodric		58	M	Farmer	NC
Issabella		52	F		NC
John		26	M	Farmer	TN
Martha E.		18	F		TN
James		11	M		TN
Susan	(Twin)	8	F		TN
Emily	(Twin)	8	F		TN
Byres, William W.		39	M	Farmer	SC
Jane S.		37	F		SC
Catharine L.		16	F		MS
E. L.		12	M		MS
Nancy E.		10	F		TX
William W.		8	M		TX
John A.		6	M		TX
Sarah Ann		4	F		TX
Andrew McW.		2	M		TX
Dauke, John L.		23	M	Physician	TN
Martha E.		14	F		MS
Byres, John H.		50	M	Merchant	SC
Plaster, Thomas P.		45	M	Farmer	--
Dolly B.		43	F		--
William		20	M	None	TN
John H.		21	M	None	TN
Benjamin McC.		11	M		TX
Joseph H.	(Twin)	10	M		TX
Margarett J.	(Twin)	10	F		TX
Henry F.		8	M		TX
Plaster, Thomas A.		22	M	Farmer	TN
Sarah Ann		20	F		MS
Emanuel		1	M		TX
Corner, John		49	M	Farmer	LA
Prusia		39	F		TN
Elizabeth		15	F		TX
Merellis		12	F		TX
Martha		10	F		TX
Julia		8	F		TX
Leonidas		5	M		TX
Andrew		3	M		TX
Silvester		1	M		TX
Nevill, William		13	M		LA
Western, Malikah		19	M	None	AL
Corner, James		36	M	Farmer	LA
McWhorter, Elizabeth A.		15	F		TN
Samuel		12	M		MS
John R.		8	M		TX
Eliza L.		3	F		TX
McWhorter, Andrew		22	M	Farmer	SC
Mary Mariah		21	F		TN
Sarah		4	F		AR
John		3	M		AR
Eveline		8/12	F		TX
Ship, Putnam S.		24	M	Farmer	TN
Elizabeth J.		16	F		SC
McWhorter, John		61	M	Farmer	IRE
Sarah		42	F		VA
Margarett E.		16	F		TN
Sarah L.		8	F		AR
Dickens, James		26	M	Farmer	TN
Martha		18	F		SC
Richard		1	M		AR
Lewis, Jefferson		28	M	Farmer	AL
Elizabeth		37	F		TN
Martha Jane		7	F		AL
Robert F.		5	M		MS
Chaney, Rebecca		51	F		VA
Francis S.		31	M	Farmer	VA

(continued)

GRIMES COUNTY, TEXAS

Name	Age	Sex	Occupation	Birthplace
Chaney, Kizziah	18	F		TN
Hiram	18	M	None	VA
Ellen W.	15	F		VA
Dodd, William H.	26	M	Farmer	TN
Mary Ann	26	F		TN
James K. P.	3	M		TX
George W.	1	M		TX
James	60	M	None	MD
Coleman, Alexander	22	M	Laborer	TN
Thomas, James	34	M	Farmer	TN
Amanda	24	F		TN
Phebe M.	7	F		TX
John	4	M		TX
Samuel A. J.	2	M		TX
Amanda C. J.	6/12	F		TX
Kinnard, Sarah	59	F		KY
Marcas L.	28	M	Farmer	AL
John R.	24	M	Lawyer	AL
Bone, Augusta	16	F		GER
Jones, Peter	25	M	Overseer	TN
Holms, Joshua	29	M	Laborer	TN
Warters, Clemant C.	55	M	Wagon Maker	NJ
Clemant	20	M	Carpenter	PA
Barnett, Joseph A.	6	M		TX
Hanie, D. C.	50	F		TN
Thomas J.	28	M	Farmer	TN
Mary	22	F		TN
Albert E.	22	M	Lawyer	TN
Uriah	20	M	Student	AL
Kinnard, M. M.	40	M	Farmer	TN
Mary Ann	25	F		GA
Anthony D.	7	M		TX
Susan E.	6	F		TX
Mary L.	2	F		TX
Abram W.	5/12	M		TX
Brown, William R.	63	M	Farmer	TN
Alex M.	20	M	None	TN
John H.	17	M	None	TN
Scott, James	52	M	Farmer	GA
Sarah	45	F		TN
Elizabeth R.	17	F		MS
James L.	14	M		MS
Garrett	11	M		MS
Walter	9	M		TX
Sarah	7	F		TX
Alice	3	F		TX
Perkins, J. C.	34	M	Overseer	TN
William W.	7	M		TN
Dallas	5	M		TN
Whitfield	2	M		TX
Mayfield, S. C.	36	M	Farmer	TN
Mary	24	F		NY
Nancy	7	F		TX
John	5	M		TX
(Blank)	2	M		TX
Charles	3/12	M		TX
Tucker, Edmund	45	M	Physician	GA
Ann	35	F		TN
Ann	2	F		TX
Greenwood, Henry B.	19	M	Student	TX
William J.	12	M	(Deaf & Dumb)	TX
Oliver, Egbert O.	26	M	Farmer	AL
Pauline	26	F		AL
Frances	7	F		MS
William	6	M		MS
Robert	2	M		TX
Williams, Francis	12	F		AL
Roberts, Thomas	32	M	None	TN
Morrison, Guyer	41	M	Farmer	NY
Ann	29	F		TN
Eliza Jane	10	F		TX

(continued)

Name	Age	Sex	Occupation	Birthplace
Morrison, Matilda A.	8	F		TX
John F.	6	M		TX
Mary	4	F		TX
Susan	1	F		TX
Evans, William	12	M		AL

HARRIS COUNTY, TEXAS

City of Houston

Name	Age	Sex	Occupation	Birthplace
Forrester, John	30	M	Merchant	TN
Mahoney, Michael	35	M	Clerk	IRE
Pehryock, M. H.	35	M	Merchant	VA
Jane E.	23	F		TN
Mary	5	F		TX
Elizabeth O.	2	F		TX
Wilson, Mary W.	45	F		MD
Fulton, William	30	M	Hotel Keeper	PA
Sellers, W. H.	24	M	Clerk	TN
Reeves, William B.	56	M	Justice of Peace	TN
White, Thomas	35	M	Hatter	ENG
E. A.	33	F		NJ
Thomas	9	M		TN
Lewette	12	F		IN
William W.	6	M		TN
Charles	3/12	M		TX
Snell, Martin	35	M	None	PA
Emeline	24	F		NC
Emma L.	2/12	F		TX
Smith, Mary Jane	12	F		MO
Messile, Robert B.	19	M		TN
Croppes, George W.	48	M	Farmer	VA
Sebrina	38	F		TN
Methina, Lewis L.	16	M	None	TN
Nancy S.	12	F		AR
Amelia C.	10	F		TX
Croppes, Thomas	7	M		TX
Lee R.	5	M		TX
Wise M.	3	M		TX
K–	1	F		TX
Burke, A. J.	36	M	Merchant	TN
E. L.	33	F		AL
Mat. J.	11	F		TX
A. J.	9	M		TX
Mary	4	F		TX
F. P.	2	M		TX
H. C.	6/12	F		TX
Foogood, Auguste	18	M	Clerk	SWE
Eliot, William H.	34	M	Druggist	Washington
Mary Jane	25	F		TN
Bond, Fitz H.	44	M		MA
Purcel, Francis A.	13	M		TN
Bryan, John L.	37	M	Dentist	NC
Marianne	27	F		AL
Lewis W.	14	M		MS
Mordecai A.	13	M		TN
William H.	10	M		TX
Thomas P.	10	M		TX
John L.	2	M		TX
Luissnor, Dorothea	20	F		PRU
Rottenshine, John	18	M	Florist	GER
Evans, Henry	42	M	Druggist	MA
Susannah	36	F		ENG
Joseph D.	13	M		TN
Kavenaugh, Nelson	38	M	Clerk	TN
Mary E.	32	F		MS
Charles T.	13	M		MS
Mary G.	11	F		MS
Hernus, William	22	M	Clerk	GER
Hutchins, William J.	37	M	Merchant	NY
Elvira	27	F		TN
Mary E.	5	F		TX
Rush	3	M		TX

(continued)

Name	Age	Sex	Occupation	Birthplace
Hutchins, William	3/12	M		TX
Harris, Ruth	50	F		TN
Eva	20	F		TN
Anna	12	F		GER
McIlheny, Samuel K.	41	M	Clerk	PA
Wood, William	46	M	Millright	ENG
Saunders, Jesse B.	36	M	Farmer	TN
Ingraham, Robert C.	50	M	Boatmaker	IRE
Rather, Harriet	42	F		TN
Samuel	24	M		AL
Mary J.	21	F		TX
Gentry, Charles	5	M		TX
Agat, Mary	17	F		TX
Parks, Elizabeth	11	F		GER
Turley, C. A.	34	M	Hatter	VA
E. G.	24	F		VA
Anne E.	7	F		TN
R. L.	5	F		TN
G. S.	2	M		TN
Martin, Thomas	29	M	Farmer	PA
Martha	24	F		TN
Thompson, Phillip	33	M	Black Smith	TN
Christina J.	24	F		TN
Martha Anne	7	F		TX
Catherine	6	F		TX
Mary	3	F		TX
John A.	4/12	M		TX
Henderson, Jas. W.	35	M	Lawyer	TN
Hariet L.	23	F		IN
Frank	1	M		TX
Duckworth, Samuel H.	14	M		TX
Cochran, O. J.	50	M	Farmer	GA
A.	35	F		SC
William	20	M	Clerk	AL
O. L. L.	16	M	None	TN
Swor, John	46	M	Carpenter	SC
Martha J.	38	F		NC
Harris, John	12	M		TN
Goklmann, Henry	40	M	Merchant	GER
Sophia	32	F		GER
Henrietta	13	F		SC
Theresa	10	F		MS
Betty	8	F		MS
Louisa	5	F		LA
Malina	3	F		TX
Marianne	1	F		TX
Nettles, William	40	M	Cabinet Maker	SC
Hathaway, C. D.	28	M	Hatter	TN
George, Philip	39	M	Sawmill	NH
Sheppard, J. W.	39	M	Sawmill	KY
Clark, Jas. H.	34	M	Clerk	NY
George, Henry	14	M		LA
Harris, John	35	M	Laborer	TN
Vincent, Henry	34	M	Lawyer	NY
Miers, Turner	35	M	Carpenter	TN
Mahala	26	F		TN
Parrylee	8	F		TN
Susan E.	5	F		TN
Octavia	2	F		TN
Brown, John	42	M	Brick Maker	VA
Eliza E.	39	F		TN
Franklin	30	M	Brick Maker	VA
Mary Anne	17	F		TN
Bennitta	15	F		TN
John	14	M		TN
Lavinia	12	F		TN
Joseph	10	M		TX
Edward	7	M		TX
William	3	M		TX
Brighurst, George H.	38	M	Surveyor	PA

(continued)

Name	Age	Sex	Occupation	Birthplace
Brighurst, Nancy	28	F		TN
John H.	6	M		TX
Anna M.	4	F		TX
Sarah	2	F		TX
Christine	1	F		TX
Dunn, Jane	11	F		TN
Brashier, Isaac W.	40	M	None	TN
Sarah	32	F		TN
John	13	M		TX
Henry	11	M		TX
Annie A.	3	F		TX
Elizabeth	7/12	F		TX
Plough, Charles	18	M	Laborer	GER
Middleton, David	14	M		MA
Parker, H. C.	32	M	M.D.	GA
Mary	28	F		VA
Sessions, Alexander	20	M	Clerk	TN
Conger, M. E.	23	F		TN
Anne E.	7	F		TX
Jarmon, Asa	43	M	None	TN
Anne	27	F		TN
Robert	18	M	Clerk	TN
Grott, Elizabeth P.	62	F		NC
Durry	21	M	None	TN
Dunn, James P.	11	M		TN
Eliz. M.	7	F		TX
Purcer, Caroline	26	F		NC
Laura	7	F		TN
Charles	4	M		KY
Morton, H. E.	40	F		LA
H. G.	9	F		LA
S. S.	2	F		TX
O. C.	12	M		LA
F. J.	3	M		TX
Tawkins, S. S.	34	M	Lawyer	TN
Shephard, B. A.	36	M	Merchant	VA
Mary	27	F		TN
Jos. H.	8	M		TX
Laura ?.	6	F		TX
Benjamin Milam	4	M		TX
William Hobson	3	M		TX
David	1	M		TX
Hamilton, Isaac D.	46	M	None	TN
Belles, Peter	40	M	Dairyman	PA
Susanna A.	42	F		TN
Dickenson, Angeline E.	16	F		TX
Goodbaker, R. E.	20	F		GER
Deibra, Dorothea	39	F		GER
Henry	17	M	Laborer	GER
Henrietta	14	F		GER
Charles	3	M		GER
Parkinson, Elizabeth	58	F		VA
Elvira	26	F		AL
Sarah	24	F		AL
Louisa	23	F		AL
Lorinda	21	F		AL
John	19	M	None	TN
Amanda	18	F		TN
Gay, Rhoda	34	F		TN
Jas. B.	6	M		TX
J. J.	4	M		TX
Lowes, Cath. E.	15	F		TN
William George	13	M		TN
Sarah M.	11	F		TN
Allen, Jas. A.	32	M	Tailor	IN
J. K.	34	F		TN
Thomas D.	9	M		TX
John A.	3	M		TX
Pace, John	15	M		TN
Ingram, James	38	M	None	TN
House, Sally	28	F		LA

Name	Age	Sex	Occupation	Birthplace
Connor, Elizabeth O.	35	F		TN
Nolan, B. T. A.	12	M		TX
McBaker, Moses	45	M	Farmer	TN
Eliza	42	F		PA
Tiglman A.	23	M	Farmer	OH
Charles H.	20	M	Farmer	OH
Job.	19	M	Farmer	OH
Rebecca Jane	14	F		IN
George Washington	11	F(M)		IN
Phillips, John W.	28	M	M.E. Clergyman	TN
Tuperville, A.	42	M	Merchant	FRA
Devall, E.	38	F		FRA
Beiher, John	25	M	Butcher	GER
Mina	20	F		GER
Leidel, John	15	M	Butcher	GER
Wilson, Moses G.	55	M	Farmer	VA
Margaret Anne	41	F		TN
Alexander	26	M	None	TN
Pratt, Robert	16	M	None	MO
Julianne	10	F		MO
Pamelia F.	7	F		MO
Martha C.	5	F		TX
Moses G.	2	M		TX
Rockwell, M.	33	M		TN
Caroline	11	F		LA
Ellis	9	M		TX
Sarah	7	F		TX
Henry	5	M		TX
T.	3	M		TX
Andrews, David	35	M	Wheelwright	TN
Elizabeth	25	F		NY
Amanda	7	F		TX
Samuel	2	M		TX
Blakely, Sarah	17	F		MO
Templeton, Jas. E.	30	M	Teamster	NC
Martin, August	52	M	Waggoner	FRA
End of Town of Houston				
Spears, Charles	37	M	Sawmill	PA
Elizabeth	34	F		ENG
Fergusson, James	38	M	Engineer	NY
Littlefield, J. M.	38	M	Carpt.	New Bruinswick
Loper, M	35	M	Lumber Mill	TN
Frazier, G. W.	25	M	Farmer	TN
T. F.	60	F		KY
Brown, J. T.	34	M		KY
Joseph	8	M		TN
Sarah F.	6	F		TX
John	14	M		GER
Blackgraves, Harrison	51	M	M.D.	TN
Rachael	29	F		KY
Washington	13	M		IN
Edmund	11	M		IN
Mary Eliza	4	F		IN
Esther Anne	2	F		IN
Brown, Crawford	39	M	Farmer	TN
Evelina	28	F		MS
Evelina C.	3/12	F		TX
Converse, Walter	12	M		TX
George	10	M		TX
Payne, Levi	30	M	Farmer	TN
Susan	17	F		LA
Wardie	5/12	M		TX
Oats, Jas. W.	53	M	Farmer	NC
Sophia	52	F		TN
Jas. Wyatt	25	M		NC
John	23	M	Farmer	NC
Henry	21	M	Farmer	NC
Crawford, John F.	57	M	Saw Mill	TN
M. Anne	49	F		MS
Tennessee	7	F		TX
Garrett, John F.	9	M		TX

Name	Age	Sex	Occupation	Birthplace
Epps, Isam	56	M	Farmer	VA
Sarah	55	F		VA
Elbert	27	M	Farmer	TN
Joshua	26	M	Farmer	TN
Clark, Edmund	28	M	Farmer	LA
Lucy	29	F		TN
Isam	6	M		TX
Alvira	7	F		TX
Alonzo	5	M		TX
Sarah	2	F		TX
Coaltre, James	50	M	Farmer	VA
Rachael	45	F		TN
Maria Isabella	18	F		AL
Joseph James	16	M		AL
Tate, William	40	M	Laborer	TN
Guymond, Anne	7	F		GER
Charles	5	M		GER
Barron, A. F.	37	M	Farmer	TN
Mary	22	F		TX
Mary E.	5	F		TX
Sarah Johanna	3	F		TX
Wm. George Washington	1	M		TX
Halsel, Berdiman	60	M	Farmer	TN
Temperance	60	F		TN
Halsel, David L.	30	M	Farmer	TN
Catherine	22	F		MS
Melvina E. J.	4	F		TX
Martha M.	2	F		TX
March, Wade H.	30	M	Farmer	TN
Leminda Clementine	22	F		MS
Abram	4	M		TX
Eliza C.	1	F		TX
Osborne, Edmund	36	M	Farmer	CT
Mary	30	F		NY
Dalton, Gillianne	14	F		TX
Bailey, Samuel	32	M	Farmer	TN
Franklin, Mary	57	F		VA
William R.	33	M	Farmer	VA
Sarah	19	F		TN
Long, James	20	M	Farmer	TN
Mary	17	F		LA
Lewis, Robert	31	M	Sawmill	RI
Mary	28	F		TN
Robert	8	M		TN
Mary F.	6	F		TN
Susan Anne	4	F		TN
Eliza	11/12	F		TN
Wilson, John R.	26	M	Farmer	TN
Charlotte	24	F		LA
Charlotte A.	8/12	F		TX
McCoy, Alexander	20	M	Black Smith	TN
Mary	18	F		TN
Cathrin	16	F		TN
Coffey, Henry	43	M	Farmer	NC
Isabel	28	F		TN
Mary Caroline	10	F		MO
Olivia Ann	9	F		MO
Rebecca Angeline	6	F		MO
Frances	4	F		TX
John Wesley	1	M		TX
Creagher, John	32	M	Waggoner	TN
Louisa	32	F		TN
Eliza Jane	10	F		AR
Mary Anne	7	F		TX
Mary Louisa	2	F		TX
Clarkson, Caleb	30	M	Hostler	ENG
Grigsby, William	30	M	Farmer	TN
Maria	30	F		GER
Eggering, Henry	18	M		GER
William	16	M		GER

(continued)

HARRIS COUNTY, TEXAS

Name	Age	Sex	Occupation	Birthplace
Eggering, Maria	6	F		GER
Henrietta	4	F		GER
Wheaton, Elizabeth	45	M(F)		TN
John	19	M	Farmer	TX
James	17	M	Carpenter	TX
McFarland, Mary	54	F		TN
Earl, Thomas	34	M	Farmer	NY
Ellen	19	F		MO
Elizabeth	4	F		TX
James	2	M		TX
McFarland, Marvel	35	M	Farmer	TN
Eleonora	22	F		TX
John	4	M		TX
William	2	M		TX
McDowell, John	57	M	None	AL
C.	40	F		TN
Francis, John	16	M	Teamster	TN
Edmund	14	M		TN
Antoinette	8	F		TX
Haily, Thomas	45	M	Farmer	TN
Rebecca	28	F		IL
Kelly, John	7	M		TX
Sarah	9	F		TX
Haily, John	25	M	Farmer	TN
Margaret	22	F		GER
Thomas	23	M	Farmer	TN
Wilkinson, John	23	M	Farmer	TN
Mary	20	F		GER
Louisa	2	F		TX
Elias	1/12	M		TX

HARRISON COUNTY, TEXAS

Name	Age	Sex	Occupation	Birthplace
West, B. L.	72	M	Farmer	VA
F.	82	M	None (Blind)	VA
E.	55	F		VA
William	24	M	None	TN
M. A.	15	F		TN
J. P.	10	M		TX
J. Perseville	11	M		TX
P.	21	F		TN
Ball, C. P.	32	M	Carpenter	MI
West, A.	28	M		TN
C.	21	F		TN
William	4	M		TX
?. J.	3	M		TX
?. H.	1	F		TX
Finley, J. D.	24	M	Farmer	TN
M. L.	18	F		VA
V. H.	3	F		TX
V. E.	1	F		TX
Shelborn, R. L.	14	F		TN
A. J.	12	M		AL
T. B.	9	M		AL
Bearden, N. R.	36	M	Farmer	SC
N.	36	F		TN
E. F.	16	M	None	TN
William C.	14	M		TN
M. L.	10	M		TN
J. J.	8	M		TN
C. P.	3	M		TN

Town of Marshall

Name	Age	Sex	Occupation	Birthplace
Williams, J. F.	48	M	Lawyer	GA
C. L.	26	F		MS
E. C.	18	M		MS
C. M.	16	M		MS
M. H.	13	F		MS
V. M.	12	F		MS
E. H.	10	M		MS
R. H.	8	M		MS

(continued)

Name	Age	Sex	Occupation	Birthplace
Williams, M. A.	3	F		MS
Fox, William	25	M	Overseer	TN
Taylor, William S.	30	M	Doctor	SC
V. H.	26	F		GA
J. H.	8	M		AL
D. S.	6	M		SC
L. D.	4	F		AL
S. J.	1	F		TX
Dandridge, G. W.	22	M	Overseer	TN
Hill, D.	44	M	Farmer	TN
M.	40	F		TN
R. J.	16	F		TN
E. H.	12	M		TX
N. J.	10	F		TX
D. J.	7	M		TX
M. E.	7	F		TX
J. T. Tyler	4	M		TX
Heath, T.	42	M	Dept. Surveyor	IRE
Young, G. W.	37	M	Carpenter	TN
M.	35	F		GA
A. M. H.	7	M		AL
J. R. T.	6	M		AL
M. M.	3	F		TX
L. R.	1	M		TX
R. G.	25	M	None	AL
Patillo, T. H.	44	M	Lawyer	KY
E.	47	F		TN
F. J.	21	M	Printer	AL
B. W.	18	M	Printer	AL
S. M.	16	F		AL
M. J.	14	F		AL
M. E.	9	F		AL
M. M.	7	F		AL
Chilcoate, William	24	M	None	AL
P.	22	M	None	AL
Loughery, R. W.	28	M	Printer	KY
Chilcoate, J.	7	M		AL
McCutchan, J.	39	M	Tailor	TN
M. L.	35	F		TN
A. D.	14	M		AL
M. A. E.	11	F		AL
M. P. J.	9	F		AL
S. C.	7	F		AL
M. J.	5	F		AL
N. R. G.	3	F		AL
J. D.	1	M		TX
Hill, William A.	45	M	Lawyer	MD
C.	35	F		DC
R.	12	F		TN
J.	15	F		IN
A.	8	F		DC
C. C.	1/2	F		TX
Rind, M.	72	F		IRE
Law, L.	42	M	Clerk	VT
Dickerson, T.	50	M	Lawyer	NC
C.	15	M		AR
Gregg, G. G.	28	M	Merchant	TN
E. B.	18	M	Clerk	TN
McGregor, J. R.	19	M	Clark	MD
Sanders, A.	25	M	Clark	TN
Davis, S. W.	45	M	Carpenter	SC
M. L.	38	F		SC
M. A.	14	F		AL
W. L.	11	M		TX
J. B.	10	M		TN
G. L.	9	M		TN
S. J. H.	7	F		TN
E. E.	5	F		TN
M. F.	3	F		TN
S. W.	1/2	M		TX
Miller, F. H.	36	M	Carpenter	TN
L. P.	25	F		TN
W. E.	9	M		TX
A. J.	7	F		TX
M. G.	4	M		TX
J. F.	2	M		TX

(continued)

HARRISON COUNTY, TEXAS

Name	Age	Sex	Occupation	Birthplace
Miller, S. H.	1/2	M		TX
Woods, A. G.	28	M	Merchant	TN
S. H.	18	F		TN
Barrett, J. W.	34	M	Merchant	SC
L. C.	34	F		TN
F. E.	9	F		TX
William G.	4	M		TX
M. L.	2	F		TX
Lane, G.	35	M	Lawyer	IRE
J. J.	23	F		TN
M. J.	7	F		TX
O. P.	6	F		TX
L.	4	F		TX
F.	3	F		TX
E.	1/2	F		TX
Curlin, F.	40	F		TN
M.	18	F		TN
J.	13	M		TN
Evans, William	57	M	Merchant & Farmer	TN
N. W.	42	F		TN
J. M.	17	F		TN
E. J.	12	F		TN
J. D.	15	M		TN
E. J.	9	F		TN
A. G.	7	F		TN
M. J.	5	F		TX
J. W.	2	M		TX
Gregg, J. H.	6	M		AR
William G.	3	M		TX
Friour, N. W.	3	F		TX
Malone, M.	28	M	Overseer	TN
Glover, J. M.	40	M	Tailor	TN
C. H.	28	F		TN
M. A.	7	F		MS
J. M.	5	F		MS
H. A.	3	F		TX
McReynolds, J. M.	28	M	None (Hotel)	AL
Halcomb, E. D.	38	F		VA
A. E.	19	F		TN
L. P.	17	F		TN
J. T.	15	M		TN
P.	12	M		TN
H.	10	F		TN
Wilson, J. M.	26	M	Merchant	TN
Casey, Z. W.	27	M	None	TN
Duke, T. H.	30	M	Tavern Keeper	TN
Williams, J. L.	19	M	Clerk	TN
Hawley, J. C.	55	M	Farmer	VT
E. L.	37	F		TN
T. P.	12	M		MS
D. T.	7	M		TX
D. S.	5	M		TN
E. J.	3	F		TX
J. L.	1	M		TX
T.	73	M	Farmer	VT
A.	58	F		VT
Young, B. F.	40	M	Doctor	SC
Ann E.	31	F		TN
J. W.	9	M		MS
C. F.	7	M		MS
M. E.	5	F		AR
F.	1	F		TX
Haraldson, J. C.	34	M	None	TN
M. S.	29	F		NC
S. A. L.	9	F		GA
J. E.	7	M		TX
Payne, A. J.	36	M	Tax Collector	GA
P. C.	27	F		TN
W. B.	7	M		TX
J. H.	5	M		TX
C. W.	1/2	M		TX
Z.	68	F		NC
J. W.	20	M	Farmer	AL
Stetford, R.	31	M	Merchant	KY
J. A.	28	F		NY
M. J.	7	F		KY
S. E.	5	F		KY
C.	2	F		KY
E.	1	F		OH
C.	41	M	Merchant	KY
L.	24	F		TN
A. J.	5	M		KY
B. F.	3	M		TX
L.	1/2	F		TX
Craig, William P.	40	M	Tailor	SC
M. V.	35	F		NC
A. P.	13	M		TN
C. M.	8	M		TN
F. D.	1	M		TX
Rhodes, F.	35	F		NC
Hamlet, J. E.	35	M	Merchant	TN
M. H.	28	F		MS
E. J.	11	F		MS
M. V.	7	F		MS
F. S.	5	F		AR
J. T.	1/2	M		TX
Hudson, J. M.	39	M	Merchant	TN
E.	30	F		KY
T. H.	10	M		MS
J. R.	9	M		MS
G. C.	7	M		MS
S. W.	22	M	Reformed Gambler	TN
Forehand, M.	51	M	Grocer	NC
N.	49	F		SC
M. P.	16	M	None	TN
N. V.	14	F		TN
W. D.	8	M		TN
Brown, E.	24	M	Wheelwright	VA
C.	18	F		TN
Strowd, B. F.	38	M	Raiser	TN
E.	27	F		TN
R.	5	M		TX
V.	1	F		TX
Ramsay, G.	24	M	None	TN
Murphy, T.	46	M	Farmer	NC
M.	28	F		TN
W.	22	M	None	AL
T.	16	M	None	TN
E.	10	F		TN
J.	13	M		TN
J.	9	M		TN
B.	7	F		TN
A.	5	M		TN
Cain, D.	37	M	None	TN
E.	37	F		AL
M. E.	15	F		TN
E. J.	14	F		MS
L.	11	M		AR
S. A.	8	F		AR
E. E.	6	F		AR
Cole, D. J.	34	M	Grocer	NC
C.	24	F		NC
Allen, G. W.	26	M	Carpenter	TN
Ogle, J.	48	M	None	TN
C.	50	F		TN
J.	11	F		AR
Jones, N.	24	M		IN
A.	7	M		TX
Houghton, J. A.	25	M	Lawyer	GA
C.	18	F		IN
McFail, D. C.	45	M	Watch Maker	NC
McPhail, A.	30	F		GA
J. A.	11	M		AL
William H.	8	M		AL
M. M.	4	M		AL
Parker, W. J.	31	M	Watch Maker	GA
McLears, L.	22	M	Watch Maker	AL
Stafford, R.	13	M		FL
Hyde, S.	27	M	Lawyer	TN

(continued)

Name	Age	Sex	Occupation	Birthplace
Billings, M.	40	M	Shoe Maker	VT
Summers, J.	24	M	Prof. of Music	KY
Frazier, C. A.	26	M	Lawyer	KY
H. J.	22	F		TN
Hunt, L.	36	M	None	TN
E.	22	F		TN
S.	2	M		TX
L. W.	1	M		TX
Coleman, J.	32	M	Black Smith	GA
C.	31	F		TN
William	10	M		TX
M. J.	4	F		TX
N. W.	2	F		TX
Thompson, A.	35	M	Black Smith	VA
Sullivan, S.	22	M	None	KY
Allen, W. S.	33	M	Gin Wright	AL
J.	22	F		TN
S. E.	2	F		TX
Harris, T. A.	32	M	Printer	TN
A. E.	31	F		TN
Lancaster, M. F.	11	F		TN
S. J.	8	F		TN
M. J.	6	M		TN
W. H.	4	M		TX
R. J.	2	M		TX
M.	56	M	J.P.	NC
J. C.	21	M	Printer	TN
Wortham, W. H.	20	M	Printer	TN
Martin, E. L. A.	22	M	Printer	TN
White, W. R.	21	M	Printer	AL
Ford, S. T.	34	M	Carpenter	MD
J. J.	26	F		TN
J. C.	7	M		TX
M. J.	5	F		TX
S. W. H.	2	M		TX
Solomon, William H.	21	M	Carpenter	TN
Smith, J.	23	M	Carpenter	SC
Curtis, J.	18	M	Carpenter	TN
Adams, J.	16	M	Carpenter	AL
Knight, T. R.	24	M	Painter	TN
Hardwick, L.	50	M	Butcher	BEL
S.	33	F		TN
T. J.	7	F		MS
L.	5	M		MS
W.	3	M		MS
Layne, M.	40	M	None	TN
M. H.	15	F		TN
P. H.	12	M		TN
Dandridge, E.	18	F	Teacher of Music	AL
Wigfall, L. T.	35	M	Lawyer	SC
C. M.	30	F		SC
F. H.	6	M		SC
S. L.	3	F		RI
Brittain, W. B.	45	M	Carpenter	NC
L.	32	F		MS
G. W.	11	M		MS
J. M.	1	F		TX
Cooper, E. A.	28	F	None	MS
Boon, E.	27	M	Carpenter	TN
Lewis, A.	22	M	Lawyer	GA
Dunnaway, G. O.	33	M	Saddler	TN
A.	32	F		TN
M.	9	M		MS
G. B.	2	M		TX
Thomas, D.	18	M	Saddler	TN
Branon, C.	26	M	None	SC
Stuart, J. S.	26	M	Saddler	VA
N. J.	22	F		TN
W. L.	4	M		TX
V. A.	2	F		TX
S. E.	1	M		TX
Hodges, J.	44	M	None	SC
Ramsay, W.	23	M	Ox Driver	IL

Name	Age	Sex	Occupation	Birthplace
Brewer, C. C.	29	M	Grocer	LA
E. A.	22	F		GA
C.	3	M		TX
Holland, B.	29	M	Merchant	TN
Heath, J.	30	M	Carpenter	IRE
S. A.	20	F		MD
Finley, A.	28	M	Carpenter	GA
Robinson, M.	21	M	Painter	GA
Hebbart, J. U(V).	22	M	Tanner	ENG
Armstrong, William	35	M	Black Smith	TN
Brewer, (Blank)	1/2	M		TX
Witt, H. B.	22	M	Brick Mason	VA
E.	21	M	Carpenter	VA
L. R.	10	M		VA
Price, J. C.	23	M	Carpenter	TN
Clark, E.	32	M	Lawyer	LA
M. H.	21	F		TN
William E.	1/2	M		TX
M. H.	62	F		GA
Taylor, S. E.	16	F		SC
S.	14	F		SC
Askew, C.	30	M	Lawyer	GA
C. J.	25	F		TN
H. G.	5	M		TX
Roberson, J. H.	29	M	Carpenter	NC
J. C.	20	F		NC
S. E.	2	F		TN
William F.	1/4	M		TX
Hudsbeth, R.	22	M	Carpenter	TN
Erwin, J.	26	M	Carpenter	TN
E.	25	F		AL
D. B.	3	M		MS
Staples, M. W.	25	M	Presby. Preacher	NY
H. T.	20	F		NY
F.	1	F		TN
Goode, R. N.	38	M	Lawyer	TN
E. V.	28	F		MS
M. V.	11	F		MS
E. H.	7	F		MS
R. P.	5	M		TX
J. W.	1	M		TX
Mahan, Obit	39	M	Carpenter	NC
Gooff, T. H.	5	F		LA
Kelsey, S. H.	51	F		SC
T. A.	16	F		TN
B. G.	12	M		TN
F. M.	7	M		TN
Cromer, J.	43	M	Farmer	SC
Burriss, E.	38	F		PA
Kesler, E.	7	F		FL
McMillan, J. A.	23	M	Cabinet Maker	TN
L. J.	21	F		TN
Stuart, J.	26	M	None	TN
Harris, J. C.	32	M	Carpenter	VA
R. J.	25	F		TN
Frazier, B. M.	25	M	Carpenter	TN
Barker, G.	30	M	Butcher	TN
H.	20	F		SCO
E.	3	F		AL
Watkins, A. E.	33	F	None	TN
C. F.	13	M		TN
J. R.	11	M		TN
McCowan, J.	41	M	Farmer	TN
E. H.	33	F		SC
D. C.	17	M	None	AL
E. M. F.	15	F		AL
J.	11	M		AL
J.	3	M		TX
Briston(?), William H.	26	M	Lawyer	ENG

HARRISON COUNTY, TEXAS

Name	Age	Sex	Occupation	Birthplace
Martin, A. C.	35	M	Dentist	PA
M.	28	F		GA
Wilson, T. B.	41	M	C.P.B. Minister	TN
M. E.	50	F		GA
H. A.	18	F	Asst. Teacher	AL
T. B.	9	M		AL
Mason, J.	50	M	Farmer	VA
M. A.	40	F		TN
William H.	17	M	None	AL
M. J.	15	F		AL
M. E.	13	F		TN
V. A.	11	F		MS
J. T.	9	F		TX
Gaines, William M.	21	M	Farmer	AL
Strowd, F.	16	M	Mail Rider	TN
Austin, R. H.	35	M	Farmer	TN
H.	6	M		TX
H. G.	3	M		TX
Darden, J. C.	21	M	None	TN
Granberry, S. W.	49	M	Farmer	NC
N. B.	46	F		NC
C. H.	16	M		NC
C.	14	M		NC
C. A.	11	F		TN
L.	9	F		TN
R.	3	M		TN
Lancaster, J. B.	24	M	Doctor	NC
Gotting, R. B.	34	M	Farmer	NC
S. E.	21	F		NC
Kellum, J.	55	M	Farmer	VA
E.	31	F		TN
E. V.	12	F		TX
R.	10	M		TX
T.	8	M		TX
E.	6	M		TX
E.	2	M		TX
Steger, L.	45	F	Farming	TN
Mayberry, A. J.	25	F		MS
L.	6	F		LA
Long, H. J.	16	M		MS
Mayberry, H.	4	M		TX
C.	2	F		TX
Steger, William	10	M		TX
Thompson, T. W.	35	M	Farmer	NC
M.	31	F		TN
E. J.	10	F		TN
M. A.	8	F		TN
J.	5	F		TN
B. S.	3	M		TN
Sherrod, L.	23	M	Medical Student	TN
Irwin, J. W.	46	M	Farmer	TN
S.	44	F		TN
J.	19	M	Farmer	TN
S.	17	M	Farmer	TN
S.	14	M		TN
J.	11	M		TN
W.	9	M		TN
T.	7	M		TN
E.	5	F		TN
R.	2	M		TX
Rodgers, A. T.	38	M	Farmer	TN
P.	36	F		TN
S. E.	15	M		TN
L.	13	M		TN
J. E.	11	M		TN
T. C.	8	M		TN
S. H.	6	F		TN
W. W.	4	M		TN
M. M.	2	F		TN
Gilmore, J. P.	49	M	Farmer	KY
S.	54	F		TN
C. C.	24	M	Farmer	AL
J. P.	19	M	Farmer	AL

(continued)

Name	Age	Sex	Occupation	Birthplace
Gilmore, H.	13	F		TN
P. A.	10	F		TN
West, A.	25	M	None	??
Copeland, E. F.	25	M	Farmer	TN
J. H.	25	M	Farmer	TN
M.	60	F		SC
E.	20	F		AL
Wiley, J.	28	M	Farmer	TN
T. A.	27	F		TN
Stevenson, J.	52	M		TN
N.	41	M		TN
E. M.	26	M		AL
William H.	21	M		AL
A.	18	M		AL
D.	16	M		AL
J.	14	M		AL
J. L.	10	M		AL
J. C.	12	F		AL
T. J.	6	M		AL
Copeland, William M.	29	M	Farmer	TN
Montgomery, R.	41	M	Farmer	TN
E.	29	F		AL
E. J.	11	F		AL
R.	8	M		AL
J. H.	5	M		AL
L. H.	3	F		MS
Allen, J.	15	M		AL
Ellis, C.	40	M	Farmer	KY
E. C.	40	F		TN
M.	11	M		MS
C. C.	6	M		TX
A. G.	1/2	M		TX
S. H.	15	F		MS
T. H.	10	F		TX
H.	5	F		TX
A. E.	3	F		TX
Ellis, M. W.	19	M	Farmer	TN
H. D.	18	F		TN
Wilder, E. M.	44	M	Farmer	NC
S.	45	F		GA
F.	16	F		TN
F.	14	F		TN
William J.	12	M		TN
McDonald, J. F.	24	M	Doctor	TN
Collier, J. Y.	41	M	Farmer	NC
R.	37	F		NC
T. H. R.	10	M		TN
Brown, R. J.	27	M	Farmer	GA
Morgan, J.	39	M	Farmer	SC
C. B.	30	F		TN
D. F.	8	M		MS
William T.	7	M		MS
S. E.	4	F		MS
M. L.	2	F		MS
McDonald, A.	27	M	Farmer	AL
L.	16	F		TN
Bell, T.	25	M	Farmer	SC
L.	25	F		TN
S. A.	4	F		TN
M. J.	2	F		TN
William J.	1	M		TX
Jetters, J.	22	M	Farmer	AL
Beard, R.	28	M	Farmer	KY
J.	20	F		TN
M. E.	1	F		TX
Henderson, L. R.	55	M	Farmer	SC
N.	45	F		VA
H. J.	13	F		TN
E.	10	M		TN
Wiley, William	30	M	None	SC

Name	Age	Sex	Occupation	Birthplace
Anderson, J.	25	M	Wagon Maker	NC
M.	22	F		TN
M. J.	2	F		TX
M. H.	1	F		TX
Lynch, T.	24	M	Farmer	TN
E.	21	F		TN
F. M.	3	F		TX
William H.	1	M		TX
Moore, J. D.	43	M	Farmer	SC
S.	38	F		TN
B. F.	12	M		TX
D. C.	2	F		TX
M.	1/2	F		TX
Craig, E. T.	37	M	Farmer	TN
N. M.	40	F		NC
J. M.	12	M		TN
J. Y.	10	F		TN
T. H.	8	M		TN
J. L.	7	M		TN
William A.	6	M		TN
Kimble, T.	50	F		TN
Nethary, A. M.	25	M	Overseer	AL
Long, J. M.	40	M	Farmer	SC
M.	38	F		SC
N. E.	17	F		SC
P. H.	16	M		SC
M. J.	13	F		SC
C. M.	12	F		AR
J. T.	11	M		TX
C. L.	10	M		TX
J. M.	9	M		TX
S. H.	7	M		TX
F. M.	4	F		TX
R. T.	3	F		TX
M. H.	1/2	F		TX
Slaughter, E.	44	M		NC
J. A. E.	18	M		TN
Montgomery, William	34	M	Carpenter	KY
Slaughter, J. R.	12	M		TN
J. A.	11	F		TN
R.	7	F		TN
S. A.	69	F		NC
Jones, William N.	28	M	Farmer	AL
A. F.	26	F		AL
C. E.	8	F		TN
S. R.	4	F		TX
H.	2	F		TX
T.	1/2	F		TX
Landrum, W. H.	44	M	Farmer	TN
E.	34	F		LA
M. E.	12	F		TX
B. P.	9	F		TX
L. A.	7	F		TX
J.	5	F		TX
T. M.	4	M		TX
H.	3	F		TX
Thomas, J.	27	M	Overseer	GA
Cooper, M.	20	F		TN
Harrison, S.	31	M	Farmer	TN
M.	20	F		MS
J. J.	4	M		TX
W.	1/2	M		TX
Martin, G. W.	28	M	Farmer	AL
M. Anna	8	F		TX
S.	63	F		SC
Jones, J. P.	21	M	Farmer	TN
Martin, J.	26	M	Farmer	AL
Austin, G. J.	35	M	Farmer	NC
Wall, E.	40	F		NC
N.	16	F		TN
E. F.	14	F		TN
J. A.	12	M		TN

(continued)

Name	Age	Sex	Occupation	Birthplace
Wall, J.	10	F		TN
A. M.	8	F		TN
Harrison, E.	60	F	Farmer	VA
T.	20	M	Farmer	TN
G.	17	M	Farmer	TN
A.	12	M		TN
Murrell, J.	47	M	Farmer	VA
L.	34	F		SC
J. T.	5	M		TN
Stuart, R.	38	M	Farmer	TN
S. J.	22	F		TX
P. M.	4	F		TX
S.	1	F		TX
M. J.	15	F		TX
Roberts, G. J.	32	M	Farmer	VA
S. E.	26	F		VA
William	10	M		VA
J. S.	9	M		TN
C.	6	M		TN
N.	3	F		TN
McGraw, J. H.	27	M	Farmer	TN
E.	25	F		TN
M.	2	F		TX
R.	1	M		TX
Saunders, R.	70	M	Farmer	NC
S.	65	F		NC
B. F.	21	M	Farmer	TN
Blackwell, E.	40	M	Farmer	TN
M.	37	F		TN
S. J.	17	F		TN
R. B.	15	M		TN
J. N.	13	M		TN
J. D.	11	M		TN
E. C.	9	F		TN
N. M.	7	F		TN
L. A.	1/2	F		TX
Finley, T.	55	M	Farmer	TN
F.	46	F		IN
A.	22	M	Farmer	AR
D.	14	M		AR
G.	12	M		AR
P.	7	M		AR
L. H.	17	F		AR
S. A.	10	F		AR
A. E.	3	F		TX
Finley, F.	25	M	Farmer	AR
P.	18	F		TN
Rogers, C. J.	25	M	Farmer	TN
M. ?.	23	F		TN
M. A.	1	F		TX
Beatty, R.	35	M	Farmer	TN
D.	30	F		TN
J.	10	M		TN
L.	8	F		TN
H.	6	F		TN
C.	4	F		TN
N.	1	M		TX
Saunders, William	42	M	Farmer	TN
M.	38	F		TN
S. E.	19	F		TN
R. T.	17	M	Farmer	TN
M. F.	15	F		TN
M. E.	12	F		TN
T. H.	10	F		TN
A. V.	8	F		TN
William	6	M		TN
G. B.	4	M		TX
E.	2	F		TX
Roberts, J.	2	F		MS
Lockett, Z.	35	M	Mechanic	VA
C. E.	21	F		VA
Stuart, L. H.	13	F		TN

HARRISON COUNTY, TEXAS

Name	Age	Sex	Occupation	Birthplace
Young, J. J.	30	M	Farmer	KY
N. H.	30	F		TN
S. T.	7	F		TN
N. E.	5	F		TX
J. R.	1	M		TX
Clark, T.	44	M	Farmer	KY
R.	14	F		IL
S.	21	M	Farmer	TN
J. N.	14	M		IL
P.	14	F		IL
J.	12	M		IL
H.	11	F		IL
N.	10	F		IL
Crawford, J. M.	36	M	Farmer	TN
Parr, J. O.	32	M	C.P. Minister	TN
A. P.	33	F	Tailoress	TN
J. C.	7	M		TN
L. G.	3	F		TN
A. C.	1	M		MO
Howell, J.	21	M	Farmer	AL
Gather, M.	20	M	Farmer	TN
McLerrin, A. J.	35	M	Farmer	TN
M. J.	--	F		AL
D. F.	8	M		TN
W.	6	M		TN
M. H.	2	F		TX
King, William J.	34	M	Farmer	NC
H. H.	24	F		NC
M. J.	3	F		TN
Mangrum, A.	42	M	Overseer	TN
M.	35	F		TN
M.	11	F		TN
T.	9	F		TN
M.	4	F		TN
Woods, M. L.	42	M	Farmer	TN
E. C.	35	F		VA
M. J.	15	F		TN
A. L.	13	F		TN
S. E.	10	F		TN
S. R.	9	F		TX
Pernick, S.	9	F	(Deaf & Dumb)	AL
Hagler, R.	30	M	Overseer	NC
Fields, J. W.	32	M	Farmer	GA
M. E.	30	F		TN
William W.	7	M		TX
S. E.	6	F		TX
J. N.	1	F		TX
R. C.	1/2	F		TX
Arnold, J. R.	36	M	Farmer	TN
M.	25	F		TN
J. L.	5	M		AR
M. E.	4	F		TX
R. M.	2	F		TX
Vosier, A. F.	28	M	Farmer	FRA
Ferguson, W. H.	19	M	Farmer	KY
Price, S. B.	25	M	Farmer	TN
C. K.	26	F		TN
S. E.	5	F		TN
J. R.	3	M		TX
A. R.	1	F		TX
West, J.	26	M	None	MS
Gilmore, William	29	M	Farmer	TN
M. E.	22	F		TN
Claunch, William	32	M	Farmer	TN
J.	26	F		TN
M.	6	F		TN
J.	4	M		TX
C. C.	2	M		TX
Rodgers, J.	50	M	Farmer	TN
E.	54	F		VA
E. J.	33	F		TN

(continued)

Name	Age	Sex	Occupation	Birthplace
Rodgers, R. E.	16	F		TN
T. O.	18	F		TN
R. E.	12	F		TN
J. H.	12	F		TN
F. M. C.	7	M		TN
Price, William	18	M		TN
Ground, P. D.	20	M	Farmer	TN
J. R.	24	F		TN
William S.	4	M		TX
M. M.	1	F		TX
Bond, M.	50	F		TN
Smith, J.	37	M	Overseer	TN
M.	20	F		TN
(Blank)	1	F		AR
Milligan, (Blank)	50	M	None	TN
Mrs.	45	F		TN
William	12	M		AR
Garrison, E.	45	F		TN
M. R.	20	F		TN
H. H.	14	M		TN
J. L.	12	M		TN
Mitchell, A.	26	M	Farmer	KY
Gibson, William J.	35	M	Overseer	TN
S.	28	F		GA
M.	8	F		GA
J.	6	F		GA
M.	4	F		GA
J.	2	M		GA
Hall, M. V.	31	M	Lawyer	TN
M. A.	31	F		SC
T.	9	M		TX
M. J.	4	M		TX
O. V.	2	F		TX
Roberts, T. W.	26	M	Overseer	GA
Richardson, L.	42	F		VA
E. J.	16	F		AL
M. L.	14	F		AL
E. V.	5	F		TX
F. H.	3	F		TX
Donaway, J.	30	M	Overseer	TN
Whitfield, D. B.	32	M	Farmer	TN
L.	25	F		MS
J. B.	9	M		MS
N. C.	7	F		MS
C. W.	3	M		MS
Lay, J.	30	M	Overseer	SC
E.	24	F		TN
E.	5	F		MS
T.	3	M		MS
Williams, B.	11	F		MS
Broome, C.	35	M	Gin Maker	NC
A. H.	32	F		GA
M.	12	M		AL
J.	9	F		AL
A.	7	M		AL
B.	5	F		AL
L. J.	2	F		AL
Alexander, J. S.	34	M	Gin Maker	NC
Crawford, William J.	22	M	Carpenter	GA
Ross, A. J.	21	M	None	TN
Hall, J. B.	28	M	Farmer	TN
M. L.	32	F		SC
Henderson, J. G. Hall	16	M	Farmer	SC
M. J.	14	F		SC
W. W.	9	M		SC
L. T.	6	M		SC
J. F.	1	M		TX
Moore, T. M.	15	M		??
Henley, L. W.	35	M	Farmer	VA
S.	32	F		TN
M. A.	7	F		TN
William W.	4	M		TN
M. J.	1	M		TN
Wadkins, R.	18	M	None	TN

Name	Age	Sex	Occupation	Birthplace
Mangrum, A. W.	41	M	Farmer	NC
W.	43	F		NC
A. T.	10	F		TN
M. S.	8	F		TN
M. W.	2	F		TN
Dalahite, W.	52	M	Farmer	NC
S.	50	F		GA
E.	18	F		TN
S.	17	M	None	TN
S.	14	F		TN
R.	11	F		TN
L. A.	8	F		MS
Taylor, R. P.	38	M	Farmer	MS
A.	21	F		TN
F. N.	11	F		AR
V. V.	8	F		AR
R. P.	7	M		AR
William H.	1	M		TX
Blaylock, R. W.	32	M	Farmer	NC
E.	27	F		TN
C.	10	M		AL
N.	7	F		AL
A.	3	M		TX
R.	2	M		TX
Price, J. H.	24	M	Farmer	TN
E.	18	F		TN
N.	56	F		GA
M.	25	F		TN
Murrel, E.	52	M	Farmer	VA
C.	36	F		TN
R.	20	M	None	TN
William	16	M	None	TN
E.	11	M		TN
A.	7	M		TN
Noland, M.	7	F		TN
Murrel, R.	1	F		TX
Crane, R. T.	52	M	Farmer	GA
C.	37	F		TN
C.	24	M	None	TN
A.	22	M		TN
N.	20	F		TN
G.	18	M		TN
R.	16	F		MS
M.	14	F		MS
A.	6	M		TX
T.	4	M		TX
A. C.	3	F		TX
J.	1/2	M		TX
McDonough, A. J.	35	M	Farmer	VA
J.	32	F		TN
E.	40	M	Farmer (Insane)	VA
Richard, J.	22	F		TN
McDonough, H. A.	8	F		AL
Rogers, J. W.	52	M	Farmer	NC
P.	48	F		NC
Rodgers, J. E.	17	M	None	TN
M. C.	18	F		TN
J. V.	14	M		TN
H. J.	12	F		TN
M. P.	10	F		TN
J. W.	9	M		TN
L. P.	7	F		TN
Jones, J. W.	30	M	Farmer	KY
S. J.	21	F		TN
Thompson, J. W.	26	M	Overseer	NC
Cochran, L. D.	20	M	Brick Mason	TN
Patterson, J.	36	M	Farmer	TN
N. H.	10	F		AL
R.	26	M	Farmer	AL
A.	23	M	Farmer	AL
A.	21	M	Farmer	AL
E. A.	18	F		AL
Vincent, A. P.	49	M	Farmer	NC

(continued)

Name	Age	Sex	Occupation	Birthplace
Vincent, S.	40	F		VA
A. L. A.	19	F		TN
C.	13	M		TN
T.	11	M		TN
A.	10	M		TN
S.	8	F		TN
J.	6	M		TN
J.	4	M		TN
H.	2	F		TX
Ferguson, J. P.	25	M	Farmer	IL
Armstrong, J.	23	F		TN
G.	4	M		AL
William	1/4	M		TX
S. H.	24	M	Farmer	AL
Smith, C.	57	M	Carpenter	NC
A.	19	M	Farmer	TN
P.	15	F		AL
B.	12	M		AL
C.	7	M		AL
Ferguson, J.	10	M		TX
A.	9	M		LA
Sorrelle, J. M.	42	M	Farmer	AL
M. A.	22	F		TN
Pile, C. R.	44	M	Farmer	KY
J. A.	42	F		KY
Freeman, William Pile	15	M		TN
M.	12	M		TN
J.	10	F		TN
Pile, William	10	M		TN
S. L.	5	F		TN
M. J.	3	M		TN
T. C.	1	M		TX
Skiles, E. L.	45	M	Farmer	TN
M.	45	F		TN
R.	21	M	Farmer	TN
D.	19	M	Farmer	TN
A.	15	M		TN
M.	12	M		TN
V.	10	M		TN
C.	9	M		TN
H.	8	M		TN
M. A.	5	F		TN
T.	4	M		GA
G. W.	3	M		GA
Washington, William B.	49	M	Farmer	GA
J.	35	F		GA
William	22	M	Farmer	AL
A.	19	F		AL
J.	11	M		MS
H.	9	M		MS
Bennett, J.	29	M	Black Smith	TN
Halbert, L.	22	M	Black Smith	TN
Jones, A.	42	M	Farmer	NC
H. M.	25	F		NC
F. L.	2	F		TN
J. P.	25	M	Farmer	NC
Freeman, H. B.	21	M	Farmer	TN
T.	17	F		TN
W.	1/2	M		TX
Clark, T. W.	45	M	Farmer	VA
H. A.	18	F		TN
B. H.	5	F		TX
P. R.	4	F		TX
Raines, M. E.	11	F		TX
Pearson, O.	21	M	Farmer	GA
Forrest, E.	66	M	Farmer	NC
S.	38	F		NC
C. J.	27	M	Farmer	TN
R. O.	22	M	Farmer	TN
O. P.	21	M	Farmer	TN
E. K.	19	M	Farmer	TN
H.	21	F		TN
Jones, C.	19	M		TN
E.	19	F		GA

HARRISON COUNTY, TEXAS

Name	Age	Sex	Occupation	Birthplace
Broome, J. G.	34	M	Farmer	NC
E. K.	30	F		TN
J. P.	12	M		MO
H. J.	7	M		TN
J. R.	5	M		TN
B. F.	4	M		TX
S. A. E.	2	F		TX
M. H.	1/2	F		TX
Chilcoat, C. C.	33	M	Farmer	TN
M.	34	F		TN
M. E.	7	F		AL
S. C.	3	F		TX
Chandler, N.	16	F		GA
King, J.	48	M	Farmer	NC
M. E.	24	F		SC
A. C.	17	M		TN
A. H.	15	F		TN
Watkins, J. W.	21	M	Farmer	TN
Pool, R.	66	M	Farmer	SC
King, E. H.	21	M	Overseer	TN
Landers, L.	34	M		TN
J.	27	F		TN
M. A.	11	F		TX
E.	8	F		TX
E. F.	5	F		TX
J.	4	F		TX
Martin, M.	17	M	Farmer	TN
Beck, J.	21	M	Farmer	AL
M.	20	F		TN
Parchman, W. J.	35	M	Farmer	TN
E.	33	F		SC
W. C.	11	M		TN
C. M.	9	M		TN
R. A.	7	F		TX
J. L.	5	M		TX
M. J.	2	F		TX
J. A.	1/2	M		TX
Parchman, J. W.	34	M	Farmer	TN
E.	30	F		SC
J.	9	M		TN
A. B.	8	M		TX
J.	8	F		TX
M. E.	5	F		TX
William J.	3	M		TX
B. B.	1/4	M		TX
Woods, William C.	44	M	Farmer	TN
A. H.	30	M	None	TN
N. E.	25	F		TN
G. B.	24	M	Farmer	TN
M. J.	22	F		TN
Presceville, J.	14	M		PA
Woods, J. P.	6	M		TX
Henley, H.	42	M	Farmer	TN
S.	32	F		TN
T.	13	M		TN
M. A.	11	M		TN
M.	10	F		TN
Fox, William	47	M	Farmer	(Lower) CAN
J.	42	F		TN
William	22	M	Farmer	TN
J.	21	M	Farmer	TN
H.	19	M	Farmer	TN
M.	13	F		TN
M. J.	11	F		TN
Stinson, S.	37	M	Farmer	TN
C.	38	F		TN
J.	2	M		TX
Burton, E.	18	F		TN
S.	16	F		MS
S. J.	14	M		MS
M.	10	F		MS
F.	4	F		TX

Name	Age	Sex	Occupation	Birthplace
Hallaburton, L.	24	M	Farmer	TN
M.	25	F		TN
V.	4	F		TN
O. G.	1	M		TN
Hughs, N.	48	F		VA
Stroud, T. P.	51	M	Md. Preacher	VA
N. M.	50	F		VA
Davault, E.	24	F		VA
A. V.	4	F		TN
Goodwin, S. B.	24	M	Carpenter	NC
M. A.	22	F		VA
Stroud, F. H.	15	M		VA
L. C.	12	F		VA
S. T.	16	F		VA
Eperson, J.	28	M	None	TN
L.	23	F		AL
F. M.	6	M		TN
M. L.	3	F		TN
Houston	1/2	M		TX
Smith, J. T.	26	M	Brick Maker	KY
A.	25	F		TN
M. J.	6	F		TN
William G.	5	M		TN
Sheller, C.	17	F		AL
J. C.	20	M	None	AL
Ellis, C. H.	32	M	Farmer	GA
T. O.	2	M		TX
G. L.	1/3	M		TX
West, A.	27	M	Carpenter	TN
J.	25	M		TN
Spraddling, M.	28	F		TN
C.	5	M		MS
William	3	M		AR
Williams, O. F.	42	M	Farmer	NC
H. M.	38	F		NC
G.	14	M		TN
O. F.	12	M		TN
E. V.	9	F		TN
Predgens, B. J.	21	M	Farmer	NC
M. H.	18	F		--
Garrett, R. C.	25	M	Farmer	TN
S. A.	26	F		NC
R.	2	M		TX
McCarty, J. R.	37	M	Farmer	TN
A.	6	M		TN
G. R.	4	M		TN
Perry, S.	19	M	School Teacher	??
Cowan, M.	42	M		TN
M.	15	F		MS
M.	11	F		MS
A.	9	M		MS
S.	7	F		MS
S.	5	F		MS
Long, B.	44	M	Farmer	NC
H. E.	24	F		TN
G.	13	M		MS
L.	11	F		MS
F. E.	4	F		TX
B.	2	M		TX
Nolen, T.	27	M	Farmer	AL
K.	29	F		TN
M. A.	5	F		TX
T.	2	M		TX
Fowler, J.	10	M		TX
E.	7	F		TX
Davis, William B.	30	M	Doctor	TN
M.	25	F		AL
J.	2	M		TX
Sparks, William P.	53	M	Farmer	SC
M.	38	F		TN
M. E.	17	F		MS
R.	15	M		MS
G. P.	13	M		MS

(continued)

Name	Age	Sex	Occupation	Birthplace
Sparks, M.	11	F		TX
J. E.	5	M		TX
F.	3	F		TX
Coyle, M.	21	M	Farmer	AR
M. J.	22	F		TN
M.	15	F		AR
Woodson, William	46	M	Farmer	VA
T.	40	F		TN
William	17	M		TN
C.	12	M		TN
A. S.	11	F		TN
L.	8	M		TN
L.	6	F		TN
J.	5	M		TN
Lowe, J.	34	M	Farmer	TN
A. A.	24	F		GA
D. H.	1/2	F		TX
Wilson, T. D.	36	M	Farmer	TN
R. J.	24	F		TN
L.	6	F		TX
R. D.	5	M		TX
A. F.	3	M		TX
M. F.	1/2	F		TX
Powell, J. S.	32	M		GA
M. A.	23	F		AL
William	10	M		TX
S.	8	F		TX
M. E.	5	F		TX
C.	2	F		TX
Moffett, S.	35	M	Overseer	AL
Scott, William W.	26	M	Mechanic	LA
Harris, J.	25	M	None	GA
Swink, A.	30	M	None	TN
Pogue, J.	28	M	Farmer	SC
E.	19	F		TN
William T.	1	M		TX
McCowan, S.	33	M	Farmer	AL
J.	27	F		TN
E. S.	2	M		--
Crump, J. W.	63	M	Farmer	VA
H.	25	M	Farmer	TN
William	22	M	Farmer	TN
N.	18	F		TN
E. R.	15	F		TN
McCullock, J.	28	M	Carpenter	TN
Harrison, William P.	25	M	Farmer	TN
C.	20	F		TN
J. T.	4	M		TX
T.	1	F		TX
Fields, J.	20	M	Carpenter	TX
Harrison, E.	55	M	Farmer	NC
G. P.	38	M	Farmer	TN
J. H.	33	M	Farmer	TN
T.	29	M	Farmer	TN
C. P.	18	M	Farmer	TN
J. A.	15	M	Farmer	TN
O. E.	13	F		TN
Curtis, (Blank)	45	M	Brick Mason	IRE
Ramsey, R.	68	M	Farmer	VA
M.	65	F		NC
M.	27	M	Farmer	TN
E. G.	18	F		GA
R. J. M.	1	M		TX
Horne, William H.	14	M		TX
Downs, J.	39	M	Farmer	TN
E.	38	F		GA
E.	18	F		AL
J. W.	16	M		AL
F. E.	12	F		AL
E.	10	F		AL
F.	10	F		AL
C.	8	M		AL

(continued)

Name	Age	Sex	Occupation	Birthplace
Downs, E.	8	M		AL
J.	3	M		MS
Parham, J.	40	M	Farmer	TN
M.	36	F		GA
J.	14	M		GA
E.	12	F		GA
M.	4	F		GA
Child Infant	1/4	M		LA
Kenzenie, L.	53	M	Farmer	SC
J.	36	F		KY
E.	11	F		TN
C.	8	M		TX
J. A.	5	F		TX
S. F.	1	-		TX
S. William	20	M		TN
Anderson, S.	18	F		TN
Adams, H.	59	M	Farmer	NC
E.	52	F		TN
H.	20	M	Farmer	TN
S.	18	M		TN
K.	16	F		TN
J.	15	M		TN
H.	12	F		TN
Fields, J.	59	M	Farmer	VA
J. H.	53	F		VA
C. W.	31	M	Doctor	VA
J(I).	22	M	Lawyer	TN
Campbell, E.	13	F		TX
Hightower, R.	14	M		TN
S.	10	F		LA
J.	8	M		TX
Bramer, L.	13	F		AL
Parchman, J.	57	M	Farmer	TN
J.	50	F		SC
W.	25	M	Farmer	TN
William	19	M	Farmer	TN
J. M.	16	M		TN
M. V. B.	14	M		TN
J.	12	F		TN
S.	10	F		TN
L. H.	7	M		TN
M. P.	4	F		TN
W.	21	M	Farmer	TN
Vivion, V. H.	28	M	Farmer	GA
S. E.	22	F		MS
W. S.	1	M		TX
Parchman, J. D.	31	M	Farmer	TN
J.	25	F		MS
M. P.	2	F		TX
S.	1/2	M		TX
McCarty, D. F.	40	M	Farmer	TN
A. F.	30	F		AL
J. E.	11	F		MS
N. C.	9	F		MS
S. A.	7	F		TX
R.	5	F		TX
D. F.	3	M		TX
Mathews, T. D.	52	M	Farmer	NC
M. M.	51	F		SC
T. E.	12	M		LA
Guthery, D.	20	M	Farmer	TN
M. E.	15	F		--
Elliott, William A.	28	M	Farmer	AL
A.	25	F		TN
William G.	6	M		TX
E. J.	2	F		TX
Grayhand, J. R.	46	M	Farmer	TN
E.	22	F		SC
Haines, R. P.	22	M	Grocer	GA
Smith, F.	35	M	Grocer	TN
Upton, H.	27	M	Farmer	TN
S.	22	F		GA

HARRISON COUNTY, TEXAS

Name	Age	Sex	Occupation	Birthplace
Watson, William H.	30	M	Clerk	MD
V. J.	23	F		TN
E. A.	3	M		TN
Shaw, J. A.	25	M	Clerk	NC
Anderson, H.	30	M	Farmer	TN
M. W.	25	F		AL
William V.	6	M		TX
W. H.	4	M		TX
J.	2	F		TX
Rutledge, M. H.	31	F		TN
M. J.	13	F		AL
C. E.	6	M		TX
Campbell, F. M.	27	M	Farmer	--
E. M.	38	F		TN
Russum, T. Reyne	17	M	Farmer	AL
A. S. Reyne	14	F		AL
William C.	8	M		AL
Downs, M.	70	F		NC
C.	26	M		TN
Downs, W. R.	42	M	Doctor	NC
H.	36	F		TN
M. J.	15	F		AL
H. F.	14	F		AL
E. M.	12	F		AL
D. N.	10	M		AL
J. A.	8	M		AL
B. A.	1	F		TX
Price, W.	21	M	Carpenter	TN
Deir, R.	56	M	Farmer	KY
W.	20	M	Farmer	TN
E.	16	F		TN
R. D.	11	M		TN
Young, S. L.	39	M	Farmer	SC
M.	35	F		TN
S. C(E).	13	F		MS
N. J.	12	F		MS
S. H.	9	F		AR
M. L.	8	F		TX
H. T.	4	F		TX
A.	1	F		TX
Williamson, J. B.	25	M	School Teacher	PA
Huggins, J.	22	M	Farmer	FL
Shaw, D.	58	M	Farmer	NC
H.	45	F		NC
D.	23	M	Farmer	NC
D.	21	M	Farmer	NC
A.	17	F		NC
M. C.	15	F		NC
S. E.	14	F		NC
C. J.	13	F		NC
J. A.	9	M		TN
A. G.	24	M	Med. Student	NC
Boissean, J. W.	47	M	Farmer	VA
J. H.	45	F		VA
R.	17	M	Farmer	VA
M.	14	F		TN
William	11	M		TN
J.	9	M		TN
J. A.	7	F		TN
Wheeler, J.	34	M	Farmer	VA
P.	32	F		TN
S.	15	F		TN
G.	13	M		TN
J.	7	M		TN
T.	6	M		TN
A.	3	F		TN
G. W.	1	M		TX
O'Neal, H. F.	20	M	Farmer	MS
M. E.	18	F		NC
F.	50	M	Farmer	VA
Cowden, B. W.	35	M	School Teacher	TN

Name	Age	Sex	Occupation	Birthplace
Vanzandt, F. C.	32	F	Farmer	VA
Clough, J. M.	29	M	Lawyer	NH
L.	16	F		TN
Vanzandt, H.	14	M		TN
L.	11	M		TX
F. C.	9	F		TX
E.	7	F		Washington City
Walton, R.	16	F		MS
Parchman, M.	55	F	Farmer	MS
M.	21	F		TN
M. J.	19	F		TN
P.	25	M	Farmer	TN
B.	23	M	Farmer	TN
H. C.	29	M	Farmer	TN
Holland, G. B.	39	M	Racing	TN
L. H.	41	F		TN
G.	6	M		MS
Child	1	F		TX
Pitts, J.	18	M	Race Rider	TN
Blackwell, M.	30	M	Overseer	TN
Mrs.	25	F		TN
(Blank)	8	F		TN
(Blank)	6	F		TN
(Blank)	4	F		TN
(Blank)	2	F		TX
Mitchell, R. T.	49	M	School Teacher	TN
M. W.	43	F		GA
G. C.	12	M		TX
Hall, C. M.	34	M	Farmer	TN
A. H.	24	F		AL
C. O.	10	M		AL
J. W.	7	M		AL
M. C.	3	F		TX
C. M.	1	M		TX
Taylor, J.	19	M	Farmer	MO
Wells, J. G.	28	M	Farmer	TN
E. C.	26	F		TN
M. V.	7	F		TN
F. E.	6	F		MO
C. W.	4	M		TX
T. P.	2	M		TX
A. O.	1/4	F		TX
Reeves, P. H.	23	M	Overseer	TN
Hunter, J. A.	38	M	School Teacher	TN
M. A.	32	F		TN
W.	17	M	Farmer	TN
R.	15	F		TN
S.	13	F		TN
S.	11	F		TN
N.	9	F		TN
S.	7	M		TN
M.	2	F		TX
Newton, R.	60	F	Farmer	TN
A.	19	F		TN
R.	18	M	Farmer	TN
J.	16	M		TN
Spear, Mrs.	32	F	None	TN
W. Henry	6	M		TN
M.	2	F		TX
Gill, J. M.	43	M	Carpenter	SC
S.	38	F		TN
Middleton, A.	12	F		MS
Alexander, W. R.	40	M	Doctor	TN
J.	25	M	Doctor	TN
M.	17	F		TN
Alexander, Silas	54	M	Farmer	TN
M.	47	F		KY
T.	25	M	Lawyer	TN
M. A.	21	F		TN
L.	19	M	Farmer	TN
R.	16	M	Farmer	TN
W.	14	M		TN
J.	12	M		TN

(continued)

HARRISON COUNTY, TEXAS

Alexander, J.	10	M		TN
L.	7	M		TN
L.	4	M		TN
E.	1	M		TN
Hunt, B. F.	30	M	Farmer	TN
M. F.	26	F		KY
C. E.	4	M		KY
E. C.	1	F		KY
Aaiken, A.	41	M	Black Smith & Farmer	SC
M.	36	F		TN
J.	16	M	Farmer	AL
M. J.	14	F		AL
G.	12	M		AL
J. B.	10	M		AL
F.	7	F		AL
J.	1	F		TX
Slater, C.	34	M	Farmer	TN
E.	25	F		TN
M.	5	F		TN
E.	2	F		TN
Thadeus	25	M	Farmer	TN
Bell, E.	25	M	Farmer	GA
Wright, A. B.	50	M	Farmer	VA
L. B.	40	F		NC
M. R.	16	F		KY
A. E.	13	F		KY
R. R.	11	M		KY
L. A.	8	F		KY
E. G.	5	F		KY
E. F.	1	F		TX
Webb, J. F.	28	M		TN
Clopton, R. J.	36	M	Farmer	GA
M. W.	26	F		AL
R. E.	9	M		AL
Witt, R.	26	F		TN
Clopton, R.	12	M		TX
Willson, J. S.	37	M	Farmer	TN
M. A.	28	F		TN
E.	7	F		TN
L.	2	F		TX
Alexander, S. G.	37	M	Farmer	TN
N.	32	F		KY
W. F.	13	M		MS
J.	12	M		TX
R.	9	M		TX
A.	7	F		TX
L.	5	F		TX
L.	2	M		TX
Kelly, S.	49	M	Carpenter	SC
D.	29	F		SC
J.	19	M	Carpenter	GA
W.	17	M		AL
F.	14	M		AL
A.	11	F		AL
P.	9	F		AL
M.	7	F		AL
P.	8	F		AL
W.	6	M		AL
E.	6	M		AL
R.	2	M		AL
Stevenson, S.	45	F	Farmer	TN
J.	19	F		TN
J.	17	M	Farmer	TN
Crawford, W. C.	35	M	Farmer	TN
E.	22	F		AL
Tool, D. L.	21	M	Farmer	AL
Price, J. A.	33	M	Farmer	TN
C.	25	F		AL
S.	5	F		AL
W. E.	2	F		AL
M.	1	F		TX
Knox, O.	33	M	Doctor	NC

(continued)

Knox, M.	25	F		TN
E.	7	F		TN
R.	5	M		TN
E.	2	F		TX
Taylor, W.	38	M	Carpenter	GA
Smith, G. W.	26	M	Overseer	AL
M.	30	F		AL
McCall, M.	10	F		TN
J. A.	6	M		TN
William C.	4	M		MS
Cain, J. A.	42	M	Farmer	VA
P.	39	F		TN
A.	17	F		TN
E.	16	F		TN
N. C.	15	F		TN
D.	13	F		TN
L.	12	F		MS
J.	7	M		TX
E.	5	F		TX
R.	2	M		TX
Beatty, J.	48	M	Farmer	TN
S.	44	F		TN
A. C.	22	M	Farmer	MS
N.	21	F		TN
J. D.	18	M	Farmer	TN
J. F.	16	M		MS
S. A.	9	F		TX
M.	4	F		TX
Rector, William	44	M	Carpenter	SC
Nesbitt, R. J.	40	M	Farmer	TN
S. A.	23	F		TN
N. L.	2	M		AR
N.	40	M		TN
S. A.	24	F		TN
S. Bradford	5	M		AR
J. C. B.	4	M		AR
M. A.	2	F		AR
Baty, J.	37	M	Farmer	TN
S.	69	F		VA
A. N.	12	M		MS
R. G. E.	10	F		TX
L. C.	9	F		TX
H. M.	4	F		TX
Jackson, W. W.	63	M	Farmer	NC
F.	61	F		NC
Mahone, R.	27	F		NC
Jackson, W.	23	M	Overseer	TN
Wortham, J. W.	1	M		TX
Johnston, J. M.	36	M	Farmer	KY
N.	40	F		TN
J. H.	11	M		AL
W. M.	8	M		AL
J. V. B.	6	M		AL
S. W.	2	M		AL
Mathews, L. H.	27	M	Farmer	LA
N.	17	F		TN
J.	1/4	M		TX
Richardson, C.	36	M	Farmer	TN
R.	32	F		TN
M. J.	14	F		TN
S. R.	12	F		TN
J. R.	10	F		TN
W.	8	F		TN
J.	5	M		TN
S. A.	3	F		TN
Shoat, S.	45	M	Farmer	TN
M.	44	F		TN
O.	16	F		TN
J.	18	M	Farmer	TN
A.	14	M		TN
C.	9	M		TN
M.	12	F		TN
W.	7	M		TN
J. A.	2	F		TX

Name	Age	Sex	Occupation	Birthplace
Shoat, A.	26	M	Farmer	TN
J. A.	24	F		TN
P. H.	8	M		TN
B. L.	6	F		TN
J. M.	2	M		TX
T. J.	2	M		TX
Hardin, P.	38	M	Farmer	TN
A.	36	F		KY
R. H.	13	M		MS
J.	12	M		MS
P.	8	M		TX
J.	7	M		TX
J.	4	M		TX
N. J.	2	F		TX
Snowden, L. H.	59	M	Farmer	NC
M.	25	F		MS
Frazier, A. W.	23	M	Overseer	TN
Thomas, E.	11	F		AR
Draper, M.	59	M	Farmer	TN
S.	38	F		NC
L.	10	M		TX
J.	8	M		TX
N.	6	F		TX
J.	4	M		TX
G.	3	M		TX
S. E.	1	F		TX
Richardson, William	25	M	Farmer	TN
J.	25	F		MS
E.	1/4	F		TX
Sullivan, William	46	M	Farmer	GA
H.	46	F		TN
W. J.	22	M	Farmer	TN
L. C.	20	M	Farmer	TN
D.	18	M	Farmer	TN
J. W.	16	M	Farmer	TN
F. M.	14	M		TN
S. C.	12	F		MS
G. W.	10	M		AR
P.	8	M		AR
H.	6	M		TX
M. J.	4	F		TX
Moses, A.	35	M	Farmer	TN
M.	25	F		TN
Die, T. N.	56	M	Tailor	MA
Blaylock, T.	60	M	None	NC
Leming, E.	38	M	Doctor	TN
M. A.	31	F		TN
G. W.	8	M		TN
J. A.	6	F		TN
N. J.	4	F		TN
G. A.	1	M		TX
L.	23	M		TN
Thompson, A.	36	M	Farmer	MS
M.	38	F		TN
M.	8	F		TX
J.	1/6	F		TX
Blythe, J.	65	F		TN
Stephenson, T.	50	M	Farmer	SC
E.	47	F		NC
J. R.	25	M	Farmer	SC
T. Thomas	22	M		TN
C.	27	F		SC
A.	22	F		TN
M.	16	F		TN
Cobb, H. S.	25	M	Farmer	AL
Saunders, Thomas	31	M	Farmer	TN
E.	27	F		VA
Walters, H.	35	M	Farmer	OH
M.	33	F		TN
H.	18	M	Farmer	IL
J. N.	16	M	Farmer	IL
M. J.	11	F		TX

(continued)

Name	Age	Sex	Occupation	Birthplace
Walters, J. M.	7	M		TX
P. A.	2	F		TX
Foshee, O.	24	M	Farmer	AL
N.	30	F		TN
C. W.	1	M		TX
Davis, V. A.	37	M	Farmer	TN
J.	27	F		VA
E.	10	F		TN
B.	8	M		TN
M.	6	F		TN
F.	4	F		TX
V.	2	F		TX
Turmon, G.	26	M	Farmer	NC
N.	28	F		TN
M.	6	F		TN
J.	5	M		TN
S. J.	3	F		TN
W. R.	2	M		TX
Harmon, C.	31	M	Farmer	TN
T. T.	25	F		AL
J. T.	6	M		AL
P. E.	2	M		AL
M. J.	2	M		AL
Blythe, S. T.	22	M	None	AL
Landers, C. C.	39	M	Farmer	TN
B.	40	F		GA
H. A.	15	M	Farmer	TN
L.	16	M		MO
J.	11	F		MO
A.	9	F		MO
S.	6	F		MO
M.	5	F		MO
J.	1	M		TX
Benson, J.	25	M	Farmer	AL
Bird, J.	28	M	Farmer	AL
J.	22	F		TN
O. P.	2	M		AR
J.	21	M		AL
Saunders, S.	46	F	Farmer	TN
S.	21	M	Farmer	TN
W.	18	M	Farmer	TN
S.	15	M	Farmer	TN
S. J.	13	F		TN
M.	6	F		AR
Landers, F. G.	30	M		TN
A.	21	F		NC
L.	4	F		TX
P.	1/6	F		TX
Chilwell, O.	19	M	Farmer	TN
McAdams, F. G.	35	M	Farmer	TN
M.	26	F		TN
S. E.	11	F		IL
W.	5	M		IL
Bass, L. L.	36	M	Farmer	NC
M.	38	F		TN
J. F.	19	M	Farmer	AL
M. J.	14	F		AL
A. E.	11	F		AL
T. J.	7	M		AL
H.	6	M		AL
C. A.	4	F		AL
G. W.	2	M	(Blind)	TX
Ford, J. G.	35	M	Farmer	SC
E.	26	F		AL
W. C.	7	M		AL
S. E.	4	M		AL
J. J.	2	M		TX
Davis, William	40	M	None	TN
M. A.	10	F		AL
M. E.	8	F		--
Schooler, S.	56	M	Farmer	KY
P.	52	F		TN
W.	26	M	Farmer	KY

(continued)

Name	Age	Sex	Occupation	Birthplace
Schooler, J.	18	M	Farmer	MS
S.	11	F		MS
Richardson, T. J.	31	M	Farmer	KY
N. G.	25	F		KY
J. H.	8	M		TX
E. A.	6	F		TX
G. D.	4	M		TX
J.	1/6	M		TX
Brooks, M.	29	M	Farmer	TN
Smith, J.	55	M	Farmer	KY
P.	54	F		SC
Eddings, B.	22	M	Farmer	TN
Glover, E.	42	M	Carpenter	TN
S.	45	F		NC
J. A.	10	M		TN
Davis, H.	40	M	Farmer	TN
F.	36	F		TN
P. A.	12	M		AL
W. A.	11	M		AL
M. E.	9	F		AL
L. F.	7	M		AL
S. A.	5	F		AL
H. C.	3	M		AL
Jones, W.	31	M	Mechanic	SC
Gibbs, P.	22	M	Farmer	AL
M. A. M.	18	F		TN
Jones, A.	25	M	Farmer	OH
S.	25	F		OH
W. A.	8	M		TN
L. J.	6	F		TN
G. W.	4	M		TN
N. E.	3	F		TN
D. M. L.	1	M		TN
Hufman, G. M.	26	M	Farmer	TN
J.	22	F		TN
J. W.	5	M		TN
E. G.	3	F		TN
G. S.	2	M		TN
A. M.	1	M		TN
Rodgers, N.	51	M	None	GA
G. W.	22	M		TN
J.	19	M		TN
E. E.	16	F		TN
J. N.	10	M		TN
Starr, L.	50	F	None	NC
B.	23	F		TN
H.	19	F		TN
J.	16	F		TN
M. A.	12	F		TN
J.	18	M		TN
P. A.	11	F		TN
J. Calvin	3	M		TN
J. W.	21	M	Black Smith	TN
C.	1	M		TX
Starr, R.	60	M	Farmer	GA
S.	39	F		OH
H.	26	F		TN
J.	23	M	None	TN
J.	21	M	None	TN
A.	19	M	None	TN
J.	17	M		TN
R. P.	11	M		TN
L.	8	F		TN
J.	10	M		TN
E. J.	6	F		TN
S. L.	4	M		TN
M.	2	F		TX
Jackson, J.	34	M	Farmer	TN
S.	30	F		TN
H.	9	M		TN
M.	8	F		TN
R.	6	M		TN

(continued)

Name	Age	Sex	Occupation	Birthplace
Jackson, M.	4	M		TN
E.	3	F		TN
J. Y.	1	M		TN
Oney, H.	40	M	Farmer	VA
L.	38	F		NC
W.	17	M	None	TN
H.	15	M	None	TN
J.	14	M		TN
M.	10	F		TN
H.	9	M		TN
H.	7	M		TN
L.	5	F		TN
E.	2	F		TN
Hay, J. K.	28	M	Farmer	TN
J.	19	F		NC
M. E.	4	F		TN
W. D.	2	M		TN
J. R.	25	M	School Teacher	TN
Brown, D.	49	M	Farmer	NC
L.	34	F		GA
S.	12	M		TN
W.	10	M		TN
J.	8	M		TN
J.	6	M		TN
J.	4	M		TN
S.	1	F		TN
W.	14	M		NC
Spencer, E.	31	M	Farmer	TN
T.	26	F		NC
W. A.	9	M		TN
M.	7	F		TN
R. W.	5	M		TX
T. F.	3	M		TX
Meadow, J. H.	19	M	Farmer	TN
Curtis, J.	21	M	Farmer	TN
R.	20	F		TN
Medcalfe, P. D.	46	M	Farmer	TN
E.	35	F		NC
S. A.	10	F		TX
H. T.	8	M		TX
S. S.	6	F		TX
M.	4	F		TX
C. E.	1	F		TX
Watkins, W.	24	M	Farmer	??
Cannon, H. E.	53	M	Farmer	GA
L.	20	F		TN
J.	20	M	Farmer	TN
J.	11	F		TN
L.	10	F		TN
C.	7	F		TX
W.	4	F		TX
Short, A. W. M.	25	M	Black Smith	TN
M.	22	F		TN
M.	1	F		TX
Thomas, W.	53	M	Farmer	KY
J. F.	21	M	Farmer	MS
M. H.	18	F		TN
L. J.	16	F		TN
J. R.	14	M		TN
M. A.	12	F		TX
W. H.	10	M		TX
James, F.	25	M	Farmer	AR
E.	32	F		TN
Flint, M.	9	F		AR
G. A.	8	F		TX
F.	4	M		TX
W.	2	M		TX
F.	6	M		TX
Jackson, J.	40	M	Miller & Farmer	SC
L.	35	F		TN
J. T.	21	M	None	MS
J. G.	19	M	None	MS
M.	16	F		MS
J. W.	11	M		MS

(continued)

HARRISON COUNTY, TEXAS

Jackson, J. N. 9 M MS
L. E. 7 F LA
J. C. 4 M LA
R. M. 1/6 F TX

Jackson, Isam 46 M Farmer NC
B. 35 F NC
N. 22 F TN
S. 20 F TN
H. 17 M Farmer TN
E. 15 M MS
J. 13 M MS
P. 12 F MS
J. 9 M MS
E. 3 M MS
M. 1/6 F TX

Jackson, J. 41 M Farmer OH
M. 39 F NC
A. 22 M Farmer TN
J. 18 M Farmer TN
O. 20 F TN
S. 16 M Farmer TN
E. 14 F MS
H. 12 F TX
M. 10 M TX
W. 8 M TX
S. J. 2 F TX
Rogers, P. 20 F TN

Jackson, H. 60 M Farmer NC
P. 60 F MS
R. 28 M Black Smith GA
P. 22 F GA
T. 14 M (Idiot) TN
S. 45 M Farmer NC

Jackson, B. 24 M Farmer TN
J. 18 F TN
N. 17 F TN
R. 3 M TN
M. 1/6 F AR

Dooley, W. 37 M Wagon Maker TN
S. 30 F GA
E. 10 F AL
S. 9 F AL
C. 7 F AL
J. 6 M AL
M. 1 F AL

Bryant, T. 31 M Farmer TN
E. M. 26 F GA
H. R. 10 F AL
C. B. 6 M AL
W. A. 5 M AL
E. M. 3 F AL
E. H. 1 F AL

Sowders, A. J. 35 M Farmer IN
J. 30 F TN
W. 15 M Farmer TN
E. 14 F TN
B. 13 M TN
S. H. 11 F TN
J. A. 9 M TN
E. 6 M TN
P. L. 4 M TN
Allen, M. 39 M Farmer GA
M. 39 F GA
H. 14 M GA
E. 12 F AL
R. 10 F AL
A. 8 F AL
A. 5 M AL
Turner, J. 26 M Farmer TN

Brothers, J. 35 M Farmer TN
M. 25 F TN
J. 6 M TX
M. 4 M TX
W. 2 M TX
M. 1/2 F TX
Turner, P. 25 M Laborer TN

Ward, L. 32 M Farmer TN
L. 25 F GA
W. 1 M TX
Manahan, C. 27 M Farmer KY
M. 26 F KY
J. F. 6 M MO
C. S. 1/2 M TX
Poman, D. 40 M Carpenter PA.

Mauldin, R. 26 M Farmer TN
S. 24 F SC
P. 4 M TX
A. 2 F TX

Pinkard, E. 30 M Farmer TN

McFarland, S. H. 28 M Steam Miller PA
Chase, S. 25 M Laborer NY
Williamson, H. 20 M Laborer TN
Breedlove, T. 20 M Laborer TN

Massie, A. D. 37 M Farmer TN
R. J. 30 F VA
J. W. 7 M TX
M. D. 5 F TX
M. J. 4 F TX

Campbell, W. C. 34 M Farmer TN
M. E. 23 F AL
M. R. 5 F TN
J. M. 3 M TN
J. A. 2 F TN
S. 50 F NC
F. 21 M TN

Sharp, H. 50 M Farmer VA
J. 46 F TN
J. 21 M Farmer AL
J. 19 M Farmer AL
G. 17 M Farmer AL
H. 16 M Farmer AL
M. 11 F AL
R. 10 F AL
S. 8 F AL
W. 6 M TN
N. 5 F TN
M. 3 F TN

Tarwick, N. 40 M Doctor & Farmer TN
S. A. 29 F LA
L. E. 13 F LA
W. W. 10 M MS
J. A. 7 F LA
N. R. 5 F LA
F. L. 3 F TX
Payne, W. A. 24 M Laborer AL

Whitfield, G. W. 50 M Farmer TN
S. 30 F TN
V. 5 F TN
D. 3 M TN
J. 1/2 M TX

Frazier, J. C. 42 M Black Smith SC
E. 32 F TN
J. M. 13 M MS
M. 10 F MS
L. J. 3 F MS
A. C. 24 M None TN

Burress, A. D. 42 M Carpt. Engineer & Farmer KY
E. 35 F AR
E. S. 16 M None AR
L. J. 16 F AR
L. V. 12 F AR
M. J. 9 F AR
H. M. 6 F TX
William D. 4 M TX
J. A. 1/6 M TX
B. 70 F VA
G. W. 36 M Farmer KY
M. 31 F KY
J. W. 19 M None AR
Stuart, J. N. 26 M Carpenter SC
Logan, J. N. 26 M Carpenter NC
(continued)

HARRISON COUNTY, TEXAS

Name	Age	Sex	Occupation	Birthplace
Bagley, J. T.	23	M	Cabinet Maker	TN
McTalbee, H.	25	M	Engineer	VA
Brantley, D.	28	M	Ox Driver	KY
Shout, J. F.	49	M	Painter	SWI
McKinsey, J. B.	24	M	Cabinet Worker	TN
M. E.	20	F		TN
J.	5	F		TN
M. J.	2	F		TX
Martin, H.	54	M	Farmer	TN
E. J.	49	F		VA
Wortham, L. M	25	M	Farmer	TN
J.	2	M		TX
Frazier, E.	50	M	Farmer	MD
J.	25	F		NC
N.	4	M		TX
J.	2	F		TX
E.	22	M		GA
F. D.	19	M	Farmer	TN
D.	16	F		TN
Wortham, J.	48	M	Farmer	TN
Neil, A.	32	M	Farmer	TN
M.	30	F		GA
S.	6	F		TX
S.	3	F		TX
Smithshire, J. C.	35	M	Millwright	TN
S. R.	35	F		TN
Smithson, P. M.	13	M		AL
T.	11	F		AL
H.	10	M		AL
M.	9	M		MS
A.	7	M		AL
F.	5	F		AL
M.	2	F		AL
W.	1	M		AL
Sawyers, B.	30	M	Farmer	TN
M.	25	F		TN
V.	4	F		TN
W.	3	M		TN
Patton, H.	53	M	Farmer	SC
R.	30	M	Methodist Preacher	MS
C.	17	F		TN
Henley, R.	32	F		MS
Patton, S. B.	22	M	Farmer	MS
G. W.	16	M	Farmer	MS
Griffin, L.	15	F		MS
M.	11	F		MS
J. G.	4	F		TX
Pope, J.	67	M	Farmer	VA
W. M.	25	M	Farmer	TN
M. E.	26	F		TN
Burress, D.	24	M	Farmer	TN
L.	35	F		SC
M.	1	F		TX
Farley, J. T.	30	M	Farmer	TN
E.	26	F		TN
J. M.	15	M		TN
M. A.	13	F		TN
A. J.	9	M		TN
W. L.	6	M		TN
J. H.	4	M		TN
T.	2	M		TX
West, J. M.	20	M	Merchant	TN
Tomalson, S.	55	M	Farmer	TN
E. J.	26	M	Farmer	TN
S.	23	M	Farmer	TN
J.	18	M	Farmer	TN
Laingham, William	24	M	Overseer	AL
E.	24	F		TN
M. N.	1	M		TX
Maloy, W. E.	42	M	Plasterer	OH

(continued)

Name	Age	Sex	Occupation	Birthplace
Maloy, S.	32	F		TN
J.	10	M		MO
J.	8	M		MO
McKinney, A.	13	F		SC
M. J.	12	F		SC
B.	10	F		AL
M.	7	M		TX
R.	5	M		TX
Lacy, R. J.	35	M	Farmer	VA
C.	22	F		TN
V.	3	F		TX
Franklin, J.	31	M	Farmer	KY
L.	27	F		SC
J.	6	M		TX
W. W.	4	M		TX
B.	1	M		TX
Cole, N.	21	F		TN
Sims, A. B.	36	M	Carpenter	VA
J.	29	F		TN
T. J.	8	M		MS
V. E.	6	F		MS
T. T.	3	M		TX
McDonald, J.	64	M	Farmer	VA
E.	52	F		SC
M. E.	18	F		AL
E.	19	M	Farmer	AL
S. T.	17	F		AL
William	15	M	Farmer	AL
W. M.	13	M		AL
F. E.	11	F		AL
T. W.	9	M		AL
Sewell, M. A.	12	F		TN
J.	8	M		TN
S.	6	F		TN
M. F.	2	F		TN
Walker, R. H.	46	M	Farmer	TN
M.	44	F		GA
J.	21	M	Farmer	MS
A. A.	17	F		MS
M. J.	16	F		MS
C. M.	13	F		MS
A. T.	11	M		MS
M. A.	9	F		TX
R. H.	8	M		TX
L. C.	6	F		TX
F. J.	4	M		TX
L. A.	2	F		TX
Palmer, H. O.	28	M	Farmer	VA
E. M.	22	F		TN
J. W.	8	M		TN
E. G.	7	F		TN
Cochran, D.	53	F		VA
L. D.	20	M	Brick Mason	TN
N. A.	16	F		TN
S. M.	13	F		TN
McKinney, S.	55	M	Farmer	NC
R.	55	F		TN
G. D.	28	M	Farmer	AL
G. A.	25	M	Farmer	AL
C. L.	23	M	Black Smith	AL
S. A.	20	F		AL
J. S.	18	M	Farmer	AL
William	16	M	Farmer	AL
M. J.	11	F		AL
Thompson, G. B.	44	M	Farmer	GA
P. T.	40	F		TN
A. D.	15	F		TN
N. T.	13	F		TN
E. J.	10	F		TN
William A.	6	M		TN
Agnes	84	F		VA
Quellen, J.	40	M	Farmer	VA
E.	37	F		TN
J.	18	M	Farmer	VA
E.	16	F		VA

(continued)

HARRISON COUNTY, TEXAS

Name	Age	Sex	Occupation	Birthplace
Quellen, H.	13	M		VA
B.	11	F		VA
J.	8	M		GA
M.	6	F		GA
E.	4	F		GA
M.	2	F		TX
Smith, William H.	31	M	Doctor	VA
L.	21	F		TN
F. A.	4	F		TN
Jackson, A. W.	21	M	Doctor	TN
Whitehorn, J. M.	55	M	Farmer	VA
E.	51	F		VA
J. E.	23	M	Farmer	TN
V.	17	F		TN
Land, W.	55	M	None	VA
White, T.	23	M	School Teacher	TN
Hindman, R. A.	35	M	School Teacher	SC
C.	29	F		NC
N. E.	13	F		TN
L. J.	8	F		TN
C. C.	5	M		TN
William H.	1	M		TX
Norwood, A.	70	M	Farmer	SC
R.	49	F		GA
R.	20	M	Farmer	TN
C. C.	17	F		AL
M. E.	15	F		AL
Thompson, A.	17	M	Farmer	AL
M.	17	M		AL
Owen, J. L.	44	M	Farmer	SC
L.	43	F		TN
J.	20	M	Farmer	AL
E.	17	F		AL
William E.	16	M	Farmer	AL
J.	14	M		AL
M. A.	10	F		AL
H. J.	8	M		MS
M. F.	6	F		MS
L.	3	F		TX
Hudspeth, S.	56	M	Farmer	VA
A. J.	30	F		AL
J. J.	1	M		TX
E.	18	F		TN
T. H.	17	M	Farmer	TN
S.	15	M	Farmer	TN
S.	11	F		TN
Harris, N. J.	26	M	Farmer	AL
F.	20	F		TN
Burnett, D. H.	22	M	Farmer	TN
S.	22	F		TN
J.	9	M		TX
G.	7	M		TX
J.	5	M		TX
E.	3	F		TX
N.	1/3	M		TX
P. C.	20	M		TN
Winn, L.	60	M	Farmer	AL
C.	44	F		TN
J.	18	M	Farmer	TN
T.	16	M		TN
D.	9	M		TN
P. A.	23	F		TN
E.	18	F		TN
S.	14	F		TN
J.	22	M	Carpenter	TN
Greer, J. T.	19	M	Farmer	TN
S. J.	16	F		MS
J.	50	M	Farmer	TN
C.	46	F		NC
C. R.	15	F		TN
C. M.	13	F		TN
M. M.	10	F		TX
J.	6	F		TX
Dillingham, A.	68	F		NC

Name	Age	Sex	Occupation	Birthplace
Alexander, E.	49	F	Farmer	NC
Burnett, T. J.	21	M	Farmer	TN
Ferguson, A.	27	M	Farmer	AR
S. C.	20	F		TN
M. J.	1½	F		TX
Winn, W.	35	M	Farmer	TN
C.	28	F		TN
M.	9	F		TN
M. A.	7	F		TN
L.	3	F		TN
Barrett, N.	47	M	Farmer	KY
E.	46	F		TN
A. M.	18	F		TN
J. H.	16	M		TN
A. F.	14	F		TN
A. E.	12	F		TN
O. A.	9	F		TN
C. P.	7	M		TN
M.	4	M		TX
P.	1	M		TX
Ferguson, J.	35	M	Farmer	MO
A.	22	F		TN
Foshee, O.	24	M	Farmer	AL
N.	25	F		TN
C.	2	M		TX
Finch, J. H.	28	M	Farmer	NC
C.	20	F		AR
M.	5	F		TN
H.	3	M		TN
M.	1/4	F		TX
A.	20	M	Farmer	TN
Harris, J.	25	M		AR
Stanfield, W. W. O.	40	M	Black Smith	VA
M. A.	28	F		ENG
T. L.	12	M		TX
M. B.	10	M		TX
A. L.	8	F		TX
M. V.	6	F		TX
W. F.	1	M		TX
McLemore, P. P.	21	M	None	TN
Montgomery, A.	34	M	Farmer	TN
M.	24	F		AL
M. J.	4	F		AL
J.	2	M		TN
J.	1/2	M		TX
Roberson, W. B.	50	M	Farmer	TN
S.	38	F		KY
W.	28	M	Farmer	TN
W. C.	20	M	Farmer	IN
Maloy, William C.	4	M		AR
S. J.	1/2	F		TX
Talifero, J. R.	54	M	Farmer	NC
S.	49	F		NC
C. C.	26	M	Farmer	TN
C.	19	F		TN
G. W.	18	M	None	TN
W. D.	16	M	None	TN
A. J.	15	M	None	TN
J. M.	11	M		TN
L. B.	9	M		TN
C. W.	6	M		TN
A. G.	22	M	None	TX
Hanks, E. J.	23	F		TN
Dandridge, N. W.	28	M	Farmer	VA
N. W.	60	M	Farmer	VA
E.	58	F		VA
M.	18	F		AL
E.	16	F		TN
Laster, J.	50	F	Farmer	NC
J.	16	F		TN
S.	14	M		TN
Green, T.	28	M	Mechanic	TN

(continued)

Name	Age	Sex	Occupation	Birthplace
Green, C.	23	F		AL
S.	5	F		TN
M.	4	F		TN
N.	3	F		TN
Smith, S. M.	40	M	Farmer	VA
A.	38	F		TN
L.	13	F		AL
J. A.	12	M		AL
F.	10	F		AL
G. A.	8	F		AL
A.	7	F		AL
J. T.	6	M		AL
E.	4	F		AL
W.	1	M		AL
Hall, W.	50	M	Farmer	TN
O.	18	F		AL
E.	15	F		AL
W.	12	M		AL
T.	10	M		AL
R.	8	F		AL
M.	6	F		AL
F.	4	F		AL
Smith, J.	54	M	Farmer	VA
J. M.	40	F		TN
D. N.	18	M	None	AL
E.	16	F		AL
J.	15	M		AL
M.	13	F		AL
J.	11	F		AL
J.	7	F		AL
Roach, A. M.	40	M	Farmer	TN
E. M.	38	F		TN
Conrow, T. C.	16	F		AL
A.	14	F		AL
C.	12	M		AL
M.	9	F		AL
Roach, T.	15	M		AL
S.	12	F		AL
F.	10	F		AL
J.	8	M		AL
E.	6	F		AL
M. A.	4	F		AL
A.	2	F		TX
E.	1/2	M		TX
Williford, B.	34	M	Farmer	TN
J.	35	F		TN
B. F.	14	M		TN
M. R.	12	M		TN
H. C.	11	F		TN
S. L.	9	M		TN
M. J.	7	F		TN
J. W.	5	M		TN
W. L.	3	M		TX
T. A.	1	M		TX
Peck, E.	42	M	Farmer	VT
M.	26	F		TN
T.	2	F		TX
Shed, C.	16	M	Farmer	TN
Hill, A.	50	M	Farmer	SC
S.	35	F		TN
A.	7	F		AL
W.	6	M		AL
M.	3	F		TX
J. T.	1/6	M		TX
Larkin, J.	50	F	None	IL
E.	20	F		IL
M. J.	16	F		IL
E. P.	18	F		IL
S.	14	M		IL
W.	22	M	Brick Maker	IL
E.	22	F		LA
T. J.	3	F		TX
W. R.	2	M		TX
Walker, A. B.	39	M	Farmer	KY
S.	32	F		TN

(continued)

Name	Age	Sex	Occupation	Birthplace
Walker, M. A.	14	F		TN
J.	12	M		TN
A. D.	10	M		MS
B. P.	7	M		MS
D. A.	5	M		MS
J. M.	3	M		MS
Pruit, J.	20	M	Overseer	TN
Harris, T. T.	40	M	Farmer	GA
M.	38	F		GA
Marshaw, M. T.	16	F		GA
Harris, M. L.	8	F		AL
M. E.	6	F		AL
S. T.	3	F		TX
H. L.	1/4	M		TX
Briggs, E.	45	M	Farming	VA
R.	19	M	Farmer	VA
T.	17	M	Farmer	TN
J.	8	M		TN
Doil, R.	28	M	Carpenter	VA
Andrews, C. K.	39	M	Farmer	TN
T. T.	18	F		AL
M. R.	1/2	M		TX
Edwards, G. C.	9	M		TX
Webb, E. W.	25	M	Overseer	TN
Frazier, B.	42	M	Farmer	SC
N. J.	27	F		MO
K. P.	1/2	M		TX
Reese, T. J.	20	M	waggoner	TN
McCathern, J. M.	55	M	Black Smith	NC
A. E.	24	F		TN
M. J.	1	F		TX
Penny, J.	35	M	Black Smith	TN
McCathern, S. J.	1	F		TX
Wetherby, L.	47	M	Carpenter	NC
T.	17	M	None	TN
E.	15	F		MS
L. A.	12	F		MS

End of Town of Marshall

Town of Port Caddo

Name	Age	Sex	Occupation	Birthplace
Perry, N. B.	28	M	Merchant	NC
S. J.	24	F		TN
J. H.	2	M		TX
Spell, F. M.	21	M	Clerk	MS
Cobb, William H.	35	M	Merchant	TN
Richie, V.	22	M	Clerk	ENG
M.	25	F		ENG
Layne, K.	19	M	Clerk	MS
Morrison, B. F.	30	M	None	TN
M.	21	F		TN
J. D.	3	F		TN
M. A.	21	F		IL
J.	24	M	None	MO
Moore, W.	20	M	None	TN

End of Town of Port Caddo

Name	Age	Sex	Occupation	Birthplace
Hope, R.	35	F	Farmer	GA
A.	12	M		MS
A. P.	9	M		MS
H. E.	7	F		MS
K. A.	4	F		TX
O.	2	M		AR
Hood, J.	44	F		TN
Watson, A. M.	30	M	Overseer	SC
Cotton, C. W.	41	M	Farmer	GA
C. E.	28	F		GA
M. C. W.	12	F		AL
S.	9	F		AL
A.	8	F		AL
C.	7	F		AR
J. P.	6	M		AR
D.	4	F		AR
Lucky, J.	19	M	Farmer	TN
Browning, J. A.	35	M	Blk. Smith & Farmer	NC
S. J.	20	F		TN

HARRISON COUNTY, TEXAS

Massie, M.	30	F		VA
Garrett, G.	28	M	Farmer	VA
W.	24	M	Farmer	VA
House, W.	24	M	None	TN
S.	20	F		TN
Sanders, D. T.	40	M	None	TN
E.	33	M	Farmer	TN
Swanson, J. M.	30	M	Farmer	TN
E.	22	F		TN
Swanson, A.	62	F	Farmer	NC
T. F.	19	M	Farmer	TN
Paterson, W.	28	M	Farmer	NC
S.	36	F		VA
S. F.	3	M		TN
J. L.	1	M		TX
Gandy, M. E.	17	F		VA
E. A.	15	F		VA
L. E.	11	M		TN
Montgomery, S. A.	36	M	Farmer	AL
T.	28	F		TN
A.	10	F		TN
J.	8	M		TN
J.	4	M		TX
Knox, R.	70	M	Farmer	NC
E.	54	F		NC
E.	19	F		NC
R.	16	M	None	TN
R.	12	F		TN
Lester, F.	33	M	Farmer	TN
M. A.	23	F		NC
H.	15	M	None	TN
A. W.	12	F		TN
S. H.	7	M		TN
W. S.	5	M		TN
R.	1	M		LA
Lester, F.	69	M	Farmer	VA
S. F.	64	F		GA
W. T.	22	M	Farmer	TN
Wallace, D. F.	36	M	Wheelwright	TN
Swanson, W. C.	40	M	Doctor	TN
A. E.	38	F		TN
H.	16	F		TN
V. B.	11	M		TN
M. J.	9	F		TN
C. E.	6	M		TN
S. W.	4	M		TN
A. S.	3	F		TN
Long, J.	23	M	Overseer	TN
Moseley, D.	23	M	Farmer	AL
L.	23	F		TN
D. D.	3	M		TX
M. A.	1	F		TX
Wagnor, E. S.	26	M	None	TN
Womack, E. P.	37	M	Farmer	NC
R.	25	F		TN
M. E.	8	F		TN
T. M.	6	F		TX
A.	3	F		TX
E.	1	F		TX
Womack, W. T.	31	M	Clerk	NC
S.	28	F		TN
M. A.	7	F		TX
W.	4	M		TX
J.	1/6	M		TX
Womack, J.	28	M	Farmer	NC
L. A.	21	F		TN
A.	7	M		TN
J.	4	F		TX
O. J.	3	M		TX
W.	1	M		TX

(continued)

Fife, J. H.	52	M	Farmer	NC
N.	47	F		TN
M.	29	M	Farmer	TN
S.	18	M		TN
A.	16	M		TN
W.	14	M		TN
L.	12	F		TN
J.	10	M		TN
J.	7	M		TN
C.	5	M		TX
S.	2	F		TX
Dial, H.	45	M	Farmer	SC
M.	26	F		TN
E.	9	F		LA
H.	6	M		TX
J.	5	F		TX
Wagnor, M.	45	F	Farmer	TN
T.	28	M	Farmer	TN
A.	20	M	None	TN
D.	16	M	None	TN
E.	19	F		TN
C.	14	M		TN
G.	12	M		TN
F.	8	M		TN
W.	22	M	Farmer	TN
J. P.	26	M	Farmer	TN
R.	80	F		TN
Edwards, J.	27	M	Farmer	VA
F.	6	M		TN
Horton, J. B.	34	M		TN
J.	31	F		TN
R.	9	M		TX
E.	7	F		TX
Haralson, S.	44	M	Farmer	TN
S.	47	F		NC
W. T.	16	M	Farmer	MS
J. H.	14	M		TN
M. J.	11	F		TX
Blades, R. M.	30	M	Farmer	KY
S. E.	20	F		TN
S. T.	1	F		TX
Lee, J. H.	40	M	Farmer	AL
A. M.	40	F		TN
C. A.	18	F		AL
A.	12	M		AL
J. E.	10	M		AL
E. M.	7	F		AL
Fife, J. R.	23	M	Farmer	TN
Smith, B. S.	38	M	Farmer	NC
C.	30	F		NC
A.	9	M		TN
L.	8	F		TN
L.	7	F		MO
W.	5	M		TX
A.	4	F		TX
M.	2	F		TX
Jones, T.	22	M	Carpenter	TN

HAYS COUNTY, TEXAS

Town of St. Marcos

Durham, John L.	30	M	Farmer	TN
Martha B.	31	F		TN
Lewilla B.	2/12	F		TX
Johns, Robert B.	8	M		TX
Clement R., Jr.	13	M		TN
Johns, Clenent R.	34	M	Farmer	TN
Edmond G.	31	M	Farmer	TN
Kyle, Claiborn	50	M	Farmer	TN
Lucy	49	F		TN
William	19	M	Student	AL
Emma	18	F		MS

(continued)

HAYS COUNTY, TEXAS

Name	Age	Sex	Occupation	Birthplace
Kyle, Fergus	16	M	Student	MS
Polk Roger	14	M		MS
Cass	12	F		MS
Curan	10	M		MS
Dallas	9	F		MS
Andrew Jackson	6	M		MS
Wright, Charles	37	M	Botanist	CT
Hamblin, William M.	35	M	Farmer	TN
Harrison, Thomas	30	M	Wagon Maker	VA
Allen, Phillip J.	38	M	Farmer	TN
Mary	35	F		TN
William	13	M		TN
John	10	M		TX
Nancy	7	F		TX
James	4	M		TX
Phillip	2	M		TX
Cannon, William	25	M	Farmer	TN
Susan	22	F		TN
Robert	4	M		TX
Jane	2	F		TX
Sowell, Andrew J.	35	M	Farmer	TN
Lucinda	23	F		TN
Asa J. L.	7	M		TX
Rachel C.	5	F		TX
Mary Ann	3	F		TX
Virginia	1/12	F		TX
Sessons, Michael	39	M	Black Smith	TN
Elizabeth	29	F		AL
John	13	M		TX
David	10	M		TX
Edward	9	M		TX
Juliann	4	F		TX
Grace	2	F		TX
John	13	M		TX
Owens, Bird	23	M	Laborer	AL
Stevenson, J. C.	26	M	Farmer	KY
Mary Jane	27	F		TN
Barbor, Edward	7	M		TX
Ann B.	5	F		TX
Lobenski, J. L.	40	M	Farmer	POL
R.	35	F		MO
Sarah	14	F		TX
James	10	M		TX
Fleming	8	F		TX
Ray Ann	6	F		TX
Robert	5	M		TX
Yell, Rev. Pleasant M.	31	M	M.E. Minister, S.	TN
Owen, Nelson F.	29	M	Farmer	TN
Sarah J.	21	F		TN
Addison L.	1	M		TN
Owen, William E.	30	M	Farmer	AL
Martha Ann	16	F		TX
Elizabeth	2/12	F		TX
Graham, Eliza C.	17	F		NC
Owen, David J.	22	M	Ranging Service	TN
Durham, Thomas	55	M	Hotel Keeper	NC
Pauline	3-	F		KY
Ann	30	F		NC
Samuel	22	M	Clerk	TN
Caroline	20	F		TN
Amanda F.	17	F		TN
Cassiliana	10	F		MS
Riense	5	M		TX
Rinalus	3	M		TX
Letherwood, Miles A.	27	M	Carpenter	NC
Donaldson, G. G.	26	M	Trader	KY
Moore, James W.	35	M	Farmer	TN
Eliza J.	30	F		MO
Robert M.	12	M		AR
William M.	10	M		AR
Mary E.	6	F		AR
James W.	4	M		AR
Debora	6/12	F		TX
Robert C.	66	M	Farmer	NC
Carr, James	43	M	Farmer	TN
Rowena	32	F		TN
Burleson, Edward	48	M	Farmer	MS
Sarah G.	54	F		SC
Edward G.	23	M	Farmer	TN
Joseph R.	21	M		TN
Kyle, Grace	18	F		TX
Felix	22	M		TN
Burleson, David C.	13	M		TX
Elizabeth	10	F		TX
Edward	14	M		TX
Flanagan, Robert A.	36	M	Gin Wright	NC
Mary D.	35	F		TN
William J.	11	M		TN
Sarah J.	8	F		TN
Asynthie	6	F		TN
Esther A.	1	F		TN
Marshall, Jeremiah D.	28	M	Farmer	GA
Mary E.	23	F		TN
Nancy E.	3	F		TX
Eliza Ann	8/12	F		TX

HENDERSON COUNTY, TEXAS

Name	Age	Sex	Occupation	Birthplace
Hunter, Martha	39	F		TN
Jonathan	16	M	Farmer	MO
S. W.	14	M	Farmer	MO
Serepta R.	12	F		MO
Abraham M.	11	M		MO
Thomas J.	7	M		MO
Henrietta	3	F		TX
Martha M.	2	F		TX
A. J.	23	M	Farmer	TN
Ranson, James	39	M	Farmer	TN
Eliza	34	F		TN
Ataway, Mary	5	F		MS
Wilson, Jonathan J.	20	M	Farmer	TN
Nancy E.	19	F		TN
Montgomery, John L.	37	M	Farmer	TN
Matilda	27	F		KY
Mary J.	10	F		MO
Eliza Ann	8	F		MO
Margaret M.	5	F		MO
William W.	3	M		TX
Mills, Thomas	27	M	Farmer	IN
Sarah	18	F		TN
James H.	3	M		TX
Sarah E.	2	F		TX
Walters, George S.	56	M	Farmer	GA
Susan	65	F		SC
Wolf, William S.	16	M	Farmer	TN
Elizabeth	13	F		AR
Craft, Samuel	48	M	Farmer	TN
Barbary	35	F		MS
Lucinda	9	F		TX
Elizabeth	6	F		TX
Nancy J.	4	F		TX
Georgiann	1½	F		TX
McManners, Joab	32	M	Farmer	TN
Rebecca	27	F		KY
Emeline	9	F		IL
Mary E.	7	F		MO
Sterman, William W.	28	M	Farmer	KY
Mary Ann	21	F		TN
Mary A.	2	F		TX
Sarah E.	1	F		TX
Chandler, Joseph	25	M	Farmer	??
Shoat, C.	44	M	Farmer	TN
Ana	39	F		KY
Elizabeth	17	F		TN
Vade	15	M	Farmer	AR

(continued)

Name	Age	Sex	Occupation	Birthplace
Shoat, Mary	13	F		AR
Eliza	12	F		AR
Christopher	9	M		TX
Elvira	7	F		TX
Marion	5	M		TX
John H.	2	M		TX
McManners, Thomas P.	35	M	Mechanic	TN
Nancy	33	F		IL
Solomon M.	15	M	Farmer	IL
James Y.	13	M		IL
Louisa	7	F		IL
John B.	5	M		AR
William F.	2	M		MO
McAdams, Deaton	35	M	Farmer	SC
Ann E.	26	F		TN
Martha V. E.	5	F		GA
Waldrup, William	38	M	Farmer	TN
Alfred J.	16	M	Farmer	TN
Seaburn H.	13	M		MS
Sintha E.	11	F		MS
Napoleon C.	8	M		MS
Mary E.	5	F		MS
Lusania	28	F		TN
Rebecca	65	F		SC
Missouri N.	10	F		MS
Steel, William	33	M	Farmer	TN
Mary	30	F		TN
Mary E.	11	F		AR
John B.	10	M		AR
Thomas R.	5	M		AR
Martha A.	2	F		TX
Wood, Nancy	16	F		GA
Cavett, Moses	64	M	Farmer	TN
Susan	36	F		TN
Georgeann	9	F		MS
Margret	7	F		TX
Richard D.	5	M		TN
John W.	4	M		TX
Martha E.	3	F		TX
James A.	2	M		TX
Curtis, E. M.	34	M		MA
Avant, William	24	M	Farmer	TN
Rutha	25	F		MO
Wiley W.	5	M		TX
Lanford, James	2	M		TX
Avant, Deram	52	M	Farmer	SC
Susan	42	F		TN
Mason	18	M	Farmer	AL
Lewis	16	M	Farmer	TX
Jane	13	F		TX
Susan	11	F		TX
James	8	M		TX
John	6	M		TX
Lesander	3	M		TX
Bucham, John	63	M	Farmer	KY
Dina	32	F		TN
Alexander	8	M		AR
Jasper N.	4	M		AR
John	2	M		AR
Nancy J.	3/12	F		TX
Perkins, James	40	M	Farmer	KY
Elizabeth	26	F		TN
Mary E.	10	F		AR
Joseph R.	8	M		AR
Daniel W.	5	M		TX
Isaac	2	M		TX
Oliver J.	2/12	M		TX
Bobo, William C(E).	25	M	Farmer	TN
Amanda	17	F		KY
Blue, M. D.	38	M	Farmer	NC
Leah	27	F		TN
Martha A.	6	F		MO
Margret J.	6	F		MO

(continued)

Name	Age	Sex	Occupation	Birthplace
Blue, Peter	2	M		TX
Franics	5/12	M		TX
Martin, James	38	M	Farmer	NC
Mary	32	F		NC
Perlina	13	F		NC
Enoch	10	M		TN
William	8	M		TN
Sarah	6	F		TN
Valentine	4	M		TN
Jasper	1	M		TN
Winchester, Harvy	17	M	Farmer	NC
Jones, Jonathan	38	M	Farmer	TN
Elizabeth	38	F		TN
James	17	M	Farmer	TN
Mary J.	15	F		TN
Robert ?.	12	M		TN
William	10	M		TN
Jacob	8	M		TN
Elizabeth E.	5	F		TN
Helm, William	33	M	Farmer	TN
Unity	33	F		AL
Elizabeth	12	F		TN
Frances	11	F		KY
Messer L.	9	M		KY
Lucinda D.	5	F		KY
Jordenia	2	F		TX
Eli	4/12	M		TX
Parson, Robert H.	32	M	Farmer	TN
Nancy E.	21	F		TN
James L.	2	M		KY
Mary E.	1	F		TX
Goodnight, Joseph	39	M	Farmer	TN
Elizabeth	37	F		AL
Catharine	14	F		TN
Thomas	13	M		TN
Tabitha	11	F		TN
Nancy	10	F		KY
Henry	8	M		KY
John M. L.	2	M		AR
William D.	2	M		AR
Whitehead, Samuel	46	M	Farmer	NC
Asenith	31	F		TN
M. Leroy	13	M		AR
James R.	7	M		AR
Elizabeth L.	5	F		AR
Martha A.	3	F		TX
Box, Thomas	45	M	Farmer	TN
Charkey	38	F		VA
Thomas M.	11	M		MS
William J.	3	M		TX
Josephine	1	F		TX
Stever, L. D.	40	M	Farmer	TN
Ann	38	F		SC
Amelia	15	F		AL
McMillion	13	M		AL
Elizabeth	11	F		AL
Margret S.	7	F		AL
Martha J.	7	F		AL
Cornela	1	F		TX
Phillips, Jackson	42	M	Farmer	TN
Eliza J.	27	F		IL
Marcus L.	21	M	Farmer	TN
Martha J.	16	F		IL
James S.	15	M	Farmer	IL
William C.	13	M		IL
Washington	9	M		IL
Harriet	8	F		IL
Sarah	4	F		TX
Andrew B.	1	M		TX
Buie, Daniel	42	M	Farmer	NC
Frances	36	F		NC
Mary C.	16	F		TN
William R.	14	M		TN
John A.	12	M		TN
Susan E.	9	F		TN

(continued)

HENDERSON COUNTY, TEXAS

Name	Age	Sex	Occupation	Birthplace
Buie, Robert D.	7	M		TN
Margret E.	5	F		TX
Alfred	1	M		TX
Cavett, Leroy	17	M	Farmer	KY
Harrison, Samuel M.	30	M	Farmer	TN
Sarah A.	29	F		TN
Mary M.	7	F		MS
Elizabeth C.	5	F		MS
Marthy E.	2	F		TX
Teel, James W.	37	M	Farmer	TN
Margret	36	F		KY
Elizabeth J.	13	F		MO
Humphry M.	11	M		MO
Thomas M.	10	M		MO
James L.	7	M		IL
Andrew J.	5	M		IL
George W.	5	M		IL
Mary	3	F		MO
Poly Ann	1	F		MO
Dickerson, N. T.	36	M	Farmer	TN
Barbary	40	F		TN
William A.	20	M	Farmer	TN
Dencilla	14	F		AR
King, Edley	24	M	Farmer	TN
Rebecca	23	F		TN
Sarah A.	4	F		TN
Samuel	3	M		TN
George W.	1	M		TX
Bufford, P. J.	36	M	Farmer	TN
Nancy C. W.	30	F		TN
Isabella J.	7	F		MO
William A.	5	M		MO
Margret A.	3	F		TX
Mary E.	17	F		MS
Marthy A. L.	15	F		TN
John W.	24	M	Boatsman	MS
Reagan, John H.	32	M	Attorney	TN
Morris R.	22	M	Student	TN
William R.	19	M	Student	TN
Sarah R.	17	F		TN
Mary J.	5	F		TN
Adams, Howel C.	36	M	Farmer	TN
Sarah A.	28	F		AL
Isabelia	13	F		AL
Washington J.	10	M		AL
Jesse H.	8	M		MS
Elizabeth M.	6	F		MS
Sarah J.	4	F		MS
William E.	2	M		MS
Sanders, Lucy	58	F		VA
Charles R.	26	M	Farmer	MO
Lucy A.	19	F		AR
Lizia J.	22	F		AR
David W.	17	M	Farmer	AR
Drucilla B.	15	F		AR
Guthrie, E. M.	44	M	Farmer	SC
Sinai	33	F		TN
John C.	13	M		AR
James T.	10	M		AR
Rachel M.	8	F		AR
Samuel H.	6	M		AR
Bartlett, Joseph	46	M	Farmer	KY
Elizabeth	44	F		TN
Mildry	24	F		TN
John	20	M	Farmer	TN
Joshua	18	M	Farmer	TN
William	16	M	Farmer	TN
Nathan	12	M		MO
John Dabney	10	M		AR
Jones, Wiley	60	M	Farmer	NC
Johanna	60	F		GA
Holman, John	26	M	Farmer	TN
Carrell, Amand	35	M	Farmer	VA
Wilkerson, William M.	16	M	Farmer	MS
Carrell, Mary F.	12	F		TN
Shankle, B. L.	40	M	Farmer	TN
Jane	38	F		SC
Sintha J.	16	F		AL
Lucinda	12	F		AL
Christiana	9	F		AL
Mary R.	7	F		TX
John T.	4	M		TX
Sophronia	1	F		TX
Scott, Perran	13	M		AL
Bird, Christiana	66	F		NC
Dickens, Richard	22	M	Farmer	TN
Mary	20	F		IN
William	1	M		TX
King, John	28	M	Farmer	TN
Mary	21	F		IL
Margret	1	F		TX
Baker, John	51	M	Farmer	TN
Eliza	41	F		TN
Emeline	17	F		IL
Joseph	13	M		TX
James	10	M		TX
Eliza	9	F		TX
John	6	M		TX
Allen, H. L.	52	M	Farmer	GA
Elizabeth	50	F		TN
Sarah E.	23	F		AL
Claiborn M.	21	M		AL
Catharine	15	F		AL
Nancy M.	12	F		MS
Malenia	8	F		MS
Hiram D.	4	M		MS
McCarty, P. M.	4-	M	Farmer	KY
Malinda M.	26	F		TN
Margret M.	11	F		MO
Thomas, R. B.	42	M	Farmer	TN
Susana	43	F		TN
Rody	18	F		MO
Lafayette	16	M	Farmer	MO
Martha	14	F		MO
Catharine	13	F		MO
Mary	10	F		MO
Nella	8	F		MO
Susania	3	F		TX
Doctor R. B.	3	M		TX
Eliza J.	2/12	F		TX
Estrage, Corral	14	M		AR
Leonard	13	M		AR
White, William T.	34	M	Farmer	KY
Sarania	24	F		TN
James F.	5	M		MO
John P.	3	M		TX
William J.	1	M		TX
Sarah C.	3/12	F		TX
Frey, William	21	M	Farmer	TN
Mary A.	22	F		TN
John G.	1	M		AR
Blue, Moses H.	58	M	Farmer	TN
July Ann	38	F		TN
William H.	20	M	Black Smith	TN
Sarah B.	16	F		AR
Blancet, John W.	15	M	Farmer	AL
Blue, Elizabeth C.	14	F		AR
John J.	11	M		AR
Douglas A.	8	M		AR
Blancet, America A.	5	F		AR
Blue, Moses H.	2	M		AR
Wingfield S.	1/12	M		TX
Gray, R. W.	45	M	Med. Doctor	KY
Elizabeth	38	F		TN
Hutchins	17	M	Farmer	MO
Lafayette B.	10	M		MO

(continued)

Name	Age	Sex	Occupation	Birthplace
Gray, Mary C.	8	F		MO
Elizabeth A.	6	F		MO
Eliza J.	4	F		MO
Martha A.	1	F		TX
Gray, Nea. H.	41	M	Sheriff	KY
Lucinda	35	F		TN
Mary E.	12	F		MO
Robert M.	9	M		MO
John T.	8	M		MO
Susan A.	5	F		MO
Martha H.	4/12	F		TX
Stockton, Elzey	28	M	Farmer	KY
Ana L.	29	F		IL
Lacrew, William W.	9	M		MO
James G.	7	M		MO
Mary M.	4	F		MO
Benjamin F.	2	M		MO
Smith, Sarah A.	18	F		TN
Damron, John	59	M	Farmer	VA
Sarah	57	F		KY
George W.	20	M	Farmer	TN
William M.	17	M	Farmer	TN
Sarah M.	14	F		MO
Sintha E.	12	F		MO
Joseph W.	9	M		MO
Shultz, John B.	81	M	Cooper	NC
Seitz, Thomas	25	M	Farmer	TN
Isabella	22	F		TN
Artimelia	8/12	F		TX
Thetford, Dennis	44	M	Farmer	TN
Hester M.	39	F		KY
Robert G.	19	M	Farmer	TN
John G.	17	M	Farmer	TN
N. H. G.	14	M		TN
William E.	10	M		MO
Daniel G.	8	M		MO
Reason A.	4	M		MO
Wilson H.	2	M		TX
Sawyer, G. N.	25	M	Farmer	MA
Martha J.	19	F		TN
Brock, George W.	36	M	Farmer	TN
Martha	32	F		TN
Charles D.	10	M		TN
Thomas H.	8	M		TN
Ann E.	6	F		TN
Richard A.	3	M		TN
Martha J.	2/12	F		TX
Flinn, James	30	M		KY
Hartgraves, Preston	34	M	Farmer	TN
Jane	26	F		TN
Preston T.	6/12	M		TX
Damron, John L.	32	M	Farmer	TN
Sally	32	F		IN
Nathaniel C.	1	M		TX
Laury L.	5/12	F		TX
Daugharty, And. J.	33	M	Trader	TN
Dianna	22	F		AL
Missouri A.	4	F		AR
Larissa J.	2	F		TX
Obadiah	8/12	M		TX
Leman, Olave E.	39	M	Carpenter	MA
Luton, J. M.	50	M	Farmer	NC
Mary P.	39	F		VA
Lilla A.	20	F		TN
Henry C.	13	M		TN
Narcissa	12	F		TN
Mary E.	9	F		TN
George W.	7	M		TN
Constantine	4	M		TN
William Penn	2	M		TN
Seitz, George	47	M	Farmer	NC

(continued)

Name	Age	Sex	Occupation	Birthplace
Seitz, Elizabeth	46	F		NC
John L.	24	M	Farmer	TN
A. J.	21	M	Farmer	TN
Ann M.	18	F		TN
George W.	16	M	Farmer	TN
Thabitha A.	14	F		TN
Luisa E.	12	F		TN
Leander M.	10	M		TN
Louisa O.	5	F		TN
Coldiron, Jacob	25	M	Farmer	KY
Leafy C.	21	F		MS
George W.	2	M		TX
Margret F.	5/12	F		TX
Williams, John	37	M	Farmer	TN
Elizabeth	35	F		TN
Florina	18	F		TN
Nancy	15	F		TN
Elias	13	M		TN
James	11	M		MO
William A.	9	M		MO
Mary A.	7	F		MO
Eliza J.	6	F		MO
Elizabeth	4	F		MO
Blacke, Daniel	37	M	Farmer	KY
Michael	35	M	Farmer	KY
John H.	15	M	Farmer	TN
Elizabeth J.	14	F		AR
George W.	12	M		AR
Marthy C.	9	F		AR
William L.	6	M		AR
James M.	4	M		AR
Rebecca A.	1	F		TX
Reynolds, E. B.	50	M	Farmer	SC
Gibbs, L. O.	42	M	Farmer	NC
Lurana	41	F		TN
J. W. W.	18	M	Farmer	TN
J. G.	16	M	Farmer	TN
Stephen O.	11	M		MS
N. J. B.	9	M		MS
Sarah A.	6	F		MS
M. M.	3	M		MS
Walker, JOhn	34	M	Carpenter	KY
Stephenson, O.	45	M	Merchant	??
Parnell, Victor	50	M	Black Smith	SC
Barsheba	39	F		NC
Elizabeth	18	F		IL
Lucinda	16	F		IL
Samuel R. G.	14	M		MO
Malinda	11	F		MO
Thomas J.	8	M		MO
Malona B.	4	F		TX
Victor M.	2	M		TX
Brikle, Henry	20	M	Farmer	GER
Williams, David	33	M	Herdsman	TN
Bersheba E.	1	F		TX
Case, Victor P. H.	4	M		TX
Mayfield, Alexander	30	M	Sportsman	NC
Lee, Lewis	36	M	Black Smith	IN
Carter, J. M.	35	M	Farmer	AL
Anna	36	F		TN
Elizabeth	14	F		TN
Hiram C.	2	M		TX
Amanda	1	F		TX
Willm. H.	2/12	M		TX
Carter, Willm. H.	35	M	Farmer	GA
Sarah	63	F		SC
Locklier, Thomas	53	M	Farmer	SC
Tinnin, E. C.	25	M	Surveyor	TN
Carter, M. J.	21	M	Farmer	AL
Walton, Jesse S.	42	M	Farmer	VA
Elizabeth	18	F		TN
James L.	13	M		TN
Thomas N.	11	M		AR
Jesse S.	11	M		AR
Gentry, Rolley	37	M	Farmer	SC
Mary	36	F		TN
Gilford	19	M	Farmer	GA

(continued)

HENDERSON COUNTY, TEXAS

Gentry, William 17 M Farmer GA
Martha A. 15 F GA
Mary 12 F GA
Allen 11 M GA
George W. 7 M GA
Lucinda 3 F TX
Andrew J. 11/12 M TX

Lovell, Washington 32 M Farmer TN
Sarah 24 F AR
Franklin 8 M AR
Mary 6 F AR

McDonald, M. 35 M Tailor NC
Mary J. 21 F TN
Nancy J. 5 F MS
Angus G. 3 M MS
Sarah E. 8/12 F TX

Mason, G. B. 43 M Farmer TN
Nancy H. 38 F VA
William C. 19 M Farmer TN
Elizabeth M. 15 F IL
Zelpha C. 13 F IL
Dampsey A. 10 M IL
Nancy E. 6 F IL
Surmantha J. 2 F TX

Vanhooser, Isaack 50 M Farmer TN
Elizabeth 46 F TN
Carmel A. 22 M Farmer TN
William C. 20 M Farmer TN
Ambrose B. 13 M TN
Moses 11 M TN

Ford, Levy 26 M Farmer TN
Mary Ann 24 F TN
Nancy E. 1 F TX

Morrow, A. M. 49 M Med. Doctor NC
Mary E. 37 F KY
Texania 9 F TX
Emily F. 7 F TX
Andrew J. 4 M TX
John M. 1 M TX
Jenkins, Eveline 17 F TN
Long, J. G. 47 M Teacher VA

Davenport, John M. 23 M Sportsman VA
Mary J. 26 F TN
Elkins, Mary A. 7 F TX
Davenport, Margret C. 7/12 F TX

Kyser, John H. 24 M Farmer TN
Sarah F. 18 F TN
Amanda C. 4 F TX
Mary E. 1 F TX

Harrison, James M. 32 M Ass. & Collector TN
Elizabeth 29 F TN
William M. 7 M MS
George W. 3 M TX
Mary M. 1 F TX

HOPKINS COUNTY, TEXAS

8th Judicial District

Mathews, Robert E. 30 M Farmer KY
Mary H(A). 25 F TN
John E. 19 M Farmer TN
Zepaniah 17 M Farmer TN
Mary P. 14 F TN
Drusilla 12 F TX
Caroline 9 F TX
Joseph 6 M TX
Mansil W. 3 M TX
Robert E. 1 M TX

McClarice, James 24 M Farmer TN
Jane 26 F KY
Daniel E. 5 M KY
Archy T. 3 M KY

Helvy, Andrew 43 M Farmer VA
Malinda 23 F TN
John H. 4 M TN
Daniel J. 2 M TX

Ramsey, Isaac 27 M Farmer (E)TN
Cynthia A. 29 F TN
Pierce, Abraham I. 20 M Farmer TN
Levi G. 6 M TN
George W. 4 M TN
John T. 2 M TN
Pleasant A. 1 M TX

McClarice, Bennet 23 M Farmer TN
Elizabeth 23 F KY
Kizziah 5 F KY
Dorcas 3 F KY
Burnetta J. 1 F TX

Hooten, Elijah 32 M Physician TN
Ellen A. 31 F TN
John B. 12 M TN
Sarah J. 10 F TN
James W. 9 M TN
Martha M. 7 F TN
Andrew J. 5 M TN
William D. 4 M TN

Landers, John C. 39 M Black Smith TN
Jane L. 28 F IN
Andrew 7 M AR
George 3 M AR
John 9/12 M TX

Ramsey, George 65 M None (E)TN
Patience 60 F SC
Mary 21 F (E)TN

Ramsey, John 36 M Black Smith (E)TN
Stacy 31 F TN
John 11 M TN
George 10 M TN
Patience 7 F TN
Ruth 6 F TN
Martha 4 F TN
Mary 2 F TX

Brechen, William 39 M Farmer TN
Elizabeth 20 F AL
Jas. M. 16 M Farmer TN
Lemuel 15 M Farmer TN
William T. 10 M MO
Mary J. 9 F TX
Nancy C. 6 F TX
Sarah E. 4 F TX
Robert E. 1/2 M TX

Ashmore, Baily 28 M Farmer (W)TN
Matilda A. 21 F AR
Lewis, Lucinda 15 F AR
Wiley 51 M KY

Spain, John D. 42 M Farmer AL
Margaret 39 F KY
Susan 14 F TN
Matilda 13 F AL
Tomas 11 M TX
Daniel 8 M TX
Olivia 5 F TX
Almira 9/12 F TX

Mason, William 46 M Farmer TN
Matilda 43 F KY
Randolph 21 M Farmer AL
Wiley 19 M Farmer AL
Susan 17 F TN
Charlotte 14 F TN
Cason 7 M TN
William W. 2 M TX

Matthews, Cyntha 50 F SC
Barton W. 26 M Farmer AL
John C. 23 M Farmer AL
Caroline 21 F TN
Mary 19 F TN
(continued)

HOPKINS COUNTY, TEXAS

Name	Age	Sex	Occupation	Birthplace
Matthews, Joseph	17	M	Farmer	TN
Mansil	15	M	Farmer	TN
Thomison, Alphus	39	M	Farmer	GA
Lucretia	30	F		TN
William Henry	7	M		MO
John	4	M		TX
George	1	M		TX
Trenon, Pathias	21	M	Farmer	MS
Emison, Josiah	50	M	Farmer	GA
Dicy	43	F		GA
Mary	10	F		AL
Eliza	6	F		TX
Daniel	3	M		TX
Cavanaugh, Hugh	29	M	Farmer	(E)TN
Wardlow, Milton	38	M	Farmer	NC
Jane	33	F		AL
John	11	M		MS
Susan E.	10	F		MS
Samuel S.	8	M		MS
David H.	6	M		MS
Matilda	4	F		TN
Milton L.	1	M		TX
Lucy A.	1	F		TX
Nalls, John	24	M	Farmer	TX
Polly Ann	20	F		TN
Emeline R.	6	F		TX
Lafayette	4	M		TX
Elizabeth	2	F		TX
George W.	9/12	M		TX
Castleberry, Mitchel	40	M	Farmer	KY
Matilda A.	40	F		KY
James B.	18	M	Farmer	TN
John W.	16	M	Farmer	TN
Thomas M.	11	M		TN
Robert M.	8	M		TX
Jefferson J.	5	M		TX
Mariah J.	3	F		TX
Morgan, Zachariah	26	M	Farmer	VA
Isabella	24	F		TN
Margaret	2	F		TX
Joseph	1	M		TX
Thomas, Washington	26	M	Farmer	TN
Ann	26	F		TN
Sarah A.	4	F		TN
Thomas, George	28	M	Farmer	TN
Eddy T.	18	F		TN
McLaughlin, John	24	M	Farmer	IL
Alice	18	F		IL
Bridgeman, Moriah	30	F		TN
Nancy	8	F		NC
McLaughlin, Jas.	22	M	Farmer	IL
Narcissa J.	16	F		TN
Long, Edward	40	M	Farmer	AL
Alsy L.	36	F		TN
Elizabeth	17	F		TN
Joh--	15	M	Farmer	TN
Reuben	13	M		TN
Polly	11	F		TN
Catharine	9	F		TN
Solomon	6	M		TN
John	2	M		TN
Junelle, Robert	24	M	Farmer	TN
Mary	25	F		TN
Sarah	7	F		TN
William	4	M		TN
Thomas	1	M		TX
Morgan, John	22	M	Farmer	GA
Elizabeth	20	F		TN
William	1	M		TX

Name	Age	Sex	Occupation	Birthplace
Burden, Hawkins	30	M	Farmer	TN
Elizabeth	26	F		TN
John	10	M		TN
Perry H.	9/12	M		TX
Bromley, Willis	60	M	Farmer	NC
Sarah	55	F		VA
Berry	19	M	Farmer	TN
Nelson	15	M	Farmer	TN
Willis	12	M		TN
Burden, John	33	M	Farmer	AL
Nancy	58	F		NC
Joseph	10	M		TN
Nancy A.	8	F		TN
Henry	5	M		TN
George	3	M		TN
Elizabeth	1	F		TX
Bradly, Robert	28	M	Farmer	TN
Lucinda	25	F		TN
Richard C.	7	M		TN
William B.	4	M		TN
George W.	1	M		TX
Berry, Jas.	46	M	Farmer	TN
Nancy	44	F		KY
Major	19	M	Farmer	AL
Andrew J.	18	M	Farmer	AL
Francis M.	16	M	Farmer	AL
Eliza Jane	13	F		AL
Elizabeth	11	F		AL
Sarah	9	F		AL
Nancy A.	7	F		TX
Jas. W.	5	M		TX
John W.	3	M		TX
Hugh	1	M		TX
Arnold, E. A.	26	M	Farmer	TN
Esther E.	25	F		TN
Sarah A.	5	F		TX
William A.	4	M		TX
Martha	1	F		TX
Deckard, John	57	M	Farmer	VA
Martha	45	F		VA
Martha J.	19	F		TN
Diana	16	F		TN
John R.	14	M		TN
Stephen T.	12	M		TN
Atchley, Jefferson	21	M	Farmer	TN
Matthews, M. W.	44	M	Lawyer	KY
Sarah A.	40	F		VA
Joseph J.	20	M	Farmer	AL
Nancy P.	20	F		AL
Thomas W.	15	M	Farmer	TN
Elizabeth	13	F		TX
John M.	10	M		TX
Helen M.	7	F		TX
O. C.	4	M		TX
Robert E.	1	M		TX
Alexander	1	M		TX
Matthews, Joseph	83	M	None	SC
Permina	76	F		NC
Young, Margaret	18	F		TN
Joseph	14	M		TX
Ramsey, Thomas	25	M	Farmer	TN
Mary E.	34	F		NC
Margaret A.	6/12	F		TX
Stephenson, John T.	31	M	Farmer	NC
Ruth C.	23	F		TN
Mary C.	1	F		TX
Brookshire, Jesse	23	M	Farmer	TN
Martha	28	F		TN
Carrol, F.	34	M	Farmer	TN
Rosanna	28	F		VA
William H.	10	M		AL
Columbia	8	F		AL

(continued)

HOPKINS COUNTY, TEXAS

Name	Age	Sex	Occupation	Birthplace
Carrol, Sarah J.	6	F		AL
Thomas	4	M		AL
Lorance	3	M		TX
Samuel	1	M		TX
Coffe(e), Larkin,	32	M	Farmer	TN
Amanda	25	F		KY
William E.	3	M		TN
James A.	1	M		TX
Odum, Allen	41	M	Farmer	NC
Mary	37	F		TN
John O.	18	M	Farmer	IN
Lucinda	14	F		TN
Jacob	13	M		TN
Nancy	11	F		TN
Martin	10	M		TN
Wily J.	8	M		TN
George W.	6/12	M		TN
Berry, Nelson	24	M	Farmer	AL
Needy	20	F		TN
Emerson, D. K.	30	M	Farmer	TN
Linda J.	25	F		TN
Jos.	6	M		IL
Benton	4	M		IL
Cynna	3	F		IL
Levi S.	2	M		IL
Martha S.	1	F		TX
Harris, Newton	30	M	Farmer	TN
Data	26	F		TN
Mary B.	9	F		TN
Louisa	2	F		TX
Bolt(?), John	21	M	Farmer	AR
Smith, Drury	24	M	Farmer	TN
Elizabeth	26	F		TN
Elizabeth J.	8	F		AR
John G.	6	M		AR
Joanna	3	F		TX
Sarah A.	6/12	F		TX
Hannah, Samuel	43	M	Farmer	TN
Rebecca	30	F		TN
Ann M.	6	F		TN
Andrew J.	5	M		TN
Thomas J.	3	M		TN
Francis E.	1	F		GA
Box, Thomas W.	29	M	Physician	AL
Sarah H.	16	F		TN
Jos. G.	6/12	M		TX
Byrd, Jesse	45	M	Farmer	TN
Shelton, John	50	M	Farmer	TN
Nancy J.	50	F		VA
Tory, Robert C.	22	M	Farmer	TN
Charlotte	24	F		TN
Sarah	1	F		TX
Crowder, G. H.	29	M	Merchant	KY
Virginia C.	20	F		AL
Sarah J.	6/12	F		TX
Ashman, Barton	25	M	Farmer	TN
Hopkins, Eldridge	43	M	Farmer	IL
Harriet	41	F		KY
Minerva	15	F		IN
Matilda	12	F		IN
Jos. E.	8	M		TX
Sophrona	6	F		TX
Rachael	4	F		TX
Stephen R.	2	M		TX
Sutherland, George	18	M	Farmer	IN
Lee, David	35	M	Farmer	VA
Grant, Isaac	25	M	Merchant	VA
Neal, Daniel	22	M	Clerk	TN
Russell, J. C.	26	M	Farmer	TN
Ellen	17	F		IN

(continued)

Name	Age	Sex	Occupation	Birthplace
Russell, Tennessee	6/12	F		TX
Watson, John	9	M		KY
Russell, Macomb	18	M	Farmer	IA
Clapp, David	60	M	Farmer	TN
Eliza	32	F		IL
Lucinda	25	F		TX
Mary	22	F		TX
John	20	M	Farmer	TX
Elisha	17	M	Farmer	TX
Ellmore, J. M.	33	M	Farmer	TN
Mary	32	F		TN
H. E. J.	9	F		MO
Mary A.	4	F		TX
Margaret	2	F		TX
Long, Christopher C.	15	M	Farmer	MO
Lindly, Eli	39	M	Farmer	KY
Sarah	29	F		MO
Jacob M.	12	M		MO
Redding G.	10	M		MO
Elizabeth	8	F		MO
Jno. W.	7	M		MO
Missouri R.	6	F		TX
T--- S.	1	M		TX
Sarah M. J.	1	F		TX
Prince, John	23	M	Teacher	TN
Harriet C.	21	F		TN
Ellmore, M. C. C.	31	M	Farmer	TN
Blyth, William	28	M	Merchant	TN
Amanda	22	F		GA
Mary	1/12	F		TX
Doherty, F. W.	28	M	Clerk	_ Carolina
Blyth, E. A.	19	M	Clerk	TN
Young, Ernest	22	M	Farmer	TN
Davis, R.	30	M	Farmer	TN
D'Spain, William R.	37	M	Farmer	AL
Ann	33	F		IL
Thomas	16	M	Farmer	TN
William M.	12	M		MO
Martha	10	F		TX
Mary	8	F		TX
Sarah	5	F		TX
Moriah	3	F		TX
Berry, William	25	M	Farmer	TN
Malinda	22	F		TN
Sarah E.	1	F		TX
Ashmore, James B.	53	M	Farmer	KY
Polly A.	60	F		VA
John	24	M	Farmer	TN
Amos	22	M	Farmer	TN
James M.	20	M	Farmer	TN
Margaret H.	18	F		TN
Prell, Edward O.	25	M	Farmer	PA
Araminta D.	20	F		TN
Alexander C.	2	M		TX
Jones, Richard	27	M	Farmer	VA
Eliza	22	F		TN
John J.	9/12	M		TX
Tadlock, Jos.	46	M	Farmer	KY
Martha	43	F		KY
Louis B.	22	M	Farmer	KY
John M.	17	M	Farmer	TN
James	15	M	Farmer	KY
Louisa	13	F		KY
Margaret	11	F		KY
Mary	9	F		KY
Franklin C.	7	M		KY
Nancy E.	5	F		KY
Martha	3	F		KY
Susan L.	3/12	F		TX
Crisp, Ruthy	64	F		TN
Carril	26	M	Farmer	MO
McMese	22	M	Farmer	MO
Redding	18	M	Farmer	MO

(continued)

HOPKINS COUNTY, TEXAS

Name	Age	Sex	Occupation	Birthplace
Collins, Jas.	20	M	Farmer	MO
Redding	17	M	Farmer	MO
Lindley, John	7	M		MO
Adkins, Owen	40	M	Merchant	TN
Eliza	39	F		NC
Jesse	17	M		IL
Elizabeth J.	14	F		MO
Sarah A.	12	F		MO
James	10	M		MO
William	8	M		MO
Isaac N.	6	M		MO
Edward	4	M		MO
Artemussa	2	F		MO
Solomon, John	24	M	Farmer	KY
Smith, William W.	24	M	Cabinet Maker	TN
Talitha	21	F		IL
Hankins, William	27	M	Farmer	TN
Esther	30	F		TN
John B.	12	M		AR
William A.	10	M		AR
Benjamin F.	8	M		AR
Rebecca	8	F		AR
Sarah Ann	3	F		AR
Frances C.	1/12	F		TX
Hankins, Joseph	27	M	Farmer	TN
Moses, John	1	M		TX
Garret, Thomas	23	M	Farmer	AL
Itson, David	29	M	Merchant	TN
Martha	26	F		KY
William	8	M		MO
Mary Jane	7	F		MO
Sarah	3	F		MO
Nancy A.	8/12	F		TX
Skinner, Wiley	36	M		KY
Carrel, William	23	M	Farmer	KY
Bledsoe, William	30	M	Farmer	TN
Lucinda J.	34	F		TN
Fry, Louis	11	M		MO
Peter	10	M		TX
Caroline	5	F		TX
William	2	M		TX
Nethery, Abner	36	M	Farmer	NC
Louisa	38	F		TN
Sarah J.	10	F		TX
Matilda	7	F		TX
Robert	4	M		TX
Louis C.	2	M		TX
Cook, Andrew	37	M	Farmer	(E)TN
Mary	35	F		TN
John	16	M	Farmer	IN
Anna	14	F		IN
Uriah	13	M		MO
Justin	12	F		MO
Polly	10	F		MO
Ann	8	F		MO
Evan	6	M		AR
Elizabeth J.	5	F		AR
Cele S.	2	F		TX
George W.	1	M		TX
Nancy	6/12	F		TX
Abram	23	M	Farmer	IN
Crook, Richard	42	M	Farmer	KY
Mary F.	33	F		TN
Louis M.	12	M		TN
Medeline	10	F		TX
Sarah Jane	1	F		TX
Haws, Thomas	51	M	Farmer	KY
Walker, Z. C.	38	M	Farmer	TN
Elizabeth	33	F		TN
James C.	12	M		TX
John D.	10	M		TX
Jane	8	F		TX
Susan	6	F		TX
Sarah	4	F		TX
Mary	1	F		TX

Name	Age	Sex	Occupation	Birthplace
Paine, Abram	39	M	Farmer	NC
Matilda	30	F		TN
Barnabas	21	M	Farmer	IN
Elizabeth	17	F		IN
Margaret	12	F		IN
William D.	4	M		TX
Harris, John	44	M	Farmer	TN
Sevilla	39	F		KY
James	21	M	Farmer	TN
Elliot N.	19	M	Farmer	TN
Elzira	16	F		TN
Fredome	14	M		TN
Stephen	12	M		TX
William	10	M		MO
John	8	M		MO
Lucretia	6	F		TX
Mary	4	F		TX
Columbus	2	M		TX
Lucy	2/12	F		TX
Johnson, Wesley	25	M	Farmer	KY
Eliza	15	F		TN
John	6/12	M		TX
Matthews, John	54	M	Farmer	SC
Sarah A.	52	F		TN
Margaret P.	14	F		TN
Joseph M.	10	M		TX
Helem, Emily	8	F		TX
Bingham, Henry	49	M	Farmer	PA
Nancy	50	F		TN
Jabus E.	20	M	Farmer	KY
Alphus C.	19	M	Farmer	KY
Henry A.	16	M	Farmer	TN
Benjamin R.	10	M		TX
Susan A.	6	F		TX
Farr, Jane	16	F		IRE
Kounts, B.	40	M	Physician	VA
Amanda	26	F		TN
Clarence	7	M		MO
Charles A.	5	M		MO
Syntha	3	F		MO
Susan	1	F		TX
Groce, Joseph	22	M	Farmer	TN
Virginia N.	16	F		MO
Maxwell, James	48	M	Merchant	NC
Martha	55	F		NC
Joseph ?.	25	M	Farmer	TN
Emaline	13	F		LA
Cole, D. W.	30	M	Merchant	KY
Rebecca Ann	28	F		TN
Ophelia Ann	1	F		TX
King, John	70	M	Farmer	NC
Martha	69	F		NC
Pett, Edwin	35	M	Farmer	TN
Edward	30	M	Farmer	NC
Halbrook, John M.	35	M	Farmer	TN
Katharine	33	F		TN
James A.	19	M	Farmer	TN
George W.	11	M		AR
Lodouka(?)	4	F		AR
Solomon	6/12	M		TX
Findley, David	35	M	Farmer	MO
Margaret	32	F		TN
Rachel	12	F		MO
John	8	M		MO
Katharine	4	F		MO
Campbell, E. G.	47	M	Farmer	TN
Charlotte	40	F		(E)TN
Charles	22	M	Farmer	AR
Rachel	20	F		AR
George	18	M	Farmer	AR
Jane	15	F		AR
Louisa	9	F		AR
Turner, William	10	M		AR
Samuel	6	M		AR

HOPKINS COUNTY, TEXAS

Name	Age	Sex	Occupation	Birthplace
King, Norris	30	M	Farmer	TN
Lavinia	28	F		TN
Mary	6	F		TX
Robert	1	M		TX
Graves, Robert	33	M	Farmer	TN
Soprona Ann	26	F		TN
Martha V.	7	F		TX
Joseph N.	5	M		TX
Nancy J.	3	F		TX
Mary E.	6/12	F		TX
Paterson, Charles	18	M	Farmer	TN
Groce, Benjamin J.	28	M	Black Smith	TN
Mary	24	F		AR
Matilda J.	5	F		AR
Louisa A.	3	F		TX
Minta E.	1	F		TX
Findley, Lewis	25	M	Farmer	MO
Letticia	35	F		TN
Katharine	65	F		VA
Edmund	63	M		KY
Netherly, Syntha	18	F		MO
Findley, Edmund	6/12	M		TX
Rollins, E. A.	37	M	Farmer	NC
Delila	34	F		TN
James C.	15	M	Farmer	TN
Mary E.	12	F		TN
John H.	8	M		TX
Harrison	6	M		TX
Berry F.	4	M		TX
William D.	2	M		TX
Martha J.	1	F		TX
Hill, James	23	M	Saddler	AL
Sary Ann	22	F		TN
Annia Jane	3	F		TX
Young, Thomas J.	33	M	Farmer	TN
Elizabeth E.	32	F		TN
Pleasant P.	5	M		AR
Josephus	4	M		AR
Thomas B.	2	M		AR
Manervy E.	1	F		AR
Gilbreth, James H.	17	M	Farmer	MO
Murry, Samuel	48	M	Teacher	VA
Elizabeth J.	27	F		TN
Thomas J.	14	M		AR
Andrew J.	13	M		AR
Mary J.	11	F		AR
Virginia	5	F		AR
Margaret A. S.	3	F		AR
Victory	1	F		TX
Russell, Henry	29	M	Farmer	AR
Clarissa	26	F		TN
Margaret J.	7	F		AR
Delila E.	1	F		TX
Groce, George W.	58	M	Farmer	TN
Martha J.	52	F		NC
James	30	M		TN
Matilda	17	F		IL
Mary	14	F		TN
Sary C.	10	F		AR
George W. McGee	7	M		AR
Riley	4	M		AR
Hill, Thomas	52	M	Farmer	GA
Matilda	46	F		GA
Julian	17	F		TN
Abner R.	15	M	Farmer	TN
William M.	13	M		TX
Martha J.	11	F		TX
Mary Ann	9	F		TX
George R.	6	M		TX
Hill, Joshua B.	40	M	Farmer	TN
Syntha	37	F		GA
Abner A.	14	M		TN

(continued)

Name	Age	Sex	Occupation	Birthplace
Hill, Elizabeth	12	F		TX
Jane	10	F		TX
Sary B.	8	F		TX
Eliza Ann	6	F		TX
William F.	4	M		TX
Malissa(?)	2	M		TX
No name	5/12	M		TX
Hill, Abner	60	M	Farmer	TN
Nancy	46	F		KY
Bailey, William W.	21	M	Farmer	AL
Mansel	17	M	Farmer	TN
Robert	14	M		TN
Sary	13	F		TX
George	10	M		TX
Martha	8	F		TX
Helen	6	F		TX
Deal, John	25	M	Farmer	TN
Mary	45	F		GA
Martha	21	F		KY
Calvin S.	18	M		TN
Samuel W.	15	M	Farmer	TN
Benjamin M.	10	M		TN
William Lewis	8	M		TN
Birdwell, Henry	24	M	Farmer	AL
Syntha C.	20	F		TN
Thomas M.	3/12	M		TX
Barnes, William	31	M	Farmer	TN
Rebecca	31	F		TN
William J.	9	M		MO
John B.	8	M		MO
Marian C.	6	M		MS
Jasper L.	4	M		AR
Virginia	2	F		TX
Tennessee	1	F		TX
Wagoner, Martha	44	F		TN
Daniel	22	M	Farmer	TN
John	19	M	Farmer	TN
Luther	18	M	Farmer	MO
Martha J.	13	F		MO
Elizabeth	10	F		MO
Mary M.	8	F		TX
Sary F.	6	F		TX
Bonapart	4	M		TX
Williams, William W.	27	M	Farmer	TN
Lucy	27	F		AL
Martha	4	F		TN
James C.	1	M		TN
Jourdan, James	60	M	Farmer	SC
Anna	39	F		NC
Daniel	21	M	Farmer	IL
Sary J.	16	F		TN
James A.	14	M		TN
Mary F.	2	F		TX
Voss, John	42	M	Farmer	TN
Lucinda	39	F		TN
Elizabeth J.	16	F		MS
Milina C.	14	F		MS
Lucinda M.	10	F		MS
Malvina	8	F		MS
George C.	6	M		MS
John M.	3	M		TX
Susana P.	6/12	F		TX
next to:				
Voss, William	72	M	None	NC
Elizabeth	70	F		NC
next to:				
Voss, Eli	25	M	Farmer	TN
Francis	23	F		??
Ratliff, David	45	M	Farmer	NC
Malinda	36	F		TN
Elizabeth J.	19	F		TN
Angeline	18	F		TN
Isabella	16	F		TN
Sarah	14	F		MS
John W.	10	M		MS
Henderson, Elihu	26	M	Farmer	TN

Name		Age	Sex	Occupation	Birthplace
Click, Calvin		35	M	Farmer	TN
Sally		34	F		TN
Harvey		11	M		TX
Martha		9	F		TX
Emily		7	F		TX
Rufus		5	M		TX
Cloud, Joseph		47	M	Farmer	TN
Nancy		46	F		TN
Frank		22	M	Farmer	AL
John		21	M	Farmer	TN
Mary J.		18	F		TN
Emeline		16	F		TN
Eliza		14	F		TN
Sarah		12	F		TN
Jacob		10	M		TN
Lucy A.		5	F		MS
Morgan, Thomas		27	M	Farmer	TN
Marion		21	F		NC
Elizabeth		13	F		TX
Malvina		5	F		TX
Rufus A.		2	M		TX
Leaky, William		36	M	Farmer	IRE
Nancy R.		20	F		TN
Martha		6/12	F		TX
Small, A. M.		43	M	Farmer	TN
Mary		41	F		TN
Tolbert		17	M	Farmer	TN
Lucinda		15	M	Farmer	MS
Sophronia		13	F		MS
America		12	F		MS
Campbell		9	M		MS
George W.		6	M		MS
Amos T.	(Twin)	3	M		MS
Mary M.	(Twin)	3	F		MS
Posey, L. P.		57	M	Farmer	GA
Sarah		43	F		SC
Eli M.		22	M	Black Smith	TN
Edwin		20	M	Farmer	MO
Emily		17	F		MO
Polly		16	F		MO
Martha		12	F		MO
Bethane		10	F		MO
Susanah		9	F		MO
Louisa		8	F		MO
Leander		6	M		MO
Sarah E.		4	F		MO
Oliver		3	M		TX
Lindley, John		38	M	Farmer	KY
Ruth		29	F		KY
Redellum(?)		14	M		MO
Clary Ann		10	F		MO
Alcy		8	F		MO
Lewis, Richard		18	M	Farmer	TN
Barret, Thomas		40	M	Farmer	NC
Alcy		23	F		KY
Flavius J.		14	M		TN
Ellen M.		12	F		TN
Monroe T.		8	M		TN
Leonidas C.		4	M		MO
Marlina E. J.		3	F		MO
Thomas J.		9/12	M		TX
Flewharty, Mathew		52	M	Farmer	MD
Hariet		40	F		SC
Robert		16	M	Farmer	SC
William		12	M		TN
Thomas		9	M		AR
Lucy		3	F		AR
Moore, William		38	M	Farmer	AL
Mary		20	F		TN
John		19	M	Farmer	MS
Nancy		13	F		MS
Sary		10	F		AL
Jane		6/12	F		TX
Priest, Christopher		32	M	Farmer	KY
Lydia		25	F		TN
Alsey		54	F		NC
Solomon		24	M	Farmer	TN
Alsey		14	F		TN
Alcy Jane		6	F		MO
Calvin L-----		4	M		TX
Sary Ann		2	F		TX
Posey, Silas		31	M	Farmer	MO
Nancy		22	F		TN
Lucretia		7	F		MO
Sary		6	F		MO
Louisa		5	F		MO
Polly		3	F		TX
Not named		4/12	F		TX
Vaden, William		44	M	Farmer	TN
Lodwick J.		18	M	Farmer	TN
Elizabeth		16	F		TN
William		14	M		TN
Matilda		13	F		TN
Katharine		11	F		TN
Martha L.		8	F		TN
Leonidas		6	M		TN
Mahala		1	F		TX
Vaden, Loderick		33	M	Farmer	TN
Emaline		30	F		SC
Mary		7	F		MS
Allen		5	M		MS
Woodson		2	M		TX
D'Spain, Benjamin		45	M	Farmer	KY
Narcissa		48	F		SC
Martha A.		18	F		TN
Mary A.		16	F		TN
Julia A.		11	F		MS
Nancy		9	F		TN
Abbot, Francis		23	M	Farmer	TN
Margaret		28	F		TN
Sarah Ann		5	F		MS
Vernetta		1	F		TX
Ewing, Wilson		50	M	Farmer	TN
Hannah		47	F		KY
Jno.		26	M	Farmer	AL
Andrew		22	M	Farmer	AL
James		20	M	Farmer	TN
Felix		19	M	Farmer	TN
Emily		17	F		TN
Henry		13	M		TX
Travis		11	M		TX
Thadeus		10	M		TX
Hetty		8	F		TX
Mary		6	F		TX
Edly		4	M		TX
Crowder, Elizabeth		25	F		TN
James O.		4	M		TX
Louisa		3	F		TX
William L.		1	M		TX
Hamilton, Thomas R.		22	M	Farmer	TN
Mary Jane		19	F		KY
Margaret O.		1	F		TX
Hamilton, Mary		48	F		TN
Perry		17	M	Farmer	TN
Margaret		15	F		TN
Alexander		11	M		TX
Daniel		8	M		TX
Robinet, Jno. J.		32	M	Black Smith	KY
Averilla		25	F		TN
William D.		12	M		TX
Mary C.		4	F		TX
George		2	M		TX
Hamilton, Jos.		29	M	Farmer	TN
Isabella		26	F		NC
Averilla		7	F		TX
Darcas		6	F		TX
Mary		3	F		TX
Amanda		6/12	F		TX

HOPKINS COUNTY, TEXAS

Name	Age	Sex	Occupation	Birthplace
Short, Jno.	28	M	Farmer	KY
Elvira	22	F		TN
Jernigan, Felix	25	M	Farmer	TN
Asa	3	M		TX
Jackson, Josiah H.	29	M	Farmer	KY
Sarah A.	25	F		TN
Lavina	8	F		TX
Jane	5	F		TX
Elijah G.	3	M		TX
Eliza A.	4/12	F		TX
Williams, Ephraim	30	M	Farmer	TN
America	28	F		VA
Francis G.	3	M		TX
Mary	1	F		TX
Williams, C. A.	35	M	Farmer	TN
Alsey	25	F		TN
Cordelia	3	F		TX
Nancy	6/12	F		TX
Bills, Isaac W.	23	M	Farmer	TN
Charlotte	28	F		KY
Josephine B.	1	F		TX
Collins, James	39	M	Farmer	KY
Elizabeth	30	F		TN
Mary M.	12	F		TN
Susan C. M.	7	F		TN
Delitha	5	F		TN
Hunt, John	25	M	Farmer	KY
Nancy	35	F		TN
Frances	11	F		MO
William	8	M		MO
Hooten, James	30	M	Farmer	TN
Susan	22	F		TN
Andrew J.	10	M		TN
William A.	8	M		TN
Robert C.	6	M		TN
Thomas W.	4	M		TN
Martha A.	1	F		TX
Cox, Edward	40	M	Farmer	TN
Hannah	36	F		KY
Alfred	16	M	Farmer	MO
Sary E.	13	F		MO
Jerucia	10	F		MO
Jane	7	F		MO
Lucy C.	4	F		MO
Ollizary	2	F		MO
Zilpha M.	2/12	F		TX
Bills, D. B.	53	M	Black Smith	NC
Martha	52	F		NC
Martha A. C.	12	F		TN
Bills, Jonathan E.	28	M	Farmer	TN
Erilda	26	F		KY
Daniel C.	3	M		TN
Williams, James W. J.	15	M	Farmer	IN
Allard, Aron	50	M	Farmer	AL
Polly	50	F		TN
John	15	M	Farmer	MO
Aron	13	M		MO
George W.	4	M		MO
Armstrong, Jesse	61	M	Farmer	NC
Hannah	33	F		TN
Hugh	26	M	Farmer	IL
James	13	M		AR
Aron	7	M		MO
Jane	14	F		TN
Bird	12	M		TN
Martha	1	F		AR
Robison, James C.	26	M	Farmer	KY
Mary Ann	23	F		TN
Malvina L.	4	F		TX
Katharine	1	F		TX
Kaufon, Lorenzo D.	25	M	Farmer	TN
Sarah Ann	25	F		TN
Franklin L.	8	M		MS
James C. C.	6	M		MS
Thomas W.	4	M		MS
Robert M.	3	M		TX
Venetta L.	9/12	F		TX
Craig, Jno. B.	56	M		NC
Nancy	35	F		TN
John	17	M	Farmer	AL
Darcas A.	10	F		TX
Mary T.	8	F		TX
Thomas B. D.	4	M		TX
Sarah J.	2	F		TX
Russell, George	49	M	Farmer	NC
Polly	44	F		TN
Washington	20	M	Farmer	IL
Fanny J.	16	F		IL
Elizabeth	15	F		IL
Sarah Ann	13	F		IL
Evaline	10	F		IL
Matilda	8	F		TX
John	4	M		TX
Elmore, A. W.	22	M	Farmer	MO
Henrietta	21	F		TN
William A. M.	1	M		TX
Waid, George	46	M	Farmer	TN
Thomas	18	M	Farmer	MO
James S.	13	M		MO
George	11	M		MO
Blackwell, Joel	44	M		SC
Jane	45	F		TN
Joel P.	21	M	Farmer	IL
Page	19	M	Farmer	IL
Lucinda	16	F		IL
Martha E.	14	F		IL
Erastus	12	M		IL
Sarah Jane	9	F		IL
Polly Ann	6	F		IL
Oxford, Claiborne	44	M	Farmer	NC
Louisa	40	F		TN
George W.	20	M	Farmer	AR
Brinkley	17	M	Farmer	AR
Nancy	15	F		AR
Mary J.	13	F		AR
Abel	10	M		AR
Claiborne	8	M		AR
Delilah	5	F		TX
Sarah E.	1	F		TX
Vezier, Peter	59	M	Farmer	VA
Abigail	49	F		PA
Peter	26	M	Farmer	AL
Fulsom, Elry P.	23	M	Farmer	TN
Julia Ann	20	F		TN
Jefferson M.	13	M		TX
Jno.	11	M		TX
Nancy Jane	8	F		TX
Prince, Thomas	45	M	Farmer	TN
Nancy	40	F		AL
Levinia	22	F		AR
Clark	19	M	Farmer	AR
Thompson	16	M	Farmer	AR
Albert	10	M		AR
Yates, William G.	29	M	Farmer	TN
Julian	24	F		TN
Mary Avis	1	F		TX
Russel, James	45	M	Farmer	NC
Frances	45	F		VA
George	20	M	Farmer	TN
Nancy Ann	17	F		IL
Malvina	15	F		IL
William P.	12	M		IL
Jno. W.	10	M		TX
Watson, Jno. A.	9	M		KY

HOPKINS COUNTY, TEXAS

Name	Age	Sex	Occupation	Birthplace
McDonald, Madison	32	M	Farmer	TN
Patsy	25	F		MO
Terrill, John	55	M	Farmer	KY
Zachariah	23	M	Farmer	KY
Elizabeth	17	F		IL
Hero C.	16	F		TN
George	7	M		IL
Herron, Ferdinand	50	M	Farmer	NC
Samantha	31	F		TN
Lotty Ann	17	F		MO
Berry O.	13	M		MO
Lewis	11	M		MO
James M.	9	M		MO
Silas	7	M		AR
Abraham	3	M		TX
Hemby, J. W.	24	M	Farmer	MO
Carter, John	49	M	Farmer	TN
Bottoms, Matilda	29	F		TN
Nancy	13	F		TN
Thomas	10	M		TN
Elmira	8	F		TN
Louisa	6	F		AR
Ratten, Daniel	27	M	Farmer	IL
Russian, Abel B.	32	M	Farmer	(E)TN
Lucinda	28	F		(E)TN
Sary	9	F		TN
William	7	M		AR
Philip C.	5	M		TX
Jonathan	2/12	M		TX
Barcler, Andrew	35	M	Farmer	MO
Cela	27	F		TN
Hugh	7	M		MO
Jane	5	F		MO
Beller, Allen	25	M	Farmer	TN
Martha	32	F		TN
Elizabeth	12	F		AR
James	11	M		AR
Sarah	10	F		AR
William C.	6	M		AR
Nancy	4	F		AR
Samuel	2	M		TX
George W.	1	M		TX
Neely, Green leaf	43	M	Farmer	VT
Nancy	36	F		TN
Sarah J.	18	F		IN
Mathew H.	14	M		IN
Mary Ann	12	F		IN
Randolph	10	M		IN
Harison L.	7	M		IN
Reubin W.	3	M		IN
Hanah	4/12	F		TX
Kates, James	27	M	Farmer	TN
Sarah A.	23	F		TN
Malinda J.	7	F		AR
July Ann	4	F		AR
Cassy C.	2	F		AR
Burkham, James	45	M	Farmer	KY
Matilda	35	F		TN
Elliott	17	M	Farmer	TX
Charles	15	M	Farmer	TX
William ?.	12	M		TX
Thursay Ann	9	F		TX
Thomas	6	M		TX
Voss, George	48	M	Farmer	TN
Mary	46	F		TN
Louisa M.	19	F		TN
Calvin H.	17	M	Farmer	TN
Mary A.	15	F		TN
Mealla, Henry	37	M	Farmer	TN
Clarissa	35	F		TN
Mary E.	10	F		MS
Elmyra	6	F		MS

(continued)

Name	Age	Sex	Occupation	Birthplace
Mealla, Ely	5	M		MS
George C.	3	M		MS
James H.	2	M		TX
Weaver, Linsley H.	28	M	Farmer	TN
Elizabeth Ann	17	F		AL
Sowell, William H.	28	M	Farmer	TN
Caroline	26	F		AR
James	20	M	Farmer	AL
Alfred L.	17	M	Farmer	AL
Mary F.	7	F		AR
Nancy E.	5	F		AR
Jones J.	2	M		AR
Martha Ann	2/12	F		TX
Clifton, Nathaniel	41	M	Farmer	TN
Polly	25	F		IL
Mary J.	15	F		TN
Nancy E.	14	F		MO
George H.	11	M		MO
John H.	6	M		TX
Daniel W.	4	M		TX
Amanda	3	F		TX
Mariah	1	F		TX
Weaver, Green	54	M	Farmer	NC
Nancy	27	F		SC
John	25	M	Farmer	TN
Shadrack	20	M	Farmer	IL
William ?. G.	18	M	Farmer	IL
Mary J.	8	F		TX
Samuel H.	6	M		TX
Shephard, David	8/12	M		TX
Withe, Charles	19	M	Farmer	GA
Merony, Edmonia	10	F		MO
Ward, James	58	M	Black Smith	SC
Elizabeth	51	F		KY
Farell, Nancy	31	F		IL
P--kins(Perkins), Allen	27	M	Black Smith	TN
Ward, John	20	M	Farmer	IN
Iry	18	M	Farmer	IN
Narcissa	14	F		MO
Elias L.	10	M		TX
William E.	7	M		TX
Withers, Steven E.	31	M	Farmer	TN
Sarah	28	F		IL
Susan P.	8	F		TX
Redly R.	6	M		TX
Jasper M.	4	M		TX
James A.	2	M		TX
Nancy	6/12	M		TX
Grey, Hanson L.	30	M	Farmer	MO
Julian	26	F		TN
John	4	M		TX
Sarah E.	2	F		TX
Mars, Franklin	30	M	Farmer	??
Juliann	28	F		GA
Ragin, Berry	30	M		TN
Mary Elizabeth	11	F		IL
James H.	9	M		MO
John W. (Twin)	5/12	M		TX
Eliza V. (Twin)	5/12	F		TX
Webb, Benjamin	46	M	Farmer	TN
Catherine	39	F		TN
John	17	M	Farmer	MO
William	15	M	Farmer	MO
George W.	11	M		MO
Robert	9	M		MO
Jacob	7	M		MO
Sally Ann	4	F		TX
Martha	2	F		TX
Cheek, Edly	29	M	Farmer	TN
Margaret	31	F		IL
Vincent, Margarette	12	F		MO
Sarah E.	10	F		MO
Roda	7	F		MO
Hugh	7	M		MO
James	2	M		TX

Name	Age	Sex	Occupation	Birthplace
Clendenon, Daniel F.	50	M	Farmer	VA
Susanah	34	F		TN
John	15	M		MO
James	11	M		MO
Sarah	8	F		MO
Elizabeth	3	F		TX
Robert	8/12	M		TX
Falk, Elizabeth	48	F		TN
Paulina E.	18	F		MO
Lucy E.	16	F		MO
Edward M.	13	M		MO
John J.	10	M		MO
Mary J.	8	F		MO
Elisha E.	6	M		AR
Daniel W.	3	M		TX
Borin, Moses	35	M	Farmer	TN
Nancy	32	F		TN
Thomas	9	M		TX
Nancy E.	2	F		TX
Lee, Robert	34	M	Farmer	IL
Phebe	32	F		TN
John	12	M		MO
Jeremiah	7	M		MO
Martha	4	F		TX
Isaac	1	M		TX
Williams, Hansford T.	28	M	Farmer	TN
Polly	26	F		TN
Mary B.	4	F		AR
Elzada H.	2	F		AR
Syntha Ann	6/12	F		TX
Crofford, Marshel	27	M	Farmer	KY
Rebecca	46	F		TN
Thomas B.	18	M	Farmer	AR
Martha	16	F		AR
Amanda	14	F		AR
Caroline	11	F		AR
Charles	8	M		AR
Carter, Thomas	25	M	Farmer	AR
Nancy E.	18	F		TN
Tollet, Elija	40	M	Farmer	TN
Sary	28	F		AR
Lynch, Experience	70	F		MS
Tollet, William	9	M		TX
Manervy	7	F		TX
Margaret	5	F		TX
Sary Susan	3	F		TX
John W.	6/12	M		TX
Williams, Keeland	57	M	Farmer	(E)TN
Mary	55	F		TN
Alexander	12	M		AR
Hampton	10	M		AR
Williams, James	31	M	Farmer	TN
Samantha	29	F		AL
Tamazine	2	F		TX
Proctor, Thomas	39	M	Farmer	MO
Elizabeth	40	F		TN
Mary Ann	16	F		MO
John	14	M		MO
Mitchel	12	M		MO
Richard	8	M		MO
William	6	M		TX
James	3	M		TX
Charles	1	M		TX
Deaton, John	55	M	Farmer	NC
Sary	45	F		IL
Elias	18	M	Farmer	TN
John C.	14	M		TN
Sary C.	12	F		TN
Sylvester	11	M		TX
Victory	8	F		TX
Jennings, Stephen	32	M	Farmer	TN

(continued)

Name	Age	Sex	Occupation	Birthplace
Jennings, Barby	29	F		NC
William J.	9	M		TN
James R.	7	M		MS
Stephen A.	4	M		TX
Nancy M.	1	F		TX
Welch, Thomas	64	M	Farmer	NC
Hetty	61	F		SC
Thomas L.	23	M	Farmer	TN
Emily	18	F		TN
Haney H.	16	F		TN
Welch, Levi	34	M	Farmer	TN
Sary	23	F		AL
Mary	2	F		TX
Aseneth	6/12	F		TX
Garret, William H.	23	M	Farmer	AL
Lucinda	24	F		TN
Clifton, Wilson	48	M	Farmer	NC
Sary	39	F		TN
Elvira D.	20	F		TN
Mary S.	19	F		TN
James A. H.	16	M	Farmer	TN
Theophilus	13	M		TN
John D. C.	12	M		TN
Thomas J. W.	9	M		MO
Wilson A. B.	7	M		MO
Mary N.	4	F		TX
William F. M.	6/12	M		TX
Vandoer, George	28	M	Farmer	TN
Hannah	36	F		TN
Nancy J.	11	F		TN
Mariam S.	9	F		TN
Martha E.	6	F		AR
Melinda E.	4	F		TX
Shores, Wiley B.	40	M	Farmer	GA
Frances	46	F		KY
William G.	17	M	Farmer	TN
Thomas G.	14	M	Farmer	IL
Sophrona J.	12	F		MO
Amanda R.	9	F		MO
Elizabeth M.	6	F		MO
Curly, James	40	M	Teacher	GA
Watters, John L.	39	M	Farmer	KY
Emaline	25	F		TN
Mary E.	14	F		LA
Ruthy A.	2	F		TX
Narcissa J.	3/12	F		TX
McRee, James H. H.	39	M	Farmer	NC
Nancy L.	32	F		AL
Edward H.	32	F(M)	Doctor	TN
Sally	6	F		MS
William F.	3	M		TX
James F.	9/12	M		TX
Ketrand, John M.	21	M	Farmer	TN
Killgore, Martin	27	M	Farmer	TN
Elizabeth J.	18	F		AL
Woodard, Mary	43	F		NC
Josiah	15	M	Farmer	AL
Margret A.	13	F		AL
Richard T.	10	M		MS
Wiles R.	7	M		MS
John D.	4	M		MS
Mary Ann	6/12	F		TX
James R.	6/12	M		TX
Armstrong, Matthew	39	M	Farmer	KY
America	29	F		IN
Permelia J.	1	F		TX
Martin, Andrew J.	34	M	Farmer	TN
Sary	30	F		TN
Elizabeth	14	F		TN
James M.	12	M		TN
William	10	M		TN
Margaret F.	8	F		TN
Rufus A.	4	M		LA
Andrew J.	1	M		TX

HOPKINS COUNTY, TEXAS

Name	Age/Sex/Occupation	Birthplace
Martin, Zadok	30 M Farmer	TN
Eleanor	38 F	SC
Thomas	16 M Farmer	TN
James	13 M	TN
William H.	11 M	TN
Mary	9 F	TN
John	6 M	TN
Green	5 M	TN
William	4 M	LA
America J.	2 F	TX
Blackman, Levi	28 M Farmer	TN
Nancy	25 F	TN
William H.	12 M	TN
Andrew J.	11 M	TN
James P.	4 M	TN
Martha J.	3 F	TN
Parton, Elizabeth	54 F	NC
Ann	25 F	NC
James L.	23 M Farmer	NC
Delila	19 F	TN
Nancy	18 F	TN
Mary	15 F	TN
Burton, Sherod	40 M Wagon Maker	KY
Mary C.	18 F	TN
Miller, Henry M.	18 M Farmer	TN
Sary M.	24 F	TN
Allasabina	3/12 F	TX
Willis, Benjamin J.	30 M Farmer	TN
Ally Frances	28 F	AL
William T.	9 M	AL
Caroline	7 F	AL
Elizabeth J.	4 F	TX
Pierce, Franklin G.	26 M Farmer	TN
Luranda	19 F	IL
William	1 M	TX
Harris, Nathaniel	45 M Farmer	NC
Elizabeth	49 F	NC
William C.	23 M Farmer	TN
Elisha G.	14 M	TN
Louisa J.	11 F	TN
John B.	8 M	TX
Bishop, Oliver	36 M Farmer	TN
Margaret	39 F	TN
Milly S.	16 F	TN
David	15 M Farmer	TN
Charles	12 M	TN
Robert G.	8 M	TX
Frances	4 F	TX
Oliver H.	2 M	TX
McCartney, Barclay H.	22 M Farmer	(E)TN
Elizabeth	20 F	TN
Elizabeth	30 F	TN
Hance	23 M Farmer	TN
McNiel, Larkin	13 M	AL
McCartney, Nancy C.	12 F	TN
George	10 M	AL
Mary	6 F	AL
John	6/12 M	TX
James	6/12 M	TX
Ringo, Samuel	22 M Farmer	MO
Nancy H.	19 F	TN
Westerman, Daniel	26 M Farmer	TN
Hannah M.	28 F	TN
Esther S.	4 F	TN
Westerman, N. B.	22 M Farmer	TN
Frances M.	23 F	TN
James S.	3 M	TX
Samuel J.	1 M	TX
Hopper, Seaborn	47 M Farmer	GA
Elizabeth	42 F	TN

(continued)

Name	Age/Sex/Occupation	Birthplace
Fields, Mariam	19 F	AR
William J.	13 M	AR
Elizabeth	11 F	AR
Hopper, Alexander J.	8 M	AR
Gustavus C.	6 M	TX
Erastus	3 M	TX
Lafayette H.	6/12 M	TX

HOUSTON COUNTY, TEXAS

Name	Age/Sex/Occupation	Birthplace
Thomas, Joseph W.	48 M Mechanic	GA
Elizabeth	49 F	GA
Groomes, Elizabeth	17 F	TN
George	15 M (Montgomery Co.)	TX
Alexander	11 M (Montgomery Co.)	TX
Medlock, Thomas	42 M Farmer	SC
Rebecca	33 F	TN
Charles	16 M	IN
Mary A.	7 F	MO
Thomas R.	6 M	MO
John C.	4 M (Houston Co.)	TX
Rebecca	2 F (Houston Co.)	TX
Miller, Mary J.	13 F	TN
Medlock, Henry	1 M (Houston Co.)	TX
Glenn, Nathan	54 M Farmer	VA
Mary L.	51 F	VA
Thomas J.	16 M	TN
John M.	13 M	TN
Steward, James	24 M Farmer	TN
Lucy A.	24 F	TN
William E.	2 M (Anderson Co.)	TX
Nancy J.	3/12 F (Houston Co.)	TX
Steward, Joseph	35 M Farmer	AL
Margarett	31 F	TN
Hariett	12 F	TN
Elizabeth	9 F	TN
David	6 M	TN
Lucinda	4 F	TN
Minerva	3 F (Houston Co.)	TX
Valentine	3/12 M (Houston Co.)	TX
Flippo, John	35 M Farmer	TN
Nancy	30 F	MS
Elizabeth C.	7 F	LA
Wheeler, Elijah	36 M Farmer	TN
Margarett	24 F	MO
Elmira	11 F (Houston Co.)	TX
Edward	10 M (Houston Co.)	TX
Jane	7 F (Houston Co.)	TX
George	4/12 M (Houston Co.)	TX
Hartley, Eliza	32 F	TN
Samuel	18 M Farmer	MS
William	6 M (Montgomery Co.)	TX
Bunyard, Larkin L.	39 M Mechanic	NC
Franks	33 F	TN
Adeline O.	14 F	TN
Mary J.	12 F	TN
William C.	10 M	TN
James B.	8 M	TN
Hariett	6 F	TN
Daniel J.	4 M (Houston Co.)	TX
Ruddell, Isaac	39 M Farmer	MO
Mary	24 F	TN
James	8 M (Houston Co.)	TX
Elizabeth	6 F (Houston Co.)	TX
John	4 M (Houston Co.)	TX
Benjamin	3 M (Houston Co.)	TX
Jackson	1 M (Houston Co.)	TX
Rozell, Milton	21 M Farmer	TN
Henrietta	16 F	TX
Duren, Jesse	46 M Farmer	SC
Margarett	33 F	TN
Nancy	18 F	AL
Susan	16 F	AL
Benjamin F.	15 M	AL

(continued)

HOUSTON COUNTY, TEXAS

Duren, William	13	M		AL
Phillip	11	M		AL
Margarett	9	F		AL
Caroline	7	F		AL
Lavenia	5	F		MS
Mary	3	F	(Red River Co.)	TX
Wall, Charles L.	35	M		TN
Eliza	24	F		TX
Josephine E.	4	F	(Harrison Co.)	TX
Earls, Mary	20	F		LA
Bodenhamer, Peter	10	M		TN
Bodenhamer, John W.	57	M	Farmer	NC
Mary	39	F		TN
William W.	16	M		TN
Hugh C.	14	M		TN
Sarah C.	12	F		TN
Mary E.	9	F		TN
Charity A.	6	F		TN
John P.	1	M	(Houston Co.)	TX
Franklin S.	36	M		NC
Jones, Jesse R.	61	M	Farmer	SC
Hannah	58	F		GA
Levenia	18	F		TN
Francis M.	17	M		TN
Jesse	16	M		TN
Elizabeth A.	14	F		TN
Martin V.	12	M		MS
Roberts, Isaac H.	27	M	Farmer	TN
Eliza D.	22	F		LA
John D.	6	M	(Houston Co.)	TX
Martha P.	4	F	(Houston Co.)	TX
Sarah E.	2	F	(Houston Co.)	TX
Edins, John S.	29	M	Farmer	AR
Amanda G.	21	F		TN
John J.	3	M	(Houston Co.)	TX
Mary C.	4/12	F	(Houston Co.)	TX
Brown, Ruben	45	M	Farmer	GA
Sarah	45	F		TN
Eliza	16	F		TX
John	13	M	(Houston Co.)	TX
Parkes, Mary A.	6	F	(Houston Co.)	TX
Whitaker, Meriday W.	49	M	Farmer	TN
Rachael	49	F		TN
George B.	28	M		AL
Lewis	25	M		TN
Martha	15	F		TN
James L.	13	M		TN
Meriday	6	M	(Houston Co.)	TX
Blair, John	44	M	Farmer	TN
Malinda	35	F		KY
Sarah A. E.	14	F		TN
Stephen J.	13	M		TN
William J.	11	M		MS
John K.	9	M		MS
Hannah C.	7	F		MS
Nancy J.	5	F		MS
Mary M.	4	F		MS
Grounds, George	46	M	Farmer	MO
Catherine	42	F		TN
Louisa	21	F		TX
Lemuel	19	M		TX
George	17	M		TX
Ann	15	F		TX
Catherine	12	F		LA
Eliza	10	F		LA
William J.	8	M		LA
Joshua	5	M	(Houston Co.)	TX
Joseph	2	M	(Houston Co.)	TX
John W.	23	M	Farmer	LA
Cintha A.	18	F		LA
Catherine	7/12	F	(Houston Co.)	TX
Clark, Pleasant	48	M	Farmer	TN
Margarett	45	F		TN
John	13	M		AL

Goolsbey, Thomas J.	35	M	Farmer	GA
Catherine L.	17	F		TN
Clark, Thomas B.	21	M	Farmer	AL
Sarah E.	20	F		TN
William V. R.	1	M	(Houston Co.)	TX
Dickerson, William	54	M	Farmer	TN
Jane	43	F		KY
Van Ransuler G.	21	M		AL
William B.	15	M		MS
Derias A.	10	M	(Houston Co.)	TX
Arthusa M.	11	F	(Houston Co.)	TX
Areta C.	5	F	(Houston Co.)	TX
John H.	2	M	(Houston Co.)	TX
Huntsman, James F. B.	19	M	Farmer	TN
Sarah	21	F		AL
Allen, Clinton	39	M	Farmer	NC
Nancy	37	F		TN
Harnell(Harrell), Keziah	17	F		AL
Pond, Carlile	32	M		AL
Martha	26	F		TN
Joshua	2	M	(Leon Co.)	TX
Mordica	1	M	(Walker Co.)	TX
Grist, Margarett	7	F	(Grimes Co.)	TX
Martha	7	F	(Grimes Co.)	TX
Rebecca	4	F	(Grimes Co.)	TX
Cornwell, Matilda	41	F		VA
John	14	M		TN
Brent, Sarah	60	F		NC
Peter E.	17	M		TN
Innman, Joseph H.	34	M	Physician	TN
Jennett H.	24	F		MO
Benjamin R.	2	M	(Houston Co.)	TX
Cristene A.	1/12	F	(Houston Co.)	TX
Davenport, John	46	M	Farmer	TN
Ellen	24	F		TN
Mary	20	F		AL
Sarah	18	F		AL
Mahala	16	F		AL
James	12	M		MO
Thomas	10	M		MO
Missouri	5	F	(Houston Co.)	TX
Martha	1	F	(Houston Co.)	TX
Burton, William H.	33	M	Farmer	LA
Constance	33	F		TN
John J.	10	M		AL
Elizabeth J.	8	F	(Houston Co.)	TX
Samuel H.	4	M	(Houston Co.)	TX
Nancy J.	2	F	(Houston Co.)	TX
Adams, Thomas J.	28	M		AL

Town of Crockett

Hefflin, James T.	34	M	Mechanic	TN
Mary C.	30	F		AL
Franklin O.	4	M		AL
Ryley V.	2	M	(Houston Co.)	TX
Randolph, Cyrus H.	32	M	Lawyer	IL
Martha	27	F		TN
Laura	4/12	F	(Houston Co.)	TX
Wood, Charles	38	M	Physician	MA
Margarett	29	F		TN
Martin, Georgianna	5	F		MS
McConner, John	28	M	Black Smith	IRE
Mary J.	17	F		TN
Collard, James H.	34	M	M.E. Minister	MO
Julia L.	32	F		MO
Edward O.	12	M	(Walker Co.)	TX
William E.	10	M	(Walker Co.)	TX
Lousina E.	9	F	(Walker Co.)	TX
Sarah E.	7	F	(Walker Co.)	TX
Ann E.	5	F	(Walker Co.)	TX

(continued)

Name	Age	Sex	Occupation / Birthplace	State
Collard, Margrett	3	F	(Walker Co.)	TX
Elijah	25	M	Mechanic	MO
Mayfield, Samuel B.	25	M	Clerk	TN
James, Washington M.	24	M		AL
Long, John	57	M	Hotel Keeper	TN
Elizabeth	62	F		NC
Hearly, Andrew	33	M	Lawyer	SC
Love, Andrew C.	50	M	Physician	TN
Peck, William	27	M	School Teacher	TN
Sarah V.	27	F		TN
Lee, John	42	M	Carpenter	NC
Long, William E.	34	M		TN
Martha	30	F		LA
John	4	M	(Houston Co.)	TX
Monroe, Armstead J.	32	M	Mechanic	VA
Rachal J.	22	F		TN
Sarah J.	2	F	(Houston Co.)	TX
Elizabeth M.	2/12	F	(Houston Co.)	TX
Bennett, George E. W.	21	M	Clerk	NC
Kinchoffer, John H.	39	M	Mechanic	IRE
Catharine	40	F		AL
Sarah	7	F	(Houston Co.)	TX
Elizabeth	5	F	(Houston Co.)	TX
Logan, Solomon	10	M	(Houston Co.)	TX
Warden, Moses	34	M	Clerk	TN
Edmiston, Mathew B.	33	M		TN
Mary A.	28	F		AL
Hendrix, Thomas D.	35	M		KY
Louisa	27	F		KY
Elizabeth	5	F	(Houston Co.)	TX
Carey A.	1	F	(Houston Co.)	TX
Taylor, William	19	M		TX
Hall, John L.	40	M	Hotel Keeper	MD
Lucinda L.	31	F		LA
Nancy B.	5	F	(Houston Co.)	TX
Silvester V.	2	M	(Houston Co.)	TX
Montgomery, John	61	M	Brick Mason	SCO
Bennett, Joseph	38	M		SC
Wall, Franklin	20	M	Clerk	TN
Short, George S.	41	M	Printer	MD

* End of Town of Crockett

Name	Age	Sex	Occupation / Birthplace	State
Nevills, David S.	42	M	C.P. Minister	TN
Mary A.	38	F		TN
Edward	15	M		AL
John C.	10	M		AL
Paul J.	6	M		AL
Rice, Clinton A.	39	M	Black Smith	TN
Jane	40	F		TN
Elen	18	F		TX
Virginia	4	F	(Houston Co.)	TX
Susan H.	2	F	(Houston Co.)	TX
Conner, William R.	38	M	Farmer	SC
McCarns, Archibald	60	M		SC
Hall, John B.	40	M		TN
Rice, Joseph	45	M	Farmer	TN
Willie	40	F		KY
Elizabeth	15	F		TX
John	12	M	(Houston Co.)	TX
Francis M.	9	M	(Houston Co.)	TX
Joseph	6	M	(Houston Co.)	TX
George R.	2	M	(Houston Co.)	TX
Thornbury, John	20	M		LA
Gossett, Lee	27	M	Farmer	TN
Lucindy	24	F		LA
James L.	2	M	(Houston Co.)	TX
John W.	2	M	(Houston Co.)	TX
Albright, Solomon	34	M	Farmer	TN
Frances	32	F		MO
Rachal E.	10	F	(Houston Co.)	TX
John H.	9	M	(Houston Co.)	TX
Eliza A.	7	F	(Houston Co.)	TX
Mary A.	5	F	(Houston Co.)	TX

(continued)

Name	Age	Sex	Occupation / Birthplace	State
Albright, Willie	4	F	(Houston Co.)	TX
Jacob E.	2	M	(Houston Co.)	TX
Margarett W.	3/12	F	(Houston Co.)	TX
Johnson, Marshal H.	25	M	Farmer	TN
Sarah	21	F		AR
Elizabeth	14	F	(Houston Co.)	TX
Russel, Rheuben R.	42	M	Farmer	KY
Louisianna	41	F		TN
Jobee, Parmelia	21	F		AR
Emily	16	F		TX
Sarah	15	F		TX
Travis	11	M	(Houston Co.)	TX
Thomas	8	M	(Houston Co.)	TX
Lidey	5	F	(Houston Co.)	TX
Mary	3	F	(Houston Co.)	TX
James	25	M	School Teacher	VA
Chapman, Robert D.	34	M	Farmer	TN
Rebecca	34	F		TN
Martha F.	13	F	(Houston Co.)	TX
John H.	10	M	(Shelby Co.)	TX
Robert W.	9	M	(Houston Co.)	TX
Hetty	7	F	(Houston Co.)	TX
Sarah E.	6	F	(Rusk Co.)	TX
Isaac J.	4	M	(Houston Co.)	TX
Abel	2	M	(Houston Co.)	TX
Hodges, Abel	31	M	Farmer	TN
Sarah J.	13	F	(Shelby Co.)	TX
James F.	11	M	(Houston Co.)	TX
Hetty	10	F	(Houston Co.)	TX
Robert C.	8	M		TN
Isaac T.	3	M	(Houston Co.)	TX
Sarah	52	F		GA
Long, Anna	56	F		NC
Hugh	20	M	Farmer	TN
Simon	18	M		TN
Hodges, Isaac J.	28	M	Farmer	TN
Alcinda	25	F		OH
Jacob W.	1	M	(Houston Co.)	TX
Walker, Henderson	38	M	Farmer	TN
Sophia	32	F		AL
John	16	M		AR
Nancy	13	F		AR
Charles	13	M		AR
Pleasant	6	M	(Fannin Co.)	TX
Sarah	3	F	(Houston Co.)	TX
Narcissa	1	F	(Houston Co.)	TX
Odum, Wade	36	M		MS
Patton, Samuel	30	M	Farmer	SC
Elizabeth	22	F		TN
Elizabeth J.	5	F	(Harrison Co.)	TX
Samuel J.	3	M	(Houston Co.)	TX
William T.	5/12	M	(Houston Co.)	TX
George W.	19	M		AL
Lucinda C.	21	F		AL
Harrison, William D.	36	M	Farmer	TN
Jincy A.	27	F		SC
Martha J.	7	F	(Houston Co.)	TX
Lucinda C.	3	F	(Harrison Co.)	TX
Keer, Bird F.	32	M	Farmer	TN
Louisa	35	F		TN
Dorinda	10	F	(Houston Co.)	TX
William	8	M	(Houston Co.)	TX
James M.	6	M	(Houston Co.)	TX
Mary A.	5	F	(Houston Co.)	TX
Elizabeth A.	4	F	(Houston Co.)	TX
Reca	1	M	(Houston Co.)	TX
Cecil, Tinvil	22	M	Farmer	TN
Martha J.	19	F		TN
Nancy J.	2	F	(Rusk Co.)	TX
Brown, Columbus	21	M		TN
Colthorp, Eli	27	M	Farmer	TN
Eliza J.	18	F		IL
John	4/12	M	(Houston Co.)	TX

(continued)

HOUSTON COUNTY, TEXAS

Name	Age	Sex	Occupation / County	Birthplace
Gregg, Jacob	29	M		IL
Chapman, William D.	32	M	Farmer	TN
Sarah B.	25	F		VA
Mary J.	2	F	(Houston Co.)	TX
Robert J.	5/12	M	(Houston Co.)	TX
Martha N.	34	F		TN
Madison	3	M		TN
Foster, Rufus	42	M	Farmer	NC
Mary A.	39	F		GA
Betsey A.	14	F		TN
Rebecca M.	12	F	(Houston Co.)	TX
Jennett	10	F	(Houston Co.)	TX
Louisa	6	F	(Houston Co.)	TX
Sarah L.	5/12	F	(Houston Co.)	TX
McClane, William Z.	37	M	Farmer	TN
Rhodey D.	25	F		LA
William R.	5	M	(Houston Co.)	TX
James A.	4	M	(Houston Co.)	TX
Julian M.	3	M	(Houston Co.)	TX
Sam H.	1	M	(Houston Co.)	TX
Smith, Luther	44	M	Farmer	MA
Nancy T.	31	F		TN
Alexander	9	M	(Houston Co.)	TX
Henry	8	M	(Houston Co.)	TX
Hannah	6	F	(Houston Co.)	TX
Luther	6	M	(Houston Co.)	TX
Manier, Malissa	12	F		TN
Martha	6	F		TN
Mary E.	4	F		TN
Upton, Joseph	31	M	Farmer	AR
Mary	28	F		TN
John	10	M		AR
Isaah T.	7	M		AR
Josephus	4	M		AR
Nancy	1	F	(Houston Co.)	TX
James	16	M		AR
Pervis, Mayburn	38	M	Farmer	NC
Melvina	25	F		TN
John	7	M		MS
Antony	6	M		MS
Sarah	1	F	(Houston Co.)	TX
Creed, Charles	37	M	Farmer	NY
Martha C.	38	F		TN
Joseph G.	19	M		MS
Silas B.	15	M		MS
Paralee	11	F		MS
James	9	M	(Newton Co.)	TX
Leanna C.	6	F	(Newton Co.)	TX
Wiley H.	12	M		MS
Newman, Alexander M.	46	M	Farmer	GA
Soperisa D.	36	F		TN
Maddison H.	15	M		MS
Mary J.	14	F		MS
Louisa L.	13	F		MS
Anderson T.	3	M	(Polk Co.)	TX
John A.	1	M	(Houston Co.)	TX
Hay, William W.	59	M	Farmer	SC
Sarah	44	F		TN
James, Jesse	48	M	Farmer	NC
Nancy	50	F		KY
John	17	M		TN
Gallion, John C.	45	M	Farmer	OH
Sarah	45	F		OH
Lucy C.	18	F		IN
Phebe	17	F		IN
Dollhern J.	15	F		TX
Eliza N.	14	F		LA
Spear, Andrew	22	M	Farmer	TN
Catherine	22	F		TN
Benjamin	2	M	(Houston Co.)	TX
Masters, Sarah	45	F		NC

Name	Age	Sex	Occupation / County	Birthplace
Goodwin, William	28	M	Farmer	TN
Elizabeth	28	F		TN
John	7	M	(Houston Co.)	TX
Sarah J.	5	F	(Houston Co.)	TX
William A.	3	M	(Houston Co.)	TX
Eliza A.	6/12	F	(Houston Co.)	TX
Hallmark, James	20	M		??
Sarah	19	F		TN
Hodges, Sarah	34	F		GA
McGee, Duncan	38	M	Farmer	TN
Sarah	23	F		LA
Sampson	7	M		LA
Agnes	5	F		LA
Nancy	1	F	(Houston Co.)	TX
Hale, Robert	34	M	Farmer	AL
Julia A.	33	F		TN
George	11	M		TN
Drury	9	M		GA
Peter	7	M		GA
John	5	M		GA
William	4	M	(Rusk Co.)	TX
Elizabeth	1/12	F	(Houston Co.)	TX
English, Archey H.	36	M	Farmer	??
Mary J.	23	F		TN
George	4	M	(Houston Co.)	TX
Susan	3	F	(Houston Co.)	TX
Elizabeth	1	F	(Houston Co.)	TX
Shirman, Ellen	12	F	(Houston Co.)	TX
English, George	40	M		??
Irvin, John	39	M	Farmer	TN
Elizabeth	24	F		IN
William H.	5	M	(Houston Co.)	TX
Charles F.	3	M	(Houston Co.)	TX
John R.	10/12	M	(Houston Co.)	TX
Masters, Jacob	44	M	Farmer	NC
Louisa	23	F		TN
Eliza J.	11	F	(Houston Co.)	TX
Jacob F.	9	M	(Houston Co.)	TX
Henry F.	7	M	(Houston Co.)	TX
Robert	5	M	(Houston Co.)	TX
Jerutha	3	F	(Houston Co.)	TX
Ford, William J. B.	42	M		ENG
Hartgroves, Sarah	34	F		KY
Benjamin G.	18	M	Farmer	TN
Charles A. W.	17	M		MS
Samantha J.	14	F		MS
Francis J.	12	M		MS
Asa J.	8	M	(Houston Co.)	TX
John D.	4	M	(Houston Co.)	TX
Hallmark, George W.	44	M	Farmer	TN
Jane	38	F		SC
Elisha C.	21	M		AL
Sarah A.	18	F		AL
Mary A.	11	F	(Houston Co.)	TX
Rufus L.	8	M	(Houston Co.)	TX
Nancy E.	5	F	(Houston Co.)	TX
Rutha J. W.	1	F	(Houston Co.)	TX
Shaver, James M.	23	M	Farmer	LA
Hallmark, Amey	65	F		TN
George	45	M	Farmer	GA
John T. W. J.	21	M		GA
John	20	M		GA
Thomas G.	16	M		GA
Eliza A.	12	F	(Houston Co.)	TX
Crowsen, Rhodey	45	F		TN
Louisa	24	F		AL
Obed	19	M	Farmer	AL
Martha	16	F		AL
Cobb, Henry	6	M		MS
Fredonia A.	4	F		MS
Askins, William	28	M	Farmer	??
Elizabeth E.	21	F		TN
Mary J.	3	F	(Tyler Co.)	TX
Nancy A.	1	F	(Houston Co.)	TX

HOUSTON COUNTY, TEXAS

Name	Age	Sex	Occupation / Born	State
Box, Thomas G.	33	M	Farmer	TN
Rachal P.	28	F		TN
John P.	10	M	(Houston Co.)	TX
Felix M.	8	M	(Houston Co.)	TX
Keziah A.	4	F	(Houston Co.)	TX
Franklin H.	3	M	(Houston Co.)	TX
Sarah A.	2	F	(Houston Co.)	TX
Almanza J.	10/12	F	(Houston Co.)	TX
Ellis, Benjamin J.	9	M	(Houston Co.)	TX
Ellis, Charles M. H.	33	M	Farmer	TN
Elizabeth	28	F		AL
Bayantha W.	12	M		MS
Obed C.	11	M	(Houston Co.)	TX
Christian C.	9	F	(Houston Co.)	TX
Hannah T.	7	F	(Houston Co.)	TX
Mary J.	5	F	(Houston Co.)	TX
John J.	3	M	(Houston Co.)	TX
Sarah L.	1	F	(Houston Co.)	TX
Goolsby, Charles M.	25	M		AL
Moore, James H.	29	M	Farmer	AL
Amanda L.	20	F		TN
Margarett A.	4	F	(Houston Co.)	TX
Mary E.	2	F	(Houston Co.)	TX
Hart, James R.	41	M	Farmer	GA
Eliza	33	F		GA
Isum J.	6	M	(Houston Co.)	TX
James M.	4	M	(Houston Co.)	TX
Green H.	11/12	M	(Houston Co.)	TX
Lovelady, Henry L.	14	M		MS
Martha A.	12	F		MS
Milliken, John C.	30	M	Farmer	KY
Nancy M.	23	F		TN
Frances A.	1	F	(Houston Co.)	TX
Hagin, John C.	51	M	Farmer	VA
Rosanna	40	F		VA
Adelia	14	F	(Houston Co.)	TX
Lucy A.	12	F	(Houston Co.)	TX
Grant, William	21	M		TN
Finch, Edward	5	M	(Houston Co.)	TX
Nancy E.	4	F	(Houston Co.)	TX
Runels, Elizabeth	38	F		TN
James	18	M	Farmer	TN
Mary	15	F		TN
George	13	M		TN
Carrol	7	M	(Houston Co.)	TX
Lucy A.	5	F	(Houston Co.)	TX
Flora	2	F	(Houston Co.)	TX
Young, Ann	46	F		VA
Peter	25	M		VA
Nancy	23	F		VA
Elizabeth	18	F		TN
Joshua	15	M		TN
Ann C.	13	F		TN
Harper, Benjamin J.	41	M	Farmer	VA
Nancy J.	20	F		TN
Morrow, William	30	M	Black Smith	TN
Margarett	22	F		AL
William J.	4	M		AL
Malinda A.	3	F		AL
Lucy	2	F		AL
James	11/12	M	(Walker Co.)	TX
Tryon, Seldon	37	M	Farmer	CT
Patience E.	33	F		NC
Ezra	13	M		NC
Laura	7	F	(Montgomery Co.)	TX
Seldon	4	M	(Houston Co.)	TX
Sophronia	1	F	(Houston Co.)	TX
Sarah Spencer	60	F		NC
Buckingham, John A.	29	M		TN
Tompkins, Mary	31	M		TN
Jane	11	F	(Houston Co.)	TX
Sophia	9	F	(Houston Co.)	TX
George	7	M	(Houston Co.)	TX

(continued)

Name	Age	Sex	Occupation / Born	State
Tompkins, Frances	4	F	(Houston Co.)	TX
Galloway, James W.	34	M	Mechanic	GA
Caroline E.	24	F		TN
William T. W.	2	M	(Houston Co.)	TX
Dillard, William M. L.	19	M		TN
Trabuca A.	17	F		TN
William	57	M		TN
Jane	57	F		VA
Sarah A. M.	5	F	(Houston Co.)	TX
Nevill, James	57	M	Farmer	SC
Melviny	30	F		TN
Parker, John R.	34	M	Farmer	VA
Mary	30	F		GA
Henry	8	M		TN
Elizabeth	6	F	(Houston Co.)	TX
Marion	4	F	(Houston Co.)	TX
Sarah	1/12	F	(Houston Co.)	TX
McCurley, James	10	M		TN
Box, John	46	M	Farmer	TN
Lucindey	29	F		AR
Keziah	19	F		AL
Lina	18	F		AL
Texana	12	F	(Houston Co.)	TX
Stephen	10	M	(Houston Co.)	TX
Mary	8	F	(Houston Co.)	TX
John	4	M	(Houston Co.)	TX
Louisa E.	1	F	(Houston Co.)	TX
Keziah	75	F		NC
Williams, Henry G.	27	M	Black Smith	TN
Isa M.	18	F		AL
Mary A.	3	F	(Houston Co.)	TX
Martha J.	5/12	F	(Houston Co.)	TX
Pendergrass, John	23	M		TN
Allbright, Edward	50	M	Farmer	NC
Tappenious	35	F		TN
Mary J.	19	F		TN
John E.	17	M		TN
Rachael	15	F		TN
Susan T.	11	F	(Houston Co.)	TX
Missouri E.	8	F	(Houston Co.)	TX
Jacob F.	4	M	(Houston Co.)	TX
George W.	2	M	(Houston Co.)	TX
Hallmark, William C.	46	M	Farmer	TN
Leanah	47	F		TN
Stephen B.	19	M		AL
Keziah C.	17	F		AL
George G.	16	M		AL
Eliza C.	11	F	(Houston Co.)	TX
Manila	9	F	(Houston Co.)	TX
Bynum, Griffin A.	22	M	Farmer	AL
Sarah J.	17	F		TN
Huntsman, James B.	19	M	Farmer	TN
Sarah	20	F		TX
Huntsman, Lemuel	62	M	Farmer	VA
John	8	M		TN
Madison	5	M		TN
Rennaugh, James F.	28	M		??
Elizabeth	24	F		TN
George W.	1	M	(Houston Co.)	TX
John	30	M		??
Click, George	54	M	Farmer	TN
Augusta	25	F		GER
George L.	7/12	M	(Houston Co.)	TX
Eldridge S.	18	M		TN
James L.	16	M		AL
Birmingham, Mary J.	10	F	(Houston Co.)	TX
Edward	8	M	(Houston Co.)	TX
Click, Malachia	28	M	Farmer	TN
Rhodey	18	F		TN
James L.	1/12	M	(Houston Co.)	TX
Shanks, Charles	4	M	(Houston Co.)	TX

HOUSTON COUNTY, TEXAS

Name	Age	Sex	Occupation / Birthplace	State
Click, Nathan	24	M	Farmer	TN
Landrum, Nancy	32	F		TN
Birmingham, Nathan	4	M	(Houston Co.)	TX
Dupree, William E.	25	M	Farmer	TN
Mary A.	18	F		TN
James A.	9/12	M	(Houston Co.)	TX
Albright, Jacob	43	M	Ass. & Collector	TN
Sarah L.	39	F		TN
Margarett V.	15	F	(Houston Co.)	TX
Amanda L.	9	F	(Houston Co.)	TX
Frances C.	4	F	(Houston Co.)	TX
William F.	20	M		AL
Mayse, James	19	M		MS
Prewitt, George W.	28	M	Farmer	TN
Elizabeth L.	23	F		TN
James H.	2	M	(Houston Co.)	TX
Elizabeth D.	7/12	F	(Houston Co.)	TX
Prewitt, George H.	76	M	Farmer	TN
Elizabeth D.	65	F		NC
Leech, John	35	M	Carpenter	NC
Mary	35	F		TN
Elizabeth	3	F	(Houston Co.)	TX
William	1	M	(Houston Co.)	TX
Prewitt, Jesse T.	26	M	Farmer	TN
Nancy	21	F		AL
John H.	3	M	(Houston Co.)	TX
Dupree, James C.	47	M	Farmer	TN
Frances	32	F		AL
Franklin	17	M		KY
Samuel	16	M		KY
Victoria	13	F		KY
Charlott	11	F		KY
Robert	9	M		KY
Mary	6	F		KY
James M.	2	M	(Houston Co.)	TX
Andrew	2/12	M	(Houston Co.)	TX
Nelson, Mary A.	13	F		IL
Charles	10	M	(Houston Co.)	TX
Ralph	8	M	(Houston Co.)	TX
Moirs, John	62	M	Farmer	TN
Eli M.	19	M		AR
Andrew	17	M		TX
Elenor	58	F		NC
Elvina	14	F	(Houston Co.)	TX
Adeline	11	F	(Houston Co.)	TX
Susan	9	F	(Houston Co.)	TX
Green	7	M	(Houston Co.)	TX
Lamuel	5	M	(Houston Co.)	TX
James, Edmond B.	53	M	Farmer	TN
Hannah	55	F		GA
Sarah	24	F		AL
Allen B.	15	M		AL
Thompson, Jesse	38	M	Farmer	AL
Malinda	20	F		TN
George M.	13	M	(Shelby Co.)	TX
Mary A.	10	F	(Jackson Co.)	TX
Jesse	7	M	(Colorado Co.)	TX
William	3	M	(Lavaca Co.)	TX
James	7/12	M	(Houston Co.)	TX
Meredith, Green W.	30	M	Farmer	NC
Caroline	25	F		NC
Jonathan	3	M	(Houston Co.)	TX
Nancy	2	F	(Houston Co.)	TX
James M.	1	M	(Houston Co.)	TX
Rone, Malinda R.	24	F		NC
James M.	20	M		NC
George W.	17	M		NC
Marsh, Jonas	23	M		TN
Oliver, John C.	38	M	Farmer	KY
Elizabeth	36	F		KY
Mary J.	18	F		TN

(continued)

Name	Age	Sex	Occupation / Birthplace	State
Oliver, John W.	9	M	(Houston Co.)	TX
Malina A.	6	F	(Houston Co.)	TX
Nancy P.	4	F	(Houston Co.)	TX
Sam H.	2	M	(Houston Co.)	TX
Martin C.	1/12	M	(Houston Co.)	TX
Jarett P.	25	M		TN
Atchison, Serginal	31	M	Farmer	KY
Sarah J.	28	F		NC
Mary C.	5	F		TN
Elizabeth J.	3	F		TN
William J.	1	M		TN
Gossett, Andrew E.	38	M	Farmer	TN
Rhodey D.	38	F		NC
Eveline S.	16	F		TX
Galveston M.	13	M	(Houston Co.)	TX
Zebedee	8	M	(Houston Co.)	TX
Kelvy L.	6	M	(Houston Co.)	TX
Albert R.(?)	3	M	(Houston Co.)	TX
Antoinett	1	F	(Houston Co.)	TX
Manus, James M.	23	M		KY
Eliza S.	21	F		TN
Elijah	4	M	(Houston Co.)	TX
JOhn V. D.	1	M	(Anderson Co.)	TX
Dodd, Mary	36	F		AL
Benge, William J.	19	M	Farmer	TN
Amelia A.	15	F		TN
Araminta	14	F	(Houston Co.)	TX
Adeline R.	12	F	(Houston Co.)	TX
Clinton A.	9	F(M)	(Houston Co.)	TX
Dodds, John W.	2	M	(Houston Co.)	TX
Willson, Benjamin N.	37	M	Farmer	TN
Margarett	36	F		TN
Mary C.	13	F		TN
Thomas D.	11	M		MS
Parilla A.	8	F		MS
Ritchard M.	7	M		MS
Lucy A.	5	F		MS
John M.	3	M		MS
Margarett A.	1	F		AR
Nevills, Calvin	24	M		AL
Murchison, Daniel	45	M	Farmer	NC
Mary	43	F		TN
Thomas F.	21	M		TN
Angeline C.	15	F		TN
Mary W.	14	F		TN
William J.	12	M		MS
Daniel M.	8	M		MS
Arabella W.	6	F		MS
Walker, George W.	9	M	(Houston Co.)	TX
Robert P.	6	M	(Houston Co.)	TX
Melling, Robert	31	M	Farmer	SC
Amanda J.	21	F		TN
Mary J.	4	F		MS
Catherine A.	3	F		MS
Julia A.	1	F	(Houston Co.)	TX
Murchison, Merdock	24	M		TN
Wortham, John	45	M	Farmer	NC
Carey A.	26	F		AL
William	17	M		TN
Ritchard	15	M		TN
Rebecca	13	F	(Houston Co.)	TX
John	4	M	(Houston Co.)	TX
Andrew	1	M	(Houston Co.)	TX
Seals, Nancy	36	F		NC
Walker, Martin	35	M		TN
Kenterling, James R.	30	M		OH
Vaughan, Thomas L.	12	M	(Houston Co.)	TX
Lacey, William	28	M	Farmer	AL
Elizabeth T.	21	F		TN
John D.	1/12	M	(Houston Co.)	TX
Walker, Martin	9	M		TN
John	6	M	(Houston Co.)	TX
Marsh, Elizabeth	40	F		NC
William	25	M	Mechanic	TN
Newton B.	17	M		TN

(continued)

HOUSTON COUNTY, TEXAS

Name	Age	Sex	Occupation / Birthplace Detail	State
Marsh, Lucious	16	M		TN
Maretta	12	F		TN
George W.	7	M		TN
Araminta	4	F		TN
Daniel V.	1	M	(Houston Co.)	TX
Barbee, James G.	36	M	Physician	NC
Miranda	26	F		TN
Virginia	15	F		TN
Napoleon	13	M		TN
Mary	9	F		TN
Banks	8	M		TN
John	3	M	(Shelby Co.)	TX
Allison, William F.	50	M	Farmer	SC
Sarah	49	F		SC
Margarett	22	F		TN
Thomas J.	17	M		AR
James N.	15	M		AR
Sarah	14	F	(Nacogdoches Co.)	TX
Jacob	10	M	(Houston Co.)	TX
Sam H.	7	M	(Houston Co.)	TX
John	76	M		SC
Smith, Stephen	35	M		TN
James	12	M	(Hopkins Co.)	TX
Sylvester	3	M	(Hopkins Co.)	TX
Pervis, Hayden	32	M	Farmer	AL
Mary A.	26	F		TN
Margarett V.	3	F	(Houston Co.)	TX
Milley	30	F		AL
Crow, Joshua W.	42	M	Farmer	TN
Martha	29	F		AL
Robert D.	13	M		TN
Frances S.	6	F	(Houston Co.)	TX
Martin J.	4	M	(Houston Co.)	TX
John W.	4	M	(Houston Co.)	TX
Walling, James	38	M	Farmer	TN
Martha	37	F		TN
Amanda	14	F		TN
Robert	13	M	(Houston Co.)	TX
Hosea	11	M	(Houston Co.)	TX
Elisha	8	M	(Houston Co.)	TX
Ritchard	6	M	(Houston Co.)	TX
Elizabeth	3	F	(Houston Co.)	TX
Sarah J.	1	F	(Houston Co.)	TX
Walling, Elisha	27	M	Farmer	TN
Penington, Ritchard	41	M	Farmer	KY
Polly	36	F		TN
Catherine	15	F		TN
Gaines	13	M		TN
Lawson J.	4	M	(Houston Co.)	TX
Jane	3	F	(Houston Co.)	TX
Luzana	1/12	F	(Houston Co.)	TX

HUNT COUNTY, TEXAS

Name	Age	Sex	Occupation	State
Boran, Tarlton	38	M	Farmer	TN
Martha	38	F		KY
William E.	15	M	Farmer	KY
James M.	14	M		KY
Martha E.	12	F		KY
Henry F.	10	M		KY
Louisa J.	6	F		KY
Joseph L.	4	M		KY
Malina J.	2	F		KY
Hale, Joshua	50	M	House Carpenter	TN
Nancy	40	F		KY
Luoratio(?)	19	M	Farmer	TN
Matthias	17	M	Farmer	TN
Margarett	10	F		KY
Mandy	8	F		KY
Adam	5	M		KY
Mary	1	F		TX
Boran, Richard	46	M	Farmer	SC

(continued)

Name	Age	Sex	Occupation	State
Boran, Laney	19	F		TN
Laurinda	16	F		TN
Preston	13	M		KY
Louisa	10	F		KY
Lovel, Jane	23	F		TN
Lavina	2	F		KY
Moore, James	53	M	Farmer	SC
Rebecca	50	F		NC
John W.	19	M	Farmer	TN
Milton J.	17	M	Farmer	TN
Napoleon	15	M	Farmer	TN
M. M. M.	10	F		TX
Rebecca L. J.	8	F		TX
Stanley, Elbert E.	27	M	Farmer	AR
Martha E.	21	F		TN
Moore, J. T.	22	M	Farmer	TN
Peneca Ann	19	F		NC
Moore, Samuel P.	25	M	Cabinet Maker	TN
Nancy	24	F		TN
Rebecca	3	F		TX
Texas	2	F		TX
Monday, Benjamin	54	M	Farmer	NC
Polly	40	F		TN
Angaline	16	F		MO
Atchison	14	M		MO
Jefferson	11	M		MO
Mary	8	F		MO
James	5	M		TX
Sarah	2	F		TX
Foster, George	23	M		AL
William	20	M		AL
Green, A. W.	20	M	Farmer	IL
Elizabeth	17	F		TN
Havans, James	50	M	Farmer	TN
Polly	48	F		GA
Catherine	21	F		AL
Hayes	18	M	Farmer	MO
Caroline	15	F		MO
Adaline	13	F		MO
Rice	8	M		MO
Havans, John	24	M	Farmer	AL
Jane	24	F		TN
Kizer, Samuel	42	M	Farmer	VA
Syntha	33	F		TN
Malinda	17	F		TN
Enoch	15	M	Farmer	TN
Valentine	13	M		TN
Frances	11	F		TN
Syntha Ann	10	F		TN
John	7	M		TN
William	5	M		TN
Hosea	1	M		TX
Kizer, William	52	M	Farmer	VA
Jane	49	F		NC
John	25	M	Farmer	TN
William	22	M	Farmer	TN
Mary	20	F		TN
Alfred	16	M	Farmer	TN
Enoch	14	M		MO
Caroline	12	F		MO
Elina	9	F		TX
Havans, John	2	M		TX
William	5/12	M		TX
Polk, Jesse	44	M	Cabinet Maker	SC
Tempy	13	F		TN
Martha	11	F		TN
Elizabeth	9	F		TN
Emily	7	F		AR
Polk, Levy	20	M	Farmer	TN
Anna	21	F		TN
Swagarty, Joseph	40	M	Farmer	TN
Laney, Culbert	25	M	Farmer	TN

(continued)

HUNT COUNTY, TEXAS

Name	Age	Sex	Occupation	Birthplace
Laney, Sarah	23	F		TN
Patterson, M. K.	34	M	Farmer	TN
Lucinda	32	F		TN
Clary M.	10	F		TN
Mary W.	8	F		IL
Sarah E.	6	F		TN
David H.	5	M		TN
Nancy E.	2	F		TX
Frances E.	2	F		TX
Wilson, Joseph	67	M	Farmer	NC
Sarah B.	57	F		NC
James	22	M	Farmer	TN
Sarah B.	20	F		TN
Joseph	14	M		TN
Ann Eliza	12	F		TN
Clinton	8	M		TX
Williams, Jonas	32	M	Shoe Maker	VA
Manerva Ann	20	F		TN
John	5/12	M		TX
Merick, J. C.	30	M	Farmer	TN
Nancy Ann	24	F		TN
Sarah A.	8	F		TX
Emily	5	F		TX
Mary E.	3	F		TX
Griffith K.	1/12	M		TX
Hutchison, George W.	40	M	School Teacher	VA
Moore, James C.	24	M	Farmer	TN
Mary Ann	19	F		GA
Pemila M.	9/12	F		TX
Williams, Jno. D.	39	M	House Plasterer	VA
Martha	32	F		TN
Elizabeth	13	F		IA
Martha J.	10	F		IA
George	6	M		TX
Angeline	4	F		TX
Ruth	2	F		TX
Rebecca	7/12	F		TX
Kizer, Enoch	38	M	Farmer	TN
Nancy	35	F		TN
George	13	M		TN
Martha	11	F		TN
John	8	M		TN
William	1	M		TX
Briscoe, John	35	M	Black Smith	TN
Rebecca	34	F		VA
Mary Jane	11	F		MO
Caroline	9	F		MO
Isaac N.	6	M		MO
John D.	4	M		TX
Ephraim W.	1	M		TX
Hill, Thomas C.	39	M	Farmer	TN
Mary	35	F		TN
John C.	18	M	Farmer	TN
Catharine	13	F		TN
Andy B.	11	M		TN
William	8	M		TN
Mary	6	F		TN
Margarett	3	F		TN
James	2	M		TN
Elizabeth	15	F		TN
Hargus, John	37	M	Farmer	TN
Anna	36	F		TN
James	17	M	Farmer	TN
Catharine	11	F		IL
Martha	6	F		MO
Murpy, Green B.	48	M	Farmer	VA
Gonail J.	22	M	Farmer	KY
Elizabeth	18	F		TN
Enoch	7	M		TN
Parilee	5	F		TN
Caskin, Robert (continued)	24	M	Farmer	TN
Caskin, America	24	F		KY
Mary	7	F		TN
John	5	M		TX
Daniel, William G.	43	M	Farmer	VA
Holly	38	F		TN
Hugh L.	20	M	Farmer	TN
John P.	16	M	Farmer	TN
Sarah Ann	13	F		TN
Enoch E.	11	M		TN
Nancy	9	F		TN
Elizabeth	7	F		TN
Bee L.	2	F		TX
Chapman, J. W.	38	M	Farmer	KY
Martha Ann	27	F		TN
Malina	8	F		KY
William	7	M		KY
Samuel	5	M		KY
James	3	M		TX
Green	6/12	M		TX
Smith, Joseph	20	M	Farmer	TN
Old, P. H.	34	M	Farmer	VA
Mahala	26	F		TN
Smith J.	1	M		TX
Clark, Henry	50	M	Farmer	TN
Lidy	46	F		KY
Louisa	18	F		AR
Mary	17	F		AR
Catharine	15	F		AR
Caroline	12	F		AR
Lewis	10	M		AR
Ridla, Henry	25	M	Farmer	NC
Mary E.	19	F		TN
William A.	1	M		TX
Sarah E.	6/12	F		TX
Guest, J. C.	26	M	Farmer	TN
Sarah	23	F		TN
McFarling, Albert	23	M	Farmer	MO
Cyntha	20	F		TN
Elizabeth J.	4/12	F		TX
Mitchell, Samuel	22	M	School Teacher	TN
Mainard, Jefferson	25	M	Farmer	TN
Ellender	18	F		AR
Rily, Isaac	27	M	Farmer	IN
Nancy	22	F		TN
Sally	7	F		AR
Meredith	4	M		TX
Malisa	1	F		TX
Dorras, Elias	28	M	Chair Maker	TN
Efi	28	F		TN
Mary	8	F		TN
James E.	6	M		TN
Francis M.	5	M		TN
Orpha L.	4	M		TN
Ripy, William P.	44	M	Farmer	NC
Mary	29	F		NC
William	10	M		MO
Calvin	8	M		MO
Eliza J.	5	F		TX
Susan	2	F		TX
James M.	5/12	M		TX
Watherby, Milton	14	M		TN
Mason, John	33	M	Farmer	TN
Elizabeth	30	F		AR
Mary	10	F		AR
--za	8	F		AR
William	5	M		AR
Sarah C.	5	F		AR
Phoeba	1	F		TX
Bowman, E. S.	34	M	Farmer	KY
Roxanna	17	F		TN
Goodner, Susanah	50	F		VA

HUNT COUNTY, TEXAS

Name	Age	Sex	Occupation	Birthplace
Horton, James R.	38	M	Farmer	NC
Mary	33	F		KY
Susannah	13	F		TN
William B.	12	M		TN
Parilee	10	F		TN
Sarah	8	F		TX
Austin	6	M		TX
Alphanagan(?)	4	F		TX
John	5/12	M		TX
Mattox, Wiley A.	30	M	Farmer	TN
Sarah	20	F		GA
Mary	1	F		TX
P. W.	27	M	Farmer	TN
Williams, John D.	51	M	Farmer	KY
Sarah	18	F		MO
Susanah	16	F		MO
Manda	15	F		TN
Roman	13	M		AR
John B.	11	M		AR
Kuykendall, Elizabeth	42	F		TN
William H.	22	M	None	AL
Jesse	21	M	Farmer	AL
James	18	M		AL
Joseph	16	M	Farmer	AL
Sarah A.	14	F		AL
Ludica	12	F		MS
James	10	M		MS
Anderson, Archibald	22	M	Farmer	TN
Emily	18	F		KY
James F.	7/12	M		TX
Odell, John	40	M	Farmer	TN
Catharine	27	F		AR
William	15	M	Farmer	MO
Reuben	11	M		MO
Simon	7	M		MO
Anna	3	F		TX
Andrew	4/12	M		TX
Riley, Jacob	35	M	Farmer	IN
Rebecca	24	F		TN
Owen	3	M		TX
David	6/12	M		TX
Merick, John	25	M	Black Smith	TN
Mary	22	F		TN
Lucindy E.	2	F		TX
Askey, John A.	30	M	Farmer	AR
Casander	25	F		TN
James H.	8	M		TX
John W.	5	M		TX
Abner N.	3	M		TX
Kimbro, Joseph T.	29	M	Farmer	TN
J. Rachael	25	F		MO
Amanda	7	F		TX
Isabella R.	6	F		TX
Norass, John B(R).	25	M	Farmer	KY
Catharine	23	F		TN
Nancy C.	1	F		TX
Norass, Pillop H.	30	M	Farmer	KY
Angaline	30	F		TN
Lucinda	3	F		TX
Keith, Elijah	33	M	Farmer	TN
Adaline	30	F		TN
Martha E.	10	F		AR
Nancy C.	9	F		AR
Mary L.	7	F		AR
Sarah R.	5	F		TX
Charles J.	3	M		TX
Taylor, Mathew M.	45	M	Brick Mason	TN
Anna	43	F		KY
Thurman	23	M	Farmer	IL
Rebeca	21	F		IL
(continued)				
Taylor, Zedic	20	M	Farmer	IL
William	17	M	Farmer	IL
Hester Ann	15	F		IL
Harry(Henry)	12	M		IL
James	10	M		IL
Permelia	5	F		AR
Keith, John J.	27	M	Farmer	TN
Isabella	26	F		VA
William B.	9	M		AR
Elizabeth J.	8	F		AR
Sarah A.	6	F		AR
Thomas E.	4	M		TX
David R.	2	M		TX
Stone, William	32	M	Farmer	TN
Malinda	24	F		AR
Martha J.	12	F		MO
Margarett	9	F		MO
Roads, Willis	18	M	Farmer	AR
Hamer, J. C.	38	M	Farmer	TN
Mary Ann	30	F		NC
Mary H.	9	F		TX
Edy	6	F		TX
Eveline M.	3	F		TX
Masick, John	45	M	Stock Raiser	MO
Matilda	35	F		TN
Virginia	16	F		AR
Elizabeth	14	F		AR
--el	12	M		AR
Josafine	10	F		AR
Stephen N.	8	M		AR
J. Maline	4	F		AR
Moore, William	26	M	Black Smith	KY
Sarah Ann	23	F		TN
Nancy E.	1	F		TX
Culver, S. G.	43	M	D.D.Meth.	NC
Mary	49	F		VA
Thomas	18	M	Farmer	TN
Margarett	16	F		KY
Martha A.	15	F		KY
Ofelia E.	11	F		KY
Downing, William	35	M	Farmer	IL
Charity	33	F		TN
Roady C.	15	F		MO
Rebecca	11	F		MO
Thomas B.	9	M		MO
William J.	6	M		TX
John B.	4	M		TX
Mary E.	2	F		TX
Bowerner, James P.	30	M	Farmer	TN
Malinda M.	29	F		KY
Jno. T.	3	M		TX
William H.	2	M		TX
Henry P.	1/12	M		TX
Harrison, Littlebury L.	38	M	Farmer	VA
Mary	25	F		MS
Harriett J.	9	F		TN
Richard J.	5	M		MS
Joel	3	M		TX
William D.	6/12	M		TX
Downey, Obediah L.	38	M	Farmer	IL
Sarah	37	F		TN
Goodson, Abigail	8	F		MO
Kitchen, William	45	M	Farmer	TN
Charlotte	50	F		SC
Thomas D.	21	M	Farmer	TN
Sarah W.	19	F		TN
Mariah H.	17	F		MO
James W.	14	M		MO
Ruth A.	11	F		MO
Margarett B.	9	F		MO
William M.	--			MO
Ealam, William	53	M	Farmer	TN
Malinda F.	14	F		IL
Mary	12	F		IL

Name	Age	Sex	Occupation	Birthplace
Hogan, Robert	31	M	None	TN
Susan A.	19	F		AR
Margarett E.	6	F		TX
McMahan, Isabella	40	F		KY
Jonathan	23	M	Farmer	TN
John R.	21	M		TN
Mary E.	19	F		TN
Marshall, Stephen	27	M	Farmer	TN
Laura ?.	25	F		TN
Malisa J.	9	F		AR
Malinda C.	7	F		AR
Mary E.	5	F		TX
Joel G.	3	M		TX
John T.	1	M		TX
Hart, Ranson P.	25	M	Farmer	TN
Mary	25	F		IL
Mary A.	5/12	F		TX
Hooker, James	43	M	Farmer	TN
Elizabeth	46	F		TN
Thomas L(T).	20	M	Farmer	TN
William H.	17	M	Farmer	MO
Mary J.	15	F		MO
Martha C.	12	F		MO
Elizabeth B.	10	F		TX
John W.	7	M		TX
George H.	5	M		TX
Anderson, Benjamin	45	M	Farmer	TN
Prudence	41	F		GA
Nathan	22	M	Farmer	AR
Joseph	18	M	Farmer	AR
William	16	M	Farmer	TN
Elijah	14	M	Farmer	TN
Benjamin F.	12	M		TN
Edward L.	10	M		TN
James F.	8	M		TN
John W.	6	M		TN
Mary	4	F		TX
Denton, Samuel	45	M	Farmer	SC
Polly	45	F		TN
Tipton	19	M	Farmer	MO
Roberts, Henderson	22	M	Farmer	AR
Hufft, William	33	M	Farmer	TN
Elizabeth	29	F		MO
Alexander	4	M		MO
Solomon	26	M	Farmer	KY
Parsons, Thomas	20	M	Farmer	MO
Martha	17	F		MO
Brown, Richard	45	M	House Carpenter	TN
Tilitha	29	F		GA
Almira	13	F		MO
Margarett	10	F		IL
William	8	M		IL
Emaline	6	F		MO
Susan	2	F		TX
Keith, Green W.	22	M	Farmer	MO
Sarah G.	15	F		MO
next to				
Keith, Jno. B.	64	M	Farmer	TN
George W.	21	M	Farmer	MO
Margarett G.	18	F		MO
Rebecca M.	15	F		MO
Matilda E.	13	F		MO
Calhoun, John	40	M	School Teacher	SC
Gilentine, Nicholas	40	M	Farmer	TN
Louisa	35	F		TN
John	14	M		TN
Sarah Ann	12	F		AR
Rachael	10	F		AR
Mathew	6	M		AR
Mary	4	F		TX
Mandy	1	F		TX
Brumlow, Oma	16	F		TN

Name	Age	Sex	Occupation	Birthplace
Keith, Nicadamus	29	M	Farmer	TN
Elizabeth	26	F		TN
Elijah	8	M		TX
Stephen	6	M		TX
John W.	4	M		TX
Wright, M. H.	37	M	Farmer	TN
Americus T.	40	F		KY
Edward P.	6	M		TX
Martha F.	2	F		TX
Virginia	3/12	F		TX
Harrison, William R.	26	M		TN
Callion(?), Benjamin	21	M	Teamster	KY
Bradley, James	40	M	Clerk	TN
Sarah Ann	27	F		NC
Medorah M.	2	F		TX
Fanning, William	25	M	Farmer	MO
Mary	23	F		TN
Martha	5/12	F		TX
Elgam, Elijah	30	M	Preacher of ----	IN
Margarett	27	F		IL
Nancy	4	F		TX
Jesse	3	M		TX
King, Mary Ann	21	F		TN
Permela	2	F		TX
Merill, Richmond	23	M	Laborer	TN
Borrow, Peter	48	M	Farmer	KY
Nancy	46	F		TN
Simpson	20	M	Farmer	IL
Jane	18	F		IL
William	14	M		MO
Zephaniah	11	M		MO
-----	5	F		MO
Cooper, Samuel	50	M	Farmer	??
Louisa	22	F		TN
Susanah	18	F		??
Jane	16	F		IN
Peter	8	M		MO
Nancy	5	F		MO
James	2	M		TX
Brake, Elisha	57	M	Farmer	NC
Elizabeth	41	F		KY
George W.	21	M	Farmer	TN
Levy H.	14	M		KY
Mary C.	12	F		TN
Ruhaney E.	10	F		TN
Huldah J.	6	F		TN
Amanda L.	5	F		TN
Cyrus C.	2	M		TX
Hugh A.	3/12	M		TX
Millerons(?), Michael	47	M	Shoe Maker	KY
Nancy	35	F		TN
Warran, John	35	M	Farmer	TN
Manervy	33	F		TN
Thomas	13	M		IL
William W.	8	M		IL
Columbus	2	M		TX
Handlin, Jacob	25	M	Laborer	VA
Isaac	19	M	Farmer	VA
Moses	16	M	Farmer	VA
Hart, Charles	55	M	Farmer	KY
Eliza	34	F		TN
John	14	M		IL
William	11	M		IL
Cyrus	10	M		IL
Delilah	8	F		IL
George	7	M		IL
Charles	4	M		IL
Cyrena	1/12	F		TX
Waterford, Maney	43	M	Farmer	TN
Nancy	43	F		TN
John H.	21	M	Farmer	AL
Manda M.	9	F		IL
Thomas T.	6	F(M)		IL
James M.	3	M		TX

HUNT COUNTY, TEXAS

Name	Age	Sex	Occupation	State
Helt, Susannah	60	F		TN
Jacob	24	M	Farmer	KY
Gabriel	23	M	Farmer (Blind)	KY
Ambrose	8	M		MO
Riley, Thomas	29	M	Farmer	IN
Sally	24	F		TN
William	8	M		AR
Henry	4	M		TX
Abraham	4/12	M		TX
Odell, Simon	63	M	Farmer	TN
Elizabeth	57	F		TN
Gabriel	22	M	Farmer	MO
Clevinger, John	18	M	Farmer	MO
Odell, Joel	26	M	Farmer	MO
John	6	M		MO
Simon	4	M		TX
Moses	1	M		TX
Finly, John	40	M	Farmer	TN
Sarah	34	F		TN
John	9	M		AR
Julia Ann	6	F		AR
Edmund	4	M		AR
Nancy	3	F		TX
Martha	2	F		TX
Elizabeth	21	F		IN
Harris, Robert	20	M	Farmer	TN
Elizabeth	62	F		GA
Cook, Mary	13	F		MO
Breeding, James M.	28	M	Farmer	MS
Elizabeth H.	21	F		TN
Margarett P.	3	F		MO
Mary C.	2	F		MO
Elijah A.	28	M	Farmer	TN
Lynch, James	30	M	Farmer	VA
Frances	23	F		TN
John	2	M		TX
Mary	1	F		TX
Harris, Virgil H.	55	M	Farmer	TN
Lucretia	28	F		TN
Cristin	11	F		TX
Susan	7	F		TX
Sam H.	3	M		TX
Louisa	1	F		TX
Harris, William A.	31	M	Farmer	TN
Sarah	21	F		TN
James A.	5	M		TX
George R.	2	M		TX
Winston, John G.	25	M	Farmer	TN
Strickland, Thomas	30	M	Farmer	TN
Elizabeth	25	F		AL
Stephen	7	M		AR
John	2	M		TX
William	3/12	M		TX
Fanning, George W.	37	M	Farmer	TN
Mary	15	F		IL
John	14	M		IL
Nancy J.	10	F		IL
Andrew J.	8	M		IL
Lucretia	5	F		IL
Peter	3	M		TX
Williams, Cintha	52	F		SC
William P.	22	M	Farmer	TN
Margarett E.	16	F		TN
Henry M.	12	M		TN
Susan A.	7	F		TN
Nancy	20	F		TN
Martha	18	F		TN
Hayse, Francis M.	28	M	Farmer	TN
Mary	29	F		MO
James	10	M		AR

Name	Age	Sex	Occupation	State
Clevinger, Thomas	50	M	Farmer	TN
Elizabeth	30	F		TN
Abigail	7	F		IL
Elias	4	M		TX
Jesse	3	M		TX
Newell, Samuel	51	M	Farmer	TN
Sally	41	F		MO
Haynes, Joshua	40	M	Farmer	TN
Delilah	42	F		KY
William	17	M	Farmer	IL
Robert	14	M		MO
Sally	11	F		MO
Joshua T.	7	M		MO
Williamson, John	65	M	Farmer	NC
Jane	55	F		NC
Margarett	18	F		IL
Martha	15	F		MO
Malinda	10	F		MO
Leroy	28	M	Farmer	TN
Chany, Stokley R.	30	M	Farmer	TN
Nancy A.	26	F		TN
Mary E.	5	F		MO
George	3	M		TX
Hobbs, William W.	53	M	Farmer	TN
Esther H.	27	F		IL
John E.	9	M		MO
Roda E.	7	F		MO
Silas O.	5	M		TX
William B.	1	M		TX
Elizabeth	55	F		KY
Quillin, E. H.	27	M	School Teacher	TN
Elizabeth J.	22	F		NC
Leroy	2	M		AR
Lucretia	6/12	F		TX
Arnold, Levi	30	M	Cabinet Maker	SC
Canzada	27	F		AL
Elenor	7	F		TN
Mahala	6	F		TN
John	4	M		TN
Margarett	6/12	F		TN
Lane, John W.	50	M	Miller	TN
Catharine	28	F		AL
Wilson	11	M		TX
Henry	9	M		TX
William	7	M		TX
Robert	5	M		TX
Ann	3	F		TX
Hariett	6/12	F		TX
Hale, Ann	30	F		VA
Thomas	18	M	Farmer	TN
James	16	M	Farmer	TN
Moody, Lewis	29	M	Merchant (Hotel)	KY
Permelia	25	F		AL
Wilson, John C.	22	M	Lawyer	MD
Potts, T. C.	27	M	Clerk	KY
Cates, James A.	23	M	Physician	TN
Hirly, Henry	52	M	Farmer	NC
July	48	F		TN
Jane	16	F		TN
Eglentine	14	F		TN
William	12	M		MO
Rachael	8	F		MO
Robert	7	M		MO
Wofield, Charus A.	50	M	Farmer	MD
Martha P.	26	F		TN
Char. A. H.	5	M		TX
George W.	3	M		TX
Sarah C.	6/12	F		TX
Louisa	22	F	(M)	AR
George	1	M	(M)	TX
Elliff, E. G.	40	M	Farmer	TN
Mariah	30	F		TN

(continued)

HUNT COUNTY, TEXAS

Name	Age	Sex	Occupation	Birthplace
Elliff, Nancy E.	3	F		TN
Harrison, Mary	49	F		NC
Robertson, E. G.	26	M	Farmer	TN
Watson, Abram	35	M	Farmer	IN
Matilda	35	F		TN
William	9	M		MO
Lucinda	2	F		TX
Henry	73	M	A.D.Crist.	??
Parsons, John	54	M	Farmer	TN
Precilla	45	F		VA
Syvana	17	F		VA
Nancy	15	F		VA
Elizabeth	13	F		IN
John	7	M		TX
William	4	M		TX
Meredith	2	M		TX
White, W. J.	25	M	Farmer	TN
Nancy	18	F		MO
Martin	8	M		MO
John	10	M		MO
Henry, Andrew	25	M	Farmer	TN
Sarah A.	19	F		MO
James E.	2	M		TX
Bowden, John T.	38	M	Farmer	KY
Elizabeth	29	F		TN
William C.	8	M		MO
Amanda F.	6	F		MO
Mary J.	4	F		TX
S. E.	2	F		TX
Findly, William	33	M	Farmer	IN
Elizabeth	26	F		TN
Eliza C.	8	F		TX
Manerva	6	F		TX
David M.	2	M		TX
Price, Isaac	43	M	Farmer	TN
Elender J.	38	F		KY
Eliza J.	14	F		AR
Thomas	11	M		MO
Isaac	8	M		MO
Telitha	6	F		MO
Andrew	4	M		TX
Manerva	1	F		TX
Shephard, C. C.	32	M	Farmer	TN
Agnes	31	F		??
Mary M.	10	F		AR
David	7	M		AR
C. C.	1	M		TX
Plumard, William	38	M	Farmer	TN
Sarah	32	F		TN
Elizabeth	11	F		AR
Arkansa	5	F		TX
Taylor, Thomas	54	M	School Teacher	SC
Bowen, Hyram	36	M	Farmer	TN
Elizabeth	26	F		TN
Amelia	7	F		AR
Robert	4	M		TX
Jesse	2	M		TX
William	6/12	M		TX
Watson, John	17	M	Farmer	IL
Bowen, George	17	M	Farmer	TN
Hogan, Robert	49	M	Farmer	KY
Phoebe	44	F		KY
John	22	M	Farmer	TN
William	19	M	Farmer	IL
Joshua	16	M	Farmer	MO
Henry	14	M		AR
Robert	11	M		AR
Martha	8	F		AR
Shephard, Savanna	44	F		TN
Pleasant	5	M		MO
Rily, Abraham	39	M	Farmer	TN
Louisa J.	13	F		AR
Clarinda	11	F		AR
McBride, Sherwood	48	M	Farmer	TN
Catharine	47	F		NC
John	26	M	Farmer	MS
Margarett	19	F		AL
Daniel	13	M		AL
Jesse	11	M		MS
Thomas	5	M		MS
Rily, Owen	34	M	Farmer	IN
Mary	25	F		TN
J. R.	6	M		TX
Wilson, Jackson	30	M	Farmer	TN
Mary	36	F		NC
Margarett	2	F		TX
Wilson, William	25	M	Farmer	TN
Mary	29	F		TN
George	8	M		MO
Milly Ann	5	F		MO
Albert	2	M		TX
Calvin	1	M		TX
Wilson, A. D.	26	M	Physician	TN
Elizabeth	19	F		TN
Williams, William L.	30	M	Farmer	AL
Cirena	25	F		TN
Frances	11	F		TN
William B.	10	M		TN
John ?.	6	M		IL
George W.	5	M		TX
Martha	1	F		TX
Hart, Hardin	34	M	Farmer	VA
Nancy J.	22	F		IL
Sintha	6	F		TX
Thomas J.	3	M		TX
Granger, John	32	M	Surveyor	TN

JACKSON COUNTY, TEXAS

Name	Age	Sex	Occupation	Birthplace
Williams, Neel	30	M	Farmer	MO
Susan	22	F		TN
Nancy	8/12	F		TX
Job	68	M		NC
Nancy	68	F		NC
Joshua	34	M	None	MO
Loony, Henry E.	30	M	Farmer	(E)TN
Lavina	26	F		(E)TN
Jenkins, Sarah	36	F		(E)TN
Annis	12	F		(W)TN
William W.	10	M		(W)TN
Joseph L.	8	M		(W)TN
Henry	5	M		(W)TN
Mary F.	3	F		(W)TN
Menefee, George	34	M	Farmer	(E)TN
Lettitia	22	F		MS
Thomas	7	M		TX
James	5	M		TX
George	3	M		TX
Penelope	1	F		TX
Crozier, Matthew	44	M	House Joiner	PA
White, John M.	42	M	Farmer	NC
Lucinda Jane	33	F		KY
J. L. Sophronia	12	F		TX
J. Bedford	9	F(M)		TX
Margarett	7	F		TX
Ellen J.	3	M		TX
Harriet A.	1	F		TX
Jane A.	43	F		NC
Harriet M.	35	F		TN
Rogers, S. C. A.	40	M	Farmer	VA
Lucinda	31	F		TN
John A.	7	M		TX
Kernan, Adolphus R.	8	M		Europe

JACKSON COUNTY, TEXAS

Menefee, John	37 M Farmer	TN
Frances J.	34 F	TN
S. Austin	1 M	TX
Stoner, George	11 M	MO
Edwards, W. C.	34 M Farmer	VA
Amanda M. E.	24 F	TN
Indiana	4 F	TX
Teana	1 F	TX
Dever, James	33 M Farmer	TN
Heard, James	22 M Farmer	AL
Dever, Lucy	10 F	TX
Sutherland, George	62 M Farmer	VA
Frances	60 F	TN
Thomas S.	28 M Farmer	TN
Mary E.	18 F	AL
Elizabeth	20 F	AL
Tillitha A.	1 F	TX
White, Benjamin J.	57 M Mechanic	(E)TN
Sarah	47 F	KY
Heley, Maria	30 F	NH
Joel	11/12 M	TX
Hogle, Isaac	28 M Farmer	NY
Rogers, Joseph	27 M Farmer	TN
Rachel T.	21 F	Nova Scotia
Susan E.	3 F	TX
Eliza V.	1 F	TX
Neunes, Antonio	21 M Becero	TX
Williams, Malkijah	46 M Farmer	(W)TN
Cynthe Ann	37 F	MO
Julia Ann	14 F	TX
Thomas R.	12 M	TX
Lucretia	11 F	TX
John	10 M	TX
Mary	8 F	TX
Ruth	8/12 F	TX
Ford, William G.	32 M Merchant	TN
Margaret B.	22 F	MS
Zacheus W.	4 M	TX
Mary Ann	1 F	TX
Wilkins, John	37 M Cabnt. Mkr.Df & D.	VA
George, Will B.	16 M Clerk	MS
Edmiston, John R.	33 M Farmer	TN
Jane	24 F	TN
William A.	22 M	TN
R. C.	20 M	TN
Billups, G. R.	34 M Clerk & Inn Kpr.	MD
Rogers, John A.	34 M Merchant	TN
Davis, Louisiana	58 F Boarding House	(E)TN
Elizabeth F. M.	21 F	(E)TN
Georgian J.	9 F	TX
Beamont, William	49 M Farmer	ENG
Susan B.	31 F	KY
Gulielmus	12 M	TN
Alex. G.	7 M	TN
Gabriel	5 M	TN
Cook, Thomas F.	37 M Clergy Methodist	KY
Daniel S.	15 M Student	--
Valentine	13 M	--
Ella	9 F	--
White, Francis M.	38 M Farmer	TN
Margaret A.	22 F	SC
Mary E.	12 F	TX
Hugh L.	10 M	TX
Rosa L.	7 F	TX
Flora	3 F	TX
Francis M.	6/12 M	TX
Flayer, George	15 M	At Sea Foreigner
Haynes, Thomas	48 M Farmer & Lawyer	(E)TN
Celia Ann	29 F	LA
Daniel	21 M Farmer	KY

(continued)

Haynes, Sally	18 F	KY
Christopher	12 M	KY
Amos	10 M	LA
Arthur	8 M	LA
Robert	4 M	LA
Blanche	2 F	TX
Stone, James	32 M Millwright	MD
Christian, James	25 M Farmer	TN
Sopona	23 F	TN
Robert	5 M	TN
Mary A.	3 F	MS
Thomas A.	1 M	TX
Thompson, N. B.	50 M Farmer	KY
R. W.	65 F	MO
Andrews, Moran	21 M Laborer	GER
Armstrong, William	23 M	TN
------	20 F	AR
Samuel	2 M	TX
Fine, Levi	32 M Farmer	(E)TN
Clarissa	24 F	MO
Mary L.	8 F	TX
Nancy A.	3 F	TX
Sarah	1 F	TX
Kellar, Francis S.	49 M Farmer	OH
Lavina	48 F	TN
Alexander	19 M	TX
Eliza	13 F	TX
Isabella	9 F	TX
Francis M.	4 M	TX
Carlin, Daniel	50 M Laborer	IRE
McHenry, John	52 M Farmer	IRE
Rachel	38 F	TN
Catharine	18 F	TX
Sarah	12 F	TX
John	11 M	TX
Susan	9 F	TX
Mary	5 F	TX
Elizabeth	4 F	TX
Ann	2 F	TX
James	1/12 M	TX
Ryan, William M.	10 M	TX
Cook, John F.	36 M Farm. & Meth.Clrgy	KY
Caroline A.	29 F	TN
Martha J.	8 F	TN
James Given	5 M	MS
William M.	3 M	TX
Margaret A.	1 F	TX
Stewart, Robert	22 M Carpenter	KY
Duncan, James A.	26 M Farmer	VA
Myers, Thomas	49 M Farm. & Meth.Clrgy	TN
Sarah	43 F	TN

JASPER COUNTY, TEXAS

Turner, Samuel	38 M Farmer	SC
Emily	32 F	TN
Pleasant D.	12 M	TX
Elizabeth	8 F	TX
Samuel H.	4 M	TX
Emily	1 F	TX
Anglin, Drury	55 M	--
Brown, John	45 M Farmer	TN
Rebecca	36 F	MO
Martha	16 F	LA
Emily	14 F	TX
Hannibal	12 M	TX
Alexander	10 M	TX
Louisa	8 F	TX
John Tyler	6 M	TX
Edward	4 M	TX
James W.	2 M	TX
Bennett, John	35 M Farmer	IRE
Martha Ann	27 F	TN
Janency	5 F	TN
Mary Jane	3 F	TN

JASPER COUNTY, TEXAS

Name	Age	Sex	Occupation	Birthplace
Isabel, Jabez	59	M	Wheelwright	SC
Martha	42	F		TN
McGaughey, Sarah Ann	30	F		AL
Isabel, Martha S.	23	F		AL
H. M.	22	F		AL
Samuel B.	21	M	Cabinet Maker	AL
Nancy Caroline	18	F		AL
Benjamin J.	15	M		AL
John G.	14	M		AL
George W.	9	M		AL
McGaughey, Martha H.	10	F		AL
Alfred D.	8	M		AL
Anderson, William C.	51	M	Farmer	SC
Mary K.	46	F		TN
Mary Martha	8	F		TX
Veatch, Samuel H.	17	M	Student	LA
Good, Edward	67	M	Farmer	VA
Nancy C.	65	F		VA
Joseph W.	25	M	Farmer	MO
Louisa	23	F		MO
Minor P.	21	M	Farmer	TN
McGaughey, L. G.	38	M	Farmer	TN
Caroline H.	26	F		SC
Bevel, Mary J.	9	F		TX
Warren J. S.	7	M		TX
McGaughey, L. V.	4	F		TX
Jackson, Thomas	2	M		TX
Everett, William	15	M		TX
James	12	M		TX
Good, Hannibal	39	M	Carpenter	TN
Julia Ann	17	F		LA
Brown, Caroline Jane	37	F		TN
E. W.	14	M		TN
Dink	8	M		TX
Elizabeth Jane	3	F		TX
McFarland, R. C.	35	M	Merchant	TN
Mary Jane	25	F		TN
Cyntha M. A.	8	F		TN
William Monroe	6	M		TN
John F.	4	M		TN
Cleopatra Jane	6	F		TN
A. J. P.	2	M		TX
Price, Frank P.	22	M		TN
McFarland, Sarah B.	19	F		TN
Robinson, S. M.	36	M	Black Smith	TN
Sarah	32	F		TN
Christopher C.	10	M		TN
Milton McD.	8	M		TN
James M.	6	M		TN
William Wallace	4	M		TN
Frazor, Washington C.	40	M	Farmer	TN
Elizabeth H.	41	F		KY
Orphelia	18	F		TN
Mary C.	4	F		MS
Edy E.	12	F		TX
Austin E.	10	M		TX
Elizabeth	7	F		TX
John D.	5	M		TX
William C.	2	M		TX
Frazor, John	34	M	Carpenter	TN
Sarah Jane	27	F		MO
William Alexander	6	M		TX
Ann Eliza	4	F		TX
John James	2	M		TX
Frazor, William S.	33	M	Black Smith	TN
Matilda Ann	24	F		AL
James W.	7	M		MS
Amanda Victory	2	F		MS
McMahon, Friend	74	M	Clergy M.E.	VA
Margarett	69	F		KY
James	32	M	Farmer	LA
Sarah	25	F		TN

(continued)

Name	Age	Sex	Occupation	Birthplace
McMahon, Mary Matilda	8	F		TX
Friend Wilson	6	M		TX
Margarett Leona	5	F		TX
William Stephenson	3	M		TX
Nancy Irvine	1	F		TX
Saxton, William C.	26	M	Black Smith	TN
Elizabeth	20	F		TN
Nancy Ann	3	F		TN
James	2	M		TN
Shipman, J. W.	28	M	Clergy M.E.	TN
Mary W.	22	F		AL
Williams, T. C.	30	M	Farmer	TN
Elizabeth	39	F		MD
Ferdinand	23	M		MS
Augustus	20	M		MS
Virginia	18	F		LA
Francis	15	F		LA
Louisia	12	F		LA
William	10	M		TX
Missouri	7	F		TX
Mary Eliza	5	F		TX
Julia	2	F		TX
Lowe, B. C.	33	M	Farmer	KY
Philam P.	29	F		TN
V--- Curlock	8	M		TX
William S---	7	M		TX
Barney Napoleon	5	M		TX
Claibourn M.	3	M		TX
Smith, Jasper	44	M	Black Smith	GA
Matilda H.	41	F		NC
Joshua	21	M		TN
Elizabeth	18	F		TN
John	16	M		TN
Champion E.	15	M		TN
Amanda	13	F		TN
Eliza	12	F		TN
Matilda Agnes	8	F		TN
William Texas	5	M		TN
Jasper Oregon	5	M		TN
McFarland, Christian	56	F		VA
Lucy Caroline	25	F		TN
Martha J.	21	F		TN
Rich. James	19	M	Farmer	TN
Rebecca Paralee	17	F		TN
Josephine Louisia	13	F		TN
Bevel, John	43	M	Farmer	GA
Ann Jane	34	F		TN
George S.	14	M		TX
John M.	13	M		TX
Spicey Ann	11	F		TX
Minerva Frances	10	F		TX
Mary Ann	5	F		TX
Sitney, Lewis	53	M	Farmer	TN
Polly	54	F		KY
Ulysus K.	20	M		MO
Angelina	18	F		TX
Almeta	16	F		TX
Josephine	14	F		TX
Melvina Jane	12	F		TX
Annecinda	10	F		TX
Miles	8	M		TX
Charlotte Virginia	6	F		TX
Montiville Lewis	4	M		TX
James Harvey	1	M		TX
Shelby, A. J.	39	M	Farmer	TN
Melinda	24	F		IN
Robert	8	M		TX
Julia	5	F		TX
Evin	2	M		TX
Precilla	1/12	F		TX
Wiss, Simeon	51	M	Trader	POL
Margrett	31	F		SCO
Paulina	14	F		TX
Napoleon	12	M		TX
Mark Pole	8	M		TX

(continued)

JASPER COUNTY, TEXAS

Name	Age	Sex	Occupation	Birthplace
Wiss, William	8	M		TX
Valentine	6	M		TX
Messina	1	M		TX
Jack, Adaline	21	F		LA
Reese, James	24	M		TN
Curtis, R.	27	M	Farmer	TN
Jane	26	F		TN
Melvina	8	F		TN
Richard P.	1	M		TX
Powell, R. E.	37	M	Farmer	VA
Mary Ann	31	F		TN
M. A. Wms.	3	F		TX
Peacock, William J.	43	M	Farmer	TN
Octavo	43	F		MS
Mary	17	F		LA
Claiborn	7	M		LA
Susan	6	F		LA
William	4	M		TX
Benjamin	3	M		TX
Robert	1	M		TX
Turner, Maddison	26	M	Farmer	TN
Catherine	25	F		TN
William	4	M		TN
Creese Ann	2	F		TX
Cameron, L. R.	33	M	Farmer	VA
Mahulda	22	F		TN
William N.	7	M		TX
Tabitha Ann	4	F		TX
McVan, Daniel	50	M	Stone Cutter	NY
Mary	20	F		TN
John	3	M		TX
James	1	M		TX
Allen, John	55	M	Farmer	TN
Laurmey	40	F		TN
Lewis, William (Lewis)	19	M		TX
Minerva Ann	16	F		TX
John Allen	12	M		TX
Clementine	11	F		TX
George	8	M		TX
Martha	6	F		TX
Nathaniel	4	M		TX
Eliza	2	F		TX
Huling, Thomas B.	46	M	Merchant	PA
Elizabeth	30	F		KY
Thomas	17	M	Student	TN
Izabella V.	9	F		TX
Rebecca D.	7	F		TX
Arietta	5	F		TX
Robert A.	3	M		TX
Walters, Henry	27	M	Laborer	LA
Norris, Joseph T.	37	M	Laborer	TN
Sarah	32	F		MO
Sorengo Dow	2	M		TX
Black, Jonathan	47	M	Farmer	TN
Melvina	48	F		TN
R. E. Augustus	20	M		AR
Melvina E.	15	F		AR
Edwin S.	12	M		AR
Sarah	9	F		AR
Carver, George W.	29	M	Laborer	TN
Mary Ann	19	F		LA
Thomas William	1	M		LA
McCallister, William B.	39	M	Merchant	TN
Izabella	39	F		TN
Mathew	14	M		AL
Susan S.	12	F		AL
Mary Ann	10	F		AL
Sarah C.	8	F		AL
Frances J.	6	F		AL
Andrew S.	4	M		AL
Smith, Andrew F.	33	M	Farmer	TN
Emily	23	F		KY
Nancy	4	F		TX
Susan	3	F		TX
Araminta	2	F		TX
George W.	1/12	M		TX
Vaughn, A. A.	26	M		LA
Lynch, John R.	52	M	Farmer	PA
Siney	34	F		TN
Edward	21	M	Laborer	MS
William	17	M	Laborer	MS
Margrett	15	F		MS
David	12	M		TX
Jesse	9	M		TX
John	6	M		TX
Elizabeth	4	F		TX
George	2	M		TX
Nancy	1	F		TX
Pearce, Aaron	25	M	Farmer	TN
Elizabeth	22	F		LA

JEFFERSON COUNTY, TEXAS

Name	Age	Sex	Occupation	Birthplace
Marble, John S.	34	M	Farmer	MS
Martha	25	F		TN
Celestine	10	F		MS
J. A.	8	M		MS
Sarah	6	F		MS
John S., Jr.	5	M		MS
Drusilla	3	F		MS
Houston, John	45	M	Farmer	TN
Ann G.	40	F		VA
Martha W.	19	F		TN
Ann E. H.	17	F		TN
Sophrona	15	F		TN
Mary Jane	9	F		TX
Esther P.	6	F		TX
Samuel L.	2	M		TX
Brown, Samuel W.	25	M	Tanner & Currier	TN
Rees, Drucilla	42	F		VA
James	23	M	Laborer	TN
Sarah Jane	16	F		TN
Franklin, Allen	46	M	Farmer	SC
Nancy	41	F		TN
James M.	23	M	Farmer	LA
Benjamin A.	21	M	Farmer	MS
Eliza	19	F		MS
Thomas	17	M	Farmer	MS
William	15	M		MS
Riley	13	M		MS
Allen	11	M		MS
Emily	9	F		MS
John	8	M		AL
Caroline	6	F		AL
Ralph	5	M		AL
Richard	1	M		TX
Safford, John	50	M	Farmer	TN
Evans, Richard	35	M	Farmer	GA
Elizabeth	22	F		TN
Thomas J.	3	M		LA
Evandy	1	M		LA
Colder, Alexander	44	M	Lawyer	NY
Luanza	38	F		MS
Sarah L.	12	F		TN
Celestine E.	9	F		TX
Lucinda H.	6	F		TX
Phebe M.	11/12	F		TX
Benjamin	25	M	Laborer	OH
Mexon, Jeremiah	51	M	Carpenter	NC
Morgan, Charles	47	M	Farmer	TN
Jemima	40	F		LA
Elijah A.	13	M		TX
William O.	7	M		TX
Sarah E.	4	F		TX
White, Nancy	31	F		VA

(continued)

JEFFERSON COUNTY, TEXAS

Name	Age	Sex	Remarks	Birthplace
White, Mary	15	F		TN
William A.	8	M		TX
Nancy J.	6	F	(Idiot)	TX
Martha Ann	3	F		TX
James H.	3	M		TX
Samuel F.	1	M		TX
Johnson, Cave	25	M	Farmer	TN
Margaret E.	18	F		LA
Sarah W.	1	F		TX
Berry, William B.	39	M	Carpenter	TN
Sarah	29	F		MS
James S.	10	M		TX
William J.	7	M		LA
Sarah C.	4	F		TX
John H.	5/12	M		TX
Reading, A. H.	45	M	Millwright	NJ
Julia Ann	35	F		NH
Juliaette	6	F		LA
Angenette	6	F		LA
Mariette	4	F		LA
Davis, William	26	M	Laborer	MS
Gates, Benjamin P.	37	M	Laborer	TN
Alexander, T. K.	27	M	Laborer	TN
Josephine	16	F		LA
Berwick, William	21	M	Laborer	LA
Sarah	16	F	(M)	TX
Harris, V. N.	48	M	Farmer	TN
Ann	49	F		SC
Charles N.	14	M		MS
Sarah E.	9	F		TX
Benjamin L. D. S.	7	M		TX
Lewis, Daniel	46	M	Farmer	NC
Esther	42	F		TN
Sarah C.	7	F		LA
Nancy Ann	6	F		LA
Martha M.	4	F		TX
Emily E.	2	F		TX
Margaret	7/12	F		TX
Naul, Elizabeth J.	19	F		LA
Albert P.	16	M	Laborer	LA
Brown, Allen	31	M	Carpenter	ME
Betsy R.	31	F		ME
Hannah P.	8	F		ME
Green B.	6	M		ME
Wilday, Joseph	25	M	Black Smith	PA
Moore, James J.	24	M	Laborer	TN
Haddling, James	31	M	Farmer	ENG
Franklin, Benjamin	38	M	Farmer	TN
Prescilla	49*	F		LA
John Orr	17	M	Farmer	TX
Joanna	15	F		TX
Sparks, Solomon	30	M	Laborer	TN
Martha C.	30	F		SC
Lucy Ann	8	F		TN
John L.	6	M		TN
James E.	3	M		LA
Mary Susan	1	F		TX
Jacob	22	M	Laborer	TN
Sparks, John S.	39	M	Farmer	NC
Melinda	29	F		TN
Albert	9	M		TX
Eliza J.	7	F		TX
John F.	4	M		TX
Sarah C.	1	F		TX
Court, James	22	M	Farmer	LA
Julia Ann	14	F		TN
Clubb, Thomas B.	32	M	Laborer	SC
Maria	24	F		TX
William C.	4	M		TX
Sarah	1	F		TX
Burris, Enos	49	M	Black Smith	CAN
Gibson, Robert	20	M	Laborer	ENG

(continued)

Name	Age	Sex	Remarks	Birthplace
Willis, John	16	M	Laborer	TX
William	49	M	Laborer	PA
William. Jr.	14	M		LA
Wilson, John	27	M	Laborer	LA
Taylor, John	39	M	Laborer	TN
Smith, Thomas F.	31	M	Carpenter	TN
Ella A.	26	F		PA
Nancy F.	4	F		LA
William H.	2	M		TX
Lowrey, Sarah L.	14	F		OH
Penrod, James	18	M	Laborer	IL
Dyson, James	57	M	Saddler	MS
McFaddin, William	31	M	Farmer	LA
Rachel	29	F		LA
James A.	10	M		TX
John A.	6	M		TX
Sarah L.	4	F		TX
David H.	3	M		TX
Drucilla	1	F		TX
Tanner, R. A.	24	M	School Teacher	TN
Stephenson, John	37	M	Farmer	LA
Sarah	42	F		LA
Sermintha	13	F		TX
Gilbert W.	9	M		TX
John W.	7	M		TX
White, J. F.	21	M	Farmer	TN
Jane	14	F		TX
Lawhon, David E.	37	M	Farmer	TN
Nancy	28	F		LA
Martha	8	F		TX
John C.	6	M		TX
William J.	5	M		TX
Caroline M.	3	F		TX
David B.	1	M		TX
Patridge, Worthy	32	M	Ass. & Collector	NY
Clementine	23	F		LA
Rosalie L.	4	F		TX
Laura Ann	11/12	F		TX
Delano, Norman	31	M	Laborer	OH
Mustin, John C.	55	M	Carpenter	NY
Yenz, Elvine	15	F		GER
Coliar, John	46	M	Grocery Keeper	SC
Myers, Mary	58	F		TN
James	22	M	Saddler	TX
Robert	13	M		TX
Kavanough, A. L.	30	M	School Teacher	TN
Martha A.	25	F		TN
Mary Jane	4	F		AR
John H.	1	M		TX
Susan	64	F		TN

KAUFMAN COUNTY, TEXAS

Name	Age	Sex	Remarks	Birthplace
Ralls, Madison	31	M	Saddler	TN
Elizabeth	24	F		IL
Joseph Monroe	8	M		TX
Mary J.	5	F		TX
Alfred B.	3	M		TX
John M.	10/12	M		TX
Lankford, Cecil B.	39	M	Farmer	SC
Sarah A.	39	F		TN
Joseph G.	8	M		TN
Benjamin F.	7	M		TN
McEnturf, David R.	28	M	Farmer	TN
Elizabeth	32	F		??
Friend, Peter	13	M		AR
John C.	11	M		AR
Hughton	7	M		MO
McEnturf, Isadore	3	F		TX
Morgan	1	M		TX
Wells, William	45	M	Farmer	TN
Mary	39	F		TN
Elizabeth M.	15	F		TN
Mary J. L. W.	12	F		TN

(continued)

Name	Age	Sex	Occupation	Birthplace
Wells, William H.	6	M		TN
Finas C.	4	M		TN
Martha T.	1	F		TX
Becket, C.	29	M	Farmer	KY
Eliza J.	27	F		TN
Sarah E.	12	F		MO
Hester A.	10	F		MO
Thomas B.	8	M		MO
John A.	5	M		TX
David B.	9/12	M		TX
George J.	4	M		TX
Jones, Elizabeth	30	F		TN
John	15	M	Farmer	TN
James L.	13	M		TN
Johile	11	M		AL
Aaron F.	9	M		AL
Mary A.	7	F		AL
Moses	5	M		TX
McEnturf, George	61	M	Farmer	TN
Sarah	56	F		SC
Sarah M.	15	F		MO
James F.	12	M		MO
Robinet, Virginia E.	10	F		MO
Gray, James	56	M	Farmer	TN
Elizabeth	64	F		NC
Holt, Nancy Jane	18	F		AL
Anderson, Thomas W.	52	M	Farmer	VA
Naphonia	45	F		TN
Isaac	22	M	Farmer	AR
Hartwel B.	19	M	Farmer	AR
Martha N.	15	F		AR
Benjamin M.	12	M		AR
George W.	7	M		AR
Anderson, Joseph	24	M	Ferryman	AR
Dosa R.	23	F		TN
Sarah A.	8/12	F		TX
Spears, Sevilia	47	F		TN
Raing, Wyett	19	M	Farmer	AR
Virginia	17	F		MO
Gore, Martha	24	F		SC
James	3	M		TX
Newman, Anda	15	F		MO
Teel, Isaac M.	33	M	Farmer	IN
Barbara E.	19	F		TN
John	15	M	Farmer	IL
Peter	8	M		MO
Eli	5	M		MO
Elliot, Emily	54	F		NC
Sarah	7	F		NC
John	27	M	Farmer	TN
Van Buren	13	M		TN
White, Mary T.	8/12	F		TX
Welsh, Lewis	32	M	Farmer	KY
Elliot, John	25	M	Farmer	KY
Arnold, L. V.	30	M	Farmer	TN
Lucinda	25	F		MO
William R.	8	M		AR
Mary E.	3	F		TX
Asa	5/12	M		TX
Johnson, R. J.	22	M	Farmer	TN
Susanna	21	F		MO
Thomas A.	1	M		TX
Nall, Margret	14	F		MO
Welsh, James	43	M	Farmer	KY
Elizabeth	16	F		TN
Elizabeth	75	F		SC
Welsh, Richard	36	M	Farmer	KY
Adeline	23	F		GA
James	11	M		TN

Name	Age	Sex	Occupation	Birthplace
Austin, J. Larken	30	M	Farmer	AL
Edness	30	F		TN
Mary M.	9	F		AL
Martha J.	7	F		AL
John S. P.	4	M		TX
Albert J.	1	M		TX
Moor, Z. W.	25	M	Farmer	TN
L. L.	7/12	F		TX
Dempsey	20	M	Farmer	TN
Hardin T.	17	M		TN
Mary P.	12	F		TN
Mary H.	47	F		TN
McCasland, J. D. F.	32	M	Farmer	AL
Nancy	54	F		KY
James A. F.	19	M	Farmer	TN
Washington L.	13	M		GA
McCasland, Andrew J.	30	M	Farmer	AL
Rebecca	21	F		TN
James A. F.	1	M		TX
Beard, William H.	30	M	Mechanic	AL
Margret H.	22	F		TN
Mary E.	3	F		TX
Alfred	11/12	M		TX
McAlroy, Martinlet	20	M	Farmer	MO
Jones, William F.	30	M	Farmer	TN
Charity	20	F		MO
Easter M.	4	F		MO
Montgomery, Eveline	18	F		MO
Ward, William	11	M		MO
Jones, Zintha A.	1	F		MO
Jordan, Lewis	23	M	Farmer	TN
Emeline E.	18	F		MO
Dorcas	8/12	F		MO
Jones, James	39	M	Farmer	NC
Sally	42	F		TN
Easter E.	16	F		MO
Lavina	15	F		MO
Louisa M.	10	F		MO
Zintha M.	8	F		MO
Franky E.	6	F		MO
James P.	4	M		MO
Nancy A.	2	F		MO
Newton, J. P.	29	M	Farmer	TN
Zillitha	28	F		TN
John J.	1	M		TX
Mary E.	4/12	F		TX
Elizabeth	31	F		TN
Wisdom, Thomas	48	M	Farmer	TN
Charity	38	F		NC
Charity E.	15	F		MO
David F.	13	M		MO
William J.	10	M		MO
Margret L.	7	F		MO
Sarah L.	5	F		MO
Thomas J.	2	M		MO
Jones, Jackson C.	28	M	Farmer	TN
Ruthy M.	18	F		MO
Zintha A.	5/12	F		TX
Rader, G. W.	41	M	Farmer	TN
Larinda	31	F		NC
Josephine	9	F		AL
Sophilia	7	F		MS
Mary E.	5	F		MS
John H.	3	M		TX
Yadon, William P.	26	M	Farmer	TN
Harriet	21	F		KY
Rutha A.	5	F		MO
Thomas A.	2	M		MO
Nancy J.	3/12	F		TX
Wilson, John A.	25	M	Farmer	TN
Mary J.	23	F		TN
William	6	M		KY

(continued)

KAUFMAN COUNTY, TEXAS

Name	Age	Sex	Occupation	Birthplace
Wilson, Thomas	4	M		IL
Martha A.	2	F		TX
Ward, Jesse	21	M	Farmer	TN
Brinkley, Leroy	38	M	Farmer	TN
Polly	39	F		TN
Wesley	14	M		KY
David	12	M		KY
Saralisa	10	F		KY
Henry Clay	7	M		KY
William	20	M	Farmer	TN
Nancy	16	F		KY
Maston, Thomas (Maston)	14	M		KY
Caroll, Allen (Caroll)	12	M		KY
Cummins, James	57	M	Farmer	KY
Elizabeth	40	F		TN
James	17	M	Farmer	KY
Alfred	14	M		KY
Casebold, James S.	16	M	Farmer	MO
Andrew J.	9	M		MO
Elizabeth J.	7	F		MO
Boyd, Joel	40	M	Farmer	TN
Narcissa	31	F		SC
Jenkins, Lauretta	24	F		TN
Weaver, J. D.	23	M	Farmer	IN
Elizabeth	27	F		KY
James C.	9/12	M		TX
Robberts, Raymond N.	9	M		TN
Ratts, Henry	28	M	Farmer	TN
Hugh	26	M	Farmer	IN
Turner, Elisha	62	M	Saddler	GA
Z. N.	39	M	Farmer	TN
Martha	30	F		SC
Rachel	12	F		LA
Mary	10	F		LA
Elisha R.	8	M		TX
Samuel W.	6	M		TX
Frances	4	F		TX
Zintha	2	F		TX
Eagan, James	45	M	Farmer	PA
Mary	36	F		AR
Sarah J.	17	F		AR
George W.	13	M		AR
Mary A.	11	F		AR
William	9	M		AR
Margret	7	F		TX
James	5	M		TX
John	2	M		TX
Dempsey, David	17	M	Farmer	TN
Scroggin, Henry	40	M	Farmer	IL
Mary	36	F		TN
Daniel W.	19	M	Farmer	IL
Thibitha A.	15	F		IL
Sophia	13	F		IL
Julia M.	7	F		AR
Sanford B.	4	M		AR
Wood, Samuel D.	20	M	None	GA
Sidney A.	15	M		GA
Chism, Enoch P.	37	M	M.E. Preacher, S.	TN
Amanda A. T.	30	F		AL
Lucinda P.	11	F		TX
John A.	9	M		TX
Missouri A. C.	6	F		TX
Luarene E. J.	2	F		TX
Joseph M. H.	31	M	Ass. & Collector	TN
Alexander, James L.	35	M	Carpenter	TN
Minerva	30	F		MO
James L.	6	M		TX
Joseph M.	2	M		TX
Robert T.	2/12	M		TX
Love, William	64	M	Farmer	SC
Nancy	57	F		VA
Alexander	30	M	Farmer	KY
(continued)				
Love, John K.	21	M	Farmer	TN
Nancy A.	18	F		TN
Margret M.	16	F		TN
Tabor, Frances A.	35	F		KY
Ezell, Frederick	49	M	Farmer	VA
Matilda	43	F		TN
Hubert C.	24	M	Farmer	TN
Phillip W.	20	M	farmer	TN
Caroline F.	17	F		KY
Candamia N. F.	14	F		KY
Eldridge F.	12	M		KY
Matilda C. V.	8	F		KY
Terrell, R. A.	30	M	Surveyor	TN
Emily L.	23	F		TX
Christopher J.	4	M		TX
Mary M.	2	F		TX
Rayel, W. W.	23	M	Black Smith	TN
Asteon, William G.	32	M	Farmer	TN
Alfrey	27	F		TN
Elizabeth	10	F		TN
James	8	M		TN
Wiley T.	5	M		TN
Alfred	4	M		AR
John	2	M		TX
Fare(Fore), W.	26	M	Farmer	TN
Elinor	23	F		AR
Sarah J.	5	F		AR
Alfrey C.	2	F		AR
Butler, Alexander M.	34	M	Farmer	TN
Catharine D.	34	F		KY
Rebecca A.	8	F		LA
Richard M.	7	M		LA
Houston, Isaac	31	M	Farmer	IL
Nancy	32	F		TN
Mary A.	12	F		TX
Linzy	11	M		TX
Claiburn	7	M		TX
William	5	M		TX
Sarah J.	5	F		TX
Permelia	4	F		TX
James	3	M		TX
John	1/12	M		TX
Irwin, William D.	28	M	Farmer	TN
Jane	61	F		NC
John L.	6	M		TX
Peter ?.	23	M	Farmer	TN
Bailey, John H.	42	M	Farmer	SC
Ellenor M.	38	F		TN
Frances A.	21	F		TN
Absalom R. B.	17	M	Farmer	AR
James A.	15	M	Farmer	AR
Zintha A. J.	11	F		AR
Samuel S.	9	M		AR
Delania B.	7	F		AR
Martha W.	4	F		TX
Elizabeth B.	2	F		TX
Elinor M.	3	F		TX
John R.	1	M		TX
McCurry, Samuel T.	40	M	Farmer	TN
Susania	31	F		TN
Fisher, Nancy J.	6	F		TN
James K.	5	M		TN
Harrison, P. Bruce	50	M	Farmer	VA
Niles, Frederick	31	M	Laborer	GER
King, Samuel	34	M	Farmer	TN
Martha A.	23	F		AR
Nancy A.	7	F		AR
Truett, James	28	M	Farmer	KY
Dean, Thomas	56	M	Farmer	VA
Jane	40	F		IN
Polly	13	F		AR
M----	9	F		AR
Doggett, (Blank)	30	M	Laborer	TN
Jacobs, Cornealeous	40	M	Farmer	GA
(continued)				

Name	Age	Sex	Occupation	Birthplace
Jacobs, Lavisa	39	F		TN
Elizabeth	20	F		TN
Symons, James	23	M	Farmer	NC
Williamson, Charles	31	M	Farmer	TN
Nancy K.	23	F		TN
Arva L.	4	F		AR
George M. H.	2	M		TX
Shaw, Dicy E.	36	F		TN
William M.	18	M	Farmer	TN
James K. P.	16	M	Farmer	TN
Margret L.	14	F		TN
Lucy A.	12	F		TN
Emily P.	9	F		TN
Hugh D.	7	M		TN
Thomas F.	4	M		TN
Wilson, Robert B.	21	M	Black Smith	TN
Kysiar, James	50	M	Farmer	SC
Fanny	50	F		NC
Lucinda	20	F		TN
Berry	15	M		TN
Wade	12	M		TN
Melford	11	M		TN
James K. P.	5	M		TN
Goodwin, C. P.	32	M	Farmer	KY
Maranda	25	F		TN
Louisa	8	F		AR
William C.	5	M		AR
Rebecca J.	8/12	F		TX
Green, Willy B.	55	M	Farmer	TN
Elizabeth	46	F		TN
Farmer, Willy B.	32	M	Farmer	TN
Connor, John R.	34	M	Farmer	PA
Maria	26	F		TN
Baker, J. L. M.	32	M	Carpenter	PA
Julia A.	27	F		TN
Marina A.	7	F		KY
Henry C.	5	M		TN
John L.	3	M		TN
Francis M.	3/12	M		TX
Barnes, Sterling R.	51	M	Wagon Maker	TN
Martha A.	39	F		VA
William H.	20	M	Farmer	AL
Marcus L.	18	M	Farmer	AL
Willy T.	16	M		AL
Mary V.	14	F		MS
Robert E.	12	M		MS
Thomas W.	10	M		MS
George M.	7	M		MS
Lucy Ann	5	F		MS
Thompson, James	37	M	Farmer	KY
Nancy	27	F		TN
Nancy A.	16	F		IN
John	10	M		IN
Tilman	6	M		IN
Lucinda R.	3	F		IN
Thomas A.	2	M		TX
Marton, Jacob	16	M	Farmer	IL
Butler, Thomas	30	M	Farmer	KY
Eady	29	F		TN
Sarah E.	11	F		KY
Polly A.	9	F		KY
Mary A.	5	F		KY
Malinda J.	3	F		KY
William M.	1	M		TX
Briscoe, Isaac	61	M	Farmer	VA
Hester	55	F		VA
Robert K.	25	M	Farmer	TN
Mildred	22	F		TN
Isaac J.	17	M	Farmer	MO
Briscoe, Susania	35	F		TN

(continued)

Name	Age	Sex	Occupation	Birthplace
Briscoe, Nancy J.	8	F		MO
William J.	6	M		MO
Robert	4	M		TX
Larkin W.	21	M	Farmer	TN
Elizabeth	15	F		TN
Briscoe, Thomas	37	M	Farmer	TN
Prasilla	25	F		NC
Sarah A.	7	F		MO
Mary H.	5	F		MO
Missouri R.	3	F		TX
Martha A.	10/12	F		TX
Briscoe, James R.	25	M	Farmer	TN
Sarah	15	F		AR
Thomas J.	10/12	M		TX
Merriman, Jemiah	36	M	Farmer	GA
Narcissa H.	26	F		TN
Thomas E.	9	M		AR
Robert P.	6	M		TX
William J.	1	M		TX
McBee, John	22	M	Farmer	TN
Elizabeth	22	F		TN
Narcissa J.	1	F		TX
Reeves, William C.	21	M	Farmer	TN
Sullivan, William E.	40	M	Farmer	TN
Mary A.	35	F		TN
Lurany A.	17	F		MS
Louisa C.	14	F		MS
James H.	12	M		MS
Elisa E.	10	F		MS
Jasper	7	M		MS
Newton	4	M		MS
Peel, James E.	59	M	Farmer	TN
Louisa	32	F		TN
Thomas	13	M		AR
Malinda	12	F		AR
Clarinda	12	F		AR
Mary J.	10	F		AR
Frederick B.	8	M		AR
James	6	M		AR
Zilphia A.	3	F		TX
Robert W. P.	3/12	M		TX
Samuel	19	M	Farmer	AR
Balls, Rolin	49	M	Farmer	NC
Oma E.	48	F		GA
F. M.	24	M	Farmer	TN
John W.	22	M	Farmer	AL
Jane	17	F		AL
Levi D.	13	M		MS
Elizabeth M.	12	F		MS
Sinderilla	9	F		MS
Williams, Thomas L.	39	M	Farmer	TN
Franky	39	F		TN
Permelia A.	17	F		TN
Polly	15	F		TN
Alanda	9	F		TN
Ira	7	F		TN
Tilda	5	F		MO
Howard, Ephraim	69	M	Farmer	CT
Silas	50	M	Farmer	TN
Libby	43	F		TN
William C.	32	M		MO
Howard, Charlton	39	M	Farmer	KY
Margret	40	F		KY
William J.	7	M		MO
Silas	4	M		MO
Edgeman, Mary	18	F		KY
Vanpool, Obed	25	M	Farmer	TN
Allen, Joseph E.	28	M	Carpenter	TN
Mary A.	23	F		LA
Mary L.	2	F		TX
Karber, Peter	69	M	Farmer	NY
Rebecca	27	F		TN
Henry	4	M		TX
Jasper N.	10/12	M		TX

(continued)

KAUFMAN COUNTY, TEXAS

Name	Age	Sex	Occupation	Birthplace
Ballard, Nancy J.	23	F		TN
Mary J.	3	F		TX
McBee, William N.	18	M	Farmer	TN
Allen, William A.	42	M	Physician	VA
John	19	M	Farmer	TN
Susan	13	F		MO
William R.	9	M		MO
Allen, James M.	22	M	Farmer	TN
Elizabeth	20	F		MS
William B.	11/12	M		TX
Simmons, Obediah	27	M	Farmer	TN
Mary A.	20	F		TN
James M.	5	M		TX
John A.	2	M		TX
Ford, Hazel P.	37	M	Farmer	TN
Susan	28	F		LA
Lucinda	9	F		TX
Ellinor	5	F		TX
Jerome	2	M		TX

LAMAR COUNTY, TEXAS

Precinct No. 1

Name	Age	Sex	Occupation	Birthplace
Reynolds, Ruben W.	50	M	Farmer	TN
Lucinda R.	42	F		TN
Ledbetter, Archibald	20	M	Ox Driver	AL
Literal, Jerry	18	M	Ox Driver	MO
Doss, Willis H.	8	M		TX
Tubbs, William	36	M	Black Smith	TN
Mary	21	F		TN
Frances	2	F		TX
Harman, John T.	59	M	Farmer	PA
James W.	25	M	Physician	TN
Lewis G.	23	M	Surveyor	TN
John T.	19	M	School Boy	TN
Graham, James	44	M	Farmer	TN
Eliza A.	28	F		AL
William S.	8	M		TX
Joseph R.	6	M		TX
Nancy J.	4	F		TX
Cynthia A.	3	F		TX
Mary L.	2	F		TX
Casbeer, John	44	M	Farmer	TN
Lucinda	43	F		TN
Malina T.	17	F		AR
Thomas A.	15	M		AR
Joseph L.	11	M		TX
William M.	7	M		TX
John R.	2	M		TX
Bonner, George S.	38	M	Farmer	TN
Elizabeth D.	34	F		TN
Mary E.	14	F		TN
Martha M.	9	F		TX
Sarah E.	6	F		TX
Margaret L. T.	4	F		TX
Minerva D.	1/12	F		TX
Casbeer, James	34	M	Farmer	TN
Melissa	34	F		TN
Thomas M.	15	M		AR
Josiah C.	13	M		AR
James	9	M		AR
Elizabeth	7	F		AR
Mary J.	5	F		AR
Lucinda	4	F		TX
Caroline	2	F		TX
Emily	1	F		TX
Cause, Isaac	53	M	Farmer	SC
Margaret	48	F		SC
Elizabeth J.	21	F		TN
Ellander J.	20	F		TN

(continued)

Name	Age	Sex	Occupation	Birthplace
Cause, William R.	17	M	Farmer	TN
Mary M.	15	F		TX
Isaac	13	M		TX
Margaret	11	F		TX
Stephenson, Sewright	21	M	Laborer	TN
Butler, John J.	25	M	Farmer	TN
Christiana	20	F		AL
Joseph	2	M		MS
Davis, Joseph	74	M	Farmer	VA
Nichelson, James	40	M	Farmer	TN
Margaret	30	F		AR
William	10	M		TX
Jane	7	F		TX
James	4	M		TX
Graham, Alexander N.	32	M	Farmer	TN
Mary J.	25	F		AL
Mary E.	5	F		TX
James H.	3	M		TX
Thomas A.	1	M		TX
Stephens, Alexander	55	M	Farmer	SC
Margaret	55	F		SC
Narcissa H.	30	F		SC
Jacob	19	M	Farmer	SC
Isaiah	25	M	Farmer	SC
George	16	M		TN
George H.	6	M		TX
Sewright, John	56	M	Farmer	SC
Caroline	45	F		SC
William	26	M	Mechanic	SC
John	18	M	Farmer	SC
Sarah	14	F		SC
Martha	12	F		TN
George	10	M		TX
Narcissa	2	F		TX
Jeffries, Samuel	60	M	Farmer	GA
Jenny	55	F		GA
Houston	19	M	Farmer	TN
Jeffries, James	36	M	Farmer	TN
Sarah	30	F		AL
Benjamin	8	M		TX
Caroline	6	F		TX
Jane	4	F		TX
James	2	M		TX
Catharine	6/12	F		TX
Jeffries, Alexander M.	27	M	Farmer	TN
Elizabeth	26	F		TN
John	3	M		TX
Allison L.	2/12	M		TX
Harman, Lewis	54	M	Black Smith	TN
Harman, Lewis	54	M	Black Smith	TN
Jacob	49	M	Farmer	TN
Elizabeth	74	F		VA
Mary A.	52	F		TN
William	22	M	Farmer	TN
Sears, John S.	28	M	Black Smith	NC
Caroline	24	F		TN
Elizabeth J.	6	F		TN
Mary C.	1	F		TX
Harman, John	43	M	Farmer	TN
Harriet	38	F		TN
Jacob W.	19	M	Farmer	TN
Margaret T.	17	F		TN
Thomas N.	15	M		TN
Lewis	13	M		TN
Henry J.	11	M		TX
James	9	M		AR
John P.	8	M		AR
Elizabeth	6	F		AR
Nancy A.	4	F		AR
Juliann	2	F		TX
Lewis, Lacy T.	38	M	(Insane)	NC
Susan	35	F		TN

(continued)

Name	Age	Sex	Occupation	Birthplace
Lewis, Martha	11	F		TX
John J.	9	M		TX
Mary	7	F		TX
Sarah	5	F		TX
Robert H. T.	2	M		TX
Julia S. M.	9/12	F		TX
Patton, Andrew B.	38	M	Farmer	TN
Elizabeth A.	37	F		GA
Sarah E.	17	F		AL
Nancy A.	15	F		AL
John Robert	12	M		AL
Patton, William B.	44	M	Farmer	TN
Elizabeth	50	F		VA
Robert J.	17	M	Farmer	AL
Salina A.	15	F		AL
Nancy E. S.	13	F		AL
Pettus, John ?.	27	M	Physician	NC
Hardison, Theophilus	49	M	Farmer	NC
Selina A.	43	F		VA
Mary A.	16	F		AL
Martha F.	14	F		AL
James W.	6	M		TX
Philley, Bartis	28	M	Farmer	TN
Westerman, John	25	M	Farmer	TN
Elizabeth	24	F		TN
John W.	4	M		TN
Jacob W.	2	M		TX
Oliver, W. James	24	M	Farmer	AL
Martha E.	18	F		TN
Harriet E.	1	F		TX
Miller, Richard G.	55	M	Farmer	NC
Rebecca	52	F		TN
Laura E.	16	F		TN
Henry P.	9	M		TX
Lawson, William	27	M	Farmer	AL
Miller, Hezekiah T.	24	M	Farmer	AL
Sarah J.	19	F		TN
Ann T.	1	F		TX
Williams, Sterling E.	39	M	Farmer	TN
Elizabeth E.	28	F		AL
Frances L.	14	F		TN
Albert N.	12	M		TN
Nancy E.	7	F		TX
Martha E.	5	F		TX
Margaret J.	2	F		TX
Mary A.	9/12	F		TX
Scales, James D.	25	M	Physician	TN
Amanda	21	F		TN
Thomas H.	5	M		TN
William James	3	M		TN
Neal, Matthias G.	40	M	Farmer	SC
Malina	28	F		TN
Celestia O.	8	F		TN
Sarah E.	5	F		TN
Josephine	3	F		TX
Marian H.	1	F		TX
Brown, Pedandrum	40	M	Farmer	AL
Rebecca	38	F		SC
Charles M.	14	M		TN
Leonidas	12	M		TN
Malinda	10	F		TN
Alphira	8	F		TN
Thomas B.	6	M		TN
George W.	4	M		TX
James	2	M		TX
Graves, Edmund	40	M	Farmer	TN
Zilpha	31	F		TN
Cornela	3	F		TN
Mary E.	1/12	F		TX
Harris, George W.	62	M	Farmer	NC

(continued)

Name	Age	Sex	Occupation	Birthplace
Harris, Julia A.	55	F		TN
Lewis H.	29	M	Farmer	TN
Nancy C.	16	F		TN
John V.	15	M		TN
Jacob C.	27	M	Farmer	TN
Stone, Benjamin S.	45	M	Farmer	MO
Rebecca	39	F		MO
Robert	18	M	Farmer	MO
Martin	5	M		TX
James W.	3	M		TX
Patterson, John	55	M	Farmer	TN
James	19	M	Farmer	AR
Harman, Michael	45	M	Farmer	TN
Phile	48	F		TN
Doctor G.	18	M	Farmer	TN
Dickson, James C.	30	M	Farmer	TN
Elizabeth	21	F		TN
Martin	7	M		TX
James	5	M		TX
Mathias	2	M		TX
Leroy	8/12	M		TX
Donald, Allen	46	M	Farmer	NC
Elizabeth	45	F		NC
Mary E.	20	F		TN
Josephine	9	F		TN
Tennessee P.	4	F		TN
Samuel H.	3	M		TX
Burris, William M.	50	M	Farmer	TN
Matilda	45	F		TN
Sarah H.	20	F		AL
Mariah	9	F		TX
Catharine C.	6	F		TX
John W.	4	M		TX
McGill, James	53	M	Farmer	TN
Mahala	31	F		AL
Andrew J.	4	M		AL
John	1	M		TX
Mary E.	7	F		AL
Wilson, Martin	24	M	Farmer	TN
Eliza	18	F		KY
Collins, James	36	M	Farmer	TN
Nancy	30	F		TN
William H.	10	M		TN
George	8	M		TN
Elizabeth	6	F		TN
Mariah	4	F		TX

Precinct No. 2

Name	Age	Sex	Occupation	Birthplace
Still, George W., Sr.	57	M	Farmer (Deaf)	VA
James W.	24	M	Farmer	TN
Mary	21	F		TN
Dennis J.	20	M	Farmer	TN
William W.	17	M	Farmer	TN
Andrew J.	13	M		TN
John T. H.	11	M		TX
Still, George W., Jr.	26	M	Farmer	TN
Martha E.	19	F		AL
Andrew M.	1	M		TX
Eubanks, James	35	M	Farmer	NC
Elizabeth	33	F		TN
George	15	M		TN
James	11	M		TN
Sarah	8	F		TX
William B.	5	M		TX
Calvin C.	2	M		TX
Crook, John H.	39	M	Farmer	TN
Martha J.	34	F		TN
Jeremiah	14	M		TN
William L.	12	M		TN
Mary C.	10	F		TX
George J. McK.	7	M		TX
Margaret D.	2	F		TX

Name	Age	Sex	Occupation	Birthplace
McCuistion, Anthony	50	M	Farmer	TN
Nancy P.	44	F		TN
Benjamin F.	15	M		MO
Elisha H.	13	M		MO
Bedford L.	11	M		MO
Harrison M.	3	M		TX
Pace, Jesse R. H.	35	M	Farmer	TN
Elizabeth B.	38	F		NC
Mahala A.	16	F		AL
David W.	14	M		AL
John H.	13	M		AL
Mary C.	11	F		TX
Martha	8	F		TX
Jane	2	F		TX
Edmondson, Ann E.	36	F		TN
Angeline	16	F		MS
Winny J.	11	F		MS
Martha E.	7	F		TX
Mary S.	1	F		TX
Crook, Lewis J.	33	M	Farmer	TN
Sarah E.	17	F		AL
Snell, Stephen	50	M	Farmer	NC
Emily D.	38	F		NC
Christopher C.	20	M	Farmer	TN
Stephen F.	16	M	Farmer	TN
Lewis D.	9	M		TN
Martha E.	6	F		TN
William Henry	1	M		TX
Fuller, Edmund	53	M	Farmer	NC
Hannah	52	F		SC
John	20	M	School Boy	TN
Rebecca	17	F		AL
Riley D.	14	M		AL
Woods, Martha	11	F		TX
Edmund R.	11	M		AL
Webb, Milton	36	M	Mechanic	TN
Elizabeth M.	28	F		TN
John W.	8	M		TN
Lavina J.	11	F		TN
James M.	7	M		TN
Elizabeth S.	4	F		TN
Jasper N.	1	M		TX
Webb, Sarah	63	F		NC
Melinda Fanney	17	F		TN
Chunn, Lavina	52	F		TN
Benjamin F. S.	17	M	Farmer	AL
Carroll	22	M	Farmer	AL
Matheny, John	38	M	Farmer	TN
Massa	38	F		TN
George Glasscock	16	M	Farmer	MO
Binnions(?), John	25	M	Farmer	TN
Clementine	20	F		TN
John R.	4	M		MO
James	1	M		TX
Skidmore, Abraham	52	M	Farmer	KY
Emily	32	F		TN
William	21	M	Farmer	AL
John	19	M	Farmer	AL
Nancy	9	F		TX
Mary E.	7	F		TX
Lucy A.	6/12	F		TX
Alexander, Daniel T.	38	M	Farmer	TN
Frances	33	F		TN
John B.	16	M	Farmer	AR
James H.	11	M		TX
Elizabeth E.	9	F		TX
Mary Ann C.	7	F		TX
Abert T.	5	M		TX
Frank T.	2	M		TX
Crabtree, Alexander C.	8	M		MO
Sarah A.	6	F		MO
John S.	4	M		TX
Spulin(Spulan), Alex. C.	30	M	Laborer	NC
Steelay(Stulay), Jane	15	F		MO

Name	Age	Sex	Occupation	Birthplace
Hemby, James	50	M	Farmer	NC
Susan	35	F		TN
Sarah A.	12	F		AR
Alfred	6	M		AR
Richard	4	M		TX
Mary A.	1	F		TX
Acard, Jacob	33	M	Farmer	VA
Mary ?.	30	F		TN
William	10	M		VA
Frederick	8	M		VA
Henry	6	M		VA
Sary A.	4	F		TX
Jacob	1	M		TX
Piper, William	30	M	Farmer	TN
Rachel	26	F		TN
Caroline	10	F		TN
Amanda	8	F		TN
Harriet	6	F		TN
Leonidas	4	M		TX
Sarah E.	2	F		TX
Bracken, Thomas H.	29	M	Farmer	TN
Sarah A.	22	F		AL
James E.	2	M		TX
Julia E.	1	F		TX
Beard, Andrew J.	37	M	Farmer	TN
Delila	41	F		TN
James M.	16	M	Farmer	AL
John W. C.	14	M		AL
William G.	12	M		AL
Pleasant C.	10	M		AL
Matilda A. L.	6	F		AL
Thomas J.	6/12	M		TX
Poteet, Thomas R.	44	M	Farmer	VA
Susan	37	F		TN
Fenton	15	M		TN
Pembroke	14	M		TN
Nancy J.	12	F		TN
Nancy A.	10	F		TN
Parale D.	8	F		TX
Samuel H.	5	M		TX
Susan E.	4	F		TX
Tennessee F.	2	F		TX
Hester A. R.	1	F		TX
Beard, William W.	38	M	Farmer	TN
Amanda M.	32	F		AL
John W.	9	M		AL
Joseph V.	7	M		AL
Tolbert F.	5	M		AL
Sam H.	4	M		TX
Harriet J. E.	2	F		TX
Stevenson, George H.	28	M	Farmer	AL
Fuller, William J.	32	M	School Teacher	TN
Jones, Lewis S.	57	M	Farmer	KY
Sarah	50	F		TN
Martha A.	17	F		TN
Adalaid	15	F		MS
Kiziah	12	F		MS
Paralee	10	F		MS
Lewis	8	M		MS
Skipper, William	25	M	Farmer	TN
Mary	22	F		TN
Rufus	8	M		TN
John	6	M		TN
James P.	1	M		TX
Hannan, Samuel	21	M	Farmer	AL
William	21	M	Farmer	AL
Freeman, Minerva	28	F		TN
William J.	12	M		AL
Carroll	8	M		AL
Samuel	7	m		AL
Almira	14	F		AL
Narcissa A.	5	F		MS
Dill, Archibald	30	M	Farmer	AL
Elenor	26	F		TN

(continued)

LAMAR COUNTY, TEXAS

Name	Age	Sex	Occupation	Birthplace
Dill, William	9	M		AR
Sarah J.	7	F		AR
Eliza N.	5	F		AR
Charles W.	3	M		TX
Kimes, Charles	23	M	Farmer	TN
Elizabeth	26	F		KY
Kimes, Elenor	58	F		TN
Columbus C.	17	M	Farmer	IL
Minerva	13	F		AR
Ambros M.	8	M		AR
Craft, William	54	M	Farmer	TN
Elizabeth B.	47	F		NC
Permelia T.	16	F		KY
Mary L.	14	F		KY
Celestile	10	F		KY
Isabella C.	8	F		KY
Boren, William	62	M	Farmer	SC
Julia A.	57	F		KY
Danold, James W.	25	M	Farmer	TN
Miriam	20	F		AR
Bracken, William	64	M	Minister B. C.	NC
Elizabeth	31	F		TN
Eliza A. J.	12	F		MO
Martha J. B.	10	F		TX
Allen H.	8	M		TX
Nancy A. J. K. P.	6	F		TX
John V. B.	9/12	M		TX
Oshield, Caroline	22	F		GA

Precinct No. 3

Name	Age	Sex	Occupation	Birthplace
Rice, F. B.	41	M	Farmer	AL
Margaret A.	40	F		NC
Cynthia A.	16	F		TN
Sarah J.	12	F		TX
Margaret	11	F		TX
Sam	3	M		TX
Evans, Edmund	5	M		TX
Miller, S. A.	35	M	Farmer	NC
Edney	28	F		TN
John R.	9	M		TX
Mary A.	8	F		TX
Henry R.	3	M		TX
Margaret E.	1	F		TX
Burton, Matilda	16	F		AR
Emeline	19	F		TN
Campbell, David S.	31	M	Farmer	TN
Frances	31	F		AL
James E.	8	M		TX
Sarah J.	7	F		TX
Margaret A.	5	F		TX
Martha E.	3	F		TX
Paul, James	46	M	Minister, Baptist	TN
Agnes	28	F		SC
Harriet	20	F		MO
Ann E.	18	F		MO
Ira	16	M		MO
Anderson	14	M		MO
Emiline	12	F		MO
James	10	M		MO
Thomas	8	M		MO
Davis, Isaiah	67	M	Farmer	NC
Unicy	63	F		NC
Trask, John	30	M	Farmer	TN
Josiah B.	26	M	Farmer	TN
Virgil A.	16	M		TN
Griffin, John F.	49	M	Farmer	LA
Sarah D.	42	F		TN
Catharine	22	F		AR
William	21	M	School Boy	AR
Eveline	19	F		AR
Samuel	15	M		AR
Mary	13	F		AR

(continued)

Name	Age	Sex	Occupation	Birthplace
Griffin, John M.	11	M		TX
Sarah	9	F		TX
Burton, Eli	35	M	Farmer	AR
Eliza	31	F		TN
Mira E.	10	F		AR
Sarah A.	6	F		AR
Ellen	3	F		TX
Onstot, John	48	M	Farmer	NC
Mary	44	F		SC
William	26	M	Farmer	TN
Elizabeth	25	F		TN
John	20	M	Farmer	IL
Henderson	17	M	Farmer	IL
Jefferson	15	M		TX
Wesley	12	M		TX
Thomas	7	M		TX
Lee, Herbert J.	57	M	Farmer	VA
Melinda	43	F		VA
Herbert	25	M	Farmer	AL
Nathaniel	20	M	Farmer	AL
Lucy A.	18	F		AL
Martha	18	F		AL
Matthew	15	M		AL
James	12	M		AL
Jane	10	F		TN
Mary	6	F		TN
Wallis, Lucy A.	16	F		AL
Wallace, Elizabeth	14	F		AL
Engeline	9	F		AL
Lee, Cincinnatus	4	M		TN
Leonidas	6/12	M		TX
Wallace, George	17	M	Farmer	AL
Latimer, H. R.	32	M	Farmer	TN
Lucinda A.	21	F		AR
Mary G.	6	F		TX
James M.	3	M		TX
Lamartine	3/12	M		TX
Yates, William	33	M	Farmer	TN
Minerva	32	F		OH
James M.	11	M		TX
Agnes J.	10	F		TX
Mary L.	9	F		TX
John H.	6	M		TX
William A.	2	M		TX
Elizabeth	3/12	F		TX
Yates, Mary	60	F		VA
Bracken, William G.	33	M	Farmer	TN
Harriet	30	F		TN
William M.	11	M		MO
Mary J.	10	F		TX
Allen, Hiram	31	M	Farmer	AL
Elizabeth	33	F		TN
John	12	M		AL
Joseph	11	M		AL
Melinda J.	9	F		AL
Martin	7	M		AL
Sarah A.	5	F		AL
Mary E.	3	F		AL
McDonald, H. G.	44	M	Farmer	TN
Sarah	37	F		TN
Mary	17	F		TN
John	14	M		TN
William	5	M		TX
Henry	3	M		TX
James	5/12	M		TX
Bledsoe, Lucinda	31	F		TN
James	28	M	Farmer	TN
Luell(Suell)	22	M	Farmer	TN
William	17	M	Farmer	MO
Cherry, Malinda	35	F		VA
Eliza J.	16	F		TN
William	13	M		MO
Susannah E.	10	F		MO
Izri M.	7	M		TX
Mary M.	2	F		TX

LAMAR COUNTY, TEXAS

Name	Age	Sex	Occupation	Birthplace
Yates, Thomas	52	M	Farmer	TN
Avis	52	M		SC
Kielon	21	M	Farmer	MO
Larkin	19	M	Farmer	AR
James	17	M	Farmer	AR
William	10	M		MO
Meads	8	M		TX
Isabella	6	F		TX
Johnson, William C.	23	M	Farmer	TN
Ophelia A.	20	F		TN
Elizabeth	6/12	F		TX
Bracken, James M.	38	M	Farmer	TN
Sarah	30	F		West India Island
William	16	M	Farmer	TN
Susan	10	F		TX
Eli	8	M		TX
Nancy	6	F		TX
Frances	4	F		TX
Ella	1	F		TX
Holt, Eliza	13	F		NY
Mallory, James	41	M	Farmer	TN
Magdalene	25	F		KY
Young	4	M		AR
James	2	M		AR
Sarah	8/12	F		TX
Thomas, John D.	34	M	Farmer	TN
Lavina	26	F		TN
Richard	7	M		TX
Mary	5	M		TX
James	3	M		TX
Dawson	1	M		TX
Draper, William	24	M	Farmer	MS
Eliot, Matthias	64	M	Farmer	TN
Lucy	60	F		TN
Terril	26	M	Farmer	AR
Henry	24	M	Farmer	AR
Eldridge	20	M	Farmer	AR
John	17	M	Farmer	AR
Dunigan, Absolum	27	M	Farmer	TN
Margaret F.	17	F		NC
Compton, Thomas	59	M	Black Smith	SC
Elizabeth	54	F		SC
Malissa	32	F		TN
Jane S(L).	24	F		TN
Susan P.	20	F		TN
Colnes C. M.	15	F		TN
John W.	14	M		TN
Willey	12	M		TN
George L.	8	M		TX
Hoosier, Noah	41	M	Farmer	NC
Rebecca C.	28	F		NC
Henry B.	9	M		TN
Amanda E.	7	F		TN
Sarah F.	5	F		TN
Charles J.	3	M		TN
James	1/12	M		TX
Ray, James M.	45	M	Farmer	VA
Sarah	43	F		OH
Alsa A. E.	18	F		TN
Sarah	15	F		TN
Mary	11	F		TX
Lethe	9	F		TX
Susannah	7	F		TX
William	4	M		TX
James	2	M		TX
Shook, Daniel	38	M	Farmer	MO
Emily	28	F		TN
Martha E.	8	F		AR
Jacob A.	6	M		AR
Serina J.	4	F		TX
Edwin J.	2	M		TX
Burgher, Young	30	M	Farmer	KY

(continued)

Name	Age	Sex	Occupation	Birthplace
Burgher, Mary A.	22	F		TN
Elizabeth	4	F		TX
Mary	2	F		TX
John	1	M		TX

Precinct No. 4

Name	Age	Sex	Occupation	Birthplace
Denton, William C.	48	M	Black Smith	TN
Nancy	39	F		AL
Elizabeth	23	F		AL
William F.	17	M	Laborer	AR
Mary	13	F		AR
John A.	11	M		TX
Byron M.	8	M		TX
Nancy J.	6	F		TX
James	3	M		TX
Orton, Samuel B.	50	M	Farmer	TN
Harriet M.	43	F		AL
James H.	18	M	Laborer	AL
Hezekiah H.	16	M	Laborer	AL
Sarah A.	5	F		TX
Mills, Richard	25	M	Farmer	TN
Nancy	19	F		TN
Foreman, W. W.	42	M	Farmer	SC
Isabella A.	41	F		--
Margaret D.	19	F		TN
Martha O.	17	F		TN
Emily R.	12	F		TN
James S.	10	M		TX
Mary J.	8	F		TX
Louisa A.	6	F		TX
William R.	4	M		TX
Boliver, Washington	31	M	Tailor	TN
Elizabeth A.	30	F		KY
William S.	8	M		KY
David W.	6	M		KY
Early, Elbert	38	M	Farmer	KY
Mary A.	26	F		TN
Emaline C.	10	F		TN
Matthias J. P.	6	M		TX
Selden Y.	4	M		TX
James C.	2	M		TX
Elbert M.	1	M		TX
Day, Samuel	28	M	Farmer	TN
Nancy J.	20	F		TN
Abbot, Larkin	24	M	Farmer	TN
Caroline	21	F		TN
Rebecca	5	F		TX
Jemima J.	4	F		TX
Francis A.	2	M		TX
Day, Franklin M.	24	M	Farmer	TN
Missouri M.	20	F		TN
Ragsdale, Martin H.	36	M	Merchant	TN
Thomas M.	10	M		TN
John C.	8	M		TX
Mary J.	4	F		TX
Calloway, Joshua	48	M	Farmer	GA
Sarah J.	21	F		GA
Margaret E.	19	F		GA
Thomas J.	15	M	Laborer	TN
Rebecca	13	F		TN
John	11	M		TN
Nancy A.	9	F		TN
Joseph R.	6	M		TN
Mary A.	3	F		TX
Dowell, David T.	25	M	Farmer	SC
Mary	60	F		SC
Wheeler, Rufus	22	M	Farmer	TN
Piland, Miles	57	M	Farmer	NC
Pennina	53	F		NC
Elisha	20	M	Laborer	NC
Rheuben	19	M		NC
George W.	15	M		NC
Mary F.	14	F		TN

(continued)

Name	Age	Sex	Occupation	Birthplace
Piland, Pennina	12	F		TN
Harrison, Zada	45	F	Farmer	SC
John M.	18	M	Laborer	TN
James C.	16	M		TN
Newton	14	M		TN
Needum	9	M		TX
Valsane G.	6	M		TX
Kennedy, Thomas D.	52	M	Farmer	KY
Louisa A.	38	F		TN
Elizabeth A.	17	F		TN
James S.	15	M	Laborer	TN
William S.	13	M		TN
John Thomas	11	M		TN
Marion W.	9	F		TN
Aurila C.	7	F		TN
Robert B.	3	M		TX
Smith, G.	36	M	Farmer	TN
Araminta P.	30	F		TN
Samuel P.	12	M		TN
Lucinda A. H.	10	F		TN
Mary N. S.	8	F		TN
Drura C. R.	5	M		TN
Martha M. E.	2	F		TX
Telitha C. R.	1	F		TX
Hobbs, John	30	M	Farmer	TN
Sarah D.	23	F		--
Whitenburg, Daniel	59	M	Farmer	TN
Nancy	54	F		TN
Shafer, Susanah	33	F		TN
Margaret H.	26	F		TN
Sarah A.	23	F		TN
Elizabeth M.	13	F		TN
Shaffer, Mary E.	9	F		TN
Whitenburg, Benjamin W.	35	M	Farmer	TN
Rebecca A.	24	F		TN
James A.	7	M		TN
John A.	4	M		TN
Joseph B.	1	M		TX
Davis, Benjamin B.	33	M	Farmer	TN
Eliza A.	24	F		TN
William	1/3	M		TX
Williams, John W.	23	M	Farmer	TN
Elizabeth F.	25	F		TN
Mary A.	2	F		TX
Marzee M.	1	F		TX
Simmons, Joseph	40	M	Farmer	TN
Martha A.	37	F		TN
George W.	17	M	Laborer	TN
Elizabeth C.	15	F		TN
Mary J.	13	F		TN
William C.	11	M		AR
Margaret E.	9	F		AR
John N.	7	M		AR
Benjamin F.	5	M		TX
Joseph	2	M		TX
Moore, Isaac	38	M	Farmer	GA
Cary H.	36	F		GA
Robert H.	13	M		TN
Martha A.	11	F		TN
Louisa C.	9	F		TX
Samuel T.	7	M		TX
John G.	5	M		TX
Mary J.	3	F		TX
George P.	1	M		TX
Mary J.	22	F		TX
Little, Marcus G.	32	M	Farmer	TN
Irena W.	32	F		TN
Joshua M.	12	M		TN
Mary A.	10	F		TN
William H.	8	M		TX
Marcus C.	6	M		TX
Wesley E.	4	M		TX

(continued)

Name	Age	Sex	Occupation	Birthplace
Little, James J.	3	M		TX
John W.	1/2	M		TX
Chaffin, Toliver B.	40	M	Farmer	NC
Angenet	36	F		TN
William	17	M	Laborer	TN
Green	15	M	Laborer	TN
Lucy	14	F		TN
Emaline	10	F		TN
Caroline	7	F		TX
Nancy	2	F		TX
Nedever, John	54	M	Farmer	TN
Mary K.	45	F		TN
George	25	M	Laborer	TN
Ebenezer	22	M	Laborer	TN
Mark	20	M	Laborer	TN
Andrew J.	18	M	Laborer	TN
David A.	16	M	Laborer	MO
John M.	13	M		MO
Elizabeth	11	F		MO
Nancy A.	9	F		MO
Mary C.	7	F		MO
Jacob	5	M		MO
Rebecca	3	F		MO
Mark	9	M		MO
Nedever, Nioma	41	F	Farmer	TN
George W.	21	M	Laborer	TN
Charles	19	M	Laborer	TN
Mary	18	F		TN
Louisa J.	14	F		TN
Jacob	13	M		TN
Allen	9	M		TN
Franklin	8	M		TN
Marion	6	M		TX
Henry	3	M		TX
Simmons, Benjamin F.	25	M	Farmer	TN
Grider, Granville	32	M	Farmer	IL
Elizabeth	40	F		TN
Robert	12	M		IL
Darinda	16	F		IL
Simmons, John B.	30	M	Farmer	TN
Mary	25	F		TN
Joel	6	M		TN
Louisiana	5	F		TN
Benjamin J.	4	M		TX
William C.	2	M		TX

Precinct No. 5

Name	Age	Sex	Occupation	Birthplace
Civeles, John	36	M	Wagon Maker	AR
Talitha	27	F		TN
John	10	M		AR
Washington	8	M		AR
Lucinda	7	F		AR
George D.	1	M		TX
Lenox, Rutha	55	M	Farmer	GA
Elizabeth B.	22	F		TN
Rachel M.	15	F		MO
Maxwell, Robert H.	20	M	Farmer	AL
Sarah	2	F		IL
Dilingham, John	42	M	Farmer	TN
Jane	31	F		KY
Reed, Easter	39	F	Farmer	TN
Sarah	16	F		AL
Jenny	14	F		AL
William	11	M		AL
Alexander	10	M		AL
Martin D.	5	M		TX
Frances	1	F		TX
Risener, George	34	M	Farmer	TN
Rebecca	33	F		TN
Joel	13	M		TN
William	11	M		TN
Tennessee	8	F		TN
Elizabeth	6	F		TN
Martha	4	F		TN
Mary S.	1	F		TX

LAMAR COUNTY, TEXAS

Name	Age	Sex	Occupation	Birthplace
Miller, James	30	M	Physician	TN
Martha	18	F		TN
Josephine	1/2	F		TX
Foster, Lee	50	M	Farmer	NC
Martha	39	F		TN
Rebecca	18	F		AR
Robert	12	M		AR
Leander	9	M		AR
Texaselina	7	F		TX
Arlethe	5	F		TX
Emaline	2	F		TX
Brewer, Will C.	37	M	Farmer	TN
Milly	32	F		IL
Mathew	17	M		MO
Green	12	M		MO
Mary	14	F		MO
Charles	10	M		MO
Edward	6	M		MO
Snowder, Martha	16	F		AR
Anderson, Frost	40	M	Farmer	TN
Matilda	38	F		TN
William	19	F		TN
George W.	15	M		TN
Jessee	13	M		AR
Susan E.	5	F		TX
Mary A.	3	F		TX
Thomas D.	1	M		TX
Davis, Abner	37	M	Farmer	KY
Sarah A.	35	F		TN
George	12	M		AR
James	11	M		AR
Margaret	7	F		AR
Lucinda	6	F		MO
John	5	M		TX
William	2	M		TX
Snow, Henry	26	M	Farmer	TN
Catherine	24	F		MS
William H.	5	M		TX
Malinda	3	F		TX
John	1/4	M		TX
Brown, William	28	M	Farmer	MS
Davis, Nancy	2	F		TX
Eliza	29	F		TN
Susan	13	F		AL
Thomas	10	M		AL
Nancy	8	F		TX
Matilda	7	F		TX
Polly A.	5	F		TX
Martha	3	F		TX
Elizabeth	1	F		TX
McFarlane, Robert	37	M	Farmer	VA
Washington	31	M	Farmer	TN
Joseph L.	2	M		TX
Huse(?), Nicholas S.	16	M		AL
Gregs, Lucy P.	9	F		AL
Davis, Thomas	39	M	Farmer	MS
Elizabeth	38	F		TN
Mary J.	16	F		AR
John M.	15	M		AR
James	10	M		AR
Virginia	9	F		AR
William	8	M		TX
Doctor R.	3	M		TX
Baker, Alexander	39	M	Farmer	TN
Zepphora	39	F		TN
Amanda P.	14	F		TN
Freeman, Jeremiah	62	M	Farmer (Idiot)	NC
Jane	55	F		KY
Jeremiah	28	M		TN
Eliza R.	20	F		SC
Louisa R.	15	F		SC
Andrew J.	16	M		SC
Francis M.	11	M		AR
Chisum, Van R.	37	M	Farmer	TN
Elizabeth	34	F		TN
Sarah R.	13	F		TN
Miller, James	15	M		TN
Dilingham, John A.	40	M	Wagon Maker	TN
William F.	4	M		TX
Georgia Ann	18	F		TX
Havens, Thomas	56	M	Farmer	TN
Sarah	50	F		TN
John	26	M	Laborer	TN
Sarena	16	F		TN
Fowler, John	53	M	Farmer	TN
Susan C.	12	F		TX
John L.	10	M		TX
Glover, Joel	30	M	Black Smith	GA
Dubly A.	24	F		GA
Nancy E.	13	F		AL
Sarah J.	5	F		TX
Mary E.	4	F		TX
William B.	2	F		TX
Robison, William	23	M	Farmer	TN
Baugus, Franklin	43	M	Carpenter	TN
Matilda	32	F		TN
John W.	13	M		TN
Martha M.	10	F		TN
Lucy A.	8	F		TN
Polly A.	5	F		TN
James K.	3	M		TN
Jane	1	F		TX
Johnson, E. R.	30	M	Farmer	TN
Lydia	24	F		TN
John C.	4	M		TN
Jane A.	2	F		TX
McAmis, James	38	M	Farmer	TN
Martiner	35	F		TN
John H.	14	M		TN
Louisa A.	12	F		TN
Thomas B.	10	M		TN
William C.	6	M		TN
James K.	4	M		TX
Lafeat	2	M		TX
Campbell, David L.	45	M	Laborer	TN
Robert E.	10	M		TN
John H.	2	M		TX
Thom, N. C.	35	M	Farmer	NC
Elizabeth	36	F		TN
David H.	13	M		TN
Malinda A.	7	F		TN
Elizabeth C.	5	F		TN
Kackham, A.	31	M	Farmer	TN
Jane	27	F		KY
William	10	M		TN
John H.	9	M		TN
Emaline M.	2	F		KY
Roberts, William	44	M	Farmer	TN
Piety	44	F		NC
Samuel	21	M		TN
William	19	M		IL
John	19	M		IL
Isabella	16	F		MS
Thomas	10	M		MS
Henry	7	M		MS
Stewart, Daniel	25	M	Farmer	TN
Nancy	21	F		KY
Margaret M.	2	F		TX
Wood, John	30	M	Farmer	IL
Rebecca	35	F		TN
William B.	8	M		SC
James	4	M		TX
George	1	M		TX
James	28	M	Farmer	SC

Name	Age	Sex	Occupation	Birthplace
Hamilton, A. F.	23	M	Farmer	TN
Eliza J.	20	F		TN
Sarah F.	1	F		TX
Dodson, Permelia	38	F		TN
Mathew	22	M	Farmer	TN
Spence	19	M	Farmer	TN
Mary	17	F		TN
Billy	15	F		TN
Nancy	13	F		MO
Eveline	11	F		MO
Elizabeth	9	F		MO
Frances	7	F		MO
Henry	5	M		MO
McCarr, John	39	M	Farmer	TN
Mary	24	F		AL
Susan	5	F		TX
Charles	3	M		TX
Franklin	1	M		TX

Precinct No. 6

Name	Age	Sex	Occupation	Birthplace
Wright, George W.	39	M	Farmer	TN
Sarah J.	28	F		TN
William T.	12	M		TX
Emily B.	11	F		TX
James H.	8	M		TX
Mary E.	3	F		TX
Orton, Benjamin O.	19	M	School Boy	TN
Graham, James	35	M	School Teacher	PA
Eliza A.	25	F		TN
John P.	5	M		TX
Robert W.	3	M		TX
Davidson, Hopkins	36	M	Cattleman(?)	TN
Easter A.	32	F		KY
Samuel M.	11	M		TN
Essenethis E.	7	F		TX
Luticia C.	6	F		TX
Larky J.	3	F		TX
Bluford D.	9/12	M		TX
Ross, Francis W.	35	M	Farmer	TN
Elizabeth	30	F		TN
Edney E.	9	F		TX
Lewis W.	7	M		TX
Martha L.	5	F		TX
Nancy	70	F		IRE
Fowler, H. V.	44	M	Farmer	GA
Sarah W.	29	F		TN
M. Caladonia	18	F		AL
John T.	16	M		AL
Letitia A.	12	F		AL
Emily A.	7	F		MS
Craddock, John R.	42	M	Clerk C.C.	SC
Louisa E.	27	F		TN
Mary E.	4	F		TX
John F.	2	M		TX
Skidmore, William	37	M	Mechanic	KY
Caroline	34	F		TN
John J.	11	M		TX
Joseph W.	9	M		TX
Mary A.	7	F		TX
George W.	5	M		TX
Edward U.	1½	M		TX
Gresham, John	19	M	Apprentice	KY
Glasscock, Richard M.	32	M	Physician	VA
Peacock, Wilson	29	M	Lawyer	TN
Martha C.	26	F		TN
Mary F.	4	F		TN
Jack	1½	M		TX
Pugh, Francis	33	M	Physician	NC
Mary C.	22	F		TN
Catharine D.	2	F		KY
Miles, Francis	28	M	Carpenter	KY

(continued)

Name	Age	Sex	Occupation	Birthplace
Miles, Martha A.	22	F		TN
Mary J.	1½	F		TX
Frank	1	M		TX
Coles, William T. F.	34	M	Physician	TN
Martha A.	21	F		KY
William H.	2	M		TX
Mary N.	1	F		TX
Hunt, Larkin B.	23	M	Wagon Maker	TN
McCuistion, Mitchel H.	22	M	School Teacher	TN
Gresham, James A.	24	M	Constable	KY
Morgan, William T. F.	28	M	Printer	TN
Sarah A. S.	23	F		AR
Mary R.	10/12	F		TX
Moody, James H.	22	M	Printer	IL
Sutton, Cary S.	18	M	Apprentice	AL
Luck, Joseph	67	M	Farmer	PA
Nancy	51	F		TN
Theodore	19	M	Farmer	TN
Alonzo L.	16	M	Farmer	TN
Jenkins, Lexy	18	F		TN
Caroline	16	F		TN
Junior	10	M		TN
Elbert	7	M		TN
Glenn, James B.	36	M	Miller	TN
Elizabeth	50	F		VA
Sarah A.	12	F		MO
Roothy J.	10	F		MO
Susan R.	9	F		MO
Silas K.	8	M		MO
James N.	4	M		TX
Eubanks, George W.	26	M	Grocer	TN
George N.	5	M		TN
James W.	3	M		TN
Mary E.	2	F		TN
Carpenter, Nancy	40	F		TN
Eubanks, Nathaniel	37	M	Grocer	TN
Cooper, Calvin C.	33	M	Physician	KY
Amanda M.	22	F		TN
James M.	5	M		TX
Nancy C.	4/12	F		TX
Long, Jacob	39	M	Clerk, D.C.	NC
Mary D.	29	F		TN
William H. H.	10	M		AR
Margaret A.	8	F		AR
Mary F.	6	F		TX
Laura	4	F		TX
James R. ?.	1	M		TX
Young, Harriet E.	13	F	School Girl	AR
Willson, William H.	31	M	Lawyer	SC
Martha M. W.	18	F		AL
Ann Eliza	2/12	F		TX
Towery, William	21	M	Saddler	TN
Willson, William D.	13	M	School Boy	AL
Anderson, Cornelius R. B.	35	M	Mechanic	TN
Nancy	24	F		IL
Sarah L.	15	F		TN
Eliza C.	12	F		AR
Edward W.	5	M		TX
William D.	3	M		TX
Wright, Alexander W.	30	M	Farmer	AR
Nancy C.	31	F		TN
Mary C.	6	F		TX
Martha H.	2	F		TX
Rhine, Abraham	25	M	Merchant	GER
Telitha C.	22	F		TN
Record, John J.	19	M	Clerk	TN
Ragsdale, Thomas	37	M	Farmer	TN
Amanda M.	27	F		NC
John M.	9	M		TX
Mary J.	8	F		TX
George W.	7	M		TX
William H.	5	M		TX
Ann E.	3	F		TX

(continued)

Name	Age	Sex / Occupation	Birthplace
Ragsdale, Travis W.	1	M	TX
Callaway, William R.	25	M Student	TX
Skidmore, Charles B.	35	M Clerk	KY
Sarah	28	F	TN
Thomas F.	8	M	TX
Stephen R.	5	M	TX
David O.	3	M	TX
Mary B.	9/12	F	TX
Fowler, B. C.	39	M Lawyer	KY
Mary A.	24	F	TN
Pitt, Edmund R.	63	M Taylor (Tailor)	VA
Dorothy	50	F	NC
Elizabeth	16	F	TN
Eliza	14	F	TN
Nowell(?), B. G.	31	M Farmer	TN
Christian E.	27	F	TN
William A.	9	M	TX
Susan A.	8	F	TX
Thomas H.	2	M	TX
Eubanks, William	50	M Farmer	NC
Jane T.	50	F	TN
Larrance	18	M Farmer	TN
Madolena	15	F	TN
Nancy A.	13	F	TN
Winey	11	F	TN
Nathaniel	7	M	TN
Guffey, John	40	M Farmer	NC
Malinda	36	F	TN
Margaret C.	12	F	TX
John H.	19	M	TX
Nancy E.	8	F	TX
Susan A.	4	F	TX
Hamblin L.	2	M	TX
Miller, E. M.	25	M Farmer	TN
Jerusha E.	31	F	TN
Robert C.	3	M	TX
William J.	1	M	TX
Joseph P.	1/2	M	TX
Castleberry, Nancy	30	F	??
Elizabeth	10	F	IL
Martha J.	4	F	TX
Travelsted, Anthony	47	M Minister C.P.	KY
Eliza	45	F	TN
Jasper N.	22	M Carpenter	KY
Smith, James J. K.	8	M	MO
Nowell, Amos S.	21	M Farmer	MO
Araminda	20	F	TN
Sarah E.	2/12	F	TX
Glass, Robert	44	M Waggoner	TN
Jane E.	30	F	AL
Amanda M.	11	F	TX
Laura A.	9	F	TX
Richard C.	6	M	TX
John T.	4	M	TX
Madora M.	2	F	TX
Little, Josephus	41	M Mechanic	KY
Susan	41	F	NC
Elizabeth M.	16	F	TN
Mary K.	6	F	TN
Martha J. M.	1	F	TX
Francis, Edmund	42	M Carpenter	VA
Jane	35	F	VA
Elizabeth	17	F	TN
James	15	M	TN
Lock, Leander	39	M Farmer	TN
Sarah	40	F	MO
Amanda	13	F	AR
Martha A.	12	F	AR
Mary E.	10	F	AR
Melissa	8	F	AR
Eliza	3	F	TX

Name	Age	Sex / Occupation	Birthplace
Hutchinson, Jane M.	44	F	TN
Nancy	19	F	AL
Elizabeth	16	F	AL
Samuel	14	M Farmer	AL
Jacob S.	12	M	AL
Rebecca	8	F	AL
John W.	5	M	AL
Duff, Dennis	38	M Farmer	TN
Foeoby M.	37	F	TN
William M.	15	M	IL
Rebecca A.	10	F	IL
Mary J.	5	F	TX
Howell, Mariah	45	F	NC
Francis M.	14	M	TN
Guane	12	M	TN
Evans, William	53	M Surveyor	KY
Rebecca	49	F	NC
Silas	29	M Farmer	KY
Martin, Martha	2	F	TX
Howell, William C.	30	M Farmer	TN
Herrill, W----	49	M Farmer	NC
Holmes, George T.	26	M Farmer	VA
Nancy	22	F	VA
Davidson, Andy P.	29	M Farmer	TN
Elmira E.	26	F	NC
Scott, Nehemiah	66	M Farmer	NC
Sarah	33	F	TN
Ester	16	F	TN
Daniel	13	M	TN
Samuel	10	M	TN
Alfred	10	M	TN
Thomas	7	M	TN
Benjamin	4	M	TN
Robert	2	M	TN
Telitha	6/12	F	TX
Moore, L. V.	41	M Farmer	GA
Elizabeth	41	F	GA
William G.	20	M Farmer	TN
Bradford C.	16	M Farmer	TN
Mary C.	13	F	TX
Stephen	11	M	TX
Sarah S.	8	F	TX
Sophronia	6	F	TX
Elinor J.	4	F	TX
George W.	2	M	TX
Elvira H.	1/12	F	TX
Williams, M. D.	47	M Farmer	GA
Lucinda W.	34	F	GA
Edwin O.	14	M	TN
William M.	10	M	TX
Harriet A.	5	F	TX
Draper, Hannah O.	16	F	AR
Wynne, William H.	43	M Mechanic	NC
Catherine G.	42	F	TN
Dashira E. H.	19	F	TN
Malvina A.	16	F	TN
William H.	13	M	TN
Mary J.	11	F	--
James G.	8	M	--
Argile B.	5	M	--
Babb, Isaac	34	M Wagon Maker	TN
Margaret E.	22	F	TN
Harriet A.	5	F	TX
Babb, Jesse F.	26	M Wagon Maker	TN
Stephens, William	23	M Farmer	AL
Elizabeth	22	F	TN
Julia R.	9/12	F	TX
Click, Andrew J.	41	M Farmer	TN
Mary A.	18	F	TN
Matthias	8	M	TX
Sarah F.	4	F	TX
Wortham, James R. G.	41	M Farmer	TN
Francis	36	F	TN
Mary E. G.	14	F	TN

(continued)

Name	Age	Sex	Occupation	Birthplace
Wortham, E. J.	21	M	Farmer	TN
Baird, Mary H.	6	F		AL
Bracken, Francis E.	4	M		TX
Reed, Matthew G.	24	M	Farmer	TN
Missouri	16	F		TN
Reed, Phereby	32	F		TN
Reed, William M.	35	M	Farmer	TN
Jane	30	F		TN
Tilford	10	M		IL
Gardener	7	M		IL
John G.	5	M		IL
Lewis C.	2	M		TX
Wortham, Robert M.	42	M	Farmer	NC
Wortham, Nancy	75	F		VA
Smith, Elizabeth	18	F		TN
Wortham, Edward	15	M		TN
Smith, Ellen	5	F		TN
Johnson, John	60	M	Farmer	NC
Mary	55	F		TN
Margaret	18	F		TN
Frances	15	F		TN
Wheat, John	35	M	Laborer	AL
Light, William	40	M	Farmer	TN
Ann	41	F		TN
Mary J.	21	F		TN
Louisa F.	18	F		TN
Michael D.	16	M	Laborer	TN
Elizabeth	15	F		TN
William	12	M		AR
Matilda	10	F		TX
Thomas	6	M		TX
Rufus	1	M		TX
Dennis, Thomas	47	M	Farmer	TN
Lydia	41	F		IL
Henry B.	22	M	Farmer	AR
Martha A. C.	16	F		AR
George W.	14	M		AR
Lucinda P.	12	F		TX
Thomas R.	9	M		TX
Colly F.	8	M		TX
Matthew M.	5	M		TX
Baron D. K.	2	M		TX
Rutherford, John A.	42	M	Farmer	TN
Jane	36	F		TN
Clinton P.	21	M	Farmer	TN
Milton	18	M		TN
Calvin	12	M		TX
Franklin	7	M		TX
Jackson	6	M		TX
Kerr, M. C.	24	M	Farmer	TN
Emberson, Elijah	24	M	Farmer	AR
Margaret	21	F		TN
Henry W.	3	M		TX
Elizabeth	1	F		TX
Higgs, William	46	M	Farmer	NC
Virginia	36	F		TN
Nancy P.	3	F		TX
Melvina	2	F		TX
Wortham, Creed T.	46	M	Farmer	NC
Harriet	43	F		NC
Minerva	18	F		TN
Mary	15	F		TN
Zelida A.	12	F		TN
Cornelia F.	8	F		TN
Thomas	3	M		TX
Baird, Gaines	40	M	Stone Mason	AL
Craine, Jasper	26	M	Farmer	IL
Mary C.	22	F		TN
Joel M.	2	M		TX
Telitha A.	6/12	F		TX
Click, Richard	18	M	Farmer	AR
Emiline	17	F		TN
Fielder, James	29	M	Farmer	VA
Monica	27	F		TN
Brunetta	10	F		MO
Bartley	9	M		MO
Mary	6	F		MO
Ellen	3	F		TX
Fama	1	F		TX
Pitt, Comey	42	M	Farmer	TN
Martha	27	F		VA
L----	16	F		IL
Bedford	10	M		IL
Moton(?)	11	F		MO
Susan	10	F		MO
Sophronia	6	F		AR
Margaret	2	F		TX
Sadler, William S.	39	M	Farmer	TN
Sarah G.	32	F		AL
Mary J.	6	F		TX
Martha F.	4	F		TX
Margaret P.	1	F		TX
Saran, James H.	25	M	Farmer	PA
Sidda E.	24	F		KY
Sarah L.	40	F		VA
John P.	22	M	Farmer	TN
Charles G.	20	M	Farmer	TN
Penelope	13	F		TN
Isaac	10	M		TN
Abraham	5	M		TX
Hamilton, William L.	32	M	Farmer	TN
Melissa A.	21	F		AL
Polly A.	17	F		AL
James G.	15	M		AL
David H.	13	M		AL
Richison, Thomas	24	M	Farmer	IL
Jane	18	F		TN
Wallace, Robert	38	M	Farmer	TN
Charlotte	38	F		TN
Sadler, Martha A.	16	F		TX
Lucy J.	14	F		TX
Elizabeth	8	F		TX
William C.	4	M		TX
James F.	4	M		TX
Henrietta	5	F		TX
Robert	2	M		TX
Housted, Titus	36	M	Farmer	NY
Eliza J.	26	F		MO
Caroline	9	F		MO
Nancy J.	7	F		AR
Sarah	3	F		TX
Brewer, Francis	19	M	Farmer	TN
Sadler, Hiram	42	M	Farmer	TN
Polly	48	F		TN
Elizabeth	7	F		TX
McKincurf, Nancy	38	F		TN
Docia	9	F		TX
Caroline	8	F		TX
John	3	M		TX
Martha	2	F		TX
Davis, Raph	31	M	Farmer	KY
Mary A.	27	F		TN
Samuel	9	M		TX
Thomas	7	M		TX
Mary E.	4	F		TX
John	1	M		TX
Taylor, Mary A.	54	F		TN
Richison, Littlery(?)	22	M	Farmer	IL
Martha J.	23	F		AL
Julia A.	11/12	F		TX

Precinct No. 8

Name	Age	Sex	Occupation	Birthplace
Smith, Dennis G.	42	M	Farmer	NC
Anny M.	35	F		TN

(continued)

LAMAR COUNTY, TEXAS

Name	Age	Sex	Occupation	Birthplace
Smith, William M.	18	M	Farmer	TN
Joseph B.	16	M	Farmer	TN
Margaret J.	14	F		TN
Isaac H.	12	M		TN
Sarah J.	9	F		TN
Henry A.	8	M		TN
Frances A.	7	F		TN
Dennis G.	3	M		TN
James T.	1	M		TX
Bryant, John S.	30	M	Farmer	TN
Arthaann	28	F		KY
Joseph H.	7	M		TX
John B.	5	M		TX
Francis J.	3	M		TX
Mary E.	3/12	F		TX
Scott, William	36	M	Farmer	TN
Sarah J.	32	F		TN
Abraham M. W.	14	M		TN
Christian E.	10	F		TX
Leadora	5	F		TX
Benjamin B.	2	M		TX
Williams, Joseph R.	20	M	Laborer	TN
Williams, A. M.	35	M	Farmer	TN
Jennetta	30	F		TN
Thomas	11	M		TX
Sarah J.	7	F		TX
Cassander	5	F		TX
Nemiah	3	M		TX
Louisa	6/12	F		TX
Wilson, Henry	56	M	Farmer	NC
Nancy	44	F		TN
William	16	M		MO
N----	15	F		MO
Mary	14	F		MO
Thomas	12	M		MO
John	9	M		MO
Jane	7	F		MO
Ellen	4	F		MO
Baker, Nathan B.	34	M	Farmer	TN
Elizabeth A.	34	F		GA
Ladona	5	F		TX
Margaret A.	4	F		TX
Mary J.	2	F		TX
Julia A.	6/12	F		TX
Davis, Ashberry	11	M		TX
Lacy, Larance	36	M	Black Smith	KY
Mary J.	34	F		TN
Elizabeth	12	F		MO
Susan A.	10	F		MO
John J.	8	M		MO
Elias P.	6	M		MO
Robert C.	3	M		MO
George A.	2	M		TX
Cosby, James	50	M	Farmer	NC
Penelope	48	F		KY
Daniel M.	26	M	Carpenter	AL
Mary A.	22	F		AL
James A.	20	M	Farmer	TN
Elizabeth E.	18	F		TN
Isaiah W.	17	M	Farmer	TN
Julia F.	14	F		TN
Penelope C.	9	F		AL
Cayle, Robert	65	M	Laborer	TN
Robert, Jr.	7	M		C?
Burks, Samuel	22	M	Farmer	TN
Rhoda A.	32	F		TN
John	10	M		IL
Mary A.	8	F		IL
Elizabeth	6	F		AR
Richard	4	M		TX
Preston	1	M		TX
Mobley, Mires	41	M	Black Smith	KY
Mary	35	F		TN

(continued)

Name	Age	Sex	Occupation	Birthplace
Mobley, George W.	6	M		TX
William	5	M		TX
Elizabeth	2	F		TX
Phebe A.	1/12	F		TX
Wilson, William	18	M	Black Smith	MS
Shookey, Elizabeth	33	F		KY
Squire	15	M		KY
George	9	M		KY
Mary A.	5	F		KY
Wilson, George	24	M	Laborer	KY
Staton, John	26	M	Farmer	KY
Elizabeth J.	24	F		TN
John W.	3	M		TX
Serrin T.	4/12	M		TX
Brummitt, Harrison	35	M	Farmer	AR
Theodocia	31	F		TN
Samuel	10	M		TX
Hannah R.	4	F		TX
Mary E.	1	F		TX
Gordon, John	21	M	Laborer	AR
McFarland, Ira	21	M	Shoe Maker	AR
St. Clair, Samuel	30	M	Mechanic	IL
Mary A.	30	F		MI
Cordelia	9	F		TX
Sarah A.	5	F		TX
Harrison	2	M		TX
David	1	M		TX
Bogart, Mary	16	F		??
James	14	M		??
Brummitt, Langston	57	M	Farmer	VA
Delila	56	F		TN
Robert T.	23	M	Farmer	AR
William F.	14	M		AR
Jasper N.	7	M		AR
Marberry, William P.	10	M		AR
Cyntha A.	10	F		AR
Amanda M.	9	F		AR
Majors, Hannah	63	F		NC
Reese M.	21	M	Farmer	TN
Hodge, Ann E.	35	F		KY
Mary M.	12	F		MS
Lucinda A.	10	F		KY
Eliza J.	8	F		TX
Alex. M.	5	M		TX
Harris, Sam	20	M	Farmer	AL
Carn, William	52	M	Farmer	TN
Eliza	40	F		TN
William	17	M	Farmer	MO
Merrick	15	M		MO
John	11	M		MO
Houston	5	M		TX
Adline	14	F		MO
Lock, J. W. T.	29	M	Farmer	TN
Deannah	24	F		IL
Emily R.	9	F		AR
Ann Eliza R.	1	F		TX
Wilson, Elisha T.	26	M	Farmer	TN
Mary A.	24	F		TN
Martha	3	F		TX
Bishop, William K.	25	M	Farmer	TN
Whitney, Adaline	41	F		VA
Jason W.	21	M		--
Elizabeth	16	F		--
Samuel E.	15	M		TN
Mary E.	12	F		TN
Reid, Harman	30	M	Wagon Maker	TN
Rebecca E.	23	F		TN
Amanda	16½	F		TX
Record, James C.	53	M	Farmer	NC
Nancy R.	47	F		KY
James K. P.	16	M	Clerk	TN
George W.	13	M		TN
Sion S.	10	M		TN
Mary A. C.	8	F		TN
William T.	2	M		TX

LAMAR COUNTY, TEXAS

Name	Age	Sex	Occupation	Birthplace
Price, Robert	40	M	Assessor	TN
McQuin, E. W.	22	M	Farmer	AL
Evans, E. J.	21	M	Farmer	KY
Ethany C.	20	F		TN
William F.	1	M		TX
King, John	40	M	Farmer	TN
Rachael	34	F		TN
Jacob	12	M		TN
Catharine	9	F		TN
Susannah	6	F		TN
Arcenitt	6	F		TN
Louisa	2	F		TN
Gibbons, Epps	64	M	Farmer	TN
Nancy	60	F		TN
Edmund	22	M	Laborer	TN
Thomas	20	M	Laborer	TN
John	16	M	Laborer	TN
Mary	14	F		TN
Vanlandingham, A. M.	27	M	Farmer	MO
Nancy	24	F		TN
Poindexter, Thomas P.	33	M	Mechanic	TN
Nancy	33	F		VA
James	9	M		TN
Fanny E.	9	F		TN
Benjamin	8	M		MO
Angeline	6	F		MO
Gilliam	4	M		TX
Mary	1	F		TX
White, Louisa	17	F		TN
Brown, Daniel T.	42	M	Mechanic	TN
Elizabeth	38	F		TN
Jackey A.	17	F		TN
Catherine	15	F		TN
Jasper	14	M		TN
Elizabeth	13	F		TN
Bede F.	11	F		TN
Nancy	6	F		TN
Tennessee J.	1	F		TN
Petty, Abigail	40	F		TN
Nancy W.	19	F		AL
Sarah E.	18	F		TN
William H.	17	M	School Boy	TN
Bourland, William H.	38	M	Farmer	KY
Rachael C.	37	F		KY
Margarie S.	17	F		TN
Mary E.	15	F		KY
Benjamin T.	13	M		MS
Nancy A.	10	F		MS
Amanda B.	7	F		TX
Matilda	5	F		TX
Bardexter(?) W.	2	F		TX
Chisum, Claborn	53	M	Farmer	TN
Cintha	35	F		TN
Jefferson	19	M	Laborer	TN
Alexander	17	M	Laborer	TN
P------(?)	16	M	Laborer	TN
R------(?)	14	M		TN
Robert	8	M		TX
Laura	7	F		TX
Mary	6	F		TX
William C.	1	M		TX
Williams, James H.	39	M	Farmer	TN
Mary	30	F		TN
William	12	M		TX
Louisa E.	10	F		TX
Sarah H.	7	F		TX
James H.	4	M		TX
Mary J.	2	F		TX
Tinnin, William	56	M	Farmer	TN
Elzira	28	F		TN
William	22	M	Farmer	MS
Lawrance W.	12	M		MS
David	9	M		MS

(continued)

Name	Age	Sex	Occupation	Birthplace
Tinnin, Martha J.	6	F		TX
H. F.	3	M		TX
Mary A.	20	F		MS
Alexander	14	M		MS
Lawrance W.	12	M		TX
Leslie, James S.	25	M	Physician	AL
Ellen S.	20	F		TN
Lucy J.	1	F		TX
McKinn(?), John	40	M	Farmer	KY
Emeline	27	F		TN
Lawrance T.	7	M		TX
Milton P.	5	M		TX
Mary J.	1	F		TX
Mebane, John A.	26	M	Farmer	TN
Joseph H.	36	M	Farmer	TN
Nathaniel H.	20	M	Farmer	TN
Mebane, Robert W.	31	M	Farmer	TN
Nancy E.	22	F		AL
Samuel R.	23	M	Farmer	TN
Harrison, William C.	58	M	Farmer	VA
Louisa K.	31	F		TN
Martha N.	8	F		TX
Mary L.	5	F		TX
Nancy C.	3	F		TX
Pauline E.	2/12	F		TX
Mebane, Ann ?.	14	F		MS
Ritchey, James	47	M	Physician	SC
Mary	40	F		TN
Caroline	11	F		AR
Thomas	8	M		AR
Andrew J.	6	M		AR
Tinnin, James G.	27	M	Farmer	TN
Lamb, Littleton P.	9	M		TX
John H.	2	M		TX
Burnett, John T.	42	M	Shoe Maker	TN
Susana	31	F		TN
James	20	M	Farmer	TN
Nathan	17	M	Shoe Maker	TN
Louisa	15	F		TN
John T.	8	M		TN
James K. P.	6	M		TX
Samuel O.	4	M		TX
William A.	1	M		TX
Lamb, Eliza J.	10	F		TX
Fulton, Samuel M.	40	M	Farmer	VA
Charity	47	F		TN
William	11	M		TX
Mary	8	F		TX
Nancy	5	F		TX
Albert McK.	4	M		TX
Mariah T.	3	F		TX
Lorenzo C.	7/12	M		TX
Roberts, Thomas	29	M	Farmer	TN
Hunt, William	30	M	Farmer	AL
Mary	18	F		IN

LAVACA COUNTY, TEXAS

Name	Age	Sex	Occupation	Birthplace
Vivion, Thacker	58	M	Farmer	KY
Rosanna	53	F		TN
Frances Ann	19	F		MO
Tryon	17	M	None	MO
Eugenia	14	F		MO
Calvin Riggs	7	M		MO
Boring, Mary Jane	19	F		AR
George W.	14	M		AR
Moffit, Enoch	23	M		NY
Virginia	23	F		AL
Joseph B.	1	M		TX
Ezra	1	M		--
Rains, Ezekiel	33	M	Black Smith & Farm	TN
Mary L.	27	F		SC
Virginia D.	9/12	F		TX

LAVACA COUNTY, TEXAS

Name	Age	Sex	Occupation	Birthplace
Cheny, L. R.	31	M	Farmer	GA
Martha S.	31	F		TN
Boatright, Martin	23	M	Farmer	AR
Nancy A.	17	F		TN
Morrow, Alfred	44	M	Farmer	TN
N. A.	35	F		VA
Mary J.	15	F		AL
Frances A.	12	F		TX
Elvira C.	11	F		TX
James L.	9	M		TX
Walton H.	7	M		TX
Ann	4	F		TX
Isaac	2	M		TX
Anderson, A. J.	50	M	Farmer	NC
Winneyfred	47	F		NC
Joseph H. J.	14	M		TN
Sarry E.	12	F		TN
Bershaba A.	9	F		TN
Alfred	8	M		TN
Blundell, David	24	M	Farmer	LA
Rachael	17	F		TN
Mathew	2/12	M		TX
Bowers, Jno. H.	33	M	Farmer	LA
Melissa	20	F		NY
Clarissa	7	F		TX
Hanises, Thomas	60	M		TN
Smith, Henry	33	M	Farmer	TN
Susan	25	F		FL
Coffee, Wilson	25	M	Shepherd	KY
Buker, Elizabeth	75	F		GER
Fenamlty, Terresa	27	F		GER
Joseph	4	M		GER
Smith, Louisa	5/12	F		TX
Chrismon, Wallace	32	M	Farmer	NC
Biddy	38	F		TN
Mary Jane	16	F		TN
Edward ?.	6	M		TN
Boatright, Lewis	56	M	Farmer	NC
Lavina	46	F		TN
Honeycut, George	19	M	Farmer	TN
Foley, H. S.	31	M	Farmer	TN
Myerson, John	30	M	Farmer	GER
Arnold, W. W.	27	M	Wheelwright	MS
Eleanor F.	21	F		TN
Missouri	3	F		TX
Mason	1	M		TX
McKiney, Martha	18	F		TN
McKiney, John	50	M	Farmer	TN
Narcissa	44	F		TN
James	20	M	Farmer	TN
Martha	18	F		TN
Narcissa	15	F		MS
Mary	12	F		MS
Sarah	10	F		MS
William	8	M		MS
Tennessee	4	F		MS
Jane	2	F		TX
Hanna, Silas H.	19	M	Farmer	LA
Elizabeth	18	F		TN
Walter	6/12	M		TX
Mays, George	52	M		NC
Mary	45	F		TN
Josephine	18	F		TX
Samuel A.	12	M		TX
John	10	M		TX
Mary Jane	8	F		TX
Sarah V----	6	F		TX
Charles V.	6	M		TX
Worthing, Fabian	24	M	Farmer	MO

(continued)

Name	Age	Sex	Occupation	Birthplace
Worthing, Martha Jane	18	F		TN
McElroy, William	41	M	Farmer	AL
Ellenor	41	F		TN
Jane	20	F		TN
Henry	17	M	Farmer	TN
John	15	M		AL
Abagail	12	F		MS
Martha A.	11	F		MS
Susan C.	7	F		MS
Isaac V.	4	M		TX
Abner	1	M		TX
Tolleson, Hebron	28	M	School Teacher	TN
Amanda	18	F		TN
Hix, A. W.	42	M	Inn Keeper	TN
Fredonia	25	F		TN
Boyce	4	M		TX
John	2	M		TX
Robert	9/12	M		TX
McKempton, Joseph	34	M	Carpenter	PA
Rice, Eliz.	44	F	Tailoress	TN
White, William B.	18	M		MO
Rice, Jas. H.	7	M		TX
Heppeman, Jno.	24	M	Farmer	NY
Matilda F.	23	F		TN
John M.	2	M		TX
Morris, Mary H.	20	F		TN
McLaughlin, S.	39	M	Farmer	TN
Martha	4	F		TX
Saunders, J. L.	32	F(M)	Farmer	TN
Margaret C.	32	F		TN
Zadah S.	9	F		TN
George G.	7	M		TN
Paralle	2	F		TX
Shewld, Arthur	42	M	Inn Keeper	TN
Mary W.	46	F		NC
Brown, Elizabeth C.	24	F		GA
Hinich, Mary J.	19	F		GA
Sherill, Georgane	12	F		TX
Treat, Archibald	45	M	Merchant	VA
Rhine, D. H.	28	M	Book Seller	NC
Danson, J. L.	50	M	Lawyer	VT
Lucien	14	M		AR
Townsend, Spencer	37	M	Inn Keeper & Merch.	SC
Louisa	27	F		TN
Spencer B.	7	M		TX
Elizabeth J.	5	F		TX
Florida	3	F		TX
A. Stapleton	1	M		TX
Wills, W. R. B.	40	M	Lawyer	KY
Derrby, Josiah	27	M	Clk. Cty. Ct.	PA
Sanders, L. F.	29	M	Carpenter	TN
Bishop, Thomas	30	M	Clk. Dist. Ct.	VA
Perkins, A. N.	23	M	Doctor	GA
Sarah	22	F		GA
Bibb, W. R.	26	M		AL
Gass, Calvin M.	34	M	Farmer	TN
Eliza	35	F		TN
Sarah	13	F		AR
Robert C.	11	M		AR
Polly	8	F		AR
Rhoda	5	F		AR
William	2	M		AR
Blackburn, G. B.	33	M	Farmer	TN
Mary A.	24	F		MO
Margaret A.	1	F		TX
R. J.	19	M	Farmer	TX
Jones, James	45	M	Farmer	TN
Elmira	34	F		LA
John Kelly	14	M		TX
William	13	M		TX
Leonard	11	M		TX
Sarah A.	9	F		TX
Napoleon	8	M		TX

(continued)

LAVACA COUNTY, TEXAS

Name	Age	Sex	Occupation	Birthplace
Jones, Mary Ann	6	F		TX
Oliver	1	M		TX
John	18	M	Farmer	TX
Guthre, Orim	45	M	Farmer	KY
Louisa	35	F		TN
William	19	M		KY
Elizabeth	12	F		MS
Mary A.	10	F		MS
Cyntha A.	8	F		MS
Vick, William	25	M	Farmer	NC
York, Jas. A.	40	M	Farmer	TN
Eliza	28	F		TN
Mary J.	7	F		TX
Sarah M.	4	F		TX
Emma	1	F		TX
Heath, Richard	44	M	Farmer	TN
Rebecca	37	F		TN
Fred Perry	14	M		LA
Manetta	12	F		TX
Eleanor A.	10	F		TX
Mason Foley	8	M		TX
Sarah F. C.	1	F		TX
Bridges, Henry N.	25	M	Farmer	PA
Tankesley, Green	55	M	Farmer	TN
Emily	45	F		TN
George	17	M		AL
Mary	15	F		AL
Benjamin	13	M		AL
Rebecca	10	F		AR
Emma	8	F		AL
John M.	5	M		AR
Simmons, James	30	M	Farmer	TN
Sarah F.	20	F		KY
Emily	2	F		TX
Letitia	6/12	F		TX
Mayo, K.	44	M	Farmer	NC
Nancy	45	F		NC
William H.	22	M	Farmer	TN
Micajah	17	M		MS
Harmon	14	M		MS
James ?.	12	M		MS
K. R.	7	M		MS
Mary E.	5	F		MS
Catharine	4	F		MS
Harless, Hyram	37	M	Farmer	TN
Mary	28	F		AL
Charles B.	17	M		AL
William B.	15	M		AL
John H.	13	M		AL
Ann E.	9	F		MS
Felix	7	M		MS
Isaac N.	2	M		TX
Long, Samuel A.	34	M	Farmer	TN
Louisa	25	F		TN
Martha A.	11	F		TX
William H.	6	M		TX
Andrew J.	2	M		TX
Long, John	26	M	Farmer	TN
Sarah	25	F		TN
Mary	5	F		TN
Samuel	3	M		TN
George W.	1/12	M		TX
Long, James	24	M	Farmer	TN
Eliza	16	F		TN
Long, Henry	53	M	Black Smith	VA
Rachael	51	F		KY
Elizabeth	18	F		TN
John C.	15	M		TN
Susan G.	13	F		AL
Hix, Stephen	40	M	Farmer	NC
Elizabeth	34	F		TN
G. Cummings	12	M		TX

(continued)

Name	Age	Sex	Occupation	Birthplace
Hix, Sarah A.	15	F		TX
William R.	10	M		TX
Mary Y.	8	F		TX
Susan	6	F		TX

LEON COUNTY, TEXAS

Name	Age	Sex	Occupation	Birthplace
Williams, William	30	M	Farmer	NC
Jane	23	F		AL
Sarah J.	4	F		TN
Joseph	2	M		MS
William	6/12	M		MS
Hunt, Noah E.	38	M	Farmer	NC
Rebecca A.	21	F		TN
William	17	M	Farmer	NC
Asalie	6	F		TX
Reinhardt, Jacob	76	M	None	PA
Sophronia	24	F		NC
Hunt, Eliza A.	8/12	F		TX
Rogers, Albert G.	29	M	Farmer	AL
Martha R.	27	F		NC
Frances J.	6	F		TX
Stephen J.	4	M		TX
William J.	1	M		TX
John W.	1/12	M		TX
Hunter, Charles B.	16	M	Student	TN
Julia	14	F		TN
Pruitt, Augustus	17	M	Student	TN
Tennessee	14	F		TN
Clapp, Elisha	47	M	Farmer	TN
Elizabeth	43	F		TN
John	21	M	Student	TX
Lavina	18	F		TX
Mary	13	F		TX
Elisha	7	M		TX
Lucinda	5	F		TX
William	2	M		TX
Price, Elisha	35	M	Black Smith	??
Robinson, William	28	M	Laborer (Idiot)	PA
Clapp, William	29	M	Wagon Maker	IL
Elizabeth	26	F		TN
Sydney	3	M		IL
Charles	1	M		IL
Conner, Robert M.	28	M	Farmer	TN
Martha	29	F		AL
Sarah E.	5/12	F		TX
Cobb, Catharine A.	15	F		AL
Jerucia J. A.	9	F		AL
Powell, James B.	36	M	Tanner	TN
William	35	M	Saddler	TN
Langston, Jacob	45	M	Farmer	TN
Margaret A.	23	F		AL
Sarah A. (Twin)	7	F		TX
Mary A. (Twin)	7	F		TX
Moses	2	M		TX
Frances E.	8/12	F		TX
Yarbrough, Elizabeth	47	M		TN
Elizabeth	17	F		AL
Braydon, A. G.	51	M	Farmer	TN
Mary G.	42	F		TN
Gabriel	18	M	Farmer	TN
Mary M.	13	F		TN
James H.	11	M		TX
Rebecca E.	7	F		TX
Frances A.	3	F		TX
Smith, Moses B.	3	M		TX
Gardner, Mary J.	1	F		TX
King, William, Sr.	54	M	Farmer	GA
Sarah	45	F		KY
William, Jr.	27	M	Farmer	TN
Peter B.	23	M	Farmer	TN
Mordicai	20	M	Farmer	AL
Thomas	18	M	Farmer	AL
Elizabeth	16	F		AL
Mary	13	F		AL

(continued)

LEON COUNTY, TEXAS

Name	Age	Sex	Occupation	Birthplace
King, Richard S.	9	M		TX
Sarah A.	7	F		TX
Arnst, John	20	M	Laborer	GER
Rogers, Joseph	26	M	Farmer	TN
Jane	21	F		AL
Frances E.	2	F		TX
Patrick, George W.	21	M	Farmer	KY
Norton, William C.	23	M	Farmer	TN
Orrell, William	37	M	Farmer	NC
Cynthia	38	F		NC
Thomas A.	12	M		TN
John H.	10	M		TN
Nancy A.	6	F		TN
Roonzo(?)	1	M		TX
Bloodworth, James C.	36	M	Farmer	TN
Mary J.	27	F		TN
William T.	7	M		TX
James M.	5	M		TX
Finley	1	M		TX
Taylor, Martin D.	29	M	Farmer	AL
Isabella	27	F		IL
Nancy J.	7	F		TX
Charles J.	5	M		TX
James D.	4	M		TX
Tyler, John	22	M	Farmer	TX
Taylor, Franklin J.	21	M	Farmer	TN
Self, David	19	M	Laborer	AL
Breshear, Isabella	16	F		AR
Choat, Stokeley	50	M	Farmer	TN
John C.	9	M		MS
Trimble, John	21	M	Farmer	IL
Jane	20	F		TN
William	2	M		TX
Sinai	7/12	F		TX
Hardin, A. B., Jr.	30	M	Farmer	TN
Mary	22	F		LA
Swan	5	M		TX
Thomas	3	M		TX
Infant	2/12	M		TX
Baker, John	21	M	Laborer	IN
Mayfield, Sterling	35	M	House Carpenter	SC
Wicard, Samuel	59	M	Farmer	KY
Sarah	43	F		TN
Sarah T.	9	F		TX
Sperry, Jackson	27	M	Shoe Maker	??
Choat, James M.	27	M	Farmer	TN
Elizabeth	29	F		TN
John H.	2	M		TX
Elizabeth	7/12	F		TX
Robeanto, Hosea	23	M	Laborer	LA
Smart, Sion	42	M	Farmer	TN
Jane	38	F		TN
William	18	M	Farmer	TN
Hetty C.	15	F		AL
Peter J.	12	M		AL
James E.	11	M		AL
John F.	7	M		MS
Benjamin J.	3	M		MS
Burlison, David	64	M	Farmer	NC
Sarah	65	F		NC
Isaac	37	M	Farmer	TN
David F.	21	M	Farmer	AL
Matthews, Naoma	38	F		TN
John S.	16	M	Farmer	AL
Mary	12	F		AL
Margaret Green	4	F		AL
Burlison, Rebecca	22	F		AL
Brashear, George N.	40	M	Wagon Maker	KY
Candis	37	F		TN
William	12	M		IL
James	10	M		IL
Caroline	8	F		TX

(continued)

Name	Age	Sex	Occupation	Birthplace
Breshear, George	4	M		TX
Mary J.	3/12	F		TX
Brown, David M.	42	M	Farmer	TN
Lavina A.	28	F		AL
Mary A.	8	F		TX
Matilda J.	6	F		TX
George M.	4	M		TX
Mary J.	3/12	F		TX
Boyd, Richard W.	26	M	Farmer	TN
Lamyramiss A.	21	F		TN
Richard P.	1	M		TX
Mary F.	1/12	F		TX
Anthony, Francis A.	22	F		TN
Hanrey, William R.	27	M	Farmer	TN
Mary	27	F		TN
John S.	6	M		TX
Snailum, Thomas C.	36	M	Farmer	NY
Mary A.	25	F		TN
Bethany	7	F		TX
Mary A.	4	F		TX
Victoria	11/12	F		TX
Rogers, Robert	50	M	Farmer	TN
Delia	46	F		GA
Andrew J.	20	M	Farmer	MO
Missouri	18	F		MO
Elizabeth	15	F		TX
Tipton	10	M		TX
Maranda	7	F		TX
Martha J.	5	F		TX
White, Robert	60	M	Farmer	NC
Nancy	55	F		NC
Sanders	21	M	Farmer	TN
Patterson, John M.	31	M	Farmer	TN
Ruth R.	31	F		TN
William A.	9	M		TN
Arthur F.	8	M		MS
John W.	6	M		MS
Willie J.	4	M		MS
Susan M.	8/12	F		TX
Newton H. C.	12	M		TN
Josiah W.	23	M	Farmer(Deaf-Dumb)	TN
Reinhardt, Isreal P.	36	M	Farmer	NC
Sibell	22	F		TN
Eugenia	2	F		TX
Georganna	1	F		TX
Evans, Edward	42	M	Farmer	TN
Isabella	36	F		SC
Mary A.	14	F		AL
Louisa E.	13	F		AL
Frances J.	11	F		AL
William T.	10	M		AL
Martha J.	8	F		AL
Julia E.	2	F		AL
Simpson, William	28	M	Farmer	AL
Smith, Manean	40	M	Farmer	LA
Matilda	31	F		TN
Nancy	6	F		TX
Thomas	1	M		TX
Copeland, Joseph	39	M	Farmer	TN
Jeremiah	14	M		TX
John	10	M		TX
Smith, Charles	33	M	Farmer	MO
Thomas, William	43	M	Farmer	SC
Cynthia	35	F		TN
Jones, Andrew R.	25	M	Farmer	TX
Ethaline	24	F		TN
Mary E.	4/12	F		TX
Richard	19	M	Farmer	TX
Jervis, William	30	M	House Carpenter	??
Jewett, Henry J.	35	M	Lawyer	ME
Rachel R.	25	F		TN

(continued)

LEON COUNTY, TEXAS

Name	Age	Sex	Occupation	Birthplace
Jewett, Mary R.	1	F		TX
Bole, James H.	7	M		TX
Smith, Eleanor	56	F		SC
Ezekiel S.	29	F	Farmer	AL
Amana	18	M	Farmer	AL
Joshua A. G.	16	M	Farmer	AL
Lydian	13	F		AL
Gibbs, Alonzo Y.	24	M	Laborer	TN
Beck, James E.	46	M	Farmer	NC
Elizabeth	46	F		NC
William M.	23	M	Farmer	TN
Taliferro	19	M	Student	TN
Thomas R.	17	M	Student	MO
Cynthia C.	13	F		MO
Malissa	11	F		MO
James R.	7	M		MO
Perry H.	3	M		TX
Martin, Peter T.	61	M	Teacher	SC
Haley, Charles Y.	30	M	Farmer	MS
Elizabeth J.	20	F		AL
Arrington, M. H.	22	M	Laborer	TN
Haley, John	26	M	Farmer	LA
Susan J.	23	F		TN
John	1	M		TX
Goodwin, Joseph P.	25	M	Farmer	TN
Cooper, William	29	M	Saddletree	TN
Louisa	19	F		TX
Mary E.	4	F		TX
Haley, Allen	43	M	Farmer	TN
Mary A.	42	F		TN
James	21	M	Farmer	LA
Richard	9	M		TX
Sellers, Matthew	16	M	Laborer	LA
Goodman, John J.	50	M	Farmer	SC
Sarah W.	45	F		VA
George C.	25	M	Carpenter	TN
Benjamin S.	23	M	Carpenter	TN
Samuel F.	20	M	Farmer	TN
Lucy C.	15	F		TN
Malinda J.	11	F		TN
Virginia W.	9	F		TN
James K. Polk	7	M		TN
Harrison, John J.	30	M	None	GA
Mary E.	21	F		TN
Elizabeth J.	1	F		TX
Glaze, John H.	48	M	Farmer	TN
Cooper, Elizabeth	54	F		NC
Allen H.	21	M	Farmer	TN
Doctor J.	16	M		TN
Harvey J.	14	M		TN
George C.	12	M		TN
Mary J.	4	F		TX
Cooper, John G.	30	M	Farmer	TN
Cooper, Mark S.	24	M	Farmer	TN
Nancy	19	F		TN
Elizabeth A.	5/12	F		TX
Higgins, Benjamin	14	M		TX
Arnold, Bird	34	M	Farmer	SC
Elvira	26	F		IL
Lucy A.	4	F		TX
Levy F.	2	M		TX
Nathaniel T.	6/12	M		TX
Clark, Edmund A.	27	M	Farmer	TX
Lucy A.	30	F		TN
Albina D.	7	F		TX
Isham E.	6	M		TX
Alonzo W.	4	M		TX
Sarah R.	1	F		TX
McDonald, Nicholas	30	M	Farmer	IRE
Elizabeth	33	F		TN
Patterson, Mary A. J.	10	F		TN
Reaggons, George W.	22	M	Farmer	TX
Jane	19	F		TN
Nancy J.	6/12	F		TX
Miller, Frederick	30	M	Physician	GER
Mary J.	22	F		TN
Pruitt, Lucy	6	F		MS
Fowler, William, Sr.	55	M	Land Lord	SC
Jane	60	F		SC
William, Jr.	23	M	Farmer	AL
Pitts(Potts), John H.	30	M	Clk Cty Court	KY
Culbertson, Theodore	25	M	Cabinet Maker	AL
William A.	23	M		KY
Gardner, Alfred J.	26	M	Black Smith	KY
McKnight, Samuel B.	32	M	Carpenter	AL
Young, Patrick T.	27	M	Physician	MS
Wheelock, William H.	22	M	Grocer	IL
Graham, Duncan P.	26	M	None	TN
Heffington, David	32	M	Trainer	KY
Clark, John M.	43	M	House Carpenter	OH
L----- A.	30	F		TN
James	9	M		AR
Ellen A.	4	F		TX
McCullough, James D.	22	M	Teacher	TN
Elizabeth	18	F		TN
Young, Theodore J.	37	M	Farmer	TN
Elvira	23	F		TN
Margaret	1	F		TX
Giddings, Erastus	32	M	None	OH
Crane, Hiram H.	35	M	Farmer	KY
Mary A.	30	F		TN
William H.	6/12	M		TX
Dotson, Christopher J.	31	M	Farmer	TN
Mary	29	F		AL
James J.	8	M		TX
Sarah E.	6	F		TX
Nancy J.	4	F		TX
Virginia A.	2	F		TX
Mary C.	6/12	F		TX
Parker, Andrew	20	M	Laborer	MS
Shearman, Parsons M.	36	M	Farmer	NC
Rebecca J.	29	F		NC
Mary E.	12	F		TN
Thomas T.	10	M		AR
Martha J.	5	F		TN
James D.	2	M		TN
Holliman, William	22	M	Farmer	NC
King, Richard B.	37	M	Farmer	TN
Polly A.	22	F		IL
Mary A.	8/12	F		TX
Reavis, William	25	M	Farmer	KY
Nelson, Esther A.	39	F		TN
Elizabeth F.	17	F		MS
Mary ?. J.	10	F		TX
Samuel H.	7	M		TX
Marcus D. F.	6	M		TX
Granville	3	M		TX
Burlison, Benjamin	35	M	Black Smith	TN
Kessiah	36	F		AL
David W.	14	M		AL
Kessiah J.	8	F		AL
Oliver W.	4	M		AL
Hopson M.	3	M		AL
Nancy R.	1	F		TX
James E.	2/12	M		TX
Evans, William	31	M	Farmer	TN
Rebecca	31	F		AL
Edward M.	9	M		AL
Joseph A.	7	M		AL
Lydia J.	5	F		AL
Julia A. F.	3	F		AL
Mary H.	1	F		TX
Boggs, James C.	41	M	Merchant	KY

(continued)

LEON COUNTY, TEXAS

Name	Age	Sex	Occupation	Birthplace
Boggs, Elizabeth M.	27	F		AL
Alon D.	8	M		MS
Harriet C.	6	F		MS
Alice J.	5/12	F		TX
Williams, Thomas J.	21	M	Clerk	TN
Ganny, John	23	M	Mail Contractor	FRA
McEuckers, James	35	M	None	??
Holliman, Mark P.	50	M	Farmer	TN
Eliza	40	F		TN
Elizabeth	17	F		TN
Yancey	15	M	Student	TN
Alfred	13	M		TN
Robert	11	M		MS
William	8	M		TX
Roberts, Eli	30	M	Laborer	MS
Nelms, William	45	M	Millwright	NC
Ann	38	F		AL
McRuffin	22	M	Farmer	TN
James	21	M	Farmer	TN
Alexander P.	2	M		TX
Caroline	18	F		AL
Choat, Prudence D.	47	F		TN
Thomas	24	M	Farmer	TN
Cinai	17	F		TN
Parallee	12	F		MS
Sarah	9	F		MS
Cothen, Jackson	24	M	Farmer	MS
Eleanor	22	F		TN
Ann J.	2	F		MS
Lamb, Richard S.	65	M	None	NC
Franklin	20	M	Student	TN
David	18	M	Student	MS
Nanna, Charles W.	30	M	Farmer	TN
Rebecca	20	F		??
Isaac	4	M		TX
William	1	M		TX
Menefee, William O.	22	M	Farmer	AL
Mary J.	15	F		LA
Orville	1	M		TX
Franklin	19	M	Farmer	TN
Sample, Samuel	41	M	Farmer	TN
Amanda J.	47	F		NC
Menefee, Artamesia	12	F		TX
Rosetta E.	9	F		TX
Truett, William	30	M	Stock Keeper	TN
Louisa	29	F		TN
Sarah A.	8	F		AR
Mary	6	F		AR
Louisa	4	F		AR
Sophronia A.	2	F		TX
Alphaus P.	5/12	M		TX
Perkins, Berry W.	34	M	Stock Keeper	TN
Faney	37	F		TN
Sarah	11	F		TN
Mary E.	5	F		TX
George D.	4	M		TX
Evans, James C.	28	M	Farmer	AL
Charlotte	58	F		TN
William M. J.	25	M	Farmer	AL
Newberry, Alexander	53	M	Farmer	TN
Ann	50	F		SC
John	28	M	Farmer	AL
Eleanor	22	F		AL
Mary A.	16	F		AL
Sarah M.	14	F		AL
Melvina	12	F		AL
Charlotte	10	F		AL
Henry W.	7	M		AL
Williams, Fletcher B.	21	M	Farmer	NC
Mary J.	37	F		TN
Moore, Thomas R.	16	M	Farmer	MS

(continued)

Name	Age	Sex	Occupation	Birthplace
Moore, Martin Van B.	11	M		MS
Rufus B.	9	M		MS
Columbus J.	5	M		TX
Margaret C. J.	3	F		TX
Powell, James	31	M	Farmer	AL
Elizabeth	35	F		MS
Mary J.	11	F		TX
John G.	9	M		TX
Elam, Felix	23	M	Farmer	TN
Baker, Yarbrough	34	M	Merchant	TN
James	6	M		TX
Hines, F. M.	22	M	Clerk	--
Engledon, J. W.	25	M	Farmer	TN
Caroline	17	F		TN
Langham, Madison H.	38	M	Farmer	AL
James M.	8	M		TX
Pruitt, William	48	M	Farmer	NC
Nancy	44	F		NC
Amanda	21	F		TN
Herod B.	19	M	Farmer	TN
Hughs, Richard	23	M	Laborer	SC
Pruitt, John	15	M	Student	TN
Patrick, Nancy	22	F		KY
Nancy W.	12	F		MS
George F.	10	M		MS
James M.	8	M		MS
Lucy A.	6	F		MS
Robert E.	1	M		TX
White, Henry	31	M	Farmer	TN
Martha R.	15	F		AL
Robert	5	M		TX
Isaac B.	2	M		TX
Brimberry, Alfred	26	M	Wheelwright	IL
Talitha	25	F		TN
Mary F.	4/12	F		TX
Jones, Joseph A.	6	M		TX
Margaret A.	4	F		TX
Nancy J.	3	F		TX
Estill, Parthenia B.	54	F		TN
Bird W.	16	M	Farmer	LA
Hardy P.	12	M		LA
Perry, Ransom	21	M	Farmer	LA
Page, Parthenia	15	F		LA
McAnally, Elizabeth	48	F		SC
Van Buren	19	M	Student	AL
Mary	16	F		TN
Anthony, A. B.	43	M	Farmer	TN
Lavissa	27	F		TN
Laura	12	F		AR
Cecil	9	F(?)		IL
Trinity	6	F		TX
Brazonia	5	F		TX
Medina	2	F		TX
Drennan, David	33	M	Carpenter	TN
Sarah	30	F		TN
James	11	M		TN
John	5	M		AR
William T.	2	M		AR
Beaver, Pleasant B.	39	M	Carpenter	GA
Buys, George W.	35	M	Black Smith	GA
Elizabeth	22	F		TN
William	4	M		AL
Martha J.	10	F		AL
Isabella	1	F		AL
Collins, William S.	24	M	Black Smith	TN
Delaney	17	F		TN
Hunter, Charles	46	M	Farmer	NC
Henrietta	35	F		NC
Marcus A.	11	M		TN
Mary R.	5	F		TX
Samuel S.	1	M		TX
Robert	35	M	Gold Digger	NC

(continued)

LEON COUNTY, TEXAS

Name	Age	Sex	Occupation	Birthplace
Hunter, Robert P.	14	M		TN
Wallace	11	M		TN

LIBERTY COUNTY, TEXAS

Name	Age	Sex	Occupation	Birthplace
Gresham, J. J.	35	M	Accountant	TN
Penelope C. B.	27	F		MO
John H.	12	M		MS
Long, William	30	M	Sailor	NY
Janey A.	24	F		TN
Elizabeth	7	F		TX
Garner	5	M		TX
Mayes, Garner	75	M	Farmer	VA
Elizabeth	65	F		VA
John J.	32	M	Farmer	TN
Abner	30	M	Farmer	TN
Joshua	27	M	Farmer	TN
George	25	M	Farmer	TN
Stephenson, Lydia	63	F		TN
Warren	17	M	Stock Raiser	TX
Fields, William	40	M	Printer	NC
Minerva	37	F		TN
Sarah	14	F		TN
William	11	M		TX
Leonidas	8	M		TX
Joshua	3	M		TX
Janey	5/12	F		TX
Hartwell, T.	47	M	Farmer	MA
Martha N.	34	F		TN
Gibbons, William K.	11	M		TX
Wallis, Francis M.	6	M		TX
Hansell R.	4	M		TX
Hartwell, Albert H.	1	M		TX
Shelton	1/12	M		TX
Shelton, Amos	25	M	Farmer	TN
Caroline	19	F		LA
Winfield	1/12	M		TX
Shelton, George W.	45	M	Farmer	TN
Cordelia	18	F		TN
Thomas	16	M	Farmer	TN
Maria	8	F		TX
Amos	6	M		TX
Carraway, C. M.	27	M		TN
Thomas J.	6	M		TX
Patrick H.	4	M		TX
Martha J. L.	2	F		TX
Shelton, John W.	10	M		TX
Seely, T. T.	29	M	Tanner	NY
Tabitha	21	F		TN
John J.	1	M		TX
McCurty, Edward	38	M	Farmer	TN
Esther	37	F		GA
James	16	M	Farmer	TN
William	15	M		TN
George	9	M		TX
Edward	7	M		TX
Jesse	4	M		TX
Rhodes, Thomas	59	M	Farmer	NC
Elizabeth	50	F		GA
William	25	M	Farmer	TN
Mary	22	F		TN
James	21	M	Farmer	TN
Thomas	17	M	Farmer	TN
Eliza	14	F		TN
Martha	12	F		TN
Elizabeth	11	F		TN
Rhodes, Marshal	30	M	Farmer	TN
Susan	21	F		MS
George M.	3	M		TX
Sarah P.	11/12	F		TX
Brooks, Wilson	33	M	Farmer	GA

(continued)

Name	Age	Sex	Occupation	Birthplace
Brooks, Jarusha	27	F		TN
Benjamin F.	7	M		TX
James H.	4	M		TX
Mary E.	3	F		TX
Amanda M. F.	2	F		TX
Spinks, Elizabeth	18	F		TX
Gilbert, William	40	M	Laborer	SCO
Gill, William	42	M	Farmer	MD
Sarah W.	33	F		TN
Margaret	10	F		TX
William	7	M		TX
Andrew M.	5	M		TX
Charles M.	3	M		TX
Mary Jane	1	F		TX
Bouch, Ernest	19	M	Laborer	GER
Rogers, Thomas G.	35	M	Saddler	TN
Elizabeth	25	F		LA
Griffin, J. H.	32	M	Farmer	MS
Louisa	25	F		TX
Mary Ann	4	F		TX
James W.	2	M		TX
Martin, Penelope	10	F		TX
Randall P.	18	M	Student	TX
Orin F.	14	M		TX
Shook, Jefferson	30	M	Clergyman, M.	MO
Mary A.	20	F		TN
Andrew ?.	3	M		TX
Elizabeth	2	F		TX
Lurens W.	1/12	F		TX
Land, Charles C.	30	M	Merchant	DEN
Mary K.	25	F		TN
Caroline A.	5	F		TX
Margaret	3	F		TX
Smith, Margaret	35	F		GER
Day, J. C.	37	M	Farmer	TN
Louisana	6	F		TX
Mary E.	4	F		TX
James H.	2	M		TX
Mordere, John A.	29	M	Farmer	MS
Sarah J.	20	F		TN
Xachary T.	1	M		TX
John, Thomas	29	M	Physician	PA
Amanda	18	F		TN
Shelby, J. T.	24	M	Physician	TN
R. S.	20	F		TN
Chambers, J. H.	19	M	Druggist	TN
Howel, A. B.	17	M	Medical Student	TN
Whitlock, G. S.	24	M	Physician	AR
Goodhand, W.	48	M	Carpenter	MD
Brame, John B. T.	51	M	Plasterer	VA
Lucy	40	F		TN
Miller, John J.	17	M	Student	TX
James M.	15	M	Student	TX
Benjamin F.	13	M		TX
Cope, Charles W.	3	M		TX
Sears, Henry	41	M	Farmer	MA
Sopha	35	F		TN
Fitzgerald, Algernon	16	M	Farmer	MS
Anna	14	F		MS
Sophronia	12	F		TX
Lucins	10	M		TX
Ellena	8	F		TX
Leroy	6	M		TX
John	4	M		TX
Sears, Margaret J.	11	F		AR
Henry C.	6/12	M		TX
Boothe, Sarah	40	F		TN
Abraham	24	M	Farmer	TN
David	23	M	Farmer	TN
Lucinda	16	F		TN
Frederick	12	M		TN
Tarkenton, Burton	69	M	Farmer	NC
Sarah	56	F		TN

(continued)

LIBERTY COUNTY, TEXAS

Name	Age	Sex	Occupation	Birthplace
Tarkenton, Harrison	23	M	Farmer	IN
Eliza	16	F		TX
Amanda	13	F		TX
John	11	M		TX
Elizabeth	7	F		TX
Lane, Alfred	40	M	Farmer	NC
Elizabeth	30	F		TN
Polly	16	F		TN
Eliza	13	F		TX
Nancy	10	F		TX
Julia Ann	7	F		TX
James	5	M		TX
Patsey	3	F		TX
Walker, R. T.	28	M	Physician	TN
E. Sidney	24	F		VA
Edgar F.	1	M		TX
Smith, C.	25	M	Farmer	TN
Elizabeth	20	F		TN
David	2	M		TX
McLane, Harrison	30	M	Farmer	TN
Rachel A.	30	F		AL
Cynthia A.	7	F		TX
Austin	5	M		TX
William	2	M		TX
Mary E. & Sarah	3/12	F		TX
Cooper, William	28	M	Laborer	NY
Mary	17	F		TN
Dake, Lewis W.	30	M	Merchant	NY
Alpha Anna	21	F		TN
Lewis	1	M		TX
Smith, James M.	41	M	Carpenter	MS
Eliza Ann	31	F		TN
Prestwood J.	12	M		MS
Ann E.	9	F		LA
John P.	7	M		TX
Francis M.	4	M		TX
William A.	1	M		TX
Rhodes, Franklin	28	M	Farmer	TN
C. D------	30	M	Farmer	LA
Truman	23	M	Farmer	TX

LIMESTONE COUNTY, TEXAS

Precinct No. 1

Name	Age	Sex	Occupation	Birthplace
Baker, Walter	23	M	Farmer	KY
Lucinda	18	F		TN
Udosa	*2	F		TX
Richards, Esther	9	F		TX
Seawright, John	56	M	Farmer	NC
Sinthy	41	F		NC
William	24	M	Farmer	SC
John	18	M	Farmer	TN
Sarah J.	14	F		TN
Synthy C.	12	F		TX
George W.	6	M		TX
Martha	4	F		TX
Narcissa	2	F		TX
Cargile, Robert	34	M	Farmer	GA
John	10	M		AR
William	8	M		AR
Mary Ann	3	F		AR
Stephenson, Seawright	21	M	Farmer	TN
Lauderdale, Jeremiah	57	M	Farmer	TN
Elizabeth	48	F		TN
Simpson J.	30	M	Farmer	AL
T. J.	17	M		AL
J. L.	19	M	Farmer	AL
Saryann	14	F		AL
E. F.	12	F		TX
J. H.	11	M		TX
Jos. L.	9	M		TX

Name	Age	Sex	Occupation	Birthplace
Henderson, Francis H.	37	M	Farmer	TN
Elizabeth M.	32	F		AL
Hugh W.	13	M		TN
John M.	11	M		TX
William H.	7	M		TX
Thomas L.	7	M		TX
S. A.	2	F		TX
Wills, James S.	41	M	Physician	TN
Margaret	72	F		VA
Emily	40	F		TN
Angaline A.	15	F		TN
J. A.	13	F		TN
Margaret D.	6/12	F		TX
Denton, Malchi	28	M	Farmer	NC
Bell, G. W.	22	M	Cabinet Maker	TN
Wills, J. H.	25	M	Farmer	TN
Mary	25	F		TN
G. M.	3	F		TN
William T.	1	M		TN
Freeman, B. F.	19	M	Farmer	MS
Patteon, E. J.	26	F		AL
Campbell, Henry C.	60	M	Farmer	VA
Mary	57	F		VA
Elizabeth	26	F		IN
M. M.	24	F		TN
Matilda R.	19	F		TN
Ann P.	16	F		AR
Robert B.	13	F		AR
Charles C.	11	M		AR
Virginia S.	9	F		AR
Love, James M.	45	M	Farmer	TN
T. A.	42	F		TN
Joseph A.	21	M	Farmer	TN
Siras W.	19	M	Farmer	TN
Martha A.	17	F		TN
Mary E.	15	F		TN
M. J.	15	F		TN
James A.	13	M		TN
Samuel B.	10	M		TN
John W.	9	M		TX
Terrissa G.	7	F		TX
Robert	4	M		TX
Tennessee A.	10/12	F		TX
Ongburn, Mary	35	F		TN
Henry	12	M		TX
Lucy C.	10	F		TX
Samuel S.	8	M		TX
John T.	6	M		TX
William	2	M		TX
Dickson, W. W.	44	M	Farmer	TN
Elizabeth	39	F		TN
L. D.	12	F		KY
Hale, Jefferson	20	M	Farmer	TN
Mary R.	18	F		TN
William D.	1	M		TX
Love, D. H.	34	M	School Teacher	TN
Mary F.	30	F		IRE
A. C.	8	M		TN
Robertson, F. F.	8	M		TX
Love, Patric H.	1	M		TX
Cornelia F.	16	F		TX
Longbottom, R. B.	55	M		ENG
Lucy	54	F		TN
Campbell, Ellis	36	M	Farmer	TN
C. T.	13	M		AL
Ware, James J.	33	M	Farmer	TN
Margaret	28	F		AL
Mary	12	F		TX
Nancy	4	F		TX
Jrey	2	M		TX
Linley, Joseph	57	M	Farmer	NC
Ann	49	F		TN
John	24	M	Black Smith	TN

(continued)

Name	Age	Sex	Occupation	Birthplace
Linley, Joseph	17	M		TX
John	15	M		TX
Simon T.	13	M		TX
Linn, B. F.	46	M	Farmer	TN
Julietha F.	43	F		KY
Joseph	18	M	Farmer	TN
Sary P.	16	F		TN
Texana F.	12	F		TX
John M.	7	M		TX
Haney, George	57	M	Farmer	TN
Sidnia	42	F		TN
George	16	M	Farmer	TN
William	14	M		TN
John	9	M		TN
Mary	5	M		TN
Phifer, Forest	36	M	Farmer	TN
Nancy L.	15	F		TN
William J.	14	M		TN
Susan L.	12	F		TX
M. J.	10	F		TX
Mila E.	7	F		TX
John	3	M		TX
Calvin	6/12	M		TX
Burns, William	33	M	Farmer	TN
Sinthy	34	F		TN
Ausker	10	M		TX
M. S.	7	M		TX
William D.	5	M		TX
M. C.	3	F		TX
S. L.	1	F		TX
Davis, John V.	25	M	Farmer	IN
Sarah E.	23	F		TN
Brinkley	10/12	M		TN
Bates, Silas H.	36	M	Farmer	OH
E. A.	25	F		TN
John A.	11	M		TX
Seth H.	9	M		TX
A.	7	M		TX
Adron	5	M		TX
Elizabeth A.	2	F		TX
Seth H.	68	M	Farmer	NJ
James, Sarah Ann	20	F	(Deaf)	IL
Carsin B.	18	M	Farmer	IL
Galloway, Hetty C.	13	F		AR
Anglin, Abraham	32	M	Farmer	KY
Rebecca	31	F		TN
John	8	M		TX
Eli	6	M		TX
James C.	3	M		TX
Abraham	8/12	M		TX
Hamilton, Isac	36	M	Farmer	TN
Rebecca	36	F		NC
John	9	M		TN
James	1	M		TX
Daugherty, William	26	M	Farmer	TN
Jackson	20	M	Farmer	TN
John	18	M	Farmer	IL
Harrison	14	M		AR
Rachael	11	F		IL
Anglin, William	29	M	Farmer	IL
Sarah	29	F		IN
Elisha	11	M		TX
William L.	7	M		TX
Tincher, James	21	M	Farmer	TN
Olliver, W. W.	20	M	Merchant	TN

Precinct No. 2

Name	Age	Sex	Occupation	Birthplace
Potter, Daniell	34	M	Farmer	TN
Elizabeth B.	29	F		MO
John C.	10	M		AR
Hannah	8	F		MO
Lucinda A.	6	F		MO
Claypool, Stephen J.	34	M	Farmer	KY
Disa	35	F		TN
Hannah M.	10	F		AR
William C.	6	M		MO
G. W.	2	M		TX
Epps, Robert C.	35	M	Farmer	TN
Lucinda A.	27	F		MO
Barbee, Joseph	45	M	Farmer	TN
Delila	45	F		TN
Elizabeth A.	22	F		TN
John Z.	18	M	Farmer	TN
William D.	16	M	Farmer	AL
Andrew J.	14	M		AL
Odle, J. B.	30	M	Farmer	TN
Mahala	22	F		TN
Margaret	2	F		TX
Barrons, Joseph	28	M	Farmer	TN
Powell, Nathan	36	M	Farmer	TN
Mary	23	F		TN
William	6	M		TN
Samuel	3	M		TN
Adaline	1	F		TX
Dunnigin, Charles G.	24	M	Farmer	MS
Gracy	21	F		MS
John W.	3	M		MS
Lucy E.	1	F		TX
Miers, William	26	M	Farmer	MS
Self, William	18	M	Farmer	TN
Webb, Edmond	35	M	Farmer	VA
Manerva	27	F		TN
James H.	6	M		TN
Eastton, Henry	23	M	Farmer	??
Hunt, Robert	28	M	Farmer	TN
Mary J.	27	F		MO
Mary E.	6/12	F		TX
Nettle, William B.	24	M	Farmer	TN
Margaret	23	F		AL
Joel	3/12	M		TX
Bankhead, William C.	22	M	Farmer	TN
Elizabeth	19	F		TN
Richard	1	M		TX
Clements, Emanuell	36	M	Farmer	KY
Martha	34	F		TN
Benjamin	13	M		MS
William	11	M		TX
Batey, Sarah A.	28	F		IL
Thomas	4	M		TX
William L.	1	M		TX
Freeman, Manerva	13	F		TN
Batey, Rebecca	71	F		VA

Precinct No. 3

Name	Age	Sex	Occupation	Birthplace
Dowdy, Howell B.	29	M	Farmer	TN
Minerva E.	25	F		AL
John C.	2	M		TX
Napoleon B.	1	M		TX
Walker, Landon	55	M	Farmer	TN
Catharine	55	F		GA
Henderson C.	25	M	Farmer	AL
Henson B.	23	M	Farmer	AL
Bennett K.	20	M	Farmer	AL
Smith, Bartholuma	56	M	Farmer	TN
Nancy	45	F		TN
Sindrilla	25	F		AL
Mary	20	F		IL
Hetta	13	F		AL
Newton P.	9	M		TN
Sarah	9	F		TN
Nancy J.	4	F		TN
Wells, Samuel G.	38	M	Farmer	KY

(continued)

LIMESTONE COUNTY, TEXAS

Name	Age	Sex	Occupation	Birthplace
Wells, Phebe	33	F		TN
Sarah C.	14	F		TX
Daniell P.	12	M		TX
Newton D.	11	M		TX
Martha E.	9	F		TX
Louisiana V.	5	F		TX
John P.	3	M		TX
Tyns, Robert	39	M	Farmer	VA
Amanda	18	F		TN
Jones, G. J.	46	M	Farmer	TN
Sarah	47	F		TN
James M.	20	M	Farmer	AL
Jeremiah D.	17	M	Farmer	AL
Joseph L.	15	M		AL
William M.	13	M		AL
George W.	12	M		TX
Sarah Ann A.	8	F		TX
Clapp, Joel	49	M	Farmer	NC
Malinda	49	F		GA
Martha L.	22	F		AL
Francis M.	14	M		TX
Caladona	13	F		TX
Texana	10	F		TX
Roberts, Edward	25	M	Farmer	GA
Mary A. R.	19	F		TN
Charles	68	M	Farmer	SC
Harris, Isom H.	50	M	Farmer	TN
Eliza	47	F		VA
Thomas R.	20	M	Farmer	AR
Samuel N.	15	M		AR
William H.	13	M		AR
Mary O.	10	F		AR
Dove S.	8	F		MO
Florence	6	F		TX
Hobbs, Elisha	33	M	Farmer	NC
Disey	31	F		NC
Eliza	9	M(?)		TN
Nancy	5	F		TN
Jas. W.	2/12	M		TX
McDurmet, Thomas H.	24	M		PA
Deborah	22	F		IL
William	3	M		TX
Cova	1	F		TX
Batey, Isah	36	M	Farmer	TN
Lenen, Charles W.	38	M	Farmer	TN
Mary A.	33	F		MS
Charles	11	M		AL
Adams, William L.	36	M	Merchant	VA
L. A.	32	F		TN
Goodman, Sarah	53	F		NC
Goodwin, Mary M.	13	F		TN
Samuel H.	15	M		TN
Williams, F. F.	38	M	Mill Builder	NC
Martha A.	40	F		KY
J. F.	18	M	Farmer	TN
M. A.	17	F		TN
M. E.	15	F		TN
E. J.	14	F		TN
C. A. A.	12	M		TN
M. E.	11	F		TN
A. L.	10	F		TN
A. J.	8	M		TN
S. A.	6	F		TN
R. F.	4	M		TN
Hardin, Joseph	46	M	Tavern Keeper	TN
An	40	F		MO
Criswell, Mara L.	19	F		LA
Hardin, Martha B.	18	F		AR
Margaret H.	15	F		MS
Nancy G.	9	F		TX
Barnett, John	14	M		TN

(continued)

Name	Age	Sex	Occupation	Birthplace
Barnett, Saryan	11	F		TN
Franklin	9	M		TN
James	7	M		TN
Matilda	3/12	F		TN
Martha	3/12	F		TN
Harper, Thomas J.	43	M	Farmer	VA
Martha A.	26	F		TN
William	1	M		TX
Barnett, Samuel	66	M	Farmer	SC
Sarah	60	F		NC
Francis A.	25	M	Farmer	KY
Salina	23	F		KY
Malinda	16	F		TN
Susan	14	F		TN
Vest, Reuben B.	49	M	Black Smith	VA
Mary A.	35	F		VA
Mary J.	15	F		AR
Matilda	13	F		AR
John	10	M		AR
Margaret	4	F		AR
Caroline	2	F		TX
Ramsey, Solomon	25	M	Farmer	TN
Long, William C.	27	M	Black Smith	TN
Mary	25	F		MO
Reubin	2/12	M		TX
Tarver, Nelson	44	M	Farmer	NC
Green M.	20	M	Farmer	TN
William B.	14	M		TN
John W.	12	M		TN
Martha C.	10	F		TN
Nancy J.	7	F		TN
Triart(?), Francis M.	22	M		AL
Tarver, Margaret A.	17	F		TN
Davis, Andrew	24	M	M. Minister	TN
Mariah S.	22	F		TN
John E.	2	M		TX
Julietta M.	1	F		TX
Canada, Allen B.	24	M	Farmer	SC
Olliver, Rodric	50	M	Farmer	NC
Temperance	51	F		KY
John E.	24	M	Farmer	TN
Thomas J.	17	M	Farmer	TN
Lucy A.	13	F		TN
Rosena	11	F		MS
Malone, Isac	36	M	Farmer	KY
Pretia	33	F		LA
Amanda	17	F		MS
Manerva	14	F		MS
Martha A.	8	F		MS
William B.	6	M		MS
Narcissa	2	F		TX
Hasher(?), William	23	M	Farmer	TN
Weaver, William	25	M	Farmer	AL
Lucinda	25	F		TN
Adaline	5	F		TX
James M.	5/12	M		TX
Youree, James	31	M	Farmer	TN
Lucin M.	34	F		VA
M. J. M.	12	F		MO
Drucilla E.	9	F		MO
William T.	7	M		MO
A. J.	3	M		MO
Willson, L. F.	28	M	Black Smith	SC
Gates, James O.	24	M	Black Smith	MS
Conclin, Samuel	34	M	Stone Cutter	NJ
Henderson, James M.	37	M	Clerk	GA
F. M.	21	F		TN
George N.	1	M		TX
Clapp, Lewis	22	M	Farmer	AL
Rebecca	21	F		TN
Benjamin	2	M		KY
Kalb, Georgian	18	F		GA
William	17	M		GA

(continued)

Name	Age	Sex	Occupation	Birthplace
Kalb, Martha J.	15	F		GA
Americus C.	13	F		GA
Hugh W.	10	M		GA
Milton L. V.	5	M		GA
Blardy, Fredoric	40	M	Farmer	VA
Wells, Moses	34	M	Farmer	KY
Eliza J.	21	F		TN
Margaret	1	F		TX
Bankhead, Margaret	20	F		AL
A---	2	F		TX
Cleridge, James	34	M	Farmer	TN
Devila	25	F		IL
Bly	5	M		IL
David	3	M		IL
Catharine	1	F		IL

Precinct No. 4

Name	Age	Sex	Occupation	Birthplace
McCallister, Thomas	24	M	Farmer	AL
Perlina	20	F		TN
Serena	1	F		TX
Walker, Gideon	25	M	Farmer	TN
Sarah L.	24	F		IL
Owens, Jefferson	35	M	Farmer	TN
Polly Ann	24	F		TN
James H.	6	M		TN
Anglin, John	27	M	Farmer	IL
Missouri	25	F		TN
Litha	7	F		TX
Nancy V.	5	F		TX
James	2	M		TX
Parker, Payton	30	M	Farmer	TN
Nancy G.	20	F		TN
Darinda	3	F		TX
Betsey	1	F		TX
Galloway, Joanna	11	F		AR
Faulkenberry, Eli	28	M	Farmer	TN
Phebe	24	F		IL
David	5	M		TX
Zachus H.	3	M		TX
John T.	1	M		TX
Faulkenberry, John T.	26	M	Farmer	TN
Elizabeth	19	F		MO
Nancy	54	F		TN
Owens, William	33	M	Farmer	TN
Elizabeth	30	F		TN
Eli	2	M		TX
Miro, James	23	M	Farmer	AR
Martha Ann	14	F		TN
McCallister, J. R.	38	M	Farmer	TN
Catherine	27	F		IN
Louisa	15	F		MS
George W.	13	M		AR
Daniell B.	3	M		TX
Margaret E.	8/12	F		TX
James, Sarah Ann	20	F		IL
Usery, Benjamin	13	M		TX
Anglin, Rebecca	14	F		TX
Elisha	13	M		TX
Seth B.	11	M		TX
Silas	7	M		TX
Emaline	3	F		TX
Trent, J.	31	M	Farmer	KY
Retta	22	F		TN
Obediah	3	M		TN
George W.	1	M		TN
Welch, William	36	M	Farmer	TN
Elizabeth	33	F		IL
M. C.	16	F		TX
John	13	M		TX

(continued)

Name	Age	Sex	Occupation	Birthplace
Welch, M. R. J.	9	F		TX
William	8	M		TX
Elizabeth	6	F		TX
Harvey	4	M		TX
Haretta	2	F		TX
Charles	9/12	M		TX
Culp, Joseph	32	M	Farmer	TN
Rachael	30	F		IL
Richard	8	M		TX
Benjamin	6	M		TX
John R.	4	M		TX
Lucinda	2	F		TX
Elizabeth	1/12	F		TX
Cox, Thomas	34	M	Farmer	KY
Martha	33	F		TN
Randolph	15	M	Farmer	MO
Eli	13	M		AR
Jeremiah	12	M		AR
Obediah	10	M		AR
Saryann	8	F		AR
Deborah	4	F		TX
James	1	M		TX
Sylvester, James	37	M		TN
Deborah	24	F		MO
William	10	M		AR
Nancy	8	F		AR
Martha	6	F		TX
Maryan	4	F		TX
Thomas	3	M		TX
Calep	3/12	M		TX
Anglin, John	24	M	Farmer	VA
E. A.	19	F		IL
Lavina	1	F		TX
Phifer, Martha J.	17	F		TN
Eaton, Benjamin	44	M	Farmer	KY
Malinda	45	F		TN
Silas	23	M	Farmer	IL
John	21	M	Farmer	IL
Richard	17	M	Farmer	IL
Benjamin	14	M		IL
William	5	M		IL
Mary	12	F		IL
Malinda	7	F		TX
James H.	2	M		TX
Anglin, John W.	4	M		TX
Margaret	2	F		TX

Town of Springfield

Name	Age	Sex	Occupation	Birthplace
Henry, J. R.	34	M	Merchant	TN
Sarah O.	17	F		AL
Callett, J. H.	24	M	Clerk	NC
Moore, James W.	26	M	Tavern Keeper	NC
Mary J.	33	F		TN
W. W.	13	M		TX
Emaline	8	F		TX
Mary	6	F		TX
Eugene	2	F		TX
Josephine	6/12	F		TX
Smith, R. K.	30	M	Physician	AL
Angaline	21	F		TN
William S.	1	M		TX
McCutchen, Joseph D.	27	M	Attorney at Law	TN
E. T.	19	F		AL
J. D.	1/12	M		TX
Johnson, G. W.	38	M	Merchant	TN
Mahulda	34	F		AL
Ann E.	14	F		MS
J. L.	12	F		MS
William J.	8	M		MS
E. M.	6	F		MS
A. J.	5	M		MS
D. E.	3	M		MS
Mortimore, Thomas V.	45	M	Attorney at Law	ME
Herenden, H. H.	46	M	House Carpenter	TN

(continued)

Name	Age	Sex	Occupation	Birthplace
Herenden, Louisa	33	F		TN
Mary	14	F		TN
John	13	M		TN
Sinthy	11	F		TN
Thomas	8	M		KY
William	6	M		KY
James	4	M		KY
(Blank)	3	M		KY

Precinct No. 1 (continued)

Name	Age	Sex	Occupation	Birthplace
Capps, Harvy	27	M	Farmer	MS
Catharine	20	F		TN
Mary	60	F		MD
Ridgell, D. P.	22	M	Farmer	AL
Capps, Elkana	24	M	Farmer	MS
Brown, Joseph R.	33	M	Farmer	SC
Lucy E.	22	F		TN
Maryann	3/12	F		TX
Allan, Joseph M.	26	M	Farmer	TN
Boyd, John	54	M	Farmer	TN
Elizabeth	53	F		KY
J. P.	24	M	Farmer	KY

Precinct No. 4 (continued)

Name	Age	Sex	Occupation	Birthplace
Pendergast, L. B.	42	M	Farmer	TN
Elizabeth	37	F		TN
H. D.	15	M		TN
M. K.	14	F		TN
S. E.	12	F		TN
Jos. B.	7	M		TX
A. T.	5	M		TX
William L.	3	M		TX
McClane, James B.	31	M	Carpenter	TN
Tiabout, Henry	30	M	Clerk	PA
M. A.	17	F		TN
Pendergast, David M.	33	M	Attorney at Law	TN
M. E.	20	F		TN
Zell, Mordiciah	41	M	Me. Minister	TN
L. M.	28	F		TN
Sarah J.	4	F		TX
M.	1	M		TX
P.	78	M	Farmer	NC
Stroud, Mandred	31	M	Farmer	AL
N.	25	F		TN
E. B.	1/12	M		TX
Gray, Jessy	38	M	Farmer	NC
E.	35	F		NC
M. E.	12	F		TN
James W.	8	M		TN
J. C.	6	M		TN
Tilley, D. H.	32	M	Farmer	NC
Martha	29	F		TN
Lucinda B.	2	F		TX
Durinda	2	F		TX
Price, Willis A.	30	M	Farmer	TN
Mary	30	F		AL
Sarah J.	7	F		TX
Mary R.	2	F		TX
Drew	2/12	M		TX
Richason, Elija	30	M	Wagon Maker	TN
Sarah	47	F		SC
Mary	28	F		MO
Sampson	23	M	Farmer	MO
Robert	21	M	Farmer	MO
James	18	M	Farmer	MO
Edward	16	M	Farmer	MO
Loranzou	13	M		MO
James	10	M		MO
N. J.	8	M		MO
Phifer, Permanis	24	M	Farmer	TN

(continued)

Name	Age	Sex	Occupation	Birthplace
Phifer, Aglentine	22	F		TN
Bradley	4	M		TX
Juda E.	17	F		TN
Townsend, William	57	M	Tavern Keeper	KY
Sarah	55	F		KY
Thomas	24	M	Farmer	TN
Olliver, Franklin C.	23	M	Merchant	TN
Lucretia	18	F		TX
Nicks, Anderson T.	21	M	Farmer	TN
Mary	21	F		NC
Eliza E.	2	F		TX
Susan	1/12	F		TX
Dunaway, John	41	M	Farmer	VA
Mary V.	35	F		TN
Newton M.	8	M		MO
McKee, Timothy	20	M	Farmer	MO
Archibald, S. N.	38	M	Farmer	SC
Mary Ann	35	F		TN
Robert C.	12	M		AL
Martha M.	10	F		AL
Nancy E.	8	F		AL
Andrew B.	6	M		AL
Thomas M.	4	M		AL
Mary E.	2	F		TX
Map, A. F.	38	M	Farmer	NC
Nancy J.	21	F		TN
John W.	4	M		TX
Bennett, Townsend	45	M	Farmer	KY
Mary	44	F		KY
James T.	23	M	Sheriff	AL
William	19	M	Farmer	TN
Betsy J.	16	F		AL
Lucinda	11	F		AL
G. W.	3	M		TX
Wiles K.	1	M		TX
Hume, Elizabeth	38	F		VA
Randolph	14	M		AR
Angaline	6	F		TX
James	3	M		TX
Prue B.	12	M		AR
Milton, Stroud	44	M	School Teacher	GA
Vanmeter, William P.	21	M	Farmer	KY
Prior, Richard	29	M	waggoner	VA
Evett, Moses S.	22	M	Laborer	TN
McKie, B. D.	26	M	M. Physician	TN

Town of Springfield (continued)

Name	Age	Sex	Occupation	Birthplace
Jackson, G. W.	26	M	Farmer	AL
Malinda	20	F		TN
Mary Ann	2	F		TX
Lethy J.	6/12	F		TX
Adamson, William	34	M	Farmer	TN
Hannah	30	F		TN
Syntha	13	F		TN
Matilda	11	F		TN
Bluford	8	M		MO
Elizabeth	6	F		MO
Olley	4	F		MO
Mary	7/12	F		TX
Cook, Wiles K.	31	M	Physician	KY
Mary D.	21	F		AL
Mary	10	F		TX
Virginia B.	7	F		TX
Louis P.	4	M		TX
Alexander, Joseph	27	M	Taylor(Tailor)	TN
Glaze, Trey	27	M	Farmer	TN
Nancy	15	F		MO
Galaway, Thomas C.	26	M	Farmer	TN
Walker, G. W.	40	M	Taylor(Tailor)	VA
Martha J.	31	F		KY
Green, Parley	54	M	Waggoner	VT
Philpott, J. P.	33	M	Surveyor	TN

(continued)

LIMESTONE COUNTY, TEXAS

Name	Age	Sex	Occupation	Birthplace
Nelson, Manerva J.	4	F		TX
Williba	2	M		TX

End of Town of Springfield

Precinct No. 5

Name	Age	Sex	Occupation	Birthplace
Polk, Thomas A.	40	M	Farmer	SC
Eliza	37	F		SC
Nancy J.	12	F		TN
Mary L.	10	F		TN
Elizabeth C.	8	F		TN
Margaret A.	6	F		TN
Harriett T.	4	F		TX
Sarah V.	1	F		TX
Slone, David	70	M	Farmer	TN
J. M.	30	M	Carpenter	TN
Robert	23	M	Farmer	MO
Alexander	40	M	Physician	TN
Smith, Pleasant	43	M	Farmer	TN
Lucinda	38	F		TN
Hinton C.	20	M	Farmer	TN
Evaline	18	F		TN
Eudorah	16	F		TN
Archibald H.	15	M		TN
Duncan, Thomas	27	M	Farmer	SC
Maryann	25	F		AL
Francis C.	4	F		TX
Mahala	2	F		TX
Williams, Martha	14	F		AL
Duncan, William S.	23	M	A Rounder	TN
Brown, James	54	M	Farmer	NC
Mary	30	F		TN
Columbus	11	M		AR
Mary L.	13	F		AR
Elender A.	8	F		AR
Diana	6	F		AR
Cornelis F.	3	F		TX
Warren, D. S.	30	M	Farmer	KY
Sarah Ann	29	F		MO
Thomas H.	2	M		TX
Charles F.	6/12	M		TX
Dority, John B.	23	M	Farmer	TN
Fretwell, Jefferson	22	M	Farmer	AL
Williams, Benjamin	24	M	Farmer	TN
Caroline	15	F		AR
Jane	14	F		AR
Cook, James B.	45	M	Wagon Maker	TN
Mary	13	F		TX
Henry	11	M		TX
Andrew J.	8	M		TX
Marinda	6	F		TX
Donahoo, Mott	40	M	Farmer	TN
Easter	29	F		KY
Angaline	11	F		TX
Archibald	7	M		TX
William	5	M		TX
Franklin	3	M		TX
Osten	8/12	M		TX
Barton, John	29	M	Farmer	TN
David	27	M	Farmer	TN
Elizabeth	16	F		MO
James	21	M	Farmer	TN
Spencer, Eliphus	47	M	Attorney at Law	PA
Catharine A.	27	F		PA
Emaly M.	2	F		TX
Dodd, Jessee	20	M	Farmer	TN
Savier, A. H.	31	M	Farmer	TN
Nancy	25	F		TN
William B.	11	M		TN
Francis B.	3	F		TX
Morgan, William J.	33	M	Farmer	AL

(continued)

Name	Age	Sex	Occupation	Birthplace
Morgan, Stasa Ann	30	F		TN
Nancy A.	11	F		TX
Louisa E.	7	F		TX
Martin	5	M		TX
Hessie Jane	3	F		TX
Barton, L. B. H.	30	M	Farmer	TN
Jane	31	F		SC
Johnson, James H.	42	M	Farmer	TN
Ruth F.	42	F		SC
Columbus C.	12	M		MS
David	11	M		MS
Mary S.	10	F		MS
Rosalinda	6	F		MS
Ruth W.	3	F		MS
Puckett, Andrew J.	32	M	Farmer	TN
Sarah	31	F		TN
Andrew J.	6	M		AR
Georgia A.	2	F		TX
Tennessee	1	F		TX
Richason, Sarah	16	F		AR
Lock, Jonas	31	M	Farmer	TN
Sarah	23	F		OH
John G.	4	M		MO
Tennessee	9/12	F		TX
Stringer, F.	25	M	Farmer	TN
Marlin, William N. P.	28	M	Farmer	AL
Rebecca J.	23	F		TN
John	1	M		TX
Shelton, A. M.	44	M	Farmer	TN
Elizabeth	40	F		TN
William	19	M		TN
Edmond	16	M	Farmer	TN
James	14	M		TN
Alfred	10	M		TX
Dred	8	M		TX
John	5	M		TX
Paidro	2	M		TX
Self, Eliza	9	F		AL
Church, Loyd	11	M		MO
Madison	9	M		MO
Sarah	9	F		MO
Rebecca	7	F		MO
Smith, Charles	34	M	Farmer	TN
Rebecca	30	F		TN
Robert E.	12	M		TX
John H.	10	M		TX
Samuel C.	9	M		TX
Ruphis	7	M		TX
Emily	5	F		TX
Luisa	3	F		TX
Charles	1	M		TX
Barton, Fleming	25	M	Farmer	TN
Elizabeth	23	F		TN
Covington, John	47	M	Farmer	TN
Jane	47	F		TN
Larkin A.	18	M	Farmer	TN
John H.	15	M	Farmer	TN
James C.	12	M		TN
Marcus L.	10	M		TN
Marlin, Rachael	85	F		NC
Crouch, Newton	25	M	Farmer	TN
Rachael L.	24	F		TN
Isabel J.	3	F		TX
William W.	1	M		TX
Crouch, William W.	24	M	Farmer	TN
Mary L.	17	F		TN
Mitchell, John	26	M		TN
Martha	19	F		TN
Araminta	4	F		TX
Thomas	1	M		TX
Duncan, John	61	M	House Carpenter	VA
Margaret	51	F		VA

(continued)

Name	Age	Sex	Occupation	Birthplace
Duncan, Alvira	18	F		TN
James	12	M		TX
Powers, Lewis	30	M	Farmer	TN
Nancy	23	F		AR
John	3	M		TX
Sarah	2	F		TX
Thomas	2/12	M		TX
Powers, Elija	26	M	Farmer	TN
Powers, Francis M.	24	M	Farmer	TN
Penelope	18	F		TX
Powers, Elija	57	M	Physician	TN
Sarah	40	F		TN
Hufman, Henry	19	M	Farmer	TN
Blunt K.	17	M	Farmer	TN
Jane	13	F		TN
Nicholas	11	M		TN
Eliza	8	F		TX
Sofrona	2	F		TX
Drake, Alfred	33	M	Farmer	TN
Sanaro	21	F		TN
Analiza	2	F		TX
Rice, David	36	M	Farmer	MA
Leona	38	F		NC
Travis, William	22	M	Farmer	TN
Ethridge, William	25	M	Carpenter	FL
Brandwell, George	37	M	Carpenter	NC
Springfield, James M.	37	M	Farmer	SC
Susan F.	17	F		TN
Nancy E.	8/12	F		TX
Welch, Charles	48	M	Farmer	NC
Elizabeth	22	F		TN
John	19	M	Farmer	MO
Charles	17	M	Farmer	MO
Patterson, Patteon	7	M		TN
Robert	5	M		TN
Martha J.	3	F		TX
Ann H.	2	F		TX
Welch, Joseph	22	M	Farmer	MO
Eliza	19	F		TN
Mary J.	2	F		TX
John	1	M		TX
Fulenton, Martha	21	F		TN
Jane	5	F		TX
John	3	M		TX
William	1	M		TX
Thermon, M. J.	36	M	Farmer	GA
Tina M.	32	F		TN
John W.	15	M		TN
Barton, William A.	8	M		MS
Sarah E.	7	F		AL
John D.	6	M		AL
Mary J.	4	F		AL
David A.	2	M		AL
Barton, S. H.	28	M	Farmer	TN
Mary	22	F		AL
Nancy	1	F		TX
David	65	M	Farmer	VA
Barton, Isac M.	32	M	Farmer	TN
Mary E.	26	F		SC
James A.	8	M		AL
Hariett	7	F		AL
Sarah M.	5	F		AL
Juliana C.	3	F		AL
Merchant, Wesly	21	M	Farmer	SC
Crouch, Alonzo	30	M	Farmer	TN
Elizabeth A.	17	F		TN
Capps, F. W.	44	M	Farmer	TN
Mary A.	30	F		TN

(continued)

Name	Age	Sex	Occupation	Birthplace
Capps, James	23	M	Farmer	AL
Elizabeth	10	F		MS
Silicia	8	F		TX
William	6	M		TX
Jenett	4	F		TX
George	3	M		TX
Church, Luke	44	M	Farmer	VA
Mary F.	36	F		KY
Susan F.	13	F		MO
Rodgers, Nathaniel	22	M	Farmer	AL
Tennessee	15	F		TN
Padier, John	2	M		TX
Sebern	1/12	M		TX
Morris, Spencer	32	M	Farmer	TN
Sarah	26	F		IL
Eliza J.	5	F		TX
Henry M.	3	M		TX
Mary A.	2	F		TX
Killgore, Charles	40	M	Black Smith	TN
Mary	18	F		TX
Mary T.	1	F		TX
Burleson, James	41	M	Farmer	TN
Matilda	39	F		TN
William B.	20	M	Farmer	AL
Wiley N.	17	M		AL
Sarah	18	F		AL
Francis	15	M		AL
John J.	11	M		AL
Carline	9	F		AL
Cager	7	M		AL
Cintha M.	4	F		AL
Mary B.	3	F		AL
Edward F.	1	M		TX
Clark, William	58	M	Bapt. Minister	TN
Malinda	48	F		TN
Clark, Samuel	32	M	Farmer	TN
Elizabeth	28	F		TN
Amanda	9	F		TN
Juley	7	F		TN
Charles	5	M		MS
William	3	M		MS
Clark J.	1	M		MS
McCanlis, James	25	M	Farmer	TN
Manerva	18	F		MS
Gentry, Emaline	37	F		TN
Martha	12	F		TN
Sarah	10	F		TN
Thomas	4	M		TX
John	1	M		TX
Gentry, George	75	M	Farmer	SC
Martha	57	F		VA
Elias	17	M	Farmer	TN
William	14	M		TN
Nelson, Samuel	42	M	Farmer	TN
Sarah	37	F		TN
Sion F.	14	M		TX
Lidia F.	11	F		TX
Sarah Ann	8	F		TX
Hill, William	14	M		TX
Sarah	13	F		TX
Howard, William R.	30	M	Farmer	TN
Drucilla	20	F		TN
Martha E.	4	F		TX
James W.	2	M		TX
Duncan, G. B.	27	M	Farmer	TN
Rebecca A.	22	F		AL
Jordin, John	33	M	Farmer	TN
Manerva	24	F		AL
Lucinda	9	F		TX
Mannin	4	M		TX
Joseph	2	M		TX

LIMESTONE COUNTY, TEXAS

Name	Age	Sex	Occupation	Birthplace
Sparks, Williba	47	M	Farmer	GA
Mary	40	F		IL
Levi	25	M	Farmer	AR
William	17	M	Farmer	AR
Tilman	13	M		AR
Clarinda	9	F		TN
Nancy C.	7	F		TN
Bagley M.	3	M		TN
John	1	M		TN
Jones, William	31	M	Merchant	??
Loup, Anna K.	14	F		GER
Shringler, George	16	M	None	GER
Blain, S. A.	33	M	Farmer	TN
Lucsa	28	F		TN
William B.	8	M		TX
John M.	7	M		TX
Mary F.	4	F		TX
George M.	11/12	M		TX
Pevahouse, A.	38	M	Farmer	TN
Mary	28	F		AR
Andrew	9	M		TX
John	6	M		TX
Elsey	5	F		TX
Jacob	9/12	M		TX
Hogg, William	34	M	Farmer	AR
Elizabeth	24	F		TN
Alicy A.	2	F		TX
John	10/12	M		TX
Forbes, Robert	44	M	Physician	KY
Abziney(?)	44	F		KY
Liourgus W.	15	M		TN
Nancy E.	13	F		TN
Barclay, David	52	M	Farmer	NC
Darcus	50	F		KY
Charles	23	M	Farmer	TN
William	21	M	Farmer	TN
Davis	19	M	Farmer	AL
Samuel	17	M	Farmer	TN
Martha	16	F		TN
Lucinda	11	F		TX
Tabitha	13	F		TX
Eliza	9	F		TX
Algiers	3	F		TX
Menifee, Strother	30	M	Farmer	TN
William	25	M	(Blind)	TN
Elizabeth	20	F		AL
John	22	M	Farmer	AL
Beasley, Nancy	24	F		TN
Stephen	8	M		TX
John	6	M		TX
Sarah	3	F		TX
Rodgers, Larkin	48	M	Farmer	TN
Mary	50	F		GA
Henry A.	20	M	Farmer	AL
Lucy F.	13	F		AL
John	8	M		AL
Mary E.	6	F		AL
McDowell, John	21	M	Farmer	AL

MATAGORGA COUNTY, TEXAS

Name	Age	Sex	Occupation	Birthplace
McCarnes(?), John W.	39	M	Land Lord (Hotel)	NY
Sarah F.	24	F		TN
W. A.	1	M		TX
Basher, Mrs.	29	F		GER
R.	10	M		GER
Williams, Edward	30	M	Gun Smith	CT
Lills(Sills), J.	30	M	Merchant	VA
McGowgal, J. C.	26	M	Lawyer	TN
Schmake, M.	30	M	Clerk	GER
Parks, D. J.	37	M	Carpenter	TN
Nancy A.	28	F		TN
James T.	12	M		TX
F. A.	10	M		TX
Parks, Harriet A.	7	F		TX
John D.	4	M		TX
Alvira J.	2	F		TX
Mary C.	1	F		TX
Graham, John G.	41	M	Boatman	ENG
Louisa M.	24	F		TN
John G. C.	1	M		TX
Williamson, Ann	41	F		TN
Annie	12	F		TX
Hellen	10	F		TX
Hodges, Galen	37	M	Land Lord (Hotel)	RI
Amelia	38	F		NY
Julia A.	4	F		TX
Austin, William	22	M	None	NY
Collinsworth, Margaret	28	F		TN
Huttner, J. F.	60	M	Physician (illegible)	
Turley, T. J.	40	M	Physician	??
Mrs.	34	F		NJ
Rush, I. G.	30	M	Painter	OH
Russell, William	40	M	Ass. & Collector	SCO
Casnahan, J. B.	28	M	Lawyer	SC
Mrs.	26	F		VA
Roberta	6	F		AL
J. W.	3	M		AL
Mary	3/12	F		AL
Bertrand, G. A.	28	M	Planter	AL
Eliza J.	22	F		TN
G. A., Jr.	2	M		TX
Jamison, Thomas	56	M	Planter	TN
Harriet B.	40	F		TN
Viser, Napoleon B.	26	M	Physician	MS
Lewis, Charles S.	45	M	Weaver	ENG
Hardeman, Samuel W.	29	M	Planter	TN
Sally A.	23	F		TN
Ellen	6/12	F		TX
Maxey, Mr.	45	M	Overseer	TN
Brewster, H. P.	30	M	Lawyer	SC
Ann E.	26	F		TN
Phebe H.	7	F		TX
Nancy	5	F		TX
Elizabeth	2	F		TX
Royall, Manerva V.	18	F		AL
Iles, Perry B.	49	M	Farmer	VA
Elizabeth	50	F		TN
Benjamin	10	M		TX
James	6	M		TX
Page, Harrison	29	M	Farmer	MS
Ramsey, Lawrence	49	M	Gin Wright	NY
Hardeman, D.	34	M	Planter	TN
S. A.	32	F		NC
Bethenia	17	F		TN
Udora	13	F		TN
D.	12	M		TN
Dickerson	9	M		MS
Evelyn	6	F		LA
M.	4	M		TX
P.	1	M		TX
H. H.	5	F		AR
Dinsmore, Amanda F.	55	F		CT
Davis, H. T.	35	M	School Teacher	TN
Demoss, Peter	50	M		OH
Susanna	47	F		TN
Elizabeth	17	F		TX
A. J.	11	F		TX
Thomas	4	M		TX
Flowers, Romulus	27	M	Waggoner	KY
Thomas, Samuel	50	M	Farmer	GA
Ellen	36	F		TN
Albert	5	M		TX
Theophalus	15	M		GA
Taylor	3	M		TX
Robert	1	M		TX
Kinney, Mary B.	31	F		GA

(continued)

MATAGORDA COUNTY, TEXAS

Name	Age	Sex	Occupation	Birthplace
Herbert, P. W.	16	M	None	AL
Rowena	9	F		AL
Theresa	4	F		TX
Black, Theresa	20	F		TN
Keller, Jas. W.	31	M	Farmer	MS
M. A.	27	F		TN
Noland	6	M		TX
Welburn	5	M		TX
Crittenden	2	M		TX
Williams, Robert H.	53	M	Planter	NC
Mary L.	34	F		TN
C. H.	12	M		TX
L. E.	10	F		TX
M. L.	8	F		TX
L. R.	5	F		TX
Bains, Mr.	30	M	Overseer	VA
Muner, John	55	M	School Teacher	IRE
Stephenson, Eliza	18	F		TN
Wheeler, Daniel	28	M	Farmer	TN
Levenia	25	F		TX
Eli H.	7	M		TX
John J.	5	M		TX
Wadsmith, Albert	36	M	Merchant	NC
Mary	32	F		TN
C. E.	10	F		TX
Mary W.	8	F		TX
William B.	6	M		TX
Thomas M.	5	M		TX
S. H.	3	F		TX
Edward	9/12	M		TX
Mackey, Ruth	50	F		VA

MEDINA COUNTY, TEXAS

Castorville

Name	Age	Sex	Occupation	Birthplace
Randatz, Henry	26	M	Saw Mill	LA
Turner, Daniel	35	M	Laborer	KY
Zimmerle, Jacob	40	M	Laborer	GER
Fitzgerald, John	33	M	Laborer	IRE
Burkhart, Christian	30	M	Laborer	GER
Pingernot, August	20	M	Laborer	FRA
Brooks, Adam	35	M	Laborer	TN

Fort Lincoln

Name	Age	Sex	Occupation	Birthplace
Robertson, Richard	24	M	Private, U.S.A.	TN

The Medina River

Name	Age	Sex	Occupation	Birthplace
Harrison, Bernard H.	21	M	1st Sgt. Vol Co.	TN
Kirkpatrick, James G.	28	M	Farrier, Vol Co.	TN
Anderson, Jeptha	21	M	Pvt. Ranging Co.	TN
Dempsey, William	29	M	Pvt. Ranging Co.	TN
Folk, Benjamin	23	M	Pvt. Ranging Co.	TN
Graham, James	24	M	Pvt. Ranging Co.	TN
Lane, John J.	28	M	Pvt. Ranging Co.	TN
Madden, James F.	26	M	Pvt. Ranging Co.	TN
Schaver, James	18	M	Pvt. Ranging Co.	TN
Wamble, Sidney	23	M	Pvt. Ranging Co.	TN
Ward, Armstead	20	M	Pvt. Ranging Co.	TN
Bandelen, Jacob	50	M	Farmer	GER
Catherine	56	F		GER
Jacob	21	M	Laborer	GER
Andrew	18	M	Laborer	GER
Wallace, Benjamin	25	M	Laborer	TN

MILAM COUNTY, TEXAS

Name	Age	Sex	Occupation	Birthplace
Stiles, Seaborn	38	M	Farmer	NC
Matilda	34	F		TN
James E.	17	M	Farmer	TN
Sarah J.	15	F		TN
Francis N.	12	M		TN

(continued)

Name	Age	Sex	Occupation	Birthplace
Stiles, Margaret E.	10	F		TN
Thomas S.	6	M		MO
Jesse L.	3	M		MO
Mary C.	1	F		TX
Kuykendall, Lewis	65	M	Farmer	TN
Margaret	55	F		SC
Louisa	18	F		IL
Walters, Alexander	34	M	Farmer	TN
Sarah	36	F		TN
Tillman W.	15	M		MS
Matilda	12	F		TX
Louisa	9	F		TX
Nancy	7	F		TX
Mathews	6	M		TX
Mary	4	F		TX
Andrew J.	3	M		TX
Stevens, James	65	M	Farmer	VA
Sarah	56	F		TN
James	26	M	Farmer	KY
William	22	M	Farmer	KY
Francis	19	M	Farmer	KY
Henderson, Nicholas	31	M	Farmer	SC
Mahaley	27	F		TN
Samuel H.	2	M		TX
Perkins, David	49	M	Farmer	KY
Cynthia	45	F		TN
Lucy A.	21	F		AR
Silas D.	18	M	Farmer	AR
Melinda	16	F		MO
Delilah	13	F		AR
William R.	10	M		AR
Francis M.	8	M		AR
Cynthia C.	2	F		TX
Pennington, John	50	M	Farmer	VA
Catharine	50	F		TN
Levi	26	M	None	TN
John	22	M	Farmer	TN
Elizabeth	12	F		MO
David	11	M		MO
Rebecca	9	F		MO
Elijah	45	M	Farmer	VA
Damron, Menton W.	26	M	Farmer	TN
Sarah	18	F		MO
Sarah	11/12	F		TX
Mills, John	38	M	Farmer	KY
Jane	28	F		TN
Fisher, Moses	42	M	Farmer	IL
Amelia	27	F		TN
Joshua	18	M	Farmer	AR
Martha	13	F		AR
Mary	10	F		AR
Delila	5	F		TX
James	2	M		TX
Havens, Thomas	57	M	Farmer	TN
Abigail	56	F		NC
Asa S.	20	M	Farmer	MO
Alvin B.	17	M	Farmer	MO
Sarah	14	F		MO
Purdon, Hannah E.	21	F		AL
Roberts, Cornelius B.	43	M	Farmer	TN
Rhoda	41	F		GA
William J.	20	M	Farmer	AL
Nathan T.	19	M	Farmer	AL
David P.	17	M	Farmer	AL
John M.	15	M		MS
Mary A.	14	F		MS
Cornelius B.	12	M		MS
James T.	11	M		MS
Emily C.	9	F		MS
Abram M.	7	M		MS
Jeremiah J.	2	M		TX
Jesse R.	4/12	M		TX
Dennis, Joseph	39	M	Farmer	TN

(continued)

MILAM COUNTY, TEXAS

Name	Age	Sex	Occupation	Birthplace
Dennis, Peg	32	F		TN
Disa	12	F		TN
Joseph T.	11	M		AR
Cleopatra	8	F		AR
Margaret J.	7	F		AR
William N.	5	M		AR
Sarah T.	3	F		AR
Lawson	2/12	M		TX
Wilkinson, Melville	32	M	Farmer	TN
Eveline	28	F		TN
Nancy E.	6	F		TX
Sarah M.	4	F		TX
Ruth	20	F		TX
Green, James	26	M	Farmer	MO
Anderson, John	32	M	Farmer	SC
Elizabeth E.	20	F		TX
Lewis W.	1	M		TX
Warren, Amanda	11	F		TN
Stillman, James	21	M	Laborer	AL
Danley, John	30	M	Black Smith	TN
Mary	29	F		KY
Charles W.	9	M		MO
Nathan B.	6	M		MO
Sarah J.	5	F		MO
Campbell	3	M		TX
Andrew	1	M		TX
Carr, Jacob	21	M	Carpenter	TN
Reed, Michael	62	M	Farmer	TN
Martha	64	F		VA
Michael	12	M		MS
Birdshaw, William	21	M	School Teacher	SC
Cathey, John	26	M	Farmer	TN
Hannah	17	F		IL
William J.	2	M		AR
Fulcher, John	52	M	Farmer	TN
Mary	43	F		LA
Willis	18	M	Farmer	TX
Henry C.	15	M		TX
Martha A.	12	F		TX
Francis F.	10	M		TX
Nathaniel	7	M		TX
John E.	3	M		TX
Mary A.	1	F		TX
Shields, Nathaniel	28	M	Farmer	LA
Samantha	20	F		TN
Catharine	2	F		TX
Williams, Jesse	11	M		TX
Cates, John	28	M	Farmer	TN
Comfort	26	F		TN
Susan J.	9	F		AR
Mary	7	F		AR
Adaline	5	F		AR
Margaret	3	F		AR
John K.	2	M		AR
Hannah	6/12	F		TX
Clary, Ransom	40	M	Carpenter	TN
Mary	30	F		TN
Jane	14	F		AR
John	12	M		AR
George	10	M		AR
Franklin J.	8	M		AR
Alexander	2	M		AR
Margaret J.	2	F		AR
Stevens, William	52	M	Farmer	KY
Agnes	44	F		TN
Job	21	M	Farmer	AR
John	19	M	Farmer	AR
Nancy	14	F		MO
Mahaley	12	F		MO
Peter	10	M		MO
Mary	8	F		TX
William	6	M		TX
Amanda	3	F		TX

Name	Age	Sex	Occupation	Birthplace
McDaniel, Granger	50	M	Farmer	VA
Mary	36	F		TN
Abner	21	M	Farmer	TN
Elizabeth	18	F		TN
Stacey	17	M	Farmer	TN
David	15	M		TN
Sarah	12	F		TX
Mary A.	10	F		TX
Mahaley	8	F		TX
Matilda	7	F		TX
Lewis	4	M		TX
Genette	2	F		TX
John	6/12	M		TX
Marshall, John	42	M	Farmer	IL
Elizabeth	46	F		TN
William	17	M	Farmer	AR
Martha J.	15	F		AR
Robert P.	13	M		AR
Sarah E.	10	F		AR
James C.	9	M		AR
Marshall, Robert	75	M	Farmer	SC
Elizabeth	66	F		TN
Margaret	44	F		IL
Elizabeth	34	F		IL
Giddins, Calvary	29	M	Farmer	KY
Mary	32	F		TN
John W.	11	M		MO
Absalom M.	9	M		TX
William E.	7	M		TX
Rebecca A.	4	F		TX
James N.	2	M		TX
Crabtree, John	52	M	Black Smith	TN
Rebecca	47	F		TN
James A.	18	M	Farmer	IL
Rebecca M.	14	F		MO
John F.	12	M		AR
William N.	10	M		MO
Ephraim J.	7	M		TX
Crabtree, Job	36	M	Farmer	TN
Malinda	19	F		TX
Peppers, William	33	M	Farmer	TN
Eveline	27	F		AL
Mary J.	9	F		AR
Ross, Shupley	39	M	Hotel Keeper	KY
Catherine	38	F		VA
Mary R.	18	F		MO
Margaret B.	16	F		MO
Peter F.	13	M		IA
Sullivan	12	M		IA
Ann	8	F		TX
James M.	6	M		TX
Robert S.	2	M		TX
Boykin, Joseph	25	M	Physician	TN
Hill, Frederick A.	27	M	Lawyer	NC
Pucket, Leyton	23	M	Grocer	TN
Illingworth, James O.	27	M	County Clerk	ENG
Jones, Thomas	21	M	Laborer	AR
Weeks, William	23	M	Laborer	AR
Barnes, Anselm	58	M	Farmer	NC
Mary	50	F		NC
Franklin	25	M	Farmer	TN
Ammon	23	M	Farmer	TN
Samuel	19	M	Farmer	IL
Emeline	12	F		AR
Bible, Adam	52	M	Farmer	TN
Eliza	36	F		GA
Philip	20	M	Farmer	TN
Christopher	18	M	Farmer	TN
George	12	M		AR
Rebecca	9	F		AR
Eleander	7	F		AR
Lewis	4	M		AR
Ave	9	M		AR
Mosier, Thomas	42	M	Mason	NY
Walker, William B.	39	M	Merchant	VA
Toole, James	26	M	Merchant	TN

MILAM COUNTY, TEXAS

Name	Age	Sex	Occupation	Birthplace
Clark, Isaac D.	36	M	Farmer	TN
Ann D.	28	F		FL
Sealy, Martha J.	15	F		FL
Hubby, Spencer	22	M	Cabinet Maker	NY
Sally	21	F		ENG
Charles M.	1	M		TX
Menzell, James B.	25	M	Carpenter	TN
Arnett, John H.	34	M	Carpenter	VA
Blair, John S.	48	M	Hotel Keeper	TN
Elizabeth L.	42	F		TN
Riggs, William	13	M		AR
Leonidas	11	M		AR
Moreland, Thomas	45	M	Shoe Maker	NC
Miller, John	35	M	Laborer	GER
Davis, William	24	M	Shoe Maker	VT
Townsand, THomas	19	M	Clerk	IA
Meek, Jacob C.	23	M	Farmer	TN
Mary A.	17	F		MS
Moore, Allen P.	35	M	Farmer	TN
Mary A.	19	F		GA
Henrietta	4	F		MO
Absalom P.	5/12	M		TX
Dawson, Francis	28	M	Farmer	IN
Maddon, Absalom D.	35	M	Farmer	TN
Barron, Thomas H.	54	M	Farmer	VA
Mary J.	20	F		TN
Milam	11	M		TX
Travis	11	M		TX
David S.	7	M		TX
Dink	2	M		TX
Mosella	4/12	F		TX
Hulme, Robert S.	49	M	Tailor	NC
Bible, John	22	M	Farmer	TN
Mary J.	17	F		TX
Long, John J.	40	M	Carpenter	TN
Elizabeth	27	F		TN
Maria	3	F		TN
Francis	1	M		TX
Holman, George W.	23	M	Farmer	TN
Mary	18	F		TN
Dice	3	F		TN
Lucy	1	F		TX
Smith, Wiley	45	M	Farmer	GA
Nancy	35	F		TN
William P.	20	M	Farmer	AL
Mary	17	F		AL
Elizabeth	15	F		AL
Prudence C.	13	F		MS
Nancy	11	F		TX
Thomas H.	9	M		TX
Stephen S.	6	M		TX
John D.	4	M		TX
George W.	1	M		TX
Jones, Robert P.	40	M	Laborer	Wales
Cook, Isaac W. H.	31	M	Cooper	TN
Nancy	23	F		MO
James K.	5	M		LA
Jasper N.	2/12	M		TX
Morrison, Samuel	36	M	Farmer	TN
Rebecca A.	34	F		KY
Mary E.	15	F		MS
Jane	13	F		IA
John W.	11	M		IA
Emily C.	9	F		IL
James A.	4	M		IL
Rosanna	2	F		TX
Oakes, Susan	40	F		TN
William	21	M	Farmer	TN
Allen	19	M	Farmer	TN
America	15	F		TN
Sarah	12	F		TN
Housten	10	M		TN

(continued)

Name	Age	Sex	Occupation	Birthplace
Oakes, Francis	7	M		TN
Jackson, Milton	5	M		TN
Barton, Albert	30	M	Farmer	AL
Elizabeth	26	F		TN
Robert J.	1	M		TX
Susan	1/12	F		TX
Smith, John	25	M	Farmer	KY
Stephen, John M.	34	M	Farmer	MO
Miranda	30	F		KY
Mary A.	10	F		TX
Samuel W.	8	M		TX
James M.	4	M		TX
England, James	22	M	Farmer	TN
Eubank, John T.	40	M	Farmer	VA
Martha K.	30	F		TN
John T.	7	M		TX
Charles	5	M		TX
Elizabeth T.	3	F		TX
Mason, Alfred	30	M	Laborer	IL
Bowen, William R.	30	M	Farmer	TN
Elizabeth S.	24	F		TN
Leonidas S.	6	M		TX
Sarah	4	F		TX
Mary H.	3	F		TX
Adam L.	6/12	M		TX
Hearn, James	21	M	Laborer	TN
Bishop, David	26	M	Farmer	TN
Elizabeth	24	F		TN
Milly E.	4	F		TX
Harriet S.	1/12	F		TX
Davis, Lee R.	38	M	Farmer	TN
Catharine	27	F		FL
John	7	M		TX
Richard	4	M		TX
William	3	M		TX
Henry	1	M		TX
Barnes, Robert S.	33	M	Farmer	TN
Richardson, Isaac	18	M	Farmer	MO
Morris, Thomas	28	M	Farmer	TN
Mary A.	19	F		MO
James W.	1	M		MO
Beller, George	15	M		AR
Stembridge, Henry R.	41	M	Farmer	TN
Celina	41	F		TN
William	14	M		AR
Lilly A.	12	F		AR
Mary A.	10	F		AR
John H.	21	M	Farmer	TN
Eliza	20	F		TN
Celina J.	1	F		AR
Bible, John	33	M	Farmer	TN
Minerva	20	F		AR
Susanna	8	F		AR
James A.	1	M		TX
Jackson, Esaw A.	37	M	Farmer	TN
Charlotte	32	F		TN
Milly J.	14	F		AR
James A.	6	M		AR
William R.	4	M		TX
Graham	25	M	Farmer	TN
Speegle, Isreal W.	39	M	Farmer	NC
Susanna	37	F		TN
Philip B.	16	M	Farmer	AL
Adam	14	M		TN
George J.	12	M		TN
Ary A.	9	F		MO
Henry W.	6	M		MO
Levy A.	4	F		MO
Sullivan, William	37	M	Farmer	KY
Letha	36	F		TN
James F.	16	M	Farmer	TN
John F.	14	M		TN
William H.	12	M		MO

(continued)

MILAM COUNTY, TEXAS

Name	Age	Sex	Occupation	Birthplace
Sullivan, George R.	10	M		MO
Polly A.	9	F		MO
Elias S.	7	M		MO
Amanda M.	5	F		MO
Martha	2	F		MO
Beller, Elizabeth	17	F		AR
Rhodes, John	38	M	Farmer	TN
Barbary	37	F		GER
Jones, Lafayette	18	M	Laborer	MO
Niess, Hester	40	F		GER
William	13	M		GER
Edwards, Joseph S.	48	M	Farmer	KY
Susanna	39	F		TN
Andrew J.	19	M	Farmer	AR
Samuel	17	M	Farmer	AR
Mary A.	16	F		AR
Thomas J.	14	M		AR
Susanna	12	F		AR
Margaret J.	10	F		AR
Jasper N.	8	M		AR
Micajah H.	5	M		AR
Virginia	3	F		AR
Smith, John M.	27	M	Guide in Garrison	TN
Childers, Robert	33	M	Hotel Keeper	KY
Adaline	23	F		AL
Thomas P.	3	M		TX
Goldsby	55	M	Farmer	VA
Caroline	21	F		KY
William	14	M		TX
Tyler, Orville T.	40	M	Farmer	MA
Smith, David	50	M	Farmer	TN
Cantrell, Pinkney	25	M	Farmer	TN
Jane	24	F		TN
Genzentist M.	5	M		TN
Mary	3/12	F		TX
Jones, Mary	39	F		TN
Wilson	22	M	Farmer	TN
Nancy	15	F		TN
Louisa	12	F		TN
Thomas	11	M		TN
Martin	9	M		TN
Callis, John	23	M	Farmer	VA
Hart, Josiah	55	M	Farmer	KY
Milly	42	F		KY
Aaron	18	M	Clerk	AR
Moses	16	M	Farmer	AR
Isaac	13	M		AR
Martin	11	M		AR
Joseph	6	M		TX
Meridith	4	M		TX
Burks, Emily T.	14	F		AR
Oliver	11	M		AR
Miller, John	48	M	Farmer	TN
Elliott, Henry B.	37	M	Farmer	TN
Matilda	28	F		MS
Sarah M.	2	F		TX
Mary E.	1	F		TX
Dennis, Neal M.	47	M	Farmer	KY
Charity	46	F		KY
John J.	22	M	Farmer	TN
Andly H.	20	M	Farmer	TN
Joseph	19	M	Farmer	TN
George	17	M	Farmer	TN
Maria	13	F		TN
Mary C.	12	F		TN
Amanda	10	F		TN
Mildred	8	F		AR
Livonia	7	F		AR
Serphronia	7	F		AR
Neal	4	M		AR
Hall, Winny	60	F		KY
Townsend, Joseph	20	M	Grocer	TN
Mary	17	F		AL

Name	Age	Sex	Occupation	Birthplace
Blair, Joel D.	42	M	Farmer	TN
Feriba	26	F		KY
James S.	1	M		TX
Riggs, Marze	15	F		TN
Paine, John	24	M	Merchant	TN
Coleman, John	23	M	Physician	GA
Bryan, William J.	52	M	Lawyer	VA
Glenn, James M.	27	M	Black Smith	TN
Sarah	16	F		TN
Blair, James R.	46	M	Farmer	TN
Elizabeth R.	47	F		VA
Solomon	22	M	Farmer	TN
William	16	M	Farmer	TN
Joel	14	M		AR
John	12	M		AR
Alfred	10	M		AR
Albert	10	M		AR
Martha J.	8	F		AR
George E.	5	M		AR
Zachariah T.	4/12	M		TX
Lawler, Sarah	41	F		TN
Levi T.	24	M	Carpenter	AL
John J.	22	M	Farmer	AL
Newton	16	M	Farmer	AL
Tabitha J.	14	F		AL
Crawford, Thomas G.	25	M	School Teacher	AL
Stewart, Benjamin S.	28	M	Carpenter	TN
Sarah	20	F		IL
James I.	4/12	M		TX
Bowles, John	48	M	Farmer	MS
Milly C.	42	F		TN
Hiram R.	23	M	Farmer	AL
James F.	21	M	Farmer	AL
John B.	18	M	Farmer	AL
Caroline	15	F		MS
William	13	M		AL
Greenville P.	12	M		MS
Emeline	11	F		MS
David C.	10	M		MS
Maria	8	F		MS
Cross, James M.	39	M	Farmer	TN
Lucy	38	F		VA
Riley	21	M	Farmer	TN
William	18	M		TN
Marion	16	M		MS
Saluda	13	F		MO
James	11	M		MO
Vergil A.	9	M		MO
Joshua	7	M		MO
Ewing	4	M		TX
Bailey, William	85	M	Farmer	VA
Casey, Joel	45	M	Farmer	VA
Charlotte	35	F		TN
John H.	15	M		AR
Preston	13	M		AR
William	9	M		TX
Margaret J.	8	F		TX
Elijah	6	M		AR
Flora	5	F		AR
Taylor	3	M		TX
Magness, Thomas H.	51	M	Farmer	TN
Cassander	30	F		IN
Mary	11	F		AR
Catharine	10	F		AR
Thomas T.	6	M		AR
Alvin	5	M		TX
Robert	2	M		TX
Odell, Simeon	26	M	Farmer	MO
Malinda	23	F		TN
Mary E.	1	F		TX
Wheat, Joseph	35	M	Farmer	AL
Malitta	36	F		TN
Drewry N.	13	M		AR
Samuel D.	11	M		AR
William J.	9	M		AR

(continued)

Name	Age/Sex	Occupation	Birthplace
Wheat, Adaline	6 F		AR
Peter	2 M		TX
Isibel C.	5/12 F		TX
Slater, Stephen T.	28 M	Farmer	TN
Mary	21 F		AR
Eugene	4 M		TX
Thomas	3 M		TX
Hantippe	1/12 F		TX
Lavina	64 F		KY
Davis, David G.	25 M	Farmer	TN
Amanda	25 F		TN
Lafayette	4 M		TX
Floyd	1 M		TX
Moss, Matthew	74 M	Farmer	VA
Mary	50 F		TN
Overton	20 M	Farmer	AR
George	18 M	Farmer	AR
Jane	16 F		AR
James	14 M		AR
Thomas	12 M		AR
Lucinda	10 F		AR
Sarah	8 F		AR
Williams, Curtis	39 M	Farmer	TN
Elizabeth	24 F		IN
Nancy	21 F		IL
Aaron	10 M		AR
Mary A.	6 F		AR
Andrew J.	3 M		TX
Spillers, Jeremiah	26 M	Farmer	LA
Tennessee J.	20 F		TN
George F.	1 M		TX
Hamblin, John W.	30 M	Farmer	TN
Sarah	24 F		AL
Claiborne A.	26 M	Farmer	KY
Josephine G.	19 F		TX
Thorp, Joseph L.	48 M	Farmer	VA
David C.	17 M	Farmer	TN
James	14 M		TN
George	10 M		TN
Margaret	8 F		TN
Gideon	6 M		TN
Elizabeth	4 F		TN
Harris, Green B.	32 M	Stone Mason	TN
Arnett, Cullen	36 M	Farmer	TN
Elizabeth	34 F		TN
William T.	13 M		MS
Alonzo M.	11 M		MS
Rebecca E.	8 F		TX
George C.	6 M		TX
David N.	4 M		TX
Mary J.	1 F		TX
Norred, James C.	17 M	Farmer	AL
Patterson, Samuel	57 M	Physician	NC
Cassandra	45 F		TN
James P.	25 M	Carpenter	MS
John	22 M	Farmer	MS
Iredell	16 M		LA
Pliney	14 M		LA
Roberts, Aaron	55 M	Farmer	TN
Sally	44 F		NC
Benjamin	22 M	Farmer	TN
Asa P.	20 M	Farmer	MO
Amanda	18 F		MO
William	14 M		AR
Matilda	12 F		AR
Richard	10 M		AR
Edwin	8 M		TX
Aaron	4 M		TX
Bruton, David E.	36 M	Farmer	TN
Martha	26 F		KY
Arrena	6 F		TX
Levi C.	3 M		TX
Eli J.	1 M		TX

Name	Age/Sex	Occupation	Birthplace
Roberts, Henry J.	32 M	Farmer	TN
Elizabeth	24 F		SC
Rachel P.	8 F		AR
Elizabeth	7 F		AR
Harriet S.	4 F		TX
Nancy J.	2 F		TX
Blevins, John	33 M	Farmer	TN
Nancy	28 F		TN
Luke	11 M		AR
Sarah	9 F		AR
William	7 M		AR
Jacob	4 M		TX
Jane	4 F		TX
Missinine(?)	1 F		TX
Blevins, Luke	37 M	Farmer	NC
Margaret	37 F		TN
Richard	20 M	Farmer	TN
Isham	14 M		AR
Diana	13 F		AR
Hugh L.	10 M		AR
John	20 M	Farmer	AL
Shipman, Jacob	32 M	Farmer	TN
Sarah	25 F		TN
Luke	4 M		AR
Martha J.	3 F		TX
Blevins, Squire	26 M	Farmer	TN
Elizabeth	30 F		TN
Margaret	3 F		TX
George W.	1 M		TX
Richard	2/12 M		TX
Walker, Lewis	45 M	Farmer	AL
Elizabeth	43 F		TN
Samuel H.	23 M	Farmer	LA
Martha A.	20 F		LA
William T.	14 M		TX
Mary J.	7 F		TX
Matilda E.	4 F		TX
Oxsheer, William W.	35 M	Farmer	TN
Martha E.	26 F		TN
Fountain G.	6/12 M		TX
McLanahan, Samuel O.	13 M		TN
Kinke, Ann R.	46 F		NC
William C.	24 M	Farmer	TN
Sylvester	22 M	Farmer	TN
Winship S.	14 M		TN
Gustavus A.	12 M		MS
McKinney, William	36 M	Farmer	TN
Eliza	33 F		TN
Hubby, Caleb M.	33 M	Merchant	NY
Jennet	22 F		NY
Chalmers, Albert	25 M	Clerk	NY
Gregory, William J.	23 M	Laborer	TN
Murrey, Alfred L.	39 M	Farmer	TN
Mary F.	23 F		GA
Ann P.	4 F		TX
Emily C.	1 F		TX
Avard, Augustus	37 M	Carpenter	SWI
Margaret	21 F		TN
Frederick W.	4 M		AR
John	4/12 M		TX
Trotter, Harvey	36 M	Gun Smith	IRE
Amerellus	22 F		TN
Mary A.	12 F		NY
William A.	1 M		TX
Shullburne, William H.	35 M	Hotel Keeper	KY
Eliza	31 F		MS
Mary J. E.	9 F		TX
George	7 M		TX
McCown, Joshua W.	20 M	Clerk	TN
Buckholtz, Charles	25 M	Lawyer	MS
Horton, George M.	35 M	Lawyer	TN
Alexander, Daniel	50 M	Mason	ME

(continued)

Name	Age	Sex	Occupation	Birthplace
Farley, Massillon	36	M	Lawyer	MA
Smith, Pickens D.	28	M	Merchant	NC
McCanless, David P.	26	M	Farmer	TN
Minerva	19	F		IL
Napoleon	8/12	M		TX
Gregory, Hiram C.	31	M	Black Smith	KY
Amoryllis	19	F		TN
William L.	1	M		TX
Riggs, James B.	47	M	Farmer	TN
Harmon, John G.	45	M	Farmer	TN
Harriet H.	35	F		AL
Georgia A.	17	F		TN
Applewite	12	F		MS
Josephine	10	F		AR
John	4	M		AR
William	8/12	M		TX
Meek, John	44	M	Farmer	TN
Jinny	30	F		TN
Harriet M.	15	F		AR
Elizabeth	13	F		AR
Jeremiah	11	M		AR
Thomas J.	9	M		AR
Squire G.	7	M		AR
Mary J.	1	F		TX
Meek, Lewis	32	M	Farmer	TN
Mary	25	F		AR
Moses	9	M		AR
Jeremiah	7	M		AR
Henry J.	5	M		TX
William R.	3	M		TX
Elizabeth	2/12	F		TX
Burney, George E.	35	M	Hotel Keeper	TN
Sarah A.	30	F		TN
John M.	12	M		AR
Martha E.	10	F		AR
Mary L.	9	F		AR
William R.	7	M		AR
Emma J.	4	F		AR
James C.	1	M		TX
Duffon, Francis T.	38	M	County Clerk	NY
Snead, George K.	38	M	Physician	TN
Fleming, Patrick R.	32	M	Physician	SCO
Moore, Lewis	35	M	Merchant	MO
Harris, Francis M.	31	M	Merchant	AL
Hancocke, John A.	24	M	Lawyer	MS
William	20	M	Student	MS
Rice, Benjamin F.	26	M	Lawyer	NY
Givins, Christopher	35	M	Laborer	TN
Moore, Carroll	24	M	Laborer	TN
Kennedy, Prior	37	M	Cabinet Maker	TN
Margaret E.	36	F		TN
Thomas M.	13	M		TN
Van Hook, Benjamin	37	M	Farmer	KY
Mary A.	22	F		TN
John T.	2	M		AR
Green	9/12	M		TX
Stokes, Abner	52	M	Farmer	SC
Elizabeth	53	F		TN
William J.	22	M	Farmer	TN
Umpries, John	14	M		TN
McDonald, Elisha	36	M	Farmer	TN
Rebecca	42	F		TN
William D.	11	M		TX
Elisha M.	8	M		TX
Daniel	5	M		TX
House, John W.	19	M	Farmer	MS
Joseph D.	17	M	Farmer	MS
Sarah A.	11	F		TX
Lewis, William W.	66	M	Farmer	NC
Lewis, Joseph D.	45	M	Farmer	TN
Joel S.	20	M	Farmer	MS
Jackson	14	M		MS

(continued)

Name	Age	Sex	Occupation	Birthplace
Lewis, Nancy	12	F		MS
Mary	10	F		MS
Scott	8	M		MS
Minerva	6	F		MS
Farmer, John	24	M	Farmer	TN
Mary	20	F		NC
Arledge, Moses D.	27	M	Farmer	AL
Elizabeth	17	F		TN
Eliza J.	1	F		TX
McManny, Thomas	17	M	Laborer	VT
Bowen, Gideon B.	59	M	Farmer	TN
Therressee	20	F		TX
Columbus	1	M		TX
Laura	4/12	F		TX
Jennet	68	F		PA
St. Clair, Stephen	14	M		TX
Wilson, Margaret	51	F		NC
Greenberry J.	24	M	Farmer	AL
John	20	M	Farmer	AL
Thomas H. B.	16	M	Farmer	AL
Cross, Richard	72	M	Farmer	SC
McLanahan, Mary	12	F		TN
Sarah A.	10	F		TN
Roberts, William R.	21	M	Black Smith	TN
Phebe E.	18	F		TN
William	3/12	M		TX
Bruce, Willis H.	38	M	Peddler	TN
Elizabeth	40	F		TN
Mary	11	F		TN
William	8	M		AR
Adaline	5	F		AR
John	1	M		TX
Harris, Emily J.	16	F		TN
Isabella	14	F		AR
Bowles, Jesse P.	28	M	Merchant	MO
Ann	20	F		TN
Elizabeth J.	25	F		MO
Hodson, John	36	M	Farmer	TN
Eliza J.	25	F		TN
William	8	M		TX
John	6	M		TX
Thomas	2	M		TX
William	19	M	Farmer	TN
Rodgers, Armstead	33	M	Farmer	TN
Polly	22	F		IL
Caroline	2	F		TX
Beller, Jackson	8	M		TX
Keller, Elijah E.	33	M	Farmer	TN
Rebecca	22	F		GA
William T.	4	M		TX
James F.	1	M		TX
Pewitt, Elizabeth	14	F		GA
White, Joseph	25	M	Farmer	TN
Mary	26	F		LA
Henry	4	M		TX
Albert	2	M		TX
Willis, Manoah	40	M	Farmer	NC
Rebecca	40	F		TN
Jesse B.	18	M	Farmer	TN
America B.	12	F		MS
James D.	9	M		AR
Narcissa L.	6	F		AR
Thomas J.	4	M		AR
Darwin P.	2	M		TX
Ophelia	2/12	F		TX
Brown, Wilson	20	M	Farmer	KY
Rodgers, James B.	43	M	Farmer	TN
Nancy	43	F		TN
Jeremiah J.	22	M	Farmer	TN
William W.	20	M	Farmer	TN
Emily J.	18	F		TN
Elizabeth M.	16	F		AL

(continued)

Name	Age	Sex	Occupation	Birthplace
Rodgers, Joseph D.	14	M		AL
Mary A.	12	F		AL
John P.	10	M		AL
James McF.	8	M		AL
Robert M.	5	M		AL
Jones, Aquilla	42	M	Farmer	TN
Dilley	41	F		AL
Caleb	19	M	Farmer	AL
Martha C.	12	F		AL
Martin H.	10	M		AL
Mary E.	5	F		AL
Ann E.	8/12	F		TX
Standifer, Isaac	48	M	Farmer	TN
Dorcas	40	F		TN
Matilda	14	F		AL
Cynthia	12	F		TX
Delia	9	F		TX
William W.	4	M		TX
Jackson, Peter	42	M	Farmer	TN
Susanna R.	35	F		NC
Gilbert H.	18	M	Farmer	AL
William A.	12	M		AL
Columbus J.	10	M		TX
Hugh C.	8	M		TX
Susanna R.	6	F		TX
Rebecca E.	4	F		TX
Standifer, Isreal B.	30	M	Farmer	TN
Elizabeth M.	27	F		TN
William R.	4	M		AL
Mary J.	2	F		TX
Sarah A.	6/12	F		TX
Lewis, Thomas J.	24	M	Laborer	TN
Bailey, Elijah	34	M	Farmer	AL
Celia	37	F		TN
James C.	12	M		TX
Winfred G.	10	M		TX
George T.	8	M		TX
Susanna	6	F		TX
Thomas E.	4	M		TX
Long, George E.	23	M	Farmer	MD
John T.	21	M	Farmer	MD
Moore, George W.	22	M	Farmer	TN
Abram	20	M	Clerk	TN
Thompson, William D.	43	M	Farmer	GA
Permelia A. R.	38	F		TN
Alexander C.	17	M	Student	TN
Daniel D.	15	M		TN
Louisa R.	12	F		TX
Kemper M.	7	M		TX
Elizabeth P.	4	F		TX
Lucinda L.	3	F		TX
Freemont K.	1	M		TX
Slaughter, William W.	17	M	Student	TN
Colburg, George	28	M	Merchant	FRA
Beckham, Charles L.	26	M	Wheelwright	TN
Pool, John C.	32	M	Farmer	TX
Caroline	31	F		TN
Jonathan	8	M		TX
Nancy	6	F		TX
Thomas	1	M		TX
McKinney, Rolin	44	M	Farmer	TN
Rachel	41	F		NC
John W.	20	M	Farmer	AL
Elizabeth	4	F		TX
Jacqueline	2	F		TX
Neal, John H.	37	M	Farmer	TN
Frances	37	F		NC
William A.	17	M	Farmer	AL
Mary A.	12	F		TX
Martha J.	6	F		TX
McKinney, Uriah	25	M	Farmer	TN
Elizabeth	24	F		IL
Minerva	6	F		TX

(continued)

Name	Age	Sex	Occupation	Birthplace
McKinney, Rebecca	3	F		TX
Amanda H.	1	F		TX
Nickson, Peter	10	M		TX
White, Elijah	27	M	Farmer	TN
Julia E.	26	F		IL
Sarah J.	6	F		TX
Calvin	3	M		TX
Joseph P.	1	M		TX
Meek, Moses	39	M	Farmer	TN
Rhoda	18	F		AR
John W.	16	M	Farmer	AR
Henry	12	M		AR
Sally	10	F		AR
Lewis	7	M		AR
Rachel	5	F		AR
Lydia M.	1	F		AR
Noah	2/12	M		AR
Aarons, John	27	M	Farmer	TN
Dicy	19	F		AL
Thomas	6/12	M		AR
Meek, Squire	23	M	Farmer	TN
Louisa	19	F		MO
Lucinda	1/12	F		TX
Langston, Lydia	50	F		TN
Catharine	13	F		AR
Lydia M.	9	F		AR
William	3	M		AR
Bethell, Payton	35	M	Farmer	NC
Martha	26	F		TN
John	8	M		MS
Martha F.	5	F		AR
Louisa	3	F		AR
Mary	1	F		AR
Bass, Mary	19	F		TN
Standifer, Luke P.	26	M	Farmer	TN
Margaret	25	F		AL
Margaret E.	1	F		TX
Riggs, Lycideous	21	M	Farmer	TN
Standifer. Alfred	45	M	Farmer	TN
William C.	19	M	Farmer	TN
Mordacai H.	14	M		TN
Green, Francis	29	M	Farmer	KY
Moore, Morris	30	M	Farmer	AR
Jacqueline	17	F		TN
Nicholas, William	40	M	Farmer	TN
Delila	37	F		TN
Drusilla	16	F		MS
Jacob	14	M		MS
Mary	12	F		MS
Delila	10	F		LA
William	8	M		LA
Catharine	5	F		LA
Wade	2	M		LA
Karnes, William K.	48	M	Farmer	TN
Rebecca	48	F		TN
Ellen M.	18	F		AR
Narcissa H.	16	F		AR
Penelope	13	F		AR
Annis O.	11	F		AR
William E.	8	M		AR
Alparitta	3	F		AR
Hash, James	30	M	Laborer	IL
Elliott, Robert L.	40	M		TN
Mary E.	32	F		AL
Henry B.	14	M		AL
James C.	12	M		AL
Martha E.	9	F		TN
Thomas W.	7	M		TN
Mary	5	F		TN
William N.	2	M		TN
Sherrod, James	27	M	Farmer	TN
Catharine	23	F		TN
Rebecca J.	4	F		AR

MILAM COUNTY, TEXAS

Name	Age	Sex	Occupation	Birthplace
Karnes, Claudius W.	22	M	Farmer	TN
Jane	19	F		IN
William	1	M		AR
Reid, John C.	36	M	Farmer	TN
Mary	24	F		TN
James C.	9	M		TX
Ann R.	2	F		TX
Louisa F.	1/12	F		TX
Williams, Isaac W.	46	M	Farmer	KY
Mary	41	F		TN
John W.	15	M		AR
William J.	5	M		AR
Shelton, Horatio	37	M	Carpenter	TN
Matilda	36	F		SC
Sophia J.	13	F		AL
Susanna	7	F		IL
Marcus	6	M		IL
James R.	3	M		TX
Reeves, Joshua	30	M	Farmer	TN
Mahala	24	F		TN
James R.	4	M		AR
Tabitha D.	1	F		AR
Grinder, Robert	21	M	Laborer	TN
Ballard, William R.	29	M	Farmer	VA
Jane	29	F		TN
Jacob	8	M		AR
Martha S.	1	F		AR
Elam, Joel	29	M	Farmer	NC
Sarah A.	29	F		VA
John	7	M		TN
Sarah	5	F		TN
Taylor M.	3	M		TN
Tabitha A.	1	F		TX
Callis, David	18	M	Farmer	VA
Ashley, James	35	M	Farmer	KY
Ann S.	28	F		TN
Mary H.	1	F		TX
Yarbrough, Absalom	35	M	Farmer	TN
Eliza J.	11	F		TN
Elizabeth	8	F		AR
John B.	6	M		AR
Nancy C.	3	F		TX
Warren, Galena	12	F		TN
Christina	10	F		TN
Glenn, Alexander	64	M	Black Smith	SC
Rebecca	52	F		NC
Louisa	25	F		TN
Margaret	23	F		TN
Alexander	20	M	Farmer	TN
Jason	18	M	Farmer	TN
Rebecca	14	F		MO
Welch, William	50	M	Farmer	MO
Elizabeth	48	F		TN
Tipton	21	M	Farmer	MO
John	19	M	Farmer	MO
Martha	16	F		MO
Elizabeth	12	F		MO
William	10	M		MO
Daniel	8	M		MO
David	6	M		MO
Overton, James D.	32	M	School Teacher	TN
Ann	22	F		AL
Texanna	1	F		TX
Ellison, Jane	18	F		AL
Bellers, Sarah	10	F		AR
Samuel	8	M		TX
Wiggins, William	25	M	Teacher	TN
Julia	21	F		IL
Webb, Reuben	47	M	Farmer	TN
Nancy	27	F		TN

(continued)

Name	Age	Sex	Occupation	Birthplace
Webb, Reuben	15	M		TN
Gray	13	M		AR
Clarissa	11	F		AR
Davis, Stephen M.	27	M	Black Smith	TN
Mary	21	F		TN
Mary E.	4	F		TN
William H.	1	M		TX

MONTGOMERY COUNTY, TEXAS

Name	Age	Sex	Occupation	Birthplace
Dorris, Anderson	39	M	Mechanic	TN
Elizabeth	38	F		TN
William	18	M	Chair Maker	TN
Hiram	17	M	Chair Maker	TN
John	14	M		TN
Monroe	13	M		TN
Gillian, William L.	34	M	Black Smith	NC
Margaret	26	F		TN
Lennie	29	M	Wagon Maker	NC
Monroe Goodrich	28	M	School Teacher	TN
Robertson, Jesse W.	27	M	Mechanic	TN
Elizabeth	22	F		TN
Lewis Thomas	6	M		TN
A. Burret	4	M		TN
Harriet Alice	2	F		TN
Bosten, H. B.	32	M	County Clerk	TN
Mary C.	17	F		TX
Dorris, Stephen J.	22	M	Farmer	TN
Elizabeth	22	F		TN
Washington E.	2	M		TN
Boyt B.	7/12	M		TX
Charlotte	24	F		TN
Oliver, R. F.	33	M	Saddler	TN
Martha	29	F		AL
Rachel Ann	12	F		AL
Nancy E.	10	F		AL
Martha S.	8	F		TX
Marietta V.	5	F		TX
Olivia C.	3	F		TX
Infant	3/12	F		TX
Elkins, Miles	31	M	Farmer	TN
Garelda J.	28	F		AL
Bill	4	M		TX
Roxanna	2	F		TX
Jim	1	M		TX
Williams, Hesekiah G.	9	M		TX
William E.	11	M		TX
James, George W.	38	M	Farmer	TN
Julia F.	36	F		NC
Elizabeth F.	7	F		TX
Whitten, A.	52	M	Farmer	SC
Nancy Ann	30	F		TN
Sarah Elen	15	F		TN
John D. G.	14	M		TN
James F.	12	M		TN
Marthan	10	F		TN
Harriet L.	8	F		TN
Alice A.	5	F		TN
Helen Josephine	3	F		TN
Clepper, Lem G.	37	M	Dentist	TN
Mary Ann	21	F		ENG
James	1	M		TX
Joseph	18	M	Farmer	TN
Francis Fortner	17	F		ENG
Albert	15	M		ENG
Davlin, Thomas	26	M	Farmer	TN
Margaret Ann	23	F		IL
Mary James	6	F		TX
Margarett Ann	4	F		TX
Collier, E. G.	48	M	Hotel Keeper	VA
Senai	45	F		TN
A. B.	24	M	Farmer	AL

(continued)

MONTGOMERY COUNTY, TEXAS

Name	Age	Sex	Occupation	Birthplace
Collier, Emily H.	18	F		AL
Arthur H.	16	M		AL
Amanda E.	13	F		AL
Elia Celess	10	F		AL
Medora	7	F		AL
Baby	3	F		TX
Bradley, Ralph	31	M	None	AL
Johnson, H. G.	53	M	Farmer	SC
Elizabeth F.	51	F		TN
William	26	M	Farmer	TN
James	21	M	Farmer	AL
Narcissa	23	F		AL
Maldanetta(?)	15	F		AL
John	17	M	Farmer	AL
Alabama	13	F		TX
Nancy	11	F		TX
Ulysis	6	M		TX
McCabee, Jesse	23	M	Farmer	TN
Darcus	20	F		AL
Alfred Jackson	1	M		TX
Zill	4/12	M		TX
McCleb, George	25	M	Farmer	TN
Mary	18	F		AL
Zill T.	1	M		TX
McCaleb, Zill	51	M	Farmer	NC
Mary	44	F		TN
Pauline Jane	20	F		TN
Sophia	18	F		TN
Frances	14	F		TN
James	17	M		TN
Eliza	10	F		TX
Luisa	6	F		TX
Thomason, Jabez S.	23	M	Farmer	AL
Matilda	40	F		TN
James	18	M	Farmer	AL
Harriet	14	F		AL
Amanda C.	12	F		AL
Georgiana	10	F		AL
Francis M.	6	M		TX
Martha	4	F		TX
Burks, John	50	M		TN
Park, John W.	25	M	Farmer	IL
Eliza M.	19	F		AL
George M.	3/12	M		TX
Ephraim	15	M		TN
Houston, Hugh	24	M	Farmer	TN
Phebe	65	F		NC
Frederick C.	30	M	Farmer	NC
Narcissa	23	F		MS
Frederick S.	1	M		TX
Callard, T. L.	43	M	Farmer	KY
Nancy Ann	28	F		TN
Felix	7	M		TX
Martha Caroline	5	F		TX
James	3	M		TX
Elizabeth Talbert	18	F		MO
Helen Besser	18	F		MO
Chambers, Thomas	38	M	Farmer	TN
William H.	18	M	Farmer	TN
Pleasant A.	16	M	Farmer	TN
Nancy Ann	15	F		TX
Sythia S.	13	F		TX
John H.	12	M		TX
James J.	11	M		TX
Daniel L.	9	M		TX
Thomas	8	M		TX
Frederick H.	6	M		TX
Oliver P.	6	M		TX
Reding, Iredel	59	M	Farmer	NC
Nancy	60	F		VA
Elizabeth C.	18	F		TN
John B.	32	M	Farmer	TN

Name	Age	Sex	Occupation	Birthplace
Eding, Elizabeth L.	29	F		TN
Jubloren(?)	9	M		TN
Elizabeth C.	7	F		TN
Brooks, J. C.	25	M	Farmer	TN
Emily Y.	20	F		TN
Sarah E.	3/12	F		TX
Reding L.	18	M	Farmer	TN
William H.	16	M	Farmer	TN
Montgomery L.	14	M		TN
Reding, George W.	26	M	Farmer	TN
Bety Ann	23	F		IL
Hulda Jane	4	F		TX
William Henry	1	M		TX
Passmore, G. L.	26	M	Carpenter	KY
Strother, James H.	25	M	Farmer	TN
W. G.	30	M	Farmer	TN
Graham, Moss	23	M	Farmer	IL
Conn, Hulda	62	F		NC
Redding, James A.	25	M	Farmer	TN
Martha Ann	18	F		AL
Conn, John S.	34	M	Farmer	KY
Nancy	32	F		TN
Malone, Thomas Monroe	15	M	Farmer	TN
Saddler, John	40	M	Farmer	TN
Basheby	39	F		IL
James	17	M	Farmer	TX
Sarah	15	F		TX
Sam	11	M		TX
Elizabeth	8	F		TX
Henry	7	M		TX
Mary	5	F		TX
Robert	2	M		TX
Baby	1/12	M		TX
Cumming	30	M	Farmer	LA
Parker, Francis	57	M	Farmer	NC
Priscilla	57	F		NC
James	21	M	Farmer	TN
David	17	M	Farmer	IL
Matilda	15	M		IL
Franklin	10	M		IL
Viser, William W.	21	M	Merchant	TN
Cumming, James F.	27	M	Mechanic	LA
Hoover, Dan C.	28	M	Carpenter	OH
Pusly, G. B.	23	M	Black Smith	IL
Mary	21	F		TN
Lydia	4	F		IL
Samuel	2	M		TX
Davis, M. H.	27	M	Saddler	TN
Grigsby, A. J.	28	M	Physician	VA
McGilberry, J. M.	38	M	Farmer	NC
Elenor	35	F		NC
William S.	11	M		TN
Mary K.	10	F		TN
Elizabeth A.	8	F		TN
Alexander M.	6	M		TN
John C.	3	M		TX
Agus T.	1	M		TX
Daughter	1/12	F		TX
Boyd, Antinette	32	F	Instructor	AL
Edwards, Charles O.	40	M	Farmer	GA
Lyllia E.	30	F		TN
Mary E.	11	F		TX
James A.	9	M		TX
Susan J.	7	F		TX
John D.	6	M		TX
Henry	4	M		TX
Charles O.	1	M		TX
Adams, Bellentine T.	12	M		TX
Coode, Alfred J.	10	M		TX
Richard D.	8	M		TX
Willis F.	6	M		TX
Timothy	4	M		TX
Tobias	25	M		TX

MONTGOMERY COUNTY, TEXAS

Name	Age	Sex	Occupation	Birthplace
Wright, J. B.	29	M	Physician	AL
Elizabeth Ann	23	F		MS
Augustus P.	2	M		TX
Elizabeth	6/12	F		TX
Wright, W. T.	29	M	Physician	AL
Mary C.	26	F		TN
Alston, Henry	37	M	Farmer	TN
Elizabeth	20	F		TN
Sophronia	1	F		TX
Coode, Timothy	46	M	Farmer	TN
Serena	36	F		GA
William J.	14	M		TX
James H.	12	M		TX
Lucy	9	F		TX
Timothy	7	M		TX
George T.	5	M		TX
John W.	3	M		TX
Minerva C.	1	F		TX
Hyett, Francis M.	12	M		TX
Ridgeway, Johnathan H.	42	M	Farmer	TN
Elizabeth	78	F		KY
Shayman, James	38	M		IRE
Elkins, William	57	M	Farmer	VA
Sarah	46	F		TN
William H.	12	M		TN
Drucilla	10	F		TN
Smith, Henry	30	M		TN
Susan	20	F		TN
Orr, John	70	M	Farmer	NY
Elizabeth	70	F		NC
Rebecca	26	F		TN
Susan	24	F		TN
Blankenship, Clarrisa	22	F		TN
Josephine	4	F		TX
Springer, A. M.	39	M	Farmer	GA
Elizabeth	49	F		TN
Job	11	M		TX
Emmet	8	M		TX
Leeberry	6	M		TX
Rabia, James	28	M	Farmer	AL
Martha J.	22	F		TN
Elizabeth A.	4	F		AL
Samuel	2	M		TX
Mellise O.	6/12	F		TX
Cooksey, Enoch	37	M	Farmer	TN
Mary	35	F		KY
Andrew J.	17	M	Farmer	AL
Clarrisa H.	13	F		AL
Emma E.	4	F		TX
Sarah Jane	9/12	F		TX
Greer, Aquilla	34	M	Farmer	VA
Martha	26	F		TN
Rosanna	3	F		TN
Sarah L.	1	F		TN
Thomas, John	67	M	Farmer	GA
Samuel	25	F	Farmer	GA
Simeon	21	M	Farmer	GA
Lang, D. P.	28	M	Black Smith	TN
Sylvana	30	F		GA
Simeon	3/12	M		TX
Lemaster, Robert	34	M	Farmer	TN
Susanna	30	F		GA
Mary	6	F		TX
William	4	M		TX
Nancy	1	F		TX
McCown, Alexander	45	M	Trader	TN
Nancy	32	F		TN
Stewart, Lucia	6	F		TX
Beard, Samuel M.	32	M	Farmer	TN
Rebecca J.	23	F		SC

(continued)

Name	Age	Sex	Occupation	Birthplace
Beard, Albert	11	M		TX
Athelia Anna	7/12	F		TX
Slaughter, Mary E.	24	F		TN
Henry Travis	6	M		TX
Pearce, Lewis	45	M	Farmer	TN
Alsey	35	F		MO
Lewis	18	M	Farmer	AR
Robert	14	M		AR
Mary	10	F		AR
Hugh	8	M		TX
David	7	M		TX
Matilda	6	F		TX
Thursa Ann	2	F		TX
Baker, Basie	46	M	Farmer	VA
Mary	36	F		TN
Katherine	16	F		TN
James T.	12	M		TX
William H.	9	M		TX
Franklin	4	M		TX
Newton	1	M		TX
John W.	5	M		TX
Luna, James	21	M	Farmer	TN
Cox, S. H.	45	M	Farmer	TN
Roseann	34	F		OH
William A.	17	M	Farmer	IN
Emily J.	13	F		IL
Rebecca S.	10	F		IN
Minerva R.	4	F		TX
Maria L.	2	F		TX
Elizabeth M.	4/12	F		TX
Elkins, James, Jr.	28	M	Farmer	TN
Lucy	17	F		AL
Chessure, J. B.	60	M	Farmer	VA
Louisa A.	49	F		TN
Benson B.	16	M	Farmer	TN
D. Simpson	14	M		TN
Sarah Gales	11	F		TX
James Fletcher	7	M		TX
John	25	M		TN
Sanders, R. M.	33	M	Farmer	TN
Mary M.	25	F		AL
Elizabeth M.	8	F		AL
George B.	6	M		AL
Paulina Jane	4	F		AL
Medra Ann	3	F		AL
Len	1/12	M		TX
Rogers, Raleigh	58	M	Farmer	TN
Mary Ann	46	F		TN
Mary D.	24	F		LA
Iasiah	22	M	Farmer	LA
George	18	M	Farmer	TX
Lafayette	16	M	Farmer	TX
James	14	M	Farmer	TX
Lewis	12	M		TX
Angelina	10	F		TX
William	4	M		TX
Burlesson, John	33	M	Farmer	TN
Mary	25	F		LA
Amanda	7	F		TX
Mary	2	F		TX

NACOGDOCHES COUNTY, TEXAS

Name	Age	Sex	Occupation	Birthplace
Boyakin, O. H.	49	M	Physician	TN
Eliza	44	F		TN
Franklin	1	M		TN
John	16	M	Student	TN
Orsborn	14	M		TN
Thomas	12	M		TN
Henry	10	M		TN
Sarah	8	F		TN
Emaline	6	F		MS
Orton, S. M.	41	M	Black Smith	TN
Louisa	29	F		NC
Mary	11	F		TN

(continued)

NACOGDOCHES COUNTY, TEXAS

Orton, Richard	9	M		TX
Winfrey	7	F		TX
John	3	M		TX
Simpson, J. J.	52	M	Tavern Keeper	SC
Jane	50	F		NC
John	22	M	None	LA
Frances	17	F		TX
Sarah	15	F		TX
Franance	13	F		TX
Augustus	11	M		TX
Isaac	9	M		TX
Thompkins, Walter	25	M	Teacher	NY
Mary	19	F		NY
Sharlot	21	M		NY
Shanks, John	20	M	Clerk	TN
Morrison, John C.	49	M	Carpenter	NC
White, Mariah	22	F		IRE
Josephine	2	F		TX
Marshal, Francis	21	M	Carpenter	TN
Nelson, Horatio	30	M	Lawyer	ME
Nickesson, Thomas D.	34	M	Teacher	ME
Johnson, H. A.	34	M	Carpenter	KY
Jane	24	F		TN
Samuel	5	M		TX
Henrietta	7	F		TX
Eugenia	3	F		TX
Ophelia	1	F		TX
Fry, B. F.	37	M	Cabinet Maker	NC
Lyons, L. P.	30	M	Black Smith	NY
Akins, J. M.	53	M	Black Smith	SC
Elizabeth	20	F		TN
James	16	M	None	TN
McElroy, J. H.	22	M	Merchant	TN
Amanda	18	F		TN
Clayton, J. G. W.	54	M	Shoe Maker	SC
Elizabeth	35	F		TN
Mary	14	F		TX
William	11	M		TX
Joseph	10	M		TX
Moore, William M.	36	M	Carpenter	TN
Sary Ann	32	F		MO
Elizabeth	10	F		TX
Artimecin	8	F		TX
Mary	6	F		TX
William	4	M		TX
Lavina	2	F		TX
Alonso	1	M		TX
Moore, N. J.	34	M	None	GA
Eliza	25	F		TN
Mary	6	F		TX
Sarah	4	F		TX
Bondis, George	36	M	Merchant	DEN
Catharine	20	F		TN
George	1	M		TX
Garrison, F.	4	M		DEN
Rohte, T.	2	M		GER
Federson, J.	32	M	Clerk	DEN
Grayyard, Christopher	--	M	Clerk	NOR
Jennings, T. J.	43	M	Lawyer	VA
Sarah	32	F		TN
Thomas	4	M		TX
Monroe	2	M		TX
Lawrence	1	M		TX
Hyde, William	25	M	Student	TN
Gray, Sarah	50	F		KY
Clark, Amos	54	M	Lawyer	MA
Asenath	53	F		NY
Walker, R. S.	25	M	Lawyer	KY
Eliza	22	F		IN
John	1	M		TX
John	21	M	Student	TN
Scott, Martha	22	F		VA
Chevaillin, Charles	37	M	Merchant	FRA
Sarah	19	F		MA
Gregory, Mariah	25	F		NOR
Thomas	14	M		NOR
Barrett, W. W.	21	M	Store Clerk	VA
Kees, Howard	19	M	Store Clerk	TN
Roundes, Rapale	50	M	Laborer	MEX
Hyde, J. H.	74	M	None	VA
William F.	24	M	Farmer	TN
Housson R.	21	M	Farmer	TN
Hoge, R. K.	29	M	Lawyer	TN
Mary E.	27	F		TN
Fany M.	2	F		TX
Mariah B.	6	F		TN
Irion, R. A.	45	M	Physician	TN
Anna	32	F		PA
Sam S.	8	M		TX
Harriet D.	6	F		TX
Julia H.	4	F		TX
Robert H.	1	M		TX
Redin, Nancy	37	F		GA
Garr, Malinda	18	F		TN
Sarah	3	F		TX
Nancy	1	F		TX
Arnold, George	16	M	None	AL
Briley, Shaderick	62	M	Farmer	NC
Cina	44	F		KY
Lucenia	7	F		TX
Goblin, Emaline	15	F		TN
James	12	M		TN
Clementine	10	F		TX
Anderson, Howard	27	M	Farmer	AL
Jackson	23	M	Farmer	AL
Benjamin	3	M		TX
Gamblin, John	18	M	Laborer	TN
Butt, W. L.	24	M	Farmer	TN
Louisa	18	F		TN
Campbell, A. G.	45	M	Farmer	SC
Sarah	32	F		VA
John	15	M	Farmer	TN
Elizabeth	14	F		TN
Margaret	11	F		TX
Sarah	9	F		TX
James	7	M		TX
William	5	M		TX
Cyntha	3	F		TX
Washington	1	M		TX
Horn, W. B.	27	M	Farmer	NC
Rebecca	25	F		TN
James	4	M		TX
Andrew	2	M		TX
William	1	M		TX
Rugle, Solomon	35	M	Farmer	TN
Jane	32	F		GA
William	6	M		TX
Stephen	1	M		TX
John	17	M	Student in School	AR
Wilson, William J.	42	M	Clergyman	GA
Caroline E.	25	F		FL
Harriet	1	F		TX
John	1/12	M		TX
Wilson, John H.	26	M	Farmer	TN
McMean, Eleazor	44	M	Farmer	SC
Catharine	42	F		TN
Martha	19	F		TN
John	14	M		TN
Emaline	12	F		TX
Viola	9	F		TX
Gustavus	8	M		TX
Emarietta	4	F		TX
Gode, Orsborn	39	M	Farmer	TN
Judith	36	F		TN
John	16	M	Farmer	TN

(continued)

NACOGDOCHES COUNTY, TEXAS

Name	Age	Sex	Occupation	Birthplace
Gode, Emily	14	F		TN
James	12	M		TN
George	9	M		TN
Robert	8	M		TN
Catharine	4	F		TN
McAnalty, John E.	39	M	Gun Smith	VA
Elizabeth	39	F		VA
Henry	15	M	Farmer	TN
Willia	13	M		TN
Ivins	12	M		TN
Mary	7	F		TX
Pryor	6	M		TX
John	5	M		TX
Henderson	2	M		TX
William	1	M		TX
Barnett, J. P.	19	M	Farmer	AL
Martha	17	F		TN
Beaman, Miles	49	M	Farmer	NC
Sarah	49	F		TN
Josiah	20	M	Farmer	AL
Louisa	13	F		AR
Hellen	9	F		AR
Sarah	7	F		TX
Elizabeth	5	F		TX
Thomas	3	M		TX
Lorane	2	F		TX
Davis, Roda	29	F		NC
Oliver	10	M		AR
James	7	M		AR
Freeman	3	M		AR
Daniels, William	51	M	Farmer	TN
Martha	40	F		TN
William	20	M	Farmer	TN
Randolph	17	F	Farmer	AL
Martha	11	F		TX
John	4	M		TX
Larabee, James V.	39	M	Farmer	VT
Martha	27	F		VA
Charles	8	M		AR
Mary	5	F		AR
George	1	M		TX
Mathews, Sarah	55	F		SC
Moon, William M.	22	M	Teacher	TN
Wilson, A. T.	27	M	Farmer	TN
Sarah	24	F		AL
William	7	M		TX
Jane	5	F		TX
Casbey	2	M		TX
James	6/12	M		TX
Rutherford, William	21	M	Laborer	AL
Shannon, A. F.	26	M	Farmer	TN
Frances	19	F		TX
Thomas	2	M		TX
Hamby, T. G.	34	M	Black Smith	TN
Rose Ann	30	F		MS
Isaac	14	M		LA
Sarah	13	F		TX
John	12	M		TX
Fanny	7	F		TX
Thomas	5	M		TX
Louisa	3	F		TX
Martha	3/12	F		TX
Hamby, John	74	M	Farmer	SC
Roda	61	F		SC
Isaac	32	M	Farmer	AL
Samuel	28	M	Farmer	AL
Enos	23	M	Farmer	LA
Marshall	19	M		LA
Hamby, Harvey J.	38	M	Carpenter	TN
Elizabeth	31	F		LA
Martha	12	F		TX
Roda	10	F		TX
Samuel	5	M		TX

(continued)

Name	Age	Sex	Occupation	Birthplace
Hamby, Mary	2	F		TX
Isaac	2/12	M		TX
Windham, J. D.	34	M	Physician	AL
Frances	34	F		TN
Samuel	8	M		TX
Jesse	4	M		TX
Mary	3	F		TX
Calvin	1	M		TX
Granad, William	22	M	Farmer	GA
Mantieth, Mary	60	F		NC
Jesse	37	M	Farmer	TN
John	28	M	Farmer	TN
Elizabeth	22	F		TN
Jane	20	F		TN
Malissa	18	F		TN
Kerkingdol, James	31	M	Farmer	TN
Martha	28	M		TN
Abraham	5	M		TX
Sarah	3	F		TX
Joshua	8/12	M		TX
William L.	33	M	Farmer	TN
Palmer, H. D.	38	M	Clergyman	TN
Jane R.	31	F		TN
William	5	M		TX
Littleton	3	M		TX
James	4/12	M		TX
Renfro, Isaac P.	21	M	Student	MO
Wilson, H. P.	14	M		TN
Mathews, Martin	27	M	Farmer	AL
Barnet, John C.	37	M	Clergyman	TN
Mary E.	38	F		KY
William	17	M	Farmer	TN
Samuel	15	M	Farmer	TN
James	13	M		TN
John	11	M		MS
Robert	9	M		MS
Martha	8	F		TX
Phineas	6	M		TX
Robinson, J. S.	34	M	Farmer	TN
Nancy	21	F		SC
Sarah	6/12	F		TX
Gowen, Benajor	21	M	Farmer	TN
Mary	20	F		TN
James	1	M		TX
Odle, Abraham	45	M	Farmer	TN
Jane	45	F		TN
Matilda	22	F		TN
John	12	M		TN
Phillip	7	M		TX
Matice, William	30	M	Farmer	GA
Harriet	18	F		TN
Hamil, William H.	38	M	Black Smith	TN
Mary	31	F		VA
William	4	M		TN
Jones, Jane	16	F		TN
Susan	15	F		TN
Richann	13	F		TN
Fall, John N.	38	M	Merchant	GA
Susan	35	F		GA
Eliza	17	F		GA
Lavona	14	F		GA
Mary	12	F		GA
Calvin	9	M		TX
Vale	6	M		TX
Zach	3	M		TX
William	1	M		TX
Fall, A. B.	36	M	School Teacher	GA
Permelia	24	F		SC
John	4	M		AL
Cooper, James	21	M	Clerk in Store	GA
Moore, W. B.	27	M	Black Smith	GA
Sharp, J. H.	33	M	Physician	TN
Swift, Willis	31	M	Farmer	SC
Mary	30	F		TN

(continued)

Name	Age	Sex	Occupation	Born
Swift, William	7	M		TX
Polly	4	F		TX
Sarah	2	F		TX
Martha	1	F		TX
Newsom, N. L.	23	M	Farmer	AL
Hubbard, Silas P.	20	M	Farmer	NH
Hardeman, Constantine	26	M	Farmer	TN
Elizabeth	28	F		TN
William	1	M		TX
Goen, Jackson	23	M	Carpenter	SC
Duffield, W. C.	36	M	Lawyer	VA
Prucilla	28	F		TN
Rose P.	3	F		TX
Flournoy, Samuel M.	51	M	Farmer	KY
Minerva A.	40	F		KY
Warren	18	M	Farmer	MS
Mercer	16	M	Student	MS
Nancy	14	F		MS
Mary	13	F		MS
Narcissa	11	F		MS
Robert	9	M		TX
Samuel	8	M		TX
Thomas	6	M		TX
Dee	4	M		TX
Isabella	3	F		TX
William	3/12	M		TX
Thompson, Bartlet T.	37	M	Stock Keeper	VA
Fallis, Samuel	22	M	Stone Mason	KY
Floyd, Elijah	27	M	Farmer	TN
Montgomery, Farris	54	M	Farmer	SC
John	18	M	Student	TN
Lucinda	16	F		TN
Harriet	15	F		TN
Sarah	14	F		TN
Angeline	9	F		TX
Hamilton	10	M		TX
Alexander	8	M		TX
Robert	6	M		TX
Sophia	1	F		TX
Wood, Sophia E.	23	F		AL
Susan	20	F		AL
Skillian, J. C.	44	M	Black Smith	KY
Lucy	36	F		TN
Sabrina	18	F		TN
William	16	M	Farmer	TN
Charles	15	M	None	TX
Elizabeth	12	F		TX
James	8	M		TX
Radford	6	M		TX
Hardy	5	M		TX
Isaac	4	M		TX
Sarah	2	F		TX
Gains, Edmond	39	M	Mill Draper	VA
Jane	25	F		TN
Raleigh	1	M		TX
Walling, A. G.	32	M	Farmer	TN
Rebecca	29	F		IL
William	10	M		TX
Amelia	8	F		TX
John	7	M		TX
Alford	5	M		TX
Elizabeth	3	F		TX
Eliza	1	F		TX
Simpson, Martha	15	F		TX
Easley, Benjamin	32	M	Farmer	TN
Nancy	23	F		AL
James	3	M		TX
John	9/12	M		TX
Killian, William	40	M	Farmer	TN
Delila	39	F		SC
Lucinda	19	F		AL
Mary	17	F		AL
Levi	7	M		TX
Elizabeth	5	F		TX

(continued)

Name	Age	Sex	Occupation	Born
Killian, Nancy	2	F		TX
Temperance	3/12	F		TX
Wood, William	42	M	Farmer	TN
Nancy	34	F		GA
Reaves, Frances	18	F		AL
Shederick	18	M	Farmer	AL
Elizabeth	10	F		AL
Malichiah	6	M		AL
Wood, Elbert	16	M	Farmer	MS
Joseph	13	M		MS
Jane	12	F		MS
Alphanso	8	M		MS
Susan	3	F		AL
Terrice	1	F		AL
Curl, Thomas J.	42	M	Farmer	TN
Laurena	42	F		TN
Julet	15	F		AR
Mary	13	F		AR
Henry	11	M		AR
James	6	M		TX
Cronch, William	24	M	Carpenter	AR
Claborne	22	M	Farmer	AR
Matilda	20	F		AR
Albert	18	M	Student	AR
Anderson, R. G.	39	M	Farmer	TN
Ann	35	F		TN
William	16	M	Student	MS
Emily	14	F		MS
Maranda	11	F		MS
Pate, William F.	22	M	Farmer	GA
Moore, William J.	29	M	Farmer	TN
Mariah	27	F		AL
James	16	M	Farmer	TN
Henry	12	M		TN
Milton	6	M		TX
Judd, Hamilton B.	31	M	Farmer	NC
Nancy	20	F		TN
Zachariah	2	M		TX
Lewis	7/12	M		TX
Nathaniel	35	M	Clerk	NC
Koonce, J. C.	35	M	Farmer	TN
Susanna	35	F		LA
Christopher	16	M	Farmer	LA
John	14	M		LA
Thomas	13	M		LA
Daniel	11	M		LA
Sarah	8	F		LA
William	7	M		LA
Phillip	3	M		LA
Amanda	3/12	F		TX
Wilson, R. P.	42	M	Farmer	GA
Mary	40	F		TN
Randle	3	M		TX
James	2/12	M		TX
Hightower, Carrol	21	M	Farmer	TN
McGowan, Joseph	28	M	Farmer	TN
Milla	23	F		TN
Louisa	4	F		TX
Holderman, William	24	M	Farmer	TN
Henry	18	M	Farmer	TN
Elizabeth	17	F		TN
John	11	M		TN
Erasmus	10	M		TX
Constantine, Richard L.	55	M	Farmer	ENG
Levina	22	F		TN
Dryer, G. J.	33	M	Farmer	TN
Eliza	36	F		SC
John	6	M		TX
William	4	M		TX
Elliot, John	30	M	Carpenter	AL
Elizabeth	27	F		TN
William	8	M		AL
Amos	7	M		AL

(continued)

Name	Age	Sex	Occupation	Birthplace
Elliot, Charles	5	M		AR
James	2	M		TX
Lucintha	4/12	F		TX
Rector, John	60	M	Farmer	NC
Martha	45	F		NC
Franklin	20	M	Farmer	NC
Joseph	15	M	Farmer	GA
Nancy	16	F		TN
Elizabeth	12	F		TX
Alexander	9	M		TX
Martha	6	F		TX
Samuel	5	M		TX
Thomas	4	M		TX
Mathews, William	31	M	Farmer	AL
Catharine	20	F		TN
James	3	M		TX
Elias	1	M		TX
Stivers, William B.	28	M	Miller	TN
Emily	23	F		VA
Stivers, Samuel	50	M	Physician	NJ
Sarah	45	F		TN
Samuel	18	M	Student	AR
Stivers, Samuel	12	M		TN
Chisum, Elijah	79	M	Farmer	VA
Salina	45	F		TN
Thomason	14	M		TN
Rebecca	12	F		TX
Andrew	5	M		TX
Jacobs, James	44	M	Farmer	VA
Mary	42	F		TN
Elijah	21	M	Farmer	TN
William	19	M	Farmer	TN
John	17	M	Farmer	TN
Madison	15	M	Farmer	TN
Claborn	13	M		TN
Russel	11	M		TX
Martha	9	F		TX
Johnson	6	M		TX
Summaranies(?)	4	F		TX
Mary	2	F		TX
James	2/12	M		TX
Chisum, Claborn	31	M	Farmer	MS
Hobbs, E. W.	37	M	Farmer	GA
Caroline	28	F		TN
Susan	18	F		AL
Eli	9	M		AL
John	7	M		AL
James	2	M		TX
Alders, Thomas	50	M	Farmer	VA
Lucy	46	F		VA
Elizabeth	20	F		TN
Nancy	17	F		TN
William	17	M		TN
Mary	16	F		TN
James	16	M		TN
Catharine	15	F		TN
Henry	13	M		TN
Pranecy(?)	8	F		TX
McDaniel, J. T.	30	M		AL
Evalina	26	F		TN
Sarah	8	F		TX
William	6	M		TX
Marion	3	M		TX
Jackson	3	M		TX
Mary	4	F		TX
Hall, Simpson	26	M	None	TN
Jackson	24	M	Farmer	TN
Jabes	17	M	Farmer	TN
Mathews, Mary A.	59	M		SC
Mary	20	F		TN
Harlan	17	M	Laborer	TN
Haynes, Elenor	52	F		TN
Mary	22	F		TN
William	16	M	Farmer	TN

Name	Age	Sex	Occupation	Birthplace
Wilson, Morgan	36	M	Tailor	VA
Sarah	24	F		TN
Joseph	6	M		TX
Francis	3	M		TX
Edward	4/12	M		TX
Pike, M. D.	30	M	Farmer	TN
Mary	32	F		TN
Isaac	5	M		TN
Patrick	3	M		TN
James	11/12	M		TN
Pike, Samuel	26	M	Farmer	TN
James	2	M		TN
Hardeman, Blackston	28	M	Merchant	TN
Rebecca	25	F		NC
Bunch	5	M		TX
Emma	4	F		TX
Angelina	3	F		TX
Samuel	10/12	M		TX
Hardeman, William N.	32	M		TN
Balch, John	37	M	Black Smith	TN
Elizabeth	23	F		AL
Joseph	7	M		TX
Hannah	4	F		TX
Hezekiah	2	M		TX
Shoftner, Acton	33	M	Farmer	TN
Sarah	26	F		AL
George	2	M		TX
Mary	1	F		TX
Shoftner, Elvira	50	F		TN
Shoftner, J. N.	30	M	Farmer	TN
Ann	21	F		AL
William	1	M		TX
Long, John	60	M	Farmer	SC
Nancy	60	F		VA
Mary Ann	18	F		TN
John	17	M	Farmer	TN
Nancy	15	F		TN
McClure, Ama	66	F		TN
Alexander	13	M		TN
Minchen, Lorenzo D.	24	M	Farmer	AL
Hannah	25	F		TN
Stephens, Augustis	39	M	Merchant	NY
Elizabeth	26	F		TN
Augustis	9	M		TX
James	7	M		TX
Mary	3	F		TX
Par, Jeremiah	32	M	Farmer	TN
Eliza	31	F		TN
Martha	7	F		TX
Mary	5	F		TX
Elizabeth	3	F		TX
Thomas	8/12	M		TX
Walker, William	43	M	Farmer	TN
Charles	20	M	Farmer	TN
Martha	17	F		TN
Sarah	13	F		TN
Joseph	12	M		TX
William	9	M		TX
James	7	M		TX
Ezekiel	3	M		MO
Fuel(?), P. B.	32	M	Farmer	NC
Eliza	31	F		TN
Sarah	12	F		TN
James	8	M		TX
Martha	6	F		TX
Mary	4	F		TX
John	2	M		TX
Thomason, David	51	M	Farmer	VA
Jane	41	F		TN
William	22	M	Farmer	TN
Martha	20	F		TN
Robert	18	M	Farmer	TN
Harriet	14	F		TN

(continued)

Name	Age	Sex	Occupation	Birthplace
Thomason, James	12	M		LA
Samelia	6	F		TX
Caladonia	2	F		TX
Bently, Whitmal	40	M	Farmer	NC
Margaret	39	F		TN
John	11	M		TX
Jane	5	F		TX
Roena	3	F		TX
Mary	2	F		TX
Robert	1	M		TX
Thomason, Jacob	24	M	Farmer	TN
Pleasants, Benjamin	53	M	Farmer	NC
Mary	50	F		NC
Thomas	22	M	Farmer	TN
Benford	20	M	Farmer	TN
John	16	M	Farmer	TN
Monroe	14	M		TN
Elizabeth	9	F		TN
Haynes, M. H.	28	M	Farmer	TN
Mary	17	F		TN
James	8/12	M		TX
Pate, John	54	M	Stone Mason	VA
Frances	54	F		VA
Mary	18	F		TN
Bonapart	16	M	Farmer	TN
Cook, William	35	M	Farmer	SC
Minerva	24	F		TN
John	7	M		TX
Mary	2	F		TX
Travis	2/12	M		TX
McKnight, James	36	M	Farmer	TN
Louisa	29	F		TN
Mary	15	F		TN
Jane	13	F		TN
Frances	8	F		TX
Jacob	6	M		TX
Daniel	5	M		TX
Lucinda	4	F		TX
Elizabeth	1	F		TX
Bates, Daniel	39	M	Farmer	IL
Sally	35	F		TN
Levi	15	M		AL
Atametia	13	F		AL
William	11	M		MS
Daniel	8	M		MS
James	4	M		MS
Mary	11/12	F		MS
Simpson, Bartlett	55	M	Farmer	VA
Nancy	41	F		TN
Mahilda	21	F		TN
John	16	M	Farmer	TX
Haufman	11	M		TX
Thomas	7	M		TX
Frances	5	F		TX
Josephine	2	F		TX
Price, Thomas W.	25	M	Farmer	TN
Juliann	18	F		TN
Yarborough, Asa	42	M	Farmer	TN
Sarah	36	F		NC
Tennessee	15	F		TN
William	13	M		MS
Elizabeth	12	F		TX
Georgia	9	F		TX
Amanda	4	F		TX
Arnold, William	24	M	Farmer	TN
Martha	25	F		AR
Susann	6	F		TX
Ama	4	F		TX
John	2	M		TX
Sarah	1	F		TX
Terry, James C.	21	M	Farmer	TX
Merchant, John D.	50	M	Farmer	SC
Sarah	45	F		TN

(continued)

Name	Age	Sex	Occupation	Birthplace
Merchant, John	14	M		TX
Claborn	14	M		TX
Richard	12	M		TX
Weedin, J. M.	24	M	Farmer	TN
Eliza	24	F		TN
William	4	M		TX
James	3	M		TX
Malisa	1	F		TX
McClure, H. S.	23	M	Farmer	TN
Hannah	20	F		TN
Neal, Samuel	61	M	Farmer	VA
Ring, M. T.	27	M	Farmer	TN
Sarah	20	F		TN
Mary	2/12	F		TX
King, Davis	50	M	Farmer	GA
Polly	46	F		TN
Anderson	25	M	Farmer	TN
Hellen	12	F		TN
Ruphis	9	M		TX
Richard	6	M		TX
Houston	4/12	M		TX
Choat, R. C.	28	M	Farmer	TN
Rebecca	25	F		AR
Mary	4	F		AR
Elizabeth	3	F		AR
John	2	M		AR
Christopher	26	M	Farmer	TN
Music, Samuel	20	M	Farmer	AR
Roena	23	F		TN
Choat, Mary	66	F		GA
Parson, Elizabeth	62	F		AL
Noling, Peter	61	M	Farmer	NC
Nancy	46	F		GA
Cornelia	21	F		AL
Henry	19	M		AL
Bentley, Daniel	27	M	Farmer	AL
Martha	23	F		AL
Peter	3	M		AL
Paul	2	M		TN
Mise, William	22	M	Farmer	MS
Rainbolt, W. H.	35	M	Farmer	AL
Mary	35	F		AL
Francis	13	M		TN
Walter	11	M		AL
Mary	9	F		MS
Sarah	4	F		MS
Nancy	1	F		TX
Glenn, W. C.	26	M	Farmer	TN
Eliza	21	F		AR
Frances	2	F		TX
Glenn, William	55	M	Farmer	NC
Elizabeth	47	F		TN
Amanda	18	F		KY
Mary	16	F		MO
Jacob	14	M		MO
William	12	M		MO
Missouri	10	F		MO
Humphreys, Bryant	36	M	Brick Mason	TN
Parthena	36	F		VA
Mary	9	F		TX
Thomas	7	M		TX
Martha	5	F		TX
Adaline	4	F		TX
Dianah	3	F		TX
Michael	1	M		TX
Craig, J. B.	41	M	Farmer	NC
Viceanna	40	F		TN
William	19	M	Farmer	AL
Sarah	16	F		AL
Martha	15	F		MS
Emily	14	F		MS
Nancy	11	F		TX
Amanda	8	F		TX
Patience	7	F		TX

(continued)

Name	Age	Sex	Occupation	Birthplace
Craig, Maturia	5	F		TX
Jesse	1	M		TX
Fenton, Joseph	69	M	Farmer	KY
Catharine	28	F		TN
Miles	8	M		TX
Cenderila	7	F		TX
Thomas	5	M		TX
Russel	4	M		TX
Silas	3	M		TX
Sally	1	F		TX
Knight, Lewis	40	M	Farmer	NC
Emily	35	F		TN
Martha	12	F		TX
Elizabeth	10	F		TX
John	8	M		TX
Walton	6	M		TX
Newel	4	M		TX
Laura	2	F		TX
Crawford, Simon B.	23	M	Farmer	AL
Elizabeth	19	F		TN
Mary	8/12	F		TX
Crain, Newel	23	M	Farmer	AL
Elizabeth	20	F		AL
Crain, Ambrose	61	M	Farmer	GA
Mary	58	F		SC
John	21	M	None	TN
Newel	15	M	None	TN
Martha	17	F		TN
Brown, J. W.	38	M	Carpenter	TN
July Ann	23	F		TX
Elias	5	M		TX
John	1	M		TX
Fenton, Washington	22	M	Laborer	AR
Stephens, William	22	M	Farmer	MS
Martha	20	F		TN
Anderson, John W.	32	M	Farmer	GA
Elizabeth	27	F		TN
Andrew	8	M		TX
Mary	6	F		TX
Mariah	5	F		TX
William	4	M		TX
Benjamin	2	M		TX
Sarah	4/12	F		TX
Jewel, Jane	15	F		TX
Blackshear, James F.	34	M	Millwright	TN
Mahalia	29	F		MS
William	9	M		TN
Mary	7	F		TN
Simpson, John	56	M	Farmer	NC
Elizabeth	51	F		OH
G. W.	26	M	Farmer	MS
Thomas	21	M	Farmer	TN
Alford	17	M	Farmer	TN
Nancy	11	F		TX
White, Sarah	63	F		NC
Harrel, Emily	15	F		TN
William	10	M		MS
Sarah	8	F		MS
Martha	6	F		MS
Penelope	5	F		MS
Moore, Asa	35	M	Farmer	NC
Elizabeth	22	F		TN
Ann	2	F		TX
Rosan	1	F		TX
Walling, Richard	20	M	Farmer	TN
White, C. B.	6	M		TN
Willis, James	22	M	Farmer	TN
Catharine	16	F		SC
Silas	3	M		AL
Milla	1	F		TX
Davis, Margaret	12	F		AL
Patterson, Eliza	1	F		AL
Patterson, Lewis	27	M	Farmer	SC
Liddy	37	F		TN
Mary	6	F		AL
James	3	M		TX
Nancy	1	F		TX
Albert	7	M		AL
Jane	5	F		AL
Walker, M. D.	38	M	Farmer	TN
Elizabeth	39	F		SC
Nancy	6	F		TX
James	5	M		TX
William	3	M		TX
Lusk, Mary E.	1-	F		AL
Swift, Jonathan	60	M	Wheelwright	SC
Stewart, John	27	M	Farmer	GA
Rachael	25	F		TN
Charles	6	M		AR
Virgil	4	M		AR
Mary	2	F		TX
William	7/12	M		TX
Thomas, C. C.	42	M	Farmer	VA
Elizabeth	42	F		TN
James	20	M	None	AL
William	17	M	None	AL
Mary	15	F		AL
Madison	12	M		AL
Ann	10	F		AL
Sumners, William	46	M	Farmer	KY
Tempa	46	F		TN
John	23	M	Farmer	IN
Sarah	19	F		IN
Moses	15	M		IN
Franklin	12	M		IN
William	10	M		IN
Martha	7	F		IN
Williams, S. C. Z.	23	M	None	MS
Charlton, James M.	32	M	Farmer	TN
Gabrella	19	F		AL
Lewis	1	M		TX
George	4/12	M		TX
Goodwin, James K.	30	M	Farmer	TN
Nancy	28	F		GA
Elizabeth	7	F		TN
James	5	M		TN
Ann	4	F		TN
Sarah	2	F		TN
Willaby	2/12	M		TN
Cockran, William	20	M	Farmer	GA
McElroy, David	26	M	Farmer	TN
Rebecca	25	F		SC
Elijah	3	M		AL
John	1	M		AL
Grayham, John F.	41	M	Farmer	TN
Nancy	31	F		TN
Elizabeth	17	F		TN
Martha	15	F		TN
John	13	M		TN
Hopkins	11	M		TX
Finas	6	M		TX
Eddy	5	M		TX
One not named	1	F		TX
Archibald C.	35	M	Farmer	TN
Seeaters, David	21	M	Farmer	AL
Lawson, Joseph	31	M	Farmer	TN
P. L.	21	M	Farmer	TN
Gordin, James	44	M	Farmer	SC
Margaret	35	F		TN
John	19	M	Farmer	TN
William	17	M	Farmer	TN
Hutchinson	15	M	Farmer	TN
Sarah	12	F		TN
James	8	M		TN
Eliza	6	F		TN
Solomon	2	M		TN
Dougherty, John F. F.	29	M	Farmer	KY

(continued)

NACOGDOCHES COUNTY, TEXAS

Name	Age	Sex	Occupation	Birthplace
Dougherty, Elizabeth	26	F		TN
James	1	M		TX
Mariah	2/12	F		TX
McElroy, David	45	M	Farmer	GA
Sarah	44	F		TN
Alexander	19	M	Farmer	TN
Elizabeth	17	F		TN
Mary	14	F		TN
Emily	8	F		TX
Harriet	5	F		TX
David	5/12	M		TX
Covington, Jefferson	30	M	Farmer	TN
Whitaker, Isaac	35	M	None	TN
Parrish, David	59	M	Farmer	VA
Margaret	60	F		VA
Elizabeth	24	F		VA
Lucy	22	F		VA
William	22	M		VA
David	19	M	Farmer	VA
Charles	17	M	None	TN
Sumers, Ava Ann	27	F		VA
Margaret	7	F		TN
David	4	M		TN
William	2	M		TN
Easley, William C.	5	M		TN
Parrish, Jane	67	F		VA
Clevenger, George C.	55	M	Black Smith	VA
Rebecca	34	F		TN
James	4	M		TX
Rebecca	1	F		TX
Langhan, Thomas	14	M		TN
Frances	12	F		TX
Mary	10	F		TX
Mayfield, W. E.	27	M	Farmer	TN
Eliza	28	F		TN
Joseph	8	M		TN
William	5	M		TN
Mary	1	F		TX
Weedin, Robin	33	M	Farmer	GA
Julia	32	F		TN
John	13	M		TN
Eliza	9	F		MS
James	7	M		MS
Martha	4	F		MS
Sarah	1	F		TX
Poe, Jedethan	70	M	Farmer	VA
Mary	52	F		SC
Stephen	21	M	Farmer	TN
Abner	8	M		TX
Atkins, Daniel	39	M	Farmer	SC
Jane	25	F		TN
Engledown, Elvira	38	F		TN
Sarah	16	F		MO
John	13	M		TX
Creed	11	M		TX
McElroy, James	50	M	Farmer	TN
Elender	34	F		SC
Sarah	13	F		TX
Hugh	10	M		TX
John	9	M		TX
Susanna	7	F		TX
Elizabeth	4	F		TX
Margaret	4/12	F		TX
Arnold, James R.	25	M	Merchant	TN
Sarah	19	F		TN
Adelia	3	F		TX
Hayden	13	M		TX
Campbell, Joseph	37	M	Farmer	TN
Piera	35	F		TN
Rebecca	11	F		TN
Mary	9	F		LA
Joana	7	F		TX
Tennessee	5	F		TX
Piera	1	F		TX

Name	Age	Sex	Occupation	Birthplace
Williams, Ezekiel	50	M	Farmer	KY
Polly	54	F		KY
John	22	M	None	TN
Thadius	20	M	None	TN
Sarah	18	F		TN
Emily	13	F		TN
James	14	M		TN
Hotchkiss, Charles	50	M	Miller	NY
Eliza	41	F		ENG
Joseph	9	M		TX
Mary	2	F		TX
Archibald	55	M	None	NY
Mariah	53	F		NY
Kid, Jackson C.	20	M	Farmer	TN
Bell, Ebenezer	19	M	Laborer	NC
Whitaker, M. G.	39	M	Farmer	TN
Henrietta	27	F		SC
Edward	6	M		TX
John	4	M		TX
Richard	2	M		TX
Ariadne	1	F		TX
Hicks, John	45	M	Farmer	VA
Sarah	48	F		TN
Joseph	20	M	Farmer	TN
Margaret	17	F		TN
Robert	14	M		TN
John	9	M		TN
George	7	M		TN
Comadore	5	M		TN
Mann, Furgason F.	50	M	Farmer	TN
Elizabeth	42	F		TN
John	8	M		TN
Randle, Polly	25	F		TN
Alford	7	M		TX
Nathaniel	5	M		TX
Winneford	3	F		TX
William	1	M		TX
McDonald, William C.	42	M	Laborer	TN
Drucilla	32	F		TN
Rebecca	10	F		AR
David	8	M		AR
Micajah	6	M		AR
Jasper	5	M		AR
Elizabeth	1	F		TX
Clifton, Redie	32	M	Laborer	NC
Margaret	25	F		??
Alford	2	M		TN
Riley	1	M		TN
Simon	27	M	Laborer	NC
Sarah	24	F		KY
Robert	1/12	M		TX
Thomas	23	M	Laborer	NC
Robert	20	M	Laborer	TN
Crain, Joel B.	35	M	Farmer	TN
Sarah	31	F		TN
William	11	M		TX
James	9	M		TX
Patience	8	F		TX
Martha	5	F		TX
Ambrose	3	M		TX
Newton	1	M		TX
White, Henry H.	42	M	Farmer	NC
Minerva	40	F		TN
William	12	M		MS
Burrel	5	M		TX
Isabella	1	F		TX
Looper, Jackson J.	32	M	Farmer	??
White, James D.	21	M	Farmer	TN
Rebecca	25	F		LA
Elizabeth	10	F		LA
America	4	F		LA
Sarah	2	F		LA
Davidson, L. G.	37	M	Farmer	TN
Harriet	33	F		VA
John	7	M		AL
Osco	5	M		AL

(continued)

NACOGDOCHES COUNTY, TEXAS

Name	Age	Sex	Occupation	Birthplace
Davidson, Martha	4	F		AL
George	4	M		AL
William	1	M		AL
Fulgium, Allice	69	F		NC
Crain, William	12	M		TN
Liles	11	M		TN
Legg, Edward	44	M	Farmer	TN
Mary	40	F		TN
James	18	M	Farmer	AL
Martha	7	F		AL
Mary	4	F		AL
Eliza	2	F		AL
Willis, J. G. B.	21	M	Farmer	TN
Mary	43	F		NC
Rutha	16	F		TN
Sewart, John	33	M	Farmer	TN
Adaline	28	F		TN
Sarah	11	F		TX
John	9	M		TX
James	4	M		TX
Mary	2	F		TX
Rodgers, Henry	35	M	Farmer	TN
Harriet	33	F		AL
Margaret	1	F		TX
Whitaker, Clinton	10	M		TX
John	9	M		TX
William	6	M		TX
Charles	4	M		TX
Bradshaw, James	39	M	Farmer	NC
John A.	29	M	Farmer	TN
Asanath	41	F		NC
Louisa	37	F		NC
Mary	27	F		TN
Clarinda	22	F		TN
Sophia	20	F		TN
Parmalee, E. M.	35	M	Farmer	AL
Margaret	23	F		TN
Alabama	8	F		TN
Tennessee	6	F		TN
Rebecca	4	F		TX
George	1	M		TX
Parmalee, John	41	M	Farmer	KY
Joana	33	F		SC
Carlisle	8	M		TN
Lorra	6	F		TN
Joana	2	F		TN
Martha	9/12	F		TX
Parmalee, Samuel	31	M	Farmer	TN
Mary	24	F		TN
James	6	M		TN
John	4	M		TX
Louisa	1	F		TX
Sharp, James M.	38	M	Farmer	TN
Margaret	26	F		AL
Elizabeth	9	F		TX
Emaline	8	F		TX
Joseph	6	M		TX
Mary	4	F		TX
Rodgers, Thomas H.	49	M	Farmer	NC
Elizabeth	45	F		TN
Samuel	22	M	Farmer	TN
Eliza	20	F		TN
Madison	19	M		MS
Rebecca	17	F		MS
John	16	M	Farmer	MS
Matilda	12	F		MS
Elizabeth	10	F		MS
Thomas	9	M		TX
Martha	8	F		TX
Clabourn	3	M		TX
Boyd, James J.	19	M	Farmer	TN
Murphy, Thomas B.	18	M	Farmer	AL
Craig, William	21	M	Farmer	TN

Name	Age	Sex	Occupation	Birthplace
Crowel, Nancy	43	F		NY
Almira	14	F		NY
Sally	9	F		NY
Baley, John	28	M	Farmer	TN
Hayton, John J.	61	M	Farmer	VA
Samuel	34	M	Farmer	TN
William	39	M	Farmer	VA
Elizabeth	24	F		TN
Ann	2	F		TX
Finch, Matt S.	27	M	Farmer	TN
Man, George W.	23	M	Laborer	TN
Burk, Thomas	23	M	Farmer	TN
Mary	20	F		TN
Levi	5/12	M		TX
Sparks, Phereby	19	F		TN
Berry, Joseph	26	M	Farmer	AL
Nancy	18	F		AL
Jourdice, Label	13	M		TN
Fulgium, Peace	44	M	Farmer	NC
Hester	37	F		NC
Mary	17	F		TN
James	14	M		TN
Amanda	11	F		TN
Donalson, Stephen	51	M	Carpenter	KY
Matilda	41	F		TN
Mary	20	F		KY
Lewis	18	M	Carpenter	KY
James	16	M	Carpenter	TN
Martha	12	F		TX
Milton	9	M		TX
Elizabeth	7	F		TX
Charles	5	M		TX
Frances	2	F		TX
Fowler, James	44	M	Cabinet Maker	SC
Polly	40	F		TN
Sarah	13	F		TN
Martha	10	F		TN
George	8	M		TN
Mary	4	F		AL
James	1	M		TX
Greer, Alexander	45	M	Farmer	TN
Martha	24	F		TN
John	17	M	Farmer	TN
Joseph	15	M	Farmer	TN
Mary	10	F		TX
Sarah	7	F		TX
Vansickle, Samuel	3	M		TX
Clark, J. M.	27	M	Laborer	NC
Catharine	5	F		TX
Susan	3	F		TX
Stone, Wilie	50	M	Farmer	TN
James	18	M	Farmer	TN
Mary	16	F		TN
Joseph	14	M		TN
Samuel	12	M		TX
Calidonia	8	F		TX
Daniel, William M.	56	M	Farmer	SC
Martha	35	F		TN
William	26	M	Farmer	AL
Rebecca	20	F		AL
James	17	M	None	AL
Bartlet	15	M	None	MS
Josephine	8	F		TX
Roberta	7	F		TX
Andrew	5	M		TX
Sarah	3	F		TX
Taylor	2	M		TX
Crain, A. H.	28	M	Farmer	AL
Adaline	28	F		TN
Croft, William	20	M	Laborer	TN
Baley, Henry	59	M	Farmer	VA
Sally	52	F		NC
Reubin	24	M	Farmer	TN

(continued)

NACOGDOCHES COUNTY, TEXAS

Name	Age	Sex	Occupation	Birthplace
Baley, Jery	54	M	Farmer	VA
Elizabeth	24	F		GA
Frealy, A. J.	32	M	Farmer	AL
Rebecca	30	F		TN
Sarah	7	F		TN
Nancy	6	F		TN
Eliza	4	F		TX
Martin	2	M		TX
John	4/12	M		TX
Sills, Isiah	54	M	Farmer	NC
Nancy	44	F		TN
Franklin	23	M	None	TN
Newnan	21	M	Farmer	TN
Eliza	19	F		TN
Madison	17	M	Farmer	TN
Clarinda	16	F		TN
Clarisa	11	F		TN
Williamson	9	M		TN
Nancy	5	F		TN
Weatherly, J. A.	49	M	Farmer	NC
Cyntha	37	F		TN
Samuel	18	M	Farmer	AL
John	17	M	farmer	TN
Edward	15	M	Farmer	TN
Jobe	14	M		TN
Kyle	11	M		TN
William	5	M		TN
Weatherly, Jobe P.	45	M	Farmer	NC
Lucinda	41	F		KY
Edward	18	M	Farmer	TN
French	17	M	Farmer	TN
Jobe	16	M	Farmer	TN
Samuel	15	M	Farmer	MS
James	12	M		MS
John	7	M		MS
Lucinda	1	F		TX
McGlohan, Thomas	30	M	Farmer	IRE
Avaline	26	F		TN
John	7/12	M		TX
McCormac, David	30	M	Farmer	TN
Sarah	40	F		NC
Smith, Barnet	45	M	Laborer	VA
Cole, Andrew	24	M	Black Smith	TN
Frances	19	F		TN
Rebecca	1	F		TX
John	21	M	Black Smith	TN
Nichols, Stephen	52	M	Farmer	SC
Martha	50	F		TN
Orval	21	M	Farmer	AR
Henry	18	M	Farmer	AR
Sarah	13	F		AR
Francis	7	M		TX
Reaves, F. W.	24	M	Farmer	AR
Eliza	18	F		TN
Spivey, Enoch	51	M	Farmer	NC
Zilpha	49	F		NC
Temple	25	M	Farmer	AL
John	21	M	Farmer	AL
James	20	M	Farmer	AL
Elias	16	M	Farmer	TN
Jane	15	F		TN
Amanda	6	F		TX
Sturdivant, Marian	23	M	Laborer	TN
Casson, H. H.	38	M	Black Smith	TN
Sarah	26	F		TN
Margaret	7	F		TX
Mary	4	F		TX
Thomas	1	M		TX
Harris, William	30	M	Farmer	TN
Jackson, Dolason	27	M	Farmer	TN
Shotwell, Thomas	19	M	Farmer	GA
Jones, G. B.	29	M	Farmer	TN
Jane	26	F		TN

(continued)

Name	Age	Sex	Occupation	Birthplace
Jones, John	8	M		TN
Pricey	6	F		TN
Martha	4	F		TN
Ivcassa	3	F		TN
Porter	4/12	M		TX
Daniel, Richard	19	M	Farmer	TN
Grayson, Jackson	44	M	Farmer	VA
Anna	43	F		TN
Lourenna	17	F		AL
Samuel	15	M	Farmer	LA
George	11	M		TX
Sarah	7	F		TX
Mary	5	F		TX
Harris, James	20	M	Farmer	AL
Bugg, Edmond	25	M	Laborer	GA
Hughes, D. H.	36	M	Farmer	KY
Nancy	32	F		TN
Polly	15	F		TN
Rolland	10	M		TX
Martha	8	F		TX
William	5	M		TX
Susan	2	F		TX
Eliza	1/12	F		TX
White, H. H.	34	M	Farmer	TN
Mary	27	F		TN
Deverux	13	M		TN
Roda	11	F		TN
Hardy	9	M		TN
Malvina	5	F		TX
Edmond	1	M		TX
Button, L. M.	27	M	Farmer	KY
Winn, Devraux	80	M	None	VA
Roday	72	F		TN
James	47	M	Farmer	TN
Ann	1	F		TX
Baxter, J. W.	40	M	Farmer	NC
Vernitha	34	F		TN
Susan	12	F		TN
Elizabeth	10	F		TX
Martha	8	F		TX
Joseph	5	M		TX
Oscar	3	M		TX
Mary	6/12	F		TX
Blackburn, James G.	22	M	Farmer	TN
Elizabeth	17	F		AL
Stewart, John V.	30	M	Farmer	TN
Margaret	31	F		AR
George	5	M		TX
Robert	2	M		TX
John	6/12	M		TX
Johnson, Clabourne	37	M	Farmer	TN
Elizabeth	32	F		TN
Mary	13	F		TN
Tabitha	10	F		MS
Blackburn, James	63	M	Farmer	NC
Louisa	40	F		TN
Louisa	19	F		TN
Andrew	17	M	Farmer	TN
Joseph	15	M	Farmer	MS
Jason	13	M		MS
William	11	M		MS
Robert	8	M		TX
George	6	M		TX
Green	4	M		TX
Thomas	2	M		TX
Painter, William	41	M	Laborer	SC
Byrd, Shelby	52	M	Carpenter	TN
Rye, Baswell	18	M	Teacher	GA
King, W. H.	34	M	Farmer	TN
Martha	33	F		TN
James	12	M		TN
John	10	M		TX
Ann	8	F		TX
Frances	5	F		TX
Martha	4	F		TX
Mary	4	F		TX

(continued)

Name	Age	Sex	Occupation	Birthplace
King, Robert	2	M		TX
Nancy	3/12	F		TX
Whitaker, L. S.	29	M	Farmer	TN
Eliza	24	F		TN
William	3	M		TN
Isaac	5/12	M		TX
King, Rufus F.	18	M	Farmer	TN
Jones, J. Y	39	M	Farmer	TN
Frances	39	F		NC
Unicy	15	F		TN
George	13	M		TN
Thomas	12	M		TN
Nancy	8	F		TX
Jesse	6	M		TX
Martha	3	F		TX
Lucas, John	25	M	Farmer	TN
Loyd, J. B.	25	M	Farmer	TN
George	20	M	Farmer	TN
Eubanks, J. L.	21	M	Farmer	TN
Lucas, Newton	23	M	Farmer	TN
King, A. C.	25	M	Farmer	TN
Finetta	22	F		TN
Sarah	4	F		TN
Martha	2	F		TN
Mary	5/12	F		TX
Casle--(?), Milford	18	M	Farmer	TN
Bullock, William N.	30	M	Farmer	MS
Margaret	18	F		TN
Durret, W. H.	30	M	Farmer	TN
Elizabeth	21	F		GA
Martha	3	F		TX
Reas	1	M		TX
Durret, Elizabeth	33	F		TN
Catharine	18	F		MS
Albert	22	M	Farmer	MS
Franklin	17	M	Farmer	MS
Tarlton	10	M		TX
Tate, S. W.	27	M	Farmer	TN
Martha	24	F		TN
Adaline	3	F		TN
Susan	1	F		TX
Grayson, Malvina	19	F		TN
Williams, L. P.	17	M	Laborer	TN
Tate, Alford	52	M	Farmer	TN
Mirena	49	F		KY
Minerva	15	F		TN
Robert	13	M		TN
Clabourn	11	M		TN
James	9	M		TN
Murphy, J. L.	38	M	Farmer	TN
Caroline	37	F		SC
Thomas	17	M	Farmer	AL
Mary	15	F		AL
Andrew	13	M		AL
Benjamin	11	M		AL
William	9	M		AL
John	6	M		AL
James	5	M		AL
Arvah	2	M		AL
Polk, John	65	M	Farmer	NC
Elizabeth	55	F		KY
Nancy	16	F		TN
Elizabeth	11	F		TX
Wadkins, John M.	37	M	Farmer	TN
Malvina	26	F		MS
Robert	6	M		TX
William	4	M		TX
John	11/12	M		TX
Clifton, Robert E.	19	M	Laborer	TN
Wadkins, Mary W.	60	F		SC
Jesse J.	21	M	Farmer	TN
Aly, John	32	M	Farmer	TN
Agnes	31	F		TN
Samuel	8	M		TN
Rebecca	5	F		TN
George	2	M		TN
Cole, James	23	M		TN
Sarah	23	F		TN
Emaline	2	F		TN
Cyntha	1/12	F		TX
Sarah	3	F		TN
Kirk, S. W.	32	M	Physician	TN
Mary	22	F		TN
John	5	M		TN
William	4	M		TN
Mary	2	F		TX
Liles, John	20	M	Overseer	AL
Winn, R. E.	41	M	Saddler	TN
Sarah	40	F		TN
Joel	15	M	Saddler	TN
Mary	13	F		TN
Jesse	10	M		MS
William	5	M		TX
Sarah	3	F		TX
McKnight, William	29	M	Farmer	TN
Susan	18	F		TN
Watkins, R. C.	34	M	C.P. Presbyterian	TN
Amanda	29	F		TN
John	9	M		TX
Jesse	6	M		TX
Richard	3	M		TX
William	1	M		TX
Watkins, Robert	30	M	Farmer	TN
Sarah	20	F		AL
John	3	M		TX
Mary	1	F		TX
Harrison, D. ?.	32	M	Shop Joiner	VA
Permelia	19	F		TN
James	10	M		VA
Martha	5	F		MS
Mary	3/12	F		TX
Smith, Sarah J.	51	F		TN
Susan	15	F		TN
Robert	13	M		AL
Gunner, William	30	M	Farmer	MS
James	2	M		MS
Deel, Milton	62	M	Farmer	VA
Mima	43	F		SC
Tennessee	12	F		TN
Cypert, W. C.	40	M	Teacher	TN
Permelia	31	F		TN
Samantha	10	F		TX
William	9	M		TX
Joseph	6	M		TN
Mary	3	F		TN
Eliza	1	F		TN
McKnight, Alexander C.	33	M	Farmer	AL
Clarasey	34	F		AL
Reubin	9	M		TX
Pernita	7	F		TX
Henry	5	M		TX
Susan	3	F		TX
Pelina	1	F		TX
Brock, Jesse	19	M	Laborer	TN
Brewer, Henry	73	M	Farmer	NC
Susan	73	F		NC
Parker, Ira	23	M	Laborer	MS
Alsey	21	F		TN
William	3/12	M		TX
Brewer, Jefferson	17	M	Laborer	MS
George	13	M		MS
Bowers, L. A.	39	M	Farmer	TN
Amanda	36	F		TN
William	17	M	Farmer	TN

(continued)

NACOGDOCHES COUNTY, TEXAS

Name	Age	Sex	Occupation	Birthplace
Bowers, Gilliann	13	F		TN
Leroy	11	M		TN
John	6	M		TX
Isaac	1	M		TX
Burk, James	30	M	Farmer	TN
Anna	29	F		TN
Minerva	10	F		TN
Samantha	7	F		TN
Martha	5	F		TN
John	3	M		TN
Britain	5/12	M		TX
Burk, William	32	M	Farmer	SC
Oney	27	F		TN
Martha	9	F		TN
John	4	M		TN
Martin	2	M		TN
Burk, A. J.	18	M	Farmer	TN
Mary	21	F		TN
Louisa	7/12	F		TN
Burk, John	36	M	Farmer	SC
Martha	26	F		TN
Martin	9	M		TN
William	6	M		TN
James	5	M		TN
Mary	2	F		TX
White, Charles	64	M	Farmer	NC
Sarah	64	F		NC
Berry	24	M	Farmer	TN
Johnson, Jabus	22	M	Farmer	GA
Spires, Benjamin	57	M	Farmer	TN
Prudence	23	F		AL
Charlot	21	F		AL
Vernetta	12	F		MS
Benjamin	17	M	Farmer	AL
John	14	M		MS
Vernon, Nancy	28	F		TN
Mary	12	F		MS
Amanda	10	F		MS
William	9	M		TX
Martha	7	F		TX
Meders, William	32	M	Laborer	AL
Mitchel, William	25	M	Laborer	AL
Garret, T. B.	55	M	Farmer	TN
Luica	44	F		TN
Elizabeth	22	F		TN
Nobles, Mary	20	F		TN
Garret, Felix	17	M	Farmer	TN
Charles	15	M	Farmer	TN
Evaline	14	F		TX
Tennessee	12	F		TX
Louisa	10	F		TX
John	7	M		TX
Wallis, Susana	45	F		TN
Sebourn	25	M	Farmer	AL
Calvin	24	M	Farmer	AL
Samuel	22	M	Farmer	AL
William	19	M	farmer	AL
Mary	17	F		AL
David	15	M	Farmer	AL
Clifton	11	M		AL
Ables, John	35	M	Farmer	MS
Nancy	35	F		TN
Thomas	13	M		TX
Mary	11	F		TX
Ezekiel	9	M		TX
Sarah	7	F		TX
John	2	M		TX
John	11/12	M		TX
Whitaker, J. H.	32	M	Farmer	TN
Tesy	21	F		TN
Martha	3	F		TX
Olivia	1	F		TX
Rodgers, Lewis	23	M	Laborer	TN
Taylor, W. C.	28	M	Farmer	AL
Mary	30	F		TN
Charles	6	M		AL
Nancy	4	F		AL
Malissa	8/12	F		TX
Taylor, C. M.	52	M	Farmer	TN
Sarah	45	F		SC
Thomas	23	M	Farmer	AL
Jane	21	F		AL
Levi	17	M	Farmer	AL
Nancy	15	F		AL
Charlotta	14	F		AL
Charles	12	M		AL
Martin	11	M		AL
John	8	M		AL
George	6	M		AL
James	4	M		AL
Renfrow, John	30	M	Farmer	TN
Jane	21	F		AL
Nancy	3	F		TX
Jesse	2	M		TX
Susanna	1	F		TX
Clute, John R.	47	M	Farmer	NY
Adaline	28	F		TN
Cora	12	F		TX
Spencer, T. C.	31	M	Merchant	TN
Amanda	22	F		TN
William	5	M		TX
Simpson, W. P.	39	M	Silver Smith	NC
Tabitha	33	F		KY
Susan	9	F		TX
Thomas	5	M		TX
Mary	2/12	F		TX
Stewart, Mary J.	17	F		TN
Henderson, D. M.	47	M	Black Smith	TN
Eliza	22	F		AL
Sarah	9/12	F		TX
Allen, Elijah	48	M	Physician	TN
Acenith	36	F		GA
Benjamin	12	M		AL
Sparks, A. J.	23	M	Farmer	MS
Mary	19	F		TN
Thomas	11/12	M		TX
Thomas	21	M	Farmer	MS
John	17	M	Farmer	MS
Bigham, M. M.	34	M	Farmer	KY
Mary	42	F		TN
Wimberly, R. E.	32	M	Teacher	GA
Henry, John	30	M	Mail Carrier	NC
Armstrong, Robert	24	M	Student	TN
McKnight, F. C.	30	M	None	TN
Charity	21	F		TN
Mary	1	F		TX
Sharp, J. P.	37	M	Physician	TN
Mary	34	F		TN
James	13	M		TN
Frances	6	F		TX
Susana	4	F		TX
Joseph	2	M		TX
Gopartner, George	9	M		IN
McKnight, James	21	M	Student	TN
Rook, Henry	28	M	Farmer	OH
Elizabeth	23	F		TN
Joseph	4	M		TX
King, Nancy	52	F		NC
John	19	M	Farmer	TN
Nancy	17	F		TN
Thomas	14	M		TN
William	11	M		MS
Chancelor, Abraham	30	M	Farmer	SC
Margaret	26	F		TN

(continued)

Name	Age	Sex	Occupation	Birthplace
Chancelor, Nancy	6	F		AL
John	5	M		AL
William	2	M		AL
Mary	6/12	F		TX
Sears, Mary	76	F		NC
Winser, Leonard	25	M	Farmer	AL
Elizabeth	24	F		TN
Mary	3	F		TX
David	1	M		TX
Sarah	7/12	F		TX
Gunter, Martin	29	M	Farmer	TN
Prudence	20	F		MS
William	1	M		TX
Cessna, G. K.	45	M	Farmer	TN
Nancy	38	F		SC
Walter	16	M	Student	GA
Susan	18	F		NC
Theodothia	19	F		TN
James	14	M		GA
Green	12	M		GA
John	7	M		TX
Daniel	3	M		TX
Mariah	2	F		TX
Nancy	6/12	F		TX
Mary	17	F		AL
Neelana	10	F		MS
Burk, Jesse	25	M	Farmer	TN
Susana	24	F		TN
Amanda	2	F		TN
Thomas	1	M		TN
Tucker, Burton	23	M	Farmer	TN
Burk, Martin	50	M	Black Smith	SC
Mary	45	F		SC
Levi	21	M	Farmer	TN
Joshua	15	M	Farmer	TN
Josiah	12	M		TN
Selman, W. P.	39	M	Farmer	TN
Rutha	35	F		AL
Louisa	11	F		AL
Robert	10	M		AL
Laura	8	F		TX
Phineas	1	M		TX
Red, J. B.	25	M		GA
Bingham, Vilot	31	F		NC
Martha	8	F		TN
William	4	M		TN
Haynes, E. J. C.	42	M		NC
Bingham, Mathias	63	M	Wheelwright	NC
Tabitha	62	F		NC
James	24	M	Farmer	TN
Tabitha	22	F		TN
Knox, G. W.	38	M	Farmer	TN
Rebecca	39	F		TN
William	11	M		TX
Susana	8	F		TX
Mary	7	F		TX
James	6	M		TX
Naoma	3	F		TX
George	1	M		TX
McKnight, James	77	M	Farmer	NC
Susana	54	F		SC
Felix	17	M	Farmer	TN
John	16	M	Farmer	TN
Margaret	15	F		TN
Sparkes, J. H.	35	M	Farmer	MS
Elizabeth	27	F		TN
Rebecca	12	F		TX
Martha	8	F		TX
Isabella	6	F		TX
Nancy	2	F		TX
Davis, Wiley	25	M	Clerk in Store	MS

Name	Age	Sex	Occupation	Birthplace
Norris, A. S.	21	M	Farmer	TN
Malinda	21	F		TN
Dike, Levi	49	M	Farmer	GA
America	33	F		TN
Elizabeth	15	F		TX
Amanda	14	F		TX
Simeon	10	M		TX
Green	8	M		TX
Jackson	6	M		TX
Joseph	4	M		TX
Sarah	1	F		TX
Conner, Hamilton	17	M	None	MO
Osco	14	M		MO
Dallis, Josephine	10	F		MO
Rowe, Elix	30	M	Farmer	AL
Martha	26	F		TN
William	6	M		AL
Franklin	4	M		AL
Rachael	2	F		AL
Walker, Y. G.	40	M	Farmer	TN
Sarah	20	F		TN
Evaline	18	F		MO
Abagil	17	F		MO
Marquis	16	M	None	MO
Matilda	14	F		MO
Mary	12	F		MO
Martin	10	M		MO
John	8	M		MO
Elizabeth	6	F		MO
Young	4	M		MO
Sarah	2	F		TX
Nale, B. S.	40	M	Farmer	TN
Anna	41	F		TN
Christopher	18	M	None	MO
Mary	16	F		MO
Nancy	15	F		MO
Julia	13	F		MO
Benjamin	9	M		MO
Elizabeth	6	F		MO
Maxwell, W. H.	25	M	Farmer	TN
Frances	22	F		TN
Margaret	1	F		TX
Wisener, William	38	M	Farmer	TN
Mary	31	F		TN
William	7	M		TX
Richard	6	M		TX
Sydna	4	M		TX
Nancy	2	F		TX
Bone, J. F.	25	M	Farmer	TN
Louisa	20	F		NC
Payn, J. W.	27	M	Farmer	TN
Asenath	23	F		TN
James	8	M		TX
Frances	3	F		TX
Robert	2	M		TX
Bone, Robert	17	M	Laborer	TN
Samuel	15	M	Laborer	TN
John	14	M		TN
Levicy	12	F		TN
Sheril, Lampkin	49	M	Laborer	TN
Mary	45	F		TN
James	17	M	Laborer	TN
Elizabeth	16	F		TN
Arthur	12	M		AL
Nancy	11	F		GA
Mary	8	F		GA
Jane	7	F		GA
Samuel	7	M		GA
Delila	2	F		AR
Hill, A. A.	43	M	Farmer	SC
Levicy	(?) 4	F		NC
Helena	9	F		TN
Mary	8	F		TX
Hill, William	39	M	Farmer	TN

(continued)

NACOGDOCHES COUNTY, TEXAS

Hill, Mary 37 F SC
Alexander 12 M TN
Nancy 10 F TN
John 9 M TN
James 8 M TX
Elijah 7 M TX
William 5 M TX
Thomas 2 M TX

Smith, W. J. 34 M Farmer TN
Nancy 26 F TN
James 7 M TX
Mary 5 F TX
Martha 3 F TX
Sarah 1 F TX
Long, Mary M. 53 F TN
Akins, Mary E. 13 F TX
Baker, Edward F. 22 M Laborer AL

Boller, S. H. 39 M Farmer TN
Sarah 28 F TN
James 11 M TX
Benjamin 9 M TX
Martha 7 F TX
Julia 5 F TX
Mary 3 F TX
Ammons, William 35 M Farmer MS

Hyde, G. C. 39 M Physician TN
Ann J. 24 F NY

Johnson, William 60 M Farmer NC
Margaret 45 F TN
Robert 20 M Farmer AL
Sarah 13 F AL
John 11 M AL
Elizabeth 6 F AL
George 3 M LA
Dunkin 2 M TX

Simpson, L. W. 42 M Gin Maker TN
Unicey 22 F AL
Thomas 17 M None AL
James 14 M AL
William 12 M AL
Andrew 11 M TX
John 9 M TX
Samuel 7 M TX
Benjamin 5 M TX
David 3 M TX

Langford, J. M. 24 M Farmer TN
Alabama 19 F MS
Ira 10/12 M MS

Gray, W. W. 43 M Farmer KY
Dunham, Elizabeth 45 F KY
Gray, J. S. 66 M None VA
Hayde, A. G. 27 M Farmer TN
Mary 17 F TN

Poe, John 34 M Laborer TN
Margaret 20 F IL
William 13 M IL
Larkin 7 M TX
Isaac 4 M TX
Sarah 7/12 F TX

Hall, B. M. 36 M Farmer TN
Harriet 34 F TN
William 16 M Farmer TN
Jane 13 F TN
Elizabeth 7 F TX
Frances 5 F TX
Henry 3 M TX
Bartlet 2 M TX
John 2/12 M TX
Glass, William 21 M Laborer LA

Engledown, Elizabeth 38 F TN
William 23 M Farmer TN
Nancy 24 F AL
Robert 19 M Farmer TN

Engledown, Oscar 40 M Farmer VA
Julia 30 F TN
Euphemia 11 F TX

Pate, D. M. 26 M Farmer AL
Lucinda 24 F TN
James 1 M TX

Brasher, E. P. 28 M None TN
Achsah 32 F VA
Parthenia 6 F TX
Liberty 5 M TX
Montgomery 3 M TX
Medora 1 F TX

Brasher, Benjamin 32 M Farmer TN
Mary 25 F TN
Elizabeth 4 F TX
John 2 M TX

Hamil, S. H. 42 M Farmer TN
Minerva 47 F VA
Amanda A. 16 F TN
Arabella H. 9 F TX
Blackwell, T. J. 25 M Farmer VA

Hamil, R. C. 36 M Farmer TN
Pokahantas 27 F VA
Samuel W. 14 M TN

NAVERRO COUNTY, TEXAS

Mathews, Martha 45 F NC
Newton 18 M Farmer TN
Martha P. 15 F TN
William B. 12 M TN
Joseph 10 M TX
T. P. 7 M TX
Flint, David P. 25 M Ferryman TN
Morgan, J. P. 41 M Physician CT

Goodman, Francis 22 M Black Smith VA
Fanny 17 F TN
Pulse, Elisha 31 M Black Smith TN

Landers, Levi B. 33 M Merchant AL
Martha 30 F TN
C. S. 14 M AR
Mary J. 12 F AR
Eveline 9 F AR
Martha B. 6 F AR
Emily F. 2/12 F TX

Smith, Eli 35 M Farmer TN
Olive 25 F NY
John (E)A. 4 M TX
Jane P. 2 F TX
Landers, John 19 M Laborer TN

Hamilton, James 43 M Farm & Mechanic TN
Margaret T. 46 F TN
John H. 15 M Farmer AR
James 12 M AR
Nancy 6 F AR

Bundy, William H. 30 M Farmer NC
Elizabeth U. 20 F TN
Young, George 50 M Physician ENG

Bragg, Joseph 37 M Farmer TN
Ann Eliza 27 F TN
William L. 6/12 M TX
Hamilton, Elizabeth 64 F PA

Baird, Alvin 43 M M.E. Minoster TN
Maria B. 39 F MD
Laura J. 12 F MO
Robert N. 9 M MO
Elizabeth R. 8 F AR
Lucretia C. 7 F AR
John C. L. 3 M TX
Mariah 1 F TX

Allen, H. M. 29 M Physician TN

(continued)

NAVERRO COUNTY, TEXAS

Name	Age	Sex	Occupation	Birthplace
Allen, Lucy A.	21	F		MA
Appleby, William	28	M	Ins. Maker London	ENG
Donaldson, R. C.	27	M	Merchant	KS
Thompson, Gabriel L.	31	M	Grocer	SC
Sarah Ann	31	F		TN
Inahilda C.	7	F		TX
Parker	4	M		TX
Oliver	1	M		TX
Leak, Samuel	27	M	Grocer	KY
Elizabeth J.	21	F		TN
Jones, John C.	26	M	Wagon Maker	AL
Scott, James D.	41	M	None	TN
King, James	26	M	Laborer	IRE
Bartlett, Joseph C.	35	M	Farmer	TN
Amanda M.	25	F		TN
Frances C.	9	F		TX
Jesse M.	8	M		TX
Thomas S.	6	M		TX
James E.	4	M		TX
Henderson, D. B.	23	M	School Teacher	TN
Wood, William P.	34	M	Farmer	SC
Brown, William	26	M	Farmer	OH
Williams, E. R.	26	M	None	AL
Mulky, T.	23	M	Farmer	IL
Tate, Frances E.	25	F		TN
R. S.	32	M	Physician	AL
Porter, Frances	8	F		TX
Parker, Louisa	5	F		TX
Bartlett, L. L.	20	M	Merchant	IL
M.	28	M	Merchant	IL
Merriman, A. P.	40	M	Farmer	TN
Sarah	36	F		KY
Louisa J.	13	F		KY
Doretha	8	F		KY
Ladd, William J.	35	M	Hotel Keeper	IN
Emeline	30	F		IN
Levi D.	10	M		AR
Abram S.	8	M		TX
Mary Ann	6	F		TX
Amanda C.	3	F		TX
Louisa J.	10/12	F		TX
Moody, Thomas	33	M	Carpenter	AL
Powell, William S.	35	M	Merchant	TN
Hedick, Albert P.	37	M	Tailor	PA
Woothen, J. A.	28	M	Physician	GA
Craft, William	23	M	Attorney at Law	AL
Vennoy, Cornelius	40	M	Saddler	NY
Wheeland, Dennis	40	M	Brick Mason	IRE
McKinney, Hampton	53	M	M.E. Minister	NC
Mary B.	53	F		TN
Johnathan	22	M	None	IL
William M.	20	M	None	IL
Elizabeth J.	18	F		IL
Ann C.	16	F		IL
Mary	12	F		IL
Elliot, J. M.	24	M	School Teacher	IL
Wear, U. H.	22	M	Physician	TN
Henderson, William H.	33	M	Attorney at Law	NC
Mary P.	25	F		TN
Henry M.	1	M		TX
Morrel, Jno. M.	28	M	Merchant	TN
Winkler, C. M.	28	M	Attorney at Law	NC
Louisa	29	F		TN
Neil, Frances E.	9	F		TX
Winkler, Martha L.	3/12	F		TX
Petty, George V.	47	M	Farmer	SC
Mary	42	F		TN
John T.	25	M	Farmer	TN
Kisine	22	F		TN
Sarah	18	F		TN
Nancy H.	16	F		TN
Elizabeth E.	14	F		TN
Mary L.	10	F		TN

(continued)

Name	Age	Sex	Occupation	Birthplace
Petty, George W.	8	M		TN
Eliza L.	5	F		TN
Duncan, James N.	22	M	Farmer	TN
Lucy Jane	23	F		TN
Mary Jane	2	F		TN
Choat, Luke	24	M	Laborer	TN
Ham, Berry L.	37	M	Farmer	TN
D. M.	27	F		TN
Nancy J.	11	F		TX
Martha A.	9	F		TX
Abner L.	7	M		TX
Jenett	5	F		TX
Elizabeth	2	F		TX
McKinney, Thomas H.	22	M	Farmer	IL
Mary L.	19	F		TN
Beoden, Alex	27	M	Attorney at Law	SCO
McCabe, W. B.	30	M	Grocer	KY
Mahilda D.	29	F		IN
Mary E.	7	F		MO
John G. W.	6	M		MO
William B.	5	M		TX
Packwood, Travis C.	9	M	Orphan	TX
Brown, John P.	28	M	Clerk	TN
Phiffer, W. A.	21	M	waggoner	TN
Rains, John	40	M	Laborer	TN
Elizabeth	40	F		TN
Talitha	6	F		AR
John	2	M		TX
Gray, Moses	25	M	Farmer	AR
Eliza	21	F		TN
Elizabeth	2	F		AR
Mary Ann	1	F		AR
George	17	M	Farmer	TN
Morrel, H. R.	22	M	Farmer	TN
Sarah	21	F		MS
Morrel, Reece V.	55	M	Farmer	SC
R. D.	18	M	Farmer	TN
Green W. W.	13	M		TN
Margaret E.	9	F		TN
Nancy A. C.	6	F		TN
Hamilton, William	31	M	Merchant	TN
Elizabeth J.	30	F		TN
James D.	6	M		AR
N. A. E.	4	F		TN
Susanna E.	1	F		TX
Story, Samuel H.	23	M	Not Known	TN
Nancy L.	24	F		TN
Matlock, E. M.	42	M	Merchant	TN
Morrel, William H.	27	M	Merchant	TN
Martha L.	17	F		TN
Hartswell, D. B.	22	M	Merchant	OH
Riggs, J. M.	41	M	Dist. Clerk	TN
M. K.	33	F		TN
Maria A.	13	F		TN
Stephen M.	9	M		MO
Lucinda J.	5	F		MO
E. R.	6/12	F		TX
Hooper, Absalom A.	38	M	Laborer	TN
Jane	25	F		TN
Isaac N.	3	M		TN
Cross, S. C.	30	M	Attorney at Law	TN
Arraminta	22	F		SC
Pochontas	4	F		TX
Mary T.	1	F		TX
Ragen, James	30	M	Farmer	TN
Emily	21	F		IL
William A.	5	M		TX
Margaret E.	3	F		TX
Mary J.	7/12	F		TX
Linsey, Alfred	29	M	Farmer	AL

(continued)

NAVERRO COUNTY, TEXAS

Name	Age	Sex	Occupation	Born
Linsey, Emeline H.	20	F		TN
William B.	1	M		TX
Wantland, Marshall	55	M	Farmer	VA
Charles	23	M	Farmer	TN
Mary E.	21	F		TN
E. Susan	18	F		IL
E. M.	16	M	Farmer	IL
Rutha J.	11	F		IL
Richardson, John	47	M	Farmer	VA
Elmyra	41	F		SC
Jonathan	23	M	Farmer	TN
Telitha	20	F		TN
Sally A.	16	F		TN
Dennis	14	M		AR
Joshua	12	M		AR
Lucy A.	7	F		AR
Melinda C.	3	F		TX
Eliza J.	4/12	F		TX
Martin, Y. L.	32	M	Attorney at Law	VA
Mary Ann	28	F		TN
Mary F.	12	F		AR
E. A.	9	F		TX
Julia Adel	7	F		TX
Eliza E.	5	F		TX
Lycurg L. J.	2	M		TX
Hampton, Mary	73	F		SC
Hodges, N. C.	38	M	Farmer	TN
D.	35	F		KY
C. J.	13	M		TX
Benjamin F.	11	M		TX
Thomas M.	9	M		TX
Green	6	M		TX
George A.	5	M		TX
Isaac N. (Twin)	2	M		TX
William J. (Twin)	2	M		TX
Brittain, Benjamin	23	M	Farmer	TN
Ligna J.	20	F		DE
Barker, William	6	M		MO
Haggard, William	24	M	Farmer	KY
Perlina	19	F		TN
Cintha J.	1	F		TX
Smith, Green L.	36	M	Farmer	KY
Amanda M.	33	F		TN
Collins, John B.	20	M	Farmer	AR
Harris, Russina	14	F		TN
Beaman, William H.	32	M	Farmer	IN
Sarah A.	25	F		TN
Elijah M.	8	M		IL
Charles W.	7	M		IL
Melissa J.	4	F		IL
Emily R.	4	F		TX
Hamilton, Samuel	30	M	Farmer	TN
Nancy T.	28	F		TN
James A.	7	M		TN
Samuel W.	4	M		AR
William C.	3	M		TX
Williamson V.	1	M		TX
Good, Richard	23	M	Laborer	TN
Burrow, William	28	M	Farmer	TN
Mary	31	F		VA
Elizabeth	6	F		MO
Margaret E.	3	F		TX
Alfuhant, William Taylor	3	M		MO
Burrow, Mary J.	6/12	F		TX
Petty, William	25	M	Farmer	TN
Susan	23	F		TN
Mary T.	1	F		TX
Anderson, Mark	52	M	Farmer	TN
Polly	52	F		TN
Willis	21	M	Farmer	IL
Eliza	18	F		IL

(continued)

Name	Age	Sex	Occupation	Born
Anderson, William	17	M	Farmer	IL
Courtney	13	F		IL
Amazi	9	M		IL
Johnson, James M.	24	M	Farmer	NC
McKinney, Jubilee	40	M	Mechanic	IL
Landers, Phebe	41	F		TN
Richard	23	M	Farmer	TN
Elijah	21	M	Waggoner	TN
Benjamin	19	M	Waggoner	TN
William	17	M	Farmer	AR
Jonathan	15	M	Farmer	AR
Charity	9	F		AR
Philip	7	M		AR
Catharine	5	F		AR
Nancy A.	3	F		TX
Dearman, James	49	M	Farmer	KY
Mary	50	F		KY
Sally Ann	28	F		KY
Horace H.	22	M	Farmer	TN
Jonathan	19	M	Farmer	TN
Ury Isabel	16	F		AL
Joseph W.	11	M		AL
Jonas M.	9	M		AL
Harris, Harden E.	43	M	Farmer	NC
Mary	40	F		TN
Emeline B.	20	F		AL
Calvin G.	18	M	Farmer	AL
Nancy J.	14	F		MS
Mary Ann	12	F		MS
William H.	11	M		MS
Lucinda	7	F		MS
Frances	4	F		MS
Telitha	2	F		MS
Tharp, Elizabeth	20	F		AL
Wasson, James	42	M	Farmer	TN
Mary	21	F		AL
Frances E.	5	F		MS
Ephraim	6/12	M		TX
McFadden, John M.	21	M	Farmer	TN
S. E.	19	F		SC
John M.	1	M		TX
Jackson, Molly	64	F		SC
Hamilton, John	40	M	Farmer	IL
Caroline	31	F		AL
Jesse L.	14	M		TN
Elisa J.	11	F		AR
Sarah E.	10	F		AR
James	8	M		AR
John	6	M		AR
Isaac	3	M		TX
Nancy C.	1	F		TX
Beasley, Jesse	45	M	Farmer	TN
Elizabeth	39	F		TN
Wiatt	19	M	Farmer	AL
Mathew	16	M	Farmer	MS
Elijah	14	M		MS
John T.	13	M		MS
James T.	10	M		MS
Martha A.	11	F		MS
Jesse R.	9	M		MS
Lucy A.	6	F		MS
Samuel B.	4	M		MS
William P.	2	M		MS
Sarah M.	4/12	F		TX
Bragg, Waney	54	F		TN
Benjamin	22	M		AL
Alfred C.	20	M		AL
James C.	17	M		AL
Caddell, Martin	42	M	Farm & Mechanic	NC
Mary	40	F		TN
Lankford, Berry	21	M		AL
Louisa J.	21	F		TN
William G.	1	M		TX
Browning, William L.	47	M	Farmer	GA

(continued)

NAVERRO COUNTY, TEXAS

Name	Age	Sex	Occupation	Birthplace
Browning, Hardena	41	F		GA
Benjamin F.	22	M	Farmer	TN
Eliza J.	19	F		TN
Almeda A.	16	F		TN
Josephus	11	M		TX
Nancy A.	9	F		TX
Elizabeth	5	F		TX
Martha	3	F		TX
Loggins, Littleton	37	M	Farmer	TN
Elizabeth	36	F		TN
Susan P.	12	F		MS
Nancy P.	11	F		MS
William H.	3	M		MS
Mary Ann	8/12	F		TX
Dearman, Jonas	47	M	Farmer	KY
Susanna	45	F		VA
Melvina	20	F		TN
Parthena C.	15	F		AL
Telitha Emeline	12	F		AL
John Spartin	9	M		AL
Reice W.	7	M		AL
Hury Eveline	5	F		AL
Dearman, James R.	22	M		TN
Martha L.	22	F		AL
Sloan, Thomas E.	27	M	Farmer	TN
Mary J.	24	F		TN
Alex.	5	M		AR
Eliza M.	3	F		TX
Archibald M.	33	M	Farmer & Saddler	TN
Boid, Robert D.	14	M		MO
Mary L.	13	F		MO
Eliza	12	F		MO
Kelly, Reuben	33	M	Farmer	TN
Louisa A.	28	F		TN
Cassanda E.	4	F		TN
John A.	3	M		TN
George Thomas	1	M		TN
Meck, Jacob, Sr.	85	M	Farmer	??
Jacob, Jr.	27	M	Farmer	TN
Sally	23	F		TN
Meck, Washington	43	M	Farmer	TN
Elizabeth	40	F		NC
Sarah	15	F		AR
Nancy	12	F		AR
Enoch	9	M		AR
Marian	6	M		AR
Blevins, Ormsteadt	39	M	Farmer	TN
Delila	33	F		AL
Missouri	13	F		MO
Monroe	12	M		MO
Martin	10	M		MO
Wade H.	8	M		AR
Meck, Wesley	36	M	Farmer	TN
Nancy	23	F		TN
Polly	6	F		AR
Elizabeth	4	F		TX
Mahilda	1/12	F		TX
Meck, Polly	36	F		TN
Elizabeth	13	F		AR
Jacob	11	M		AR
Sarah	8	F		AR
Roda	5	F		AR
Perlina	1	F		AR
Donighee, Thomas R.	28	M	Farmer	MO
Nancy J.	22	F		TN
Meck, Lorenz D.	37	M	Farmer	TN
Roda	36	F		KY
Sarah	13	F		AR
Elizabeth	9	F		AR
Jacob	6	M		AR
Roda	4	F		TX
Hammons, John J.	48	M	Farmer	KY
Nancy M.	41	F		TN
Rachael M.	19	F		AR
Mary R. T.	16	F		AR
Isaac M.	14	M		TX
Amanda P.	10	F		TX
John C.	8	M		TX
Melinda	3	F		TX
Burrow, T. J.	62	M	Farmer	NC
Nameless Boy	14	M		TN
Zachariah	12	M		TN
Runion, James	52	M	Laborer	NC
Bidwell, Christopher	32	M	Wagon Maker	TN
Elizabeth	31	F		KY
Missouri C.	11	F		MO
Barbara	8	F		MO
Nancy	4	F		MO
Sarah F.	21	F		MO
Cole, William T.	34	M	Farmer	MO
Martha J.	21	F		TN
Andrew J.	8	M		MO
William Stephen	5/12	M		TX
Burrow, Elizabeth	19	F		TN
Allina J. E.	6	F		MO
Brittain, Joseph	34	M	Farmer	(E)TN
Marthena	32	F		NC
Louisa J.	12	F		IL
David L.	10	M		IL
James M.	9	M		MO
Nancy M.	7	F		IL
Joseph B.	4	M		MO
Benjamin M.	1	M		TX
Cowen, Benjamin L.	12	M		IL
Blevins, Jackson	35	M	Farmer	TN
Susan	31	F		AL
William R.	12	M		AR
Squire E.	10	M		AR
Armsteadt	7	M		AR
Sally	4	F		AR
James M.	2	M		TX
Parris, William	34	M	Farmer	TN
Mary	24	F		IN
Louisa	9	F		IN
Amanda	7	F		TX
Delila	4	F		TX
Nathaniel	2	M		TX
Fletcher, William	61	M		VA
Anderson, Elijah	48	M	Farmer	SC
Ruth	44	F		TN
John P.	18	M	Farmer	MO
McNulty, Margaret	24	F	Widow	AL
Richard E.	2	M		TX
Carroll, Nathaniel	50	M	Farmer & Waggoner	SC
Susanna	41	F		MS
Elias J.	21	M	Farmer	LA
Joseph W.	17	M	Farmer	TN
Harriet	15	F		LA
Eliza J.	13	F		TX
Samuel	9	M		TX
Mary	7	F		TX
Ammons, Jesse	35	M	Farmer	NC
Carroll, Joseph	46	M	Farmer	SC
Nathaniel H.	7	M		TN
John W.	5	M		TX
Samuel	4	M		TN
Carroll, Samuel, Sr.	36	M	None	SC
Anderson, John	60	M	Farmer	(E)TN
Williams, David	50	M	Farmer	NY
Laura A.	22	F		IL
Jones, Thomas	45	M	Farmer	MS
Delila	25	F		TN
William J.	5	M		AR
Levise E.	2	F		TX

NAVERRO COUNTY, TEXAS

Name	Age	Sex	Occupation	Birthplace
Cadwell, John W.	27	M	Farmer	TN
Aletha Ann	19	F		OH
Sarah E.	1	F		TX
Jeffers, J. P.	22	M	Farmer	OH
Levina	22	F		TN
Matilda	8/12	F		TX
Donighee, William G.	33	M	Farmer	IN
Mary A.	34	F		TN
John J.	8	M		MO
Hugh M.	4	M		TX
William	1	M		TX
Caudle, John	22	M	Laborer	TN
McDonald, John P.	20	M	Laborer	AL
Jones, Reuben	50	M	Farmer	GA
Ruth M.	44	F		SC
McFadden, Thomas L.	10	M		TN
Humphrey, Owen	49	M	Farmer	KY
Jane	45	F		KY
Benjamin F.	21	M	Farmer	TN
John J.	18	M	Farmer	AR
William K.	13	M		LA
David N.	11	M		AR
Francis M.	9	M		AR
Owen P.	5	M		TX
Jones, James C.	35	M	Farmer	TN
Lucinda	20	F		TN
Martha Jane	9	F		AR
Mary Ann	7	F		AR
Joanna E.	4	F		TX
James L.	1	M		TX
Hilburn, John	49	M	Farmer	SC
Nancy	45	F		VA
John	25	M	Farmer	TN
James C.	23	M	Farmer	TN
Samuel R.	18	M	Farmer	TN
Robert L.	14	M		GA
Rebecca M.	12	F		GA
Dealtha	11	F		GA
Seburn W.	9	M		GA
Edward A.	7	M		GA
Perry V.	6	M		MO
Martha E.	2	F		TX
Nathaniel	9/12	M		TX
Mitchell, David R.	53	M	Farmer & Surveyor	NC
William Y. H.	18	M	Farmer	TN
McCracken, William H.	23	M	Farmer	TN
Pillow, William B.	49	M	Farmer	TN
John	24	M	Farmer	TN
H.	19	M	Farmer	TN
Johnson, James A.	34	M	Farmer	TN
Nancy	24	F		AL
Rebecca	12	F		MS
S. P.	10	M		MS
Elizabeth	8	F		AR
Elijah	6	M		AR
Moses H. (Twin)	3	M		TX
R. F. (Twin)	3	M		TX
James A.	1	M		TX
Johnson, Moses	65	M	Farmer	TN
Younger, Alexander	63	M	Farmer	NC
Jane M.	52	F		KY
Robert A.	20	M	Farmer	TN
Thomas H.	12	M		MO
Allen, Margaret E.	22	F		TN
John A.	5	M		MO
Sterlin B.	3	M		MO
Lansford, J. R.	32	M	Trader	NC
Sally	19	F		TN
Elizabeth	4	F		TX
Hyram	2	M		TX
Tinery, Thomas J.	34	M	Farmer	TN
Nancy	26	F		MS
Golston, James M.	27	M	Farmer	TN
Mary A.	22	F		TN
Wiley J.	1	M		TX
Howard, William	27	M	Farmer	MO
Lucinda	23	F		MO
Francis M.	4	M		TX
George	1	M		TX
Lee, Abner	47	M	Mechanic	TN
Crabtree, William	27	M	Black Smith	TN
Mary	25	F		MO
Naoma	6	F		MO
William D.	3	M		TX
John	1	M		TX
Pace, William	50	M	Farmer	TN
Nancy	41	F		TN
Martha J.	20	F		TN
Hugh B.	19	M	Farmer	TN
Elizabeth P.	17	F		TN
William R.	16	M		TN
Elijah A.	13	M		AR
Cintha Ann	10	F		AR
Henning A.	8	M		AR
Gideon J.	5	M		AR
Mary A.	3	F		AR
Joel H.	5/12	M		TX
Newby, Jonathan	47	M	Farmer	TN
Dorothea	45	F		TN
John H.	18	M	Farmer	MO
Jeremiah	12	M		MO
Louisa	9	F		MO
Isabella	7	F		MO
Swinney, Hannah M.	26	M		TN
William R.	9	M		MO
Mary L.	6	F		MO
Jeremiah	1	M		TX
Biles, Daniel	55	M	Farmer	KY
Sarah	46	F		TN
George W.	14	M		MO
William M.	12	M		MO
Martin V.	10	M		MO
Dawson, Brittain	30	M	Farmer	FL
Susanna	20	F		TN
Nancy	1/12	F		TX
Sarah	9	F		TX
Henry	6	M		TX
Elizabeth	4	M		TX
George, Perlia J.	23	M	Farmer	IN
Nancy E.	20	F		TN
McClelland, John J.	26	M	Farmer	TN
Susan J.	21	F		AL
William J.	1/12	M		TX
January, Benjamin	31	M	Tailor	(E)TN
Sarah	19	F		MO
John	5	M		TX
Marcus D. L.	3	M		TX
William	1	M		TX
Meck, Simeon	33	M	Farmer	TN
Laura A.	24	F		AL
William	10	M		AR
Jacob	8	M		AR
John S.	6	M		AR
Mary Ann	5	F		AR
James M.	3	M		TX
Jackson, Elizabeth	18	F		MO
Wright, Samuel	34	M	Farmer	TN
Prudence	34	F		TN
Robert J.	13	M		TN
Joseph S.	11	M		TN
Newton M.	8	M		TN
Samuel F.	7	M		TN
Wilkinson B.	5	M		TN
John L.	4	M		TN
M. C. J.	7/12	F		TX

NAVERRO COUNTY, TEXAS

Name	Age	Sex	Occupation	Birthplace
Roberts, Evans	43	M	Farmer	TN
Susanna	43	F		TN
Barbara M.	16	F		IL
Lydia M.	14	F		IL
Evans S.	12	M		IL
Mary	10	F		IL
Martha P.	4	F		IL
Williams, Fred W.	29	M	Farmer	TN
Mahaley	33	F		IN
John David	8	M		MO
Mary E.	6	F		MO
Nancy E.	4	F		TX
Thomas Jacob	2	M		TX
Sarah	7/12	F		TX
Onstatt, David	46	M	Farmer	NC
Elizabeth	34	F		TN
Leroy	17	M	Farmer	MO
William R.	15	M	Farmer	MO
John W.	13	M		MO
Mary Jane	11	F		MO
Thomas B.	8	M		MO
James L.	7	M		MO
Joshua K. P.	5	M		MO
George W.	3	M		TX
Nancy Hood	6/12	F		TX
Onstatt, Joshua	48	M	Farmer	NC
Mary M. C. D.	31	F		TN
John A. H.	15	M	Farmer	AR
Francis M.	8	M		MO
Nancy J.	3	F		TX
Lee, Grisham	30	M	Farmer	TN
Mary J.	27	F		MO
Leanora	7	F		MO
George D.	5	M		MO
Abigail	2	F		TX
Naoma	1	F		TX
Richy, William	46	M	Farmer	SC
Mary	38	F		TN
Mary	7	F		TX
James B.	5	M		TX
Melissee P.	3/12	F		TX
Cannon, William P.	19	M		TN
Hutson, Dicy	11	F		TX
Richey, George W.	2	M		TX
Williams, Thomas	62	M	Farmer	NC
Nancy	53	F		NC
Thomas M.	27	M	M.E. Minister	TN
James V.	17	M		MO
Ann V.	14	F		MO
Carroll M.	12	M		MO
L. L.	25	M		TN
Mary Ann	22	F		IN
Muncy A. V.	4/12	F		TX
Hollis, H. T.	33	M	Farmer	IN
Elvira	29	F		TN
Andrew S.	10	M		TX
William M.	8	M		AR
James S.	7	M		TX
John H.	5	M		TX
Harry T.	1	M		TX
Mayfield, Benjamin	18	M	Farmer	TN
Burns, Mahaly	25	F		AL
James	5	M		AL
Sarah	3	M		AL
Daniel	1	M		TX
McKey, Sarah	55	F		TN
Foreman, Ranson	45	M	Farmer	NC
Darcus	40	F		NC
John A.	21	M		TN
Sarah	15	F		TN
Rebecca	12	F		TN
William W.	9	M		TX
Darcus	7	F		TX
Martha E.	10/12	F		TX
Duncan	6	M		TX
Foreman, Augustus L.	23	M		TN
Nancy S.	20	F		AL
Amanda F.	3	F		TX
Sutton, Jesse	43	M	Black Smith	TN
Frances	39	F		SC
Elizabeth	16	F		TN
James M.	14	M		TN
Abel	12	M		TN
Sarah J.	10	F		AR
George B.	7	M		TX
Frances	2	F		TX
Hudson, Dicy	10	F		TX
Lee, Ephraim	65	M	Farmer	(E)TN
Nancy B.	49	F		GA
Brook W.	24	M	Carpenter	TN
Barlow, Naoma F.	7	F		MO
Lee, L. K.	33	M	Farmer	TN
Fanny E.	30	F		MO
Hyron	10	M		MO
Palmyra	8	F		MO
Lenny	4	F		TX
Ward, William	51	M	Farmer	GA
Rebecca	47	F		GA
Ind.	25	F(?)	Farmer	AL
Mary E.	25	F		TN
Roberts, Benjamin	32	M	Farmer	TN
Anna	33	F		NC
Evan	10	M		IL
Clarissa J.	8	F		IL
Jacob R.	6	M		IL
James M.	1	M		TX
Carroll, Abner	57	M	Farmer	SC
Ann	57	F		SC
Sarah E.	20	F		SC
Abner M.	19	M		SC
Rachael L.	16	F		TN
Jesiah M.	14	M		TN
Mary Ann	12	F		TN
John W.	10	M		MS
Samuel P.	9	M		MS
James Y.	8	M		MS
Martha T.	3	F		MS
Pickett, William	50	M	Farmer	NC
Mary A.	25	F		TN
Leatha	20	F		TN
Louisa	18	F		AL
Permelia	16	F		TN
John	14	M		AL
Permina	12	F		AL
Mary Jane	10	F		TX
Wesley N.	7	M		TX
George W.	4	M		TX
M. Isabinda	1/12	F		TX
Dunn, Martha Ann	8	F		AR
Tutt, Marissa E.	4	F		TX
Cintha	1	F		TX
Measles, Moses	54	M	Farmer	NC
Mary	50	F		TN
George	18	M	Farmer	IN
Andrew J.	16	M	Farmer	IN
Moses M.	13	M		IN
Emeline E.	8	F		AR
Jones, Simeon	20	M	Farmer	IL
Martin	16	M	Farmer	IL
Jacob	13	M		IL
Anderson, William N.	44	M	Physician	TN
Susanna L.	29	F		IN
Sarah	9	F		??
Thomas J.	7	M		??
Jno. J.	5	M		TX
William N.	2	M		TX
Alex. H.	1	M		TX
Hargas, Larry	37	M	Farmer	NC
Mary M.	27	F		TN
James M.	8	M		TX

(continued)

NAVERRO COUNTY, TEXAS

Name	Age	Sex	Occupation	Birthplace
Hargas, Martha Jane	7	F		TX
Frances Ann	4	F		TX
Minerva Ann	1	F		TX
Ross, Samuel	26	M	Farmer	TN
Jane	20	F		TN
Mary Thankful	3	F		AR
Susan	7/12	F		TX
Williams, James J.	26	M	Farmer	NC
Eleanor	21	F		TN
Fred N.	6/12	M		TX
Williams, Fred L.	48	M	Farmer	NC
Sally J.	36	F		TN
McGeehe, Henry	30	M	Farmer & Trader	TN
Mary	24	F		TN
George	5	M		TX
James	3	M		TX
Thomas	1	M		TX
Peoples, Jehue	67	M	Tailor & Farmer	PA
Eleanor	63	F		PA
George	19	M		TN
Bowman, Samuel	44	M	Farmer	TN
Lucinda	20	F		AR
M. A. A.	6	F		TX
Orlena G. H.	3	F		TX
M. L. L.	2	F		TX
Clarissa S.	1	F		TX
White, David	50	M	Farmer	NC
Mary	48	F		NC
Sarah Jane	18	F		TN
Zachariah	8	M		TX
Russian, Caswell	21	M		TN
White, Martin	29	M	Farmer	TN
Missouri J.	21	F		MO
Celia E.	3	F		TX
Sarah Ann	8/12	F		TX
Frasin, Elizabeth	10	F		AR
Hill, George W.	35	M	Physician	TN
Catharine M.	34	F		TN
Slaughter, R. F.	12	M		TX
Mary J.	9	F		TN
L. M.	6	F		TX
Hill, B. J. C.	20	M	Farmer	TN
G. W.	19	M	Farmer	TN
Benjamin F.	10	M		TX
Pernetha	8	F		TX
Beeda	6	F		TX
Jno.	10	M		TX
Reed, John	19	M		NH
Hill, Rebecca	67	F		SC
Mather, R. H.	30	M	Farmer	TN
Harper, Benjamin	63	M	Carpenter	VA
Binum, N. G.	32	M	Far.-Stockraiser	TN
Richard G.	5	M		TX
Bohannon, Jno. P.	19	M	Farmer	IL
Eleanor	21	F		KY
Jno. H.	1	M		IL
Ramsey, Francis	48	F		GA
Martha	28	F		KY
Donnel, Elizabeth	14	F		KY
Mann, Jno.	24	M		TN
Shelton, Louis H.	26	M	Farmer	AL
Nancy Ann	22	F		TN
Elias D.	1	M		TX
Tankesley, William	46	M	Far.-Stockraiser	(E)TN
Elizabeth	45	F		NC
Edward W.	18	M		TN
Mary A.	13	F		TN
Jesse Ellis	12	M		LA
Clara	8	F		TX
Becky	4	F		TX

(continued)

Name	Age	Sex	Occupation	Birthplace
Tankesley, J. B. W.	2	M		TX
Howell, Walton B.	17	M	None	TN
Asa	54	M	Merchant	TN
Anderson, Q. N.	34	M		TN
Mary J.	25	F		TN
William T.	5	M		AR
John A.	3	M		TX
Sarah E.	1	F		TX
Thomas M.	21	M	Farmer	TN
Love, William M.	35	M	Land Speculator	TN
Jno. W.	19	M	Farmer	TN
Acuff, Calvin	32	M	Farmer	(E)TN
Rachael	34	F		KY
Laughlin, David	56	M		VA
Adams, Elvira	21	F		TN
Martha E.	11/12	F		TX
Bennett, Seburn J.	28	M	Farmer	AL
Mary Ann	24	F		TN
Gge. Etta	6	F		TX
Elizabeth	3	F		TX
Joseph	11/12	M		TX
Young, Richard	50	M	Farmer	VA
Henry, Conrad	17	M	Farmer	GER
Epps, H. B.	22	M		TN
Salina	21	F		AL
George	8/12	M		TX
Jackson, R. R.	28	M	Farmer	TN
A. C.	23	F		AL
Irena E.	2	F		TX
Martha A.	10/12	F		TX

NEWTON COUNTY, TEXAS

Name	Age	Sex	Occupation	Birthplace
Williams, Robert S.	48	M	Farmer	TN
Sarah	39	F		AR
Houston	19	M		LA
John	16	M		LA
Robert Young	14	M		LA
Louisia	12	F		LA
Wiley	10	M		TX
Mary	9	F		TX
Amanda	7	F		TX
Oliver Perry	5	M		TX
Langham, Thomas	64	M	Saddler	GA
Wilmouth	72	F		VA
W. D.	34	M		AL
Elias L.	22	M		TN
Amanda	17	F		MS
Marshall, Isaac	23	M		TN
Moore, John	42	M	Carpenter	SC
Sarah H.	40	F		NC
Christiana J.	14	F		TN
Mary Jane	13	F		TN
Clementine H.	11	F		TX
Robert H.	7	M		TN
Arabella	3	F		TX
Burk, John R.	54	M	Merchant	VA
Mary W.	50	F		VA
M. W.	23	M	Clerk	TN
Mary L.	20	F		TN
Williams, Ray	31	M	Trader	TN
Brandon, William M.	39	M	Farmer	TN
Susan	27	F		TX
John	12	M		TX
William	10	M		TX
James	8	M		TX
King	6	M		TX
Nathaniel G.	4	M		TX
Rebecca	1	F		TX
Harper, Epperson	41	M	Millwright	VA
Nancy	36	F		TN
Mary Jane	16	F		TN
Elizabeth	11	F		TX

(continued)

NEWTON COUNTY, TEXAS

Name	Age	Sex / Occupation	Birthplace
Harper, Hulda	6	F	TX
Wiley M.	14	M	TN
Ferdenand M.	13	M	TX
William	12	M	TX
Moore	9	M	TX
Manning, John	31	M Carpenter	GA
Mary Jane C.	24	F	TN
William R.	3	M	FL
Ruben E.	1	M	TX
Garlington, B.	59	M	SC
Cyntha A. C.	44	F	TN
D. R.	24	M	MS
L------	18	M	MS
Selindra	11	F	LA
Sarah E.	9	F	LA
Jourdin, Henry A.	50	M Farmer	AL
Lucy	38	F	OH
Love, Joseph A.	15	M	TN
Jourdin, Albert P. M.	3	M	LA
Simmons, Richard	50	M Farmer	SC
Susan R.	43	F	TN
Nancy	21	F	MS
William W.	17	M	TX
Pleasant	13	M	TX
Thomas, John W.	52	M Farmer	NC
Perlina	37	F	TN
Martha E.	19	F	MS
Maria	17	F	MS
Mary Ann	14	F	MS
Alexander	11	M	MS
John Smart	8	M	TX
Perlina Jane	6	F	TX
Samuel North	3	M	TX
McMahon, Isaac	46	M Farmer	KY
Francis	35	F	TN
Friend R.	13	M	TX
Mary Jane	11	F	TX
Woods, Seabourn	41	M Black Smith	GA
Nancy	35	F	TN
Marinda	12	F	MS
Callaway	10	M	MS
Waltin	8	M	TX
Rayford	6	M	TX
Ransom	4	M	TX
Samuel	2	M	TX
Woods, Hiram	18	M Laborer	TN
Charlotte	20	F	LA
Marshall, Mathew	70	M Farmer	GA
Irvine, Jas. S.	31	M Farmer	TN
Nancy	26	F	LA
Margarett J.	9	F	TX
James P.	7	M	TX
William F.	5	M	TX
Nancy E. V.	3	F	TX
Rutledge, John	60	M Carpenter	TN
Sarah K.	45	F	SC
William	21	M	MS
John	19	M	MS
Ivestor	16	M	MS
Eliza Jane	12	F	MS
Edith Ann	9	F	MS
Oliver C.	8	M	MS
Cassell, Samuel	25	M Laborer	TN
Matilda	22	F	AL
Levi	8	M	AL
William	5	M	AL
Thomas Newton	6/12	M	TX
Irvine, James T. P.	35	M Clergyman, M.E.S.	TN
Susan Y.	33	F	TN
Feby Eliza	16	F	TX
Samuel D.	6	M	TX
Benjamin	3	M	TX

Name	Age	Sex / Occupation	Birthplace
Marshall, John	33	M Farmer	TN
M. Caroline	23	F	AL
Polly Ann	15	F	MS
Alson	14	M	MS
Curtis	12	M	MS
Rheuben	8	M	MS
James	4	M	AR
Daniel	2	M	TX
Steele, William A.	32	M Merchant	TN
Burks, Randolph C.	30	M Farmer	MS
Sarah	28	F	AL
Leroy	7	M	MS
Randolph A.	4	M	MS
Samuel	2	M	MS
Wardine, Jesse	39	M Laborer	TN
Moyer, Peter D.	62	M Cooper	NY
Elizabeth	60	F	TN
Cooper, W. C.	37	M Farmer	LA
Rebecca	39	F	TN
Talitha C.	11	F	MS
William Carmon	6	M	TX
Frances	4	F	TX
Martha Jane	2	F	TX
McMahon, James	32	M	LA
Sarah	25	F	TN
Mary Matilda	8	F	TX
Friend Wilson	6	M	TX
Margaret Leona	5	F	TX
William Stephenson	3	M	TX
Nancy Irvine	1	F	TX
Scott, James M.	38	M Farmer	TN
Hester Ann	31	F	AR
Mary Jane	12	F	TX
James B.	10	M	TX
Henry Carroll	8	M	TX
Margarett	6	F	TX
Felix	3	M	TX
Wortham, Sidney P.	32	M Farmer	TN
Mary	28	F	TN
Nancy	12	F	TX
Martha	10	F	TX
Sally	9	F	TX
Leonora	7	F	TX
Susan	5	F	TX
Washington	3	M	TX
Elizabeth	1	F	TX
Slaughter, Robert	60	M Farmer	NC
Easter	42	F	TN
William F.	23	M Laborer	MS
John J.	16	M Laborer	LA
James W.	14	M	LA
Amanda	8	M	TX
Melissa Jane	6	F	TX
Francis Marion	4	M	LA
Easter Delila	2	F	TX
Wright, Solomon	28	M Stockraiser	LA
Roena	23	F	TN
Frances Elizabeth	2	F	TX

NUECES COUNTY, TEXAS

Corpus Christie

Name	Age	Sex / Occupation	Birthplace
Basken, J. N.	27	M Farmer	AL
J. W. S.	19	M Farmer	AL
Tatum, Thomas T.	45	M Carpenter	TN
Bias, Jane	40	F (Black)	TN
Rodgers, Elizabeth	55	F	VA
L. M.	27	F None	AL
Denton, Louisa J.	24	F	AL
Emaline	16	F	AL
Reeves, Frances J.	8	F	TN
Denton, Elizabeth	4	F	LA

(continued)

NUECES COUNTY, TEXAS

Name	Age/Sex	Occupation	Birthplace
Denton, Patterson C.	1 M		TX
Berry, H. W.	32 M	Mason	OH
Elizabeth	17 F		AL
Robert	1 M		TN
Hulet, Laura	12 F		IL
Leech, A. W.	33 M	Cabt.	CT
Cox, J.	30 M	Laborer	NY
Haynes, Ephraym	30 M	None	PA
Mary Ann	24 F		AL
Hulet, Mary	14 F		TN
Smith, Francis	-- M	Soldier, U.S.Army	SCO
Low, John	-- M	Soldier, U.S.Army	CAN
McDaniel, George	-- M	Soldier, U.S.Army	IRE
Aikens, Charles E.	-- M	Soldier, U.S.Army	VT
Toul, James	-- M	Soldier, U.S.Army	AL
Ikard, John	-- M	Soldier, U.S.Army	TN
Graham, John	-- M	Soldier, U.S.Army	TN
Elkins, John	-- M	Soldier, U.S.Army	EUR
Henly, Patrick	-- M	Soldier, U.S.Army	IRE
Cunningham, Joseph	-- M	Soldier, U.S.Army	KY
Oliver, Dew	-- M	Soldier, U.S.Army	FL
O'Donald, J.	-- M	Soldier, U.S.Army	IRE

PANOLA COUNTY, TEXAS

Name	Age/Sex	Occupation	Birthplace
Weger, Thomas	44 M	Farmer	TN
Catharine	37 F		TN
William	18 M	Farmer	LA
Elizabeth	15 F		LA
John	13 M		LA
Alizae	12 F		LA
Mary	8 F		LA
Henry	1 M		TX
Nichols, A. T.	34 M	Farmer	TN
Susan	30 F		TN
Mary	16 F		TN
Rebecca	14 M(F)		MS
Tennessee	11 F		TN
William	7 M		TN
Virginia	4 F		TX
John	2 M		TX
Smith, H. H.	45 M	Farmer	SC
Elizabeth	45 F		TN
Mary	22 F		TN
Susan	14 F		TX
William	11 M		TX
John	9 M		TX
Emaly	6 F		TX
James	2 M		TX
Carter, Martin	21 M	Farmer	TN
Mary	45 F		??
Wade	17 M	Farmer	TN
Elizabeth	10 F		TX
Coleman, Wyatt	39 M	Black Smith	TN
Susan D.	41 F		TN
Jas. N.	18 M	Farmer	TN
Henry F.	16 M	Farmer	TN
Wilian	13 F		TN
Wyatt A.	8 M		TN
George M. D.	6 M		TN
William C.	1 M		TX
Casaty, John	38 M	Tanner	VA
Adaline M. J.	27 F		VA
Francis M.	15 M	Farmer	TN
Langford N.	14 M		TN
William S.	6 M		TX
Mary E.	4 F		TX
Nail, Peter M.	20 M	Farmer	??
Miller, Mark	40 M	Trader	TN
Erwin, Isaac N.	32 M	Farmer	TN
Pheby R.	28 F		TN
Abigal A.	9 F		TN

(continued)

Name	Age/Sex	Occupation	Birthplace
Erwin, Martha E.	5 F		TN
James K.	1 M		TX
Scott, M. P.	45 M	Farmer	KY
Elizabeth C.	34 F		TN
Jas. J.	17 M	Farmer	TN
Cyntha J.	16 F		TN
Madison F. A.	13 M		MS
Felix W.	10 M		MS
Prudence J.	8 F		MS
Marian	7 F		MS
Elizabeth L.	6 F		MS
Frances J.	2 F		TX
Jno. M.	2/12 M		TX
Pelham, Joseph M.	35 M	Farmer	GA
Mary	40 F		VA
Jeter, Jas. A.	21 M	School Teacher	VA
Lewis, Jas.	16 M	Farmer	TN
Pelham, Elisha	65 M	Mechanic	SC
Horn, M. L.	22 M	Farmer	AL
Boid, Thomas G.	40 M	Black Smith	TN
Ann E.	19 F		LA
Mary M.	3 F		TX
Jno. T.	6/12 M		TX
Waters, Martha M.	27 F		TN
Mary L. M.	10 F		AR
James J.	8 M		AR
Thomas R.	5 M		AR
Elizabeth R.	4 F		TX
Nancy C.	3 F		LA
Parry, Samuel M.	53 M	Farmer	VA
Eliza	41 F		GA
Samuel	18 M	Farmer	AL
Catharine	16 F		AL
Roseannah	14 F		AL
Jno. B.	13 M		AL
David	11 M		LA
Martha	9 F		TN
Thompson, Jno.	46 M	Farmer	TN
Eliza	32 F		TN
Catharine	15 F		TN
Samuel	13 M		TN
John	9 M		TX
Coffee	7 M		TX
Mary	5 F		TX
Sarah	2 F		TX
Dodson, Elijah	25 M		GA
Jerman, Robert	45 M	Farmer	NC
Eliza	41 F		SC
John	13 M		AL
Robert	9 M		AL
Caledona	7 F		AL
William	2 M		AL
Woods, Benjamin	22 M		TN
White, David	37 M	Farmer	TN
Martha	29 F		TN
John	8 M		TN
Paul	6 M		TN
Mary J.	4 F		TN
James H.	1 M		TX
Tutor, Jno.	36 M	Laborer	TX
Shote, Nicholas	22 M	Laborer	TN
Deal, N. ?.	27 M	Farmer	TN
Mary	19 F		TN
Cenia A. E. M.	1 F		TX
John A.	4/12 M		TX
Row, James	39 M	Tanner	NC
Mira	34 F		TN
Burnard	11 M		TX
Nancy	9 F		TX
Emaly	8 F		TX
Sarah	6 F		TX
James	4 M		--
Charles	1 M		--
Seton, Thomas	30 M	Farmer	NC
Paul, Jas.	35 M	Carpenter	??

PANOLA COUNTY, TEXAS

Name	Age	Sex	Occupation	Born
Watson, William	42	M	Farmer	KY
Nancy B.	35	F		TN
Henry	9	M		TX
Catharine	7	F		TX
John L.	5	M		TX
William W.	4	M		TX
James	2	M		TX
No Name	1	M		TX
Soap, T. M.	22	M	Farmer	TN
Elizabeth	49	F		TN
Mary	19	F		TN
Mahaly	16	F		TN
Joseph	18	M	Farmer	TN
James	15	M	Farmer	TN
Permentra	12	M		TN
Armstrong, Jas. B.	29	M	Farmer	TN
Aletha E.	22	F		TN
Sarah E.	2	F		TX
Mary A.	5/12	F		TX
Viola E.	3	F		MS
Renfro, R. W.	27	M	Farmer	TN
Elizabeth E.	24	F		MO
Mary	5	F		AR
Witherspoon, Joseph	35	M	Farmer	TN
Emily H.	24	F		TN
John	6	M		TN
Emily	2/12	F		TX
Garner, William	22	M	Farmer	AL
Renfro, J. N.	20	M	Farmer	TN
Wender, Peter	23	M	Farmer	TN
Kerren	23	F		TN
Christoper	1	M		TX
Herren, William	25	M	Farmer	TN
Mary	20	F		TN
Lemuel	3	M		TX
James	8/12	M		TX
Wender, Christopher	62	M	Black Smith	NC
Gennett	65	F		TN
Elizabeth	25	F		TN
John	16	M	Farmer	TN
Witherspoon, Jas.	40	M	Farmer	NC
America	32	F		TN
Mary	11	F		MS
Martha	9	F		MS
James	7	M		MS
Sarah	5	F		MS
Louisa	4	F		TN
George	1	M		TN
Witherspoon, Alex.	30	M	Farmer	TN
Kissiah	25	F		AL
John	6	M		TX
Anis	2	F		TX
James	1	M		TX
Sexton, Jack	18	M	Farmer	TN
Mise, Jesse	32	M	Farmer	TN
Martha	21	F		??
Lewis	5	M		LA
Benjamin	4	M		LA
William	2	M		LA
Mise, Jesse, Sr.	71	M	Methodist Minster	VA
White, William	35	M	Carpenter	NC
Catharine	25	F		AL
Frances	6	F		MS
Sarah	4	F		MS
Amla	2	F		TX
Moore, David	21	M	Farmer	TN
Graham, Jno. H.	26	M	Farmer	TN
Winey A.	23	F		NC
Mary	1	F		TX
Long, Andrew	30	M	School Teacher	TN
Alabama C.	17	F		AL

Name	Age	Sex	Occupation	Born
Finley, Jno.	49	M	farmer	TN
Elizabeth	43	F		MS
Joseph	21	M	Farmer	TX
Peter	18	M	Farmer	TX
Matilda	16	F		TX
Sarah	13	F		TX
William	10	M		TX
David	8	M		TX
John	5	M		TX
James	2	M		TX
Wallace, Allice	37	M	Farmer	TN
Mary	34	F		SC
Jno. M.	11	M		AL
Elender T.	9	F		AL
Mary	6	F		AL
Narcissa	4	F		AL
Mary	2	F		MS
Smith, Mitchel	42	M	C.P. Preacher	KY
Martha	36	F		TN
Tennessee	15	M	Farmer	AL
Edwin	14	M		AL
Fedora	13	F		AL
Eliza	12	F		TX
Caroline	11	F		TX
Balzora	10	F		TX
Mary	7	F		TX
Thomas	5	M		TX
James	1	M		TX
Dobbins, William	22	M	Farmer	AL
Soap, Abner F.	26	M	Farmer	TN
Elizabeth	28	F		TN
James	9	M		MS
Thomas	7	M		MS
Andrew	2	M		MS
Ramsey, William	66	M	Farmer	NC
Elizabeth	63	F		NC
Arabella	39	F		KY
Mary J.	21	F		TN
F. F.	20	M	Farmer	TN
Neham, Basel	33	M	Mechanic	TN
Elizabeth	36	F		KY
William L.	11	M		TN
Elizabeth T.	9	F		TN
Martha C.	8	F		TN
Mary E.	6	F		TN
James	5	M		TN
Thomas J.	3	M		TX
John	11/12	M		TX
Teppet, Catharine	58	F		NC
William	35	M	Farmer	TN
Andrew	34	M	Tax Collector	TN
Julia A.	23	F		TN
Susan	22	F		TN
Russell, Emaly	40	F		TN
Martha	11	F		TX
Teppet, Robert	38	M	Mechanic	TN
Good, B. L.	24	M	Mechanic	AL
Nancy J.	21	F		TN
Mary S.	11/12	F		LA
Hall, T. A.	38	M	Mechanic	VA
Hill, B. H.	26	M	Mechanic	NC
Philip, Jackson	26	M	Laborer	NC
Whittenton, Gadie	25	M	Clerk	AL
White, Alex.	21	M	Ostler	KY
Poag, William R.	28	M	Attorney at Law	SC
Jackson, James M.	20	M	Attorney at Law	TN
Crofford, Cyntha M.	35	F		TN
Virginia	12	F		TN
Stillwell, Milton	30	M	Farmer	GA
Martha	27	F		TN
Sarah	5	F		TX
Catharine	3	F		TX
Story, James	45	M	Farmer	??
Tenny	34	F		TN
Joseph	13	M		LA
Matilda	12	F		TX
William	8	M		TX

(continued)

PANOLA COUNTY, TEXAS

Name	Age	Sex	Occupation	Birthplace
Story, Robert	4	M		TX
Felina	2	F		TX
Fleming, Robert	29	M	Farmer	TN
Mary A.	27	F		MS
Nancy A.	11	F		LA
Thomas C.	9	M		TX
William B.	7	M		TX
James H.	1	M		TX
Akin, Newton E.	39	M	Farmer	TN
Mary	35	F		TN
Malissa	12	F		TN
John	10	M		TN
Tilford	6	M		TN
Mosura	3	F		TN
Frelen, James	34	M	Farmer	TN
Martha	18	F		TN
Elizabeth	8	F		TN
Parrish, William G.	59	M	Farmer	NC
Eliza	49	F		VA
Washington	25	M	Farmer	TN
James	23	M	Farmer	TN
Mary Jane	21	F		TN
William	18	M	Farmer	TN
Dinah	13	F		TN
Thomas	11	M		TX
Casanda	6	F		TX
Pamelia	4	F		TX
Jordan, Augustine	23	M	Farmer	??
Mary	17	F		GA
James	1	M		GA
Cook, Milton	38	M	Farmer	SC
Sofia	35	F		TN
Sofrona	2	F		TX
Mary	6/12	F		TX
Julia	15	F		TN
Ja.	9	M		TN
Kyle, Robert	44	M	Farmer	NC
Elizabeth	35	F		TN
Carmella	13	F		MS
Nancy	9	F		TX
Mary	7	F		TX
James	5	M		TX
John	2	M		TX
Barthena	2/12	F		TX
Fleming, Jas. M.	31	M	Farmer	TN
Evaline B.	27	F		TN
Thomas J.	8	M		MS
Sarah A.	5	F		TX
John	3/12	M		TX
Bartley, Richard	23	M	Farmer	TN
Armstrong, Jno. B.	25	M	Farmer	TN
Steel, William	20	M	Farmer	??
Crofford, Mary	50	F	Widow	TN
Samuel	20	M	Farmer	TN
Thomas	17	M	Farmer	TN
Stanler, Jas. M.	33	M		MS
Mary	20	F		TN
Philips, N. B.	29	M	Farmer	TN
Pamelia	22	F		AL
William	3	M		TX
Albert	1	M		TX
Nichols, Jacob	31	M	Farmer	TN
Philips, A. G.	23	M	Farmer	TN
Margaret	5	F		TN
Thomas	4	M		TN
Jesse	1	M		TX
Nichols, Newton	26	M	Farmer	MS
Sarah	18	F		TN
Nichols, J.	52	F	Widow	??
James	16	M	Farmer	TN
Westley	14	M		TN
English, William	28	M	Farmer	TN
Eliza	25	F		TN
Sarah	8	F		TX
Thomas	6	M		TX
Nathan	5	M		TX
James	1	M		TX
White, Joel	52	M	Farmer	NC
Sarah	48	F		KY
Manervy	17	F		TN
Richmond	14	M		MS
Margaret	12	F		MS
Milton	10	M		TX
Marthy	3	F		TX
Sant, Franklin	27	M	Farmer	AL
Martha	20	F		SC
Elisha	54	M		SC
Jane	48	F		SC
Jane	22	F		TN
John	20	M	Farmer	TN
Martha	18	F		TN
Nancy	14	F		AL
Taylor, William H.	31	M	Farmer	AL
Emaly	27	F		TN
Emaline A.	5	F		TX
Pamelia J.	4	F		TX
John A.	2	M		TX
George M.	1	M		TX
Person, William T.	26	M	Farmer	TN
Mary A.	26	F		AL
Tabitha E.	2	F		TX
Pamela S.	1/12	F		TX
Adams, Sarah	12	F		LA
Taylor, William	57	M	Farmer	SC
Pamela	52	F		GA
Hugh	28	M		AL
Elizabeth	19	F		AL
Trypence(?)	15	F		TX
Key, Alexander	15	M	Farmer	TX
Strange, L. J.	1	F		TX
Earley, Richard	19	M	Farmer	TN
McDonel, Peter	22	M	Farmer	??
Nail, George	29	M		TN
Mary	23	F		TX
Martha	7	F		TX
Margaret	5	F		TX
William	3	M		TX
Abner	6/12	M		TX
Nelson, William F.	30	M	Farmer	NY
Louisa	20	F		TN
Mary	2	F		TX
Joseph	11/12	M		TX
Shepherd, Hugh	47	M		NC
Elizabeth	38	F		TN
Frances	12	F		TX
Panola	9	F		TX
Isaac	6	M		TX
Samuel	3	M		TX
Richmond	9/12	M		TX
Shepherd, William J.	20	M	Farmer	TN
Eliza	17	F		TN
Samuel	5/12	M		TX
Reed, Elizabeth	71	F	Widow	SC
Lafayette	16	M	Farmer	TN
Lem	14	M		TX
James	13	M		TX
Kessiah	10	F		TX
Morris, Jno. M.	32	M	Farmer	SC
Frances	43	F		TN
Moores, John	36	M	Farmer	TN
Frances	29	F		TN
Mary	11	F		TX
Isaac	9	M		TX
Elizabeth	7	F		TX

(continued)

Name	Age	Sex	Occupation	Birthplace
Moores, Elisha	4	M		TX
Nancy	6/12	F		TX
Colyear, Isham	27	M	Farmer	??
Almona	27	F		AL
Jonathan	8	M		TN
John	6	M		AL
Martha	4	F		LA
Lucinda	3	F		TX
Thomas G.	1	M		TX
Alison, John	59	M	Farmer	NC
Nancy	52	F		NC
Robert L.	18	M	Farmer	TN
Samuel G.	15	M	Farmer	TN
Teppet, Mary G.	24	F		TN
Alison, Thomas G.	33	M	Farmer	TN
Mary E.	17	F		GA
Jos. T.	4	M		TX
Pike, Samuel	46	M	Farmer	NC
Rhoda	42	F		TN
Isaac	21	M		TN
Caroline	13	F		TN
Hannah	10	F		TN
William	8	M		TN
Henry	6	M		TN
Frances	4	F		TX
Samuel	2	M		TX
Gentry, Joseph P.	28	M	Farmer	TN
Sarah	23	F		TN
Sarah J.	1	F		TX
Nail, Pat	34	M	Mechanic	TN
Eliza C.	24	F		TN
Mary	8	F		TN
James	7	M		TN
Jerome	1	M		TX
Nail, Daniel	24	M	Mechanic	VA
McCarrell, Jno.	60	M	Mechanic	VA
Nail, Salena	21	F		VA
Halcom, Ervin	35	M	Mechanic	SC
Harris, Spencer	27	M	Farmer	NC
Sarah	25	F		TN
Francis	7	M		TN
Eveline	6	F		TN
John	3	M		TN
Prudence	1	F		TX
Harris, Alford B.	26	M	Farmer	NC
Nancy	23	F		TN
Mary	5	F		TN
Walter	2	M		TN
Allred, Stephen, Jr.	26	M	Farmer	NC
Mary	22	F		TN
James	2	M		TX
Jane	7/12	F		TX
Allred, Alford	30	M	Farmer	NC
Margaret	26	F		TN
Martha	8	F		TN
Susan	6	F		TN
Thomas	4	M		TX
Sarah	2	F		TX
William	11/12	M		TX
Robinson, J. H.	31	M	Mechanic	TN
Edia	31	F		IN
Lovenia	13	F		TN
Hester Ann	10	F		TN
Isaac	9	M		TN
James	8	M		TN
William	6	M		TN
John	4	M		TN
Amon	2	M		TN
Joel	1	M		TX
Williams, Purvine	46	M	Farmer	NC
Matilda	36	F		TN
Jas. P.	19	M	Farmer	TN
(continued)				
Williams, Robert P.	16	M	Farmer	TN
Eliza J.	15	F		TN
Sarah	14	F		TN
Benjamin	13	M		TN
Elizabeth	7	F		TX
Manerva	5	F		TX
Nancy	4	F		TX
John	3	M		TX
Susan	1	F		TX
P. W.	1/12	M		TX
Williams, William M.	21	M	Farmer	TN
Mary Ann	22	F		TN
J(G)entry, Samuel	33	M		TN
Jemima	35	F		TN
Sarah E.	10	F		AL
William	9	M		AL
Mary Ann	7	F		AL
Hugh	6	M		AL
Thomas J.	5	M		AL
Nancy	2	F		TX
Swit, Edward	35	M	Farmer	NC
Elizabeth A.	24	F		TN
George W.	10/12	M		TX
Thompson, Lorrance	24	M	Farmer	AL
Wyatt, Wash	25	M	Farmer	TN
Nancy	22	F		??
William	5	M		TX
Sarah	1	F		TX
Garison, Mitchel	45	M	Farmer	TN
Elen	33	F		TN
James	16	M	Farmer	OH
Mary	13	F		MS
Eliza	9	F		TX
Susan	7	F		TX
William	6	M		TX
John	5	M		TX
Elen Ann	3	F		TX
Emaly	2/12	F		TX
Amy	17	F		OH
Williams, George W.	41	M	Farmer	KY
Susan	31	F		TN
Mitchel G.	12	M		MS
Frazier, William	35	M	Farmer	TN
Harriet	36	F		SC
Elizabeth	7	F		TX
Nancy	6	F		TX
Charity	3	F		TX
Peterson, Cyntha	13	F		AL
James	11	M		LA
Hoskins, P. H.	29	M	Mechanic	TN
Julia Ann	25	F		TX
Malissa C.	4	F		TX
Emaly G.	1	F		TX
Magness, Caroline	19	F		TX
Jno. B.	2	M		TX
Barber, Christian	54	M	Farmer	NC
Elizabeth	45	F		GA
Julia Ann	23	F		TN
Abner	16	M		AL
Hannah	14	F		AL
Charles	9	M		TN
Eliza	6	F		TX
Scruggs, Charles	34	M	Farmer	VA
Elizabeth	28	F		TN
Lemuel	7	M		TX
Mary	5	F		TX
William	4	M		TX
Charles	1	M		TX
Goldin, H. H.	21	M	Farmer	AL
Sarah A.	18	F		TN
Cowen, Alfred	53	M	Farmer	KY
Ann	47	F		TN
Mary	24	F		TN
(continued)				

PANOLA COUNTY, TEXAS

Name	Age	Sex	Occupation	Birthplace
Cowen, William	20	M		TN
Martha	18	F		TN
Talitha	17	F		TN
Samuel	13	M		TN
Elizabeth	11	F		TN
Martha	9	F		TN
Malinda	7	F		TN
Francis	4	M		TN
Shackleford, George	26	M	Farmer	TN
Sarah	23	F		GA
Martha	6	F		AR
Carter	3	M		AR
Jonathan	10/12	M		TX
Henson, Elizabeth	39	F		NC
Eliza	10	F		AR
Jane	10	F		AR
Shackleford, Rogers	83	M	Farmer	KY
Jane	49	F		NC
Lutica	14	F		TN
Betsey	10	F		AR
Daniel	7	M		AR
Bratright, Lewis	40	M	Farmer	??
Adams, Joseph	32	M	Farmer	MA
Barbary	24	F		TN
Elizabeth	7	F		AR
Manda	5	F		AR
Sarah	4	F		AR
Persa	2	F		AR
William	11/12	M		AR
Henson, Terrell	38	M	Farmer	SC
Minerva	28	F		TN
Drucilla	4	F		TX
Joseph	2	M		TX
Sarah	1	F		TX
Wyatt, Sarah	40	F		TN
Henson, Jno.	30	M	Farmer	GA
Henry	27	M	Farmer	GA
Mary Ann	24	F		GA
Jas. W.	1	M		TX
Conner, Henderson	63	M	Farmer	NC
Wilson	27	M	Farmer	GA
Sarah	24	F		TN
Simmond, Margaret	30	F		NC
Samuel	10	M		TN
Charles Hamilton	9	M		TN
Sarah E.	3	F		TN
Conner, Peyton	26	M	Farmer	NC
Sarah	24	F		TN
Wyatt, William H.	23	M	Farmer	TN
Emaline	24	F		TN
Mary	11/12	F		TX
Barber, William H.	23	M	Farmer	TN
Wyatt, Robert	33	M	Farmer	TN
Larisa	29	F		AR
Alfred	12	M		TN
Eliza	7	F		TX
Betsey	4	F		TX
Elijah	2	M		TX
Martin, Peter C.	26	M	Farmer	NC
Abigal	23	F		TN
William H.	6	M		TX
Eliza J.	4	F		TX
Daniel B.	2	M		TX
John G.	4/12	M		TX
Martin, Daniel, Jr.	22	M	Farmer	TX
Cyntha	19	F		MS
Bradberry, Daniel R.	23	M	Farmer	TN
Metcalf, S. J.	45	M	Farmer	KY
Caroline	29	F		TN
James	18	M	Farmer	MS
Jasper	16	M	Farmer	MS
Stewart	14	M		MS

(continued)

Name	Age	Sex	Occupation	Birthplace
Metcalf, William	12	M		MS
Norris	10	M		MS
Leander	7	M		MS
Isaac	5	M		MS
Sarah	6	F		MS
Henry	4	M		TX
Mary	2	F		TX
Hough, James	38	M	Farmer	TN
Elizabeth	35	F		AR
Samuel	19	M	Farmer	AR
Polly	18	F		AR
Nelly	15	F		AR
Hannah	13	F		AR
Peter	7	M		AR
James	1	M		TX
Chapman, William G.	24	M	Farmer	TN
Mariah	23	F		KY
Edward	4	M		MS
Mary C.	1	F		TX
Hines, Sheard	45	M	Farmer	NC
Mary	22	F		TN
Sarah	5	F		TN
Jas.	4	M		TN
Robert	3	M		TX
Andrew	3/12	M		TX
Craig, Jonathan C.	42	M	Farmer	NC
Mary	22	F		TN
Sarah	5	F		TN
Jas.	4	M		TN
Robert	3	M		TX
Andrew	3/12	M		TX
Craig, Jonathan C.	42	M	Farmer	TN
Iba	43	F		NC
Elizabeth C.	18	F		TN
Iba	16	F		TN
Mary S.	13	F		TN
Jonathan B.	11	M		TN
Lora Ann	9	F		TN
Artelia	7	F		TN
William Z.	6/12	M		TX
Tisdale, Thomas H.	26	M	Farmer	AL
Roberts, George	36	M	Farmer	VA
Rosana	31	F		TN
Pheby	13	F		TN
Ingram, Jno.	22	M	Farmer	??
Atkerson, G. B.	27	M	Farmer	TN
Nancy N.	30	F		TN
George F.	8	M		TN
Jno.	6	M		TN
Richard A.	4	M		TN
William J.	2	M		TX
Maberry, Sarah	14	F		TN
Moore, Jacob	49	M	Farmer	TN
Lucy F.	24	F		TN
Louisa	5	F		MS
Ann	2	F		TX
Lewis, Edward	33	M	Farmer	TN
Elizabeth A.	30	F		VA
William H.	6	M		AL
Mary J.	4	F		TX
Lewis, Francis	26	M		TN
Clements, C. T.	36	M	Mechanic	VA
Lewis, Thomas	20	M	Farmer	AL
Darnell, Samuel B.	37	M	Farmer	KY
Elizabeth	31	F		TN
Mary	7	F		AR
Jno. W.	5	M		AR
William W.	4	M		AR
Elizabeth C.	1	F		AR
Holland, Devro D.	24	M	Farmer	TN
Eliza	22	F		TN
Joseph B.	1	M		TX
Wall, William	37	M	Farmer	VA

(continued)

PANOLA COUNTY, TEXAS

Name	Age	Sex	Occupation	Birthplace
Wall, Mary	50	F		MA
Armstrong, G. H.	19	M	Farmer	TN
Anderson, Jonathan	44	M	Sheriff	AL
Jno.	20	M	Farmer	AL
Samuel	15	M		AL
Josaphine	13	F		AL
Charlotte	11	F		AL
Clary J.	8	F		LA
Jane	3	F		TX
Mary M.	1	F		TX
Garison	23	M	Farmer	AL
Cherry, Joshua	27	M		AL
Sarah	22	F		AL
Jno. H.	3	M		TX
Charles R.	5/12	M		TX
Fite, Jno. W.	33	M	Farmer	TN
Elender	27	F		TN
Smith	7	M		TN
Lewis, Newton	35	M	Farmer	TN
Bythena	32	F		MS
Sprawls, Jane	80	F		NC
Smith, Augustus	22	M	Mechanic	MS
McNair, D.	28	M	Mechanic	??
McCartney, William W.	28	M	M.D.	TN
Manly, Jno. B.	49	M	Farmer	GA
Catharine	37	F		TN
Martha	19	F		MS
Sarah	11	F		LA
Moses	7	M		LA
Nancy	3	F		LA
Roselean B.	5/12	F		TX
Coats, Thomas	21	M	Farmer	TN
Verelia	16	F		MS
Boren, L. E.	30	M	Farmer	TN
Louisa	20	F		TN
Elizabeth	2	F		MS
Thomas	1	M		MS
James	1/12	M		TX
Anderson, Jonathan	50	M	Farmer	KY
Hannah	53	F		TN
Mahala	25	F		TX
Pink	22	M	Farmer	LA
Jas.	19	M	Farmer	TX
Arch	16	M	Farmer	TX
Elizabeth	14	F		TX
Eliza	12	F		TX
Bailey J.	9	M		TX
McLaughlin, Pat.	23	M	Laborer	IRE
Sprawls, Samuel	24	M	Laborer	MS
Herrin, Abner	31	M	Farmer	TN
Lucinda	22	F		AL
William	1	M		TX
Kessiah	70	F	Widow	??
Herrin, Louisa	37	F	Widow	TN
Mary C.	18	F		TN
James S.	12	M		TX
Sarah	10	F		TX
Browning, Jas. R.	26	M	School Teacher	TN
Smith, William	28	M	Black Smith	TN
Herrin, Grison	48	M	Farmer	GA
Martha	31	F		TN
Mary E.	10	F		TN
Ephraim	8	M		TN
Lemuel	5	M		TN
William	2	M		TX
Hamond, William S.	24	M	Farmer	TN
Margaret	16	F		TX
John	11/12	M		TX
Dorter, Ira	26	M	Farmer	VA
Mary Ann	24	F		VA
Mary E.	2	F		TN
William H.	11/12	M		TX

Name	Age	Sex	Occupation	Birthplace
Yarborough, Jas. J.	30	M	Black Smith	AL
Elizabeth	25	F		TN
William H.	3	M		TN
George H.	9/12	M		TX
G.	20	M	Black Smith	AL
George W.	5	M		MS
William L.	6/12	M		AL
Stone, Jno.	47	M	Farmer	GA
Oria J.	35	F		GA
Jno. M.	19	M	Farmer	AL
Thomas B.	18	M	Farmer	AL
Malinda F.	14	F		TN
Selvanus C.	13	M		TN
Jonna	10	F		TN
Peter W.	9	M		MS
Sarah	4	F		TX
Margaret	1	F		TX
Jones, T. L.	28	M	Mechanic	NC
Benton, P. H.	21	M	Farmer	TN
Williams, W. W.	22	M	Farmer	TN
Taylor, C. C.	18	M	School Teacher	MS
Kirkendol, Middleton	34	M	Farmer	TN
Maria	26	F		IL
Frances	12	F		TN
Mary E.	10	F		TN
William A.	8	M		TN
Henrietta	7	F		TN
George	5	M		TX
Clementina	4	F		TX
Norman	1	M		TX
Laseter, Jas.	50	M	Farmer	NC
Sarah	45	F		VA
William	23	M	Farmer	TN
Elizabeth	17	F		TN
Lafayette	14	M		TN
Mary	12	F		TN
Erwin	10	M		TN
Martha	8	F		TN
Edward	6	M		TN
Charles W.	2	M		TX
Raycroft, Caswell	31	M	Farmer	NC
Nancy	21	F		TN
Mary E.	1	F		TX
Nancy	16	F		TN
Dickson, J. P.	39	M	Farmer	GA
Matilda W.	38	F		SC
McClerden, Jas. A.	19	M	Farmer	SC
Blake	14	M		AL
Joseph	12	M		AL
Everett	10	M		AL
Williams, Joshua	23	M	Farmer	TN
Guthry, A.	18	M	Farmer	TN
Mary E.	14	F		AL
Kern, J. T.	30	M	Farmer	NC
Amanda	21	F		TN
Jas. R.	5	M		TN
Betsy	3	F		TN
Susan M.	1	F		TX
Arnold, Wesley	40	M	Mechanic	??
Catharine	17	F		TN
Twomey, Haston	26	M	Farmer	TN
Emaly	28	F		TN
J. F.	1	F		TX
R. D.	1/12	M		TX
Elliott, William K.	33	M	H. Keeper	TN
Lora C.	30	F		AL
Demetra A.	11	F		AL
Jno. A.	6	M		TX
Right W.	1	M		TX
Dozier, S. B.	28	M	Mechanic	VA
Eveline E.	14	F		TN
Fyke, H.	26	M	Attorney at Law	TN
McNair, D.	25	M	Mechanic	GA
Satty, A.	25	M	Farmer	SC
Hill, Benjamin	25	M	Mechanic	NC

Holland, S.	48	M	Farmer	TN
Nancy W.	44	F		TN
Jas. K.	28	M	Representator	TN
Spearman, Jr.	18	M	Farmer	TN
Wilson, George K.	23	M	Overseer	??
Garner, Jno.	23	M	Laborer	??
Senton, (Blank)	23	M	Laborer	??
Hill, H. H.	35	M	Farmer	KY
Jane	35	F		KY
Harison	14	M		TN
Elizabeth	12	F		LA
Jesse	10	M		TX
Mary	7	F		TX
Russell, Francis	12	F		TX
Sara	10	F		TX
Margaret	7	F		LA
William	6	M		TX
Leddy, William	58	M	Farmer	TN
Mahaly	48	F		GA
Davis, Stephen L.	52	M	Farmer	SC
Caroline	15	F		AL
Hulda	45	F		SC
Jane	12	F		AL
Cyntha A.	10	F		AL
Marian	7	F		TX
Hulda Va.	32	M	Farmer	KY
Bond, William H.	32	M	Farmer	KY
Darcus	21	F		AL
Hulda	3	F		TX
Francis	9/12	F		TX
Craig, William	54	M	Surveyor	TN
Umphries, Polly	26	F	Widow	TN
Jane	15	F		TX
Sina	13	F		TX
Manda	12	F		TX
Jonathan	10	M		TX
Andrew	9	M		TX
Polly	8	F		TX
Mahaley	4	F		TX
Russell, Jesse	37	M		KY
Darcus	47	F		KY
Nancy	18	F		TN
Gibbs, Jonathan	29	M	Farmer	AL
Nancy	22	F		TN
Lucinda	2	F		TX
Jacob E. K.	3/12	M		TX
Coats, William G.	26	M	Farmer	AL
Mary	21	F		TN
Thomas J.	1	M		LA
Andrew	9/12	M		TX
Martin, William P.	31	M	Farmer	TN
Rodan	29	F		TN
Mary	8	F		TN
Sarah	6	F		TN
Jas. P.	4	M		TN
Nancy	3	F		MS
Booker, Enoch	26	M	Farmer	TN
Johnson, Mary J.	14	F		AL
Kessiah	71	F		VA
Elizabeth	45	F		TN
Abraham	6	M		TX
Kessiah	3	F		TX
Woolf, Thomas H.	31	M	Farmer	TN
Elizabeth	19	F		TX
James M.	1	M		TX
Booker, Jno.	8	M		TX
Boit, Onny	35	M	Farmer	TN
Susan	23	F		MS
John	3	M		LA
James	7/12	M		TX
Thompson, Amos	50	M	Mechanic	NC

(continued)

Thompson, Leodora	33	F		TN
William	14	M		AR
Mary C.	9	F		LA
Susan	7	F		TX
Adelia	5	F		TX
Amos H.	2	M		TX
Thompson, Dickson	28	M	M.D.	TN
Caroline K.	24	F		AL
Augustus A.	2	M		TX
Cornelia	6/12	F		TX
Reeves, Jno. B.	39	M	Mechanic	TN
Elizabeth	32	F		NC
Sarah	11	F		TX
Barnett B.	9	M		TX
William F.	8	M		TX
Mary Ann	6	F		TX
John H.	2	M		TX
Maxam, Cyrus	40	M	Farmer	OH
Eliza	19	F		TN
Cash, Tracy	34	M	Farmer	TN
Aramenta	22	F		AL
Elen E. A.	1	F		LA
Akinson, Alford	30	M	Farmer	??
Wood, Moses	37	M	Farmer	AL
Matilda W.	35	F		TN
Nancy J.	13	F		AL
Alexander S.	11	M		AL
Mary S.	10	F		AL
Solon K.	7	M		AL
Lora J.	5	F		AL
Ala	3	F		TX
Gibbs, Isaac L.	33	M	Farmer	GA
Francis	33	F		TN
Amelia P. H.	8	F		TN
Thomas W.	5	M		AR
Almeda	3	F		TX
Rachal	3/12	F		TX
Landers, Ro.	20	M	Farmer	TX
Bound, Francis	50	M	Farmer	??
Mary	50	F		VA
Thomas	21	M		TN
Jefferson	13	M		TN
Hardna T.	11	F		TN
La-(z,y,g)rone, William A.	34	M	Farmer	TN
Martha	42	F		SC
Christiana	14	F		TX
Levi	10	M		TX
Alex. H.	9	M		TX
Sarah	7	F		TX
Oliver T.	4	M		TX
Delia A.	3	F		TX
Walton, Killis	40	M	Farmer	TN
Margaret	35	F		MS
Rebecca	15	F		MS
Mariah	10	F		MS
Margaret	9	F		MS
Killis	7	M		TX
Julia	5	F		TX
Surat, R. T.	40	M	Farmer	TN
Elizabeth A.	35	F		SC
Mary A.	7	F		AL
Joseph P.	6	M		AL
Jno. G.	4	M		AL
Martha E.	3	F		LA
Marshall	1	M		TX
Dickerson, J. R.	32	M	Farmer	AL
Mildred	12	F		AR
John	2	M		LA
George W.	26	M	Farmer	AL
Sophia	21	F		AL
Benjamin F.	2	M		LA
William	12	M		AL
Birmingham, William	24	M	Farmer	TX
Birdsong, M. J.	22	M	Student	TN
J. M.	26	M	M.D.	AL

PANOLA COUNTY, TEXAS

Walton, William W. 26 M Farmer AL
Caroline E. 20 F TN
Nancy R. 2 F TX
Alice 5/12 F TX
Cunningham, Vince 25 M KY
Walton, George 74 M GA

Jones, Ezekiel 50 M Farmer NC
Eliza J. 32 F MS
Robert 11 M MS
Mary Ann 8 F TX
George W. 6 M TX
Lora 3 F TX
Martha E. 2/12 F TX
Gideons, R. C. 25 M Grocery Keeper TN
Brison, James 21 M Grocery Keeper SC

Chumley, Right 35 M Farmer TN

Birdsong, William A. 28 M Farmer AL
Nancy C. 22 F TN
William A. 1 M TX
Frances P. 3/12 F TX
Thomas, William 58 M Mechanic NC
David R. 38 M Mechanic TN

Williams, Elisha 51 M Farmer TN
Martha 60 F NC
Sophony 22 F MS
Rosna 21 F MS

Barnes, William 37 M Farmer NC
Catharine 29 F TN
Charles J. 11 M AL
Mary E. 9 F TX
Robert P. 6 M TX
Nancy J. 3 F TX
William G. 1 M TX

Lovell, Benjamin 59 M Farmer TN
Mary F. 46 F GA
James M. 22 M Farmer MS
Queen A. 21 F AL
Peter 19 M Farmer AL
Cuff 14 M AL

Baitman, Nancy S. 40 F Widow TN
John H. 21 M Farmer TN
E. H. 18 F TN
Rosey T. 16 F TN
Lawrence 15 M Farmer TN
William S. 7 M LA
Martha L. 5 F LA
Goldsmith, A. 26 M Merchant EUR

Field, R. W. 27 M Farmer VA
R. G. 23 F TN
R. A. 4 M LA

Corzine, P. B. 21 M Farmer TN
W. R. 19 M Farmer TN

Birdsong, A. 50 M Farmer SC
Mariam B. 50 F SC
Albert G. 19 M Farmer TN
Alex. L. 15 M Farmer TN
Hulda V. 5 F TX
Bailey W. 20 M TN
Dean, William 30 M Mechanic ??
Yarber, Lewis 36 M Mechanic VA

Chisom, Leroy 37 M Mechanic TN
Ann 42 F ??
Nancy G. 12 F AL
Mary L. 7 F AL
Sarah G. 3 F TX
Hooper, W. 22 M Farmer TN

Bowers, N. D. 30 M Farmer TN
Elizabeth J. 26 F GA
Mullins, Ann 13 F ??

Bagley, W. R. 32 M Farmer NC
(continued)

Bagley, Frances 26 F TN
Jas. H. 12 M AL
Columbus S. 11 M AL
Charles W. 7 M AL
John R. 6 M AL
Richard M. 4 M AL
George R. 8/12 M AL

Crenshaw, C. 35 M Farmer TN
Elizabeth J. 27 F AL
Julia Ann 10 F LA
Mary M. 6 F TX
Richard C. 3 M TX
Catharine L. 4 F TX
John H. 2 M TX

Oden, Isreal 33 M Farmer TN
Lucinda M. 30 F AL
Mary Ann 13 F AL
Jef. 11 M AL
Eliza R. 4 F TX
Catharine E. 3 F TX
Melvira J. 1 F TX

Parker, Jno. M. 24 M Mechanic TN
Mary E. 24 F NC
John E. 2 M MS
Albright, G. W. 21 M Farmer TN
Ramsey, Jane 30 F NC

Turner, Henry 60 M Farmer VA
Martha 58 F VA
Albert G. 30 M Farmer TN
Amanda F. 18 F AL

Root, E. 30 M Farmer NY
Caroline 20 F TN
Arans 4 F TN
Kate 1 F TN
McKinney, H. 21 M Farmer ??

Rutledge, Mary H. 38 F Widow TN
Mary E. 13 F AL
Charles E. 6 M TX

Rutledge, Charles 53 M Farmer TN
Mary 52 F KY
Roberts, Susan 52 F NC
Richey, E. 45 M Farmer GA
Panter, William G. 6 M TX

Dillard, John 30 M Farmer TN
Ann S. 20 F TN
Mary C. 4 F TX
Nancy J. 2 F TX

Walton, Ro. 41 M Farmer TN
Sarah 26 F AL
Robert 1 M TX
Woodley, Amanda 20 F AL

Watson, George W. 40 M Farmer TN
Susan 34 F TN
Joseph 15 M MS
Thomas 12 M MS
Grant, J. J. 39 M Farmer TN

Weir, Dr. Andrew 49 M M.D. VA
Andrew, Jr. 23 M Clerk TN
George S. 22 M TN
Charles W. 18 M MS
Robert V. 14 M MS
Henry B. 11 M MS
Berry A. 10 M MS

Dillard, H. D. 32 M Mechanic TN
Beleda 26 F ??
Jas. M. 7 M TX
Martha F. C. L. 5 F TX
Andrew 7/12 M TX
McKain, William 35 M Mechanic GA

Vanter, A. L. 27 M Mechanic IN
Martha 20 F TN
Julia 1/12 F TX

PANOLA COUNTY, TEXAS

Name	Age	Sex	Occupation	Birthplace
Brakin, Thomas	45	M	Farmer	NC
Mary	37	F		TN
Francis M.	17	M		AL
Elijah B.	15	M		AL
George W.	12	M		TX
Narcissa	8	F		TX
Elizabeth	6	F		TX
Matthew	4	M		TX
Cina	3	F		TX
M-- N.	4/12	F		TX
Westmoreland, Joseph	32	M	Farmer	TN
Lucinda	27	F		GA
William	9	M		AL
James	7	M		TX
Thomas	4	M		TX
John	2	M		TX
Cock, Lineus	40	M	Farmer	VA
Eliza	27	F		TN
Lafayette	19	M		TN
Mary Ann	16	F		TN
John	14	M		TN
Paralee	12	F		TN
William	7	M		MS
Joseph	3	M		MS
Charles	1	M		MS
Segar, Daniel	20	M	Farmer	MS
Lyghtfoot, O.	25	M	Trainer	KY
Barnett, Elisha	21	M	Farmer	TN

POLK COUNTY, TEXAS

Name	Age	Sex	Occupation	Birthplace
Fry, Robert	33	M	Millwright	GA
Lucinda	28	F		KY
Henry	5	M		TX
Mary	3	F		TX
Christine	6/12	F		TX
Flood, George L.	23	M	Hireling	GA
Lumpkin, J.	21	M	Hireling	TN
Worthey, E.	37	F	Widow	MS
Nancy	5	F		LA
George W.	3	M		TX
Dooly, Joel	20	M	Farmer	TN
Shields, J.	14	M		TN
Holbets, Robert	55	M	Farmer	TN
Margaret	45	F		TN
Joseph	19	M		TN
Nancy	5	F		TX
John	3	M		TX
William	1	M		TX
Wyatt, Joseph	46	M	Farmer	TN
John	26	M	Farmer	AR
James	21	M		AR
Mary	19	F		AR
Elizabeth	17	F		AR
Sarah	14	F		AR
Joseph	11	M		AR
Nancy	9	F		AR
Abner	7	M		AR
Martha	5	F		AR
Louisiana	3	F		AR
Cochrane, Dan	11	M		AR
Palmer, Thomas	38	M	Farmer	TN
Rachel	35	F		TN
Serena	11	F		AR
Isam	8	M		TX
Amanda	5	F		TX
William	3	M		TX
Mary	6/12	F		TX
Alexander, John M.	32	M	Farmer & Tanner	TN
Drucilla	28	F		AL
Francis	7	M		TX
Lydia	5	F		TX
Mary	3	F		TX
Martha	1	F		TX

Name	Age	Sex	Occupation	Birthplace
Larimore, John	39	M	Farmer	TN
China	28	F		TN
Mary	12	F		TX
Isabella	8	F		TX
Elizabeth	6/12	F		TX
Abbey, James	40	M	Farmer	GA
Nancy	39	F		TN
Edward	16	M		MS
Frances	14	F		MS
Hugh	8	M		TX
Ann	5	F		TX
Emerinda	3	F		TX
Jane	1	M		TX
Bryant, Pressly	33	M	Farmer	KY
Ruth	33	F		TN
Thadeus	8	M		KY
Mary	6	F		KY
Elizabeth	3	F		TX
Calvin	2	M		TX
Lucy	1	F		TX
Beece, George	73	M	Farmer	NC
John J.	35	M		TN
Ludlow, C. M.	50	M	Farmer & Millwright	TN
Mahala	14	F		MS
Mary	10	F		MS
John	7	M		MS
Garner, J.	63	M	Farmer	NC
Nancy	56	F		NC
Amanda	14	F		TX
Milton	11	M		TX
Thompson, Andrew	25	M	Laborer	TN
Thompson, William	33	M	Farmer	TN
Minerva	26	F		KY
Margarite	7	F		TX
James	9	M		TX
John	6	M		TX
Nancy	4	F		TX
Mary	2	F		TX
Josephine	2/12	F		TX
Thompson, Jas.	29	M	Farmer	TN
Harriett	22	F		MS
Mary	6	F		TX
Arena	4	F		TX
McGowen, Leroy	33	M		MS
Cynthia	28	F		TN
Copeland, John	33	M	Farmer	SC
Adeline	28	F		TN
Elvira	12	F		MS
William	10	M		MS
Thomas	6	M		MS
Sterling	4	M		MS
Sarah	3	F		MS
Catharine	2	F		MS
John	1	M		TX
Kincade, William N.	51	M	Farmer & Tanner	KY
Drucilla	42	F		KY
David	19	M		TN
Elizabeth	15	F		TN
Serenah	12	F		TX
William	10	M		TX
James	6	M		TX
Alexander	5	M		TX
Dugan, Alonzo	12	M		TX
Butler, Charles	60	M	Farmer	NC
Mary	53	F		GA
Lucinda	20	F		TN
Martha	18	F		TN
Charles	13	M		TN
Oscar	11	M		TN
McGee, E.	1	F		TN
Key, William	48	M		TN
Sarah	34	F		MO
John	16	M		TX

(continued)

POLK COUNTY, TEXAS

Name	Age	Sex	Occupation	Birthplace
Key, James	14	M		TX
Gabriella	7	F		TX
Nancy	5	F		TX
Malinda	2	F		TX
Key, Jas.	35	M		TN
Kincade, D. G.	44	M	Farmer	KY
Tabitha	35	F		TN
James	18	M		AR
John	4	M		TX
Mary	2	F		TX
Hester	6/12	F		TX
Ann	75	F		KY
Eliza	26	F		AL
Dougan, M. A.	18	F		AR
Isabella	7	F		TX
Palestine, P.	10	M		TN
Henderson, D. F.	34	M	Farmer	TN
Mary	32	F		TN
Ann	13	F		MS
Precilla	10	F		MS
Alice	6	F		TN
Loyd, A. J.	30	M	Black Smith	TN
Desdamona	26	F		TX
Mary	2	F		TX
Loyd, T. G.	20	M	Laborer	TN
Thompson, H.	29	M		TN
Louisa	33	F		KY
Amanda	17	F		TX
Solomon	14	M		TX
Mary	9	F		TX
Washington	7	M		TX
Marion	4	M		TX
Jefferson	2	M		TX
Ralph, Nancy	46	F	Widow	KY
Castile, Frank	15	M		IRE
Harper, John	39	M	Laborer	TN
Pindexter, William	40	M	Farmer	TN
Mary	35	F		GA
Thomas	13	M		LA
Sarah	6	F		LA
Robert	3	M		LA
Reams, Ransom	50	M	Laborer	SC
Johnson, Charles	23	M	Farmer	LA
Martha	18	F		TN
Green, R. N.	22	M	Black Smith	TN
Martha	22	F		AL
Darcus	6/12	F		TX
Sharer, H. L.	38	M	Cabinet Maker	TN
Martha	28	F		TN
Parthenia	12	F		TN
William	9	M		TN
Oscar	7	M		TN
Sarah	5	F		TN
Mary	3	F		TN
Margaret	1	F		TN
Tracy, M.	39	M	Farmer	TN
Eda	25	F		LA
Mary	18	F		TN
Benjamin	14	M		MS
William	11	M		TX
Tabitha	9	F		TX
Gibson	7	M		TX
Ryans, Mahala	8	F		TX
Mary	6	F		TX
Taylor, Ben	40	M	Farmer	NC
Mary	17	F		TN
John	13	M		AL
Bryant	5	M		LA
Franklin	3	M		LA
Nancy	1	F		TX
Tipton, Eli	56	M	Farmer	TN

(continued)

Name	Age	Sex	Occupation	Birthplace
Tipton, Margaret	58	F		TN
Eli	21	M		TN
Sarah	18	F		AL
John	16	M		AL
Thomas	14	M		AL
Martha	11	F		MS
Meshac	9	M		MS
Tipton, Ed	35	M	Farmer	TN
Charity	35	F		MS
Margaret	14	F		MS
Eli	6	M		MS
Charity	1	F		TX
Tipton, William	23	M	Farmer	TN
Sarah	18	F		LA
Dunlap, J. C.	36	M	Farmer	TN
Georgia	33	F		NC
Crockett	13	M		TX
John	9	M		TX
William	6	M		TX
Frances	4	F		TX
Daniel	2	M		TX
Hurt, O. P.	30	M	Farmer	NC
Virginia	25	F		TN
Leonidas	5	M		TN
Joseph	3	M		TX
Cumings, David M.	40	M	Farmer	PA
Heelen	41	F		TN
Thomas	14	M		MS
Mary	12	F		MS
John	9	M		TX
David	5	M		TX
Harden, Martha	66	F	Widow	SC
Ben	38	M	Farmer	TN
Mary	37	F		TN
Barnet	16	M		MS
Martha	12	F		MS
Caldwell, Bates	25	M	Farmer	LA
Sarah	18	F		TN
Hudson, W. G.	40	M	Farmer	TN
Mary	38	F		TN
Sarah	14	F		TN
Edwin	11	M		TN
Adeline	5	F		TN
Tennessee	3	F		TX
Stocton, J. F.	44	M	Black Smith	KY
Margarite	47	F		TN
Thomas	20	M		TN
William	16	M		TN
Hardin, William B.	44	M	Farmer	TN
Ann	40	F		TN
Jerusha	14	F		TX
Holston, C.	36	M	Farmer	TN
Margarite	29	F		IRE
Eliza	2	F		TX
James	1	M		TX
Ann	70	F		NC
Dodd, Sarah	41	F	Widow	TN
Mary	15	F		AL
Nancy	12	F		AL
Josiah	10	M		AL
Sarah	6	F		MS
John	4	M		MS
James	2	M		AL
Hooker, Robert	46	M	Farmer	TN
Hester	25	F		TN
William	22	M		AL
James	20	M		AL
Leander	18	M		AL
Leroy	16	M		AL
Robert	3	M		TX
Susan	14	F		AL
Nancy	11	F		AL

(continued)

Name	Age	Sex	Occupation	Birthplace
Hooker, Margaret	9	F		TX
Mary	1	F		TX
Clanks, James	5	M		TX
Green, D. G.	36	M	Black Smith	TN
Matilda	34	F		KY
Henry	13	M		TX
Mary	12	F		TX
Arterberry	8	M		TX
Ellen	6	F		TX
Newton	4	M		TX
William	2	M		TX
Matilda	1	F		TX
McGee, R.	53	M	Merchant	TN
Eliza	44	F		GA
Sam	13	M		TX
Sarah	9	F		AL
Smilly, Julia	18	F		AL
Payall, William	65	M	Farmer	TN
Bilya	50	F		GA
Arcadia	24	F		MS
Arrena	20	F		MS
John	18	M		MS
William	14	M		MS
Elbert	12	M		MS
Elizabeth	9	F		MS
Lowe, Joel	32	M	Farmer	TN
Millory	26	F		LA
Ellen	7	F		TX
Isaac	5	M		TX
Mary	3	F		TX
William	1	M		TX
Lowe, Elisha	62	M	Farmer	TN
Martha	20	F		AL
Isaac	28	M	Carpenter	TN
Scott, D. B.	41	M	Farmer	TN
Mary	40	F		TN
William	10	M		AL
Andrew	8	M		AL
Sarah	6	F		TX
Catharine	4	F		TX
Martha	2	F		TX
Isaac	6/12	M		TX
Cruse, John	27	M	Farmer	TN
Sarah	17	F		AL
Shoat, William M.	56	M	Farmer	TN
Ursula	45	F		KY
Saunda	20	F		KY
Elizabeth	13	F		TX
Zerilla	10	F		TX
Rufus	8	M		TX
Louisa	18	F		TX
Fields, E. J.	26	M	Farmer	NC
Dolly	22	F		TN
Lucilles	2	F		TX
Jones, W. W.	32	M	Farmer	TN
Sarah	28	F		AL
Callaway	7	M		AR
William	6	M		AR
Jesse	4	M		TX
Emily	3	F		TX
Enich	1	M		TX
Polar, Anson	42	M	Farmer	NC
Mary	30	F		TN
Nancy	11	F		TN
Virginia	9	F		MS
-amah	6	F		TN
Josephine	4	F		TX
Napoleon	2	M		TX
Alonzo	6/12	M		TX
Jones, John H.	44	M	Farmer	TN
Lucinda	42	F		TN
(continued)				
Jones, Jesse	20	M		AL
Peter	17	M		AL
Emily	14	F		AR
James	12	M		AR
Sarah	7	F		AR
Alpha	5	F		AR
Melinda	2	F		AR
Lems, William T.	49	M	Farmer	TN
Cynthia	25	F		AL
Sam	8	M		TX
Misseline	7	F		TX
William	2	M		TX
Vincent	2	M		TX
Harrison, M.	18	F		AL
Jones, E. C.	34	M	Farmer	TN
Elizabeth	32	F		TN
William	11	M		AR
Rhoda	9	F		AR
Franklin	7	M		AR
Misseline	5	F		TX
Elish, John	50	M	Farmer	TN
Elizabeth	41	F		TN
Christopher	17	M		TX
Arrena	14	F		TX
John	11	M		TX
William	6	M		TX
James	3	M		TX
Elizabeth	1	F		TX
Dillon, William D.	36	M	Lawyer	TN
Felis	36	F		TN
Lawson, J. W.	37	M	Farmer	TN
Mary	22	F		MS
John	4	M		TX
Alphanso	1	M		TX
Weatheis, Alex.	46	M	Farmer	GER
Nancy	24	F		TN
Edward	3	M		TX
Powell, E. S.	56	M	Methodist Minister	NC
Jane	44	F		SC
McCady, M. B.	5	F		TX
Powell, Susan	14	F		TX
Sam	12	M		TN
McCady, W. L.	22	M	Farmer	TN
Martha	16	F		TN
Sanson, Jane	64	F	Widow	SC
Eliza	19	F		TN
Williams, J. V.	67	M	Farmer	NC
Matilda	45	F		TN
Robert	22	M		TN
John	16	M		TN
Matilda	14	F		TN
Susan	13	F		TN
Hill, John E.	26	M	Doctor	MS
Mary	17	F		TN
Sanson, J. W.	25	M	Farmer	TN
Martha	20	F		VA
Carr, John F.	33	M	Farmer	TN
Arrabella	29	F		TN
Anderson	9	M		TX
Mary	2	F		TX
Vickery, Mary	37	F	Widow	TN
Aaron	20	M	Farmer	MS
Mathew	16	M		MS
Hardin	9	M		MS
Vance	7	M		MS
Lucinda	5	F		MS
Jane	3	F		MS
Epperson, T. L.	33	M	Carpenter	KY
Emily	24	F		TN
Mary	2	F		TX
Rogers, Joseph P.	36	M	Wagon Maker	TN
(continued)				

POLK COUNTY, TEXAS

Name	Age	Sex	Occupation	Birthplace
Rogers, Mary	18	F		TN
John	15	M		TN
William	12	M		TN
Margaret	9	F		TN
Pace, George L.	45	M	Farmer	VA
Margaret	29	F		AL
McDonald, Caroline	18	F		TN
Sarah	13	F		TX
Baily, Nat.	51	M	Merchant	NH
Sarah	39	F		NY
Alphonso	20	M		TN
Williams, Harriet M.	24	F		MA
Hill, Elizabeth	40	F	Widow	VA
Amelia	24	F		TN
Harriet	18	F		TN
James	13	M		TN
Medows, Jacob	40	M	Farmer	SC
McClenny, S. E.	38	M	Merchant	VA
Quarts, Henry S.	23	M	Clerk	SC
McDonald, William	28	M	Black Smith	TN
House, Garret	22	M	Farmer	GA
Eran	18	F		TN
Knight, J. W.	27	M	Merchant	TN
Marietta	20	F		NY
Eliza	2	F		TX
Piece, W. J.	31	M	Merchant	NC
Lucy	34	F		TN
Sanders, Louisa B.	18	F		TN
Thomas B.	14	M		TN
Valentine	16	M		TN
Stubblefield, John	45	M	Farmer	TN
Eliza	40	F		TN
Margaret	14	F		TN
Cyntha	10	F		TX
Julia	6	F		TX
Anna	2	F		TX
Carr, B. F.	32	M	Farmer	VA
Mary	28	F		TN
Francis	6	M		TX
James	4	M		TX
Mary	3	F		TX
Westbrook, Chris	20	M		AL
Marion	22	M		AL
Williamson, R. F.	23	M	Farmer	AL
Susan	22	F		TN
Henry	6/12	M		TX
Carr, George W.	24	M	Farmer	VA
Warner, Drayton	19	M		SC
Pratt, Mary	40	F	Widow	TN
Mary	20	F		TN
Shepherd, Jno. R.	37	M	Farmer	GA
Sarah	22	F		TN
Martha	4	F		MS
Wilmuth	2	M		TX
Bass, William	35	M	Farmer	TN
Mary	4	F		TX
Robert	7	M		TX
Bass, Sarah	56	F	Widow	TN

RED RIVER COUNTY, TEXAS

Name	Age	Sex	Occupation	Birthplace
Cheek, Randolph	33	M	Farmer	TN
Nancy	25	F		AL
William	7	M		AL
John	5	M		AL
Jane	3	M		AL
Balinda	1/12	F		AL
Humphreys, William (continued)	46	M	Farmer	TN
Humphreys, Mary	42	F		SC
John	21	M	Farmer	SC
Alabama	15	F		SC
Mary	13	F		SC
James	7	M		SC
Rebecca	5	F		SC
Miller, W. G.	30	M	Farmer	KY
Nancy	33	F		TN
Martin	4	M		TN
Coldwell, S. W.	32	M	Farmer	IL
Leana	47	F		TN
Fulbright, Martin	33	M	Farmer	NC
Mary	24	F		TN
Constantine	5	M		TN
Leonidas	3	M		TN
Martha	1	F		TN
Louisa	1	F		TN
Jalissa, Marian	14	M		KY
Word, James	50	M	Farmer	TN
Catherine	44	F		TN
Elizabeth	20	F		TN
John	22	M		TN
Mary Jane	17	F		TN
Russel	12	M		TN
Thomas	11	M		TN
Martha	6	F		TN
William	4	M		TN
Thomas	1	M		TN
Davis, Abner	37	M	Meth. & Farmer	TN
Elizabeth	34	F		TN
Greenberry	13	M		TN
Amos	10	M		TN
Mary Anne	7	F		TN
William	4	M		TN
Edward	1	M		TN
Tomlinson, John	30	M	Farmer	NC
Jane	24	F		TN
July Anne	5	F		TN
Elizabeth	2	F		TN
Humphrys, William	22	M	Farmer	AR
Parthena	22	F		TN
Mary	3	F		TN
Mary Anne	1	F		TN
Humphrys, George	50	M	Farmer	NC
Polly Ann	24	F		TN
John	26	M	Farmer	TN
George	20	M	Farmer	TN
James	18	M	(Idiot)	TN
Sterling	16	M	Farmer	TN
Thomas	14	M		TN
Lucy Anne	12	F		TN
Perry	10	M		TN
Andrew	7	M		TN
Thomas	3	M		TN
Isaac	7/12	M		TN
Stephenson, Isaac	22	M	Farmer	SC
Sarilda	18	F		TN
Williams, Silvester	32	M		TN
Savilla	26	F		AL
Miles	7	M		TN
John	5	M		TN
Jane	2	F		TN
Hale, Jonah	38	M	Meth. & Farmer	CT
Roda	61	F		SC
John	25	M		TN
Mary	25	F		TN
Ward, James	67	M	Farmer	SC
Bloodworth, John	40	M	Farmer	TN
Loucinda	31	F		TN
Elizabeth	9	F		TN
John	5	M		TN
Jonah	3	M		TN
Bloodworth, Benjamin	21	M	Farmer	TN

RED RIVER COUNTY, TEXAS

Name	Age	Sex	Occupation	Birthplace
Smith, Drury	32	M	Farmer	SC
Lucinda	24	F		TN
Charles	7	M		TN
Mary	5	F		TN
Westerman, Wilson	28	M	Farmer	TN
Margaret	20	F		TN
Charles	4	M		TN
Esther	50	F		KY
Charles	16	M		KY
Guest, Martin	36	M		TN
Mary	35	F		KY
William	12	M		KY
James	7	M		KY
Elisha	4	M		KY
Sarah	3/12	F		KY
Biggs, William	25	M	Farmer	TN
Margaret	28	F		TN
Louisa	8	F		TN
William	4	M		TN
James	1	M		TN
Guest, William	35	M	Farmer	TN
Nancy	35	F		KY
Baker, Alexander	18	M		TN
Richards, William	63	M	Farmer	TN
Henrietta	32	F		AL
Mary	8	F		TN
Ellen	6	F		TN
Elizabeth	4	F		TN
Epham	3/12	M		TN
John	3	M		TN
Baley, J. C.	50	M	Farmer	TN
Lemaranis(?)	33	F		AL
Livingston	14	F(?)		TN
James	12	M		TN
John	10	M		TN
Barton	8	M		TN
Erasmus	5	M		TN
Lemaranis(?)	1	F		TN
Guest, Martin	22	M	Farmer	TN
George	16	M	Farmer	TN
Martin	16	M	Farmer	TN
Benjamin	14	M		TN
James	12	M		TN
Robert	9	M		TN
Mary	7	F		TN
Epram	6	M		TN
Blackburn, James	55	M	Farmer	SC
Nancy	43	F		TN
Morris	25	M	Laborer	TN
William	22	M	Laborer	TN
Roda	18	F		TN
Margaret	13	F		TN
John	11	M		TN
Merilda	8	F		TN
Rebecca	6	F		TN
Lewis	3	F(?)		TN
Levina	20	F		TN
Parks, James	60	M	Farmer	NC
Maria	55	F		SC
Newton	23	M	Farmer	TN
Hatchet, Edward	41	M	Laborer	NC
Roda	31	F		TN
Ellen	4	F		TN
William	3	M		TN
Malinda	1	F		TN
Hatchet, James	31	M	Laborer	TN
Scott, George	30	M	Farmer	TN
Jane	22	F		TN
Ruphus	7	M		TN
Clement, Egbert	31	M	Farmer	TN
West, James (continued)	36	M	Farmer	TN
Harris, Henry	35	M		VA
Martha	28	F		TN
Nelson	6	M		TX
Virginia	3	F		TX
Margaret	1	F		TX
Hancock, Lewis	32	M	Farmer	IN
Jane	25	F		TN
Albert	10	M		TN
Mary	8	F		TN
Charles	3	M		TN
Johnson, J. J.	32	M	Brick Mason	KY
Shrygley(?), Joseph	41	M	Black Smith	TN
Hite, Benjamin	34	M	B. Miller	VA
Caudle, Marcus	26	M	Clerk	TN
Francis	15	M		TN
Reeves, John	42	M	Doctor	TN
Mary	31	F		TN
Harriet	16	F		TN
Theodocia	14	F		TN
M--	12	F		TN
Aramit	7	F		TN
John	6	M		TN
Egbert	3	M		TN
Orville	1	M		TN
Clampette, Elisha	68	M	Farmer	DE
Mary	67	F		DE
Abraham	36	M		DE
Elisha	22	M	Farmer	TN
Sarah	18	F		TN
Henry	15	M		TN
John	13	M		TN
Lemuel	11	M		TN
Maryetta	9	F		TN
Joseph	7	M		TN
Bowers, Martha	35	F		AL
Mathews, Daniel	43	M	Farmer	KY
Huldane	42	F		TN
Newton	20	M	Farmer	TN
Charles	16	M	Farmer	TN
Mary Jane	18	F		TN
James	12	M		TN
Joseph	10	M		TN
Daniel	8	M		TN
Lea	4	F		TN
Elizabeth	3/12	F		TN
King, James	32	M	Renter	TN
Sarah	30	F		TN
McLaughlin, Jas.	48	M	Farmer	TN
Malintha	46	F		TN
Malinda	16	F		TN
Margaret	12	F		TN
John	9	M		TN
Arheart, Michal	28	M	M.D.	OH
Virginia	21	F		TN
Caudle, Eliza	13	F		AL
Parks, William	34	M	Farmer	TN
Mary	20	F		NC
William	2	M		TX
King, Catherine	54	F	Farmer	NC
Anderson	22	M		NC
Sarah	18	F		TN
Margaret	4	F		TN
Shaw, Nancy	24	F	None	TN
Ralston, William	32	M	Farmer	TN
Frances	2-	F		TN
Elvira	9	F		TN
John	8	M		TN
Mahala	6	F		TN
Nancy	4	F		TN
Mary	2	F		TN
Newton, Jacob	32	M	Miller	NC
Harriet	36	F		TN
Mary Jane	3	F		TN

RED RIVER COUNTY, TEXAS

Name	Age	Sex	Occupation	Birthplace
Adams, Jesse	43	M	Engineer	PA
Martha	43	F		PA
Evaline	22	F		TN
Louisa	15	F		TN
Mary	12	F		TN
Vanora	6	F		TN
St. Clair, Robert	25	M	Laborer	TN
Wilkins, John	35	M	Lawyer	TN
Montgomery, Leonidas	20	M	Lawyer	TN
Davis, William	28	M	Lawyer	TN
Coldwell, J. C.	39	M	Tanner	KY
Martha	35	F		TN
Martha Ann	14	F		TN
John	12	M		TN
Benjamin	10	M		TN
James	3	M		TN
Smith, Samuel	40	M	Tanner	TN
Louisa	38	F		KY
William	7	M		TX
Brown, Cicero	53	M	Miller	SC
Elizabeth	45	F		TN
Hugh	24	M	Miller	TN
Robertson	20	M	Miller	TN
Joseph	18	M	Miller	TX
Mary	16	F		TX
Harrison	14	M		TX
Elizabeth	12	F		TX
Cicero	10	M		TX
William	7	M		TX
Calhoun, Jiles	25	M	Farmer	TN
Mary	22	F		TN
Elizabeth	7	F		TN
Martha	6	F		TN
Nelle	4	F		TN
Mary	1/12	F		TN
Perry, A. D.	44	M	Farmer	NC
Mary	48	F		NC
Jane	20	F		NC
George	15	M		NC
Mariam	10	F		TN
Wright, T. G.	45	M	Farmer	TN
Mary	39	F		NC
Samuel	10	M		TN
Edmund	19	M		TN
Margaret	12	F		TN
Marler, H. W.	32	M	Overseer	NC
Wright, J.	22	M	Clerk	AR
Gamble, Isaac	28	M	Grocer	IL
Jane	17	F		TN
Gill, William	39	M	Farmer	MD
Elizabeth	32	F		TN
Johnson, William	31	M	Overseer	NC
Sabina	24	F		TN
Rebecca	7	F		TN
Mary Anne	5	F		TN
Margaret	3	F		TN
James	10/12	M		TN
Hamilton, Ruphus	23	M	Renter	TN
Mary	21	F		TN
Sarah	1/12	F		TX
Brigance, J. M.	50	M	Farmer	TN
Eliza	39	F		--
Redman	17	M	Farmer	TN
Richard	16	M	Farmer	TN
Lafayette	10	M		TN
John	8	M		TN
Moses	6	M		TN
Thomas	4	M		TN
Susan	2	F		TN
Colyer, Thomas	25	M	Merchant	SC
Elizabeth	20	F		NC

(continued)

Name	Age	Sex	Occupation	Birthplace
Williams, Polly	28	F		TN
Breasley, J. J.	18	M	Clerk	VA
Mathews, James	37	M	Farmer	TN
Sarah	31	F		VA
Jiles	3	M		TN
Humphreys, William	32	M	Renter	IL
Nancy	28	F		TN
Owen	9	M		TX
Margaret	4	F		TX
Manerva	1	F		TX
Hamilton, Robert	32	M	Farmer	TN
Hamilton, Elizabeth	53	F		SC
John	16	M		TN
McCaudle, Morgan	19	M	Farmer	TN
Hamilton, John	22	M	Laborer	TN
Catherine	18	F		AL
Baggley, George	49	M	Farmer	VA
Margaret	37	F		TN
Daniel	21	M		TN
William	19	M		TN
Lucy	17	F		TN
Ballard	13	M		TN
Madison	11	M		TN
Henry	8	F		TN
Georgeann	6	F		TN
Susan	4	F		TN
William	2/12	M		TN
Spencer, Oliver	40	M	Overseer	SC
Curry, Thomas	40	M	Weaver	IRE
Latimer, James	68	M	Farmer	CT
Jane	68	F		NC
Elizabeth	28	F		TN
Robert	11	M		TN
Sarah	8	F		TN
Mary	6	F		TN
Latimer, Albert	47	M	Farmer	TN
Elizabeth	37	F		KY
John	18	M		TN
Tennessee	15	F		TN
Daniel	13	M		TN
Henry	8	M		TN
Dallas	6	M		TN
Maranda	4	F		TN
Louisa	2	F		TN
Davidson, Jos.	50	M	Farmer	NC
Margaret	39	F		TN
Edward	18	M		TN
Abigail	13	F		TN
Daniel	11	M		TN
Crocket	9	M		TN
Louisa	.5	F		TN
Lawden, Amanda	19	F		TN
Ramsdale, Oliver	60	M	Gardner	NY
Ervine, Richard	33	M	School Teacher	NY
Elizabeth	26	F		TN
Benjamin	11	M		TN
William	5	M		TN
Susan	1	F		TN
Morton, William	26	M	Shoe Maker	TN
Jane	25	F		TN
Cyntha	4	F		TN
Joseph	2	M		TN
Remington, Daniel	39	M	Gun Smith	MA
Susan	29	F		TN
Huser, William	24	M	Farmer	TN
Joana	20	F		TN
Harrison, William	30	M	Farmer	KY
Elizabeth	20	F		TN
Madora	2	F		TN
Montgomery, Ge-anna	40	F	Farmer	TN
Elizabeth	18	F		TN

(continued)

Name	Age	Sex	Occupation	Birthplace
Montgomery, Thomas	12	M		TN
Hugh	10	M		TN
William	8	M		TN
Forbes, T. C.	37	M	Farmer	(City)NY
Elizabeth	25	F		AR
Adalana	8	F		TN
Laura	6	F		TN
Malcum	4	F		TN
Jane	3	F		TN
Clasane(?)	3	F		TN
Dodson, James	35	M	Overseer	TN
Griggs, Daniel	39	M	Farmer	MO
Louisa	30	F		TN
Daniel	7	M		TN
Lavisa	5	F		TN
Margaret	2	F		TN
Kaufman, Lovel	47	M	Farmer	TN
Catherine	46	F		TN
James	25	M	Mechanic	TN
Leburn	22	M	Waggoner	TN
William	17	M	Farmer	TN
Jackson	14	M		TN
Warren	9	M		TX
Mary	10	F		TX
Word, Lenasa	34	M	Farmer	TN
Malinda	33	F		TN
William	14	M		TN
Joseph	9	M		TN
James	7	M		TN
John	4	M		TX
Mary	3	F		TX
Ellen	1	F		TX
Bell, Elijah	40	M	Laborer	TN
Mary	30	F		TN
Jane	17	F		TN
William	15	M		TN
Elizabeth	11	F		TN
James	9	M		TN
Elizah	7	F		TN
Lewis	5	M		TX

In Young Men's Retreat, Methodist

Name	Age	Sex	Occupation	Birthplace
Thorton, Fayette	18	M		TN
Hale, James	16	M		TN
Fuller, Benjamin	23	M		TN
Lida, Simeon	18	M		TN
Tirus	18	M		TN
Love, John	22	M		TN
Lewis, Josua	22	M		TN
Embry, Talton	12	M		TN
Steel, Clark	18	M		TN
Thomas, John	16	M		TN

End of Retreat

Name	Age	Sex	Occupation	Birthplace
Barry, Hardy	32	M	Farmer	TN
Violet	37	F		TN
Jane	19	F		TN
Nancy	14	F		TN
Mary	10	M		TN
Laura	5	F		TN
John	6	M		TN
Fanny	3	F		TN
Harriet	3/12	F		TX
Burton, Nancy	26	F		TN
Anne	6	F		TN
Howard	4	M		TN
Barry, D. N.	41	M	Trader	NC
Martha	35	F		NC
Jasper	18	M	School Teacher	TN
Joseph	11	M		TN
Samuel	8	M		TN
John	5	M		TX
Mary	4	F		TX
Martha	3	F		TX
Doak, Nelson	44	M	Farmer	KY

(continued)

Name	Age	Sex	Occupation	Birthplace
Doak, Jane	44	F		NC
Margaret	13	F		TN
John	9	M		TN
Doak, John	75	M	None	(VA)TN
Doak, Hugh	50	M		KY
Elizabeth	45	F		KY
Logan	16	M		KY
Mary Jane	14	F		KY
Grant, Stephen	28	M	Farmer	TN
Margaret	27	F		TN
Mary	3	F		TX
George	2	M		TX
Joseph	1	M		TX
Sims, Samuel	22	M	Laborer	KY
Dickson, A. R.	23	M	Farmer	TN
Sarah	22	F		TN
James	2	M		TX
Tomlinson, Richard	35	M	Farmer	NC
Sarah	22	F		TN
William	4	M		TX
Mary Jane	2	F		TX
Dickson, Abigail	50	F	Farmer	TN
George	20	M		TN
Joseph	18	M		TN
E. Jane	16	F		TN
Mary	14	F		TN
John	12	M		TN
Martha	9	F		TX
Snell, J. T.	26	M	Farmer	TN
Melinda	24	F		AL
Alince	4	F		AL
Mary Ade	22	F		TX
Tolbert, Harriet	16	F		LA
Butler, Lucy	28	F		TN
George	4	M		TX
John	3	M		TX
Dickson, Albert	37	M	Waggoner	IN
Joseph	25	M		TN
Jamison, S. K.	47	M	Farmer	KY
Jane	31	F		TN
John	10	M		TN
Elizabeth	18	F		TX
Susan	8	F		TX
Samuel	6	M		TX
James	4	M		TX
Bunavista	2	F		TX
George	1	M		TX
Moor, G. F.	57	M	Farmer	KY
Sally	47	F		TN
Samuel	16	M		TN
Rissel	13	M		TX
Wa---, Kisiah	50	F		TN
Doak, John	50	M	Farmer	NC
Sarah	50	F		TN
Thomas	21	M		TN
Susan	22	F		TN
Joseph	19	M		TN
James	14	M		TN
Floyd, Joseph	32	M	Farmer	TN
Eliza	30	F		TN
Fletcher	4	M		TN
Richard	1	M		TN
Cardwell, Eliza	25	F		TN
Chesier, Daniel	26	M	Shoe Maker	VA
Sally	24	F		VA
James	4	M		TN
Margaret	1	F		TX
Ritchey, William	40	M	Farmer	KY
Eryha	34	F		TN
Jane	15	F		TN
John D.	13	M		TX
Susan	8	F		TX
Harriet	4	F		TX

RED RIVER COUNTY, TEXAS

Name	Age	Sex	Occupation	Birthplace
Duty, Phillip	57	M	Farmer	NC
Sally	41	F		TN
Richard	20	M		TN
Benjamin	18	M		TN
Samuel	14	M		TN
John	11	M		TX
Nancy	10	F		TX
Phillip	7	M		TX
Russel, Anne	19	F		TN
Sarah	1	F		TX
Barnet, Alex	34	M	Farmer	TN
Sarah Jane	29	F		KY
Lafayette	9	M		KY
John Mary	8	M		KY
Martin	5	M		TX
Mary	5	F		TX
George	3/12	M		TX
Dillard, Thomas	45	M	None	TN
Polly	32	F		IL
Joseph	11	M		IL
Jane	4	F		IL
Phillip	2	M		IL
Taylor, Claricy	46	F	Farmer	KY
John	19	M		KY
Elizabeth	16	F		KY
James	14	M		KY
Martha	10	F		KY
Sarah	8	F		TX
Olivia	6	F		TX
Claricy	3	F		TN
Dean, Levi	43	M	Farmer	TN
Leticia	39	F		AR
Elias	22	M		AR
Martha	15	F		AR
George	12	M		AR
Lafayette	10	F		AR
Susan	8	F		AR
Mary	5	F		AR
Albert	2	M		AR
Susan	1	F		AR
Neathery, Robert	5-	M		NC
Rebecca	33	F		TN
James	9	M		TN
Nancy	7	F		TN
Elizabeth	4	F		TX
John	1	F		TX
Cranle, Richard	39	M	Farmer	TN
Rosena	27	F		TN
Charles	10	M		TN
Margaret	8	F		TN
George	8	M		TN
John	4	M		TX
James	2	M		TX
Fedric	8	M		TX
Laney, G. W.	22	M	Farmer	NC
Elizabeth	17	F		TN
Bateman, Irvin	41	M	Farmer	NC
Nancy	41	F		TN
Isaac	12	M		TN
Johnathan	7	F		TN
Evaline	4	F		TX
Esaus	4	M		TX
Elizabeth	2/12	F		TX
Butts, G. W.	21	M	Farmer	TN
Evaline	17	F		TN
Pope, James	39	M	Farmer	TN
Lucy Jane	33	F		TN
Anne	15	F		TN
Mary Jane	15	F		TN
James	11	M		TN
Wiley	8	M		TN
Benjamin	7	M		TX
Catherine	5	F		TX
Lewis	1	M		TX
Lamberson, William	23	M	None	TN
Martha	18	F		TN
Murphy	47	M		TN
Stephen	20	M		TN
Johnathan	12	M		TN
Sarah Anne	4	F		TN
Mathews, D. R.	37	M	Farmer	VA
Florandine	23	F		TN
Rebecca	14	F		TN
July Anne	9	F		TX
Anne	6	F		TX
Martha	3	F		TX
Sarah	1	F		TX
Bascum, Alijah	28	M	Farmer	TX
Louisa	24	F	None	TN
Elizabeth	0/12	F		--
Sipe, Moses	36	M	Farmer	NC
Ellina	34	F		TN
Perry	3	M		TN
Thomas	3/12	M		TX
Ridley, Reuben	36	M	Renter	NC
Susanna	40	F		TN
Samuel	10	M		TN
Nancy	8	F		TN
Ridley, Barbary	61	F	None	NC
Bauster(?), B. F.	45	M	Farmer	PA
Luvica	44	F		KY
Grey, Hannah	39	F		TN
Margaret	16	F		TN
Samuel	13	M		TN
Oscar	9	M		TN
Sarah	8	F		TN
Amanda	6	F		TN
Jesse	4	M		TN
Porter, William	28	M	Renter	SC
Feriba	18	F		TN
Isabella	1	F		TX
Stalling, Abram	33	M	None	IL
Pamelia	33	F		TN
Sarah	6	F		TX
Mary	4	F		TX
Deering, E. H.	23	M	Farmer	TN
Lucy Jane	21	F		IN
Rebecca	1	F		TN
Stalling, William	25	M	None	TX
Parmer, Thomas	22	M	Farmer	AR
Sarah	36	F		AR
William	18	M	None	AR
Sarah	15	F		AR
Mahala	10	F		AR
Loucinda	7	F		TX
Thomas	3	M		TX
George	1	M		TX
Joice, Henry	33	M		GA
Potter, William	26	M	Laborer	TN
Sarah	46	F		SC
George	20	M		GA
Andrew	17	M		GA
Sally Anne	14	F		GA
Mary	14	F		GA
Charlotte	11	F		GA
John	6	M		TX
Henry	2	M		TX
Jefferson, Thomas	29	M	Miller	GA
Patterson, J. A.	28	M	Farmer	TN
Susan	28	F		NC
Martha	9	F		NC
Nancy	7	F		NC
James	5	M		TX
John	3	M		TX
William	3/12	M		TX
Pruette, M.	33	M	Farmer	TN
Temperance	30	F		TN

(continued)

Name	Age	Sex	Occupation	Birthplace
Pruette, Martha	10	F		TN
Matilda	8	F		TN
William	7	M		TN
Nancy	4	F		TX
Janetta	10/12	F		TX
Burge, J. C.	33	M	Farmer	TN
Annice	33	F		TN
Sarah	10	F		TN
Mary Jane	8	F		TN
John	4	M		TX
Martha	2	F		TX
Wood, Elizabeth	50	F	Farmer	SC
Metilda	50	F		SC
Jeremiah	26	M	Farmer	TN
Lewis	23	M	Farmer	TN
Buford	24	M	Farmer	TN
Nancy	10	F		TN
Jane	9	F		TN
Kimbly	13	M		TN
Leonidas	11	M		TN
Dillard, W. N.	30	M	Farmer	NC
Mary Anne	27	F		TN
Frances	9	F		TN
Robert	6	F		TX
Louisa	3	F		TX
Jesse	1	M		TX
Peters, Richard	35	M	Farmer	TN
Eliza	21	F		TX
Louisa	1	M(F)		TX
Peters, S. M.	42	F(M)	None	VT
Catherine	30	M		TN
Charles	8	M		TX
Samuel	6	F		TX
Julia	2	F		TX
William	1	M		TX
Farris, G. W.	31	M	Farmer	TN
Eliza Jane	31	F		NC
Angarene	5	F		TX
Martha	3	F		TX
Adaline	1	F		TX
Wood, Robert	21	M	None	??
Hobbs, William	45	M	Farmer	TN
Elizabeth	8	M		TN
Johnathan	5	M		TX
Matilda	4	F		TX
Edith	2	F		TX
Bernet, Mark	31	M	Black Smith	TN
Mary	31	F		TN
Ruben	10	M		TN
John	8	M		TN
Martha	6	F		TX
Manerva	2	F		TX
Gilliam, James	46	M	Mechanic	VA
Margaret	38	F		TN
Martha	18	F		TN
William	16	M		TN
Mary	14	F		TN
Ellen	10	F		TN
Jesame	8	F		TN
Margaret	6	F		TN
James	1	M		TN
Williams, Lorance	45	M	Farmer	NC
Polly	30	F		TN
Esther	20	F		TN
Ema	16	F		TN
Elizabeth	14	F		TN
Catherine	12	F		TN
William	14	M		TN
Joa---	8	M		TX
Mary	6	F		TX
Thomas	4	M		TX
Lorance, Margaret	60	F	None	NC

Name	Age	Sex	Occupation	Birthplace
Titus, A. J.	36	M	Farmer	AL
Jane	32	F		TN
Ebenezer	12	M		TX
Anne	10	F		TX
Titus, T. F.	38	M	M.D.	AL
Sarah Anne	33	F		AL
James	1	M		AL
Breeding, W. H.	34	M	Overseer	TN
Augusta	22	F		GER
Taylor, J. J.	22	M		MS
Beaty, Ellen	47	M	Farmer	TN
John	20	M	Student	TN
Samuel	19	M		TN
Robert	14	M		TN
William	9	M		TN
Robert	9/12	M		TN
Glass, W. B.	51	M	Farmer	TN
Jane	43	F		TN
Emily	19	F		TN
Elizabeth	13	F		TN
Lar---dus	12	M		TN
Harrison	10	M		TN
Thomas	8	M		TN
Henry Clay	6	M		TN
Duke, W. C.	45	M	Meth. & Farmer	TN
Nancy	46	F		AR
Mary Anne	16	F		AR
Robert	13	M		AR
William	12	M		TX
Nancy	9	F		TX
Sam	7	M		TX
Nevels, T.	55	M	School Teacher	PA
Furgason, W. M.	25	M	Laborer	TN
Martha	25	F		MO
Wesley	2	M		MO
William	1	M		MO
Ritchey, Samuel	28	M	Farmer	KY
Martha	26	F		TN
James	6	M		TN
John	4/12	M		TN
Parkes, G. W.	43	M	Farmer	TN
Rebecca	42	F		TN
John	19	M		TN
Margaret	14	F		TN
Evaline	11	F		TN
Kate	7	F		TN
Sally	10	F		TN
Furling, L. K.	32	M	Black Smith	TN
Susan	32	F		TN
Box, Stephen	51	M	Farmer	TN
Darcus	46	F		KY
Rebecca	16	F		IL
Margaret	12	F		MO
Lafayette	5	M		MO
Joabella	4	F		MO
John	1	M		MO
Jenkins, J. K.	20	M	None	IL
Hale, Thomas	27	M	Overseer	TN
Frances	25	F		TN
John	1	M		TN
Williams, Sarah	38	F	None	TN
Austin, A. J.	44	M	Renter	AR
Elizabeth	32	F		NC
John	11	M		TN
Mary	9	F		MS
Young, W. C.	38	M	Attorney	TN
Pernicianne	19	F		TN
Jane	15	F		TN
Mary Anne	11	F		TN
Nancy	8	F		TN
John	5	M		TN
Sopha	1	F		TN
Young, Nancy	56	F		NC
Sarah	13	F		TN

Name	Age	Sex	Occupation	Birthplace
Ervine, Elizabeth	49	F	None	VA
Aris-a	18	F		TN
William	22	M		TN
Alexander	17	M		TN
Nancy	13	F		TN
John	12	M		TN
Virginia	10	F		TN
Martha	8	F		TN
Bruton, David	38	M	Farmer	TN
Marium	28	F		KY
Alonzo	7	M		TX
Lucy Jane	6	F		TX
Mary	3	F		TX
Martha	4/12	F		TX
Hamlin, H.	50	M	Surveyor	TN
Mary	50	F		TN
Martha	21	F		TN
Welch, James	28	M	Farmer	TN
William	7	M		MS
John	4	M		TN
Sarah	2	F		TX
Bryant, Nelson	47	M	Overseer	VA
Jane	44	F		TN
Mary Elizabeth	9	F		TN
Stanley, Furna	54	M	Farmer	TN
Elizabeth	30	F		TN
Matilda	17	F		TN
Mahala	15	F		TN
Caralinlene	13	F		TN
Samuel	14	M		TN
James	13	M		TN
Angalina	11	M(F)		TN
Isabella	9	F		TN
Elizabeth	2	F		TX
Mary	36	F	None	KY
Welch, William	47	M	Farmer	NC
Cyntha	47	F		KY
Martin	12	M		TN
Martha	19	F		TN
Welch, Clark	21	M	Waggoner	TN
Mary	16	F		AL
Sims, F. M.	35	M	Carpenter	VA
Mary	35	F		TN
Martha Jane	7	F		TX
Caroline	10	F		TX
Emily	5	F		TX
Mahala	1	F		TX
Orr, William	55	M	County Surveyor	NC
Margaret	41	F		TN
Alfred	22	M	Carpenter	TN
Sarah	18	F		TN
Nancy	16	F		TN
Elizabeth	12	F		TN
John	12	M		TN
Henry	8	M		TN
Word, James	43	M	Farmer	TN
Lavina	40	F		TN
George	14	M		TX
Sarah	10	F		TX
Humphreys, Lucy	3	F		TX
Richardson, James	48	M	Overseer	??
Nolls, M. G.	44	M	Farmer	TN
Cyntha	41	F		TN
Loucinda	24	F		TX
Marley	17	F		TX
Robert	12	M		TX
Elizabeth	10	F		TX
Lafayette	7	M		TX
Artamecia	6	F		TX
Louisa	4	F		TX
James	3/12	M		TX
Bass, William (continued)	45	M	Farmer	KY
Bass, Margaret	31	F		TN
William	7	M		TX
David	10	M		AR
Absalom	6	M		AR
John	2	M		AR
Nolls, Elizabeth	70	F	None	PA
Guest, Isaac	66	M	Farmer	NC
Mary	10	F		TN
Isaac	8	M		TN
McAnese, A.	50	M	Farmer	SC
Elizabeth	40	F		TN
Isaac	21	M		AL
Polly	18	F		AL
July Ane	17	F		AL
Jackson	13	M		AL
Jane	14	F		TX
Emily	13	F		TX
Sarah	12	F		TX
John	10	M		TX
David	9	M		TX
Ruth	8	F		TX
Nancy	6	F		TX
Catherine	1	F		TX
Ritchey, Henry	28	M	Farmer	KY
Martha	24	F		TN
Charles	2	M		TX
Smith, Sampson	70	M	Farmer	NC
Hillis, Samuel	38	M		KY
Jane	28	F		TN
Isaquena	4/12	F		TX
Vandyke, L. D.	33	M	Farmer	PA
Adelia	23	F		TN
James	3	M		TX
William	8/12	M		TX
West, Edward	48	M	Farmer	VA
Susan	41	F		TN
John	21	M		TX
Wade	10	M		TX
Martha	8	F		TX
Lucy	3	F		TX
Sanders, John	52	M	None	VA
Ritchey, James	38	M	Farmer	KY
Louisa	30	F		TN
Jeralene	11	F		TX
Mary Jane	8	F		TX
Anne	1	F		TX
Biles, Thomas	30	M	Farmer	KY
Prucilla	27	F		TN
Jane	11	F		TX
Dallas	6	M		TX
Martha	4	F		TX
Zach Taylor	1	M		TX
Carter, R. A.	30	M	Renter	KY
Malinda	34	F		VA
Mary Jane	11	F		KY
James	10	M		KY
Josephine	7	F		KY
David	4	M		KY
Amelia	1	F		TX
Biles, John	37	M	Laborer	TN
Eperson, B. H.	26	M	Attorney	MS
Harriet	16	F		TN
Corah	4/12	F		TX
Searry, Richard	39	M	Attorney	TN
Evantha	27	F		LA
Catherine	6	F		TX
Foster	4	M		TX
Worth	2	M		TX
Dale, John	44	M	Tailor	TN
Adline	26	F		TX
Mary Anne	8	F		TX
Charles	6	M		TX
Louisa	4	F		TX

RED RIVER COUNTY, TEXAS

Name	Age	Sex	Occupation	Birthplace
Murry, J. A. M.	28	M	Attorney	TN
Amelia	17	F		MS
Denwida, J. H. B.	22	M	Merchant	TN
Sarah Jane	19	F		TN
Vithada(?)	1	F		TX
Cornelius, W. P.	25	M	Merchant	AL
Arabella	17	F		TN
Ellette, A. K.	41	M	M.D.	NJ
Ame	38	F		NJ
William	16	M	Student	TN
Rosah	10	F		TN
Anteonette	8	F		AR
Betsy Anne	5	F		TN
James	3	M		TN
Mary	1/2	F		TN
Osteen, George	22	M	Mail Rider	TN
Clarksville Female Inst.				
Case, Mary T.	11	F		TN
Jewet, Sarah	14	F		TN
Couly, Louisa	11	F		TN
James, Frances	15	F		TN
Francis, Mary	11	F		TN
James, Elizabeth	15	F		TN
End of Female Inst.				
Yeager, L. W.	36	M	Painter/Plasterer	TN
Louisa	32	F		TN
Mary Jane	12	F		TN
John	10	M		TN
Theodocia	7	F		TN
Thomas	5	M		TN
Lewis	2	M		TN
Smith, S. H.	44	M	Wagonwright	CT
Morgan, S. H.	29	M	Atty in Eagle Hotel	TN
Dickson, W. P.	40	M		TN
Susan	34	F		SC
William	10	M		SC
Mary	13	F		TN
Sarah	1	F		TX
Darnell, William	21	M	Clerk	SC
Fleming, J.	43	M	Deputy Clerk	NC
Sampson, James	55	M	C. Preacher	NC
Mary	48	F		NC
Paralee	17	F		TN
Mary	13	F		TN
Ultimata	15	F		TN
Clarksville Female Academy				
McAllen, Elizabeth	13	F		TN
Lewis, Maria	16	F		TN
Latima, Tennessee	16	F		TN
Nail, Isabella	15	F		TN
Brown, Mary	15	F		TN
Dickson, Diana	15	F		TN
Ellett, Resetta	12	F		TN
Aramita	9	F		TN
End of Clarksville Female Academy				
Smith, B. P.	26	M	Attorney	TN
Sarah	19	F		KY
Malinda	10/12	F		TX
Carter, J. C.	33	M	Merchant	TN
Mary	22	F		TN
Thomas	15	M		TN
Virgil	12	M		TN
Mary	9	F		TN
Susan	7	F		TN
Fuqua, Joshua	32	M	Black Smith	TN
Catherine	26	F		AL
Mary	7/12	F		TX
Rebbele, Joseph	73	M	Wagonwright	MD

Name	Age	Sex	Occupation	Birthplace
Wilson, T. R.	29	M	Saddler	TN
Jane	27	F		TN
Nancy	3	F		TN
William	2	M		TN
Parton, Milbury	21	M	Apprentice	TN
Patrick, Lemuel	16	M		AR
Wilson, T. C.	21	M		TN
Hane, Mary	26	F	None	AL
Catherine	16	F		AL
John	3	M		TN
Clark, Agnes W.	36	F	None	VA
James	17	M	Student	TN
William	15	M		TN
Demorse, Charles	33	M	Editor	MA
Lesly	9	M		TX
Ida	7	M		TX
Isabella	2	F		TX
Dannell, J. E.	19	M	Apprentice Printer	TN
Clark, W. W.	15	M	Apprentice Printer	TN
Crook, Thomas	17	M	Apprentice Printer	TN
Morrill, Amos	45	M	Attorney	MA
Maranda	25	F		TN
John	43	M		MA
Dickson, Joseph	20	M		TN
Bryant, Sarah	10	F		TN
Lawton, G. F.	46	M	Clerk C.C.	RI
Maria	23	F		TN
George	3	M		TN
Mary	1	F		TN
Stacy, Thomas	21	M	Constable	TN
Kayton, Cyntha	55	F	Landlady	NC
Lafayette	18	M		TN
John M.	25	M	None	TN
Nancy	18	F		TN
Gillet, Henry	45	M	Factor	PA
Cotheran, John	20	M	Shoe Maker	PA
Sims, James	44	M	Farmer	TN
Susan	44	F		LA
Robert	13	M		TX
Roggers, Frances	47	F		AL
Nancy	19	F		AL
Louisa	18	F		AL
Julia	15	F		AL
Thomas	13	M		AL
John	16	M		AL
Halley, G. E.	25	M	Carpenter	MS
Roggers, Thomas	43	M		TN
Gordon, George	44	M	M.D.	KY
Isabella	45	F		KY
Patrick	15	M		TX
Clark, Frank	20	M	Law Student/C. Nation	
James John	12	M		TN
Isabella	10	F		TN
Richard	7	M		TN
James	6	M		TN
Brown, James C.	30	M	Trader	KY
Mary	22	F		AL
Presh	1	F		TX
Rochell, Pinkney	19	M		SC
Carter, Martha	16	F M		SC
Covington, Peter	22	M	Overseer	AL
Huchins, Thomas	22	M	Law Student	VA
Graham, Robert H.	33	M	District Clerk	TN
Mareva	25	F		C. Nation
Willie	5	M		TX
Robert	2	M		TX
Stanley, William	23	M	Ass. & Collector	TN
Walker, R. W.	38	M	M.D.	NC
Eliza	36	F		TN
Hannah	16	F		TN
Mary Anne	14	F		TN
Tabitha	10	F		TN
Eliza	10	F		TN
Duke, John H.	38	M		TN

(continued)

RED RIVER COUNTY, TEXAS

Name	Age	Sex / Occupation	Birthplace
Duke, Mary	37	F	MO
Ellen	12	F	TX
James	10	M	TX
Mary Jane	7	F	TX
Julia	4	F	TX
John	2	M	TX
Montgomery, W. T.	42	M Gentleman	TN
Nancy Jane	32	F	TN
John	12	M	TN
Rebecca	11	F	TX
Maryetta	7	F	TX
Exine	4	F	TX
Scurry, Richard	38	M Attorney	TN
Evantha	27	F	LA
Kate	6	F	TX
Foster	4	F(M)	TX
Worth	2	M	TX
Murry, Martha	44	F Seamstress	TN
Felix	19	M None	TN
Margaret	16	F	TN
Newton	14	M	TN
Luther	12	M	TN
Jefferson	9	M	TN
McCallay, Charles	39	M Clerk	IRE
Hopkins, Richard	41	M Farmer	KY
Nancy	35	F	TN
Mary Anne	10	F	TX
James	4	M	TX

REFUGIO COUNTY, TEXAS

St. Joseph's Island

Name	Age	Sex / Occupation	Birthplace
Jones, William H.	40	M Col of Costumes	CT
J.	33	F	CT
Catharine	12	F	CT
William	10	M	TN
Severs	6	M	TN
Charles E.	2	M	TN
Glen, Severs	22	F(?)	CT
Agery, C. W.	43	M Farmer	MA
Mary R.	35	F	TN
Elliss, Sarah E.	12	F	AR
Agery, George C.	9/12	M	TX
William R.	23	M	MS
Snively, David	43	M Surveyor	PA
Ozell, T. W.	36	M Farmer	TN
Manerva Ann	35	F	IL
Mary	11	F	IL
John A.	7	M	TX
Malinda	5	F	TX
William A.	1	M	TX

ROBERTSON COUNTY, TEXAS

Name	Age	Sex / Occupation	Birthplace
Irvine, L. J.	33	M Farmer	TN
Nancy	28	F	AL
Mary M.	10	F	TX
Lucinda	9	F	TX
William A.	7	M	TX
James J.	4	M	TX
King, Miles	28	M Farmer	TN
Eppatha	24	F	AL
Anjaline	17	F	TX
Manda	4	F	TX
Mary E.	2	F	TX
Baggis, Leroy	40	M Farmer	IL
Mary	25	F	TN
Graves, Ralph	51	M M.E. Minister	NC
Adaline	45	F	NY
William	24	M Farmer	TN
Gilbert	18	M Farmer	TN
(continued)			
Graves, James	16	M Farmer	TN
Adaline	6	F	TX
George	4	M	TX
Andrew	4	M	TX
Graves, George W.	42	M Farmer	TN
Mary E.	40	F	VA
Lucy E.	12	F	TN
Ann M	10	F	TN
Sarah J.	8	F	TN
Joseph	1	M	TN
Bratton, C. W.	31	M Farmer	TN
Sarah A.	20	F	TN
Mary N.	3	F	TX
Lafyett	2	M	TX
Margaret	5/12	F	TX
Rains, Elija	36	M Farmer	NC
Satire	36	F	SC
Margaret J.	13	F	TN
Isac N.	11	M	TN
Caleb C.	9	M	TN
Aaron C.	7	M	TN
James J.	6	M	TN
Martha A.	4	F	TN
Boon, James M.	35	M Farmer	TN
Bethina	21	F	MO
Stephen	1	M	TX
Boon, Mordica	76	M Black Smith	VA
Lankford, William M.	22	M Farmer	AL
Elizabeth E.	22	F	TN
Reed, Henry	49	M Attorney at Law	TN
Cobb, Clay	30	M Farmer	AL
Charlotta	26	F	TN
Mila	9	F	TX
Isabella	6	F	TX
Williamson	2	M	TX
Dunn, James	31	M Farmer	SC
Misouriann	20	F	TN
Henderson, M. C.	33	M Farmer	NC
Sarah	24	F	TN
Wood, D. S.	30	M Farmer	KY
Safronia V.	22	F	LA
Sarra	7	F	TX
Ralph S.	4	M	TX
Amalva C.	3	F	TX
Prim, Mary Ann E.	12	F	LA
McFarlin, William	21	M Farmer	TN
McMellon, Edward	35	M Farmer	IRE
Mary	32	F	TN
Mary J.	8	F	TX
James J.	6	M	TX
Robert	4	M	TX
Lethe	3	F	TX
Cintha	2	F	TX
Hunter, G. M.	25	M	TN
Neoma	23	F	TN
Jos. D. F.	2	M	TX
Barzilla J.	7/12	M	TX
Powell, Enoch	23	M Farmer	AL
Nancy	24	F	TN
McCuistion, James	32	M Farmer	TN
Noah	12	M	TN
Hannah	11	F	TN
Martha D.	7	F	TX
Joshua	20	M Farmer	TN
Rice, William S.	39	M Farmer	TN
Milla	33	F	TN
Elisha P.	6	M	TX
Elija W. M.	4	M	TX
Babe	2	M	TX
Catharine	6/12	F	TX

Name	Age	Sex	Occupation	Birthplace
Price, Rufus	27	M	Farmer	TN
Diadem	28	F		TN
William S.	5	M		TN
Brunetta A.	2	F		TX
Sam Houston	4/12	M		TX
Powell, Wiley	52	M	Farmer	GA
Mary E.	16	F		TN
Strother, John L.	41	M	Farmer	TN
Susan	36	F		TN
Aylcy A.	14	F		TX
James L.	9	M		TX
Sarah J.	7	F		TX
Vitalee	4	F		TX
Caroline K.	9/12	F		TX
Owen, Elizabeth	57	F		GA
Samuel F. E.	19	M	Farmer	TN
John B.	18	M	Farmer	TN
Sarah Ann	14	F		TN
Owen, Small Wood	37	M	Farmer	TN
Jane	42	F		SC
Mary Ann	17	F		TN
William	15	M		TN
Oliver J.	13	M		TN
Sterlin B.	11	M		TX
Turner B.	5	M		TX
James S.	8/12	M		TX
Anderson, Mathew	44	M	Farmer	TN
Febe	30	F		TN
James P.	10	M		TX
Polk	2	M		TX
Margaret	1	F		TX
Milligan, Willis	35	M	Stock Raiser	SC
Luisa M.	34	F		TN
Sarah V.	4	F		TX
Elizabeth	3	F		TX
Luticia A.	11	F		TX
Summerville, Marcis	35	M	Farmer	TN
Mary	35	F		TN
Susan J.	9	F		TN
Martha A.	6	F		TX
Joseph	4	M		TX
Phebe	3	F		TX
Norton Write	22	M	Wagon Maker	TN
McDaniel, Richard	25	M	Farmer	TN
Sarah	25	F		TN
Elizabeth	3	F		TN
Eaton, Thomas	34	M	Farmer	IL
Eliza Jane	28	F		TN
John T.	8	M		TX
Sarah	4	F		TX
Margaret	2	F		TX
Graham, John	53	M	Farmer	NC
Margaret	49	F		VA
Mary	19	F		TN
Catharine	16	F		TN
Martha	11	F		TX
Margaret J.	7	F		TX
Charles	2	M		TX
Bedford, William	29	M	Farmer	GA
Nancy	21	F		TN
Margy	1	F		TX
Stokes, John	33	M	Farmer	TN
Elizabeth	30	F		IRE
Young, David	25	M	Farmer	TN
Cook, Green B.	30	M	Cooper	TN
Martha	28	F		IL
Francis M.	13	M		TX
Leonidas	7	M		TX
Ira	3	M		TX
Alonzo	1	M		TX
Malisa	1	F		TX

Name	Age	Sex	Occupation	Birthplace
Cavitt, Volney	26	M	Farmer	TN
Sheridin	32	M	Farmer	TN
Arnett, Greenville	36	M	None	VA
Chandler, Eli	52	M	Farmer	SC
Mary	55	F		NC
Susan C.	18	F		TN
Amanda	17	F		TN
Lowery	14	F(M)		TN
Sloat, Narcissa	24	F		TN
Spence, Isac	41	M	Merchant	TN
Martha A.	33	F		TN
Julias J.	14	M		IL
William T.	8	M		TX
Hortense D. B. H.	4	F		TX
Frances J.	1	F		TX
Milhanks, John	34	M	waggoner	TN
Lewis, William J.	31	M	Carpenter	TN
Allan, Johnathan	37	M	Carpenter	IN
Beet, Abraham	45	M	Farmer	TN
Coley, John G.	25	M	Farmer	AL
Arnett, William	23	M	Waggoner	TN
Richards, Andrew	56	M	Carpenter	TN
Rosanah	53	F		KY
William	23	M	Farmer	KY
Andrew	19	M		KY
Nancy J.	17	F		IL
Anthony, Juliuseazer	40	M	School Teacher	MA
Mary	50	F		VA
Cox, Frances	25	F		TN
Collins, Martha	18	F		TN
Manurva	15	F		TN
Thomas	12	M		TN
Kellogg, Samuel W.	45	M	Merchant	CT
Caroline	45	F		PA
Francis	15	M		IN
Charles	10	M		IN
Cornelia	7	F		TX
Henry	4	M		TX
Crockett, George	35	M	Farmer	TN
Eliza	18	F		TN
Collins, C. C.	22	M	Farmer	TN
Hill, J. L.	30	M	Physician	TN
Phebe	36	F		TN
Moore, William	20	M	Farmer	TN
Thomas	15	M		TN
Dawson	13	M		TN
Brooks, B.	16	M	Physician	NC
Armstrong, Cavitt	44	M	Farmer	TN
Ann	50	F		TN
Thomas E.	10	M		TN
Kelough, S. B.	37	M	Farmer	TN
Annett	29	F		IL
Nancy J.	5	F		TX
Lucy E.	3	F		TX
Annett	9/12	F		TX
Pierce, Earl	56	M	None	VA
Cavitt, Josephis	23	M	Farmer	TN
Catharine	23	F		AL
William R.	1	M		TX
Camfield, Henry	22	M	None	AL
McCanlis, David	58	M	Farmer	NC
Lawrence, James	26	M	Farmer	TN
Macca	19	F		TN
Moody, John D.	45	M	Black Smith	SCO
Tabitha	34	F		IL
Walker, Eliza	57	F		IRE
Alice	18	F		MS
Susan	11	F		TN
Webb, James M.	27	M	Farmer	VA
Elizabeth	58	F		VA
Mary Jane	16	F		TN

ROBERTSON COUNTY, TEXAS

Name	Age	Sex	Occupation	Birthplace
Navarro, Lidia	44	F		AL
John	22	M	Farmer	TN
Emaline	18	F		TN
William	12	M		TN
Williams, Thomas B.	34	M	Farmer	GA
Loduskey	28	F		TN
Stone, David	12	M		TN
Walker, James	30	M	Farmer	IRE
Precilla	18	F		TN
William J.	7/12	M		TX
Lawrance, William	35	M	Farmer	TN
Darcus	31	F		TN
Isabel	10	F		TN
James C.	8	M		TN
Sarah J.	4	F		TN
John W.	1	M		TN
Galaway, William	35	M	Farmer	KY
Elizabeth	21	F		TN
Dickson, James M.	40	M	Farmer	VA
John J.	12	M		TN
William H.	10	M		TN
James L.	8	M		TN
Mary J.	5	F		TN
Hinson, David	26	M	Farmer	TN
Alexander	24	M	Farmer	TN
Richard	23	M	Farmer	TN
Eliza	16	F		TN
Mary	15	F		TN
Moss, Samuel R.	40	M	Farmer	NC
Lida L.	24	F		TN
Hartwell W.	2	M		TX
Sarah J.	10/12	F		TX
McCraccin, John	26	M	Farmer	SC
Liston, James C.	59	M	Farmer	NC
Dove	44	F		GA
Levey	12	F		FL
Dickson, Samuel L.	6	M		TN
French, James	30	M	Farmer	KY
Sirena	30	F		TN
Magrew, Janett	11	F		TX
John	8	M		TX
Paralee	7	F		TX
French, William	1	M		TX
Morell, A. H.	25	M	Mechanic	TN
Cardwell, Samuel	33	M	Farmer	VA
Mary A.	25	F		IN
Mahala J.	9	F		IN
Key, Joseph	28	M	House Carpenter	TN
Lain, Mary	51	F		KY
Alfred	22	M	Farmer	TN
Mary	15	F		TN
James	13	M		TX
Franklin	8	M		TX
Martha	7	F		TX
Iron, Van	32	M	Farmer	GA
Madora C.	24	F		TN
Van	1	M		TX
Robertson, James R.	56	M	Farmer	TN
Susan R.	47	F		VA
Fredoric D.	31	M	None	TN
Hosiah H.	27	M	None	TN
James R.	13	M		TN
Andrew J.	6	M		TX
Webb, Thomas R.	37	M	Farmer	GA
Calistine	32	F		TN
Thomas	10	M		MO
Frances	9	F		TX
Livingston	7	M		TX
Mary E.	3	F		TX
Hardin, Jonathan	50	M	Farmer	SC
William	26	M	Farmer	VA
Martha	16	F		TN
Jonathan	1/12	M		TX
Webb, Jesse J.	31	M	Farmer	TN
Webb, William M.	32	M	Farmer	TN
Elizabeth	24	F		AL
Mary A.	8	F		TX
Marthy E.	5	F		TX
Jesse J.	2	F		TX
Webb, Joseph	41	M	Farmer	GA
Martha H.	29	F		TN
Jesse	25	M	Farmer	TN
Susan H.	11	F		TX
Andrew J.	7	M		TX
Martha	4	F		TX
Joseph W.	1	M		TX
McClines, Richard	18	M	None	AL
Anderson, Joseph H.	25	M	Farmer	TN
Elizabeth	19	F		TN
Hariett J.	3/12	F		TX
Barns, Eliza A.	3	F		TX
Anderson, Harriett	49	F		GA
William T.	21	M	Farmer	TN
George W.	15	M		TX
Handford A.	10	M		TX
Reubin S.	8	M		TX
Jackson R.	5	M		TX
Hill, Josiah	31	M	Farmer	NC
Louisa	26	F		NC
Nancy	10	F		TN
Elizabeth	6	F		AR
Sarah	3	F		TX
William	3	M		TX
Sion	2/12	M		TX
McKnight, William	63	M	Farmer	KY
Rachael H.	63	F		SC
Johnathan P.	34	M	Farmer	TN
Elizabeth	22	F		TN
Flint, Franklin	14	M		AR
Henson, Henry	10	M		TX
Melton, David	26	M	Farmer	MS
Caroline	21	F		TN
George W.	3	M		TX
Josiah	2	M		TX
Mary E.	7/12	F		TX
Morrow, John	25	M	Farmer	AR
Manerva	38	F		TN
George	18	M	Farmer	TN
James	15	M		TN
Nancy	10	F		TN
Henderson	8	M		TN
John M.	6	M		TN
Richard	9/12	M		TX

RUSK COUNTY, TEXAS

Name	Age	Sex	Occupation	Birthplace
Wheeler, Richard C.	29	M	Printer	KY
Mary E.	25	F		KY
Mary	4/12	F		TX
Wilson, Nancy	60	F		VA
Bigney, James	25	M	Artist	Nova Scotia
Mysinger, William	23	M	Printer	TN
Crawford, Colby W.	39	M	Merchant	TN
Malone, Robert	23	M	Farmer	TN
Miller, John C.	41	M	Farmer	SC
Isabella	40	F		SC
Emila	19	F		GA
Josaphine	14	F		GA
William	12	M		GA
Henry	7	M		TX
Robinson, William	25	M	Farmer	TN
Basinger, Martin	39	M	Farmer	NC
Adaline	34	F		TN

(continued)

RUSK COUNTY, TEXAS

Name	Age	Sex	Occupation	Birthplace
Basinger, Sarah	16	F		TN
Henry	10	M		TX
Lavisa	7	F		TX
Amanda	4	F		TX
William	2	M		TX
Blythe, Thomas	45	M	Trader	TN
Nancy	43	F		KY
James	23	M	Clerk	TN
Eliza	19	F		IL
Elizabeth	17	F		IL
Sarah	13	F		TN
George	10	M		TN
Benjamin	5	M		TX
Susan	2	F		TX
McWilliams, James	36	M	City Clerk	TN
Martha	26	F		TN
Robinson, Andrew C.	49	M	Black Smith	TN
Elizabeth	53	F		TN
William	29	M	Gun Smith	TN
Henry	23	M	Black Smith	TN
Caroline	20	F		TN
James	18	M	Farmer	TN
Harris	17	M	Farmer	TN
Thomas	15	M	Farmer	AL
Azariah	13	M		AL
Alexander, Charles M.	25	M	Farmer	GA
Diadema	27	F		TN
John	5	M		AL
William	3	M		AL
Mary	1	F		TX
Wingfield, William W.	37	M	Farmer	VA
Eliza	29	F		TN
Mary	12	F		TN
Hamilton, James E.	24	M	Farmer	TN
McCline, Elisha	30	M	Farmer	SC
Phillips, Z. R.	30	M	Tailor	KY
Emila	27	F		TN
Ann	7	F		TN
Frances	3	F		TN
Mary	1	F		TN
Swan, S. G.	24	M	Lawyer	TN
John L.	22	M	Lawyer	TN
Spencer, William	28	M	Printer	MS
Wood, John	24	M	Trader	TN
Easley, John	34	M	Farmer	TN
Mary	38	F		NC
Caroline	14	F		TN
James	13	M		TN
David	11	M		TN
Jane	8	F		TN
William	5	M		TN
Armstrong, James R.	27	M	Lawyer	TN
Jane	23	F		TN
Barton, James M.	30	M	Sheriff	SC
Jane	18	F		MS
George	2	M		TX
Infant	1/12	M		TX
Miller, Thompson B.	24	M	Deputy Sheriff	TN
Willson, Nancy	60	F		VA
Hawith, F. C.	30	M	Farmer	TN
Matilda	25	F		MS
Susan	6	F		TX
Ambrose	4	M		TX
Francis	2	M		TX
Johnson, William H.	29	M	M.E. Clergyman	TN
Sarah	21	F		TN
America	2	F		TX
William	1/12	M		TX
Thompson, Martha	56	F		IRE
Vansickle, Elias S.	31	M	Farmer	AR
Mary	27	F		TN
Martha	6	F		TX
Leah	4	F		TX
King	2	M		TX
Hawith, William	32	M	Farmer	TN
Harriet	24	F		TN
Thomas	7	M		TX
Louisa	5	F		TX
William	3	M		TX
Virgil	1	M		TX
Bell, John	14	M		AL
Millinda	8	F		TX
William	18	M	Farmer	TN
Wilson, William H.	27	M	Merchant	TN
Emeline	24	F		TN
Hollingsworth, Stephen P.	35	M	Lawyer	GA
Martha	19	F		GA
Mary	3	F		TX
John	1	M		TX
Oran, John	21	M	Farmer	TN
Eaton, John C.	31	M	Grocer Merchant	TN
Cincinnatti	24	F		TN
Joel	8	M		TX
George	5	M		TX
James	4	M		TX
Thomas	6/12	M		TX
Pitner, Thomas R.	23	M	Lawyer	TN
Wood, David	32	M	Farmer	TN
Martha	29	F		GA
William	12	M		AL
James	3	M		TX
Smith, James	56	M	Farmer	SC
Hannah	47	F		SC
William Jasper	22	M	Farmer	TN
Marian	17	M		TN
Burt	13	M		TX
Kilgore, Willis	45	M	Carpenter	GA
Isabella	44	F		GA
Mary	21	F		GA
Andrew	19	M	Farmer	GA
William	17	M	Farmer	GA
Constantine	15	M	Farmer	GA
Ann	13	F		GA
Willis	11	M		GA
John	9	M		GA
Jane	7	F		GA
Adaline	5	F		GA
James	3	M		TX
Lathum, John	22	M	Farmer	TN
Grigsby, James P.	36	M	District Clerk	SC
Frances	24	F		TN
Hamilton, Young H.	23	M	Tavern Keeper	TN
Martha	7	F		TX
Cairy, James	23	M	School Teacher	AL
Sumners, John	24	M	Vocalist	KY
Smither, Bryant	24	M	Lawyer	KY
Hyde, S. M.	27	M	Lawyer	MS
Ramsaur, Hosea	30	M	Millwright	NC
Archibald	24	M	Millwright	NC
Seagle, James	20	M	Millwright	NC
Smith, James	22	M	Farmer	TN
Kimbrell, Ransom	22	M	Wagon Maker	GA
Manning	27	M	Carpenter	GA
Robertson, John	55	M	Farmer	SC
Corsia	45	F		SC
Charles	27	M		GA
Margaret	23	F		TN
John	20	M	Farmer	TN
William	17	M	Farmer	TN
Mary	15	F		TN
Sarah	13	F		AL
Joseph	9	M		AL
Ellen	4	F		AL

Name	Age	Sex	Occupation	Birthplace
Hamilton, John D.	28	M	Farmer	TN
Hamilton, Amanus	55	M	Farmer	SC
Delila	50	F		SC
Andrew J.	5	M		TX
Mary	18	F		TN
Cornelius, Thomas J.	35	M	Merchant	AL
Maria	26	F		TN
William	10	M		AL
Ellen	11	F		AL
Lucy	13	F		AL
Frances	5	F		TX
Thomas	3	M		IL
Maria	1	F		TX
King, Joseph S.	21	M	Clerk	TN
McGuire, George W.	35	M	Farmer	TN
Elizabeth	30	F		AL
Jane	13	F		TN
Charles	11	M		TN
Amanda	8	F		TX
Thomas	4	M		TX
Jasper	1	M		TX
Dennis, John	46	M	Farmer	NC
Delila	28	F		AL
Eli	18	M	Farmer	TN
Cynthia	16	F		KY
Louisiana	14	F		KY
William	12	M		TN
Caroline	9	F		TN
John	4	M		TN
Lettitia	2	F		TX
Thomas	1	M		TX
Parsons, James A. S.	43	M	Physician	TN
Cosan, Larkin	55	M	Farmer	NC
Sarah	50	F		TN
Wilmot	13	F		TN
William	10	M		TX
Turner, William B.	40	M	Lawyer	TN
Mary	38	F		VA
Idella	17	F		TN
Saloam	16	F		TN
George	14	M		TN
William B., Jr.	12	M		TN
Lewirka	10	F		TN
Hallissa	8	F		TN
Mary	5	F		TN
Osborn, William T.	23	M	Carpenter	TN
Garrett, Robert O.	23	M	Farmer	AL
Hollingsworth, Joice	58	F		GA
Benjamin	22	M	Surveyor	TN
Benton	20	M	Farmer	TN
Orlando	13	M		AL
Smith, Robert W.	40	M	Farmer	NC
Mary	29	F		TN
Alfred	13	M		TX
Joseph	11	M		TX
Mary	9	F		TX
James	7	M		TX
Alvira	5	F		TX
Brown, Seaborn H.	45	M	Gun Smith	SC
Assenth	35	F		GA
Thadius	12	M		TN
Leven	8	M		TN
Susan	5	F		AR
George	2	M		TX
Lucitta	5/12	F		TX
Tucker, William	20	M	Farmer	TN
Husband, Harmon	46	M	Farmer	NC
Nancy	43	F		GA
M. H.	24	M	Farmer	TN
William M.	20	M	Farmer	TN
Sanders	18	M	Farmer	TN
(continued)				

Name	Age	Sex	Occupation	Birthplace
Husband, Millissa	15	F		TN
James	13	M		TN
Windle, J. W.	23	M	Farmer	AL
Lucinda	20	F		TN
James	2	M		TX
Nancy	5/12	F		TX
Willis, Charles	23	M	Farmer	TN
Beggers, Giles S.	53	M	Ass. & Collector	TN
Sarah	50	F		TN
Milton	18	M	Student	GA
Vasta	16	F		GA
William	13	M		GA
Ruth	11	F		GA
Brazilla	8	M		GA
Smith, Isaac N.	22	M	Engineer	TN
Mary	15	F		AL
Smith, Andrew J.	24	M	Surveyor	TN
Cumby, R. H.	25	M	Farmer	VA
Nancy	28	F		TN
Elizabeth	45	F		TN
Adriana	3	F		MS
Cruse, Andrew	27	M	Black Smith	NC
Eliza	23	F		TN
Modina	4/12	F		TX
Cruse, John F.	23	M	Black Smith	TN
Johnston, C. M.	26	M	Black Smith	TN
Jennings, James	45	M	House Painter	KY
Gilla	25	F		TN
Thomas	4	M		TX
James	2	M		TX
Charles	8/12	M		TX
Forsyth, James B.	16	M	Mail Carrier	TN
Chaney, C. W.	34	M	House Painter	TN
Susan	24	F		TN
Leonadus	11/12	M		TX
Cruse, Adam	35	M	Carpenter	NC
Kelly, William C.	35	M	Farmer	TN
Mary	30	F		TN
Drayton	10	M		AL
Texanna	8	F		AL
Laura	4	F		AL
Mary	1	F		AL
Kelly, James S.	21	M		TN
Lakey, William B.	40	M	Brick Mason	TN
Lavinia	40	F		TN
David	13	M		TN
Sarah	11	F		TN
William	9	M		TN
Monroe	7	M		TN
Mary	7	F		TN
Emeline	3	F		TN
Martha	1	F		AR
Spear, George W.	43	M	Plow Maker	NC
Caroline	37	F		NC
Margaret	16	F		NC
James	4	M		TN
John	4/12	M		TX
Cogburn, Headly	35	M	Farmer	NC
Eliza	35	F		TN
Isaac	15	M	Farmer	AL
Anville	13	M		TN
Leonora	11	F		TN
Eliza	9	F		MS
Esther	7	F		TN
William	5	M		TN
Thomas	3	M		TX
Henry C.	3/12	M		TX
Bachellor, John	30	M	Black Smith	TN
Elizabeth	27	F		TN
John	6	M		TN
Thomas	3	M		TN
Wilson	3/12	M		TX
(continued)				

RUSK COUNTY, TEXAS

Name	Age	Sex	Occupation	Birthplace
Hardne, William	28	M	Farmer	VA
Lawder, Thomas	22	M	Farmer	TN
Rucker, George C.	30	M	Teamster	VA
Pugh, Andrew	21	M	Teamster	TN
Berry, Henry	43	M	Farmer	NC
Eliza	37	F		TN
James	17	M	Farmer	TN
Silas	12	M		TN
Samuel	10	M		TN
Hannah	8	F		TN
George	6	M		TN
Henry	1	M		TX
McCoy, James	21	M	Farmer	TN
Williams, Elkana	40	M	Farmer	TN
Cynthia	21	F		TN
George	7/12	M		TX
Ash, Hiram	36	M	Farmer	NC
Sarah	37	F		TN
Mary	13	F		TN
James	11	M		TN
John	9	M		TN
William	2	M		TX
Brown, Richard	40	M	Farmer	PA
Nancy	18	F		TN
Mary	1	F		TX
Osbourn, E. M.	22	M	Farmer	GA
Murry, Joseph	35	M	Farmer	GA
Louisa	30	F		TN
Wyly	10	M		AL
Martha	5	F		AL
Ruth	2	F		AL
Mary	6/12	F		AL
Timmons, Thomas	35	M	Farmer	TN
Frances	27	F		TN
Mary	12	F		TX
Hannah	6	F		TX
Julia	2	F		TX
Miller, James W.	32	M	Farmer	TN
Frances	22	F		GA
Andrew	7	M		AL
James	5	M		AL
John	3	M		AL
Robert	2	M		AL
Emila	1	F		TX
Oliver, Martha	69	F		SC
McLanahan, William A.	35	M	Tailor	TN
Cynthia	38	F		SC
William	12	M		MS
Ann	7	F		TX
Charles	5	M		TX
James	3	M		TX
Elizabeth	3/12	F		TX
Johnston, Joseph	39	M	Farmer	TN
Eliza	32	F		GA
Frances	13	F		AL
George	10	M		AL
Emory	8	M		AL
Eli	5	M		MS
Florida	1	F		TX
Caruthers, John	37	M	Merchant	TN
Sarah	23	F		AL
Mary	16	F		AL
Catherine	14	F		AL
James	11	M		TX
Susan	9	F		TX
Isabella	7	F		TX
Martha	5	F		TX
Alexander, Joseph W.	31	M	Farmer	TN
Violet	31	F		AL
Wells, Joseph A.	18	M	Farmer	KY

Name	Age	Sex	Occupation	Birthplace
Brown, David B.	50	M	Farmer	GA
Elizabeth	42	F		TN
David	15	M	Farmer	AL
Julia	19	F		AL
Robert	13	M		AL
John	11	M		AL
Sarah	14	F		AL
James	9	M		TX
Stuart, Pleasant	24	M	Farmer	TN
Sarah	20	F		TN
William	5	M		TN
Sarah	4	F		TN
Ann	2	F		TN
Infant	4/12	M		TX
Moore, William	50	M	Farmer	TN
Catherine	49	F		TN
Julia	28	F		AL
Martha	16	F		AL
Mary	14	F		AL
Thomas	10	M		AL
James	8	M		AL
J. W.	6	M		AL
Yancey, James	30	M	Farmer	VA
Mary	30	F		KY
Elizabeth	7	F		TN
Disartemus, Patrick	65	M	Farmer	SC
Sarah	47	F		GA
Warren	23	M		GA
Brown, Sarah	13	F		AL
Howel, Richard	20	M	Farmer	TN
Oliver, Milton	23	M	Farmer	TN
Banks, Sarah	20	F		GA
Elizabeth	4	F		GA
Lloyd, James	27	M	Farmer	AL
Permelia	18	F		TN
Glasscock, James E.	37	M	Chief Justice	TN
Mary	31	F		MS
Sarah	6	F		TX
James	2	M		TX
William	4	M		TX
Francis Penn	10	M		TX
Robert Pearce	21	M	Farmer	GA
Walling, P. M.	28	M	Farmer	MS
Elizabeth	26	F		TN
Jesse	6	M		TX
Martha	4	F		TX
Mary	1	F		TX
Tipps, L. E.	31	M	Merchant	TN
Amelia	23	F		AL
Colby	6	M		TX
Ervin	2	M		TX
Tipps, Peter	66	M	Farmer	NC
Sarah	62	F		KY
Jacob	17	M	Farmer	TN
Windle, J. A.	46	M	Farmer	VA
Permelia	36	F		SC
James	21	M	Farmer	TN
Elizabeth	14	F		LA
David	4	M		TX
Mary	2	F		TX
Carney, William	26	M	Farmer	TN
Eveline	21	F		TN
Silas	2/12	M		TX
White, William	27	M	Carpenter	TN
Smith, Bennet	44	M	Farmer	NC
Susan	27	F		TN
Mary	6	F		TX
Althia	5	F		TX
C---	3	M		TX
Brumet, S. J.	27	M	Farmer	TN
Smith, Samuel	85	M	None	VA
Mary	75	F		NC

RUSK COUNTY, TEXAS

Name	Age	Sex	Occupation	Birthplace
Smith, Joseph	25	M	Farmer	TN
Minerva	21	F		TN
James	2	M		TX
Weldon, William T.	57	M	Farmer	TN
Sarah	58	F		VA
Gabriel	18	M	Farmer	AL
Millinda	10	F		AL
Golman, William	22	M	farmer	TN
McMurry, W. L.	29	M	Merchant	TN
Elizabeth	19	F		AL
Taylor	1	M		TX
Isam, W. B.	29	M	Farmer	TN
E. A.	24	M	Farmer	TN
S. F.	25	M	Farmer	TN
Eliza	18	F		TN
Martha	2	F		TN
James	5/12	M		TX
Ogletree, Edmund	54	M	Farmer	GA
Martha	54	F		NC
Jasper	20	M	Farmer	TN
Clarissa	14	F		AL
Martha	10	F		AL
Mundy, Tipton	41	M	Farmer	TN
Eliza	32	F		GA
Elizabeth	18	F		TN
Martha	15	F		AL
Millinda	13	F		AL
Margaret	12	F		AL
William	8	M		AL
Hariet	6	F		AL
Jane	5	F		AL
Mary	4	F		AL
Susan	2	F		AL
Casky, Robert	45	M	Carpenter	SC
Delila	45	F		SC
Mary	19	F		TN
Lucinda	17	F		AL
Benjamin	10	M		AL
Frances	10	F		AL
Malvina	7	F		AL
John	4	M		AL
Dodson, Thomas S.	23	M	Farmer	TN
Martha	18	F		KY
Williams, John	30	M	Farmer	??
Dodson, Labon	51	M	Farmer	TN
Margaret	45	F		NC
Jones, Rebecca	17	F		TN
Heidleburg, Samuel	21	M	Carpenter	TN
Johnston, A. G.	31	M	Farmer	TN
Louisa	25	F		TX
John	9	M		TX
Samuel	7	M		TX
Thomas	4	M		TX
Phillip H. B.	1	M		TX
Grider, Enos	22	M	Farmer	TN
Burk, S. P.	45	M	Carpenter	KY
Ann	37	F		KY
Albert	18	M	Farmer	TN
Vaden	16	M	Farmer	TN
Rachael	12	F		MS
Sarah	14	F		MS
William	9	M		TX
Samuel	6	M		TX
John	4	M		TX
Walters, D. D.	30	M	School Teacher	GA
Lowrie, A. H.	32	M	Farmer	TN
Priscilla	22	F		AL
Amelia	1	F		TX
Henry	1/12	M		TX
Amelia	65	F		IRE
Lowrie, S. H. (continued)	39	M	Farmer	??
Lowrie, Susan	28	F		NC
William	7	M		TN
Smitha	5	F		TN
Alexander	3	M		TX
Ben.	1	M		TX
Gentry, M. T.	27	M	School Teacher	VA
Collins, Mary Ann	9	F		??
Savage, Wyley B.	36	M	Laborer	TN
Thomas	12	M		TN
Louisa	10	F		TN
Elizabeth	8	F		TN
William	5	M		TN
Robert	1	M		TN
Hawith, Thomas	53	M	Farmer	TN
Nancy	52	F		TN
Thomas	20	M	Farmer	TN
Marthy	22	F		TN
Jefferson	18	M	Farmer	TN
Cornelius	15	M	Farmer	TN
Catherine	13	F		AL
Louis	11	M		AL
Bryan	10	M		AL
Franklin	9	M		TX
Pearce, James	42	M	Farmer	TN
Elizabeth	38	F		GA
Louisa	10	F		AL
Albert	18	M	Farmer	AL
Samuel	15	M		AL
George	13	M		MS
William	8	M		MS
James S.	4	M		MS
John H.	2	M		TX
Dodson, Jesse	49	M	Butcher	TN
Amanda	37	F		TN
Robinson, James P.	30	M	Farmer	TN
Jarittel(?)	28	F		SC
Louis C.	3	M		TX
Isaac Stephen	9/12	M		TX
Matlock, Robert	37	M	Laborer	TN
Churchwell, William C.	39	M	Farmer	TN
Manerva	24	F		AL
Elizabeth	7	F		MS
Mahala	5	F		MS
George W.	4	M		MS
Berthena	2	F		MS
Josephus	10/12	M		TX
Wood, Eli	32	M	Farmer	AL
Ann	31	F		TN
Hart, Thadeus	23	M	Farmer	TN
Margaret	48	F		KY
Theodore	21	M	Farmer	TN
Armenia	18	F		TN
Blackburn, Eli	38	M	Brick Layer	TN
Anna	22	F		AL
James	13	M		MS
Frances J.	14	F		TN
Edward M.	9	M		TX
William W.	7	M		TX
Gideon	3	M		TX
Mary Ann	1	F		TX
Langston, Hiram	55	M		SC
Elenor	44	F		TN
Martha	20	F		IL
Elizabeth	15	F		AR
Jesse	17	M		IL
James	9	M		MO
William	8	M		MO
Andrew S.	5	M		TX
Telitha	2	F		TX
Emiline	1/12	F		TX
Martha	6	F		MO
Delila	24	F		TN
Brakeman, Tunis	74	M		NY

RUSK COUNTY, TEXAS

Name	Age	Sex	Occupation	Birthplace
James, Thomas	37	M	Farmer	TN
Narcissa	33	F		AL
Charles	9	M		TN
Victoria	5	F		TN
Julia	4	F		TN
Sarah	2	F		TX
Hudson, Julia	30	F		TN
Mahala	9	F		AR
Rufus	8	M		AR
Francis	4	M		AR
Charles	3	M		AR
Robert	2	M		AR
Smith, George	33	M	Carpenter	TN
Catharine	32	F		TN
Washington L.	9	M		AL
Robert W.	7	M		AL
William C.	5	M		AL
Joseph M.	3	M		AL
John C.	1	M		TX
Grisham, John M.	27	M	Saddler	TN
Frances	25	F		SC
Thomas A.	3	M		TN
Jonathan	11/12	F(M)		TX
Nichols, John T.	26	M	Waggoner	TN
Gant, Mathew	62	M	Farmer	TN
Delilah	40	F		SC
James B.	36	M	Farmer	TN
Samuel	34	M	Black Smith	TN
Jane H.	13	F		AL
Eliza E.	12	F		AL
George M. H.	12	M		AL
Nancy	10	F		AL
Nancy Ann	10	F		AL
William M.	10	M		AL
Love, Wade	55	M	Farmer	SC
Jane	52	F		SC
Alexander	18	M	Farmer	GA
Westley	15	M		TN
Leonard	11	M		MS
Miller, A. T.	43	M	Farmer	SC
Lucretia	45	F		TN
James T.	16	M		TN
John B.	14	M		AL
Elizabeth	13	F		AL
Delilah J.	11	F		AL
Wiley J.	9	M		AL
Esther B.	7	F		AL
William P.	5	M		AL
Shomaley, Samuel	48	M		TN
Haynes, J. C.	26	M		TN
Caroline	19	F		TN
Haynes, Ally	3	M		TX
William T.	8/12	M		TX
Chisum, Thomas G.	45	M	Farmer	TN
Malinda	40	F		TN
Parilee	17	F		TN
Talbot	15	M	Student	TN
William	13	M		TX
Andrew	11	M		TX
Sis	9	F		TX
Paxham	7	M		TX
Adaline	5	F		TX
John	2	M		TX
Buckhanon, Samuel D.	34	M	Farmer	TN
Celia Ann	30	F		TN
Mary	11	F		TN
Sarah Jane	9	F		TN
Edwin	7	M		TN
John N. M.	4	M		TN
Leticia C.	2	F		TN
Renow, R. T.	22	M	Farmer	TN
Lindsey, Thomas R. (continued)	42	M	Farmer	KY

Name	Age	Sex	Occupation	Birthplace
Lindsey, Jane	38	F		TN
William T.	15	M		TN
Margaret	14	F		MS
Malvina	12	F		MS
John	10	M		MS
Charles	8	M		MS
Eliza	6	F		MS
Sarah	2	F		MS
Carter, Josiah	23	M	Wagon Maker	TN
Gray, Robert	63	M	Farmer	NC
Cynthia	63	F		TN
Mary H.	34	F		TN
Cynthia C.	17	F		TN
Gray, William	36	M	Millwright	TN
Robert N.	10	M		AL
Mary	8	F		AL
Susan	5	F		AL
Alexander, T. S.	22	M	Farmer	TN
Birch, Leroy	25	M	Farmer	TN
Edith	22	F		TN
Birch, Hardy	50	M	Farmer	??
Hannah	50	F		??
John C.	21	M	Farmer	TN
Catherine	16	F		TN
Rhoda Ann	14	F		TN
George M.	10	M		TN
Thomas J.	8	M		TN
Woodward, Dabney	49	M	Farmer	NC
Sarah	50	F		NC
John	20	M	Farmer	TN
Sarah	15	F		TN
Clarissa	13	F		TN
Joseph	10	M		MS
Stone, Martin	34	M	Farmer	TN
Nancy	26	F		TN
Sarah	9	F		MO
James	8	M		MO
Margaret	7	F		MO
Elizabeth	5	F		TX
Malinda Ann	1	F		TX
Head, Madison	21	M	Farmer	TN
Collins, Hesekiah	30	M	Farmer	TN
Mary	23	F		TN
Priddle, George W.	28	M	Farmer	TN
Jane	27	F		TN
Emiline	2	F		TX
Reed, W. T.	19	M	Farmer	TN
Gurley, John	28	M	Farmer	TN
Louis	49	M	Farmer	NC
Eda	49	F		NC
Willis	23	M	Farmer	TN
Jacob	20	M	Farmer	TN
Jesse	17	M	Farmer	TN
Daniel	15	M		TN
James	13	M		TN
Louis	10	M		TN
Stancel	8	M		TN
Mary	8	F		TN
Callahan, Caroline	4	F		MS
Helton, J. H.	33	M	Farmer	TN
Lucinda	33	F		TN
David M.	10	M		MS
James	8	M		TX
Cynthia E.	6	F		TX
Joseph N.	4	M		TX
Isabella J.	2	F		TX
Wade, Isaac M.	29	M	Farmer	TN
Susan	29	F		VA
James H.	9	M		TN
Milton M.	6	M		GA
Mary Ann	2	F		GA
William W.	16	M		GA

RUSK COUNTY, TEXAS

Name	Age	Sex	Occupation	Birthplace
Lantz, John G.	42	M	Carpenter	NC
Teressa L.	32	F		TN
Jacob B.	8	M		AL
John D.	6	M		AL
Sarah F.	4	F		AL
Marion	2	M		TX
Lantz, Henry	45	M	Farmer	NC
Hoke, Daniel	24	M	Carpenter	NC
Ghinn, James	25	M	Farmer	??
Bagget, Silas	28	M	Farmer	AL
Ellen	20	F		TN
James M.	4	M		TX
Eli B.	3	M		TX
Letticia Ann	1	F		TX
Bagget, Joel	23	M	Farmer	AL
Wiley B.	18	M	Farmer	AL
Eliza J.	16	F		AL
Mary	13	F		AL
Susan	10	F		AL
Murrell, Lemuel	30	M	Farmer	AL
Louisa	20	F		TN
Pendleton, John	25	M	Brick Layer	TN
Lakey, John	30	M	Brick Layer	TN
Rollins, Benjamin	20	M		TN
Cox, John H.	22	M	Farmer	AL
Lee, William	39	M	Millwright	TN
Nancy	18	F		TN
James J.	17	M	Farmer	TN
Amanda J.	15	F		TN
George W.	13	M		AL
Ruben J.	13	M		AL
Margaret E.	12	F		AL
William H. H.	9	M		AL
Sarah F.	7	F		AL
Christopher	5	M		AL
Warren P.	3	M		AL
Neelen, James W.	38	M	Farmer	TN
Elizabeth	39	F		TN
John S.	13	M		AL
Rufua R.	12	M		AL
George A.	6	M		GA
A. A.	5	M		AL
Victoria H.	2	F		AL
Rogers, Henry T.	24	M	Farmer	TN
Martha	26	F		AL
Mary B.	67	F		??
Dice	13	F		MS
Louisiana	11	F		MS
Hinke, Henry	34	M	Brick Layer	TN
Sarah Ann	6	F		MS
Crow, Thomas	45	M	Cabinet Maker	VA
Mary Ann	35	F		TN
Phebe Ann	14	F		IL
Robert	10	M		IN
William T.	8	M		IN
Mary E.	4	F		LA
Slaughter, Calvin	26	M	Cabinet Maker	AL
Mullins, Barkley	50	M	Carpenter	GA
Elizabeth	46	F		TN
Barkley	16	M		MS
Carr, J. D.	32	M	None	TN
Maria E.	32	F		TN
Eudora A.	12	F		MS
William L.	8	M		MS
Jesse D.	4	M		MS
Albert S.	11/12	M		LA
Redden, G. C.	21	M	Black Smith	TN
Williams, S. O.	22	M	Black Smith	AL
Habard, William C.	24	M	Farmer	AR
Hodges, William	33	M	Farmer	TN
Jane	27	F		KY
Elizabeth	13	F		TN
Frances	11	F		TN

(continued)

Name	Age	Sex	Occupation	Birthplace
Hodges, Susan	9	F		MS
Martha	7	F		MS
Joel	6	M		MS
Tabitha	4	F		MS
Hariet	1	F		MS
Montgomery, Robert	53	M	Farmer	TN
Maria R.	47	F		TN
James A.	26	M	Farmer	TN
Isaac R.	24	M	Farmer	TN
Stephen D.	22	M	Farmer	TN
Harshaw, George	25	M	Farmer	TN
Simpson, Joshua	45	M	Farmer	KY
Sarah	44	F		KY
Rolden H.	19	M	Farmer	TN
Rachael	13	F		??
William T.	14	M		AR
Columbus	10	M		AR
Polly Ann	6	F		AR
Balzora Lee	2	F		TX
Anderson, Thomas J.	30	M	Farmer	GA
Margaret Ann	32	F		TN
Mary Ellen	12	F		MS
Thomas Jefferson	8	M		TX
Sarah A.	7	F		TX
Enoch Kuter	5	M		TX
Margaret E.	2	F		TX
Georgeanna T.	1	F		TX
Guthrie, James S.	55	M	C.P. Clergyman	TN
Burnes, Robert	18	M	Farmer	AL
Mary Anny	13	F		AL
Vienna	10	F		AL
Gray, Huston J.	22	M	Farmer	TN
Arelia P.	21	F		AL
Wood, Elizabeth	40	F		SC
Hiram	25	M	Farmer	AL
Jane Maria	16	F		AL
Francis Jackson	13	M		AL
Frances Elizabeth	11	F		AL
Pleasant S.	6	M		MS
Sparks, Luvisa R.	28	F		TN
Wynn, William B.	33	M	Farmer	TN
Sarah A.	26	F		TN
Mary Rhoda	12	F		TN
Virginia	10	F		TN
Richard	8	M		TN
James	6	M		TX
Deverix S.	4	M		TX
Thomas	1	M		TX
Beene, Caleb S.	29	M	Farmer	TN
Mary Ann	23	F		GA
Ruth Ann	4	F		AR
John F.	2	M		AR
Rooter, Andrew	20	M	None	AR
Sutton, Jack	22	M		GA
Carter, David	55	M		TN
Jane	50	F		TN
Eliza	18	F		TN
Susan	15	F		TN
Robert	13	M		TN
Sarah	11	F		TN
Permelia	9	F		TN
Bradshaw, Joseph	39	M	Farmer	TN
Nancy	26	F		TN
Sally	7	F		TN
Elisha	5	M		TN
James K. P.	4	M		TN
Albert, Infant	8/12	M		TX
Hicks, John	4	M		TN
Stubblefield, Anderson	35	M	Overseer	TN
Martha Eliza	30	F		TN
James Mark	2	M		MS
Julius Mc.	10	M		MS
Mary E.	8	F		MS
Thomas J.	4	M		MS
Martha Ann	7/12	F		TX

Name	Age	Sex	Occupation	Birthplace
Dixon, James	45	M		TN
Margaret	26	F		KY
Grisham, John M.	27	M	Saddler	TN
Frances	25	F		SC
Archibald T.	3	M		TN
Samantha	1	F		TX
Walker, W.	60	M	Wagon Maker	VA
Haden, Charles A.	33	M	Shoe-Boot Maker	MA
Hannah Balyora	27	F		TN
Thomas Glenroy	7/12	M		TX
Box, Salina	48	F		TN
Benjamin B.	28	F	Farmer	TN
Joseph Gooden	25	M	Farmer	TN
Franklin	18	M	Farmer	TN
Mary	16	F		TN
James Robert	14	M		AL
Andrew J.	11	M		AL
Stephen Jones	60	M	None	TN
Harmon, George W.	39	M	Carpenter	TN
Ellender	30	F		TN
Sarah Jane	12	F		AR
Dynersey(?)	10	F		AR
James A. M.	7	M		AR
Martha Ann	5	F		AR
Ward, Noah H.	37	M	Farmer	SC
Elizabeth	26	F		TN
Redson	15	M		AL
Virgil	13	M		AL
Malvina	10	F		AL
Sam	4	M		TX
William	2	M		TX
Martha	1	F		TX
McVay, Mary	24	F		TN
Davis, J. T.	38	M	Farmer	GA
Martha Ann	30	F		TN
Lee, William C.	45	M	Physician	KY
Cynthia	46	F		NC
Thadeus C.	22	M	Medical Student	AL
Thomas W.	20	M	Farmer	AL
William C.	18	M	Farmer	AL
Sarah B.	16	F		AL
Margaret E.	14	F		AL
Joseph	11	M		AL
Cynthia P.	9	F		AL
Lee, William	83	M	Farmer	VA
Margaret	81	F		VA
Snoddy, L. B.	23	M	Teacher	TN
Benson, M. L.	23	M	Farmer	GA
Dooley, Littleton J.	49	M	Farmer	TN
Susan	35	F		VA
Thomas	23	M	Farmer	TN
M. A. E. J.	17	F		LA
Matilda	14	F		MS
George	13	M		TX
John	11	M		TX
James	6	M		TX
Christiana	5	F		TX
Corilda	3	F		TX
William	1	M		TX
Cobb, William	25	M	Farmer	GA
Gant, Mathew	62	M	Farmer	TN
Delila	42	F		SC
Samuel	35	M	Black Smith	TN
George M. H.	13	M		AL
Nancy A. A.	11	F		AL
Gant, Jane	14	F		AL
Eliza	12	F		AL
Nancy Ann	9	F		AL
Gant, James B.	36	M		TN
William A.	10	M		AL
Ackins, James M.	37	M	Farmer	TN
Nancy	38	F		??
(continued)				
Ackins, Robert	6	M		AL
Jane	4	F		AL
Caroline	1	F		TX
Yates, Caroline	20	F		??
Kersey, David	23	M	Farmer	GA
Mary Ann	25	F		TN
Mary E.	2	F		TX
John Madison	1	F		TX
Couch, Clamoy	38	M	Farmer	SC
Isabella C.	41	F		KY
Elizabeth C.	17	F		TN
Margaret Ann	8	F		TX
Anderson, W. W.	33	M	Farmer	KY
Mary	27	F		TN
Irvin	9	M		AR
William	7	M		AR
Hugh	5	M		TX
Mary	2	F		TX
Kate	1	F		TX
Murchison, Isabella	21	F		TN
Dixon, Sarah	12	F		AR
Murchison, John M.	28	M	Teacher	TN
Wright, W. C.	27	M	Farmer	TN
Martha Jane	1	F		TX
Cole, William H.	24	M	Student	TN
Howell, Edward	46	M	Farmer	TN
Amanda	23	F		AL
David B.	1	M		TX
Howell, Walter	16	M	Farmer	--
Rounsville, Amos H.	39	M	Farmer	TN
Susan F.	37	F		TN
James K.	13	M		TN
Sarah Jane	11	F		MS
Mary E.	9	F		MS
Susan F.	7	F		MS
Amos H.	5	M		TX
Ellen T.	2	F		TX
Husbands, Miles H.	24	M	Farmer	TN
Beasley, James	28	M	Farmer	TN
Brown, George W.	25	M	Farmer	AL
Letitia Ann	19	F		TN
Wiley, C. M.	38	M	Farmer	GA
Nancy	30	F		TN
Charles F.	13	M		AL
Thomas J.	10	M		MS
Virlinda E.	7	F		MS
Dudley W.	5	M		MS
Missouri F.	2	F		MS
Wiley, Taylor	57	M	Cabinet Maker	NC
Leroy W.	19	M	Cabinet Maker	AL
Lowrie, Robert G.	44	M	Farmer	TN
Elizabeth	44	F		GA
Joana Amelia	15	F		TN
George A.	13	M		MS
Mary P.	4	F		AR
Phillips, Charles	22	M	Laborer	TN
Payne, William B.	47	M	Farmer	NC
Rhoda G.	45	F		NC
William G. B.	23	M	Farmer	TN
Sterling S.	19	M	Farmer	TN
Charles H.	15	M	Farmer	TN
Mary E.	13	F		TN
Julia	9	F		TN
Nancy R. A.	5	F		TN
Loyd, Mary	55	F		NC
Paine, McKenzie L.	25	M	Farmer	TN
Hetty	25	F		AL
William H.	5	M		TN
Sarah E.	2	F		TX
James P.	7/12	M		TX
Meredith, James L. P.	43	M	Farmer	TN
(continued)				

Name	Age	Sex	Occupation	Birthplace
Meredith, Amelia	27	F		TN
Joseph	11	M		TN
John V.	8	M		TX
Sarah J.	6	F		TX
Minerva A.	4	F		TX
William T.	2	M		TX
Day, John R.	21	M	Farmer	TN
Mary Ann	17	F		TN
Day, Emily	23	F		TN
Lawrence, Jeptha	3	M		TX
Bragg, William	55	M	Farmer	TN
Patience	25	F		TN
Elizabeth	9	F		TN
Amanda	7	F		TN
Martha	5	F		TN
Columbus	3	M		TN
Konce, Benjamin F.	28	M	Farmer	KY
Sevier	59	F		TN
Roberts, James	25	M	Farmer	TN
Irene	21	F		TN
Evan	2	M		TN
Missouri Ann	2/12	F		TX
Copeland, Wiley	46	M	Farmer	TN
Nancy	42	F		KY
Mary	15	F		MS
James	18	M	Farmer	AL
Martha	12	F		MS
John	14	M		MS
Francis M.	10	M		MS
Fletcher	8	M		MS
Nancy	6	F		MS
William	4	M		MS
Hodges, William	33	M	Farmer	TN
Jane	32	F		KY
Elizabeth	12	F		TN
Frances	11	F		TN
Susan	8	F		MS
Martha	7	F		MS
Joel	5	M		MS
Tabitha	3	F		MS
Hariet	1	F		MS
Murchison, Simeon	49	M	Farmer	NC
Elizabeth	39	F		TN
M. R. H.	22	M	Farmer	TN
Lucy Ann	20	F		TN
Mary M.	17	F		TN
Elizabeth	15	F		TN
Martha E.	11	F		TN
George R.	1	M		TN
Hestey, Daniel	36	M	Farmer	AL
Emiline F.	21	F		TN
Sarah J.	4	F		TX
Mary Ann	2	F		TX
Nancy E.	7/12	F		TX
Simpson, Marshal	21	M	Laborer	TN
Jones, Angeline	26	F		SC
Susan L.	9	F		TN
William M.	4	M		TN
Nancy B.	2	F		TN
Lawyer, William G.	40	M	Farmer	NC
Sarah A. F.	32	F		SC
Enoch W.	9	M		TN
Marshal N.	5	M		TN
Jesse E.	4	M		TN
Sp----	1	M		TX
Jones, Joseph	20	M	Farmer	TN
Rountree, Thomas P.	33	M	Farmer	AL
Eveline	26	F		TN
Thomas	8	M		AR
Leonidas A.	6	M		TN
James O.	1	M		TX
Murchison, Murdock	50	M	Farmer	NC
Sarah	51	F		TN

(continued)

Name	Age	Sex	Occupation	Birthplace
Murchison, George S.	26	M	Farmer	TN
Morgan H.	24	M	Farmer	TN
Elizabeth J.	22	F		TN
Nancy Ann	20	F		TN
Ellen F.	18	F		TN
Catherine	17	F		TN
Rebecca	15	F		MS
Margaret	11	F		MS
Robert W.	9	M		MS
Murchison, John Mc.	28	M	School Teacher	TN
Isabella M.	22	F		TN
Murchison, Kenneth	40	M	Farmer	TN
Mary	30	F		NC
Nancy J.	13	F		TN
John W.	12	M		MS
William M.	7	M		TN
Sarah E.	2	F		TN
Margaret J.	6/12	F		TX
Dereberry, Tapley	30	M	Farmer	TN
Elizabeth A.	26	F		TN
Henrietta E.	4	F		TN
William H.	2	M		TN
Amanda G.	5/12	F		TX
Angel, John	50	M	None	NC
Mahala	47	F		KY
Caroline	25	F		AL
James L.	22	M	M.E. Clergyman	AL
John W.	20	M	Farmer	AL
James R.	18	M	Farmer	AL
Charles	16	M		AL
Martha E.	9	F		MS
Mary H.	7	F		MS
Tiner, J. M. C.	26	M	House Carpenter	TN
Logan, W. H.	30	M	House Carpenter	GA
Alexander, Lafayette	25	M	Farmer	NC
Lawler, Henry	39	M	Farmer	TN
Jane	41	F		KY
Orange, Frederick	16	M		GER
Sartin, James R.	52	M	Farmer	GA
Matilda	45	F		TN
John F.	26	M	Farmer	TN
Martha Jane	17	F		AL
Charles J.	12	M		TN
Easton, Joel	27	M	Farmer	TN
Scates, Elizabeth	42	F		TN
George W.	21	M	Farmer	TN
John W.	12	M		TN
Starr, George H.	44	M	Farmer	TN
Nancy	36	F		GA
Jane	19	F		TN
John W.	8	M		AR
Mary	6	F		AR
George	3	M		AR
Ezekiel	1	M		TX
Hawkins, James	32	M	Overseer	KY
Smith, H. M.	32	M	Farmer	SC
Sarah	26	F		TN
Green Lafayette	9	M		TX
James DeKalb	7	M		TX
Susan	5	F		TX
John	4	M		TX
Joseph	3	M		TX
Morison, Alfred	35	M	Farmer	GA
Scott, James	38	M	Black Smith	TN
Parker, Isaac G.	47	M	Clerk	SC
Rucker, Robert D.	21	M	Farmer	VA
Mary Jane	18	F		TN
Latham, Sterling	26	M	Farmer	TN
Farmer, Samuel	30	M	Farmer	TN
Sarah	27	F		NC
Ford, Timothy	49	M	House Carpenter	NC

(continued)

RUSK COUNTY, TEXAS

Name	Age	Sex	Occupation	Birthplace
Ford, Hariet	38	F		GA
Elizabeth	10	F		AL
Florena	8	F		AL
Emmah H.	6	F		AL
McKenzie, E. A.	24	M	Farmer	AL
Eaton, Alfred	24	M	None	TN
Wright, George H.	37	M	Farmer	TN
Elizabeth J.	37	F		SC
Rebecca	5	F		TX
Nancy Jane	3	F		TX
William H.	1	M		TX
Churchill, William	24	M	Student	TN
Alfred	22	M	Student	TN
Stone, Nancy	45	F		TN
Catharine E.	21	F		KY
Montgomery, William	30	M	Farmer	TN
George W.	16	M	Student	KY
Mary	14	F		KY
William	12	M		KY
Samuel	10	M		TX
Robert L.	8	M		TX
Hooker, Jesse	35	M	Shoe Maker	TN
Catharine	32	F		TN
John Long	14	M		TX
Sarah	5	F		TX
Hearst, William W.	34	M	Farmer	TN
Mary Ann	30	F		TN
Elizabeth Jane	8	F		TN
William M.	7	M		TN
Bailey Paton	6	M		TN
Gurley, Lewis	51	M	Farmer	NC
Eden	51	F		NC
John	24	M	Farmer	TN
Willis	22	M	Farmer	TN
Jacob	20	M	Farmer	TN
Daniel	16	M	Farmer	TN
James	14	M		TN
William S.	10	M		TN
Mary	10	F		TN
Caroline	5	F		MS
McClure, Thomas B.	48	M	Farmer	NC
Linville	43	F		GA
Catharine	12	F		TN
Sophia	17	F		TN
Fatima	14	F		TN
Roxana	12	F		GA
Lyons, Thomas	29	M	Tanner	GA
Linville	?7	F		TN
Claiborne	6	M		TN
Martha	4	F		TN
Nowlin, Lewis	40	M	Farmer	NC
Eliza	32	F		NC
Martha Ann	14	F		TN
Louisa	9	F		TN
Joana Josephine	6	F		TX
Doctor	12	M		TN
Watson, Dempsey	58	M	Farmer	NC
Mary	54	F		SC
Wyley	33	M	None	SC
Dempsey M.	23	M		TN
Mary G.	18	F		TN
Martha L.	16	F		TN
Elias	25	M	Farmer	TN
Smith, Elisha A.	46	M	M.E.C. Clergyman	MO
Elizabeth	33	F		TN
Adaline	11	F		LA
Melissa	9	F		TX
Allen	7	M		TX
Presley	5	M		TX
Margaret	3	F		TX
Wilbanks, Gardiner	53	M	Farmer	SC
Sally	36	F		TN
William	20	M	Farmer	TN
Allen	19	M	Farmer	TN
Hiram	17	M	Farmer	TN
Calvin	16	M	Farmer	TN
Jesse	13	M		TN
Benjamin	12	M		AR
Doctor	11	M		TX
Daniel H.	7	M		TX
Susan	5	F		TX
Sarah C.	4	F		TX
Stockton, Thomas P.	35	M	Farmer	TN
Martha E.	29	F		TN
James T.	10	M		TN
Jane	8	F		MO
Hariet	6	F		TN
Sarah	4	F		TN
Jones, William	45	M	Farmer	SC
Catharine	36	F		TN
Britton	19	M		MS
Alexander	17	M		MS
Mary Jane	15	F		MS
Adeline	13	F		MS
Clarissa	11	F		MS
Amanda	7	F		MS
David R.	8/12	M		TX
Jones, Brittan	75	M	None	NC
James Alexander C.	12	M		TN
Davis, William C.	38	M	Farmer	MD
Caroline	35	F		TN
Hamilton, James	14	M		TN
Mary L.	12	F		TX
Davis, Permelia	7	F		TX
Lewis A.	6	M		TX
Elizabeth	3	F		TX
Thomas J.	1	M		TX
Cash, John S.	39	M	Farmer	NC
Rebecca	39	F		TN
Susan	13	F		AL
William W.	11	M		AL
Catharine	9	F		AL
Joel Thomas	6	M		AL
John G.	5	M		AL
Rebecca L.	2	F		AL
Estill, William H.	36	M	Lawyer	TN
Amanda L. L.	26	F		TN
Mary C.	9	F		AL
James Thomas	6	M		AL
Julia Hester	3	F		AL
Likens, Thomas M.	50	M	Lawyer	TN
Hester L.	55	F		MD
John T.	23	M	Farmer	TN
James B.	21	M	Lawyer	GA
Carnes, Thomas	43	M	Farmer	TN
Mary	28	F		TN
Martha K.	2	F		TX
John Henry	6/12	M		TX
McGowan, P. H.	25	M	Farmer	TN
McGowan, Brown	--	M		TN
Martin, Jane	35	F		TN
Lafayette	14	M		TN
Jeraline	10	F		TN
John James	8	M		TN
Spinks, John	43	M	Farmer	TN
Sarah	47	F		NC
Samuel	19	M	Farmer	TN
Martha Jane	17	F		TN
Sarah Ann	14	F		TN
John M.	10	M		TN
Mary A.	6	F		TN
Penn, George	40	M	None	VA
Benjamin F.	13	M		MS
Lee, John	21	M	Farmer	TN
Nicholson, James	23	M	None	PA

(continued)

RUSK COUNTY, TEXAS

Name	Age	Sex	Occupation	Birthplace
Nicholson, Walter C.	24	M	Farmer	--
Nancy E.	17	F		TN
Farmer, Hulet	39	M	Farmer	KY
Anna	38	F		KY
Frederick	18	M	Farmer	TN
Ewel	16	M	Farmer	TN
Marian	14	M		TX
Rosalthia	12	F		TX
Mary Jane	11	F		TX
George M.	5	M		TX
McGraw, Robert H.	35	M	Farmer	TN
Elizabeth	35	F		TN
John H.	8	M		MS
Sarah Jane	5	F		MS
Buffington, Ellis	27	M	Farmer	GA
Elizabeth	26	F		TN
Ezekiel S.	8	M		AR
Susan Jane	5	F		AR
Joshua	3	M		AR
Ellis B.	2	M		AR
Sabira E.	3/12	F		TX
Starr, Jane	16	F		TN
Arnold, Elisha	30	M	Overseer	MS
Martha	34	F		TN
Jonathan	11	M		MS
Thomas	9	M		MS
Margaret	7	F		MS
Sarah	5	F		MS
Martha	4	F		MS
Mary Ann	2	F		TX
Mayfield, Wilson	23	M	Farmer	TN
Sarah	24	F		TN
Ezekiel	3	M		AR
Penelope	2	F		TX
Starr, Ellis	20	M	None	TN
Spence, Henry B.	23	M	Farmer	TN
Harriet	18	F		AL
Ray, D. L.	50	M	Farmer	KY
Mary	49	F		TN
Nancy	22	F		TN
Eliza	18	F		TN
Joseph	15	M		TN
James	9	M		TN
Wright, Thomas L.	34	M	Farmer	TN
Izetta E.	25	F		SC
Daniel	8	M		TX
Izetta	7	F		TX
Martha	5	F		TX
Delila E.	1	F		TX
Mary A.	1	F		TX
Wright, Hansel	77	M	None	VA
Elizabeth	70	F		NC
Sarah C.	40	F		TN
Walling, Thomas J.	39	M	Farmer	TN
Nancy Ann	37	F		TN
Edward T.	17	M	Farmer	TN
John H.	15	M	Farmer	TN
Thomas J.	12	M		TX
Charles T.	10	M		TX
Sarah Ann	8	F		TX
Cynthia	6	F		TX
Pauliney V.	4	M		TX
William F.	1	M		TX
Nisuet(?), Michael	21	M	Black Smith	GER
Reagan, William	50	M	Farmer	TN
Matilda	44	F		TN
Adaline	23	F		TN
James	21	M		TN
Amanda	19	F		TN
Robert	16	M		GA
Caroline	14	F		TX
Noble	11	M		TX
Emily	9	F		TX
(continued)				
Reagan, Hellen	5	F		TX
Allenia	1	F		TX
Todd, Jackson	33	M	Farmer	LA
Martha Ann	25	F		TN
Eliza Letitia	8	F		TX
Sarah Ann	6	F		TX
Nancy Jane	4	F		TX
Elizabeth Jane	4	F		TX
James C.	2	M		TX
Jesse W.	6/12	M		TX
Pitner, Andrew H.	38	M	Farmer	TN
Margaret	35	F		TN
Eliza Ann	19/12	F		TX
Kelley, Nancy	78	F		NC
Barnes, Roswell	21	M	Farmer	TN
Greenwood, Thomas B.	42	M	Farmer	TN
Elizabeth	30	F		GA
Wiley, Collin F.	24	M	Farmer	AL
Sarah	22	F		MS
Reese, John K.	45	M	Farmer	TN
Angeline	22	F		AL
Sophia	18	F		AL
Sampson	16	M		AL
William	14	M		AL
Louisa	12	F		AL
Rachel	10	F		AL
Alsey	1	F		AL
Simpson, Hariet	42	F		TN
David	15	M	Laborer	AL
Martha	11	F		AL
Rachel	7	F		AL
Amanda	5	F		AL
Levina	3	F		AL
Reese, James M.	28	M	Laborer	AL
Reese, David	25	M	Laborer	AL
Forbus, James	55	M	Farmer	SC
Jane	64	F		IRE
David	25	M	None	AL
Octavus	22	M	Farmer	AL
William J.	17	M	None	MS
Anderson, C. C.	22	M	Laborer	TN
Phillips, William P.	10	M		MS
Lemons	8	M		MS
Gardner, George W.	28	M	Farmer	TN
Mary	23	F		TN
Brown, Aron V.	5	M		TN
William T.	2	M		TX
Abner L.	8/12	M		TX
Seamore, Isaac H.	30	M	Farmer	TN
Mary	29	F		TN
Lucinda A.	8	F		TN
William W.	6	M		TN
Jacob H.	5	M		TN
James H.	2	M		TX
Sarah E.	1	F		TX
Daniels, Abraham	38	M	Farmer	GA
Mary Ann	28	F		SC
Eugenia A.	12	F		FL
Penn, Sarah	7	F		TN
Richardson, Mary	76	F		SC
Hicks, Agnes	36	F		TN
Moore, Jesse	19	M		TN
Saline	13	F		TN
Lusetta	11	F		TN
Caldeone	15	M	Laborer	TN
Louisa	9	F		TN
Crockett	7	M		TN
Mark Banks	5	M		TN
Sugar	3	M		TN
Myres, Josiah T.	31	M	Black Smith	TN
Dicy	32	F		TN
John E.	9	M		TN
Samuel S.	7	M		TN
Sarah E.	5	F		TN
(continued)				

Myres, Cyrus P.	2	M		TX
Myres, Jacob G.	24	M	Farmer	TN
Seamore, William	65	M	Farmer	NC
Sarah	55	F		VA
David P.	27	M	Farmer	TN
William H.	25	M	Farmer	TN
R. L.	21	M	Farmer	TN
Mathews, Lewis A.	23	M	Farmer	TN
Britenia	31	F		AL
Ruth	51	F		NC
Samuel B.	31	M	Farmer	AL
James S.	27	M	Farmer	TN
John H.	17	M	Farmer	TN
Hicks, John	56	M	Farmer	KY
Mary	45	F		TN
Tabitha	26	F		TN
Elizabeth	20	F		TN
Martha	19	F		TN
Theressa	22	F		TN
Jane	17	F		TN
Huldy	15	F		TN
Guines	10	M		GA
Julian	8	F		GA
James K. P.	5	M		TN
Tennessee	5	F		TN
Alvisa	20	M	Farmer	TN
Elijah	18	M	Farmer	TN
Hogue, Lewis T.	31	M	Farmer	NC
Esther	31	F		NC
William D.	9	M		NC
Julian H.	6	F		GA
Sarah A.	4	F		TN
John L. K. Polk	3	M		TX
David J.	1	M		TX
Presnel, Luke	40	M	Farmer	SC
Rhoda	21	F		TN
Mary	1	F		TX
Gailey, Andrew	60	M	Carpenter	TN
Catharine	45	F		AL
Langston, John P.	21	M	Farmer	TN
Rebecca	27	F		TN
C. Perry	3/12	M		TX
Julian L.	2	F		TX
Hammonds, John G.	25	M	Carpenter	GA
Margaret E.	23	F		TN
Belcher, Edward H.	32	M	Farmer	GA
Mary	21	F		TN
Thomas J.	3	M		TX
Edward P.	1	M		TX
Barnes, James	23	M	Farmer	KY
Elizabeth	18	F		SC
Ebenezer	1/12	M		TX
Hicks, Ann	23	F		TN
Elizabeth	9/12	F		TX
Wade, James M.	27	M	Merchant	TN
Martha W. H.	20	F		TN
Bragg, Lydia Ann	25	F		TN
Davenport, William	17	M	Clerk	AL
Baines, William	50	M	Farmer	GA
Celia	34	F		TN
Isam	9	M		MS
Charlotte T.	6	F		MS
Mary L.	3	F		MS
Fatima E.	5	F		MS
Baines, Lunsford	21	M	Laborer	KY
Harwood, William T.	22	M	Laborer	TN
Nancy	19	F		TN
Hunt, Thomas	23	M	Farmer	TN
Hariet	21	F		KY

(continued)

Hunt, Sarah F.	3	F		TX
John A.	2	M		TX
Hurt, John C.	52	M	Farmer	NC
Martha	50	F		VA
Lucy	21	F		TN
Rachel A. L.	17	F		TN
Daniel	14	M		TN
John C., Jr.	10	M		TN
Henry G.	5	M		TN
Gilbreath, Amos	28	M	Farmer	TN
Juda	29	F		TN
Martha J.	6	F		TN
Mary T.	3	F		MS
Andrew J.	2	M		TX
Margaret A. H.	21	F		TX
Hurt, William C.	27	M	Farmer	TN
Elizabeth	24	F		TN
Fatima	5	F		TX
Susan C.	3	F		TX
Lucy	2	F		TX
John Thomas	1	M		TX
Forister, Edward	44	M	Farmer	NC
Alsey	27	F		TN
Lock S.	6	M		TN
Hoss	4	M		TN
Ruch	2	M		TN
Infant	2/12	F		TX
Stubblefield, William	37	M	Farmer	TN
Melisa	40	F		SC
John	17	M		TN
Betsey Ann	14	F		MS
Wyatt	12	M		MS
Martha Jane	11	F		TN
Polly Ann	9	F		MS
Samuel	8	M		MS
Betsey Jane	6	F		MS
Thomas	5	M		MS
Stephen	4	M		TX
Willis T.	2	F		TX
Stubblefield, Dixon	30	M	Farmer	TN
Eliza	30	F		TN
Robison, William	29	M	Farmer	TN
Hariet	20	F		TN
Zachariah W.	5	M		TN
Eliza	2/12	F		TX
Gross, George W.	45	M	Farmer	TN
Lucinda	35	F		TN
James	10	M		TX
Mary Ann	7	F		TX
George W.	5	M		TX
William	1	M		TX
Strickland, Henry	45	M	Laborer	MS
Moore, John	25	M	Farmer	TN
Mary Ann	25	F		TN
Margaret E.	7	F		TN
Sarah E.	2	F		TX
George W.	7/12	M		TX
Harwood, Sally	45	F		TN
Joseph	14	M		TN
Catharine	12	F		TN
Boggy	10	M		TN
Moore, William	50	M	Farmer	TN
Sarah	45	F		TN
William, Jr.	19	M	Farmer	TN
Thomas	18	M	Farmer	TN
James H.	16	M	Farmer	TN
Sam Huston	15	M	Farmer	TN
George W.	13	M		TN
Robert C.	8	M		TN
Thompson A.	6	M		TN
John	27	M	Laborer	AL
Henry	25	M	Farmer	AL
Thomas M.	22	M	Laborer	AL
James M.	19	M	Farmer	AL

(continued)

RUSK COUNTY, TEXAS

Name	Age	Sex	Occupation	Birthplace
Moore, Calvin	7	M		AL
Polly Ann	11	F		AL
Hargrave, Edward	24	M	Laborer	TN
Duncan, George W.	38	M	Farmer	NC
Angeline	25	F		TN
Elizabeth	15	F		TN
George H.	14	M		TN
James A.	9	M		TN
Mary Ann	9	F		TN
William T.	7	M		MS
Sarah C.	4	F		MS
Joseph	1	M		MS
Irans, G. S.	31	M	Black Smith	GA
Louisa	23	F		MO
Amanda	3/12	F		TX
Hambright, F. A.	21	M	Laborer	TN
Simpson, James	34	M	Farmer	TN
Lucy Ann	23	F		VA
Susan R.	3	F		TX
Laura	1	F		TX
Woolsey, Thomas	47	M	Farmer	TN
Elizabeth	46	F		TN
Mary	20	F		TN
Stephen M.	18	M	Farmer	NC
Nathan R.	16	M	Farmer	NC
Robert L.	14	M		NC
Thomas J.	12	M		NC
Sarah Jane	10	F		NC
Harriet C. P.	8	F		NC
Elizabeth L.	6	F		NC
Hester Ann	2	F		NC
Roberts, Patsey	20	F		NC
Screws, Nathan	55	M	Farmer	TN
Matilda R.	31	F		NC
Henry Elbert	15	M		AL
Mary M.	11	F		TX
Christopher C.	1	M		TX
Lavina Jane	4	F		TX
John Wesley	2	M		TX
Nowlin, James	72	M	None	VA
Harris, Thomas L.	22	M	Farmer	MS
Mary Ann	21	F		AL
Beck, William	39	M	Farmer	TN
Polly	43	F		TN
Thomas	7	M		TN
William	5	M		TN
Beck, Samuel M.	34	M	Farmer	TN
Darthula A.	21	F		TN
George W.	2	M		TX
Zilinda	3/12	F		TX
Geor, Leonard G.	19	M	Farmer	TN
Ben B.	17	M	Farmer	TN
Phebe E.	15	F		TN
Harris, Loving P.	39	M	Carpenter	MA
Susan C.	30	F		TN
Edward C.	6	M		AR
Nancy J.	4	F		AR
Susan E.	2	F		AR
Walden, John	40	M	Farmer	TN
Nancy	32	F		OH
Ann	10	F		AR
Melinda	8	F		AR
Solomon	4	M		AR
Isreal	2	M		AR
Farington, A. H.	24	M	Carriage Maker	NC
Aveana	28	F		TN
T. W. R.	4	M		TN
Leonidas P.	2	M		TN
Hugh	1/12	M		TX
Brown, James N.	33	M	Farmer	GA
Lucinda J.	23	F		TN
John W.	6	M		TX
Letitia Minerva	5	F		TX
(continued)				

Name	Age	Sex	Occupation	Birthplace
Brown, Margaret Ellen	4	F		TX
James N., Jr.	3	M		TX
Nancy Ann	2	F		TX
Tucker, Henry	30	M	Farmer	NC
Sarah	25	F		NC
Harnage, George W.	35	M	Farmer	GA
Nancy	30	F		TN
John	3	M		AR
Reuben Thomas	19	M	Farmer	TN
David	17	M		TN
Burrell	15	M		TN
Elizabeth	14	F		TN
Allen	11	M		TN
Lacy, Griffith	49	M	Farmer	NC
Elizabeth	42	F		NC
Sarah	20	F		TN
Elizabeth	18	F		TN
John	13	M		TN
James	12	M		TN
Frances	8	F		TN
Westbrook, Stephen	22	M		TN
Stone, Lemuel	23	M	Farmer	TN
Margaret A.	21	F		TN
Thomas A.	1	M		TX
Jones, M. H.	47	M	Teacher	TN
Mary	48	F		KY
Milton	14	M		MS
Martha E.	12	F		MS
Benjamin F.	11	M		MS
Wyley	6	M		TX
Lee, William L.	20	M	Farmer	IL
Crawford, William N.	33	M	Farmer	TN
Lucinda	29	F		TN
Samuel A.	9	M		TN
Thomas J.	7	M		TN
Ambrose	2	M		TX
George	5	M		TN
Williams, William	52	M	Farmer	TN
Gerrilla	41	F		GA
William	20	M	Farmer	TX
Thomas	19	M	Farmer	TX
Russel	16	M	Farmer	TX
Mary	17	F		TX
Lidia	14	F		TX
Gerilla	12	F		TX
Prescilla	11	F		TX
Leonard	9	M		TX
Leander	8	M		TX
Aditha	7	F		TX
Infant	6/12	F		TX
Reasonover, Early B.	36	M	Farmer	TN
Levina	36	F		TN
William T.	14	M		TN
Nancy Jane	8	F		MS
Thomas, James	64	M	Farmer	TN
Nancy	56	F		VA
Wesley G.	23	M	Farmer	TN
William C. M.	15	M	Farmer	TX
Wyatt, Elijah	58	M	Farmer	VA
Nancy	22	F		MS
Edward J.	19	M	Farmer	TN
Joseph	17	M	Farmer	TN
Thomas J.	4	M		TN
Elijah	2	M		TX
George, James	47	M	Farmer	SC
Sarah	39	F		TN
Martha R.	24	F		GA
Lucinda E.	21	F		GA
Nancy	18	F		GA
William T.	17	M	Farmer	GA
Emila	16	F		GA
Eliza	15	F		GA
Phebe	12	F		GA
Amanda	6	F		GA
Heath, Richard	23	M	Farmer	SC
Gentry, Elisha	1	M		GA
Boyd, Alexander	8/12	M		MS

RUSK COUNTY, TEXAS

Yell, Benjamin B.	21	M	Farmer	TN
Ame	19	F		TN
Lydia	1	F		TX
Howett, Andrew	25	M	Farmer	TN
Eliza	19	F		AL
Mary E.	8/12	F		TX
Wiley, Anne	33	F		SC
Mary E.	10	F		TN
Candor M.	8	M		TN
Mary F.	6	F		TN
William E.	5	M		TN
Isaac P.	4	M		TN
Cates, James K.	25	M	Farmer	AL
Mary Ann	23	F		AR
Sarah E.	3	F		TX
Elizabeth	1	F		TX
Smith, Peter	24	M	Farmer	TN
Edmondson, Waddy	48	M	Farmer	SC
Nancy	40	F		SC
William	17	M	Farmer	AL
Adaline	15	F		AL
John	11	M		AL
Jane	8	F		AL
James K. P.	6	M		AL
Martha	3	F		AL
George M. D.	1	M		TX
Bowlin, William B.	20	M	Farmer	TN
Yarborough, Benjamin F.	20	M	Farmer	TN
Crawford	43	M	Farmer	TN
Elizabeth	26	F		TN
Riggs, Josiah	26	M	Farmer	NC
Rebecca	26	F		SC
William H.	7	M		TN
David	4	M		TN
John W.	2	M		TX
Jones, Robert P.	31	M	Carriage Maker	VA
Cloiann	24	F		TN
Amanda J.	9	F		TN
Elizabeth P.	6	F		TN
Samuel	4	M		TN
John R.	2	M		TN
Welch, Robert	30	M	Farmer	NC
Mary Ann	52	F		TN
Sarah E.	10	F		TN
Amanda T.	8	F		TN
Nancy M.	5	M(F)		TN
Buena Vista	3	F		TN
Infant	1	F		TX
McLeod, Angus	50	M	Saddler	SCO
Elizabeth	33	F		NC
William	10	M		TN
Isabell	5	F		AR
Mary	4	F		AR
John	2	M		TX
Caroline	2	F		TX
Allen, Sam T.	49	M	Merchant	VT
Lucretia	50	F		NC
Montgomery	25	M	Clerk	TN
Nelson	24	M	Farmer	??
Sanders, John	26	M	Farmer	NC
Nancy	28	F		NC
Letitia	6	F		TN
William R.	4	M		TN
Joseph H.	2	M		TN
Caine, William	34	M	None	TN
Eleander J.	27	F		TN
Mary E.	9	F		AL
John	8	M		AL
Andrew	6	M		AR
William	5	M		AR
Hugh	2	M		AR
Koonce, Daniel	73	M	Farmer	NC
Mary	50	F		KY
John Ky	18	M		TN
Lock, James	68	M	Farmer	VT
Lucinda	65	F		VT
James D.	21	M	Farmer	TN
John M.	19	M	Farmer	AL
Milton	16	M	Farmer	AL
Furgueson, Elizabeth	63	F		KY
Nicholas	21	M	Farmer	IL
Eveline	17	M		TN
Mary	2	F		TX
Patterson, John	22	M	Farmer	GA
Bond, Samuel	48	M	Farmer	KY
James J.	20	M	Farmer	TN
Sarah J.	17	F		TN
Elizabeth	14	F		TN
Rebecca	11	F		TN
John F.	10	M		TN
Mary M.	6	F		TN
Joel, James A.	50	M	Farmer	SC
Tabitha	35	F		TN
John R.	17	M		AL
Mary C.	16	F		AL
Rebecca E.	14	F		AL
George R.	12	M		AL
James C.	10	M		AL
Cynthia A.	8	F		AL
Sarah T.	4	F		TX
Jeremiah T.	1	M		TX
Latimer, Robert W.	36	M	Carpenter	TN
Nancy	33	F		IL
James R.	13	M		TN
John G.	11	M		TN
Thomas	9	M		TX
Margaret	7	F		TX
Martha	6	F		TX
Samuel H.	4	M		TX
Nicholas	2	M		TX
Moss, Hardin	35	M	Farmer	SC
Mary	35	F		TN
Thomas W.	10/12	M		TX
Brinson, Allen T.	23	M	Farmer	AL
Laura	19	F		TN
Virginia	2	F		TX
King, W. G.	28	M	Physician	TN
Rhoda E.	19	F		GA
Easley, John	63	M	Farmer	SC
Nancy	46	F		TN
John, Jr.	23	M	Farmer	TN
Susan	21	F		TN
James	22	M		TN
Richard	19	M		AL
Edward	16	M		AL
Thomas	14	M		AL
Andrew J.	12	M		AL
Newton J.	10	M		AL
Louis	6	M		TX
Ferguson, Joseph	27	M	Farmer	MO
Mary	27	F		TN
Alston	3	M		TX
Margaret	1	F		TX
Cates, Henry	25	M	Farmer	AL
Vannoy, Jesse	47	M	Farmer	NC
Elizabeth	43	F		TN
John	20	M	Medical Student	TN
Isaac	18	M	Farmer	TN
Archibald	12	M		TN
Susan	7	F		TN
Catharine	4	F		TX
Mary	2	F		TX
Dixon, Eliza	36	F		NC
Edwin	13	M		TN
Elvin	13	M		TN

RUSK COUNTY, TEXAS

Name	Age	Sex	Occupation	Birthplace
Biggs, Benjamin F.	35	M	Farmer	TN
Jane	22	F		IL
Eliza J.	12	F		MS
Martha	7	F		MS
Benjamin F.	5	M		TX
Robert	1	M		TX
Woolwine, William	36	M	Physician	VA
Mary	31	F		TN
Margaret	12	F		TN
Maria L.	9	F		TX
Hariet	6	F		TX
Nancy E.	5	F		TX
Virginia T.	2	F		TX
Fields, William	25	M	Farmer	TX
Kizziah	28	F		TN
Elliott, William	56	M	Farmer	DE
Polly	43	F		TN
Thomas	20	M	Farmer	TX
Louis	17	M	Farmer	TX
Edward	13	M		TX
Eliza J.	9	F		TX
Permelia	7	F		TX
Brewer, William	60	M	None	??
Elliott, John T.	22	M	Farmer	TX
Charles Anna	15	F		TN
Smith, James H.	45	M	Farmer	VA
Jane	40	F		TN
Lorinda	20	F		IL
Burton	16	M	Laborer	TN
Peyton	14	M		TN
Betsey	11	F		TN
Caroline	10	F		TN
George	8	M		TN
Jonathan	6	M		TN
Nancy	4	F		TN
Smith, Calvin	22	M	Laborer	TN
Sarah	24	F		TN
Haltom, Robert R.	26	M	Farmer	TN
Mary Ann	17	F		GA
Haltom, Thomas	22	M	Farmer	TN
James	15	M	Farmer	TN
Sarah	18	F		TN
Gentry, William	45	M		TN
Polly	35	F		TN
Jane	18	F		TN
James	16	M	Farmer	TN
Joseph	14	M		TN
Betsey	12	F		TN
Ann	10	F		TN
Peter	8	M		TN
John	6	M		TN
Margaret	4	F		AL
Washington	1	M		TX
Wren, Washington	23	M	None	TN
Stovall, F. M.	30	M	M.E. Clergyman	TN
Maria Jane	30	F		KY
Samuel Fulton	6	M		AR
Martha Jane	4	F		AR
Papham, William	18	M	Student of Divinity	MO
Ohare, Washington	36	M	Farmer	KY
Patsey Jane	35	F		TN
Sarah E.	14	F		IL
John T.	12	M		IL
Robert	10	M		TX
Amanda J.	8	F		TX
William W.	5	M		TX
Siba E.	3	F		TX
Nancy C.	4/12	F		TX
Ray, Robert	35	M	None	NC
Lucretia	30	F		TN
Ellen	8	F		TN
Sarah A.	6	F		TN

(Continued)

Name	Age	Sex	Occupation	Birthplace
Ray, Penila J.	4	F		TN
Infant	6/12	F		TN
Stroud, Mark	38	M	Farmer	GA
Sarah A.	36	F		GA
Ethan A.	13	M		AL
A. D.	11	M		AL
Susan	5	F		TX
Sarah J.	2	F		TX
Williams, John S.	23	M	Farmer	VA
Wolverton, Greenville	38	M	Farmer	TN
Permelia	35	F		TN
John J.	13	M		TN
William T.	11	M		TN
Mary A. E.	9	F		TN
Elijah H.	8	M		TN
Thornton B.	4	M		TN
Milinda J.	3	F		TX
Sarah C.	1	F		TX
Wood, Mathew	59	M	None	GA
Hannah	59	F		GA
Birdwell, George	23	M	Overseer	TN
Williams, William G.	33	M	Farmer	GA
Sarah	22	F		TN
Hiram J.	1	M		TX
Reed, Lemuel	50	M	Farmer	MS
Mary	44	F		TN
William T.	22	M	Farmer	TN
Wesley	16	M	Farmer	MS
John F.	14	M		MS
Mary A.	12	F		MS
Christopher	10	M		MS
Nancy E.	8	F		MS
Lemuel M.	6	M		MS
James Robert	4	M		MS
Rebecca A.	3	F		MS
Burton, Alexander	21	M	Farmer	TN
Talier, Shipman	35	M	Farmer	TN
Elizabeth	33	F		TN
David C.	11	M		TN
Martha	7	F		AR
William	5	M		AR
James	8/12	M		TX
Donald, James M.	55	M	C.P. Clergyman	TN
Margaret	55	F		NC
William	17	M	Farmer	TN
Thomas	15	M		TN
Mitchel	12	M		TN
Balis, Nancy	37	F		TN
Adella	16	F		TN
James C.	14	M		TN
Carson, Tennessee	23	F		TN
Margaret C.	1	F		TX
Terey, Claiborn	30	M	Farmer	TN
Levina	30	F		TN
John	12	M		TN
Joseph	10	M		TN
Newton	8	M		TN
Elizabeth	6	F		AR
Margaret	4	F		AR
Drucilla	19	F		TN
Nail, (Blank)	30	M	Farmer	TN
Sylvestine	30	F		TN
Studvant, Marion	21	M	Farmer	TN
Mary J.	18	F		TN
McDaniel, Andrew J.	35	M	Farmer	AL
Elizabeth	24	F		TN
John	12	M		AL
Mary Jane	5	F		AL
Josephine	2	F		TX
Lawrance, James	30	M	Laborer	GA
Harris, James	21	M	Laborer	AL
Cogborne, T. F.	32	M	Potter	GA
Sarah	17	F		TN

(continued)

RUSK COUNTY, TEXAS

Name	Age	Sex	Occupation	Birthplace
Cogborne, Taylor	2	M		TX
Cyrus	68	M	None	NC
Weeks, Daniel	36	M	Black Smith	VT
Elizabeth	28	F		TN
Sarah	9	F		TX
William	8	M		TX
Ellen	6	F		TX
John	5	M		TX
Eliza	3	F		TX
Susan	1/12	F		TX
Hicks, Newton	21	M	Black Smith	TN
Cogburn, Jackson	34	M	Potter	GA
Martha	28	F		GA
Elizabeth	11	F		GA
Desdimina	9	F		AL
Mary	7	F		AL
Ophelia	5	F		AR
Jane C.	3	F		TX
Jackson, Donaldson	35	M	Laborer	TN
Branch, Asher	53	M	Farmer	VT
Nancy	43	F		TN
George W.	24	M	Farmer	TN
Marian	27	F		IL
Norman	22	M	Laborer	TN
Oliver	19	M	Laborer	TN
Sarah	17	F		TN
Miles	14	M		TN
Virginia	12	F		TN
Lafayette	8	M		TN
Culbreth, Mary	70	F		NC
Loller, Isaac	40	M	Farmer	TN
Susan	35	F		TN
Lindsey L.	17	M	Laborer	AL
Mary M.	14	F		AL
Semantha	13	F		AR
Handy	11	M		TX
John	9	M		TX
Ewen	7	M		TX
Martha	4	F		TX
Williams, William	21	M	Farmer	AL
Martha	22	F		TN
George W.	6/12	M		TX
Williams, James	23	M	Farmer	AL
Sarah J.	9	F		TN
Moore, P. C.	40	M	Farmer	TN
Elizabeth	40	F		TN
Mary	14	F		TN
Susan	11	F		TN
Ellen	9	F		TN
William	5½	M		TN
Mabray, Joseph	30	M	Farmer	TN
Hester A.	28	F		TN
Andrew E.	12	M		TN
Elizabeth	11	F		TN
Sarah Ann	10	F		TN
John F.	8	M		TN
Nancy C.	6	F		TN
Margaret E.	4	F		TN
Susan J.	3	F		TX
Mary C.	1	F		TX
Miller, Elizabeth	43	F		TN
Robert C.	9	M		TX
Brown, Richard	57	M	Farmer	PA
Nancy J.	18	F		TN
Mary E.	1	F		TX
Osborne, Elias	23	M	Laborer	GA
George	18	M	Laborer	GA
Clifford, Nasay M.	25	M	Farmer	TN
Eliza J.	21	F		TN
James Henry	1	M		TX
Clifford, John C.	22	M	Laborer	TX

Name	Age	Sex	Occupation	Birthplace
March, S. W.	25	M	Physician	TN
Martha	--	-		AL
Virzent, Charles	34	M	Merchant	GER
Caroline A.	20	F		NOR
Frederick	1	M		TX
Collins, A. B.	26	M	Clerk	TN
Cake, Lafayette F.	25	M	Clerk	TN
Moore, Elbert C.	23	M	Wool Carder	AL
Williamson, Isaac	25	M	Laborer	AL
Loop, Charles	23	M	Black Smith	GER
Frickey, Earnest	24	M	Cabinet Maker	GER
Rolly, Gerald	40	M	Black Smith	GER
Heiniman, Arnold	24	M	Tinner	GER
Hoffman, Charles	45	M	Tanner	GER
Thorison, William	30	M	Tanner	GER
Echols, Champness T.	45	M	Farmer	VA
Agness	45	F		VA
Odiah	17	M	Farmer	TN
William	15	M	Farmer	TN
Benjamin	13	M		TN
Sarah	11	F		TN
Nancy A.	4	F		TN
Thomas	15	M	Farmer	TN
Polly	13	F		TN
James M.	10	M		TN
William G.	8	M		TN
Sarah E.	5	F		TN
Nancy J.	1	F		TX
Bedford, Polly	71	F		NC
Curtis, Benjamin	33	M	Farmer	TN
Elizabeth	32	F		TN
William F.	6	M		TN
George W.	4	M		TN
Curtis, Samuel M.	23	M	Farmer	TN
Curtis, John	27	M	Farmer	TN
Martha	20	F		TN
Robert	1	M		TN
Curtis, Robert	27	M	Farmer	TN
Watson, Jefferson S.	49	M	Physician	TN
Sarah Ann	29	F		TN
Hodges, George W.	8	M		TN
Ross, James H.	40	M	Farmer	TN
Jane	28	F		GA
Ross, Robert	66	M	None	VA
Polly	55	F		TN
Robert R.	25	M	Farmer	TN
Samuel O.	21	M	Farmer	TN
Blackburn, William	48	M	M.E. Clergyman	TN
Sarah	46	F		TN
James C.	21	M	Farmer	TN
David M.	10	M		MS
Jones, Hardy	23	M	Farmer	TN
Martha C.	22	F		TN
Sarah J.	4	F		TX
Rebecca	1	F		TX
Seaborn, Francis M.	25	M	Laborer	TN
Polly	26	F		TN
John	6	M		TN
Mary Jane	4	F		TN
William	2	M		TN
George	1	M		TN
McDowell, Brad	18	M	Laborer	TN
Little, William D.	42	M	Farmer	SC
Amanda C.	23	F		TN
Jason B.	18	M	Farmer	TN
James W.	16	M	Farmer	TN
Mediann J.	14	F		TN
Melinda J.	2	F		TX
Samuel H.	1	M		TX
Bragg, William T.	29	M	Farmer	NC
Frances P.	22	F		TN
Mary E.	10	F		TN
Frances A.	8	F		TN

(continued)

RUSK COUNTY, TEXAS

Name	Age	Sex	Occupation	Birthplace
Bragg, Martha E.	6	F		TN
William C.	3	M		TN
Serica, Margaret	56	F		TN
Barksdale, P. C.	31	M	Farmer	VA
Eliza	24	F		TN
Rhoda M.	10	F		TX
Gray, William	47	M	Farmer	SC
Mary	43	F		NC
Rebecca	20	F		TN
Jesse	18	M	Farmer	TN
Ephraim	15	M		TN
John W.	13	M		TN
Mary F.	11	F		TN
William F.	7	M		TN
Martha E.	3	F		TN
Gray, Samuel	35	M	Farmer	TN
Elizabeth	32	F		TN
Zachariah	10	M		TN
Margaret	7	F		TN
Caroline	4	F		TN
John	3	M		TN
Sarah E.	3/12	F		TX
Delilah	70	F		SC
Young, Charles	28	M	Farmer	TN
Elizabeth	25	F		TN
James K.	5	M		TN
Mary E.	3	F		TN
Wright, William P.	45	M	Farmer	NC
Mary	38	F		TN
Elizabeth	19	F		TN
Samuel P.	17	M	Farmer	KY
John H. R.	16	M		KY
Franklin G.	14	M		KY
William G.	12	M		KY
Sarah C.	8	F		TX
Tennessee H.	5	F		TX
Mary E.	3	F		TN
James, Abner C.	23	M		TN
Stone, Nancy	50	F		NC
George W.	16	M	Farmer	KY
Mary J.	15	F		KY
William J.	13	M		TX
Samuel A.	11	M		TX
Robert L.	8	M		TX
Stanley, George W.	36	M	Farmer	KY
Margaret	35	F		TN
William	15	M		TN
George R.	11	M		TN
Elizabeth	7	F		TN
Charles W.	1	M		TX
Goodwin, E. T.	47	M	Farmer	NC
Nancy	38	F		TN
Ducallon A.	18	M	Farmer	AL
Sarah N.	17	F		AL
James P.	14	M		AL
Temperance	11	F		AL
Elijah T.	7	M		AL
Mary Ann	6	F		MS
Amanda	4	F		TX
John W.	4/12	M		TX
Wills, Elias	27	M	Farmer	KY
Price, Charles L.	29	M	Farmer	AL
Rebecca	21	F		GA
John Wesley	10/12	M		TX
Daniel J.	23	M	Farmer	TN
Paschal M.	21	M	Farmer	TN
Elisha M.	31	M	Black Smith	AL
Mary Ann	17	F		TN
Weaver, Posey P.	27	M	Farmer	SC
Elizabeth	27	F		TN
Mary F.	8	F		MS
Nancy Jane	7	F		MS
Martha A.	5	F		MS
Elizabeth	1	F		TX
Peters, Hutson	30	M	Farmer	AL
Caroline	26	F		AL
Walling, Thomas J.	35	M	Farmer	TN
Nancy	32	F		AL
Edmond	16	M	Farmer	TN
John H.	15	M		TN
Thomas J.	13	M		TX
Charles T.	12	M		TX
Sarah A. C.	7	F		TX
Cynthia	6	F		TX
Vance P.	5	M		TX
William F.	1	M		TX
Mann, Alen J.	43	M	Farmer	TN
Elizabeth	42	F		NC
Henry W.	18	M	Farmer	GA
Thompson, H. M.	23	M	None	TN
Mary	17	F		MS
Sarah M.	1	F		TX
Davidson, J. F.	40	M	Farmer	TN
Mary	35	F		TN
Otey	3	M		MS
Davidson, Thomas J.	22	M	Farmer	TN
Phillips, David	28	M	Farmer	IRE
Rutha	24	F		TN
Charles E.	4	M		AL
John L.	2	M		AL
Madaux, John	36	M	Brick Layer	TN
Mary	26	F		TN
Olivia J.	5	F		MS
William	2	M		TX
Bell, Robert	36	M	Farmer	TN
Mary	31	F		TN
Hannah E.	12	F		TN
Hariet E.	10	F		AL
Mary L.	6	F		TN
William H.	4	M		TN
Mary Ann	4	F		TN
Margaret	2	F		TN
Reasonover, Burson	44	M	Farmer	TN
Naoma E.	32	F		TN
Peru	21	M	Student	TN
Sam S.	19	M	Farmer	TX
Sarah C.	13	F		TX
Jorden	10	M		TX
Margaret E.	6	F		TX
Jacob	4	M		TX
Cynthia J.	1	F		TX
Stephens, Margaret	9	F		TX
Newton R.	9	M		TX
Jasper	7	M		TX
Harris	5	M		TX
Sarah	4	F		TX
Nancy	2/12	F		TX
Gibson, William	21	M	Farmer	TN
Watson, William	35	M	Farmer	TN
Emily	32	F		TN
Miranda	14	F		TN
James	12	M		TN
Henry	10	M		TN
Sarah	8	F		TN
Zachariah	6	M		AR
John	3	M		TX
Montgomery, William	26	M	Farmer	TN
Catharine	18	F		KY
Samuel	4	M		TN
Walling, John	47	M	Farmer	KY
Rhoda	44	F		TN
William A.	12	M		TX
Rhoda	9	F		TX
John	7	M		TX
Thompson, William T.	40	M	Carpenter	GA
Sarah Ann	23	F		GA
Bethian Ann	5	F		TX
Phillip S.	2	M		TX

(continued)

RUSK COUNTY, TEXAS

Name	Age	Sex	Occupation	Birthplace
Fair, Thomas	36	M	Millwright	TN
Nancy	25	F		AL
Mary A.	1	F		FL
Parsons, L. B.	30	M	Miller	TN
Louisa	28	F		TN
John	5	M		TN
Nancy A.	4	F		TN
White, Allen	28	M	Merchant	TN
Bell, James	39	M	Shoe Maker	SC
Cynthia	30	F		MS
Elizabeth	13	F		TX
John C.	9	M		TX
Jesse M.	7	M		TX
Walling, William	21	M	Farmer	TN
Casey, Martin	30	M	School Teacher	IRE
Mossey, John W.	42	M	Physician	VA
Jane	27	F		TN
Smith, Virginia	3	F		TX
Martha E.	1	F		TX
Mary M.	1	F		TX
Alston, Ciscero D.	10	M		MS
Mary Ann	8	F		TX
Payne, Thomas T.	38	M	Farmer	NC
Nancy	38	F		TN
Henry W.	17	M	Farmer	TN
William F.	15	M	Farmer	TN
Charity Ann	14	F		TN
Thomas B.	12	M		TN
Jeremiah E.	10	M		TN
Johnston, John	50	M	Carpenter	GA
Eliza Ann	33	F		TN
Moses	20	M		TN
Nancy J.	17	F		TN
Mary	15	F		TN
Tubles, John L.	13	M		MS
Sarah L.	11	F		MS
Johnston, Ann E.	8	F		MS
Robert C.	5	M		MS
James H.	2	M		MS
Stubblefield, Stephen	62	M	Farmer	(E)TN
Betsey	58	F		VA
Wilson	24	M	Farmer	TN
Thomas	18	M	Farmer	TN
Stephen, Jr.	17	M	Farmer	MS
Shot, Nancy	23	F		TN
Stubblefield, R. L.	28	M	Farmer	TN
Susan	26	F		TN
Joel	4	M		TX
Stephen	2	M		TX
Kennard, Charles H.	41	M	Farmer	TN
Mary J.	36	M(F)		AL
James W.	15	M	Farmer	AL
Balsonia E.	13	F		MS
Mary E.	11	F		MS
Louisa A.	9	F		MS
Josephus G.	7	M		AL
George T.	5	M		AL
Taylor E.	3	M		AL
Sarah A.	1	F		MS
Graham, Jesse	45	M	B.C. Clergyman	NC
Martha	39	F		TN
Jackson, Isaac	21	M	School Teacher	AL
Curtis B.	18	M	Farmer	AL
John	16	M	Farmer	AL
Ozius D.	14	M		AL
Martha Jane	11	F		AL
William F. L.	9	M		AL
Jesse	7	M		AL
Hulda A.	4	F		AL
Ben F.	1	M		AL
Coats, Solomon	49	M	Farmer	NC
Delilah	38	F		TN

(continued)

Name	Age	Sex	Occupation	Birthplace
Coats, Martha	21	F		TN
Needham	18	M	Farmer	TN
Mary A.	15	F		TN
Martin V.	12	M		TN
Mary Jane	10	F		TN
Samuel H.	7	M		TN
Temps V.	5	-		TN
Baker, Wilson W.	35	M	Carpenter	GA
Nancy	23	F		TN
Frances	6	F		TX
McAlister, Peter	3	M		TX
Miller, John	55	M	Farmer	TN
Ann	50	F		TN
Hollaway, Polly	36	F		TN
Lafayette	18	M	Farmer	TN
Mary	15	F		TN
William	12	M		AL
Thompson	10	M		AL
Wallace	6	M		AL
Louisiana Texas	8/12	F		TX
Yandle, Miles	35	M	Farmer	NC
Elizabeth M.	29	F		TN
Mary C.	5	F		TX
Sarah J.	3	F		TX
Elizabeth P.	1	F		TX
Moorman, John B.	33	M	Farmer	NC
Lucinda	20	F		TN
Ross, William M.	34	M	Farmer	TN
Mary Ann	30	F		TN
Lucretia A.	12	F		MS
Margaret	8	F		TX
Kizziah T.	3	F		TX
William C.	3/12	M		TX
McKneley, Martin	22	M	Laborer	AL
Moses	4/12	M		TX
Carson, James	32	M	Farmer	TN
Tennessee	23	F		TN
Clinton	1	M		TX
Carson, Catherine	62	F		KY
Matilda	37	F		TN
Birdwell, Andrew	28	M	Farmer	TN
Elizabeth	20	F		IL
Robert R.	2	M		TX
Jones, Thomas	44	M	Farmer	KY
Ellen J.	44	F		TN
Mary A.	16	F		IL
Nancy J.	13	F		IL
Thomas P.	9	M		TX
James M.	8	M		TX
Ellen P.	5	F		TX
Eliza	3	F		TX
Infant	1/12	F		TX
Shoffit, Littleton	54	M	Farmer	VA
Sally	40	F		SC
Littleton	20	M	Laborer	TN
Josiah	18	M	Laborer	AL
William H.	15	M	Laborer	AL
Noah W.	11	M		AL
Louisa	9	F		TN
Tyra H.	7	M		AL
Henry A.	4	M		AL
Lewis S.	1	M		TX
Shoffit, John	25	M	Farmer	TN
Ann	21	F		AL
Mary E.	1	F		TX
Manning, James	33	M	Farmer	SC
Minerva A.	23	F		TN
Sarah J.	4	F		LA
Mary A.	2	F		TX
Josiah F.	1	M		TX
Sharpton, Mary G.	43	F		MO
Lock, Jacob	34	M	Farmer	VA
Elizabeth J.	22	F		AL

(continued)

Name	Age/Sex	Occupation	Birthplace
Lock, James M.	6 M		AL
William W.	3 M		TX
Lock, Libbon	24 M	Farmer	TN
Moore, Ruben	46 M	Carpenter	NC
Thomas	21 M	Carpenter	TN
Stephens, Naoma	3 F		TX
Reed, William B.	52 M	Farmer	SC
Sarah	50 F		TN
John	23 M	Farmer	TN
James	20 M	Farmer	TN
Margaret	18 F		TN
Lydia F.	16 F		TN
Bridget	13 F		TX
Catharine	10 F		TX
Amanda	6 F		TX
Reed, Pleasant	32 M	Farmer	TN
Amanda	32 F		TN
William H.	6 M		TX
Lemuel	4 M		TX
Mary	2 F		TX
James	6/12 M		TX
Reed, Isaac	25 M	Farmer	TN
Eliza	23 F		TN
Nancy	4 F		TX
Elizabeth	2 F		TX
John	1 M		TX
Martha	7/12 F		TX
Morris, Isreal	32 M	Farmer	AL
Elizabeth	30 F		TN
Jesse	9 M		TX
William	7 M		TX
David	5 M		TX
Mary	3 F		TX
Henry	1 M		TX
Awalt, Henry	44 M	Farmer	TN
Mary	45 F		TN
Isreal	20 M	Farmer	TN
George	18 M	Farmer	TN
Jesse	15 M	Farmer	TX
Permilla	10 F		TX
Lemuel	8 M		TX
Dolahite, Jesse	26 M	Farmer	MS
Rachael	21 F		TN
John Wiley	3 M		TX
William H.	1 M		TX
Samuel	17 M	Farmer	MS
Franklin, R. L.	30 M	Farmer	GA
Nancy	28 F		TN
Mary E.	3 F		TX
Avon	1 M		TX
Kukendall, John	52 M	Farmer	KY
Mary	41 F		TN
Nancy	22 F		TN
Mary	13 F		MS
Rebecca	11 F		MS
William	16 M		TN
John	5 M		MS
George	4 M		TX
Hutson, George	18 M	Farmer	TN
Martin, James	30 M	Farmer	AL
Sarah	25 F		AR
Lucinda	9 F		AR
Peter	8 M		AR
William V.	6 M		AR
Charlotte	5 F		AR
James W.	3 M		AR
Sarah E.	2 F		TX
Catharine	13 F		AR
Kuykendal, James	50 M	Farmer	KY
Dorcas	46 F		TN
Mathew	18 M	Farmer	TN
Nancy A.	15 F		TN

(continued)

Name	Age/Sex	Occupation	Birthplace
Kuykendal, Drucilla M.	13 F		MS
George	10 M		MS
Kukendal, William T.	21 M	Farmer	TN
Elizabeth	17 F		AL
Lovel C.	1/12 M		TX
James S.	6 M		MS
Martin, Sarah A.	6 F		TX
Drucilla S.	3 F		TX
Kukendal, Eli	27 M	Farmer	TN
Elizabeth	31 F		TN
Dorcas	7 F		TX
Spencer	5 M		TX
Sarah	3 F		TX
James	1 M		TX
Bennett, F. H.	40 M	Farmer	TN
Margaret	31 F		OH
George M.	5 M		AR
Sarah M.	2 F		AR
William R.	4/12 M		TX
Pennywright, Tarver	65 M	None	OH
Kykendal, Owen	26 M	Farmer	MS
Eveline	30 F		TN
Sarah	10 F		TN
Sarah Ann	4 F		TX
James W.	1 M		TX
Joel L.	17 M	Farmer	GA
James	14 M		GA
William	11 M		GA
Alfred	9 M		GA
Edmund T.	7 M		GA
Elizabeth J.	3 F		GA
Robertson, Cullen A.	55 M	Farmer	NC
Jane E.	60 F		NC
Catharine P.	20 F		TN
Sarah E.	18 F		TN
Albert T.	18 M	Farmer	TN
Berry, E. S.	32 M	Farmer	NC
Elizabeth	31 F		TN
John A.	13 M		IL
George H.	8 M		IL
Mary Ann	4 F		IL
Eliza J.	3/12 F		TX
Staton, Everett	48 M	Farmer	NC
Kissiah	39 F		NC
William R.	21 M	Farmer	TN
Bennett	19 M		TN
Everett	16 M	Farmer	TN
Sarah Ann	15 F		MS
Mary Jane	13 F		TN
George H.	10 M		IL
Hariet E.	8 F		IL
Joseph	6 M		IL
Thomas E.	4 M		IL
Emily A.	2 F		IL
Vardiman, William	41 M	Farmer	GA
Alcy D.	41 F		GA
Alcy	15 F		TX
James S.	13 M		TX
Sarah J.	10 F		TX
John H.	7 M		TX
Martha E.	5 F		TX
Bradberry, Daniel	30 M	Farmer	TN
Waller, Peter E.	27 M	Farmer	VA
Eliza M.	18 F		TN
Milton L.	3 M		MS
Kuykendall, A.	26 M	Farmer	MS
Martha A.	23 F		TN
George W.	3 M		TX
Goulden, Ruben	34 M	Farmer	SC
Ann	29 F		TN
Newton A.	9 M		MS
Jasper E.	7 M		MS
William	6 M		AR
Sarah J.	3 F		AR
Cullen	1 M		TX

Name	Age	Sex	Occupation	Birthplace
Hicks, Isaac	57	M		VA
Mary	50	F		KY
William L.	24	M	Farmer	AL
Joshua	17	M	Farmer	TN
Isaac R.	15	M		TN
John	11	M		LA
Thomas S.	8	M		TX
Hannah	5	F		TX
Miles, William	22	M	Farmer	TN
Martin, Lucien D.	23	M	Millwright	TN
Ruth Ann	21	F		TN
Christopher L.	5/12	M		TX
Rice, John N.	33	M	Farmer	AL
Mary W.	24	F		TN
Margaret E.	3	F		TX
Seaborn J.	1	M		TX
Matlock, Lewis J.	24	M	Farmer	AL
Amanda	26	F		TN
Thomas J.	5	M		MS
James M.	3	M		MS
Henry	2	M		MS
Nancy	1/12	F		TX
Matlock, Manuel	23	M	Farmer	AL
Bell, Jasper	23	M	Farmer	TN
Vaught, Lucinda	38	F		TN
Sarah J.	17	F		TN
Mary A.	15	F		AL
William M.	14	M		AL
Susan C.	10	F		AL
Roman T.	9	M		AL
Lucinda B.	8	F		AL
Margaret	7	F		AL
James P.	5	M		TX
Bell, Joel	60	M	Farmer	TN
Elizabeth	50	F		TN
Osar	25	M	Farmer	TN
Josiah	20	M	Farmer	TN
Thompson	18	M	Laborer	TN
Mary	15	F		TN
Licurgus	13	M		TN
Wiley	8	M		MS
Birdwell, Allen	48	M	Farmer	TN
Sarah J.	30	F		TN
James R.	17	M	Farmer	AL
William R.	15	M	Farmer	AL
George P.	13	M		AL
Charles A.	11	M		AL
Benjamin F.	8	M		MS
Joel V.	2	M		TX
Henry H.	1/12	M		TX
Birdwell, John	80	M	None	VA
Ferguson, William	25	M	Overseer	SC
Haltom, William	58	M	Farmer	NC
Priscilla L.	53	F		NC
Noah G.	21	M	Farmer	TN
Martha M.	18	F		TN
Balzera V.	1	F		TX
James G.	12	M		MS
Josephine A.	8	F		TX
McCormack, John M.	24	M	School Teacher	NC
Swank, Daniel	23	M	Farmer	PA
Haltom, Edmund W.	34	M	Farmer	TN
Martha A.	24	F		AL
Mary T.	2	F		MS
Sarah H.	2/12	F		TX
Jackson, Cordelia E.	8	F		MS
Sorry, John	33	M	Farmer	TN
Jane C.	29	F		TN
Amantha	10	F		TX
Jamison M.	8	M		TX
Priscilla	6	F		TX
Leenda T.	4	F		TX
William H.	6/12	M		TX
Birdwell, John	22	M	Farmer	AL
Adaline	19	F		TN
Jeremiah A.	2/12	M		TX
Haltom, William F.	24	M	Farmer	TN
Sarah	18	F		TN
Murphy, Martha	28	F		TN
Mary	1	F		LA
Vannoy, Andrew	37	M	Black Smith	NC
Margaret J.	27	F		TN
Joel R.	8	M		TX
John W.	5	M		TX
Eliza E.	1	F		TX
Ray, William D.	43	M	Farmer	NC
Ellinor	23	F		TN
John R.	18	M	Farmer	TN
Margaret	12	F		TN
Josephine	8	F		TN
Robert	5	M		TN
Thomas	3	M		TN
Simmons, James B.	25	M	Farmer	VA
Mary Jane	23	F		TN
Sarah Jane	4	F		AL
William W.	2	M		AL
Ferguson, Alston	56	M	Farmer	TN
Mary	47	F		KY
George W.	19	M	Farmer	MS
John	17	M	Farmer	MS
Alston	15	M		TX
Mary	13	F		TX
Lucinda	11	F		TX
Elizabeth A.	8	F		TX
Millinda	4	F		TX
Bramlee, William	50	M	Farmer	VA
Elizabeth	46	F		TN
Mary Ann	26	F		TN
Eliza Jane	22	F		TN
Martha A.	20	F		TN
John T.	17	M	Farmer	TN
Elizabeth	14	F		TN
Margaret S.	13	F		TN
Sarah	11	F		TX
Texana	4	F		TX
Sam H.	1	M		TX
Amanda	12	F		TX
Mayfield, Jesse	51	M	Farmer	SC
Sarah	46	F		TN
Walker	16	M	Student	TN
Alvira	13	F		TN
Salvina	10	F		AR
Victoria	8	F		AR
Wilbanks, Marshal	31	M	Farmer	SC
Mary M.	20	F		TN
Joseph	9	M		TN
William S.	7	M		TN
Lemuel H.	9/12	M		TX
Hiram	40	M	Farmer	SC
Northart, Augustus	39	M	Farmer	NC
Drucilla	46	F		NC
George	19	M	Farmer	NC
Eliza	13	F		TN
Francis	8	F		MS
McCormack, Archibald W.	29	M	Farmer	TN
Elizabeth	38	F		KY
John W.	8	M		TN
Virginia F.	3	F		TN
Telitha C.	1	F		TN
Sarah E.	15	F		TN
King, Perlina	25	F		TN
Nancy Ann	5	F		TX
Salina S.	2	M		TX
Cruise, Jacob	22	M	Farmer	KY
Isaac	22	M	Farmer	KY
Chitwood, James O.	18	M	Farmer	TN

Name	Age	Sex	Occupation	Birthplace
Ice, Andrew	54	M	Farmer	TN
Sarah P.	19	F		AL
Eliza Jane	17	F		AL
Matilda C.	15	F		AL
Frederick B.	10	M		AL
Martha C.	8	F		AL
Josanna C.	7	F		AL
Betsey Ann	6	F		AL
Isaac N.	5	M		AL
Isabella	2	F		AL
Duncan, David H.	25	M	Black Smith	TN
John T.	27	M	Farmer	TN
Rossin, William	33	M	Farmer	TN
Elizabeth	33	F		TN
James M.	10	M		TN
Thomas J.	8	M		TN
Rebecca Jane	6	F		TN
Mary E.	3	F		TX
Joseph B.	6/12	M		TX
Lee, John C.	24	M	Farmer	NC
McCormick, John	13	M		TN
Utzman, George V.	27	M	Carpenter	TN
Emily M.	24	F		TN
James M.	4	M		TN
Nancy Jane	2	F		TX
McMillan, N. P.	56	M	Farmer	VA
Catharine	48	F		TN
Asberry, Jane J.	13	F		MS
N. M.	11	M		MS
Virgil	9	M		MS
Asberry, Thomas J.	45	M	Wagon Maker	TN
Haddox, Henry	25	M	Farmer	AL
Louisa W.	18	F		TN
Wilmoth Ann	1	F		MS
Doherty, James W.	48	M	Farmer	KY
Isabella	42	F		KY
Robert N.	24	M	Farmer	KY
Julian Clay	16	F		KY
James P.	20	M	Farmer	KY
Mary Jane	13	F		KY
Araminta	11	F		KY
Nancy M.	9	F		KY
Rachael S.	7	F		KY
Almedia	4	F		TX
John	6/12	M		TX
Wiseman, Martin	22	M	Farmer	TN
Hargrove, Edward	22	M	Laborer	TN
Utzman, Thomas	29	M	Black Smith	TN
Elizabeth A.	21	F		TN
Margaret Jane	1	F		TX
McCormick, James	15	M	Laborer	TN
Utzman, Jacob	48	M	Farmer	NC
Nancy	45	F		TN
John L.	26	M	Farmer	TN
Mumford	23	M	Farmer	TN
William	21	M	None	TN
Martha	15	F		TN
Jacob	12	M		TN
James F.	10	M		TN
Margaret L.	7	F		TN
Barnett, John	48	M	Farmer	KY
Adaline	21	F		KY
Ruphus Penn	5	M		TX
Elliott, A.	28	M	Physician	TN
Hamilton, A. R.	23	M	Physician	TN
Barnett, S. Slade	43	M	Farmer	KY
Telitha C.	40	F		KY
Eliza	15	F		KY
Frances Young	12	F		KY
Salin	4	M		TX
Eugene Mury	2	M		TX
Bertha C.	10/12	F		TX

(continued)

Name	Age	Sex	Occupation	Birthplace
Woff, Mary	17	F		TN
Edward Penn	10	M		TX
Williams, John	18	M	Laborer	??
Lockridge, James	53	M	Farmer	SC
Martha	51	F		TN
Ann A.	1/12	F		TX
Bryan, R. S.	45	M	Farmer	NC
Pheraby	48	F		NC
Elizabeth	14	F		TN
John L.	13	M		TN
William	10	M		TN
Thomas	8	M		TN
Pyles, Joseph	37	M	Farmer	GA
Martha	27	F		GA
Sarah J.	11	F		AL
Samuel J.	7	M		LA
William T.	5	M		TX
Mary Ann	2	F		TX
Logan, M.	28	M	Farmer	TN
Etheridge, T. H.	32	M		NC
Elizabeth	21	F		TN
Caroline	4	F		TN
Mary Ann	2	F		TX
Triplett, E.	27	M	Saddler	KY
Cochran, O. L.	24	M	None	KY
Hicks, C. J.	30	M	None	NC
Jones, John S.	30	M	Farmer	KY
Yarborough, J. N.	32	M	Carpenter	SC
Elizabeth	22	F		TN
Josephine	2	F		TX
Crooms, Jessie	17	M		TN
Sykes, D. R.	37	M	Carpenter	VT
Mary Ann	24	F		TN
Napoleon B.	6	M		TN
William	4	M		TN
Elizabeth	1	F		TX
Dodson, Thomas	23	M	Farmer	TN
Eliza	18	F		SC
Clay, Marcus D.	26	M	Farmer	TN
Mary J.	23	F		TN
James C.	4	M		TX
Sarah E.	1	F		TX
Richardson, Amos	38	M	Farmer	??
Susannah	36	F		SC
Eliza	18	F		TN
Henry	16	M		TN
Elizabeth	15	F		TN
Franklin	12	M		TN
Arthur	10	M		TN
William	8	M		TN
Sarah	6	F		TN
George	3	M		TN
Roark, James	44	M	Farmer	TN
Martha	38	F		SC
James	18	M		TN
Louisa	16	F		TN
Jasper	14	M		TN
Nancy	7	F		TN
Catharine	4	F		TN
Newton	1/12	M		TN
Roark, William	22	M	Farmer	TN
Ann M.	26	F		TN
Gillum, Charles	38	M	Farmer	TN
Rebecca	37	F		TN
Eliza	16	F		TN
Arthur	14	M		TN
Martha	13	F		TN
James K.	11	M		TN
Gray, George	48	M	Farmer	NC
Margaret	45	F		SC
John A.	23	M	Farmer	TN
Ruben W.	21	M	Farmer	TN

(continued)

Name	Age	Sex	Occupation	Birthplace
Gray, Nancy	17	F		TN
Susan	15	F		AL
George	11	M		MS
William F.	7	M		MS
Victory, W. P.	33	M	Farmer	KY
Cynthia J.	27	F		TN
James T.	5	M		TN
Agnes E.	3	F		TN
William	1	M		TX
Scott, Dicy	49	F		NC
Logsden, John	53	M		KY
Anna S.	48	F		KY
Catharine	14	F		MO
John S.	12	M		MO
Tennessee A.	9	F		TX
Mary Ann	28	F		MO
Scott, William M.	26	M	Farmer	TN
Sarah O.	20	F		TN
James R.	4	M		TN
Frances	1	F		TX
Taylor, Mordica R.	20	M		TN
Grant, James D.	32	M	Farmer	TN
Sarah	25	F		TN
Elizabeth J.	8	F		MS
Sarah P.	6	F		MS
Nancy L.	5	F		MS
Flowers, John	20	M	Farmer	AL
Clay, Dawson	19	M	Farmer	TN
Tally, Christine D.	35	F		TN
James W.	6	M		MS
Moodey, John G.	35	M	Carpenter	VT
Misadora	30	F		MS
Susan	11	F		TN
Mary	8	F		TN
Sarah	4	F		TN
Caulder, William W.	26	M	M.E. Clergyman	AL
Elizabeth C.	20	F		TN
Lunora V.	2	F		MS
T. C. W.	3/12	M		TX
Kykendal, Charles	30	M	Farmer	TN
Caroline L.	26	F		SC
John A.	7	M		MS
Susan J.	4	F		TX
James M.	3	M		TX
Mary Frances	3/12	F		TX
Smith, George W.	48	M	Farmer	TN
Mary	46	F		KY
Andrew J.	20	M	Farmer	TN
Adaline	15	F		TN
Sindrella	13	F		TN
Virginia A.	10	F		TN
Jerome M.	5	M		GA
Houston	3	M		GA
Smith, John W.	26	M	Farmer	TN
Nancy	26	F		TN
George A.	4	M		GA
Francis M.	1	M		GA
Childress, Benjamin	32	M	Farmer	TN
Mary	32	F		TN
Susan G. M.	7	F		TX
Smith, Marion	23	M	Farmer	TN
Taylor, Jacob	37	M	Farmer	TN
Maryann	33	F		AR
Martha Jane	15	F		AR
Delila	12	F		TX
George A.	8	M		TX
Artimesia	4	F		TX
Robert Bruce	2	M		TX
Taylor, Robert M.	46	M	Farmer	SC
Elizabeth	36	F		SC
Frances	15	F		TN
Martha	9	F		TN

(continued)

Name	Age	Sex	Occupation	Birthplace
Taylor, Eliza	8	F		TN
Ross, Johnson	25	M	Overseer	AL
Moore, William	20	M	Hack Driver	AL
Lucy, Donald R.	47	M	Farmer	NC
Jane	40	F		KY
Catharine	18	F		TN
James	16	M	Farmer	TN
Thomas	12	M		TN
Stephen	10	M		TN
Hugh	8	M		TN
John	6	M		TN
Donald	4	M		TN
Eliza	2	F		TN
Stone, Lemuel	24	M	Farmer	TN
Margaret	20	F		TN
Thomas	3/12	M		TX
Renfro, John B.	33	M	B.C. Clergyman	TN
Nancy	26	F		AL
Virgil	11	M		AL
Mary	7	F		AL
Martha	5	F		AL
William	3	M		AL
Frances	1	F		TX
McClure, William	75	M	None	NC
Nancy	50	F		TN
Hays, William	44	M	Farmer	SC
Mary	44	F		NC
James	20	M	Farmer	TN
Cunningham	17	M	Farmer	TN
Daniel	16	M	Farmer	TN
Benjamin	14	M		TN
William	11	M		TN
John	8	M		TN
Mary	6	F		MS
Christopher, John	22	M	Farmer	TN
Minton, Joseph G.	38	M	None	NC
Elizabeth	38	F		TN
Joseph Hambrick	14	M		TN
Nancy C.	12	F		TN
Thomas	9	M		TN
Leah	11	F		TN
Elizabeth	8	F		TN
William	6	M		TN
John	1	M		TX
Lee, John A.	31	M		TN
Cairy	30	F		TN
William	9	M		TN
Elizabeth	6	F		TN
Sarah	4	F		TN
John	1	M		TX
Sykes, William	30	M	Farmer	NC
Emily	20	F		FL
Napoleon	4	M		FL
James	3	M		FL
Nancy	9/12	F		FL
Scarborough, W. L.	28	M	Farmer	NC
Millinda	28	F		TN
Charles	6	M		TN
Elizabeth	4	F		TN
Armintha	2	F		TN
Walkup, William	32	M	None	MO
Maria	23	F		TN
William	5	M		TN
John	4	M		TN
Sarah	2	F		TN
Wilson, G. W.	24	M	Student	AL
Lawrie, George R.	35	M	Farmer	GA
Mary	28	F		TN
Samuel	15	M		TN
Robert	12	M		TN
John	10	M		TN
Nancy	7	F		TX
David B.	4	M		TX
Amelia	2	F		TX
Zachariah T.	2/12	M		TX
Harris, Alora	30	F		TN

RUSK COUNTY, TEXAS

Name	Age	Sex	Occupation	Birthplace
Barran, Mary	44	F		TN
Isaac	25	M	Farmer	AL
Ann	20	F		AL
Henry	18	M	Farmer	AL
William	16	M	Farmer	AL
James	14	M		AL
Martha	12	F		AL
Emiline	10	F		MS
Frances	8	F		MS
Hoover, John	46	M		VA
Nancy	42	F		VA
William	14	M		TN
Thomas	10	M		TN
Mary	8	F		TN
Benjamin	6	M		TN
James	5	M		TN
Andrew J.	1	M		TN
George W.	1	M		TN
O'Hair, A. W.	36	M	Farmer	KY
Martha	35	F		TN
Sarah	14	F		IL
John	11	M		IL
Robert	10	M		TX
Amanda	8	F		TX
William	5	M		TX
Eleanor	4	F		TX
Nancy	5/12	F		TX
Westbrook, Samuel H.	30	M	Farmer	NC
Amelia	30	F		NC
William	8	M		TN
Margaret	5	F		TN
John	3	M		TN
Watkins, Archibald H.	38	M	C.P. Clergyman	TN
Mary A.	31	F		TN
Nancy F.	13	F		TN
James	9	M		TX
Jesse	6	M		TX
Jane	4	M		TX
George	4	M		TX
Murphy, John M.	26	M	Physician	TN
Poe, John S.	31	M	Farmer	GA
Lucretia	30	F		TN
Mary A.	13	F		AL
James	11	M		AL
William	9	M		AL
John	7	M		AL
Frances	5	F		AL
Henry	2	M		TX
Malaley, William	22	M	Farmer	AL
Reed, J. B.	54	M	Farmer	NC
James	18	M		AL
Rebecca	50	F		TN
Mary	13	F		TN
Margaret	11	F		TX
Martha	6	F		TX
Gooden, William	37	M		KY
Birdwell, Elizabeth	52	F		TN
Mathew	33	M	Farmer	TN
George	24	M	Farmer	TN
John	23	M	Farmer	TN
Mary	17	F		TN
Robert	15	M	Farmer	TN
Cynthia	14	F		AL
Sarah	12	F		AL
Henry	10	M		AL
William	8	M		AL
Benjamin	6	M		TX
Birdwell, Henderson	31	M	Farmer	TN
Margaret A.	20	F		TN
Mary	3	F		TX
George	1	M		TX
Wood, James	26	M	Farmer	??
Kerbo, James	31	M		GA
Elizabeth	32	F		TN

(continued)

Name	Age	Sex	Occupation	Birthplace
Kerbo, Thomas	9	M		TN
Hannah	7	F		TN
Martha	3	F		TN
Nicholas, J. T.	26	M	Teamster	TN
Kerbo, Nathaniel	36	M	Teamster	GA
Lucinda	30	F		TN
Thomas	14	M		TN
Willis	10	M		TN
Louisa	8	F		TN
Margaret	7	F		TN
Leander	3	M		TX
Infant	5/12	F		TX
Scott, John	33	M	Farmer	TN
Martha	19	F		TX
James	1	M		TX
Heath, Thomas	33	M	Farmer	NC
Mary	27	F		TN
James	11	M		TN
Burrell	9	M		TX
Carroll	7	M		TX
Sarah	5	F		TX
Susan	5	F		TX
Mary	4	F		TX
John	1	M		TX
Heath, Burrell	31	M	Farmer	NC
Wolf, Jacob	39	M	Farmer	TN
Adaline	28	F		TN
William	17	M	Farmer	TN
Lafayette	12	M		TN
Sarah	10	F		TN
Ace	8	M		TN
Thomas	5	M		TN
George	3	M		TN
Pennington, John	22	M	Brick Layer	TN
Jones, Elizabeth	41	F		NC
Rebecca	21	F		TN
Mark	17	M	Farmer	TN
Mary	15	F		TN
Jacob	14	M		TN
Sarah	12	F		TN
Temperance	10	M		TX
Reason	8	M		TX
Dinisa	6	F		TX
George	1	M		TX
Sanlin, T. A.	30	M	Farmer	NC
Lucinda	21	F		TN
William	1	M		TX
James	3/12	M		TX
Medford, John A.	32	M	Farmer	AL
Nancy	27	F		TN
Margaret	9	F		TX
Isam	5	M		TX
Levi	3	M		TX
James	1	M		TX
Kellum, A. G.	23	M	Black Smith	AL
Rebecca	19	F		TN
John	4/12	M		TX
Nance, R. W.	29	M	Laborer	AL
Sylvestra	30	F		AL
Benjamin	7	M		AL
Samuel	3	M		AL
John	6/12	M		TX
McVey, William	35	M	Trader	TN
Blair, Vinson	30	M	Farmer	TN
Mary	27	F		TN
Ann	2	F		TN
Mary E.	4/12	F		TX
McCray, Miles	25	M		NC
Blair, Hugh	26	M	Laborer	TN
Sarah	25	F		TN
Tennessee	10/12	F		TN
Smith, Robert	15	M	None	TN
Ables, H.	30	M	Farmer	TN

(continued)

RUSK COUNTY, TEXAS

Name	Age	Sex	Occupation	Birthplace
Ables, Mary	30	F		TN
Eliza	13	F		TX
William	8	M		TX
Amanda	8	F		TX
Henderson	6	M		TX
John	3	M		TX
James	2/12	M		TX
Adams, Quincey	26	M	None	AR
Low, William H.	29	M	Carpenter	TN
Walker, Dixon	46	M	Farmer	TN
John	11	M		TN
Parr, Henry D.	32	M	School Teacher	MO
Lucy	21	F		TN
Leatherman, Graves	45	M	Farmer	KY
Mary	30	F		TN
David	16	M		LA
Thomas	14	M		AR
Elkins	12	M		LA
Cyrus	10	M		LA
Martha	8	F		LA
Henry	3	M		LA
Sarah	2	F		LA
Arthur, G. S.	27	M	Farmer	TN
Malinda	23	F		SC
Elizabeth	2	F		TX
William	11/12	M		TX
Miles, A. F.	33	M	Farmer	TN
Elizabeth	25	F		NC
Berry	8	M		LA
William	6	M		LA
Margaret	5	F		TX
Robert	4	M		TX
Martha	1	F		TX
William	12	M		AL
Adline	7	F		AL
Nelson, John C.	34	M	Merchant	MD
Frances	24	F		TN
Marie	4	F		TX
Nelson, H. F.	23	M	Merchant	MD
Samuel	23	M	Carpenter	MD
Gilbert, Emily	18	F		TX
O'hair, William	29	M	Merchant	AL
Annice	18	F		TN
John	8	M		TX
Elizabeth	6	F		TX
Martha	4	F		TX
Jonathan	25	M	Clerk	IL
Underwood, G. W.	28	M	Farmer	AL
Eliza	21	F		AR
John	9/12	M		TX
Wade, Isabella	60	F		TN
Worrel, William R.	61	M	Farmer	KY
Judah	48	F		SC
John	21	M	Farmer	TN
David	14	M		MS
Isabella	10	F		TX
Emily	9	F		TX
Sawyer, Nancy	16	F		LA
Hester, Alexander	25	F(M)		TN
Mary	6	F		TX
William R.	4	M		TX
Allen	2	M		TX
Champion, James	30	M	Carpenter	SC
Mitchell, John	35	M		GER
Lyles, James H.	28	M	Laborer	SC
Christian, G. A.	38	M	Miller	TN
Nancy	36	F		AL
John	8	M		TX
Pyera	7	F		TX
Missouri	5	F		TX
Elizabeth	3	F		TX
Georgia A.	2	F		TX

(continued)

Name	Age	Sex	Occupation	Birthplace
Christian, William	4/12	M		TX
Evens, Hariet	18	F		AL
Lyles, William	33	M	Teamster	TN
Eliza	28	F		TN
Malissa	13	F		TN
Martha	9	F		TX
Levisa	6	F		TX
Robert	3	M		TX
Amos	1/12	M		TX
Smith, W. T.	42	M	Farmer	TN
Sarah	40	F		GA
Schoto, Julius	20	M	Farmer	AR
Cardney, Charlott	30	F		GA
Sarah	8	F		TX
David	6	M		TX
Harl, William	38	M	Physician	TN
Hariet N.	28	F		TN
Robert	12	M		TN
James	9	M		TN
William	5	M		TN
Emily	2	F		TX
Tunney, Emily	25	F		TN
Vaughan, E. H.	41	M	Farmer	SC
Mary	33	F		TN
Mary A.	8/12	F		TX
Baker, Morris	27	M	None	TN
Cox, James	37	M	Merchant	VA
Martha	23	F		TN
Frances	4	F		TX
Celeste	1	F		TX
Chisum, G.	27	M	None	TN
Loftess, James H.	35	M	Farmer	SC
Leannah	29	F		TN
Thomas	14	M		AL
Loftess, Elizabeth	57	F		SC
Martha	30	F		AL
Lilly, Frances	32	F		AL
Martha	8	F		TX
James	7	M		TX
Lucy	3	F		TX
Boyd, O. H. P.	31	M	Farmer	TN
Crawford, Edmund	45	M	School Teacher	VA
Harmon, John	44	M	Farmer	TN
Sylvester	42	F		SC
Franklin	17	M	Farmer	AL
Elizabeth	15	F		AL
William	13	M		AL
Winnia	10	F		AL
James	8	M		AL
John	6	M		AL
Polk	5	M		AL
Andrew	4	M		AL
Barbara	2	F		AL
Foreman, Dempsey	25	M	Black Smith	TN
Sarah Nancy	14	F		SC
Henry, Cynthia	35	F		TN
Martin	20	M	Farmer	MS
Martha	15	F		MS
William	11	M		MS
James	10	M		MS
Sarah	8	F		MS
Nancy	7	F		MS
John	5	M		MS
Manerva	5/12	F		TX
Rhodes, William C.	28	M	Farmer	TN
Sarah	19	F		TN
Thomas	10/12	M		TX
Bagley, James	58	M	Farmer	NC
Martha	43	F		NC
Elisha	31	M	Farmer	TN
Nathan	29	M	Lawyer	AL
Henry	27	M	Farmer	AL
Joab	12	M		AL

(continued)

RUSK COUNTY, TEXAS

Name	Age	Sex	Occupation	Birthplace
Bagley, Josiah	4	M		AL
Elizabeth	11	F		AL
Martha	7	F		AL
Emeline	2	F		AL
Evans, John	30	M	Farmer	NC
Sims, Alfred	39	M	Farmer	TN
Ann	30	F		TN
John	11	M		TX
Elizabeth	6	F		TX
Mary	4	F		TX
Alfred	2	M		TX
Fitzhugh, L--	25	M	None	VA
Everett, Joshua	49	M	Black Smith	TN
Fitzhugh, John S.	25	M	Farmer	VA
Mary	23	F		TN
William	2	M		TX
Izara	1	F		TX
Reagan, John	62	M	Farmer	TN
Mary	55	F		TN
Mary, Jr.	30	F		TN
Narcissa	22	F		TN
Malvira	18	F		AR
Zenas	11	M		AR
John	6	M		AR
William	10	M		AR
Anderson, Henry	25	M	Farmer	TN
Fitzhugh, Rowland	40	M	Laborer	VA
Buckner, G. D.	41	M	Farmer	NC
Sarah	37	F		KY
Moses	21	M		TN
Adaline	19	F		TN
Catherine	17	F		TN
Green Clay	13	M		TN
Elvira	5	F		GA
Robert	3	M		TX
Mary	6/12	F		TX
Aiken, Mary	35	F		TN
William	9	M		TN
Blackwell, Joel	28	M	Farmer	NC
Sarah	23	F		AL
Martha	6	F		AL
John	4	M		AL
George	3	M		AL
Blackwell, Amos	23	M	Farmer	TN
Payne, William	18	M	Farmer	TN
Moore, Ransom J.	49	M	Farmer	NC
Nancy	45	F		SC
Lemuel	23	M	Farmer	NC
Elvira	20	F		NC
Alanson	19	M	Farmer	NC
O---	17	M	Farmer	TN
Isabella	13	F		TN
Salina	11	F		TN
Henry	6	M		TN
Emily	4	F		TN
Connally, Drewry M.	61	M	Farmer	VA
Dianah	36	F		NC
George	22	M	Farmer	TN
Drewry	21	M	Farmer	TN
Amanda	10	F		TN
James K. P.	5	M		TN

SABINE COUNTY, TEXAS

Name	Age	Sex	Occupation	Birthplace
Green, William	45	M		TN
Marinda	36	F		TN
John	8	M		TX
William	7	M		TX
Cytha Allise	5	F		TX
Emily Jane	3	F		TX
Susan	4	F		TX
(Blank)	1	F		TX
Hemby, Cornelius S.	21	M	Farmer	TN
Caladonia	--	F		MS
Speights, William M.	36	M	Farmer	GA
Eliza R.	36	F		TN
Conway, Nathaniel J.	15	M		MS
William R.	12	M		MS
Ellen E.	10	F		MS
Speights, John H. H.	7/12	M		TX
Caradine, Robert P.	37	M	Farmer	TN
Nancy	33	F		AL
Henry	14	M		TX
Polly Ann	10	F		TX
William	12	M		TX
Isaac	6	M		TX
Robert	3	M		TX
Sarah V.	10/12	F		TX
Martin, James	17	M		TX
Crawford, Jacob	58	M	Farmer	SC
Huldeth	55	F		SC
Joseph M.	22	M		TN
Elizabeth	17	F		SC
Mary	17	F		TN
Mary Ann	10	F		TX
Lane, Isaac	69	M	Farmer	TN
Elizabeth	65	F		VA
Margaret Ann	20	F		TX
Thomas M.	22	M		TN
Cook, Rebeca	35	F		TN
Millany	14	F		LA
William Riley	13	M		LA
Rice, Joseph	44	M	Farmer	SC
Catharine	34	F		TN
Mathias	18	M	Farmer	MS
Jesse	11	M		MS
Mary	9	F		MS
Samantha	7	F		MS
Eliza	6	F		MS
Elizabeth	2	F		MS
Delila	1	F		TX
Davis, Milly	50	F		TN
James	17	M	Farmer	LA
Thomas	15	M		TX
Mayo, Thomas	49	M	Farmer	TN
Watson, Thomas B.	24	M	Farmer	GA
Deanah Lucinda	21	F		TN
Wofford, James C.	41	M	shoe Maker	KY
Elizabeth Ann	27	F		TN
John Henderson	7	M		TX
Margaret A. A.	2	F		TX
Frances E.	3/12	F		TX
Davidson, William M.	42	M	Farmer	TN
Martha	35	F		VA
Mary J.	8	F		AL
William R.	6	M		AL
Jefferson O.	4	M		AL
Ane Adney	2	F		AL
McGowen, George W.	49	M	Farmer	KY
Margaret	47	F		GA
Margaret A.	23	F		TN
Evaline	17	F		TN
James J.	14	M		TN
John F.	12	M		MS
Frances R.	7	F		TX
McGowen, Alexander H.	25	M	Farmer	TN
Elizabeth	22	F		TN
George W.	1/12	M		TX
McMahon, James B.	35	M	Farmer	TN
Matilda	34	F		AL
James D.	14	M		TX
Charles F.	9	M		TX
Manerva S.	6/12	F		TX

SABINE COUNTY, TEXAS

Name	Age	Sex	Occupation	Birthplace
Smith, Mary	35	F		KY
Joseph	17	M	Farmer	TN
Mary	12	F		TN
Ellen Ora	10	F		TX
Sarah	8	F		TX
Miller, James P.	29	M	Wagon Maker	MO
Frances Ann	30	F		TN
Susan	10	F		MO
Lucy	3	F		TX
Parker, Joseph B.	45	M	Gun Smith	NC
Eliza	32	F		TN
Caroline	16	F		TN
John	12	M		TX
Elvira	8	F		TX
Mary Ann	10	F		TX
Joseph	6	M		TX
Louisa	2	F		TX
George W.	1/12	M		TX
Scruggs, Jesse T.	51	M	Farmer	VA
Mary A. F.	31	F		KY
Finch P.	25	M	Farmer	AL
Nathaniel S.	22	M	Farmer	AL
Sarah A.	24	F		AL
William A.	20	M		TN
Nancy L.	18	F		TN
Jesse T.	14	M		TN
Lawrence M.	13	M		TX
Hembleton M.	11	M		TX
George W.	8	M		TX
Charles A.	5	M		TX
Mary S.	2	F		TX
Sanders, Spotswood H.	36	M	Farmer	VA
Nancy E.	30	F		SC
Francis A.	10	M		TN
Susan E.	6/12	F		TX
McGuin, Hambleton B.	41	M	Farmer	KY
Malinda	34	F		KY
Thomas	16	M		TN
Margaret S.	12	F		TX
Mary L.	10	F		TX
Arabella	8	F		TX
Nancy L.	6	F		TX
Martha	4	F		TX
Lawrence B.	2	M		TX
Amanda V.	2/12	F		TX
Lowe, Moses	56	M	Farmer	TN
Rube	47	F		TN
John W. DeL. F	23	M		TN
Mary A. M.	21	F		TN
Hester Ann J. R.	23	F		TN
Rebeca A. A.	20	F		TN
Euclyd F. A.	15	M		TN
Elizabeth E.	13	F		TN
Abagil D.	11	F		TN
Haney, Robert S.	24	M	Farmer	NC
Arabella	24	F		TN
Mazy Ann Z.	2	F		TX
Robert J.	1	M		TX
Easley, Daniel	58	M	Farmer	GA
Jane	44	F		GA
Clement	23	M		TN
John Baker	9	M		TX
James	7	M		TX
William Lemmons	6	M		LA
Eaton, George W.	44	M	Farmer	KY
Malinda	38	F		TN
Longrage, John	12	M		LA
Westbrook, William	8	M		TX
Eaton, Ellen	6	F		LA
McKirby, Mary	5	F		TX
Ruddell, John	35	M	Farmer	LA
Margarett	25	F		TN
Frazer, Andrew J.	15	M		TN
(continued)				

Name	Age	Sex	Occupation	Birthplace
Ruddell, Isaac N.	9	M		TX
Archer G.	7	M		TX
James P.	4	M		TX
Mary	2	F		TX
Biddo, Earl P.	28	M	Saddler & Tanner	TN
Martha C.	22	F		TN
Malvina P.	5	F		TN
Ann E. M.	3	F		TX
(Blank)	1	F		TX
Veranah H. A.	1	F		TX
Biddo, Philip H.	23	M	Saddler & Tanner	TN
Martha	13	F		TX
Ennis, James	39	M	Black Smith	ENG
Mary Ann	22	F		TN
Mary	1/12	F		TX
Oliver, Ananias G.	28	M	Farmer	TN
Cornelia L.	26	F		MS
Caroline E.	6	F		TX
James A.	1	M		TX
Houghton, Kenedy	56	M	Farmer	NC
Elizabeth	28	F		TN
Manervia	21	F		NC
C---	20	F		NC
Malaki	15	M		NC
Pleasant	12	M		NC
John	10	M		NC
George	1	M		TX
Jonathan E.	3	M		TX
Housman, William D.	32	M	Farmer	TN
Elizabeth	35	F		TN
Tenison, Temperance A.	15	F		TN
Housman, John A.	8	M		KY
James F.	6	M		KY
William H.	3	M		TX
Martha D.	1	F		TX
Cartwright, Clementine	4	F		TX
Virginia A.	2	F		TX
McGuire, Lawrence	56	M	Physician	VA
Frazer, William G.	19	M		TN
John	14	M		TN
Douththat, Latitia	14	F		TN
Lucentia	14	F		TN
Neeley, John E.	29	M	Farmer	TN
Nancy R. A.	21	F		TX
Sarah M.	10/12	F		TX
McMahon, Samuel D.	60	M	Farmer	TN
Phebe R.	59	F		VA
Crawford, Rebeca	4	F		TX
Gaines, John B.	32	M	Farmer	TX
Nancy H.	26	F		TN
Virginia M.	8	F		TX
Phebe A. V.	4	F		TX
Margaret T. A.	10/12	F		TX
Young, Acton	28	M	Preacher	TN
Margaret T.	18	F		TN
Phebe N.	1	F		TX
Pillow, Missouri M.	42	F		KY
Fowler, Mary	11	F		TX
Littleton M.	9	M		TX
Vanderpool, John	15	M		TN
Tipps, John	28	M	Farmer	GER
Warren, James	38	M	Farmer	NC
Amanda L.	32	F		TN
Martha M.	6	F		TX
Susan C.	1	F		TX
Kohn, George	70	M		PA
Susanah	66	F		TN
Myers, George	20	M	Farmer	MS
Kohn, Elias M.	25	M	Farmer	MS
Mary Jane	18	F		TN
Amanda M.	1	F		TX

Name	Age	Sex	Occupation	Birthplace
Delany, Isaac N.	23	M	Farmer	TN
Higgins, James	33	M	Farmer	TN
Rhoda C.	38	F		OH
Rebecca	17	F		OH
George	10	M		OH
James	6	M		TX
William	4	M		TX
Harriett	2	F		TX
Frances	7/12	F		TX
Delany, Isaac	56	M	Farmer	TN
Milanda	47	F		VA
Newton	22	M	Farmer	TN
Jasper	21	M	Farmer	TN
Rebeca	18	F		TN
Frances	14	F		TX
Samuel H.	12	M		TX
B-----	10	F		TX
Missouri	8	F		TX
Virginia	5	F		TX
Jenell, David	50	M		MO
Sophiah	44	F		TN
Stagnus, Henry	94	M		PA
Barfield, Judith	20	F		IL
Kyle, Absolom S.	34	M	Farmer	TN
James M.	9	M		TX
Ema Jane	5	F		TX
Martha L.	3	F		TX
Oliphant, Alfred D.	51	M	Farmer	KY
Martha Ann	32	F		MS
Sarah M.	24	F		TN
Frances V.	8	F		TX
Alfred Jackson	5	M		TX
Emily E. K.	3	F		TX
Candy, Thomas W.	26	M	Overseer	MS
Wiltshire, Benjamin	40	M	Farmer	MS
Martha	38	F		TN
Eliza	4	F		TX
Louisa	4	F		TX
Martha D.	2	F		TX
Robert B.	12	M		MS
Halbert, Joel	40	M	Farmer	TN
Tabitha	36	F		TN
Louisa	16	F		AL
Martha	14	F		AL
Washington	11	M		TX
Amanda	9	F		TX
Susan	6	F		TX
Rebeca	4	F		TX
Westhand, James M.	40	M	Grocer	TN
Elvira	30	F		TN
Sarah Agness	13	F		TN
Frances Ann	10	F		TX
George M.	8	M		TX
James Napoleon	2	M		TX
Neely, Mary	20	F		TN
Damewood, Henry	30	M	Farmer	TN
Lean S. L.	20	F		AL
Harriett Ann	2	F		TX
Easley, James	30	M	Farmer	TN
Nancy N.	20	F		TX
William C.	4	M		TX
Pamelia	3	F		TX
Matilda	9/12	F		TX
Green, Thomas J.	32	M	Farmer	TN
Nancy J.	20	F		MS
John M.	1	M		TX
Lane, John C.	28	M	Farmer	TN
Sarah J.	22	F		AL
Samuel T.	4	M		TX
Hudson, Jackson	31	M	Farmer	TN
(continued)				
Hudson, Sarah A. A.	26	F		MS
Lucinda E.	7	F		TX
Thomas	5	M		TX
Eliza J.	3	F		TX
Salina	1	F		TX
Summers, William S.	36	M	Cabinet Maker	TN
Mary Jane	21	F		TN
Frank	3/12	M		TX
Gowen, Augustus C.	26	M	Farmer	TN
Manerva	18	F		TX
Millions, George S.	34	M	Tavern Keeper	NY
Sarah A.	32	F		TN
Sarah E. J.	10	F		TX
Frederic R.	7	M		TX
Isabella R.	5	F		TX
Benjamin L.	3	M		TX
Fountleroy, Frederic W.	26	M	Attorney at Law	IN
Boyd, James C.	22	M	Grocer	TN
Hanes, Abram	20	M	Clerk	POL
Oliphant, Joseph B.	21	M	Clerk	MS
Newman, David	19	M	Clerk	POL
Westhand, Benjamin F.	37	M	Farmer	TN
Sarah M.	27	F		MS
Lema Ann	2/12	F		TX
Oliphant, Milford	48	M	Farmer	SC
Martha	44	F		GA
Abigal A.	17	F		MS
Robert	14	M		MS
John Houston	11	M		TX
Milford	8	M		TX
Seaborn H.	6	M		TX
Martha Jane	4	F		TX
Alfred D.	1	M		TX
Milford M.	17	M	Farmer	TN
Hicks, Robert	26	M	Overseer	MS
Austin, N---	39	M	Merchant	PA
Mary S.	65	F		PA
E---	32	F		PA
Mary	12	F		PA
Lonis	9	M		PA
Peter	6	M		TX
Nancy	3	F		TX
Alexander, Whitson C.	20	M	Clerk	TN
Hicks, Thomas	63	M	Farmer	SC
Elizabeth	48	F		SC
James M.	28	M	Farmer	TN
Thomas	18	M		MS
Weath---d, Francis M.	67	M	Hotel Keeper	VA
Nancy	58	F		VA
William C.	35	M		TN
Mary A.	23	F		MS
William A.	6	M		TX
Ema Jane	3	F		TX
Frazer, William B.	32	M	Clerk	TN
Mahon, James	33	M	Carpenter	AL
Gunter, William W.	23	M		TN
Myers, James J.	31	M	Carpenter	KY
Norford, Gideon A.	31	M	Carpenter	VA
Mildred	42	F		TN
James F. W.	8	M		TX
John F.	5	M		TX
Ellen E.	1	F		TX
Weath---d, Francis M.	31	M	Clerk	TN
Frances E.	20	F		TN
Madora	3/12	F		TX
Lucas, Bazil E.	41	M	Wagon Maker	PA
Lavica W.	35	F		GA
Elizabeth F.	16	F		TN
Phineas F. M.	11	M		AL
James M. S.	8	M		GA
George M. M.	5	M		GA
Susan R.	2	F		TX
Bazil M.	1	M		TX

SABINE COUNTY, TEXAS

Name	Age	Sex	Occupation	Birthplace
Lorge, Abraham	43	M	Farmer	TN
Drucilla	33	F		AR
Isaam	14	M		TN
Sarah J.	12	F		TN
David C.	10	M		TN
Ann M.	4	F		TN
Mary C.	3	F		TN
Latham, Lewis W.	16	M		AR
Lorge, Mary M.	1	F		TX
Banks, Benjamin G.	52	M	Attorney at Law	KY
Caroline	29	F		TN
William S.	25	M	Medical Student	KY
Benjamin F.	17	M		KY
Crawford, Jacob, Jr.	32	M	Minister & Farmer	NC
Maryann D.	25	F		TN
Mary M.	2	F		TX
Huldah O.	1	F		TX
Griffin, Thomas J.	30	M	Farmer	TN
Rebeca	24	F		TX
Louisa F.	5	F		TX
Nancy J.	3	F		TX
Thomas F.	1	M		TX

SAN AUGUSTINE COUNTY, TEXAS

Name	Age	Sex	Occupation	Birthplace
Bate, Humphrey	71	M	Farmer	NC
Ann	46	F		VA
Willey Ann	21	F		TN
William	19	M	Farmer	TN
Agness E.	16	F		TN
Amanda	14	F		TN
Henry	10	M		TN
Humphrey	7	M		TN
Aaron	4	M		TN
Warren, David O.	41	M	Farmer	SC
Eliza S.	34	F		TN
Thomas R.	17	M	Farmer	AL
William H.	14	M		TX
Henry M.	12	M		TX
Susan A.	10	F		TX
David O.	4	M		TX
Richard D.	1	M		TX
Swinggs, E.	29	M	Overseer	GA
Polk, Margaret	51	F		NC
Lucius	27	M	Farmer	TN
Jane	15	F		TN
Green	15	M		TN
Robina	11	F		TN
Thomas, Theophilus	35	M	Farmer	AL
Susan	28	F		TN
Amanda	8	F		TX
Virginia	5	F		TX
Robert	4	M		TX
Edwin	2	M		TX
Gilbert, David W.	26	M	Farmer	TN
R. N.	24	M	Farmer	TN
Wilson, Frances	55	F		NC
Robinson, Richard O.	27	M	Farmer	TN
Melown, Elizabeth	22	F		TN
Robinson, Charles H.	16	M		TN
James M.	34	M	Farmer	TN
James A.	13	M		TN
Hail, Wilson E.	24	M	Farmer	TN
Mary	24	F		TN
Benjamin	4	M		TX
Zacary T.	3	M		TX
Moore, Elizabeth	13	F		TX
Cartwright, Richard H.	22	M	Farmer	TX
Ann E.	16	F		TN
Sandford	5	M		TX
Polk, Alfred	42	M	Farmer	TN

(continued)

Name	Age	Sex	Occupation	Birthplace
Polk, Nancy	39	F		NC
Charles (Twin)	19	M	Farmer	TN
John (Twin)	19	M	Farmer	TN
Ann	16	F		TN
Silas	14	M		TN
Drew	12	M		TX
Margaret	10	F		TX
Mary	8	F		TX
William	8	M		TX
Tyler	6	M		TX
Isabella	4	F		TX
Pool, A. N.	28	M	Farmer	SC
Anthony, Roddy	45	M	Farmer	NC
Sintha	45	F		TN
Catharine	23	F		TN
Samuel	18	M	Farmer	TN
Lavilla	16	F		TN
Elvira	14	F		TX
Sintha	12	F		TX
William F.	8	M		TX
McNeill, Neill	57	M	Farmer	NC
Delila	45	F		TN
Jane	15	F		NC
Fry, Isaac	20	M	Farmer	TN
Thomas	17	M	Farmer	TN
Jerome	15	M	Farmer	TN
John	10	M		TX
Bartlett	8	M		TX
Burlison, James	27	M	Farmer	MO
Margaret	21	F		TN
Priscilla	3	F		TX
Jerome E.	1	M		TX
Defee, William	50	M	Brick Mason	SC
Nancy	46	F		NC
Joseph S.	19	M	Farmer	TN
Martha	17	F		TX
Permelia	15	F		TX
Evaline	12	F		TX
William	10	M		TX
Nancy	8	F		TX
Tennessee	6	F		TX
Kitty	3	F		TX
Keel, Jerre V.	33	M	Farmer	KY
Elizabeth	25	F		TN
Joseph	5	M		TX
Mary	3	F		TX
Leona	5/12	F		TX
James	2	M		TX
Chumney, Thomas	33	M	Farmer	TX
Nancy	23	F		TN
James	6	M		TX
Isabella	4	F		TX
John	3	M		TX
Mary	1	F		TX
Igo, Garrett	39	M	Farmer	KY
Nancy	36	F		KY
Pleasant	15	M	Farmer	KY
Lewis	11	M		KY
Mary	12	F		KY
Harrison	7	M		KY
Emily	5	F		KY
Greenberry	4	M		KY
Ephraim	3	M		KY
Garrett	3	M		KY
William	2	M		TN
Nicholson, John	46	M	Farmer	NC
Mary	73	F		NC
Mary	45	F		NC
Margaret	30	F		NC
Archibald	20	M	Farmer	TN
John	18	M	Farmer	TN
Peter	16	M	Farmer	TN
Kenneth	15	M	Farmer	TN
Margaret	13	F		TN
Sarah	11	F		TX
Daniel	9	M		TX

(continued)

SAN AUGUSTINE COUNTY, TEXAS

Name	Age	Sex	Occupation	Birthplace
Nicholson, Lewis	7	M		TX
James R.	6	M		TX
Adaline	4	F		TX
Martin	3	M		TX
Bobbett, R. R.	38	M	Farmer	VA
Permelia	29	F		MS
Louisa	12	F		MS
George	10	M		MS
Amanda	8	F		TX
Alfonzo	4	M		TX
Mary	2	F		TX
Susan	6/12	F		TX
Argus	28	M	Farmer	TN
Nash, John D.	34	M	Sheriff	TN
Ellen	25	F		AL
Oscar	10	M		TX
Lucretia	7	F		TX
Frances	5	F		TX
John D.	8/12	M		TX
Heffington, D. C.	40	M	Trainer	KY
Jones, John	27	M	Trainer	KY
Hail, Jonas J.	48	M	Farmer	NC
Amanda	41	F		TN
James	19	M	Farmer	TN
Edley	18	M	Farmer	TN
Jesse	15	M	Farmer	TX
Frances	13	F		TX
Jonas	11	M		TX
Amanda	9	F		TX
Oscar	7	M		TX
Mary J.	5	F		TX
Moore, Elizabeth	14	F		TX
Susan	12	F		TX
Deen, Calaway	39	M	Farmer	TN
Mary	38	F		TN
Oliver	29	M	Farmer	TN
Richard	12	M		TX
Mary	8	F		TX
James	6	M		TX
Caroline	4	F		TX
Joanna	6/12	F		TX
Williams, Samuel A.	46	M	Methodist Minister	TN
Terressy	28	F		TN
Jesse A.	26	M	Farmer	AL
Samuel F.	3	M		TX
Kellogg, Ebenezer	10	M		TX
Roher, Jacob	45	M	Waggoner	MD
Rebecca	46	F		TN
James	4	M		TX
Davis, Jeptha	26	M	Waggoner	TN
Sublett, Henry W.	34	M	Lawyer	KY
Jane	17	F		TN
Anderson, Theophilus	16	M	None	TN
Sharp, B. F.	31	M	Physician	TN
Martha	28	F		TN
Phebe	8	F		TN
William H.	6	M		TN
Mary	4	F		TN
Lafayette	2	M		TN
James	1/12	M		TX
Hale, John	25	M	Farmer	TN
Bate, Humphrey	23	M	Farmer	TN
Sharp, John M.	21	M	Farmer	TN
Perkins, James	49	M	Farmer	VA
Mary S.	41	F		TN
James	3	M		TX
Davenport, James	21	M	Lawyer	TN
Smith, James	47	M	Farmer	VA
Evaline	43	F		VA
Benjamin	18	M	Clerk	TN
James C.	15	M	Farmer	TN
Robert	11	M		TN
George	10	M		TN
Charles S.	3	M		TX

Name	Age	Sex	Occupation	Birthplace
Brown, Richard O.	45	M	Farmer	TN
Nancy W.	40	F		VA
John E.	18	M	Farmer	TN
George W.	16	M	Farmer	TN
William	15	M	Farmer	MS
R. O.	12	M		TX
Mary	9	F		TX
Alvis, James A.	23	M	Farmer	VA
Alexander, H. G.	72	M	Carpenter	PA
Mary	48	F		MS
Francis A.	30	M	Carpenter	TN
Lewis	24	M	Farmer	TN
John R.	22	M	Farmer	TN
Cartwright, Amanda	5	F		TX
Brown, Ezekiel W.	54	M	Farmer	SC
Mary	50	F		NC
Ezicl(?)	18	M	Farmer	TN
Manes, William H.	35	M	Farmer	AL
Matilda	20	F		TN
Kenner, James	54	M	Farmer	TN
Martha	40	F		LA
Winder	18	M	Farmer	LA
Elizabeth	20	F		LA
William	16	M	None	LA
Rodham	14	M		LA
Jonathan	12	M		LA
Francis	10	M		LA
Daniel	7	M		LA
Maria	4	F		LA
Nancy	1	F		TX
Platt, James	29	M	Farmer	NJ
Rosetta	21	F		TN
Elizabeth	1	F		TX
Hollis, William	49	M	Farmer	TN
Elizabeth	38	F		TN
Thomas H.	20	M	Farmer	TN
Jane	16	F		TN
Watson, William	14	M		TX
William	11	M		AR
Mary Jane	8	F		AR
Crouch, Charles W.	43	M	Farmer	VA
Amanda	20	F		NC
John	18	M	Farmer	TN
William	16	M	Farmer	TN
Elizabeth	13	F		MS
Lucretia	4	F		TX
Martha	2	F		TX
Allen, Richard M.	36	M	Carpenter	VA
Susan	27	F		TN
William	6	M		TX
Lucy	5	F		TX
John	6/12	M		TX
Jones, George W.	38	M	Farmer	TN
Malinda	25	F		TN
George	5	M		TX
Malinda	10	F		TX
William	3	M		TX
Thomas	1	M		TX
Stovall, James	20	M	Farmer	TN
Curl, Henry H.	39	M	Farmer	TN
Nancy	29	F		TN
Malissy	19	F		TN
Missouri	16	F		AR
Clementine	14	F		AR
Eudora	12	F		AR
Charlotte	9	F		MO
Henry	3	M		TX
James	1	M		TX
Cartwright, William	12	M		TN
Julia	9	F		TX
John	7	M		TX
Wood, Reuben	39	M	Farmer	TN
Martha	39	F		NC
Susan	17	F		TX
Sophia	14	F		TX

(continued)

SAN AUGUSTINE COUNTY, TEXAS

Name	Age	Sex	Occupation	Birthplace
Wood, Horton	10	M		TX
Mariam	7	F		TX
Kenneth	5	M		TX
Joseph	61	M	Physician	NC
Duncan, Thomas	22	M	Farmer	NC
Franklin	17	M	Farmer	NC
Barnes, Moses	35	M	Farmer	TN
Brooks, James H.	55	M	Farmer	TN
Ann	43	F		GA
William F.	15	M	Farmer	LA
Angeline	13	F		LA
Adaline	12	F		LA
Eliza	7	F		LA
James	5	M		LA
Thomas N.	3	M		LA
Garrett, William	38	M	Farmer	TN
Lucett	22	F		TX
Clementine	14	F		TX
Mary	12	F		TX
Holman, Anna	10	F		TX
William	8	M		TX
Fitzgerald, Jackson	34	M	Farmer	VA
Catharine	30	F		TN
Mary	18	F		TN
Jackson	17	M	Farmer	TN
Edmund	15	M	Farmer	TN
Francis	13	M		TN
Henry, John	39	M	Farmer	VA
Rebecca	22	F		TN
Augustus	6	M		TX
Malinda	4	F		TX
Edward	2	M		TX
No Name	5/12	M		TX
No Name	5/12	M		TX
Stovall, Malinda	52	F		TN
William A.	20	M	Farmer	TN
Sims	17	M	Farmer	TN
Mary Ann	9	F		TX
Matilda	13	F		LA
Malinda	3	F		TX
Roberts, Isaac	56	M	Farmer	TN
Elizabeth	55	F		GA
Thomas B.	29	M	School Teacher	LA
Washington	25	M	Medical Student	LA
Abner	23	M	Farmer	LA
Isaac	20	M	Farmer	LA
Cornelius	17	M	Farmer	LA
Elisha	14	M		LA
Elizabeth	9	F		TX
Coulter, Sampson	25	M	Farmer	NC
Adaline	20	F		TN
Bullock, Jesse T.	32	M	Farmer	MS
Harriet	30	F		TN
Manerva	12	F		MS
Nathan	7	M		TX
David	5	M		TX
Martha	2	F		TX
Coulter, Henson	61	M	Farmer	NC
Jelany	61	F		NC
Carney	28	M	Farmer	NC
Alexander	26	M	Farmer	NC
Sarah	20	F		NC
Thomas	17	M	Farmer	TN
Love, John G.	62	M	Farmer	TN
Margaret	40	F		TN
Joseph	21	M	Farmer	TX
John	19	M	Farmer	TX
William	17	M	Farmer	TX
Ann	15	F		TX
Randal, Leonard	50	M	Physician	NC
Sarah	40	F		NC
Almedia	18	F		TN

(continued)

Name	Age	Sex	Occupation	Birthplace
Randal, Horace	17	M	Cadet	TN
Susan	15	F		TN
Mary	13	F		TN
Leonard	11	M		TX
Sarah	6	F		TX
Eliza	3	F		TX
Solan	1	M		TX
Deen, Russel	21	M	Farmer	TN
Elizabeth	21	F		TN
Williams, James W.	30	M	Farmer	AL
Sarah	26	F		TN
Newton	5	M		TX
McKee, Isaac V.	44	M	Notary & J.P.	IA
Mary	27	F		TN
Shannon	9	M		TX
Josiah	7	M		TX
Samuel	5	M		TX
Wesley	3	M		TX
Archibald	1	M		TX
Rankin, John M.	49	M	Money Linder	KY
Sarah	32	F		TN
Martha	15	F		TN
John	13	M		TN
Ellen	9	F		TX
Louisa	6	F		TX
Henry	1	M		TX
Smith, Daniel D.	34	M	Farmer	TN
Ann	31	F		MS
Susan	12	F		MS
Benjamin	10	M		TX
James	8	M		TX
Catharine	5	F		TX
David	1	M		TX
Martin, Robert W.	42	M	Tailor	VA
Eliza	44	F		VA
John S.	18	M	Carpenter	TN
George	16	M	Dept. Clerk	AL
Robert	15	M	Saddler	AL
James	14	M		AL
Tennessee	13	F		AL
Alabama	11	F		TX
Albert S.	10	M		TX
Daniel G.	8	M		TX
Rachael	6	F		TX
Charles	4	M		TX
Manes(?), A. J.	25	M	Farmer	AL
Martha	24	F		TN
McAlister, Josiah	12	M		TN
Slaughter, William H.	52	M	Gun Smith	TN
Richard	21	M	None	TN
William	18	M	None	TN
Winn, John A.	33	M	Merchant	TN
Evaline	25	F		LA
Frances	9	F		TX
Cora	7	F		TX
Mary	5	F		TX
John	3	M		TX
Puss	1	F		TX
McCarroll, Ame	28	F		NC
Johnson, J. B.	33	M	Merchant	VA
Louisa	22	F		TN
Henry H.	3	M		TX
Smith O.	1	M		TX
Rankin, Henry L.	30	M	Clerk	KY
Jordan, Samuel	37	M	Deputy Sheriff	VA
Lucy Ann	22	F		TN
Lucy	5	F		TX
Mary	3	F		TX
Sarah	2	F		TX
John	1	M		TX
Lockheart, William	50	M	Grocery Keeper	VA
Roberts, J. J.	30	M	Physician	LA
Jordan, John F.	45	M	None	VA

Name	Age	Sex	Occupation	Birthplace
Plunkett, E. J.	41	M	Hotel Keeper	NC
Susan	29	F		ENG
Walter	5	M		TX
Littleton	3	M		TX
Alice	1	F		TX
Thorn, J. F.	27	M	Clerk	NH
Rhote, John C.	22	M	Merchant	GER
King, William	19	M	Clerk	TN
Reilly, Bernard	36	M	Shoe Maker	IRE
FitzAllen, Oscar	40	M	Physician	PA
Ochilton, Hugh	30	M	Clerk	NC
Margaret	25	F		TN
Eliza	4	F		TX
Margaret	1	F		TX
Patton, Anthony B.	34	M	Saddler	AL
Mary	22	F		TN
Priscilla	7	F		TX
Thomas	5	M		TX
John	4	M		TX
Catharine	1	F		TX
Martin, Brown	15	M	Saddler	AL
Nicks, James	21	M	Saddler	AL
Martin, James	28	M	Saddler	NY
Scott, Robert	13	M		TX
Watson, Simeon C.	32	M	Grocer	GA
Mary	28	F		TN
Margaret	6	F		TX
Simeon	4	M		TX
Aran	2	M		TX
Thomas	6/12	M		TX
Burleson, Joseph	49	M	Farmer	TN
Mary	48	F		KY
Edward	21	M	Farmer	TN
Joseph	20	M	Farmer	TN
Margaret	16	F		TN
Augustus	14	M		TX
John	12	M		TX
Thomas	10	M		TX
Mary	8	F		TX
Sarah	5	F		TX
Bullock, James W.	62	M	Farmer	NC
Nancy	50	F		NC
Ann	14	F		TX
Henry P.	12	M		TX
Uriah	9	M		TX
Amanda	7	F		TX
Thaddeus	21	M	Farmer	TN
Sarah	18	F		TX
James W.	3/12	M		TX
Berry, John G.	49	M	Farmer	NC
Harriet	42	F		TN
William	19	M	Farmer	TN
Elisha	13	M		TX
John	8	M		TX
Caroline	11	F		TX
Kenneth	6	M		TX
Rush	4	M		TX
Watson, James	34	M	Farmer	TN
Clark, John	30	M	Farmer	TN
Sossaman, Charles R.	33	M	Merchant	SC
Cornelia	25	F		NC
Charles R.	4	M		TX
Albert P.	1/12	M		TX
Hudnell, Leroy	31	M	Laborer	TN
Newton, Elizabeth	35	F		PA
Laura	4	F		TX
Sossaman, Cornelia E.	2	F		TX
McKnight, James H.	48	M	Tailor	NC
Mary J.	20	F		TN
James M.	18	M	Tailor	TN
William H.	16	M	Tailor	TN
Robert C.	12	M		TN
James B.	7	M		TX
Helen E.	4	F		TX

Name	Age	Sex	Occupation	Birthplace
Teal, Edward	84	M	Farmer	MD
Noland, Edward	26	M	Farmer	TN
Lumpkins, William M.	49	M	Farmer	VA
Polina	38	F		KY
Christney	21	F		TN
John	20	M	Farmer	TN
David	18	M	Farmer	TN
William	16	M	Farmer	TX
Elizabeth	13	F		TX
Nancy J.	8	F		TX
Martha	6	F		TX
George W.	2	M		TX
McKinney, Henry	44	M	Farmer	TN
Permelia	35	F		LA
Newman	10	M		TX
Frederick	8	M		TX
Nancy	6	F		TX
Navaline	5	F		TX
James	4	M		TX
Betty	2	F		TX
Hunt, Henry	27	M	Farmer	TN
Mary G.	18	F		MS
Nathaniel	1	M		TX
Franklin, Willis	25	M	Farmer	MS
Brooks, Henry	39	M	Farmer	NC
Mary J.	28	F		TN
Josephus	13	M		TN
Julia	28	F		NC
Sarah	10	F		TX
Elizabeth	2	F		TX
Bacon, Elizabeth	40	F		NC
Jonathan	12	M		TX
Mary Ann (Twin)	9	F		TX
Frances (Twin)	9	F		TX
Rountree, Joseph	22	M	Farmer	TN
Silema A.	17	F		MS
Thomas, J. D.	44	M	Merchant	NC
Elizabeth	35	F		TN
Almedia	18	F		TX
Mary	16	F		TX
Loena	13	F		TX
Penelope	11	F		TX
Victoria	9	F		TX
William	14	M		TX
Iredel	8	M		TX
James E.	6	M		TX
Miller, Leroy	40	M	Farmer	AL
Trephena	30	F		TN
Theophilus	9	M		TX
Samuel	4	M		TX
Not Named	2/12	M		TX
Johnson, James A.	22	M	Farmer	VA
America	18	F		TN
King, Samuel H.	24	M	Farmer	TN
George W.	17	M	Farmer	TN
Nash, William	41	M	Farmer	TN
Louisa	41	F		TN
William D.	22	M	Farmer	TN
Lewellen	21	M	Farmer	TN
Charles	16	M	Farmer	TN
Napoleon	12	M		TX
Lucy	10	F		TX
Herbert	8	M		TX
Politha	2	F		TX
Mary L.	6	F		TX
Bissett, R. B.	55	M	School Teacher	SCO
Vanderpool, Sampson	55	M	Stone Mason	SC
Arilla	30	F		TN
John	15	M	Farmer	TN
Lafayette	11	M		TN
Martha	5	F.		TN
Elihu	4	M		TN
Samuel	2	M		TN

SAN AUGUSTINE COUNTY, TEXAS

Name	Age	Sex	Occupation	Birthplace
Crow, James M.	31	M	Farmer	TN
Susan E.	21	F		TN
Emily	3	F		TX
Ellen	9/12	F		TX
Sanders, John	29	M	Farmer	SC
Elizabeth	23	F		TN
John	6	M		TX
Charity	4	F		TX
Charles	2	M		TX
Davis, Henry S.	32	M	Farmer	NC
Lindsey, Isaac	63	M	Farmer	SC
Esther	65	F		SC
Davis, Jesse	10	M		TX
Runnels, John	25	M	Farmer	TN
Spears, Andrew	86	M	Farmer	MD
Mary	58	F		PA
John	30	M	Farmer	TN
James	25	M	Farmer	AL
John	14	M		TX
Andrew	11	M		TX
Solomon	10	M		TX
Lakey, William	52	M	Farmer	NC
Sarah	52	F		NC
John V.	15	M	Farmer	LA
Sam Houston	13	M		TX
Noah	12	M		TX
Mary E.	19	F		TN
William C.	22	M	Farmer	TN
Wood, Charles A.	44	M	Farmer	NJ
Elizabeth	37	F		NC
George W.	16	M	Farmer	TN
Frances	12	F		TX
Charles	11	M		TX
Margaret	9	F		TX
Izreal	9	M		TX
Edwin	6	M		TX
Stephen	3	M		TX
Levi	2	M		TX
Williams, Greenbury	28	M	Farmer	TN
Elizabeth	25	F		MS
Mary	1	F		TX
Martha	4	F		TX
Hobdey, Joses	53	M	Farmer	NC
Lizetta	46	F		TN
Martha	21	F		TX
Clementine	19	F		TX
Amanda	16	F		TX
Tabitha	14	F		TX
Malissy	11	F		TX
Abram	5	M		TX
Robert	8	M		TX
John	3	M		TX
Miller, Robert F.	27	M	Farmer	TN
Eliza	18	F		GA
Fondren, John	36	M	Farmer	GA
Eliza	25	F		TN
Sophia	8	F		MS
Nancy	7	F		AR
Columbus	4	M		TX
Richard	2	M		TX
Marshal	3/12	M		TX
Crow, Levi M.	35	M	Farmer	TN
Mary L.	29	F		TN
Ellison, Marison	28	M	Farmer	GA
Hunt, Thomas	34	M	Farmer	TN
Jane	27	F		MS
Elizabeth	9	F		TX
America	7	F		TX
Thomas	5	M		TX
Prunia	3	F		TX
Frances	1	F		TX

Name	Age	Sex	Occupation	Birthplace
Hunt, Elizabeth	56	F		GA
Neely, Clarrissy	36	F		TN
Matilda	6	F		TX
Nathaniel	4	M		TX
Loggins, Susan	58	F		SC
William Henry	26	M	Farmer	TN
Lewis	18	M	Farmer	TN
Richard	16	M	Farmer	MS
William D.	12	M		TX
Loggins, Samuel	40	M	Farmer	TN
Calpernia	16	F		MS
Helen	14	F		MS
James T.	12	M		TX
Argi	10	M		TX
Malissy Ann	8	F		TX
Samuel	6	M		TX
Vashary, John	40	M	None	MS
Mary	26	F		TN
Nancy	12	F		TX
Anthony	8	M		TX
Susan	5	F		TX
Greenbury	3	M		TX
John	2/12	M		TX
Pinson, Harvey H.	19	M	Farmer	TN
Elizabeth	20	M(F)		MS
Hereford, William H.	41	M	Farmer	TN
Amanda	28	F		MS
Clarinda	13	F		TX
Marion	11	M		TX
Drewry	8	M		TX
Missouri	5	F		TX
Dandy	3	M		TX
Winborne, David	34	M	Farmer	MS
America	28	F		TN
Lorado	3	F		TX
Sally	2	F		TX
Ham, Orange	55	M	Farmer	NC
Brison, Ferview	25	F		TN
Margaret	10	F		TN
Martha	7	F		TN
Amanda	5	F		TN
Butler, Hampton	53	M	Farmer	NC
Sarah	46	F		VA
Polley	30	F		TN
Samuel	23	M	Farmer	TN
James	18	M	Farmer	TN
Nancy	16	F		TN
Milly	14	F		TN
Jane	11	F		TN
Hampton	7	M		TN
Goddard, Larkin	30	M	Farmer	TN
Elizabeth	21	F		TN
Jane	1/12	F		TX
Ellison, Thomas	24	M	Farmer	TN
Selia	23	F		TN
Ellison, James H.	30	M	Farmer	TN
Nancy	22	F		TN
George	19	M		TN
Stewart, Charles	42	M	Merchant	MD
Ann S.	36	F		TN
Ellen	13	F		IA
John	12	M		IA
Marian	5	F		TX
Catharine	2	F		TX
Charles	3/12	M		TX
Garner, Virginia	15	F		AL
Mary	13	F		AL
Martha	11	F		AL
James	9	M		TX
Broocks, T. G.	41	M	Farmer	VA
Elizabeth	35	F		AL
John H.	20	M	Merchant	TN

(continued)

SAN AUGUSTINE COUNTY, TEXAS

Name	Age	Sex	Occupation	Birthplace
Broocks, Moses A.	17	M	Student	TN
James A.	15	M	Student	TN
Lycurgus	9	M		TX
Kenneth L.	5	M		TX
Elizabeth H.	2	F		TX
King, John R.	21	M	Clerk	TN
Garner, John	49	M	Farmer	NC
Mary	47	F		SC
Thomas R.	22	M	Farmer	TN
John T.	18	M	Farmer	TN
James S.	11	M		TX
Raines, John D.	42	M	Carpenter	TN
Rheudy	30	F		SC
William S.	7	M		TX
Thomas R.	5	M		TX
Mary C.	3	F		TX
Laura	8/12	F		TX
Phillips, William	33	M	Merchant	TN
Virginia	23	F		VA
William L.	9/12	M		TX
Kimbro, William	40	M	Farmer	TN
Sarah	42	F		TN
Benjamin	11	M		TX
Price, Albert G.	26	M	Farmer	AL
Sarah E.	24	F		TN
William W.	3	M		TX
Horn, Ransom	27	M	Gin Wright	TN
Sarah	25	F		AL
Henry	4	M		MS
Nancy J.	2	F		TX
Deen, C.	26	M	Black Smith	TN
Susan	20	F		TN
Mary Ann	3	F		TN
Celia E.	1	F		TX
Bullock, Frances	47	F		VA
Solomon	19	M	Farmer	TN
Araminta	16	F		TN
William	15	M	Farmer	TN
Arthissa	11	F		TN
Arjarah	9	F		TN
Argera	8	F		TN
Arletta	6	F		TN
Thomas J.	4	M		TN
Francois, Emily M.	20	F		TN
Poline	4	F		TX
Mary	2	F		TX
Anderson, Mary S.	40	F		GA
Mary E.	14	F		AL
Oliver Z.	12	M		TX
Martha	8	F		TX
James C.	1	M		TX
Chillies, J. F.	29	M	Lawyer	NY
Anderson, Malcom G.	21	M	Lawyer	TN
Teal, George	51	M	Farmer	MD
Rebecca	47	F		MO
Wyatt	21	M	Farmer	TX
Eliza	16	F		TX
Olive	12	F		TX
Wilson, Ewing	30	M	Farmer	TN
Polk, John	51	M	Farmer	NC
Cynthia	47	F		TN
Isaac C.	22	M	Farmer	TN
Jerome	16	F		TN
Eugenia	14	F		TN
John D.	11	M		TX
Benjamin	7	M		TX
Simpson, William M.	30	M	Trader	TN
Letitia	34	F		SC
Buford, Thomas R.	18	M	Farmer	TN
Mary B.	32	F		TN

(continued)

Name	Age	Sex	Occupation	Birthplace
Buford, Mary T.	10	F		TX
John	7	M		TX
Elizabeth C.	5	F		TX
Burnes, Samuel T.	37	M	Trader	GA
Eliza B.	26	F		TN
Lafayette	19	M	Farmer	TN
Mary Ann	9	F		TX
Almedia	6	F		TX
Rachel	3	F		TX
Samuel T.	2/12	M		TX
Payne, Charlton	31	M	Lawyer	TN
Elizabeth	28	F		SC
Rosealtha	7	F		TX
William W.	5	M		TX
Charlton	3	M		TX
Lucas, David	55	M	Stock Keeper	VA
Samuel	30	M	Farmer	TN
Mitchell	28	M	Farmer	TN
Mary	23	F		TN
Elvira	21	F		TN
Benton, Mary	58	F		NC
Jesse	36	M	Lawyer	TN
B. F.	22	M	Editor	TN
Anderson, William C.	38	M	Lawyer	KY
Elizabeth	31	F		TN
William S.	13	M		TX
Sam Houston	11	M		TX
Mary S.	4	F		TX
Laura J.	2	F		TX
Willington, Edward	50	M	Farmer	MS
Isabella	40	F		MS
Barnett	24	M	Farmer	MS
Henderson	23	M	Farmer	TN
Thomas	19	M	Farmer	TN
Sarah	15	F		TN
Isaac	12	M		TX
John W.	5	M		TX
Edward	7	M		TX
Shirley, Felix C.	38	M	Farmer	KY
Levonia	32	F		TN
James	6	M		TX
William W.	4	M		TX
Rebecca J.	3	F		TX
Baines, John	33	M	Farmer	VA
Childers, J. T.	32	M	Saddler	VA
Emily	23	F		TN
Mary E.	3	F		TX
John T.	1	M		TX
Fry, George	50	M	Tanner & Currier	PA
Johnson, George	17	M	Apprentice	IA
Colia, James	18	M	Apprentice	ENG
Holloway, Daniel	48	M	Farmer	SC
Elizabeth	26	F		TN
Gray, Anthony F.	55	M	Farmer	KY
Lucinda C.	43	F		TN
John H.	22	M	Farmer	TN
William W.	20	M	Farmer	TN
Margaret E.	17	F		TN
Mary Ann	15	F		TN
Lawrence	14	M		TN
Edmund	12	M		TX
Martha	10	F		TX
Samuel	6	M		TX
James R.	4	M		TX
Eliza J.	1/12	F		TX
Gray, Thomas S.	26	M	Farmer	TN
Elizabeth	23	F		AR
Sarah L.	2	F		TX
Weare, Catharine	38	F		SC
Louisa	14	F		AL
James E.	13	M		TN
Theophilus	11	M		TX
Frances	1	F		TX

SAN AUGUSTINE COUNTY, TEXAS

Name	Age	Sex	Occupation	Birthplace
Stovall, Thomas S.	49	M	Farmer	GA
Sarah	46	F		VA
Mary Ann	22	F		TN
Thomas	15	M	Farmer	TN
Susan	12	F		TN
George	10	M		TN
Jefferson	7	M		TN
Malinda	4	F		TN
Lewis, Precious	2	F		TX
Wheeler, Otis M.	37	M	Farmer	MA
Elvira	25	F		TN
Otis	5/12	M		TX
Polley, John	27	M	Overseer	TN
Kelly, John	26	M	Laborer	OH
Cartwright, William	4	M		TX
Payne, Thomas P.	34	M	Farmer	TN
John A.	7	M		TX
James P.	4	M		TX
Adams, Hopewell H.	25	M	Farmer	AL
Jane	21	F		TN
Caroline	5	F		TX
Crocket	4	M		TX
Nancy	3	F		TX
Levona	8/12	F		TX
Lambert, Thomas	49	M	Cooper	TN
Sarah	28	F		TN
Joseph	13	M		TN
Martha	8	F		TN
Amon	6	M		TN
Taylor	2	M		TN
David	1	M		TX
Dixon, Felix B.	32	M	Wagon Maker	OH
Lavina	22	F		TN
Mary	3	F		TX
Sarah	1	F		TX
Shanks, Helen	16	F		TN
Horn, Eunicy J.	46	F		NC
Columbus	17	M	Farmer	TN
John	13	M		TX
Robert	11	M		TX
Fitzgerald, Calvin	24	M	Farmer	TN
Nancy A.	20	F		TN
Jane	5	F		TN
James	3	M		TX
Martin	5/12	M		TX
Mitchell, Jesse A.	30	M	Farmer	AL
Sarah	22	F		TN
Sarah	2	F		TX
Mary	8/12	F		TX
Garrett, Milton	46	M	Farmer	TN
Elizabeth	33	F		TN
Robert M.	2	M		TX
Samuel	1	M		TX
Duncan, Jane	32	F		TN
Sidney	12	F		TX
Amanda	10	F		TX
Adaline	7	F		TX
Susan	4	F		TX
Dilliard, Allen	60	M	Farmer	NC
Lucretia	47	F		NC
John D.	15	M	Farmer	TN
Merritt	13	M		TX
Mary Ann	10	F		TX
Ward, William H.	26	M	Farmer	NC
Baker, James A. L.	26	M	Farmer	TN
Martha	27	F		TN
William	5	M		TX
Mary	3	F		TX
James	1	M		TX
Pumphrey	17	M	Farmer	TN
Samuel	11	M		TX
Cushman, Joshua	54	M	School Teacher	IA
Smith, Solomon	45	M	Farmer	NC
Martha	20	F		KY
James	11	M		TN
Nancy	9	F		TN
Louisa	4	F		TN
Texanna	6/12	F		TX
Greer, Lewis V.	44	M	Farmer	TN
John A.	48	M	Lt. Governor	TN
Hultz, Silas	43	M	Carpenter	PA
Malinda	35	F		TN
Howard, Jane	19	F		IL
Sutton, Green	39	M	Farmer	AL
Ginsey	36	F		TN
Frances	11	F		MS
Elizabeth	7	F		AL
John G.	3	M		AL
Mary	1	F		TX
Cartwright, Matthew	42	M	Trader	TN
Amanda	33	F		TN
Columbus	13	M		TX
Americus	10	M		TX
Leonadas	8	M		TX
Anna	6	F		TX
Mary	4	F		TX
Anthony, Patterson	25	M	Farmer	TN
Mary	16	F		MS

SAN PATRICIO COUNTY, TEXAS

Name	Age	Sex	Occupation	Birthplace
Fadden, Patrick	42	M	Farmer	IRE
Ellen	22	F		IRE
John	13	M		TN
Ellen	12	F		TN
Bridget	8	F		TN
Mary Ann	4	F		TN
Henry	4/12	M		TN
Hallacon, Ann	16	F		TN
Mahoney, Peter	42	M		IRE
Rose	34	F		IRE
Thomas	10	M		TN
John L.	9	M		TN
Maryann	7	F		TN
Michael	5	M		TX
James	4	M		TX
Jane	1	F		TX

SHELBY COUNTY, TEXAS

Name	Age	Sex	Occupation	Birthplace
Cooper, Jobe	50	M	Farmer	TN
Elizabeth	43	F		TN
M. L.	20	M	Farmer	TN
J. An	16	F		TN
J. D.	14	M		TN
J. B.	12	M		TN
E. H.	8	M		TX
Mary T.	5	F		TX
Jobe	3	M		TX
Sary Z.	8/12	F		TX
Landrum, A. K.	28	M	House Carpenter	TN
Estes, Bethleham	33	M	Farmer	TN
July An	35	F		TN
Louisa	14	F		TN
Faithy	13	F		TN
Calhoune	11	M		TX
Cornelius	9	M		TX
Catherine	7	F		TX
Matthew C.	5	M		TX
Mary J.	3	F		TX
A. D.	1	M		TX
Hill, Edmund	40	M	School Teacher	VA
Sary	22	F		TN
Phillip	4	M		TX
Charles	3	M		TX
Mary	2	F		TX
Nancy	8/12	F		TX

SHELBY COUNTY, TEXAS

Name	Age	Sex	Occupation	Birthplace
Handley, A. E.	31	M	Farmer	TN
Susan	23	F		FL
Eliza	6	F		TX
Inman, Hiram	28	M	Farmer	TN
Nancy	24	F		AL
Frances M.	6	F		TX
Thomas J.	3	M		TX
Delily A.	2	F		TX
John G.	11/12	M		TX
Graves, R. R.	36	M	Farmer	GA
Esther E.	35	F		TN
William J.	7	M		TX
Davy	5	M		AL
Elizabeth	9/12	F		TX
Dickason, Sary	25	F		TN
Edwin H.	8	M		TN
Graves, Cornelia	8	F		AL
Georgie E.	5	F		AL
Barron, John	23	M	Farmer	SC
Alvis, William C.	38	M	Cabinet Maker	TN
Elizabeth	37	F		TN
Margret	15	F		TN
Louisa J.	13	F		TN
Elizabeth	11	F		TN
William W.	9	M		TX
Lucindy A.	7	F		TX
Martha E.	2	F		TX
McClelland, Sam C.	39	M	Farmer	TN
Jane C.	26	F		SC
Mary E. N.	2	F		TX
Nancy K.	11/12	F		TX
Slaughter, Jno.	64	M	Farmer	GA
Mary	30	F		TN
Robert	16	M	Farmer	GA
Rubin	24	M	Farmer	GA
George	21	M	Farmer	GA
Westly	12	M		GA
Nancy	1/12	F		TX
Myrick, John E.	42	M	Farmer	TN
Beck, John	24	M	Farmer	GA
Frances	18	F		TN
Benge, Marthy	8	F		TN
Henderson, Ambrose	47	M	Black Smith	TN
Lorinda	28	F		AR
William	10	M		TX
Margret J.	8	F		TX
Moses W.	6	M		TX
Mary A.	4	F		TX
Lucretia	2	F		TX
Callahan, R. P.	33	M	Farmer	TN
Mary	25	F		TN
Sary J.	4	F		MS
Frances A. P.	2	F		TX
Knight, Thomas J.	25	M	Farmer	TN
Marthy A.	17	F		TN
William A.	5/12	M		TX
Latham, John	53	M	Farmer	TN
Susan	42	F		KY
Jno.	18	M	Farmer	TX
Houston	14	M		TX
Stephen	12	M		TX
Malindy	6	F		TX
Jerome	4	M		TX
Alvin	2	M		TX
Jas.	21	M	Farmer	TX
Kirkpatrick, Lewis	69	M	Farmer	NC
Mahaly	36	F		TN
Robert	26	M	Farmer	TN
F. M.	24	M	Farmer	TN
Elizabeth	20	F		TN
Mary S.	4	F		TX
Dewit	8/12	M		TX
Rains, Emory	50	M	Farmer	TN
Rainy	48	F		KY
Mary A.	23	F		TX
Manervy	21	F		TX
James D.	19	M	Farmer	TX
Sary	18	F		TX
Presly P.	14	M		TX
Elizabeth	12	F		TX
M--	10	F		TX
Cathrine	8	F		TX
Ellenor	6	F		TX
Porter, Samuel	51	M	Farmer	VA
Mary	45	F		TN
Mahaly	15	F		TX
Caroline	13	F		TX
Malindy	8	F		TX
Andrew J.	4	M		TX
English, Joshua	43	M	Farmer	TN
Candis	33	F		GA
Matildy E.	14	F		TX
James M.	12	M		TX
William T.	7	M		TX
A---	6	F		TX
Marthy A.	4	F		TX
Elizabeth	2	F		TX
Gray, James	23	M	Farmer	AR
Runnels, Stephen S.	28	M	Grocer	TN
Mary A.	23	F		AL
Robert	7	M		TX
Susan C.	4	F		TX
Margret E.	10/12	F		TX
Turner, Thomas M.	22	M	Grocer	AL
Payne, John	33	M	Farmer	TN
Nancy	28	F		TN
Rebecca	11	F		TX
Mary	8	F		TX
Amandy	5	F		TX
Elviry	3	F		TX
James A.	11/12	M		TX
Ervin, James	45	M	Farmer	TN
Terecy	27	F		AL
Robert B.	10	M		TX
Asa G.	7	M		TX
Thomas L.	3	M		TX
Dudley	1	M		TX
Wheeller, William	60	M	Farmer	TN
Nancy	55	F		??
Alford	35	M	Farmer	TN
Martin	29	M	Farmer	TN
Patsey	25	F		TN
Modeny	23	F		TN
Ellen	21	F		TN
Lusindy	18	F		TN
Preston	11	M		AR
Anderson	7	M		TN
Henry	5	M		TN
Payne, Sary	32	F		TN
Elizabeth	8	F		AR
William	6	M		AR
Raines, George R.	40	M	Farmer	TN
Hannah J.	35	F		TN
Cathrine	12	F		TX
George R.	7	M		TX
Mary	5	F		TX
Carroll	4	M		TX
Lewis C.	2	M		TX
Longacre, Uriah	44	M	Farmer	TN
Harriet E.	28	F		TN
Eliza	1	F		TX
Dial, Anna	56	F	Hotel Keeper	NC
John C.	23	M	Farmer	TN
Hamilton C.	17	M		TN
Runnels, John	25	M	Grocer	TN
Hewit, William M.	28	M	Clerk	AL
Williams, F. G.	27	M	Physician	GA
Lester, S. T.	22	M	Clerk	AL

(continued)

SHELBY COUNTY, TEXAS

Name	Age	Sex	Occupation	Birthplace
Armstrong, John	24	M	House Carpenter	ENG
Booth, Zach.	20	M	Clerk	GA
Loony, J. C.	23	M	House Carpenter	TN
Boles, Albert	18	M	House Carpenter	AL
Huddleston, Pleasant	60	M	Farmer	VA
Elizabeth	25	F		VA
Willaba, Andrew	27	M	illegible--	
John P.	6	M		TN
William W.	5	M		TN
Cathrine	1	F		TX
Hall, Marthy	3	F		TX
Turner, Charles	27	M	Merchant	MS
Amandy	18	F		AL
William C.	4	M		TX
Ephraim M.	1	M		TX
Longacre, Elliott	32	M	Overseer	TN
Smith, Logan L.	27	M	Farmer	TN
Mariah	21	F		IN
Marthy A.	3	F		TX
Alford M. H.	1	M		TX
Snider, Joel	45	M	Farmer	SC
Jennette	51	F		NC
Ellany L.	17	M	Farmer	AL
Epsey D.	15	F		AL
Matildy T.	12	F		AL
Margret E.	10	F		AL
Pernecy M.	8	F		TX
Hutson, William R.	18	M	Farmer	TN
J. D.	16	M	Farmer	TN
Susan J.	10	F		TX
Georgie A.	7	F		TX
Tatum, A. J. G.	34	M	Farmer	VA
Susan E.	26	F		TN
Mary A.	9	F		TN
Nancy V.	7	F		TN
Susan F.	5	F		TX
Samuel F.	10/12	M		TX
Grady, Sary A.	22	F		AR
Spencer, Henry	35	M	School Teacher	NY
Middleton, Jno. W.	43	M	Farmer	TN
Mary A.	41	F		NC
Washington	17	M	Student	TN
Marthy E.	10	F		TN
Drury L.	13	M		TN
William C.	9	M		TX
Nathan A.	7	M		TX
Sary L.	2	F		TX
Smith, William S.	29	M	Grocer	TN
Ann	24	F		NC
Seline	11	F		TN
William R.	5	M		TX
Mary A.	2	F		TX
Moore, Matthew	20	M	Grocer	TN
Harris, Ira	65	M	Farmer	NC
Margret	50	F		KY
Runnels, Eliza	13	F		TN
Henry H.	12	M		TN
Joshua	11	M		TN
Day, William W.	22	M		TN
Mahaly C.	17	F		TN
Porter, William P.	29	M		AL
Margaret C.	22	F		TN
Jane A.	8	F		TX
Mary E.	6	F		TX
Manervy C.	4	F		TX
Sary E.	1	F		TX
Dial, Joseph	30	M	Farmer	TN
Marthy E.	22	F		SC
Beatrice E. A.	6	F		TX
Marcilly J.	4	F		TX
Elenor M. T.	2	F		TX
Hall, John	44	M	Laborer	SC

Name	Age	Sex	Occupation	Birthplace
Johnston, A. R.	44	M	Farmer	NC
Rody D.	40	F		TN
Jos. L.	20	M	Farmer	AR
Ellinor	18	F		TX
Milam	13	M		TX
Elizabeth	10	F		TX
A. R., Jr.	8	M		TX
Eli	4	M		TX
Samuel	2	M		TX
Preston	20	M	Farmer	AR
Wadkins, B. D. S.	45	M	Farmer	SC
Jane	44	F		TN
David H.	18	M	Farmer	AL
Rachal	17	F		AL
Marthy E.	13	F		AL
Louis C.	12	M	Farmer	TX
William C.	8	M		TX
Margret	4	F		TX
Scinthy	18	F		AL
Ross, William H.	35	M	Farmer	TN
Elizabeth	27	F		LA
Mary J.	11	F		MS
Robert	10	M		MS
Henry	8	M		MS
John	4	M		TX
William B.	3	M		TX
Amandy L.	10/12	F		TX
Withers, Vallentine	29	M	Farmer	KY
Angeling	24	F		MS
William J.	9/12	M		TX
Statts, Mary	45	F		TN
Washington	15	M	Farmer	MS
Susan	75	F		MS
Hemby, Joseph	38	M	Farmer	TN
Elizabeth	37	F		TN
Bradley, Mortimer W.	9	M		TX
Malindy H.	8	F		TX
Tate, Jno.	22	M	Farmer	AR
Amandy F.	6	F		TX
Malviney D.	5	F		TX
Webb, Meredith	47	M	Farmer	NC
Rebecca	19	F		AL
Antony	22	M	Farmer	TN
Seliny	15	F		TN
Laviny	15	F		TN
Milton	13	M		TN
Orelnous(?)	11	F		TN
John	8	M		TX
Elizabeth	3	F		TX
Jacob W.	1	M		TX
Hooper, J. J.	38	M	Farmer	TN
Allazara	34	F		AL
Frances	11	F		TN
Marion	10	M		TX
Washington	9	M		TX
Elizabeth	8	F		TX
Marthy Ann	7	F		TX
Mahaly	6	F		TX
Adaline	5	F		TX
Richard	2/12	M		TX
Hooper, Richard	67	M	Surveyor	VA
Isable	62	F		NC
Lafayette	25	M	Farmer	TN
Collumbus	20	M	Farmer	TN
Wiseman, Caroline	30	F		TN
Mariah	12	F		TX
Amandy	6	F		TX
John R. P.	3	M		TX
Meeks, J.	28	M	Farmer	TN
Darnell, N. H.	43	M	Merchant	TN
Isabella	42	F		NC
Henderson	15	M	Student	TN
Nicholas	11	M		TX
Nancy	9	F		TX
Adaline	7	F		TX
Algernon	5	M		TX

SHELBY COUNTY, TEXAS

Name	Age	Sex	Occupation	Birthplace
Smith, E. F.	26	M	Farmer	TN
Elviry	21	F		NC
Alford	9	M		TX
Lucy	5	F		TX
William	1	M		TX
Truett, Susan	14	F		NC
Nancy	13	F		TX
Isaac	18	M	Laborer	NC
Ameson, Jesse	46	M	Farmer	GA
Sary A.	26	F		TN
William J.	12	M		TX
Hiram	10	M		TX
Mary E.	8	F		TX
John W.	6	M		TX
Sophrony P.	1	F		TX
M. T. J.	1/12	M		TX
Cullen	30	M		AL
Cravans, William	42	M	Farmer	TN
Mary R.	32	F		ENG
Sanderson, Arthur	21	M	Cripple	ENG
Kirkpatrick, Jahu	25	M	Farmer	TN
Strong, Elizabeth	20	F		TN
Sanford, Eleony	41	M	Black Smith	SC
Devilly A.	21	F		TN
Joab	20	M	Farmer	AL
George A.	16	M		AL
Rebecca S.	15	F		AL
Balindy C.	13	F		AL
Pernecia S.	12	F		AL
David L.	2	M		TX
Wadkins, William P.	38	M	Farmer	GA
Mary	35	F		TN
Mary E.	15	F		AL
Jos. P.	13	M		AL
Betsey J.	10	F		AL
Nancy A.	8	F		AL
Susan C.	6	F		AL
Jas. M. M.	1	M		AL
Eldridge, Samuel	44	M	Farmer	TN
Matildy	45	F		TN
Arrington, Susan	7	F		TX
William	4	M		TX
Beaucamp, Bennedict	36	M		KY
White, F. G.	27	M		TN
Sary	34	F		NC
Hutson, Ann	14	F		MS
Marthy	12	F		MS
Semintha	9	F		TX
Mansfield	7	M		TX
Sophrony	4	F		TX
Powdrill, John W.	24	M	Farmer	TN
Margret	22	F		TN
John T.	2	M		TX
Mary J. E.	5/12	F		TX
Haresign, Thomas	22	M	Laborer	ENG
Choat, John	48	M	Farmer	TN
Mary	38	F		TN
Holt, Solomon	29	M	Farmer	SC
Rhody M.	22	F		MS
Mary R.	2	F		TX
Leach, Rachel	55	F		NC
Wiggans, Harbard	6	M		TX
Bounds, Frank B.	22	M	Farmer	TN
Sary E.	22	F		AL
Merill B.	1/12	M		TX
Hooper, Benjamin F.	30	M	Farmer	TN
Laury A.	28	F		TN
Frances	11	F		TN
John	7	M		TX
Mary	4	F		TX
Myrah	2	F		TX
Pittman, Edward	47	M	Gin Wright	CT
(continued)				
Pittman, Mary E.	31	F		TN
Quinn, Sary A.	11	F		TN
William M.	8	M		TN
Mary F.	5	F		TN
Pittman, Benjamin F.	2	M		TX
English, R. B.	35	M	Farmer	TN
Frances	30	F		VA
James A.	8	M		TX
Mary	1	F		TX
Landrum, William P.	31	M	Physician	TN
Cathrine	30	F		TN
M. E.	7	M		TX
Hicks, Jane A.	12	F		TX
Robberts, William E.	25	M	Clerk	TN
Hargrove, Porter	25	M	Laborer	TN
Bell, Collumbus	27	M	Farmer	TN
Amandy	27	F		MS
Margret E.	1	F		TX
Thomas	74	M		MD
F. Washington	17	M		TN
Hooper, George W.	42	M	Farmer	GA
Mary E.	28	F		GA
Sary A.	17	F		TN
Elizabeth	16	F		TN
James	10	M		TX
Marthy	9	F		TX
Samuel	7	M		TX
Hetty	5	F		TX
George W.	2	M		TX
Sinclair, Leland	26	M	Farmer	TN
McKee, Louisa	26	F		TN
Adolphus	10	M		TN
Pierson, Martin	22	M	Laborer	TN
McWilliams, Robert	51	M	Farmer	IRE
Mary A.	43	F		SC
William F.	15	M	Student	SC
George M.	13	M		SC
Mary A.	12	F		SC
Nancy E.	10	F		TX
Robert	8	M		TX
Ellenora C.	3	F		TX
Sary A.	1/12	F		TX
Ray, William	20	M	Laborer	TN
Rains, Joel D.	38	M	Farmer	TN
Elizabeth	28	F		LA
James	12	M		TX
Emory	10	M		TX
Mariah	8	F		TX
America	2	F		TX
Scina	8/12	F		TX
Walker, Phillip	32	M	Farmer	SC
Elizabeth	22	F		TN
Marthy	1	F		TX
Davis, Harrison	35	M	Farmer	IL
Elizabeth	31	F		TN
Nathan	11	M		TX
Sary	10	F		TX
Jane	6	F		TX
Thomas	3	M		TX
John	4/12	M		TX
Tate, Allen	27	M		MO
Margrett	27	F		AR
Robbison, Jas.	38	M	Farmer	KY
Rebecca	22	F		AR
James	2	M		TN
John	11/12	M		TN
Lewis, Elizabeth	16	F		AR
Robert	10	M		AR
English, Jonas	45	M	Nothing	TN
Marthy	28	F		GA
Caroline	13	F		TX
Jas.	10	M		TX
Mary	6	F		TX
William	4	M		TX
(continued)				

Name	Age	Sex	Occupation	Birthplace
English, Johnathan	1	M		TX
Samuel	2/12	M		TX
Choat, Redmon	51	M	Farmer	TN
Sary	40	F		KY
Squire	21	M	Farmer	TN
Alexander	20	M	Farmer	TN
David	18	M	Farmer	TN
Joseph	15	M	Farmer	TN
Elizabeth	13	F		TX
Margrett	12	F		TX
James	9	M		TX
Susan	8	F		TX
Sary	6	F		TX
Andrew B.	2	M		TX
Morrison, Jas. P.	25	M	Farmer	AL
Liddy N.	19	F		TN
S. M.	2	M		TN
Mauldin, E. C.	40	M	Physician	SC
Elisa	36	F		TN
William B.	20	M	Farmer	TN
Asa J.	18	M	Student	TN
Jno. W.	16	M	Student	TN
Mary W.	12	F		TN
George H.	8	M		TX
James W.	30	M	Teacher	AL
McCoy, David	60	M	Farmer	VA
Jincy	50	F		TN
Stephen R.	22	M	Farmer	TX
Nathan	16	M	Farmer	TX
Thomas	14	M		TX
T. T.	12	F		TX
Malissa	9	F		TX
Biggers, Robert	25	M	Farmer	MO
M. Jane	20	F		TN
Mary M.	1	F		TX
Martin, J. M. H.	25	M	Student	TN
E. F.	24	F		TN
S. A.	18	F		TN
E. L. A.	22	M	Printer	TN
C. M. B.	16	M	Student	TN
Middleton, J. R.	35	M	Farmer	TN
Mary	13	F		MS
Marthy	10	F		MS
Sary A.	7	F		MS
Andrew	5	M		MS
Anderson, Felix A. E.	40	M	Farmer	TN
Susan C.	38	F		SC
Mary	16	F		MS
William	14	M		MS
Eliza E.	10	F		MS
Elonzo M.	9	M		MS
Della J.	7	F		MS
Henry H.	4	M		TX
Mary E.	1	F		TX
Matthew	70	M	Farmer	VA
Smith, J. M.	38	M	Farmer	TN
Amandy	28	F		TN
Moore, John L.	24	M	Farmer	TN
Sanford, William A.	22	M	Farmer	AL
Sary J.	18	F		TN
Laviney J.	3/12	F		TX
Dysart, E. B.	40	M	Farmer	TN
Mary D.	35	F		KY
Black, Susan A.	13	F		AR
Larooe, Abram	23	M	Farmer	TN
Biggers, R. S.	33	M	Farmer	MO
Delily	32	F		TN
B. F.	6	M		TX
Lorey	4	F		TX
Margret E.	3	F		TX
James G.	1	M		TX
Wiggins, R. R.	38	M	Merchant	KY
Elizabeth	22	F		TN
Ellenor	17	F	Student	TX
Mariah	14	F		TX
Washington	11	M		TX
Hannah	7	F		TX
Emma C.	1/12	F		TX
Inman, John H.	25	M	Farmer	TN
Frances	25	F		TX
Susan J.	4	F		TX
Sophrony	1	F		TX
Prudence	2/12	F		TX
Childers, Wiett	36	M	Bapt. Clergyman	TN
Mariah	31	F		TN
Mary T.	10	F		TN
Hiram T.	9	M		TN
Margret C.	7	F		TN
William R.	5	M		TN
G. W.	1	M		TX
Sanders, David M.	20	M	Farmer	TN
Adaline	16	F		GA
Tatum, J. C.	36	M	Grocer	KY
Mary A.	27	F		TN
Marthy C.	7	F		TX
Mary A.	5	F		TX
Bozaris R.	3	M		TX
Leuellen, Amon	34	M	Tax Collector	NC
Mary H.	25	F		TN
Susan A. F.	8	F		TX
Almedia M.	5	F		TX
Mary C.	1	F		TX
Yates, Mark	17	M	Farmer	NY
English, Denton	17	M	Farmer	TN
Fielder, John	27	M	Farmer	MO
Echells, William F.	50	M	Farmer	GA
Eliza P.	40	F		TN
Sherod, George W.	29	M	Farmer	AL
Sophia	22	F		AL
William W.	4	M		LA
Morgan M.	2	M		LA
Morgan, Elizabeth	40	F		TN
Willaba, Wallis	38	M	Farmer	KY
Henrietta	34	F		TN
Jane E.	14	F		TN
John T.	12	M		TN
William H.	9	M		TN
Mary C.	7	F		TN
Sary E.	5	F		TN
Jas. D.	2	M		TN
Houston, Rufus	38	M	Mill Wright	MA
McCray, Henry	20	M	Farmer	TN
Schooler, R. A. J.	35	M	Farmer	KY
Narcissy	24	F		SC
Jas.	4	M		TX
William L.	2	M		TX
Jno.	17	M		TN
Schooler, Benjamin H.	23	M	Black Smith	TN
Rosanna	21	F		AR
Benjamin	1	M		TX
Sublett, William S.	51	M	Farmer	VA
Ann	48	F		TN
John W.	24	M	Saddler	TN
J. P.	23	M	Saddler	TN
Susan	26	F		VA
Sary E.	14	F		TN
Susan A.	13	F		TN
Daniel W.	11	M		TN
Francis A.	1	F		TN
Cravens, J. J.	35	M	Farmer	TN
Mary A.	32	F		TN
William G.	10	M		TX

SHELBY COUNTY, TEXAS

Name	Age	Sex	Occupation	Birthplace
Smith, James	59	M	Farmer	NC
Permelia	39	F		SC
Mary A.	18	F		TX
Rachel	16	F		TX
William	12	M		TX
John	9	M		TX
Charles	5	M		TX
Cathrine	4	F		TX
Stephen	25	M	Farmer	TN
Narcissa	20	F		AL
Peoples, Thomas	25	M	Farmer	TN
Sary E.	20	F		TN
Stephen	6	M		TX
Robert	3	M		TX
Mary A.	2/12	F		TX
Jordon, William H.	37	M	Farmer	VA
July A.	28	F		AL
Thomas B.	9	M		TN
Mary F.	5	F		TX
Adelbert	2	M		TX
Elizabeth	1	F		TX
Smith, Rachel	46	F		TN
Mary J.	20	F		TN
Jas. M.	18	M	Farmer	TN
Thomas M.	16	M	Farmer	TN
Margret H.	14	F		TN
Yates, William	69	M	Farmer	NC
Sary	53	F		NC
Noah	36	M	Farmer	NC
Anna	50	F		NC
Westly, William	26	M	Farmer	TN
Duncan, William B.	25	M	Farmer	AL
Margret J.	19	F		TN
Thomas L.	2/12	M		TX
Thomas A. R.	16	M		TN
Benge, Elizabeth A.	14	F		TN
Graves, William	39	M	Farmer	KY
Elizabeth	29	F		TN
Elizabeth	6	F		LA
Sary J.	5	F		LA
Roxanna	3	F		TX
William B.	1/12	M		TX
Biggs, Henry H.	25	M	Farmer	TN
Sary	25	F		AL
Willy B.	2	F		TX
Mary W.	2/12	F		TX
Biggs, Wilson H.	35	M	Farmer	TN
Scillia	34	F		SC
Mary E.	15	F		TN
Susan A.	10	F		TX
David A.	9	M		TX
Jas. H.	5	M		TX
Elizabeth	3	F		TX
Amandy	6/12	F		TX
Clark, Dred.	46	M	Farmer	TN
Rebecca	16	F		AL
Texanna	1	F		TX
Glass, Shelby	25	M	Laborer	TX
Huckaby, William R.	25	M	Farmer	TN
Elizabeth	36	F		AL
Liddy A.	5	F		AR
Elizabeth	3	F		TX
Mary C.	3/12	F		TX
Tanner, James	17	M	Farmer	IN
Raburn, Hodge	48	M	Farmer	NC
Susan	36	F		TN
James	18	M	Farmer	GA
Mary C.	13	F		GA
William	11	M		TN
Howel A.	9	M		TN
Milton	7	M		AL
Robert L.	1	M		TX

Name	Age	Sex	Occupation	Birthplace
Lamance, A. J.	33	M		TN
Nancy C.	27	F		TN
Jas. L.	6	M		GA
Benjamin F.	11/12	M		TN
Rayburn, Hodge, Jr.	27	M	Farmer	NC
Biggs, Asa	62	M	Reg. Bpt. Clerk	NC
Winneford	63	F		NC
Bird, James M.	25	M	Farmer	TN
Amandy W.	18	F		TN
William T.	1	M		TX
Groomes, William	31	M	Laborer	TN
Kirksey, John M.	30	M	Farmer	AL
Elizabeth	24	F		VA
Elihu L.	3	M		TN
Jno. B.	1	M		TN
Brown, Jno.	60	M	Farmer	NC
Lusindy	51	F		SC
Mary C.	14	F		TN
Samuel E.	8	M		TN
Sary L.	4	F		TN
Mauldin, James	76	M	None	NC
White, Rubin B.	40	M	Carpenter	GA
Marthy A.	25	F		TN
Marthy	12	F		MS
Bowden, Bennet H.	53	M	Farmer	NC
Nancy	46	F		TN
Allen B.	5	M		TX
John B.	3	M		TX
Clark, Levy	14	M		TX
Eddings, Robert	29	M	Farmer	TN
Mary	23	F		AL
Sary	2/12	F		TX
Ray, John L.	46	M	Farmer	NC
Rebecca	49	F		NC
Mary F.	16	F		NC
Rufus H.	14	M		NC
Marthy H.	12	F		NC
Jas. M.	10	M		NC
Rudy A.	8	F		TN
Brown, Franklin	27	M	Farmer	NC
Emily C.	23	F		NC
Elizabeth M.	3	F		TN
Marthy A.	4/12	F		TX
Sanders, Jno.	30	M	Farmer	KY
Rachal	31	F		VA
James	9	M		TN
Ann E.	8	F		TN
Elenora	7	F		TN
John	4	M		TX
Elizabeth	3	F		TX
Robert	1	M		TX
McGuffey, R. M.	40	M	Farmer	NC
Chaley E.	34	F		SC
William J.	18	M	Farmer	TN
Mary A.	16	F		TN
Coleman L.	9	M		MS
Rufus M.	6	M		TX
M. Eliza	3	F		TX
Susan C.	1	F		TX
Hill, Marthy L.	25	F		SC
Emma C.	6	F		TX
Sanders, Francis L. A.	11	M		TN
Goodwin, Robert, Jr.	49	M	Farmer	GA
Eliza A.	42	F		TN
Goodwin, Thomas R.	26	M	Farmer	AL
L. A.	25	F		TN
Sary E.	10/12	F		TX
Williams, James	35	M	Ferryman	TN
Sary	27	F		MS
Alexander	9	M		LA
Toby	7	M		LA
John	4	M		TX
George W.	5/12	M		TX

Haly, Richard 40 M Farmer TN
Sareny 40 F MS
Susan 17 F TX
Mary 15 F TX
Jno. 12 M TX
Scinthy 9 F TX
Smith, William 21 M LA
Daniel P. 6 M TX
Arvilla (Twin) 2 F TX
Vinetta (Twin) 2 F TX
Allice 4/12 F TX

Wooten, Nathan D. 22 M Farmer LA
Amandy 19 F TN
Moses 6/12 M TX

Robberts, Moses F. 47 F Farmer TN
Nancy N. 40 F SC
Christopher 7 M TX
Amandy 5 F TX
Scinthy 4 F TX
Littleton F. 4 M TX
McI---- 1 M TX

Cook, William R. 43 M Farmer TN
Rachal 25 F MS
Charles W. 9 M TX
Benjamin F. 11 M TX
Rebecca 5 F TX

Fain, Mercer 63 M Farmer SC
Louisa 39 F TN
Josiah 17 M Farmer MO
Maddison 15 M Farmer MO
Charlton 13 M TX
Sidney 11 M TX

Shires, Nancy A. 55 F NC
Sary 24 F TN
Jane 20 F TN
George 18 M Farmer TN
Mary 16 F TX
Rachal 14 F TX
Thomas, W. Jackson 30 M Farmer TN
Elijah 28 M Farmer TN

Kirkpatrick, Hiram 41 M Farmer TN
Adaline 33 F TN
Mary L. D. 13 F AL
Amandy T. 11 F TX
Sary J. 9 F TX
Albert H. 7 M TX
Louis A. 5 M TX
Marthy M. 4/12 F TX
Bragg, James 23 M House Carpenter NC

Applegate, Mary 61*F TN
James C. 21 M Farmer LA

Golding, Joel F. 23 M Farmer SC
Elizabeth 20 F TN
Rebecca E. 1 F TX

Edwards, Jno. 60 M Farmer NC
Julia 48 F NC
Sara 16 F TN
William 13 M TN
Elviry 12 F TN
Elizabeth J. K. P. 9 F TX

Farrar, Sam 40 M Farmer NC
Manervy 43 F TN
Thomas J. 18 M Farmer TN
Alexander 12 M MS
Sinthy R. 9 F MS
Robert 6 M TX
Elizabeth A. 4 F TX

Rhoodes, William R. 35 M Farmer TN
Amanda 30 F AL
Charity A. 8 F TX
Charles 6 M TX
Sary A. 3 F TX
(continued)

Rhoodes, James 1 M TX
Lindsey, Samuel 35 M Farmer SC

Wilcocks, Allen R. 26 M Farmer TN
Marthy 24 F TX
Elizabeth 4 F TX
Jno. A. 10/12 M TX

Ballard, James W. 26 M Farmer LA
Sary E. 23 F TN

Updegraff, Samuel 49 M Farmer PA
Ruthy 34 F TN
Still, Walton T. 14 M TN
Mary A. 12 F TX
Elizabeth 9 F TX

Tribble, Jas. H. 38 M Carpenter TN
Eliza R. 31 F TN
Debringan 7 M AL
George N. 5 M AL
Robert 2 M TX
Samuel, Elisha 22 M Farmer AL

Netherley, William 44 M Carpenter TN
Elviry S. 38 F TN
Jas. R. 21 M Carpenter AL
Thomas 20 M Farmer AL
Paralee 18 F AL
Alex. M. 16 M AL
Benjamin 13 M AL
William 10 M AL
Thaddeus 7 M TX
Amandy 5 F TX
Alford 3 M TX
Carshaw, George W. 21 M Carpenter LA

Davis, John W. 38 M Farmer NC
Hanna E. 37 F TN
Mary J. 19 F NC
Sary L. 15 F TN
Phillip 13 M TN
James R. 10 M TX
Hannah E. 6 F TX
Francis E. 2 F TX

Stephens, Caswell 30 M Laborer TN
Nancy 26 F TN
Thomas A. 14 M LA
Adaline 4/12 F LA

Harding, John D. 31 M Farmer NC
Susan 35 F NC
Sary 16 F TN
Rufus 11 M MS
Jorden 6 M TX
Pleasant B. 2 M TX
Henderson S. 2/12 M TX

Kennedy, Fedrick 49 M Farmer NC
Mary 46 F NC
Truax, Marthy 28 F NC
Permelia 9 F TX
Leander W. 4 M TX
Mary A. 1 F TX
White, Jackson 25 M Farmer TN

White, Josiah 57 M Farmer NC
Pheby 60 F NC
Samuel 30 M None (Idiot) TN
Pharby 32 F TN
John 25 M Farmer TN
Westly 21 M Farmer TN
Isaac 22 M Farmer TN
Joseph 19 M Farmer TN

Clark, William 45 M Farmer Atlantic Ocean
Elizabeth 37 F TN
William 12 M TX
Flecher 9 M TX
Pheby 7 F TX
John 4 M TX
David 2/12 M TX

Reddet, William 30 M Farmer TN
(continued)

SHELBY COUNTY, TEXAS

Name	Age	Sex	Occupation	Birthplace
Reddet, Ruthy	23	F		TN
William J.	7	M		MS
Mary C.	4	F		MS
MIddleton, D. C.	30	M	Farmer	TN
Frances	30	F		KY
John W.	12	M		TN
James B.	10	M		TN
Mary E.	8	F		TN
Marthy	6	F		TN
Nancy A.	4	F		TN
Drury W. H.	1	M		TX
Barnet, Mary	57	F		VA
Middleton, Nathan	21	M	Farmer	TN
Susanna	21	F		MS
Augustus	1	M		MS
Marthy	63	F		SC
White, William H.	38	M	Meth. Clergyman	TN
Elizabeth	38	F		TN
May, John	53	M	Farmer	MS
Elizabeth	38	F		TN
Dempsy	21	M	Farmer	MS
James S.	17	M	Farmer	MS
Lucy A.	13	F		TX
William H.	9	M		TX
Mary	7	F		TX
Fabre, William	30	M	Farmer	AR
John	18	M	Farmer	MS
Nancy	51	F		TN
Parker, Mary	3	F		TX
Stephen, L. H.	27	M	Farmer	TN
Sary L.	24	F		NC
John H.	2	M		TX
James T.	5/12	M		TX
George H.	22	M		TN
Choat, Joab	21	M	School Teacher	TN
Hay, John	20	M	Waggoner	TN
Freeland, James D.	67	M	Farmer	PA
Nancy	65	F		NC
George W.	27	M	Farmer	TN
Weaver, Joseph N.	21	M	Farmer	TN
Whitten, William E.	27	M	Farmer	GA
Ethelindy	25	F		AL
Sary	7	F		AL
William L.	5	M		AL
Nancy A. E.	3	F		AL
Edward T.	1	M		AL
Weaver, Marthy	23	F		TN
Smith, A. N.	35	M	Farmer	TN
Sary N.	33	F		TN
Ambrose W.	15	M		TN
Harriet	13	F		TN
Amandy	11	F		TN
Margret N.	16	F		TN
James P.	8	M		TN
Neal	6	M		TN
Joseph M.	4	M		TN
Marthy	1	F		TN
Smith, Malcom	29	M	Farmer	TN
Jane	30	F		NC
William P.	4	M		TN
Williams, James B.	27	M	Farmer	TN
Drusilla R.	21	F		TN
Marthy J.	3	F		TN
Williams, C. T.	46	M	Farmer	SC
Elizabeth	44	F		NC
Sary A.	16	F		TN
Clayburn	12	M		TN
Alexander	10	M		TN
Texannas	8	M		MS
Elizabeth	6	F		TX
Misouri	5	F		TX
John D.	1	M		TX
Arnold, Fresueus	26	M	Physician	SC

Name	Age	Sex	Occupation	Birthplace
Cochran, William W.	49	M	Meth. Clergyman	GA
Dove F.	46	F		SC
Freeland, Elizabeth	8	F		TN
McCaddams, James E.	25	M	Farmer	AL
Hannah	22	F		TN
John	2	M		AL
Geton, Hiram	25	M	Farmer	TN
Louisa	22	F		AL
Landon	19	M	Farmer	TN
Floyd, William	40	M	Cabinet Maker	TN
M.	25	F		TN
Joseph	5	M		TN
Reed, Alex. A.	33	M	Black Smith	TN
Louisa	29	F		AR
Sary	9	F		TX
Mary	7	F		TX
Marthy	5	F		TX
John	3	M		TX
Child unnamed	7/12	F		TX
Nybit, Henry C.	29	M	Black Smith	TN
Reed, Richard G.	27	M	Black Smith	TN
Nancy C.	19	F		TN
Sary L.	2	F		TX
Childers, Hiram H.	38	M	Meth. Clergyman	TN
Tens.	32	F		TN
Margret	12	F		TN
William R.	10	M		TN
Laury E.	7	F		TX
Rufus E.	4	M		TX
Asberry M.	1	M		TX
Miller, G. W.	40	M	Farmer	TN
Savage, James	32	M	Farmer	IRE
Mary E.	30	F		TN
David L.	12	M		TN
Elizabeth	10	F		TN
Marthy	8	F		TN
Mary A.	6	F		TN
Harriett	4	F		TN
Nancy A.	1	F		TX
Beaucamp, Jerebram	45	M	Farmer	KY
Mary E.	30	F		TN
William	12	M		TX
Mary A.	10	F		TX
Jerebram	7	M		TX
Hilliard	5	M		TX
George	4	M		TX
Nepoleon	2	M		TX
Lester, Zion F.	29	M	Farmer	TN
Marthy F.	34	F		GA
William T.	5	M		TX
Gruer, David	53	M	Farmer	TN
Frances ?.	44	F		NC
Louis N.	15	M		TN
Mary V.	13	F		TN
Cathrine	11	F		TX
Jno. W.	8	M		TX
Frances	5	F		TX
Thomas J.	1	M		TX
Newville, Stephen	32	M	Farmer	FRA
Ham, Joel	45	M	Farmer	SC
Nancy	37	F		TN
William	17	M	Farmer	TN
John	15	M	Farmer	TN
Mary	13	F		TX
Edward	11	M		TX
Isabel	9	F		TX
Amandy	6	F		TX
James	4	M		TX
Vanrapper, Gooley	19	F		TN
Lewis, David C.	30	M	Farmer	TN
Mary J.	26	F		TN
David A.	5	M		TX
Marthy A.	7	F		TX
Lucrecia	3	F		TX

SHELBY COUNTY, TEXAS

Name		Age	Sex	Occupation	Birthplace
Henning, Lewis		37	M	Farmer	VA
Rebecca		31	F		AL
Isabella A.		12	F		MS
Pernecy M.		10	F		TX
John L.		8	M		TX
Amandy		6	F		TX
Albert L.		2	M		TX
Rebecca		2/12	F		TX
Pierson, Martin		25	M	Farmer	TN
Dean, William		49	M	Wagon Maker	TN
Marthy		45	F		VA
Thomas C.		24	M	Farmer	TN
William G.		16	M	Farmer	TN
John S.		14	M		TN
Marthy		12	F		TN
Wayman A.		8	M		TX
Deen, John		44	M	Farmer	TN
Elizabeth		40	F		TN
Ezekiel		17	M	Farmer	TN
Marthy		7	F		TN
Thornburg, Alexander		63	M	Mill Wright	??
Mary		37	F		TN
Napkins, Ruthy E.		18	F		TN
Nancy C.		15	F		TN
John T.		11	M		TN
James T.		8	M		TN
Solomon		5	M		TN
William L.		3	M		TN
Wheeler, Ransom		37	M	Farmer	TN
Laviney		33	F		TN
Caroline		15	F		TN
Leonidas		13	M		TN
Fernando		12	M		TN
Parron		10	M		TX
Francis		9	F		TX
Minervy		8	F		TX
Lyacurges		5	M		TX
Marthy		4	F		TX
Massy		2	F		TX
William S.		2/12	M		TX
Davis, John		31	M	Farmer	TN
Elizabeth		27	F		TN
Nancy		9	F		TX
Sary A.	(Twin)	2	F		TX
Rody J.	(Twin)	2	F		TX
William		2/12	M		TX
Poppin, James		25	M	Farmer	KY
Nancy		24	F		TN
Mary J.		5	F		TX
William C.		7/12	M		TX
Music, Samuel		20	M		AR
Ro--my		23	F		TN
Hancock, Hardy		29	M	Farmer	TN
Ireny		29	F		SC
Thomas J.		7	M		AL
Nancy J.		5	F		AL
Susan D.		1/12	F		TX
Haly, B. F.		23	M	Farmer	TN
Harriett		22	F		TN
Newton		1	M		TN
Rion, Richard		60	M	Farmer	GA
Miraim		51	F		GA
Elizabeth		21	F		GA
Mary		15	F		IN
L. D.		13	M		TN
Reason J.		11	M		TX
Luisia		8	F		TX
Powdrell, Thomas		56	M	Farmer	SCO
Eliza		45	F		NC
Richard		26	M	Merchant	TN
Thomas J.		22	M	Merchant	TN
Sary A.		20	F		TN
Catharine		18	F		TN

(continued)

Name	Age	Sex	Occupation	Birthplace
Powdrell, William	13	M		TN
George L.	25	M	Farmer	ENG
Willows, Phillip	21	M	Farmer	ENG
Rennolds, William	43	M	Black Smith	TN
Sary	40	F		TN
Gilford	16	M	Farmer	AR
Thomas B.	12	M		AR
Mary	8	F		TX
John D.	5	M		TX
James C.	5	M		TX
William	1	M		TX
Choat, Mary	63	F		GA
McCoy, Pargetty	20	F		TN
Newton J.	4	M		TX
Simon W.	2	M		TX
Walker, Simeon	75	M	Old Man	VA
Mitchel, Ephraim M.	36	M	Farmer	TN
Rebecca	32	F		TN
Sary J.	14	F		MS
John K.	12	M		MS
Mary E.	10	F		TX
Wilson J.	9	M		TX
Marthy	7	F		TX
Sam H.	6	M		TX
Ephraim	2	M		TX
Bryant, John	35	M	Farmer	AL
Lavicy	26	F		TN
Elizabeth A.	4	F		TX
Jobe A.	2	M		TX
Emaly C.	1/12	F		TX
Pounds, William	38	M	Farmer	NC
Nancy	35	F		TN
Mary	14	F		TN
J. M.	12	M		TN
Laviny C.	10	F		TN
Amandy R.	8	F		TN
Collumbus S.	5	M		TN
Elizabeth	2	F		TX
Olliver, Malachi	41	M	Farmer	KY
Elizabeth	29	F		TN
Mary A. E.	6	F		TX
Thomas J.	5	M		TX
Andrew J.	2	M		TX
William A.	2/12	M		TX
Dillard, H. H.	28	M	Farmer	NC
Sam	7	M		TN
Joseph C.	34	M	Farmer	NC
Frances H.	59	F		NC
Holeman, Jeremiah	36	M		TN
Mary	44	F		SC
Hughes, John J.	25	M	Farmer	TN
Permelia	28	F		AL
Mary J.	10/12	F		TX
Mysic, Robert J.	3	M		TX
Hughes, Mary	49	F		TN
W. P.	24	M	Farmer	TN
Andrew F.	21	M	Farmer	TN
Ennis C.	20	M		AR
Ennis	5	M		TX
Palmer, William	21	M		AR
Hughes, Robert T.	25	M	Farmer	TN
Dorothea	17	F		AR
Eleany S.	1/12	M		TX
Harkaness, Benjamin	40	M	House Carpenter	KY
Ann	41	F		SC
Elizabeth	18	F		TN
Mary J.	13	F		TN
Jane E.	8	F		TX
Margret A.	6	F		TX
Ben F.	3	M		TX
Thomas C.	3/12	M		TX
Eakin, Elizabeth	74	F		SC

SHELBY COUNTY, TEXAS

Harcaness, William B. 21 M Farmer TN
Rachal 19 F AL

Inman, John 50 M Farmer SC
Prudence D. 44 F TN
James C. 20 M TN
Clayburn C. 16 M MO
Suoty J. 14 F TX
Joseph A. 10 M TX
Leonard R. 7 M TX
Edith P. E. 4/12 F TX
Wood, Jno. R. 20 M School Master TN
Walker, Edith 66 F TN

Sanders, Richard 22 M Farmer TN
Sary 17 F IN

Straw, Leonard 59 M Farmer VA
Elizabeth 49 F SC
William 9 M TX
John B. 7 M TX
Buckner, Thomas 23 M House Carpenter MO
Francis 14 F MO
Straw, J. J. 35 M Farmer VA
Hooper, J. M. 30 M Farmer TN
Susan A. 21 F MO
Marthy 2 F TX
Margaret E. 2 F TX
Biggers, George W. 16 M Farmer AR

Cartwright, Robert G. 41 M Farmer TN
Mary H. 31 F TN
Amandy 7 F TX
Matthew 2 M TX
Robert 6/12 M TX
Lanier, Clement W. 17 M Farmer TN
McBride, Pvt. H. 43 M Chair Maker KY
Martin, Easter 28 F ??
Dick William 9 M TX
Bennet 7 M TX
Alford 5 M TX
Perkins, William 19 M Farmer AL

Lanier, William W. 34 M Farmer TN
Matildy 26 F KY
William 4 M TX
Robert 2 M TX
Sary 7/12 F TX
Middleton, Drury 63 M Farmer SC

Oliver, Alex 51 M Farmer SC
Jane 45 F TN
David 24 M Farmer TN
Andrew J. 17 M Farmer TN
Washington L. 11 M TN
Sary C. 7 F TN
James K. P. 3 M MS

McKelvy, Hesekiah 44 M Farmer TN
Elizabeth 44 F NC
Willis 15 M Farmer TX
Mahaly 21 F LA
Jesse 17 M TX
H. Dennis 14 M TX
Wade H. 6 M TX
Burson, Joseph 50 M School Teacher GA

Olliver, Andrew 32 M Farmer TN
Amandy 23 F AR
William N. 4 M TX
Jonston, John R. 11 M AR
Oliver, Andrew, Sr. 77 M Farmer GA

Muse, Thomas J. 34 M Farmer TN
Sary 33 F TN
Thomas H. 13 M TN
Amandy J. 12 F TN
Frances A. 9 F TN
Joab D. 7 M TN
Tabitha 4 F TN
Ireny M. 2 F TN

Collins, Elizabeth 51 F TN
William R. 19 M Farmer TN

Childers, Moses B. 45 M Farmer TN
Jane 35 F TN
Andrew K. 14 M TN
Mary A. 11 F TN
Lusindy 9 F TN
Sary S. 7 F TN
Jno. T. 2 M TN

Smith, David 45 M Farmer NC
William A. 18 M Farmer TN
Moses B. 15 M Farmer TN
Sary 7 F TN
Margret 6 F TN
James T. 1 M TX

Walker, William C. 36 M Farmer TN
Nancy 46 F PA
Seth B. 12 M Farmer MO
Rebecca J. 14 F MO
Sary 11 F TX
William P. 8 M TX

Strickland, David 20 M Farmer TX
Marthy L. 19 F TN
Jesse M. 10/12 M TX
Amos 22 M Farmer TX
James 18 M Farmer TX
Rachel 15 F TX
Stanfield, Elizabeth 12 F IN

Daniels, Henry 40 M Farmer NC
Sinthy 22 F CT
Louisa 15 F TN
James 13 M TN
Harriett 10 F TX
William 8 M TX
John 7 M TX
Rebecca J. 1 F TX

Yarborough, Richard 45 M Farmer SC
Hannah 45 F NC
Elizabeth 18 F TN
John 17 M Farmer TN
Mary J. 17 F TN
James 15 M TN
G. Gains 13 M TN
Sary E. 11 F TX
Joel 9 M TX
Gilbert 7 M TX
Amandy 1 F TX
Mary 69 F NC

Burrus, Henry C. 22 M Farmer GA
Marthy 20 F IL
Mary J. 2 F TN
Elizabeth 1/12 F TX

Williams, James 30 M Farmer TN
Susan D. 19 F TN
Marthy J. 4 F TN

Crowson, J. W. 44 M Farmer TN
Elizabeth 41 F TN
James E. 18 M Farmer GA
Robert F. 14 M Farmer AL
Huldy E. 11 F AL
Rachel M. 10 F AL
Jefferson W. 9 M AL
David F. 8 M AL
William L. 7 M AL
Lucrecia L. 3 F AL

Wright, Nathaniel C. 20 M Farmer MS
Elizabeth 18 F TN
John H. 1 M TX

Wright, Harding 39 M Farmer TN
Hepsebeth 28 F TN
Andrew J. 15 M Farmer TX
Harding 14 M LA
Mary L. 12 F LA
John M. 11 M TX
Nancy C. 8 F TX
Sary J. 7 F TX
Eliza R. 1 F TX
(continued)

Name	Age	Sex	Occupation	Birthplace
Wright, Matildy E.	1/12	F		TX
Iley, Marthy	7	F		TN
William S.	6	M		MS
Mary V.	4	F		MS
Ruth P.	2	M(F)		TX
Morris, J. W.	29	M	Farmer	NC
Violett	29	F		TN
Margret E.	11	F		TX
Mary	7	F		TX
Boland, James	41	M	Farmer	TN
Eliza	31	F		AL
William M.	15	M	Farmer	TX
Jeremiah	13	M		TX
Mary R.	10	F		TX
Manervy	8	F		TX
James F.	6	M		TX
Solomon	4	M		TX
Sary	2	F		TX
Dianna E.	4/12	F		TX
Reed, Sary J.	52	F		VA
John F.	22	M		TN
Sary	19	F		TN
Lemuel	18	M	Farmer	TN
Jesse	11	M		TN
Morrison, John E.	35	M	Merchant	TN
Eliza J.	29	F		AL
Ely R.	11	M		AR
Margret	8	F		AR
Oby	2	M		TX
Infant unnamed	1/12	F		TX
Hammilton, H. B.	28	M	M.E. Clergyman	AL
Euny	25	F		AL
Morgan, H. C.	30	M	Clerk	TN
Wiet, William	30	M	None	TN
Morgan, R. W.	20	M	School Teacher	TN
Sapp, S. H.	48	M	Farmer	GA
Elizabeth	37	F		TN
Mary E.	1/24	F		TX
Jno.	86	M	Clock Maker	MD
Winneford	60	F		NC
Eluphis	18	M	Farmer	AL
Demarius	20	M		--
Boland, William R.	49	M	Farmer	TN
Rhody	46	F		NC
G. C.	17	M		TN
R. J.	7	M		AR
Charity M.	5	F		AR
Porter, Samuel B.	20	M		IL
Porter, Loranse D.	25	M	Farmer	IL
Marthy	24	F		TN
James K. P.	5	M		AR
W. D.	3	M		AR
Rachel E.	4/12	F		TX
Rachel	60	F		NC
Williams, Benjamin	25	M	Farmer	TX
Mary E.	18	F		TX
Mahaly J.	4/12	F		TX
Turpin, William	42	M	Farmer	GA
Elizabeth	35	F		GA
George V.	17	M	Farmer	GA
Sally A.	14	F		GA
Seely J.	12	F		TN
William C.	11	M		TX
Mary E.	8	F		TX
Louisa	2	F		TX
Hammers, Elisha	30	M	Farmer	MO
Catherine	27	F		TN
Calvin	12	M		TN
Amandy P.	10	F		TX
John	7	M		TX
William	5	M		TX
Mary A.	3	F		TX
T--l A.	1	M		TX
Richards, John S.	31	M	Farmer	AL
Nancy S.	24	F		TN
Mary E.	5	F		TX
John	4	M		TX
Francis M.	3	M		TX
Josephus	1	M		TX
King, John	39	M	Merchant	OH
Susan	39	F		GA
Clayton C.	12	M		TN
Thomas	9	M		TN
Sophrony	7	F		TN
Mary A.	6	F		TN
John	4	M		TN
Angeling	2	F		TN
Laury	1/12	F		TN
Richards, Hampton	24	M	Farmer	AL
Elenor C.	24	F		TN
Charles H.	3	M		TX
Mary E.	1	F		TX
Freeland, John B.	40	M	Farmer	TN
Margret	39	F		TN
Davis P.	17	M		MS
William J.	16	M		TN
Mary E.	5	F		TN
Caladona	10/12	F		TX
Nail, A. J.	35	M	Farmer	TN
Mary	34	F		TN
George T.	12	M		TX
Louisa	9	F		TX
Frances	6	F		TX
Emily P.	5	F		TX
Marthy	2	F		TX
Child unnamed	4/12	M		TX
Redders, Nancy	13	F		LA
Mouser, David	29	M	Farmer	MO
Sary	24	F		TN
John H.	6	M		TX
Mary E.	5	F		TX
Sary J.	2	F		TX
James	1/12	M		TX
Frasier, Hartwell,	37	M	Farmer	TN
Harriet	25	F		PA
George W.	9	M		TX
Milton A.	4	M		TX
Malindy	2	F		TX
Sary E.	4/12	F		TX
Wilson, Henry	27	M	Farmer	NC
Mary A.	24	F		TN
John B.	7	M		TN
William C.	4	M		TN
Henry R.	5/12	M		TX
Dillon, James M.	32	M	Farmer	NC
Marthy	24	F		NC
Andrew R.	5	M		TN
John D.	3	M		TN
Son unnamed	11/12	M		TX
Harenlons, E. W.	28	M	Farmer	VA
Ferenecious(?)	19	F		TN
Sary	2	F		TX
James	1	M		TX
Statum, William	20	M	Farmer	TN
Mary A.	22	F		TN
Starky, John	31	M	Farmer	TN
Mary T.	24	F		GA
Mary A.	5	F		TX
Joel J.	2	M		TX
Rhody J.	2/12	F		TX
Milstead, Joseph	31	M	Farmer	TN
Farthy A.	31	F		NC
James F.	8	M		TN
Mary E.	7	F		TN
Sary M.	5	F		TN
Daniel A.	2	M		TN
Marthy J.	16	F		TN
Ely	28	M	Farmer	TN

Name	Age	Sex	Occupation	Birthplace
Corder, Marthy	49	F		SC
Rubin F.	30	F	Farmer	TN
Thomas F.	17	M	Farmer	TN
Malindy	15	F		LA
Elizabeth	13	F		TX
Rachel	11	F		TX
S. H. P.	8	M		TX
Sary A.	5	F		TX
William D.	21	M		TN
Mary A.	18	F		TN
Persons, Benjamin D.	33	M	Farmer	NC
Marthy A.	24	F		TN
Alford T.	8	M		TN
Louis B.	7	M		TX
Georgian	5	F		TX
E. H.	3	M		TX
Susan J.	1	F		TX
Donnahoo, Thomas	35	M	Farmer	IRE
Corder, William A.	58	M	Farmer	SC
Clay, John	45	M	Farmer	VA
Sary L.	44	F		TN
M.	10	M		TN
C. B. D.	7	M		TN
Birras, Albert	23	M	Farmer	TN
Elizabeth	23	F		GA
Marthy V.	8/12	F		TX
Hey, John	55	M		GA
Marthy	16	F		GA
Askins, Charles	62	M	Farmer	TN
Elizabeth	39	F		MO
Francus M.	10	M		TX
Jane	7	F		TX
Charles M.	5	M		TX
Mary F.	5/12	F		TX
Alviry	22	F		TN
George W.	3	M		TX
Mary M.	1	F		TX
Spencer, Martin V.	15	M	Farmer	TX
Askins, James W.	33	M	Farmer	TN
Nancy L.	26	F		GA
William C.	6	M		TX
Mary J.	4	F		TX
Henry H.	1	M		TX
P. H. P. M.	5	M		TX
Mills, Ellender	40	F		SC
Askins, Henry N.	24	M	Farmer	TN
Sary J.	23	F		GA
Delily A.	1/12	F		TX
Palmer, Wilson L.	50	M	Farmer	TN
Sary	39	F		TN
William J.	20	M	Farmer	AR
David A.	15	M	Farmer	AR
Mary A.	13	F		TX
James W.	10	M		LA
Thomas G.	8	M		LA
Sary E.	6	F		LA
Julia F.	2	F		TX
Mays, Matthew	51	M	Farmer	TN
Mary	35	F		TX
Mary A.	19	F		AR
George	17	M	Farmer	AR
Francine	7	F		TX
Nicey	4	F		TX
Eliza J.	1	F		TX
Smith, V.	15	M	Farmer	TX
Amandy	9	F		TX
Palmer, John	37	M	Farmer	AL
Rebecca	39	F		TN
William H.	15	M	Farmer	AR
Nancy J.	14	F		TX
Elizabeth L.	13	F		LA
Mary M.	9	F		TX
James M.	7	M		TX
Marthy	4	F		TX
Burdett, Jessy C.	28	M	Farmer	TN
Marthy A.	25	F		TN
Elizabeth	7	F		TX
Williamson R.	5	M		TX
John S.	3	M		TX
Gaines, William H.	30	M	Cabinet Maker	AL
Elizabeth	27	F		TN
James	5	M		TX
Louise	1	F		TX
Sapp, Jasper N.	31	M	Farmer	TN
Mary A.	22	F		AL
Manervy	5	F		AL
Thomas J.	3	M		AL
John A.	1	M		TX
Marcus	22	M	Farmer	TN
Richards, John D.	40	M	Cabinet Maker	TN
Nancy	30	F		MO
Mary J.	11	F		TX
John D. A.	8	M		TX
Susan A.	4	F		TX
Charles L.	2	M		TX
Foster, John F.	55	M	Farmer	??
Elizabeth	53	F		VA
John	20	M	Farmer	TN
Lucy	15	F		TN
Tims, John	38	M	Farmer	SC
Sary	38	F		SC
Jerome F.	8	M		TN
Araminta	1	F		TX
Johnston, Mary A.	40	F		TN
Jeremiah	13	M		LA
Obidiah	11	M		TX
Washington	9	M		TX
Elizabeth	6	F		TX
Mary A.	5	F		TX
Child unnamed	1	F		TX
Loyd, William	47	M	Saddler	VA
Susan	30	F		TN
William T.	6	M		AL
Hubbert	2/12	M		TX
Lee, Elizabeth	25	F		AL
Riddle, William	46	M	Farmer	VA
Sary	46	F		NC
Elmina	8	F		TX
English, James	27	M	Farmer	TN
John	25	M		TN
Stephen	21	M	Farmer	TN
Jonas	17	M	Farmer	TX
Castleberry, Sary C.	54	F		TN
James	28	M	Farmer	AL
Edward	25	M	Farmer	AL
Richard	22	M	Farmer	AL
Andrew	20	M	Farmer	AL
Angeline	18	F		AL
Sary An	16	F		AL
Amanda	14	F		TX
Robison, N. T.	29	M	Farmer	TN
Susan M.	25	F		GA
Levony J.	2	F		TX
Reavis, William F.	25	M	Farmer	NC
Dorothy	19	F		TN
Crawford, William C.	45	M	M.E. Clergyman	NC
Rhody	32	F		IL
Mary E.	12	F		TX
Charles W.	9	M		TX
Sary J.	7	F		TX
William C.	5	M		TX
Margret T.	2	F		TX
Louis F.	9/12	M		TX
Harcaness, James	20	M	Farmer	TN
July A.	15	F		TX
Hicks, A. W. O.	33	M	Lawyer	TN

(continued)

SHELBY COUNTY, TEXAS

Name	Age	Sex	Occupation	Birthplace
Hicks, Margret C.	26	F		TN
Izora	6	F		TX
John N.	4	M		TX
William B.	3	M		TX
Harper, William	22	M	Farmer	TN
Sollomon, Samuel	27	M	Farmer	TN
Marthy	24	F		TN
Pleasant W.	6	M		TN
Eliza R.	5	F		TN
Sary G.	3	M(F)		TN
Rachel	1	F		TN
Margrett V.	10/12	F		TN
Tubbs, Abraham	38	M	Farmer	TN
Emaly	34	F		SC
Nancy	15	F		AL
Jane	13	F		AL
Robert	12	M		AL
Rosanna	10	F		AL
Henry B.	9	M		AL
Malissy	7	F		AL
Marthy F.	5/12	F		AL
Stevens, Enoch	28	M	Farmer	TN
Vincy	25	F		TN
Alziny	10	F		TN
Holston	4	M		TN
Susan	2	F		TN
Webb, Jefferson N.	22	M	Farmer	TN
Mary M.	20	F		TN
Boyd, Huldy	31	F		TN
Strong, Isam	48	M	Farmer	VA
Susan	46	F		TN
Emaly	16	F		TN
Alexander	13	M		TN
Wiett	11	M		MS
John	7	M		TX
Mary	3	F		TX

SMITH COUNTY, TEXAS

Name	Age	Sex	Occupation	Birthplace
Daniel, James W.	32	M	Farmer	NC
Louisa H.	20	F		TN
Margaret J.	3	F		TN
Mary E.	4/12	F		TX
Lovett, Samuel S.	32	M	Farmer	AL
Johanna	24	F		TN
John	11	M		TN
Levi	8	M		TN
Mary	6	F		TN
Charity	2*	F		TN
Waldrup, Andrew B.	28	M	Farmer	TN
Matilda E.	23	F		TN
Mary E.	8	F		MS
James S.	6	M		MS
Andrew	4	M		TX
Merchant, James B.	40	M	Farmer	TN
Mahulda	41	F		TN
Nancy C.	19	F		TN
John W.	17	M	Farmer	TN
Catharine E.	14	F		TN
Matilda L. J.	12	F		MS
Rachel L.	10	F		MS
William W.	8	M		MS
Margaret A.	6	F		MS
Caleb H. B.	4	M		MS
Martha S.	2	F		TX
Waldrup, Anderson M.	23	M	Farmer	TN
Barcroft, Elisha H.	41	M	Farmer	TN
Margaret B.	37	F		TN
Maranda C.	16	F		TN
Loranzo O.	14	M		TN
William H.	13	M		TN
James D.	11	M		TX

(continued)

Name	Age	Sex	Occupation	Birthplace
Barcroft, Joshua T.	9	M		TX
Margaret J.	5	F		TX
Sarah C.	1	F		TX
Clarey, William P.	50	M	Farmer	TN
Sarah	46	F		TN
Solomon	20	M	Farmer	IL
Jackson	18	M	Farmer	IL
Washington	15	M		AR
Joseph	13	M		AR
Sarah	11	F		AR
Martin	9	M		AR
Jasper	6	M		AR
Abigail	18	F		NY
Hays, William B.	47	M	Farmer	NC
Rachel	48	F		TN
Cyrus C.	15	M		MO
Rebecca J.	13	F		MO
Harrison	11	M		AR
Elizabeth	9	F		AR
Virginia	7	F		MO
Hays, William C.	25	M	Farmer	TN
Amanda	25	F		TN
James	8	M		MO
William	6	M		MO
Gilbert	2	M		TX
Hester, Robert H.	39	M	Farmer	NC
Margaret A.	38	F		TN
Absalum	18	M	Farmer	TN
Martha	16	F		TN
Avery	14	M		TN
Elitha	12	F		MS
Franklin	10	M		MS
Elizabeth	8	F		MS
Sarah J.	7	F		MS
James P.	3	M		TX
Susan	11/12	F		TX
Lewis, James J.	25	M	Farmer	TN
Lurane	21	F		??*
James D.	6	M		AL
Mary J.	5	F		MS
Ira D.	4	M		MS
Elizabeth	3	F		MS
Matilda A.	3/12	F		TX
Barber, Majors E.	56	M	Farmer	NC
Susan P.	45	F		VA
Thomas S.	28	M	Farmer	KY
John P.	21	M	Farmer	MS
Henry B.	17	M	Farmer	TN
Wilkerson, John C.	31	M	Farmer	TN
Editha	31	F		TN
William L.	9	M		TN
Sarah E.	7	F		TN
Ann E.	5	F		MO
Euphima	3	F		TN
John W.	1	M		TX
Blackwell, Richard	31	M	Farmer	TN
Mary A.	30	F		NC
Myra	8	F		TN
Evelina	6	F		TN
Elmore	4	M		TN
Eliza J.	2	F		TN
Mack, Edward	38	M	Farmer	IRE
Mary	39	F		TN
Sarah E.	13	F		AL
Jesse	11	M		AL
George W.	9	M		AL
John	7	M		AR
Rebecca A.	5	F		TX
Susan C.	3	F		TX
Mary J.	3/12	F		TX
Williams, John M.	36	M	Farmer	GA
Rhoda	31	F		TN
Mary Ann	13	F		MS
Robert	11	M		MS
Lucinda	9	F		MS

(continued)

SMITH COUNTY, TEXAS

Name	Age	Sex	Occupation	Birthplace
Williams, Elizabeth	6	F		MS
William	4	M		TX
John	5/12	M		TX
Williams, A. C.	21	M	Farmer	TN
Samuel	18	M	Farmer	TN
David	16	M	Farmer	TN
Sprewell, John	18	M	Laborer	NC
Henry, Woodson D.	32	M	Farmer	TN
Levissa	30	F		AL
James C.	12	M		TX
Nancy C.	10	F		AL
Permelia F.	7	F		TX
Ezekiel L.	5	M		TX
Hugh W.	2	M		TX
Lawler, John	32	M	Farmer	TN
Elizabeth	33	F		TN
Eli	11	M		TX
Mary (Twin)	8	F		TX
William W. (Twin)	8	M		TX
Charlotta T.	5	F		TX
Elizabeth	3	F		TX
America	3/12	F		TX
James	68	M	Farmer	NC
Ward, William	45	M	Teacher	??
Hand, James C.	56	M	Farmer	SC
Nelley	42	F		TN
Johnson, Robert	19	M	Farmer	AL
Hand, Samuel	19	M	Farmer	TN
Emeline	17	F		TN
John B.	16	M	Farmer	TN
Eliza	14	F		TN
Henry	11	M		TN
Johnson, George	12	M		TN
Dollahite, James	50	M	Farmer	NC
Tilley	48	F		TN
Isabella	14	F		TN
Averrilla	13	F		TN
James C.	10	M		MS
Martha	8	F		TX
Mary E. J.	3	F		TX
Blount, George W.	19	M	Laborer	??
Dollahite, Charles W.	26	M	Teacher	TN
Jackson, Francis C.	25	M	Farmer	GA
N. Caroline	20	F		TN
Archibald A.	3	M		TN
Calloway H.	11/12	M		TN
Moore, David	40	M	Farmer	TN
Sarah	34	F		TN
Joseph	9	M		TN
Lucinda M.	5	F		TN
Lemuel	3	M		TN
Elizabeth J.	21	F		TN
Gilbert, Wilson	55	M	Farmer	NC
Martha M.	53	F		PA
James M.	31	M	Farmer	TN
Carrey Ann	18	F		TN
Martha M.	1	F		TX
Bond, Jesse	24	M	Farmer	MS
Mary Ann	20	F		TN
Lewis Cass	1	M		TX
Cates, Hyram	30	M	Farmer	TN
Mary C.	20	F		TN
Priscilla	6	F		TN
Thomas J.	4	M		TX
George W.	2	M		TX
Hill, James C.	43	M	Farmer	TN
Rebecca M.	39	F		AL
Mary	15	F		AL
Hellen M.	13	F		AL
John A.	12	M		AL
Margaret	8	F		TX
Sarah	7	F		TX
Thomas R.	5	M		TX

(continued)

Name	Age	Sex	Occupation	Birthplace
Hill, Charles G.	4	M		TX
Rebecca	3	F		TX
Samuel H.	1	M		TX
Hill, Andrew J.	27	M	Farmer	TN
Farmer, Samuel W.	60	M	Teacher	GA
Wooton, William	42	M	Farmer	TN
Martha	43	F		NC
Pollett, Martha	6	F		TX
Leming, Jesse	63	M	Bapt. Clergyman	TN
Nancy	64	F		TN
Polley	20	F		TN
Rustin, E. B.	28	M	Brick Mason	TN
Nancy E.	24	F		TN
Henry S.	3	M		TN
Alexander B.	2	M		TN
Hariet E.	11/12	F		TX
Luckey, N. B.	24	M	Laborer	TX
Coxey, A. P.	24	M	Laborer	TX
Harten, N. S.	52	M	Laborer	TX
Pierce, Michael	20	M	Laborer	TX
Henry, John C.	24	M	Laborer	TX
Stubblefield, George W.	27	M	Farmer	TN
Susan J.	23	F		TN
Sabol C.	2	M		TN
Robert J. C.	1/12	M		TX
Harper, John M.	41	M	Farmer	TN
Malinda	42	F		NC
John W.	20	M	Farmer	TN
Thomas J.	19	M	Farmer	TN
Samuel G.	14	M		TN
George McD.	6	M		TN
Mary Eliza	5	F		TN
Martha Ann	3	F		TN
England, Elizabeth	12	F		TN
Benson, William W.	32	M	Grocer	GA
Mary E.	25	F		TN
Joseph W.	6	M		GA
Holman, Hardy	50	M	Tavern-Hotel Keeper	NC
Sarah	45	F		SC
Alexander S.	25	M	Grocer	TN
John C.	18	M	Farmer	MO
Martha A.	16	F		MO
William A.	14	M		MO
Hardy S.	11	M		MO
Sigler, Rufus B.	22	M	Lawyer	AL
McLemore, Daniel J.	22	M	Lawyer	TN
Bell, Francis M.	25	M	Land Trader	NC
Lindsey, Harvey	24	M	Physician	TN
Pate, John W.	21	M	Dry Goods Clerk	TN
Hatley, T. B.	33	M	Grocer	TN
Bartlett, Robert	53	M	Laborer	CT
Ellis, Morgan P.	35	M	Trader	KY
Butler, Thomas	36	M	Farmer	IL
Mary Ann	34	F		TN
Jerome	13	M		AR
Crittendon	11	M		AR
Marion	9	M		AR
Mary	7	F		AR
Jasper	5	M		AR
Sarah	3	F		AR
Martha	2	F		TX
Edwards, William N.	30	M	Farmer	AR
Martha E.	30	F		TN
Morning	9	F		AR
Mary	8	F		AR
Joseph S.	7	M		AR
James H.	5	M		AR
John W.	3	M		AR
Louisa	1	F		TX
Short, Robert L.	28	M	Farmer	TN
Frances	25	F		MO
William J.	5	M		MO
Narcissa E.	3	F		MO
Nancy E.	1	F		TX

SMITH COUNTY, TEXAS

Name	Age	Sex	Occupation	Birthplace
Butler, Marrietta L.	46	F		KY
Argent	15	F		TN
Mary A.	13	F		AL
Osbourn, Noble	25	M	Farmer	TN
Winniford E.	23	F		TN
Nancy A.	1	F		TX
Nelson, Hugh	30	M	Farmer	TN
Nancy L.	24	F		AL
John E.	7	M		MO
Marrietta J.	5	F		MO
Mary C.	2	F		TX
Kutch, Daniel	42	M	Farmer	KY
Mary	36	F		TN
Margery	18	F		TN
William C.	17	M	Farmer	TN
Bowlin Lee F.	15	M		TN
Cyrus W.	13	M		TN
Mary F.	11	F		TX
Hannah E.	9	F		TX
Benjamin F.	7	M		TX
Virginia J.	6	F		TX
Moses S.	3	M		TX
John F.	1	M		TX
Dillard, A. B.	25	M	Farmer	TN
Elizabeth	18	F		AL
A. George	2	M		TX
Joseph	31	M	Farmer	TN
Patterson, Newman M. C.	24	M	Farmer	AL
Lucy Ann	19	F		TN
John W.	10/12	M		TX
Fleming, Andrew J.	45	M	Farmer	TN
Elizabeth	38	F		TN
Margaret	9	F		TN
Susan	7	F		TN
Burrel W.	4	M		TN
Tennessee	1	F		TN
Sneed, Warren	22	M	Farmer	TN
Baylass, Milton	32	M	Farmer	TN
Elizabeth J.	21	F		MS
Sarah	60	F		TN
Stephen A.	2	M		TX
Mary A.	1	F		TX
Hoover, Joseph P.	24	M	Farmer	TN
Elizabeth	25	F		TN
John	7	M		TN
McDowall, Thomas	49	M	Farmer	SC
Yarborough, Nathaniel	46	M	Farmer	NC
Sophronia	42	F		GA
C. Narcissa	21	F		TN
Elizabeth T.	19	F		TN
George P.	17	M	Farmer	TN
Nancy W.	15	F		TN
James Henry	13	M		AR
Harriet C.	11	F		AR
Samuel E.	9	M		AR
Alfred W.	7	M		AR
Sophrona J.	5	F		AR
Mary J.	3	F		AR
Nathaniel W.	3/12	M		TX
Wallace, Holmes	44	M	Black Smith	--
Gwin, Malcom	42	M	Farmer	TN
Mary	53	F		TN
James S.	20	M	Farmer	TN
Malcom	18	M	Farmer	TN
Mary E.	16	F		TN
Thomas J.	14	M		TN
Hamilton, Fredonia	17	F		TN
Cambern, James B.	37	M	Teacher	KY
Margery C.	22	F		TN
Luther H.	4	M		TX
William J.	2	M		TX
Thomas	1	M		TX

Name	Age	Sex	Occupation	Birthplace
Lemming, William	30	M	Farmer	TN
Sarah	26	F		GA
Joel	4	M		TN
Thomas J.	1	M		TX
Jenkins, David	47	M	Farmer	GA
Nancy	37	F		NC
William	12	M		TN
Nancy	9	F		TN
Celia	5	F		TN
Tilmon	3	M		TN
Burnam, Henry T.	33	M	Cabinet Maker	TN
Elizabeth A.	26	F		NC
Mary J.	4	F		AL
Joseph S.	2	M		AL
Louisa A.	1	F		TX
Griffin, Columbus	19	M	Laborer	GA
Meador, Elijah	30	M	Farmer	SC
Laura N.	19	F		TN
Sarah L.	4	F		TX
Mary L.	3	F		TX
Laura R.	1	F		TX
Stephens, Elias W.	35	M	Farmer	KY
Elsey E.	32	F		TN
Absalum	10	M		GA
Louisa	8	F		AL
William W.	5	M		AL
Frances	4	F		AL
Bethanie	2	F		AL
Joseph W.	2/12	M		TX
Collins, Joseph	34	M	Farmer	SC
Angeline	28	F		TN
Marthena	9	F		AR
Lavena	7	F		AR
Rutha Ann	5	F		TX
James B.	3	M		TX
Joseph F.	1	M		TX
Coltrell, Jesse H.	35	M	Farmer	TN
Mahulda	24	F		TN
Mary Ann	7	F		AR
Levenia	5	F		TX
Sarah C.	2	F		TX
Elliott, John	57	M	Farmer	GA
Anna	49	F		GA
J. Jackson	23	M	Farmer	TN
Tennessee J.	21	F		TN
Francis M.	18	M	Farmer	TN
Thomas L. F.	16	M	Farmer	TN
Elizabeth K.	14	F		AR
Augusta	10	F		AR
America	7	F		TX
Prather, Thomas H.	24	M	Farmer	SC
Elizabeth	16	F		TN
Pigg, Susan	11	F		TN
Sarah	9	F		TN
McHenry, Samuel	45	M	Merchant	VA
Mary	20	F		TN
Francisco, Jacob	55	M	Laborer	KY
Kincannon, Jesse C.	38	M	Farmer	VA
Verlinder	38	F		KY
David R.	19	M	Farmer	TN
William P. K.	15	M		TN
Jesse C.	12	M		TX
Beane E.	10	M		TX
F. Elizabeth (Twin)	5	F		TX
Susannah M. (Twin)	5	F		TX
Robert R.	1	M		TX
McKinney, John N.	34	M	County Sheriff	NC
Tabitha	33	F		TN
Mary C.	14	F		MS
James W.	12	M		MS
Robert J.	10	M		MS
Margaret A.	8	F		MS
Elizabeth T.	5	F		MS
Lucinda A.	3	F		TX
John N.	1/12	M		TX

SMITH COUNTY, TEXAS

Name	Age	Sex	Occupation	Birthplace
Sensibaugh, Jacob	42	M	Farmer	TN
Jane	36	F		TN
Daniel H.	10	M		TN
William L.	6	M		TN
Henry	84	M	Farmer	VA
Lucinda	48	F		TN
Smith, Drury	40	M	Farmer	TN
Harriet E.	21	F		TN
Hopper, John	27	M	Laborer	TN
Graham, Arthur M.	43	M	Farmer	TN
Celia	37	F		TN
Elizabeth A.	17	F		TN
Mary J.	15	F		TN
Speer, John	34	M	Farmer	KY
Elizabeth	28	F		TN
Levi L.	10	M		TN
Melvina	8	F		TN
John D. W.	6	M		TN
Penelope	4	F		TN
Grimes, James A.	28	M	Farmer	TN
Angeline E.	23	F		AL
Mary E. (Twin)	2	F		TX
Nancy J. (Twin)	2	F		TX
Merchant, John T.	20	M	Farmer	TN
Sarah	21	F		TN
Younger, Eliza	4	F		TN
William	2	M		TX
Britton, Mathew A.	32	M	Farmer	TN
Elizabeth	26	F		AL
James E.	9	M		MS
William M.	7	M		MS
Martha A.	5	F		MS
Newton H.	2	M		TX
Green, Berry	28	M	Farmer	TN
Irena	22	F		IL
Mary	6	F		TX
John	4	M		TX
George W.	1	M		TX
Davis, John L.	35	M	Farmer	TN
Elizabeth	33	F		TN
Hannah D.	15	F		TN
Martha E.	11	F		MS
James E.	9	M		MS
Robert H.	5	M		MS
Jeremiah Z. T.	2	M		MS
Marrow, James	17	M		TN
Rogers, James C.	31	M		TN
Parker, William G.	47	M	Farmer	NC
Sylvia	44	F		TN
Leroy S.	22	M	Farmer	KY
Jacob D.	21	M	Farmer	MS
Mary E.	16	F		MS
Archibald G.	12	M		MS
Andrew J.	10	M		MS
Martha A.	8	F		MS
Thomas J.	6	M		MS
Rush, James M.	43	M	Farmer	GA
Tennessee	42	F		TN
Seeton, James M.	20	M	Farmer	TN
Anna A. D.	17	F		TN
Rush, Henderson C.	18	M	Farmer	GA
Seeton, William M.	16	M	Mail Carrier	TN
Martha R.	14	F		TN
Rush, Piety	14	F		GA
Arretta	12	F		GA
Seeton, Nancy P.	12	F		MS
Rush, Van Burena	3	F		TX
Secrest, Harrison	26	M	Farmer	TN
Martha C.	22	F		GA
McIntosh, George	36	M	Farmer	TN
Elizabeth A.	22	F		MS

(continued)

Name	Age	Sex	Occupation	Birthplace
McIntosh, Charles A.	4	M		MS
Susan J.	3	F		MS
Alexander W.	2	M		MS
Kidd, Thomas D.	49	M	Farmer	SC
Susan	40	F		TN
William W.	15	M		TN
Benjamin F.	9	M		MS
George W.	7	M		MS
Patric H.	5	M		MS
Copeland, Elisha	43	M	Farmer	KY
Rebecca	38	F		KY
Susannah	16	F		AL
Mary A.	14	F		AL
Johanna E.	12	F		AL
Martha A.	10	F		AL
William H.	8	M		AL
James A.	6	M		TN
Jonathan C.	4	M		TX
Dancy, Thomas P.	41	M	Farmer	ENG
Nancy A.	29	F		TN
Mary E.	8	F		TX
Narcissa L.	6	F		TX
Nancy E.	4	F		TX
James H.	6/12	M		TX
Steele, J. J.	29	M	Farmer	IN
Eliza J.	26	F		TN
James F.	3	M		TX
Jane C.	7/12	F		TX
Davidson, J. L.	33	M	Physician	TN
Scott, Mary	60	F		GA
Lukenbill, Michael	24	M	Farmer	IN
David	22	M	Farmer	IN
Powell, James	52	M	Farmer	VA
Elizabeth	50	F		NC
James W.	22	M	Farmer	TN
William	20	M	Farmer	TN
Hezekiah	17	M	Farmer	TX
Elizabeth	11	F		TX
Jesse	8	M		TX
John	6	M		TX
Lassiter, Merriman	39	M	Farmer	NC
Mary	35	F		TN
Rebecca	18	F		TN
Jane	16	F		TN
Amos	14	M		TN
Frances	12	F		TN
Andrew	10	M		TN
Susan	8	F		MS
Joel	6	M		MS
Hugh	5	M		MS
Perryman, William	39	M	Farmer	KY
Elizabeth	34	F		KY
Lucy A.	13	F		TN
James	12	M		TN
Sarah C.	10	F		TN
Gabriel	8	M		MS
Sarah E.	10	F	(Blind)	MS
Alley	7	F		MS
William	5	M		MS
Jennetta	3	F		MS
Rebecca M.	1	F		TX
Welch, John	35	M	Farmer	TN
Margaret	22	F		AL
California	11	F		MO
John	10	M		MO
Henry B.	7	M		MO
Salley	6	F		TX
Flournoy	4	M		TX
Sebra	2	F		TX
Beverley T.	1/12	M		TX
Prickett, James T.	30	M	Farmer	AL
Juda	29	F		TN
William J.	6	M		AL
Mary A. L.	5	F		AL
Nancy A. E.	4	F		AL
Hester, Zachariah T.	3	M		TN
Prickett, Martha J.	10/12	F		TX

Name	Age	Sex	Occupation	Birthplace
Taylor, Josephus	37	M	Farmer	TN
Martha M.	22	F		AL
Mary M.	3	F		MS
Davis, William	20	M	Laborer	MS
Spier, Dennis	29	M	Farmer	KY
Lucinda	27	F		TN
John H.	10	M		TN
Ellen A. E.	8	F		TN
James T.	5	M		TN
Dennis T.	3	M		TX
Francis M.	8/12	M		TX
Watts, Bartlett S.	33	M	Farmer	MS
Thomas	79	M	Farmer	SC
Dicey	31	F		TN
Whitson	10	M		MS
Margaret	8	F		TX
Sarah	5	F		TX
Thomas	1	M		TX
Lorance, Hyram	53	M	Farmer	NC
McDonald	25	M	Farmer	TN
Sarah J.	20	F		TN
Pernica	18	F		TN
Thomas	16	M	Farmer	TN
Laurissa	14	F		TN
Hendric, William	3	M		TX
Steane, John	25	M	Farmer	AL
Mary	22	F		TN
Malissa J.	5	F		TX
William T.	3	M		TX
McLure, Samuel L.	41	M	Farmer	NC
Margaret	34	F		TN
Warren J.	15	M		AL
Martha J.	13	F		AL
John A.	11	M		AL
Arthur	9	M		AL
Ann	7	F		AL
Adeline	3	F		TX
White, John T.	24	M	Laborer	AL
Davis, William	25	M	Laborer	TN
Pitman, James W.	38	M	Farmer	NC
Matilda	37	F		TN
Jane	14	F		MS
Caroline	12	F		MS
Malissa	8	F		MS
Martha	6	F		MS
William C.	6/12	M		TX
White, Alexander W.	40	M	Teacher	SC
Margaret E.	34	F		TN
Sarah A. R.	14	F		AL
Susan E.	12	F		AL
Frances E.	10	F		MS
Caroline H.	8	F		MS
Mary J.	6	F		MS
Eliza T.	3	F		MS
Yarborough, Harvey	35	M	Farmer	TN
Margaret A.	24	F		NC
William M.	1	M		TX
Lott, Arthur	62	M	Farmer	GA
Elizabeth	42	F		GA
Elizabeth	19	F		MS
Adaline	18	F		MS
Rebecca	5	F		TX
Nancy A.	5/12	F		TX
McClung, Cowen	30	M	Merchant	TN
Stevenson, W. H.	43	M	Farmer	KY
Elizabeth S.	43	F		AL
James F.	19	M		AL
Mary A.	16	F		AL
Isam H.	14	M		AL
Matilda L.	12	F		AL
William H.	10	M		AL
Susan E.	9	F		AL
Nancy E. (Twin)	7	F		TN
(continued)				
Stevenson, John P. (Twin)	7	M		TN
Margaret L.	5	F		TX
Calvin, John	45	M	Farmer	MO
Lucy	21	F		TN
Hester, Elizabeth	7	F		TN
Talbot, Eliza E.	2	F		TX
Thompson, Allen	34	M	Farmer	TN
Elvira	28	F		AL
John A.	9	M		MS
Ann E.	8	F		MS
Susanah A.	6	F		MS
Jeptha T.	3	M		TX
Thompson, Burrell W.	45	M	Farmer	TN
Serena M.	37	F		TN
William F.	19	M	Farmer	MS
Samuel A.	11	M		MS
Cassander	8	F		MS
Thomas G.	5	M		MS
Emerilla	2	F		MS
Thompson, William B.	46	M	Farmer	TN
Minerva	36	F		TN
Nancy E.	17	F		MS
Mary C.	15	F		MS
William H.	11	M		MS
Samuel N.	8	M		MS
Harriet B.	6	F		MS
Martha J.	4	F		TX
Ervin L.	1	M		TX
Thompson, Stephen E.	47	M	Farmer	TN
Pheba A.	35	F		TN
John H.	18	M	Farmer	MS
James	16	M	Farmer	MS
Serena	14	F		MS
William H.	10	M		MS
Samuel E.	2	M		TX
Beckerstaff, William S.	40	M	Farmer	GA
Nancy	33	F		TN
Elizabeth A.	14	F		MS
Nancy E.	7	F		MS
William A.	3	M		TX
Samuel B.	2/12	M		TX
Byers, Isaac	27	M	Farmer	AL
Elizabeth	20	F		TN
Martha	3/12	F		TX
Lawrence, J. P.	32	M	Farmer	NC
Amanda J.	24	F		TN
William N.	5	M		MS
Henry C.	2	M		TX
Thompson, Harvey M.	39	M	Farmer	TN
Martha	40	F		TN
Susan	11	F		MS
John P.	9	M		MS
Ann M.	7	M		MS
William M.	5	M		MS
S. Jasper	3	M		TX
James N.	1	M		TX
McKinley, William L.	44	M	Farmer	NC
Elizabeth	29	F		TN
Leonidas LaF.	21	M		MS
John L.	18	M		MS
Mary E.	15	F		MS
Sarah A.	12	F		MS
Margaret C.	8	F		MS
Martha C.	6	F		MS
Nancy A.	4	F		TX
Tabitha A.	1	F		TX
Hamilton, Nancy	41	F		TN
Robert	15	M		TN
Rufus H.	14	M		TN
Eupheme S.	11	F		MS
William H. H.	8	M		TX
Malcom	4	M		TX

Name	Age	Sex	Occupation	Birthplace
Thomas, John W.	46	M	Farmer	GA
Caroline	38	F		TN
John C.	20	M	Farmer	MS
Isaac N.	16	M	Farmer	MS
Benjamin F.	14	M		MS
Sarah A.	12	F		MS
James W.	10	M		MS
Susan J.	5	F		TX
Louis G.	1	M		TX
Farmer, Christopher	39	M	Farmer	TN
Jane E.	28	F		GA
Cynthia A.	7	F		TN
Dorothy B.	4	F		TN
Hellen E.	2	F		GA
Robert H. (Twin)	4/12	M		TX
Joseph L. (Twin)	4/12	M		TX
Parten, James	65	M	Farmer	KY
Frances	65	F		VA
James M.	27	M	Farmer	TN
Holloway	23	M	Farmer	TN
Weaver, Jonathan	49	M	Farmer	NC
Ferriba	41	F		TN
Jane	24	F		TN
Anna	17	F		AL
Mark	19	M	Farmer	AL
Stephen	12	M		AL
Matthews, Jacob	51	M	Farmer	GA
Virginia	40	F		TN
Sarah E.	14	F		MS
Adaline	12	F		TX
Julia O.	9	F		TX
Atlantic M.	7	F		TX
Hester A.	4	F		TX
Milton F.	1	M		TX
Waggoner, Peter	65	M	Farmer	TN
Sarah	52	F		SC
Edmund A.	21	M	Farmer	TN
Ellis	18	M	Farmer	TN
Martha A.	12	F		TN
George W.	11	M		MO
Nancy J.	9	F		MO
Amanda M.	7	F		MO
McClure, William F.	32	M	Farmer	TN
Elizabeth P.	31	F		TN
Henshaw, Jesse	50	M	Farmer	TN
Nancy	30	F		KY
James M.	16	M	Farmer	MO
Jane	12	F		MO
Amanda	10	F		IL
Margaret	8	F		IL
Penina	6	F		TX
Marthana	4	F		TX
Brittain, Joel	27	M	Farmer	TN
C------	25	F		MO
James L.	5	M		AL
Elizabeth A.	3	F		TX
Little Berry	1	M		TX
Spier, Bennet	43	M	Farmer	NC
Susan	37	F		NC
Martha A.	14	F		TN
Anderson, Mary E.	10	F		AR
Spier, Edward	8	M		AR
Rebecca	6	F		AR
John	1/12	M		TX
Williams, Richard	23	M	Farmer	AR
Camp, L. E.	31	M	Millwright	GA
Sarah G.	23	F		GA
Sarah A. E.	1	F		TX
Merchant, Mahulda J.	18	F		TN
Randolph, John	42	M	Farmer	TN
Jane	40	F		NC
Joseph	17	M	Farmer	AL
William	15	M		AL

Name	Age	Sex	Occupation	Birthplace
Farris, Sarah	60	F		??
Andrew	22	M	Farmer	TN
Joseph	19	M	Farmer	MO
Chancellor, Jesse G.	25	M	Farmer	AL
Dorothy	20	F		TN
William M.	2	M		AL
Allen, Robert R.	49	M	Farmer	TN
Mary	46	F		TN
Elizabeth	16	F		TN
Alexander	14	M		GA
John	11	M		GA
William	7	M		AR
Margaret	5	F		AR
Beard, William	26	M	Laborer	SC
Hay, William S.	33	M	Wagon Maker	KY
Amanda	32	F		NC
Miles F.	12	M		TN
Joel D.	22	M	Black Smith	TN
Fuller, Henry P.	22	M	Laborer	TN
Taylor, F. M.	24	M	Farmer	TN
Malissa V.	19	F		TN
Taylor, Thomas J.	32	M	Farmer	TN
Levonia	24	F		TN
Julius	4	M		TN
Robert M.	2	M		TN
Wells, Rice, Sr.	68	M	Farmer	GA
Chaney	56	F		GA
Calvin	23	M	Farmer	LA
Rice	22	M	Dry Goods Clerk	LA
Thompson	18	M	Farmer	MS
Hancel F.	3	M		TX
Swan, Thomas R.	24	M	Merchant	AL
McCorkle, (Blank)	30	M	Physician	??
Turner, Phillip	23	M	Laborer	TN
Brown, James	19	M	Student	AL
Wells, Louisa	20	F	Student	MS
Martha A.	12	F	Student	MS
Beene, F. H.	35	M	Farmer	TN
Jesse	76	M	Farmer	VA
Mary	65	F		NC
Mary J.	19	F		TN
Huggins, William	26	M	Farmer	KY
Mary Ann	25	F		TN
Christopher	3	M		TX
Josephine	2	F		TX
Reuben	16	M	Farmer	KY
Lucinda	23	F		KY
Louisa	19	F		KY
Mayfield, Battle	42	M	Farmer	GA
Cynthia	38	F		KY
John	20	M	Farmer	IN
Lewis	13	M		IN
George	10	M		IN
Jasper	7	M		IN
Chandler	5	M		TX
James	3	M		TX
Stephen	1	M		TX
Davis, James	19	M	Farmer	TN
Bates, Robert L.	36	M	Farmer	TN
Margaret Ann	34	F		TN
Beene, Robert O.	43	M	Farmer	TN
Lavina	38	F		VA
Mary E.	16	F		TN
Martha J.	14	F		MS
Sarah C.	12	F		MS
Ann Eliza	9	F		TX
Thomas F.	7	M		TX
Lavina	4	F		TX
Louisa	6/12	F		TX
Howell, Joseph	24	M	Laborer	TN
Pollett, Edgar	30	M	Farmer	KY
Mary	20	F		TN
Martha	7	F		TX

(continued)

Pollett, Elizabeth 6 F TX
Susan 3 F TX
Caroline 4/12 F TX
Frost T. 17 M Farmer TX

Dixon, James G. 39 M Farmer KY
Ann 27 F TN
Sarah E. 9/12 F TX
Gilley, G. D. 22 M Farmer TN

Jackson, Zachariah 50 M Farmer SC
Sarah 45 F TN
Samantha 18 F TN
Mary 16 F TN
Ann 14 F TN
Margaret 12 F TN
Harriet 10 F TX
William 8 M TX
Martha 6 F TX

Baird, John 56 M Farmer NC
Mahala 44 F TN
Robert J. 19 M Farmer NC
John S. L. 5 M AR
Sarah P. 2 F AR

Johnson, Rodolphus E. 44 M Farmer TN
William R. 24 M Farmer AL
Sarah Ann 20 F AL
Jarusha 18 F AL

Lanham, Solomon 62 M Farmer TN
Mary 60 F SC
Bedford 20 M Farmer AL
Cynthia 17 F MS
Daniel, William 18 M Laborer GA
Lanham, Minerva 20 F AL
Margaret 18 F AL
Robert 14 M AL
William 11 M AL

Holbrook, Thomas P. 30 M Farmer GA
Hetty 28 F TN
Sarah A. E. 7 F MS
Arminda C. 5 F MS
Permelia A. 3 F MS
Hyram D. 2 M TX

Wilson, William C. 29 M Farmer AL
Nancy 27 F NC
John 6 F MS
Perry 6/12 M TX
Hodges, J. H. 25 M Farmer TN

Pendergrass, M. 44 M Farmer SC
Juda 44 F TN
James 19 M Waggoner AL
Polly Ann 17 F AL
Larinda T. 15 F AL
Joseph W. 13 M AL
Maranda M. 11 F AL
Emeline 9 F AL
Susa Ann 7 F AL
Moses M. 5 M AL
Melvina 3 F TX

Flinchum, George W. 19 M Farmer IN
Irving, Susannah 55 F NC
Flinchum, Andrew J. 13 M IN
Irving, Susannah E. 5 F TN
James 21 M Farmer TN

Adams, Ichabod 39 M Farmer TN
Ann C. C. 34 F TN
Sylvester 16 M Farmer TN
Hooper, Amanda 18 F TN
Adams, Fredonia 14 F TN
Ennis 12 M TN
Kizziah 10 F TN
George 8 M TN
Rebecca J. 6 F TN
Amanda 4 F TN
Philander 8/12 M TN
Averey, James 25 M Farmer TN

Wright, John 29 M Painter VA
Mary 65 F VA
Rachel 25 F VA
Richard 6 M TN
Josephine 3 F TN
Richard M. 21 M Painter VA
John T. 12 M VA

Pierce, David 27 M Farmer TN
Mary 28 F TN
William H. 6 M TN
Lewis M. 4 M TN
John W. 3 M TN

Green, Jonathan 62 M Farmer NC
Anna 57 F NC
David 20 M Farmer TN
Stephen 17 M Farmer TN
Johanna 14 F TN

Jeffers, Elijah 50 M Farmer SC

Riddle, Thomas W. 25 M Farmer TN
Mary A. 25 F NC
Lucinda G. 4 F MS
James B. 2 M MS

Green, Shaderic W. 33 M Farmer NC
Rebecca C. 35 F TN
Nancy J. 13 F TN
James J. 11 M TN
Joseph M. 10 M TN
Andrew J. 8 M TN
David N. 7 M TN
Lucinda A. E. P. 5 F TN
Lydia C. 3 F TN
William T. 1 M TX

Brooks, Francis 25 M Farmer TN
Flora 23 F Nova Scotia
Mary J. 1/12 F TX

Weatherbee, Thomas H. 44 M Farmer GA
George W. 74 M Saddler NJ
Margaret 37 F TN
Sarah C. 12 F MS
Mary K. 10 F MS
Louisa ?. 6 F MS
Flora G. 3 F TX
William A. 8/12 M TX
Middleton, John G. 27 M Dry Goods Clerk AL

Rucker, James E. 33 M Farmer TN
Elizabeth 28 F TN
Nancy 11 F TN
Mary 10 F TN
Martha M. 8 F TN
Marinda 7 F TN
William J. 4 M TN
James W. 3 M TN
John M. 1 M TN
Cole, Charles 24 M Farmer TN

Rucker, James C. 20 M Farmer TN
Virginia C. 20 F SC

Wilson, Samuel 58 M Farmer TN
Mary 54 F GA
James 16 M Farmer MS
Mary J. 13 F MS
Moore, Henry 30 M Farmer NC
Nancy 19 F TN

Wilshire, Josiah S. 24 M Farmer AL
Martha 21 F TN
William R. 1 M TX

Nelson, Horatio 41 M Physician TN
Angeline F. 21 F LA
Adeline L. 8/12 F TX

Wilson, John F. 24 M Farmer TN
Ellen 17 F TN

Prewett, Archibald 41 M Farmer SC
(continued)

Name	Age	Sex	Occupation	Birthplace
Prewett, Eliza	33	F		TN
Mary R.	17	F		AL
James W.	14	M		AL
John E.	11	M		AL
Martha J. E.	9	F		AL
Nancy Ann	6	F		AL
Robert F.	5	F		AL
Harriet D.	4	F		AL
Samuel	1/12	M		TX
Hodges, William T.	30	M	Farmer	TN
Harriet	30	F		AL
Frances	8	F		TN
Emily	5	F		TN
Luda	3	M		TN
Martha A.	6/12	F		TX
Hodges, James	39	M	Farmer	TN
Boisen, Wyley N.	38	M	Farmer	SC
Elizabeth	32	F		TN
Samuel W.	14	M		MS
William C.	13	M		MS
Ewen	11	M		MS
Lucinda	10	F		MS
Mary E.	7	F		MS
Matilda	5	F		MS
George W.	2	M		TX
Stone, Isaac	36	M	Farmer	VA
Almeda H.	30	F		TN
William H.	10	M		TN
Rebecca F.	7	F		TN
John T.	5	M		TN
James J.	3	M		TN
Mary E.	1	F		TN
Cougins, Peter G.	44	M	Farmer	VA
Edna	38	F		VA
William	21	M	Farmer	VA
John	16	M	Farmer	VA
Ann	13	F		VA
Isaac	10	M		TN
James K. P.	6	M		TN
Mary	3	F		TN
Eliza V.	4/12	F		TX
Smith, Samuel	50	M	Farmer	SWI
Eney	46	F		TN
Julius B.	21	M	Silver Smith	TN
Hannah	12	F		TN
Rufus	7	M		TN
Fradey, Asberry	21	M	Farmer	NC
Sarah	19	F		TN
Armstrong, William	54	M	Farmer	SC
Jane	48	F		SC
George	23	M	Farmer	TN
Wilson	21	M	Farmer	TN
Joseph	19	M	Farmer	TN
Jesse	17	M	Farmer	TN
Elizabeth	15	F		TN
James	12	M		MO
Henry	9	M		TN
Moore, Elisha	56	M	Farmer	VA
Harriet	52	F		TN
Elisha	14	M		AL
Burrow, Elizabeth	10	F		LA
Starns, William	48	M	Farmer	KY
John	34	M	Farmer	TN
Manilla	12	F		AL
Clarke, William	54	M	Farmer	TN
Anna	46	F		GA
David	25	M	Farmer	GA
Jane	19	F		GA
Elizabeth	17	F		GA
Benjamin	15	M		GA
Thomas	13	M		GA
L.	11	M		GA
John	9	M		GA
George W.	6	M		GA

Name	Age	Sex	Occupation	Birthplace
Whitemore, John	54	M	Farmer	MD
Elizabeth	50	F		VA
James M.	23	M	Teacher	TN
John H.	21	M	Farmer	TN
Franklin P.	15	M		TN
William H.	14	M		TN
Mary L. (Twin)	12	F		TN
Martha E. (Twin)	12	F		TN
Eaton, George	25	M	Farmer	TN
Tempey Ann	23	F		GA
Elizabeth J.	9/12	F		TX
Dodson, Jehu	23	M	Farmer	TN
Ann	20	F		GA
James M.	10/12	M		TX
Sosebey, Lafayette J.	29	M	Farmer	GA
Tempey	28	F		GA
William J.	7	M		GA
James K. P.	5	M		TN
David LaF.	4	M		TN
Alfred M.	2	M		TX
Sarah G. A.	1/12	F		TX
Robison, Moses	65	M	Farmer	TN
Mary	63	F		VA
Mahulda	38	F		TN
Seba	37	F		TN
Pheba	34	F		TN
James	32	M	Farmer	AL
Polley L.	28	F		IN
Sarah	30	F		IN
Samuel	26	M	Farmer	IN
Roberson, Arthur	42	M	Farmer	TN
Elizabeth	33	F		TN
William	10	M		TN
Jesse	7	M		TN
Sarah	5	F		TN
Vina	3	F		TX
Ritta Ann	1	F		TX
Roberson, Alfred	40	M	Farmer	TN
Eliza	36	F		TN
Sargant Jasper	14	M		TN
Samuel G.	11	M		TN
Nancy E.	10	F		TN
James N.	8	M		TN
Polley Ann	6	F		TN
Sarah M.	1	F		TX
Thomas, Benjamin	50	M	Farmer	VA
Mary	49	F		VA
James H.	19	M	Farmer	TN
Nancy E.	17	F		MO
Margaret J.	13	F		TX
Donald, Mathew B.	40	M	Farmer	TN
Isabell D.	38	F		TN
Holman B.	15	M		AL
Blecher C.	14	M		AL
Mary E.	12	F		AL
Julia E.	11	F		AL
Robert	9	M		AL
Nancy J.	8	F		AL
Elizabeth F.	6	F		AL
John R. (Twin)	3	M		TX
Margaret A. (Twin)	3	M		TX
Dealpha T.	1	F		TX
Ginn, James A.	21	M	Laborer	GA
Kirkpatric, John	55	M	Farmer	NC
Catharine	46	F		NC
Margaret J.	19	F		GA
James H.	14	M		GA
John	12	M		GA
Lindley, Emily	8	F		TN
Carruthers, Bowlin	38	M	Farmer	TN
Sarah	30	F		AL
Calafornia	13	F		MO
John	11	M		MO
Tunnell, James	38	M	Farmer	TN

(continued)

Name	Age	Sex	Occupation	Birthplace
Tunnell, Elizabeth	35	M(F)		AL
Eliza Jane	14	F		AL
Josiah T.	12	M		AL
Perry W.	11	M		AL
Hannah C.	8	F		AL
Jesse E.	4	M		AL
John B.	2	M		AL
Little, Catharine	60	F		AL
Tunnell, Enoch	34	M	Farmer	TN
Louisiana	29	F		SC
Perry O.	11	M		AL
Martha J.	10	F		AL
William B.	8	M		AL
John W.	6	M		AL
Milton R.	4	M		AL
Benson M.	2	M		AL
Prewett, Carroll W.	28	M	Farmer	TN
Hannah	22	F		MO
Perry, Solloman	26	M	Farmer	TN
Elizabeth	21	F		TN
Thomas J.	4	M		TN
Louisa E.	2	F		TN
Maxfield, William	29	M	Farmer	TN
Kizziah	19	F		TN
Mary J.	2	F		TX
Landers, Henry G.	29	M	Farmer	TN
Angeline	27	F		TN
Calloway D.	5	M		TX
Rachel A.	4/12	F		TX
Dean, James	47	M	Carpenter	TN
Dicey	43	F		KY
Eliza A.	17	F		TN
Jefferson C.	15	M		TN
John H.	12	M		TN
Mary J.	9	F		TN
Oliver H. P.	6	M		TN
Hamilton R.	4	M		TN
Asberry M.	27	M	Farmer	TN
Landers, Logan	22	M	Farmer	TN
Frances	16	F		TN
Farmer, Isaac	26	M	Farmer	TN
Sarah D.	27	F		NC
John B. H.	5	M		TN
William H.	3	M		TN
Lindley, James A.	16	M	Farmer	TN
Thompson, Wyley M.	27	M	Farmer	TN
Louisa	24	F		AL
Nancy E.	4	F		AL
Julia A.	1	F		TX
Cromwell, James S.	52	M	Farmer	NC
Margaret	42	F		TN
Sarah M.	14	F		GA
William B.	11	M		GA
Isaac N.	9	M		GA
Julius S.	6	M		GA
Nancy J.	3	F		TN
Mary E.	1	F		TN
Baker, Melvina	39	F		TN
Doyle, John	64	M	Farmer	PA
Theodore G.	33	M	Millwright	TN
William W.	27	M	Carpenter	TN
Russell H.	18	M	Farmer	TN
Columbus C.	16	M	Farmer	TN
Drucilla	24	F		TN
Harriet	22	F		TN
Martha	14	F		AL
Doyle, Albert B.	25	M	Farmer	TN
Malinda	19	F		GA
Farmer, Burdine	28	M	Farmer	TN
Luvenia	18	F		TN

Name	Age	Sex	Occupation	Birthplace
Parker, Harris	26	M	Farmer	TN
Martha	30	F		TN
Martha E.	3	F		TN
Billington, Hardy	26	M	Farmer	TN
Elizabeth Jane	19	F		TN
Ellison W.	1	M		TX
Wolf, Sarah	15	F		TN
Dodson, Nicholas P.	42	M	Farmer	TN
Martha	42	F		TN
Mary Jane	18	F		TN
George	11	M		TN
Lourinda	9	F		TN
Sarah Ann	6	F		TN
Adams, Samuel P.	25	M	Farmer	TN
Martha A. F.	25	F		GA
Aurelius G.	2/12	M		TX
Adams, A. J.	35	M	Farmer	TN
Eliza	30	F		IN
Wilson	7	M		IN
John ?.	5	M		IN
Martha J.	3	F		TX
Nutt, Marvin A.	21	M	Farmer	TN
Sarah E. A.	18	F		TN
Mary E.	1	F		TN
Brown, George	16	M		TN
Keating, Warner	50	M	Farmer	VA
Polley Ann	41	F		GA
Emily	13	F		TN
Elijah	8	M		AR
Patsey M.	4	F		TX
Benjamin C.	2	M		TX
Burrows, Wyley W.	32	M	Farmer	TN
Burrows, Elias W.	23	M	Farmer	TN
Jane	28	F		AL
Ishmael H.	7	M		AL
Emily A.	4	F		TX
Leonidas W.	2	M		TX
Mason, Andrew	43	M	Farmer	KY
Malissa	40	F		TN
Sarah	16	F		IN
Stephen	13	M		IN
Rosanna	12	F		IN
Owen	10	M		IN
Mary Ann	8	F		IN
Margaret J.	6	F		IN
Henrietta	5	F		IN
Andrew J.	3	M		TX
John M.	1	M		TX
Martin	33	M	Farmer	IN
Overton, John F.	34	M	Farmer	TN
John	1	M		TX
Alden A.	19	M	Teacher	TN
McDonald, William	28	M	Farmer	AL
Charity	27	F		TN
Albert T.	6	M		MS
Martha M.	4	F		TX
Samuel P.	2	M		TX
McKay, Joseph L.	44	M	Farmer	TN
Margaret C.	36	F		TN
Martha J.	14	F		TN
Harvey J.	12	M		TN
Susan N.	10	F		TX
Rebecca A.	8	F		TX
William O.	4	M		TX
Thomas C.	1	M		TX
Lewelling, John	55	M	Farmer	NC
Nancy	55	F		NC
Nancy	21	F		TN
Dovey	18	F		TN
John	12	M		IL
Ellison, William	27	M	Farmer	TN

(continued)

Name		Age	Sex	Occupation	Birthplace
Ellison, Louisa		25	F		TN
George W.		3	M		TX
Louisa J.		2	F		TX
Slaven, Nancy A.		8	F		TX
Gordon, Abram		38	M	Farmer	TN
Tabitha		30	F		NC
William		13	M		IL
Alfred		10	M		IL
David		7	M		MO
Abraham		3	M		TX
Eli	(Twin)	6/12	M		TX
Levi	(Twin)	6/12	M		TX
Lewelling, Wyley		22	M	Farmer	TN
Johnson, Tilley		38	M	Laborer	NOR
Bell, John		34	M	Farmer	TN
Nancy		29	F		TN
Amanda		12	F		TN
Elizabeth		10	F		TN
Allen		8	M		TN
Mary Ann		7	F		TN
Louisa		5	F		TN
Martha		4	F		TN
Joel		2	M		TX
Wilson		6/12	M		TX
Fisher, David		18	M	Farmer	IL
Suton, Samuel		36	M	Farmer	TN
Nancy R.		30	F		TN
Sarah L.		9	M(F)		TN
James C. D.		7	M		TN
Priscilla C.		2	F		TX
McBryde, Daniel		23	M	Farmer	TN
Hale, John		25	M	Farmer	TN
McBryde, Margaret		30	F		TN
Martha		28	F		TN
Lucinda		26	F		TN
Delila		21	F		TN
Jemima		19	F		TN
McBryde, William		33	M	Farmer	TN
Levisa		30	F		TN
Sarah		9	F		TN
Pleasant		7	M		TN
William		4	M		TN
John A.		1	M		TX
Smith, Hiel		43	M	Farmer	TN
Permelia A.		32	F		MS
William M.		12	M		MS
Robert J.		10	M		MS
Elizabeth J.		8	F		MS
Mary R.		6	F		MS
Martha F.		4	F		MS
Drury W.		2	M		MS
Hiel		4/12	M		TX
Davis, John		33	M	Farmer	TN
Carter		33	F		AR
James		14	M		TX
Vincent		10	M		TX
Andrew		7	M		TX
Melvina		5	F		TX
Green		3	M		TX
Hiel		4/12	M		TX
Pendergrass, William		32	M	Farmer	TN
Emeline		31	F		TN
Mary S.		7	F		TN
Marion D.		6	M		TN
Fanny B.		4	F		TN
John W.		2	M		TN
Myra E.		4/12	F		TX
Ellison, James		37	M	Farmer	TN
Nancy		32	F		GA
Sarah A.		13	F		AL
James M.		10	M		AL
John		8	M		AR
Not named		4	F		AR
Lewis C.		1	M		TX
Baird, John		40	M	Farmer	GA
Hill, James		68	M	Farmer	VA
Elizabeth		65	F		TN
Hill, David		36	M	Farmer	TN
Carger, Thomas		21	M	Farmer	TN
Sadler, Rachel		44	F		TN
Sarena A.		8	F		TX
Arnold, William C.		18	M	Farmer	TN
Sadler, America A.		6	F		TX
Mary M. R.		3	F		TX
Chisum, William		28	M	Farmer	TN
Elizah J.		23	F		IN
John W.		6	M		TX
Nancy J.		4	F		TX
Tabitha		10/12	F		TX
Samuel		3	M		TX
Crockett, Thomas A.		38	M	Farmer	GA
Eliza		34	F		TN
Henry J.		14	M		MS
Daniel W.		12	M		MS
Marcus LaF.		6	M		TX
Harvey P.		10/12	M		TX
Bell, George		25	M	Farmer	GA
Hill, Massano(?)		32	M	Farmer	TN
Julia A.		19	F		MO
Mary A.		2/12	F		TX
Nutt, Mary A.		16	F		AR
Louisa J.		11	F		LA
Potter, William		50	M	Farmer	TN
Jane		47	F		KY
John P.		24	M	Farmer	TN
Elijah J.		21	M	Farmer	TN
Josephus E. V. B.		15	M		TN
Daniel H.		12	M		TN
Sarah J.		8	F		TN
Potter, James D.		25	M	Farmer	TN
Elizabeth B.		22	F		TN
Margaret J.		1	F		TN
Findley, John		22	M	Farmer	TN
Austin, John		59	M	Farmer	VA
Delila		50	F		VA
Lucinda		17	F		TN
Robert		12	M		TN
Henry		5	M		TN
Jones, Willis		27	M	Farmer	GA
Mary		24	F		TN
Narcissa J.		3	F		GA
Samuel		2	M		GA
Jones, Samuel		22	M	Farmer	GA
Beene, James K.		33	M	Farmer	TN
Ellen		32	F		TN
Jessee M.		4	M		TX
John S.		2	M		TX
Terry, John		37	M	Farmer	TN
Nancy		30	F		AL
Jessee C.		11	M		MS
Mary E.		8	F		TX
Juda		4	F		TX
Benjamin F.		1	M		TX
Beene, Jessee E.		53	M	Physician	TN
Sarah M.		37	M		SC
Jenkins, Jesse		67	M	Farmer	NC
Sarah		65	F		VA
John		33	M	Farmer	TN
Susan		31	F		TN
Rebecca		28	F		TN
Jacob		22	M	Farmer	AL
Samuel S.		19	M	Farmer	AL
James C.		15	M		AL
Weatherford, Permelia		7	F		GA
Shaw, Jonathan		46	M	Farmer	TN
Malinda		42	F		MO

(continued)

SMITH COUNTY, TEXAS

Name	Age	Sex	Occupation	Birthplace
Shaw, William	15	M		MO
Margaret J.	13	F		MO
Robert	11	M		AR
Levi	5	M		TX
Thomas J.	2	M		TX
Not named	1/12	M		TX
Wilkerson, James H.	29	M	Farmer	TN
Sarah C.	20	F		TN
Monroe L.	11/12	M		TX
Keath, William	49	M	Farmer	TN
Gilbert, James	38	M	Farmer	SC
Lucy	38	F		KY
John	18	M	Farmer	TN
Mary A.	16	F		TN
Andrew	14	M		TN
William	12	M		TN
Samuel	10	M		MS
Elizabeth	7	F		MS
Nancy	4	F		MS
Rosa	2	F		MS
Lucinda	8/12	F		TX
Boyd, Ephraim L.	40	M	Farmer	TN
Martha	40	F		TN
William	16	M	Farmer	TN
Joseph	13	M		TN
Jefferson (Twin)	10	M		GA
Alexander (Twin)	10	M		GA
Elizabeth	6	F		GA
Mary	2	F		TX
Dillard, James	51	M	Farmer	NC
Cassa	49	F		TN
James M.	22	M	Farmer	TN
John L.	20	M	Farmer	TN
Lorenzo D.	13	M		TN
Francis M.	10	M		TN
Isaac V.	6	M		TN
George W.	3	M		TN
Dillard, Enoch W.	25	M	Farmer	TN
Josephine	21	F		NC
Mary L.	1	F		TN
Cook, Henry	38	M	Farmer	TN
Mary A.	27	F		TN
Cassander	10	F		TN
Mary J.	8	F		TN
Martha F.	4	F		TN
America W.	1	F		TN
Warren, George W.	35	M	Farmer	NC
Maria L.	21	F		NC
Nancy L. J.	2/12	F		TN
Claibourne, George W.	23	M	Farmer	TN
Martha	20	F		TN
James M.	9/12	M		TN
Perdue, Philemon	63	M	Farmer	NC
Elizabeth	68	F		NC
Bennet	27	M	Farmer	NC
Elbert	24	M	Farmer	TN
Elizabeth	22	F		NC
William	3/12	M		TN
McGee, R. A.	31	M	Lawyer	NC
Mary	30	F		TN
Henry A.	6	M		MS
John J.	4	M		MS
Davis, Ann E.	15	F		MS
Nancy J.	13	F		MS
Yarborough, Joseph	29	M	Farmer	NC
Sarah	32	F		NC
Sarah F.	3	F		TN
William	11/12	M		TX
Morris, Jesse	45	M	Farmer	NC
Violet	41	F		TN
John C.	21	M	Farmer	TN

(continued)

Name	Age	Sex	Occupation	Birthplace
Morris, Thomas R.	18	M	Farmer	TN
Lorenzo H.	16	M	Farmer	TN
Mary Jane	11	F		TN
Nancy M.	10	F		TN
Eliza A. A.	8	F		TN
William E.	6	M		TN
Stacey E.	5	M		TN
Robert G.	3	M		TN
Gilley, John, Sr.	56	M	Farmer	VA
Sarah	56	F		VA
John B.	31	M	Farmer	TN
William	24	M	Farmer	TN
Charles	29	M	Farmer	AL
Susan	16	F		TN
James	14	M		TN
Taylor, Christopher C.	28	M	Dry Goods Clerk	TN
Sarah J.	21	F		TN
Wren, Craig	35	M	Farmer	TN
Josephine B.	31	F		TN
Thomas L.	11	M		TN
Mariah L.	9	F		TN
Campbell M.	3	M		TX
Nicholas I.(?)	1	M		TX
James C.	6	M		TN
Neal, William	48	M	Farmer	VA
Mary Ann	48	F		NC
John L.	22	M	Farmer	TN
Thomas D.	16	M	Farmer	TN
Charles W.	14	M		TN
Martha J.	13	F		TN
Duncan McF.	11	M		TN
Drury R.	9	M		TN
William E.	7	M		TN
Mary Ann	3	F		TN
McCullough, William	46	M	Black Smith	TN
Lucinda	40	F		TN
Tabitha	2	F		TN
Nancy	1	F		TN
Carter, James A.	25	M	Farmer	TN
Mary	24	F		TN
Emily F.	6	F		TN
Reed, Allen	50	M	Farmer	TN
Sarah Ann	16	F		IL
Isaiah	15	M		IL
Warren	14	M		IL
Martha C.	12	F		IL
William L.	10	M		IL
John A.	7	M		IL
Sarah	75	F		IL
Walters, Mary	40	F		TN
George T.	20	M	Farmer	MS
Whitson H.	19	M	Farmer	MS
Lurinda	17	F		MS
Moses	15	M		MS
Robert	13	M		TX
Margaret	11	F		TX
Milly	9	F		TX
Leah E.	7	F		TX
Cynthia M.	5	F		TX
Neal, James H.	25	M	Farmer	TN
Sarah F.	26	F		NC
John D.	3	M		TN
Ervin A.	1	M		TX
Daniel, Thomas G.	21	M	Farmer	NC
McPeters, Jonathan	35	M	Farmer	TN
Mary	30	F		TN
Luzzephia	12	F		AR
Sarah Jane	10	F		AR
Luiza Ann	8	F		MO
Martha M.	5	F		TX
Artemesia C.	2	F		TX
Mary E.	6/12	F		TX
Richardson, Sylpha	57	F		TN
Malinda	25	F		TN

(continued)

SMITH COUNTY, TEXAS

Name	Age	Sex	Occupation	Birthplace
Peel, Elizabeth	21	F		AR
Dougherty, J. Nelson	20	M	Farmer	TN
Pearson, John	32	M	Grocer	NJ
Carter, Henry J.	23	M	Farmer	TN
Mary C.	20	F		TN
James W.	7/12	M		TX
Hughs, Mariah	38	F		TN
Eliza	13	F		AR
Frances	12	F		AR
Calvet, E. S.	30	M	Farmer	SC
Taylor, David	22	M	Farmer	TN
Mary	35	F		KY
Sarah An	10/12	F		TX
Nancy	14	F		TN
Young, William	33	M	Millwright	TN
Julia Ann	20	F		KY
John W.	12	M		TN
Lewis M.	8	M		MS
Elizabeth F.	6	F		TN
Young, Mordicai A.	30	M	Farmer	TN
Louisa B.	28	F		TN
Ann E.	10	F		MS
Attilla V.	8	F		TX
Eliza J.	5	F		TX
Amanda M.	3	F		TX
Lovett, John	60	M	Farmer	NC
Eli H.	26	M	Farmer	TN
Jasper N.	22	M	Grocer	TN
Andrew J.	19	M	Farmer	TN
Sarah	57	F		NC
Martin V. B.	13	M		TN
Speer, James	59	M	Farmer	NC
Penelope	56	F		NC
Nancy	20	F		TN
Coker, Leonard F.	22	M	Farmer	??
Sarah	32	F		AL
Nutt, Penelope	15	F		TN
Mary J.	13	F		TN
Coker, William M.	2	M		TX
John D. W.	7/12	M		TX
Favers, Elizabeth F.	17	F		GA
Argerbright, Arthur A.	38	M	Farmer	TN
Amanda	31	F		TN
Henderson	3	M		TN
Sarah F.	1	F		TN
Argerbright, George	72	M	Farmer	TN
Adaline	28	F		TN
Eldridge H.	20	M	Farmer	TN
Sarah	7	F		TN
Wolf, John	30	M	Farmer	TN
Mary Ann	27	F		NC
Malinda E.	4	F		TX
Louisa J.	2	F		TX
Thomas	1/12	M		TX
Andrew	44	M	Farmer	TN
Wells, Albert	38	M	Farmer	LA
Rebecca	18	F		TN
Martha Ann	13	F		MS
Bear Arnold	11	M		MS
William M.	6	M		TX
Floyd H.	4	M		TX
McGuffin, William W.	46	M	Farmer	SC
Nancy	39	F		MS
John W.	14	M		MS
Jensey E.	12	F		TN
Charles B.	10	M		IL
William S.	8	M		IL
James H.	5	M		MO
Joseph D.	2	M		MO
Kelly, James	44	M	Farmer	SC
Elizabeth	41	F		TN
Derinda P.	20	F		TN
Abner R.	18	M	Farmer	TN
Nancy C.	16	F		TN
Elijah A.	14	M		TN
Mary E.	12	F		TN
Martha E.	10	F		TX
James	5	M		TX
John	2	M		TX
Sarah	7/12	F		TX
Pierce, Nancy	42	F		TN
Riley W.	20	M	Farmer	AL
Elizabeth J.	16	F		AL
Nancy S. M.	14	F		AL
Merchant, William R.	20	M	Farmer	TN
Alexander, Christopher C.	39	M	Trader	TN
Margaret	37	F		NC
Armisa F.	12	F		TN
Rogers, Everett	80	M	Farmer	NC
Tinkle, J. P.	48	M	Carpenter	TN
Navina	29	F		AL
Learner	9	M		MS
Susan Jane	6	F		MS
Matilda S.	4	F		MS
Rebecca Ann	1	F		TX
Bell, Thomas W.	48	M	Farmer	TN
Susanna	42	F		VT
Benjamin R.	22	M		TN
Mary Jane	20	F		TN
Sarah C.	14	F		TN
Harriet C.	7	F		TN
James K. P.	4	M		TN
Thomas J. G.	2	M		TN
McKinley, Robert L.	30	M	Farmer	MS
Ailsey	20	F		TN
John N.	10	M		MS
Excellona	4	F		MS
Cass	2	M		TX
Enlow, William S.	23	M	Farmer	IN
Lucretia	19	F		TN
Mary J.	10/12	F		TX

TITUS COUNTY, TEXAS

Name	Age	Sex	Occupation	Birthplace
Moore, Thomas C.	32	M	Farmer	TN
M.	25	F		TN
M.	10	F		AL
E.	9	F		AL
James	4	M		AL
Smith, Jesse	47	M	Farmer	VA
Sarah	37	F		TN
Presley, William	17	M		MO
James	14	M		MO
Mary	12	F		MO
James	10	M		MO
John	8	M		MO
Louisa	6	F		MO
Smith, Nancy	3	F		MO
Jesse	1	M		TX
Russell, George	45	M	Farmer	TN
Salina	37	F		LA
Carolline	13	F		AR
William	12	M		AR
Nathania	9	F		AR
Carrol	5	M		AR
Baby	9/12	M		TX
Watson, John M.	36	M	Farmer	TN
Paralee	22	F		TN
Joseph	12	M		TX
Caroline	6	F		TX
Mary	10/12	F		TX
Cochrane, Joseph	19	M	Farmer	AL
George	14	M		AL

(continued)

Name	Age	Sex	Occupation	Birthplace
Cochrane, Rose	11	F		MS
Amanda	4	F		TX
Ward, Robinson	37	M	Farmer	TN
Susan	38	F		SC
Philip	14	M		AL
Sarah	13	F		AL
Frances	11	F		AL
John	9	M		AL
Stephen	7	M		AL
Nathan	5	M		TX
William	1	M		TX
Cook, William	33	M	Farmer	TN
Emily	33	F		TN
John	10	M		TN
William	9	M		TN
Frances	6	F		TN
Jefferson	4	M		TN
Sarah	3	F		TN
P. A.	1	F		TN
Clark, Joseph	31	M	Farmer	NC
Elizabeth	33	F		TN
James	6	M		TX
Joseph	4	M		TX
David	21	M	House Painter	NC
Smith, Isaac	26	M	Farmer	TN
Mary	27	F		AL
Charles	7	M		MO
Isaac	1	M		TX
A. D.	4/12	M		TX
Frank, Henry	42	M	Farmer	TN
Rebecca	34	F		TN
E. J.	14	F		AL
Eliza	8	F		AL
Nancy	6	F		AL
William	4	M		AL
Stephen	1	M		TX
Snodgrass, David	45	M	Farmer	VA
Emiline	38	F		TN
William	21	M	Farmer	AL
John	19	M	Farmer	AL
Mary	17	F		AL
Thomas	15	M		AL
George	14	M		AL
Ann	12	F		AL
Caroline	11	F		AL
Nancy	9	F		AL
Frances	7	F		AL
David	2	M		AL
Griffith, John M.	23	M	Farmer	NC
Rachel	17	F		TN
Margaret	11/12	F		TX
D'Spain, David	19	M	Farmer	AL
Hetty	10	F		TN
Griffith, Evan	57	M	Farmer	NC
Elizabeth	58	F		NC
Daniel	17	M	Farmer	TN
Amos	14	M		TN
Wardlow, James	43	M	Farmer	KY
Eliza	42	F		TN
James	13	M		TN
David	11	M		TX
Nancy	6	F		TX
Henderson, Hugh G.	53	M	Farmer	NC
Mary	45	F		TN
Michael	20	M	Farmer	AL
James	15	M	Farmer	AL
Johnson	12	M		MS
Mary	10	F		MS
Lydia	6	F		MS
Eliza	4	F		MS
Allread, Mrs.	24	F		AL
James	13	M		MS
(continued)				
Allread, Mary	10	F		MS
Emily	8	F		MS
James	3	M		TN
Biddle, Joseph	39	M	P.B. Clergyman	KY
Nancy	40	F		KY
Emily	20	F		KY
John	18	M	Farmer	KY
Sarah	18	F		KY
Isaac	17	M	Farmer	KY
James	15	M		KY
Thomas	12	M		KY
Joseph	9	M		TN
William	7	M		TN
Adaline	5	F		TN
Ann	3	F		TX
Mary	1	F		TX
Biddle, Isaac	74	M	Farmer	VA
Ann	65	F		NC
Isaac	21	M	Farmer	KY
Biddle, James G.	37	M	Farmer	KY
Mrs.	39	F		KY
Nancy	14	F		TN
John	12	M		KY
James	10	M		KY
Elam	9	M		KY
C. E.	5	F		TX
Isaac	3	M		TX
Walker, James T.	48	M	Carpenter	NC
Mary	36	F		NC
Sarah	12	F		TN
C. M.	11	M		TN
D. W.	11	M		TN
J. E.	8	M		TN
R. E.	7	F		TN
James	3	M		TX
Dove, James T.	40	M	Carpenter	TN
Amanda	14	F		AL
James	13	M		AL
John	10	M		AL
Paralee	9	F		AL
Lilly, Joseph D.	33	M	Farmer	TN
Sarah	22	F		GA
Mary	1	F		TX
Martha	1/12	F		TX
Lilly, Hugh B.	30	M	Farmer	TN
Bolivar	22	M	Farmer	TN
Mary	17	F		TN
Webster, William	50	M	Farmer	NC
Hannah	50	F		GA
Frances	21	F		AL
William	20	M	Farmer	TN
Amanda	19	F		TN
Alexander	17	M	Farmer	TN
Greenbury	15	M		MS
Arminda	12	F		MS
Emmet	10	M		MS
Donaldson, Elizabeth	53	F		VA
Emeline	23	F		TN
John	22	M	Farmer	TN
James	18	M	Farmer	TN
Marshal	17	M	Farmer	TN
Louisa	15	F		TN
Flinn, William F.	26	M	Farmer	MS
Sarah	24	F		TN
Charles	1	M		TX
Mays, Stephen	46	M	Farmer	NC
Rosana	32	F		NC
Emiline	13	F		TN
Joel	11	M		TN
Munroe	9	M		TN
Thomas	5	M		TN
Mary	3	F		TN
Baby	3/12	F		TX

TITUS COUNTY, TEXAS

Name	Age	Sex	Occupation	Birthplace
Conner, Johnathan	33	M	Farmer	NC
Letitia	30	F		VA
Judith	2	F		TN
Baby	5/12	F		TX
Ryan, Harris	28	M	Farmer	AL
Sarah	30	F		TN
Alex	8	M		AL
Andrew	7	M		AL
Martha	6	F		AL
Mary	4	F		AL
M. M.	2	F		AL
Doriss, Samuel	45	M	Farmer	TN
Linny	41	F		SC
William	18	M	Farmer	AL
James	16	M	Farmer	AL
Sarah	13	F		AL
Thomas	11	M		AL
Polina	8	F		AL
Nancy	6	F		AL
John	2	M		AL
Smith, Hiram	30	M	Farmer	SC
Nancy	26	F		AL
Jane	10	F		TN
Mary	6	F		TN
Carroll	4	M		TN
Ann	2	F		TN
Houston, James	30	M	Farmer	TN
Ann	25	F		TN
Mary	2	F		AR
Margaret	6/12	F		AR
Price, John W.	43	M	Farmer	KY
Mary	42	F		NC
Martha	17	F		TN
Elizabeth	15	F		TN
Henry	12	M		TN
Hayes	10	M		TN
Amanda	8	F		TN
Sarah	6	F		TN
James	5	M		TN
Charles	3	M		TX
George	1	M		TX
Hinson, Robert	37	M	Farmer	TN
Harriet	28	F		AL
Felix	13	M		AL
William	11	M		AL
Daniel	9	M		TX
Jeremiah	7	M		TX
John	4	M		TX
Tracy	1	F		TX
Johnson, George	25	M	Farmer	TN
Cynthia	21	F		AL
Thomas	6	M		TX
Melinda	3	F		TX
George	1	M		TX
Sam	26	M	Farmer	TN
Bush, James	17	M	Farmer	TN
Little, Robert	46	M	Farmer	TN
Susan	46	F		NC
Caroline	22	F		TN
Arline	21	F		TN
George	19	M	Farmer	TN
Louisa	17	F		TN
Lavina	15	F		TN
Mary	14	F		TN
Robert	12	M		TN
Paralee	10	F		TN
Zachariah	10	M		TN
Eliza	8	F		AR
Henry	7	M		AR
Sweeny, Susan	5	F		AR
Ed	3	M		AR
Frances	2	F		AR
Willis, William B.	45	M	Farmer (Hotel)	NC
Rebecca	43	F		TN

(continued)

Name	Age	Sex	Occupation	Birthplace
Willis, Margaret	17	F		TN
Lucinda	16	F		TN
Andrew	14	M		TN
Sarah	11	F		TN
Brison	9	M		AR
David	7	M		AR
Julia	5	F		AR
George	3	M		TX
Thompson, Benjamin	27	M	Black Smith	AL
Riley, William	33	M	Carpenter	NC
Powell, Frank	28	F	Carpenter	TN
Moore, Burell	36	M	Farmer	TN
Lucinda	30	F		AL
Eliza	12	F		AL
B. A.	11	F		AL
J. T.	9	M		MS
Sarah	6	F		TX
Nancy	4	F		TX
Richard	2	M		TX
Moore, Richard	28	M	Farmer	TN
Sarah	24	F		AL
William	7	M		TX
Burrell	5	M		TX
C. T.	2	M		TX
Hughes, Robert	32	M	Farmer	TN
Sarah	22	F		GA
Nancy	6	F		TX
Julia	1	F		TX
Rutherford, James	45	M	Physician	TN
Jane	47	F		KY
James	21	M	Farmer	TN
Zebediah	13	M		AR
Brooks, William	32	M	Merchant	NC
Matilda	20	F		AL
Marshal	2/12	M		TX
McNairy, Lewis	21	M	Clerk	TN
King, David	29	M	Saddler	IA
Emily	23	F		TN
Deborah	4	F		TX
Charles	2	M		TX
Philips, Burrell	27	M	Farmer	TN
Elizabeth	24	F		AL
Mary	3	F		TN
Jane	4/12	F		TX
Cowan, Thomas L.	38	M	School Teacher	GA
Catharine	30	F		TN
Senica	8	M		TX
Sweeny, L. W.	30	M	Saddler	TN
Bridges, James	30	M	Carpenter	KY
Eliza	26	F		TN
Martha	3	F		TN
Frances	6/12	F		TX
White, Eliza	12	F		AL
Caroline	10	F		AL
Cowan, Caroline	12	F		TX
Baily, James	23	M	Farmer	TN
Angeline	19	F		AL
Ann	4/12	F		TX
Holder, Presley	37	M	Farmer	VA
Mary	32	F		TN
John	13	M		AL
William	12	M		AL
Thomas	9	M		AL
Emily	6	F		AL
Robert	4	M		AL
Presly	1	M		TX
Hargus, Alexander	48	M	Farmer	SC
Mahala	40	F		TN
Margaret	16	F		AL
Catharine	8	F		TX
Thomas	4	M		TX
Riddle, T. M.	35	M	Farmer	TN

(continued)

TITUS COUNTY, TEXAS

Name	Age	Sex	Occupation	Birthplace
Riddle, Mrs.	32	F		TN
Polina	18	F		TN
Mary	8	F		TX
Conner, Orange	57	M	Farmer	NC
Judith	55	F		SC
Susana	21	F		AL
Cicero	20	M	Clerk	TN
William	18	M	Farmer	TN
Munroe	16	M	Farmer	TN
Mary	12	F		TN
Norwood, J. P.	35	M	Farmer	TN
Pamelia	36	F		TN
Mary	14	F		AL
Emily	12	F		AL
Henry	9	M		AL
Martha	5	F		AL
Jane	3	F		AL
Kate, Mary	35	F		TN
Mary	15	F		TN
Louisa	12	F		TN
Elizabeth	10	F		TN
John	9	M		TN
Martha	1	F		MS
Titsworth, C. G.	39	M	Christian Clergy	KY
Louisa	37	F		KY
Levi	19	M	Farmer	TN
Peyton	15	M	Farmer	TN
John	13	M		TN
Sarah	11	F		AR
Lemuel	9	M		AR
Minerva	4	F		AR
Ragland, James T.	32	M	Farmer	TN
Dorah	28	F		TN
Eliza	4	F		TX
Alva	2	F		TX
Gist, Joseph	30	M	Farmer	TN
Dorcas	28	F		TN
Jane	9	F		AL
Martha	7	F		TX
William	5	M		TX
Robert	3	M		TX
Emily	4	F		TX
Darwin, J. C.	34	M	Farmer	TN
Lucinda	24	F		AL
Lewis	7	M		TX
Nancy	5	F		TX
Lucinda	2	F		TX
Linam, Thomas	36	M	Farmer	SC
Sarah	30	F		TN
William	11	M		TN
John	9	M		AR
Levi	5	M		AR
Andrew	3	M		TX
Sarah	1	F		TX
Hamilton, Elizabeth	60	F		VA
James	40	M	Farmer	VA
Wiley	36	M	Farmer	VA
Bennet	30	M	Farmer	TN
Ann	17	F		AL
Darwin, Sarah	11	F		AL
Ferguson, Clark C.	9	M		TX
Womack, William	20	M	Farmer	AL
Coffee, William S.	53	M	Farmer	KY
Elizabeth	45	F		KY
Mary	23	F		AL
Eliza	21	F		AL
Emiline	18	F		AL
Catharine	16	F		AL
Henrietta	12	F		AL
Margaret	6	F		TX
John	3	M		TX
McCain, William	31	M	Farmer	TN
Ragland, Burrell	33	M	Farmer	TN
Matilda	32	F		TN
Ann	9	F		AL
Calvin	7	M		TX
Arthur	4	M		TX
James	2	M		TX
Jopling, Benjamin	55	M	Farmer	VA
Melinda	35	F		TN
John	27	M	Farmer	VA
William	19	M	Farmer	AL
George	16	M	Farmer	AL
Lucinda	14	F		AL
Lewis	4	M		AL
Jane	1	F		TX
Massey, John	30	M	Farmer	TN
Emily	28	F		NC
Orrell, Eliza	8	F		IL
Boren, J. R.	29	M	Laborer	KY
Holbrook, William	40	M	Farmer	NC
Mary	33	F		NC
Columbus	15	M	Farmer	TN
Elizabeth	12	F		TN
Jane	10	F		TN
Thomas	8	M		MS
Cordelia	6	F		TN
Fredonia	1	F		TX
Green, Rolin	24	M	Farmer	VA
Sarah	16	F		TN
St. Clair, Paschal	49	M	Farmer	VA
Jane	36	F		TN
Tilman	15	M		AL
Caleb	9	M		AL
William	7	M		TX
James	5	M		TX
Winfield S.	2	M		TX
Burell	1	M		TX
Williams, Polly	40	F		TN
John	19	M	Farmer	TN
Hayes, William	30	M	Farmer	NC
Emiline	18	F		AL
Margaret	9	F		TN
James K.	5	M		TN
Milly	3	F		TX
George	6/12	M		TX
Butler, John P.	30	M	Farmer	NC
Judith	25	F		NC
Solomon	6	M		TN
Emily	5	F		TN
Margaret	2	F		TX
Flippin, Henderson	24	M	Black Smith	TN
Mary	19	F		IA
Flippin, Allan	50	M	Black Smith	KY
Rosanna	48	F		KY
Thomas	20	M	Farmer	TN
Brittey Ann	16	F		TN
James	14	M		TN
Mary	12	F		AR
Elizabeth	9	F		AR
Rhoda	7	F		AR
Jenkins, James	32	M	Farmer	KY
Laura	23	F		TN
William	1	M		TX
Jenkins, Benjamin	28	M	Farmer	TN
Ann	18	F		TN
Allan	1	M		TX
Beaver, Thomas	42	M	Farmer	TN
Mrs.	40	F		KY
Benjamin	21	M	Farmer	TN
Evan	19	M	Farmer	TN
Nancy	17	F		TN
William	15	M	Farmer	TN
Sarah	12	F		TN
Mary	10	F		TN
Lucinda	8	F		AR

(continued)

TITUS COUNTY, TEXAS

Name	Age	Sex	Occupation	Birthplace
Beaver, Frances	7	F		AR
Susan	5	F		AR
Hamilton, Robert	51	M	Farmer	SC
Mrs.	50	F		SC
Mary	27	F		SC
Robert	20	M	Farmer	GA
Thomas	6	M		AL
Stinnett, David	26	M	Farmer	TN
Stinnett, Sam	27	M	Farmer	TN
Mrs.	27	F		TN
James	7	M		TN
Martha	7	F		TN
Rufus	5	M		TN
Sarah	1	F		TX
Lilly, William	25	M	Farmer	TN
Mrs.	19	F		GA
M. L.	1	F		TX
Cherry, Nancy	40	F		TN
J. P.	20	M	Farmer	TN
Margaret	18	F		TN
Jackson	14	M		TN
Adaline	12	F		TN
Hugh	9	M		TN
Washington	4	M		TX
Galbreth, J. B.	35	M	Physician	VA
Mrs.	37	F		TN
Ursery, Franklin	20	M	None	TN
Calvin	16	M	Farmer	MS
Theodore	14	M		LA
Anthony	7	M		LA
Adaline	1	F		LA
Harrison, Sam	24	M	Farmer	TN
Emily	24	F		TN
Farmer, Mr.	5	M		AL
A. L.	3	F		AL
Hawkins, James	20	M	Farmer	TN
Mary	17	F		NC
Brison, Elam	40	M	Farmer	NC
Mrs.	45	F		TN
John	13	M		TN
Henry	10	M		TN
Mary	8	F		TN
Martha	8	F		TN
Thomas	4	M		TN
Mary	2	F		TN
Hale, Sam	37	M	Farmer	TN
Mrs.	36	F		TN
William	12	M		TN
John	9	M		TN
Susan	7	F		TN
Robert	1	M		TN
Martin, John	77	M	Farmer	TN
Nancy	62	F		VA
C. T.	34	M	Farmer	TN
Jane	24	F		AL
A. J.	15	F		TN
Akeman, Nancy	23	F		AL
Johnston, William	30	M	Farmer	TN
Mrs.	25	F		AL
Sarah	4	F		TX
Georgia	3	F		TX
Farris, Y(Z). C.	32	M	Farmer	TN
Mrs.	30	F		KY
William	8	M		TX
Lucy	4	F		TX
George	1	M		TX
Davis, Isham	31	M	Farmer	TN
Julia	21	F		AL
John	4	M		TX
Dotia	2	F		TX

(continued)

Name	Age	Sex	Occupation	Birthplace
Trammell, M. C.	23	M	Laborer	LA
Hannah, Lewis	20	M	Laborer	LA
Johnson, William	42	M	Farmer	TN
Sarah	26	F		LA
Thomas	25	M	Farmer	IL
William	23	M	Farmer	LA
Milton	20	M	Farmer	LA
Abner	18	M	Farmer	LA
Louisa	16	F		LA
Henry	13	M		LA
Hulen, Nancy	4	F		LA
D. A.	3	F		LA
Johnson, Mary	5/12	F		LA
Finley, William	36	M	Farmer	AL
Mrs.	26	F		TN
Mary	3	F		TX
Alva	4	F		TX
Bates, Sarah	52	F		TN
Caroline	27	F		TN
Catharine	18	F		TN
Harriet	13	F		TN
Martin	11	M		TN
Eliza	9	F		TX
William	4	M		TX
Dove, John	35	M	Farmer	TN
Mrs.	46	F		NC
Theophilus	19	M	Farmer	TN
Mary	16	F		TN
H. A.	14	F		TN
L. C.	11	F		TN
A. J.	7	M		TN
E. E.	8/12	F		TX
Dove, Alden	25	M		TN
D.	29	F		TN
Lilly, Harris	36	M	Farmer	TN
Jane	20	F		AL
John	7	M		TX
Martha	1	F		TX
Cheatham, Edward	36	M	Farmer	TN
Mrs.	24	F		GA
George	3	M		TX
Thomas	1	M		TX
Hughes, Martha	74	F		SC
Scott, Fanny	16	F		AL
Jane	9	F		AL
Thomas	6	M		TX
John	6	M		TX
Beall, W. P.	28	M	Physician	KY
Myrtilla	24	F		TN
Dixon, John B.	56	M	Farmer	NC
Mrs.	48	F		NC
McKisick, A. C.	21	F		TN
William	13	M		TN
Dixon, John	17	M		AR
Albert	9	M		AR
Powel	7	M		AR
Nichols, A.	25	M	Farmer	GA
Adaline	23	F		TN
L. H.	6	M		AR
M. H.	4	M		AR
S. E.	1	F		TX
Clayton, Ewing	42	M	Farmer	TN
Mrs.	39	F		TN
Sarah	15	F		AL
William	13	M		AL
Louisa	13	F		AL
John	9	M		AL
Mary	7	F		AL
S. S.	5	M		TX
M. A.	3	F		TX
A. P.	1	F		TX
E.	1/12	M		TX
Truitt, Wingate	49	M	Farmer	MD

(continued)

TITUS COUNTY, TEXAS

Name	Age	Sex	Occupation	Birthplace
Truitt, Mrs.	46	F		TN
William	21	M	Farmer	TN
E.	20	M	Farmer	TN
Sarah	17	F		TN
Edward	14	M		TN
M. Martha	13	F		AL
James	10	M		AL
Nancy	7	F		TX
Wingate	1	M		TX
Holbrook, Robert J.	42	M	Merchant	NC
Mary	32	F		TN
Georgiana	11	F		MS
Lavenia	9	F		TX
Mary	5	F		TX
Robert	3	M		TX
Nancy	8/12	F		TX
Cooper, William	23	M	Laborer	TN
Orrell, Cornelius	12	M		IL
Cherry, Nancy	38	F		TN
John	10	M		TX
Mary	8	F		TX
James	6	M		TX
Nancy	4	F		TX
Coffman, Barton	25	M	Farmer	TN
Frankly	23	F		NC
Mary	4	F		TN
M. Ann	2	F		TX
Cherry, William	23	M	Farmer	GA
Mrs.	20	F		TN
John	3/12	M		TX
Caudle, Melinda	50	F		TN
William	19	M	None	TN
George	17	M	None	TN
Caroline	15	F		TN
Henry	13	M		TN
M. B.	11	M		TN
Sarah	10	F		TN
Smith, James	25	M	Farmer	TN
Mrs.	24	F		AR
William	6	M		TX
B. F.	4	M		TX
Mary	2	F		TX
Boase, J. W.	27	M	Farmer	AL
Martha	29	F		TN
Rosa	8	F		TN
Mary	6	F		TN
Frank	3	M		TN
Rutherford, Nancy	71	F		NC
John	35	M	Farmer	TN
Wright, William C.	29	M	Physician	SC
Mary	21	F		TN
Griffith	1	M		TN
Hall, William A.	23	M	Farmer	KY
Nancy E.	23	F		TN
Sullens, Jesse	42	M	Farmer	TN
Mary	42	F		TN
Elizabeth	16	F		AR
Zachariah	13	M		IL
Rutha	11	F		TX
Nancy	9	F		TX
William	7	M		TX
Martha	5	F		TX
Mary	3	F		TX
Martin, Osborne	32	M	Farmer	TN
Mary	29	F		AL
John	6	M		AL
A. J.	4	F		TX
Mary	2	F		TX
Lackay, William	35	M	Farmer	SC
Jane	40	F		TN
Moore, F. A.	7	F		TN

Name	Age	Sex	Occupation	Birthplace
Haynes, G. W. L.	42	M	Farmer	VA
Sarah	34	F		GA
F. H.	13	M		TN
Cleopatra	10	F		TN
Martha	6	F		TN
Andrew	3	M		TX
James	1	M		TX
Rogers, Ransom	26	M	Farmer	NC
Jane	24	F		NC
John	4	M		TN
J. K.	1	M		TX
Rogers, Benjamin	22	M	Farmer	NC
Lydia	21	F		TN
Elizabeth	3	F		TN
Nancy	4/12	F		TX
Reed, Isaac	41	M	Farmer	GA
Charity	47	F		TN
Smith, Charity	15	F		LA
Napoleon	11	M		LA
Precious	8	F		TX
Spencer, James	45	M	Farmer	NC
Mrs.	30	F		NC
John	14	M		TN
Willis	12	M		TN
Celia	11	F		TN
Eliza	8	M		TN
James	6	M		TN
Elizabeth	5	F		TN
Nancy	3	F		TN
Heath, William	53	M	Farmer	SC
Abigail	48	F		NC
James	26	M	Farmer	TN
Castleman, Andrew	16	M	Farmer	TX
Spencer, E.	38	F		NC
Cantrell, Haris	24	M	Farmer	TN
Young, David	43	M		KY
Eliza	37	F		TN
Nancy	15	F		KY
Jane	13	F		KY
William	10	M		MO
James	7	M		MO
Sarah	5	F		TX
Mary	3	F		TX
John	1	M		TX
Nix, John	21	M	Farmer	KY
King, Carter B.	36	M		TN
Caroline	33	F		TN
Mary	12	F		GA
Harriet	9	F		TN
J. H.	7	M		TX
William	2	M		TX
Pryor, Seth	50	M	Farmer	NC
Dorcas	39	F		KY
Eliza	17	F		TN
George	15	M		TN
James	14	M		TN
Polly	12	F		MO
Sally	9	F		MO
Harvy	7	M		TN
F. M.	5	M		TN
C. C.	1/12	M		TX
Shoate, John	25	M	Farmer	TN
Amelia	24	F		TN
Martha	5	F		TN
Sina	2	F		TX
Andrew	4/12	M		TX
Nevill, Alex.	45	M	Farmer	KY
Elizabeth	35	F		TN
Thomas	17	M	Farmer	TN
Napoleon	15	M	Farmer	TN
Margaret	12	F		TN
Mary	11	F		TN
Andrew	9	M		TN
Martha	7	F		TX
William	5	M		TX

(continued)

Name	Age	Sex	Occupation	Birthplace
Nevill, Patience	3	F		TX
Julia	1	F		TX
Nevill, Talefario	48	M	Farmer	KY
Sina	38	F		TN
James	15	M	Farmer	AL
Mary	12	F		AL
Barker	10	M		AL
Helen	9	F		AL
William	5	M		TX
Nevill, Thomas	34	M	Farmer	KY
Mrs.	34	F		TN
Talefario	10	M		AL
William	8	M		AL
Joseph	5	M		TX
Martha	3	F		TX
Mary	9/12	F		TX
Rowland, Joseph	28	M	Farmer	TN
Polly	28	F		TN
James	4	M		TN
Mary	1	F		TX
Dixon, Robert W.	34	M	Lawyer	VA
F. A. F.	22	F		TN
Sarah	1	F		TX
Hays, James	25	M	Laborer	TN
Elizabeth	30	F		TN
William	12	M		TN
Jesse	8	M		KY
Amanda	5	F		MS
Nancy	2	F		TX
Husky, Silas	43	M	Merchant	TN
Elizabeth	23	F		MO
Lewis	13	M		MO
Melissa	2	F		TX
Louisa	7/12	F		TX
Nash, Joseph	23	M	Laborer	MO
Nancy	17	F		MO
Beck, Henry H.	26	M	Physician	TN
Mary	18	F		IL
Gregg, Sam	40	M	Farmer	IL
Cinderilla	30	F		TN
John	10	M		TX
William	10	M		TX
Mary	7	F		TX
Elizabeth	5	F		TX
Margaret	3	F		TX
Harman	1/12	M		TX
Proctor, William	57	M	Farmer	NC
Sarah	37	F		KY
W. R.	10	M		AL
F. C.	12	F		AL
D. N.	4	M		TN
E. A.	2	F		TN
Saylors, N.	28	M	Farmer	TN
Nancy	21	F		TN
John	2	M		TN
James, Isaac	24	M	Clerking	TN
Rebecca	14	F		TX
Kinsey, Peter	33	M	Merchant	TN
Louisa	18	F		MO
John	8	M		AR
Martha	6	F		AR
Ardell	1	F		TX
Riddle, Elam	45	M	Farmer	TN
Matilda	41	F		NC
William	22	M	Farmer	KY
Eliza	14	F		TN
John	17	M	Farmer	KY
Martha	12	F		TN
Charlotte	10	F		KY
Jesse	8	M		KY
David	5	M		KY

Name	Age	Sex	Occupation	Birthplace
Binnion, Isaac	50	M	Farmer	KY
Joseph	19	M	Farmer	TN
Sarah	15	F		MS
Caroline	13	F		MO
Evins, Henry	29	M	Farmer	KY
L. J.	24	F		TN
P. E.	2	F		TX
John	6/12	M		TX
Taylor, Mr. L.	19	M	Farmer	TN
Orrell, Elizabeth	15	F		VA
Lancaster, John	26	M	Farmer	TN
P. M.	17	F		GA
Martha	3/12	F		TX
Lancaster, N.	38	M	Farmer	TN
Mary	33	F		TN
William	15	M		TN
Ulyssus	11	M		TN
Josiah	9	M		TN
Martha	5	F		TN
J. W.	3	M		TN
Jones, Henry W.	32	M	Farmer	KY
Patience	60	F		SC
M. E.	11	M		TN
D. W.	9	M		TX
Sarah	5	F		TX
Henry	2	M		TX
Easley, Lavinia	25	F		MS
Pace, Dempsy	35	M	Farmer	TN
Mrs.	24	F		AR
Leann	7	F		AR
David	3	M		TX
Gray, B. W.	25	M	Lawyer	TN
Rebecca	19	F		TN
Mary	3/12	F		TX
Evins, Edward	31	M	Farmer	KY
Waggoner, Francis	26	M	Farmer	TN
Overton, R.	37	M	Farmer	NC
Henry	21	F		AL
John	16	M	Farmer	TN
Mary	5	F		TX
Evins, Sarah A.	25	F		TN
Smith, Mary	10	F		MO
Brooks, Z.	40	M	Farmer	TN
Sarah	38	F		SC
J. A.	16	M	Farmer	AL
Jesse	13	M		AL
A. W.	10	M		AL
C. C.	8	M		AL
M. J.	6	F		TX
Cook, J. C.	28	M	Farmer	AL
Harriet	28	F		TN
Mary	14	F		MS
Rebecca	12	F		MS
Daniel	7	M		MS
Emily	5	F		MS
Sarah	1	F		MS
Jones, Martin G.	27	M	Farmer	TN
Elizabeth	22	F		MO
Missouri	1	F		TX
Copeland, Solomon	21	M	Farmer	TN
White, J. R.	24	M	Farmer	GA
Bouge, Johnathan	32	M	Farmer	TN
Frances	30	F		GA
Marion	7	M		LA
Sarah	3	F		AR
Jason	2	M		TX
Brooks, J. V.	3	M		TX
McNiece, Mrs.	50	F		GA
Fairchild, Jesse	53	M	Farmer	SC
McNiece, Nancy	18	F		LA
Amanda	14	F		TN

(continued)

TITUS COUNTY, TEXAS

Name	Age	Sex	Occupation	Birthplace
McNiece, Susan	12	F		LA
James	10	M		LA
Stewart, Nancy	47	F		TN
E. J.	16	F		AL
Thomas	14	M		AL
William	12	M		TX
Samuel	10	M		TX
John	8	M		TX
Phoebe	5	F		TX
Peacock, William	31	M	Farmer	NC
Mrs.	28	F		TN
John	4	M		TX
Caroline	3	F		TX
Colier, A.	21	M	Farmer	TN
Mrs.	22	F		TN
J. W. C.	2	M		TN
George	6/12	M		TN
Colier, H.	57	M	Farmer	VA
Mrs.	57	F		TN
H. C.	24	M	None	TN
Gray, James N.	39	M	Farmer	TN
Mrs.	21	F		TN
McCain, Robert	59	M	Farmer	TN
Mrs.	54	F		TN
Nancy	29	F		TN
Martha	21	F		TN
Isaac	22	M	Farmer	TN
L. Mc.	19	F		KY
Lucinda	17	F		KY
Robert	15	M		KY
William	12	M		MS
Bridges, James	4	M		MS
Woods, Mary	2	F		AR
Bennion, Peyton	55	M	Farmer	VA
Lucilla	56	F		VA
James	22	M		TN
Eveline	19	F		TN
Morris, Hiram	25	M	Farmer	TN
Ellender	18	F		TN
John	2	M		TN
Mitchell, Mary	28	F		TN
John	12	M		TN
Louisa	10	F		TN
Rosilla	9	F		TN
Mary	7	F		TN
Adaline	5	F		TN
Henry	4	M		TN
Hiram	1	M		TN
Porter, Benjamin	33	M	Farmer	TN
Rebecca	32	F		AL
William	12	M		AL
Reese	11	M		AL
Charles	9	M		AL
George	8	M		AL
Nancy	7	F		TX
Benjamin	6	M		TX
Frances	4	F		TX
James	2/12	M		TX
Saylors, John	26	M	Farmer	TN
Melinda	23	F		TN
Francis	5	M		TN
Sally	2	F		TN
Porter, Samuel	30	M	Farmer	TN
Sarah	28	F		AL
Mary	7	F		AL
Parmer, James	9	M		LA
Thomas	7	M		LA
Melvina	5	F		LA
Lettitia	3	F		LA
Charles	1	M		LA
Richard	11/12	M		LA

Name	Age	Sex	Occupation	Birthplace
Clifton, George	27	M	Farmer	TN
Mary	23	F		TN
William	2	M		TX
Mary	29	F		TN
Bennion, Martin	39	M	Farmer	TN
Elizabeth	39	F		VA
James	13	M		TN
Mary	11	F		TN
William	9	M		TX
Thomas	7	M		TX
Milton	5	M		TX
Munroe	3	M		TX
Martin	1	M		TX
Stewart, Cynthia	46	F		KY
John	24	M	Farmer	AL
Hugh	19	M	Farmer	TN
Margaret	18	F		TN
Richard	15	M		TN
Susan	13	F		TN
Tennessee	9	F		TN
Martin, M. C.	49	M	Black Smith	NC
Margaret	26	F		TN
Ferguson, Caroline	10	F		AL
Mary	6	F		TX
Martin, Amanda	2	F		TX
Bennion, John	40	M	Farmer	TN
Minerva	29	F		AL
Robert	9	M		MO
Samuel	6	M		TX
Isabella	1	F		TX
Burns, Thomas L.	38	M	Merchant	TN
Mary	32	F		KY
Sylvanus	14	M		MS
Amanda	8	F		TX
John	5	M		TX
Mary	1	F		TX
Bickerstaff, John M.	35	M	Farmer	TN
Mary	77	F		MD
Marshal, Parmelia	47	F		NC
Mary	16	F		TN
Martha	14	F		TN
Amanda	13	F		TN
Nancy	11	F		TN
Jasper	10	M		MS
Caroline	8	F		AR
Marion	5	M		AR
Owens, Elizabeth	85	F		NC
Hickey, Isaac	31	M	Farmer	TN
Melinda	27	F		TN
John	10	M		MS
Sarah	8	F		AR
West	6	M		AR
Louisa	5	F		AR
William	4	M		TX
Mary	2	F		TX
Isaac	3/12	M		TX
Rosh, N. L.	43	M	Farmer	TN
Elizabeth	23	F		TN
Amanda	4	F		AR
John	2	M		TX
Hood, Mary	83	F		IRE
Talbott, A. G.	43	M	Farmer	TN
Tempe	29	F		TN
Romulus	9	M		TN
William	7	M		TN
Sarah	6	F		TN
Kesiah	4	F		TN
Reuben	2	M		TX
Ore, John H.	28	,	Methodist Clergy	TN
Hodges, Albert	16	M	Farmer	TN
Hodges, James	36	M	Farmer	TN
Margaret	32	F		TN
Overton	11	M		TN
William	9	M		TN

(continued)

TITUS COUNTY, TEXAS

Name	Age	Sex	Occupation	Birthplace
Hodges, Caloway	7	M		TN
George	4	M		TN
Mary	2	F		TN
Hodge, Jeremiah	40	M	Farmer	TN
Mary	32	F		NC
Elizabeth	12	F		TN
Lettia	6	F		TN
Malissa	2	F		TN
Graham, John D.	38	M	Farmer	TN
Mary	40	F		TN
William	7	M		TN
Barsheba	11	F		TN
Amanda	5	F		TX
Anzonetta	3	F		TX
James	1	M		TX
Johnson, Thomas	30	M	Farmer	NC
Lucy	31	F		NC
George	10	M		TN
Charles	7	M		TN
Lavonia	5	F		TN
William	3	M		TN
Burton, Elisha	44	M	Farmer	SC
Nancy	34	F		TN
Armstead	13	M		TX
Mary	11	F		TX
Lawsannet	9	M		TX
Nancy	7	F		TX
Sarah	1	F		TX
Burk, Lindzey	54	M	Farmer	VA
Nancy	45	F		TN
Nancy	14	F		MO
Temperance	12	F		MO
Benjamin	9	M		MO
Martha	7	F		MO
Draper, Charles	25	M	Farmer	TN
Mary	25	F		TN
Virginia	2	F		TN
John	1/12	M		TX
James	7	M		TN
More, David	40	M	Farmer	KY
Eliza	35	F		TN
Rebecca	17	F		IL
John	16	M	Farmer	IL
Drury	13	M		MO
Minerva	11	F		MO
Melissa	8	F		MO
Martha	6	F		TX
Sidney	4	M		TX
Sarah	1	F		TX
Harper, Enos	55	M	Farmer	GA
Mary	46	F		TN
John	21	M	Farmer	TN
Mary	18	F		TN
Martha	16	F		TN
Thomas	14	M		TN
Elizabeth	13	F		TN
Rebecca	10	F		TN
Nancy	6	F		MO
Margaret	1	F		TX
More, Stanford	53	M	Farmer	NC
Minerva	43	F		TN
Alston	20	M	Farmer	IL
Anne	18	F		IL
McCoy	15	M		IL
Haywood	12	M		IL
Narcissa	10	F		MO
Alexander	6	M		AR
Eliza	1	F		TX
Hughes, William	60	M	Farmer	NC
Ellendor	64	F		GA
Calvin	22	M	Farmer	TN
Blake	20	M	Farmer	TN
Silas	18	M	Farmer	TN

(continued)

Name	Age	Sex	Occupation	Birthplace
Hughes, Harman	16	M		TN
Mary	14	F		MS
Elizabeth	12	F		MS
Harriet	10	F		MS
Johnson, William	35	M	Farmer	VA
Caroline	25	F		TN
Sarah	1	F		TX
Charlotte	7/12	F		TX
Campbell, William	68	M	Farmer	TN
Martha	51	F		VA
Franklin, Edward	19	M		AL
Campbell, Charles	13	M		AL
Martha	9	F		TX
Mary	7	F		TX
Franklin, William	26	M	Farmer	VA
Davis, Jacob	40	M	Farmer	NC
Elizabeth	35	F		GA
Jesse	22	M	Farmer	TN
Gabriel	14	M		MO
James	11	M		MO
Morton, Cynthia	53	F		TN
Rufus	28	M	Farmer	TX
Louisa	20	F		TX
Rosanna	18	F		TX
John	15	M		TX
Wilson, Thomas R.	39	M	Surveyor	MO
Baker, William C.	28	M	Farmer	TN
Sarah	29	F		AR
Wilber	6	M		TX
Mary	1	F		TX
Bullard, Coleman	33	M	Farmer	TN
Fanny	24	F		KY
Gordon, Joseph	36	M	Farmer	TN
Elizabeth	22	F		GA
Charles	3	M		TX
Campbell, Crockett	33	M	Farmer	TN
Elizabeth	21	F		AR
Sarah	4	F		TX
Robert	3	M		TX
Reddin	2	M		TX
William	3/12	M		TX
Gregg, Jacob	36	M	Farmer	IL
Margaret	32	F		TN
Isaiah	7	M		TX
Mary	6	F		TX
Catharine	4	F		TX
Celia	2	F		TX
Harman, Nat	18	M	Farmer	TN
Dobbs, J. W.	41	M	Toll Bridge Keeper	SC
Sarah	47	F		SC
William	17	M	None	TN
Sarah	15	F		TN
Ann	13	F		TN
Senora	10	F		TX
Paralee	8	F		TX
Harrison, John	66	M	Farmer	NC
Nancy	44	F		KY
Paralee	15	F		TN
Minerva	10	F		MO
Charles	8	M		MO
Franklin	6	M		TX
James	4	M		TX
Reuben	1	M		TX
Wheeler, Ambrose	28	M	Farmer	TN
Martha	29	F		TN
Nancy	9	F		MO
Mary	11	F		TN
John	7	M		MO
Martha	5	F		TX
William	3	M		TX
Sirena	8/12	F		TX
Yates, George	31	M	Stock Raiser	TN

(continued)

TITUS COUNTY, TEXAS

Name	Age	Sex	Occupation	Birthplace
Yates, Kesiah	31	F		KY
William	9	M		AR
John	7	M		TX
Mary	4	F		TX
George	1	M		TX
Ward, Andrew	62	M		NC
James	27	F		TN
Temperance	18	F		TN
John	15	M		TN
Parthena	12	F		TN
Thomas	11	M		TN
Harmon, Joseph	48	M	P.B. Clergyman	NC
Mary	32	F		TN
Lydia	11	F		TN
Esperan	7	F		TX
Caudle, Mary	69	F		NC
Caudle, John W.	21	M	Farmer	TN
Margaret	17	F		TN
James	5/12	M		TX
Cowan, James	34	M	Farmer	TN
Louisa	31	F		TN
John	7	M		AL
Nancy	6	F		AL
James	4	M		TX
Wade	1	M		TX
Weir, John	31	M	Black Smith	MO
Jane	29	F		TN
William	3	M		TX
Laura	1	F		TX
Bickerstaff, Seborn	38	M	Carpenter	GA
Frances	37	F		TN
James	15	M		AL
Amanda	13	F		MS
Benjamin	11	M		MS
Miller, Lodabar	38	M	Farmer	TN
Martha	23	F		NC
William	8/12	M		TX
Gray, William	32	M	Merchant	TN
Leah	20	F		AL
Ephraim	10	M		TN
Hannah	4	F		TX
Mary	4	F		TX
O'Neal, Wilson	33	M	Stock Raiser	TN
Eveline	27	F		TN
Louisa	11	F		MS
Mary	9	F		MS
Amanda	7	F		MS
Sarah	5	F		MS
John	2	M		TX
Sheek, Joseph	23	M	Farmer	NC
Sarah	20	F		TN
Martha	1/12	F		TX
Keith, William	37	M	Farmer	TN
Nancy	37	F		TN
Mary	13	F		TN
Sarah	11	F		TN
William	10	M		MS
Emily	8	F		MS
Nicodemus	6	M		MS
Johnathan	4	M		TX
Elizabeth	2	F		TX
Reed, Joseph	58	M	Farmer	SC
Mary	48	F		NC
David	14	M		TN
Caroline	13	F		TX
Benjamin	12	M		TX
Pamelia	7	F		TX
Ealy, Henry	29	M	Farmer	VA
Sarah	33	F		VA
David	11	M		TN
(continued)				
Ealy, Thomas	9	M		AR
Melinda	7	F		AR
Rachel	3	F		TX
O'Neal, George W.	44	M	Farmer	TN
Mary	42	F		TN
Robert	19	M	Farmer	TN
Cornelius	17	M	Farmer	TN
Hardin	15	M	Farmer	TN
Sarah	13	F		TN
Margaret	11	F		TN
Nancy	9	F		TN
Georgge	6	M		TN
John	3	M		TX
James	3	M		TX
Grant, James	30	M	Farmer	TN
Ezzyriah	22	F		AL
Joseph	2	M		TX
Gregg, Milton	31	M	None	AR
Sarah	26	F		TN
Koonce, Mary	8	F		TN
Hester	6	F		TN
Margaret	4	F		TN
Arrington, Joel	33	M	Farmer	NC
Sarah	20	F		TN
William	7	M		TX
James	5	M		TX
Robert	4	M		TX
Nancy	3	F		TX
Jane	8/12	F		TX
Caudle, Mark	44	M	Farmer	NC
Rebecca	46	F		NC
James	20	M	Farmer	TN
Louisa	18	F		TN
Mary	16	F		TN
William	14	M		KY
Martha	12	F		KY
Elizabeth	10	F		KY
Joseph	8	M		TN
Newton	7	M		TX
Matilda	5	F		TX
Richard	3	M		TX
George	2	M		TX
Lofton, Charles	50	M	Ostler	KY
Burns, Wiley	37	M	Farmer	TN
Indiana	20	F		TN
Jackson, James W.	25	M	Physician	AL
Wise, George J.	22	M	Student	MS
Patterson, William	20	M	Student	TN
Hightower, John	39	M	Farmer	SC
Nancy	28	F		TN
James	16	M		TN
Mary	13	F		TN
Emiline	12	F		TN
John	4	M		TX
Gabriel	2	M		TX
Jane	9/12	F		TX
Campbell, B. M.	23	M	Carpenter	AL
Godwin, H. W.	27	M	Laborer	KY
Flemming, Thomas	22	M	Farmer	TN
Celia	18	F		PA
Amanda	6/12	F		TX
Keith, William S.	36	M	Farmer	TN
Nancy	34	F		TN
Caroline	15	F		AR
Elizabeth	13	F		AR
Mahala	11	F		TX
George	9	M		TX
David	5	M		TX
Charles	3	M		TX
Amanda	3/12	F		TX
Hickey, W. W.	28	M	Farmer	TN
Elizabeth	20	F		AR
Christan	3	F		TX
John	5/12	M		TX

Name	Age	Sex	Occupation	Birthplace
Wilson, William	66	M	Farmer	NC
Hester	47	F		NC
Martha	15	F		TN
Garret, James	25	M	Farmer	SC
Pope, Thomas	56	M	Farmer	NC
Cynthia	48	F		NC
Thomas	18	M	Farmer	TN
Peter	16	M	Farmer	TN
Jane	14	F		TN
James	11	M		TN
Ulyssus	7	M		TX
Cynthia	6	F		TX
Vica	6	F		TX
John	4	M		TX
Ash, John L.	22	M	Farmer	LA
Angeline	20	F		TN
Miller, Martin	28	M	Farmer	TN
Rebecca	30	F		AL
Lodabar	5	M		TX
Charles	2	M		TX
Denny, James	53	M	Farmer	TN
Lavina	49	F		TN
George	24	M	Farmer	TN
James	21	M		TN
Amanda	17	F		MO
Adelia	16	F		MO
Margaret	12	F		MO
Susan	10	F		MO
Whitesides, John	32	M		IL
Elizabeth	28	F		TN
William	8	M		IL
Margaret	4	F		IL
Ellen	2	F		IL
Rice, Elias	40	M		TN
Mary	26	F		IL
John	9	M		MO
Eli	8	M		MO
Sarah	5	F		IL
Martha	2	F		TX
Elizabeth	1	F		TX
Ringo, A.	24	M	Farmer	MO
Sarah	19	F		TN
Bishop, Luna	54	M	Farmer	TN
Elizabeth	38	F		AL
Oritha	18	F		AL
Jane	3	F		AR
East, William	39	M	Farmer	TN
Burnetta	31	F		IL
Samuel	8	M		IL
Emily	6	F		IL
Priscilla	5	F		TX
Francis	3	M		TX
Kelly, Hugh	26	M	Farmer	AL
Morrison, Andrew	48	M	Farmer	SC
Elizabeth	49	F		NC
James	21	M	Farmer	TN
William	19	M	Farmer	TN
Alabama	15	F		TN
Andrew	13	M		TN
Thomas	12	M		TN
John	9	M		TX
Caroline	6	F		TX
George	3	M		TX
Vaught, Andrew	30	M	Farmer	AL
Louisa	25	F		TN
Martha	7	F		TX
William	4	M		TX
Nancy	3	F		TX
Bryanly, Thomas F.	41	M	Farmer	VA
Minerva	36	F		KY
Joseph	18	M	Clerk	VA

(continued)

Name	Age	Sex	Occupation	Birthplace
Bryanly, Susan	16	F		VA
Hester	13	F		OH
Mary	11	F		OH
Thomas	7	M		TX
Samuel	6	M		TX
Lucy	4	F		TX
James	2	M		TX
Oliver, William	17	M	Farmer	TN
John	15	M		MS
Johnson, Joshua F.	25	M	Farmer	TN
Amanda	20	F		TN
Ida M.	2	F		TX
Clarence	8/12	M		TX
Stanfield, Henry	40	M	Farmer	TN
Minerva	33	F		TN
William	12	M		AR
Mary	10	F		AR
Margaret	7	F		TX
Allan	5	F(M)		TX
Minerva	1	F		TX
Joseph	1	M		TX
Knowles, Laura	18	F		TN
Mack	10	M		TN
Sarah	7	F		TN
Clarinda	5	F		TN
Merchant, Berry	30	M	Farmer	TN
Nancy	25	F		TN
Silas	11	M		TX
Eliza	9	F		TX
Martha	7	F		TX
Rachel	5	F		TX
Sarah	2	F		TX
James	3/12	M		TX
Barton, John	30	M	Farmer	AL
Mary	25	F		TN
Barland, James	20	M		TX
William	17	M	Farmer	TX
Bell, James	24	M	Farmer	GA
Frances	19	F		TN
Matilda	2	F		TX
Maria	5/12	F		TX
Sheek, Adam	48	M	Farmer	NC
Jemima	49	F		NC
James	21	M	Farmer	NC
John	18	M	Farmer	TN
Susan	16	F		TN
Lucinda	12	F		TX
Martha	8	F		TX
Melton, Joseph	20	M	Laborer	AL
Ward, Isaac	20	M	Laborer	TN
Crane, Joel	26	M	Farmer	TN
Melinda	25	F		TN
Annice	7	F		TX
George	5	M		TX
John	4	M		TX
Mary	1	F		TX
Crane, William	56	M	Farmer	GA
Mary	55	F		TN
George	12	M		TX
Shoemaker, Evan	48	M	Farmer	AL
Matilda	30	F		TN
Fanny	20	F		TN
Jackson	15	M	Farmer	TN
Elizabeth	14	F		TX
Mary	10	F		TX
Martha	9	F		TX
Joel	6	M		TX
Stephen	3	M		TX
Mayfield, G. F.	30	M	Carpenter	TN
Henrietta	27	F		TN
Abe	4	M		MS
Eliza	2	M(F)		MS
Crane, John	33	M	Farmer	TN

(continued)

Name	Age	Sex	Occupation	Birthplace
Crane, Minerva	33	F		TN
Mary	14	F		MS
Nancy	11	F		TX
Caroline	6	F		TX
William	4	M		TX
Rachel	1	F		TX
Keith, Stephen	61	M	Farmer	TN
Rebecca	52	F		GA
Martin	10	M		AR
Keith, Elija	22	M	Farmer	TN
Marinda	21	F		GA
Louisa	1/12	F		TX
Leslie, Martha	13	F		GA
Arnold, William B.	46	M	Black Smith	SC
Mary	46	F		SC
Oliver	22	M	Student	SC
Absolam	17	M	Student	TN
Koots, Aynthia	5	F		MO
Trummer, A. B.	25	M	Laborer	MS
Montgomery, Eliza	39	F		TN
Samuel	11	M		TN
Emily	8	F		TN
Harrietta	6	F		TX
Cowan, William	38	M	Farmer	TN
Sally	33	F		TN
James	16	M	Farmer	TN
Polly	14	F		MS
John	12	M		MS
Delila	10	F		AL
West	8	M		AL
Isaac	4	M		MS
Elizabeth	2	F		TX
Stanfield, James	25	M	Farmer	TN
Lotta	22	F		TN
William	3	M		TN
Flemming, Berry	25	M	Farmer	TN
Lydia	22	F		TN
William	3/12	M		TX
Denny, James	21	M	Grocer	TN
McGee, M. J.	25	M	Physician	NC
Flora	24	F		TN
Texana	1	F		TX
Hambrick, James	19	M	Farmer	TN
Wilson, M. B.	15	F		TN
Koonce, Mary	8	F		TN
Spicer, William	48	M	Farmer	NC
Caroline	36	F		GA
John	17	M		GA
Valentine	14	M		GA
Rowan	9	M		GA
George	6	M		GA
Emily	4	F		GA
Sarah	2	F		GA
Davis, Caroline	14	F		TN
Dosson, Martin	27	M		TN
Eliza	21	F		TN
Mullens, Cynthia	39	F		KY
William	21	M	Laborer	KY
Daniel	15	M		TN
Sarah	13	F		TN
Jane	11	F		TN
James	9	M		TN
Bennet	7	M		TX
Louisa	2	F		TX
Duncan, John	45	M		VA
Leah	44	F		TN
Eliza	20	F		IL
Robert	17	M	Farmer	IL
Catharine	12	F		AR
Mary	7	F		AR
John	4	M		AR
Cowan, Samuel	25	M	Farmer	TN
Polly	22	F		TN
Majors, Berry	48	M	Farmer	VA
Martha	47	F		TN
Nelson	20	M	Farmer	TN
Riley	17	M	Farmer	TN
Ephraim	16	M		TN
Alexander	13	M		TN
William	11	M		TN
Pleasant	8	M		TN
James	6	M		TN
Elizabeth	4	F		TN
Sarah	2	F		TN
Keith, Eli	62	M	Farmer	VA
Elizabeth	55	F		TN
James	31	M	Farmer	TN
Jacob	25	M		TN
Isaac	21	M		TN
Marshal, Margaret	38	F		TN
John	19	F(M)	None	TN
Mary	17	F		TN
Delila	15	F		TN
Jasper	13	M		TN
Newton	12	M		TN
Marion	10	M		AR
Elizabeth	8	F		AR
Brumley, James C.	39	M	Farmer	TN
Melinda	38	F		TN
William	17	M	Farmer	TN
Jasper	15	M		TN
Nancy	13	F		TN
Calvin	10	M		TN
Nelson	8	M		TN
Henderson	6	M		TN
Henry	2	M		TX
Hale, Margaret	29	F		NC
William	22	M	Farmer	NC
Hugh	20	M	Farmer	NC
Jane	18	F		TN
Betsy	14	F		TN
Kenneth	13	M		TN
Henry	5	M		TN
Brumley, Carol	29	M	Farmer	TN
Delila	29	F		TN
Louisa	9	F		TN
John	7	M		TN
Hetty	5	F		TN
Sally	3	F		AR
William	6/12	M		TX
Smith, William	29	M	Farmer	TN
Ann	26	F		TN
Sarah	9	F		TN
Mary	2	F		TX
Bibb, John	60	M	Farmer	NC
Sarah	51	F		KY
William	18	M	Farmer	TN
Mary	16	F		TN
Letitia	14	F		TN
Emiline	11	F		TN
Miller, Greenbury	38	M	Farmer	TN
Mary	34	F		TN
Robert	15	M		TN
Pleasant	12	M		TN
Bethena	7	F		AR
Adaline	5	F		TX
Frank	2	M		TX
Turly, William	47	M	Farmer	TN
Minta	47	F		NC
Allan	23	M	Farmer	AL
William	21	M	Farmer	AL
John	19	M	Farmer	IL
Martha	14	F		IL
George	9	M		MO
Mary	7	F		TX
Nancy	4	F		TX

Name	Age/Sex/Occupation	Birthplace
Stroud, Abram	38 M Farmer	NC
Elizabeth	37 F	TN
Benjamin	12 M	TX
Sarah	8 F	TX
George	4 M	TX
Lamb, James	40 M Farmer	TX
Reddin, John	42 M	NC
Elizabeth	44 F	SC
Johnathan	24 M Farmer	TN
William	21 M Farmer	TN
Henry	13 M	TN
Nancy	11 F	TN
John	7 M	TN
James	9/12 M	TX
Autwell, John	24 M	IL
Milly	19 F	TN
William	2 M	TX
Reddin, Ann	16 F	TN
Johnson, John	40 M Black Smith	TN
Sydney	40 F	TN
Levi	17 M Farmer	TN
William	14 M	TN
Mary	11 F	TN
Eliza	9 F	MS
Sarah	5 F	MS
Arena	2 F	TX
Rebecca	3/12 F	TX
Canada, Jarman	38 M Farmer	NC
Polly	34 F	AL
David	15 M Farmer	TN
Sarah	15 F	TN
William	31 M Farmer	NC
Canada, James	25 M	TN
D-------	12 M	TN
Stephen	10 M	TN
Margaret	7 F	TN
Brunson, Samuel	30 M Farmer	AL
Polly	33 F	TN
Susan	12 F	TN
Margaret	10 F	MS
Eliza Jane	5 F	MS
Matthew	1 M	TX
O'Neal, John	21 M Farmer	TN
Nancy	20 F	TN
Miranda	1 F	TX
Berry	19 M Farmer	TN
Johnson, Thomas	62 M	TN
Sarah	60 F	TN
Thomas	23 M	AL
Arena	22 F	AL
John	21 M	TN
Francis	18 M Farmer	TN
Louisa	15 F	TN
Thomas, William	23 M Farmer	TN
Nancy	20 F	GA
Shoemaker, Jacob	30 M Millwright	GER
Abigail	32 F	TN
John	6 M	TN
Andrew	2 M	TX
Cunningham, L.	31 M Farmer	TN
Sena	28 F	TN
William	12 M	AR
Mary	10 F	LA
David	9 M	LA
Sarah	7 F	AR
Martha	6 F	AR
Alexander	4 M	TX
Lem	1 M	TX
Barnes, Lofton	74 M Farmer	VA
Polly	58 F	SC
Polly	21 F	TN

(continued)

Name	Age/Sex/Occupation	Birthplace
Barnes, Martha	18 F	MS
Thomas, William	24 M Farmer	TN
Nancy	21 F	GA
Yates, Berry	7 M	TX
Simmonds, Thomas	53 M Farmer	SC
Sarah	35 F	NC
Holt, Giles	8 M	TN
Reed, James	1 M	TX
Holt, Albert	39 M	TN
Mary	37 F	TN
James	11 M	TN
George	9 M	TN
Mary	7 F	TN
The Baby	1 F	TX
Holt, Tilman	29 M	TN
Louisa	27 F	TN
Giles	7 M	TN
Holt, D. P.	29 M Farmer	TN
Nancy	18 F	TN
Mary	1 F	TX
Andrew	20 M Laborer	TN
Thomas	17 M Laborer	TN
Long, James	29 M Farmer	TN
Mary	23 F	TN
Sarah	5 F	TN
Virginia	2 F	TX
Waters, James	22 M Farmer	IL
Elizabeth	22 F	TN
William	3 M	TX
Elizabeth	6/12 F	TX
Sells, Susan	18 F	TN
Plunk, Peter	48 M Farmer	TN
Trasdy(?)	39 F	TN
John	19 M Farmer	TN
George	16 M Farmer	TN
Nancy	12 F	TN
Jacob	11 M	TN
Mary	7 F	TN
Susan	3 F	TN
Stewart, William	26 M Farmer	TN
Margaret	25 F	MO
Payne, Wilson	25 M School Teacher	AL
Rachel	23 F	TN
Godwin, Rufus	32 M Farmer	TN
Mary	23 F	MO
William	3 M	TX
Mary	7/12 F	TX
Garrison, Daniel	26 M	??
Triplet, Nancy	13 F	MO
Edgar, Thomas	22 M Farmer	??
Martha	19 F	TN
A Boy	2 M	TX
William	1/12 M	TX
Myers, Gibson	32 M Miller	LA
Jane	27 F	TN
Henry	6 M	TX
Marion	4 M	TX
Hale, Jesse P.	26 M Miller	TN
Hutson, Sarah	47 F	TN
Hardiman	18 M Laborer	TN
William	10 M	TN
Thomas	8 M	TX
Lindsey, James	37 M Farmer	TN
Martha	36 F	GA
Elizabeth	14 F	AL
John	15 M	AL
William	12 M	AL
Thomas	10 M	AL
Lindsey, Elisha	35 M Farmer	TN

(continued)

TITUS COUNTY, TEXAS

Name	Age	Sex	Occupation	Birthplace
Lindsey, Catharine	37	F		AL
Charles	10	M		AL
Melvina	8	F		AL
James	6	M		MS
Mary	4	F		AL
Jesse	3	M		AL
Martha	1	F		AL
Smith, Jesse	44	M	Miller	AL
Nancy	29	F		TN
Arthur	23	M	Miller	AL
Green	17	M	Miller	AL
Thomas	15	M		AL
John	10	M		AL
Jesse	8	M		AL
McNiece, William	25	M	Farmer	TN
Diana	27	F		TN
Mary	9	F		TX
Abram	7	M		TX
Marion	7/12	M		TX
Gibson, John	40	M	Farmer	TN
Tabitha	34	F		TN
Benjamin	11	M		LA
Marion	7	M		LA
Sarah	5	F		LA
Mary	2	F		TX
Celia	2/12	F		TX
Dayton, Mary	15	F		OH
Hitchins, Almon	3	M		TX
Koots, Margaret	30	F		TN
George	10	M		TX
Munroe	8	M		TX
Matilda	6	F		TX
Martha	5	F		TX
Marion	1	M		TX
Eason, William	39	M	Farmer	NC
Rebecca	33	F		TN
Bethena	14	F		TN
Mills	11	M		MO
Minerva	9	M		MO
William	1	M		TX
Tatom, Richard	29	M	Farmer	TN
McCaskey, Andrew	30	M	Farmer	Atlantic Ocean
Martha	10	F		TN
Hicklin, Martha	44	F		TN
Johnathan	18	M	Farmer	TN
Return	15	M		TN
Nancy	12	F		MO
Bethena	10	F		MO
Riggins, Johnathan	32	M	Black Smith	TN
Mary	29	F		GA
Sarah	9	F		TN
Newton	6	F		TN
Matilda	4	F		TN
John	3	M		AL
Mary	8/12	F		TX
Garret, Jacob	30	M	Carpenter	TN
William	10	M		TN
Pruit, Hezekiah	21	M	Farmer	GA
Murphy, Lewellan	33	M	School Teacher	??
McBroom, Isaac	46	M	Black Smith	NC
Musgrove, Bushrod	24	M	Merchant	AL
Sarah	21	F		TN
Edward	3	M		TX
Goodman, William	25	M	Farmer	TN
Jane	18	F		AL
Copeland, Pamelia	47	F		SC
John	16	M		AL
Goodman, George	68	M	Farmer	VA
Elizabeth	63	F		TN
Frank	22	M	Farmer	AR
William	13	M		AR
Isabella	11	F		AR

Name	Age	Sex	Occupation	Birthplace
COffee, Milton	28	M	Farmer	TN
Nancy	29	F		TN
Newton	4	M		TX
William	1	M		TX
Rutherford, Thomas	43	M	Farmer	TN
Letitia	33	F		KY
Julia	13	F		TN
Griffith	12	M		AR
Mary	10	F		AR
Angeline	6	F		TX
Alfred	5	M		TX
Sarah	2	F		TX
Eliza	10/12	F		TX
McCarty, Andrew	38	M	Farmer	TN
Melinda	25	F		KY
Landon	14	M		AL
James	12	M		AL
Elizabeth	10	F		LA
Welch, William	36	M	Farmer	KY
Susan	38	F		TN
Charles	14	M		AL
James	7	M		AL
John	5	M		TX
Ann	4	F		TX
Nancy	2	F		TX
Box, James F.	52	M	Farmer	TN
Sarah	18	F		TN
John	21	M	Farmer	TN
Watson, Joseph	12	M		TX
Hayes, Solomon	56	M	Farmer	NC
Milly	45	F		NC
Candace	18	F		TN
Nancy	16	F		TN
Milly	11	F		TN
Hayes, James	21	M	None	TN
Cynthia	22	F		TN
Lydia	2	F		TX
Edwards, James	22	M	Farmer	TN
Rogers, James H.	38	M	Lawyer	GA
Barbara	32	F		TN
Albert	11	M		GA
Theophilus	7	M		AL
Mary	3	F		TX
Charlotte	1	F		TX
King, Nathaniel	31	M	Grocer	TN
Nancy	24	F		TN
Sophronia	3	F		TX
Argyle	1	M		TX
Moore, Cyrus H.	30	M	Farmer	TN
Elizabeth	20	F		CT
Minerva	7	F		TX
Henry	5	M		TX
Jane	9/12	F		TX
Hamilton, James	33	M	Farmer	TN
Catharine	29	F		CT
Elizabeth	7	F		TX
Marcus	2	M		TX
Miller, Richard	12	M		MS
Ewing, William M.	30	M	Farmer	AL
Viola	24	F		TN
Wilson	7	M		TX
Clarence	5	M		TX
Emily Ann	9/12	F		TX
Andrew B.	22	M	Farmer	TN

TRAVIS COUNTY, TEXAS

City of Austin

Name	Age	Sex	Occupation	Birthplace
Parkerson, M. M.	46	M	Wagon Maker	TN
Martha	24	F		IN
Lavinia	4	F		TX
Harriet	3	F		TX
John	2	M		TX
Martha Jane	8/12	F		TX

Name	Age	Sex	Occupation	Birthplace
Haynie, S. A. J.	35	M	Farmer	TN
Martha	26	F		TN
Scott, Robert	5	M		AR
Haynie, Jack	4/12	M		TX
Allen, William	25	M	Farmer	TN
Adams, Alsy	48	F		SC
Camp, Martha A.	12	F		AL
Virlina	12	F		AL
Rebecca	10	F		AL
Manor, J. J.	32	M	Farmer	TN
Caroline	20	F		IN
Texana	2	F		TX
Josaphine	1	F		TX
Shepherd, Eli	41	M	Farmer	NC
Hamilton, William	39	M	Farmer	OH
Louiza	28	F		TN
Eliza Jane	11	F		TX
Ben	10	M		TX
William	8	M		TX
John O.	6	M		TX
Adeline	3	F		TX
Mary	1	F		TX
Hopkins, Dicy	39	F		TN
Harriet	22	F		IN
Mary	18	F		IN
Martha	14	F		IN
Gregory, David	40	M	Farmer	NC
Martha	28	F		TN
Margarett	9	F		MO
Susan	8	F		MO
Mary Jane	5	F		MO
Sarah	2	F		TX
Hamilton, John	40	M	Farmer	OH
Lavina	38	F		TN
Charles	18	M	Farmer	IN
Margarett	16	F		IN
Mary	13	F		IN
John	11	M		TX
Wayne	8	M		TX
George	7	M		TX
Ann	4	F		TX
Andrew	3	M		TX
James	6/12	M		TX
Brown, Albert	31	M	Mechanic	NY
Jane	17	F		AL
Casander	10/12	F		TX
Montgomery, W. C.	28	M	Mechanic	TN
Forehance, Blake	40	M	Black Smith	TN
Julia	17	F		TN
John	14	M		TN
Hugh	12	M		TN
Mary	8	F		TN
Sarah	6	F		MS
Martha	4	F		MS
Dodd, James L.	32	M	Farmer	TN
Willson, John C.	24	M	Farmer	TN
Thomas, Alexander	21	M	Laborer	VA
Woods, William	27	M	Farmer	AL
Louisa	24	F		AL
Silas	7	M		AL
Elizabeth	5	F		AL
Calvin	3	M		AL
James	3/12	M		TX
James	19	M	Laborer	AL
Pruett, Mac	17	M	Laborer	TN
Duty, Joseph	51	M	Farmer	TN
Louisa	38	F		MO
Franklin	19	M	Farmer	TX
Milton	14	M		TX
Sarah	11	F		TX
Milam	8	M		TX
Albert	5	M		TX

(continued)

Name	Age	Sex	Occupation	Birthplace
Duty, Elen	2	F		TX
William	2/12	M		TX
Haslet, Eliza G.	12	F		TX
Highsmith, Senica	41	F		TN
Malkijah	21	M	Farmer	TX
Sarah	18	F		TX
Amanda	15	F		TX
Albert	7	M		TX
Edwin	5	M		TX
Meeks, John	44	M	Farmer	KY
Mary	43	F		AL
Sudduth	18	M	Farmer	MO
Francis	16	M	Farmer	MO
Ambroze	15	M	Farmer	MO
Randolph	13	M		MO
William	11	M		MO
Richard	10	M		MO
Eudora	9	F		MO
Amanda	7	F		MO
Charles	6	M		MO
Martha	3	F		MO
Mary	3	F		MO
John	1	M		MO
Van Cleave, Jonathan	25	M	Black Smith	PA
John C.	23	M	Black Smith	PA
Driskall, Jonathan	23	M	Laborer	TN
Leedam, Anthony W.	34	M	Physician	PA
Mary	20	F		TN
Aribella	3	F		AR
William A.	5/12	M		TX
Pierce, James	50	M	Farmer	TN
Elizabeth	26	F		AL
James	7	M		AL
Susan Jane	5	F		AL
George W.	4	M		AL
Louisa E.	1	F		TX
Miligan, Thomas	31	M	Laborer	TN
Mahala	24	F		TN
Matilda	8	F		TX
Margaret	6	F		TX
Mary	4	F		TX
Brock, William	23	M	Farmer	TN
Susan	21	F		MO
Andrew L.	21	M	Farmer	TN
King, John L.	40	M	Farmer	TN
Elizabeth	29	F		TN
James	8	M		MO
William T.	6	M		MO
Sarah A.	4	F		MO
Susan	2	F		MO
Ellison, Rufus P.	19	M	Farmer	AL
Mary	17	F		TN
Osborn, John L.	42	M	Farmer	TN
Claiborn	24	M	Farmer	TX
Hanley, Elias	41	M	Farmer	SC
Lurane	41	F		GA
Adeline	18	F		TN
Mary	16	F		MS
Narcissa	13	F		MS
James	11	M		MS
Martha	9	F		MS
William	7	F		MS
John	5	M		MS
Elias	4	M		MS
Clarinda	2	F		MS
Chandler, William	52	M	Farmer	VA
Martha	44	F		VA
Drake, Benjamin C.	40	M	Farmer	TN
Mary Jane	22	F		VA
Francis C.	6	M		TN
Hamilton	3	M		TN
Strayhorne, Newel T.	27	M	Farmer	NC
Lucy	23	F		TN

(continued)

TRAVIS COUNTY, TEXAS

Name	Age	Sex	Occupation	Birthplace
Strayhorne, Aribella	6	F		TN
Samellen	4	F		TN
Nancy	1	F		TX
Smith, William	25	M	Trader	TN
Strayhorne, Sam M.	18	M	Laborer	NC
Parris, William	30	M	Farmer	TN
Sarah	21	F		AL
Eli	4	M		TX
Hariett	2	F		TX
Love, Martin	33	M	Waggoner	SC
Sarinda	27	F		GA
Calvin	6	M		TX
Were, William	27	M	Carpenter	TN
Yait, Thomas	54	M	Farmer	NC
Mary	51	F		NC
Munroe	25	M	Waggoner	NC
Cornelia	20	F		NC
Mary	19	F		NC
Margaret J.	17	F		NC
Joseph	16	M	Farmer	NC
Martha	13	F		NC
Thomas	12	M		NC
Hariett	10	F		TN
Graves, Decater	30	M	Peddler	AL
Sarah E.	24	F		NC
Chamberland, James	41	M	Farmer	TN
Sarah	26	F		TN
Jeremiah	7	M		MO
John	4	M		MO
Thomas	2	M		MO
Barton, Hannah	66	F		TN
McFarlin, William L.	10	M		MO
Glasscock, Thomas	22	M	Farmer	VA
Eliza	18	F		FL
Biron	1	M		TX
Richardson, John	25	M	Laborer	TN
Stratton, A---	40	F		AL
Duncan, Josephine	17	F		AL
Ayres, Daniel R.	34	M	Farmer	TN
Julina	26	F		AL
Alcemeda	6	F		TX
Susan	5/12	F		TX
Haynes, Thomas J.	33	M	Farmer	TN
Hulda	23	F		IN
Martha	4	F		AR
James	1/12	M		TX
Conway, W. T.	50	M	Farmer	TN
Levina	38	F		TN
Joseph	19	M	Laborer	MO
James	18	M	Laborer	MO
Mariah	13	F		MO
Plesant	12	M		MO
Isac	9	M		MO
Louisa	7	F		MO
Alexander	2	M		MO
Bacon, John B.	42	M	Physician	TN
Rogers, Jesse W.	39	M	Farmer	TN
Mary	40	F		GA
Catharine	14	F		MS
Elizabeth	12	F		MS
Susan	11	F		MS
William	10	M		MS
James	9	M		MS
Matilda	8	F		MS
John	7	M		MS
Andrew	6	M		MS
Benjamin	4	M		MS
Casner, Martin	35	M	Farmer	TN
Jane	35	F		AL
Sarah	12	F		AL
Telitha	9	F		AL
Martin	6	M		TX

(continued)

Name	Age	Sex	Occupation	Birthplace
Casner, Francis	6	M		TX
Louiza	4	F		TX
Thomas	2	M		TX
Montgomery, R. C.	50	M	Farmer	TN
Lewis	8	M		TX
Henry	6	M		TX
Casner, James	26	M	Farmer	AL
Sarah	20	F		GA
Houston, A. D.	43	M	Farmer	TN
Emily	35	F		GA
Thomas	15	M	Laborer	TX
Cyntha	13	F		TX
William	10	M		TX
Rosa	8	F		TX
Barnhill, Cyntha	64	F		PA
Shelby, Evan W.	49	M	Physician	TN
Judith L.	46	F		GA
McDaniel, Thomas	10	M		TN
Small, James	28	M	Laborer	PA
McClellan, Thomas	21	M	School Teacher	TN
McClary, M---	20	M	Laborer	TN
Craft, John S.	41	M	Farmer	TN
Abigail	36	F		TN
Jasper	16	M	None	TN
James	12	M		TX
John	10	M		TX
Russle	8	M		TX
Charles	5/12	M		TX
Self, George	41	M	Laborer	SC
Fort, Wiley D.	30	M	Laborer	SC
Willson, Edward	32	M	Farmer	AL
Elizabeth	24	F		TN
Thomas	3	M		TX
George	1	M		TX
McCutcheon, William	36	M	Farmer	TN
Elizabeth	29	F		MS
Willis	14	M		TX
Mary	12	F		TX
John	10	M		TX
Jesse	8	M		TX
Sarah	6	F		TX
Joseph	5	M		TX
George	1	M		TX
Clark, Joseph	21	M	Laborer	AR
Denison, T. L.	36	M	Laborer	TN
Mary	28	F		TN
Robert	17	M	Laborer	TN
William	6	M		TN
Martha	4	F		TN
Sarah	2	F		TN
Burnam, Martha	66	F		TN
Eliza	28	F		TN
Baker, James	50	M	Farmer	TN
Frances	46	F		VA
William	25	M	Farmer	TN
John	24	M	Farmer	TN
James	21	M	Farmer	TN
Sarah	18	F		TN
Martha	16	F		TN
Mary	14	F		TN
George	11	M		TX
Peter	6	M		TX
Nicli, Francis	33	M	Cabinet Maker	GER
Simpson, Thomas	44	M	Farmer	TN
Nancy	40	F		TN
Wallace, Mary A.	28	F		IRE
John	10	M		TX
William	6	M		TX
Elizabeth	2	F		TX
Simpson, James	25	M	Laborer	TN
Martin, Enoch	31	M	Laborer	Long Island
Elizabeth	21	F		TN
Joel M.	6/12	M		TX

TRAVIS COUNTY, TEXAS

Name	Age	Sex	Occupation	Birthplace
Montgomery, James	30	M	Farmer	IL
Almira	28	F		TN
Charles	7	M		MO
Richard	4	M		MO
Silas	2	M		MO
Charles, Alfred B.	26	M	Carpenter	TN
Pace, Gideon G.	35	M	Farmer	TN
Nailor, C. H.	21	M	Farmer	TN
Susan	18	F		TN
Charles	1	M		TN
Nailor, C. P.	23	M	Farmer	TN
Turley, James M.	32	M	Carpenter	TN
Loucinda	21	F		MO
Mary Jane	6	F		TX
Desdemoney	4	F		TX
Nancy	2	F		TX
Smith, Samuel	27	M	Laborer	MO
Araline	25	F		TN
Louiza	10	F		TX
Manerva	8	F		TX
Henry	6	M		MS
Anna	3	F		TX
Elizabeth	6/12	F		TX
Brown, Mathew	43	M	Farmer	OH
Mary	40	F		TN
William	18	M	Farmer	IL
Catharine	17	F		IL
Jacob	15	M	Laborer	IL
James	13	M		IL
Elizabeth	11	F		IL
Margarett	9	F		IA
Jane	6	F		TX
Susan	4	F		TX
Sarah	1	F		TX
McChristen, John	26	M	Farmer	TN
Rebecca	25	F		VA
Susan	4	F		TX
Martha	2	F		TX
John	2/12	M		TX
Edwards, John	53	M	Farmer	GA
Martha	49	F		GA
Emily	20	F		FL
John	14	M		FL
Callim	10	M		TX
McCustian, Elija	32	M	Laborer	TN
Nichols, Wily	50	M	Farmer	TN
Sarah	40	F		TN
Sarah	15	F		AL
Hanibal	13	M		AL
John	9	M		AL
George	7	M		AL
Nail, George	37	M	Farmer	TN
Mary	25	F		MO
Mary	2	F		TX
James	2/12	M		TX
Higgy	2/12	M		TX
Bird, Luannia	19	F		MO
Chote, Benjamin	35	M	Laborer	TN
Mary	33	F		TN
Misouri	7	F		AR
Virginia	5	F		AR
Corine	2	F		AR
Stanly, Thomas E.	47	M	Farmer	SC
Holland	50	F		TN
John	20	M	Laborer	TN
Thomas	18	M	Laborer	TN
Booker	17	M	Laborer	TN
William	16	M	Laborer	MS
Joseph	13	M		MS
Jefferson	12	M		MS
George	10	M		MS
Henry	8	M		MS
Elias	6	M		MS
Nolan, Thomas W.	30	M	Farmer	NC
Sarah	22	F		TN
Mary	2	F		MS
William	9/12	M		MS
Wood, Joseph P.	33	M	Laborer	IN
Hariett	19	F		TN
Cox, Benjamin	59	M	Laborer	??
Elizabeth	50	F		TN
Hanah	19	F		IN
Delila	16	F		IN
Tempa	10	F		AR
Cyntha	9	F		AR
Sutton, James	17	M	Laborer	AR
William	15	M	Laborer	AR
Burdet, William	39	M	Farmer	TN
Caroline	39	F		TN
Martha	16	F		TN
John	13	M		TX
Jesse	11	M		TX
Ann	4	F		TX
William	2	M		TX
Patience	1/12	F		TX
Davidson, Andrew	37	M	Farmer	TN
Elizabeth	34	F		TN
Lavina	16	F		TN
James	13	M		TN
Margaret	11	F		TX
John	6	M		TX
Almeda	4	F		TX
Henry, John D.	44	M	Farmer	TN
Elizabeth	39	F		TN
Merideth	19	M	Farmer	TN
Elizabeth	17	F		TN
Hugh	16	M	Laborer	TN
David	15	M	Laborer	TN
John	14	M		TN
Mary	12	F		TN
Amanda	10	F		TN
Thomas	8	M		TN
James	6	M		TN
Franklin	3	M		TN
Hutchins, James H.	36	M	School Teacher	NC
Francas	26	F		TN
James	6	M		MS
Amelia	4	F		MS
Albert	1	M		MS
Burdet, Joel	35	M	Farmer	TN
Elizabeth	29	F		AL
Martha	10	F		MS
Giles	7	M		MS
Jane	2	F		TN
McArthur, Nicholas	38	M	Farmer	KY
Lodoisky	27	F		GA
James	8	M		TX
John	5	M		TX
Mary	2	F		TX
Doyle, James	52	M	Brick Mason	IRE
Mary	45	F		GA
Upchurch, Henderson	32	M	Farmer	TN
Henry	22	M		AL
Rowe, Joseph	48	M	Physician	NC
Lavina	38	F		TN
Josaphine	12	F		TX
Jesse	7	M		TX
Hatt, John	27	M	Farmer	AL
Rowe, H. H.	25	M	Farmer	NC
Jane	20	F		TN
Martha	18	F		IN
Vincent, Elizabeth	7	F		TN
Cook, James	7	M		TX
Duggins, Franklin	35	M	Millwright	VA
Burdet, Jesse	62	M	Farmer	SC
Mildred	60	F		GA
Night, Edwin	17	M	Farmer	TN

Name	Age	Sex	Occupation	Birthplace
Burdett, Minus C.	27	M	Farmer	AL
Sarah	21	F		MO
Mildred	1	F		TX
Vincent, Emaline	10	F		TN
Mary	3	F		TX
Jones, Thomas H.	37	M	Farmer	NC
Mariah	28	F		TN
Emily	11	F		TN
Rufus	9	M		TN
Isac	8	M		TN
Lucy	3	F		TX
C---	1	M		TX
Barnard, Levi	28	M	Farmer	TN
Vincent, Margaret	5	F		TN
Davis, Emily	32	F		TN
Wofford, Jacob	14	M		TN
Davis, Ann	11	F		MS
Thomas	10	M		MS
Isabella	9	F		MS
Isac	7	M		MS
Robert	5	M		MS
William	2	M		TX
Gracy, John N.	29	M	Farmer	TN
Harriet	25	F		TN
William	6	M		MO
John	5	M		MO
James	3	M		MO
Mary	1	F		MO
Roundtree, James	44	M	Farmer	TN
Martha	(44)14	F		MS
Martha	14	F		TN
Louiza	11	F		TN
Amanda	8	F		TX
Alvina	5	F		TX
Robert	4	M		TX
Josephine	2	F		TX
Rowe, Thomas E.	28	M	Farmer	NC
Catharine	40	F		TN
Joseph	4	M		TX
Thomas	1	M		TX
Furgeson, Robert	24	M	Farmer	AL
Sarah	10	F		MS
Mary	8	F		MS
Boyce, James	50	M	Farmer	TN
Harriett	47	F		VA
Malinda	15	F		WI
James	12	M		WI
Henry	11	M		TX
Albert	8	M		TX
Marella	7	F		TX
Pope	*1	M		TX
Atwood, William W.	45	M	Farmer	ME
Mary C.	39	F		TN
Mary J.	20	F		TN
Adela	12	F		TN
Rufus	9	M		TX
Jane	7	F		TX
Octovia	3	F		TX
Charles	1	M		TX
Elison, John H.	34	M	Laborer	VA
Ruth	33	F		TN
Martha	13	F		VA
Elizabeth	12	F		VA
Margarett	11	F		VA
Mary	9	F		VA
Louiza	7	F		MO
Misouri	6	F		MO
Cunningham, James	35	M	Farmer	TN
Susan	31	F		TN
Aaron	14	M		AL
Elison, Harris	4	M		MO
Elizabeth	9	F		AL
David	7	M		TX
Richard	5	M		TX

(continued)

Name	Age	Sex	Occupation	Birthplace
Elison, John	3	M		TX
William	1	M		TX
Bowers, Mary	4	F		TX
Rowlet, Joseph O.	23	M	Laborer	TN
Elizabeth	23	F		TN
John	9	M		AR
Mary	7	F		AR
William	2	M		TX
Elizabeth	2/12	F		TX
Hays, Nicholas	45	M	Laborer	KY
Zilly	45	F		SC
Martha	20	F		TN
James	15	M		MO
McHarrison	12	M		MO
Elizabeth	10	F		MO
Thomas	8	M		MO
Petty, Nathan	41	M	None	TN
Elizabeth	41	F		SC
Mary	14	F		AR
Elizabeth	12	F		AR
Albert	7	M		TX
Sarah	1	F		TX
Petty, John	21	M	None	TN
Serilda J.	17	F		IL
Brachene, Lemuel	52	M	Farmer	NC
Mary	50	F		KY
John	13	M		MO
Mathews, Emoline	17	F		TN
Joseph	8	M		TX
Elizabeth	6	F		TX
Robert	4	M		TX
William	1	M		TX
Davis, George W.	42	M	Farmer	TN
Emoline	40	F		KY
James	16	M	Farmer	TN
Blackston	15	M	Farmer	TN
Sarah	11	F		TX
Richard	10	M		TX
William	6	M		TX
Glen	4	M		TX
Mary	1	F		TX
Riley, James W.	50	M	Farmer	KY
Sarah	44	F		TN
William	24	M	Farmer	IN
Delfia	21	F		IN
James	19	M	Farmer	IN
David	17	M	Laborer	IL
George	14	M		IL
Richard	13	M		IL
Sarah	10	F		MO
Mary	8	F		MO
Phebe	6	F		TX
John	4	M		TX
Elkin, Preston	38	M	Farmer	TN
Nancy	27	F		IN
Mary	3	F		TX
Zerilda	1	F		TX
Parris, N. G.	31	M	Farmer	TN
Elizabeth	22	F		VA
Virginia	7/12	F		TX
Robertson, Loucinda	29	F		TN
William	12	M		AR
Elizabeth	10	F		AR
James	7	M		AR
Mary	4	F		TX
Compton, Charles	38	M	Farmer	NJ
Eliza	32	F		TN
Amanda	10	F		MO
Doxy, James D.	25	M	Farmer	MO
Elizabeth	21	F		MO
Bradford, James C.	34	M	Laborer	KY
Mahilda	28	F		TN
Jasper	9	M		MO
John	8	M		MO

TRAVIS COUNTY, TEXAS

Adams, Thomas	47	M	Farmer	VA
Ruth	48	F		TN
Francis	17	M	Farmer	MO
Parnecia	21	F		MO
Margaret	13	F		MO
Dancer, James	46	M	Meth. Preacher	TN
Jane	51	F		NC
Mariah	19	F		TN
Clementine	17	F		TN
Jonas	14	M		TN
Tennessee	11	F		TX
Bedford, James	70	M	None	NC
Elen	50	F		NC
George	28	M	None	TN
Bedford, James F.	42	M	Laborer	TN
Lucy	29	F		AL
Thomas	13	M		MS
George	11	M		MS
Julia	9	F		MO
Elen	7	F		MO
Jonas	4	M		MO
Masse	2	M		TX
Moore, Mississippi	17	F		AL
Hudson, Wily	26	M	Laborer	AR
Catharine	24	F		TN
James	7	M		AR
Jane	1	F		TX
Baker, Elijah	35	M	Laborer	??
Thomas, David	37	M	None	TN
John	12	M		TN
Mary Jane	10	F		TX
Ann	8	F		TX
Nathan	5	M		TX
Nancy	3	F		TX
Enochs, Jason A.	26	M	Farmer	TN
Hariett	19	F		AL
Lokely	2	M		TX
Forbus, Colin	53	M	C.P. Preacher	GA
Mary	49	F		KY
Cyntha	25	F		TN
John	18	M	Farmer	TN
Sarah	16	F		TN
Margaret	13	F		MS
Harvy	10	M		MS
Emily	8	F		MS
Brazill, Abram	19	M	Laborer	AR
Starr, Solomon	24	M	Farmer	TN
Margaret	23	F		TN
William	2	M		MO
James	1	M		MO
James, Martin	28	M	Carpenter	AL
Mary	23	F		TN
Elizabeth	1	F		TX
Hurst, Edward M.	36	M	Farmer	TN
Charlotte	40	F		IL
James	18	M	Farmer	AR
Joab	13	M		AR
Margaret	12	F		AR
Rody	8	F		AR
John	6	M		AR
Zarada	3	F		TX
Ballard, William R.	28	M	Laborer	AL
Jane	25	F		TN
Jacob	7	M		AR
Susan	1	F		AR
John	1/12	M		TX
Aynesworth, J. H.	53	M	Farmer	SC
Nancy	43	F		TN
William	19	M	Farmer	AL
Isah	15	M	Farmer	TN
Ally	12	F		TN

(continued)

Aynesworth, George	10	M		TN
Andrew	8	M		TN
Manerva	1	F		TX
Minnelle, Mary	27	F		TN
Mary	9	F		TX
William	11	M		TX
James	8	M		TX
Anna	3	M		TX
Burdet, Giles M.	32	M	Farmer	AL
Mary	29	F		TN
Almeda	9	F		TX
Levina	6	F		TX
Margaret	4	F		TX
William	2	M		TX
James	2/12	M		TX
Burdet, Newel	30	M	Farmer	TN
Misouri	26	F		SC
William	10	M		TX
Thomas	8	M		TX
Minus	5	M		TX
George	2	M		TX
Mildred	1/12	F		TX
Hormerly, William W.	33	M	Farmer	MS
Loucinda	30	F		TN
Margarett	9	F		TX
Macomb	8	M		TX
Rebecca	6	F		TX
Helen	4	F		TX
Sarah	2	F		TX
Cane, Shugars M.	28	M	Farmer	TN
Susannah	23	F		TN
Lane, Addison	46	M	Farmer	TN
Sally	46	F		TN
William	23	M	Clerk	IN
James	15	M	Laborer	IN
Addison	12	M		IN
F---	6	M		IN
Ferrando	1	M		AR
Upright, David	33	M	Mechanic	PA
Mary	29	F		MO
Catharine	4	F		MO
Mary	2	F		TX
Martha	2/12	F		TX
Oliver, John	39	M	Farmer	TN
Farlee, James	31	M	Black Smith	NC
Gilliland, Diana	44	F		TN
Nathaniel	22	M	Farmer	AR
Sarah	15	F		TX
Dianah	13	F		TX
James	10	M		TX
Moore, Thomas A.	42	M	Farmer	TN
Mary	39	F		AR
Robert	16	M	Farmer	TX
Ann	14	F		TX
Nancy	12	F		TX
Mary	10	F		TX
Jackson	8	M		TX
Jane	6	F		TX
Thomas	1	M		TX
Williams, Nancy	77	F		VA
Miles, William	24	M	Horse Trainer	VA
Sartin, Granville	21	M	Horse Trainer	MO
Burleson, John	45	M	Farmer	TN
Bell	19	F		TN
Martha Ann	17	F		MS
Martha Jane	14	F		TX
Manerva	8	F		TX
John	5	M		TX
Bauchman, William R.	26	M	Farmer	TN
Sarah	21	F		AL
Williams, John R.	22	M	Farmer	TN
Elizabeth	22	F		AL
Sarah Ann	1	F		TN

TRAVIS COUNTY, TEXAS

Name	Age	Sex	Occupation	Birthplace
Warren, Jeff	38	M	Farmer	KY
Elizabeth	33	F		AL
Thadeus	17	M	Farmer	TN
Ezekels	15	M	Farmer	TN
Margarett	13	F		TN
Henry	11	M		TN
Valley	8	F		TN
Benjamin	6	M		TN
Martha	4	F		TN
Joseph	2	M		TX
Chamberland, Thompson	53	M	Farmer	TN
Mary	51	F		TN
Andrew	14	M		MO
Sterling	9	M		MO
Chamberland, Sam W.	26	M	Farmer	TN
Margaret	19	F		MO
Ureal	6/12	M		TX
Sterling, James	33	M	Farmer	TN
Elizabeth	31	F		TN
Joseph	8	M		MO
Catharine	1	F		MO
Elgin, John	34	M	Physician	TN
Mary	27	F		TN
Elizabeth	3	F		TX
Haney, Mary	27	F		TN
Elgin, Robert M.	24	M	Clerk	TN
Thomas C.	21	M	None	TN
Browning, Columbus	38	M	None	GA
Penina	38	F		TN
Glasscock, Phile Ann	19	F		AL
Texas	3	F		TX
Henry, Wade	26	M	Black Smith	TN
Mary	20	F		TN
Foster, James	36	M	Black Smith	SCO
Beasly, Houston	26	M	Laborer	GA
Turner, Samuel	33	M	Mechanic	ENG
Jacobs, Aaron	32	M	Mechanic	GA
Wortham, John	30	M	Mechanic	VA
Forsyth, Andrew	25	M	Mechanic	SC
Minor, Joel	45	M	Printer	VT
Cyntha	23	F		TN
Arther	4	M		TX
Farr, David H.	30	M	Brick Mason	TN
Martha	30	F		AL
Robert	3	M		TX
Mary	1	F		TX
Canfield, James	42	M	Mechanic	TN
Ruth	15	F		MO
Eliza	13	F		MO
John	10	M		MO
James	8	M		TX
Josephine	5	F		TX
William	2	M		TX
Tucker, Jeff T.	20	M	Mechanic	NC
Chalmers, Mary W.	40	F		NC
Alexander	18	M	None	VA
William L.	17	M	None	TN
Eliza	13	F		TN
Sarah	9	F		TX
Ann	6	F		TX
Fanny	3	F		TX
Hancock, George	39	M	Mechanic	VA
Hamilton, Morgan	40	M	Mechanic	AL
Collins, Thomas	33	M	Confectioner	SC
Lee, Joel	53	M	Mechanic	KY
Emily	31	F		TN
George	9	M		TX
Laura	8	F		TX
Josaphine	5	F		TX
Mary	4	F		TX
Charles	3	M		TX
Richard	1/12	M		TX
Osburn, Ann E.	31	F		SCO

Name	Age	Sex	Occupation	Birthplace
Fox(Fore), Augustus	36	M	None	NC
Elizabeth	30	F		TN
Sarah	10	F		MO
Calvin, John	35	M	Farmer	TN
Elizabeth	21	F		AR
Horne, Andrew O.	56	M	School Teacher	TN
Elizabeth	52	F		NC
Archibald	23	M	None	AL
Mary	16	F		AL
Andrew	18	M	Clerk	AL
Lampkins, George F.	21	M	Painter	VA
Skinner, Jeremiah	25	M	Carpenter	GA
Carroll, John	22	M	Clerk	MD
Taylor, George	26	M	Carpenter	GA
Foster, Finus U.	36	M	C.P. Preacher	TN
Malvina	28	F		AL
Thomas	3	M		TX
Twisher, John M.	31	M	Auditor	TN
Mariah	30	F		VA
Mary	5	F		TX
Louiza	1	F		TX
Hall, Martha G.	40	F		VA
Smith, Elizabeth	38	F		NC
John	12	M		TN
Mary	8	F		TX
Susan	4	F		TX
Brown, Sidny	30	M	Clerk	AL
Caroline	18	F		NC
Tarbox, Lyman	37	M	Stage Contractor	NY
Jane	22	F		TN
Gertrude	3	F		TX
Kimbell, Sarah C.	24	F		TN
John	7	M		TX
Mary	6	F		TX
William	3	M		TX
Albert	1	M		TX
Kimbell, William	28	M	Clerk	TN
Rebecca	17	F		TN
Temperance	1	F		TX
Oldham, Overton	34	M	None	TN
Nancy	26	F		TN
William	7	M		MO
Mary	5	F		MO
Archibald	3	M		AR
Sarah	3/12	F		TX
Long, James M.	35	M	Merchant	NC
Mary	29	F		TN
Sneed, Sebron G.	48	M	Lawyer	KY
Maranda	37	F		TN
Edward	20	M	None	MO
Thomas	17	M	None	AR
Sebron	13	M		AR
Maranda	12	F		AR
Isable	9	F		AR
William	8	M		AR
Matilda	3	F		AR
Oldham, William S.	37	M	Lawyer	TN
Williamson	8	M		AR
Sarah	12	F		AR
Mary	10	F		AR
Letitia	6	F		AR
Ada	3	F		AR
Ward, Thomas W.	25	M	Clerk	TN
Laura C.	20	F		AL
Laura E.	2/12	F		TX
Allen, Henry P.	27	M	Printer	NH
Ann	23	F		ME
Melora	7	F		ME
Edwin	2	M		TX
Brown, Frank	17	M	Printer	TN
Evans, Alexander	45	M	Painter	SC
Mary	35	F		TN

(continued)

TRAVIS COUNTY, TEXAS

Name	Age	Sex	Occupation	Birthplace
Evans, Sarah	16	F		TN
Silvester	14	F		TN
Hugh	12	M		MS
Thomas	10	M		MS
Henry	8	M		MS
Cook, Abner H.	36	M	Mechanic	NC
Eliza	37	F		TN
George	16	M	None	MS
Alonzo	12	M		MS
Abner	6	M		TX
Frank	3	M		TX
Banks, William M.	25	M	Preacher	DC
Susan	16	F		VA
Carr, John A. P.	49	M	None	TN
Jane	39	F		TN
Robert	18	M	None	MS
Elizabeth	13	F		MS
Marilda	11	F		AR
Martha	11	F		AR
Mary	6	F		AR
Cartwell, Thomas P.	23	M	Clerk	TN
Mabey, Lela	45	F	(B)	TN
Haynie, Samuel G.	45	M	Physician	TN
Hanah	39	F		NY
Thomas	8	M		TX
Loucinda	6	F		TX
George	4	M		TX
Mariah	1	F		TX
Hugh	21	M	Clerk-Land Office	AL
Dix, William	20	M	Asst. P.M.	MI
Dety, John	27	M	Mechanic	SWI
Dix, Mary	19	F		MI
Marshall, Peter	31	M	Black Smith	TN
Martha	26	F		TN
William	8	M		AR
John	6	M		AR
Wiley	4	M		AR
Latitia	1	F		AR
Holms, Sarah	8	F		TN
Phineus	4	M		TX
Whinrey, Carol	22	M	None	TN
Blaylock, William	26	M	None	KY
Marshall, Wiley	26	M	None	TN
Duncan, John M.	30	M	Black Smith	TN
Barbary	22	F		AR
Fitzsimmons, John	40	M	Mechanic	NY
Robertson, E. Sterling C.	30	M	Clerk-Land Office	TN
Eliza	25	F		TN
Sterling	1	M		TX
Farly, Mr.	28	M	School Teacher	CT
Robertson, James	13	M		TX
Porterfield, Mathew	33	M	Carpenter	TN
Elizabeth	28	F		TN
Franklin	6	M		MS
Mary	4	F		TX
Charles	2	M		TX
William	2/12	M		TX
Piper, Benjamin	57	M	Farmer	TN
Susan	42	F		GA
Alexander	25	M	Farmer	TN
William	16	M	Farmer	TN
Nancy	13	F		TN
Susan	11	F		TN
Samuel	8	M		TN
Benjamin	6	M		MO
Edgar, Mr.	30	M	Laborer	??
Moore, Asanah	35	M	Carpenter	DC
Nancy	32	F		TN
James	3	M		TX
Robertson, Jane	52	F	Boarding House	KY
William	21	M	Farmer	AR

(continued)

Name	Age	Sex	Occupation	Birthplace
Cace, William	25	M	Mechanic	??
McAnella, Robert	40	M	None	AL
Basford, Mr.	40	M	None	??
Rankin, Mr.	35	M	Printer	TN
Gosler, Mr.	28	M	Printer	OH
McCuskny, William H.	31	M	Editor-Boarding Hse.	NY
Jane	20	F		TN
Mary	2	F		TX
William	1/12	M		TX
Brown, Sarah	41	F		TN
Elen	18	F		TN
Frank	17	M	Printer	TN
Mary	14	F		TX
Thomas, Warren L.	23	M	Printer	NY
Dun, John J.	27	M	Printer	AL
Rankin, Daniel H.	30	M	Printer	KY
Miller, David J.	20	M	Printer	AL
Castley, James	15	M	Printer	TX
Turley, Flavus	19	M	Printer	MS
Gasley, John J.	27	M	Printer	PA
McKesic, John W.	31	M	Printer	TN
Swisher, James G.	55	M	Tavern Keeper	TN
Elizabeth	53	F		TN
James M.	27	M	Tavern Keeper	TN
Ann	14	F		TX
Edward	10	M		TX
Batt, J. J.	28	M	Clerk	MO
McSham, Paul	22	M	Clerk	TN
Harns, Frank	30	M	Clerk	AL
Forest, William	20	M	Stage Driver	MS
Anderson, Thomas	60	M	Physician	VA
Handcock, John	30	M	Lawyer	TN
Peters, George	30	M	Stage Driver	TN
Merphn, John	20	M	Tailor	VA
Toskiss, Louiza	25	F		DC
O'Brien, Owen	41	M	Tavern Keeper	IRE
Hall, James W. W.	42	M	Tavern Keeper	NY
Honor	36	F		MS
William	5	M		TX
Sunderland, William	22	M	Bar Keeper	NY
Cardova, J. D.	40	M	Editor	PA
Nichols, Samuel	25	M	None	SCO
White, Robert	25	M	None	??
Jester, John	30	M	None	??
Caltell, Cass	35	M	None	??
Marshall, Wily	24	M	None	AR
Nangermin, Albert	20	M	None	GER
Brass, John	30	M	None	??
Anderson, Charles	35	M	None	TN
G---, John M.	30	M	Grocery Keeper	TN
Parker, P. F.	25	M	Merchant	NY
Muray, A.	21	M	None	??
Matler, Samuel	18	M	(illegible)	GER
Pace, James R.	35	M	Surveyor	TN
Smith, Hary	34	M	Sheriff	TN
Valguine, John	35	M	None	SWI
Hodgekiss, William	30	M	Clerk-Land Office	TN
Hanah	28	F		IN
Martha	7	F		TX
Daniel	6	M		TX
Mary	4	F		TX
Roger, William	28	M	Farmer	VA
Hopkins, Andrew	60	M	Mechanic	TN
Jane	50	F		TN
Constantine	19	M	Mechanic	TN
Jason	17	M	Laborer	TN
Preston	13	M		TN
Desman	11	M		TN
Albina	4	F		TN

End of Austin

Name	Age	Sex	Occupation	Birthplace
Miller, William S.	35	M	Laborer	DC
Palmine	25	F		TN
Peter	2	M		TN
Nowlin, Peyton W.	47	M	Farmer	KY
Martha	43	F		TN
Susan	20	F		MO

(continued)

TRAVIS COUNTY, TEXAS

Name	Age	Sex	Occupation	Birthplace
Nowlin, Ann	16	F		MO
Martha	15	F		MO
Mary	12	F		MO
Peyton	11	M		MO
Adeline	7	F		MO
Mathews, Abner	57	M	Farmer	NC
Aseneth	57	F		NC
James W.	29	M	Farmer	TN
John	26	M	Farmer	TN
Easter	24	F		TN
Stephen	21	M	Waggoner	TN
Amanda	16	F		TN
Franklin	14	M		TN
Paine, Banian	23	M	Farmer	AL
Elizabeth	19	F		TN
Darling	26	M	Farmer	AL
Giles, Edward	52	M	Farmer	TN
Nancy	52	F		TN
Elizabeth	19	F		TN
William	18	M	Farmer	TN
Loucelus	11	M		TN
Valenus	8	M		TN
Henry, William	20	M	Laborer	TN
Howard, Shadric	44	M	Farmer	SC
Sarah	38	F		KY
Eli	26	M	Farmer	MS
Chapman	19	M	Farmer	TN
Valentine	13	M		LA
Sarah	10	F		LA
Leroy	7	M		LA
Smith, Alfred	35	M	Farmer	NC
Ann	24	F		TN
Amelia	8	F		TX
James	19	M	None	NC
Burleson, Aaron	35	M	Farmer	MO
Nerva	30	F		AL
Fayett	18	M	Laborer	TN
Aaron	17	M	Laborer	TN
Jeff	9	M		TX
John	6	M		TX
Elizabeth	5	F		TX
Nancy	3	F		TX
Margaret	1/12	F		TX

TYLER COUNTY, TEXAS

Name	Age	Sex	Occupation	Birthplace
Parsons, Edward J.	29	M	County Clerk	TN
Mary A.	20	F		MS
Virginia A.	4	F		TX
E. J. W.	1	M		TX
Charlton, N. B.	35	M	Farmer	TN
Sarah L.	27	F		GA
Rachael A.	5	F		TX
Josephine	4	F		TX
Catharine	3	F		TX
McDaniel, William G.	42	M	Farmer	TN
Susan A.	28	F		MS
Mary A.	8	F		TX
William P.	5	M		TX
E. L.	3	M		TX
Mariah A.	1	F		TX
McAllister, S. B.	38	M	Wagon Maker	TN
Mary L.	30	F		AL
Nathan S.	13	M		AL
Lucy A.	11	F		AL
William J.	7	M		AL
Sarah P.	4	F		AL
George W.	9/12	M		TX
McAllister, D. E.	41	M	Farmer	TN
Mary E.	29	F		AL
John H.	10	M		AL
R. P.	8	F		AL
McAllister, Mathew D.	6	M		AL
Nancy P.	4	F		AL
Johnson, A. L.	21	M	Farmer	AL
Margaret A.	16	F		AL
Parks, William S.	30	M	Black Smith	TN
Mary E.	20	F		TX
Milton C.	3	M		TN
Susan B.	1	F		TN
Lansom, Samuel D., Jr.	34	M	Farmer	TN
Sarah A.	26	F		TN
Mary E.	6	F		MO
Martha A.	4	F		TX
Willey, M. M.	36	M	Carpenter	GA
Eliza A.	20	F		TN
Mary P.	4	F		TX
Sarah E.	2	M(F)		TX
James P.	5/12	M		TX
Willey, James	31	M	Farmer	GA
Rahal	28	F		GA
Bean, Milton J.	26	M	Farmer	TN
Rotan, Rufus	16	M	Farmer	AL
Trim, John G.	30	M	Farmer	KY
Barclay, Anderson	43	M	Farmer	TN
Sarah A.	34	F		LA
William W.	19	M	Farmer	TX
Elizabeth	11	F		TX
Mahaly F.	9	F		TX
Anderson, Jr.	5	M		TX
Jerry	3	M		TX
Barclay, James	34	M	Farmer	TN
Virginia	22	F		GA
Jane E.	9	F		TX
Aravilla	7	F		TX
Mary L.	5	F		TX
Sarah A.	3	F		TX
James W.	1	M		TX
Barclay, Lacy M.	24	M	Farmer	AR
Nancy	16	F		TN
Nelson, William N.	24	M	Farmer	GA
McQueen, Milton	42	M	Farmer	TN
Susan	36	F		TN
Tranqulla	18	F		TN
John	13	M		TN
Susan J.	10	F		TN
Amanda M.	8	F		TN
Catharine	6	M(F)		TN
James P.	3	M		TN
Tennessee A.	2	F		TN
Rock, Thomas	27	M	School Teacher	LA
Bean, Jane	29	F		KY
Daniel M.	29	M	Farmer	TN
James W.	17	M	Farmer	TN
Martha M.	15	F		TN
Hooker, Robert D.	6	M		TX
Mary J.	4	F		TX
Ratcliff, E. L.	43	M	Farmer	MS
Almyra A.	25	F		TN
James A.	18	M	Farmer	LA
E. T.	5	M		TX
Peter	3	M		TX
Emily	11/12	F		TX
Walters, Sam	31	M	Black Smith	SC
Elizabeth A.	24	F		TN
James T.	4	M		TX
David M.	2	M		TX
Bean, George P.	32	M	Farmer	TN
Elleanor	22	F		AR
Pierce, William D.	31	M	Farmer	GA
Williametta	25	F		TN
Sarah J.	7	F		TX
George W.	5	M		TX
John O.	3	M		TX

(continued)

Name	Age	Sex	Occupation	Birthplace
Pierce, Martha H.	2/12	F		TX
Tompkins, A. N. B.	41	M	Black Smith	TN
Susan	29	F		NC
John W.	10	M		TX
Margarite	8	F		TX
Malina J.	6	F		TX
Mary E.	5	F		TX
Robert W. B.	1	M		TX
Waters, Elizabeth O.	23	F		SC
Taylor, John M.	38	M	Farmer	TN
Nancy A. P.	38	F		TN
Elgina	11	F		TX
Susana	10	F		TX
Henryetta N.	8	F		TX
John Mc.	2	M		TX
Isbell, B. W.	40	M	Farmer	TN
Susan	36	F		TN
James M.	16	M	Farmer	AL
Susan F.	13	F		AL
Mary J.	11	F		AL
Louisa V.	7	F		AL
Claudius B.	4	M		AL
George C.	8/12	M		TX
Parker, A. G.	42	M	Farmer	NC
Elgina	41	F		TN
Pruett, N. M.	28	M		TN
Elizabeth	12	F		TX
A. P.	8	M		TX
John B.	6	M		TX
Willis	4	M		TX
George O.	1	M		TX
Enloe, Benjamin	53	M	Farmer	TN
Sarah	42	F		TN
David C.	27	M	Farmer	AL
Amanda	14	F		MS
Jones, Johnathan	32	M	Farmer	GA
Amanda	19	F		TX
Sarah F.	1	F		TX
Williams, Charles	28	M	Farmer	GA
Bayley, Dudly	21	M	Farmer	TN
Journagan, Stephen	36	M	Ferryman	GA
Cruise, Squire	56	M	Farmer	KY
Piety	46	F		TN
William	16	M	Farmer	TX
Clementine	13	F		TX
Elender	10	F		TX
Pulina	8	F		TX
Anderson	4	M		TX
Franklin	2	M		TX
Wheat, James	28	M	Farmer	AL
Elizabeth	19	F		TN
Martha Ann E.	3	F		TX
Mary J.	1	F		TX
Ratcliff, William	47	M	Carpenter	TN
Abagail	41	F		CAN
William R.	18	M	Farmer	MS
E. D. B.	16	M	Farmer	MS
Olivea	12	F		MS
Nowlin, Milly	45	F		TN
Edward T.	26	M	Farmer	AL
Henry N.	18	M	Farmer	TX
Manervy J.	15	F		TX
Phebe B.	13	M		TX
Charles	11	M		TX
John	8	M		TX
Bean, John T.	33	M	Farmer	TN
Nancy	26	F		GA
M. Lafayette	7	M		TX
Lewis F.	6	M		TX
John T., Jr.	5	M		TX
George M.	4	M		TX
Franklin T.	3	M		TX
David T.	1	M		TX

Name	Age	Sex	Occupation	Birthplace
Young, William	32	M	Black Smith	TN
Delila E.	24	F		AL
William A.	5	M		TX
Emily M.	4	F		TX
Mahaly E.	2	F		TX
Virginia A.	1	F		TX
Sims, George A.	33	M	Farmer	GA
Beet, Samuel T.	48	M	Farmer	MD
Hellen	36	F		TN
John M.	15	M	Farmer	TX
Elizabeth T.	13	F		TX
Spicy M.	10	F		TX
Musidora A.(?)	8	F		TX
A. P.	4	M		TX
Susan M.	1	F		TX
Nowlin, Light	56	M	Farmer	SC
Elizabeth	46	F		TN
Elizabeth T.	17	F		TN
Judith A.	15	F		MS
Lucy A.	10	F		MS
Light, Jr.	8	M		MS
Sansom, Robert P.	30	M	Farmer	TN
Susan	17	F		TX
Parsons, Zenus	37	M	Farmer	TN
Sarah A.	32	F		GA
Mary E.	10	F		AL
William T. J.	8	M		AL
Jaret J. S.	6	M		TX
James C.	4	M		TX
Virginia A.	9/12	F		TX
Parsons, Edmon	73	M	Farmer	NC
Elizabeth	69	F		SC
Wilson, Margarite	46	F		SC
Parsons, Jason H.	33	M	Farmer	TN
Gibson, R. T.	54	M	Coach Maker	TN
Mahaly	42	F		TN
Thomas D.	17	M	Farmer	AL
Nancy J.	15	F		AL
Huldah M.	14	F		AL
William W.	12	M		TX
Elizabeth C.	10	F		TX
Leonidas D.	9	M		TX
Decater J.	7	M		TX
Ruthvan N.	6	M		TX
Cicero L.	2	M		TX
Gibson, Marion M.	22	M	Farmer	AL
Lydia D.	17	F		TN
Wallace, G. B.	28	M	Farmer	AL
Nancy B.	28	F		TN
Elphida B.	8	F		AL
Mary C.	7	F		MS
John P.	5	M		MS
Zalmona V.	3	F		MS
Marquis L.	1	M		TX
Coopwood, Benjamin F.	28	M	Farmer	TN
Eliza A.	24	F		TN
Sansom, William P.	38	M	Minister	TN
Mary A.	32	F		TN
Samuel F.	15	M	Farmer	TN
Eliza J.	13	F		TN
William M.	11	M		TX
Sarah B.	9	F		TX
Elizabeth E.	7	F		TX
John W.	4	M		TX
Mary L.	2	F		TX
Sansom, Samuel D., Sr.	74	M	Minister	SC
Amanda L.	16	F		TN
Sansom, Thomas L.	32	M	Farmer	AL
Mary	32	F		NC
Elizabeth J.	10	F		TN
Martha M.	8	F		TN
Thomas L., Jr.	6	M		TX
Amanda C.	5	F		TX
Sarah A. G.	4	F		TX
Mary E.	2	F		TX

TYLER COUNTY, TEXAS

Name	Age	Sex	Occupation	Born
Barnes, William R.	37	M	Farmer	MS
Isabella	30	F		TN
William E.	14	M		MS
Eli J.	12	M		MS
John H.	10	M		TX
Andrew J.	8	M		TX
Margaritt A.	6	F		TX
Nancy J.	4	F		TX
Mary A.	2	F		TX
Cauble, John M.	37	M	Farmer	TN
Mariah J.	20	F		AL
Samantha	14	F		TN
Sarah	12	F		TN
Green, Ellis	40	M	Farmer	TN
Martha J.	15	F		AL
Green, Joseph	40	M	Farmer	TN
Eliza J.	38	F		KY
George W.	14	M		MS
Martha A.	12	F		MS
Henryetta	9	F		TX
William E.	4	M		TX
Parilee A.	2	F		TX
Green, Aaron	46	M	Farmer	VA
Mary W.	46	F		KY
Thomas L.	25	M	Farmer	AL
John	21	M	Farmer	TN
Ellis	18	M	Farmer	TN
Ann	16	F		TN
Alfred G.	14	M		MS
Catherine	13	F		MS
Benjamin F.	10	M		TX
Nancy E.	7	F		TX
Mary W.	7	F		TX
Green, John, Sr.	52	M	Farmer	VA
Sarah	46	F		SC
John, Jr.	16	M	Farmer	TN
Nancy	13	F		MS
Benjamin	8	M		TX
Laann(?)	7	M		TX
Amanda E.	6	F		TX
Rosilas	4	F		TX
Parks, Nathan J.	18	M	Farmer	TN
Stephen	12	M		TX
Jones, Allen	50	M	Farmer	VA
Nancy	45	F		TN
Jackson	20	M	Farmer	MS
Mary	18	F		MS
Henry	17	M	Farmer	MS
Matilda	16	F		MS
Levina A.	15	F		MS
Calvin	14	M		MS
George	13	M		MS
Kazan	12	F		MS
Washington	11	M		MS
Nancy	4	F		MS
Puss	2	F		TX
Wilson, Hiram A.	28	M	Farmer	GA
Mary	22	F		TN
Stephen E.	3	M		TX
H. A., Jr.	1	M		TX
Samuel	1	M		TX
Cauble, John W.	34	M	Farmer	TN
Eliza	26	F		VA
Mary R.	12	F		TX
Elvira	8	F		TX
John W., Jr.	6	M		TX
James K. P.	4	M		TX
N. B.	2	M		TX
Payne, G. W.	31	M	Merchant	TN
Julia A.	25	F		AR
Mary E.	2	F		TX
Harriett A.	1/12	F		TX
Tipton, J. W.	24	M	Farmer	TN
(continued)				
Tipton, Isabella	19	F		AL
William J.	2	M		TX
West, Henry	23	M	Farmer	TN
Emily C.	19	F		AR
Caroline L.	2	F		TX
Green, Benjamin	56	M	Farmer	VA
Mary	53	F		KY
George W.	18	M	Farmer	AL
William L.	17	M	Farmer	AL
Mary J.	16	F		AL
Rachael M.	12	F		AL
Priest, William	22	M	Farmer	TN
Sumnars, Benjamin	1	M		TX
Walker, John	29	M	Farmer	TN
Ann	24	F		TN
Thomas S.	4	M		TN
William J.	2	M		TN
Cauble, D. B.	30	M	Farmer	TN
Sarah E.	28	F		AL
James Mc.	7	M		TX
John P.	5	M		TX
Thomas F.	3	M		TX
Sarah E., Jr.	1	F		TX
Wilson, William	28	M	Farmer	TN
John A.	4	M		TX
Clerence	1	M		TX
Wilson, Jane	49	F		KY
Shelby	25	M	Farmer	TN
John	23	M	Farmer	TN
Wainn	21	M	Farmer	TN
Elisha	18	M	Farmer	AL
Susanna	19	F		AL
Adaline	16	F		AL
Oliver, Alfred	49	M	Farmer	SC
Amanda	39	F		TN
Allson T.	20	M	Farmer	FL
Eveline	18	F		FL
Alfred, Jr.	14	M		FL
Hughs, Robert	58	M	Hatter	TN
Jesse C.	19	M	Farmer	AL
Butler	12	M		AL
Hoffman, M. L.	43	M	Millwright	TN
Feriby	33	F		KY
Mary A. E.	10	F		LA
Francis M.	8	M		LA
Jane W.	7	F		LA
Penelope	4	F		LA
John J.	2	M		TX
Nowlin, Asa T.	29	M	Farmer	TN
Delila B.	25	F		AL
A. J.	1	M		TX
Jutson, John	26	M	Farmer	IL
Talitha	22	F		TN
Missouri A. R.	6/12	F		TX
Green, James, Jr.	34	M	Farmer	AL
Nancy A.	28	F		TN
Joseph B.	4	M		TX
George W.	2	M		TX
Smith, William H.	53	M	Farmer	KY
Elizabeth	20	F		MO
William J.	8	M		TN
Sarah A. M.	4	F		TX
Welch, Samuel D.	14	M		TN
Smith, Eliza Ann	1	F		TX
Watts, Hiram	33	M	Farmer	LA
Elizabeth	27	F		TN
Carroll	6	M		TX
Louranda	4	F		TX
John	2	M		TX
Caroline	2/12	F		TX

TYLER COUNTY, TEXAS

Name	Age	Sex	Occupation	Birthplace
Allison, J. B.	57	M	Farmer	SC
S.	48	F		SC
Jas. J.	18	M	Farmer	TN
Martha A.	21	F		TN
Robert	15	M	Farmer	TN
Calvin	14	M		MS
Sarah	12	F		MS
Malissa A.	10	F		MS
Daniel B.	6	M		MS
Jenning, Temp S.	29	M	Farmer	TN
Nancy	19	F		MS
Horton, C. J.	35	M	Farmer	NC
Rhoda	17	F		TN
Corsey, V. A.	32	M	Farmer	AL
Nancy	30	F		AL
Eliza A.	8	F		TX
Sarah P. J.	6	F		TX
Charlotte H.	5	F		TX
William T.	4	M		TX
Zilpha	2	F		TX
Benjamin M. F.	4/12	M		TX
Ceacrest, Cyntha	17	F		TN
Ferrill, M. H.	24	M	Farmer	GA
Jane	20	F		TN
Moore, Malinda	35	F		TN
Daniel B.	12	M		MS
Wilmeth A.	9	F		MS
Rhoda A.	7	F		MS
Josephus	6	M		MS
Hanks, Wyett	56	M	Farmer	KY
Hannah	55	F		TN
George T.	18	M	Farmer	TX
Susan T.	16	F		TX
Wyett, Jr.	15	M	Farmer	TX
Rich S.	12	M		TX
Pemberton, J. J.	46	M	Farmer	TN
Mary A.	28	F		KY
J. A.	24	M	Farmer	TN
Tisdell G.	21	M	Farmer	TN
Roland P.	18	M	Farmer	TN
Mary J.	13	F		TX
William J.	10	M		TX
James C.	5	M		TX
Elbrady C.	3	F		TX
Moses L.	1	M		TX
Allison, Isaac	48	M	Farmer	SC
Lourany	43	F		TN
Thomas J.	22	M	Farmer	TN
George W.	20	M	Farmer	TN
Clarinda	16	F		TN
Jefferson	15	M		MS
Marion	13	M		MS
John T.	11	M		MS
Louisa	9	F		MS
Ann P.	7	F		MS
Lurany J.	3	F		TX
Wheat, John	37	M	Farmer	AL
Mary J.	22	F		TN
James D.	5	M		TX
Calaslia A.	4/12	F		TX
Durham, Elizabeth	52	F		VA
America	14	F		TN
Joicy	12	F		TX
Jerushy	9	F		TX
Parsons, Cragg	44	M	Farmer	SC
Mary D.	38	F		TN
Margarett E.	18	F		AL
E. C. D.	16	M	Farmer	TN
Nancy A.	14	F		TN
Lem J. H.	12	M		TN
Sarah T.	10	F		TN
William T. J.	8	M		TN

(continued)

Name	Age	Sex	Occupation	Birthplace
Parsons, Jas. Q. W.	6	M		TX
Mary T.	4	F		TX
Martha C.	1/12	F		TX
Lea, Mjr.	54	M	Farmer	TN
Elizabeth	49	F		TN
Elsy	25	F		MS
F. M.	21	M	Farmer	MS
Angeline	17	F		MS
Adaline	12	F		MS
Priest, M.	41	M	Lawyer	AL
Mary A.	35	F		TN
Margarett J.	16	F		AL
Susan E.	14	F		AL
Henry M.	12	M		AL
Elisha M.	10	M		AL
William H.	8	M		AL
Mejamin D.	6	M		AL
Mary A. T.	2	F		TX
Jewell, E.	41	M		NY
Sarah W.	31	F		TN
William E.	7	M		TX
Eliza A.	4	F		TX
Anna M.	4	F		TX
Ferguson, Lewis	30	M	Farmer	AL
Elizabeth	28	F		TN
E.	8	F		TX
M. N.	6	F		TX
W. M.	2	M		TX
Barclay, John M.	36	M	Farmer	TN
Louisa J.	19	F		TN
Sarah E.	2	F		TX

UPSHUR COUNTY, TEXAS

Name	Age	Sex	Occupation	Birthplace
Ward, William	46	M	Doctor	GA
S.	41	F		TN
M.	18	F		AR
Samuel	15	M		TN
William	12	M		TX
Thomas	2	M		TX
Trowel, Thomas	45	M	Black Smith	SC
S.	27	F		TN
Slayton, Thomas	24	M	Dentist	TN
E. A.	17	F		MO
Barcroft, D. F.	37	M	Merchant	TN
E. G.	26	F		TN
Franklin	7	M		TX
S.	4	F		TX
V.	2	F		TX
Hammer, J.	22	M	Tavern Keeper	TN
Norman, Jno.	37	M	Cabinet Maker	TN
M.	30	F		TN
W.	8	M		TX
J. M.	6	M		TX
E.	3	F		TX
Warren, E.	61	F		TN
G. E.	26	M	Trader	TN
S.	21	F		MO
Richardson, James W.	35	M	District Clerk	SC
Louisa	25	F		TN
M.	5	F		TX
J. P.	4	M		TX
William N.	1	M		TX
Patillo, G. C.	35	M	Chief Justice	TN
L.	26	F		NC
M.	1	F		TX
Martin, William L.	31	M	Farmer	TN
S. B.	20	F		GA
G.	3	M		TX
M. E.	1	F		TX

UPSHUR COUNTY, TEXAS

Name	Age	Sex	Occupation	Birthplace
Yeary, C. H.	25	M	Workman	AL
Mary	16	F		TN
Sharp, R. S.	22	M	Clerk	AL
Warren, R. S.	35	M	County Clerk	TN
A.	23	F		MO
L.	5	F		TX
C.	2	M		TX
Isabel, P.	34	M	(illegible)	AL
A.	36	F		TN
S.	13	F		AL
R. A.	9	F		AL
E.	6	M		AL
A. E.	3	F		AL
Stinson, David	40	M	Lawyer	TN
S. R.	25	F		AL
A. W.	3	M		TX
A.	3	F		TX
P.	20	F		TN
Millow, M.	19	F		TN
Addington, J.	34	M	Cabinet Maker	TN
M. C.	28	F		AL
S. S.	10	M		AL
S. E.	8	F		MS
T. T.	6	F		MS
J. R.	4	M		MS
C. T.	2	F		TX
S. G.	6	F		TX
Hurley, T. N.	27	M	Carpenter	TN
M.	39	F		TN
W.	12	F		TN
S.	8	F		TN
R.	12	M		TN
Hart, J. A.	22	M	Medical Student	TN
Beasley, B. C.	39	M	Medical Student	AL
Derrick, A. C.	57	F		SC
J. A.	23	M	Carpenter	SC
Durard, N. B.	21	M	Carpenter	TN
Smith, S. G.	22	M	Hunter	FL
Moncrief, A.	31	M	Carpenter	GA
C.	29	F		TN
L. A.	2	F		TN
Clarke, J. L.	36	M	Merchant	VA
L.	65	F		NC
Slayton, L.	12	F		TN
E.	14	M		TN
Martin, P. C.	35	M	Carpenter	TN
E.	38	F		TN
M. J.	10	F		TX
W. H.	8	M		TX
G. W.	4	M		TX
M. C.	2	F		TX
S. P.	2/12	M		TX
Starkie, James	37	M	Loafer	TN
Sarah	26	F		TN
E.	6	F		TN
C.	4	M		TN
M.	12	F		TN
Griggs, M.	52	F		GA
Roberts, A.	18	M		TN
A.	15	F		AR
Moore, E.	1	F		TX
Griggs, D.	10	M		AR
Slider, Richard	50	M	Wagon Maker	IN
R.	48	F		VA
E.	27	M		TN
A.	12	M		TN
W.	10	M		TN
Ray, E.	25	F		IN
J.	3	M		TN
Bell, A.	19	M	Cow Driver	TN
Stiles, John R.	27	M	Farmer	TN
N. E.	26	F		TN
S. R.	4	M		TX
W. L.	3	M		TX
L. R.	2	M		TX
Lynch, Samuel	31	M	M.E. Preacher	VA
M.	26	F		TN
Humphreys, Joseph	51	M	Farmer	GA
Martha	28	F		TN
N.	6	M		TX
A.	3	F		TX
M.	1	F		TX
Stocton, Samuel	36	M	Farmer	TN
S.	23	F		TN
M. A.	6	F		MS
S. M.	4	F		MS
J. Y.	3	F		MS
G. H.	2	M		MS
William	4/12	M		TX
Henson, Geremiah	75	M	Farmer	SC
T.	60	F		SC
T. M.	19	M		TN
Davis, P.	33	M	Farmer	TN
D.	32	F		TN
G. A.	7	M		TX
S. S.	5	F		TX
E.	4	F		TX
S.	2	F		TX
Horn, W. A.	25	M	Farmer	TN
N. W.	24	F		TN
M. M.	5	F		MS
S. M.	3	F		MS
G. E.	1	M		MS
Long, Tobias	52	M	Farmer	NC
H.	30	F		TN
W.	18	M		TN
R.	16	M		TN
George	14	M		TN
Martin	12	F(M)		TN
Darcas	10	F		TN
Morris, Jno.	40	M	Farmer	NC
M.	38	F		NC
William	17	M		NC
S.	14	F		NC
H.	10	M		NC
Susan	8	F		NC
N.	7	F		NC
R.	5	F		NC
Martha	3	F		NC
George	2	M		NC
S.	1/12	F		TX
Reynolds, James	28	M	Farmer	TN
S. R.	23	F		AL
F.	5	M		AL
M.	2	F		AL
M. T.	6/12	M		AL
Hays, Rachael	50	F	Widow	NC
R. S.	23	M		AL
R.	22	F		TN
R. G.	20	M		TN
W.	17	M		TN
Meek, Jno.	44	M	Farmer	NC
M.	32	F		TN
Orlena	16	F		TN
Rachael	14	F		TN
C. C.	12	M		TN
M.	8	F		TN
R. G.	7	M		TN
S.	4	F		TN
C.	2	F		TX
Knight, Solomon	40	M	Farmer	TN

(continued)

Name	Age	Sex	Occupation	Birthplace
Knight, Sarah	58	F		KY
Mary	16	F		TN
James ?.	14	M		TN
M.	12	F		MS
R. G.	10	M		MS
S.	8	F		MS
T. G.	5	M		MS
Jno. N.	2	M		TX
Walker, Johnson	23	M	Farmer	MO
Jane	18	F		TN
Weaver, Simeon	41	M	Presby. Preacher	TN
M. C. A.	38	F		TN
S. G.	12	F		MS
S. A.	6	M		AR
G. B.	9	F		TX
M. V.	4	F		TX
E. B.	3/12	M		TX
Holt, A. G.	61	M	Farmer	SC
E.	55	F		SC
William	31	M	Farmer	TN
George M.	15	M		AL
T. S.	17	F		AL
Thomas	13	M		AL
R.	10	F		AL
Henderson, William P.	55	M	Farmer	MD
N. M.	35	F		TN
James	21	M	Farmer	MO
S. P.	19	M		MO
Mary	16	F		MO
Jno.	13	M		MO
V. A.	11	F		MO
D.	2	F		TX
Hill, Hexley	46	M	Farmer	SC
E.	41	F		TN
G.	19	F		AL
A. A.	16	M		AL
Louisa	14	F		AL
Levi	12	M		TX
James	10	M		TX
Jas.	5	M		TX
W. M.	2	M		TX
Edwards, Howard	37	M	Farmer	TN
M.	34	F		TN
T. S.	16	M		IL
W. G.	13	M		IL
N. M.	6	F		MS
S. A.	4	F		TX
R. C.	3	M		TX
M. C.	1/12	M		TX
Stiles, A.	48	M	Farmer	SC
E.	45	F		SC
R.	20	M		TN
S.	15	M		AL
M. S.	13	F		AL
R.	16	F		AL
S. A.	6	F		AL
V. N.	17	F		TN
Stiles, W.	22	M	Farmer	TN
N. M.	16	F		??
Grigory, S.	44	M	Farmer	TN
M.	44	F		SC
S. A.	21	F		AL
R. S.	19	F		AL
N. C.	16	F		AL
M. E.	14	F		AL
N. P.	4	F		TX
W. S. P.	3/12	M		TX
Edwards, W.	34	M	Farmer	TN
M. A.	30	F		NC
M. H.	13	M		MS
M. T.	12	F		MS
William B.	10	M		MS
M.	6	F		MS

(continued)

Name	Age	Sex	Occupation	Birthplace
Edwards, S.	5	F		MS
E. W.	4	F		MS
J. G.	1	M		TX
Allen, M. M.	24	M	Farmer	TN
S. G.	22	M	Farmer	TN
Bullion, T.	46	M	Farmer	SC
E.	46	F		TN
Carroll, C.	60	F		NC
Bullion, R.	15	F		AL
M.	10	M		AL
M. G.	8	F		AL
Hellems, W.	29	M	Farmer	NC
M.	23	F		TN
M. E.	3	F		AL
W. C.	2	M		AL
Coffman, James	48	M	Farmer	TN
S.	45	F		VA
Connally, C. P.	25	M	Farmer	TN
V.	22	F		AL
M. A.	3	F		AL
J. M.	1/12	M		TX
S.	42	F		SC
Crawford, Joel	30	M	Farmer	NC
E.	23	F		TN
G. B.	6	M		AL
William W.	2	M		AL
Collier, Thomas	50	M	Farmer	NC
S.	37	F		NC
G.	23	M		NC
J.	19	F		NC
R. T.	17	F		TN
M. A.	14	F		TN
J.	13	F		TN
Thomas	8	M		MS
S.	3	F		TX
Davis, James	41	M	Farmer	NC
E.	25	F		GA
Smith, M.	63	F		VA
Davis, M. P.	18	F		SC
D.	12	F		AL
S. A.	6	F		TX
J. T.	4	M		TX
M. A. E.	2	F		TX
McCrackin, S.	39	M	Farmer	SC
J. S.	16	M		SC
V. G.	14	F		AL
G. M.	11	M		AL
M. T.	9	F		AR
Christopher, G. C.	21	M	Farmer	TN
Lee, Nathan	31	M	Farmer	TN
S. A.	27	F		AL
S. W.	10	M		AL
S. A.	9	F		AL
Isam	6	M		AL
M. E.	4	F		AL
Z. T.	1	M		AL
Martin, S. B. B.	33	M	Farmer	AL
S. G.	32	F		AL
W. C.	9	M		TX
S. N.	7	M		TX
S. E.	6	F		TX
G. F.	4	M		TX
E. E.	1/12	M		TX
Reavis, D. M.	31	M		TN
Jones, P. A.	45	F		TN
R. P.	20	M	Farmer	TN
R.	28	M	Farmer	TN
G.	17	M		TN
James	15	M		MS
E.	5	F		MS
B. F.	2	M		AR
Wyatt, S.	52	M	Farmer	SC
M.	50	F		NC

(continued)

UPSHUR COUNTY, TEXAS

Name	Age	Sex	Occupation	Birthplace
Wyatt, A.	25	M	Farmer	TN
N.	20	F		TN
R.	18	F		TN
Richard	17	M		TN
M.	14	F		TN
A.	12	M		MS
E. A.	8	F		TX
Shipman, Jno.	28	M	Farmer	TN
S.	22	F		TN
Daniel, C.	34	M	Farmer	NC
M.	33	F		NC
M.	7	F		TN
James	5	M		TX
W.	1/12	M		TX
Brown, R.	32	M	Farmer	??
J.	21	F		TN
R.	2	M		TX
R. G.	1	M		TX
Loyd, William	54	M	Farmer	KY
M.	48	F		SC
J.	19	M		TN
Vincent	17	M		TN
William	15	M		TN
Vine	12	F		AR
M.	10	F		MO
S.	25	M		TN
Loyd, Simpson	25	M	Farmer	TN
Olif	18	F		TN
Loyd, Jackson	25	M	Farmer	TN
M.	22	F		TN
Yancey, S. M.	38	M	Farmer	NC
M.	24	F		TN
S. F.	5	F		TX
W. H.	4	M		TX
M. E.	5	F		TX
G. A.	6/12	M		TX
Robertson, J. F.	45	M	Farmer	SC
M.	43	F		NC
W. M.	22	M	Farmer	TN
C. C.	20	M	Farmer	TN
M. S.	15	M		TN
E. D.	18	M	Farmer	TN
G. W.	13	M		TN
G. P.	11	M		TN
D. F.	9	M		TN
P. N.	8	M		TX
M. E.	7	F		TX
E.	5	F		TX
W. P.	1	M		TX
Robertson, W. M.	22	M	Farmer	TN
N. A.	20	F		--
Atkinson, S. G.	34	M	Black Smith	TN
M.	30	F		KY
A.	10	M		KY
T.	7	M		KY
M. E.	6	F		KY
S. E.	3	F		KY
Robertson, W. M.	41	M	Farmer	SC
E.	30	F		NC
C. F.	16	M		TN
C.	14	M		TN
M. A.	12	F		TN
M.	10	F		TN
A.	8	M		TX
T.	6	M		TX
S.	4	F		TX
M.	1	F		TX
Robertson, C.	83	M	Farmer	MD
S.	63	F		NC
Newman, S. C.	52	M	Merchant	SC

(continued)

Name	Age	Sex	Occupation	Birthplace
Newman, A.	54	F		SC
M. A.	17	F		TN
G.	16	M		TN
M.	14	M		AL
Beggs, G. D.	23	M	Farmer	IL
M. H.	19	F		TN
W. N.	9/12	M		TX
Minor, Thomas	21	M	Farmer	TN
M.	21	F		TN
N. E.	1	F		TX
McLain, W.	52	M	Farmer	TN
N. C.	26	F		AL
S. E.	17	F		AL
W. G.	15	M		AL
L. H.	13	M		AL
M. C.	11	F		AL
R. A.	8	M		MS
P. A.	6	F		MS
White, L. B.	27	M	Farmer	MS
N. C.	26	F		AL
S. B.	3/12	M		TX
G. C.	27	M		TN
McNairy, J. H.	45	M	Farmer	NC
S.	26	F		TN
R. D.	22	M	Farmer	TN
D. H.	21	M	Farmer	TN
C. H.	15	F		TN
L.	16	M		TN
S.	12	F		MS
N. A.	7	F		TX
A.	5	F		TX
E. S.	3	F		TX
M. M.	3	F		TX
E. P.	10/12	F		TX
Holt, L. E.	26	M	Farmer	TN
E.	28	F		TN
Parker, E.	49	M	Farmer	NC
S. A.	49	F		PA
D.	18	M		TN
M.	15	M		TN
S.	13	F		TN
P.	12	F		TN
T.	9	M		TN
S. A.	7	F		TN
Gardener, A.	24	M	Farmer	TN
N. N.	24	F		TN
Holt, William H.	30	M	Farmer	TN
E.	30	F		TN
S.	10	M		TN
E.	8	F		TN
S. M.	4	F		TN
W. S.	6	M		TN
M.	2	F		TN
Stephen, J. S.	45	M	Farmer	NY
M.	35	F		TN
W. C.	15	M		TN
D. S.	12	M		TN
G. W.	10	M		TN
S. C.	8	M		TN
A. J.	3	M		TN
M. A.	3	F		TN
Hanley, S.	50	M	Farmer	TN
M.	38	F		GA
W.	12	M		TN
R.	10	M		TN
Clark, R. G.	44	M	Farmer	SC
M. G.	40	F		SC
S.	21	M	Farmer	SC
T.	18	M		TN
J.	15	F		SC
James	12	M		TN
S.	11	F		AL
A.	9	F		AL

(continued)

UPSHUR COUNTY, TEXAS

Name	Age	Sex	Occupation	Birthplace
Clark, B.	8	F		AL
Jno.	4	M		MS
Latimer, J.	25	M	Farmer	TN
H.	19	F		TN
M. C.	5/12	F		TX
Clayton, John	22	M	Farmer	TN
S.	31	F		AL
M. A.	11	F		LA
M. W.	8	M		LA
G. R.	5	M		LA
N.	3	M		AR
S.	7/12	F		AR
Clark, Jonathan	36	M	Farmer	KY
S. M.	37	F		TN
N. L.	14	F		TN
E. M.	12	F		TN
M. M.	10	F		MS
S. E.	8	F		MS
S. V.	5	F		MS
M. S.	2	M		MS
Medlin, G. B.	52	M	Farmer	NC
N.	32	F		OH
M. J.	15	F		TN
S. E.	11	M		TX
J. S.	9	M		TX
N. A.	6	M		TX
L. E.	3	F		TX
R. C.	1	F		TX
Morris, J. H.	22	M		TN
N.	19	F		TN
Hambright, William	34	M	Farmer	SC
E.	30	F		TN
G. W.	9	M		MO
S. E.	6	F		TX
M. C.	4	F		TX
J. G.	6/12	M		TX
Williams, J.	50	M	Cabinet Maker	PA
Star, William	24	M	Farmer	OH
J.	27	F		OH
J. A.	2	M		TN
Jackson, A.	33	M	Farmer	NC
J.	17	M		TN
N. J.	11	F		TX
G.	7	M		TX
M.	5	M		TX
Whittaker, William	46	M	Farmer	MS
N.	30	F		TN
E.	21	M		TX
R.	20	M		TX
C.	17	F		TX
M. A.	6	F		TX
E. H.	6/12	F		TX
Moodey, A.	33	M	Farmer	AL
N.	32	F		TN
Thomas	14	M		TX
M.	10	M		TX
J.	7	M		TX
H.	5	M		TX
N. A.	4	F		TX
Jas.	2	M		TX
Taylor, J. R.	43	M	Farmer	MS
E.	35	F		TN
Thomas	13	M		TX
J. H.	12	M		TX
M. J.	6	F		TX
B.	5	M		TX
N. E.	1	F		TX
Brewer, P. W.	19	M	Farmer	MS
Burtin, E.	33	M	Farmer	MS
S.	30	F		TN
M. J.	12	F		AR

(continued)

Name	Age	Sex	Occupation	Birthplace
Burtin, S.	10	F		AR
E.	8	M		AR
S.	6	F		AR
B.	4	F		AR
E.	1	M		TX
Mottock, Jno.	29	M	Farmer	TN
M.	28	F		AL
J. P.	8	M		MS
J. S.	6	M		TX
J. M.	4	M		TX
S. W.	1	M		TX
Glasco, J. M.	32	M	Surveyor	TN
S. M.	26	F		AL
M. E.	3	F		TX
S. M.	1	M		TX
Craft, J.	54	M	Farmer	TN
M.	45	F		GA
J.	19	M		MS
M.	17	F		MS
Thomas	15	M		MS
R.	13	M		MS
G.	11	M		MS
M.	9	F		MS
E.	7	F		MS
R.	5	M		MS
Galihight, T. H.	26	M	Farmer	TN
S.	27	F		TN
C.	4	F		TN
Maloy, A.	30	M	Farmer	GA
S. S.	19	F		TN
Dotson, C.	32	M	Farmer	AL
S. A.	30	F		TN
N. A.	6	F		TX
W. R.	5	M		TX
S. T.	3	F		TX
M. A.	27	F		TX
E. R.	20	M	Farmer	TN
Walker, M.	38	F		TN
J.	18	M	Farmer	TN
S.	16	F		TN
M.	14	F		MS
S.	12	F		MS
W.	10	M		MS
Knight, S. R.	46	M	Farmer	NC
J. A.	35	F		NC
R. C.	15	F		TN
W. C.	11	M		MS
S. A.	10	F		TX
T. M.	7	M		TX
M. E.	6	F		TX
J. J.	4	M		TX
A.	3/12	M		TX
Farensworth, S.	54	M	Farmer	TN
M.	44	F		KY
J.	21	M		TN
S.	17	M		TN
M. A.	14	F		TN
W.	12	M		TN
H.	8	M		AL
T. A.	6	M		TX
S.	4	F		TX
E.	1/12	F		TX
Calbert, D. C.	32	M	Farmer	IL
M.	33	F		NC
T. C.	11	M		TN
S. A.	9	F		TN
W. C.	7	M		TN
A. C.	5	F		MS
G. H.	3	M		MS
Barnes, N. C.	28	M		SC
Try, William	26	M	Farmer	TN
E.	27	F		TN
Alexander, S. S.	36	M	Farmer	AL

(continued)

UPSHUR COUNTY, TEXAS

Alexander, E. M.	25	F		NC
S. R.	3	F		TN
J. C.	6/12	M		TX
Hart, J. D.	30	M	Farmer	NC
C. C.	22	F		NC
S.	65	F		NC
G. W.	18	M	Farmer	TN
Turner, W. W.	30	M	Farmer	TN
S.	35	F		KY
J. R.	4	M		TN
M. S.	2	F		TX
W. W.	1	M		TX
S. J.	1/12	M		TX
Kelsey, W.	20	M	Teacher	TN
Patison, R. H.	46	M	Farmer	TN
P. E.	28	F		TN
S. C.	5	F		TN
J. H.	3	M		TX
Hamilton, A. L.	30	M	Cabinet Maker	TN
M. J.	24	F		TN
W. W.	3	M		TX
J. H.	3/12	M		TX
Spencer, E.	37	M	Farmer	NC
J. A.	10	F		TN
P. M.	9	F		TN
R.	28	M	Farmer	NC
Brown, J.	24	M	Farmer	AL
M. A.	17	F		TN
Larkington, B. W.	42	M	Farmer	TN
M.	4	F		TN
B.	18	M		TN
L.	14	F		TN
J.	11	F		TN
N.	8	F		TN
F.	6	F		TN
A.	3	F		TX
J.	6/12	M		TX
Stubblefield, J. L.	41	M	Farmer	TN
N.	33	F		AL
R. E.	15	M		MS
M. E.	11	F		MS
H. E.	8	F		TN
S. J.	6	F		TX
S. J.	3	F		TX
Walker, R. M.	36	M	Farmer	GA
E.	28	F		TN
Nation, J.	14	F		TN
W.	18	M		TX
Stovall, E.	34	M	Farmer	IL
N.	22	F		TN
Bell, E.	50	F		NC
Moore, J. W.	30	M	Farmer	TN
S.	25	F		KY
J. M.	4/12	M		TX
Edwards, T. L.	30	M	Farmer	TN
M. L.	18	F		IL
J. W.	12	M		TX
Russel, D.	28	M	Farmer	AL
S.	28	F		TN
R.	6/12	F		TX
Edwards, H. H.	32	M	Farmer	TN
E.	23	F		TN
L.	4	M		TX
N. R.	2	M		TX
Edwards, S.	62	M	B. Minister	NC
S.	60	F		NC
M. H.	25	M		TN
G. B.	21	M		TN

(continued)

Edwards, W.	19	M		TN
M. L.	23	F		TN
Smith, G. P.	40	M	Doctor	TN
Price, R. E.	47	M	Miller	NC
P. N.	17	M		TN
E. A.	13	F		TN
R. E.	11	M		TX
R. M.	6	M		TX
N. C.	3	F		TX
Price, P. P.	23	M		TN
M. E.	18	F		GA
R. R.	1	F		TX
Starnes, E. R.	28	M	Miller	GA
S. E.	20	F		TN
R. A.	1	M		TX
N. J.	4/12	M		TX
H. C.	15	M		GA
L. C.	9	F		TX
N. E.	6	F		TX
J. H.	24	M		GA
Head, E. S.	30	M		TN
M. A.	3	F		TX
Moore, J. W.	53	M	Farmer	NC
S.	55	F		NC
G. W.	25	M		TN
M. E.	23	F		TN
Chapin, P. S.	25	M	Farmer	TN
S. C.	22	F		TN
M. E.	3	F		TX
J. A.	1	M		TX
Milligan, W.	35	M	Farmer	TN
A.	24	F		SC
S.	10	F		TX
E.	8	F		TX
A.	4	M		TX
S.	6/12	F		TX
T.	25	M	Farmer	TN
Lam, J.	25	M	Teacher	LA
Benson, Jerre	24	M	Farmer	TN
M. J.	23	F		TN
M. A. E.	1	F		TX
W. C.	3/12	M		TX
Jones, R.	32	M	Farmer	TN
M.	20	F		MS
J.	2	M		TX
T.	11	M		MO
N.	9	F		MO
J.	4	M		TX
Allen, A.	34	M	Farmer	TN
S.	24	F		AR
W. B.	13	M		TN
T. B.	11	M		TN
M. J.	9	F		TN
R. P.	7	M		TN
R. E.	5	F		TX
J. H.	2	M		TX
Norwood, W. C.	43	M	Farmer	TN
S.	32	F		GA
W.	10	M		TN
D.	8	M		TN
J. W.	6	M		TX
H.	3	F		TX
E.	1	F		TX
Mitchel, John	63	M	Farmer	GA
J.	23	M		TN
J. B.	18	M		TN
L. A.	18	F		--
Mitchel, H.	37	M		GA
S.	37	F		TN
M. A.	14	F		TN
L.	12	M		TN
E.	10	F		TN
C.	8	F		TN

(continued)

Name	Age	Sex	Occupation	Birthplace
Mitchel, S.	6	F		TN
M.	3	F		TN
Holt, E.	50	F		NC
Porter, B. J.	44	M	Farmer	GA
D.	39	F		SC
E. N.	17	F		TN
C. M.	15	F		MS
M. M.	13	F		MS
S. E.	11	F		TX
H.	9	M		TX
J.	6	M		TX
S.	4	F		TX
N.	1	F		TX
Lank, J. H.	23	M	Teacher	LA
Thornton, J.	42	M		GA
M.	34	F		TN
S.	15	F		AL
B.	11	M		AL
J.	9	M		AL
A. M.	1	F		AL
Davis, B.	60	M	Farmer	TN
L.	53	F		NC
M.	21	F		AL
Thomas	20	M		AL
E.	17	F		AL
J.	13	M		AL
N.	9	F		AL
Mahaffy, M. C.	24	M	Farmer	TN
E. J.	19	F		TN
J. T.	1/12	M		TX
Hill, J. T.	44	M	Farmer	NC
N.	44	F		TN
W. H.	20	M		AL
J. H.	14	M		AL
E. A.	11	M		AL
L. G.	9	F		MS
S. C.	5	F		MS
Maning, D. S.	30	M		OH
S.	21	F		TN
S.	5	F		AR
S. E.	3	F		AR
A. W.	2	M		AR
W. W.	2/12	M		TX
Lore, W.	25	M	Farmer	TN
S. A.	25	F		AL
Gilliand, Allen	46	M	Farmer	AL
M.	36	F		TN
W.	18	M		AR
M. A.	15	F		AR
M.	11	F		AR
J. W.	9	M		AR
J.	7	M		AR
S. J.	3	F		TX
Ray, James	28	M	B. Minister	KY
M.	26	F		TN
L. S.	6	F		LA
M. A.	2	F		LA
S. J.	6/12	F		TX
S.	60	F		KY
C.	19	F		IL
M. V.	14	F		IL
Gipson, S. S.	25	M	Farmer	AL
N.	24	F		TN
M. A.	3	F		LA
M.	6/12	F		TX
M. E.	14	F		TN
T.	62	M		NC
Gipson, Leroy	27	M		TN
S.	29	F		IL
L. H.	5	M		LA
J.	3	M		KY
M. A.	1	F		LA

(continued)

Name	Age	Sex	Occupation	Birthplace
Davis, B.	21	M	Farmer	GA
Morris, B. M.	16	M		TN
Dial, Martin	36	M	Farmer	TN
M.	34	F		TN
A. J.	12	M		AR
J. R.	10	M		AR
M.	7	F		LA
M. S.	9/12	F		TX
Dial, Jonathan	23	M	Farmer	TN
R.	20	F		AR
J. W.	2	M		TX
J. E.	2/12	M		TX
Tidwell, M.	36	M	Farmer	TN
M.	36	F		TN
J.	12	M		TN
M.	10	F		TN
D. H.	8	M		TN
L. C.	2	F		TN
Sears, M.	28	M		TX
Rodgers, A. G.	46	M	Farmer	TN
K.	35	F		TN
A.	20	M	Farmer	MS
L. J.	19	M	Farmer	MS
M. A.	15	M		MS
B. G.	10	M		MS
K.	7	F		MS
V.	6	F		MS
S. E.	4	F		MS
S.	1	F		TX
Crow, J. W.	29	M	Farmer	NC
M.	39	F		TN
Davison, Thomas	27	M	Farmer	TN
Henrel, J.	27	M	Carpenter	TN
Neasbet, R.	22	M	Farmer	TN
McLaughlin, William	42	M	Farmer	TN
M.	32	F		TN
A.	12	F		AR
Smith, M.	7	F		AR
Carrol, Thomas	50	M	Meth. Preacher	MS
P.	42	F		TN
M.	22	F		LA
S.	20	F		LA
J.	19	M	Farmer	LA
W.	17	M	Farmer	LA
Thomas	15	M		LA
A. J.	13	M		LA
H. H.	10	M		LA
C.	8	M		LA
N.	11	F		LA
P.	6	F		LA
E.	4	M		LA
Decker, E.	25	M	Farmer	KY
M.	17	F		TN
S. M.	1	F		TX
Pettey, John M.	45	M	Farmer	SC
S. M.	43	F		TN
L. M.	18	M	Farmer	TN
L. W.	16	M	farmer	TN
B. J.	13	M		TN
J. S.	11	M		TN
F. M.	9	F		TN
Richardson, G. T.	17	M		MS
A.	16	F		MS
S. P.	11	M		MS
S. J.	9	M		MS
M. J.	4	M		MS
S. C.	3	F		TX
West, J.	25	M	Farmer	TN
M. E.	18	F		TN
Long, Mathew	29	M	Farmer	TN
E.	18	F		TN
N.	3	F		TX
M. C.	1	F		TX
W. W.	10	M		TX
J. J.	3/12	M		TX

UPSHUR COUNTY, TEXAS

Name	Age	Sex	Occupation	Birthplace
Benton, Nathan	29	M	Farmer	TN
L.	29	F		TN
M. J.	6	F		TN
N. A.	4	F		TX
S.	1	F		TX
Mann, John	43	M	Farmer	TN
D.	42	F		TN
James	21	M	Farmer	TN
M.	20	F		TN
N.	18	F		TN
W.	16	M	Farmer	TN
S.	14	M		TN
L.	12	M		TN
E.	10	F		TN
John	8	M		TN
Rice	6	M		TN
Henry	4	M		TN
L. J.	2	F		TN
Webb, W. M.	32	M	Farmer	TN
E.	28	F		MO
S. E.	4	F		TX
S. M.	2	M		TX
Davis, O.	37	M	Farmer	TN
N.	40	F		TN
J. W.	14	M		TN
S. S.	9	M		TN
L. L.	6	F		TN
L. M.	4	M		TN
M. W.	3	F		TX
P.	1	M		TX
Benton, T.	53	M	Farmer	SC
N.	48	F		VA
James	20	M	Farmer	TN
T. M.	16	M		GA
J.	15	M		GA
S. A.	13	F		TN
E.	11	F		TN
A.	9	M		TN
P. J.	7	M		TN
M.	5	F		TN
N.	2	F		TX
M.	18	F		GA
Snow, S.	31	M	Farmer	TN
E.	50	F		NC
J. H.	4	M		TN
W. M.	2	M		TN
J.	6/12	M		TX
Curry, S.	29	M	Farmer	TN
J.	18	F		TN
F. M.	3/12	M		TN
Green, B. M.	25	M	Farmer	TN
N. A.	25	F		TN
B. F.	2	M		TN
J.	1/12	M		TX
Marsh, Alexander	22	M	Farmer	VA
F.	24	F		TN
S.	2	F		TN
Taylor, M.	29	M	Farmer	LA
S.	21	F		TN
S. N.	6	M		TX
W. J.	3	M		TX
J. A.	2	M		TX
Tridel, H.	13	M		TX
Taylor, Mary	57	F		VA
Stokely, Mary	16	F		TN
H.	23	M	Farmer	TX
Denton, B.	48	M	Farmer	TN
L.	38	F		AL
S. A.	18	F		TN
J.	17	M		TN
Lewis	15	M		TN
J. C.	14	M		TN
W. C.	10	M		TN
P. S.	8	M		TN

(continued)

Name	Age	Sex	Occupation	Birthplace
Denton, G. W.	5	M		TN
C.	2	F		TX
Earp, James	52	M	Farmer	GA
M.	48	F		TN
R.	22	M	Farmer	AL
P.	19	M	Farmer	AL
James	16	M	Farmer	AL
E.	12	F		TX
N.	11	F		AL
Wilson, W.	23	M	Farmer	AL
Earp, R.	30	M	Farmer	AL
M.	27	F		AR
M.	6	F		TX
R.	4	M		TX
B.	21	M	Farmer	TN
Humphreys, J. T.	34	M	Farmer	TN
M. J.	21	F		TN
M. V.	5	F		TN
J. H.	3	M		TN
G. P.	2/12	M		TX
G. P.	26	M	Farmer	TN
Ellis, T. O.	47	M	Doctor	MO
E.	30	F		TN
James W.	14	M		IL
S. J.	11	F		MS
Thomas U.	9	M		MS
M. S.	7	F		MS
L. A.	6	F		MS
M. S.	4	F		MS
M. C.	2	F		TX
E. J.	1	F		TX
Gray, V. B.	18	M	Farmer	IL
Ellis, N. B.	29	M	Doctor	TN
Ellis, G. J.	31	M	Farmer	TN
M. C.	27	F		TN
J.	8	M		TX
C.	6	F		TX
G. J.	1	M		TX
Morgan, G.	30	M	Farmer	AL
E.	23	F		TN
Halbert, C.	30	M	Farmer	TN
D.	63	F		SC
Greer, Mikel	25	M	Farmer	MO
M.	25	F		IL
H.	9	F		TX
J.	7	M		TX
Thomas	5	M		TX
Newton	2	M		TX
Dellinham, A.	65	F		TN
McNut, H.	46	M	Farmer	TN
E.	46	F		TN
M.	20	F		AL
Alex	18	M		AL
W.	16	M		AL
W.	12	M		TX
Jane	9	F		TX
M. E.	7	F		TX
J.	5	F		TX
T. A. A.	2	M		TX
Lamascus, William	25	M	(illegible)	AL
N. C.	21	F		TN
J. R.	1	M		TX
Wilson, Robert	32	M	Farmer	AL
R. C.	20	F		TN
J.	5	M		AL
W.	4	M		AL
G. W.	1	M		TX
Brewer, John W.	30	M	Farmer	NC
L.	30	F		TN
W. R.	9	M		TN
J. W.	9	M		MS
G. W.	1	M		TX
Hester, J.	16	F		MS

UPSHUR COUNTY, TEXAS

Name	Age	Sex	Occupation	Birthplace
Crain, Lewis	53	M	Farmer	GA
M.	58	F		NC
Alexander, James	32	M	Farmer	GA
C.	27	F		AL
M. J.	13	F		MS
Crain, Juda	21	F		MS
Howel, John	55	M	Farmer	TN
Jane	55	F		NC
Josaphine	19	F		TN
M. A.	15	F		TN
W. H.	13	M		TN
Vesrey, R. L.	28	M	Farmer	TN
M. J.	25	F		TN
N. J.	4	F		TN
E.	5	F		TX
Wilborn, William	59	M	Farmer	NC
N.	56	F		NC
James	20	M	Farmer	TN
L.	17	M		TN
Awalt, S.	39	M	C.P. Preacher	NC
A. E.	28	F		NC
W. J.	11	M		TN
N. C.	6	F		TN
L. H.	1	M		TX
Fisher, John	51	M	Farmer	VA
S. S.	45	F		SC
L. P.	22	M	Farmer	TN
M. C.	18	F		TN
James L.	16	M		TN
J. A.	12	F		TN
C. D.	8	F		TN
Rodden, John	55	M	Farmer	VA
A.	45	F		GA
M. A.	23	F		AL
N. J.	19	F		AL
A.	18	F		AL
J.	15	M		AL
J. H.	12	M		AL
W. J.	8	M		TX
Templeton, G. S.	32	M	C.P. Preacher	KY
Spencer, Benjamin	24	M	C.P. Preacher	TN
Ward, J. A.	41	M	Farmer	TN
M. W.	35	F		TN
L. A.	16	M		TN
Jas.	13	M		MS
N. H.	9	F		TN
J. A.	8	M		TN
J.	4	M		TN
M. M.	3/12	F		TX
McGee, James J.	51	M	Doctor	TN
E. A.	24	F		TN
J. A.	6	M		AR
J. L.	2	M		TX
M(N)ight, Levi	17	M	Farmer	KY
Templeton, Thomas	29	M	Farmer	AL
E. C.	24	F		TN
J. D.	4	M		TN
Jas. D.	3	M		TN
J. W.	2	M		TN
Dickson, M. E.	10	F		TN
Barber, M.	30	M	Farmer	VA
C. H.	30	F		TN
H. B.	7	M		TN
Sally	4	F		TN
Jane	2	F		TN
Aleup(?), John	25	M	Chair Maker	AL
Cooper, Sam M.	26	M	Farmer	TN
F.	25	F		TN
E. J.	4	F		TN
John	2	M		TN
V.	5/12	F		TN
Wagner, Jane	55	F		NC

Name	Age	Sex	Occupation	Birthplace
Moorse, W.	26	M	Farmer	TN
E.	25	F		TN
H.	6	M		TN
M.	5	F		TN
John	3	M		TN
C. H.	8	M		TN
Pearce, W.	17	M		TN
Echols, J. T.	42	M	Merchant	GA
M. C.	41	F		TN
G.	8	M		TX
Robert	4	M		TX
Houstin, S. A.	40	M	Merchant	TN
W. T.	14	M		TN
M.	7	F		TN
Payne, W. H.	41	M	Farmer	TN
A.	33	F		GA
Davis, S. H.	7	M		TX
James R.	4	M		TX
Payne, A. E.	6/12	F		TX
Casselbury, Jas.	42	M	None	GA
Casselbury, Stephen	38	M	Farmer	GA
M.	37	F		TN
A.	14	M		AL
M.	11	F		TX
Felix	8	M		TX
A.	6	F		TX
S.	3	F		TX
Jane	2/12	F		TX
M.	8	F		TX
Casselbury, A. L.	35	M		GA
E.	26	F		TN
Jas.	10	M		TX
A.	8	M		TX
R.	6	M		TX
M.	4	F		TX
James	1	M		TX
A.	21	M	None	AL
John	18	M	None	AL
Hambelton, J. P.	33	M	Farmer	TN
M. J.	27	F		TN
R. S.	8	M		TN
J. L.	4	M		TN
S. A.	2	F		TN
S. E.	11/12	F		TX
Denton, A. B.	32	M	Farmer	TN
M. A.	21	F		AL
S. M.	4	F		TX
H. H.	2	F		TX
Jordin, Elias	30	M	Farmer	MS
James	11	M		MS
H.	9	M		MS
M.	7	F		MS
Manda	5	F		MS
Elias	3	M		MS
E.	1	F		MS
John	50	M	Farmer	TN
E.	45	F		GA
John	27	M	Farmer	MS
E.	20	F		MS
M.	18	F		MS
A.	16	M	Farmer	MS
V.	13	M		MS
V.	12	M		MS
Maranda	10	F		MS
Wilborn, William T.	27	M	Farmer	TN
J.	24	F		TN
S. A.	3	F		TX
J. M.	1	M		TX
Cist, L.	40	M	Black Smith	TN
Luce	37	F		TN
Winifred	17	F		TN
E.	15	F		TN
J. P.	10	M		TN
M. A.	6	F		TN
M. J.	4	F		TX
M. C.	2	M		TX

UPSHUR COUNTY, TEXAS

Name	Age	Sex	Occupation	Birthplace
Smith, David	30	M	Farmer	TN
E.	45	F		TN
Crier, Elijah	45	M	Farmer	KY
E.	36	F		VA
J.	16	M	Farmer	TN
D. J.	12	M		TN
S.	8	F		TN
L. W.	7	M		AL
Jane	5	F		AL
John B.	2	M		TX
Smart, G. B.	21	M	Farmer	TN
M. C.	18	F		MS
Smart, M.	41	F		TN
Silas A.	17	M	Farmer	TN
Milton	16	M	Farmer	TN
W. W.	12	M		TN
M. C.	9	F		MS
Joshua	8	M		MS
E.	6	M		MS
M. L.	2	F		MS
M. A.	13	F		MS
Mackey, J. J.	49	M	Farmer	TN
M.	49	F		NC
R.	15	F		TN
W. L.	13	M		TN
J. B.	11	M		TN
Landingham, William	25	M	Farmer	AL
E.	25	F		TN
N.	4/12	M		TX
Barnes, William	25	M	Farmer	TN
Eveline	18	F		TN
Mackey, Alex	23	M	Farmer	TN
L. T.	22	M	Farmer	TN
Right, A. L.	39	M	Farmer	GA
A.	29	F		SC
L.	19	F		AL
W. H.	17	M		AL
John B.	14	M		AL
S.	13	F		AL
H.	11	M		AL
J. L.	10	M		AL
Landingham, W.	24	M		AL
Martin, E. L. A.	22	M	Printer	TN
Boyd, Mary	43	F		VA
J. M.	23	M	Farmer	TN
S. A.	21	F		TN
James	17	M	Farmer	TN
E.	15	F		TN
M.	13	F		TN
R.	11	F		GA
William	9	M		GA
Thomas H.	7	M		GA
M. J.	5	F		GA
Mosley, August	35	M	Farmer	SC
M. A. E.	28	F		GA
M. A. E.	7	F		AL
P.	2	F		TX
Abney, A. H.	28	M	School Teacher	VA
L. H.	5	M		GA
Dickson, J. D.	24	M	Farmer	TN
Beavers, Joseph	40	M	Farmer	VA
S.	40	F		NC
Jessee	16	M		TN
Wilson	14	M		TX
M.	10	F		TX
W.	6	M		TX
Underwood, A.	50	M	Farmer	NC
C.	44	F		NC
A. A.	18	F		TN
P. H.	16	F		TN
N. E.	13	F		GA
S. A.	10	M		TN

(continued)

Name	Age	Sex	Occupation	Birthplace
Underwood, A. J.	8	M		TN
G. W.	4	M		TN
S. A.	3/12	F		TX
Reynolds, M.	50	F		TN
N.	24	F		TN
C.	20	M		TN
C.	18	F		TN
William	16	M		TN
B.	14	M		TN
S.	12	M		TN
C.	9	M		TN
Reynolds, John G.	25	M	Farmer	TN
Frances	22	F		TN
W. D.	3/12	M		TX
White, David	30	M	Farmer	TN
F.	21	F		TN
James	23	M	Farmer	TN
Hendrick, James	44	M	Merchant	VA
E.	43	F		KY
P.	16	F		KY
Robert	13	M		IL
Jas.	12	M		KY
T.	5	F		KY
H.	4	M		KY
F.	1	F		TX
Williams, A. C.	34	M	Miller	TN
Walters, William	38	M	Farmer	VA
M.	36	F		VA
P.	17	M	Farmer	TN
John	15	M		TN
W.	10	M		TN
A.	8	F		TN
Arthur	6	M		TN
M.	4	F		TN
Sam	1	M		TX
Walker, Robert	46	M	Farmer	VA
M.	40	F		VA
W.	24	M		VA
N.	17	F		VA
M.	15	F		TN
L.	12	F		TN
Robert	10	M		TN
L.	5	F		TN
S.	3	F		TN
Vannoy, Isaac R.	41	M	Meth. Preacher	NC
P. J.	23	F		TN
M. H.	6	F		TX
W. H.	4	M		TX
R. P.	2	M		TX
Collier, W. M.	23	M		NC
Pearce, James	21	M		AL
Methvin, Sam	20	M		AL
Bristo, C. F.	--	M	Merchant	ENG
Parker, S.	60	F		NC
Lock, Thomas	35	M	Farmer	TN
L.	23	F		TN
L.	7	F		TN
A.	4	M		TN
E.	7/12	F		TN
Geare, Alex	45	M	Farmer	TN
N.	32	F		TN
C.	8	F		TN
L.	1	F		TX
Marsh, James	29	M	Farmer	VA
E.	29	F		TN
Orlena	5	F		TN
Sanders, Ira	31	M	Farmer	TN
E.	35	F		TN
J. A.	13	M		TN
L.	11	F		TN
L. R.	9	F		TN
A.	7	M		TN
W.	5	M		TN
Ira	2	M		TX

UPSHUR COUNTY, TEXAS

Name	Age	Sex	Occupation	Birthplace
Heaslet, James A.	44	M	Farmer	TN
C.	41	F		GA
N. R. C.	5	M		AL
Randal, E. E.	8	F		AL
Melam, W. B.	38	M	Farmer	AL
E.	40	F		AL
N. A.	18	F		AL
L.	11	F		AL
John	12	M		TN
M.	10	F		TN
B. Y.	8	M		AL
W. P.	6	M		AL
James W.	3	M		MS
L. W.	2	F		MS
Galaspy, W. C.	38	M	Farmer	TN
M. M.	33	F		AL
M. E.	13	F		MS
S. F.	7	F		TX
W. C.	5	M		TX
Alex	3	M		LA
A. E.	27	F		KY
John	7	M		TX
S. J.	5	F		TX
L. A.	4	F		TX
Slider, James	27	M	Millwright	IA
E.	27	F		TN
James D.	10	M		TN
John M.	9	M		TN
C. V.	9/12	F		TX
R. J.	5	F		TN
Thomas, E.	31	M	Farmer	SC
L.	25	F		TN
J.	9	M		TN
M.	5	F		TN
Martha	4	F		TN
J.	1	F		TX
H.	3	M		TX
Youngblood, J. L.	38	M	Brick Mason	TN
E.	38	F		TN
A.	10	F		AL
Jack	9	M		MS
Jane	6	F		MS
M.	2	M		MS
Nicholson, M.	30	F		TN
Mahaffey, J. M.	33	M	Farmer	TN
N.	36	F		SC
M. J.	9	F		MS
A. C.	7	M		MS
V. A.	4	F		MS
M. E.	1	F		MS
McHary, Robert	24	M	Farmer	TN
M.	16	F		AL
Lambinson, Ben	40	M	Farmer	GA
S. R.	16	F		TN
S. R.	9/12	F		TX
Johnson, L. A.	61	M	Farmer	NC
S.	31	F		GA
W. L.	4	M		TX
S.	11/12	F		TX
Waggoner, Jacob	29	M	Farmer	TN
Davidson, A.	58	M	Farmer	VA
M.	49	F		TN
Richard	20	M	Farmer	AL
E.	18	F		AL
Y(?).	17	F		AL
A. J.	16	F		AL
Miller, Jessee	35	M	Farmer	TN
M.	26	F		TN
George	13	M		AL
M.	12	F		MS
C. S.	10	M		MS
Charles	8	M		MS

(continued)

Name	Age	Sex	Occupation	Birthplace
Miller, D.	6	M		MS
R. A.	5	F		MS
N.	4	F		AR
J.	2	M		TX
Stone, John	18	M	Farmer	AL
M.	17	M	Farmer	AL
H.	22	F		AL
H.	5	M		AR
V.	3	F		AR
Marshall, John	62	M	Farmer	SC
A.	59	F		NC
M.	37	F		TN
J. C.	30	M	Farmer	KY
Jane	20	F		KY
J. C.	10	M		TX
J. P.	7	M		TX

VAN ZANDT COUNTY, TEXAS

Name	Age	Sex	Occupation	Birthplace
Harper, John	29	M	Farmer(Smith Co.)	TN
Phoeby	21	F		AR
H. H.	1 10/12	F	(VZ)	TX
Tumbleston, James	36	M	Farmer (Rone Co.)	TN
Mary	25	F		KY
E. J.	5	F	(N.C.)	TX
A. E.	4	F	(Chk.)	TX
J. M.	2	M	(VZ)	TX
Johnson, John	21	M	Farmer (Mon)	TN
Sarah	17	F		YN
Catsharp, James	40	M	Farmer(Greene Co.)	TN
Johanah	39	F	(Ch. Co.)	KY
William H.	21	M	Farmer(Mov. Co.)	TN
S. C.	16	F	(Ctt. Co.)	GA
S. A.	13	F	"	GA
A. R.	10	M	"	GA
M. C.	1 6/12	F	(R. Co.)	TX
Grisom, James	18	M	Farmer(Mor. Co.)	TN
McSpadin, L. J.	14	F	"	TN
P. C.	11	F	(Caps. Co.)	GA
William G.	8	M	"	GA
Beall, A. C.	30	M	Farmer(Frk. Co.)	GA
E. C.	19	F	(Mero Co.)	TN
Thomas F.	2	M	(Buck Co.)	TX
Sulivan, J. N.	44	M	Farmer	VA
J. D.	31	F	(B. Co.)	TN
Kilaw, J. S.	11	M	(Nc. Co.)	TX
Sulivan, W. H. S.	9	M	(Nt. Co.)	LA
R. A. G.	7	M	(Ne. Co.)	TX
E. S. W.	5	M	"	TX
S. A. C.	4	F	(Chk. Co.)	TX
J. S. K.	4/12	F	(VZ Co.)	TX
Montgomery, Thomas J.	47	M	Farmer(S. Co.)	TN
Elizabeth	44	F	(Mt. Co.)	TN
Scott, William F.	63	M	Farmer(Carrell Co)	SC
Sarah	55	F	(Emlo Co.)	NC
Reubin	31	M	Widow/Farmer(M Co)	TN
A. W.	24	M	Farmer "	TN
R. H.	23	M	Farmer (N. Co.)	TN
W. D.	18	M	Farmer (Ob. Co.)	TN
Scott, Tilford	27	M	Farmer (M. Co.)	TN
Lavina	22	F	(Hn. Co.)	TN
S. T.	5	M	(St. L. Co)	MO
M. J.	2	F	(Hess Co.)	TX
Edwards, Lousinda	34	F	Widow (M. Co.)	TN
William L.	16	M	Farmer (Ob. Co.)	TN
S. H.	14	F	"	TN
J. J.	11	M	(Pt. Co.)	MS
E. M.	7	M	"	MS
J. W.	6	M	"	MS
D. R.	3	M	(St. L. Co)	MO
Cook, Obediah	43	M	Farmer (Lc. Co.)	NC
Sarah	39	F	(Hd. Co.)	NC
Tabitha	16	F	(McM. Co.)	TN

(continued)

VAN ZANDT COUNTY, TEXAS

Name	Age	Sex	Occupation / Birthplace	State
Cook, Jane	12	F	(Cm. Co.)	MO
J. R.	10	M	"	MO
William T.	8	M	"	MO
Josephine	3	F	(VZ Co.)	TX
L. A.	1	F	"	TN
Snider, John	34	M	Carpenter(Mr. Co.)	KY
S. F.	26	F	(H. Co.)	AR
Henry	8	M	"	AR
William	6	M	"	AR
John	4	M	(R. R. Co.)	TX
Margarett	2	F	"	TX
James	21	M	Carpenter (W. Co.)	MO
Orr, A. M.	22	M	Daily Laborer(B.Co)	TN
Solomon, Sarah	18	F		AR
Parks, Felix	25	M	Farmer(Shelby Co)	TN
Synthy	17	F		TN
Leroy	23	M	Farmer "	TN
Henry, J. N.	60	M	Farmer	TN
Sarah	52	F		GA
H. A.	21	M	Farmer (Ma. Co.)	AL
L. S.	18	M	Farmer (Wash. Co.)	AR
John	12	M	"	AR
Upton, Monroe	31	M	Farmer (Wray Co.)	TN
E. C.	20	F	(Jeff. Co)	AL
Anny	5	F	(Pauldan Co.)	GA
E. E.	3	F	(Tala. Co.)	AL
B.	4/12	F	(Smith Co.)	TX
Bandy, James	51	M	Farmer (Jack. Co.)	GA
Nancy	47	F	(Wmson Co.)	TN
J. T.	26	M	Carpenter "	TN
E. C.	24	F	"	TN
William H.	22	M	Farmer "	TN
N. A.	20	F	"	TN
D. T.	19	M	Farmer "	TN
M. F.	16	F	"	TN
R. P.	9	F	"	TN
M. C.	11	F	"	TN
S. C.	6	F	"	TN
Strasner, Benjamin	34	M	Farmer (Sinc. Co.)	AL
Nancy	30	F	(Frank. Co.)	TN
William H.	10	M	(Aust. Co.)	TX
M. A. S.	8	F	(NC Co.)	TX
Ellen	3	F	(Smith Co.)	TX
M. A.	16/12	F	(VZ Co.)	TX
McInturf, Abraham	30	M	Farmer	TN
M. A.	25	F	(Pick. Co.)	AL
E. A.	9	F	(NF Co.)	AR
Y. W.	6	M	(VZ Co.)	TX
M. J.	3	F	"	TX
J. M. F.	6/12	M	"	TX
Petty, Robert	41	M	Farmer	TN
Sarah	42	F	(David. Co)	TN
Isam	21	M	Farmer (McNai. Co)	TN
J. W.	19	M	Farmer (Fayet. Co)	IL
Thomas	13	M	(Carr. Co.)	AR
Elizabeth	11	F	"	AR
E. J.	9	M	(Mar. Co.)	AR
William C.	8	M	"	AR
Abigal	3	F	"	AR
Outon, Mahaly	18	F	(Wash. Co.)	MO
Shirley, John	55	M	Farmer (David. Co)	TN
House, Kitty	46	F	Widow (David. Co)	TN
William H.	22	M	Farmer (Marac. Co)	MS
Catharine	20	F	(McNai. Co)	TN
Elizabeth	18	F	(Hend. Co.)	TN
F. A.	16	F	(Wayne Co)	TN
Artamia	14	F	(Stad. Co)	MO
T. J.	12	M	"	MO
Edward	10	M	"	MO
Robertson, David	44	M	Farmer (Wms. Co)	TN
M. A.	25	F	(Laud. Co)	AL
J. B.	8	M	"	AL
David	4	M	"	AL
Sarah	6	F	"	AL

Name	Age	Sex	Occupation / Birthplace	State
Jones, Elizabeth	30	F	Widow (Hick. Co)	TN
John	15	M	Farmer (McNai. Co)	TN
James	13	M		AL
Jahial	12	M	(Laud. Co.)	AL
A. F.	10	M	"	AL
M. A.	8	F	"	AL
Maris	2	M	(VZ Co.)	TX
Benton, P. S.	40	M	Farmer (Greene Co.)	TN
Martha	41	F	(Jeff. Co.)	TN
William	20	M	Farmer (Morgan Co.)	IL
Abert	16	M	Farmer	MO
Malindy	12	F		MO
Mary	10	F	(Ander. Co.)	MO
Thomas H.	6	M	(Platt Co.)	MO
James	2	M	(VZ Co.)	TX
Willhight, J. A.	21	F	(Jeff. Co.)	TN
J. J.	20	M	Farmer (Morgan Co)	IL
Smith, Redin	44	M	Farmer	VA
Brown, Lenard	39	M	Farmer (Hump. Co.)	TN
Elizabeth	32	F		IL
J. E.	15	M	Farmer (Searcy Co)	AR
M. A.	12	F	"	AR
M. J.	10	F	(Barry Co.)	MO
O---	8	M	(Newt. Co.)	MO
F. M.	5	M	(Hopk. Co.)	TX
Shumate, L. H.	26	M	Farmer (Clab. Co.)	TN
Nancy	26	F	(Wash. Co.)	AR
M. C.	2	F	(Carr. Co.)	AR
Blair, Allen	43	M	Farmer (Roan Co.)	TN
Sinderela	36	F	(Gren. Co.)	TN
J. W.	12	M	(Brad. Co.)	TN
E. J.	10	F	"	TN
P. A.	8	F	"	TN
M. E.	6	F	"	TN
S. E.	2	F	(VZ Co.)	TX
Crawford, C. P.	30	M	Farmer (Gren. Co.)	TN
Scates, Joseph C.	24	M	Farmer (Munro Co)	TN
S. M.	22	F	(Clark Co)	GA
M. E.	1	F	(Rusk Co)	TX
McKinney, C. C.	27	M	Farmer (Munro Co)	MS
E. C.	20	F		IL
E. C.	1	F	(Smith Co)	TX
Anderson, William A.	22	M	Farmer	TN
Cragle, Henry	36	M	(illegible)	GER
Sarah	22	F		TN
Catharine	1	F	(VZ Co)	TX
Cox, Thomas	32	M	Farmer (Hawk. Co)	TN
Permela	31	F		TN
J. R.	5	M	(S Co)	TX
Pickle, J. R.	9	M	(R. Riv Co)	TX
Raby, J. W.	38	M	Farmer (Charl Co)	SC
E. E.	27	F	(Hawk Co)	TN
Simpson, Nathaniel	7	M		TN
Witherford, B. W.	39	M	Far./ Widow (Ch.Co)	VA
Permelia	7	F	(Hamt. Co)	TN
Kuykendall, Peter	40	M	Farmer	SC
Prudence	37	F	(Jack Co)	TN
J. J.	22	M	Farmer "	TN
N. H.	18	M	Farmer "	TN
M. J.	16	F	"	TN
E. R.	14	M	"	TN
Nancy	12	F	"	TN
S. J.	10	F	"	TN
L. L.	8	F	"	TN
Catharine	6	F	"	TN
E. P.	2	M	"	TN
M. C.	1	M	(VZ Co)	TX
Hadlock, J.	26	M		TN
M.	22	F		TN
S.	2	M		TN
Cox, Joseph	53	M	Farmer	SC
Catharine	50	F	(Green Co)	TN

(continued)

VAN ZANDT COUNTY, TEXAS

Name	Age	Sex	Occupation	County	State
Cox, J. A.	18	M	Farmer	(Bedf. Co)	TN
William C.	15	M	Farmer	(Hard. Co)	TN
Thomas	12	M		(Hems. Co)	AR
P---	6	F		(Lama. Co)	TX
Moore, Ely	5	M		"	TX
T---	3	F		(Coff. Co)	TX
Hayse, J. M.	28	M	Farmer	(Linc. Co)	TN
M. J.	17	F			TN
Arsula	1	F		(VZ Co)	TX
Kuykendall, J. Y.	30	M	Farmer	(Over. Co)	TN
Nancy	26	F		(Jack. Co)	TN
E. J.	10	F		"	TN
C. C.	8	F		"	TN
Peter	6	M		"	TN
N. M.	4	F		"	TN
Tankesly, William W.	42	M	Farmer	(Pemd. Co)	SC
Elizabeth	37	F		(Wilk. Co)	NC
Richard	19	M	Farmer	(Mur. Co)	GA
Matildy	14	F		"	GA
Milton	14	M		"	GA
Barbry	12	F		(Brad. Co)	TN
Elizabeth	9	F		"	TN
Sarah	7	F		(Titus Co)	TX
William	5	M		"	TX
Larkin	3	M		"	TX
Clarisy	1	F		(VZ Co)	TX
Smith, Jackson	23	M	Farmer	(Bunc. Co)	NC
Catharine	21	F		(Over. Co)	TN
E. J.	2	F		(VZ Co)	TX
Greer, Adam	30	M	Farmer	(Warrn Co)	TN
M. C.	21	F		(Walk. Co)	AL
M. D.	3	M		(VZ Co)	TX
Josephine	1 8/12	F		"	TX
Greer, Joseph	22	M	Farmer	(Over. Co)	TN
Armilla	19	F		(Walk. Co)	AL
M. J.	9/12	F		(VZ Co)	TX
Greer, James	25	M	Farmer	(Over. Co)	TN
Indiana	17	F		(Bras. Co)	TX
Lamans, John	39	M	Farmer	(Linc. Co)	TN
Elizabeth	24	F		(Morg. Co)	AL
M. A.	7	F		"	AL
T. J.	6	M		"	AL
S. J.	4	F		"	AL
J. H.	2	M		"	AL
Malcome	30	M	None	"	AL
Greer, J. W.	52	M	Farmer	(Over. Co)	TN
Elizabeth	54	F		(Cart. Co)	TN
J. N.	17	M	Farmer	(Wain Co)	MO
N. G.	15	F			AR
Stout, Henry	50	M	Farmer	(Wash. Co)	TN
S. J.	48	F		(Pula. Co)	KY
Henry H.	5	M		(Upsh. Co)	TX
Smith, William	13	M		(Nact. Co)	LA
S. C.	9	F		(Harr. Co)	TX
Boyd, John	22	M	Day Laborer		TN
Lovell, Rebecka	65	F	Widow	(Rock. Co)	NC
D. F.	23	M	Farmer	(illeg.)	TN
William	26	M	Farmer	"	TN
Rebecka	16	F		"	TN
J. H.	9	M		(Shel. Co)	TN
Garrett, Nathan	44	M	Farmer	(Bedf. Co)	VA
Nancy	42	F			VA
Joseph	21	M	Farmer	(Jack. Co)	TN
Lucinda	20	F		"	TN
Hanah	18	F		"	TN
S. A.	16	F		"	TN
James	14	M		"	TN
William	11	M		"	TN
John	9	M		"	TN
Mary	7	F		"	TN
Franklin	3/12	M		(Upsh. Co)	TX

Name	Age	Sex	Occupation	County	State
McDaugh, John	58	M	Farmer	(Ruth. Co)	NC
Elizabeth	62	F			VA
Clarisy	26	F		(Jack. Co)	AL
James	21	M	Farmer	(McNai. Co)	TN
Davis, Hillery	25	M	Farmer	(Jack. Co)	AL
S. A.	21	F			TN
M. J.	2	F		(Harr. Co)	TX
Dave, William	23	M	Farmer		AL
Nancy	19	F		(Walk. Co)	AL
J. M.	1	M		(VZ Co)	TX
T. A.	18	M		(Faye. Co)	TN
Edwards, John	26	M	Farmer	(Mars. Co)	AL
M. A.	26	F		(Warr. Co)	TN
M. J.	4	F		(Cret. Co)	AR
R. G.	1	M		(VZ Co)	TX
Elledge, D. C.	27	M	Farmer	(Warr. Co)	TN
Allen, Robert	32	M	Farmer	(Hard. Co)	TN
C. F.	25	F		(Jeff. Co)	AL
M. R.	7	F		(R. Riv. Co)	TX
J. W.	5	F		(Green Co)	MO
S. H.	3	M		"	MO
E. A.	1	F		"	MO
Attaway, David	45	M	Farmer	(Spart. Co)	SC
Rebeka	45	F		(Edgef. Co)	SC
James	18	M	Farmer	(Ander. Co)	TN
Letha	16	F		"	TN
Nicy	14	F		"	TN
Mabery	13	F		"	TN
Elbert	11	M		"	TN
Martha	9	F		"	TN
Mary	7	F		(Itawa. Co)	MS
Basel, Peter	47	M	Farmer	(David. Co)	TN
Frances	46	F		(Frank. Co)	TN
Mary A.	21	F		(Jack. Co)	AL
J. M.	18	M	Farmer	"	AL
G. W.	16	M	Farmer	"	AL
S. M.	15	F		"	AL
J. M. P.	12	M		"	AL
William J.	11	M		"	AL
T. B.	8	M		(Newt. Co)	MO
J. W.	6	M		(Barry Co)	MO
N. A.	4	F		(Newt. Co)	MO
Vaden, Oliver	22	M	Farmer		LA
Willson, Hugh	63	M	Farmer	(illeg.)	VA
J. M.	22	M	Farmer	(Greene Co)	TN
Susanah	17	F		"	TN
Benton, William M.	26	M	Farmer	(Roane Co)	TN
Arsula	29	F		(Greene Co)	TN
Susan	5	F		(Roane Co)	TN
S. J.	1	F		(Upshur Co)	TX
Williams, Isam	44	M	Farmer		TN
J. E.	32	F		(Fairf. Co)	SC
S. A.	14	F		(Pike Co)	AR
J. W.	10	M		(Nc Co)	TX
William Y.	8	M		(Harr. Co)	TX
N. C.	5	F		"	TX
Rutha	4	F		(Upshur Co)	TX
M. A.	1	F		"	TX
Etherdge, Thomas	33	M	Widow	(Camp. Co)	NC
M. A.	16	F		(Madis. Co)	TN
N. C.	14	F		(Newt. Co)	MO
M. L.	12	M		"	MO
DeCalf	10	M		"	MO
S. J.	7	F		"	MO
William A.	2	M		(Harr. Co)	TX
S. M.	1	M		(VZ Co)	TX
Williams, W. L.	29	M	Black Smith	(Blnt Co)	TN
A. A.	24	F		(Chact. Co)	GA
E. A. J.	16/12	F		(Upshur Co)	TX
Hearn, J. B.	15	M	Farmer	(Tala. Co)	AL
Norton, D. O.	33	M	Merchant	(Bedf. Co)	TN
C. A.	25	F		(Greene Co)	TN

(continued)

VAN ZANDT COUNTY, TEXAS

Name	Age	Sex	Occupation	Place	State
Norton, J. F.	5	M		(Hopk. Co)	TX
M. R.	3	F		"	TX
T. E.	1	F		"	TX
Watson, James	17	M	Farmer		KY
M. A.	11	F			KY
Hillhouse, James	33	M	Daily Laborer		TN
Fitzgerald, Aratus	37	M	Daily Laborer		IL
George, E. B.	24	M	Lawyer	(Fayet. Co)	PA
Norton, H. W.	39	M	Surveyor	(Bedf. Co)	TN
Elizabeth	27	F		(Greene Co)	TN
F. L.	6/12	F		(Vaught Co)	TX
Carter, Malinda	25	F		(Greene Co)	TN
Duncan, Robert	50	M	Farmer	(Adam Co)	KY
Elizabeth	49	F		"	KY
J. R.	17	M	Farmer	(Jack. Co)	TN
L. F.	14	F		(Jack. Co)	AL
Robert	12	M		"	AL
M. J.	9	F		"	AL
Elizabeth	1	F		(Bent. Co)	MO
Duncan, J. P.	21	M	Farmer	(Jack. Co)	AL
M. L. A.	24	F		(illeg.)	AL
Duncan, Silas	28	M	Farmer	(Bedf. Co)	TN
Elizabeth	21	F		(Jack. Co)	AL
J. K. P.	4	M		(Berry Co)	MO
S. M.	1 6/12	M		(VZ Co)	TX
Crockett, James	22	M	Farmer	(Clay Co)	MO
S. E.	22	F		(Sumn Co)	TN
M. J.	1	F		(VZ Co)	TX
Crockett, Joseph	63	M	Farmer	(Sull. Co)	TN
Martha	60	F			SC
Drusiller	13	F		(Clin. Co)	MO
M. A.	11	F			MO
Clark, Isam	53	M	Farmer		SC
Jane	45	F		(Hayw. Co)	NC
B. M. C.	21	M	Farmer	(Sevi. Co)	TN
Isam	16	M	Farmer	"	TN
J. B.	13	M		(Brad. Co)	TN
J. A.	10	M		(illeg.)	MO
M. M.	9	F		"	MO
R. M.	7	F		"	MO
H. H. T.	3	M		(Coll. Co)	TX
Willcox, E.	26	F	Widow	(Sevi. Co)	TN
A. J.	6/12	M		(VZ Co)	TX
Williams, David	40	M	Farmer	(Hayw. Co)	NC
Clark, Joseph	25	M	Farmer	(Sevi. Co)	TN
M. J.	25	F		(Waba. Co)	IN
B. F.	3	M		(Reyn. Co)	MO
E. J.	1	F		(Gray. Co)	TX
Brustle, Benjamin	21*	M	Daily Lab.	(Wash Co)	IN
Clark, J. O.	32	M	Farmer	(Sevi. Co)	TN
Eviline	26	F			KY
G. W.	6	M		(Reyn. Co)	MO
W. M.	4	M		"	MO
E. J.	1	F		(VZ Co)	TX
Williams, John	22	M	Farmer	(Sevi. Co)	TN
M. J.	15	F		"	TN
Greer, Walter	30	M	Farmer	(Over. Co)	TN
M. A.	30	F		(Linc. Co)	NC
M. M.	15	F		(Mari. Co)	TN
D. ?.	1	M		(VZ Co)	TX
J. D.	1	M		(Vaug. Co)	TX
Samuel	28	M	Farmer	(Over. Co)	TN
Centers, David	41	M	Farmer (widowed)	(Sinc. Co)	NC
N. T.	13	F		(Mari. Co)	TN
William J.	12	M		"	TN
L. C.	11	F		"	TN
J. M.	1	M		(Vaug. Co)	TX
Sarah	61	F	Widowed	(Linc. Co)	NC

Name	Age	Sex	Occupation	Place	State
Simpkins, J. E.	24	M	Farmer	(Cumb. Co)	NC
Mary	20	F			TN
Zachariah	2	M		(VZ Co)	TX
Susan	5/12	F		"	TX
Esry, Andrew	23	M	Farmer	(Perry Co)	TN
Nancy	15	F		(Bent. Co)	AL
John	1	M		(VZ Co)	TX
McCarrell, William	29	M	Farmer	(Blou. Co)	TN
Elizabeth	29	F			KY
M. J.	7	F		(Rusk Co)	TX
Eveline	6	F		(VZ Co)	TX
Elizabeth	3	F		(Vaug. Co)	TX
William M.	2	M		"	TX
Nicey	1	F		"	TX
Adams, Plesant	19	M	Farmer		KY
Cyrena	20	F			TN
Yarborough, Lidy	19	F	Widow		TN
M. E.	6/12	F		(VZ Co)	TX
Danby, Andrew	25	M	Farmer	(Willms Co)	TN
Elmira	39	F		(Nashv.)	TN
Johnson, Christopher	20	M	Farmer	(Chero. Co)	AL
Havans, Jahon	36	M	Farmer		TN
Nancy	37	F			TN
A. J.	13	M		(Newt. Co)	MO
T. J.	12	M		"	MO
B. F.	9	M		"	MO
Mary	8	F		"	MO
Elizabeth	5	F		(Hopk. Co)	TX
Ira	4	M		"	TX
Eliza	2	F		"	TX
Freeman, J. D.	30	M	Farmer	(Dicks. Co)	TN
Sarah	32	F		"	TN
Alexandria	10	M		(Wash. Co)	AR
?. M.	3	M		(Lamar Co)	TX
Truman, Jackson	22	M	Farmer	(Rando. Co)	MO
Elizabeth	21	F			TN
Fitzgerald, Nicey	60	F	Widow		TN
Fitzgerald, Ambry	23	M	Farmer		TN
Mary	20	F			TN
William	3	M		(VZ Co)	TX
Sarah	6/12	F		"	TX
Lacey, J. R.	31	M	Black Smith	(Log. Co)	KY
Mary	21	F			TN
M. A.	9	F		(Bowie Co)	TX
N. C.	7	F		"	TX
M. E.	6/12	F		(Vaugh. Co)	TX
Brewer, Thomas P.	24	M	Farmer	(Jack. Co)	TN
Susanah	17	F		(Pike Co)	KY
J. A.	2	M		"	KY
J. M.	7/12	M		"	KY
Rushin, Mark	38	M	Farmer	(Stew. Co)	TN
Elizabeth	37	F			KY
William	12	M		(Tish. Co)	MS
Elizabeth	14	F			TN
Martha	9	F		(Tish. Co)	MS
John	8	M		"	MS
Fitzgerald, Julian	9	F		(Newt. Co)	MO
John	8	M		"	MO
Evans, William	22	M	Farmer	(Newt. Co)	MO
N. A.	19	F		(Madi. Co)	TN
M. L.	1	M		(Vaug. Co)	TX
Yarborough, Gilbert	49	M	Farmer		NC
Ellen	41	F		(Warr. Co)	TN
Catharine	19	F		(Perry Co)	TN
William	17	M	Farmer	"	TN
Manervy	15	F		(Newt. Co)	MO
James	12	M		"	MO
Lacy, Lucy	22	F	Widow	(Perry Co)	TN
Ellen	3	F		(Vaug. Co)	TX
Adams, Benjamin	22	M	None	(Simp. Co)	KY

VAN ZANDT COUNTY, TEXAS

Name	Age	Sex	Occupation	County	State
Johnson, Rheubin	45	M	Farmer		TN
Mary	35	F			TN
Jackson	18	M	Farmer		TN
Martha	13	F			TN
Lusinda	10	F			TN
Adaline	8	F			TN
John	6	M			TN
Clanton, James	32	M	Farmer		KY
Louisa	34	F		(Ander. Co)	TN
E. A.	9	M		(Wash. Co)	AR
M. J.	7	F		(Barry Co)	MO
E. C.	5	F		(Lamar Co)	TX
Artamis	2	F		"	TX
William	3/12	M		(VZ Co)	TX
Lagett, William	33	M	Farmer	(Mont. Co)	NC
Anny	30	F		(Newt. Co)	AR
Rebecka	11	F		(Sevi. Co)	AR
Martha	9	F		"	AR
David	3	M		(VZ Co)	TX
Nancy	10/12	F		"	TX
Talbott, John	36	M	Farmer		TN
Stephens, John	41	M	Farmer	(Pend. Co)	SC
E. A.	20	F			TN
Rains, Joab	33	M	Farmer		TN
Elizabeth	33	F		(Willms. Co)	TN
William	13	M		(Newt. Co)	MO
Mary	11	F		"	MO
Caroline	10	F		"	MO
Margaret	8	F		"	MO
Louisa	6	F		(Rusk Co)	TX
John	4	M		"	TX
Danby, E. J.	21	F		(Faye. Co)	IL
James	17	M	Farmer		AR
O'Kelly, F. D.	32	M	Farmer		NC
Molly	29	F			GA
John	9	M		(Berry Co)	MO
J. S.	7	M		"	MO
F. M.	6	M		"	MO
Penelope	5	F		"	MO
S. E.	1	F		(VZ Co)	TX
Fitzgerald, Milly	14	F		(Meigs Co)	TN
Carr, Sarah	40	F	Widow		--
Jacob	22	M	Farmer	(Monro. Co)	TN
Riley	18	M	Farmer	"	TN
Jefferson	16	M	Farmer	"	TN
William	14	M		(Meigs Co)	TN
Jenette	12	F		"	TN
P. A.	10	F		"	TN
David	6	M		(Newt. Co)	MO
James	4	M			AR
Sarah	11/12	F		(VZ Co)	TX
Lee, John	26	M	Farmer	(Linc. Co)	TN
S. A.	19	F		(Scott Co)	AR
W. M.	1	M		(Hopk. Co)	TX
Riley, Jackson	17	M	Farmer	(Scott Co)	AR
William	22	M	Farmer		IN
Dement, J. R.	37	M	Black Smith	(Sum.Co)	TN
D. A.	24	F		(Blount Co)	AL
Rebecka	13	F		(Limes. Co)	AL
William	12	M		"	AL
John	10	M		"	AL
Charles	8	M		"	AL
George	6	M		"	AL
James	4	M		"	AL
Sarah	2	F		"	AL
Moss, William M. C.	20	M	Laborer	"	AL
Barne, Nancy	47	F	Widow		TN
Moss, W. A.	23	M	Farmer	(Limes. Co)	AL
J. D.	15	M	Farmer	"	AL
S. W.	13	M		"	AL
Adams, J. M. D.	21	M	Farmer	(Wayne Co)	TN
Huggins, R. F.	23	M	Farmer	(Fayet. Co)	TN
S. A. L.	18	F		"	TN

(continued)

Name	Age	Sex	Occupation	County	State
Huggins, S. A.	6/12	F		(VZ Co)	TX
Garrett, James	28	M	Farmer		TN
Amanda	20	F		(Lawr. Co)	TN
William	8	M		(Frank. Co)	AR
Julia	6	F		"	AR
M. A.	17	F		(Lime. Co)	AL
Warren	4	M		(Frank. Co)	AR
Gill, J. T.	27	M	Farmer		VA
B. D.	17	F		(Hends. Co)	TN
Balwin, John	27	M	Farmer	(Lawr. Co)	TN
M. A.	25	F		"	TN
C. C.	5	M		(Lamar Co)	TX
Sells, Benjamin	59	M	Farmer		PA
Dudia	49	F		(Cald. Co)	NC
J. P.	25	M	Farmer	(McNa. Co)	TN
Thomas	20	M	Farmer	"	TN
J. A.	22	F		"	TN
Susan	18	F		"	TN
Dianna	14	F		"	TN
Mary	11	F		"	TN
Marthy	8	F		"	TN
Smith, J. R.	19	M	Farmer	(Blount Co)	AL
Mary	20	F			TN
M. J.	14	F			AL
Gillm, David	31	M	Farmer		TN
Mary	33	F		(Green Co)	IL
Mordica	10	M		(Panola Co)	TX
John	12	M		"	TX
Martha	8	F		"	TX
Elvira	6	F		(VZ Co)	TX
Samuel	3	M		"	TX
J. M.	1	M		(Upshur Co)	TX
Elzina	13	F		(Green Co)	IL
William	18	M	Farmer	"	IL
Davis, S. H.	43	M	Farmer	(Sevier Co)	TN
E. C.	45	F		"	TN
A. J.	15	F		(Roane Co)	TN
S. J.	13	M		(Hamil. Co)	TN
C. F.	10	M		(Harri. Co)	TX
S. A.	6	M		"	TX
J. M.	11	M		"	TX
Davis, Isaac	80	M	Farmer	(Lawrn. Co)	SC
Lucy	77	F		(Edgef. Co)	SC
Walker, Marthy	19	F		(Roane Co)	TN
Moore, Joseph	38	M	Laborer		TN
Nancy	35	F			TN
M. E.	10	F			MS
James	7	M			MS
Dimpsey	5	M			MS
Joseph	2	M		(Upshur Co)	TX
James	40	M	Millwright		AL
Benton, John	24	M	Farmer	(Roane Co)	TN
Julian	15	F			MS
Saunders, Joseph	38	M	Farmer	(Gilford Co)	NC
Sarah	18	F			AL
Jessey	1	M			TX
Susanah	65	F		(Roane Co)	NC
David	20	M	Farmer	(Hawk. Co)	TN
Gergerlly, A. J.	28	M	Farmer	(Jeff. Co)	TN
McClane, J. W.	23	M	Farmer	(Marian Co)	IN

VICTORIA COUNTY, TEXAS

Name	Age	Sex	Occupation	State
Wright, George W.	39	M	Farmer-Hotel	TN
Amanda	29	F		TN
Dorothy	10	F		TX
Lalura	3	F		TX
Izora	1/12	F		TX
Fitzpatrick, (Blank)	35	M	Laborer	IRE
Newner, John	24	M	None	AR
Holland, A. D.	17	F		GER
Neave, Francis	30	M	Merchant	ENG
Smith, John	40	M	Carpenter	NC

VICTORIA COUNTY, TEXAS

Name	Age	Sex	Occupation	Birthplace
Linc, Anto	23	M	Laborer	GER
Ana	22	F		GER
Amelia	2	F		TX
Henry	1	M		TX
Shives, John L.	30	M	Teacher	NC
V. H.	30	F		VA
Friar, Susan	12	F		TX
Smith, Martha	12	F		TN
Cock, Medora	10	F		VA
Lansing, Evalina	13	F		TX
Charles Ana	11	F		TX
Vanoman, Stephen K.	25	M	Laborer	IN
Mary	21	F		IL
Joseph M.	3	M		IL
L. E.	3/12	F		TN
Lansing, Julia	9	F		TN
Butts(Bates), Jackson	38	M	Laborer	MO
Cathrin	21	F		TN
Margaret	13	F		MO
John W.	9	M		MO
A. J.	7	M		TX
Ragland, John B.	35	M	M.D.	NC
R. S.	30	F		NC
Martha	4	F		MS
John	2	M		TN
Wilkins, James L.	36	M	Teacher	NC
Edgar, William G.	30	M	Mechanic	LA
Hathaway, Woodbery	24	M	None	ME
Ann	20	F		IRE
John	1	M		TN
John	21	M	None	ME
Hardy, Milton	33	M	Farmer	TN
Margaret	25	F		NY
Mary	5	F		TX
Julia	2	F		TX
Smith, Elizabeth	23	F		TX
DeSoto, Ferdenand	16	M	Laborer	GER
Cunningham, John	50	M	Farmer	TN
Frances	44	F		IL
Sarah	21	F		AL
Vickery, C. W.	44	M	Farmer	NY
Napoleon	15	M	Farmer	NY
Mexon, Samuel B.	40	M	Farmer	TN
Harriet R.	38	F		TN
Atkinson, Dassey	46	M	Farmer	VA
Mary Ann	40	F		TN
W. P.	15	F		TN
Palmyra	13	F		TN
Frances E.	10	F		TN
J. H. D.	9	M		TN
M. C.	2	F		TN
Patton, John W.	43	M	M.D.	TN
Malinda	39	F		TN
E. A.	17	F		TN
Margaretta J.	15	F		TN
Isaac A.	12	M		TN
John A.	10	M		TN
David M. G.	8	M		TN
Atkinson, M. F.	15	M	Farmer	TN
Land, J. R.	43	M	Farmer	TN
Martha	32	F		TN
Sebrina	13	F		TN
Martha M.	9	F		TX
Thomas D.	5	M		TX
Temperance	2	F		TX
Glass, William S.	26	M	Lawyer	TN
Mary	19	F		IRE
Wheeler, J. O.	35	M	Merchant	OH
Mary	29	F		TN
J. O.	7	M		TN

(continued)

Name	Age	Sex	Occupation	Birthplace
Wheeler, Loring	5	M		TN
Mary	6/12	F		TN
Thornton, Abner E.	40	M	Merchant	TN
Mary A.	40	F		SC
Eba	18	M	Clerk	AR
John	14	M		AR
Lafayette	12	M		AR
William J.	10	M		AR
Rozell, J.	30	M	Tailor	OH
Eliza J.	31	F		TN
Christopher C.	12	M		TX
Alfred	10	M		TX
Mary C.	8	F		TX
Junita R.	2	F		TX
Fell, Catharine	12	F		GER
James, Ashbery	56	M	Farmer	VA
Catharine	56	F		NC
B. F.	21	M	Farmer	TN
Leary, Rhetta	6	F		TX
Murphrie, D.	39	M	Farmer	TN
Margaretta	22	F		KY
Alex.	5	M		TX
James O.	3	M		TX
Gaines, G. W.	37	M	Clark	VA
Mary Ann	27	F		TN
Harrel	7	M		TX
Mary F.	3	F		TX
George W.	6/12	M		TX
Webb, Felix D.	53	M	M.D.	KY
Catharine	50	F		TN
Nelco, Ferdenande	10	M		GER
Rogers, G. F.	38	M	Merchant	TN
Mariah	26	F		NC
L. C.	28	M	Merchant	TN
Harrison, W. L.	19	M	Clerk	VA
Lochra, John	15	M	Laborer	GER
Lovelady, James	53	M	Farmer	TN
Nancy	50	F		SC
Allice, Alfred	30	M	Mechanic	PA
Baty, Archibald	38	M	Farmer	NC
Amyra	28	F		NC
Mary Jane	7	F		TX
James, Benjamin	21	M	Farmer	TN
Patton, John	45	M	Farmer	NC
Polly	42	F		VA
Jasper	19	M	Farmer	TN
Brazoria	16	F		TN
Louisa	14	F		TX
Mary	11	F		TX
Manerva (Twin)	6	F		TX
Martha (Twin)	6	F		TX
John	4	M		TX
White, L. A.	45	M	Farmer	NC
Susan A.	30	F		TN
B. M.	7	M		TX
Pellham, William	45	M	Farmer	KY
Mary Ann	35	F		TN
Charles T.	13	M		AR
Isabela A.	11	F		AR
Patton, Isaac	73	M	Farmer	SC
Ann H.	60	F		NC
Blanton, Susan J.	20	F		TN
Malinda	20	F		TN
Ann J.	60	F		NC
Davidson, Quncy	36	M	Farmer	NC
George W.	74	M	Farmer	NC
L. C.	19	M	Farmer	TN
Mary	63	F		NC
Lucy R.	40	F		NC
Caroline	22	F		NC
Mary F.	20	F		NC

VICTORIA COUNTY, TEXAS

Name	Age	Sex	Occupation	Birthplace
Cobler, John D.	34	M	Farmer	TN
Julia L.	32	F		NC
Mary L.	11	F		TN
Cornelia	9	F		TN
Gaston D.	7	M		TN
John I.	4	M		TN
Harris, George	2	M		TX
Mitchell, Isaac N.	38	M	Lawyer	TN
Isabella	26	F		ENG
Mary	9	F		MS
Thiereh(?)	4	M		MS
Thomas	1	M		TX
Cain, Margaret	45	F		IRE
Wright, John J.	47	M	Farmer	TN
Ema A.	20	F		TX
Tennessee	16	F		TX
Wright, Franklin M.	35	M	Farmer	TN
Ethalge, Francis	70	M	Herdsman	MEX
Joana	25	F		TN
Oliviana	3	F		TX
Bennett, Elijah	37	M	Farmer	KY
Elizabeth	35	F		TN
Sarah A.	8	F		TX
Gaudalaupe	2	F		TX
Luda J.	3/12	F		TX
Tharper, Luderick	11	M		GER
Stinson, Rhodham	15	M	Farmer	MO
Moderly, Henry	30	M	Farmer	LA
Donalson, Mary	40	M		TN
Mary J.	10	F		TX
Edward	8	M		TX
Adison W.	2	M		TX
Hogan, Jno. W.	45	M	Farmer	TN
Louisa	33	F		AL
Robert	12	M		AR
James	10	M		AR
Frank	8	M		AR
Granville	6	M		TN
Lafayette	3	M		TN
Swann, Robert	55	M		NY
Leven, Elbridge	36	M	Farmer	TN
Louisa	28	F		LA
Hughes, James	13	M		TX
Mary	11	F		TX
Leven, Margaret	8	F		TX
Elen	6	F		TX
Elizabeth	3	F		TX
John E.	4/12	M		TX
Sadoc, Mary	47	F		TX
Teal, Peter	38	M	Farmer	TN
Ann	36	F		IRE
Mary Ann	15	F		TX
William	12	M		TX
Nicholas	10	M		TX
Catharine	6	F		TX
Rosana	4	F		TX
James	2	M		TX
Whillington, Weston	41	M	Farmer	NC
Lucy Ann	39	F		NC
John R.	18	M	Farmer	NC
James W.	13	M		TN
Sarah C.	10	F		TN
George M.	7	M		TN

WALKER COUNTY, TEXAS

Name	Age	Sex	Occupation	Birthplace
Cumings, Uriah	52	M	Farmer	PA
Lucinda	34	F		VA
Isabella	16	F		TN
Pettny	14	F		TN
Celia	6	F		TX
William	26	M	Farmer	TN
Cumings, Sidney	28	M	Farmer	TN
Lenorah	17	F		MS
Judge	4	M		TX
Steven	2	M		TX
Ford, William	43	M	Farmer	TN
Harriet	33	F		NC
William	15	M	Farmer	TN
John	10	M		TN
Morto	8	M		TX
Jas.	4	M		TX
Sarah	13	F		TX
Ford, Sarah	70	F		NC
Davis, David R.	41	M	Farmer	TN
Sarah	39	F		TN
Sarah	18	F		TN
Gabrella	10	F		LA
Amanda	7	F		TX
Henry	19	M	Farmer	TN
John	13	M		MS
Parker, Nicholas	22	M	Cropper	GA
Skelton, Jas.	24	M	School Keeper	AL
Ford, John	45	M	Farmer	TN
Nancy	37	F		TN
William	14	M		TN
Moses	12	M		MS
John	10	M		MS
Susan	19	F		TN
Nancy	4	F		TX
Duberry, Thomas	28	M	Farmer	AL
Mary	22	F		TN
Maranda	3	F		TX
Mary	1/12	F		TX
Ford, Craner	33	M	Farmer	TN
Mary	25	F		NC
Jos.	2	M		TX
John	6/12	M		TX
Richardson, John	32	M	Farmer	VA
Rayburn, R. L.	45	M	Farmer	TN
Sarah	35	F		AL
Nancy	10	F		MS
Martha	7	F		MS
Robert	4	M		TX
Sarah	14	F		MS
Rayburn, Alex D.	22	M	Farmer	TN
Nancy	20	F		TX
Carson, Thomas	34	M	Black Smith	TN
Elizabeth	30	F		AL
Sarah	11	F		TX
Sophronia	9	F		TX
Mary	4	F		TX
Thomas	7	M		TX
Jas.	?	M		TX
McCan, John	27	M	Hireling	AL
Young, William F.	50	M	Farmer	AL
William C.	24	M		AL
Mary	50	F		TN
William	30	M	Farmer	TN
Evalina	20	F		TN
Elvira	18	F		TX
Page, Richard	33	M	Farmer	SC
Penelope	33	F		NC
Fredonia	15	F		TN
Texanna	10	F		TN
Tennessee	12	F		TX
Thomas	7	M		TX
John	4	M		TX
Howard, Elisha	48	M	Transient	NY
Allphine, Ransom	37	M	Farmer	KY
Elizabeth	37	F		TN
Louisa	18	F		IL
Martha	16	F		TX
Bernetta	13	F		TX
Thomas	12	M		TX
Margarette	8	F		TX

(continued)

WALKER COUNTY, TEXAS

Name	Age	Sex	Occupation	Birthplace
Allphine, Katharine	5	F		TX
Washington	2	M		TX
Clabaugh, John	72	M	Farmer	MD
Elizabeth	67	F		TN
Elizabeth	23	F		AL
Rachel	21	F		AL
Susan	8	F		AL
Haggard, Joel	81	M	Bapt. Preacher	VA
Martin, William B.	43	M	Farmer	GA
Delila	39	F		GA
Eliza	16	F		AL
Martha	10	F		TX
Delila	2	F		TX
John	21	M	Farmer	GA
William	13	M		AL
Daniel	7	M		TX
Jas.	4	M		TX
Alexander, William F.	58	M	Farmer	TN
Park, Andrew	50	M	Farmer-Black Smith	SC
Jane	47	F		SC
William	21	M	Farmer	TN
Joseph	19	M	Farmer	TN
Nathan	14	M		AL
Thomas	12	M		AL
George	10	M		AL
John (Twin)	3	M		TX
Sam (Twin)	3	M		TX
Mary	17	F		AL
Sarah	8	F		AL
Cowan, J. C.	25	M	Farmer	TN
Jane	22	F		TN
Martha	2	F		TX
Bairet, John W.	27	M	Merchant	SC
Huldah	30	F		TN
Steven	10	M		TX
William	7	M		TX
Ann	5	F		TX
Martha	3	F		TX
David (Twin)	1	M		TX
Amanda (Twin)	1	F		TX
Clarke, Jas.	38	M	Farmer	MS
Caroline	29	F		TN
Bloomfield, Robert H.	11	M		TX
George	9	M		TX
Mary	7	F		TX
Clarke, Jas. F.	4	M		TX
Martha	2	F		TX
Malvina	4/12	F		TX
Shaw, G. C.	34	M	Farmer	TN
Mary	27	F		AL
Jas.	8	M		TX
William	4	M		TX
Robert	1	M		TX
Miller, Ben L.	31	M	Hireling	AL
McKinney, Sam	42	M	Professor AC	PA
Nancy	30	F		SC
Andrew	12	M		IL
Margaret	10	F		IL
Elenor	8	F		IL
Cornelia	6	F		IL
Robert	5	M		TN
Mary	3	F		TN
Rogers, George W.	30	M	Merchant	TN
Lucinda	32	F		SC
William	4/12	M		TX
Mowery, Walter	50	M	Farmer	NC
Frances	43	F		NC
Jas.	21	M	Farmer	TN
William	23	M	Farmer	NC
Margaretta	19	F		TN
Robert	14	M		TN
Sarah	12	F		TX
Pamelia	6	F		TX

(continued)

Name	Age	Sex	Occupation	Birthplace
Mowery, Columbus	8	M		TX
Joseph	2	M		TX
Calwell, Thomas J.	38	M	Farmer	TN
Letticia	26	F		NC
Mary	1	F		TX
Alexander, Joseph B.	23	M	Hireling	AR
Fry, George	35	M	Farmer	GER
Lavinia	19	F		TN
Franklin	1	M		TX
Vaughn, Alberto	31	M	Farmer	TN
Martha	39	F		VA
Woods, John W.	24	M	Hireling	LA
Vaughn, Mary	19	F		TN
Patrick	17	M	Farmer	TN
Martha	15	F		TN
Tennessee	12	F		TX
Alberto	6	M		TX
Royal, Andrew	15	M	Farmer	TN
Hill, Sam	44	M	Farmer	ENG
Susan	32	F		NC
Calpernia	7	F		TX
Jane	4	F		TX
Josaphine	2	F		TX
Grooms, Isaac	22	M	Hireling	TN
Barnet, John	27	M	Farmer	TN
Lourinda	21	F		MS
Mary	1	F		TX
Medkiff, J. J.	40	M	Farmer	TN
Delatha	35	F		IN
Francis	16	M	Farmer	TX
Charles	13	M		TX
Isaac	12	M		TX
Sarah	6	F		TX
Pleasant	4	M		TX
Margaret	1	F		TX
Susannah	61	F		TN
Carter, John	54	M	Farmer	TN
Mary	54	F		TN
Stockman, Lewis	37	M	Farmer	TN
Charlotte	19	F		MS
John	5	M		LA
Elizabeth	2	F		LA
Alexander	1	M		TX
Jacob	48	M	Laborer	SC
Smith, John	41	M	Farmer	IL
Susan	27	F		TN
Leonard	19	M	Farmer	TN
Singleton	17	M	Farmer	TX
Martha	15	F		TX
Archibald	11	M		TX
John	6	M		TX
Calvin	4	M		TX
Frank	3	M		TX
Charles	1	M		TX
Miller, Gilbert	18	M	Farmer	LA
Woodeson, William	38	M	Cabinet-Farmer	PA
Elizabeth	27	F		TN
Isabella	10	F		TX
Julietta	5	F		TX
Elizabeth	3	F		TX
William	2	M		TX
Davis, W. H.	36	M	Farmer	TN
Narcissa	26	F		KY
Mariah	8	F		TX
Mary	6	F		TX
John	4	M		TX
Madison	1	M		TX
McAdams, John	35	M	Farmer	TN
Mary	16	F		TN
Mary	10	F		TX
William	8	M		TX
John	6	M		TX
Hiram	5	M		TX

(continued)

Name	Age	Sex	Occupation	Birthplace
MCAdams, Jas.	2	M		TX
Mills, Richard	36	M	Croper	GA
Guerrant, Dan	28	M	Farmer	KY
Edah	18	F		TN
Charles	1	M		TX
Lamb, Susan A.	13	F		TX
Birdwell, William	41	M	Farmer	TN
Jedida	25	F		TN
John	1	M		TX
Petrie, Peter	31	M	Farmer	TN
Pesorie	26	F		GA
Elizabeth	6	F		TX
Nancy	3	F		TX
Jas.	2	M		TX
Thomas	4/12	M		TX
Campbell, Joseph K.	40	M	Farmer	TN
Erzenith	29	F		MS
Netherland, Sol	48	M	Farmer	TN
Elizabeth	35	F		GA
Lewis	18	M	Farmer	MS
Mary	16	F		MS
Jas.	13	M		MS
Sarah	8	F		MS
Franklin	4	M		MS
Melicia	2	F		MS
Johnson, William	70	M	Farmer	SC
Mary	55	F		TN
Adam	37	F	Farmer	MO
Miriam	18	F		AR
Amanda	16	F		TX
Street, Sam	17	M		MO
Hoskinson, Mary	22	F		AR
Mary	2	F		TX
Maurice, Jas.	56	M	Farmer	NC
Mary	50	F		NC
Jas.	21	M	Farmer	TN
Visor, William	56	M	Farmer	VA
Rachel	52	F		NC
McKan, Katharine	19	F		AL
Andrew	17	M	Farmer	AL
Jos.	14	M		AL
Mary	13	F		AL
Word, Charles	14	M		MS
Ford, Moses	35	M	Farmer	TN
Hampton, Hugh	27	M	Farmer	TN
Ann	17	F		AL
Mary	1	F		TX
Harden, Joel F.	30	M	Farmer	TN
Susan	25	F		IL
George	2	M		TX
Branch, Anthony M.	26	M	Lawyer	VA
Amanda	22	F		TN
Roundtree, J. M.	21	M	Clerk	AL
Keenan, A. L.	11	M		TN
Jones, S. A.	30	M	Brick Mason	??
Willson, J.	40	M	Clerk, D.C.	SC
Finey, Thomas H.	32	M	Carpenter	TN
Sarah	28	F		MS
Napoleon	5	M		TX
Ellen	3	F		TX
William	6/12	M		TX
Finey, A. A.	28	M	Carpenter	TN
Leach, William	35	M	Farmer	SC
Margaret	40	F		TN
Cox, Andrew	19	M	Farmer	AR
Jas.	16	M	Student	AR
Taylor	14	M		TX
Isaac	12	M		TX
Minerva	11	F		TX

(continued)

Name	Age	Sex	Occupation	Birthplace
Cox, Lewis	8	M		TX
Nancy	7	F		TX
Katharine	5	F		TX
Scott, Hamilton	25	M	P.P. Old School	PA
Polk, Cumberland	44	M	Farmer	TN
Nancy	38	F		AR
Elias (Twin)	17	M	Farmer	AR
Jas. (Twin)	17	M	Farmer	AR
William (Twin)	15	M	Farmer	AR
Cumberland (Twin)	15	M	Farmer	AR
Jane	12	F		AR
Lewis	9	M		AR
Jennet	7	F		AR
Prudence	5	F		AR
Mary	3	F		TX
Martha	6/12	F		TX
Houston, David	47	M	Farmer	NC
Harriet	43	F		SC
Anthony	17	M	Farmer	TN
Martha	14	F		TX
Amanda	11	F		TX
Emily	8	F		TX
Frances	5	F		TX
Robert	1	M		TX
Spillers, H. N.	29	M	Farmer	IL
Rebecca	21	F		TN
Mary	5	F		TX
John	3	M		TX
Martha	2	F		TX
Lusk, A. C.	30	M	Hireling	LA
Allan, William A.	43	M	Dr.	NY
Martha	55	F		NC
Hoggs, Charles F.	30	M	Cropper	TN
Mason, Joseph	40	M	Farmer	NY
Jane	38	F		TN
Augustus	13	M		AL
Trephena (Twin)	10	F		AL
Harriet (Twin)	10	F		AL
Katharine	8	F		TX
Hightower	4	M		TX
Heath, William	26	M	(illegible)	TN
Nancy	32	F		IL
McCullah, Elizabeth	12	F		IL
Sam	10	M		IL
Robert	8	M		TX
John	6	M		TX
William	4	M		TX
Heath, John W.	2	M		TX
Rollins, Mark	68	M	Farmer	TN
Leah	40	F		GER
Elizabeth	14	F		MS
Mary	12	F		MS
Jas.	10	M		MS
Matilda	6	F		TX
Montgomery, Edley	40	M	Farmer	TN
Emaline	28	F		TN
William	7	M		TX
Emily	4	F		TX
Mary	1	F		TX
Farris, William	55	M	Farmer	VA
Jackson	17	M	Farmer	TN
Sarah	16	F		TN
Margaret	12	F		TN
Roberts, Allan	40	M	Farmer	GA
Henrietta	35	F		TN
Edwin	15	M	Farmer	TN
Elizabeth	13	F		TN
George	10	M		TX
William	8	M		TX
Thomas	4	M		TX
Ann	6	F		TX
Smith, Lemuel	40	M	Cabinet Maker	VA
Mary	35	F		TN
Thomas	10	M		TX

(continued)

Name	Age	Sex	Occupation	Birthplace
Smith, Sam	8	M		TX
Lemuel	6	M		TX
Ann	4	F		TX
Hesekiah	2	M		TX
Farris, Hesekiah	48	M	Farmer	VA
Matilda	50	F		VA
Jas.	19	M	Farmer	TN
Montgomery, John	34	M	Farmer	TN
Sarah	21	F		MS
Andrew	10	M		TX
Benjamin	7	M		TX
Julia	5	F		TX
Sarah	6/12	F		TX
Stone, Richard	38	M	Farmer	VA
Grace	37	F		TN
Margaret	10	F		AL
William	8	M		AL
Shook, Laurena	30	F	Widow	AR
Robinson, Joshua	25	M	Farmer	LA
Shook, Joshua	7	M		TX
Jas.	5	M		TX
John	3	M		TX
Mary	2	F		TX
Adison, Oscar M.	29	M	M.E.,S. Preacher	MD
Robb, George	24	M	M.E.,S. Preacher	TN
Dun, William S.	38	M	Tanner	TN
Mary	22	F		MS
Roxanna	12	F		MS
Mary	8	F		TX
Cinthia	4	F		TX
Sarah	6	F		TX
William	1	M		TX
Smither, John	71	M	Farmer	VA
Mary	61	F		VA
Joseph	17	M		TN
Ann Eliza	18	F		TN
Smith, Henry S.	50	M	Farmer	NC
Rebecca	50	F		SC
William	15	M	Farmer	LA
Robert	18	M	Farmer	LA
Jerry	26	M	Farmer	TN
Smith, William H.	24	M	Farmer	TN
Martha	22	F		LA
Frank	2	M		TX
Mary	4/12	F		TX
Cotten, John	60	M	Farmer	TN
Gincy	40	F		LA
Robert	18	M	Farmer	MS
Tasa	17	F		MS
William	16	M	Farmer	MS
Joseph	10	M		MS
John	4	M		MS
Melicia	8	F		MS
Julia	6	F		MS
Willey, H.	40	M	Tanner	NH
Mary	31	F		NC
Thomas	10	M		TN
Martha	1	F		TX
Lewis	2	M		TX
Tase, Albert G.	40	M	Farmer	TN
Ann	33	F		SC
Hull, Sarah	12	F		MS
William	11	M		MS
Tase, Mary	5	F		TX
Ronald (Twin)	6/12	M		TX
Donald (Twin)	6/12	M		TX
Bingham, Frances	12	F		MS
Margaret	9	F		TX
Tase, Elmirah	7	F		TX
Jane	5	F		TX
Tase, Sarah	63	F		GA

Name	Age	Sex	Occupation	Birthplace
Keenan, Charles G.	37	M	Doctor	TN
Eliza	20	F		TN
Charles	2	M		TX
Randolph, John	56	M	Farmer	TN
Frances	45	F		NC
Jasper	24	M	Farmer	AL
Nancy	18	F		AL
Newton	21	M	Farmer	AL
Clinton	20	M	Farmer	TX
Mansell	17	M	Farmer	AL
Green	8	M		TX
Hannah	18	F		TX
Nancy	14	F		TX
Elizabeth	11	F		TX
Davidson, Frances E.	4	F		TX
Wisdom, George W.	27	M	Carpenter	TN
Malinda	20	F		GA
Sasser, William	40	M	Carpenter	NC
Rogers, Micaja	55	M	Merchant	TN
Cintha	50	F		TN
Lafayette	21	M	Post Master	TN
Mary	16	F		TN
Minerva	14	F		TN
Ransom, D. J.	24	M	Doctor	TN
Martha	21	F		AL
John	1/12	M		TX
McCary, Jehu	20	M	Student	TN
Maddox, Z. W.	32	M	Carpenter	AR
Lorinda	25	F		TN
Leonidas	5	M		TX
Maddox, F. E.	27	M	Carpenter	AR
Randolph, Harvey	30	M	Grocery Keeper	TN
Evaline	22	F		TN
John	6/12	M		TX
Puette, Mary	15	F		TN
Caroline	19	F		TN
Perry, C. L.	24	M	Grocery Keeper	TN
Cotten, Thomas J.	50	M	Farmer	TN
Elvina	40	F		KY
Thomas	19	M		MS
Benjamin	17	M		MS
Julian	14	F		MS
John	12	M		KY
Susan	9	F		KY
Leathiann	7	F		TX
Bud	2	M		TX
Bowen, Adam R.	28	M	Tavern Keeper	KY
Trecilla	22	F		MS
William	5	M		TX
John	3	M		TX
Mary	1	F		TX
Rowe, Lewis	20	M		MS
Abbot, C. C. S. D.	35	M	Lawyer	TN
Wade, John W.	35	M	Printer	NY
Virginia	20	F		NC
Franklin	8	M		TX
Thirza	5	F		TX
Rooth	1	F		TX
Dupree, John S.	21	M	Printer	TN
Reeves, William	31	M	Saddler	TN
Caroline	24	F		AL
Jas.	6/12	M		TX
Brickhouse, Latimer	28	M	Hireling	??
Wells, Jackson	34	M	Farmer	AR
Nancy	22	F		TN
Nancy	12	F		AR
William	10	M		TX
Sarah	8	F		AR
Robert	6	M		TX
Smith, J. C.	32	M	Merchant	TN
Mary	26	F		MS
Sam	9	M		TX
Sarah	7	F		TX

(continued)

Name	Age	Sex	Occupation	Birthplace
Smith, William	5	M		TX
Clemantine	3	F		TX
Mosellah	2	F		TX
Jas.	6/12	M		TX
Smith, Sam R.	34	M	Merchant	TN
Capshaw, J. W.	23	M	Clerk	AL
Hoskins, Hugh C.	44	M	Farmer	TN
Sarah	44	F		VA
Frances	17	F		TN
William	15	M	Farmer	AL
Thomas	13	M		TN
John	11	M		TX
Alfred	9	M		TX
Barret, William M.	37	M	Carpenter	VA
Nancy	30	F		TN
Elizabeth	1	F		TX
Hamilton, John F.	8	M		TX
McGilvery, Alex	29	M	Carpenter	NC
Rentfroe, E. D.	30	M	Doctor	TN
Katharine	20	F		TN
Katharine	4/12	F		TX
Heath, Simon Peter	37	M	Farmer	TN
Lavinia	43	F		TN
Margaret	18	F		TN
Lerena	14	F		LA
Sarah	13	F		TX
Lewis	8	M		TX
Jesse	6	M		TX
Simon Peter	4	M		TX
Jas.	4/12	M		TX
Lagrove, Frances	37	F	Widow	TN
Henry	20	M	Farmer	AL
Jas.	17	M	Farmer	AL
Daniel	14	M		AL
Lucinda	13	F		AR
John	11	M		AR
David	9	M		AR
Susan	6	F		AR
Harrison, Mary	39	F		TN
William	29	M	Ranger	AL
Hiram	27	M	Ranger	AL
Avery, Ben	29	M	Miller	TN
Elizabeth	27	F		TN
Elisha	4	M		TX
Moore, John B.	40	M	Farmer	GA
Sabre	26	F		TN
Julia	10	F		TX
Alace	4	F		TX
Thomas	1	M		TX
Martha	18	F		GA
Sadler, John	39	M	Farmer	TN
Bersheba	38	F		IL
Jas.	16	M	Farmer	TX
Sally	14	F		TX
Sam	10	M		TX
Elizabeth	8	F		TX
Norvel	6	M		TX
Mary	5	F		TX
Robert	3	M		TX
Williams, Hiram	32	M	Farmer	LA
Sophronia	21	F		TN
Nancy	1	F		TX
Clanton, F. K.	45	M	(illegible)	VA
Patience	30	F		TN
Oliver	9	M		TX
Sarah	6	F		TX
Horton	3	M		TX
Winters, John	30	M	Black Smith	TN
Tillice	30	F		MS
Hampton	12	M		TX
Josephus	8	M		TX
Marion	6	M		TX
Adaline	3	F		TX

Name	Age	Sex	Occupation	Birthplace
Keys, Reuben	33	M	Farmer-Stockraiser	GA
Martha	31	F		TN
John	14	M		TN
Rachel	11	F		AR
Jas.	9	M		AR
Malinda	7	F		AR
Susan	5	F		TX
Sarah	1	F		TX
Winters, Oran L.	37	M	Farmer	TN
Susannah	37	F		TN
Alfred	14	M		TN
Frances	11	F		TX
Daniel	7	M		TX
Elizabeth	5	F		TX
Martha	4	F		TX
Rodah	3	F		TX
Susan	6/12	F		TX
Pursley, John	46	M	Farmer	KY
Jane	37	F		TN
William	18	M	Farmer	IL
Hiram	15	M	Farmer	IL
Lydia	10	F		IL
John	8	M		IL
Elizabeth	6	F		IL
Joseph	4	M		MO
Mary	2	F		TX
Sarah	4/12	F		TX
Halsel, Thomas	35	M	Farmer	TN
Margaret	37	F		AL
William	15	M	Farmer	AL
Elizabeth	13	F		TX
Hannah	11	F		TX
Margaret	9	F		TX
Martha	4	F		TX
Irwin	6/12	M		TX
Winters, John F.	36	M	Miller-Farmer	TN
Margaret	35	F		??
Rooth	14	F		TX
Sidney	12	M		TX
Rodah	10	F		TX
Mary	3	F		TX
Jas.	6/12	M		TX
Rodah	65	F		NC
Winters, Billington	25	M	Farmer	TN
Darcus	22	F		AL
Jas.	5	M		TX
Billington	3	M		TX
Ben	1	M		TX
Massey, William S.	36	M	Farmer	TN
Margaret	31	F		TN
John	11	M		TX
Joel	8	M		TX
Emily	6	F		TX
Charles	4	M		TX
Estill, Milton	43	M	C.P. Preacher	KY
Louisa	34	F		TN
Charles	14	M		TN
Ben	12	M		TN
Jas.	8	M		TX
Milton	6	M		TX
Edwin	3	M		TX
Crouch, Jackson	34	M	Farmer	KY
Sarah	32	F		TN
Lydia	11	F		TX
William	9	M		TX
Jas.	7	M		TX
Charles	5	M		TX
Rodah	2/12	F		TX
Cooda, Joseph	38	M	Farmer	TN
Hesther	38	F		TN
Taylor, Andrew J.	18	M	Farmer	AR
Harmer, Francis	7	M		LA
Cooda, Henry	15	M	Farmer	TN
Peter	9	M		TX
Sarah	7	F		TX
Milam	5	M		TX

Name	Age	Sex	Occupation	Birthplace
Walker, Charles	46	M	Black Smith	TN
Jeretha	38	F		TN
Hesther	19	F		AR
Barbary	15	F		AR
Elizabeth	11	F		TX
Joseph	9	M		TX
Mary	7	F		TX
Nancy	5	F		TX
Owen, Pinckney W.	32	M	Farmer	TN
Zilley	28	F		AL
Jas.	10	M		TX
John	8	M		TX
Robert	6	M		TX
Mary	3	F		TX
Sarah	6/12	F		TX
Sessums, Richard	50	M	Farmer	NC
Pamelia	40	F		NC
Blount	15	M	Student	TX
Peter	14	M		AL
George	12	M		TN
William	3	M		TX
Sims, T. S.	44	M	Farmer	MS
Mary	42	F		TN
Arranna	15	F		MS
Mary (Twin)	10	F		MS
Richard (Twin)	10	M		MS
Elizabeth	8	F		TX
Olephant, Sandford	35	M	Overseer	MS
Cato, Alfred	35	M	Farmer	TN
Sarah	35	F		LA
Webb, Elizabeth	15	F		TX
William	10	M		TX
Shaw, J. G.	25	M	School Teacher	TN
Phillips, T. R.	39	M	Farmer	TN
Hannah	36	F		TN
Erasmus	16	M	Farmer	MS
Sophronia	14	F		MS
Erastus	12	M		MS
Albert	10	M		MS
Leonorah	7	F		TX
King, A. C.	37	M	Tanner	TN
Jane	34	F		TN
Athelia	12	F		TN
Harriet	10	F		TN
Jas.	8	M		TN
John	6	M		TN
Christina	4	F		TN
David	2	M		TX
Dill, George	45	M	Presby. Preacher- Regular & Saddler	SC
Banton, G. W.	64	M	Farmer	SC
Cinthia	53	F		NC
Glover	22	M	Lawyer	TN
Joab	16	M	Student	TN
Byran	14	M		TN
Black, Livingston	20	M	Student	MS
Wilkins, W. W.	32	M	Farmer	NC
Martha	24	F		TN
Elizabeth	3	F		TX
Lewis	2	M		TX
McMillon, Thomas	27	M	Farmer	AL
Eladia	25	F		AL
Julian	4	F		TX
Isaac	2	M		TX
Dyer, B. F.	49	M	Tailor	TN
Frances	24	F		AL
Katharine	3	F		TX
Benjamin	6/12	M		TX
Gibbs, Thomas	38	M	Merchant	SC
Nancy	23	F		TN
Sandford	28	M	Merchant	SC
Powel, William R.	39	M	Carpenter	TN

(continued)

Name	Age	Sex	Occupation	Birthplace
Powel, Melicia	32	F		MEX
Mary	7	F		TX
Elen	5	F		TX
Zachariah	1	M		TX
Day, Elbert E.	50	M	Farmer	GA
Anna	40	F		TN
Dempsey	23	M	Farmer	MS
William	20	M	Farmer	MS
Elbert	14	M		MS
Jas.	12	M		MS
Jeptha	8	M		MS
Rebecca	5	F		MS
Frances	1	F		TX
Glass, J. P.	28	M	Farmer	TN
Parish, W. A.	44	M	Farmer	NC
Kathrine	26	F		TN
Joel	3	M		TX
Brown, Marion	8	M		TN
Parrish, Leonidas E.	2	M		TX
John	4/12	M		TX
Birdwell, Thomas G.	46	M	Farmer	TN
Tirza	49	F		SC
Robert	19	M	Farmer	TN
Elizabeth	17	F		TN
Thomas	16	M	Farmer	TN
Nancy	13	F		TN
McGowan, Margaret	73	F		SC
Gault, Thomas	34	M	Overseer	KY
Crane, C. P.	29	M	Farmer	TN
Susan	22	F		TN
Mary	5	F		TX
Rodah	4	F		TX
John	3	M		TX
Andrew	1	M		TX
Crane, Jackson	19	M	Farmer	TN
Wiley, A. P.	28	M	Lawyer	GA
Mary	24	F		TN
John	1	M		TX
Ford, Henry	49	M	Farmer	NC
Elizabeth	49	F		SC
Hampton, William R.	17	M	Farmer	TX
Belvidera	7	F		TX
Baker, Elizabeth	4	F		TX
J. D.	30	M	Carpenter	TN
McGowan, A. J.	33	M	C.P. Preacher	TN
Burrel D.	19	M	Printer	TN
Jenkins, William	18	M	Printer	IN
Royal, Peter	32	M	Brick Mason	VA
Vaughn, Sterling	20	M	Student	TN
Conner, David	58	M	Farmer	GA
Foreman, David	19	M	Farmer	AL
Crabb, Lowery	28	M	Farmer	TN
Angeline	20	F		MS
Brantley, J. W.	27	M	Tanner	TN
Nancy	21	F		TN
Rebecca	4	F		TN
John	1	M		TX
Briscoe, Robert	25	M	Tanner	TX
Brantley, J. J.	33	M	Misc.	TX
Harrison, J. P.	42	M	Guard to Penitentiary	NC
Emily	35	F		KY
Martha	20	F		TN
Mary	6	F		TX
Stanford	4	M		TX
Milton	1	M		TX
Paul, Andrew	70	M	Farmer	VA
Lucinda	50	F		GA
Lucinda	21	F		TN
Andrew J.	19	M	Farmer	TN
Katharine	15	F		TN
Jane	12	F		MS

(continued)

WALKER COUNTY, TEXAS

Paul, Orlena	10	F		MS
Dockery, Edward	33	M	Hireling	MD
Smith, E. M.	35	M	Miller	TN
Harriet	26	F		TN
Gransevoorte(?)	5	M		TX
Paulina	3	F		TX
Smith, J. G.	21	M	Hireling	TN
Nooner, William	24	M	Hireling	TN
Heath, William	40	M	Hireling	N ENG
Gillaspey, Margaret	58	F	Widow	MD
Jane	24	F		TN
Margaret	22	F		TN
Samuel	21	M	Waggoner	TN
Elizabeth	17	F		TN
Sarah	15	F		AL
Thornton, F. G.	30	M	Carpenter	CT
Margaret	25	F		ENG
Frank	3	M		TX
Emma	1	F		TX
Dillard, Nancy Ann	33	F	Widow	TN
Martha	9	F		TX
Gillaspey, Jas.	28	M	Warden at Penitentiary	TN
Harrison, Joseph	44	M	Sargent	NC
McGary, Isaac	50	M	Clerk of County	OH
Elizabeth	34	F		TN
Marion	7	M		TX
Austin	4	M		TX
Rachel	1	F		TX
Word, Sarah	14	F		TN
Gillaspey, James	39	M	Brick Mason	TN
Susan	21	F		TN
Oliver, Charles	21	M	Black Smith	TN
Gillaspey, Argyle C.	21	M	Tanner	TN
Reed, Sam	30	M	Brick Mason	PA
Evans, J. W.	45	M	Farmer	SC
Manurva	37	F		TN
Duncan, Josephine	16	F		AL
Harrison, J. S.	12	M		AL
Ketura	10	F		AL
Evans, Elizabeth	72	F		VA
Foreman, J. J.	30	M	Farmer	GA
Priscilla	28	F		TN
Mary	13	F		AL
William	10	M		AL
Arzena	9	F		AL
Capt.	8	M		AL
Maranda	6	F		AL
Drucilla	5	F		AL
Yokum, Henderson	40	M	Lawyer	TN
Edaline	37	F		TN
Eliza	15	F		TN
Martha	13	F		TN
Mary	11	F		TN
George	8	M		TN
Robert	6	M		TN
Anna	3	F		TX
McCrary, John	28	M	Lawyer	??
Furgason, Moses	71	M	Farmer	SC
Joice	60	F		TN
Jas.	23	M	Farmer	LA
Oliver	18	M	Farmer	LA
Isam	17	M	Farmer	LA
Parish, Joice	8	F		LA
Crane, A, J,	24	M	Farmer	TN
Mary	19	F		TN
Black, Henry	38	M	Trader	TN
Mary	38	F		MO
Jas.	10	M		TX
John	5	M		TX
Ellin	3	F		TX

(continued)

Black, Martha	1	F		TX
Cochren, Jas.	22	M	Hireling	AR
Charman, John	34	M	Farmer	TN
Margaret	28	F		LA
Frances	8	F		LA
Benjamin	6	M		LA
Mary	4	F		TX
Martha	2	F		TX
John	6/12	M		TX
Hemphill, Jas.	27	M	Farmer	AR
Eliza	24	F		TN
William	8	M		AR
Jacob	6	M		AR
Jane	3	F		AR
Kerby, Isaah	32	M	Farmer	KY
Martha	22	F		AL
Sleals, Thomas	17	M	Hireling	TN
Carver, John	25	M	Farmer	TN
Elizabeth	22	F		TN
Mary	5	F		TX
John	3	M		TX
Sarah	2	F		TX
Martha	5/12	F		TX
McMillon, Mathew	58	M	Farmer	PA
Ann	45	F		TN
Jas.	16	M	Farmer	AR
John	12	M		AR
Caroline	6	F		TX
Mary	4	F		TX
Thomas	2	M		TX
Rock, Charles	30	M	Farmer	LA
Mary	23	F		TN
Sam	2	M		TX
William	1	M		TX
Fielder, R. R.	27	M	Farmer	AL
Elizabeth	20	F		TN
William	3	M		AL
John	4/12	M		TX
Fry, William	26	M	Wagon Maker	TN
Elizabeth	27	F		TN
Carver, William	18	M	Farmer	TN
Hunter, George	53	M	Tavern Keeper	KY
Tamer	52	F		KY
Jas.	15	M	Tavern Keeper	AL
Drury, Arabella	24	F	Widow	AL
Amelia	6	F		TX
Cora	4	F		TX
Tamer	2	F		TX
Meredith, Jas.	38	M	Doctor	VA
Ross, Sterling B.	30	M	Wagon Maker	TN
Aires, Andrew	20	M	Hireling	SC
Gorman, Roswell	37	M	Farmer	AL
Hart, H. P.	29	M	Grocery Keeper	TN
Delcima	19	F		TN
Mary	2/12	F		TX
Taylor, A. R.	33	M	Grocery Keeper	TN
Pomeroy, Frederick	36	M	Misc.	NY
Katharine	24	F		OH
Simeon	4	M		TX
Susannah	3	F		TX
Dolph, Letticia	60	F	Widow	MD
Noe, L. D.	30	M	Tailor	KY
Ward, Sam L.	30	M	Laborer	TN
Young, Jane	50	F	Widow	VA
Mary	20	F		TN
Tabitha	18	F		TN
Wright, Jas. S.	30	M	Merchant	SC
Davis, J. C.	40	M	Saddler	TN
Shockley, William	36	M	Carpenter	TN
Lanetta	22	F		AR
Nancy	7	F		AR
Mary	2	F		AR

WALKER COUNTY, TEXAS

Name	Age	Sex	Occupation	Birthplace
Leaks, John P.	30	M	Farmer	MS
Mary	17	F		TN
Trecilla	65	F	Widow	NC
Culp, John	42	M	Black Smith	GER
Wilkinson, H. C.	55	M	Horse Trainer	ENG
Smither, Robert	38	M	Merchant	VA
Elizabeth	30	F		SC
William	10	M		MS
John	6	M		TX
Jas.	4	M		TX
Juliet	2	F		TX
John R.	20	M	Clerk	TN
Barnett, Maleda	52	F	Widow	TN
Foster, Elizabeth	10	F		TX
Kibble, Albert	49	M	Farmer	VA
Evaline	19	F		TN
Malvina	16	F		TN
Edwin	10	M		TN
Watkins, William	25	M	Overseer	LA
McMillon, Jas.	34	M	Farmer	TN
Nancy	32	F		SC
Daniel	23	M	Farmer	AL
Martha	11	F		AL
Jas.	10	M		AL
George	8	M		AL
Abner	6	M		TX
Cordelia	4	F		TX
Drue	2	M		TX
Evans, Frances	17	F		AL
Farris, Loocy	39	F	Widow	TN
Nathan	16	M	Farmer	AL
Loocy	14	F		AL
Edward	8	M		TX
John	6	M		TX
George	3	M		TX
Gillaspey, Jas.	45	M	Farmer	TN
Sarah	33	F		TN
Jacob	12	M		TN
Jas.	10	M		TN
Salena	4	F		TX
John	2	M		TX
McCaleb, Ephraim	64	M	Farmer	NC
Ruston, John	30	M	Misc.	TN
Caroline	18	F		NC
Susan	12	F		TX
Mary	10	F		TX
Infant	1/12	-		TX
Lithrust, Lavenia	15	F		TX
Palmer, William	45	M	Farmer	KY
Lucinda	43	F		TN
Mary	16	F		LA
Roark, Reed	45	M	Carpenter	GA
Dunn, Narcissa	25	F		AR
Gray, Hannah	41	F	Widow	NC
John	20	M	Misc.	TN
Oliver	16	M	Student	TX
David	12	M		TX
Amanda	10	F		TX
Mary	6	F		TX
Elizabeth	4	F		TX
Moore, S. A.	52	M	Farmer	VA
Issabella	22	F		TN
Elizabeth	20	F		TN
William	17	M		TN

WASHINGTON COUNTY, TEXAS

Name	Age	Sex	Occupation	Birthplace
Cody, Moses	30	M	Mechanic	IRE
Lucinda	20	F		TX
Price, Williamson	45	M	Mechanic	TN
Petty, J. T.	25	M		TN
H. V.	20	F		AR

(continued)

Name	Age	Sex	Occupation	Birthplace
Petty, N. A.	5	F		TX
M. D.	1	F		TX
Tucker, William	14	M		TX
Petty, A.	23	M		TN
Josephine	19	F		TX
D. C.	1	M		TX
Pullin, B. S.	25	M	Inn Keeper	TN
J. M.	20	F		IL
J. J.	1	F		TX
William	20	M		TN
Rippetoe, A. J.	33	M	Inn Keeper	NC
Sergent, W. L.	26	M	Mechanic	TN
Williams, Noah	35	M	Farmer	NC
Pullin, M. G.	1	F		TX
Cloy, T. T.	26	M	Farmer	KY
Barnhill, T. W.	34	M	Farmer	AL
Elizabeth	19	F		TX
M. D.	3	M		TX
J. D.	2	M		TX
Plesant	11	M		TN
J. A.	9	F		TN
Berry, Thomas	48	M		TN
R. C.	22	M	Farmer	TN
Crumpler, D. D.	35	M		VA
M. E.	25	F		TN
Lusk, P. H.	26	M	Lawyer	TN
Mary	1	F		TX
Isreal, W. T.	22	M	Clerk	GA
Stocton, Emily	48	F		SC
James	18	M	Farmer	TN
Augustus	15	M		TN
Hayden	13	M		TN
Money, J. H.	55	M	Farmer	TN
Galspn, B.	45	M	Lawyer	TN
Emily B.	30	F		TN
Lane, Thomas	62	M		VA
Sayles, John	25	M	Lawyer	NY
M. E.	17	F		TN
Atkinson, Nat.	44	M	Farmer	VA
A. E.	33	F		TN
J. S.	11	M		TN
L. A.	9	F		TN
J. M.	6	M		TN
J.	3	F		TX
Brown, J. H.	25	M		MO
H.	17	M		MO
Sneed, J. P.	44	M	Farmer	TN
A.	26	F		TN
Emily	5	F		TX
J. W.	4	M		TX
Joseph	3	M		TX
Rogers, William	25	M	Farmer	LA
Toxey, Asa O.	50	M		GA
Elizabeth	47	F		CT
S. A.	16	F		TX
Thomas	12	M		TX
Jelet, Frank	27	M	Lawyer	CT
Miller, James	24	M	Mechanic	GA
S. A.	15	F		TN
Mayfield, Jno. N.	42	M	Farmer	TN
Louisa	36	F		TN
Sarah	16	F		TN
James	15	M		TN
Martha	13	F		TN
Hester	12	F		TN
William	11	M		TN
Lucinda	9	F		TN
N.	6	F		TN
M.	1	F		TX
Laura	2	F		TN
Blackburn, T. B.	24	M	Farmer	SC

WASHINGTON COUNTY, TEXAS

Name	Age	Sex	Occupation	Birthplace
West, Isaac	45	M	Farmer	TN
Sarah	27	F		TN
E. C.	10	F		TN
L. N.	15	F		TN
J. W.	13	F		TN
J.	8	M		TN
D. M.	6	M		TN
G. R.	4	M		TX
D. E.	18	F		TN
Griffith, J.	36	M	Farmer	TN
Cranshaw, J. C.	35	M	Farmer	TN
A. M.	28	F		TN
L. A.	5	F		TX
M. T.	4	F		TX
T. W.	1	F		TX
E.	60	F		TN
Thomas, James	28	M	Farmer	TN
Nunn, Margaret	21	F		KY
William L.	3	M		TX
S. G.	1	F		TX
Mary	52	F	Farmer	GA
Nancy	14	F		TN
Burns, Leander	45	M	Farmer	SC
Nancy	35	F		TN
L. Y.	16	M	Farmer	GA
Sarah	13	F		AL
Jas.	11	M		TX
J.	8	M		TX
L.	4	M		TX
L. A.	2	F		TX
T.	65	M	Mechanic	GA
Irving, Thomas	30	M	Farmer	GA
Caroline	20	F		TN
James	7	M		TX
J. L.	2	M		TX
Harrell, J. A.	40	M	Farmer	NC
E.	40	F		TN
J. A.	16	F		TN
M. D.	14	F		TN
Matilda	12	F		TN
Isabella	10	F		TX
Elizabeth	6	F		TX
Piplin, M. R.	30	M	Farmer	TN
Elizabeth	22	F		GA
Pipkin, S. M.	35	M	Farmer	TN
Watson, James	26	M	Farmer	MO
Mary	24	F		MS
Syford, John	45	M	Mechanic	NC
Gentry, G. M.	42	M	Farmer	TN
Jane	20	F		MO
G. V.	1	M		TX
S. E.	1	F		TX
Coatson, J. S.	38	M	Farmer	VA
Nancy	38	F		VA
Thomas	14	M		TN
Martha	12	F		AR
Henry	10	M		TN
Richard	8	M		TN
Elizabeth	6	F		TN
Jane	4	F		TN
John	2	M		TX
McCaleb, Alson	38	M	Farmer	TN
K. K.	36	F		TN
Jas. C. C.	8	M		AR
Martha E.	6	F		AR
Bishop, W. S.	32	M	Merchant	KY
Snodgrass, J. A.	36	M	Farmer	TN
Elma	28	F		TN
Leroy	9	M		TN
Jackson, Jno.	7	M		TN
Dallas, G. M.	5	M		TN
Snodgrass, M. P.	2	M		TN
Albert	3	M		TN

Name	Age	Sex	Occupation	Birthplace
Williams, Samuel	26	M	Farmer	MO
A. B.	55	M	Farmer	TN
David	18	M		MO
Robert	22	M		TN
M. A.	20	F		MO
Catharine	16	F		TX
Murphy, J. B.	32	M	Farmer	TN
J. A.	24	F		TN
A. E.	2	F		TX
M. J.	1	F		TX
Cary, F.	16	M	Farmer	GA
Clemens, A. J.	29	M		KY
J. A.	20	F		TN
James	3	M		TX
William	1	M		TX
Mundine, J. C.	46	M	Farmer	TN
E. M.	41	F		TN
T.	24	M	Farmer	AL
Petty, G. M.	28	M	Farmer	TN
Marion	23	M		TN
James	13	M		TX
J.	9	M		TX
Sophia	6	F		TX
Ambrose	3	M		TX
Rheuben	1	M		TX
House, J. J.	50	M	Farmer	TN
Frances	38	F		TN
Marion	18	F		TN
George	15	M		TX
Joseph	13	M		TX
James	11	M		TX
J. J.	5	F		TX
Samuel	3	M		TX
William	2	M		TX
Dykes, M. W. D.	38	M	Farmer	TN
Dinah	26	F		MS
A. J.	6	F		TX
C. J.	4	M		TX
Malinda	1	F		TX
Perry, James	50	M		MS
Fisher, John	30	M	Farmer	TN
Anny	12	F		TX
Dinah	8	F		TX
James	6	M		TX
M. Taylor	4	M		TX
Estes, James	18	M	Farmer	TN
W.	60	F		KY
West, John	9	M		TN
Shipman, Moses G.	32	M	Farmer	TN
J. J.	21	M		TN
Melinda	6	F		TX
James	3	M		TX
Mary	1	F		TX
Mills, J. B.	55	M	Farmer	TN
Anna	48	F		TN
Wilson	24	M	Farmer	TN
Archibald	11	M		MO
Alexander	7	M		TX
C. H.	15	M		GER
Hope, Jasper	47	M	Farmer	NY
Julia	22	F		TN
M. E.	9	F		TX
R. A.	7	M		TX
Cyrus	5	M		TX
A. A.	2	F		TX
Robert P.	1	M		TX
Hensley, John	44	M	Mechanic	TN
Sarah	28	F		LA
J. A.	12	F		TX
J. H.	5	M		TX
L. E.	3	F		TX
Elizabeth	1	F		TX
Gray, William	60	M		IRE

WASHINGTON COUNTY, TEXAS

Name	Age	Sex	Occupation	Birthplace
Farrell, Irvin	36	M	Farmer	TN
M. C.	37	F		SC
D. C.	13	M		TN
J. W. F.	10	M		TX
J.	8	M		TX
J. A.	7	M		TX
J. J.	5	M		TX
Hensley, Jackson	34	M	Farmer	TN
Jane	39	F		GA
B.	6	M		TX
D. M.	5	M		TX
Charles	3	M		TX
M. S.	1	M		TX
Shaw, J.	29	M	Farmer	TX
A. E.	24	F		TN
Charles	6	M		TX
John	4	M		TX
William	1	M		TX
James	21	M	Farmer	TX
Lucas, Samuel	19	M	Farmer	TN
Cooper, Martha	29	F		TN
Ashley	9	M		TX
Susan	6	F		TX
M.	4	F		TX
Charles	1	M		TX
Hughes, Thomas M.	35	M	Farmer	TN
Elizabeth	32	F		TX
Eliza	9	F		TX
Elizabeth	8	F		TX
Hensley, Charles	36	M	Farmer	TN
Indiana	25	F		TN
Alex	8	M		TX
Rankin	5	M		TX
Solden	2	M		TX
William	1	M		TX
Owans, Brady	5	F		TX
Frances	5	F		TX
Lucas, E. M.	25	M		TN
Harriet	22	F		TX
James	25	M	Farmer	TN
Alexander, M. F.	37	M	Farmer	TN
S.	32	F		TN
M. A.	9	M		TX
J. C.	7	M		TX
L. M.	5	F		TX
S. F.	2	M		TX
J. H.	1	M		TX
Harman, Jos.	16	M	Farmer	GER
Hunt, William	41	M	Farmer	TN
Murphy, Rebecca	60	F		NC
Virginia	19	F		TN
White, Mary	8	F		TX
Martha	7	F		TX
V.	1	F		TX
Lester, E. J.	31	M	Farmer	TX
Elizabeth	25	F		TN
S. A. S.	5	F		TX
E. E.	2	F		TX
Evetts, J. H.	44	M	Mechanic	TN
A.	38	F		MO
Milton	20	M		TN
Miligan, P. D.	20	M		TX
J. M.	16	M		TX
B. F.	11	M		TX
Evetts, S. A.	4	M		TX
N. C.	10	M		TX
Snodgrass, William	50	M	Farmer	TN
Catharine	52	F		SC
Nancy	25	F		TN
Malinda	22	F		SC
Hodge	20	M		TN
J. N.	19	M		TN
M. J.	14	F		TN

Name	Age	Sex	Occupation	Birthplace
Mills, E. T.	26	M	School Teacher	TN
M. M.	1	M		KY
N.	4	F		TN
Barnhill, P. F.	22	M	Farmer	TN
Mary A.	18	F		TX
Kelly, S. C.	3	F		TX
Mayatt, J. W.	30	M	Farmer	SC
Elizabeth	24	F		TN
Harriette	3	F		TX
L.	1	F		TX
Lyel, William	43	M	Farmer	VA
E.	30	F		TN
G. W.	11	M		TN
J. J.	17	F		TN
S. C.	5	F		TN
Elizabeth	3	F		TN
Julian	7	F		TN
Watson, Aron D.	36	M	Farmer	TN
M.	31	F		TN
Gambal, E. J.	11	F		TX
John	9	M		TX
Green	7	M		TX
Key, James P.	39	M	Doctor	VA
S. E.	20	F		TN
L. A.	1/12	F		TX
McDods, Jas. W.	30	M	Farmer	AL
C. F.	26	F		TN
William M.	9	M		TX
J. M.	7	M		TX
Elizabeth	5	F		TX
Robert	3	M		TX
Alexander	23	M	Farmer	TX
Tom, Joseph	21	M	Saddle Maker	TN
Higgins, Clabe	20	M		TN
Geddings, J. D.	30	M	Attorney	PA
A. M.	29	F		TN
E. F.	5	M		TX
James C.	3	M		TX
F. D.	1	M		TX
Barber, C. F.	27	M	Attorney	NY
Testard, Adrain	60	M		FRA
Mary	61	F		LA
Adolph	24	M	Grocer	LA
C.	18	F		TN
A.	14	M	Grocer	KY
McIntre, H. C.	44	M	Farmer	NC
Sarah	36	F		TN
J. B.	18	M		TN
H. E.	15	F		TN
S. E.	13	F		TN
D. M.	6	M		TX
Daniel	4	M		TX
Hugh	2	M		TX
Clark, James	60	M	Farmer	RI
Rhody	53	F		TN
Nester	18	M		TX
Elizabeth	14	F		TX
John	8	M		TX
McDonaldson, S. M.	10	M		TX
Brown, James, Sr.	46	M	Farmer	SC
Margaret	45	F		KY
Sandford	18	M		TN
Hamilton	10	M		TX
Marion	9	M		TX
Ann	5	F		TX
Adeline	12	F		TX
Lusk, P. H.	27	M	Attorney	TN
Estes, John	42	M	Farmer	TN
Elizabeth	28	F		KY
John	10	F(M)		TN
L.	9	M		TN

(continued)

Name	Age	Sex	Occupation	Birthplace
Estes, James E.	8	F(M)		TN
A. A.	5	F		TN
Shannon, Martha J.	4	F		TN
Furgua(Furqua), Stephen	41	M	Farmer	VA
Caroline	39	F		TN
M. E.	15	M		TN
Martha	15	F		TN
Nancy	11	F		TX
George	9	M		TX
Emily	7	F		TX
James	3	M		TX
McCain, Abraham	24	M	Farmer	AR
Susan	21	F		TN
Sarah M.	1	F		TX
Armstrong, James C.	33	M		TN
Francis	10	M		KY
V. M.	4	M		TX
S. G.	2	M		TX
P. T.	7	F		TX
Hogan, James	21	M	Farmer	TN
Nunn, T. R.	33	M	Farmer	TN
Mary	31	F		TN
William	11	F		TN
Martha	9	F		TN
John	7	M		TX
Mary	5	F		TX
A.	3	F		TX
T. N.	1	M		TX
Ferral, Griffin	31	M		NC
Ariste	21	F		TN
J. H.	1	M		TX
McClelland, William B.	46	M	Farmer	TN
Juliette	46	F		VA
A. G.	18	M		TN
T. B.	16	M		TN
S. H.	14	M		TN
Mary	10	F		TN
W. N.	5	M		TN
Gentry, Mary	50	F	Farmer	SC
Gentry, Thomas	27	M	Farmer	TN
Rebecca	17	F		TN
Louisa	14	F		TN
E. A.	12	F		TN
Gentry, James	30	M	Farmer	TN
Amanda	25	F		KY
W. N.	½	M		TN
J. J.	30	M		NC
W. B.	20	M		TN
Nunn, Simpson H.	27	M	Merchant	TN
Ann	17	F		AL
Richard	½	M		TX
Jane	17	F		TN
Higgins, Henry	54	M	Farmer	NC
Jane	40	F		SC
William	28	M	Attorney	TN
James	24	M		TN
Charles	22	M		TN
Bell, Elizabeth	25	F		TN
West, Mary	10	M(F)		TX
Higgins, Jane	3	F		TN
E. T.	19	F		TX
Stamps, John	51	M		TN
Jane	48	F		MS
J. C.	26	M		MS
Maria	11	F		MS
M.	7	F		TX
Pillow, Richard	45	M	Farmer	VA
Elizabeth	37	F		TN
Alonzo	20	M		TN
Martha	18	F		TN

(continued)

Name	Age	Sex	Occupation	Birthplace
Pillow, Elizabeth	16	F		TX
Paralee	14	F		TX
Louisa	12	F		TX
Eliza	10	F		TX
Jas. H.	7	M		TX
Elben	5	F		TX
A.	3	F		TX
Richard	6/12	M		TX
Hackworth, W. W.	36	M	Mechanic	TN
Eliza J.	28	F		IL
Stephen	10	M		TX
Adeline	8	F		TX
Julian	4	F		TX
John	6	M		TX
Mary	6/12	F		TX
Lockridge, Isaac P.	21	M	Farmer	TN
William	16	M		TN
Blackborn	15	M		TN
Margaret	12	F		TN
Louisa	9	F		TX
Rebecca	44	F		TN
Johnson, F. A.	28	M	Farmer	TN
M. J.	19	F		TN
W. A.	½	M		TX
Davis, J.	31	M	Farmer	TN
Sarah	35	F		TX
Joseph	1	M		TX
Graham, J. T.	44	M	Black Smith	NC
Mary	45	F		NC
Betsey	17	F		NC
E. F.	14	M		NC
H. C.	7	F		TN
J. E.	5	F		TN
Hawkins, Jesse B.	35	M	Mechanic	VA
Margaret	35	F		TN
Alonzo	14	M		TX
Mary	12	M(F)		TX
B.	9	M		TX
A. A.	6	M		TX
Samuel	3	M		TX
Jesse	1	M		TX
Banner, Joseph	50	M	Farmer	--
Martin	24	F(M)		--
T. T.	22	F		--
Eliza	20	M(F)		--
Martin	18	M		--
S. J.	16	F		--
Minerva	14	F		TN
Montgomery, James	35	M		TX
Mary	5	F		TN
Flord, A. W.	33	M	Tavern Keeper	NC
Elizabeth	35	F		NC
Lydia	26	F		NC
Margaret	23	F		NC
Robert	17	M		AL
W. S.	14	M		AL
Lucy	3	F		TN
Covington, Charles	40	M	Grocer	TN
E.	40	F		VA
James	13	M		TX
William	11	M		TX
S. A.	7	F		TX
Robertson, J. B.	35	M	M.D.	KY
M. E.	33	F		KY
F. H.	11	M		TX
Julia	7	F		TX
Barton, J. E.	19	M		TN
Hill, C.	19	M		TN
Devreaux, Benjamin	17	M		AL
White, Susan	14	F		AL
Brown, Martha	7	F		TX
Reese, James	73	M		NC
Robinson, F. W.	35	M	Merchant	TN
Susan	25	F		KY

(continued)

Name	Age	Sex	Occupation	Birthplace
Robinson, E.	10	F		LA
Boynton, Winston	28	M	Farmer	GA
M. A.	25	F		GA
J. E.	5	M		GA
Woodban, Eliza	65	F		TN
Crosby, J. F.	22	M	Attorney	SC
A. ?.	18	F		KY
Fral, Eliza	15	F		TN
Good, G.	45	M	Farmer	NC
Juliana	47	F		TN
W. S.	22	M		TN
J. B.	19	M		TN
E. L.	11	M		TN
Isabella	8	F		TN
Hamilton, John	44	M		SCO
H.	37	F		TN
William	12	M		AL
Maria	10	F		TX
Ann	8	F		TX
John	3	M		TX
Hursby, Johnson	43	M	Well Digger	TN
Sarah	43	F		TN
William	17	M		TX
S.	13	F		TX
A.	11	F		TX
E.	7	F		TX
French, ?. J.	31	M	Merchant	GA
A. A.	21	F		MD
M. F.	6	F		TX
Alice	2/12	F		TX
J. P.	22	M	Clerk	GA
Wilson, G. H.	17	M	Clerk	MD
Scott, Henry	39	M	Mechanic	TN
Wynne, J. W.	25	M	Lawyer	TN
Cheek, Noah	32	M	Merchant	SC
Evaline	24	F		TN
Levy, L.	56	F		MA
James	56	M	Farmer	MA
Robert	22	M	Farmer	TN
A. L.	19	M	Farmer	TN
Rebecca	18	F		TN
Tennessee	16	F		TN
Sarah	14	F		TN
Kell, William	33	M	Farmer	TN
H. E.	33	F		TN
D. E.	10	M		TN
Dorothy	9	F		TN
H. J.	7	F		TN
W. C.	4	F		TN
G. ?.	3	M		MS
M. J.	3/12	M		TX
Middleton, Jno.	48	M	Farmer	NC
Aldridge, A. A.	9	F		TN
Catharine	7	F		TN
Bussey, John	27	M	Mechanic	TN
J. E.	29	F		TN
James H.	6	M		AR
Mary F.	3	F		TX
Harper, R. H.	52	M	Farmer	NC
E. J.	19	F		NC
S. A.	18	F		NC
Julia	24	F		NC
Leonidas	20	M		NC
R. J.	18	M		NC
R. G.	9	M		TN
Mary E.	7	F		TN
Wells, Lewis	33	M	Merchant	TN
George, Mary E.	41	F	Farmer	TN
Louisa	13	F		AL

(continued)

Name	Age	Sex	Occupation	Birthplace
George, Joel	10	M		AL
Pleasant, M. J.	38	M	Clerk	GA
M. F.	22	F		TN
Roberts, Luke	33	M	Farmer	TN
Eleanor	37	F		LA
Gay, G. E.	16	M		TX
William	14	M		TX
Milam	12	M		TX
Mary	10	F		TX
J. F.	5	M		TX
Austin, W. T.	37	M	Merchant	CT
E.	31	F		TN
Emma	8	F		TX
S.	6	F		TX
Mary	4	F		TX
W. T.	5/12	M		TX
Aldridge, L. B.	37	M	Farmer	TN
L. B., Jr.	4	M		TN
Thomas	1	M		TN
Susan	32	F		TN
Elizabeth	79	F		TN
Middleton, Sarah	45	F		TN
T. J.	27	M		MS
Nancy	19	F		AL
Adena	17	F		AL
J. B.	13	M		--
S. A.	11	M		--
Frances A.	5	F		--
Jackson, Nancy	25	F		--
Jane	19	F		TX
Carothers, T. J.	26	M	Farmer	TN
Margaret	24	F		TN
William	2	M		AL
Glass, A. H.	25	M	Clerk	AL
Upshaw, M. A.	46	M	Farmer	VA
A. H.	40	F		TN
R. J.	17	M		TN
A. Y.	14	M		TN
S. C.	10	M		AR
J.	6	F		IA
H.	4	M		IA
A. L.	1 2/12	M		IA
Chappell, G. T.	33	M	Farmer	TN
Kell, William	40	M	Farmer	TN
Peggy	40	F		TN
Andrew	10	M		TN
Henry	8	M		TN
Mary	6	F		TN
Elizabeth	4	F		TN
Harriette	2	F		TN
Gutham, William	40	M	Farmer	SC
Frank	10	M		TN
M. E.	35	F		TN
Ann	12	F		TN
William	8	M		TN
John M.	6	M		TX
Martha	4	F		TX
Nancy	2	F		TX
Vinson, W. H.	25	M	Lawyer	TN
Mary	19	F		AL
Nancy	1	F		TX
Surley, J. G.	29	M	Lawyer	TN
Ashman, C.	30	M	Farmer	TN
Cooke, N. B.	25	M	Farmer	TN
Glenn, Thomas J.	37	M	Farmer	SC
Margaret	30	F		SC
Leth	10	M		SC
Gray	8	M		SC
James	6	M		SC
Taylor, A. G.	43	M	Farmer	TN
Martha	38	F		TN
William	18	M		AL
J. W.	15	M		AL

(continued)

WASHINGTON COUNTY, TEXAS

Name	Age	Sex	Occupation	Birthplace
Taylor, A. C.	13	M		AL
J. B.	8	M		AL
G. B.	4	M		MS
J. M.	6/12	M		TX
Chappell, William	40	M	Farmer	TN
H. C.	32	F		TN
R. H.	16	M		AL
M. J.	10	F		AL
C. C.	7	M		TX
E. P.	5	F		TX
H. B.	3	F		TX
M. C.	1	F		TX
Chappell, Robert	38	M	Farmer	TN
S. J.	2	F		TX
Thomas, B. R.	43	M	Farmer	NC
Mary A.	40	F		VA
Jno. W.	18	M	Farmer	TN
W. T.	6/12	M		TX
Elgin, S. B.	16	F		TN
Mary	14	F		TN
Martha	13	F		TN
Thomas	9	M		TN
Frances	11	F		TN
Robert	8	M		TN
Harborough, Mary	35	F		MO
Silvery	30	F		TN
Jackson, Joseph	35	M		TN
Precilla	30	F		TN
James	8	M		TX
William	6	M		TX
A. G. J.	4	M		TX
Nancy	2	F		TX
Allen, M. C.	50	M	Farmer	TN
Melissa	45	F		TN
John	21	M	Farmer	TN
Margaret	19	F		TN
Harriette	17	F		TN
S. A.	15	F		TN
William	12	M		TN
Robert	10	M		TN
Richard	8	M		TN
McMillen, A.	34	M	Farmer	TN
Nancy	27	F		TN
Jno. C.	8	M		TN
M. E.	6	F		TN
W. I.	4	F		TN
Georgianna	2	F		TX
Eslinger, James	30	M	Merchant	TN
McGahae, J. S.	34	M	Merchant	TN
Martha	12	F		TN
Ellen	30	F		TN
Nancy	10	F		TN
Mariah	8	F		TX
Rachel	4	F		TX
Emily	2	F		TX
Ballen, J. A.	35	M	Shepherd	AR
Wimberly, Pleasant	30	M	Farmer	NC
Julian	22	F		TN
Dallas, M. L.	28	M	Farmer	TN
Milton	19	M		TX
Precilla	16	F		TX
Mary	24	F		--
Rhody	58	F		MA
Clayton, J. A.	33	M	Farmer	TN
Indiana	20	F		TN
Mary Jane	3	F		TN
Pitts, John C.	35	M	Farmer	TN
Mary	28	F		AR
Levi	9	M		TX
Joseph	7	M		TX
Mariah	5	F		TX
Sarah	3	F		TX
Estes, D. M.	34	M	Inn Keeper	TN
Frances	30	F		TN
J. C.	15	F		TN
Robert	12	M		TN
Arabella	10	F		TX
Thomas	8	M		TX
Henry	4	M		TX
Williams, A. G.	35	M	Mechanic	MS
Davis, A.	31	M	Teamster	OH
Armstrong, M. F.	31	M	Farmer	TN
Woodlief, Thomas C.	40	M	Farmer	MA
Lebetha	34	F		TN
E. C.	12	M		TX
E. R.	12	M		TX
D. S.	10	M		TX
Ellen	8	F		TX
Jennett	6	F		TX
Hale, H. P.	33	M	Farmer	TN
A. G.	14	M		AL
Lucinda	28	F		GA
Margaret	12	F		AL
James	10	M		AL
L. C.	8	F		AL
G. P.	6	M		AL
Amos	4	M		AL
J. R.	2	M		TX
Harris, T. J.	18	M	Farmer	TN
Nat.	16	M		TN
Buntlinger, William	32	M	Seaman	TN
Bouldin, E. G.	26	M		TN
Bolden, Mary E.	30	F		TN
McCrackin, J. L.	45	M		KY
A. F.	40	F		KY
Mary	14	F		KY
John	16	M		KY
Vabella	6	F		KY
James L.	10/12	M		KY
Alexander, James	30	M	Merchant	TN
Wilhaim, James	29	M	Farmer	TN
Precilla	22	F		TN
Allen	6	M		TX
Flintgin, Henry	8	M		GER
Maria	6	F		GER
Patoine(?)	4	F		GER
William	1	M		TX
Harrison, Henry	23	M	Farmer	TN
W. A.	9	M		TN
Lucy	43	F		TN
Harris, R.	50	M	Farmer	TN
Henrietta	45	F		TN
F. J.	23	M	Farmer	TN
William	20	M	Farmer	TN
Williams, William	4	M		TX
Jno.	2	M		TX
Ray, L. P.	24	M	Clerk	TN
Glass, W.	22	M	Farmer	MS
Canley, Isaac	48	M	Farmer	TN
S. A.	35	F		AL
J. C.	10	M		TX
Margaret	15	F		TX
Marthy L.	12	F		TX
Willingham, A.	60	M	Farmer	MO
Kate	50	F		TN
W. C.	20	M	Farmer	AR
Marion	32	M	Farmer	AR
W. S.	16	M	Farmer	GA
Mary	28	F		MO
Willie, James	27	M	Lawyer	GA
S. L.	15	F		TN
Ware, Jno. R.	38	M	Physician	TN
Elizabeth	28	F		GA

(continued)

Name	Age/Sex/Occupation	Birthplace
Ware, M. L.	14 F	AL
C. C.	12 F	AL
Ellen	9 F	AL
Frances	5 F	TX
D.	2 M	TX
Lile, B.	53 M Farmer	NC
E.	40 F	NC
M. L.	6 M	TN
C. C.	4 F	TN
W. E.	3 F	TX
Oneal, James	16 M Farmer	AR
Mary	14 F	AR
Julia	12 F	AR
Brown, James	30 M Farmer	TN
Mary	24 F	TN
George	2 M	TX
Crutcherfield, Jno.	26 M Mechanic	AL
Glass, J. H.	26 M Farmer	MS
Cooper, James	60 M Farmer	TN
Martha	58 F	TN
J. D.	33 M	TN
Martha	18 F	TN
Love, Robert	33 M	TN
S. A.	25 F	TN
Allen	10 M	TX
James	8 M	TX
William	6 M	TX
Cooper, Thomas	35 M Farmer	TN
Mary	28 F	TN
James	6 M	TX
John	4 M	TX
Margaret	8 F	TX
Caroline	2 F	TX
Gee, Alfred	50 M Farmer	VA
Sarah	45 F	VA
William	20 M Merchant	TN
M. C.	18 M	TN
James	16 M	TN
Elizabeth	15 F	TN
Nancy	70 F	VA
Rachell	8 F	TX
Hardman, J. M.	40 M Farmer	TN
Jane	37 F	TN
Ann	18 F	TN
Block	16 M	TN
Thomas	15 M	TN
H. V.	14 M	TN
William	12 M	TN
J. B.	11 M	TN
Mary	10 F	TN
Margaret	9 F	TN
Elizabeth	7 F	TX
Seth	4 M	TX
Dealk, William	34 M Mechanic	TN
Julia	34 F	TN
George	14 M	TN
Martha	12 F	TN
John	10 M	TX
Mary Ann	8 F	TX
Dean, J.	38 M Mechanic	TN
Margaret	30 F	TN
Robert	15 M	TN
William	13 M	TN
Eliza	10 M	TN
H.	8 M	TN
Mary	6 F	TX
Yermenn, Mary	20 F	SC
Hill, M. M.	25 M Mechanic	MS
Bright	23 M Mechanic	MS
R. J.	21 M Farmer	MS
William	18 M Farmer	MS
John	16 M Farmer	MS
Cade, James	23 M Farmer	TN

Name	Age/Sex/Occupation	Birthplace
Hope, Richard	35 M Farmer	TN
Harriette	20 F	MO
Hope, A.	40 M Mechanic	TN
Elizabeth	25 F	MS
Rucker, B. F.	35 F(M) Druggist	TN
Adeline	35 F	AL
Martha	13 F	TX
Mary A.	11 F	AL
Margaret	9 F	AL
Ellen	7 F	AL
Melinda	5 F	TX
Robert	1 M	TX
Brown, William	29 M Farmer	TN
Nancy	22 F	TN
Alexander	5 M	TX
N. A.	3 M	TX
R. P.	1 M	TX
Grisham, E. H.	45 M Mechanic	TN
Frances	40 F	TN
George	15 M	TN
Esom	13 M	TN
M. E.	11 F	TN
J. C.	8 F	TX
L. C.	6 F	TX
Elizabeth	3 F	TX
Deaver, William	50 M Farmer	TN
Caroline	40 F	TN
Lind	16 F	TX
M. Ann	14 F	TX
Nancy	12 F	TX
Jane	12 F	TX
J. E.	9 M	TX
Thomas	7 M	TX
R. E. B.	5 M	TX
William	3 M	TX
Jas.	1 M	TX
Smith, Nancy	51 F	TN
Jane	18 F	TN
Mary	13 F	TN
Charles	16 M Clerk	TN
Wiley	10 M	TX
Franklin, J. R.	40 M Farmer	TN
Brown, George	29 M Farmer	TN
Adeline	24 F	TN
Alexander	4 M	TN
Erving	2 M	TN
Robertson, H. V.	48 M Farmer	TN
Fanny	40 F	TN
William	19 M	TN
Felix	19 M	TN
J. B.	15 M	TX
S. C.	13 M	TX
Randal	3 M	TX
Ann	11 F	TX
M. E.	9 F	TX
Caroline	7 F	TX
Harriette	3 F	TX
Robertson, W. A. T.	32 M Farmer	TN
S. V.	10 M	TN
Jenett	27 F	TN
Lucinda	8 F	TN
Mary A.	6 F	TN
W. A.	2 M	TX
Brown, Jno. M.	38 M Farmer	MS
Harriette E.	28 F	NC
Lensobey, William	30 M Farmer	TN
Scurry, W.	35 M Lawyer	TN
Jenett	19 F	AL
E. J.	3 F	TX
Walton, Thomas	35 M Farmer	TN
Peggy	30 F	TN
Henry	12 M	TN

(continued)

WASHINGTON COUNTY, TEXAS

Name	Age	Sex	Occupation	Birthplace
Walton, Hester	10	F		TN
Frances	8	F		TN
Ann	6	F		TN
Gate, Amos	49	M	Farmer	TN
Nancy	45	F		TN
Amy	16	F		TX
Jenny	14	F		TX
Mary	12	F		TX
Ellen	10	F		TX
Catharine	4	F		TX
Samuel	17	M	Farmer	TX
Harborough, Mary	73	F		MO
Harborough, G. W.	35	M	Farmer	MO
Silvey	30	F		TN
Jackson, Joseph	35	M	Farmer	TN
Priscilla	30	F		TN
William	8	M		TX
James	6	M		TX
A. G.	4	M		TX
Nancy	2	F		TX
Kell, William	40	M	Farmer	TN
Peggy	40	F		TN
Anderson	10	M		TN
Henry	8	M		TN
Mary	6	F		TN
Elizabeth	4	F		TN
Harriette	2	F		TX
Cooke, F. J.	35	M	Merchant	NC
E.	19	F		TN
Hugh	3	M		TX
E., Jr.	9/12	F		TX
McFadden, N. A.	46	M	Farmer	TN
Eliza	38	F		TN
E. M.	18	F		TX
J. B.	12	M		TX
C. J.	10	M		TX
S. H.	7	F		TX
N. A.	5	M		TX
H. C.	2	M		TX
White, C. M.	48	M	Farmer	TN
N. M.	46	F		VA
T. M.	21	M	Farmer	TN
R. M.	22	M		TN
J. H.	20	M		TN
W. A.	15	M		TN
B. S.	12	M		TN
J. H.	9	M		TX
Cochrel, J. H.	4	M		TX
White, Emeline	28	F		TN
Keser, William	40	M	Farmer	TN
M. C.	39	F		TN
G. M.	19	M		AL
R. M.	17	M		AL
William, Jr.	16	M		AL
W. J.	15	F		AL
Thomas	13	M		TX
G.	12	M		TX
William	7	M		TX
Emiline	5	F		TX
J. C.	3	M		TX
E.	2	M		TX
Hannoy, J. A.	37	M	Farmer	TN
P. A.	25	F		AL
M. A.	5	F		TX
B. R.	3	M		TX
Rucker, L. P.	35	M	Clergyman	TN
H. M.	30	F		TN
W. P.	12	M		TN
E. S.	9	M		TX
Jas. E.	6	M		TX
Mary E.	1 6/12	F		TX

Name	Age	Sex	Occupation	Birthplace
Pearson, C. C.	30	M	Farmer	TN
M. A. E.	20	F		AL
L. M.	1	F		TX
Blackmore, J. A.	50	M	Farmer	TN
D. L.	43	F		VA
A. J.	20	M	Farmer	TN
Basey, Martha	3	F		TN
Washington	1	M		TX
Daniel, J. B.	30	M	Gentleman	SC
E.	21	F		TN
M. L.	4	F		TX
M. M.	2	F		TX
Lynch, G. P.	26	M	Clerk	KY
Carnes, R. W.	30	M	Farmer	TN
W. M.	6	M		TN
M. C.	4	F		TN
R. S.	9/12	M		TN
Houston, R.	40	M	Farmer	SC
Catharine	31	F		GA
P.	14	F		AL
Mary	13	F		AL
Martha	11	F		AL
Harriette	9	F		AL
Allen	7	M		TX
John	5	M		TX
Amos	4	M		TX
James	3	M		TX
Glenn, Eugenia	5	F		TN
Charles	3	M		TN
Austry, R.	32	M	Farmer	TN
H. R.	33	F		TN
Mary	2	F		TX
P. B.	12	M		TN
Watson, Jno.	10	M		TN
Sam	8	M		TX
Tennessee	5	F		TX
Maxey, John	35	M	Farmer	MO
Jane	30	F		MO
Wood, A. H.	35	M	Farmer	TN
M. E.	22	F		NC
Y. F.	2	F		TX
Ann	60	F		NC
Jones, J. M.	22	M	Farmer	GA
Byer, Isaac	34	M	Farmer	TN
Ann	33	F		TN
James H.	13	M		MS
E. V.	18	F		MS
Sarah	15	F		MS
Basey, Mary	12	F		MS
J. L.	9	M		MS
Harrison	6	M		MS
Cooper, E.	30	F		TN
S. A.	14	F		TN
N. S.	7	F		TN
James	3	M		TX
Ren--(?), Edwin	38	M	Farmer	KY
Autry, Lewis	27	M	Farmer	TN
Mary	22	F		AL
Farril, Thomas P.	26		Mechanic	TN
Rutledge, M.	35	M	Mechanic	TN
Susan	23	F		AL
William	8	M		TX
S. H.	4	M		TX
E. J.	1	F		TX
O.	13	M		GER
Sanderson, G. E.	50	M	Farmer	VA
M.	49	F		TN
Robert	23	M		TN
Lucas	19	M		TN
Jane	20	F		TN
Martha	17	F		TN
Glenn, Thomas	39	M	Inn Keeper	VA
J.	30	F		VA
L. M.	15	F		TN

(continued)

WASHINGTON COUNTY, TEXAS

Name	Age	Sex	Occupation	Birthplace
Glenn, N. A.	13	M		TN
J. T.	11	M		TN
E. E.	9	F		TN
Thomas, Houston	3/12	M		TX
Jackson, E. D.	44	M	Farmer	CAN
Anna	38	F		TN
Martha	15	F		TX
L.	13	F		TX
Hugh	10	M		TX
Nancy	8	F		TX
James	6	M		TX
Elisha	4	M		TX
Amanda	2	F		TX
Amos	1 8/12	M		TX
Heard, T. J.	38	M	M.D.	GA
Frances	25	F		TN
Harman, F.	45	M	Gardner	PRU
Baley, Henry	40	M	Mechanic	RI
M.	38	F		MA
C. F.	16	M		RI
A. E.	14	M		MA
F. A.	10	M		RI
Carrett, Jno.	23	M	Mechanic	IL
Sam	20	M	Mechanic	IL
Powlston, Jno.	20	M	Mechanic	IL
James	14	M		GER
Clarke, Jesse	20	M	Farmer	AR
Doran, Jno.	39	M	Clark	IRE
Minerva	23	F		TN
Walters, Jas.	22	M	Baker	IRE
Quinn, M. C.	11	M		TX
Roberts, S. R.	57	M	Farmer	TN
Elizabeth	53	F		TN
Dade, J. A.	31	M	Farmer	AL
Margaret	21	F		TN
Huston, J. M.	6	M		MS
Cobler, E. S.	40	M	Farmer	TN
Rebecca	40	F		TN
Martha	16	F		TN
E. J.	13	F		TX
E. J.	2	F		TX
White, Anderson	31	M	Grocer	TN
Quinn, E.	33	M	Mechanic	KY
Cappel, J. B.	33	M	Mechanic	GA
Roberts, B.	49	M	Butcher	MA
Elizabeth	23	F		TX
Collins, S. G.	28	M	Farmer	NY
Blakeman, D. E.	15	M		TN
John	10	M		TN
F. C.	5	F		TN
Willford, W. J.	24	M	Mechanic	MS
Gorman, P.	47	M		IRE
Evans, Moses	38	M	Land Agent	KY
Calvert, H. H.	45	M	Farmer	SC
Louisa	39	F		TN
Jesse A.	22	M		SC
Jane	12	F		SC
L. C.	5	F		TX
A. C.	3	F		AL
John W.	2	M		TX
D. S.	19	M		TX
Hale, Jno.	44	M	Farmer	KY
Lucinda	27	F		TN
Thomas J.	8	M		TX
C. V.	5	F		TX
M. A.	1	F		TX
Harborough, G. H.	30	M	Farmer	AR
B. A.	25	F		TN
Cocke, J. H.	50	M	Farmer	VA
E. J.	40	F		MO
M. D.	15	F		AL

(continued)

Name	Age	Sex	Occupation	Birthplace
Bates, M. E.	22	F		VA
McGregor, E.	38	F		VA
J. H.	21	M	Clerk	TN
S. M.	15	F		MS
M. B.	12	M		TN
E. S.	10	F		MS
J. M.	6	M		TX
D. A.	3	M		TX
White, Harden	34	M	Farmer	TN
Louisiana	20	F		MS
Ewing, J. T.	28	M	Merchant	GA
Bullard, A.	50	M	Baker	FRA
Nelly	28	F		LA
Frances	10	F		LA
Edward	5	M		TX
McNight, J. A.	43	M	Merchant	VA
A. E. T.	11	F		MS
Prestell, Charles	25	M	Merchant	GER
Kenly, S.	16	M	Merchant	TN
Taylor, William	28	M	Merchant	TN
Winder, J. A.	29	M	Mechanic	VA
Indiania	26	F		TN
Moore, M. A.	7	F		TX
Virginia	5	F		TX
Flenry, A. B.	37	M	Merchant	NJ
M. L.	33	F		TN
James	10	M		TX
Robert	7	M		TX
Cooper, S. M.	38	M	Farmer	TN
H. A.	21	F		TN
Cooper, Thomas M.	34	M	Farmer	TN
Lile, S. D.	4/12	F		TX
Stockton, M. B.	25	M	Farmer	TN
Dallas, J. S.	32	M	Farmer	TN
Nancy V.	33	F		TN
James W.	7	M		TX
Jenett	5	F		TX
W. P.	1	M		TX
Terry, J. S.	43	M	Mechanic	VA
Hester	33	F		AL
William	12	M		AL
Nathaniel	10	M		AL
Nancy	8	F		TN
M. E.	6	F		TN
Mary	2	F		TN
Shepherd, J. P.	50	M	Farmer	TN
M.	45	F		TN
Joshua	23	M		TN
S. A.	15	F		TN
Mary A.	13	F		TN
James	9	M		--
N.	7	M		--
Thomas	5	M		--
Marsh, S.	50	M	Farmer	KY
Caroline	45	F		TN
Harriette	14	F		TX
Jane	12	F		TX
Elizabeth	10	F		TX
Thomas	16	M		TX
Joseph	8	M		TX
J. P.	6	M		TX
Samuel	4	M		TX

WHARTON COUNTY, TEXAS

Name	Age	Sex	Occupation	Birthplace
Guinan, George	30	M	Lawyer	IRE
Mary A.	27	F		TN
Jackson, Alen	10	M		TX
Blythe, Eliz.	2	F		TX
Kincheloe, D. R.	32	M	Tavern Keeper	MS
Martha	20	F		MS
William	4	M		TX
George	6	M		TX

(continued)

WHARTON COUNTY, TEXAS

Name	Age	Sex	Occupation	Birthplace
Kincheloe, Lawrence	24	M	Stockraiser	TX
Beaumont, C. W.	53	M	Dr. of Medicine	ENG
Birdsong, William	23	M	Clerk	VA
Watson, Lewis	43	M	Farmer	SC
Thurmond, G. W.	26	M	Merchant	SC
Johnson, Thomas T.	26	M	Stockraiser	TN
Higley, H. H.	40	M	Carpenter	CT
Wright, Ralph	45	M	Farmer	TN
Mary A.	17	F		AR
Graves, J. B.	25	M	Farmer	LA
Cayce, John	24	M	Farmer	TN
Cayce, Shad.	32	M	Farmer	TN
Mary E.	17	F		GA
Toliver, B.	42	M	Dr. of Medicine	TN
A. B.	10	M		AL
J. O.	8	M		TN
Cage, B.	35	M	Farmer	TN
Baker, J. A.	11	F		TX
D. D.	8	M		TX
E.	6	F		TX
S. J.	4	F		TX
T. J.	1	M		TX
Cayce, H. P.	31	M	Farmer	TN
M. F.	23	F		VA
G. W.	7	M		TX
H. P., Jr.	4	M		TX
C. B.	1	F		TX
Slade, H.	12	F		VA
Newman, William R.	40	M	Farmer	IL
M. A.	26	F		TN
J. A.	9	M		TX
A. F.	5	M		TX
R. A.	2	F		TX
Gilbert, M.	19	M		TX
W.	14	M		TX
Osburn, Jas.	50	M	Farmer	NC
P. G.	49	F		TN
J. M.	20	M	Farmer	MS
E. G.	11	F		MS
Green, William	14	M		MS
Mercer, Levi	33	M	Farmer	MS
S.	23	F		TN
M.	10	F		TX
A.	8	F		TX
L.	4	M		TX
W.	2	M		TX
J.	1/12	M		TX
Mercer, E. G.	32	M	Farmer	MS
G. A.	28	F		AL
C.	7	M		TX
J.	5	F		TX
H.	3	M		TX
P.	2	M		TN
Reed, Thomas J.	42	M	Farmer	TN
M. J.	38	F		TN
M.	13	F		TX
T. J.	12	M		TX
William H.	10	M		TX
J. P.	8	M		TX
E. J.	5	F		TX
T. A.	3	F		TX
M. F.	2	F		TX
S. A.	4/12	M		TX
Stewart, V. A.	41	M	Farmer	GA
L.	36	F		MS
Flowers, C.	11	M		MS
J. S.	7	F		TX
Hatcher, Thomas	3	M		TX
Hunt, T. G.	26	M	Doctor	TN
Howard, H.	25	M	Farmer	GA
Davis, S. S.	30	M	Farmer	GER
Henry	45	M	Farmer	TN
Barnes, Eli	53	M	Farmer	TN
William	32	M	Farmer	MS
Jos.	26	M	Farmer	AL
Myers, Jas. O.	23	M	Farmer	MS
D. V.	21	M	Farmer	MS
Core, W. B.	24	M	Overseer	TN
Moore, Alex	57	M	Farmer	TN
Polk, E. S.	21	F		MS
Moore, Lucy	18	F		MS
Brown, H.	27	M	Overseer	NC
Gallagher, Ed.	50	M	Farmer	IRE
N. C.	38	F		TN
S.	13	M		TX
Jas.	9	M		TX
Mentor	6	M		TX
Joe	4	M		TX
F. C.	2	F		TX
Hamilton, E.	22	F		TN
Copeland, J.	47	M	Stockraiser	TN
N.	46	F		TN
M.	7	M	Stockraiser	AR
G.	15	M		AR
R. P.	13	M		TX
S.	11	M		TX
J.	7	M		TX
Heard, W. J. E.	49	M	Farmer	TN
A.	42	F		TN
I. M.	17	M	Farmer	TX
G. S.	12	M		TX
Sutherland, Dav. K.	27	M	Farmer	TN
E.	18	F		--
D.	1	F		TX
Heard, Jen.	70	F		TN
Jones, Sarah	34	F		TN
B(?).	6	F		TX
G.	4	M		TX
McLaughlin, L.	17	M	Farmer	TX
Newell, John D.	45	M	Farmer	NC
T. V.	35	F		TN
A. W.	13	F		TX
V. A.	11	F		TX
E. S.	9	F		TX
J. E.	7	M		TX
H. B.	5	F		TX
Anderson, J. S.	32	M	Farmer	VA
E. M.	30	F		TN
Sweeney, T. M.	13	M		LA
E. V.	10	F		TX
Anderson, J. E.	3	M		TX
T.	1	F		TX
Monroe, Jas.	38	M	Laborer	IRE
Hancock, Jas.	37	M	Farmer	NC
Deaderick, Jo H.	31	M	Merchant	TN
T. S.	23	M	Merchant	TN
Eagan, G.	40	M	County Clerk	TN
Horton, A. C.	52	M	Farmer	GA
E.	47	F		NC
P. L. T.	13	F		AL
B. W.	5	M		TX
Hawks, T. H.	27	M	Doctor	NC
Lawson, W. K.	30	M	Overseer	AL
Ryon, H. E.	42	M	Carpenter	SC
Jamison, C. H.	42	M	Bricklayer	KY
Harvey, J. H.	24	M	Bricklayer	AL
Craig, J. H.	28	M	Carpenter	TN
Henning, H.	19	M	Shoemaker	GER
Dance, J. T.	23	M	Bricklayer	AL
Gatch, (Blank)	32	M	Tailor	GER
Connor, Jas.	33	M	Painter	IRE

WHARTON COUNTY, TEXAS

Brandon, Alex W. 26 M Farmer TN

WILLIAMSON COUNTY, TEXAS

Ricketts, Reuben W. 39 M Farmer TN
Sarah 33 F IN
William A. 10 M IN
Christopher C. 8 M IN
Reuben C. 7 M IN
John L. 5 M IN
Hannah 3 F IN
Joseph S. 1 M IN

Barton, John 32 M Farmer IN
Melissa A. 22 F TN
Jerome B. 2 M TX
Elizabeth A. 6/12 F TX

Kelly, Isaac 30 M Farmer IN
Nancy J. 18 F IN
Barton, Nancy 63 F TN

Allison, Elihu 42 M Farmer AL
Margaret M. 41 F SC
James F. 20 M Farmer TN
Mary S. 17 F AR
Sarah J. 15 F TX
Elizabeth A. 12 F TX
Margaret M. 10 F TX
Elihu P. 5 M TX
Samuel M. 4 M TX
Russel J. C. 1 M TX

Allison, James 40 M Farmer TN
Delila 38 F TN
David 19 M Farmer TN
Elihu C. 19 M Farmer TN
John 17 M Farmer AR
Sarah J. 13 F TX
Elizabeth 11 F TX
Thomas J. 9 M TX
James 7 M TX
William F. 4 M TX
Jemima 10/12 F TX

Dyches, William 51 M Farmer SC
Jane 48 F SC
Elias P. 20 M LA
Jerusha J. 15 F TX
Lucinderilla 10 F TX
Mary E. 5 F TX
Bingham, James 21 M Farmer MO
Lavica 18 F LA
Lewis, Harman 40 M Cooper TN

Dawson, Samuel 66 M Farmer SC
Anna 63 F TN

Dawson, Samuel R. 25 M Farmer TN
Margaret 20 F TN
Mary A. 4 F AR
Elizabeth P. 7/12 F TX

Burris, James M. 34 M Farmer MO
Nancy C. 25 F TN
Richard J. 11 M TX
William M. 7 M TX
James H. 5 M TX
Sarah J. 2 F TX
Ellenor L. 2/12 F TX
Lackey, William 25 M Farmer IL

Cook, Charles C. 45 M Farmer SC
Mary 44 F NC
Royal A. 22 M Farmer NC
Malachiah M. 17 M Farmer TN
Thomas J. 15 M MO
Susan M. 12 F MO
Sarah A. E. 9 F MO
John W. 4 M TX

Chapman, James 33 M Farmer TN
(continued)

Chapman, Celinda 29 F TN
Eda J. 13 F AR
Isaac S. 11 M AR
Gilford R. 9 M AR
Benjamin L. 6 M AR
William H. 4 M AR
Elizabeth 1 F TX

Dennis, Osro 23 M Farmer AR
Rebecca T. 22 F TN

Cowen, David C. 44 M Farmer VA
Elizabeth 39 F VA
Ruth 18 F TN
Luther H. 16 M Farmer TN
Margaret H. 12 F TN
Thomas J. 10 M TN
Gideon P. 4 M TX
Gideon P. 28 M Farmer TN
Ruth 65 F MD
Berns, John 17 M Laborer GER
Throp, Margaret R. 8 F TN
Ella E. 3 F TN

Allen, Huelson 57 M School Teacher GA
Deborah 54 F GA
Joseph 25 M Farmer TN
Mary A. 18 F TN

Allen, Thomas P. 26 M Farmer TN
Eliza 21 F AL
John L. 2 M TX

Russell, David W. 24 M Farmer TN
Mahaley 19 F IL
Milam B. 1 M AR

House, Daniel Bolting 21 M Farmer IL
Mary J. 22 F TN
Andrew J. 1 M AR

Russell, John H. 47 M Bapt. Clergyman NC
Sarah S. 42 F TN
Cornelius A. 19 M Farmer AR
John H. 12 M TX
Genette 3 F AR

Anderson, Uriah H. 38 M Farmer TN
Elizabeth E. 26 F AL
George 5 M TN
Thomas 2 M TX

Smith, Taylor 40 M Farmer GA
Sarah 35 F NC
Taylor 15 M TN
Elizabeth 13 F TX
Rebecca 11 F TX

Gregg, Abner 53 M Farmer TN
Rebecca J. 17 F MO
William R. 16 M Farmer MO
Martha A. 11 F MO
John 9 M MO

Smelser, Harmon 52 M Farmer TN
Elizabeth 44 F OH
Abram J. 17 M Farmer MO
Eliza A. 13 F MO
Rebecca A. 10 F MO
Melissa E. 6 F MO
John B. 4 M MO

Love, David 28 M Farmer SC
Mary J. 20 F TN
William 3 M TX
Texanna 10/12 F TX

Chandler, Mary C. 65 F SC
William 40 M Farmer KY
Caroline 22 F TN
Almedia 18 F TN

Joplin, James 26 M Farmer TN
Julia A. 24 F TN
Josiah 1 M AR

WILLIAMSON COUNTY, TEXAS

Name	Age	Sex	Occupation	Birthplace
Watts, John W.	29	M	Farmer	IN
Nancy J.	26	F		TN
Parmelia M.	1	F		AR
Davis, Josiah B.	46	M	Farmer	SC
Priscilla	26	F		MO
Amzi A.	15	M		TN
William M.	12	M		TN
Robert B.	9	M		MO
Mary J.	7	F		MO
JOhn R.	4	M		MO
Glasscock, George W.	40	M	Farmer	KY
Cynthia C.	35	F		TN
Elizabeth	8	F		TX
Margaret	6	F		TX
George W.	4	M		TX
Albert H.	2	M		TX
Baker, Daniel M.	29	M	Black Smith	TN
Glasscock, Joseph	15	M		IL
Tucker, Eleazer	57	M	Carpenter	CT
Utz, Andrew	30	M	Carpenter	PA
Sherman, JOhn	26	M	Farmer	NY
Morris, Guy	21	M	Farmer	IL
McNeil, John	34	M	Millwright	NC
Elizabeth	20	F		TN
Louisa J.	4	F		TN
Alvin C.	2	M		TX
Berry, John B.	36	M	Farmer	IN
Martha E.	20	F		TN
Robbins, Aaron	46	M	Farmer	TN
Elizabeth	46	F		KY
Richard	14	M		AR
Robbins, George M.	58	M	Farmer	KY
Orry	55	F		TN
Henry	32	M	Farmer	AR
Joseph	28	M	Farmer	AR
Jane	22	F		AR
George S.	20	M	Farmer	AR
Samuel	17	M	Farmer	AR
Aury	15	F		AR
Catharine	13	F		AR
Sally	8	F		TX
Skin, Fleman	22	M	Farmer	AR
Branch, James	33	M	Farmer	TN
Nancy	32	F		MS
John W.	7	M		TX
Elizabeth J.	6	F		TX
Eliza J.	5	F		TX
Virginia A.	1	F		TX
Nicholas	37	M	Farmer	TN
Gorman, James S.	37	M	Physician	TN
Margaret	28	F		GA
Joel H.	16	M	Farmer	MS
Emily E.	10	F		TX
William T.	7	M		TX
Newton S.	5	M		TX
John	3	M		TX
Julia A.	1	F		TX
Scott, John W.	27	M	Farmer	TN
Charlotte	20	F		MO
James F.	1	M		TX
Wilkinson, John	23	M	Farmer	IL
McFaddin, David H.	34	M	Farmer	TN
Jerusha	38	F		LA
John M.	11	M		TX
William D.	9	M		TX
Irvin A.	8	M		TX
Dyches, Lucinda	75	F		SC
Lydia C.	12	F		LA
St. Clair, Duncan	66	M	Farmer	NC
Stephen	15	M		TX
Duncan	13	M		TX
Queen, Reuben	64	M	Farmer	NC

(continued)

Name	Age	Sex	Occupation	Birthplace
Queen, Mary	61	F		NC
Davis, Huldah	23	F		TN
Mary J.	6	F		AR
Laura A.	4	F		AR
Queen, William	57	M	Farmer	NC
Kiser, William	52	M	Farmer	NC
Frances	49	F		TN
John	17	M	Farmer	AR
Rebecca	14	F		AR
Ruth	13	F		AR
Martha J.	11	F		AR
Mary A.	9	F		AR
William B.	7	M		AR
Mankins, Samuel	35	M	Farmer	KY
Dotia	34	F		AL
John	15	M		AR
Nancy J.	13	F		AR
William H.	12	M		AR
Evan	11	M		AR
Sarah A.	9	F		AR
Marze	8	F		AR
Samuel J.	7	M		AR
Jasper	5	M		AR
George	3	M		AR
Celina	2	F		AR
Sherwood, William	23	M	Laborer	TN
Gooch, Benjamin	56	M	County Clerk	NC
Elizabeth R.	49	F		NC
Chism, John E.	28	M	Farmer	TN
Alexander B.	22	M	Farmer	AL
Jesse B.	21	M	Farmer	AL
Aza O.	20	M	Farmer	AL
Angeline A.	16	F		AL
Mathews, Angeline E.	10	F		TX
Vermilla M.	6	F		TX
Nancy A.	4	F		TX
Northington, Marshal W.	36	M	Farmer	NC
Jane M.	26	F		TN
Jesse A.	10	M		TX
Elizabeth A.	7	F		TX
Marshal W.	5	M		TX
John A.	3	M		TX
Rebecca J.	3/12	F		TX
McFarland, Samuel	49	M	Farmer	TN
Jane	46	F		TN
James G.	19	M	Farmer	MO
Lucinda G.	15	F		MO
Samuel K.	12	M		MO
William B.	8	M		MO
Francis M.	4	M		MO
Barton, John	28	M	Farmer	TN
Mary	27	F		MO
Margaret A.	4	F		MO
Robert T.	2	M		MO
Sarah E.	2/12	F		TX
Hill, James	23	M	Farmer	TN
Sarah A.	17	F		MO
Smith, James A.	27	M	Farmer	VA
Clarissa W.	23	F		TN
Robley D.	4	M		TX
Czarina	1	F		TX
Aubery, Henry	17	M	Laborer	MO
Williams, George T.	26	M	Farmer	AL
Jane	23	F		TN
Catherine	3	F		TX
Sarah A.	4/12	F		TX
Harrell, James G.	43	M	Black Smith	TN
Catharine	40	F		TN
Francis M.	13	M		TN
Susan A.	11	F		TN
Henry C.	6	M		TN
Jacob	4	M		TX
Dorsey, Greenberry W.	30	M	(illegible)	AL
Nancy	30	F		TN

(continued)

Name	Age	Sex	Occupation	Birthplace
Dorsey, John H.	12	M		AR
Emily	10	F		AR
Adaline	7	F		TX
William G.	4	M		TX
Mary	1	F		TX
Melchiger	23	M	Farmer	AL
Ake, William	59	M	Farmer	VA
Joseph	27	M	Farmer	TN
Castleton	24	M	Farmer	TN
Panelope	15	F		AR
Ake, John J.	35	M	Hotel Keeper	TN
Jane	28	F		AL
Panelope	10	F		AR
Royal, Jesse	38	M	Farmer	TN
Sarah E.	22	F		TN
Mary E.	4	F		AR
Charles W.	1	M		AR
Jackson, Melissa A.	4/12	F		TX
Laxson, James	35	M	Farmer	TN
Rachel	25	F		TN
Sarah J.	4	F		AR
Zelpha A. R.	1	F		AR
Walden, Hugh	27	M	Farmer	AL
Rachel	19	F		TN
James	8/12	M		AR
Gooch, John	56	M	Gun Smith	NC
Cyrus	21	M	Tanner	MO
Lloyd, James W.	36	M	Meth. Clergyman	TN
Goff, Ambrose	36	M	Farmer	TN
Guest, Joseph	25	M	Farmer	TN
Nancy A.	2	F		TX
Phillis	74	F		NC
Hudon, George B.	25	M	Stone Mason	NY
Bright, Levi	66	M	Black Smith	NJ
Mary	64	F		VA
Samuel T.	22	M	Farmer	IN
McChristian, Noah	28	M	Meth. Clergyman	TX
Ballard, James C.	17	M	Laborer	TN
Tankersley, James	25	M	Farmer	TN
Louisa	22	F		AR
Richard D.	2/12	M		TX
Chandler, Lewis	25	M	Farmer	AR
Mary	17	F		TN
James	3/12	M		TX
Bythe, Anthony W.	28	M	Farmer	TN
Cox, William	28	M	Farmer	AL
Permelia	26	F		AL
Minerva J.	6	F		AL
Adaline	4	F		AL
Gincy	2	F		AL
Harrell, Jacob M.	45	M	Black Smith	TN
Mary	47	F		NC
Emma B.	7	F		TX
Hill, Richmond	12	M		AR
Harrell, John	25	M	Farmer	TN
Elizabeth	21	F		OH
John	6/12	M		TX
Harrell, Anderson J.	27	M	Farmer	TN
Dorthea	22	F		TN
Micajah, Johnston	38	M	Black Smith	TN
Susanna	31	F		OH
Lydia	13	F		IL
Martha A.	12	F		IN
Minerva	7	F		AR
Julia A.	4	F		AR
Amanda	3	F		AR
Garner, Leroy	22	M	Farmer	LA
John	21	M	Farmer	LA

Name	Age	Sex	Occupation	Birthplace
Brown, John H.	33	M	Farmer	TN
Jane A.	29	F		TN
James M.	11	M		AL
Asa R.	9	M		AR
Savina J.	8	F		AR
Amanda C.	5	F		AR
William A.	2	M		AR
Harrell, Joab	36	M	Farmer	TN
Arretta	38	F		NC
William H.	12	M		TN
Elizabeth E.	10	F		TN
Joanna M.	8	F		TN
John W.	5	M		TN
Sarah J.	2/12	F		TX
Bailey, John C.	45	M	Farmer	TN
Mary	18	F		TN
Thomas	16	M	Farmer	TN
David	14	M		TN
Henderson	11	M		TN
Narcissa	9	F		TN
Eliza J.	7	F		TN
Turner	5	M		TN
Hyland, Joseph	37	M	Farmer	NY
Sarah E.	35	F		TN
Robert	7	M		TX
Savina A.	5	F		TX
Nancy E.	2	F		TX
Campbell, Elizabeth J.	9	F		TX
Charles T.	8	M		TX
John W.	7	M		TX
Mullens, Elizabeth	13	F		IL
Standifer, James S.	43	M	Farmer	GA
Caroline	43	F		GA
John B.	17	M	Farmer	TN
Elizabeth	14	F		AL
Mary A.	11	F		AL
Benjamin	11	M		AL
David	9	M		AL
Jemima	8	F		AL
Julia A.	6	F		AL
Harriet	4	F		AL
Champion, John	32	M	Farmer	SC
Naomi J.	16	F		TN
Gilreath, Nathan D.	25	M	Farmer	SC
Standifer, William R.	22	M	Carpenter	TN
Champion, James	30	M	Farmer	SC
Stillman, Mary A.	48	F		GA
Moss, Mathew	48	M	Farmer	TN
Mary A.	26	F		MO
Julia A.	9	F		TX
James	7	M		TX
Charles	4	M		TX
Stephen	2	M		TX
Lewis, James H.	37	M	Carpenter	TN
Malvina	28	F		KY
William H.	7	M		TX
Sarah J.	5	F		TX
John	4	M		TX
Mary A.	2	F		TX
Asher, Tobias	22	M	Farmer	IN
Maria A.	20	F		NC
Harriet J.	8/12	F		TX
Asher, William K.	42	M	Farmer	TN
Catharine	20	F		GER
Sarah A.	12	F		TX
Bacon, Thomas	23	M	Farmer	TN
Martha	21	F		TN
Margaret A.	2	F		TX
Emma	3/12	F		TX
Harrison, Daniel	33	M	Farmer	TN
Nancy	32	F		AR
Melinda E.	9	F		TX
Orry C.	6	F		TX
Mary J.	4	F		TX
William	10/12	M		TX

Name	Age/Sex	Occupation	Birthplace
Allen, James B.	39 M	Farmer	LA
Nancy	29 F		TN
William B. T.	11 M		TX
Mary E.	9 F		TX
Martha M.	7 F		TX
Benjamin B.	5 M		TX
Louisa	4 F		TX
Eliza J.	2 F		TX
Morey, Eliza E.	1 F		TX
Stearns, John	20 M	Laborer	OH
Freestone, Joseph H.	25 M	Laborer	OH
Allen, Benjamin	28 M	Farmer	LA
Martha	26 F		TN
Martin R.	6 M		TX
Anna C.	3 F		TX
William B.	1 M		TX
Freestone, Benjamin	21 M	Laborer	OH
Casner, Mary A.	50 F		NC
Elihu E.	22 M	Farmer	TN
Nancy A.	16 F		TX
Hiram	11 M		TX
Mary E.	9 F		TX
Jason	30 M	Farmer	TX
Yarborough, Matthew	35 M	Farmer	TN
Rhoda	56 F		VA
Hinds, Benjamin J.	32 M	Farmer	AL
Mary J.	23 F		MO
Walters, John	26 M	Laborer	TN
Castlebury, John	15 M		IL
Farris, Solomon	27 M	Farmer	TN
Loucinda	27 F		AL
Mary E.	7 F		AL
John B.	5 M		MS
William J.	3 M		AR
Champion N.	3 M		AR
Hinds, Margery A.	22 F		AL
Kimbro, Daniel	40 M	Wheelwright	NC
Mary	34 F		TN
Euclid W.	16 M	Farmer	TN
Lemuel G.	14 M		TN
Nitena E.	9 F		TX
Cynthia V.	6 F		TX
Crawford M.	3 M		TX
Gilbert, Cynthia	54 F		SC
Payne, John R.	34 M	Farmer	TN
Hannah E.	34 F		MS
Woodruff, Cornelia C.	6 F		TX
Key, Jesse	18 M	Laborer	GA
West, William	23 M	Laborer	IN
Simms, Bartlett	57 M	Surveyor	TN
Sarah	43 F		TN
James C.	22 M	Farmer	TX
Margaret A.	15 F		TX
William A.	12 M		TX
Thomas M.	6 M		TX
Missouri	5 F		TX
Emily V.	1 F		TX
Barker, Calvin	26 M	Farmer	MO
Nancy	25 F		TN
Margaret A.	11 F		TX
Jesse	9 M		TX
Albert	6 M		TX
Amanda	5 F		TX
Travis	2 M		TX
Eliazer	15 M		TX
Gage, William	21 M	Farmer	AL
Liffinwell, Ira	32 M	Farmer	NY
Olive, James	43 M	Farmer	NC
Julia A.	30 F		TN
Elizabeth	12 F		LA
James P.	10 M		LA
Thomas J.	7 M		LA
Mary J.	6 F		LA

(continued)

Name	Age/Sex	Occupation	Birthplace
Olive, Ira	4 M		
Elzinn	4/12 F		
Thompson, John S.	36 M	Farmer	
William G.	25 M	Farmer	

INDEX

C

D

E

F

G

H

I

M

Mc

N

Q

R

S

T

U

V

W

Y

Z

www.ingramcontent.com/pod-product-compliance
Lightning Source LLC
Chambersburg PA
CBHW080243030426
42334CB00023BA/2677